The Student's Companion to the Theologians

The Wiley-Blackwell Companions to Religion

The Wiley-Blackwell Companions to Religion series presents a collection of the most recent scholarship and knowledge about world religions. Each volume draws together newly-commissioned essays by distinguished authors in the field, and is presented in a style which is accessible to undergraduate students, as well as scholars and the interested general reader. These volumes approach the subject in a creative and forward-thinking style, providing a forum in which leading scholars in the field can make their views and research available to a wider audience.

Recently Published

The Student's Companion to the Theologians

Edited by

Ian S. Markham

A John Wiley & Sons, Ltd., Publication

This paperback edition first published 2013
© 2013 Blackwell Publishing Ltd

First published in hardback as *The Blackwell Companion to the Theologians* (Blackwell Publishing Ltd, 2009)

Blackwell Publishing was acquired by John Wiley & Sons in February 2007. Blackwell's publishing program has been merged with Wiley's global Scientific, Technical, and Medical business to form Wiley-Blackwell.

Registered Office
John Wiley & Sons, Ltd, The Atrium, Southern Gate, Chichester, West Sussex, PO19 8SQ, UK

Editorial Offices
350 Main Street, Malden, MA 02148-5020, USA
9600 Garsington Road, Oxford, OX4 2DQ, UK
The Atrium, Southern Gate, Chichester, West Sussex, PO19 8SQ, UK

For details of our global editorial offices, for customer services, and for information about how to apply for permission to reuse the copyright material in this book please see our website at www.wiley.com/wiley-blackwell.

The right of Ian S. Markham to be identified as the author of the editorial material in this work has been asserted in accordance with the UK Copyright, Designs and Patents Act 1988.

Library of Congress Cataloging-in-Publication Data

The student's companion to the theologians / edited by Ian S. Markham.
     p.   cm. — (Blackwell companions to religion)
   Includes bibliographical references and index.
   ISBN 978-1-4051-3507-8 (hardcover : alk. paper) – ISBN 978-1-118-47258-3 (pbk.)   1. Theology–History.
2. Theologians–History.   I. Markham, Ian S.   II. Title: Companion to the theologians.
   BR118.B48 2009
   230.092'2—dc22
                                                2008054911

A catalogue record for this book is available from the British Library.

Cover image: Barbara Chase/Corbis
Cover design by Nicki Averill Design

Set in 10/12pt Bembo by SPi Publisher Services, Pondicherry, India
Printed in Malaysia by Ho Printing (M) Sdn Bhd

1   2013

Contents

Notes on Contributors

Travis E. Ables is Visiting Assistant Professor of Historical Theology at Eden Theological Seminary, St. Louis, Missouri. His upcoming book studies the pneumatologies of Augustine and Karl Barth.

Efrain Agosto, PhD, is Professor of New Testament Studies at New York Theological Seminary. His book, *Servant Leadership: Jesus and Paul* (2005) studies leadership and status in the Jesus movement and Pauline Christianity. He has also published a Spanish-language lay commentary on Paul's letters to the Corinthians, Corintios (2008).

Lewis Ayres is Bede Chair in Catholic Theology at Durham University. He is currently the Henry Luce III Fellow in Theology. He has a DPhil from Oxford University and a Master's from St Andrews University. His research interests focus on Augustine and on Greek and Latin Trinitarian theology, christology, and pneumatology in the fourth and fifth centuries.

Matthew Berke was for many years the managing editor of the journal *First Things*. He has a PhD from Yale, a master's from Columbia, and a bachelor's degree from the University of Michigan. He writes on issues of politics, religion, and culture.

Augustine Casiday (PhD, University of Durham) is Senior Lecturer in Historical Theology and directs the MA program in Monastic Studies in the University of Wales, Lampeter. His research interests include patristics and Orthodox Christianity.

Gary Chartier is a faculty member at La Sierra University, California. His books include *The Analogy*

of Love: Divine and Human Love at the Center of Christian Theology (2007).

David Cheetham is Senior Lecturer in Theology and Religion at the University of Birmingham, UK. He specializes in the philosophy and theology of religions. He is the author of *John Hick* (2003) and numerous articles in journals including The *Heythrop Journal*, *Sophia*, *New lackfriars*, and *Theology*.

Kelton Cobb is a faculty member at the Oregon Extension of Eastern University. He has written on theology and popular culture in his book, *The Blackwell Guide to Theology and Popular Culture* (2005), which draws from the work of Paul Tillich in the area of theology of culture. He is a member of the North American Paul Tillich Society.

Mary E. Coleman was a specialist in Church History, a regular contributor to *Reviews in Religion and Theology* and adjunct Professor of Church History at Hartford Seminary.

Joseph Constant currently serves as the Director of Ethnic Ministries and Student Life at Virginia Theological Seminary. In this role, he is primarily responsible for co-ordinating the Seminary's Racial and Ethnic Ministries, including recruitment and outreach efforts and the development of cross-cultural campus activities.

Richard Cross is John A. O'Brien Professor of Philosophy at the University of Notre Dame, Indiana, having previously been Professor of Medieval Theology in the University of Oxford and a Fellow of

Oriel College, Oxford. His most recent books are The *Metaphysics of the Incarnation* (2002), and *Duns Scotus on God* (2005).

Minlib Dallh, OP, completed his doctoral studies at Hartford Seminary in Islamic Studies and is a Dominican friar of the Southern Province of the USA.

Ivor J. Davidson is Dean of Divinity and Professor of Systematic and Historical Theology at the University of St. Andrews. He has published widely in historical and systematic theology, and has a particular interest in patristics, in which his publications include a major critical edition of the *De officiis* of Ambrose of Milan (2 vols, 2002).

R. John Elford is the Visiting Professor of Ethics at Leeds Metropolitan University and author of *The Pastoral Nature of Theology* and *The Ethics of Uncertainty*.

Siobhán Garrigan is a Senior Lecturer on contemporary approaches to theology at the University of Exeter. She is also Director of the new Exeter Centre for Ecumenical and Practical Theology.

Katharina Greschat is Doctor of Theology (University of Münster) and Privatdozentin for Church History (University of Mainz). She holds the Professorship for Patristic Studies/Ancient Church History at Humboldt University of Berlin in proxy of the President of Humboldt University.

John W. de Gruchy is Emeritus Professor of Christian Studies at the University of Cape Town, South Africa. Editor of the 'Making of Modern Theology' series (Fortress Press), he is also author of *Christianity and Democracy* (1995) and *Christianity, Art and Transformation* (2001), among other works, and editor of the *Cambridge Companion to Dietrich Bonhoeffer*. He has translated, edited, and served on the Board for the English-language edition of Dietrich Bonhoeffer's Works.

Nathan J. Hallanger received his PhD in theology from the Graduate Theological Union. He is co-editor (with Ted Peters) of *God's Action in Nature's World: Essays in Honour of Robert John Russell* (2006). He is Special Assistant to the Vice President of Academic Affairs at Augsburg College, Minnesota.

Brian Hebblethwaite, DD, Life Fellow of Queens' College, Cambridge, formerly Lecturer in the Philosophy of Religion in the Faculty of Divinity, University of Cambridge.

Leslie Houlden has taught in the University of Oxford, where he was Fellow Chaplain of Trinity College, and at King's College, London, where he was finally Professor of Theology. He is author of some 20 books.

Thomas L. Humphries is Assistant Professor of Theology at Saint Leo University, Florida.

Molly F. James holds a BA from Tufts University, an MDiv from Yale Divinity School and Berkeley at Yale, and a PhD from the University of Exeter. She is Adjunct Professor of Theology and Ethics at Hartford Seminary, Connecticut.

Nancy C. James is priest associate at St John's Lafayette Square in Washington, DC and a professor at American University in Washington, DC. She received her MDiv from Virginia Theological Seminary and her PhD from the University of Virginia.

J'annine Jobling, PhD, is Associate Professor at Liverpool Hope University. Her interests focus on feminist theology, postmodernism, and hermeneutics. Her research is primarily centered upon feminist biblical hermeneutics in postmodern context; and this was the subject of her doctoral thesis. Jan Jobling is a graduate of Cambridge University and the University of Kent, and formerly worked as a lecturer at Canterbury Christ Church University. Dr Jobling is the author of *Feminist Biblical Interpretation in Theological Context: Restless Readings* (2002), co-editor, with Ian Markham, of *Theological Liberalism. Creative and Critical* (2000), and co-editor, with Robert Hannaford, of *Theology and the Body: Gender, Text and Ideology* (1999).

Daniel A. Keating is Associate Professor of Theology at Sacred Heart Major Seminary in Detroit, Michigan, where he teaches on Scripture, Theology, and the Church Fathers. His doctoral dissertation on Cyril of Alexandria's theology of sanctification and divinization was published as *The Appropriation of Divine Life in Cyril of Alexandria* (2004). Dr Keating is co-editor and contributor to *The Theology of St. Cyril of*

Alexandria: A Critical Appreciation (2003); *Aquinas on Doctrine: A Critical Introduction* (2004); and *Aquinas on Scripture: An Introduction to His Biblical Commentaries* (2005). He is the editor of St. Thomas Aquinas, *Commentary on Colossians* (2006), and his most recent work is *Deification and Grace* (2007).

David R. Law is the Reader in Christian Thought at the University of Manchester. With a doctorate from the University of Oxford, he has worked at the University of Manchester since 1994. He is the author of numerous books and articles, including *Inspiration* (2001).

Shannon C. Ledbetter is Community Canon at Blackburn Cathedral. She is a Process Theologian engaging in practical ministry. With degrees from the University of Louisville, Virginia Theological Seminary and a PhD from the University of Liverpool, she has contributed to *Encountering Religion* (edited by Ian Markham and Tinu Ruparell) and *Theological Liberalism* (edited by Ian Markham) and has done countless reviews for *Conversations in Religion and Theology*. She is also involved in developing resources for inter-faith dialogue and religion and the arts.

Alastair H. B. Logan is retired as Senior Lecturer in Christian Doctrine at Exeter University. He studied at Edinburgh, Harvard, and St Andrews. His main research interests are in Gnosticism, early Christian heresy, including Arius and Marcellus of Ancyra, and early Christian art and architecture.

Christy Lohr is the Associate Dean for Religious Life at Duke University Chapel, North Carolina. She served as the co-ordinator for the World Council of Churches' "Interfaith Education Project" and was a member of the North American Interfaith Network's Board of Directors.

Andrew Louth is a professor in the Department of Theology and Religion at Durham University, UK. His interests are in Patristic and Byzantine studies. His books include *Greek East and Latin West: The Church AD 681–1071* (2007) and *St John Damascene: Tradition and Originality in Byzantine Theology* (2002).

Philip McCosker is Deputy Master and Research Fellow in Theology at St Benet's Hall in Oxford. He has pursued theological studies in Oxford, Harvard,

Yale, and Cambridge where he recently completed his doctorate at Peterhouse on Christological configurations of theological paradox in mystical theologies. He teaches theology in Cambridge and Oxford. He was the editor of *What Is It That the Scripture Says?* (2006) and is co-editor (with Denys Turner) of *The Cambridge Companion to the Summa Theologiæ of Thomas Aquinas* (forthcoming 2009). He is the founding editor of the "Foreign Language Books" section of *Reviews in Religion and Theology*.

F. J. Michael McDermott is a Jesuit priest and professor of theology at Sacred Heart Major Seminary in Detroit, Michigan.

Mark McIntosh is a priest of the Episcopal Diocese of Chicago and did his undergraduate work at Yale University. After pursuing a second BA at the University of Oxford and completing his Master of Divinity degree at the General Theological Seminary of the Episcopal Church in Manhattan, he earned his PhD in Theology from the Divinity School of the University of Chicago. His work there on the christology of the Swiss theologian Hans Urs von Balthasar developed into a book, which has since been published under the title, *Christology from Within.*

Bernadette McNary-Zak is an Associate Professor in the Department of Religious Studies at Rhodes College. She holds a BA from University of Rochester, an MA from Catholic University of America, and a PhD from University of Toronto.

Kevin Magill is part-time lecturer in Theology and Religious Studies, University of Bristol, and Head of Religious Studies at Reading Blue Coat School. He completed his doctoral work at University of Bristol on Julian of Norwich's *Showings*.

Ian S. Markham is the Dean and President of Virginia Theological Seminary. He is an Associate Priest at St Paul's Episcopal Church, Alexandria, Virginia. He is the author of *Theology of Engagement* (2003) and *Understanding Christian Doctrine* (2007). Awards include the Teape Lectures of 2004 in India and the Robertson Fellow in Glasgow 2006.

Clive Marsh, BA, MEd, DPhil, is Senior Lecturer and Director of Learning and Teaching at the Institute of Lifelong Learning in the University of Leicester, UK.

Ryan A. Neal is Associate Professor & Chair of Undergraduate Programs in Christian Studies at Anderson College, South Carolina. He holds a BA from Texas Tech University, M,Div from Southwestern Baptist Theological Seminary, MTh and PhD from the University of Edinburgh (2005).

George Newlands is Professor Emeritus of Divinity and an Honorary Professorial Research Fellow at the University of Glasgow. He is a graduate of Edinburgh and Cambridge, a Fellow of the Royal Society of Arts and of the Royal Society of Edinburgh. Recent publications include *Christ and Human Rights* (2006) and *Faith and Human Rights*, with Richard Amesbury (2008).

Kenneth G. C. Newport is Pro Vice-Chancellor and Professor of Theology at Liverpool Hope University, UK. A graduate of the University of Oxford, Kenneth has a particular interest in the use and influence of biblical texts, particularly the book of Revelation. He has also published widely on the life, literature, and legacy of Charles Wesley. He has previously taught in Hong Kong and at the Universities of St Andrews and Manchester.

Eric Osborn is Emeritus Professor at the Department of History, La Trobe University and at the Department of Fine Arts, Classical Studies, and Archaeology, University of Melbourne. His books include *The Beginning of Christian Philosophy* (1981), *The Emergence of Christian Theology* (1993), and *Tertullian, First Theologian of the West* (1997).

Martyn Percy (BA Hons, MA, MEd, PhD) is the Principal of Ripon College Cuddesdon and the Oxford Ministry Course. He is also Honorary Professor of Theological Education at King's College London, an Honorary Canon of Salisbury Cathedral, and an Associate Priest in the Wheatley Team of Churches in Oxfordshire.

Craig A. Phillips, PhD, is the Rector of St Peter's Church, Arlington. He is an adjunct professor at Virginia Theological Seminary.

Andrew Radde-Gallwitz teaches in the department of theology at Loyola University, Chicago. With a doctorate from Emory University, he is the author of numerous articles.

Joanne Maguire Robinson is an Associate Professor in the Department of Religious Studies, University of North Carolina at Charlotte. She is the author of *Nobility and Annihilation in Marguerite Porete's "Mirror of Simple Souls"* (2001) and the forthcoming *If It Tarries, Wait for It: Waiting in Christian Thought and Practice*. She holds an MTS from Harvard Divinity School and a PhD from University of Chicago.

Wayne G. Rollins is currently Adjunct Professor of Scripture at Hartford Seminary, Connecticut, and Professor Emeritus of Theology at Assumption College, Worcester, Massachusetts, where he served as Director of the Ecumenical Institute and Graduate Program of Religious Studies. He received the BD, MA, and PhD degrees from Yale University, with postgraduate study at Cambridge University, Harvard University, and the Graduate Theological Union in Berkeley, California. He is the founding chair of the Psychology and Biblical Studies Section of the Society of Biblical Literature, an international organization of biblical scholars, and has published extensively in the field.

J. Elton Smith, Jr. is a PhD candidate in history at Fordham University, New York. He is an attorney and an Episcopal priest and teaches part-time at Montana Tech in Butte, Montana.

Cynthia Stewart is an elder in the African Methodist Episcopal Zion Church and holds a doctorate in the history of the AME Zion Church from the University of Exeter.

Tarmo Toom, PhD, Associate Professor of Patristics, The Catholic University of America, Washington, DC. Dr Toom is from Estonia. He is a member of the North American Patristics Society, a Regular Contributor for *Reviews in Religion and Theology*, and a member of the Steering Committee for the group "Augustine and Augustinianisms" at the American Academy of Religion. His most recent book is *Classical Trinitarian Theology: A Textbook* (2007).

Medi Ann Volpe, PhD, is Lecturer in Systematic Theology and Ethics at Cranmer Hall Theological College in Durham, UK. Her dissertation, "Make Love Your Aim: Sin and the Goal of Charity in Christian Formation," brings themes in contemporary theology into conversation with Gregory of Nyssa. Her research interests include theological method, ecclesiology, and the relationship between doctrine and practice.

Stephen H. Webb is Professor of Religion and Philosophy at Wabash College, Indiana. His books include *American Providence, The Divine Voice, The Gifting God, The Dome of Eden*, and *Jesus Christ, Eternal God*.

Christopher L. Webber is a graduate of Princeton University and has two earned degrees (STB, STM) and an honorary doctorate (DD) from the General Theological Seminary. A priest of the Episcopal Church, he has served parishes in the New York-Connecticut area and Tokyo, Japan. He is the author of some 25 books, ranging from a study of marriage (*Re-Inventing Marriage*) to an anthology of Anglican prayer (*Give Us Grace*) and *Beyond Beowulf*, the first-ever sequel to Beowulf.

Samuel Wells is the vicar of St. Martin-in-the-Fields, London. His publications include *Transforming Fate into Destiny*, *Improvisation*, and *God's Companions*.

Dr Wells received his PhD in Christian Ethics from Durham University, UK. He has written numerous books and articles on Christian social ethics. His latest book, co-edited with Sarah Coakley, is *Praying for England: The Heart of the Church* (2008).

D. H. Williams (PhD, MA University of Toronto, 1991) is currently Professor of Religion in Patristics and Historical Theology in the Department of Religion of Baylor University, Texas. Prior to 2002 he was Associate Professor of Theology at Loyola University Chicago. His major books include *Tradition, Scripture and Interpretation: A Sourcebook of the Ancient Church* (2006), *Retrieving the Tradition and Renewing Evangelicalism: A Primer for Suspicious Protestants* (1999), and *Ambrose of Milan and the End of the Nicene–Arian Conflicts* (1995).

Christian Collins Winn (BA, University of North Carolina; MDiv, Gordon Conwell Theological Seminary; PhD, Drew University) is Associate Professor of Historical and Systematic Theology at Bethel University, with special interest in post-Reformation and modern theology.

Preface

From the outside, theology looks difficult. How exactly do we reflect on ultimate questions? How can we have any confidence that our claims are true? These are obvious and legitimate questions. The temptation is to decide that these questions are impossible to answer and dismiss the entire subject area.

This is a temptation that is important to resist. From the outside the talk of space being curved sounds bizarre, but in Einstein's world the sun's gravity really does create a geometry of spheres. Naturally, it takes some time to understand the discourse. To start with it will sound odd and, in the case of Einstein, there is some complicated mathematics that one will need to grasp. However, if one does this work and gets inside a world, then it becomes intelligible.

This *Companion* is an introduction to the remarkable world of theology and theologians. You are being invited to 'understand'—to step inside—and thereby start to appreciate a discourse that those within certainly appreciate is difficult. These articles are intended to provide a way in to the connections, links, and influences that create a distinctive approach to the Christian faith. This is a book dedicated to Christian theology, although there are entries describing theologians who have been influenced by other faith traditions. It explores a world where the disclosure of God in Jesus is in some way (and as you will discover the ways are very various) a revelation to humanity about the nature of God.

Theology is not just about doctrine. Theology emerges out of life and story. So in every case, we touch on the factors in a person's life that shapes that theology. For some forms of theology (black and feminist), the experience shapes the theology in very distinctive ways.

Welcome to this world. Please step inside and learn to appreciate the challenging world of theology.

I. Purpose of This Book

The primary purpose of this reference work is to introduce the remarkable world of theology to a thoughtful interested reader. However, the approach and selection have been shaped by a particular audience in mind. This audience is the student who is taking introductory classes in theology.

As every professor knows, one never moves beyond the basics unless one can assume the basics. Depth in any discipline requires one to assume that students have learned certain key concepts and heard of certain key people. However, in a world where countless practical considerations make it difficult to insist that certain courses need to be taken in a particular order, professors find themselves constantly revisiting the basics.

The purpose of this substantial reference work is to free up the professor from this task. The professor can invite the student to read the substantial introductory articles on this or that theologian, and then assume a basic map of positions and views in the mind of the student. So the goal of this book is to provide students with accurate, informed, accessible articles on all the key people in our discipline. Articles are structured in a similar way: after a brief survey of the life, a description of the theology follows, culminating in a brief discussion of the significance of that theologian.

To help the students there is a glossary, which includes the terms that most often appear in the various articles. In addition, there is a timeline, thereby ensuring that students locate the theologian in the appropriate context of world events.

II.   Selection

It is inevitable that selection is difficult. Who precisely one includes and excludes will be hotly contested. The criterion for inclusion is the introductory theology course—theologians that are included are the ones that are likely to be mentioned in such a course. Now, given the introductory theology course comes from a variety of different perspectives, this *Companion* has attempted to make sure that key people in the main approaches are included. So, for example, Martin Luther, James Packer, and C. S. Lewis are important for the evangelicals; Julian of Norwich, Rosemary Radford Ruether, and Elizabeth Schüssler Fiorenza are important for the feminists; Thomas Aquinas, Serge Laugier de Beaurecueil, and Richard John Neuhaus are important for the Roman Catholics; and Martin Luther King Jr. and James Cone are important for those approaching the discipline from the perspective of black theology.

Naturally, all these approaches are in conversation with the broad center of the Christian tradition. So, naturally, there are some theologians who are included simply because they have shaped the tradition in a major way—Aquinas, Augustine, Luther, and Calvin. The key theologians of the New Testament are there: Paul, Matthew, Mark, Luke, John, and the author of the Apocalypse of John. Some are included because they were a particular influence at a particular time—thus John Nelson Darby and the Left Behind theology or Reinhold Niebuhr and Christian Realism. Others are included because they represent a particular approach—Richard Swinburne takes an analytical philosophical approach and Keith Ward has

produced a systematic theology which takes comparative theology seriously. Others are there because they represent a school—James Cone is the main representative of black theology and Rosemary Radford Reuther was the first to provide a feminist systematic theology.

The length of articles varies. Those in the "Early Centuries" and "Middle Ages" are longer than those in the "Enlightenment and Modern Period"; this is partly because modernity has had such a dramatic impact on the sheer variety of approaches that one needed more (and therefore shorter) articles for this period. Given that we are living in the modern period, it is especially important that students have a sense of trajectories that are currently emerging.

Inevitably there will be those who feel that this *Companion* needed to include this or that person—and a project of this nature could easily be twice the size. There are many important voices that are not included. Therefore, in certain key areas, there is a general description of a theological approach, which ensures that a range of theologians in that area are identified and described (e.g., black theology, liberal theology, and Vatican II).

III.   Invitation to Participation

Theology is not a discipline that one observes from afar. Instead, it is one that every reader is invited to join. This is the hard work of making sense of what we learn in Christ about God and God's relations to the world. Each Christian is invited to engage with these writers and join the conversation. These theologians are very diverse—from evangelical to liberal and from Catholic to Protestant. As one agrees and disagrees, one arrives at a greater sense of what one believes. This process is the act of participation in the conversation.

Ian S. Markham
Virginia Theological Seminary

Acknowledgments

It was Rebecca Harkin—the commissioning editor of Wiley-Blackwell—who had the original vision. It is one of the delights of my life to work with Rebecca: she understands the worlds of the academy, church, and publishing perfectly. I am deeply grateful to her and her team at Wiley-Blackwell.

Naturally a project of this scope is very dependent on the contributors who worked hard on their articles to capture the heart of their subject accurately and thoughtfully. I am humbled by the willingness of some of the most interesting scholars in the academy today to find time to write for the *Companion*. I am confident their willingness will enhance the value of this reference work. An edited volume of this scope—with so many contributors with different styles—requires exceptional expertise at the copy-editing stage. I wish to thank Caroline Richards and Ben Shelton for their efforts in this area.

The project evolved over several years, so various colleagues were intimately involved. It started at Hartford Seminary, with Yvonne Bowen as the assistant; then Christy Lohr took it on. As I moved to Virginia Theological Seminary, it was Katie Glover who helped keep all the various projects in my office progressing. Finally, Leslie Steffensen agreed to make sure that the manuscript was delivered to the publisher on time. For her exceptional hard work and careful attention to detail, I am extremely grateful.

For this paperback edition, I am grateful to Elizabeth Locher for helping to make appropriate adjustments and changes to the text.

When it comes to theology, my 16-year-old son Luke remains my favorite conversation partner. He has a good aptitude for the technicalities of the subject. I appreciate his endless capacity to help me see the world differently.

Finally, my delightful wife Lesley helped out with the project in countless ways. I appreciate her interest in my work very much. She is, as ever, the best.

Permissions

Ian Markham is grateful to Blackwell Publishing for permission to reproduce aspects of chapter 11 of *Theology of Engagement* (2003) for the article on Keith Ward. David Cheetham is grateful to Ashgate Publishing for permission to reprint or rework passages from his book *John Hick* (2003) for the article on John Hick.

Eric Osborn is grateful to Blackwell Publishing for permission to reproduce "Irenaeus of Lyons" from G. R. Evans (ed.), *The First Christian Theologians* (2004). Mark McIntosh is grateful to Blackwell Publishing for permission to reproduce "Von Balthasar" from Gareth Jones (ed.), *The Blackwell Companion to Modern Theology* (2004). John W. de Gruchy is grateful to Blackwell Publishing for permission to reproduce "Bonhoeffer" from Gareth Jones (ed.), *The Blackwell Companion to Modern Theology* (2004).

Timeline

Dates	Theologian	Event
c.35–c.110	Ignatius of Antioch	life of Jesus, 0–33
c.85–c.160	Marcion	
2nd century	Irenaeus of Lyons	
c.155–c.225	Tertullian	Roman Empire begins to decline, 180
c.185–254	Origen	
c.256–336	Arius	
c.295–373	Athanasius	Emp. Diocletian divides Rom. Emp. into two, 285
c.306–73)	Ephrem the Syrian	Constantine grants toleration of Christians, 313
c.329–c.524	Basil of Caesarea, Gregory of Nyssa & Gregory of Nazianzus	Council of Nicaea, 325
c.354–430	Augustine of Hippo	barbarian invasions of Europe, 360 to 600
c.378–444	Cyril of Alexandria	
c.381–c.451	Nestorius of Constantinople	Council of Constantinople, 381
		sack of Rome, 410
		St Patrick in Ireland, 430
		fall of the Western Roman Empire, 480
c.475–c.524	Boethius	Buddhism in Japan, 540

(Left margin, spanning the rows: ROMAN EMPIRE)

Empire	Dates	Person	Events
FRANKISH EMPIRE / BYZANTINE EMPIRE	580–662	Maximos the Confessor	spread of Islam to Africa and Asia, 660
			birth of Islam, 622
			Hinduism dominates over Islam in India, 700
			Charlemagne helps to spread Christianity, 780
			Charlemagne crowned Holy Roman Emperor, 800
			Monks write Anglo-Saxon Chronicle, 890
			Fatimid University founded in Cairo, 975
			Orthodox Christianity in Kiev, 990
HOLY ROMAN EMPIRE	1033–1109	St Anselm of Canterbury	Crusaders take Jerusalem, 1099
	1079–1142	Peter Abelard	
	1090–1153	Bernard of Clairvaux	
	c.1217–74	Bonaventure	Genghis Khan, Mogul ruler, 1210
	c.1224–74	Thomas Aquinas	
	c.1266–1308	Duns Scotus	
	c.1280–c.1349	William Ockham	the Black Death, 1320–60
	1342–c.1416	Julian of Norwich	
OTTOMAN EMPIRE			Joan of Arc, 1430
			Gutenberg Bible printed, 1455
			Ottomans take
			Constantinople, 1455
	1483–1546	Martin Luther	
	1497–1560	Philip Melanchthon	
	1509–64	John Calvin	Reformation begins, 1505
	1515–82	Teresa of Ávila	Tyndale translates NT into English, 1526
			Calvin starts church reform, 1535

			Henry VIII breaks from Rome, 1534
	1554–1600	Richard Hooker	Sikhs build temple at Amritsar, 1605
			Europe's 30 y. war betw. Catholics & Protestants, 1620–50
			North America settled by Europeans, 1610
	1724–1804	Immanuel Kant	
	1768–1834	Friedrich Schleiermacher	American Revolution, 1775–83
			French Revolution, 1789–99
	1770–1831	Georg Hegel	
	1800–82	John Nelson Darby	Napoleonic Wars, 1799–1815
			Francis II gives up title of Holy Roman Emp., 1800
	1801–90	John Henry Newman	Industrial Revolution begins, 1810
	1802–75	Gottfried Thomasius	
	1813–55	Søren Kierkegaard	Crimean War, 1853–56
	1851–1921	B. B. Warfield	
	1886–1968	Karl Barth	
	1886–1965	Paul Tillich	
	1886–1960	John Baillie	
	1887–1954	Donald Baillie	
	1889–1966	Emil Brunner	
	1892–1971	Reinhold Niebuhr	
	1893–1979	Georges Florovsky	

OTTOMAN EMPIRE

HOLY ROMAN EMPIRE

1898–1963	C. S. Lewis	
1904–68	A. M. Farrer	
1904–84	Karl Rahner	
1905–88	Hans Urs von Balthasar	
1906–45	Dietrich Bonhoeffer	
1913–94	Donald MacKinnon	First World War, 1914–18
1917–2005	Serge Laugier de Beaurecueil	Russian Revolution, 1917
1920–99	Charles Philip Price	Gandhi marches against British rule in India, 1920s
1922–88	Hans Frei	
1922–2012	John Hick	
1923–	George Lindbeck	
1926–	Jürgen Moltmann	
1926–	James Packer	
1928–	Gustavo Gutiérrez	
1928–	Wolfhart Pannenberg	
1929–2003	Dorothee Sölle	
1929–68	Martin Luther King, Jr.	
1934–	Richard Swinburne	
1936–	Rosemary Radford Ruether	
1936–	Richard John Neuhaus	
1938–	James Cone	
1938–	Elisabeth Schüssler Fiorenza	
1938–	Keith Ward	
1940–	Stanley Hauerwas	Second World War, 1939–45

OTTOMAN EMPIRE

1941–2003	Colin Gunton	
1941–	Elizabeth Johnson	State of Israel formed, 1948
1952–	John Milbank	USA civil rights protests, 1960s
		Vatican II, 1962–65
		Chinese Cultural Revolution, 1966 to mid-1970s

The following are the relevant dates for each empire:

Roman Empire	(pre-)zero to 480
Frankish Empire	480 to 825
Byzantine Empire	525 to 1455
Holy Roman Empire	825 to 1815
Ottoman Empire	1305 to 1910

Early Centuries

The Apocalypse of John

Kenneth G. C. Newport

Among the books of the Bible there can be few that have been so widely utilized as the Apocalypse of John. From early times this book has been a favorite for those believers and communities who wait expectantly for "the end" (however that is conceived), for it has long been assumed that this is what the Apocalypse, or "Revelation," is really all about. Down through the Christian centuries, therefore, careful attention has been paid to this book and much energy expended upon trying to understand more precisely what it is about the end that the book of "Revelation" actually reveals. The most widely accepted interpretation is that it reveals the events that will occur as the end of the world approaches; it is, in short, and to use the title of this book that has now become synonymous with its presumed contents, a timetable of the Apocalypse (Froom, 1946–54).

While it is true that interest in the book has a long and distinguished history (Sir Isaac Newton, for example, was fascinated by it, as his posthumously published *Observations upon the Prophecies* [1733] clearly shows), in recent times there has been no let-up in interpretative endeavor. And there are some extreme examples of the same: infamously, it was this book above all others that led David Koresh and his Branch Davidian community to self-destruct in Waco in 1993 (Newport, 2006). It is this book, too, which inspires much of the thinking in the now massively successful, and, one suspects, influential, *Left Behind*

series. Contemporary evidence shows also how the Apocalypse of John has left its mark on many aspects of popular culture and in the genres of music, literature, and art (Kovacs and Rowland, 2003; Newport and Walliss, forthcoming).

There has been a great deal of discussion regarding the authorship of this book. "John" is named as the author in four places (1.1, 4, 9; 22.8), with no further identifying information. Assuming that the work is not consciously pseudepigraphical, the traditional view is that the "John" in question is the author of the gospel of John (not that that book names "John" as its author), himself taken to be the brother of James, one of Jesus' disciples (see Matt. 4:21). There are problems with this view, however, not the least of which is that the Greek of the Apocalypse is a very strange Greek indeed and not at all like that found in the Gospel. In fact, it would seem that whoever the author of the Apocalypse was, he (or just perhaps she) was much more at home linguistically in a Semitic rather than Hellenistic context, thinking in Aramaic perhaps, and with a thorough acquaintance of Hebrew, but writing in Greek (Thompson, 1985). And there are other indications that a thoroughly Semitic mind is at work here. For example, although the Hebrew Scriptures are never directly quoted, more verses than not in Revelation show the influence of the Hebrew texts (Moyise, 1996). Indeed, so soaked through with Jewish thought, literature, and language is the book of

The Student's Companion to the Theologians, First Edition. Edited by Ian S. Markham.
© 2013 Blackwell Publishing Ltd. Published 2013 by Blackwell Publishing Ltd.

Revelation that some have even suggested that it originated as Jewish text that has been edited by a later Christian writer (Massyngberde Ford, 1975).

There is in fact little question that the author of the Apocalypse was a Jew. However, like Paul and most of the other early Christians, this Jew had come to the conclusion that Jesus was the Messiah and indicates that it was as a result of this belief that he had been exiled to the Isle of Patmos, a Greek Island in the Aegean Sea (Rev. 1:9). The fact that the author was an exile is important for an understanding of the text, as is the commonly held view that his exile coincided with a period of persecution of the Christian church at the hands of the Roman state. Again there is some dispute here: was this, as is most commonly thought, a period of persecution toward the end of the first century ce or an earlier one, perhaps in the 60s? In either case the experience has left its mark on the author whose theology is understandably reflective of it. This is a text born of suffering – both communal and individual. It is one also which comes from a period during which there is great external pressure to conform to society's norms. The message that comes loud and clear in response is "I [Jesus] am coming soon; hold fast to what you have, so that no one may seize your crown" (Rev. 3:11).

Certainly the "end of the world" and the return of Jesus is a theme of significant importance to the author of the Apocalypse. However, some, most famously Rowland (1972), have raised a fundamental challenge to the notion that "apocalyptic" literature really has "the end" as its principal concern. The Greek word *apocalypsis* (the word used in Rev. 1:1), it is argued, is rather about "drawing back the veil," so as to "un-cover—*apo-kaluptein*" something. This act of "uncovering" might of course include aspects of revealing what is to come (see Rev. 1:1 and 4:1), but more central to the genre's concern is the act of taking the seer "behind the scenes" of this world so as to put on show the heavenly reality behind the earthly façade. In the Apocalypse, John is hence taken through a door into heaven (Rev. 4:1, 2) and given in effect a tour of God's dwelling place, the purpose of which is to reassure him, as the one who is to speak to God's persecuted and distressed community, that whatever the outward appearance, God is in control and that all things will, in the end, work to God's

glory and achieve God's purpose. The great beasts of Revelation as depicted so graphically in chapter 13 and via the Whore of Babylon motif of Rev. 17–18, then, may appear to be in control to the untrained eye as they (in the form of the Roman state) persecute the saints; but in fact God guards every soul that is slain. They rest under the altar (Rev. 6:9) dressed in white robes awaiting vindication. Satan does his work now (Rev. 12), but he will be bound (Rev. 20); the wicked prosper in the present, but their final end is certain. The righteous suffer now, but will inherit eternal life.

It would appear, then, that the author of the Apocalypse calls for endurance in the face of two major challenges: persecution and assimilation. The people of God will suffer physically; they will be slain and trodden upon by the unrighteous who individually and collectively are instruments in the hands of Satan (for as Rev. 12 and 13 reveal, it is none other than this "old serpent" who is at work behind the scenes) and in this context the promise of reward is held out to those that endure to the end. As important as this theme is, however, perhaps an equal concern to the author is the pressure to conform to practices that, while widespread and accepted in the larger society, are not to be engaged in by the people of God. In the "letters to the seven churches" found in Rev. 2–3, there are dire warnings to those who do assimilate and compromise their distinctiveness—to those who are in danger of losing their "first love" and have become "lukewarm" (Rev. 2:4; 3:16). It is this uncompromising call to purity of faith and endurance under stress that is perhaps the most fundamental concern to the author. The "end of the world" is of course a key part of this, for by showing that God in the end will win out, that wrongs will eventually be righted, that the wicked will be slain, that Satan will be destroyed and that the righteous will be granted access to the new Jerusalem and the right to eat of the tree of life (Rev. 21), John shores up the community and gives hope and confidence for the future. But the theology of the future, with its rewards and paradisal bliss, is very much invoked to serve present needs and determine behavior in the here and now.

The author of the Apocalypse does of course have other important theological concerns which are worked out in this text. It is a contentious but nevertheless arguable view that outside of the Gospel of John, the Apocalypse contains the "highest" christology in the New Testament (though Col. 1:15ff. and perhaps Phil. 2:6–11 may be contenders here). Certainly the portrait of Jesus which the author presents is a powerful one. He is "King of Kings and Lord of Lords" (Rev. 17:14; 19:16); he is "the faithful witness, the firstborn of the dead, and the ruler of the kings of the earth" (Rev. 1:5); and the description of him in the latter part of chapter 1 is truly a description of a being the likeness of which (at the very least) borders on the divine. What is more, while the instruction from the angel to whom John offers worship is "You must not do that! ... Worship God!," when worship is offered to Christ, it is apparently appropriate and accepted (Rev. 5). And yet this is also the lamb who was slain (Rev. 5), whose blood cleanses sinners from their sins (Rev. 1:5). The Christ here is, then, recognizable as the Christ of the church: a divine Christ whose blood was spilt to bring redemption; and one ought not to underestimate the extent to which within the New Testament, 2000 years of Christian tradition notwithstanding, this reasonably clear dual testimony is distinctive.

The author of the Apocalypse is hence a figure in Christian history who should not be ignored. His influence has been significant, and not only in theological backwaters inhabited by the eschatologically obsessed, the millennially extreme, and/or the religiously volatile. The author speaks not just from the landscape of first-century Christianity in general, but from the specific context of a persecuted community and a social setting where a blurring of the boundaries between those who are "called out," "the *ekklesia*—the Church," and the society from which they are called to stand in righteous relief is a real danger, and probably an actual fact. The author's voice is a clear one, a clarion call to distinctiveness and perseverance in difficult times. It is perhaps not a voice the full impact of which is acceptable today, as Christians seek to maintain a rather more moderate balance between distinctiveness and inclusivity. But it is a voice that is worth hearing, for the questions it addresses continue to echo in contexts entirely distant from, but similar to, John's own.

References

Froom, Le Roy Edwin. 1946–54. *The Prophetic Faith of our Fathers*, 4 vols. Washington, DC: Review and Herald Publishing Association.

Kovacs, J. and Rowland, C. 2003. *Revelation through the Centuries*. Oxford: Blackwell.

Massyngberde Ford, J. 1975. *Revelation*, 2 vols. Anchor Bible vol. 38. Garden City, NY: Doubleday & Co.

Moyise, Steven. 1996. *The Old Testament in the Book of Revelation*, JSNT Testament Supplement Series 115. Sheffield: Sheffield Academic Press.

Newport, Kenneth G. C. 2000. *Apocalypse and Millennium: Studies in Biblical Eisegesis*. Cambridge: Cambridge University Press.

Newport, Kenneth G. C. 2006. *The Branch Davidians of Waco: The History and Beliefs of an Apocalyptic Sect*. Oxford: Oxford University Press.

Newport, Kenneth G. C. and Walliss, J., eds. Forthcoming, 2009. *The End All Around Us: The Apocalypse in Popular Culture*. London: Equinox.

Newton, Isaac. 1733. *Observations upon the Prophecies of Daniel and the Apocalypse of St John*.

Rowland, Christopher. 1972. *The Open Heaven: A Study of Apocalyptic in Judaism and Early Christianity*. London: SPCK.

Thompson, Steven W. 1985. *The Apocalypse and Semitic Syntax*, SNTS Monograph Series 52. Cambridge: Cambridge University Press.

Arius (*c.*256–336)

Alastair H. B. Logan

I. Life

Arius (*Areios* meaning "warlike," after the Greek god Ares) is a figure about whom we know very little for certain. What survives is preserved by his bitter opponents such as Athanasius of Alexandria (*c.*296–373 CE) and Epiphanius of Salamis (*c.*315–403 CE) or by church historians of varying degrees of objectivity writing a century or more later, such as the lawyers Socrates (380–450 CE) and Sozomen (early fifth century CE), the "Arian" Philostorgius (*c.*368–*c.*439 CE), also a layman, and the Catholic bishop Theodoret of Cyrrhus (393–466 CE). We do not know when he was born: the traditional dating of 256 seems too early even though Epiphanius calls him an "old man" at the outbreak of the controversy, a remark echoed perhaps by Emperor Constantine's abusive description of him in a letter of 333 as wasted and lifeless. We can be fairly certain that he was a Libyan, from the evidence of Epiphanius and his own testimony in a letter to Constantine. Certainly Libyan bishops were among his staunchest supporters and we find in Arius an unequivocal condemnation of the modalist heresy of the Libyan Sabellius, very widespread there in the latter part of the third century and vigorously refuted by Dionysius of Alexandria (247–64 CE).

As regards his education, both Socrates and Sozomen remark on his dialectical skill, while contemporary opponents such as Athanasius and Marcellus of Ancyra (*c.*284–*c.*374 CE) claim he got his ideas from the devil and Greek philosophy. From his description in his letter to Eusebius of Nicomedia (d. 341 CE) of the latter as a "fellow Lucianist," it has been deduced that he was a pupil of Lucian of Antioch, a shadowy figure who most probably was the presbyter, teacher, and biblical critic martyred in Nicomedia in 312. However, we know very little about Lucian. Strikingly, Philostorgius in his lists of his pupils, which include Eusebius of Nicomedia and the Cappadocian sophist Asterius and seem to center on Asia Minor, makes no mention of Arius. The idea of a Lucianic school in Antioch devoted to a literal exegesis of scripture is discounted nowadays, as is the claim that Arius learnt from it to practice such a form of exegesis. He *may* have attended lectures by Lucian but seems not to have been a devoted pupil. As we shall see, there are clear differences between his ideas and those of the Lucianists under Eusebius of Nicomedia, and his term "fellow Lucianist" may well have been intended to secure Eusebius's support for his rather different theology.

Recent scholarship has tended to focus on an Alexandrian theological and philosophical background for Arius's views. Arius sees himself in his confession to his bishop Alexander (313–28 CE) as a theological traditionalist, while the opening of his poem *Thalia* ("Banquet") presents him as standing in a line of wise sages, taught by God and inspired by the

Holy Spirit. This is very likely an allusion to the scholarly tradition of learned presbyters in Alexandria going back to Clement (*c.*150–*c.*215 CE) and Origen (185–254 CE), over against and sometimes at odds with the bishop. One is particularly reminded of Origen's role as teacher and his speculative theology and the strained relations between him and bishop Demetrius. However, there seems to have been a reaction in Alexandria both against Origen's more speculative views (such as the eternity of rational creatures) and against his allegorical interpretation. His influence on Arius seems limited.

Some scholars have sought to explain distinctive, radical features of Arius's views, particularly the absolute transcendence of God and the Son's ignorance of him and of his own being, in terms of Arius's acquaintance with contemporary philosophy, Platonic or Aristotelian. Thus Williams (2001, 209–13) and Kannengiesser (1991, I, 35–40) note the remarkable similarities between Arius and Plotinus, also an Alexandrian, if developing his Neoplatonism in Rome in the 260s. Arius would thus be one of the first Christian theologians to assimilate Neoplatonic ideas, long before the Cappadocians, Marius Victorinus, and Augustine. However, how exactly Arius might have come across such ideas is not at all clear, and some scholars still prefer to situate Arius in the milieu of late Middle Platonism as represented in Alexandria (Stead 1997, 39–52; 1999, 101–8). This would take in figures like Philo. Aspects of Arius's views also recall Jewish–Hellenistic wisdom speculation.

Most scholars discount the association of Arius with the schismatic Egyptian bishop Melitius and his ordination as deacon by him, which rests on scanty evidence. It seems most likely that Arius was ordained deacon by Peter (300–12 CE) and presbyter by Peter's successor, Achillas (312–13 CE). It was Achillas's successor, Alexander, who in all probability appointed Arius as priest of the Baucalis church with authority to expound the Scriptures. Alexandrian presbyters, as Williams points out (2001, 42–4), had particular autonomy, and we are told that they preached in their churches on Wednesdays and Fridays. Epiphanius suggests that individual presbyters by their exposition of scripture attracted rival followings. Thus he notes that Arius, tall and gaunt, with his charming speech

and garb resembling that of a philosopher and ascetic, succeeded in attracting 700 women vowed to virginity as well as seven presbyters and 12 deacons to his church and group. It was thus as a scholarly but persuasive preacher and scriptural expositor, a senior presbyter in the Alexandrian church, that Arius provoked the doctrinal controversy that was to rock and split the church, in both East and West.

Modern scholars are divided on when the controversy broke out. Besides the classic treatment of the sources by the German scholar Hans-Georg Opitz (1934), who traces the outbreak to 318 and whose ordering and dating of the material many scholars still tend to accept, Rowan Williams in his classic monograph of 1987, rearranging and redating Opitz's documents (2001, 48–58), suggests 321 for the outbreak. More recently Sara Parvis (2006, 68–9) has argued for the shortest possible time scale, suggesting the spring of 322. The evidence seems too fragmentary to decide the matter. As to how the controversy arose, the ancient church historians, Socrates and Sozomen, are divided: Socrates attributes it to a too ambitious discourse by Alexander to his clergy on Unity in Trinity, which Arius vehemently countered, thinking it smacked too much of Sabellianism, while Sozomen derives it from Arius's preaching in church, sparking protests and leading to an inquiry chaired by Alexander as judge between the two opposing groups. Both accounts have anachronistic features, though Sozomen's seems closer to Epiphanius's version which has the schismatic Melitius inform Alexander of Arius's heterodoxy, leading to Alexander's examination of him before the presbytery and some other bishops. Conversely Arius in his letter to Eusebius of Nicomedia seems to bear out Socrates' version in that he talks of Alexander as having driven him and his supporters out for not agreeing with Alexander's public preaching about the coeternity of Father and Son.

However we reconstruct the origins of the controversy, it seems that Arius was condemned, deposed, and excommunicated by an Alexandrian council and that he instigated a campaign of support from sympathizers, including Palestinian bishops such as Eusebius of Caesarea (*c.*260–339 CE). He seems to have moved to Palestine and been recognized by a council there which allowed him to function as a presbyter with his own congregation. To counter

Alexander's hostile encyclicals to eastern bishops and to widen his support he was urged to write to Eusebius of Nicomedia, who had recently got himself translated there, the seat of the eastern emperor Licinius, from Berytus. Eusebius instigated a vigorous campaign enlisting support from bishops in Bithynia, Cilicia, Syria, and Palestine, the heartlands, with Libya, of support for Arius. This probably provoked Alexander to propose a synod to deal with the issues that had arisen, theological and canonical. This was originally to have met at Ancyra, probably at the behest of its bishop, Marcellus (c.314–36 CE), who had been a target of the Arian propaganda campaign.

But Licinius's renewed campaign of persecution in 323–4, banning Christian councils from meeting, meant a postponement, and things changed radically with the arrival of Constantine in the East in 324, defeating Licinius and assuming sole rule. Faced at once with the Arian crisis, he sent Ossius of Cordoba, his advisor on church affairs, to Alexandria with an exasperated letter for both Alexander and Arius, seeking to resolve the dispute and restore peace and unity to the church. But it was too late, and, when advised by Ossius of his failure, and perhaps alerted by Eusebius of Nicomedia and others to the likely character of the council at Ancyra, he abruptly changed the venue to Nicaea, where he could himself attend and ensure an acceptable outcome. In the meantime Ossius, returning via Antioch, had held a council there in late 324 to resolve the dispute over a new bishop and deal with Arius. The council, representing largely the diocese of Antioch, and reflecting the theology of Alexander, condemned Arius and his views in a rather rambling fashion and provisionally excommunicated Eusebius of Caesarea and two other Palestinian bishops for supporting him. At the Council of Nicaea of May–June 325, attended by some 250 bishops as well as by Constantine, the views of supporters of Arius such as Eusebius of Nicomedia were shouted down although Eusebius of Caesarea was rehabilitated. The Council produced a short, biblically based creed which rejected Arius's views by positive statements (the Son is of the substance [ousia] of the Father, true God of true God, begotten, not made, consubstantial [homoousios] with the Father) and anathemas countering his supposed tenets. He was deposed and excommunicated, as were the two Libyan

bishops who had staunchly supported him and who also refused to subscribe to the creed and the anathemas, Secundus and Theonas, and all three along with an Alexandrian fellow presbyter, Euzoius, were exiled by Constantine at the end of the council, probably to Illyricum.

However, a remarkable volte-face occurred at the end of 327, when Constantine wrote to Arius summoning him to court at Nicomedia, surprised that he had not come earlier. Parvis (2006, 101–7) attributes this to the disgrace and fall of Eustathius of Antioch, a key player at Nicaea, who seems to have committed a serious sexual offense which so horrified the emperor that it opened the way for him to recall Arius. This would have to have been sanctioned by a council, probably meeting in Antioch in the fall of 327. Arius and Euzoius returned and presented the emperor with a neutral creed, which avoided all the contentious terms and issues but which satisfied Constantine and his ecclesiastical advisors. Arius was probably readmitted to communion by a local Bithynian synod and Constantine wrote to Alexander urging him to do the same. However, in the interim Alexander had died and was replaced by Athanasius (328–73 CE). He soon embarked on what was in effect a civil war with Eusebius of Nicomedia and his supporters. Thus when a Bithynian synod of late 328 under Eusebius again appealed to Athanasius to readmit Arius, the latter refused, turning away Arius himself who had returned to Alexandria, and resisting all later attempts to have him readmitted.

Arius rather drops out of sight from 328, perhaps living in Libya, accepted by the church there, but he reappears in 332 or 333, writing a despairing letter to Constantine asking what he was supposed to do if no one in Egypt would receive him back, and supplying another, rather ambiguous, confession of faith claiming the support of all of Libya for his views regarding salvation. However, the effect was far from what he had intended. Constantine, alarmed by the suggestion of a schismatic church in Libya, wrote a very blustering, venomous open letter in 333 to Arius and his supporters, ridiculing his confession, threatening divine judgment on Libya and the Libyans, contemptuously describing him as half dead, feeble in look and pale in complexion, and threatening with punishment all clergy and laity who continued to support him. His letter was accompanied by an edict comparing Arius with Porphyry, the great pagan critic of Christianity, branding his supporters Porphyrians and demanding, as with the works of Porphyry, the burning of any of his treatises discovered and capital punishment for anyone not surrendering copies. However, at the end of his letter Constantine did invite Arius to his court in Constantinople, an invitation Arius seems to have accepted, with the result that he was encouraged to make his case at a major council summoned by Constantine in 335 for the dedication of his great church in Jerusalem.

This council of about 60 bishops, having met first at Tyre to consider the charges against Athanasius, convened at Jerusalem in September and admitted Arius and Euzoius to communion, the emperor having accepted their orthodoxy and having invited the council to examine their creed. The council, as well as informing the emperor of their actions, wrote to the church in Alexandria and bishops and clergy of Egypt and Libya telling them of their decision, urging them to receive back the two and enclosing the emperor's letter of recommendation based on personal interviews. The bishops speak of Arius's "recantation," which in the light of his enigmatic statements in his letter to Constantine might suggest further concessions on his part. However, Athanasius, who had been condemned and deposed by the Tyre council, did not receive the letter, since he had taken the opportunity to travel secretly to Constantinople to confront the emperor. This ended in failure and led to his first exile. The way was thus open for Arius to return to Alexandria, but this provoked rioting and he was again refused communion. Constantine recalled him once more to Constantinople, where he had influential friends such as Eusebius, now bishop there, who probably helped him escape punishment for what had happened. Finally, in the summer of 336 a council was held in Constantinople to deal with Marcellus, the last prominent foe of Arius, who had attacked Asterius and the Eusebian party and failed to attend the Council of Jerusalem when he understood that Arius would be readmitted by it. Besides condemning and deposing Marcellus, the council pressed the elderly bishop, Alexander, to receive Arius into communion. The emperor also examined Arius who, to his surprise, agreed to subscribe on oath to the creed of Nicaea, and he ordered Alexander to readmit the penitent.

What happened next is only attested in a much later letter of Athanasius, although he claims an eyewitness, his friend the Alexandrian presbyter Macarius. According to Athanasius's account the emperor ordered Alexander on a Saturday to admit Arius at the service the next day. Alexander, accompanied by Macarius, shut himself in the episcopal church (*Hagia Irene*) fasting and praying that either he or Arius might die before morning. Arius himself, answering an urgent call of nature, found a public lavatory and suffered some kind of hemorrhage from which he died.

II.   Writings

Very little actually written by Arius survives and all of it in works of his opponents, Athanasius and Epiphanius, if also in later historians such as Socrates, Sozomen, and Theodoret. Three letters are extant: Arius's creedal statement to Alexander of perhaps 321, his letter to Eusebius of Nicomedia of later in 321 or early 322, and his joint creedal statement with Euzoius to Constantine of 327. There are also fragments of his poem, *Thalia*, preserved in two places in Athanasius: in his *First Discourse* of around 340 and his *On the Synods* of 359–61. The former shows unmistakable signs of Athanasius's editing and selection, while the latter is more obviously a unity and may well go back to Arius himself. The date of the work is disputed: it seems to have been inspired by Eusebius and his party's propaganda campaign, and shows signs of being early, perhaps before Arius left Alexandria. The beginning is preserved in Athanasius's *First Discourse* and the content seems mainly in line with what Arius says in his first two letters. With suitable caution it will be used here to supplement the information in the letters in an attempt to reconstruct the main lines of Arius's theology. In addition, phrases from a later letter of Arius of around 332–3 are quoted in Constantine's letter to him of 333. Further writings of a learned Alexandrian presbyter of Arius's stamp such as treatises or scriptural commentaries may well have been destroyed as a result of Constantine's edict of 333; we should not be surprised that what survives is in works by his opponents or others quoting them. Certainly later supposed "Arians" of both East and West appear to know little of or about his writings.

III. Theology

The very limited, sometimes problematic, evidence of Arius's views, primary and secondary, makes it very difficult to reconstruct his theology, but perhaps not impossible. Despite their bias, his opponents could not have got away with entirely misrepresenting his theology, and we have the balancing factor not only of his genuine writings but also of the evidence of other writers sympathetic to him and hostile to the Nicene party, such as Eusebius of Caesarea and Philostorgius. As noted above, the primary evidence must be the three letters, supplemented by the *Thalia* and the reports of his opponents, particularly Alexander in his two letters, *hē philarchos* of 321 and *henos sōmatos* of 324/5 (probably written by his deacon Athanasius), Constantine in his letter to Arius, and Athanasius in his *Discourses, Letter to the Bishops of Egypt and Libya* and *On the Synods*.

As a learned presbyter of Alexandria, expounding scripture regularly, claiming to be a wise teacher in a tradition of sages, Arius must surely have taught across the spectrum of Christian theology, as Clement and Origen had done and as his creedal statement and later letter to Constantine imply. Thus even though his surviving statements are almost exclusively concerned with the doctrine of God proper, *theologia* in the strict sense, and in particular with the relation of Father and Son, he also treats christology and alludes to the Holy Spirit and to a trinity of sorts. What is more, although the thesis of the American scholars Gregg and Groh (1981), identifying as central to Arianism a particular type of soteriology, namely by advance, has been strongly criticized, Richard Hanson is surely right to argue (1988, 96–8, 121–2) that Arius must have had a doctrine of salvation, even if it does not seem to feature explicitly in his surviving fragments. Thus in what follows I will sketch out what we can plausibly deduce Arius appears to have believed about (1) God, (2) Christ, and (3) salvation.

In his doctrine of *God* Arius seems to have been very perturbed by developments in Origen's view of the eternal generation of the Son, such as represented by his bishop, Alexander, and the consequent blurring of the distinctions between Father and Son, Creator and creation. Furthermore, this seemed to suggest that

God consisted of two coeternal beings, the heresy of Sabellius according to Arius, about which, as a Libyan, he was particularly sensitive. It also suggested the emanationist theories of Valentinus, and the materialist conceptions of the Son as a consubstantial part of God, which he attributes to the Manichees, who were very influential in Alexandria at this time. Such threats to the Christian doctrine of God must have seemed very real to Arius, part of the atmosphere of the cosmopolitan, pluralist city in which he lived and worked, a city which had just witnessed a powerful pagan backlash against the Christians and their God. Furthermore, the striking absence of any reference to the Logos or Word in the two early letters, and its coming last in a list of the Son's titles in the *Thalia*, might suggest Arius was wary of the Logos doctrine, concerned by certain implications of it as found in his predecessors such as Justin Martyr, with his talk of a "second God," distinct in number and so on. Thus he rejects Hieracas's analogy, echoing that of Justin, of a lamp lit from another. Although we only hear in his opponents' accounts of a distinction drawn by him between the Logos as an attribute immanent in God and the Logos as an improper or courtesy title applied to the Son because of his participation in that immanent Logos, such a view does seem to underlie the views of early supporters of Arius such as Asterius, and thus may well be a genuine feature of his beliefs. Such an idiosyncratic view, rejecting the assumed identity between the immanent and expressed Logos of the earlier Apologists, and the deduction from that of the coeternity of the Son as Word and Wisdom, may well have been designed to avoid the ditheistic implications of the traditional doctrine, and the occurrence of the term in his creed of 327 as applied to the Son may be part of his deliberate attempt to present a more traditional type of formula.

Arius is thus determined to stress the absolute unity, otherness, and transcendence of God, as is clear from his letter to Alexander, with its unparalleled piling up of attributes, negative and positive, each qualified by the adverb "alone." Significantly, the first three of these are the same, if in a different order, in the letter and the *Thalia* as quoted by Athanasius in *On the Synods* 15: "unbegotten" (*agennētos*), "eternal" (*aidios*), "unbegun" (*anarchos*). God too is "unalterable" (*atreptos*) and "unchangeable" (*analloiōtos*). God, as the cause of all things, says Arius, is unbegun and altogether sole, before all things as monad and beginning (*archē*) of all. This God begat (*gennaō*) an only (*monogenēs*) Son before eternal times, through whom he created time and the universe, begetting him truly and not in appearance, making him subsist by his own will, unalterable (*atreptos*) and unchangeable (*analloiōtos*), a perfect creature (*ktisma*) of God but not as one of the creatures, an offspring (*gennēma*) but not as one of the offspring. Arius then rejects any materialistic interpretation as found in the classic heretics, Valentinus, Mani, and Sabellius, as well as contemporaries such as Hieracas, and insists that the Son was created (note the identification of begetting and creating) by the will of God before times and ages, having his life, being, and glories from the Father, who, Arius insists, did not, in making the Son heir of everything, deprive himself of what he has ingenerately in himself, since he is the source of all things. From this Arius deduces that there are three hypostases, reflecting Origen's terminology, but as we shall see, not his Trinitarian understanding of them. Indeed Arius seems little concerned with the Holy Spirit in his surviving fragments, concentrating on Father and Son.

In his letter Arius once more stresses the uniqueness of God, as unbegun and sole, in contrast to the Son who, as begotten apart from time by the Father, and also, in a further echo of the terminology of Prov. 8.22–5, created and established before ages, did not exist before he was begotten. However, as begotten in this way he is unique, alone made to subsist by the Father, although not eternal, co-eternal or co-unoriginate with the Father. The Father is therefore— logically and perhaps even temporally, in the sense of unmeasured time (Stead 1999, 102–3)—prior to the Son as the source of his being, glories, and life; he is above him as his God. Arius claims to have heard this in Alexander's sermons. But if this account is designed to appeal to Alexander and his Origenist theological views, it also finds an echo and complement in Arius's letter to the Lucianist Eusebius of Nicomedia, similarly designed to appeal to him, a theologian of a rather different stamp. In it he attacks Alexander's Origenist teaching, which he represents as insisting on the co-eternity of Father and eternally begotten Son as both unbegotten. In contrast, Arius insists, appealing to the similar views of Eusebius of Caesarea and

other bishops of Palestine, Syria, and Cilicia, that God alone exists without beginning prior to his Son. The Son is not ingenerate, nor from any lower substrate but subsisted by the will and counsel of God before times and ages, fully God, only-begotten, unchangeable (*analloiōtos*). Arius claims he is persecuted for teaching that the Son had a beginning, while God did not, and that the Son is, therefore, out of nothing: neither a part of God nor from any lower substrate.

To this evidence from the two early letters we could add the data of the *Thalia*. Here Arius teaches that God is in his essence ineffable and invisible to all, including the Son, who only sees him in the manner appropriate to him as a creature. This seems borne out by the claim in *henos sōmatos* that the Son does not perfectly and accurately know or see the Father. Indeed the Son does not even know his own essence. This assertion, however, may also reflect the need to make some concession to the party of Eusebius of Nicomedia, for whom God was knowable through the Son as his exact image, and who, according to Athanasius, pressurized Arius to compose the *Thalia*. Here too Arius may have been forced to modify what he really thought about the incomprehensibility and ineffability of God.

Now although Arius can and does appeal to biblical texts such as Prov. 8.22–5 to demonstrate the Son's origin from and relation to the Father, this highly abstract view of God as totally transcendent and ineffable, invisible to and prior to the Son, producing him from nothing by a sheer act of will, seems to derive not so much from scripture or even tradition, despite Arius's appeal to it, as from his encounter with contemporary philosophical theology and certain problems thrown up by it. On one side, he rejects all materialistic views of God, insisting, perhaps under the influence of contemporary Platonism, on his utter transcendence, ineffability, and non-communicability. Conversely, his insistence on the absolute gulf between God as Creator and all creation, including the Son, and hence on creation as out of nothing through God's exercise of will, finds no real parallel in pagan philosophy (Hanson, 1988, 98). It may well reflect his rejection of surviving traces of Origen's doctrine of the eternity of the Son and of the created rational beings. Such a doctrine must have seemed to Arius to veer too close to Valentinian emanationism. As with so many early Christian theologians, from Justin onwards, what Arius seems to reflect is a certain eclecticism, selecting from the spectrum of pagan philosophical thinking what ideas best suited his Christian concerns and seemed to find some support from scripture.

Thus it may be that Arius was seeking a more precise and accurate definition of the terms used to describe God and the divine, distinguishing God in the strict sense (*ho theos*) from everything else created by him, starting with the Son (*theos*, or *monogenēs theos*) and his unique status as only-begotten, created directly by God's free act of will as the instrument (*organon*) by which all else, and particularly the human race, was created. At the same time Arius seems to be seeking to understand more precisely what the terms used to describe God's creative functions in scripture, such as those in Prov. 8:22–5 ("create" or "found" [*ktizō*], "beget" [*gennaō*], "establish" [*themeliō*]) can really signify. Because God cannot share his unique being with anybody else, since he is by definition unalterable and unchangeable, such language must be metaphorical and simply refer to God's creative activity by will out of nothing. Texts that refer to anyone or anything as "from God" thus cannot mean from the actual being of God. The term "beget" used of Wisdom in Proverbs 8 and traditionally interpreted in terms of the Son must be glossed as "create" in a spiritual, not material sense, ruling out any appeal to the human analogy of fathers begetting consubstantial sons from their own being.

Thus although Arius does use traditional language going back to Origen when he refers in his letter to Alexander to there being three hypostases, he departs from the Origenist tradition by at once insisting that the three are entirely dissimilar in being, with the Father as infinitely more glorious than the others. If the Son is only-begotten God, mighty God, than whom God cannot beget anyone superior, the Spirit seems much inferior, certainly not called "God" but merely the first being to be created by the Son, the illuminator of God's prophets and sages. These include Arius's teachers, mentioned in Arius's uncontentious creed of 327, which, echoing Eusebius of Caesarea's statement in his letter to his church after Nicaea, cites the baptismal formula of Matt. 28.19 to illustrate the distinction of hypostases. God in the strict sense pre-exists the Son, and only becomes Father when, before

(measured) time, he begets the Son as the beginning (*archē*) of Prov. 8:22. Therefore, as Arius states in the *Thalia*, there was when he was not Father, as there was when the Son was not.

We have already noted and suggested a reason for the virtual absence of the term "*Logos*" in the genuine early writings of Arius, apart from its inclusion as the last in a list of the Son's aspects (*epinoiai*) in the *Thalia*. However, both the encyclical *henos sōmatos* (probably the work of Athanasius) and Athanasius himself in his *First Discourse* of around 340 claim that Arius taught two Words or Wisdoms, distinguishing between the attribute coexistent with God on the one hand, and the Son on the other. The latter was named, but only by a misuse of language or by grace, as Word and Wisdom as having come into existence through and participating in the former. This seems borne out to some extent both by Arius's statement in the *Thalia* that Wisdom existed as wisdom by the will of a wise God and by his reference in his statement of faith preserved by Constantine to "an unoriginated [*anarchos*] and unending word [*logos*] of his substance," and to "the spirit of eternity … in the superior Word [*Logos*]." But such a doctrine, as indicated, is idiosyncratic and not shared by his contemporaries.

In the light of all this, how are we to understand Arius's doctrine of God, especially as regards the status of the Son? Opinion is divided on this. Some interpreters, particularly relying on the *Thalia*, have tended to stress the subordinate status of the Son in Arius's scheme, emphasizing his created and dependent nature, his not sharing the being of God and having a beginning, his being unchangeable not by nature but only by grace, his inability to see and know God perfectly and accurately or even to know his own essence, the fact that he worships God and that he was created as an instrument specifically to create us. Conversely, others have stressed his unique status as only-begotten God, fully God, mighty God, given the same attributes as God (unalterable and unchangeable) in the two early letters apparently without qualification, and someone than whom God cannot beget anyone more excellent, superior, or greater, through whom God created everything else. Even Arius's insistence in his letter to Alexander on calling the Son a creature (*ktisma*), "but not as one of the creatures," can best be interpreted as marking out the uniqueness of the Son. Everything hangs on how we evaluate the Son's status, particularly his unchangeability, especially when it comes to christology and soteriology. Is the Son immutable by nature or only by grace and effort of will? It is striking that the latter interpretation is only found in critics such as Athanasius and the authors of the statement of the Council of Antioch of 324.

That issue brings us to consider Arius's *Christology*, as far as it can be reconstructed. Certainly Alexander, in *hē philarchos*, begins his attack on Arius and his supporters by stressing how they "organized a gang to fight Christ," noting how they pick out every scriptural statement about his saving dispensation (*oikonomia*) and his humiliation to support their views, claiming they can become sons of God like him (cf. Isa. 1.2). Other texts cited are Isa. 45(44).8 on the Son's choice and anointing and Heb. 1.9 where this same verse is applied to Christ. Unfortunately there is really no allusion to christology in the early letters and *Thalia*, and we learn nothing of Arius's own distinctive views from his confession of faith to Constantine of 327. This simply echoes the scriptural language of contemporary creeds such as those of Nicaea and of Eusebius of Caesarea. However, there are, as Hanson has noted (1988, 9–10), several tantalizing phrases in Arius's statement of faith preserved in Constantine's letter to him of 333, which relate to christology. After allusions to God and apparently to the Word, Arius refers to "the alien nature of the body as regards the implementation [*oikonomia*] of the divine energies," which would seem to refer to the incarnation. Later on Constantine quotes Arius as saying, "No! I for my part do not wish God to be involved with the suffering of insults," and "whatever you take away from him, in that respect you make him less." Further on he quotes Arius as saying, "Christ suffered for us … yes, but there is a danger that we may appear to lessen him in some way." From Constantine's response he clearly interprets Arius as rejecting any suffering on the part of God as a result of the incarnation, in what seems an allusion to Phil. 2:6–8. Further, the earlier phrase about the alien body would seem to suggest Arius wanted to distinguish the body of Christ from the divine element or powers involved. On the other hand, he does affirm the suffering of Christ, seeking to distance God from it.

How are we to interpret this seeming paradox? Is he simply reflecting here the traditional Alexandrian doctrine of the interchange of properties (*communicatio idiomatum*) pioneered by Origen? In his statement of faith to Constantine of 327 he has God the Word as subject of the events of the incarnation and passion. Is he then attempting here to distinguish between the body which suffers and the divine element which does not? Or does he really believe, as Hanson argues (1988, 121–2), in a suffering God? We have seen how in his two early letters he insists, without apparent qualification, on the unchangeable nature of the Son.

Can we clarify this from other sources? Hanson (1988, 111) argues that Arius's christology involved a union of human flesh or a human body and the divine Word or Son, with no room for a human soul. He appeals to Eustathius of Antioch's claim that the Arians denied a human soul in Christ to ensure that the divine could change and suffer. He also claims that Lucian of Antioch taught such a christology of a *sōma apsuchon*, seeing Arius as undoubtedly his pupil in this, as were the later Neo-Arians. However, not all scholars are convinced (Rankin, 2000, 985) and, once again, in the light of the silence or ambiguity of our sources, it all depends on how we interpret Arius's view of the Son and also his understanding of salvation. Was the Son, as Gregg and Groh argue (1981, 14–20), essentially a mutable creature, a created Creator and saved savior, who is promoted to divine status through his obedience and saves us by his example? Or is he, as Hanson argues, a suffering God, with a reduced divinity which could become incarnate and suffer? Such a divinity, it should be noted, is nevertheless the only kind of divinity in which we can really participate and thus be saved. For if the Son cannot share in the being of God, who is infinitely superior to him, how can we, who are the creatures of that Son?

This brings us finally to the issue of Arius's *soteriology*. Hanson is surely right to insist that he must have had one even though he himself seems to make almost no explicit allusion to it in his letters and the *Thalia* excerpts. This must make questionable the claim of Gregg and Groh that a certain view of salvation as reconstructed by them was central to Arius and his theology. What is more, their reconstruction is weakened by its reliance on the claims of opponents and on the genuineness of the *Third Discourse*

(Kannengiesser, 1991, II, 470–1; Rankin, 2000, 984). Williams (2001, 258) has claimed to find no real support for their understanding of salvation by advance in earlier or contemporary thinkers. Moreover, Hanson (1988, 97) has insisted that the Son cannot give an example of human achievement of perfection because he is precisely not a human being. But he has also pointed (1988, 121–2) to what he thinks is the true rationale of Arianism, linking the doctrine of God reciprocally with the doctrine of salvation. As he notes, its elaborate theology of the relation between the Son and the Father was devised to find a way of envisaging a Christian doctrine of God that would make it possible to be faithful to the biblical witness of a God who suffers. This was done by distinguishing between the supreme God who cannot suffer and the Son, a reduced God, who could become incarnate and suffer, thereby giving humanity an example of God suffering as humans suffer.

But is this view, which Hanson dubs "exemplary," if in a different sense, any more adequate than that of Gregg and Groh? Does it do justice to Arius's repeated insistence on the unchangeability of the Son and the evidence, if ambiguous, of his statement of faith to Constantine? Arius, while rejecting any kind of suffering on God's part in the incarnation, yet allows the incarnate Son to suffer, if even here too insisting on a distinction between the body and the divine energies, and perhaps also denying any lessening of the Son's divinity. Salvation would thus seem, as with Athanasius, to involve some kind of deification—God the Son takes on a human body, to suffer and die in it but also to enable us to share in his divine life. Once more Arius seems to be attempting to define more carefully the meaning and implications of the terms "God" and "divine."

Some light may be cast on this by examining Arius's understanding of how we can know God. We have seen his stress in the *Thalia* on God's ineffability, and invisibility even to the Son, but also his qualification of that: by the power by which God sees, the Son can see the Father. A similar interpretation must apply to the Son's knowledge—it must correspond to the Son's nature as created and different in being. The Son can have, if not a comprehensive knowledge of God, yet an appropriate one. So too with us humans: we too can have a knowledge of the ineffable, transcendent God. Indeed this is exactly what Arius himself claims in the opening lines of the *Thalia* preserved by Athanasius. Arius has learned the truth from God's sage servants, via the Holy Spirit, and, what is more, he claims to have wisdom and knowledge *learned from God*. So humans can have genuine and appropriate, if not comprehensive, knowledge of God, and can do so, it would seem, through the Son and the Spirit. Such an interpretation illuminates Arius's doctrine of the three hypostases, his version of the Trinity, and explains why he needs such a doctrine. As the task of the Son, our creator, is to grasp and make known God as far as he understands him, so the task of the Spirit, his first creation, is to communicate that saving knowledge to us.

Salvation then, as with Athanasius writing not long afterwards, would seem to involve both the incarnate Son's impartation to us of true, divinely inspired wisdom, true knowledge of God, and his overcoming of the power of sin and death, enabling us to share in the divine life, an insight going back at least as far as Irenaeus. But how, for Arius, do we share in the divine life? As we have seen, while he implacably rejects any sharing of God's being by the Son, he does insist on the Son's unique status as only-begotten God, fully God, unalterable and unchangeable, who participates in God's immanent Wisdom and Word. Similarly, while the Son is not a creature like us, but divine, unique, and our creator, yet he can take on human flesh and enable us to participate in him, becoming divine by adoption, not nature. Once more Arius is seeking to clarify and distinguish levels of the divine: God at the top with his supreme unchangeable, unalterable being that cannot be shared; below him the Son, also unchangeable and unalterable (if by grace and will), who can participate in God's attributes, but who has a lesser, if unique, degree of divinity; and below him, us, his mutable creatures, who can yet participate in the immutable, unchangeable character of his divinity (if only by grace).

IV.   Significance

As contemporary scholars agree, Arius is something of a loner, a radical, who, though with a small, keen band of supporters including some significant bishops, never formed a real party and was soon forgotten. He clearly had to modify his views to find support. Moreover, the lack of evidence, as we have seen, makes it very hard to reconstruct his theological views. Nevertheless he marks a turning point in Christian theology. His protest against contemporary views of Father and Son and radical insistence on the transcendence of God, backed by appeal to scripture and tradition, led to over half a century of heated theological debate in East and West, resulting in what Hanson calls "the Christian doctrine of God." Even if the concept of "Arianism" has been shown to be dubious, the issues he raised concerning the doctrines of God, Christ, creation, and salvation exercised the greatest theological minds of several generations and led directly to the Niceno-Constantinopolitan creed of 381, one of the few threads still holding together the tattered robe of Christendom.

References

Gregg, Robert and Groh, Dennis. 1981. *Early Arianism: A View of Salvation*. London: SCM Press.

Hanson, Richard P. C. 1988. *The Search for the Christian Doctrine of God*. Edinburgh: T&T Clark.

Kannengiesser, Charles. 1991. *Arius and Athanasius: Two Alexandrian Theologians*. Hampshire: Variorum.

Opitz, Hans-Georg. 1934. *Athanasius Werke*, vol. 3.1 Urkunden zur Geschichte des arianischen Streites 318–28. Berlin and Leipzig: De Gruyter.

Parvis, Sara. 2006. *Marcellus of Ancyra and the Lost Years of the Arian Controversy 325–345*. Oxford: Oxford University Press.

Rankin, David. 2000. "Arianism." In *The Early Christian World*, 2 vols., ed. Philip F. Esler. London and New York: Routledge, pp. 975–90.

Stead, G. Christopher. 1997. "Was Arius a Neoplatonist?" *Studia Patristica* 33: 39–52.

Stead, G. Christopher. 1999. "Philosophy in Origen and Arius." In *Origeniana Septima*, ed. W. A. Bienert and U. Kühneweg. Leeuven: University Press/Peeters, pp. 101–8.

Williams, Rowan D. 2001. *Arius: Heresy and Tradition*, 2nd ed. London: SCM Press.

Athanasius (c.295–373)

Tarmo Toom

I. Life

Athanasius, a fourth-century bishop of Alexandria, was among those polarizing figures who left only very few impartial. His friends regarded him as a saint and his enemies as a despot. Gregory of Nazianzus began his panegyric with words, "In praising Athanasius, I shall be praising virtue" (*Or.* 21.1); but, in their encyclical, the bishops at the Council of Philippopolis called him a "sacrilegious plague" and "criminal" (Hilary of Poitiers, *C. Valens and Ursacius* 1.8, 14). Even today when scholars write about Athanasius, his admirers author hagiographies and his despisers demonologies. Athanasius's fame/notoriety ranges from being a staunch defender of orthodoxy to being a power-hungry gangster. Accordingly, his steadfastness is interpreted either as heroic resoluteness or autocratic obstinacy.

There are several accounts of Athanasius's career: a Syriac *Index* to his *Festal Letters*, the so-called *Historia acephala* (i.e., a chronicle of Athanasius's life), Gregory of Nazianzus' panegyric to Athanasius (*Or.* 21), and a Coptic eulogy. We also have the *Ecclesiastical Histories* of Rufinus, Socrates, Sozomen, Theodoret, Philostorgius, and the writings of Hilary of Poitiers and Epiphanius of Salamis. In addition, we have Athanasius's own reports of "how things really were," which have cast their spell over all the accounts of the early church historians, except Philostorgius. However, the friendly meta-narratives about Athanasius have

probably suppressed the other not-so-friendly shadow-narratives. Thus, Athanasius cannot be taken as the final authority on Athanasius.

Athanasius was born in the 295s CE, that is, during the persecution of Diocletian and right before the great fourth-century theological upheavals. His life turned out to be as turbulent as the times during which he lived. It is significant that the young Athanasius saw Christianity becoming a *legal* religion of the Roman Empire (in the 310s), and he almost saw Christianity becoming the *official* religion of the Roman Empire (in the 380s).

Athanasius was born in Alexandria, in one of the most important ecclesiastical centers of the ancient world (*Apol. sec.* 51). Partisan accounts of his childhood provide little historical evidence, although they can be portentous and entertaining, as is the story about young Athanasius playing baptism at the seashore (Rufinus, *Hist. eccl.* 10.15).

More reliable information begins with Athanasius's joining the episcopal household in Alexandria. In 319, he became a deacon and secretary of Alexander of Alexandria, his patron and mentor. A tenth-century Arabic *History of the Patriarchs of Alexandria* reports that, "Athanasius remained like a son with the father Alexander, who educated him with gentleness in every art." Yet, Athanasius's classical education seems to have been rather modest. Gregory mentions his "brief study of literature and philosophy," which was

The Student's Companion to the Theologians, First Edition. Edited by Ian S. Markham.
© 2013 Blackwell Publishing Ltd. Published 2013 by Blackwell Publishing Ltd.

necessary "so that he might not be utterly unskilled in such subjects, or ignorant of matters which he had determined to despise" (*Or.* 21.6). However, Athanasius's education in the Scriptures seems to have been more thorough. The above-mentioned Arabic text claims that, "[h]e memorized the gospels." Gregory reinforces the point that Athanasius understood all the books of the Scriptures "with a depth such as none else has applied even to one of them" (*Or.* 21.6). It is not to pre-judge that thereby his theology was "biblical" and that of his opponents was not. Athanasius had his theological presuppositions like any other reader of the Scriptures. But it remains true that his thought, theological discourse, and aspirations were thoroughly molded by the Scriptures (Ernest, 2004).

Athanasius emerges as the right-hand man of bishop Alexander. When the latter began to impose doctrinal unity on the Egyptian church, young Athanasius was entrusted with significant duties, including drafting Alexander's encyclicals (e.g., *Encyclical Letter of Alexander*). As a deacon, Athanasius also accompanied Alexander to the first ecumenical Council of Nicaea in 325. Eventually the young deacon became an unwavering defender of the theology of this council.

In 328, Athanasius was consecrated the bishop of Alexandria (*Index* 1). Thus wished the deceased Alexander. But the facts that Athanasius became a bishop of a major see before his canonical age (30) (*Index* 3), and that he was not even a presbyter at that time, clouded the legitimacy of his election and played into the hands of his ecclesiastical enemies. Philostorgius, an anti-Athanasian church historian, contends that Athanasius was ordained at night by two bishops (*Hist. eccl.* 2.11). (A canonical ordination would have required three bishops. All other sources mention six and seven ordaining bishops.)

As a new bishop, Athanasius had to deal with two inherited problems of the Egyptian church: Melitian schism and Arius.

Ecclesiological controversies had troubled Egypt already for some time. Although the Council of Nicaea urged the "schismatic" Melitian church to be reintegrated into the catholic church of Peter of Alexandria and his successor Alexander, the consecration of Athanasius as a new bishop undermined any plans of reconciliation. Athanasius decided to ignore

this decision of the Council of Nicaea completely, despite the warning given by the emperor himself (*Apol. sec.* 59).

On the other hand, the catholic church of Peter and Alexander experienced its own division—not about schism but about heresy. A priest called Arius had begun to spread a teaching that the Son was a lesser God than the Father. Since the Council of Nicaea had condemned Arius, Athanasius stubbornly continued to insist on *that* decision of the Council of Nicaea and refused Arius's re-admission into the Alexandrian church.

In short, Melitian resistance and "Arian" controversialists found a common goal—to get rid of the troublesome Athanasius. It is a truism that common enemies often unite better than shared convictions.

The outcry against Athanasius led to the summoning of the Synod of Tyre in 335 by Constantine (Sozomen, *Hist. eccl.* 2.25). The atmosphere was so tense that the presence of a military guard seemed necessary. This synod, which received Melitians into communion and proclaimed Arius orthodox, was anything but friendly towards Athanasius. Melitians and "Arians"—whom Athanasius now grouped as "Eusebians" (*Apol. sec.* 87; *Decr.* 1)—accused the bishop of Alexandria of sacrilege, bribery, rape, and murder. First, Athanasius was indicted for ordering his colleague Macarius to break the Melitian Ischyras's chalice and overturn his altar in order to prevent him from practicing his priestly office. Second, Athanasius was charged with giving a box of gold to an imperial officer, Philoumenus, who proved to be an enemy of Constantine. Third, Athanasius's opponents brought forth a woman who delivered "the speech she had been taught" (Rufinus, *Hist. eccl.* 10.18), saying that Athanasius had violated her. However, the woman confused presbyter Timothy with Athanasius and the scheme misfired. Fourth, Athanasius was blamed for organizing the killing of a Melitian bishop, Arsenius, and cutting off his hand in order to perform magic. This accusation did not stick, though, because Athanasius's friends managed to capture the hiding Arsenius and bring him in front of the bishops—with two perfectly healthy hands.

Those who tried to dislodge Athanasius almost always insisted that Athanasius used force to suppress his enemies. Such frequent accusations of heavy-handedness may prove indeed that Athanasius did not hesitate to use his political power whenever it suited him. Intimidation and violence have always been great silencers of opposition. A more recently discovered papyrus letter written by a Melitian called Callistus—perhaps the smoking gun?—suggests that Athanasius and his intoxicated supporters harassed, beat, and chased away Melitians and those who favored them. Considering this evidence credible, Hanson (1988) writes, "It [i.e., the papyrus letter] is a factual account written for people under persecution, a private missive not intended for publication nor propaganda, and therefore all the more damaging" (252; but see Arnold, 1991, 71–89, 179–82).

It might be safe to assume, however, that it was ugly on all sides. (One can get an idea of the low-level ecclesiastical politics from the shocking story narrated in Athanasius's *H. Ar.* 20.). "Expression of religious intolerance was part and parcel of the peculiar nature of the exercise of power in late antiquity" (Brown, 1995, 53). It is estimated that, after the Council of Nicaea, the number of deaths of "the victims of creedal differences" was roughly about 25,000 (MacMullen, 2006, 56).

At "that Synod of his enemies" (i.e., Synod of Tyre) (*Index* 8), the bishop of Alexandria was excommunicated and sent to exile to Trier, in Gaul. Perhaps the deciding factor that turned Constantine against Athanasius was a fabrication of a new accusation that Athanasius withheld grain shipments to Constantinople (*Apol. sec.* 87).

All things considered, Athanasius was accused of *ecclesiastical* disobedience, because he refused to accept Arius into communion after he was restored by his friends in 327. Moreover, defying orders and leaving Tyre before the verdict of the hostile synod was announced also brought about a dangerous accusation of *political* disobedience. His opponents tagged him as a man "who set at naught the commands of the ruler" (Sozomen, *Hist. eccl.* 2.25). That Athanasius went straight to the emperor to petition his rehabilitation and honorable return did not bring about any lasting imperial reconsiderations. But it disclosed that Athanasius had the audacity to defy hostile synods and even emperors, and also the skill to avoid the fatal consequences of such dangerous audaciousness.

As always, the death of an emperor brings drastic changes. Constantine died in 337. His son Constantinus came to know Athanasius in Trier and decided that his father had protected the bishop from his enemies by sending him to exile (*Apol. sec.* 87). Equipped with this ingenious interpretation of his exile and with an imperial letter, Athanasius returned to his see, only to face the "fire and brimstone" of "Eusebians" (i.e., the followers of Eusebius of Nicomedia whom Athanasius equated with "Arians" for polemical reasons). "Eusebians" continued to accuse Athanasius of violating the decisions of the Synod of Tyre, of using violence in his unstoppable fury against fellow Alexandrians, and of setting aside the funds meant for widows (*Apol. sec.* 3–5, 18). They also managed to install an alternative bishop according to their own liking—Gregory of Cappadocia (*Index* 11). Prefect Philagrius used his soldiers to turn the churches over to Gregory while the condemnation of Athanasius was renewed by the Council of Antioch in 339. Even the show of public solidarity by Saint Anthony did not secure Athanasius's dominance (*Vit. Ant.* 69–70). The unseated Athanasius went into hiding and then fled to Rome where he sought the protection of Pope Julius and Emperor Constans. The recent events back home provoked Athanasius to write his *Encyclical Letter*, in which he tried to rally every official of importance against Gregory and against "Arians"/"Eusebians" who stood behind the new "anti-bishop." In Rome, Athanasius also authored his mega-treatise *Orations against the Arians*, which created an impression that to support Athanasius was to support orthodoxy. "The line which divides historical integrity and theological polemic in the writings of the bishop of Alexandria is very thin indeed" (Arnold, 1991, 9).

The western emperor Constans decided to resolve the bickering of the competing theological factions, to overturn the decisions of the Council of Tyre, and to rehabilitate Athanasius by summoning the Council of Sardica (342 or 343). But Pope Julius's initiative in overturning the conciliar decisions of the eastern bishops only offended the easterners. Instead of a reconciling council, two mutually deposing councils convened in Sardica and Philippopolis. Such a sad development indicated a deep theological divide between the emerging Athanasian pro-Nicenes and their adversaries. The Council of Sardica got

Athanasius in trouble, though, because many eastern bishops came to regard him as an associate of the condemned "modalist" Marcellus of Ancyra. (Yet Athanasius was never condemned because of false teachings but always because of his behavior.)

Since Athanasius managed to plead his case personally before the eastern emperor Constantius, and since Gregory, his Alexandrian replacement, had died, Athanasius returned to his home city in 346. He was "thought worthy of a grand reception" (*Index* 18). Back in office and full of resolve, Athanasius continued his anti-"Arian" campaign. The late 340s proved to be a most prolific period in Athanasius's life. He penned various treatises and organized alliances which had the eventual effect of uniting all like-minded theologians behind the Nicene Creed.

But Constans died in 350 and Constantius, the eastern emperor, had less and less sympathy toward pro-Nicenes. His theological preferences sided with "Arians." Eventually, Emperor Constantius resorted to military force (!) to arrest Athanasius. "More than 5000 soldiers" surrounded the Church of Theonas, where Athanasius was presiding at a Vigil service (*Fug.* 24). But, having the unwavering support of his congregation and local monks, Athanasius managed to disappear into the night and flee to the desert for about the next five years. Emperor Constantius was frustrated. In one of his letters, he cursed, "For while that pestilent fellow Athanasius is driven from place to place, being convicted of basest crimes, for which he would suffer the punishment he deserves, if one were to kill him ten times over …" (*Apol. Const.* 30). Hiding in various monastic communities, Athanasius defended himself against all accusations by penning two treatises: *Defense of His Flight* and *Apology to Constantius*.

Athanasius' return to Alexandria in 361 was possible due to Emperor Julian's pardoning of all exiled bishops (*Index* 34)—for the emperor's own clever reasons. (As a believer in traditional Roman gods, Julian expected the quarrelling Christian factions to weaken each other.) It was not yet Athanasius's final return to his see, for he stayed in office for only about eight months. But almost immediately he convened an anti-"Arian" Synod of Alexandria (362), which created a powerful pro-Nicene coalition with some Homoeousians (i.e., with those who insisted that the Father and the Son are of "like essence" [*homoiousios*]. This synod published a document, *Tome to the People of Antioch*, which spelled out the pro-Nicene Trinitarian theology.

Yet Athanasius was dethroned again because Emperor Julian could not stand Athanasius's aggressive stance against "Arians" and his international activities beyond the bishop's Egyptian jurisdiction. Athanasius famously considered Julian "a small cloud which will soon pass away" (Socrates, *Hist. eccl.* 3.14). And indeed, Julian died in 363. The undefeatable patriarch was back in Alexandria. In these years, "Athanasius' prominence on the international scene faded as younger men began to do the cutting-edge theology and almost everyone lost interest in matters like chalices broken 30 years ago" (Brakke 2000, 1113).

Athanasius established good relations with the new emperor, Jovian. However, the bishop could not profit much from Jovian's favor, because the emperor died in the next year.

When Valens gained power in 364, he reinforced the banishment of all bishops exiled by Constantius (*Hist. aceph.* 10.15). Accordingly, and despite a public demonstration of solidarity, Athanasius had to pack his things once again in 365/366 and hide in his ancestral tomb (Socrates, *Hist. eccl.* 4.13). But Valens soon had greater problems on his hands (i.e., a war against a usurper, Procopius) than Athanasius. The emperor needed all the support he could get. So Athanasius was allowed to return. After spending altogether some 17 years in exile, the defiant bishop remained in possession of his see until his death in 373.

II.   Works

Athanasius is among those lucky authors whose writings have mostly survived—no doubt, because his name was associated with orthodoxy.

The five exiles had the curious effect of forcing Athanasius to grasp for his pen in order to refute his enemies and conduct the matters of his see with the help of theological treatises and *Festal Letters*. Almost all of his works bear a stamp of controversy. (Notice the word "against" in the many titles of Athanasius's treatises!) He wrote in Greek.

Against the Pagans and *On the Incarnation* are among his earliest works. These were probably written in the mid-330s and they discuss some key themes, such as how God relates to God's creation. The first treatise is an apologetic conversation with several "pagan" worldviews. It describes the human failure to remain positively related to its Creator, thus ending up in idolatry. The second treatise argues that the incarnation of the fully divine Son is the sole means of human salvation, the guarantee of restoring the relation between God and God's creation. There is also a short version of his *On the Incarnation*, but it is disputed whether Athanasius abridged this treatise himself or not.

A significant portion of Athanasius's works is constituted by his anti-"Arian" corpus. The three books of *Orations against the Arians* written in the 340s provide fragments of Arius's writings and Athanasius's exegetical and theological refutation of Arius's arguments. It also begins the polemical postulation of "Arianism" as a coherent theological position. (The third book of *Orations* was written a few years later under different circumstances. The fourth book is spurious.) *Apology against the Arians* (also called *Apologia secunda*) is a great mine of the documents of the "Arian" controversy. *Defense of the Nicene Definition*, written in the 350s, provides valuable information about the first ecumenical council and includes Athanasius's justification of the keyword "consubstantial" (*homoousios*). Next is the overly polemical/satirical *History of the Arians*. *On the Councils of Ariminum and Seleucia* was written in 362, and it includes a critical assessment of Homoean and Homoeousian doctrines of the Trinity, as well as precious documentation of the Trinitarian controversy. A dogmatic letter, *On the Opinion of Dionysius*, clears Dionysius, a former bishop of Alexandria, from accusations of being a subordinationist theologian and thereby prevents Arius from appealing to the Alexandrian tradition.

Athanasius was a significant letter writer. What he left behind, however, was not an organized collection of literary letters, but occasional writings on various topics in the forms of personal, circular, and *Festal Letters* (on liturgical and spiritual matters). (It was customary for the bishops of Alexandria to write Festal Letters each year before Lent.) His *Letters to Serapion* are significant because they defend the full divinity of the Holy Spirit, and *Letter to Epictetus* because it presents an anti-Apollinarian christology and argues that the body born from Mary was the incarnated God's own body. Athanasius's christological convictions gained prominence during the fifth-century controversies, because Cyril of Alexandria regarded them as orthodox and foundational.

Life of Anthony was composed while Athanasius was with monks in Upper Egypt. He had established good relations with "renouncers" in Alexandria, and with the emerging monastic communities during his earlier visitations as a new bishop of Alexandria (*Index* 2). *Life of Anthony* presents the desert saint as an ideal Christian. *Abba* Anthony became "the perfect instance of human appropriation of the Word's victory over sin and death" (Brakke, 1995, 13). Athanasius's *Life of Anthony*, in turn, became a "bestseller" and a prototype for many subsequent lives of saints. Its genre is protreptic; that is, it is a text which calls for imitation. Therefore, even if the basic outline of Anthony's life is credible, the strict historicity of the *Life of Anthony* is a moot point. But it is important to recognize the anti-"Arian" character of the *Life of Anthony*. The author's hidden agenda is to use the monastic hero to recruit monks for the pro-Athanasian cause.

Among his other ascetical writings, the four *Letters to Virgins*, which are extant in Coptic, Syriac, and Armenian translations, should be mentioned. Jerome reports that Athanasius also authored a whole treatise on virginity. However, several scholars doubt the authenticity of these letters and the available *On Virginity*. *Letter to Marcellinus* explains the importance of praying the Psalms and is a great example of Athanasius's authentic exegetical writings. Interestingly though, the bishop never authored a full-length commentary on a biblical book, although perhaps he started one on the Psalms shortly before his death. Nevertheless, apart from the exegesis provided in anti-"Arian" works, fragments of his catenas (i.e., collections of passages) on Genesis, Song of Songs, Job, Matthew, Luke, and First Corinthians are extant.

Since famous people always wrote "more" than they actually wrote, especially in antiquity, a significant corpus of spurious writings is attributed to Athanasius. There is an entire volume (*Patrologiae Graeca*, 28) of spurious works, in addition to those found in other volumes in the same series. The name Pseudo-Athanasius stands either for some anonymous authors, or for Apollinaris of Laodicea, Marcellus of Ancyra, Hesychius of Jerusalem, or Eusebius of Vercelli. The so-called Athanasian Creed (fifth to sixth century) is among the documents attributed to the famous bishop of Alexandria.

III. Theology

Whatever was the true character of Athanasius—the business of living and staying alive during tough times tends to make people hard—his theology deserves to be taken most seriously.

Anatolios (1998) has argued that "the center of coherence of Athanasius' theology [is] the distinction, and simultaneous relation, between God and the world" (3). God the Creator is infinite, transcendent, self-sufficient, and eternal; God's creation, however, is finite, contingent, and temporal. "Creation is not God. Nor God's contemporary, nor an emanation from God … It is the result of God's calling into being what formerly was not" (Pettersen, 1995, 22; cf. 1 Cor. 8.6). But even though the Creator God is other than the creation, God is still related to the creation. Athanasius is no cosmological dualist. Rather, he teaches that God, who is love and goodness, is the source, sustainer, and redeemer of his creation.

For Athanasius, this very distinction between the Creator and the creation was the device for constructing the "Arian heresy" (Gwynn, 2007, 231). That is, Arius's gravest category mistake was to place the Son on the side of the creation. Arius argued that the Son was not intrinsic to what God was. The Son was not born from the Father's *essence* but he was made by the Father's *will* and out of nothing (Arius, *Ep. Eus. Nic.* 1.5). The Son was created like the rest of the creation yet "before" the rest of the creation, including time (cf. Prov. 8:22; Col. 1:15).

For Athanasius, however, the Son was undoubtedly on the side of the Creator. The Son was God (John 1:1) and not a lesser mediating god between the transcendent God and the creation. Athanasius gave two good reasons for the full divinity of the Son. First, when Christians were worshiping Christ, they were not worshiping anything that was created and less than the Creator. That would have been idolatry! Second, a created and less-than-divine mediator could not save. "If being a creature, he [i.e., the Son] had become human, humanity would have remained just as it was, not joined to God" (*C. Ar.* 2.67).

Athanasius's case for the Son being on the side of the Creator consisted of several arguments. The Father and the Son are consubstantial, which means that they have the same divine essence (John 10:30). The only-begotten Son is born out of the Father's essence, and those who are born share the essence of the begetter. But the creation which is *made* rather than begotten has a different essence than its Creator. The Father and the Son are also co-eternal, for "father" and "son" are correlative terms. One implies the other. At the same time, the Father is not the Son. The Son shares all the divine properties of the Father, except paternity. "Everything that can be said of the Father can also be said of the Son, except his being called 'Father'" (*C. Ar.* 3.4). When the Scriptures indicate the inferiority of the Son (e.g., John 14:28), then such passages have to be interpreted in the light of the "double account of the Savior" (*C. Ar.* 3.29). This means that some Scriptures refer to the incarnated and others to the pre-existent Son. It is a mistake to deduce the ontological status of the pre-existent Son from his incarnational limitations. The Son was eternally "in the form of God" before his assumed human nature was "highly elevated" (Phil. 2:6–9; *C. Ar.* 1.41–3).

Athanasius was one of the first to argue that the Spirit, too, was on the side of the Creator. The actions of the Spirit prove that the Spirit is fully God. Since only God can divinize, the Spirit has to be divine. "The one who binds creation to the Word could not be among the creatures … the one in whom creation is divinized cannot be extrinsic to the divinity of the Father" (*Ep. Serap.* 1.25). Athanasius pronounced his Trinitarian doctrine of God thus: "The Trinity is holy and perfect, confessed as God in Father, Son, and Holy Spirit, having nothing foreign or extrinsic mingled with it, nor compounded of creator and created, but is wholly Creator and maker. It is identical with itself and indivisible in nature, and its activity is one" (ibid., 1.28).

Despite the fact that it was only in the 350s when Athanasius began to emphasize the importance of the Nicene pronouncements and formulas (Ayres 2004), the bishop of Alexandria was perhaps *the* defender of what was eventually considered to be the Nicene orthodoxy.

The incarnation of the Son was *God's* becoming human. But rather than providing a philosophical justification of the coexistence of human and divine natures in the person of the incarnated Son, Athanasius focused on the transformation of the human nature in this incarnated person. "Fundamentally, Athanasius'

Christology is what we might call '*hina* ["in order to"] Christology'; his Christological statements tend to be conceived in teleological terms, the *telos* ['goal'] being always our salvation" (Anatolios, 1998, 147). "He [i.e., the Son] has been manifested in a human body for this reason only … for the salvation of us human beings" (*Inc.* 1). But what kind of being did Jesus Christ have to be in order to save us? Functional christology has to answer, sooner or later, this more basic question about ontology.

Athanasius contended that the incarnated Son was fully divine and fully human, yet so that the Son of God was the subject and performer of all the acts of the incarnated Son. The body, the "instrument" through which the incarnated Son of God acted, was his own; that is, it never was a body of another human being which was then adopted (*Inc.* 8, 18; cf. *C. Ar.* 3.31). It followed that the suffering which the incarnated Son experienced was also his own suffering, although, strictly speaking, it was his human nature and not his divine nature which suffered (*C. Ar.* 3.32–4; *Ep. Epict.* 6).

But if the body of Jesus Christ was a mere "instrument," then what about the integrity of Christ's human nature? Arguably, before the 360s, Athanasius taught that Christ did not have a human mind. And because Athanasius allegedly taught a "mindless" Christ, he could not have been the author of the two books *On the Incarnation against Apollinarius*. However, such assessment rests primarily on a presumption that Athanasius follows the so-called *Logos*–flesh scheme, where flesh/body is preconceived as a mindless corpse (Dragas, 2005; but see Hanson, 1988, 645–51). However, Athanasius's use of the words "flesh" and "body" does not imply that Christ had no mind, just as the Johannine "flesh" (John 1:14) and Pauline "form of a slave" (Phil. 2:7) do not imply that Christ had no mind (cf. *Ep. Adelph.* 4–5). The Son "became man, and did not come into man" (*C. Ar.* 3.30). True, Athanasius posited an "asymmetrical christology" where the divine nature was the active and giving entity and the human nature the passive and receiving entity. But the fact that Athanasius affirmed the priority of the divine nature in the incarnated Christ in no way threatened the integrity of Christ's human nature. It could not, because if anything less than true humanity was joined to the Word, salvation would not have taken place. "What is not assumed is not saved"

(*Inc.* 54)—hence the importance of the integrity of Christ's humanity, including his having a human mind (*Tom.* 7).

The incarnation of the fully divine Son launched the restoration of the relationship between the Creator and the creation which was damaged in the Fall. The Son became a creation in order to make the created humans sons. It was an interesting process of reversal: "God, being first Creator … becomes Father of human beings … But in the case of the Word the reverse; for God, being his Father by nature, becomes afterwards his creator and maker when the Word puts on flesh which was created and made, and becomes a human being" (*C. Ar.* 2.61). The reversal is summarized in a famous dictum, "[H]e was made human so that we might be made God" (*Inc.* 54). God's becoming human was humanity's deification (cf. 2 Pet. 1:4). God's becoming human was the re-activation of the human capacity to participate in the divine life.

Incarnation is not merely the initial phase of this restoration process, which is then followed by Christ's death and resurrection. Rather, it is the comprehensive designation for the whole salvific event. It comprises Christ's birth, life, death, and resurrection (*Inc.* 19–31). Incarnation as the archetypical uniting of the divine and human natures in the person of Jesus Christ was the very basis of the soteriological effectiveness of Christ's death in the first place. The death of our Lord's body was atoning "because the Word was in it" (*Inc.* 20).

Athanasius emphasized that the restoration of the relation between the Creator and the creation began with the Creator's initiative to save the creation. God was/is the primary agent of salvation. In fact, both Pelagian and "Arian" controversies found the orthodox rebuttal in the conviction that only God could save. *God's* decision to become incarnated established the "transcendental possibility" of restoring the postlapsarian relation between the Creator and the creation.

God created humans in order to be in communion with them, but human beings sinned and turned away from their Creator. Consequently, as contingent creatures with misdirected wills and dislocated desires, humans were caught up in the process of corruption. "For the nature of things that come to be, inasmuch as they exist out of nothing, is unstable, weak, and mortal" (*C. Gent.* 41). Humans were created out of nothing (*ex nihilo*). In the Fall, they were cut off from their divine "life-line" and, therefore, tended to relapse into being nothing unless God corrected their orientation again. So, God decided to redeem the creation by drawing it again into the orbit of the divine life (*Inc.* 6). God condescended to the creation. "The Creator … put on the created body" (*Ep. Adelph.* 6).

Salvation is not an automatic process, however. "God does not effect an enforced rescue" (Pettersen, 1995, 53). Salvation requires a deliberate human appropriation. Well, can humans turn back to God, if they are corrupted by sin and fundamentally disoriented?

Athanasius's doctrine of the Fall does not constitute a radical loss of human capacity for God. It is not the Western/Protestant "total depravity," but rather a serious yet partial damaging of the prelapsarian human nature. This means that, being created according to the image and likeness of God, humans already have a gift in their constitution which enables them to participate eternally in the divine life (*C. Gent.* 2, 4.3). Humans have the capacity for God, although it needs serious restoration after the Fall. Obviously, only that which already exists to some extent can be restored (*Inc.* 14). Accordingly, God's "additional" grace offered in Christ's assumption of the human nature helped to release the salvific powers that were already within this divinely imaged nature, and which was restored to its proper functioning. Athanasius contended that "the grace of being made in His image was sufficient to give them [i.e., humans] knowledge of the Word and, through Him, of the Father" (*Inc.* 12).

This means that "[c]*haris* [i.e., 'grace'] is not an after-thought, following after God's creation of human *physis* [i.e., 'nature']" (Dragas, 2005, 38). There is no radical dichotomy between nature and grace in Athanasius's theological anthropology. Rather, there is a synergy or co-working which is made possible by the prior divine energy. This synergy is not a human work meriting salvation, but rather participating in the divine Son's victory demonstrated in the incarnation. Human response is never something autonomous and self-sufficient in the first place. It is fundamentally God-given. At the same time, the acknowledged priority of the divine energy in no

way cancels out the human part in this synergy, namely volition and striving. The "additional" divine aid enhances human effort and brings it to fruition rather than precludes it. "For in it [i.e., discipline] the Lord is our fellow-worker, as it is written, 'to all that choose the good, God works with them for good [Rom. 8:28]'" (*Vit. Ant.* 19).

Human beings have free will which can "turn either way" (*Inc.* 3). Human beings can exercise their free will either to choose life without God, which reduces them to being nothing, or life with God, which elevates them to God-likeness. "We float on this sea … through our own free will, for everyone directs his course according to his will, and either, under the pilotage of the Word, he enters into rest, or, laid hold of pleasure, he suffers shipwreck" (*Ep. fest.* 19.7). To underline the importance of individual responsibility coming from deliberate choosing, Athanasius pointed to the teaching in the parables of the Talents and the Sower (e.g., *Ep. fest.* 3.2–3).

The whole humanity (as well as the whole creation) benefits from the Son's incarnation, yet all human beings have to appropriate the benefits deliberately through reorientation of their soul's desire. It happens through prayer and *askesis*. Ascetic practice keeps the body and its desires from gaining control over the rational mind which naturally yearns to gaze at God. "We are made alive in Christ, the flesh being no longer earthly, but at last having been made rational thanks to the Word of God, who became flesh for our sake" (*C. Ar.* 3.33). Anthony, too, understood that the task was not to be "dragged down by pleasures of the body, but, on the contrary, [that] the body might be in subjection of the soul" (*Vit. Ant.* 45). Salvation is not obliteration of the body but redemption of "the whole human being, body and soul alike" (*Ep. Epic.* 7).

To conclude, the basic human connectedness to its Creator was permanently repaired by God's becoming human. "[Christ] came for this reason: that in the flesh he might suffer and the flesh be made impassible and immortal" (*C. Ar.* 3.58). Mere forgiveness of the sins of humankind would not have been enough, because it would not have restored the divine image/likeness in fallen human beings.

IV. Significance

Athanasius was a bishop of a major see, Alexandria, during one of the most dramatic times in Christian history—the messy fourth century. He saw the change of the Christian church from a persecuted illegal sect to a church of emperors and masses. He also saw the church's frantic attempts to retain its prophetic voice and independence from the dictates of the state. Athanasius became "a prominent symbol of opposition to imperially sponsored consensus theology" (McGuckin, 2004, 35). He wondered, "When did a judgment of the Church receive its validity from the emperor?" (*H. Ar.* 52). At the same time, there is also an important truth in Gwynn's (2007) reminder, "Every imperial decree hostile to his [i.e., Athanasius's] own cause is the product of the 'conspiracy' of his opponents, whereas every decision in his favour reflects the true judgement of the pious emperor himself" (151–2).

Due to his five exiles, Athanasius lived in East and West and therefore managed to mobilize representatives from all regions to support his pro-Nicene campaign. Furthermore, his ties with Rome established an important alliance between the sees of Rome and Alexandria, which was to play a major role in subsequent theological controversies. Athanasius is still honored in both East and West. His feast day is May 2.

Athanasius is among the authors quoted by medieval scholastics and spiritual writers. He belongs to the Erasmian "canon" of great authors whom the humanist translated. Athanasius's collected works were also owned and studied by Zwingli (Backus, 2001). Even today, a web page is dedicated to Athanasius: www.athanasius.theologie.uni-erlangen.de.

In 367, Athanasius was among the first to use a legal term "canon" (*kanōn*) for the Scriptures (i.e., for the Hebrew Scriptures and the 27 books of the New Testament) (Dungan, 2007). "In these [canonical Scriptures] alone is proclaimed the doctrine of godliness" (*Ep. fest.* 39). Athanasius placed the seven Catholic Epistles after the Book of Acts and Hebrews before the Pastoral letters.

Athanasius shaped the Christian and orthodox church in Egypt. He turned several "pagan" temples into Christian churches, built a church "which bears his name" (*Index* 41), established the uniformity of the celebration of Easter in his jurisdiction, was the head of the patronage and welfare systems of the rich Egyptian church, and worked tirelessly to unify the church, which had had rival bishops and competing structures for quite some time.

Athanasius witnessed the emergence of monasticism and was one of the first, if not the first, to ordain monks as bishops. His friendships and co-operation with monks prevented the separation of the monastic movement from the larger institutional church. He managed to amalgamate the ascetic virtuosi of the desert with the church hierarchs of the city. As Gregory of Nazianzus put it, "[Athanasius] reconciled the solitary with the community life" (*Or.* 21.19). Brakke (2000) has worded well the challenge of the post-Constantinian times: "Such a catholic church, one that embraced society and culture rather than stood in opposition to them, required a theology that was also 'catholic,' that is, inclusive of and intelligible to persons of a wide variety of social roles and at diverse levels of spiritual perfection" (1120). So, Athanasius, too, tried hard to keep the "more dedicated" and the "less dedicated" together in the same church. It was a tough task, because monks had left the world in protest against the imperial semi-Christianity in the first place. Yet monks were nevertheless united to the larger church through baptism. They also needed priests to celebrate the Eucharist and bishops to solve various theological and ethical questions. The larger church, in turn, could learn from monks ascetic discipline and deeper spirituality. Mutual benefits made such alliance desirable. Notice that Anthony was obedient to the clergy and that he also symbolically left one of his cloaks to bishop Athanasius (*Vit. Ant.* 20; cf. 2 Kings 2:13). Athanasius's unification plan never reached out after schismatics and heretics, though.

While Athanasius promoted several "models" of salvation, he was one of the first to clearly articulate the idea of deification, which later became the prevalent soteriological "model" for most Greek and Byzantine churches. "Athanasius is using the divinization motif to score a theological point against his Arian opponents, with the telling argument that divinization by a non-divine *Logos* is a logical and theological impossibility" (Hess, in Livingstone, 1993, 373).

Athanasius participated in the first ecumenical council in 325 and in other fourth-century councils which shaped Christian Trinitarian orthodoxy. Although his direct influence on the coining of the Nicene Creed was rather minimal, Athanasius's defense and explication of the Nicene doctrine of the Trinity was nevertheless his major achievement and the cause for his lasting fame. In time, Athanasius came to be identified with the Nicene cause, which received conciliar and imperial backing at the Council of Constantinople in 381. Even when Athanasius became more flexible with regard to the precise Trinitarian terminology, the main idea of the full divinity and consubstantiality of the Son and the Spirit with the Father remained a non-negotiable article of faith.

References

Anatolios, Khaled. 1998. *Athanasius: The Coherence of His Thought*. London: Routledge.

Anatolios, Khaled. 2004. "Athanasius." In *The Early Church Fathers*, ed. C. Harrison. London: Routledge.

Arnold, Duane W.-H. 1991. "The Early Episcopal Career of Athanasius of Alexandria." In *Christianity and Judaism in Antiquity* 6, ed. C. Kannengiesser. Notre Dame, IN: University of Notre Dame Press.

Ayres, Lewis. 2004. *Nicaea and Its Legacy: An Approach to Fourth-Century Trinitarian Theology*. Oxford: Oxford University Press.

Backus, Irena Dorota. 2001. *The Reception of the Church Fathers in the West: From the Carolingians to the Maurists*. Boston: E. J. Brill.

Barnes, Timothy D. 1993. *Athanasius and Constantius: Theology and Politics in the Constantinian Empire*. Cambridge, MA: Harvard University Press.

Behr, J. 2004. "The Nicene Faith." In *Formation of Christian Theology*, part 1, vol. 2. Crestwood: St Valdimir's Seminary Press.

Brakke, David. 1995. *Athanasius and the Politics of Asceticism*. Oxford: Oxford University Press.

Brakke, David. 2000. "Athanasius." In *The Early Christian World*, vol. 1., ed. P. F. Esler. London: Routledge, pp. 1102–27.

Brown, Peter Robert Lamont. 1995. *Authority and the Sacred: Aspects of the Christianisation of the Roman World*. New York: Cambridge University Press.

Butterweck, Christel. 1995. *Athanasius von Alexandrien Bibliographie*. Düsseldorf: Westdeutcher Verlag. (It includes a comprehensive bibliography and a list of the printed works of Athanasius since 1482.)

Dragas, George D. 2005. "Saint Athanasius: Original Research and New Perspectives." In *Patristic Theological Library* 1, eds. G. D. Dragas and D. R. Lamoureux. Rollinsford, NH: Orthodox Research Institute. (It includes a comprehensive bibliography and a list of all the works attributed to Athanasius.)

Dungan, David L. 2007. *Constantine's Bible: Politics and the Making of the New Testament*. Minneapolis: Fortress Press.

Ernest, James D. 2004. "The Bible in Athanasius of Alexandria." In *The Bible in Ancient Christianity* 2, ed. D. J. Bingham. Leiden: E. J. Brill.

Gwynn, David M. 2007. *The Eusebians: The Polemic of Athanasius of Alexandria and the Construction of the "Arian Controversy."* Oxford: Oxford University Press.

Hanson, R. P. C. 1988. *The Search for the Christian Doctrine of God: The Arian Controversy 318–381*. Edinburgh: T&T Clark.

Hess, Hamilton. 1993. "The Place of Divinization in Athanasius' Soteriology." In *Studia Patristica* 26: 369–374.

Kannengiesser, C. 1991. *Arius and Athanasius: Two Alexandrian Theologians*. Brookfield, VT: Variorum/Grower.

Leemans, J. 2000. "Thirteen Years of Athanasius' Research (1985–1998): A Survey and Bibliography," *Sacris Erudiri* 39: 105–217.

Pettersen, Alvyn. 1995. *Athanasius*. Harrisburg, PA: Morehouse Publishing.

Tetz, Martin. 1995. *Athanasiana: zu Leben und Lehre des Athanasius*, ed. W. Geerlings and D. Wyrwa. Berlin: de Gruyter.

Torrance, Thomas, F. 1995 [1973]. "Athanasius: A Study in the Foundations of Classical Theology." In *Divine Meaning: Studies in Patristic Hermeneutics*. Edinburgh: T&T Clark, pp. 179–228.

Weinandy, Thomas G. 2007. *Athanasius: A Theological Introduction*. Aldershot, UK: Ashgate.

Williams, Rowan. 2004. "Athanasius and the Arian Crisis." In *The First Christian Theologians: An Introduction to the Theology in the Early Church*, ed. G. R. Evans, London: Blackwell, pp. 157–67.

www.athanasius.theologie.uni-erlangen.de. (Critical editions of Athanasius's works and bibliography, 1982–2006.)

Augustine of Hippo (*c*.354–430)

Thomas L. Humphries

I. Life

Augustine of Hippo is an African saint and father of the church. Roman Catholics celebrate him as a Doctor of the Faith on August 28, immediately following the feast of his mother, St Monica. Augustine wrote and preached with the kind of honesty and vigor to which most theologians aspire. His grasp of vexing human problems makes his work perennially relevant. Augustine's works are numerous and are divided into a wide range of genres, from philosophical dialogues modeled on Cicero to an extensive series of sermons. His "commentaries" on the Psalms and on John's Gospel were also originally sermons or notes for sermons. The vast majority of his theological reflection occurs in the context of scriptural exegesis and, thus, understanding Augustine requires not only awareness of the history of doctrinal debates, but also attention to his methods of reading scripture. His works often demand much from their readers, but the effort proves rewarding. Many thinkers, from his fourth-century contemporaries to the twentieth-century Ludwig Wittgenstein, have found his reflections and arguments stimulating for their own.

In 354 Augustine was born to Monica and Patricius in the town of Thagaste, in present-day Algeria. We know he had a brother, Navigius, and at least one sister. He studied rhetoric, the art of persuasive speech, at Carthage and returned to Thagaste to teach in 375.

He tells us that he loved Virgil and always respected Cicero, but did not care for studying Greek (the extent of his knowledge of Greek has been the subject of much debate). He was a gifted *rhetor*, and thus demands of his readers' attention to the various ways in which arguments can be woven into different kinds of works. He became involved as an *auditor* ("hearer") in the sect of the Manichaeans (see below), but gradually grew dissatisfied with it. Augustine was appointed the professor of rhetoric and official orator in Milan in 384, a city which had been the imperial capital in the West for some time. In the summer of 386 he withdrew from his teaching position, and after a winter spent in retreat with friends at Cassiciacum, he was baptized at Easter 387.

Of his family, his mother occupies the dominant role in his own narrative of his life. The vision he had with her at Ostia, near Rome, just before her death in 387 made a profound impact on his life and his theology. Those wishing to parse Augustine's attitude toward women would do well to study the respect he had for St Monica. Before coming to Italy Augustine had lived for some years with a woman whose name is not known to us. The two had a much-loved son, Adeodatus, who died in 390 in his teenage years. Monica was instrumental in encouraging Augustine to end the relationship and to search for a socially advantageous marriage, but she was delighted when he eventually decided on a celibate life as part of his

The Student's Companion to the Theologians, First Edition. Edited by Ian S. Markham.
© 2013 Blackwell Publishing Ltd. Published 2013 by Blackwell Publishing Ltd.

conversion. In 389 Augustine returned to Africa with the intention of living a monastic life. Despite this desire he was ordained a priest in 391 during a visit to Hippo and then became the town's bishop in 395. He died in 430, during the Vandal invasion of North Africa, just before the Ecumenical Council of Ephesus (to which he had been invited). Thus, he was the contemporary of some of the other great Latin theologians, St John Cassian and St Jerome, and the (Greek) Patriarch of Alexandria, St Cyril.

It is common to divide Augustine's life into periods that correspond to his pre-conversion, his preordination, and his episcopacy. While his birth (354), ordinations to the priesthood (391) and episcopacy (395), and his death (August 28, 430) are relatively easy to date and describe, the case is not the same with his conversion. As Augustine himself makes clear in his famous and popular *Confessions*, conversion is not the experience of a single moment, but rather an intricate process of being led by God through a lifetime toward a final moment of decision. Prior to receiving baptism, he had grown dissatisfied with other, more or less religious and philosophical sects (in particular Manichaeism) and had been affected by Ambrose's preaching. In the final stages of this process he was also moved by Simplicianus's telling of the story of Marius Victorinus, a celebrated philosopher-rhetorician who converted to Christianity.

II.   Theology

Augustine was deeply influenced by the Neoplatonic approach he encountered in the preaching of Ambrose, bishop of Milan, and which he also found in the writings of non-Christian Neoplatonists. Neoplatonism provided him with a sense that the material world was undergirded by an omnipresent and ordering spiritual reality that gave the material world intelligibility and purpose. We should, however, not too easily separate the more philosophical modes of his thought from the reality of his own struggle to accept Christianity. He combined much of what he knew about *nous* (intellect) from philosophical sources with *verbum* (word) as he knew it from rhetorical sources as well as the Gospel of John. This allowed him to develop philosophical anthropology and Trinitarian theology

together. The most complete and dense treatise that achieves this synthesis is *On the Trinity*, but *On the Literal Interpretation of Genesis* should also be remembered in the context of anthropology, psychology, and creation, three themes that are commonly related in philosophical texts of this period.

It is common to divide his works according to the controversy or text which they engage. Thus, the principal categories are the anti-Manichaean, anti-Pelagian, anti-Donatist, the so-called "semi-Pelagian" or Massilian debates, and the commentaries on various books of scripture. This can be helpful for students of Augustine as long as we remember that he did not understand himself to have multiple theologies that responded to different issues. Rather, Augustine understood himself to hold the one true faith which offered critiques of the various perversions of truth he observed in some of his contemporaries. Nevertheless, Augustine shifted his position on several key elements of his understanding of the faith as he developed his theology (e.g., grace and the categories of "under the law" and "under grace," discussed below). In this sense, his theology was shaped by responding to various pastoral and doctrinal matters.

As an exegete, Augustine was both theoretically and practically very capable. His treatise *On Christian Teaching* has already served as a source for some 1,500 years of the study of rhetoric, hermeneutics, and a philosophy-theology of language. He adopted the practice of reading scripture allegorically (or mystically) from Ambrose, who was familiar with the practice at least through Origen's texts. Augustine also explains in some detail a system of semiotics and rules for how to use various interpretive methods correctly. When considering these guides for determining the meaning of scripture, Augustine allows that any interpretation which points to the command to love has not missed the mark. That is, his most basic rule of interpretation returns to the twofold Gospel principle of love of God and love of neighbor.

In his Trinitarian theology he is a Nicene Latin theologian: the Father, Son, and Spirit are irreducible persons of the Trinity that is God, but the Father retains the role, status, or position as *principium*. Each of the divine persons is entirely God such that the Son is as much God as is the Spirit and the Father together. After an extended attempt to explore this mystery analogically, Augustine eventually rejects all analogies to human experience and psychology as ways of explaining the Triune God. His famous statement that the Spirit proceeds from the Father as well as from the Son (*Trin.* 15.17.29) has merited much discussion in scholarly literature. In his christology, he champions the language of Christ as the Divine Word. In his Pneumatology, he carefully articulates the Spirit as the love and self-gift which unites Father and Son, without being subordinated to the Father and Son as though the Spirit does not also give himself (*Trin.* 15.19.36). Thus, Augustine was able to articulate a dynamic of giving and receiving at the heart of a theology of love and a theology of the Trinity.

Augustine is, perhaps, most remembered for his contributions to the theology of grace and free will. Early in his career, he relied on the position that knowledge of the good is sufficient for action. This is related to the position that the beginnings of faith belong to human free will. His mature position denies that knowledge of the good is a sufficient condition for action. Grace—the active presence of God—is required due to the effects of original and particular sin which bind and divide the human will and desires. Grace provides us with a new object of will—beyond the sinful objects that now draw us in place of the Good—and the power to follow those true and appropriate objects of desire. This shift is first clearly apparent in letters to Simplicianus which date from 396, and is developed during the controversy with Pelagius after 412. True to his form as an exegete, Augustine uses the key phrases "under the law" and "under grace" from Romans 7 to provide the terminology around which he often discusses these issues. His mature position allows for genuine struggle to lead the virtuous life even while the faithful are "under grace." Thus, justification and sanctification are life-long processes, and the faithful are never fully perfected in this life.

A theology of grace is often contrasted with a theology of merit. A strong reliance on grace is understood to argue for divine agency, while a strong reliance on merit is understood to argue for human agency. The two are then placed in competition, and some theologians attempt to articulate which party is responsible for particular types of actions. Much of the debate and even schism in the Western church involves precisely this issue: forcing a choice of divine grace or human merit over the other. Augustine's dictum, "When God crowns our merits, he crowns nothing but his own gifts" (*Ep.* 194), shows that he sees the matter differently. God gives to us what becomes our very own; God aids our own willing and loving so that it may be more fully human, more fully what it was created to be. Perhaps Augustine's greatest contribution in this regard is his appeal to the loving union of wills between Christians and God. The goal of the Christian life, according to Augustine, is to dissolve into the flow of the Triune love. In this state, it will no longer make sense to pose questions of divine agency over and against human agency, but rather to understand that a system of merit is crucial to the basic moral structure of Christianity and that such a system is rooted in God's grace, which is always prior to human action. As with many elements of his theology, Augustine argues that love resolves the tension by establishing unity.

Since the early fourth century, Christianity in North Africa was divided between two camps, one in communion with Christianity throughout the Mediterranean, and another group known by their opponents as the "Donatists" (after one of their early leaders), whose origins lay in divisions about whether those who had abandoned their Christianity in the face of Roman persecution could be readmitted to the church, and whether priests and bishops who had done so could still celebrate the sacraments. This dispute continued throughout Augustine's lifetime. He was a major figure in the attempts of the Catholic church in North Africa to heal this division. Augustine argued that the twofold love of God and neighbor lies at the heart of Christianity, and thus, schism is a failure of love. It is, then, the duty of Catholic Christians to accept Donatists back into the public and visible church. The power of the sacraments comes not from the purity of those who are ordained, but from Christ whose body the church is. For Augustine, all Christians must accept their impurity and the need for divine aid. Even the church consists of the good and bad intermingled until the final judgment. The Donatist problem proved intractable and Augustine eventually came to accept the need for legislation to decrease the hold of the Donatist clergy over their flock. This followed on a long history of both sides asking the imperial authorities to intervene.

Augustine's long and complex work *The City of God* transposes his understanding of the intertwined reality of the good and the bad onto human history as a whole and especially onto the political realm. The history of the world is the history of the two cities, one of God and the other of this world, which will only be clearly separated at the final judgment. Such an approach radically undercuts any claims of the state to an independent sphere of responsibility in the world, and Augustine's attitude to the role of governance is consequentially often ad hoc, emphasizing that God may use Christian rulers to secure peace for the fostering of the church, but not in aid of any one state in itself.

Augustine always maintained the creedal belief in "one baptism for the forgiveness of sins," especially against the Donatist practice of rebaptizing Catholics. Scholars are at pains to agree on other aspects of his sacramental theology, particularly in the cases of ordination and Eucharist, largely due to the fact that his terminology is not consistent, though it is a source for the systematic definitions and divisions made famous in medieval sacramental theology. In addition, he is willing to entertain multiple levels of meanings for key phrases, such as "the body of Christ." At times, theologians have attempted to reduce certain phrases to one meaning for the sake of clarity, but at the expense of the full value of Augustine's theology, which embraces signs that have multiple meanings.

Augustine reflected extensively on the power of sexuality, and in particular the way arousal and attraction can dominate all aspects of a human person. While he thought the asceticism of sexual abstinence a higher calling, he is notable for his positive attitude toward marriage in the debates of his day, as especially evidenced in texts like *On the Good of Marriage*. Augustine saw both as matters of divine calling and attempted to steer a middle course between the Roman Jovinian, who saw marriage as the preferable option, and figures like Jerome, who saw the married as second-class Christians. Augustine's theology of marriage is consistent with his theology of creation: he defends the Christian belief that creation is fundamentally good, though perverted by sin.

To the Manichaean doctrine of a fundamental dualism between good and evil, Augustine articulated the basic Christian notion that the divine goodness is fundamentally prior to evil. Manichaeans (also spelled Manichees) were a religious sect that originated in third-century Persia, in the area that is now Iraq. It drew both on Christianity and on the Zoroastrianism practiced within the Persian empire. Mani, its founder, was eventually martyred for his faith. Manichaeans believed in a complex mythology, but had a fundamentally simple account of the world as caught up in a struggle between two equally powerful principles: good and evil. Augustine taught a stark contrast: evil has no absolute existence, but is a privation of good. In the same vein of thought, Augustine upheld the fundamental distinction between Creator and creation, though at times the discussion is complicated by appeal to various and intricate philosophical theories popular in the third and fourth centuries.

With respect to the field of eschatology, that area of theology which defends Christian hope in a most glorious life to come, Augustine is famous for his insistence that God is our final goal. Since this final state involves radical transformation and resurrection, it is not possible to achieve heavenly perfection in this life, though this should not prevent us from attempting to become better.

III.   Writings

Experienced and first-time readers alike will find Augustine's *Tractates on 1 John* and *Tractates on the Gospel of John* fantastic introductions to the versatility, depth, and beauty of his theology. The *Confessions* is a classic well worth reading several times throughout one's life. In addition, his *Commentary on the Psalms* and the other works mentioned here, *On Christian Teaching*, *On the Trinity*, and *The City of God*, are all available in good English translations with appropriate notes. His more pointedly philosophical works include *Against the Academics* (a refutation of Academic Skepticism), *On Order* (a theodicy), *On the Happy Life* (a discussion of happiness and knowledge), and *On Free Will* (a dialogue on human choice and divine agency). The *Enchiridion on Faith, Hope and Love* written toward the end of his life offers a concise summary of his theology. *Augustine Through the Ages: An Encyclopedia* (Eerdmans, 1999), edited by Allan Fitzgerald, provides one of the best guides to his multifaceted thought and influence.

Augustine was knowledgeable about the intellectual history which preceded him, but eclipsed nearly all other authors as the source for the medieval philosophy and theology which succeeded him. His immense curiosity and intense personality drove him to success as a rhetor, involvement with the sect of Mani, appropriation of Neoplatonic systems, and, eventually, to life as a Christian pastor and theologian of great repute. His mark on Christian theology is impossible to describe comprehensively, as is his mark on philosophy. At the heart of his most impassioned preaching and most vehement arguments, we should not miss his insistence on the fundamental Gospel imperative to love.

Boethius (c.475–c.524)

Ivor J. Davidson

Anicius Manlius Severinus Boethius (c.475/80–524/6 CE) ranks among the most significant of Western Christian intellectuals in the sixth century. An obvious product of the later Roman world and the political and cultural dynamics which made that world the place it was, he was also one of the most important shapers of the discourse of philosophical theology in the Middle Ages, and a major influence upon Western thought and letters for centuries thereafter. His legacy represents at once an impressive asset and a complex interpretative challenge. An essential conduit of ancient traditions of logic and metaphysics and a methodological pioneer in his own right, Boethius epitomizes a style of sophisticated late antique Christianity that can only be appraised in its native context, an environment in which philosophy and faith, art and piety interacted in particular ways. His personal circumstances also dominate everything: his career witnessed an abrupt fall from the heights of prestige and power to disgrace, incarceration, and a violent death. His bequest includes philosophical-theological work of some depth and a final literary testament that counts among the most widely read of books ever written in Latin. Yet our access to his ideas and their motivations is complicated by the puzzling image he projects in that last text: stripped of wealth and status, falsely imprisoned for treason, he writes not of Christ but of Philosophy; his final vision of divine providence and human acceptance of adversity owes more to classical thought than it does to Christian scripture. Unjustly executed for his alleged crimes, he comes to be venerated as a Catholic martyr and eventually canonized as a saint, yet the questions about his ultimate convictions have never entirely disappeared. Boethius is an intriguing figure.

I.   Life and Context

He was born into the old aristocracy of Rome. The *gens Anicia* had been Christian for several generations, but cherished its ancient roots and enduring place among the comfortable elite of its world. The year of his birth is not certain: some suggest a date as early as 475; a likelier setting may be a little later, closer to 480. His father, who had a distinguished public career, died when Boethius was still a child, and he was adopted into an even grander household, that of Quintus Aurelius Memmius Symmachus. Consul in 485, and later urban prefect and head of the senate, Symmachus was in a position to offer his young charge the finest of cultural formation and the best of opportunities. A respected author, judge, and patron of literature and ideas, Symmachus was also a deeply committed Christian, with a strong interest in theological and ecclesiastical as well as civil politics, and his household was noted for its piety; two of his daughters would take the veil. Boethius received a thorough education in

The Student's Companion to the Theologians, First Edition. Edited by Ian S. Markham.
© 2013 Blackwell Publishing Ltd. Published 2013 by Blackwell Publishing Ltd.

classical literature and philosophy, and strong Christian instruction. His proficiency in Greek was particularly striking, so much so that it has been supposed that—like many in his social class before him, though far fewer in his day—he may have travelled to the East to study in one of the remaining great Neoplatonist schools, perhaps the one at Alexandria. The evidence is ambiguous; it is likelier that his versatility in the language was acquired at the hands of a native-speaking tutor in Rome, and his familiarity with Neoplatonist thought in particular was almost certainly encouraged by Symmachus's own intellectual tastes. He grew up to hold Symmachus in the highest esteem as a role model, and to marry another of his daughters, Rusticiana. We know nothing of the context of his earliest Christian profession, but the faith of the household was also his, and he would take some interest in church debates from an early age. Just how much Christian literature he read in his youth is hard to say. He was certainly influenced by Augustine, and by something of the Latin Christian tradition before him, but he does not evince extensive knowledge of historical or contemporary Greek theology.

The circles that shaped Boethius took pride in their heritage, but the Rome in which they gloried existed largely in the past. In August 476, a date not far removed from the time of Boethius's birth, the last emperor of the West, Romulus Augustulus, was deposed in a coup by Odoacer, commander of the Germanic forces in Italy. The truly serious blows to the integrity of the empire had already been struck in the barbarian invasions of two generations earlier, and real power had increasingly resided not in the hands of emperors but with army chiefs like Odoacer and the forces they commanded. The trappings of public life continued in Rome, but the city had long ago ceased to be the seat of meaningful Western government; that was now to be found at Ravenna, 200 miles to the northeast, whose surrounding marshes and lagoons rendered it somewhat more resistant to assault from invaders. Odoacer declared himself "king" rather than emperor, and did not disturb the Roman administrative order. In principle the emperor in Constantinople retained official sovereignty. Nevertheless, from the perspective of the Eastern court the situation was hardly ideal. There were also questions about what to do with the Ostrogoths, who were settled in Pannonia,

south and west of the Danube, under their increasingly potent leader, Theoderic. In 489, Theoderic was persuaded to invade Italy and seek a place for his people there. After four years of sporadic campaigning and a lengthy siege of Ravenna, he defeated and executed Odoacer and installed himself as king in his place.

Boethius grew up in an age of change. Nevertheless, for the class to which he belonged Theoderic's regime was as good as anything that had existed in a long time (Moorhead, 1992; Amory, 1997). Freedom and independence were respected, and there were plenty of opportunities to participate in public life. The senate continued to act under license, and the prefect of Rome served as a go between with the court in the north. Theoderic had been brought up in Constantinople, and had much respect for Rome's traditions; law was upheld, art and literature were sponsored, and splendid new buildings were constructed in Ravenna. Nor were there major religious problems. Theoderic and his Ostrogoths were "Arians"—*homoian* "Arianism," the view that God the Son is *like* (*homoios*), but not consubstantial with (*homoousios*), God the Father, had been the dominant form of Christian confession among Gothic converts since the fourth century. But there was little or no interference in the doctrinal sympathies of pro-Nicene believers, who remained in a clear majority in Italy, and relations with Catholic authorities were generally very positive (they would decline somewhat in Theoderic's latter days).

A young man with Boethius's privileges had two obvious paths before him: he could either pursue an active political career in Ravenna, or remain in Rome and devote himself to another traditional upper-class ideal: a life of learned leisure. Boethius opted for the latter, seeing literary activity as a prime means by which a publicly minded intellectual might serve his society. Scholarly work was not an alternative to direct political engagement, just a more interesting way of passing one's time; public honors would follow in any event. Conscious of the example of Cicero (106–43 BCE), whose philosophical writing had conveyed the riches of Hellenistic philosophy to Roman readers, he worked first on translating Greek thought in mathematical disciplines, then proceeded to philosophy. He conceived a grand plan to translate into Latin all the available works of Aristotle and Plato and write a commentary on every one of them; he would then demonstrate that the two giants of the Greek tradition were not in fact at odds on most matters, as was often supposed, but generally of the same mind. The youthful dream was never fulfilled, but what he did achieve was remarkable nonetheless.

While he pursued his intellectual work, Boethius's public profile continued to grow, assisted by the strong patronage of Symmachus. He became a leading member of Roman society, and was also noticed in Ravenna. Awarded the title of "patrician" before 507, in 510 he was appointed consul. His public duties did not interfere greatly with his scholarship, nor did they get in the way of some involvement in theological discussion. Ever since 484 the churches of Rome and Constantinople, whose relationship had always been liable to serious tensions, had been officially divided. The "Acacian" schism, so called after Acacius, patriarch of Constantinople 471–89, had been triggered by an imperial document of 482, the *Henotikon*, which had been intended to heal the serious divisions between Christians in the East over the christological formula issued by the Council of Chalcedon in 451; in the eyes of Rome the *Henotikon* had gone far too far in implying deficiencies in Chalcedon and its key Western influences, especially Leo's *Tome* (449). Boethius took some part in ecclesiastical affairs, and wrote a series of theological tractates, which we shall consider further below. They reveal, among other things, his commitment to the cause of restoring unity on Rome's terms. That cause was also gaining in political momentum, and in 519 the new Latin-speaking emperor Justin would persuade the Constantinopolitan hierarchy to accept peace in a way that acknowledged the supremacy of Chalcedon and the authority of Rome.

In 522 Boethius's two sons were appointed joint consuls. This was an extremely rare honor, which said as much about the father as it did about his boys: Boethius had indubitably been marked out in both Constantinople and Ravenna as a figure of great potential usefulness. On the day of their installation he delivered an encomium for Theoderic. A short time later, he agreed to move to Ravenna to serve as the king's "Master of Offices" (*Magister Officiorum*). The post had first been created in the days of Diocletian and Constantine, as a chief-of-staff position in the imperial household. Its holder controlled public appointments, oversaw the security apparatus, and acted as gatekeeper for all who sought an audience with his master. Theoderic's system retained the model. Boethius was thus appointed to a highly influential role. He must have seemed a great asset: a sophisticated intellectual with great social capital and a high level of respect in ecclesiastical circles. If the Arian king was aware of his theological views (and it seems unlikely that he was not), he perhaps calculated that these convictions were not an impediment to Boethius's worth as a public servant.

For all the promise, things quickly went wrong. Boethius appears to have exercised his authority in a vigorous manner, dealing sharply with corruption and injustice, and he rapidly made a number of enemies at court. Within just a year or so of taking office, matters came to a head. A leading senator, Albinus, was accused by Cyprian, the king's private secretary, of writing letters to persons close to the emperor Justin in Constantinople, in which there were references to Theoderic that were treasonable. Albinus denied the allegation, but the king was convinced of his guilt and condemned him without a proper trial. Boethius spoke out in Albinus's defense, and was accused by Cyprian of suppressing evidence, and of himself engaging in correspondence which included treasonous sentiments about his hopes for "Roman liberty"—presumably from Gothic control. He was also charged with engaging in black magic in order to achieve his ends. The notion sounds fairly absurd today, but such activity was regarded very seriously at the time. There was no evidence of his involvement in any of it, but Cyprian managed to stir up a powerful lobby of people who had grown deeply resentful of the Master of Offices' ways of operating.

Theoderic for his part was easily persuadable, for there were indeed various desires that his reign should come to a rapid end. Now in his seventies, he faced mounting political and strategic problems: the stability of his regime had always involved the maintenance of a coolness toward Constantinople on the part of the Western senatorial aristocracy, and he knew that if this mood were changing he would face real political crisis. He was also afraid that Constantinople would use the recent ecclesiastical rapprochement with Rome in the interests of reasserting its political authority in the West. Justin had already set about harassing Arian believers in his territories, and was showing signs of a serious will to crush the Ostrogothic dream. In Theoderic's mind, Boethius may have represented a dangerous faction of pro-Eastern sentiment that deserved to be dealt with firmly. Albinus and Boethius were both arrested and imprisoned: Albinus was perhaps executed fairly rapidly; Boethius was confined at Ticinum (modern Pavia), south of Milan, and never summoned to defend himself legally. A senatorial court was convened at Rome and passed a sentence of exile and death; his friends utterly failed to stand up for him. Boethius may well have hoped that Theoderic would grant his chief official a reprieve, and that judicial execution, which was out of character for the king, would not follow. Whatever attempted negotiations may have followed—and Theoderic conceivably had his own reasons for delaying Boethius's fate, possibly using him as a pawn in his games with the East—he was detained for some time near Pavia. During this period he wrote the remarkable work with which his name would forever be associated, the *Consolation of Philosophy*, a powerful reflection upon divine justice in the face of human suffering (Walsh, 1999; Relihan, 2001). Composed in prosimetric form (a mixture of prose and verse), it is a dialogue in five books between Boethius, the prisoner awaiting his fate, and a lady who personifies Philosophy, his teacher, as he ponders the deep questions of life. There is little reason to doubt that the basic setting is genuine, and Boethius underscores the injustice of his fall from grace at the hands of named historical actors.

There was no remission in the end. Death came by brutal torture and clubbing, Boethius's social status affording no exemption from extreme cruelty at the hands of Ostrogothic officials. The conventional date is 524, though it may have been the following year or even 526. Shortly afterwards, Symmachus, now head of the senate, also fell under suspicion and was arrested and put to death. Theoderic chose as Boethius's successor another great Catholic intellectual of the coming generation, Cassiodorus (*c*.485–580). But the king himself did not have long to go. He died in 526, his last period dominated by furious disputes with Constantinople and a breakdown in church as well as state relations (even the elderly pope was detained for disloyalty, and died before his fate was decided).

Boethius would come to be seen as an orthodox Christian martyr, executed by a vicious Arian king, and a cult in his honor at Pavia was well established by the Middle Ages; St Severinus Boethius was finally approved by Rome in 1883, with a feast day on October 23. In reality, his Catholic confession was scarcely the cause of his demise. Nor, on the other hand, is there reason to suppose that he was merely a political schemer who miscalculated the difficulties involved in siding with Constantinople against Theoderic. In all probability, he was a victim of more prosaic circumstances—lesser-order intrigues, made worse by a certain personal inflexibility and a naïve supposition that the world he represented, Rome and its traditional institutions, still mattered to those with actual power. Whatever the reasons, it was a tragic end for one whose career had been marked by unqualified prosperity until so recently.

II.   Intellectual Influences and Program

Boethius's two main philosophical influences were Aristotle and Greek Neoplatonism respectively, and the latter mediated particular interpretations of the former (Sorabji, 1990). He was familiar with the *Enneads* of Neoplatonism's founder, Plotinus (*c*.205–70), and with the development of Plotinus's ideas by his pupil Porphyry (*c*.232–305), which had given Aristotelian logic a significant place in a Neoplatonist system (a move contrary to the instincts of Plotinus himself). He also knew the writings of Porphyry's main successors, Iamblichus (*c*.250–325) and Proclus (*c*.410–85), as well as Platonist thought in his own times. Iamblichus and Proclus represented a style of Neoplatonism strongly associated with opposition to Christianity, but Boethius was equally aware of thinkers who felt they could successfully combine a Neoplatonist metaphysic with Christian orthodoxy, such as Marius Victorinus (*fl.* 350–65), the pagan rhetorician whose conversion to Christianity in later life made a notable impression on Augustine (*Confessions* 8.2.3–5.10). Augustine's own theology, though far from the unreconstructed Neoplatonism it has sometimes been accused of being, also exemplified the striking possibilities of a serious relationship between philosophical thought and Christian conviction.

Boethius's earliest literary ventures were text-books on arithmetic, music, geometry, and astronomy (Chadwick, 1981, 69–107; Masi, 1981). He was the first to call these disciplines the *quadrivium*, or "fourfold path." The term is suggestive of Neoplatonist sensibilities: the mathematical subjects open up a path beyond the realm of the senses to the "more certain" world of intelligence. Only parts of his work survive. *On Arithmetic* (trans./ed. Masi, 1983) is essentially a free translation of a text by an early second-century Greek mathematician, Nicomachus of Gerasa. Its concern is not with practical calculation but with the abstract properties of number. *Introduction to Music* (trans./ed. Bower and Palisca, 1989) follows a (now lost) work of that name by the same Nicomachus, though seemingly a little less closely than in *On Arithmetic*, for four books; in a fifth, incomplete, book it draws on another great second-century text, the *Harmonics* of Ptolemy. Boethius sketches a Pythagorean vision of the universe as constructed in accordance with harmonic ratios; it is these proportions that are his interest, though he celebrates the power of music to move and delight. *On Geometry* apparently existed in Cassiodorus's time, and there is some evidence that it may have survived later than this, but no copy is extant today. There is also no trace of *On Astronomy*.

These studies were preparatory to engagement with logic and metaphysics. In logic, Aristotle and the Peripatetic tradition held unrivalled authority. The standard guide was the *Isagoge* ("Introduction") by Porphyry, which had been translated into Latin by Marius Victorinus. Boethius first wrote a commentary on this version, but, having access to Porphyry's Greek, he was unhappy with the accuracy of the rendering and decided to start afresh, this time making his own translation. The method would be his practice thereafter, as he set about the task of translating and commenting upon Aristotle himself. He would translate a portion of text, then write commentary upon it, relying heavily upon Neoplatonist predecessors, above all Porphyry. In this way he worked through the various treatises of Aristotle's *Organon* ("Instrument of Thought"): *Categories*; *On Interpretation*; *Prior* and *Posterior*

Analytics; *Topics*; and *On Sophistical Refutations*. In a number of cases he produced two commentaries, the second more advanced than the first. By the time he was writing his second study of *On Interpretation*, he was confident that he could go on to do the same job of translation and commentary for the entire corpus of Aristotle's extant writings, and all of Plato's dialogues. He never got beyond Aristotle, or much beyond Aristotle's logic (he seems to have written some explanatory comments also on Aristotle's *Physics*, though not a translation or substantive commentary), and even this would occupy his scholarly energies for over 20 years (Ebbesen, 1990; Shiel, 1990; Asztalos, 1993; Marenbon, 2003, 17–42).

Only some of these works survive. The translations favor literalism over style; the results make for dense reading, but achieve impressive fidelity to the Greek. As a commentator, his method is typical of the Neoplatonist tradition: the scholar's task is to comment respectfully rather than use the texts as a springboard for independent thought. There is little interest in originality, or in the excavation of the extensive secondary authorities cited. In the period *c.*513–22 Boethius also wrote a series of books on specific themes arising from the Aristotelian corpus, including logical divisions, categorical and hypothetical syllogisms, and topical differences (Chadwick, 1981, 163–73; Marenbon, 2003, 43–65). Here his secondary sources were not so much Neoplatonists but the later Peripatetics and Cicero (on whose *Topics* he also wrote a commentary). His discussions are again intended not to forge his own system of formal or scientific logic, but to educate in the sorts of skills appropriate to reasoned engagement with serious questions.

Incomplete, derivative, and often leaden in style, Boethius's overall program of translating and expounding Greek philosophy nevertheless proved of lasting significance. His versions furnished the Christian West with almost all it knew of Aristotle's writings until the Middle Ages, and his commentaries provided scholars with a major expository resource long after the Western rediscovery of Aristotle's corpus in the early twelfth century (Lewry, 1981; Marenbon, 2003, 165–70). But Boethius was much more than a preserver of texts or a teacher of logic: he was also a philosophical theologian.

III. Logic in the Service of Theology

His five *Opuscula Sacra* ("Short Theological Works") were produced in the period 519–23 (Stewart, Rand, and Tester, 1973). Probably designed not for general readership but for a limited circle of mentors, family, and friends in Rome, they may have been collected by one such figure, John the Deacon, conceivably the elderly John who became pope in 523; two are addressed to him, another to Symmachus. The issues are of wider relevance in any case (Daley, 1984). The sequence of the texts as we have them does not reflect their chronological order. The earliest is probably the fourth, *On the Catholic Faith*. Its authenticity has been subject to much dispute, but most scholars now agree that, on both material and stylistic grounds, it is the work of Boethius (Bark, 1946; Chadwick, 1980). It is essentially a statement of orthodox Christian belief: Christianity is depicted as a revealed religion, with a specific historical and doctrinal content which it is heretical to dispute. Beginning with the authority of the Bible, Boethius summarizes Catholic teaching on the Trinity, then traces the course of salvation history from creation and Fall onwards, through God's relations with Israel, to the incarnation, life, death, resurrection, and ascension of Christ, the spread of the Christian message, and the hope of the world to come. The work is much influenced by Augustine, though his name appears nowhere.

Next in order came Tractate V. *Against Eutyches and Nestorius* was inspired by a letter written by a group of Eastern bishops to the church in Rome, seeking clarification on christology. Eutyches (*c.*378–454) had held that there was only one nature in Christ, that of the divine Word; Nestorius (*c.*380–451) had allegedly— the allegation was unfair—maintained that there were two distinct persons (*prosopa*), one divine and one human. Both views were condemned by Chalcedon, which spoke of one incarnate person, "acknowledged in two natures, without confusion, without change, without division, without separation." The East as a whole was, however, deeply divided between those who accepted this language and those—dubbed by their opponents Monophysites, or advocates of a "single-nature" christology insufficiently distinct from Eutyches'—who insisted that although Christ

existed *from* two natures there was in his incarnate person "one nature out of two." The bishops who wrote to Rome upheld Chalcedon's "*in* two natures," but were inclined to concede "*from* two natures" as well, as a gesture to other sensibilities currently in political ascendancy in the East; they sought guidance on what the difference might really be, and on how the Chalcedonian *via media* between the respective heresies of Eutychianism and Nestorianism made sense. Boethius was dismayed at the lack of logical rigor evident in the discussion that their letter provoked, and his treatise was an effort to sort out the issues at stake: chiefly, the definition of "natures" and "person."

Noting the different senses in which "nature" can be understood (to refer variously to everything that exists, to corporeal substances, or to incorporeal ones), Boethius favors an Aristotelian conception of a nature as "the specific difference that gives form to each thing" (*Opuscula sacra* [hereafter *OS*] V, 1.57–8). The Latin *persona* had a long history in theological discourse, to refer first to the Greek *prosopon*, used to describe each of the three divine identities, Father, Son, and Holy Spirit, then to render the Greek *hypostasis*. In Aristotelian terms, a *hypostasis* is a "substance" in the sense of a thing which acts as a substrate (*hypostasis* literally = "that which stands under") for accidents; this construal had been subject to other appraisal by the Neoplatonist tradition, but it is the one that Boethius prefers, encouraged by the fact that the Latin *substantia* is the literal equivalent of *hypostasis*. In what would become a highly influential definition for later theology, a "person," he writes, is "an individual substance of a rational nature" (*OS* V, 3.4–5). Armed with these specifications, Boethius is able to demonstrate that neither Eutychianism nor Nestorianism is logically coherent: the one implies that there can be some kind of transformation of human things into divine ones; the other suggests that there is merely a juxtaposition, not a union, of individual substances. Logical differentiation provides the key to the justification of Chalcedon's christology as the only intellectually tenable option.

Tractate III is a response to a question from John about *How Substances are Good in that they Exist yet are not Substantial Goods*. Its opening words ("You ask me to state and explain a little more clearly that obscure question in my *Hebdomads* …") have been taken to imply that John's query was generated by some lost work of Boethius so named (*Hebdomads* = "Groups of Seven"). Other explanations have also been proffered: that the nine rules that Boethius goes on to enunciate as his guiding principles in the treatise really amount to seven; that the term "Hebdomad" refers to a period of philosophical debate that John and Boethius had had; and so on. To confuse things further, in the Middle Ages Tractate III itself was mistakenly given the title *De Hebdomadibus*. The setting is probably quite simple, however: "Hebdomads," a title given to a number of intentionally heavyweight works in antiquity, may very well be a playful name used by John to refer to Boethius's philosophy in general (along the lines of, "Tell me more about that idea you have in your Grand Treatise"). The argument that follows is essentially Platonist: existence as such is a good, and all particular goods are good insofar as they are related to the ultimate source of all goodness, God, who is the source of all being. For Boethius, it is axiomatic that everything that exists tends to the good, and that everything tends to its like; hence everything is by nature good. But is this goodness acquired by participation or by substance? If the former, it appears to be an accident: existence and goodness can be conceived as separable. If the latter, there can be no distinction between things that are good and the prime good itself. The solution is to say that, in the case of things that derive their existence from the prime good, existence and goodness could conceivably be distinguished, whereas in the case of the prime good itself it is inconceivable that goodness could be mentally abstracted: in God, being and goodness are identical. The goodness in created things is not an accident, but nor is it substantial, such that these things are indistinguishable from the prime good; rather, their goodness attaches to the fact that they owe their existence to the will of the God who alone cannot exist without being good.

There follow two treatises on the Trinity. Tractate II, on *Whether Father, Son and Holy Spirit may be substantially predicated of the Divinity*, seems to have been a prior sketch for Tractate I, *The Trinity is One God, Not Three Gods*. The context was a further series of efforts to mend relations between Rome and Constantinople, this time by reviving fifth-century language about "one of the Trinity" suffering in the flesh. Such formulae raised the question of God and number: to

what extent could the members of the one Trinity be enumerated as three, and how might such differentiation be undertaken? Boethius's starting point is "the foundations of the catholic faith" (*OS* II, 5): the one divine substance cannot be separated or divided, nor does it consist of various "parts," combined into one: it is simply one. Accordingly, everything predicated of the divine substance is common to the Three, and at the same time predicable of each of the Three. Such predicates include truth, goodness, immutability, justice, and omnipotence: all these are substantial attributes. Anything predicable *only* of each of the Three and not of the Three together is not, however, substantial. The terms "Father," "Son," and "Holy Spirit" apply uniquely to particular persons of the Three, and thus cannot be predicated of the Divinity in a substantial manner, but "in some other manner" (*alio quodam modo*): they are applied in a *relative* fashion (*ad aliquid*): the Father is the Father to the Son, the Son is the Father's Son, and so on (*OS* II, 44–51).

The roots of much of this lie in Boethius's reading of Augustine's magisterial work *On the Trinity*, especially Book 5. In Tractate I, he acknowledges this debt, and expands considerably upon the line of argument thus opened up by an Augustinian construal of divine relations. As we might expect, his favored method is basically Aristotelian. Identity and otherness have to be determined in one of three ways: with reference to genus, species, or number. In the case of God, neither genus nor species is relevant for the differentiation of Father, Son, and Holy Spirit; but what about number? After all, three human beings may share a genus and a species, yet be three. Such threeness is, however, a matter of accident, illustrated by the fact that in physical terms alone three bodies cannot occupy the same place simultaneously. In theology, the point is heightened: unlike physics or mathematics, theology deals with substance which is without matter or motion, and which can only be approached by means of intellectual concepts. The divine substance is Form without matter, and, unlike all other things, is not made of separate elements in combination; its unity and its being simply coincide. The divine substance does not consist of this and that taken together, any more than it consists of this taken apart from that: "it is what it is" (*est id quod est*: *OS* I, 2.31). Accordingly, in this supreme One there is no number: nothing is present except God's own essence, and that essence cannot be a substrate of anything, for it is pure Form, to which the accidents of the material do not apply. In God there is no difference, no plurality, no multiplicity; there is simply unity alone. The names "Father," "Son," and "Holy Spirit" do not denote three different Gods; they are a "threefold predication" of the one God (*OS* I, 3.30).

Of the Aristotelian categories—substance, quality, quantity, relation, place, time, condition, situation, activity, passivity—the first three are intrinsic (they denote what a thing is); the rest, with the exception of relation, are extrinsic (they indicate the circumstances in which the thing exists). Extrinsic predications can be made about both created things and God, but while all intrinsic predications are substantial when they apply to God, extrinsic predications are not. In fact, extrinsic predications only apply to God in a qualified way: for example, to say that God is "everywhere" does not mean that God is in every place, but rather that every place is present to God for God to occupy; God is everywhere but in no place. Relation is different from all the other categories. It neither adds to nor subtracts from nor alters the essence of an object in any way (to stand on someone's "right" or "left" makes no difference to the person's essence, only to the relation of the person to oneself). Relation thus implies merely that a comparison is possible, and—crucially—the comparison may not be simply with something other than the object, but also with the object itself: a thing may have a relationship to itself, such as a relationship of equality. In the case of God, "Father" and "Son" are relational terms, again, but they are used of the one God who is not altered or changed in so relating. What is denoted by the relation is a unique kind of distinction, an "otherness of persons" (*alteritas personarum*), a phrase that tries "to interpret something that can scarcely be understood" (*OS* I, 5.33–40). God does not become Father by the addition of an accident to his substance, even though the word "Father" is relative, for the Father's generation of the Son is a matter of substance: God begets God, and there is no point of difference at which Father and Son are distinguished from God.

The upshot is that relation secures the manifoldness (*numerositas*: *OS* I, 6.4) of God, while substance speaks of God's unity. Like Augustine, Boethius is cautious about the pertinence of the word "person" in a

Trinitarian context, but accepts that it is serviceable so long as creaturely analogy is not pressed; in the case of God, we have somehow to conceive of a relation between two "persons," a Father and a Son, for whom fatherhood and filiation are reflexive: there is only one God, who is self-related in this way. Boethius is well aware that at this point human logic reaches its limits, but the challenge to reason, he suggests, may be not because logic actually breaks down but because we are overly distracted by the imagination's tendency to lead astray through its preoccupation with transient things. The Platonist overtones are clear.

The most obvious feature of the tractates is their formal register. *On the Catholic Faith* rehearses a scriptural narrative, but the other treatises engage in no exegetical reflection; analytical reason, not scripture or the history of its interpretation, lies in the foreground. Boethius is the defender of an orthodox christological and Trinitarian inheritance, a critic of heresies, the heir of a Western doctrinal tradition, yet the resources on which he draws are not those of patristic authority. Writing as a scholarly layman, aware that his intellectual training is far superior to that of many ecclesiastical disputants, he uses logic to demolish error and to set forth, calmly and confidently, the intellectual coherence of orthodox convictions. In this cause, and with an elite readership especially in mind, a certain synthesis of classical metaphysics and Christian theology can be presupposed rather than labored; Tractate III approaches its theme in terms that any Platonist, Christian or otherwise, might follow. At various points his arguments beg questions, and there are serious difficulties inherent in some of his definitions—his influential construal of "person," for example, has received a good deal of critique in modern theology for its overtly individualistic and rationalistic cast, and its role within an anthropological tradition that had baleful effects on Western thought. Overall, however, the tractates deserve respect for two things. First, Boethius is concerned to prosecute theological discussion with real rigor and clarity, not to hide doctrinal substance behind a smokescreen of merely traditional terminology, pious ambiguity, or studied agnosticism. In the process, he goes considerably further than any patristic theologian, including Augustine, in applying logical differentiation to theological questions. Second, he is exacting in his effort to show just where it is that logical classification, derived from the created world, genuinely reaches its limits in reference to God. He is aware that, for all its powers, natural reasoning will encounter challenges at some point. But the point is that theology has no grounds to appeal to mystery too soon: it can and must pursue the business of thinking in the confidence that genuine knowledge of transcendent truth is possible for finite minds. Delimiting the proper core of revealed mystery is its business.

In modeling a combination of analytical precision and commitment to tracing the far boundaries of theological predication, Boethius serves as one of the chief pioneers of medieval theological method. He had a significant impact on debates about Trinitarianism and about universals in the Carolingian period, and his work was treated as a vital resource in the twelfth century, inspiring aspects of Abélard's exposition of Trinitarian persons and attracting a major commentary from Gilbert of Poitiers (*c*.1085–1154)—though Gilbert's innovative and large-scale expansion of his Trinitarian metaphysics was itself highly controversial. With the recovery of Aristotle and the emergence of other styles of dialectics the *opuscula* gradually came to be cited in sentence-literature more than they were studied as venerable textbooks in their own right, but I and III were also the subject of notable commentaries by Aquinas (Gibson, 1981, 214–34; Marenbon, 2003, 170–2).

IV.   The *Consolation of Philosophy*

Boethius's other substantive engagement with theological themes is to be found in his final book. Translated by Alfred the Great, Jean de Meun, Geoffrey Chaucer, and Elizabeth I, commented on extensively in the medieval schools, a comfort to Dante, an inspiration to Boccaccio, recommended reading for educated people well into modern times—the *Consolation* is Boethius's greatest literary achievement (Courcelle, 1967; Minnis, 1987; Hoenen and Nauta, 1997; Kaylor and Phillips, 2007). A work of considerable learning and art (for introduction, see Crabbe, 1981; Lerer, 1985; introductions to Walsh, 1999; Relihan, 2001), it evokes a range of classical genres:

the philosophical dialogue; the *consolatio*, offering moral medicine to the grieving; and Menippean satire, a type of composition inherited by Latin writers from Greek origins, in which the follies of human existence, including its pretensions to wisdom, were deflated in a prose–verse combination.

Book 1 sets the scene, introducing Philosophy as teacher and physician of the bewildered prisoner lamenting his misfortunes. Her personification is a long-standing trope, favored by Plato, Cicero, and Seneca among others. In Book 2 Philosophy denounces Boethius's bitter complaint about his lot, and invokes an also personified Fortune to justify her ways with humans; the upshot of the argument is that Fortune, whose essence is change, actually benefits humans more when adverse than when favorable, for in adversity people are led away from specious notions of happiness toward the true good. Book 3 considers further the nature of real happiness. Quests for riches, status, and glory, or the pursuit of bodily pleasure, are false ends. The perfect good, in which genuine happiness lies, is God; God is the good which all things seek, and all things are ordered by that good, "the helm and rudder by which the frame of the world is held steady and undamaged" (3.12.14). Book 4 addresses the issue of why, if this God is in charge, there is so much apparently mixed justice in the world. It is vital, Philosophy argues, to discern the proper relationship between divine Providence, which is God's all-embracing purpose, and Fate, which is the subordinate outworking of this will at the level of earthly realities in a world of change. Every fortune, pleasant or unpleasant, is in fact (and mysterious as it may seem) good, for it serves the end of the good, rewarding or exercising virtuous people, punishing or correcting the wicked.

But how can human beings have free will if there is such a divine Providence? In Book 5 Philosophy differentiates four levels of cognition: sensation, imagination, reason, and understanding; these correspond with four levels of existence: immobile life, the life of lower animals, human life, and divine life. The apparent tension between divine foreknowledge and creaturely free will can be resolved only at the fourth: God, who is eternal, knows all things, past, present, and future, in the same way that humans, who are in time, know what is present. Since God's knowledge is always in the present, future events are necessary, in relation to their being known by God, in just the way that anything which is presently the case is necessary; yet in their own nature some future events will be necessary but others freely chosen. Divine foreknowledge does not change the nature and character of things; human free will remains. It is worth praying to God and pursuing virtue, for God dispenses rewards to the good and punishments to the wicked.

The *Consolation* raises complex questions about theodicy, evil, necessity, freedom, cognition, and time, the substance of which needs to be pursued in the secondary literature (Chadwick, 1981, 223–47; Marenbon, 2003, 96–145, citing other vital references). For the theologian, the most striking feature of the work is that there is nothing explicitly Christian about its argument. Classical figures are mentioned or evoked frequently; there is no reference to biblical models, no mention of Christ. Some of the sentiments about fortune are tinged with Stoic sentiment; the bulk of the reasoning overall is Platonist. The prisoner is led back from the darkness and falsehood of undue attention to physical circumstances toward the light and truth of the Supreme Good. True happiness is found as the soul recollects its origins in the transcendent One, and rediscovers the awareness that its end, like the end of all things, is this Good, from which it is deflected by false images of fulfillment. At the central point in the treatise, a solemn prayer to God in Book 3, chapter 9, which precedes Philosophy's turn to prescribe the true medicine that Boethius needs, the idiom is strongly evocative of Plato's *Timaeus* and of Neoplatonist sentiments. The opening to Book 4 draws on Plato's *Gorgias* for the argument that virtuous people are truly happy and strong; the theodicy that then unfolds is deeply marked by Neoplatonist ideas about evil as privation and about participation in the good as the key to freedom. In the final poem of the book, Agamemnon, Odysseus, and Hercules, not Job, David, or Paul, are cited as inspiring examples of perseverance and achievement. Book 5's discussion of contingency assumes Aristotelian ideas on absolute and incidental causality; the closing account of time as a moving image of eternity is expressly evocative of Plato.

Why would the Christian Boethius *in extremis* not have turned directly to scripture and the native logic of his faith for consolation? This question has bothered readers since at least the early tenth century, and all kinds of explanations have been offered (Chadwick, 1981, 247–53; Marenbon, 2003, 154–63): the author of the *Consolatio* was not the author of the theological tractates; Boethius lost his faith in prison; Boethius never was a genuine Christian at all, but always a Platonist first and foremost. Other construals have tended in the opposite direction: Lady Philosophy is strongly evocative of Old Testament Wisdom (Wisd. 8:1 is clearly echoed at 3.12.22), or perhaps an angel of the Christian God, sent to lead a wayward child back, slowly but surely, to his real parent; the setting for the treatise is a Christian visionary experience; the entire argument is designed not to celebrate philosophy's capacity to console, but to demonstrate its *inadequacy* so to do—and thus, by a subtle irony typical of the Menippean tradition, to invite readers to consider the superiority of Christian faith (Relihan, 1993, 187–94). Others suggest that Boethius was endeavoring to show the complementarity of Christian and non-Christian ideas: perhaps he was conscious of the example of Augustine, who, in his journey towards Christianity and in his earliest philosophical writing, found common ground in Platonism and faith; or perhaps, influenced by a certain style of Greek Neoplatonism, he saw grounds to develop a model of an essentially rational theology, distinct from but congenial to scripture's assumptions.

The work contains some biblical echoes (though none as clear as the Wisdom reference just mentioned), some probable allusions to liturgical language, and some idioms on the freedom of creation and on divine providence that may belong more with Christian than Neoplatonist logic. At the same time, there are features that are undoubtedly odd from a Christian perspective, such as the depiction of God as the World Soul in 3 m.9. The most persuasive reading is that Boethius is indeed writing as a Christian for educated Christian readers, and that he is interested neither in effecting a contrived synthesis of faith and philosophy nor in exposing the bankruptcy of philosophy: for him, there simply is no serious tension between his Christian belief and a philosophical inquiry into divine justice and human freedom. An essentially non-Christian Philosophy is his teacher and guide; some but not all of her views are congenial, and she sounds most Christian when she directly echoes the prisoner's own words; but there is no indication that her counsel as a whole is inadequate. Boethius's approach to theological issues always was via philosophical thought, and four of his five tractates are as affected by Neoplatonism as anything here. What he does in the *Consolation* is to ponder his existential plight, and the ethical conundra it presents, in keeping with those instincts, deploying polished literary form to convey a message that is in the end religious: a plea to hope in God and pray to God even in the face of the worst that life can bring.

There are arguably far greater challenges than Boethius may realize to his assumption that the Christian God's identity can be so neatly equated with the God of whom Philosophy speaks, and far greater obstacles than he supposes to a straightforward fusion of Platonist and biblical accounts of reality. Nevertheless, the ethics of the *Consolation* were deeply respected by Christian philosophers such as Aquinas, and a long line of medieval Christian

commentaries, from the overtly syncretistic Remigius of Auxerre (*c*.841–908) and William of Conches (*c*.1090–1160) to the more measured English Dominican Nicholas Trivet (*c*.1257–1334), could see the text as a subtly rich resource for Christian piety. Undoubtedly some representatives of that tradition showed too much ingenuity in their quest to align Philosophy's arguments with biblical doctrine, but the fact that they found reason to do so testifies both to the possibilities of the work and to the enduring appeal of Boethius's depiction of the God–world relation. To much Christian theology today, that vision may well appear far too generic, far too bereft of incarnational specificity, to be of serious service. But there is no reason to doubt Boethius's Christian faith. In his mind, the moral lessons of philosophical theism for human sufferers were not at odds with the doctrinal assumptions of his tractates, nor did philosophical dialogue represent a Christianly unworthy means of pondering the ultimate dilemmas of life. Whether he was right or not is a question too large to explore here; the fact that he saw things so confirms his place as a theologian entirely of his time.

References

Primary texts

Bower, Calvin M. and Palisca, Claude V., trans. and eds. 1989. *Anicius Manlius Severinus Boethius: Fundamentals of Music*. New Haven and London: Yale University Press.

Magee, John, trans. and ed. 1998. *Anicii Manlii Severini Boethii "De divisione liber"*. Leiden: Brill.

Masi, Michael, trans. and ed. 1983. *Boethian Number Theory: A Translation of the* De institutione arithmetica *(with Introduction and Notes)*. Amsterdam: Editions Rodolpi.

Moreschini, Claudio, ed. 2000. *Boethius: De Consolatione Philosophiae; Opuscula sacra*. Bibliotheca Teubneriana. Munich and Leipzig: K. G. Saur. (The most recent critical texts.)

Relihan, Joel C., trans. and ed. 2001. *Boethius:* Consolation of Philosophy. Indianapolis and Cambridge: Hackett.

Stewart, H. F., Rand, E. K., and Tester, S. J., trans. and eds. 1973. *Boethius: The Theological Tractates; The Consolation of Philosophy*. Loeb Classical Library. Cambridge, MA and London: Harvard University Press.

Walsh, P. G., trans. and ed. 1999. *Boethius: The Consolation of Philosophy*. *Oxford World's Classics*. Oxford: Oxford University Press.

Watts, V. E., trans. and ed. 1999. *Boethius:* The Consolation of Philosophy, rev. ed. Penguin Classics. Harmondsworth: Penguin.

Other Latin texts can be found in PL (*Patrologiae cursus completus, series Latina*), CSEL (*Corpus Scriptorum Ecclesiasticorum Latinorum*), Teubner and Budé series.

Secondary works

Amory, Patrick. 1997. *People and Identity in Ostrogothic Italy, 489–554*. Cambridge: Cambridge University Press.

Asztalos, Monika. 1993. "Boethius as a Transmitter of Greek Logic to the Latin West: the *Categories*," *Harvard Studies in Classical Philology* 95: 367–407.

Bark, William. 1946. "Boethius's Fourth Tractate, the so-called *De fide catholica*," *Harvard Theological Review* 39: 55–69.

Chadwick, Henry. 1980. "The Authenticity of Boethius's Fourth Tractate *De fide catholica*," *Journal of Theological Studies* n.s. 31: 551–6.

Chadwick, Henry. 1981. *Boethius: The Consolations of Music, Logic, Theology, and Philosophy*. Oxford: Clarendon Press.

Courcelle, Pierre. 1967. *La Consolation de Philosophie dans la tradition littéraire Antécedents et posterité de Boèce.* . Paris: Etudes Augustiniennes.

Courcelle, Pierre. 1969. *Late Latin Writers and Their Greek Sources*, trans. Harry E. Wedeck. Cambridge, MA: Harvard University Press.

Crabbe, Anna. 1981. "Literary Design in the *De Consolatione Philosophiae*." In *Boethius: His Life, Thought and Influence*, ed. Margaret Gibson. Oxford: Blackwell, pp. 237–74.

Daley, Brian E. 1984. "Boethius's Theological Tracts and Early Byzantine Scholasticism," *Mediaeval Studies* 46: 158–91.

Dürr, Karl. 1951. *The Propositional Logic of Boethius.* Amsterdam: North-Holland.

Ebbesen, Sten. 1990. "Boethius as an Aristotelian Commentator." In *Aristotle Transformed: The Ancient Commentators and their Influence*, ed. Richard Sorabji. London: Duckworth; Ithaca, NY: Cornell University Press, pp. 373–391.

Fuhrmann, Manfred and Gruber, Joachim, eds. 1984. *Boethius.* Darmstadt: Wissenschaftliche Buchgesellschaft.

Gibson, Margaret, ed. 1981. *Boethius: His Life, Thought and Influence.* Oxford: Blackwell.

Gruber, Joachim. 1978. *Kommentar zu Boethius De Consolatione Philosophiae.* Berlin and New York: De Gruyter.

Hoenen, Maarten J. F. M. and Nauta, Lodi, eds. 1997. *Boethius in the Middle Ages: Latin and Vernacular Traditions of the Consolatio philosophiae.* Leiden: Brill.

Kaylor, Noel Harold, Jr. 1992. *The Medieval Consolation of Philosophy. An Annotated Bibliography.* New York: Garland; London: Routledge.

Kaylor, Noel Harold, Jr. and Phillips, Philip Edward, eds. 2007. *New Directions in Boethian Studies.* Kalamazoo, MI: Western Michigan University.

Lerer, Seth. 1985. *Boethius and Dialogue: Literary Method in the Consolation of Philosophy.* Princeton, NJ: Princeton University Press.

Lewry, Osmund. 1981. "Boethian Logic in the Medieval West." In *Boethius: His Life, Thought and Influence*, ed. Margaret Gibson. Oxford: Blackwell, pp. 90–134.

Magee, John. 1989. *Boethius on Signification and Mind.* Leiden: Brill.

Marenbon, John. 2003. *Boethius.* Oxford: Oxford University Press.

Marenbon, John, ed. Forthcoming. *The Cambridge Companion to Boethius.* Cambridge: Cambridge University Press.

Masi, Michael, ed. 1981. *Boethius and the Liberal Arts: A Collection of Essays.* Bern: Peter Lang.

Minnis, Alastair J., ed. 1987. *The Medieval Boethius: Studies in the Vernacular Translations of "De Consolatione Philosophiae."* Woodbridge: Brewer.

Moorhead, John. 1992. *Theoderic in Italy.* Oxford: Clarendon Press.

Obertello, Luca. 1974. *Severino Boezio*, 2 vols. Genoa: Accademia Ligure di Scienze e Lettere.

O'Daly, Gerard. 1991. *The Poetry of Boethius.* London: Duckworth.

O'Donnell, James J., ed. 1990. *Boethius:* De Consolatione Philosophiae. Bryn Mawr, PA: Bryn Mawr College. (Commentary on Latin; also available online at http://etext.virginia.edu/latin/boethius/.)

Phillips, Philip Edward and Kaylor, Noel Harold, Jr., eds. Forthcoming. *A Companion to Boethius in the Middle Ages.* Leiden: Brill.

Reiss, Edmund. 1982. *Boethius.* Boston: Twayne.

Relihan, Joel C. 1993. *Ancient Menippean Satire.* Baltimore, MA and London: Johns Hopkins University Press.

Shiel, James. 1990. "Boethius's Commentaries on Aristotle." In *Aristotle Transformed: The Ancient Commentators and Their Influence*, ed. Richard Sorabji. London: Duckworth; Ithaca, NY: Cornell University Press, pp. 349–72.

Sorabji, Richard, ed. 1990. *Aristotle Transformed: The Ancient Commentators and Their Influence.* London: Duckworth; Ithaca, NY: Cornell University Press.

Carmina Philosophiae, the Journal of the International Boethius Society, also publishes papers of interest.

The Cappadocians (*c.*329–*c.*524)

Andrew Radde-Gallwitz

Basil of Caesarea (*c.*329–378/9), his younger brother Gregory of Nyssa (*c.*335–*c.*394), and his sometime friend Gregory of Nazianzus (*c.*330–391) emerged in the late fourth century as leading theologians and churchmen in the Greek-speaking eastern Mediterranean. They were connected by family and friendship, as well as by common doctrinal allegiances and a shared commitment to the ascetic life. These connections have led modern scholars to characterize the three together as "the Cappadocians" after the Roman province of Cappadocia (in modern Turkey), where all three were bishops for at least part of their careers. Yet it is important to note that this designation is something of a scholarly construct which goes back only to the nineteenth century, and thus does not necessarily reflect how they were perceived in their own time or in Eastern or Western calendars of saints' memorials. Still, it is not without value to treat the three together, provided one bears in mind the artificiality of the "Cappadocian" label and remains attentive to the differences among the three.

Since all three were born during the reign of Constantine the Great, none of the trio experienced official Roman hostility toward Christianity, at least not until the reign of the emperor Julian (361–363). Called "the Apostate" by Christians, Julian turned away from the pro-Christian policies of the Constantinian dynasty. Julian did not systematically put Christians to death as some pre-Constantinian

emperors like Decius and Diocletian had done. However, he did, among other things, forbid Christians from holding positions teaching rhetoric. His "persecution" (if it can be so called) was more of a struggle for the cultural soul of Roman elites. And it was a struggle the Cappadocians were eager to take up.

Basil and Gregory of Nazianzus were educated in that epicenter of Hellenism, Athens, at the same time that the young Julian was studying there. Julian's ban on Christian rhetoricians was in effect a way of asserting that there was a close link between Greek culture and traditional Greek religion. The literature of Homer, Hesiod, and Euripides, the philosophy of Plato and Pythagoras—these and many more cultural gems belong to "Greeks," a group being defined over against "Christians" (or "Nazarenes" as Julian called them).

The reply of Basil and Gregory of Nazianzus would have long-lasting influence, particularly in the Greek-speaking Byzantine Empire. They followed Origen in claiming that Christians could, like the ancient Hebrews during the exodus, "despoil the Egyptians" by appropriating the riches of the Greek literary, rhetorical, and philosophical traditions for Christian purposes—and their works are filled with erudite allusions to the classics.

Education in some of the finest schools of the late ancient world placed Basil and the Gregories in a position from which they could pursue the life of the

The Student's Companion to the Theologians, First Edition. Edited by Ian S. Markham.
© 2013 Blackwell Publishing Ltd. Published 2013 by Blackwell Publishing Ltd.

cultured rhetor, as professors or in high posts within the imperial administration. After returning from Athens, Basil became professor of rhetoric at Caesarea, following the path of his father, a grammarian at Neocaesarea in Pontus. But Basil's older sister, Macrina (d.379) had better plans for him. On Gregory of Nyssa's account in his *Life of Macrina*, she persuaded Basil to abandon such vain pursuits and pursue a monastic vocation, as she was doing at the family villa at Annisa in Pontus. Basil had another mentor in the ascetic life, the "philosopher" Eustathius, bishop of Sebasteia. Basil resigned his post and established a monastic dwelling-place near the family's estate in Annisa. He wrote to his friend, Gregory of Nazianzus, inviting him to join him in the "philosophical life" here, which he did. Together at Annisa, the two edited a collection of extracts from Origen's works called the *Philokalia* ("love of beauty"). Though Nazianzen did not share Basil's enthusiasm for this spot—he called it a "rat hole"—or for the extremes of Basil's asceticism, he did come to share his view that the lives of the professor or civil administrator and the life of the ascetic Christian were largely incompatible.

The younger Gregory of Nyssa probably spent some time with the two at the retreat in Annisa, abandoning it for a post teaching rhetoric in Cappadocian Caesarea. Nazianzen wrote to him, expressing dismay at his assumption that he could safely practice Christianity while holding such a post. The letter contains learned references to Hesiod and others. The implication is clear: a serious, baptized, ascetic Christian will not pursue the worldly honor of the secular rhetorician; but baptism is not incompatible with immersion in Greek literature. Gregory of Nyssa would eventually return to the philosophical life.

Basil and Nazianzen did not remain in seclusion, and Nyssen did not remain in his professorial post. They are best known for the work they did after being made bishops. In fact, Basil, the first to become bishop, consecrated the Gregories as bishops, a move Nazianzen resented. The friendship between Basil and Nazianzen did not survive this event and Nazianzen oscillated throughout his life between episcopal service and periods of seclusion. Unlike the secular careers they gave up, the Cappadocians did not view public roles in the church as contradictory to their ascetic commitments, but rather articulated a

theology of the monk-bishop that would become influential in later Byzantine theology. For the Cappadocians, the best bishop is one chosen not for his social status, but for his spiritual character. They advocated the mixed life of contemplation and action. The bishop who embodied ascetic virtues would lead his flock in matters of doctrinal orthodoxy and would model the central Christian virtue of philanthropy toward the poor. Their contributions in these public roles did not go unnoticed. Nazianzen became for a short time leader of the community in Constantinople that would, with the support of the emperor Theodosius, give the Christian tradition its basic confession of faith, the Nicene-Constantinopolitan Creed of 381. Though Nazianzen would fall out with this community, Nyssen would continue to enjoy imperial favor throughout the 380s.

Basil of Caesarea

Basil's principal contributions lie in two areas: his directions for monastic life and his role in the development of the doctrine of the Trinity. Basil's thoughts on the ascetic life are contained in a number of sources. In addition to letters to friends like Gregory of Nazianzus, after his ordination as priest and then bishop Basil sent instructions to communities of male and female ascetics. Throughout these works, his fundamental concern lies with the spiritual dispositions of the ascetics, rather than with offering detailed regulations of monastic practice. In his early *Letter* 2 to Nazianzen, he speaks of the need for mental tranquility and for utter separation from the world. He also recommends a method of biblical meditation in which the monk takes each major biblical holy person as an exemplar of a particular virtue. Basil's fullest instructions on the ascetic life survive under the titles of the *Shorter Rules* and *Longer Rules*, which together make up the *Great Asceticon*. The *Rules* consist of instructions given in question-and-answer format. Presumably many of them arose from real concerns among his monastic communities. It is clear that ongoing revisions of an originally shorter work (which came to be known as the *Small Asceticon*) were made throughout Basil's life. The *Longer Rules* begin with a striking interpretation of the Gospels' Double Commandment to love God and neighbor. For Basil, this commandment is utterly different from an ordinary command, in which an external authority figure imposes a law onto someone. Rather, this command is rooted in our very nature as created in God's image. The monastic life is not fundamentally about following a set of orders; it is rather a disciplined, communal process aimed at bringing to light the seeds of love which God has sown in one's deepest self. Basil's influence in this area extended beyond the East. Portions of Basil's ascetic writings made their way west and were endorsed by Benedict of Nursia in his own highly influential *Rule*, which eventually became the charter for Western monasticism. Like Benedict, Basil stresses the need for monastic *community*; both are suspicious of attempts by monks to go it alone in isolation.

Basil did not remain at the retreat in Annisa. Rather, he entered into public life, first as a priest in Caesarea and later as bishop of this metropolitan see. In these positions, he faced a series of struggles, which would also engulf Nazianzen and Nyssen, over the Christian doctrine of God. The first struggle began while Basil was a priest and involved a radical theologian named Eunomius who argued that the Father and the Son are unlike in essence. In his work entitled the *Apology*, Eunomius argued in characteristically rationalistic fashion that God's defining attribute is being without origin and "unbegotten." This clearly rules out the Son's equality with God the Father, since the Son is the "Only-Begotten." For Eunomius, the separate activities of Father and Son rule out their sharing a common substance. Basil responded to this work in a three-book work entitled *Against Eunomius*. He argued that terms like "unbegotten" do not define God, though they do reflect some truth about God. For Basil, we cannot know the essence of God, as Eunomius claimed. But we can know that certain attributes are appropriate to God, such as goodness, wisdom, power, and life.

Basil distinguishes between terms we attribute to God because of the divine activities, all of which the Father, Son, and Holy Spirit accomplish in common, and terms we attribute individually to the three "persons." (Later in his career, Basil would contribute to technical Trinitarian terminology by arguing that *hypostasis* is the best Greek word for capturing the distinct realities of Father, Son, and Spirit within the common divine nature, but that development had not yet occurred in *Against Eunomius*.) Some things we say of God "in common," such as that God is light, life, power, and goodness. No attribute of this sort is unique to one of the "persons." But each is distinguished by a peculiar feature (*idiôma* in Greek) that makes that person separate from and irreducible to the others. Basil's distinction between common and individual features in God will strongly influence the two Gregories who go on to develop a more fully Trinitarian theology. Basil also influentially argues that the Father's "begetting" of the Son is an eternal, immaterial act of causality; the word connotes no temporal or material process and does not imply that the Son is a created being. In the mid-360s when Basil wrote *Against Eunomius*, Basil speaks of the Son as "like in substance" (*homoios kat' ousian*) to the Father, a position which to some contemporaries appeared incompatible with Nicaea's confession that the Son is "of the *same* substance" (*homoousion*) with the Father. However, Basil does not seem to have viewed the two claims as incompatible.

Basil develops his Trinitarian theology further in later works, especially *On the Holy Spirit*. Here the opponent is not primarily Eunomius, but a group led by his former friend and mentor, Eustathius of Sebasteia, who have been derisively labeled "Pneumatomachians" ("Spirit-fighters"). These were former allies of Basil who accepted that the Son is like in essence to the Father, but denied the Spirit's divinity. Basil argues for ranking the Holy Spirit with the Father and the Son from the shared activities of the three. Yet, he is reticent about directly calling the Spirit "God," preferring to keep silent where scripture is silent. Basil appeals to liturgical tradition as a source for Christian doctrine, arguing that the church's practice of baptizing in the names of the Father, the Son, and the Holy Spirit must shape how the church confesses God. To deny worship to the Spirit is to deny the Spirit's saving activity in baptism, an activity which he shares inseparably with the Father and the Son.

Gregory of Nazianzus

Gregory of Nazianzus is best known for a series of five sermons he delivered in Constantinople in 380 which were published as the *Theological Orations* (numbers 27–31 in his corpus of orations). The enormous influence of these reflections on the nature of God has earned him the title "the Theologian." The *Theological Orations* begin, not by addressing doctrinal matters directly, but by offering what Lewis Ayres (2004) has called a "theology of theology": an account of the dispositions and practices a good theologian should embody. Gregory approaches theology with a sense of wonder. In the doctrinal disputes about the Trinity which had rocked the Christian population for nearly a century, Gregory perceives an unfortunate theological populism. Theology is not such a cheap thing that it can be taken up by just anyone at any time for any purpose. It demands a rigorous self-examination in light of the mystery of Christ. It is not a game in which one tries to score rhetorical points against one's opponents, but a disciplined inquiry into the fundamental language of the Christian faith. This investigation requires spiritual seriousness as much as logical rigor. Gregory is particularly concerned to argue that one must purify one's thinking of materialistic images when contemplating the divine. Thinking of God in material terms (such as trying to envision the Trinity by way of visual analogies) is just another way of committing Eunomius's error of claiming that one has comprehended and defined the undefinable.

Gregory is perhaps the clearest of the Cappadocians in his insistence on the irreducible oneness and threeness of God. He even goes so far in his 23rd Oration as to suggest that the harmony in God of what seems to be irreconcilable (simple unity and trinity) *constitutes* the divine perfection. A master rhetorician, Gregory weaves the Trinitarian paradox into the very construction of his sentences, encouraging the reader (or listener) to hold divine unity and plurality together, simultaneously encouraging faith in the saving mystery and unsettling the audience's sense of having a grasp on God. Gregory is also much more insistent than Basil had been on affirming the Spirit's consubstantiality with God.

Gregory presided for a while as bishop of Constantinople during the ecumenical Council there in 381. Under pressure from opponents, he resigned from this post before the council's end. The creed's ambiguity on the Spirit, who is not explicitly called "God" or "consubstantial" with the Father or the Son,

may well reflect the lingering influence of Basil after his death and his more *homoiousian*-leaning followers rather than the immediate influence of Nazianzen. Still, Gregory of Nazianzus's influence on subsequent generations of theological minds far outstrips that of Basil or Nyssen. In addition to his role in the development of Trinitarian theology (a development which may have outpaced the official creedal development of the church), Gregory paved the way for developments in the church's teaching about the unity of Christ's humanity and divinity. Arguing against Apollinarius, who held that in Christ the Logos replaced the human mind, Gregory famously argued that the salvation of the whole of humanity required a union of the whole humanity with God in Christ. Even outside of these doctrinal writings, his body of work is wide-ranging, including letters, orations, and the most extensive body of poetry left behind by any early Christian author. His poetry includes the first in-depth works in the genre of Christian autobiography, which Augustine will take up in his *Confessions*.

Gregory of Nyssa

While modern theologians tend to know Nyssen primarily for his "mysticism," it is important not to overlook the range of topics his writings cover. Probably not long after being ordained priest by Basil, he wrote an encomium on the life of celibacy entitled *On Virginity*, the first of his many works on ascetic themes. He was interested in theological anthropology, as evidenced in his *On the Making of Humanity* and *On the Soul and Resurrection*. He wrote several series of homilies in which biblical exegesis and philosophy interpenetrate, dealing with themes such as the Genesis account of creation, the Lord's Prayer, and the Beatitudes. Like Nazianzen, he wrote against Apollinarian christology. He wrote lengthy tomes against Eunomius, a series of short works on Trinitarian theology, a work against believing in fate, a work on the problem of why some infants die prematurely, and biographical works, including one on his sister Macrina.

Gregory sees himself as taking up Basil's legacy after the latter's death in 378 or 379, fighting against both Eunomius and Pneumatomachians. Like Basil,

Gregory counters Eunomius's presumption to know the divine essence by emphasizing the unknowability of God. But, again like Basil, Gregory also defends the reliability of human reasoning about God. For Gregory, though human reasoning is limited, it is essential as the theologian struggles to form appropriate concepts of God by contemplating God's activities in scripture. As he says in his short work *To Eustathius on the Holy Trinity*, if we could know the essence of God on its own, we would not need to engage in the complex process of forming good notions of God. If the meaning of "God" were obvious, theology would be unnecessary. But since it is not, we do not simply throw up our hands and cry "mystery"; divine mystery is not a conversation-stopper. Rather, Gregory proposes that we investigate what we *do* know of God from scripture and from looking (with eyes formed by our reading of scripture) both within ourselves as images of God and at the created world around us. In this way we can form the best possible concepts of God, all the while recognizing their ultimate inability to describe the transcendent Source of all goodness and life. We need to investigate these notions in order to ensure that our teaching about God is salutary and consistent.

But, of course, for Gregory, Christianity is not ultimately about forming concepts at all, but about participation in that newness of life which comes to us, as he likes to say, "from the Father, through the Son, in the Holy Spirit." Gregory famously argues that, since God is infinite, the finite human will never exhaust the potential for further progress in this participation in God's life. The eschatological state is not stasis. Rather, the purified human being will continue to grow "from glory to glory," being ever more fully conformed to that perfection of goodness that is the Trinity.

Reference

Ayres, Lewis. 2004. *Nicaea and Its Legacy: An Approach to Fourth-Century Theology*. Oxford: Oxford University Press, pp. 273–343, 414–25.

Cyril of Alexandria (*c.*378–444) and Nestorius of Constantinople (*c.*381–*c.*451)

Daniel A. Keating

Introduction

The names Cyril of Alexandria and Nestorius of Constantinople are forever linked in the history of Christian theology. This is perhaps inevitable given their momentous conflict in the fifth-century Christological controversies, but also regrettable for at least two reasons. First, the political rivalry between these two protagonists (and their respective cities) tends to get placed in the foreground. Genuine theological issues and concerns are often obscured. Second, preoccupation with narrow christological issues causes wider theological contributions to be neglected. When students learn about Cyril and Nestorius, they hear only of the heated debates of 429–431 and usually read just their exchange of letters concerning the propriety of calling Mary *Theotokos*. All this is essential and understandable, but when attention is given solely to events leading up to the Council of Ephesus (431), political considerations predominate and Cyril and Nestorius end up being evaluated more for their moral character (or lack thereof) than for their specific theological convictions and contributions. The simple drama of events often overshadows the theological issues that were most precious to Cyril and Nestorius themselves.

The conflict began in 428 as a local dispute in Constantinople between the newly elected bishop, Nestorius, and a set of clerics, monks, and members of the royal family. Upon hearing of the conflict, Cyril intervened by letter from Alexandria. Very quickly the fracas escalated into an empire-wide controversy involving all five of the great sees of the ancient world: Alexandria, Constantinople, Antioch, Rome, and Jerusalem (for a detailed account of this conflict, see McGuckin, 2004, 20–107, and Russell, 2000, 31–56). At the heart of the controversy between Cyril and Nestorius was not political rivalry, but a concern for Christian truth and especially for a true understanding of the incarnation. Each was convinced that the other was denying something essential to the Christian account of salvation. According to Norman Russell (2000, 39), "despite the disclaimers, each believed that heretical conclusions were necessarily implied by the logic of the other's language about Christ." The sparring between Cyril and Nestorius culminated in the Council of Ephesus in the summer of 431. The final outcome—involving two rival councils and extensive negotiation—was the deposition of Nestorius and the approval of the council presided over by Cyril that upheld Mary as *Theotokos*. A fragile reconciliation of the two parties (Cyril and the Antiochenes) only occurred two years later with Cyril's signing of the Formula of Reunion, a carefully worded statement of Antiochene origin that acknowledged Mary as *Theotokos*, but also spoke of two natures in Christ after the union.

The Student's Companion to the Theologians, First Edition. Edited by Ian S. Markham.

This summary of events—more or less detailed—is what most students of the history of Christian doctrine are taught. What they fail to learn from this standard presentation is that Cyril was one of the great biblical commentators of the ancient church and that his early doctrinal works were concerned, not with christology per se, but with the defense and exploration of the doctrine of the Trinity. His substantial commentaries on Isaiah, the Minor Prophets, John, Luke, and his treatises on the spiritual interpretation of the Old Testament remain largely unknown and untapped.

Nestorius, unfortunately, became embroiled in theological controversy from the very beginning of his public term of office, and so was never at liberty to write more widely on other topics of the Christian faith. All his extant writings are directly concerned with defending his teaching on Christ and his struggle with Cyril. Nevertheless, by probing into his wider concerns and the theological context from which he came, we can gain a more sympathetic understanding of the positions he adopted, and can more effectively assess both his contributions and his shortcomings. For both Cyril and Nestorius, the goal is to understand each figure in his own context, and to view the significance and contribution of each to Christian theology.

Cyril of Alexandria

I. Background

The early years of Cyril's life are little known to us. His birth is usually placed around the year 378 in Egypt, and the evidence from the character and quality of his writings suggests that he received both the formal rhetorical education of his day and a very intensive education in the Scriptures and selected church fathers who preceded him (Hardy, 1982; Russell, 2000, 4–5; McGuckin, 2004, 4). According to Cyril's own testimony (*Ep.* 33.7), he was a bystander at the deposition of John Chrysostom at the Synod of the Oak in 403 in the company of his uncle, Theophilus, the powerful archbishop of Alexandria. Cyril seems never to have doubted the legitimacy of Chrysostom's deposition on disciplinary grounds, though he upheld the orthodoxy of his doctrine and gradually acquiesced in the reinstatement of his reputation.

Cyril succeeded Theophilus as bishop of Alexandria in 412. The first years of his reign were marked by sharp controversies: action against the Novationist sect, quarreling with the Jewish community in Alexandria, and the mob slaying of the Neoplatonist philosopher, Hypatia. To what extent Cyril was the instigator of these events, and therefore responsible for acts of rioting and violence, is disputed by scholars. Some estimate him as largely continuing the ruthless policies of his uncle, and so implicate him directly in these actions (Chadwick, 1967, 194; Russell, 2000, 6–9). Others minimize Cyril's role and responsibility for these events (Wickham, 1983, xiii; McGuckin, 2004, 7). No one denies that Cyril was politically astute and able to wield his influence effectively in favor of his positions. He was a man of strong opinions and decisive action. However, the common portrait of Cyril as the cunning plotter whose only aim was to advance his own power—and that of the church of Alexandria—is unpersuasive. He was genuinely concerned for the truth of the Christian gospel and the promotion of the church. The effort he expended over many years in the production of biblical commentary also belies the common caricature of Cyril: a bishop interested only in furthering his own political influence does not spend his career commenting on nearly the whole of the Bible.

From the time of the early controversies (412–15) until the outbreak of the Nestorian controversy in 429 we hear very little of Cyril, though he was obviously occupied with producing an impressive written corpus. Cyril's literary production from the Nestorian controversy to the end of his life is largely concerned with justifying to his own allies his signing of the accord with the Antiochenes, and with further explaining and defending his doctrine of Christ. Cyril died on June 27, 444, despised by some but revered by many others. He left behind him an impressive theological legacy that would, in the years immediately following his death, be the subject of fierce contention leading to the Council of Chalcedon in 451.

II. Works

Cyril's extant written corpus occupies 10 volumes of the *Patrologia Graeca* (vols. 68–77), seven of which contain biblical commentary alone. We possess commentaries on the Pentateuch (*De Adoratione in Spiritu et Veritate* and the *Glaphyra*), Isaiah, the 12 Minor Prophets, Luke and John. The monumental *Commentary on John*, a pre-Nestorian work, combines biblical commentary with an anti-Arian orientation, and notably already reveals Cyril's concern with a "two-sons" christology that he later found to be so offensive in Nestorius. In addition we possess from Cyril extended fragments on Matthew, Romans, 1 Corinthians, 2 Corinthians, and Hebrews, and partial or fragmentary remains of commentaries on the books of Kings, Psalms, Proverbs, Song of Songs, Jeremiah, Ezekiel, Daniel, Acts, James, 1 Peter, 2 Peter, 1 John, and Jude. Whether Cyril composed a full commentary on all of these books is uncertain. Most of the biblical commentaries come from the pre-Nestorian period, though the *Homilies on Luke* and the fragments from 2 Corinthians and Hebrews make explicit or implicit reference to Nestorius.

Cyril wrote two anti-Arian treatises on the Trinity (*Thesaurus de sancta et consubstantiali Trinitate* and the *Dialogues on the Trinity*), several shorter treatises and letters against anthropomorphite teaching, and a massive refutation of Julian the Apostate's critique of the Christian faith (*Contra Julianum*). Of his many shorter and longer anti-Nestorian works concerning the doctrine of Christ, the most noteworthy are his second and third letters to Nestorius, his *Letter to the Monks of Egypt*, *On the Unity of Christ*, *Scholia on the Incarnation*, and the five books *Against Nestorius*. In addition, Cyril also composed a series of annual *Festal Letters* marking the date and celebration of Easter, and a wide array of letters and homilies on various topics.

III. Major influences

The chief influence on Cyril is Athanasius, his predecessor as bishop of Alexandria. From Athanasius Cyril received an approach to the interpretation of scripture, to the doctrine of the Trinity, to the person of Christ, and to the goal of salvation, namely, the full sanctification and divinization of the believer in the church. By the time Cyril came to be bishop in 412, Athanasius was firmly established as one of the pillars of orthodoxy in the wider church, and it is plain especially from Cyril's

early writings that he relied quite heavily on the theological approach of Athanasius. Yet Cyril does not merely mimic Athanasius—he genuinely brings about development of his thought, especially in the explication of the Trinity, of christology, and of divinization.

Cyril was also notably influenced by his uncle and immediate predecessor, Theophilus, and through Theophilus came the influence of Jerome and others connected with the anti-Origenist campaign of the early fifth century (see Russell, 2007). Due to a reaction against the teachings of Origen's more fervent disciples, Theophilus moderated the allegorical interpretation of Scripture derived from Origen, and handed on to Cyril a distinctive approach that clearly shaped Cyril's own treatment of the Old Testament and the spiritual sense of scripture. In Theophilus's homilies, we also find a connection between divinization and the Eucharist that will be characteristic of Cyril. Among other authorities that Cyril cites explicitly in his works, Basil of Caesarea and Gregory of Nazianzus occupy a place of special importance.

IV. Theological contribution

Biblical exegesis

In standard accounts of patristic exegesis, Cyril is often labeled as eclectic in his method, combining features of Alexandrian allegorical method with Antiochene literal and historical exegesis (Simonetti, 1994, 81). He inherited the Alexandrian tradition of allegory, but this came to him already moderated by Theophilus. From what we can ascertain, Cyril had access to and made use of a varied set of commentators. He probably possessed copies of biblical commentaries from Origen, Eusebius of Caesarea, Didymus, Apollinarius, and Jerome, and possibly had access as well to works from Basil of Caesarea, John Chrysostom, Theodore, and Theodoret (Kerrigan, 1952, 249–50).

The heart and unity of Cyril's exegetical approach, however, cannot be grasped in terms of Alexandrian and Antiochene categories. It is most aptly described as christological or christocentric exegesis. Following his mentor Athanasius, Cyril reads the Bible in terms of its overall *skopos* or purpose, which is the divine plan of salvation culminating in Christ, the incarnate Word. According to Robert Wilken (1998, 41):

> The subject of Cyril's exegesis is never simply the text that is before him, it is always the mystery of Christ. He is less interested in understanding what Moses or Zechariah or Paul or Matthew "meant" than he is in understanding what Christ means ... Christ is Cyril's true subject matter. Yet without the Bible there is no talk of Christ. Cyril knew no other way to speak of Christ than in the words of the Bible, and no other way to interpret the words of the Bible than through Christ.

In his reading of the Bible Cyril distinguishes two fundamental senses: the literal or historical sense and the spiritual sense. The literal sense pertains to things perceived by the senses, that is, to the earthly and human reference of the passage. The spiritual sense pertains to things perceived through and in the Spirit, and points in some sense to the mystery of Christ. While taking account of the contextual and historical meaning of the law and the prophets, Cyril interprets the Old Testament primarily in terms of its spiritual fulfillment in Christ, using Matt. 5:17 and John 4:24 as hermeneutical keys. Whether speaking of how the Old Testament realities foreshadow salvation in Christ, or of how the Gospels reveal the full humanity and divinity in Christ, Cyril is always concerned to manifest the unity of the plan of redemption through the incarnate Word.

Trinitarian theology

It is unclear why Cyril felt the need to write so much about the doctrine of the Trinity. On the one hand, there are grounds for concluding that he faced pastoral problems arising from unorthodox teaching on the Trinity. On the other hand, he may have wanted to make a further apologetic to educated pagans concerning the Christian distinctive regarding the Triune God (Boulnois, 2003, 77). His basic teaching on the Trinity follows the lines set down by Athanasius, and includes as well the formula of Gregory of Nazianzus accepted at the time of the Council of Constantinople, that God is one substance (*ousia*) in three hypostases. Cyril uses the terms *ousia* and nature interchangeably to denote the oneness in God, and hypostasis and prosopon to denote the Father, Son, and Holy Spirit respectively. For Cyril belief in the

Trinity is the first article of the Christian faith, and he consistently employs the formula, "from the Father through the Son in the Holy Spirit," as the guiding truth about God and his work in the world.

Cyril, however, does not merely repeat formulae inherited from Athanasius and the fourth-century councils. He develops the notion of the Trinity as the enlargement or deployment of the one divinity into three hypostases and the recapitulation of the three into one united divinity:

> We will not follow the Jewish practice of contracting the nature of the Divinity to one sole God and Father; on the contrary, we will stretch it, so to speak, into one Holy and consubstantial Trinity; and while expanding it by the quality of the Persons and the property of the hypostases we will once more contract it as one sole God because of the sameness of substance. (Boulnois, 2003, 84)

Moreover, he speaks of the Son and Spirit as both "from" and "in" the Father, and so moves further in the direction of the idea of the circumincession of the persons of the Trinity.

But Cyril's most noteworthy contribution is his account of the Holy Spirit within the Trinity. Using various formulae, Cyril speaks of the Spirit being proper, not only to the Father, but also to the Son. On occasion he speaks of the Spirit proceeding from the Father and the Son, but more commonly he uses the phrase, "from the Father through the Son." There is a continuity for Cyril between "theology" and "economy," that is, between how the divine persons operate in the world and how they relate with each other. For this reason, Cyril shows a close relation between the Son and the Spirit in his understanding of the immanent Trinity:

> The Spirit belongs properly to God the Father, and just as properly to the Son, not in the sense of two distinct substances, or one [substance] thought of and existing separately in each of the two; but because the Son is by nature from and in the Father, true fruit of his substance, he takes as a natural attribute the Spirit of his Father. (Boulnois, 2003, 104)

Because he teaches the close alignment of the Son with the Spirit's procession, Cyril has been an important figure in the debates between East and West on the question of the filioque. Though he does not follow the approach taken by Augustine and the West, he does see a role for the Son in the procession of the Spirit (see Daley, 2003, 144–8). Because he stands in a sense midway between the traditional positions of East and West on the procession of the Spirit, his theology of the Holy Spirit can potentially serve as an arbiter and bridge between them. But Cyril's statements concerning the Son's role in the Spirit's procession are not a matter of abstract theological speculation. He builds his Trinitarian theology on the practice of baptism and puts his theology of the Spirit at the service of a rich account of our share in the divine life through the indwelling Spirit of the Son.

Christology

Nestorius famously charges Cyril with beginning his narrative of the incarnation with the eternal Word and Son instead of beginning with Christ as the "prosopon of union" as Nestorius himself does (Driver and Hodgson, 1925, 153). Nestorius has in fact accurately grasped the center and starting point for Cyril's understanding of Christ and the incarnation: the eternal Word of God, consubstantial with the Father, has become a human being and died in the flesh for our sake, while remaining fully God. In his *Second Letter to Nestorius* (Norris, 1980, 132), Cyril uses the language of the Creed of Nicaea to state his position on the incarnation:

> The unique Son himself—naturally begotten out of God the Father, true God out of true God, light out of light, through whom the Father made everything that exists—descended, was enfleshed, became human, rose on the third day, and ascended into the heavens … We do not say that the Logos became flesh by having his nature changed, nor for that matter that he was transformed into a complete human being composed out of soul and body. On the contrary, we say that in an unspeakable and incomprehensible way, the Logos united to himself, in his hypostasis, flesh enlivened by a rational soul, and in this way became a human being and has been designated "Son of Man."

The central point is the identity between the eternal Word and Jesus Christ. Christ simply *is* the eternal Word now made flesh for our sake. The Word is the personal subject of Christ, and all the attributes, say-

ings, and actions of Christ can properly be attributed to the Word. This view is typically termed a "single-subject" christology, and it is the hallmark of Cyril.

It is crucial to recognize that Cyril's view is grounded in his reading of John 1:14 and Phil. 2:5–11, and that it sums up the whole biblical narrative beginning with Adam and the Fall. Cyril presents the incarnation in the context of the narrative of salvation—it is the narrative of the descent of God himself in human form for the restoration and recreation of Adam's fallen nature. For Cyril, the Word assumed human nature—became a human being—in order to restore that nature from the effects of Adam's sin and raise it to participation in God himself.

This view of the incarnation is marked by several important features. First, Christ must be confessed as both fully God (by virtue of his nature as the Word) and fully human (by virtue of assuming our full humanity). Cyril teaches the double consubstantiality of Christ—consubstantial with the Father in divinity, consubstantial with us in humanity. Second, all the human attributes of Christ can be properly applied to the Word, and all the divine attributes of the Word can be properly applied to the man Jesus, because there is one "person" (Cyril typically uses the word "hypostasis") who is both God and human. This paradoxical way of speaking is called the "exchange of attributes" or the "communication of idioms" (*communicatio idiomatum*). This is why Cyril was so adamant in defense of the title *Theotokos* for Mary. For Cyril she did not give birth to the divine nature, but she did give human birth to the one who is the divine Son of God. To deny this title for Mary is tantamount for Cyril to denying that Christ *is* the Word made flesh (Weinandy, 2003, 31–41).

Third, Cyril claims that nothing less than a full "union" (*henosis*) of the divine and human natures in the hypostasis of the Word must be maintained. In the one hypostasis of the Word the two natures are united. The humanity and divinity remain distinct, but they are fully united in the one Christ (McGuckin, 2004, 195). The natures are not somehow stuck together or intermingled directly, but are united in the hypostasis of the Word while remaining distinct in themselves. Cyril described this as the "hypostatic union," but he employs principally a set of images and analogies, mostly drawn from scripture and the relationship of the soul and body, to portray how one reality (Christ) can possess two distinct parts (humanity and divinity) and yet remain one (Wickham, 1983, xxxiv; McKinion, 2000).

The most controversial aspect of Cyril's christology is his use of the phrase, "one nature of the Incarnate Word" (or "one incarnate nature of the Word"—both were used) to describe Christ. To those who used the term "nature" to describe the humanity and divinity respectively, this sounded like Apollinarianism (and the phrase did have an Apollinarian pedigree), a fusing together of the two natures to produce a third combined nature. It appeared to them that Cyril was denying a distinct humanity and divinity in Christ. But Cyril plainly does not use the phrase in an Apollinarian sense, and he clarifies in his writings following the Council of Ephesus that he is not denying the ongoing reality of humanity and divinity in Christ. Rather, he uses the term "nature" to mean "entity" or "reality"—the point of the expression is to assert in bold language that Christ is one and not two. Despite clarifications from Cyril—and notwithstanding his readiness to sign a statement with the Antiochenes that uses "two natures" language—this phrase continued to cause confusion and proved to be an unpromising way to describe the unity in Christ (Weinandy, 2003, 38). Arguments over this language (one nature or two natures) erupted in the years following Cyril's death and proved to be the main point of contention between those who accepted the Chalcedonian statement (451) and those who rejected it.

Cyril's signal contribution to christology is his insistence on the Word as the single subject in Christ and his ability to distinguish between the hypostasis of the Word (as the basis for the union) and the full humanity and divinity that are united in the Word. Through the use of paradoxical statements and various images, Cyril was able to reveal the full biblical narrative and confession of the Word made flesh for the restoration of our nature without compromising the integrity of Christ's divinity or humanity:

> For the Word of God, even with flesh, is the divine nature, and we are his kin, even though he is God by nature, because of his taking the same flesh as ours ... For Christ is, as it were, a kind of common frontier of the supreme dignity and humanity (being both in the

same one, and as it were holding together in himself things so greatly separated); and as God by nature he is joined to God the Father, and again, as truly a man, is joined to human beings. (Keating, 2003, 178 adjusted)

Theology of divinization

Cyril's theology of divinization is firmly grounded in his christology. Cyril was intent on maintaining that Christ *is* God the Word in the flesh because of our need to be restored and recreated by intimate connection with divine life and power, as this selection from his *Commentary on John* displays (Keating, 2003, 8):

> Therefore his only-begotten Word has become a partaker of flesh and blood, that is, he has become man, though being Life by nature, and begotten of the Life that is by nature, that is, of God the Father, so that, having united himself with the flesh which perishes according to the law of its own nature ... he might restore it to his own life and render it through himself a partaker of God the Father ... And he wears our nature, refashioning it to his own life. And he himself is also in us, for we have all become partakers of him, and have him in ourselves through the Spirit. For this reason we have become "partakers of the divine nature," and are reckoned as sons, and so too have in ourselves the Father himself through the Son.

Divinization in Cyril may be understood in two senses, a strict and narrower sense, and a broad and more comprehensive one. In the strict sense, divinization is the impartation of divine life effected in us through the agency of the indwelling Spirit in baptism, and through Christ's life-giving flesh in the Eucharist. Properly speaking, Christ in us—through his Spirit and his life-giving flesh—is the source and ground of human divinization, accomplishing our justification, our sanctification, our divine filiation, and our participation in the divine nature. In the broad and more comprehensive sense, divinization includes our progressive growth into the divine image. In Cyril's view, our divinization cannot be dissociated from free and faith-filled response to God and human growth in virtue through obedience to the divine commands, yielding a way of life pleasing to God. Cyril correlates the somatic and pneumatic means of union with Christ, and impressively integrates the ontological and ethical aspects of human divinization. His account represents an advance on Athanasius and brings the patristic doctrine of deification to a new maturity (Russell, 2004, 192).

Nestorius of Constantinople

I. Background

Little is known about Nestorius's early life. He was born sometime in the 380s (the date often suggested is 381) in Syria. What can be gleaned about his education from his literary works shows that he was ably trained in the logical rhetorical school of Antioch, but that he probably did not undergo advanced rhetorical training and was no master of literary style (Wessel, 2004, 242–9). He was a student of Theodore of Mopsuestia, along with three other important Antiochene figures, John of Antioch, Andrew of Samosata, and Theodoret of Cyr. Together they form a certain "school" of Antiochene theology in the tradition of Diodore of Tarsus and Theodore. Nestorius became a monk at the monastery of Euprepios near Antioch, where he came to be known and respected for his preaching. At the probable recommendation of his friend John, bishop of Antioch, he was nominated to succeed Sisinnius as bishop of Constantinople in 428 (McGuckin, 2004, 20).

Nestorius, like Cyril, took office in the midst of controversy and factionalism. And, like Cyril, he began with an active campaign against various opponents: he made enemies of the monastic establishment by requiring them to stay within their monasteries; he provoked the Arians into burning down their own chapel, thus earning the epithet, "incendiary"; and he angered the empress Pulcheria by denying her certain special rights she had enjoyed under Sisinnius. It is useful to recognize that Nestorius was in fact very much like Cyril in personality and manner of exercising his episcopal office. Both men were strong-minded, sure of their own positions, and quick to go on the attack—this explains in part why their confrontation was so explosive. According to McGuckin (2004, 21), Nestorius was "no less dogmatic, uncompromising, and ready to use the full extent of his powers, both

political and canonical, than Cyril or any of the other leading hierarchs of the period."

Still in the first year of his reign, Nestorius was faced with a sharp disagreement between opposing parties in Constantinople: Was it was proper to call the Virgin Mary *Theotokos* (God-bearer) or *Anthropotokos* (man-bearer)? Judging that neither party was strictly heretical, he proposed his own mediating term, *Christotokos* (Christ-bearer), urging that the other terms each contained an element of potential error in them. The *Theotokos* party were offended and concluded that Nestorius was in effect denying that Jesus was really and truly God in the flesh. As the debate deepened, Nestorius and his associates began preaching more strenuously against the term *Theotokos*. A series of sermons preached and circulated by Nestorius in early 429 reached Cyril in Alexandria and provoked him to write his *Letter to the Monks of Egypt*. From this point forwards, the controversy escalated, leading to a sharp exchange of letters between Cyril and Nestorius, a mutual appeal to Pope Celestine in Rome, the condemnation of Nestorius both by Celestine (August 430) and Cyril (November 430), and the calling of an ecumenical council by the emperor Theodosius to be held in the summer of 431 at Ephesus.

The complex series of events in 431 resulted in the deposition of Nestorius as bishop of Constantinople and his life-long exile (which began in Syria, moved to Arabia, and ended at the Upper Oasis in Egypt). It appears that he died at or around the time of the Council of Chalcedon, which he expected would vindicate his teaching on Christ. Rejected outright by those of Cyril's party, he was also reluctantly abandoned by his former Antiochene friends and associates as the two contending parties worked toward a reconciliation in 433. Nestorius is a tragic figure who was in a sense "sacrificed" in order to advance the cause of peace and doctrinal clarity in the church—and he clearly saw himself in this light at the end of his life (Driver and Hodgson, 1925, 95, 291). Although even some sympathetic scholars judge that he bears a large share of the blame for his own troubles (Young, 1983, 234), he was in the end plainly dealt a hard hand. Even those critical of his account of Christ could wish that events had turned out differently for the devout monk from Antioch. He died in exile sometime around the year 451.

II. Works

Most of Nestorius's works perished in the wake of his condemnation, and much of what we possess has come down in translation, often under a pseudonym. Nestorius is credited with having written a liturgy, a tragedy, the *Book of Heraclides* (also known as the *Bazaar of Heracleides*), and a series of sermons, letters, and discourses (McGuckin, 2004, 127). His *First Sermon against the Theotokos*, and his letters to Cyril, John of Antioch, and Pope Celestine supply what we know of his early thought (from 429 to 431). His longest extant work, the *Book of Heraclides*, written principally toward the end of his life, was only discovered in the early twentieth century in a Syriac manuscript (published 1910; English translation 1925). The apology that comprises the second (and longest) part of the *Book of Heraclides* is plainly written between 449 and 451—Nestorius describes current events that match the years leading up to the Council of Chalcedon. The first part of the *Book of Heraclides*, a dialogue, is disputed. Some scholars argue that the dialogue was written after Nestorius's death; others propose that it is a genuine early work from around the time of the Ephesus Council in 431 (see Chesnut, 1978).

III. Major influences

The chief influence for Nestorius was his teacher and model, Theodore of Mopsuestia. Though their views are not always identical, there is a close correlation between them, especially in their respective exegetical approaches and accounts of Christ (McLeod, 2005, 166–8). Theodore himself plainly built upon and developed fourth-century Antiochene approaches to theology and exegesis, most notably those of Diodore, his teacher, yet with him these tendencies reach a full flowering and attain their characteristic shape. Theodore was a voluminous writer who composed commentaries on most of the books of the Bible (which have largely been lost), and who wrote numerous dogmatic, apologetic, and catechetical works. Revered widely for his preaching, he also earned a reputation as a formidable apologist against the Arians, Eunomians, Apollinarians, and Origenists. He died highly honored within his own circles

coincidentally in 428, the year of Nestorius's fateful appointment as bishop of Constantinople.

Direct influence from Diodore of Tarsus (died *c.*394) is more difficult to establish—his influence on Nestorius is probably largely filtered through Theodore. Diodore was the chief antagonist to Apollinarius in the late fourth century, and developed a highly dualistic christology that was censured by Gregory of Nazianzus as teaching "two sons"—a divine Son and a human son conjoined in Christ. Whether or not this charge is accurate, Diodore and his successors promoted a strongly dualistic account of Christ that was continually subjected to the charge of effectively teaching a "two-sons" christology.

The close theological link between Nestorius and Theodore is shown in the dispute over Theodore himself that emerged in the late 430s between the Antiochenes and Cyril. Having effectively abandoned Nestorius, the Antiochenes began publicly to praise the writings and heritage of Theodore, their common teacher. This roused Cyril to compose his treatise, *Against Theodore and Diodore*, which in turn stirred up further defense of Theodore from the Antiochene party. All this reveals that Theodore was just as central to current Antiochene theology as Athanasius was to Cyril and his associates. Close scrutiny can and should recognize differences between Theodore and Nestorius, but they are remarkably close in their overall approach and are forever bound together in the history of Christian theology.

IV. Theological contribution

Trinity and soteriology

Before turning to Nestorius's account of Christ—the centerpiece of his theology—it will be useful to examine other features of his thought that provide a context for his christology. The starting point for Nestorius—as for Cyril—is the full divinity of the Son as defined by the Council of Nicaea in 325. The theological foundation for Nestorius's thought, therefore, is the doctrine of the Trinity (inclusive of the full divine status of the Holy Spirit)—but it is an understanding of the Trinity as shaped by Antiochene emphases and concerns. For Nestorius (and the Antiochenes more generally) two truths merited special attention and preservation: that the eternal Son be confessed as fully and completely divine, and that the divine nature not be compromised in any way by an account of the incarnation. To guard and ensure these truths, the Antiochenes distinguished the Word from the humanity as far as possible without destroying the union, in order to make the human soul of Christ the principle of suffering and to remove the Word from any taint of passibility. And so they developed a highly dualistic christology.

But of equal concern to Nestorius was the full humanity of Christ the New Adam. If Arius was the great opponent of the full divinity of the Son, then Apollinarius was the arch-foe of the full humanity of the Son. Nestorius's account of Christ is really his attempt to read the biblical narrative in a way that avoids the dual errors of Arius and Apollinarius. From Nestorius's apologetic writings, we can glean a narrative of salvation that is heavily weighted toward Adam and Christ. In other words, Christ is consistently presented against the backdrop of the Adam story and the need for a renewed humanity because of Adam's Fall. In this feature Nestorius is strikingly similar to Cyril—both rely on the Adam–Christ typology as the central frame of salvation, and both see the loss of the image of God in Adam as being crucially restored in Christ. They diverge significantly, however, in how they view the endpoint of the restoration of our humanity in Christ, the New Adam. Nestorius and the Antiochene tradition more broadly have little to no place for the account of divinization that we see in Cyril's understanding of salvation (Harrison, 2001, 222).

In his *First Sermon against the Theotokos*, Nestorius writes: "Because humanity is the image of the divine nature, but the devil overthrew this image and cast it down into corruption, God grieved over this image as a king might grieve over his statue, and renewed the ruined likeness … Through a human being he brought about the revival of the human race" (Norris, 1980, 124). In a further explication of this, we see why it was so crucial for Nestorius that Christ should win our redemption through his full and complete humanity:

> Consequently, Christ assumed the person [*prosopon*] of the debt-ridden nature and by its mediation paid the debt back as a son of Adam, for it was obligatory that the

one who dissolved the debt come from the same race as he who had once contracted it. The debt had its start from a woman, and the remission had its start from a woman … Adam fell into the guilt of seeking divinity for himself in opposition to God, since he had heard the devil say, "You will be as gods" (Gen. 3:5) … Moreover, the one who made restoration on our behalf is Christ, for in him our nature discharges its debt. He had assumed a person [*prosopon*] of the same nature [as ours], whose passions were removed by his passion. (Norris, 1980, 126–7)

Christology

Two axioms undergird the christological doctrine of Nestorius: Christ must be confessed as fully divine and fully human, and the integrity and distinction of the natures must be upheld in order to safeguard the impassibility of the Logos in the incarnation, and to assure that it is genuinely by a human being that salvation is secured (McGuckin, 2004, 132–5). In *The Book of Heraclides* Nestorius lays out his own peculiar metaphysics of the incarnation in order to explain how these two axioms can be understood (Hodgson, 1925). His account builds on the use of four key terms: *ousia*, *hypostasis*, *physis*, and *prosopon*. Each *physis* has its own *ousia* (or each *ousia* is characterized by its proper *physis*, its distinguishing set of characteristics that define what it is). And each *physis* has its underlying *hypostasis*, which makes it concrete and real, and which in turn is made visible and manifested in the *prosopon*. Consequently, the humanity and the divinity in Christ each possesses its own *ousia*, *physis*, *hypostasis*, and *prosopon*. Each nature (*physis*), therefore, must have its own *hypostasis* (or else it is not real) and its own *prosopon*, that which makes it manifest. And because there must be complete human and divine natures in Christ, there must also then be two *hypostases* and two *prosopa* in Christ.

Significantly for Nestorius, the *hypostasis* of each nature concerns what is essential to it, and so cannot be either confused, mixed, or changed if the nature is to remain intact. Therefore, the union in Christ cannot be on the level of *ousia*, *physis*, or *hypostasis*, for this would involve loss to the integrity of the natures. Nestorius firmly and consistently denies any notion of a "natural" or "hypostatic" union in Christ. What is left on Nestorius's metaphysical plate is the term *prosopon*, the outward and visible manifestation of the nature. Here is where Nestorius, following Theodore, draws his line. The union of the human and divine, brought about by the good pleasure and will of God, is properly understood as a "prosopic union," whereby the fully intact divine and human natures can be predicated of the one *prosopon* of union, which *is* Christ. For Nestorius, what we see on the pages of the Gospels is Christ, the *prosopon* of union. He is not the Logos per se, nor "the man" Jesus per se, but the conjunction of the two, who is and can be properly called one Christ (see Grillmeier, 1975, 457–63).

The idea of the *prosopon* of union is plainly the crux of Nestorius's account of the incarnation, but the precise meaning of this term has been constantly debated both by Nestorius's contemporaries and by modern scholars. By the concept of prosopic union Nestorius is clearly attempting to assert something less than a substantial union (which he strictly denies) and something more than a merely moral union (which he considers inadequate). It seems that Nestorius intends the prosopic union to have a metaphysical basis (though some scholars deny this), but his account suffers from at least three problems. First, Nestorius uses a single term, *prosopon*, to refer both to what belongs properly to each nature and for the product of the union of the natures. This equivocal use of a single term is confusing and unpromising for a clear account of the incarnation. Second, it is difficult to see how the concept of *prosopon* can do the work Nestorius asks of it. If it describes a metaphysical aspect of each nature, it is difficult then to see how there can be a union of the *prosopa* without violating the integrity of each nature. But if it does not describe a metaphysical aspect of each nature, then it is equally hard to see how the union of the *prosopa* really brings about a true and effectual union. We seem to be left with mere appearance. Third and most crucially, it is unclear how the union of *prosopa* can adequately account for the "subject" who is Christ. Nestorius seems to propose a compenetration of the two *prosopa*, a kind of perichoresis, by which the two become one in Christ and show forth one Christ. But the lingering problem with this account of Christ is the question of "who" Christ is. How can the subject that appears on the pages of the Gospels be the product of a union of *prosopa* of the divine and human natures?

This brings us to the linchpin of Nestorius's christology and the main cause of the grievance against him: his refusal to make a strict identity between Christ and the eternal Word of God. In his long, rambling defense in the *Book of Heraclides*, this is the issue that constantly returns. Given his presuppositions concerning the eternal Son and the divine nature, Nestorius simply cannot allow that Christ *is* the Word of God, now in human nature. For Nestorius, the subject of the two natures must be "Christ" and not the Word of God. He writes:

> Therefore the two natures belong to Christ and not to God the Word … But if not, prove … how he [Cyril] confesses that God the Word is in two *ousias* … Of what divinity, of what humanity was God the Word perfected that God the Word should be in two natures? … Now "God the Word" and "Christ" do not indicate the same thing, either in the Divine Scriptures or as he [Cyril] has said, although Christ exists not apart from God the Word." (Driver and Hodgson, 1925, 170, 173–4)

Nestorius's efforts to exegete Philippians 2:5–11 and the Nicene Creed according to this distinction between Christ and the Word is simply not persuasive (see Driver and Hodgson, 1925, 145, 166–70).

The refusal to identify Christ with the eternal Word of God explains why Nestorius was so uneasy with the term *Theotokos*, and why he allowed for only a guarded use of the traditional *communicatio idiomatum* (Grillmeier, 1975, 452). For Nestorius, to strictly identify Christ and the Word was to implicate the divine nature in passibility, and to threaten at the same time the natural integrity of the humanity of Christ through which he won salvation for us. His *Second Letter to Cyril* neatly displays his concern in this matter:

> To attribute also to him [the Son], in the name of association, the characteristics of the flesh that has been conjoined with him—I mean birth and suffering and death—is, my brother, either the work of a mind which truly errs in the fashion of the Greeks or that of a mind diseased with the insane heresy of Arius and Apollinaris and the others. Those who are thus carried away with the idea of this association are bound, because of it, to make the divine Logos have a part in being fed with milk and participate to some degree in growth and stand

in need of angelic assistance because of his fearfulness at the time of the passion. (Norris, 1980, 139)

Nestorius's friends and colleagues (John of Antioch and Theodoret) were much quicker to see the weakness of this account, and to recognize the need to confess that Christ is the "same" as the Word—once Cyril realized that they granted this point, he was willing to allow the language of "two natures" in Christ. To the end of his days, Nestorius was never able to reconcile himself to the identity between Christ and the Word. This is the most notable feature of his christology and the crucial point on which the wider Christian tradition has found his approach wanting.

Conclusion

It was not the intricacies of his metaphysical system or his idea of "prosopic union" that stirred up opposition to Nestorius. It was his refusal to confess that Christ *is* the Word (now made flesh) and his reluctance to grant the title *Theotokos* to Mary that raised the ire of the monastic establishment, and in the end caused the Alexandrian and Roman churches to reject his teaching. When on occasion in his early writings (and following the usage of Theodore) Nestorius spoke separately of the Logos and "the man assumed," the specter of a "two-sons" christology was raised and charged against him. For example, in his *First Sermon against the Theotokos*, he confesses: "I revere the one who is borne because of the one who carries him, and I worship the one I see because of the one who is hidden … Moreover, the incarnate God did not die;

he raised up the one in whom he was incarnate" (Norris, 1980, 130–1).

In his defense written late in life, Nestorius strenuously denies that he ever taught or conceived of "two sons" in Christ. He takes great pains to state the union of humanity and divinity in the one Christ, and to assert that there is no division between them. According to the conventional understanding of "Nestorianism," Nestorius is plainly *not* Nestorian. Twentieth-century scholarship has attempted to rehabilitate Nestorius by showing what he was trying to accomplish and how he was often misunderstood (Loofs, 1914; Anastos, 1962; Braaten, 1963). Yet even among sympathizers and admirers, his doctrine of Christ is often judged to be inadequate. According to Rowan Greer (1966, 60), "On balance, I should submit that the prosopic union per se does not provide a formula adequate for stating the union of the two natures." Following the distinction between intention and achievement, Nestorius clearly *intended* to provide for a full unity that would ensure redemption in Christ, but what he *achieved* was less successful in accounting for the unity of the divine and human in Christ (Turner, 1975). It is noteworthy (and ironic) that in the church of the East where Nestorius's name came to be honored and revered, his specific christological teaching played little role (Taylor, 2004, 214–15). If it was Cyril's contribution to insist on the identity of Christ as the Word of God made flesh, and to display how a fruitful interaction between the divine and human in Christ can yield a rich doctrine of divinization, then it was Nestorius's contribution to ensure that a thick account of the full humanity of Christ would be maintained in the church's theology.

References

Anastos, M.V. 1962. "Nestorius was Orthodox," *Dumbarton Oaks Papers* 16: 119–40.

Boulnois, Marie-Odile. 2003. "The Mystery of the Trinity According to Cyril of Alexandria: the Deployment of the Triad and Its Recapitulation into the Unity of Diversity." In *The Theology of St. Cyril of Alexandria: A Critical Appreciation*, ed. Thomas G. Weinandy and Daniel A. Keating. London: T&T Clark, pp. 75–112.

Braaten, Carl E. 1963. "Modern Interpretations of Nestorius," *Church History* 32: 251–67.

Chadwick, Henry. 1967. *The Early Church.* New York: Penguin.

Chesnut, R. C. 1978. "The Two Prosopa in Nestorius' Bazaar of Heracleides," *Journal of Theological Studies* n.s. 29: 392–408.

Daley, Brian. 2003. "The Fullness of the Saving God: Cyril of Alexandria on the Holy Spirit." In *The Theology of St. Cyril of Alexandria: A Critical Appreciation*, ed. Thomas G.

Weinandy and Daniel A. Keating. London: T&T Clark, pp. 113–48.

Driver, G. R. and Hodgson, Leonard, trans. and eds. 1925. *The Bazaar of Heracleides*. Oxford: Clarendon Press.

Greer, Rowan A. 1966. "The Image of God and the Prosopic Union in Nestorius' Bazaar of Heracleides." In *Lux in lumine*, ed. R. A. Norris. New York: Seabury Press, pp. 46–61.

Grillmeier, A. 1975. *Christ in Christian Tradition: From the Apostolic Age to Chalcedon*, 2nd edn., trans. J. S. Bowden. New York: Sheed & Ward.

Hardy, E. R. 1982. "The Further Education of Cyril of Alexandria (412–44): Questions and Problems," *Studia Patristica* 17: 116–22.

Harrison, Nonna Verna. 2001. "Women, Human Identity, and the Image of God: Antiochene Interpretations," *Journal of Early Christian Studies* 9: 203–49.

Hodgson, L. 1925. "The Metaphysics of Nestorius." In *The Bazaar of Heracleides*, trans. and ed. G. R. Driver and L. Hodgson. Oxford: Clarendon Press.

Keating, Daniel A. 2003. *The Appropriation of Divine Life in Cyril of Alexandria*. Oxford: Oxford University Press.

Kerrigan, Alexander. 1952. *St. Cyril of Alexandria: Interpreter of the Old Testament*. Rome: Pontificio Istituto Biblico.

Loofs, Friedrich. 1914. *Nestorius and His Place in the History of Christian Doctrine*. Cambridge: Cambridge University Press.

McGuckin, John. 2004. *Saint Cyril of Alexandria and the Christological Controversy*. Crestwood, NY: St. Vladimir's Press.

McKinion, Steven. 2000. *Words, Imagery and the Mystery of Christ: A Reconstruction of Cyril of Alexandria's Christology*. Leiden: Brill.

McLeod, Frederick G. 2005. *The Roles of Christ's Humanity in Salvation: Insights from Theodore of Mopsuestia*. Washington DC: Catholic University of America Press.

Norris, Richard A., trans. and ed. 1980. *The Christological Controversy*. Philadelphia: Fortress Press.

Russell, Norman. 2000. *Cyril of Alexandria*. London: Routledge.

Russell, Norman. 2004. *The Doctrine of Deification in the Greek Patristic Tradition*. Oxford: Oxford University Press.

Russell, Norman. 2007. *Theophilus of Alexandria*. London: Routledge.

Simonetti, Manlio. 1994. *Biblical Interpretation in the Early Church: An Historical Introduction to Patristic Exegesis*, trans. J. A. Hughes. Edinburgh, T&T Clark.

Taylor, David G. K. 2004. "The Syriac Tradition." In *The First Christian Theologians*, ed. G. R. Evans. Oxford: Blackwell, pp. 201–24.

Turner, H. E. W. 1975. "Nestorius Reconsidered," *Studia Patristica*, vol. 13, ed. E. A. Livingstone. Berlin: Akademie-Verlag, pp. 306–21.

Weinandy, Thomas G. 2003. "Cyril and the Mystery of the Incarnation." In *The Theology of St. Cyril of Alexandria: A Critical Appreciation*, ed. Thomas G. Weinandy and Daniel A. Keating. London: T&T Clark, pp. 23–54.

Wessel, Susan. 2004. *Cyril of Alexandria and the Nestorian Controversy: The Making of a Saint and a Heretic*. Oxford: Oxford University Press.

Wickham, Lionel. 1983. *Cyril of Alexandria: Select Letters*. Oxford: Clarendon Press.

Wilken, Robert. 1998. "St. Cyril of Alexandria: Biblical Expositor," *Coptic Church Review* 19: 30–41.

Wilken, Robert. 2003. "Cyril of Alexandria as Interpreter of the Old Testament." In *The Theology of Cyril of Alexandria: A Critical Appreciation*, ed. Thomas G. Weinandy and Daniel A. Keating. Edinburgh: T&T Clark, pp. 1–21.

Young, Frances. 1983. *From Nicaea to Chalcedon: A Guide to Its Literature and Its Background*. London: SCM.

Ephrem the Syrian (*c.*306–73)

Philip McCosker

A remarkable volte-face has taken place in the last hundred years with regard to the scholarly opinion concerning Ephrem the Syrian. Just over a century ago the learned Cambridge theologian F. Crawford Burkitt (later Norris Professor of Divinity) simply could not restrain himself from making what now seem patronizing and blinkered comments:

> What has given S. Ephraim his magnificent reputation is hard to say … Ephraim is extraordinarily prolix, he repeats himself again and again, and for all the immense mass of material there seems very little to take hold of. His style is allusive and unnatural as if the thought was really deep and subtle, and yet when the thought is unravelled it is generally commonplace … it has no merit either of simplicity or of subtlety in the choice of words … Judged by any canons that we apply to religious literature, it is poor stuff … He goes on from symbol to symbol, and the points he emphasises are sometimes striking, sometimes preposterous, but always fanciful … His fatal want of intellectual seriousness helps to explain to us why his Church became strongly orthodox under Rabbûla, and yet sank permanently a hundred years later into heterodoxy and schism. (Burkitt, 2004, 95, 96, 104, 110)

Clearly these opinions were well entrenched, for 70 years later J. B. Segal could write: "His work, it must be confessed, shows little profundity or originality of thought, and his metaphors are laboured. His poems are turgid, humourless, and repetitive…"

(Segal, 1970, 89). Commensurate with these views was the total absence of Ephrem from accounts of the patristic theology of his time, and this has continued until very recently. So, for instance, he is not mentioned in R. P. C. Hanson's important work on the doctrine of God during the Arian controversy (Hanson, 1988), nor in Rowan Williams's study of the same (Williams, 1987). No doubt the absence of Ephrem from J. P. Migne's works, the *Patrologia Series Latina* and the *Patrologia Series Graeca*, did not help in this regard.

These perspectives on Ephrem—the negative and the absent—have become increasingly odd. The work of publishing Ephrem's works, initially including everything attributed to him, was undertaken particularly through the Herculean efforts of the Maronite Assemani family in Rome (Assemani, Mobarak, and Assemani, 1732–46; for more on the work of this distinguished family see Raphael, 1950, 123–44), and then T. J. Lamy (Lamy, 1882–1902), whose work probably led to Pope Benedict XV declaring Ephrem a doctor of the universal church in 1920 (Benedict XV, 1920). In the twentieth century the tide has continued turning, significantly aided by the mammoth single-handed labors of the Benedictine Edmund Beck of Metten Abbey (on whom see Haering, 1992), who has done the bulk of the work of recovering the genuine Syriac works of Ephrem and publishing them in critical editions with German

The Student's Companion to the Theologians, First Edition. Edited by Ian S. Markham.
© 2013 Blackwell Publishing Ltd. Published 2013 by Blackwell Publishing Ltd.

translations, in 38 volumes in the *Corpus Scriptorum Christianorum Orientalium* series published in Louvain. Increasingly the works are being made available in reliable translations in other modern languages too.

Now that Ephrem's genuine works are actually coming to light scholarly opinion has changed. It is becoming clear that earlier scholars were looking for the wrong kind of theology in Ephrem's works, for he is in fact a theologian-poet. Robert Murray thus can write that he sees Ephrem "as the greatest poet of the patristic age and, perhaps, the only theologian-poet to rank beside Dante" (Murray, 1962–71, 223, and reaffirmed in Murray, 2006, 32). Thanks to the work of Sebastian Brock, Sidney Griffith, and Murray amongst others in the anglophone literature over the last several decades, one now sees Ephrem's theology integrated in surveys of patristic literature (for instance, Brock, 2004), and contributing substantively to academic monographs on the same subject, particularly now in connection with Arianism, and pro-Nicene theology (see Young, 1997, 145–58; Ayres, 2004, 229–35), as well as stimulating contemporary constructive theology, for instance in Eugene Rogers's recent eclectically resourced pneumatology (Rogers, 2005, 70, 97, 125, 153–4), or Tina Beattie's exploration of "queer" mariology (Beattie, 2007, 293–4). Indeed Benedict XVI, in contrast to his eponymous predecessor, recently underlined the contribution Ephrem can make to a theology of womanhood in an audience on Ephrem's theology (Benedict XVI, 2007). We are also realizing the staggering extent of Ephrem's influence on many diverse strands of the theological tradition, from Romanos the Melodist (Petersen, 1985), to Wesley (Wakefield, 1998), to Pusey (Rowell, 1999), as well as in Anglo Saxon England (Stevenson, 1998), and the Latin and German literature of the middle ages (Schmidt, 1973, 1982). In all of these, and other, regards Ephrem's theology is of great actuality and interest. He speaks powerfully to theological efforts toward gender equality, to (postmodern) theological interest in polyvalent, "irregular dogmatics," and poetry as theology (on which see Montemaggi and Traherne, forthcoming), and particularly to contemporary interest in apophaticisms and theologies of deification, as well as concern for the environment.

I. Life

Despite a wealth of purportedly biographical materials we must in fact admit that we know very little about the life of Ephrem. His life is shrouded in the apophatic silence which he would have all good theology clothed in. Recent research has shown that the portrait painted by Greek and Latin hagiographical sources after the Syrian died are "almost totally inaccurate" (Mathews, Amar, and McVey, 1994, 23). These sources created an idealized Ephrem to suit their own ideological purposes, both imperial and ecclesial with not infrequent overlap. Notable amongst the causes for which Ephrem was claimed is early monasticism. As we will see, from the earliest account of Ephrem given by Sozomen in his *Ecclesiastical History* onwards, Ephrem was portrayed as an epitome of Byzantine world-shunning asceticism, rather than the much more interesting Syriac *îḥîdāyâ* and exemplar of early proto-monasticism which he is much more likely to have been. Given the number of personae which developed around the real Ephrem the Syrian, and the literatures which were attached to those largely fictitious figures, recent research distinguishes between a number of Ephrems: Ephrem Syrus, Latinus, and Graecus (for example Beck, Hemmerdinger-Iliadou, and Kirchmeyer, 1960, 788–822). The recovery of Ephrem's genuine Syriac works by Edmund Beck has enabled us to establish the few details of his life that can be determined from evidence internal to these genuine Syriac works.

Thus it is most likely that Ephrem was born to Christian parents, for he writes that he was "born in the path of truth" (*Hymns on Heresies*, 26), and not to a pagan priest father, as the later Syriac *vita* asserted (see Amar, 1988, 197). He was born in the early years of the fourth century in, or in the vicinity of, Nisibis in Mesopotamia (present-day Nusaybin in southeast Turkey). The conjectural date of his birth is 306. We should note that he is therefore a slightly older contemporary of the three Cappadocian fathers. Nisibis occupied a strategic position on the edge of Mesopotamia, and therefore between the Roman and Persian empires, a fact which led to its turbulent life (not much is known about Nisibis, but for a collection of the information we do have, see Russell, 2005). As a result of a pact between Diocletian and the Persian ruler Narses II in 298 Nisibis became Roman territory. It was also an economic crossroads, which led to a great diversity of religion. The lingua franca in this region was Syriac, a dialect of Aramaic, itself the language of Jesus. Ephrem is therefore an extremely important link to a very early form of semitic Christianity contemporaneous with early Greek patristic literature with which the theological literature is in general much more familiar.

Born into a Christian family, it is likely that Ephrem was baptized as a child and came under the formative influence of a number of exemplary bishops of Nisibis. He recounts their influence in the *Hymns on Nisibis*. The first of these bishops, St Jacob of Nisibis (d.338), employed Ephrem as a *mālpanâ*, or teacher, a catechist and biblical interpreter. Jacob himself was one of the 318 bishops who attended the Council of Nicaea in 325 which condemned the theology associated with Arius, which may consequently explain why the Arians, or the "scrutinisers," as Ephrem calls them, were so significant in the pro-Nicene theology of Ephrem's catechetical hymns. It is unlikely that Ephrem himself accompanied Jacob to the council, as the Syriac *vita* alleges (see Amar, 1988, 214–15). The church of St Jacob in Nisibis, in which Ephrem must have taught, has recently been excavated in Nusaybin. At some unknown point Ephrem was ordained a deacon and he continued to serve in Nisibis under bishops Babu, Vologeses, and Abraham.

The political situation changed after the death of Constantine I in 337. Shapur II of Persia led three sieges against Nisibis. The saintly bishop Jacob died after the first in 338. Further sieges followed in 346 and 350 (the latter is described by Ephrem in his first *Hymn on Nisibis*: Brock and Kiraz, 2006, 224ff.), but it was only in 362 with the death of Emperor Julian (the "Apostate"), during an incursion into Persian territory, that Nisibis finally fell. It was agreed that the Christians should be allowed to leave the city, and Ephrem, now in his fifties, left for Edessa. This marks the beginning of the second major period in his life.

At Edessa Ephrem would have found a city marked by more intellectual and theological ferment than Nisibis. Significantly, here he came into contact with a number of heretical strands of theological thought which he sought to address in his writings. Notable amongst these are the followers of Mani, Bardaisan, and

Marcion, as well as the Arians whose thought he had already encountered (on Ephrem's polemics against the various heretics see Griffith, 1999a and Bundy, 1982). The *Chronicle of Edessa* tells us that "on the ninth day of Haziran (June) the wise Mar Ephraem departed from the world" (see Russell, 1998, 79). This is one of the few relatively certain facts we have about Ephrem's life.

As already suggested, it seems likely that Ephrem was part of a Syriac proto-monastic movement as an îḥîdāyâ. Contrary to the impression given by Beck (Beck, Hemmerdinger-Iliadou, and Kirchmeyer, 1960, 788) when he writes "īḥīdâyâ = monachos," the îḥîdāyê do not in fact seem to have been monks in the sense we attach to the word today. They did not live apart, but rather lived lives of consecrated service and virginity within the world around them and were therefore an urban phenomenon. Strikingly, the movement and its title bring with it a christologically focused ascetical theology of no mean interest. The phenomenon has been thoroughly examined by AbouZayd (AbouZayd, 1993) and Griffith (Griffith, 1993b, 1995, see also Brock, 1992, chapter 8, 131–41). Contrary to the popular image of Syrian asceticism as severe, body-hating, and dramatic (as for instance popularized by Peter Brown), it seems in fact that the îḥîdāyê, the "singles," who formed the groups known as the sons/daughters of the covenant (*bnay/bnat qyama*), lived a rather unfamiliar kind of ascetic life. The main source for this way of life is to be found in the sixth *Demonstration* of Aphrahat (written in 336/7), one of Ephrem's teachers (see Pierre, 1988–9, vol. 1, 358–41). They had a special status within the church but were not ministers such as deacons, priests, or bishops. The word used to describe them, "îḥîdāyâ" (single), captures a number of concurrent senses which form a picture of this way of life (see Griffith, 1995, 224–9 as well as Murray, 2006, 13–16). They were "single" in the sense of being consecrated virgins, whether male or female, and whether previously married or not. Significantly the Syriac word is also a title of Christ, as the "only-begotten" Son of God. A third kind of singleness alluded to is "single-mindedness." The term indicates then a purposeful life of consecration in virginity and service within the church in imitation and participation of the only-begotten one, Jesus. Indeed Ephrem describes the process of becoming an îḥîdāyâ, which took place at baptism, with the same language of "putting on" (on this terminology which is so important in Ephrem's theology for linking up christology with the Christian life, see Brock, 1992):

> Here they are, coming to be baptised
> and to become Virgins and Holy Ones.
> They step down, are baptised,
> and they put on the one [Ihidaya]
> For whoever is baptised and puts on
> the Ihidaya, the Lord of the many,
> Has come to fill for him the place of the many,
> and Christ becomes for him the greatest treasure
> (*Hymn on the Nativity*: Griffith, 1995, 226)

We can say then that he espouses a christological theology of the Christian life and we see how for him this concept of îḥîdāyâ ties together, in today's terms, christology, spirituality, ecclesiology, and ethics. We should note here, too, the easy interchange between individual and corporate senses so common in semitic writings, and particularly in the Old Testament, for instance in the servant songs of Deutero-Isaiah.

As we have noted, the early biographical sources on Ephrem paint a picture of the paragon monk of Byzantium; indeed on the frontispiece of the first volume of the Assemani edition of the works of Ephrem that contains those biographical works, Ephrem is depicted in a cowl as a stereotypical *monachos*. This can be seen in the early Greek works such as Sozomen's *Ecclesiastical History* (III.16), and Palladius's strongly Evagrian *Lausiac History* (chapter 40), whose influence in turn can be traced in the Syrica *Life* of Ephrem (on the Syriac *Life* see Amar, 1988; on the influence of the Greek texts upon it see the helpful discussion of Amar, 1992). The Syriac *vita* portrays a number of fanciful events in Ephrem's life for which there is no other evidence, notably an account of a visit of Ephrem to St Basil of Caesarea, during which he miraculously received the gift of understanding Greek, and also ordination at Basil's hands (see Amar, 1988, 265–82).

A work which does not contain these later accretions but which quite likely includes accurate details about Ephrem's ministry to women is the *memre* by Jacob of Sarug on Ephrem. Although it contains little other biographical information, this verse homily contains truly remarkable passages that describe Ephrem as a new Moses empowering women, which will repay extensive quotation:

> Our sisters also were strengthened by you to give praise;
> for women were not allowed to speak in church.
> Your instruction opened the closed mouths of the daughters
> of Eve;
> and behold, the gatherings of the glorious (church) resound
> with their melodies.
> A new sight of women uttering the proclamation;
> and behold, they are called teachers among the congregations.
> Your teaching signifies an entirely new world;
> for yonder in the kingdom, men and women are equal.
> You labored to devise two harps for two groups;
> you treated men and women as one to give praise.
> You resemble Moses, leader of the tribes,
> who gave tambourines to the young girls in the wilderness.
> The Hebrew women made a joyful sound with their tambourines,
> and now (Syrian) woman sing praises with their hymns.
> (Amar, 1995, 34–7)

And again:

> Blessed (Ephrem) observed that women were silent from praise,
> and (this) wise man decided that it was right for them to sing
> praise.
> As Moses had given tambourines to the young girls,
> this discerning man composed hymns, and gave them to the
> virgins …
> He taught the swallows to chirp,
> and the church resounded with the pure voices of pious women
> (Amar, 1995, 48–9)

He goes on to give soteriological warrant for Ephrem's actions, as usual bringing out the parallelism between Eve and Mary:

> You have partaken of a single forgiving body with your brothers,
> and from a single cup of new life you have been refreshed.
> A single salvation was yours and theirs (alike); why then
> have you not learned to sing praise with a loud voice?
> Your silent mouth which your mother Eve closed,
> is now opened by Mary, your sister, to sing praise.
> The old woman (Eve) tied a cord of silence around your tongues;
> the Son of the virgin loosed your bonds that you may sing out …
>
> The married one put a muzzle of silence on your mouths;
> (but) the virgin opened the closed door of your tongues.
> Until now, your gender, was brought low because of Eve;
> but from now on, it is restored by Mary to sing Alleluia!
> Because of the wickedness of Eve, your mother, you were
> under judgement,
> but because of the child of Mary, your sister, you have been set
> free.
> (Amar, 1995, 50–3)

Jacob goes on to describe how some of the heretics Ephrem came across used hymns to spread their theologies, and how Ephrem countered them with women singing his own hymns (a claim also made by Theodoret of Cyrus in his *Ecclesiastical History* IV.26):

This man introduced women to doctrinal disputes;
with (their) soft tones he was victorious in the battle against
    all heresies…
This man hurled wonderful melodies against the evil …
… his hymns went forth like legions against falsehood
When he was barking at the wolves that attacked the flock,
he became a (watch)dog that guarded the sheep of the house
    of God.
He built enclosures of homilies and hymns
within which to keep the sheep from marauders.
                      (Amar, 1995, 64–71)

This is a remarkable account and analysis of it is only just beginning (for excellent analysis of the text see McVey, 2007). There is scope for a large-scale exploration of the role of women in Ephrem's life and theology (see the helpful partial studies in which Ephrem is discussed in Harvey, 2000, 2001, 2005, as well as Brock, 1990, 168–72). Strikingly, Ephrem preceded Julian of Norwich in describing God as "attuned to us … like a nursing woman to an infant" and repeatedly talks of God's womb for the first birth of the Son, to parallel the second from Mary (on all this see the insightful article, McVey, 2001).

The various Ephrems left a huge body of works, many of which cannot be attributed to Ephrem the Syrian (for a guide see Brock, 1990, though note the more recent translations mentioned in the bibliography below, as well as in den Biesen, 2002, 103 with references, and the useful table in Brock, 2006, 259–62). The genuine Syriac works are now conventionally divided up into four groups: verse homilies (*memre*), hymns (*madrashe*), artistic prose or *Kunstprosa*, and plain prose works. Ephrem's burgeoning reputation rests principally on works in the first two categories, which probably come largely from his Nisibene period of teaching. The prose works comprise his *Refutations*, which deal with the heretical theologies he came across in Edessa (Mitchell, 1912–21), as well as his scripture commentaries, most notably his commentary on the Diatesseron (McCarthy, 2000). In turning to look at a small selection of themes from Ephrem's theology, we will concentrate on his distinctive poetic works.

II.   Theology

Ephrem sees two principal sources for his theology: scripture and creation. Both reveal God, but in different ways. Here Ephrem resonates with our contemporary heightened appreciation of the environment, as well as the current interest in the different ways of envisioning the theological interpretation of scripture (there is an extensive literature on Ephrem's hermeneutic; see Youssif, 1983; Griffith, 1997; Russell, 2001; Brock, 2007).

In his book Moses
described the creation of the natural world,
So that both Nature and Scripture
might bear witness to the Creator:
Nature, through man's use of it,
Scripture, through his reading of it.
These are the witnesses
which reach everywhere,
They are to be found at all times,
present at every hour,
Confuting the unbeliever
who defames the Creator.
   (*Hymn on Paradise*, V: Brock, 1990, 102–3)

His theology is stretched out between Eden and Paradise and all creation bears witness to the Creator.

In every place, if you look, His symbol is there,
and when you read, you will find His types.
For by Him were created all creatures,
and He engraved His symbols upon His possessions.
When he created the world,
He gazed at it and adorned it with His images.
Streams of His symbols opened, flowed and poured forth
His symbols on His members.
   (*Hymn on Virginity* XX: McVey, 1989, 348–9)

A key word in Ephrem's vocabulary is that of *raza*, which, as with *ihidaya* above, brings out a number of resonances. It can mean symbol, mystery, and even sacrament. Central to all the senses is the sense of mixture of revelation *and* hiddenness, veiling *and* unveiling.

Absolutely central to all Ephrem's theology, and in particular to its apophaticism and polyvalent, imagistic, symbolical quality is his theology of the *chasm* between heaven and earth, God and human beings (on this theme see Koonammakkal, 1998). It is the chasm which necessitates and encourages symbolism and apophaticism, paradox and poetry: these are forms which are naturally suited to pointing across such an ontological divide and dealing with its epistemological consequences. It is also, in consequence, a central piece of ammunition in Ephrem's offensive against the Arians and their overly confident theology (a point picked up on by Young, 1997, 145 and Ayres, 2004, 231–2).

In the case of the Godhead, what created being is able to investigate Him?
For there is a great chasm between him and the Creator.
In the case of the Godhead, it is not that He is distant from his possessions,
For there exists love between Him and creation.
None of those who try to investigate God has ever drawn near to Him
—yet He is extremely close to those who have discernment.
(*Hymn on Faith* LXIX: Brock, 1990, 67)

It is because God as Trinity is located on the other side of the chasm from us that the Arian theology of the Son is too confident:

We shall not forget ourselves and plunge headstrong into our God
Let us measure our intellect, and let us balance our thought,
An [*sic*] let us know our knowledge: How small it is,
And despicable, to pry into the Knower-of-all.
Tell me how have you depicted in your mind
That birth which is far away from your inquiry?
Do you think that there is just a small range
In the middle, between you and searching (it)?
Seal your mouth with silence! Let not your tongue dare!
Know yourself, O "created," "made," son of an "earth-formed."
For the chasm is a great, limitless one,
Between you and the Son as regards investigation.
(*Hymn on Faith* XV: Koonammakkal, 1997, 175–6)

As befits a theology conscious of this chasm, and largely expressed in poetry, Ephrem's is a highly symbolical theology expressed most often in forms which capitalise on contrast and opposition, such as paradox. Ephrem never resists the opportunity to bring oppositions together when he possibly can, especially when he can summon up type and anti-type between the Old and New Testaments. He does this, for instance, when he is exploring the different ways in which Christ can be said to be the New Lamb:

For Abel was both shepherd and sacrifice,
And so our Shepherd and our Sacrifice has depicted in him
His own role as both Shepherd and Sacrifice.
Praise be to You, Depicter of symbols!
(*Hymn on the Crucifixion*, II: Brock and Kiraz, 2006, 129)

Although there has been some analysis of the logic(s) of paradox in Ephrem (see Botha, 1988, 1990 and particularly his helpful but hard to find 1990–1), there is clearly more work to be done. His use of paradox builds on the semitic penchant for parallelism which is familiar from the Psalms. As I have remarked elsewhere (McCosker, 2008, Introduction), it is important to observe carefully the operation of different kinds of opposition in paradox, in particular paying attention to the kind of negation between opposite terms. In this way one can come to distinguish between paradox which emphasizes the mutually exclusive and collectively exhaustive opposition of contradiction, and more complicated kinds of paradox which emphasize "weaker" senses of opposition and their continuing coincidence. One can see both kinds at work in Ephrem's work. In the example cited above, and frequently when treating the incarnation, Ephrem's use of paradox falls into the latter category, which may loosely be dubbed as "both/and." However, the former category (loosely, "either/or") can be seen at work when he presses biblical typology to fuel his supersessionist view of the Jews (on which see Sed, 1968):

By the shining forth of Your advent the shadows have been illuminated.
The types have come to an end, but the allusions persist.
The flash of the symbols has been swallowed up by Your rays.
Your symbols have passed away, but Your prophets have not passed away.
The [Jewish] people have erred in their reading of the prophets,
And they maintained that You were not You.
(*Hymn on Virginity* XXVIII: McVey, 1988, 387)

Ephrem's theology is resolutely christological with Christ at the center, with everything in creation pointing to him. Many of his most striking images are ones used to show different facets of the christological reality. This is true of his five famous hymns on the pearl (which are within the cycle of *Hymns on Faith*, LXXXI–LXXXV), of which he says, "it became a fountain from which I drank the mysteries of the Son" (Brock, 1992, 106). He manages to extract much from the image: the luminosity of the Son, the tastiness of scripture, the nakedness of those being baptized, the nakedness of the fishermen/apostles, the piercing of the Son/pearl, the Eucharist as medicine of life. As so often, Ephrem fully utilizes possible word plays. In this case the verb for diving (the pearl fishers) and being baptized are the same. Similarly Ephrem uses the image of oil for much christological mileage:

The face that gazes on a vessel filled with oil
Sees its reflection there, but he who gazes in a hidden way
Sees Christ in its symbols: and as the beauty of Christ is
    manifold
So too the olive's symbols are manifold.
Christ has many facets, and the oil acts as a mirror to them all:
From whatever angle I look at the oil, Christ looks out at me
    from it.
             (*Hymn on Virginity*, VII: Brock and Kiraz, 2006, 197)

One of the most striking ways in which Ephrem talks of the christological union of humanity and divinity in Christ is by using the language of mixture and mingling of the two natures:

Glorious is the Wise One Who allied and joined
Divinity with humanity,
    ane from the height and the other from the depth.
He mingled the natures like pigments
and an image came into being: the God-man.
        (*Hymn on the Nativity* VIII: McVey, 1989, 119)

Strikingly, he then uses the same language to talk of our deification:

God had seen that we worshipped creatures.
He put on a created body to catch us by our habit.

Behold by this fashioned one our Fashioner healed us,
and by this creature our Creator revived us.
His force did not govern us. Blessed is He Who came in what
    is ours
and mingled us into what is His.
            (*Hymn on the Nativity* XXI: McVey, 1988, 176)

Ephrem not only intertwines christology and deification with the language of mixture, he also adds to this the Eucharist (on the Eucharist in Ephrem see Griffith, 1999b):

His body [Christ's] was newly mixed with our bodies,
And His pure blood has been poured out into our veins,
And His voice into our ears, and his brightness into our eyes.
All of Him has been mixed into all of us by His compassion,
And since He loves His church very much,
He did not give her the manna of her rival.
He had living bread for her to eat.
            (*Hymn on Virginity* XXXVII: McVey, 1988, 425)

I have explored elsewhere in some depth the language of mixture in christological contexts in mystical theologies, both patristic and medieval, as well as the complex underlying philosophical background (McCosker, 2008, chapter 2). We cannot go into that here, but it is clearly an area which needs further treatment (there is some discussion of Ephrem's use of mixture language in Stewart, 1991, 191–8), both in terms of the contemporaneous use of this language by Ephrem and the Cappadocians, for instance (for some reflections on this see Russell 1995, 146–78), but also in terms of the analysis of the extent of Ephrem's awareness of philosophical works, started by Possekel, reversing the earlier scholarly consensus which asserted that Ephrem knew no philosophy (see Possekel, 1999).

It is to be hoped that this rapid survey of some selected key themes in the writings of Ephrem the Syrian, "Harp of the Spirit," which resonate with a number of contemporary theological interests, will whet the appetite of readers and encourage them to pick up his works for themselves.

References

Abouzayd, Shafiq. 1993. *Iḥidayutha: A Study of the Life of Singleness in the Syrian Orient. From Ignatius of Antioch to Chalcedon 451A.D.* Oxford: ARAM Society for Mesopotamian Studies.

Amar, Joseph P. 1988. "The Syrian 'Vita' Tradition of Ephrem the Syrian." Unpublished PhD thesis. Washington: Catholic University of America.

Amar, Joseph P. 1992. "Byzantine Ascetic Monachism and Greek Bias in the *Vita* Tradition of Ephrem the Syrian," *Orientalia Christiana Periodica* 58: 123–56.

Amar, Joseph P. 1995. *A Metrical Hymn on Holy Mar Ephrem by Mar Jacob of Serug: Critical Edition of the Syriac Text, Translation and Introduction.* Patrologia Orientalis 47(1), 205. Turnhout: Brepols.

Assemani, J. S., Mobarak (Benedictus), P., and Assemani, S. A., eds. 1732–46. *Sancti patris nostri Ephraem Syri opera omnia quæ exstant, Græce, Syriace, Latine, nova interpretatione, præfationibus, notis, variantibus lectionibus illustratur,* 6 vols. Rome: ex Typographia Vaticana.

Ayres, Lewis. 2004. *Nicaea and Its Legacy: An Approach to Fourth-Century Trinitarian Theology.* Oxford: Oxford University Press.

Bardy, Gustave. 1946. "Le souvenir de saint Ephrem dans le haut moyen age latin," *Revue du Moyen Age Latin* 2: 297–300.

Beattie, Tina. 2007. "Queen of Heaven." In *Queer Theology: Rethinking the Western Body*, ed Gerard Loughlin. Oxford: Blackwell, pp. 293–304.

Beck, Edmund. 1981. *Ephräms Trinitätslehre im Bild von Sonne/Feuer, Licht und Wärme.* Louvain: Peeters.

Beck, Edmund, Hemmerdinger-Iliadou, D., and Kirchmeyer, Jean. 1960. "Éphrem (saint)." In *Dictionnaire de spiritualité: Ascétique et mystique, doctrine et histoire*, ed. Marcel Villier, F. Cavallera, and J. de Guibert. Paris: Beauchesne, vol. IV, pp. 788–822.

Benedict XV, Pope. 1920. "Principi Apostolorum Petro," *Acta Apostolicae Sedis* 12(12): 457–71.

Benedict XVI, Pope. 2007. General Audience: Saint Ephrem. November 28, 2007. [online: http://www.vatican.va/holy_father/benedict_xvi/audiences/2007/documents/hf_ben-xvi_aud_20071128_en.html] Accessed January 3, 2008.

Bestul, Thomas H. 1981. "Ephraim the Syrian and Old English Poetry," *Anglia* 99: 1–24.

Biesen, Kees den. 2002. *Bibliography of Ephrem the Syrian.* Giove in Umbria: Private Publication.

Biesen, Kees den. 2006. *Simple and Bold: Ephrem's Art of Symbolic Thought.* Piscataway, NJ: Gorgias Press.

Botha, P. J. 1988. "Antithesis and Argument in the Hymns of Ephrem the Syrian," *Hervormde Teologiese Studies* 44(3): 581–95.

Botha, P. J. 1989. "Christology and Apology in Ephrem the Syrian," *Hervormde Teologiese Studies* 45(1): 19–29.

Botha, P. J. 1990. "Polarity: The Theology of Anti-Judaism in Ephrem the Syrian's Hymns on Easter," *Hervormde Teologiese Studies* 46(1–2): 36–46.

Botha, P. J. 1990–1. "The Stucture and Function of Paradox in the Hymns of Ephrem the Syrian," *Ekklesiastikos Pharos* 68: 50–62.

Bou Mansour, Tanios. 1988. *La pensée symbolique de saint Ephrem le Syrien.* Kaslik, Lebanon: Bibliothèque de l'Université Saint-Esprit.

Brock, Sebastian. 1975. *The Harp of the Spirit: Twelve Poems of Saint Ephrem.* Oxford: Fellowship of St. Alban and St. Sergius. Studies Supplementary to Sobornost. No. 4.

Brock, Sebastian. 1979. "Jewish Traditions in Syriac Sources," *Journal of Jewish Studies* 30(2): 212–32.

Brock, Sebastian. 1982. "Clothing Metaphors as a Means of Theological Expression in Syriac Tradition," In *Typus, Symbol, Allegorie bei den östlichen Vätern und ihren Parallelen im Mittelalter*, ed. Margot Schmidt with Carl Friedrich Geyer. Regensburg: Friedrich Pustet, pp. 11–38.

Brock, Sebastian. 1987. *The Syriac Fathers on Prayer and the Spiritual Life.* Kalamazoo, MI: Cistercian Publications.

Brock, Sebastian. 1988. "The Poet as Theologian: St Ephrem." In *Sebastian Brock, Studies in Syriac Spirituality*. Poona: Anita. (Reprinted from *Sobornost*.)

Brock, Sebastian. 1990. "A Brief Guide to the Main Editions and Translations of the Words of St. Ephrem," *The Harp* 3: 7–29.

Brock, Sebastian. 1992. *The Luminous Eye: The Spiritual World Vision of Saint Ephrem the Syrian.* Kalamazoo, MI: Cistercian Publications.

Brock, Sebastian. 2003. "The Changing Faces of St Ephrem as Read in the West." In *Abba: The Tradition of Orthodoxy in the West: Festschrift for Bishop Kallistos (Ware) of Diokleia*, ed. John Behr, Andrew Louth, and Dimitri Conomos. Crestwood: St Vladimir's Seminary Press, pp. 65–80.

Brock, Sebastian. 2004. "Ephrem and the Syriac Tradition." In *The Cambridge History of Early Christian Literature*, ed. Frances Young, Lewis Ayres, and Andrew Louth. Cambridge: Cambridge University Press, pp. 362–72.

Brock, Sebastian. 2007. "St Ephrem the Syrian on Reading Scripture," *Downside Review* 125(438): 37–50.

Brock, Sebastian and Kiraz, George. 2006. *Ephrem the Syrian: Select Poems.* Provo, UT: Brigham Young University Press.

Bundy, David D. 1982. "Ephrem's Critique of Mani: The Limits of Knowledge and the Nature of Language." In *Gnosticisme et monde hellénistique*, ed. Julien Ries with Yvonne Janssens and Jean-Marie Sevrin. Louvain-la-Neuve: Institut Orientaliste, pp. 289–98.

Bundy, David D. 1988. "Language and the Knowledge of God in Ephrem Syrus," *Dialogue & Alliance* 1(4): 56–64.

Burkitt, F. Crawford. [1904] 2004. *Early Eastern Christianity : St Margaret's Lectures 1904: On the Syriac Speaking Church.* Piscataway: Gorgias.

Griffith, Sidney H. 1986. "Ephraem, the Deacon of Edessa, and the Church of the Empire." In *Diakonia: Studies in Honor of Robert T. Meyer,* ed. T. Halton and J. P. Williman. Washington: Catholic University of America Press, pp. 22–52.

Griffith, Sidney H. 1993a. "The Image of the Image Maker in the Poetry of St. Ephraem the Syrian." In *Studia Patristica,* ed. E. A. Livingstone. Leuven: Peeters, pp. 258–69.

Griffith, Sidney H. 1993b. "Monks, 'Singles,' and the 'Sons of the Covenant': Reflections on Syrian Ascetic Terminology." In *ΕΥΛΟΓΗΜΑ: Studies in Honor of Robert Taft, S.J.,* ed. E. Carr, S. Parenti, A.-A. Thiermeyer, and E. Velkovska. Rome: Centro Studi S. Anselmo, pp. 141–60.

Griffith, Sidney H. 1995. "Asceticism in the Church of Syria: The Hermeneutics of Early Syrian Monasticism." In *Asceticism,* ed. Vincent Wimbush and Richard Valantasis. Oxford: Oxford University Press, pp. 220–45.

Griffith, Sidney H. 1997. "*Faith Adoring the Mystery*": *Reading the Bible with St. Ephraem the Syrian.* Milwaukee, MI: Marquette University Press.

Griffith, Sidney H. 1998. "A Spiritual Father for the Whole Church: the Universal Appeal of St. Ephraem the Syrian." *Hugoye* [online journal: http://syrcom.cua.edu/Hugoye/Vol1No2/HV1N2Griffith.html] 1/2.

Griffith, Sidney H. 1999a. "Setting Right the Church of Syria: Saint Ephraem's *Hymns against Heresies.*" In *The Limits of Ancient Christianity: Essays on Late Antique Thought and Culture in Honor of R. A. Markus,* ed. William E. Klingshirn and Mark Vessey. Ann Arbor: University of Michigan Press, pp. 97–114.

Griffith, Sidney H. 1999b. "'Spirit in the Bread; Fire in the Wine': the Eucharist as 'Living Medicine' in the Thought of Ephraem the Syrian." In *Catholicism and Catholicity: Eucharistic Communities in Historical and Contemporary Perspectives,* ed. Sarah Beckwith. Oxford: Blackwell, pp. 113–34.

Haering, Stephan. 1992. "In Memoriam: Prof. Dr. P. Edmund Beck OSB," *Studien und Mitteilungen zur Geschichte des Benediktinerorden und seiner Zweige* 103(2): 438–40.

de Halleux, André. 1983. "Saint Éphrem le Syrien," *Revue théologique de Louvain* 14: 328–55.

Hanson, R. P. C. 1988. *The Search for the Christian Doctrine of God: The Arian Controversy, 318–381.* Edinburgh: T&T Clark.

Harvey, Susan Ashbrook. 1998. "St Ephrem on the Scent of Salvation," *Journal of Theological Studies* 49(1): 109–28.

Harvey, Susan Ashbrook. 2000. "Women's Service in Ancient Syriac Christianity," *Kanon: Jahrbuch der Gesellschaft für das Recht der Ostkirchen* 16: 226–41.

Harvey, Susan Ashbrook. 2001. "Spoken Words, Voiced Silence: Biblical Women in Syriac Tradition," *Journal of Early Christian Studies* 9(1): 105–31.

Harvey, Susan Ashbrook. 2005. "On Mary's Voice: Gendered Words in Syriac Marian Tradition." In *The Cultural Turn in Late Ancient Studies: Gender, Asceticism, and Historiography,* ed. Dale B. Martin and Patricia Cox Miller. Durham, NC: Duke University Press, pp. 63–86.

Harvey, Susan Ashbrook. 2006. *Scenting Salvation: Ancient Christianity and the Olfactory Imagination.* Berkeley, CA: University of California Press.

Hausherr, Irénée. [1960] 1978. *The Name of Jesus, trans. Charles Cummings.* Kalamazoo, MI: Cistercian Publications.

Hymns of Saint Ephrem the Syrian, trans. Mary Hanbury. Oxford: SLG Press.

Koonammakkal, Thomas. 1993a. "Divine Names and Theological Language in Ephrem." In *Studia Patristica,* ed. E. A. Livingstone. Leuven: Peeters, pp. 318–23.

Koonammakkal, Thomas. 1993b. "Changing Views on Ephrem," *Christian Orient* 14(3): 113–30.

Koonammakkal, Thomas. 1998. "Ephrem's Imagery of Chasm." In *Symposium Syriacum VII,* ed. R. Lavenant, SJ. Rome: Pontificio Istituto Orientale, pp. 175–83.

Koonammakkal, Thomas. 2005. "Imagery of Dust in Ephrem," *The Harp* 18: 357–64.

Lamy, T. J., ed. 1882–1902. *Sancti Ephraem Syri Hymni et Sermones,* 4 vols. Malines: H. Dessain.

Mathews, Edward G. and Amar, Joseph P., trans., McVey, Kathleen, ed. 1994. *St. Ephrem the Syrian: Selected Prose Works: Commentary on Genesis, Commentary on Exodus, Homily on Our Lord, Letter to Publius.* Washington: Catholic University of America Press.

McCarthy, Carmel, ed. and trans. 2000. *Saint Ephrem's Commentary on Tatian's Diatessaron: An English Translation of Chester Beatty Syriac MS 709.* Oxford: Oxford University Press.

McCosker, Philip. 2008. "Parsing Paradox, Analysing 'And': Christological Configurations of Theological Paradox in Some Mystical Theologies." Unpublished PhD thesis. University of Cambridge.

McVey, Kathleen E. 1988. "Saint Ephrem's Understanding of Spiritual Progress: Some Points of Comparison with Origen of Alexandria," *The Harp* 1(2–3): 117–28.

McVey, Kathleen E., ed. and trans. 1989. *Ephrem the Syrian: Hymns.* New York: Paulist Press.

McVey, Kathleen E. 1990. "The Anti-Judaic Polemic of Ephrem Syrus' Hymns on the Nativity." In *Of Scribes and Scrolls: Studies on the Hebrew Bible, Intertestamental Judaism, and Christian Origins,* ed. Harold W. Attridge, John J. Collins, and Thomas H. Tobin, SJ. Lanham, MD: University Press of America, pp. 229–40.

McVey, Kathleen E. 2001. "Ephrem the Syrian's Usa of Female Metaphors to Describe the Deity," *Zeitschrift für antikes Christentum* 5: 261–88.

McVey, Kathleen E. 2007. "Ephrem the *Kitharode* and Proponent of Women: Jacob of Serug's Portrait of a Fourth-century Churchman for the Sixth-century Viewer and Its Significance for the Twenty-first Century Ecumenist." In *Orthodox and Wesleyan Ecclesiology*, ed. S. T. Kimbrough. Crestwood, NY: St Vladimir's Seminary Press, pp. 229–53.

Mitchell, C. W. 1912–21. *S. Ephraim's Prose Refutations of Mani, Marcion, and Bardaisan*, vols 1–2. London: Williams and Norgate.

Montemaggi, Vittorio, and Traherne, Matthew, eds. Forthcoming. *Dante's Commedia: Theology as Poetry*. Notre Dame, IN: University of Notre Dame Press.

Morris, J. B., ed. and trans. 1847. *Select Works of S. Ephrem the Syrian*. Oxford: Parker.

Murray, Robert. 1962–71. "Ephrem Syrus, St." In *Catholic Dictionary of Theology*, ed. H. Francis Davis et al. London: Nelson, part 2, pp. 220–23.

Murray, Robert. 1973. "The Lance Which Re-opened Paradise: A Mysterious Reading in the Early Syriac Fathers," *Orientalia Christiana Periodica* 39(1): 224–34.

Murray, Robert. 1975–6. "The Theory of Symbolism in St. Ephrem's Theology," *Parole de l'Orient* 6–7: 1–20.

Murray, Robert. 1980. "St Ephrem's Dialogue of Reason and Love," *Sobornost* 2(2): 26–40.

Murray, Robert. 1995. "Aramaic and Syriac Dispute-Poems and Their Connections." In *Studia Aramaica: New Sources and New Approaches*, ed. M. J. Geller, J. C. Greenfield, and M. P. Weitzman. Oxford: Oxford University Press, pp. 157–87.

Murray, Robert. 2006. *Symbols of Church and Kingdom: A Study in Early Syriac Tradition*, rev. ed. Cambridge: Cambridge University Press.

Outtier, B. 1973. "Saint Éphrem d'après ses biographies et ses œuvres," *Parole de l'Orient* 4: 11–33.

Palmer, Andrew. 1993. "'A Lyre without a Voice': The Poetics and the Politics of Ephrem the Syrian," *ARAM* 5: 371–99.

Palmer, Andrew. 1996–7. "Mind the Gap! or, A Church Father with a Sense of Fun," *Golden Horn: Journal of Byzantium [online journal*: http://www.isidore-of-seville.com/goudenhoorn.42 andrew.html] 4/2.

Palmer, Andrew. 1999. "The Influence of Ephraim the Syrian," Hugoye [online journal: http://syrcom.cua.edu/Hugoye/] 2/1.

Petersen, William L. 1985. "The Dependence of Romanos the Melodist upon the Syriac Ephrem: Its Importance for the Origin of the Kontakion," *Vigiliae Christianae* 39: 171–87.

Pierre, Marie-Joseph, ed. 1988–9. *Aphraate le sage persan: Les exposés. Sources Chrétiennes*, 349, 359. Paris: Cerf.

Possekel, Ute. 1999. *Evidence of Greek Philosophical Concepts in the Writings of Ephrem the Syrian*. Leuven: Peeters.

Raphael, Pierre. 1950. *Le rôle du Collège maronite romain dans l'orientalisme aux XVIIe et XVIIIe siècles*. Beirut: Université Saint Joseph.

Rogers Jr., Eugene. 2005. *After the Spirit: A Constructive Pneumatology from Resources outside the Modern West*. Grand Rapids, MI: Eerdmans.

Rowell, Geoffrey. 1999. "'Making the Church of England Poetical': Ephraim and the Oxford Movement," *Hugoye* [online journal: http://syrcom.cua.edu/Hugoye/] 2/1.

Russell, Paul S. 1995. *St. Ephraem the Syrian and St. Gregory the Theologian confront the Arians*. Kottayam: St Ephrem Ecumenical Research Institute.

Russell, Paul S. 1998. "A First Look at the Christology of Ephraem the Syrian." In *Symposium Syriacum VII*, ed. R. Lavenant, SJ. Rome: Pontificio Istituto Orientale, pp. 107–15.

Russell, Paul S. 2000. "Ephraem the Syrian on the Utility of Language and the Place of Silence," *Journal of Early Christian Studies* 8(1): 21–37.

Russell, Paul S. 2001. "Making Sense of Scripture: An Early Attempt by St. Ephrem the Syrian," *Communio [English edition]* 28: 171–201.

Russell, Paul S. 2005. "St Ephraem's *Carmina Nisibena 33*: A Hymn on Paganism's Place in the World," *St Vladimir's Theological Quarterly* 49(4): 395–415.

Russell, Paul S. 2005. "Nisibis as the Background to the Life of Ephrem the Syrian," *Hugoye* [online journal: http://syrcom.cua.edu/Hugoye/] 8/2.

Russell, Paul S., ed. and trans. Forthcoming. *Ephraem the Syrian. 80 Hymns on Faith*. Leuven: Peeters.

Schmidt, Margot. 1973. "Influence de saint Éphrem sur la littérature latine et allemande du début du moyen-age," *Parole de l'Orient* 4(1–2): 325–41.

Schmidt, Margot. 1982. "Die Augensymbolik bei Ephräm und Parallelen in der deutschen Mystik." In *Typus, Symbol, Allegorie bei den östlichen Vätern und ihren Parallelen im Mittelalter*, ed. Margot Schmidt with Carl Friedrich Geyer. Regensburg: Friedrich Pustet, pp. 278–301.

Séd, Nicolas. 1968. "Les hymnes sur le paradis de saint Ephrem et les traditions juives," *Le Muséon* 81(3–4): 455–501.

Segal, J. B. 1970. *Edessa: "The Blessed City"*. Oxford: Clarendon.

Stevenson, Jane. 1998. "Ephraim the Syrian in Anglo-Saxon England," *Hugoye* [online journal: http://syrcom.cua.edu/Hugoye/] 1/2.

Stewart, Columba. 1991. *"Working the Earth of the Heart":
The Messalian Controversy in History, Texts, and Language to
AD 431.* Oxford: Clarendon.

Taylor, David G. K. 1998. "St. Ephraim's Influence on the
Greeks," *Hugoye* [online journal: http://syrcom.cua.edu/
Hugoye/] 1/2.

Wakefield, Gordon. 1998. "John Wesley and Ephraem
Syrus," *Hugoye* [online journal: http://syrcom.cua.edu/
Hugoye/] 1/2.

Walsh, James. 1980. "Divine Call and Human Response:
The Syriac Tradition: St Ephrem I," *The Way* 20: 228–33.

Williams, Rowan. 1987. *Arius: Heresy and Tradition.* London:
Darton, Longman & Todd.

Young, Frances. 1997. *Biblical Exegesis and the Formation of
Christian Culture.* Cambridge: Cambridge University
Press.

Yousif, Pierre. 1977–8. "Symbolisme christologique dans la
Bible et dans la nature chez s. Ephrem de Nisibe," *Parole
de l'Orient* 8: 5–66.

Yousif, Pierre. 1983. "Exegetical Principles of St Ephrem
the Syrian," *Studia Patristica*, ed. E. A. Livingstone.
Leuven: Peeters, 18(4): 296–302.

Yousif, Pierre. 2001/2. "Parole et silence chez saint Éphrem
de Nisibe," *La Maison Dieu* 226: 95–114.

Ignatius of Antioch (*c.*35–*c.*110)

Bernadette McNary-Zak

The second-century bishop Ignatius of Antioch is remembered for his witness to the Christian faith as a disciple, a bishop, an apostolic father, and a martyr. His letters are a notable testament to his life. Furthermore, they provide insight into the intense internal process of self-definition, as Christians sought to identify themselves in distinct relation to society and empire.

Virtually nothing is known with certainty about Ignatius's birth and early life. The ecclesiastical historian Eusebius writes that Ignatius became the third bishop of Antioch in 69 CE, after the death of Evodius, successor to Peter (Eusebius, *Ecclesiastical History* 3.22). Ignatius was arrested in Antioch toward the end of the reign of Emperor Trajan (98–117 CE), under unknown circumstances, and he was taken to Rome for judgment and death as a martyr. Trajan's correspondence with Pliny, the governor of Bithynia in 112 CE, calls for this same practice to be instituted toward problem Christians of Roman citizenship. Upon his arrest, Ignatius was led by a military escort through Syria, Asia Minor, and Philadelphia. At Smyrna, Ignatius was met by delegates from the Christian communities in Tralles, Magnesia, and Ephesus, to whom he then issued letters. He also wrote a letter to the church in Rome regarding the status of his arrival. From Smyrna the escort led Ignatius to Troas where he issued three more letters, one each to the Christian communities of Philadelphia and of Smyrna, as well as a personal letter to his colleague and friend, Polycarp, the bishop

of Smyrna. From the port in Troas, Ignatius boarded a boat and was taken to Neapolis and to Philippi where, Polycarp writes, he was welcomed and encouraged by the local Christian community (Polycarp, *Letter to the Philippians* 1.1) before finally arriving in Rome where he was tried and executed. Ignatius's date of death is unknown. Eusebius situates it in the latter part of Trajan's reign; others have placed it later under the rule of Trajan's successor, Hadrian.

Ignatius's letters were influenced by contemporary epistolary models and by Pauline language. Ignatius drew upon the intellectual resources of his day. Evidence for his adoption and adaptation of common literary devices to suit his own style is found, for example, in the salutation of each letter. Here, Ignatius incorporates a standard epistolary opening by beginning with his identification as author of the letter. Whereas he follows this by a commonly employed statement of self-reference, his choice is distinctive to his cause; he is "Theophorus," ("God-bearer," "bearing God"). The salutation concludes with another standard device, a statement of "abundant" or "heartiest" greeting. Ignatius's letters are brief; their tone is direct and firm. In many cases, his issuance of a letter is an extension of continued fellowship, personalized by his stated acknowledgment of the respective delegates from each community who visited him while en route to Rome. His mention of these and other prominent persons, including the identity of the bishop, in all of

The Student's Companion to the Theologians, First Edition. Edited by Ian S. Markham.

the letters except that issued to the Romans serves to further bind the ties of these relationships.

Certainly, the personal and ecclesiastical contexts of Ignatius's authorship must bear on the interpretation of the letters. The letters are framed by Ignatius's impending death and by the circumstances of the church in the second century. The two are not mutually exclusive. As a result, the reader must balance Ignatius's statements with his concerns: his call for structural integrity offers a response to the organizational variety of the Christian communities; his appeal to unity attests to the multiplicity of forms, beliefs, and practices that divided the churches; his desire for consensus addresses the difficult state of theological dissension. Moreover, these concerns were hardly isolated to Ignatius's church in Antioch; rather, his experience as a bishop of a major urban center necessarily informed his counsel to the other Christian communities. Ignatius's arrest had significant ramifications for the members of the church in Antioch; clearly, the evidence of the letters indicates that it affected Christians in other regions of the empire as well.

Several key themes permeate the letters. Ignatius was acutely aware of the relationship between his martyrdom and his identity as a Christian, explaining that he was put "in chains for the sake of the Name" (*Eph*. 3.1). He understood his death as a form of imitation, claiming that "the faithful in love bear the stamp of God the Father through Jesus Christ, whose life is not in us unless we voluntarily choose to die into his suffering" (*Mag*. 5.2). Given this, Ignatius employs sacrificial language, writing of himself as the offering for the altar (*Rom*. 2.2). As William Schoedel has observed, in this way Ignatius "invites fellow Christians to see beyond appearances and to grasp the hidden meaning of his wretched condition. It seems obvious that Christians who had been nurtured on the story of the crucified Lord and who had experienced rejection by society in their own lives (see on *Eph*. 10) would be prepared to welcome such a figure" (Schoedel, 1985, 11).

Ignatius insists that his death is of his own free will and asks that he not be hindered in it (*Rom*. 4.1) His martyrdom is perceived as an "accomplishment," a "goal," for which he hopes God will continue to find him worthy (*Rom*. 1.1; *Rom*. 8.3). It is through his death, he maintains, that he will become a true disciple

(*Rom*. 4.2) for "a Christian has no authority over himself; rather he devotes his time to God" (*Poly*. 7.3).

If Ignatius perceived martyrdom as a means of imitation and union for the individual Christian, he envisioned a specific ecclesiastical organization as providing the same for the church. Ignatius applauds the structure of the true church as it is found in the communities to whom he writes. This structure consists of a single bishop assisted by deacons and a council of presbyters. Ignatius insists that this structure has a theological foundation. "Similarly, let everyone respect the deacons as Jesus Christ, just as they should respect the bishop, who is a model of the Father, and the presbyters as God's council and as the band of the apostles. Without these no group can be called a church" (*Tral*. 3.1). As a result, this tripartite ministerial structure, with the bishop at its center, is essential to the unity of the church. "Be subject to the bishop and to one another, as Jesus Christ in the flesh was to the Father, and as the apostles were to Christ and to the Father, that there might be unity, both physical and spiritual" (*Tral*. 13.2). Ignatius personalizes this appeal in each letter by recognizing the contributions of individual bishops, deacons, and presbyters. Since many of the delegates who met him en route to Rome included these, Ignatius is able to refer to their particular gifts. Yet, he also supplies statements of general admonishment to the members of each community regarding the bishop. Christians should know that the ministry of their "earthly" bishop is obtained in, and fostered by, a love of God (*Eph*. 1.3; *Phil*. 1.1). Their respect for the bishop is in accordance with that for "the Father of Jesus Christ, the Bishop of all" (*Mag*. 3.1). Furthermore, "the one who honors the bishop has been honored by God; the one who does anything without the bishop's knowledge serves the devil" (*Smyrn*. 9.1). The bishop was required for such marks of unity as baptism and Eucharist to be valid (*Smyrn*. 8.2). In the person of the bishop, Ignatius can see the whole Christian community (*Eph*. 1.3; *Mag*. 2; *Phil*. 1; *Smyrn*. 8.2). Indeed, he admits that he saw himself as a ransom for those who upheld such unity of the church in faith and in love (*Poly*. 6.1). Perhaps he envisioned the church in Antioch in these terms since he expresses relief that its members were able to resolve any division caused by his arrest and absence in peace (*Poly*. 7.1).

Imitation in martyrdom and solidarity in ministerial structure and sacrament were possible because of the incarnation, suffering, death, and resurrection of Jesus Christ. Ignatius writes of Christ as "both flesh and spirit, born and unborn, God in man, true life in death, both from Mary and from God, first subject to suffering and then beyond it" (*Eph.* 7.2), thereby emphasizing a unique and specific union of human and divine. Moreover, for Ignatius, the truthfulness of this reality is recognizable in the historical details and soteriological significance of the crucifixion (*Smyrn.* 1.2; *Tral.* 9). Those who do not affirm the centrality of such realities are "heretical." Ignatius confronts a variety of such views. Against the docetists, for whom Christ only appeared human and only seemed to suffer, Ignatius insists that Christ "truly suffered just as he truly raised himself" (*Smyrn.* 2.1), a view that gives meaning to his own impending death. "For if these things were done by our Lord in appearance only, then I am in chains in appearance only" (*Smyrn.* 4.2; *Tral.* 10). Other false teachings about the grace of Jesus Christ further threaten the unity of the church. Ignatius chastises those who fail to adhere to the teachings of the gospel over those of the prophets (*Phil.* 8.2). He also alerts his readers to ethical practices that characterize some heretical opinions:

They have no concern for love, none for the widow, none for the orphan, none for the oppressed, none for the prisoner or the one released, none for the hungry or thirsty. They abstain from the Eucharist and prayer, because they refuse to acknowledge that the Eucharist is the flesh of our Savior Jesus Christ, which suffered

for our sins and which the Father by his goodness raised up. (*Smyrn.* 6.2)

In contrast, Ignatius insisted, the life of the true Christian overturns these heretical opinions and practices (*Poly.* 4). He supplies a number of relevant images for the true Christian. Drawing an analogy with the good athlete, Ignatius exhorts the true Christian to be sober and always ready to struggle, to endure with patience and good judgment (*Poly.* 2, 3). Likewise, as soldiers prepared to serve, the true Christian accepts instruction to "let baptism serve as a shield, faith as a helmet, love as a spear, endurance as an armor" (*Poly.* 6).

Ignatius's letters were collected soon after his death by Polycarp and circulated widely (Polycarp, *Letter to the Philippians*, 13.2). As a result, there are several recensions of the letters; they were preserved and transmitted in a variety of languages. Their reconstruction and recognition of their authenticity is largely a product of late nineteenth-century scholarship. The influence of Ignatius and of the letters is evident in the writings of several later church fathers, including Polycarp, Irenaeus, Eusebius, and Theodoret. Ignatius's teachings had an impact on the development of theology and the institutionalization of the church. The church of his day was an apocalyptic sect of Judaism, marked by loose structures of authority and theological diversity. To this, Ignatius offered the preliminary foundations for emerging constructions of canon, creed, sacrament, and ministry that would serve to define the true Christian community united in faith and in love. As a result, the letters remain the subject of considerable study, research, and debate.

References

Corwin, Virginia. 1960. *St. Ignatius and Christianity in Antioch*. New Haven, CT: Yale University Press.

Grant, R. M. 1966. *Ignatius of Antioch*. The Apostolic Fathers, vol. 4. Camden, NJ: Nelson.

Holmes, Michael W. 1999. *The Apostolic Fathers: Greek Texts and English Translations*, ed. and rev. Grand Rapids, MI: Baker Books.

Schoedel, William R. 1985. *Ignatius of Antioch. A Commentary on the Letters of Ignatius of Antioch*. Philadelphia: Fortress Press.

Irenaeus of Lyons (2nd century)

Eric Osborn

One of the great paintings in the world is found at Rome in the Sistine Chapel where the walls and roof are covered with incidents from the Old and New Testaments. On the one side there are pictures from the life of Moses, on the other side there are incidents from the Gospels. Above, the story of creation is set out and the prophets and sibyls foretell the coming of Christ.

The front of the chapel is dominated by the figure of Christ in judgment, his raised hand revealing the wound in his side. The centrality of Christ is supported by the detail of the picture in which everything points to him. Everything that the Bible has told of God's dealing with man finds meaning in one point: the person of Jesus Christ. Splendid as is the triumph of Michelangelo, the conception is not new. From the beginning, Christians have seen their faith expressed in awareness of one God and his plan for human salvation which culminates in Jesus Christ. This is the primitive Christian *kerygma*.

No one has set out this account of the Christian message in written form more clearly than did Irenaeus, who was bishop in Lyons after the persecution of 177. He was a man of vision (*homme de voir*) who combined imagery with argument to transpose the message of scripture into public discourse. Lyons was and is a great city where the Roman forum is set on a hill overlooking the confluence of two rivers, the Rhone and the Saône. Irenaeus came here from Asia

Minor, where at Smyrna he had listened to the teaching of Polycarp, a bishop who, like Irenaeus's predecessor at Lyons, died a martyr. What Irenaeus had to say, his account of God, who created the world and guided its history and then came himself in Jesus Christ, has dominated the culture of the Christian West. Michelangelo's great painting is the clearest expression of this culture in visual form, as Handel's *Messiah* is the clearest statement in music. They attempt to express the message of the Christian Bible which shapes the puzzling narratives and the account of God. There are four things that the Bible, Michelangelo, and Handel want to tell us and Irenaeus put them better than anyone else: the goodness of God; his saving plan; its perfection in Christ; and the offer of salvation.

Irenaeus's major work, *Against the Heresies*, survives in fragments, but a translation from about 380 is complete. It is stimulated but not determined opposition to Gnosticism, a form of theosophy which today attracts interest sympathy. Some take the exuberance and composite nature of this work as an excuse for neglect, but its main ideas are powerfully clear. His *Demonstration of the Aposto Preaching* is a brief work, known in a sixth-century Armenian translation since 1907. It expresses the same themes as the longer work.

With his two criteria of logical truth (Is it logically coherent?) and aesthet fitness (Is it aesthetically harmonious?), Irenaeus develops four concepts which underpin the first comprehensive Christian theology. These concepts are the good mind of God (divine intellect), God's plan of salvation (divine economy), the summing up of all things in Christ (recapitulation), and the sharing of the believer in God's salvation (participation). The first and last point to optimism and growth while the middle concepts show the way in which growth is achieved.

Divine Intellect

For Irenaeus, God is universal intellect, holding all things in knowledge and vision, indivisible and simultaneous, entire and identical, the source of all good things: "His greatness lacks nothing, but contains all things, comes close to us and is with us" (*Haer.* 4.19.3). Instead of rejecting the philosopher's concept of God as ultimate being, Irenaeus joins philosophy with the biblical witness to develop his account of the divine intellect. We learn from scripture that God is one and three: one Father, one Son, and Holy Spirit (*Haer.* 1.10.1; 5.20.1).

Against those Gnostics who had divided the divine fullness into a multitude of eons, Irenaeus draws on the pre-Socratic philosopher Xenophanes, who supplanted the many gods of Greece with a universal mind who "sees all, thinks all and hears all" (Kirk et al., 1983, 170). Anthropomorphic subdivision of the divine mind is foolish and presumptuous. God simply is, while man "becomes." God makes, while man is made. God is always the same, while man grows from a beginning, through a middle, to an end. God's goodness is poured out on man who grows from creation to final glory.

Irenaeus identifies the concept of divine intellect with active goodness to make a theocentric optimism. God's goodness precedes his action (*Haer.* 4.39.2). Optimism springs from confidence in the goodness of Creator and creation. Irenaeus describes Gnostics as restless and dissatisfied; they are always seeking but never finding (*Haer.* 5.20.2). In contrast, Irenaeus puts forward a love of what exists. The divine perfection needs a contingent creature to receive the goodness which it gives. The diversity of the world is ordered to become a splendid harmony from the composer of a wonderful universe (*Haer.* 2.26.3; 2.25.2; 4.4.2).

Irenaeus develops the common human awareness of a divine being into the forceful claim: God is a universal, intelligent being, who sees all, who knows in advance every creature's need, and who displays his love and glory everywhere, but especially through his prophets and supremely in his Son.

Salvation History/Economy

The divine economy or plan of salvation begins with creation. To explain creation, Irenaeus use two biblical analogies: God as Wise Architect and God as Sovereign King (*Haer.* 2.11.1). The Wise Architect produces order from disordered matter; the Sovereign King produces by word, will, and power. God, not an inferior demiurge, produces the varied beauty of the world (*Haer.* 2.2.1–3). While the Architect needs material in order to create, the King does not. By joining the two images together Irenaeus formulates a concept of creation from nothing.

The divine economy is the way in which the Wise Architect, God, proceeds and "draws up the plans for the edifice of salvation" (*Haer.* 4.14.2). It is packed with artistic detail and gives order to the story of God's dealing with mankind, without losing continuity in time or comprehensiveness in space. The functions of the economy—accustoming of God to man and man to God, progressive revelation and human development—are never abstract. They all have a human orientation.

The idea of "accustoming" meets an obvious challenge to Christian belief: why had God left it so late to send his Son to save the world? Irenaeus ingeniously replies that man had to be accustomed to God and God had to be accustomed to man. Abraham, Isaac, and Jacob prefigured what was to come as God accustomed his people to live as strangers in the world and to follow his word (*Haer.* 4.21.3). The incarnation is the climax because in Christ man is able to see God, to contain God and to participate in God; at the same time God is accustomed to live in man (*Haer.* 3.20.2).

The economy thus describes the ascent of man. Irenaeus's human optimism has long excited enthusiasm. At the Renaissance he inspired Erasmus. In the twentieth century he enthused those who, like Teilhard de Chardin, were driven by science to see human evolution to Christ as the omega point.

Irenaeus's account of the ascent of man to Christ has been contrasted with the fall of man as it is later described in Augustine. This contrast is oversimplified, for Irenaeus also speaks of the fall of man in Adam, and does not diminish the catastrophe. Yet Adam was an infant and God was able to take him and bring him, even in his fallen state, to perfection in Christ. Man, a mixture of soul and flesh, is created by God through his hands, the Son and the Spirit (*Haer.* 4.20.1). Adam has never left the hands of God, who made him and finally perfected him in Christ (*Haer.* 5.1.3). Irenaeus's many-sided development of the Adam–Christ typology takes the restoration of divine sonship and immortality in new directions. He develops the Pauline defense of the flesh and of human status as creature, against the spiritualizing tendencies of Gnostics.

The economy of salvation presents a progressive revelation of God. Revelation begins with creation and continues through the law and the prophets to end in the Incarnation of the Son. Here all creation sees its King, and in the splendid flesh of the Lord, man finds and receives the light of the Father (*Haer.* 4.20.2). The plan of salvation is defined by its climax in recapitulation.

Summing up/Recapitulation

Salvation history leads to the summing up or recapitulation of all things in Christ. In this event, end is joined to beginning, omega to alpha, and death is changed to life.

The first meaning which Irenaeus links with the concept of recapitulation is that of correcting what has gone wrong with human history. With this concept of correction are linked the ideas of the liberation of captive sinners, the justification of the ungodly, repetition, restoration, and reconciliation.

God is in Christ reconciling the world to himself. The world (sinful humanity) is summed up, united, and included in Christ just as it had been included in Adam. The action is repetitive in that it returns to the point of error and replaces the wrong deed with the right deed, thereby rectifying the ancient fault.

The mass of detail which Irenaeus uses to describe recapitulation reflects his desire to include everything.

Christ is not merely Head, Chief, or Summit, but the one who unites a vast plurality. To Romans 5:12–21 (Christ as second Adam) and 1 Corinthians 15:25–8 (subjection of all things to Christ), must be added Ephesians 1:10 (summing up of all things) for an appreciation of Irenaeus's cosmic view.

Secondly, recapitulation means perfection. The whole history of salvation is resumed by the gospel, so that beginning, middle, and end are brought together (*Haer.* 3.24.1). The supremacy of Christ over all things is established; just as he reigns over the unseen world, so he is Lord of the visible world, which he supports by the axis of his cross. All things are restored, renewed, and set free. Creation achieves its purpose; it is not merely repaired but brought to perfection.

Thirdly, recapitulation means the inauguration of a new humanity: "The glory of God is a living man and the life of man is the vision of God" (*Haer.* 4.20.7). Irenaeus has his own account of man as the image and likeness of God. Because the incarnate Son is the archetypal image, every human possesses shape and flesh similar to him. At baptism every believer receives the power of assimilation (likeness) from the Holy Spirit as a dynamic which gradually transforms the image until it is finally perfected by Resurrection.

Adam was weak, incomplete, an infant, possessing by the Spirit a likeness to God which he lost through disobedience. God led Adam to penitence (*Haer.* 3.23.5), life (*Haer.* 3.23.7), immortality (*Haer.* 3.20.2; *Dem.* 15) and communion with himself (*Haer.* 5.27.2). Lost possibilities were restored by Christ whose fullness now excels what was given during his earthly life. The new life is marked by immortality, for the Father will receive the righteous into incorruption and everlasting refreshment (*Haer.* 4.6.5), as his order of salvation moves forward to liberate his servant, adopt him as son, bestow on him an incorruptible inheritance, and so perfect humanity (*Haer.* 4.11.1).

Finally, recapitulation points to resurrection. The resurrection of Christ concerns the substance of his flesh. Our resurrection, like his, must be a resurrection of the flesh, for he will raise us by the same power which he used in his own resurrection. The reality of his flesh was proved when he showed the marks of the nails and the wound in his side. Our mortal bodies will be raised as he was raised. This is the work of the Spirit, whose power we already know in his pledge which prepares us for future incorruption. Those who possess this pledge of the Spirit are subject to the Spirit and serve the Spirit rather than the flesh.

Irenaeus's millenarian eschatology is the necessary act of a God who renews creation. The return of Christ in glory will display and prove his saving work (*Haer.* 3.16.6). The restoration of human lives, which is the present concern of the Church, will be complete in a restored universe. The inauguration of a new humanity is fed by the hope of final glory. Recapitulation and final consummation are thus tied together, and the whole of recapitulation is oriented to the end when creation and redemption fulfill their purpose.

A good image for Irenaeus's exuberant thought is that of an hourglass lying on its side so that it presents a movement from left to right. God begins with creation and ends with the consummation of all things. The first half of the hourglass bears on its sides the message of the prophets. Their visions represent the mind of God, and for Irenaeus take the place of the world of Platonic forms. The narrow neck of the hourglass is the recapitulation of all things in Christ, and the second half of the hourglass bears on its side the message of the prophets and the words of Christ and the Apostles.

Participation

Participation, the fourth of Irenaeus's key concepts, takes many forms. His first three concepts, we have seen, are unitive and point to one God, one saving economy or plan of salvation, one summing up. Participation is distributive, for God shares his life, truth, beauty, and goodness with humans in many ways. Humanity cannot live without life, which comes from participation in God. True knowledge works through divine/human exchange (*Haer.* 5.1.1), God becoming what we are so that we might become what he is. Irenaeus claims that this exchange, in a single stroke, destroys the dualism of the heretics (*Haer.* 5.1.1). Moreover, God finds joy in the work of salvation. He is the good shepherd, who "regaining his own, hoists the lost sheep on his shoulders to carry it back with joy to the fold of life" (*Haer.* 5.15.2).

Humans participate in God's truth through faith and reason. A canon or rule of truth was central to Hellenistic philosophy, but Irenaeus was the first Christian theologian to speak of the rule of truth or rule of faith, which is the original true and firm knowledge of God which the Church preserves. This has been handed down in succession from the Apostles (*Haer.* 3.3.2–3). Irenaeus sets out the succession for the church of Rome as an example. Other churches have a similar succession and will agree with Rome because they too hold apostolic doctrine. Irenaeus belonged to a church which had accepted a canon of four Gospels and he was the first writer to a church which had accepted a canon of four Gospels and he was the first writer to have a complete Christian Bible before him. He sought out what was clear and unambiguous in scripture by applying the classical criteria of logic (what is true) and aesthetics (what is fitting).

Humans find beauty in the light of God's glory and participate in God's life through the breath of his Spirit. Finally, they participate in God's goodness by loving those who wrong them. God's glory shines not in supernal heights but in a living human being. From the vision of God who is light comes life. The glory of God is thus revealed in the flesh which he first made (*Haer.* 5.3.2–3) and which bears the imprint of his fingers (*Haer.* 4.39.2).

We began our account of Irenaeus with a reference to Michelangelo's great painting. This is appropriate, for Irenaeus has been called an *homme de voir*, and visual metaphors abound. We turn to a detail of that painting to explain where Irenaeus found the center in his ocean of imagery. The uplifted arm of Christ in judgment reveals the wound in his side. For Irenaeus the cross is central. Paul had found the summing up of the law in the command to love. Irenaeus has two extended passages of argument where he moves first from the summing up in Christ to the love command and then from the love command to the recapitulation of all things (*Haer.* 3.18–20; 4.13–16, 20). The end of each complex argument is to identify the apex of Christ's summing up with his utterance on the cross: "Father forgive them, they know not what they do." This is an unforgettable claim of Irenaeus. While few writers call for conceptual stamina as often as he does, few reward it so richly.

References

Behr, John. 2000. *Asceticism and Anthropology in Irenaeus and Clement of Alexandria*. Oxford.

Fantino, Jacques. 1994. *La théologie d'Irénée*. Paris.

Fernandois, R. P. 1999. *El concepto de profecía en la teología de San Irenea*. Madrid.

Grant, R. M. 1997. *Irenaeus of Lyons*. London and New York.

Hitchcock, F. R. M. 1914. *Irenaeus of Lugdunum. A Study of his Teaching*. Cambridge.

Kirk, G. S., Raven, J. E., and Schofield, M. 1983. *The Presocratic Philosophers*. Cambridge, p. 170.

Meijering, E. P. 1975. *God, Being, History: Studies in Patristic Philosophy*. Amsterdam and Oxford.

Minns, Denis. 1994. *Irenaeus*. London.

Orbe, A. 1969. *Antropologia de San Irenea*. Madrid.

Osborn, Eric 2000. "Love of Enemies and Recapitulation," *Vigiliae Christianae* 54(1): 12–31.

Osborn, Eric. 2001. *Irenaeus of Lyons*. Cambridge.

Sesböüé, B. 2000. *Tout récapituler dans le Christ, christologie et sotériologie d'Irénée de Lyons*. Paris.

Wingren, G. 1959. *Man and Incarnation. A Study in the Biblical Theology of Irenaeus*. Edinburgh.

John the Evangelist

Wayne G. Rollins

I.   Introduction

When biblical scholars in the second half of the twentieth century began intensive analysis of the literary,
historical, and theological idiosyncrasies of the four
Gospels, they were echoing an assumption that was
alive in the earliest church, namely that each gospel
spoke in the voice and venue of its writer. This recognition of difference among the Gospels was implicit
in the early titles assigned to them: "According
to Matthew," "According to Mark," "According to
Luke," and "According to John." By the second century symbols were attached to the Gospels to denote
their differences: Mark was assigned a calf, Matthew a
lion, Luke the face of a human, and John the eagle
(Irenaeus, *Adversus Haereses* [*Adv. hae.*] 3.11.8).

By the third century it became clear that John was
a distinctly different Gospel among the four. Origen
tells us it was his favorite: "We may therefore make
bold to say that the Gospels are the first fruits of all
Scriptures, but of the Gospels, that of John is the first
fruit" (Origen, *Comm. on John*, 1.6). Eusebius in the
fourth century offers a characterization of John as a
"spiritual Gospel" (Smith, 1995, 1). By the twentieth
century the characterizations multiply. John is labeled
the "maverick Gospel" (Kysar, 1976), the "mystical
Gospel" (Countryman, 1994), the "prophetic Gospel"
(Hanson, 1991), the "spiritual Gospel" (Wiles, 1960),
and for some, a quasi-proto-Gnostic Gospel (Sloyan,

1996). But in common academic parlance, the title
most commonly applied to John was the "Fourth
Gospel" (e.g., Ashton, 1991).

In comparing the Gospels, even the non-technical
reader will recognize that John thinks and writes differently. He speaks with a poet's tongue that regards
remarkable events in life as "signs" that point beyond
themselves to another level of meaning and to a continuum of "eternal life" in which the life of Jesus and
the lives of all humanity participate. He speaks of the
pre-existent "Word" as having manifested itself in
space, time, and human flesh. He tells of Jesus convers-
ing with the scholar Nicodemus on the subject of
rebirth as a necessary stage in human development. He
portrays Jesus engaging a Samaritan woman at a well
in a discussion of "living water." His language is stud-
ded with the vivid metaphorical images of light and
darkness, truth and falsehood, life and death, natural
birth and rebirth, love and hate. Like Zen Buddhist
Ko'ans, the sayings in John seem designed to fracture
ordinary consciousness, such as, "Before Abraham was,
I AM" (8:58). John also provides the most economic
description of the community that Jesus intends to
create: "In this all men will know that you are my
disciples, if you have love for one another" (13:35).

The purpose of this article is to provide a sketch of
the theology of the Fourth Gospel, focusing on three
aspects: first, the theological context and history of the
Johannine writings; second, the theological message

The Student's Companion to the Theologians, First Edition. Edited by Ian S. Markham.
© 2013 Blackwell Publishing Ltd. Published 2013 by Blackwell Publishing Ltd.

in John's method; and third, John's fourfold theological agenda, focusing on God, christology, the Spirit/ Paraclete, and the community of disciples.

II.   Theological Context and History of the Johannine Writings

Contemporary biblical scholarship suggests that the first question one should ask of the Fourth Gospel is not "Who is John?" but "What is John?" (Segovia, 1996). Though the Gospel originates in one of the most imaginative theological minds in the New Testament, it is in the end an edited literary construct. It was written over the course of a half century within the context of a "Johannine school" undergoing socio-political-theological changes that produced in time, not only the Gospel, but four additional books: three epistles of John and the book of Revelation.

Evidence of editorial and historical change within the Gospel abounds. For example, John appears to have two endings, one at the end of chapter 20 (vv. 20–21), and a second with the whole of chapter 21. Chapter 21 seems to have been added to address two developments in the life of the Johannine church. First was the crisis of the death of the Beloved Disciple, contrary to an expectation, attributed to Jesus, that the Beloved Disciple would remain alive until Jesus' return (21:20–23). Second was the death of Peter (21:19) and the issue of reinstating Peter's tarnished reputation in the Johannine church (21:15–18).

A second type of editorial tampering can be seen in several striking contradictions, e.g., Peter's question, "Lord, Where are you going? (13:36), followed by Jesus' comment three chapters later, "Yet none of you asks me, 'Where are you going?'" (16:5). Another instance of contradiction occurs in 4:1–2 with the statement that, "Jesus was baptizing more disciples than John," followed by the contradictory assertion in the next verse that "Jesus himself did not baptize," an apparent reflection of growing disaffection between John the Baptist followers and the followers of Jesus (1:6–7, 15, 19–42; 3:26–30; 4:1; 5:33; 10:41, also 12:42; 16:2).

A third type of editorial activity was generated by changes in the ethnic-religious environment in the Johannine community. Greek translations of Hebrew/ Aramaic terms (John 1:38, 41, 42) are inserted into the text to address an audience no longer conversant in Hebrew/Aramaic. A comparable environmental change is echoed in hints of a crisis that surfaced in the history of the Jewish Christians in the Johannine community: the threat of expulsion from the synagogue (9:22–23; 12:42; 16:2).

Where does such evidence leave us with respect to reconstructing the theological history and context of John's Gospel? Acknowledging the variety of scholarly opinions on the subject, the following picture emerges. Sometime between 30 and 50 CE an original unidentified author, named "John" by the early church, gathered and shaped an oral tradition about Jesus into a proto-Gospel, marked with characteristic Johannine touches, e.g., a theology of "signs," the rendering of Jesus' teaching in long discourses, the employment of a handful of favorite literary devices (paradox, misunderstanding, irony, etc.; see below), and a theology quintessentially voiced in the prologue poem on the Logos (Word). Several decades later (50 to 80 CE), the proto-Gospel of John was editorially amended, and in some instances corrected to address a changed theological and social setting in which the controversy with the John the Baptist group and the threat of expulsion from the synagogue had emerged (Martyn, 1978). A final redaction stage, perhaps as late as 100 CE, dealt with the news of the death of the Beloved Disciple, the death of of Peter, and the transition of the Johannine community from a Hebrew/ Aramaic to a Greek-speaking setting.

Can anything definite be said about "John," the real-time figure whose genius gave birth to the Johannine tradition? Raymond Brown's suggestion that he was a "disciple of the Beloved Disciple, about whom he writes in the third person," is as persuasive as any (Brown, 1998, 11). Though we do not know him by name, we have his intellectual fingerprints. He is thoroughly Judaic, manifestly familiar with Judaic feasts, lore, and religious customs. He utilizes a choice set of literary devices in the service of his theology and purports to make public (16:29) the inner world of the Messiah. He demonstrates unique geographic familiarity with Palestine, naming 12 sites not mentioned in the other gospels, which adds credence to the growing suspicion in twenty-first-century Johannine scholarship that the Fourth Gospel may be a more reliable historical source than previously supposed, and that the long-standing practice of the "de-Johannification of Jesus" and the "de-historicization of John" may stand in need of correction (Anderson, 2006).

How do the Johannine epistles and the book of Revelation fit the picture? Though one seems to be walking on familiar theological turf when reading the Johannine epistles because of their typical Johannine vocabulary (e.g., love, hate, light, darkness, life, death), it becomes clear in short order that the author of the Gospel is not the author of the epistles. Many of the key terms (e.g., *logos*, Paraclete) are used with different meanings in the epistles. The socio-religious environment has changed. The issue that once troubled the Johannine community (expulsion from the synagogue) has disappeared. A new one has taken its place, namely the emergence of a group of Gnostic agitators who deny the full humanity of Jesus and repudiate his having appeared in the flesh (cf. 2 John v. 7 and 1 John 4:2).

As for the book of Revelation and its authorship, we find that already in the third century, Dionysius of Alexandria had made the observation that "the man who wrote these things [Revelation] was John, since he himself says so. But *what* John is not clear" (Wiles and Santer, 1975, 147–51). Contemporary scholarship agrees. Granting that Revelation might be part of the Johannine school tradition, it was written at a later stage when the community was faced with persecution and found itself turning to the extravagant language of apocalyptic, to steel the faith of the oppressed and to inspire them to outlast the beasts.

III. Theological Method and Message in John

John's narratives abound with a cluster of literary devices that express in form and function theological truths implicit in the Gospel. They are the media for John's theology, but at the same time part of the message. From beginning to end, the author/editors utilize a range of calculated *misunderstandings*, *ironies*, *double meanings of words*, *pairs of opposites*, *paradoxes*, and "*signs*." These tropes have been imbedded in the text for the knowing reader to detect, in the conviction that ultimate truth requires a capacity for seeing

beyond first impressions, for challenging conventional wisdom, and for seeking out the truth hidden in apparent contradictions and ambiguities.

An example of *misunderstanding* occurs when Jesus tells Nicodemus that one must be born anew, and Nicodemus asks, "How can a man be born when he is old, can he enter a second time into his mother's womb?" (3:1–4). *Irony* is high when Philip excitedly tells Nathanael of a man named Jesus of Nazareth, and Nathanael retorts, "Can anything good come out of Nazareth?" (1:44–46). Readers then and now enjoy the *double meaning* in the word "food" when the disciples ask, "Has any one brought him food?" and Jesus responds, "My food is to do the will of him who sent me" (4:31–34).

Pairs of opposites are a trademark feature in John, highlighting the need not only to make choices in life but to cultivate a keener sense of the reality of the options, e.g., light vs. darkness (1:1ff.; 8:12; 12:35–36); rebirth vs. natural birth (3:6; 16:21); spirit vs. flesh (1:13; 3:6; 6:63); living water vs. static water (4:10; 7:38); worship in spirit and truth vs. worship in temple sanctuaries (4:23ff.); bread of heaven vs. ordinary bread (4:31; 6:32); day vs. night (9:4; 11:9–10; 13:30); the shepherd vs. the thief (10:1–18); life vs. death (11:35ff.); peace vs. tribulation (16:33); joy vs. sorrow (16:21–24); heavenly kingship vs. earthly kingship (18:36ff.).

Paradox is also a major tool in John's reserve. More than any of the other Gospels, John enlists paradox as a theological strategy for affirming the truthfulness of realities that would be seen in "the world" as contradictory. Paradox appears throughout, e.g., in the story of a blind man who now sees (ch. 9), in a dead Lazarus who lives (ch. 11), in Samaritans who are spiritual (ch. 4), in an hour that is coming and now is (5:25), in an eternal life that transcends both life and death (5:24), in a "world" that despises the faithful but is also the irresistible object of God's love (15:18–19; 3:16), in a christology that hears Jesus stating, on the one hand, "I and the Father are one" (10:30) but on the other, that "the Father is greater than I" (14:28), and in the appearance of the eternal Logos on the stage of history in a man of flesh (1:14), who knows fatigue and physical thirst (4:6–7) and profound anxiety (12:27), who weeps (11:35), who mixes mud with his spittle (9:6), and dies (19:34).

The word "*sign*" or "*signs*" occurs 17 times in John. It is the premier device in John's Gospel for making the theological-hermeneutical point, that the story itself is not the message, but that to which the story points. Scholars have labeled the first half of the Gospel "The Book of Signs," identifying seven such "signs" between chapters 2 and 12: the marriage feast in Cana (2:1–11), the healing of the official's son (4:46–54), the healing at the Pool of Bethzatha (5:1–16), the feeding of the five thousand (6:1–13), Jesus' walking on water (6:14–21), the healing of the man blind from youth (ch. 9), and the raising of Lazarus (11:1–46). It is theologically noteworthy that John recognizes three types of response to signs. One is the response of indifference—those who fail to notice or recognize the "significance" of the event (12:37; cf. Num. 14:11). A second type, far more troubling for John and for Jesus, is the response of the fire-engine chasers of signs, those who are astonished by the event but oblivious to its meaning. A classic instance is the crowd, who having witnessed the multiplication of the loaves, set out to make Jesus king (6:15). Third are those who see the significance of the event and come to "believe" (2:11), which for John implies, not credulity, but commitment and trust (Schneiders, 1999, 87–92).

With this battery of devices John invites the reader to recognize that most things require a second look and that truth lurks in the haunts of the commonplace, waiting to be caught sight of.

IV.   The Theological Agenda: Seeking the Truth

The word "truth" (Greek: *aletheia*) occurs once in Mark, three times apiece in Matthew and Luke, and 25 times in John's Gospel. It is a term at the center of John's theology, and Pilate's question posed at the conclusion of the remarkable seven-stage dialogue with Jesus could ironically serve as the theme of John's theology: "What is truth?" (18:38).

Etymologically the word *aletheia* connotes something that has been unconcealed, that has been rescued from oblivion, that has not escaped notice and has come to light. As Johannine commentators have observed, truth in John is a synonym for "reality" (Bultmann, 1955, 18; Dodd, 1968, 170–8). It is not

one truth among others, it is truth about being. It is not just perceived truth, it is experienced truth. It is a truth that brings light (3:21) and that sets free (8:32).

John's devotion to truth is reinforced with the privileged position given to the Hebrew phrase *Amen, Amen*, translated "truly, truly" or "verily, verily." It is a formula known to the Qumran authors of the Dead Sea Scrolls and rehearsed in early Christian prayers and liturgies. In John it is heard only on the lips of Jesus and used as a rhetorical seal of veracity for whatever statement that follows. It occurs 25 times in the Gospel and provides a virtual catalogue of "reality" from John's perspective.

What are the *Amen-Amen* truths or realities in John's Gospel? They range from the personal-existential ("Unless one is born anew he cannot see the Kingdom of God," 3:3); to the epistemological ("We speak of what we know and bear witness to what we have seen," 3:11); to the christological ("The Son can do nothing of his own accord but only what he sees his Father doing," 5:19); to the spiritual ("Do not labor for the food that perishes," 6:26); to the ontologically outrageous ("Before Abraham was I AM," 8:58); to the tragic ("One of you will betray me," 13:21); to the proverbially wise ("A slave is not greater than his master, nor is he who is sent, greater than he who sent him," 13:16). And they include, above all the theological.

The theology of John's Gospel focuses on four realities, which might be called the "four faces of God": the Father/Logos, christology, the Spirit-Paraclete, and the Community of Disciples, to which we now turn.

Theology and God the Father/Logos

Theology in John is radically theocentric. The goal of John's Gospel is to awaken God-consciousness. From beginning to end, "knowing" God is the one, consuming objective, as expressed in the premier theological statement in John 17:3: "This is eternal life, that they know the only true God and Jesus Christ whom you have sent." From John's standpoint the content of revelation is not a teaching, a dogma, nor a religious fact, but "knowing" a reality and a presence.

John uses three names for "God": Father, Spirit, and Word (*logos*). The term "Father" (*pater*) is a relational term, occurring 122 times, most often as the term of choice for God on the lips of Jesus (20:17).

The term "Spirit" (*pneuma*) expresses the agency of God in the life of Christ, the prophets, and the community of believers (see the discussion of spirit below). But the term that informs all the others and provides a theological substratum for the entire Gospel is "Word" (*logos*). Logos, which also can be translated "reason" or "purpose," is a term with a seasoned history in Greco-Roman and Hellenistic-Jewish theosophy. It expresses the self-disclosure of the ineffable and invisible God in God-speech that is manifest in the virtuosity of creation, in the promulgation of the divine will through dreams and visions, in the indwelling of the divine mind in human flesh, and in the accomplishment of its work in human hands.

John's Logos theology is spelled out in the Prologue (1:1–18) as a metaphysical preamble. The four strophes of the Prologue (subtracting vv. 6–8 and 15, as later interpolations on John the Baptist) describe four stages of God's self-disclosure, ranging from the beginning of time to the incarnation of the Logos in Jesus. It opens with the familiar words of the first strophe:

> In the beginning was the Logos
> And the Logos was with God
> And God was the Logos
> He was in the beginning with God.
> (1:1–2)

This opening strophe takes the reader to the heart of being in terms reminiscent of the metaphysics of the Hellenistic Judaism which spoke of the *logos endiathetos*, the inner Logos of the ineffable, invisible God, being disclosed in the form of a *logos prophorikos*, the "promulgated" Logos, that manifests itself in time and space.

The second strophe (1:3–5) moves from primordial being with God to the creation of "all things" through the creative agency of the Logos. Life is part of this; light is part of this; and, contrary to expectation, darkness does not have the last word:

> All things came into being through him
> And without him nothing came into being that was;
> In him was life,
> And the life was the light of men
> And the light shines in the darkness
> And the darkness did not consume it.

A third strophe (1:9–13) moves the camera-eye of John's Prologue from the creation of the universe to the emergence of civilization, "the "world" (*kosmos*; from the root *kosmeo*, "to order or arrange"), a term that in John does not denote earth, globe, planet, or place, but rather the adaptive social, economic, political, religious, and cultural structure into which society has organized itself and within which it understands itself. This structure, we read, has ironically failed to recognize the source of its being in the divine Logos, and has concomitantly failed to recognize that the identification of people as "children of God" is not a matter of "blood," race, or class, but of having come to know one's true parentage.

The fourth strophe (14:16–18) moves from "world" history to recent history within the storied remembrance of the Johannine community, namely the incarnation of the Logos in the flesh. For the Johannine community in its tenuous relationship with its synagogue, this final manifestation of the Logos sets the stage and theme for the story that follows: the law that "was given through Moses" is now in the presence of a new dispensation of "grace and truth" (*aletheia*) that "has come through Jesus the Messiah (Christos)," a thesis that will provide the raison d'être of virtually every episode that follows.

As a closing theological, metaphysical reprise, the last line of the Prologue reads: "No one has ever seen God; the only Son, who is in the bosom of the Father, he has made him known" (1:18). For John, the ultimate goal is the "knowing" of God.

Theology and christology

Though not all theology is christology, within the early church all christology is theology. Every statement about Jesus in John is simultaneously a statement about the activity of God. Beyond the words and acts of Jesus, Johannine christology manifests itself in two forms: "names and titles" and "I AM sayings."

A remarkable cluster of *names and titles* is gathered in John 1:19–51, immediately following the Prologue: Christ, Elijah, Prophet, Lamb of God, Son of God, Rabbi, Teacher, Messiah, Jesus, Jesus of Nazareth, Son of Joseph, "a Man," King of Israel, Son of Man, "the one who baptizes with the Holy Spirit," and by implication, " I Am" (1:20) (see below). Though most of the titles are theological in intent, they are polemical and apologetic in function. They are designed to address three sets of issues brewing on the Johannine community's front. The primary issue is the growing tension between the Johannine cultus and the synagogue community that threatens to expel them. Second, is the growing rift with the John the Baptist cultus, which in time will maintain that John the Baptist, not Jesus, is God's Messiah, developing in time into the sect of Mandaeans, continuing in Mesopotamia in the twenty-first century. The third is a creeping Gnostic Christian docetism so caught up in the spiritual that it repudiates the idea that the eternal Logos would ever appear in human flesh.

The polemic function of these terms in chapter 1 sets the tone for the 12 chapters that follow. In a series of vignettes—one following on the heels of another—John will be sending the message to his readers that Jesus displaces the religious paradigms of the past. He is the true baptizer with the Holy Spirit, superseding John's baptism with water (1:19–34; 3:22–26; 10:40–41); the true King of a New Israel (1:43–51; 12:13); the true source of purification over against the six stone jars of purification water at the Wedding at Cana (2:1–12); the true temple (2:13–22); the true teacher of Israel who tutors the scholar Nicodemus on the need for rebirth (3:1–21); the true source of living water (*pege*) vs. the water pit well (*phrear*) of the Samaritan woman at Sychar (4:1–45); the Elijah-like healer of the official's son (4:31–38); the true son of the Father who does the father's work healing the lame man at the pool of Bethzatha on the Sabbath (5:1–47); the new Moses who feeds his people with the bread of heaven (6:1–15); the true light of the world echoing the festival of lights at Tabernacles (chaps. 7–8; 8:12); the true successor and predecessor of Abraham (8:34–59); the true Son of Man who makes the blind see and exposes the blindness of the sighted (9:1–41); the true good shepherd, fulfilling the prophetic image of Ezekiel 34 (10:1–21); the true resurrection and life as opposed to the coming resurrection at the last day in Pharisaic expectation (11:24–25); and the true King of Israel entering Jerusalem (12:12–19).

The *I AM sayings* constitute a second set of christological statements. They are the most distinctive and unique of John's christological cues and, for some, the most perplexing. The phrase I AM occurs 30 times in John, 26 of the occurrences on the lips of Jesus. Its most memorable forms are seven I AM sayings: "I am the bread of life" (6:35, 48, 51); "I am the light of the world" (8:12; 9:5); "I am the door of the sheep" (10:7, 9); "I am the good shepherd" (10:11, 14); "I am the resurrection and the life" (11:25); "I am the way, the truth, and the life" (14:6); "I am the true vine" (15:1, 5).

One cannot utter I AM (Greek: *ego eimi*) in a religious Hellenistic-Jewish context without activating the echo of the I AM of Exodus. When Moses inquired of God what his name was, God replied, "Say this to the people of Israel, I AM has sent me to you" (Exod. 3:13). The paramount importance of the phrase I AM in the verbal iconography of Judaism extends across the board in the Hebrew Bible. Leviticus 19, for example, includes 11 occurrences of the phrase. Isaiah 43 repeats the phrase with powerful effect nine times.

On several occasions John adds to the mystique of the I AM phrase by deploying it without the predicate nominative—just the two words, "I AM," inserted into the narrative—with the confidence that the aural memory of the reader will make the connection, no matter how covert. For example, when the Samaritan woman tells Jesus she knows the Messiah will come, Jesus' response in Greek reads the equivalent of, "It is I AM who speaks to you" (the English translation loses the symbolism and reads: "I who speak to you am he," 4:26). Or again when Jesus, walking on the water, encounters the frightened disciples rowing against the waves, the English tells us he said, "It is I; be not afraid," but the Greek reads, "I AM. Be not afraid." The most dramatic illustration of the power with which John endows *ego eimi* appears in the passion narrative when Jesus asks the band of soldiers who have come to seize him, "Whom do you seek?" They respond, "Jesus of Nazareth." Jesus replies, in the Greek, *ego eimi*, "I AM" (the English translation reads, "I am he," 18:6). The text tells us, "When he said, 'I AM' to them, they drew back and fell to the ground."

Though these stories contain obvious legendary elements, they nevertheless raise the question of their historicity, that is, whether Jesus actually used the phrase I AM in this way, or whether the I AM format is the product of the imaginative faith of the early church, as many scholars in the past have maintained.

Until recently, main-line biblical scholars tended to the latter position on the grounds that the Synoptic gospels were more historically reliable, and that they carried only the barest trace of the I AM sayings (Mark 6:50; 13:6). Also, it seemed unseemly for psychological and cultural reasons to envision Jesus using I AM language so susceptible to the charge of delusion and even megalomania.

But in the twenty-first century scholars are beginning to ask whether we might do well to rethink the I AM sayings, not as the creation of the early church, nor as the pronouncements of an ego-inflated cult leader, especially in light of statements of Jesus, such as, "If I bear witness to myself my testimony is not true" (5:31). Instead they are beginning to consider the I AM sayings as a consciously adopted code word that Jesus employed to raise consciousness of his identity and their identity as God's offspring, initiating hearers into the mystery of the presence of God in their midst. In the Synoptic Gospels, Jesus does this with parables. In John, Jesus achieves this with the symbol, image, conundrum, and metaphor of I AM sayings, designed to fracture consciousness and give birth to a new angle of vision.

If the latter might be true, does John's Gospel offer any insight into Jesus' motivation for using the phrase I AM? A clue can be found in a collection of passages in which Jesus speaks of his mission to bring "the name" of God into public consciousness. He announces that he has come in his Father's name (5:43) and has done works in his Father's name (10:25). In the Great Prayer he proclaims, "I have manifested thy name to the men you gave me" and "have kept them in Thy name" (17:6, 12). He concludes with an epitome : "I made known to them your name, and I will make it known, that the love with which you have loved me may be in them and I in them" (cf. also 12:28).

Taking these passages as a possible index of the mind of Jesus, they offer a portrait of Jesus in John's Gospel as committed to bringing the name, and thereby the presence mediated through the name, into consciousness. When contemporary Jews speak of God as "*Ha Shem*," "The Name," they presume that even in saying the words, they are somehow mediating God's presence into the circle of faith. When Jesus says I AM the way, or the truth, or the life, or the bread of life, or the good shepherd, or the light of the world,

he is making a dual assertion. First that the I AM is the source of light, and is the way, and the truth. But second, he is suggesting that his speaking the name of the I AM mediates a presence. John portrays the historical Jesus as a man who "knows" his transparency to the I AM, and would engender this same sense in his disciples. He speaks in the hope of creating a lineage of the spiritually conscious who "know" God, who see God at work in the world around them, and who sense their participation in God's "eternal life" (17:3). "Truly, Truly, I say unto you; he who receives anyone whom I send receives me, and he who receives me receives him who sent me" (13:19–20).

Theology and the spirit/Paraclete

John is the only Gospel to offer an explicit descriptive definition of God. It occurs at the point in Jesus' conversation with the Samaritan woman where they are discussing the religious sanctuaries of the Samaritans and the Judeans. Jesus makes the statement that the hour will come when God will be worshipped in neither sanctuary. He adds, "God is spirit" (*pneuma*), and those who worship him must worship in spirit (*pneuma*) and in truth (*aletheia*) (4:24). In speaking of God as spirit, John is touching on the fundamental experiential phenomenon that gave birth to and defined earliest Christianity, the experience of being in and living out of the Spirit. Though "spirit" in John relates to the activity of the Holy Spirit (mentioned four times), John is not making a statement about the third person of the Trinity. He is making a statement about the "essential nature of God" (Taylor, 1959, 111–12).

The experience of the Spirit in the early church dominates New Testament consciousness. It is dramatized in Luke's legendary Pentecostal story in Acts 2 as the founding event of the early church, taking the gospel from Jerusalem to Rome. Paul, the earliest New Testament witness to Christian experience, identifies the gift of the spirit as that which liberated him from his "wretched body of death" under the law (Rom. 7:24; 8:2, 9–14). He confides that the spirit assists him in his weakness (8:26), fostering the psycho-spiritual gifts of love, joy, peace, patience, kindness, goodness, gentleness, faithfulness, and self-control as the marks of transformed living (Gal. 5:16–23). The four Gospels, written more than a decade after Paul, take as

foundational theological reality that a defining difference between Jesus' ministry and that of John the
Baptist is a baptism with the Spirit. John's Gospel goes
beyond this in maintaining the need to be born again
of the spirit (3:5). Spirit for John is God's immeasura-
bly bountiful gift (3:34), building up within oneself a
virtual fountain of living water (7:18), mediated in part
through the words of life that Jesus speaks (6:63), but
promised in full as a personal, transforming power that
will touch their lives when Jesus is no longer with
them (7:39). It will come as a Paraclete (Greek: *parak-
letos*), like a friend who exhorts, encourages, and counsels (14, 15), dwelling within them, guiding them to
the truth (*aletheia*) (16:13). In a post-resurrection scene,
Jesus gives birth to the new community with the
words, "Receive the holy spirit" (20:22). The primary
manifestation of God in John's Gospel is, to be sure,
the presence of Jesus in their midst. But above all, from
the standpoint of the early Christian readers in the
continuing Christian community, the primary manifestation of God is found with the sense of having
been reborn of God who is Spirit.

Theology and the community of disciples

The dictum that "all theology is anthropology" is
profoundly true of John's Gospel. In no other gospel
do we find the disciples so explicitly identified with
and incorporated in the life of God.

Four distinct features of John's portrait of "discipleship" are worth noting. First, it refers to a social unit
that differs in structure and authority from the
construct of discipleship in the Synoptics. Second,
discipleship in John is conspicuously intentional in its
inclusion of women. Third, it refers to a community
based not on rank, status, special authority, or ecclesiastical privilege, but on having passed from "death to
life," from one level of consciousness to another.
Fourth, discipleship consists of those to whom Jesus
has given the Logos for engagement in "the world."

John's portrait of the disciples differs significantly
from that of the Synoptics. "The twelve" are mentioned sparingly (6:67, 70, 71; 20:24), in a way that
suggests these passages might possibly be editorial
gloss, inserted in the interest of harmonizing the gospels. John seems to have a different idea of the type of
group the disciples represent. He leaves the impres-

sion they were a small, somewhat unstructured team.
He names a few of them: Philip, Andrew, Peter, the
sons of Zebedee, and Thomas. He advances one of
them, Nathanael, not listed in the Synoptics, as a
model of the new "Israel" of God (1:43–51), marked
by intelligence, healthy skepticism, and discernment.

John's image of discipleship includes women: the
Samaritan woman, Mary and Martha, Mary the wife
of Clopas, the Mother of Jesus, and Mary Magdalene.
Though not named "disciples," they dominate the
Gospel as models of discipleship. They do not conform to the common role of the feminine for the
times. They ask questions, dare to protest, think independently, take extraordinary initiative, and engage in
theological discussion (Schneiders, 1999, 98–101). As
feminist scholars have pointed out, women in John's
gospel function as disciples and apostles. The Samaritan
woman, for example, is said to have left her water jar
in much the same way as the Synoptic disciples left
their nets to follow Jesus. Martha's acclamation of
Jesus, "Yes, Lord, I believe that you are the Christ, the
Son of God, he who is coming into the world"
(11:27), parallels the confession of Peter in the
Synoptics (Mark 8:29; Matthew 16:16; Luke 9:20).
Most remarkably, it is Mary Magdalene, not Peter,
who is commissioned by the risen Christ in the post-
resurrection scene to "go to my brethren and say to
them, I am ascending to my Father and your Father,
to my God and your god" (20:17).

What makes a disciple? Disciples in John are
defined not in terms of status, privilege, or rank. They
are defined by their having moved from a state of
curiosity to conviction in their relation with Jesus.
The truth that they have reached is not the product of
fact finding, but arriving at a state of "believing."
Sandra Schneiders explains:

> Scholars have long recognized that John developed a
> special vocabulary for exploring and explaining what it
> means to respond to Jesus' self-revelation. The human
> pole of the revelation dynamic is "believing." It is strik-
> ing that John uses the verb "to believe" ninety-eight …
> times in comparison with the Synoptics, who together
> use it only thirty-four times. Furthermore, John never
> uses the noun "faith" or "belief." For John faith is not a
> spiritual acquisition or a state of being but an activity, an
> ever-active relationship in the present. (Schneiders, 1999,
> 51–2)

In addition to the verb "believing," John constructs a series of verbs that denote eight stages of awareness in the emerging relationship between the characters in his Gospel and Jesus. Classic examples are the story of Nathanael, the Samaritan woman at the well, and the man born blind, all describing the route from indifference to believing. Seven of the eight verbs occur in the story of seeking Jesus in John 1:18–51. The first verb is "seeking" (*zeteo*; 1:38), occurring 35 times in John. The second is "to come and see" (*erchomai* and *horao*; 1:46, 48, 50, 51). Third is "finding" (*heurisko*; 1:41, 43, 45). The fourth is "abiding" (*meno*; 1:38, 39), i.e., staying to ruminate on what you have found. The fifth is "believing" (*pisteuo*; 98 occurrences; 1:50), i.e., entrusting oneself to another. The sixth, "knowing" (*ginosko*; 56 occurrences; 1:48), in the same sense friends know friends; the seventh is "keeping" (*tereo*; 18 occurrences; cf. 14:15, 21–24), i.e., holding, guarding, treasuring; the eighth is "following" (*akoloutheo*; 1:37, 38, 40, 43), moving into action. Discipleship is intimacy, relationship, transformation, and action. Disciples have, in John's words, passed from "death to life" (5:24).

What is the present and future status of disciples from John's perspective? In chapter 17, John culminates his history of the Logos. He had begun in chapter 1 with the metaphysical trajectory of the Logos from the mind of God, to creation, to the establishment of "world," to habitation in human flesh in Jesus. In the ensuing chapters, however, the trajectory continues. Logos occurs 40 times in John. On some occasions it means simply a saying (e.g., 4:37). But in most instances Logos carries the overtones of a transcendent presence that is mediated through Jesus and is now operative through his "word" in the world. It finds place in some people but not others (8:37). It is the Logos that was at work in the words of Isaiah and the Psalms (12:38; 10:35). The Logos has transformative power; it is the mediator of truth (17:14); it makes clean (*katharos*; 15:3). Though Jesus mediates the Logos to others he maintains the Logos is not his but the Father's who sent him (14:24). The Logos is common property of all who love him and "keep" his Logos (15:20b). Jesus' mission is to "give" the Logos to others (17:14), that they in turn may "keep" it (e.g., 5:20; 8:51–52, 55; 14:23–24; 15:20; 17:6) and pass it on to others who come to believe through

their Logos (17:20). The aim of the process is, as Jesus prays in 17:21–22, "that they may all be one, even as thou, Father, art in me, and I in thee, that they also may be in us." Vincent Taylor describes this as a "'Christ Mysticism' meeting the deepest needs of men in the attainment of communion with God" (Taylor, 1959, 121–2).

Though John's theology does not include a formal ecclesiology, and never mentions the word "church" (*ekklesia* is found only in Matthew: 16:18, 18:17) it offers images that serve as substitutes for the term. Four of these would be "the vine" (15:1–11), "the flock" (10:16), the community of "one" (17:20), and society of "friends" (15:2–15). The community to which they all refer is characterized by four dimensions: a *mystical dimension* marked by the cognitive restructuring of one's vision of God, Jesus, self, and neighbor into a unity of will (4:34), work (5:15), word (14:24), and witness (8:18); a *behavioral dimension* grounded in the new commandment to love one another and be defined as disciples by this love (13:34–35); an *apostolic dimension*, acknowledging one's being sent with the Logos into the "world" (17:15–16); and a *social dimension*, espousing a nonhierarchic, democratized society of men and women, Samaritans, Galileans, and Jews, who construe the enjoinder to wash one another's feet as a symbol, neither of subservience nor of condescension, but of friendship between equals in loving service (13:1–11).

V. Postscript: Johannine Effects

For close to two millennia, John's Gospel has become a touchstone for three diverse, even adverse, theological traditions within Christendom: orthodoxy, gnosis, and popular piety.

When orthodox Christianity formulated the creeds of Nicaea and Chalcedon, it found in the tradition of John's theology the materials for building the case for the doctrine of the Trinity. Three components were crucial: John's identification of the fleshly Jesus with the pre-existent eternal Logos; John's unprecedented formulation of the role and function of the Spirit-Paraclete as a special agency within the divine economy (Taylor, 1959, 110, 119, 123); and third, John's paradoxical emphasis on the full humanity of Jesus and his "oneness" with the Father.

Christian Gnosticism found another message in John's Gospel. Though John clearly opposes docetic Gnosticism in its denial of the fleshly humanity of Jesus, it also is the only one of the four Gospels in which Gnostic Christianity would find itself at home (Sloyan, 1996). Gnosticism would clearly find a kindred voice in the Johannine prioritization of the experiential over the noetic. It would share John's resistance to Petrine hierarchical authority in favor of the spiritual authority of the individual. On sacramentalism, it would approve of John's having omitted the words of institution at the Last Supper and the record of Jesus' baptism by John.

It would also welcome John's emphasis on the wisdom of the "God-taught" and unlettered (6:45, 7:15, 9:24) over established learning (3:1–12). It would endorse John's advocacy of an ethic of conscious love over cultic legalism. It would endorse the unprecedented apostolic significance conferred on women. And it would find in the metaphysical poetry of the Logos, precedent for the cosmogonies of later Gnosis.

Popular Christian piety, whether of a fundamentalist or biblical critical strain, would also find a spiritual home in John's theology and a venue in which our better natures are summoned and our differences are superseded by the supreme mandate to be known as disciples of Christ by having love for one another.

References

Anderson, Paul N. 2006. *The Fourth Gospel and the Quest for Jesus: Modern Foundations Reconsidered.* New York: T&T Clark.

Ashton, John. 1991. *Understanding the Fourth Gospel.* Oxford: Clarendon.

Brown, Raymond E. 1966–1970. *The Gospel According to John.* Garden City, NY: Doubleday.

Brown, Raymond E. 1988. *The Gospels and Epistles of John: A Concise Commentary.* Collegeville, MI: Liturgical Press.

Brown, Raymond E. 1998. *A Retreat with John the Evangelist: That You May Have Life.* Cincinnati, OH: St. Anthony Messenger Press.

Bultmann, Rudolf. 1955. *Theology of the New Testament, trans. Kendrick Grobel*, vol. 2. New York: Charles Scribner's Sons.

Countryman, L. William. 1994. *The Mystical Way in the Fourth Gospel: Crossing Over Into God.* Valley Forge, PA: Trinity Press International.

Dodd, Charles Harold. 1954. *The Interpretation of the Fourth Gospel.* Cambridge: Cambridge University Press.

Dodd, Charles Harold. 1968. *More New Testament Studies.* Manchester: Manchester University Press.

Haenchen, Ernst. 1984. *A Commentary on the Gospel of John, I–II*, trans. Robert W. Funk. Philadelphia: Fortress.

Hanson, Anthony T. 1991. *The Prophetic Gospel: A Study of John and the Old Testament.* Edinburgh: T&T Clark.

Kysar, R. 1976. *John, the Maverick Gospel,* rev. ed. Louisville, KY: John Knox/Westminster.

Martyn, J. Louis. 1978. *The Gospel of John in Christian History: Essays and Interpretations.* New York: Paulist.

Schneiders, Sandra. 1999. *Written That You May Believe: Encountering Jesus in the Fourth Gospel.* New York: Crossroads.

Segovia, Fernando F., ed. 1996. *"What is John?" Readers and Readings of the Fourth Gospel.* Atlanta, GA: Scholars Press.

Sloyan, Gerard S. 1996. "The Gnostic Adoption of John's Gospel and Its Canonization by the Church Catholic," *BTB* 26: 125–32.

Smith, D. Moody. 1995. *The Theology of the Gospel of John.* Cambridge: Cambridge University Press.

Taylor, Vincent. 1959. *The Person of Christ in New Testament Teaching.* London: MacMillan and Co., Ltd.

Wiles, Maurice T. 1960. *The Spiritual Gospel: The Interpretation of the Fourth Gospel in the Early Church.* Cambridge: Cambridge University Press.

Wiles, Maurice T. and Santer, Mark, eds. 1975. *Documents in Early Christian Thought.* New York: Cambridge University Press.

Marcion (*c*.85–*c*.160)

Katharina Greschat

Marcion, born *c*.85 CE in the province of Pontus on the Black Sea, was a wealthy *nauclerus* (Tert. *praescr.* 30,1). About 140, when he joined the Christian community in Rome, he could give it the enormous gift of 200,000 sesterces. Whether he had been a Christian before settling in the capital of the Roman Empire or not cannot be decided. Maybe in Rome he was the disciple of a certain Cerdon, a personage of whom we know almost nothing, because all statements about his thought seem to project Marcion's teachings onto him. In 144 he caused a severe clash with the Roman church, got his money back and founded his own church, which was very successful in the West up to the fourth—and in the East up to the fifth—century. When Justin Martyr wrote his first Apologia for Christianity, Marcion was still alive, which places his death probably around the year 160.

None of Marcion's sentences or arguments is directly transmitted in one of his works. What makes things worse is that his opinions are not even handed down in an indirect way. There is only second-hand information from the writings of his opponents mixed with more or less polemics: the already mentioned Justin Martyr, Irenaeus of Lyons, Clement of Alexandria, and Origen, but first of all from Tertullian's five books against Marcion (*Adversus Marcionem*) in their third edition, which dates from 207 to 212. Other important sources are: Hippolytus of Rome, Epiphanius of Salamis in his *Panarion*

("Medicine Chest"), Adamantius, Ephrem the Syrian's *Prose Refutations of Bardesanes, Mani, and Marcion*, and the writings of Eznik of Kolb. It is not easy to separate the bits of information concerning Marcion's life from polemical items, as the following example shows. According to one tradition based on the lost Syntagma of Hippolytus, Marcion was the son of the bishop of Sinope in Pontus and was thrown out by his own father for having seduced a virgin. Evidently this detail was a later invention meant to symbolize a typical heretic who corrupted the virgin church.

This poor documentary status causes considerable problems in reconstructing what Marcion might have meant with his statements in the historical situation of the second century as well. Based on all the available source material and on the research of the nineteenth century, the famous German church historian Adolf von Harnack tried to constitute his lasting picture of Marcion. But Harnack overrated Marcion as a unique figure within his own times and one of the most important theologians of late antiquity. Everyone who reads his most important books on Marcion must bear in mind that his Marcion is not of the second century but an idealized figure Harnack made up through his benevolent interpretation.

The main difference and contentious issue between the "great church" and Marcion seemed to be the assessment of the Christian tradition, which Marcion thought to be corrupted by a long chain of people

The Student's Companion to the Theologians, First Edition. Edited by Ian S. Markham.
© 2013 Blackwell Publishing Ltd. Published 2013 by Blackwell Publishing Ltd.

who wanted to bring the true followers of Jesus Christ back to Judaism. From Paul's attacks (especially in his epistle to the Galatians) on false brethren who clung to the practices of the law and from his fervent defense of the "truth of the gospel" even against the venerated Peter (Gal. 2:11–14), Marcion drew the conclusion that even the first disciples of Jesus had no correct understanding of his preaching. Attached to Judaism and to the law, they preached Jesus as Son of the Creator, taught obedience to the law, and darkened the Gospel of Jesus who wanted his followers to be free from the suppressive power of the law and from obedience to the Creator. According to Marcion, Paul was the only reliable apostle and witness of the one authentic Gospel of Jesus Christ given to him directly and without any human falsification just at the moment of his conversion. Marcion took the record from the first chapters of Paul's epistle to the Galatians seriously. Galatians was Marcion's main document and he placed it at the beginning of the Pauline letters. Together with Paul he felt that these Judaizing disciples, apostles, or followers of the apostles were an immense danger for Christian preaching and tradition. From the first days of Christianity up to the present they threatened the church of Jesus Christ. Marcion thought he was called to remedy the situation by purifying the interpolated letters of Paul, of which he used only 10, without the Pastorals and Hebrews. Furthermore, he applied the standard methods of late antique textual criticism not only to the Pauline letters, but also to the Gospel of Jesus Christ that he identified with Luke to eliminate what he regarded as Judaizing interpolations. According to him, the result of his work was the only opportunity to find the true Gospel of Jesus Christ. Why he chose Luke is not clear: maybe he had heard of the tradition that Luke was a direct disciple of Paul; maybe he knew no other Gospel.

Many scholars, in particular Hans von Campenhausen in his classic, 1968 published study on the formation of the Christian Bible, therefore regard Marcion as the inventor of the very idea of a Christian scripture. They see the canon of the "great church" as the direct response to the collection of Marcion that contained only 10 Pauline epistles and the one Gospel. But nowadays a more subtle approach seems to be necessary, placing Marcion and his opponents from the "great

church" within the framework of a larger and more complex process, in which Christians faced the question of a reliable tradition concerning Jesus and his work, and of the criteria for identifying this tradition. This approach has to consider that a similar process was going on in Judaism during the same time. In order to differentiate themselves from the Christians the Jews solidly established the Writings as the third part of the Hebrew Bible and codified the Mishnaic traditions.

From his point of view it is obvious that Marcion rejected the Hebrew Bible, which the Christians named Old Testament because they had taken it over as part of their own scripture. Marcion concluded from his reading and meditation on the Old Testament in comparison with the Gospel that the revelation of this scripture was incompatible with the revelation brought by Jesus. According to Marcion, Jesus Christ proclaimed in his Gospel a God totally different from the God revealed to the Jews as creator and ruler of the world and of the human beings through his law. The nature of the Old Testament God can be discovered by a closer look at his work of the Creation: he wanted to exercise power over the humanity he created and for that reason he arbitrarily imposed a severe law on his chosen people of Israel. But the creator and inferior demiurge of this world is not a righteous or just judge; as Harnack puts it, he did not even respect the rules of fair play, since he was extremely jealous and took satisfaction in leading human beings into temptation. He did not even consider that Adam might fall into sin and could barely manage the consequences. His sudden rages, his changes of plan, and his unreliability show how close his relation is toward the lower world and how distant from the idea any educated person might conjure up of the supreme divinity. Furthermore, this imperfect God is ignorant of the existence of another God who is far superior to him and who is well aware of this inferior demiurge and his creation. About this supreme God, whose nature is graciousness and who is the Father of Jesus Christ, the Old Testament has nothing to say since Marcion was not willing to use any allegorical interpretation.

To bring the Pauline differences between the law and the Gospel and between the demiurge of the Old Testament and the supreme God to light, Marcion used his tool (*instrumentum*) of the so-called *Antitheses* by showing how the two revelations are irreconcilable (Adv. Marc. I,19,4). The work of Marcion's Antitheses is known merely by its title, which Tertullian mentions several times. But he gives his readers no specific idea how Marcion arranged the material so that it is at any rate impossible to reconstruct the Antitheses, even if Harnack tried to do so. Tertullian also refers to a letter of Marcion (Adv. Marc. I,1,6/IV,4), now lost, but nobody knows anything certain about its wording.

According to Marcion, the supreme God saw the distressed human beings and sent Jesus Christ, his own son, to ransom them by his death on the cross. Christ came down to earth from the transcendent realms of his Father in the fifteenth year of the Emperor Tiberius to free the souls of all people who trusted in him from the obedience to the Creator (Adv. Marc. I,19,2; III,2,2f.). After his death and before his resurrection he preached the Gospel in the world of the dead where all the souls of the depraved persons in the Old Testament ran to him since they longed for freedom from the Creator, but the righteous remained skeptical and kept waiting for their redeemer (Iren. *Adv. haer.* I,27,3). Marcion shared the conviction with other educated people that no more than the human soul can be saved while the flesh equally made by the demiurge will perish. The Marcionite Christ came directly down from the immaterial world of his Father and throughout his stay on earth he took a real, palpable body, but without nativity. Tertullian reproached Marcion with Docetism and declared that the body of his Christ had no real substance and was merely a *phantasma* (Tert. Adv. Marc. I,19,2). For Marcion things looked different: he compared the body of Jesus Christ with the angelic beings of the Creator of which the Old Testament tells, and the Christians of the "great church" had no problem in believing that they came down without nativity but nevertheless had a solid corporality which can be seen and touched (Tert. Adv. Marc. III,9,1/De carn. 3,6). Any

reader of Tertullian might feel the atmosphere of direct dispute with some Marcionites.

The scholarly debate on whether Marcion was a Gnostic teacher—which Harnack strictly denied—is still heated. Many of his late antiquity adversaries regarded him just as one of the multiheaded hydra of the Gnostics, because like most of them he made a clear distinction between a supreme God and the minor Creator of this world who is identified with the God of the Old Testament. However, Marcion lacks one key element of Gnosticism, namely the consubstantiality of the saved with the supreme divinity: in Marcionitism the saved belong entirely to the Creator, and possess nothing that comes from the Father of Jesus Christ. The strangeness of the supreme God to the world and human beings seems to be a peculiarity of Marcion.

The attractiveness of his teachings and the heavy emphasis placed on asceticism won Marcion and his church great success. All Marcionites who received the mercy of the supreme God by baptism had to flee the works of the Creator and abstain from sexual relationships (Clement str. III,12/III,105,1). Similar to the development within the "great church," the dynamic church of the Marcionites had several different schools of thought as well. Eusebius provides valuable citations from an anti-Marcionite work by a certain Rhodon (Hist. eccl. V,13), who spitefully emphasized the splintering of the Roman Marcionites and gave information on the teaching of Apelles, who was perhaps the most important Marcionite after Marcion.

Due to his rejection of the Old Testament and his refusal to find something of the supreme God in it, Marcion was seen as the adversary par excellence, and many writers challenged him and his followers in the second half of the second, and the first half of the third, century. This controversy stimulated the authors of the "great church" to hold on to the one good God as Creator and Redeemer and to the correspondence between the Old Testament and the Gospel.

References

Blackman, E. C. 1948. *Marcion and His Influence*. London: SPCK.

Campenhausen, H. von. 1984. *The Formation of the Christian Bible*, 2nd ed., trans. J. A. Baker. Philadelphia: Fortress Press.

Deakle, D. W. 1992. *The Fathers against Marcionitism: A Study of the Methods and Motives in the developing Patristic Anti-Marcionite Polemic*. Ann Arbor, MI: Ann Arbor Microfilms.

Grant, R. M. 1993. *Heresy and Criticism. The Search for the Authenticity in Early Christian Literature*. Louisville, KY: John Knox Press, pp. 33–47.

Harnack, A. von. 1924. Marcion. *Das Evangelium vom frem-den Gott. Eine Monographie zur Grundlegung der katholischen Kirche*, 2nd ed. Leipzig: Hinrichs.

Harnack, A. von. 2003. "Marcion. Der moderne Gläubige des 2. Jahrhunderts, der erste Reformator." *In Die Dorpater Preisschrift* (1870), ed. F. Steck. Berlin: Walter de Gruyter.

Head, P. 1993. "The Foreign God and the Sudden Christ: Theology and Christology in Marcion's Gospel Redaction," *Tyndale Bulletin* 44: 307–21.

May, G., Marcion. 1987/88. "In Contemporary Views: Results and Open Questions," *SecCen* 6: 129–51.

May, G. and Greschat, K., eds. 2002. *Marcion und seine kirch-engeschichtliche Wirkung* (Marcion and His Impact on Church History). Berlin: Walter de Gruyter.

Räisänen, H. 2005. "Marcion." In *A Companion to Second-Century Christian "Heretics*," ed. A. Marjanen and P. Luomanen, *Supplements to Vigiliae Christianae 76*. Leiden: Brill, pp. 100–24.

Schmid, U. 1995. *Marcion und sein Apostolos. Rekonstruktion und historische Einordnung der marcionitischen Paulusbriefausgabe*, Arbeiten zur neutestamentlichen Textforschung. Berlin: Walter de Gruyter.

Maximos the Confessor (580–662)

Andrew Louth

I. Life

Born in 580, Maximos's early years are shrouded in mystery. According to the published Greek *vita* he was the son of well-to-do parents in Constantinople, and received there a good classical education. According to the recently discovered Syriac *vita* he was the son of an irregular union between a Samaritan merchant and a Persian slave-girl, baptized Moschion, and after the early death of his parents, found his way to the Old Lavra in Palestine, where he became the monk Maximos and came under the influence of Origenism; there, too, he attracted the attention of Sophronios, later patriarch of Jerusalem. Although contemporary, the Syriac *vita* is written from a Monothelite point of view and clearly intended to blacken Maximos's name.

A final judgment on the truth of his early years awaits a thorough investigation of all the accounts of Maximos's life. According to the Greek *vita*, in 610 Maximos became the head of the new Emperor Herakleios's imperial chancery: this is difficult to reconcile with the Syriac *vita*, but gains support from Maximos's own remarks about his service in the imperial court, as well as the circle of friends he had at court and in the imperial service throughout his life. After a few years in the court Maximos left to become a monk, initially at Chrysopolis (modern Scutari), across the Bosphoros from Constantinople, and later at the monastery of St George at Kyzikos

(modern Erdek) on the south coast of the Sea of Marmara. By 618 Maximos's reputation as a monk was such that he had acquired a disciple, Anastasios, who remained with him for the rest of his life.

In 626, with the Persian advance on Constantinople, Maximos went into exile and by 630 had arrived in North Africa, having on the way passed through the islands of Crete and Cyprus. He most likely remained in North Africa for the next 15 years, and there wrote most of his theological works. Although Maximos was consulted over the monenergist controversy by none other than Pyrrhos, later patriarch of Constantinople and upholder of monothelitism, Maximos did not clearly come out against the christological compromises of monenergism and monothelitism until after the issue of the monothelite imperial *Ekthesis* in 638. The early 640s, however, saw a stream of polemical works from his hand, attacking monothelitism and expounding authentic orthodox doctrine.

In 645 Pyrrhos, the deposed patriarch, fleeing from political disgrace in Constantinople, arrived in North Africa, and there took part in a public debate on christology with Maximos, in which he conceded defeat and embraced orthodoxy. He then went to Rome with, or followed by, Maximos, who there prepared for the Lateran Council called by the new pope, Martin, in 649, which condemned the heresies of monenergism and monothelitism and the patriarchs who had espoused these doctrines—Sergios, Pyrrhos,

The Student's Companion to the Theologians, First Edition. Edited by Ian S. Markham.
© 2013 Blackwell Publishing Ltd. Published 2013 by Blackwell Publishing Ltd.

and Paul of Constantinople, Cyrus of Alexandria, and Pope Honorius. Recent research on the *acta* of the Lateran Council has shown that their original form was Greek, strongly suggesting the close involvement of Maximos. For this defiance of the imperial will, Maximos was eventually arrested and brought to Constantinople, where he was put on trial in 655, initially for sedition. He was exiled to Bizya in Thrace (modern Vize on the Turkish–Bulgarian border), where attempts were made to break his resolve. With their failure, he was exiled to Perberis, also in Thrace.

After six years there, Maximos and the two Anastasii—the disciple already mentioned, and the papal apocrisiarius who had thrown in his lot with Maximos—were brought to Constantinople for a further trial, this time for heresy. They were condemned, and, after having their tongues and right hands—the members with which they had propagated their "heresy"—amputated, they were exiled to Lazika, on the southeast shore of the Black Sea, where Maximos died on August 13, 662. Within 20 years, at the Sixth Ecumenical Council in Constantinople in 681, Maximos's doctrine, though not his person, was vindicated.

II.   Works

About 90 of Maximos's works survive, though the manner of their transmission is very complex and only recently has much progress been made in understanding it. Dom Polycarp Sherwood attempted many years ago to produce a chronology of these works, and though much that he proposed is conjectural, his resulting chronology is still largely accepted by scholars. The principles behind this chronology are the fixed points of the progress of the monenergist and monothelite controversy—the *Psephos* of 633 and the *Ekthesis* of 638—together with internal evidence, both of cross-reference and of development of Maximos's thought. There is very little that can be confidently assigned to the period before Maximos's stay at Kyzikos (that is before 624/5). While he was at Kyzikos, he certainly wrote several letters to John the Koubikoularios (the chamberlain) in Constantinople, and several other works have been placed as early as this, but most of his writing seems to have been done during his time in

North Africa, even though some of these works were conceived during his time at Kyzikos, if not actually written there.

Virtually all Maximos's works were written in response to some request for assistance or illumination, and many of them take forms that have their roots in monastic catechesis, especially his "centuries" of chapters (or paragraphs) and his collections of "questions" (*ambigua* or ἀπορίαι, or ἐρωταποκρίσεις). Many others are directly in the form of letters, including many that are called "opuscula." Given the monastic genre in which Maximos generally casts his theology, it seems best to begin consideration with his ascetical writings, a decision borne out on grounds of chronology, although with Maximos the distinction between ascetical, dogmatic, exegetic, and liturgical works is generally artificial, as these different concerns are so closely interwoven in his thought.

III.   Ascetical Works

The ascetic life

This work, dated to before Maximos left Kyzikos (626), is a series of question and answers (ἐρωταποκρίσεις) between a brother and an old man (γέρων). The "old man" appears on other occasions in Maximos's works, notably in the *Mystagogia* and at times in the *Ambigua*, and there has been speculation as to whether he is an historical person, or simply a representative of traditional monastic wisdom. On other occasions (though not here) he is a source of ideas drawn from Dionysios the Areopagite, which makes unlikely the suggestion that he is to be identified with Sophronios, who certainly stood in relation to Maximos as his γέρων. The dialogue begins with the brother asking about the purpose of the incarnation, and continues by presenting the ascetic life as the human response of love to the love of God manifest in the incarnation.

Four centuries on love

This, surely the most attractive of Maximos's ascetical writings, presents the Christian life as a purification of love. Its sources are largely Evagrian, though unlike Evagrios Maximos makes it clear that the whole human being, including the body and the irrational parts of the soul, are involved in the loving union with God that is the goal of the Christian life. Maximos also draws on Dionysios, especially when he considers the final union with God. A Latin translation was made in Hungary in the twelfth century. It was included in the *Philokalia* of Nikodimos and Makarios (1782). Several of the letters (notably ep. 2 to John the Koubikoularios, on love) should be regarded as ascetical treatises.

IV. Dogmatic Works

Quaestiones et Dubia

The title, "questions and doubts," was given to this work by its first editor, F. Combefis, but it really is a series of ἐρωταποκρίσεις, better translated "questions and answers." What Combefis edited, however, was a selection of 79 questions (one of three such selections to have been preserved) from a much longer series of questions and answers. What appears to be the original series has been discovered in a manuscript in the Vatican Library (*Vat. gr.* 1703), which is, however, missing its beginning and end: the fragment that remains contains 195 questions. Most of these questions concern the exegesis of passages of scripture, though several of them discuss passages from the fathers (e.g., a series on Gregory Nazianzen—QQ 95–105—and several on passages from Basil's *Moralia*—QQ 93–4, 107–10); there is a discussion of the phrase on the virginal conception from the creed (Q 50), and a discussion of Gregory of Nyssa's understanding of *apokatastasis* (Q 19). Sherwood, following Balthasar, discussing the selection edited by Combefis, placed *Quaestiones et Dubia* among the earliest of Maximos's works (before 626). The much longer series now available does not upset this dating: Maximos's discussion of themes important to his theology (notably the Transfiguration: Q 191) shows lack of development. It is interesting to note that the selection published by Combefis seems to have been compiled by someone acutely aware of the dangers of Origenism: to the extent that the triad of *praktikē-theoria-theologia*, so important in Maximos's own ascetical theology, is entirely absent.

Early Ambigua (Ambigua ad Ioannem)

One of the most important of Maximos's dogmatic works consists of a series of 71 *ambigua* (ἀπορίαι, or "difficulties'): discussions of difficult passages drawn almost entirely from the works of Gregory Nazianzen. There are two series: the earlier and longer, consisting of 66 *ambigua*, together with an introductory letter, addressed to John, bishop of Kyzikos; and a later and shorter series of five, together with an introductory letter, addressed to a monk called Thomas. As published by F. Oehler, these two series are run together, with the later series coming first, and the *ambigua* enumerated consecutively (not counting the introductory letters), so that *Ambigua* 1–5 constitute the later *Ambigua* and *Ambigua* 6–71 the earlier. This arrangement (and consequent enumeration) seems to go back to Maximos himself, who in *opusc. theol. et pol.* 1 (PG 91, 33A: to be dated 645/6) refers to a passage from the second of the earlier *Ambigua* (PG 91, 1076C) as from "the seventh chapter of the difficulties of the great Gregory."

The earlier *Ambigua* deal entirely with passages from Gregory Nazianzen. From the introductory letter it is clear that they arose out of discussions between Maximos and Bishop John of Kyzikos that took place when Maximos was still at the Monastery of St George, though they were not committed to paper until after Maximos's arrival in North Africa (towards 630). The difficulties are of various kinds: some deal with obscure or technical words (e.g., *Amb.* 43, 69), others with textual problems (e.g., *Amb.* 70); several of them supplement the kind of allegory that Gregory provides in his sermons (notably *Amb.* 52–9, which provide allegorical interpretations of people associated with the passion of Christ, already discussed by Gregory in his second Easter Sermon). It is striking that, in many cases, Maximos gives several alternative interpretations (θεωρίαι he calls them), and makes no claim to having a definitive solution.

Many, however, are concerned with passages that might lend themselves to an Origenist interpretation, and Maximos's response sometimes turns into a veritable treatise in which the Origenist interpretation is refuted and a more satisfactory interpretation provided (notable examples are *Amb.* 7, 10, 42). As Sherwood says of these early *Ambigua*: "it is here that one finds, perhaps alone in all Greek patristic literature, a refutation of Origenist error with a full understanding of the master" (Sherwood, 1952, 32). But on the basis of this refutation, Maximos works out his own theological vision, in which the ascetic and dogmatic traditions of the fathers are given philosophical depth, and there emerges the most searching and influential synthesis of Greek patristic theology. The early *Ambigua* (separated from the later) found its way to the West, and was translated in Latin in the latter half of the ninth century by the great theologian of Charles the Bald's court, John Scotus Eriugena. Not knowing the later *Ambigua*, John enumerated the early *Ambigua* separately, with the introductory epistle to John of Kyzikos counting as the first.

Questions to Thalassios

The *Questions to Thalassios* are a series of ἐρωτα ποκρίσεις on biblical subjects addressed to Thalassius, a friend of Maximos's who was an abbot in nearby Libya, sometime between the completion of the *Ambigua ad Ioannem* (*Thal*. 39 refers to *Amb*. 65) and the outbreak of the monenergist controversy: that is, between 630 and 633/4. Some of them are strictly exegetical, concerned with the elucidation of passages of scripture on which Thalassius had sought Maximos's opinion, but many of them are more broadly theological. Next to the *Ambigua*, this set of questions is the main source for Maximos's theological and ascetical vision. Most of the questions have appended to them scholia, which summarize the main points made in the question: it is generally thought that these are a later addition. A Latin translation was made by John Scotus Eriugena in the latter half of the ninth century.

Two centuries on theology and the incarnate dispensation of the son of god

These two centuries (the "Gnostic Centuries" or "Theological and Economic Chapters") contain a summary of Maximos's theology—its metaphysical basis, its dogmatic grounding in the incarnation, and its ascetic fulfillment in a Christian life culminating in deification—based on the principles worked out more expansively in his *Ambigua ad Ioannem* and his *Questions to Thalassios*. They are prefaced by ten paragraphs (or chapters) that, drawing on the formulations of Origen and Evagrius, succinctly state Maximos's correction of their metaphysical vision.

Fifteen chapters

These 15 chapters appear separately in several early manuscripts (Sherwood, 1952, 35–6), but otherwise form the introductory chapters of five centuries that consist of an anthology of largely Maximian inspiration, drawn especially from the *Questions to Thalassios* (for a collation of the *Questions to Thalassios* with these five centuries, see the introductions to the critical edition of *Thal.*: CCSG 7, lxxvii–lxxix; CCSG 22, xlv–xlvii). They contain a summary of Maximos's metaphysics and understanding of the Fall and incarnation. Like the *Two Gnostic Centuries*, they probably belong to the period 630–4.

Questions to Theopemptos

This elucidation of three scriptural texts (Luke 18:6; 6:29; John 20:27), addressed to an otherwise unknown Theopemptos Scholastikos, seems to form a kind of appendix to the *Questions to Thalassios*, and probably belongs to the period 630–4.

Later Ambigua (Ambigua at Thomam)

These five later *Ambigua* are addressed to Thomas, a monk whom Maximos addresses as his spiritual father and teacher, and to whom Maximos wrote another letter, known to Photios and only recently published. The first four concern passages from Gregory Nazianzen, and concern Trinitarian and christological doctrine; the fifth discusses Dionysios the Areopagite's *ep*. 4 to Gaius, and provide an orthodox interpretation of the Areopagite's notorious reference to Christ's "new theandric activity." These reflections clearly have in mind the monenergism of Cyrus of Phasi's Pact of Union of 633, though, in obedience to Sergios's *Psephos*, Maximos avoids counting the energies or activities of Christ.

Dispute with Pyrrhos

This contains an account of the public debate between Pyrrhos, the former patriarch of Constantinople, and Maximos about christology, which took place in

Carthage before Gregory, the exarch of North Africa, and other notables in July 645. It contains an important statement of Maximos's objections to monothelitism. As a result of the debate, Pyrrhos relinquished his heresy and set off to Rome to be received into the communion of the orthodox.

Thelogical and polemical opuscula

Combefis edited 27 opuscula, which are all printed in Migne's *Patrologia*. Several of them contain, or consist of, *florilegia* concerning theological and philosophical terminology, especially that needed to bring clarity to the debates provoked by monenergism and monothelitism, in matters both of christological definition and also of human psychology. Some of the *florilegia* are thought to be of later compilation, or to have been augmented after the death of the Confessor: this is true of *opuscula* 26 and 27, as well as of the *florilegia* in *opusc.* 23. Most of the *opuscula* belong to the period 640–6, when the monothelite controversy was at its height. *Opusc.* 4, 5, 13, 14, 17, 18, 20, 22, 23 are probably earlier, and perhaps 21, too. Apart from the *Dispute with Pyrrhos* (sometimes regarded as *opusc.* 28), the most important works of Maximus concerned with the refutation of monothelitism are *opusc.* 3, 6, 7, 15, and 16, all of which contain reflection on Christ's agony in the garden, and (especially *opusc.* 15) gather together patristic exegesis of this pericope. These patristic citations form the basis for the *florilegia* presented at the Lateran Council in 649 and the Sixth Ecumenical Council in 681.

V.   Exegetical Works

On Psalm 59

Maximos's verse-by-verse commentary on Psalm 59 is an early work, possibly dating from his time at St George's, Kyzikos (before 626). It is striking that in many cases, as in his dogmatic works, Maximos gives several alternative interpretations of words and verses.

On the Lord's Prayer

Maximos's *On the Lord's Prayer* is another early work, probably written at the beginning of his stay in North Africa (628–30). It is really a treatise on prayer, which passes over into a commentary on the Lord's Prayer: in this it belongs to a tradition of such patristic commentaries going back to Origen. Maximos makes marked use of Gregory of Nyssa's *Homilies on the Lord's Prayer*. The work contains a succinct account of Maximos's understanding of the life of the Christian as the response through prayer and ascetic struggle to God's love manifest in the incarnation, which leads to deification. It was highly valued in the Byzantine tradition, and was included in the *Philokalia* of SS Nikodimos and Makarios.

VI.   Liturgical Works

Mystagogia

The *Mystagogia* is a commentary on the symbolism of the liturgical ceremonies of the Eucharist. It is prefaced by a series of chapters expounding the symbolism of the church building, divided into the nave and the sanctuary, within which the altar is situated, which is seen reflected in the cosmos, in man, and in the human soul, as well as in the Christian Scriptures, which are divided into Old and New Testament and bear a literal and a spiritual meaning. There is a conclusion that consists of an appendix applying the symbolism of the ceremonies to the soul's progress through the virtues (thus making explicit the parallelism between the church building and the soul, introduced in the prefatory chapters), and a summary, drawing out the ascetical significance of the symbolism of the eucharistic action (which may well be a series of scholia, appended to the treatise at a later date). The work is presented as a supplement to the *Ecclesiastical Hierarchy* of Dionysios the Areopagite, and as containing, not ideas of Maximos's own, but what he learnt from a certain "great old man": perhaps the same to whom Maximos elsewhere acknowledges his indebtedness, especially in the *Ascetical Life* and in the *Ambigua*. It sheds light on the structure of the Byzantine liturgy in the seventh century. But its real importance lies in the way it shows how Maximos understood the interrelationship between the different dimensions in which the healing work of salvation is worked out—the cosmic, the personal, and the liturgical (the interrelationship of the first two is made clear in *Amb.* 41, with which the *Mystagogia* should be compared). Parts of the *Mystagogia* were incorporated into the expanded versions of the commentary on the liturgy, probably first compiled by Germanos of Constantinople, that formed a preface to the priest's part (the *hieratikon*) of the liturgy in the Middle Ages.

Computus ecclesiasticus

The *Computus ecclesiasticus* is addressed to Peter, the prefect of Africa, and from internal evidence can be dated to between October 5, 640 (the beginning of Herakleios's thirty-first year) and the news of Herakleios's death reaching Africa (February 11, 641). It is mainly concerned with explaining and justifying the methods of calculating Easter, but is also concerned to fit the Easter cycle into the sequence of years from the creation of the world, and to that end includes chronological material drawn from the Byzantine chronographers.

VII.   Epistles

There was no ancient collection of the letters of Maximos, but Combefis included 45 letters in his edition of Maximos's writings (*ep.* 43 and *ep.* 23 are the same, though addressed to two different people). Several of Maximos's treatises are prefaced by letters—e.g., both sets of *Ambigua* and the *Questions to Thalassios*. A further letter, mentioned by Photios (*Bibliotheca*, cod. 194), to Thomas (Photios treats the *Ambigua ad Thomam* as the first letter to Thomas) has recently been discovered; a letter to his disciple, Anastasius, is included in the documents concerning his trials, which is also preserved, along with a letter to Thalassios, in Anastasius Bibliothecarius's Latin version; an otherwise unknown letter to John the Koubikoularios is still unedited. Several of these letters are effectively treatises: e.g., *ep.* 2, to John the Koubikoularios, is an ascetical treatise on love, and *ep.* 4, also to John, on godly grief. Others constitute individual "questions": e.g., *ep.* 6, on the incorporeality of the soul in answer to a query from John, as archbishop (perhaps the John of Kyzikos, for whom Maximos wrote the early *Ambigua*), or *ep.* 10, on human equality, in response to a question from John the Koubikoularios. *Ep.* 19, to Pyrrhos, then an abbot, later patriarch of

Constantinople, responds to a question about Sergios's *Psephos* with what later seemed to Maximos excessive warmth. Several other letters expound christological doctrine. Some of the letters are letters of recommendation (e.g., *epp.* 27 and 44, both to John the Koubikoularios). *Ep.* 8, to Sophronios, is of particular importance in expressing Maximos's dismay at Herakleios's forcible conversion of the Jews.

VIII.   *Scholia* to Corpus Dionysiacum

The *scholia* to the works of Dionysios the Areopagite (CPG 6625) were long ascribed to Maximos. It is now known that the core of these *scholia* belong to the sixth-century editor of the *Corpus Dionysiacum*, John of Scythopolis. Whether any of the *scholia* not attributed to John are to be restored to Maximos may be determined by the critical edition of the *scholia*, which is currently being prepared by Beate Suchla, as part of the new edition of the Areopagite. The wider question of Maximos's dependence on Dionysios is independent of the attribution of the *scholia*, although Maximos's reputation in the Western Middle Ages as primarily the scholiast of Dionysios resulted from the attribution to him of the whole body of the *scholia*, for Maximos frequently quotes Dionysios with approval, and shows a broad knowledge of his works.

IX.   Hagiography

A *Life of the Virgin*, attributed to Maximos, survives in a Georgian translation. M.-J. van Esbroeck, who has edited the text (1986), claims it as an authentic work of the Confessor, and believes it to be a direct response to the charge, leveled at him during his trial, of having denied the Virgin Mary the title of *Theotokos*. This seems rather unlikely.

X.   Theology

Maximos's theology is expressed in an unsystematic way: his most important treatises take the form of responses to questions addressed to him. It is likely, however, that this very fact is significant for understanding

Maximos's theology, in that it suggests that his theology grew out of monastic catechesis, and that the roots of his theology are to be found in his monastic experience—both ascetic and liturgical. His fondness for the genres of both *erotapokriseis* and *centuries*—the one popular in monastic circles, the other actually created by monks, probably by Evagrios—confirms this. It was apparently only with reluctance that Maximos allowed himself to be drawn into the christological controversy provoked by imperial attempts to find an "ecumenical" solution to the long-standing division between Orthodox Chalcedonians and Monophysites in the East, attempts spurred on first by the exploitation of these divisions by the victorious Persian Shah Chosroes in the early 620s, and then by the loss of the Eastern provinces to the Arabs in the 630s. He seems to have observed the terms of Sergios's *Psephos*, which forbade any counting of the activities of Christ, and only openly opposed heresy with the publication of the imperial *Ekthesis*, which embraced monothelitism, in 638. From then on, however, his opposition was unqualified.

If one follows the development of his theology chronologically, one should, then, start with his ascetic theology, move on to explore its cosmic and liturgical dimensions, and finally turn to his christological reflections, although it is evident from Pyrrhos's seeking his advice as early as 633, the year of the *Psephos*, that he already had a reputation as a champion of Orthodox theology. It has long been recognized that, like most of the masters of Byzantine spirituality, Maximos owed a very great deal in his ascetical theology to Evagrios, despite the condemnation of the Egyptian ascetic at the Fifth Ecumenical Council in 553. The threefold pattern of *praktikē*, *physikē theoria*, *theologia*—ascetic struggle, natural contemplation, theology—is as fundamental to Maximos as to Evagrios. Like Evagrios, he uses the ultimately Platonic tripartition of the soul in his analysis of the virtues and vices, and sees the goal of ascetic struggle in terms of *apatheia*. But it is clear from his very earliest works that this indebtedness to Evagrios is not uncritical. Instead of seeing the virtues as detaching the intellect from the lower parts of the soul (and the body), the whole human person is involved in communion with God and ultimate deification. When the intellect is constantly with God, the desiring part of the soul is transformed

into *eros* and the incensive part of the soul into *agape* (*Centuries on Love* II. 48): detachment yields to transfiguration.

He again parts company with Evagrios when he considers union with God, and adopts the Dionysian language of divine darkness and ecstatic love. He also draws on the very different ascetical tradition associated with the Makarian Homilies, and, like the fifth-century Diadochos of Photikē, whose works Maximos certainly knew (and who may even have spent the latter years of his life in North Africa), he works toward a synthesis between Evagrios's spirituality of the intellect and Makarios's spirituality of the heart.

It is evident from many parts of Maximos's works, but especially from the *Ambigua ad Ioannem*, that "Origenism" was still popular among Byzantine monks. Maximos's metaphysics can be regarded as an orthodox refashioning of the Origenist vision. This is most clearly manifest in his doctrine of the *logoi* of creation. Like Origen—and others influenced by the great Alexandrian, notably Evagrios and Dionysios the Areopagite—Maximos interpreted the doctrine that the universe was created through the Logos or Word of God as entailing that everything created had its own *logos*, through which it participates in the creative Logos. As a result of sin, the cosmos has been fractured and the harmony of the universe, manifest at the level of the cosmos, has been obscured. Human beings can recover this again by attaining natural contemplation, as a result of ascetic struggle, though this is a possibility only capable of realization through human beings' responding to the love and grace of God encountered in the incarnation of the Logos of God. But it is important for Maximos that the integrity of the universe that exists at the level of the *logoi* is inviolable: the cosmos is not, as with Origen, a result of the Fall; it is, and remains, what God intended.

Maximos explains the possibility, and reality, of the Fall by making a distinction between $\lambda\acute{o}\gamma o\varsigma$ and $\tau\rho\acute{o}\pi o\varsigma$—meaning or principle and mode or manner: a distinction that he further clarifies in his christology. The distinction is founded on the Cappadocian notion of person (or $\acute{u}\pi\acute{o}\sigma\tau\alpha\sigma\iota\varsigma$) as a mode or manner of existence ($\tau\rho\acute{o}\pi o\varsigma$ $\tau\tilde{\eta}\varsigma$ $\acute{u}\pi\acute{\alpha}\rho\xi\epsilon\omega\varsigma$). Nature is what creatures are, mode of existence is how they are: and human free will means that in the case of humans it is possible either for the mode of existence to correspond to the *logos* of nature, as was the case before the Fall, or for the mode of existence to fail to correspond to the *logos* of nature, which is the result of the Fall. This failure of the mode of existence to correspond to the *logos* of being or nature also obscures from fallen human beings the harmony of the cosmos God made, which exists at the level of the *logoi*. A further consequence of Maximos's doctrine of the *logoi* is the high value he ascribes to nature and natural law, so that natural law is the same as the written law (of scripture) or the spiritual law (of the incarnate Logos): the natural law is not transcended by the spiritual law, but transfigured, so that its true worth is realized.

Along with this strong doctrine of the integrity of the created order manifest in the *logoi* of creation, Maximos has a profound belief in the providence of God, and indeed embraces Dionysios the Areopagite's identification of the *logoi* with "predeterminations and divine and good wills" (*Amb*. 7: 1085A, citing Dionysios, *Divine Names* V. 8: 824C). Understood in the light of his doctrine of Providence, the doctrine of the *logoi* acquires eschatological significance: the *logos* of each being represents its final perfection; conformity to one's *logos* entails both the restoration of one's natural state, but also deification. This sense of the created cosmos as moving toward perfection and deification finds expression in another important correction of Origenist metaphysics. Origenism had envisaged a primal state of rest, in which everything constituted an original henad or unity, from which the created rational beings had turned away, their fall resulting in the cosmos, itself a system, providentially devised, for restoring the rational beings to their original state of union with God. The state of created beings as they are now was explained by the triad, στάσις–κίνησις–γένεσις, rest–movement–coming-to-be. Maximos reverses this triad, replacing it with γένεσις–κίνησις–στάσις, for in his view created beings first come into being (through creation by God), and then move toward a final state of rest, or communion with God (see especially *Amb*. 15). This movement toward rest in God is further elucidated by another triad, εἶναι–εὐ εἶναι–ἀεὶ εἶναι, being–well-being–eternal being: of this triad Maximos remarks that both ends of the triad are gifts from God—in creation and at the end—but that well-being is within our power, and determines whether the passage from

being to eternal being is accomplished or frustrated (see *Amb*. 10: 1116B).

Even in this comparatively abstract analysis, it is evident that human free will is endowed with metaphysical significance. Elsewhere Maximos expounds the central position of the free human person within the cosmos more concretely. One way of expressing this involves the doctrine, derived from Gregory of Nyssa in particular, of the division of nature or being. The most profound division, separating God from his creation, is that between the uncreated and the created; the created in turn is divided into the intelligible and the sensible; the sensible into heaven and earth; earth into paradise and the inhabited world (οἰκουμένη); and within the inhabited world there live human beings divided into male and female. All these extremes meet in the human being, whose original function it was to hold them together, so that the human person, being in itself a miniature cosmos (microcosm), constituted the bond (σύνδεσμος) of the cosmos. As a result of the Fall, however, the human has been unable to fulfil this mediating role, and the divisions of the cosmos have become fault lines, so to speak, along which the fallen cosmos has been fractured. The human cosmic function as microcosm and bond of the cosmos is restored by the incarnate Word, who in the course of his life, from conception to ascension, recapitulates and heals all the divisions of being: in response to the incarnation, human beings can once again fulfill their cosmic role through a life of ascetic struggle. Also, as the *Mystagogia* makes clear, the Eucharist itself can be seen as a celebration and extension of the healing of the divisions of being in the incarnation.

It is the centrality of the incarnation in Maximos's theology that made the christological controversies of his time of such crucial significance. Attempts to heal the division with the Monophysites by securing their assent to the doctrine of two natures in Christ by finding the unity at the level of activity (ἐνέργεια) or will (θέλημα) inevitably led, in Maximos's eyes, to frustrating the healing of the divisions of being that it was the purpose of the incarnation to achieve. For Maximos, following Aristotelian teaching, nature and activity are correlative: activity entails nature. The same is true of will: will is a function of a rational nature. If Christ, as the Chalcedonian Definition affirms, subsists in two natures, then he must have two activities—one divine, one human—and two wills—one divine, one human. However, in his refutation of monothelitism, Maximos had to respond to the charge that two wills in Christ would both be psychologically incoherent and leave open the possibility of the two wills coming into conflict and thereby frustrating Christ's saving purpose. In response to this, Maximos developed his distinction between natural will and deliberative will (or "gnomic" will, i.e., a will that operates on the basis of an opinion, *gnōmē*, itself the produce of a process of deliberation)— $\theta\acute{\epsilon}\lambda\eta\mu\alpha$ $\varphi\upsilon\sigma\iota\kappa\acute{o}\nu$ and $\theta\acute{\epsilon}\lambda\eta\mu\alpha$ $\gamma\nu\omega\mu\iota\kappa\acute{o}\nu$. This is the distinction between will as the natural desire of the rational being for the good, and the process of deliberation by which, in our experience of willing in a fallen world, we seek to discover how our natrual will—our natural desire for the good—is to be fulfilled. But this distinction is a distinction that gives insight into what it is to be a person. The distinction between $\lambda\acute{o}\gamma o\varsigma$ and $\tau\rho\acute{o}\pi o\varsigma$, already mentioned, corresponds to the distinction between nature and person: person is manifest in the way ($\tau\rho\acute{o}\pi o\varsigma$) rational beings allow their nature (defined by $\lambda\acute{o}\gamma o\varsigma$) to exist.

When the Word became incarnate, it assumed a perfect human nature, including the natural will: the way it exercised this will belongs to the person of the Word, and differs from our exercise of natural will, because by the grace of union the incarnate Word transcends the darkness and obscurity in which, as a result of the Fall, we experience our willing. There is, then, no deliberative will in Christ, but there are two natural wills, one human, one divine (which is identical with the will of the Father and the Holy Spirit), which are in perfect harmony: the harmony of the divine purpose the incarnation is to fulfill. In his consideration of the two natural wills in Christ Maximos turns again and again to the mystery of Christ's agony in the garden. But, for the most part, all this is rather in the nature of an *ad hominem* argument against monothelite arguments, to such an extent that there are those who think that monothelitism as a heresy—in contrast to the idea that the human will in Christ was simply quiescent to the divine—is a product of Maximos's imagination. However, Maximos's fundamental objection to monothelitism and monenergism is that both entail that in the incarnation the Word assumed an incomplete, and therefore defective, human nature, something that runs utterly counter to his conviction of the integrity of the created order.

Maximos's christology, then, is of a piece with his whole theology, which in both its ascetical and cosmic dimensions bears witness to a deep respect for the integrity of God's created order.

XI.   Influence

The influence of Maximos in Byzantine and later Eastern Orthodox theology has been profound. The definition of Orthodoxy entailed by the theological "level playing field," created in the East by the rise and dominance of Islam, was worked out by Palestinian monks, who drew their inspiration from Maximos. This is such a marked feature of the Orthodoxy that finds its most renowned expression in John Damascene's *Exposition of the Orthodox Faith*—and also in the liturgical poetry that found its first flourishing among John Damascene and the Palestinian monks contemporary with him—that the Christians of the Middle East who rejected the Orthodoxy of the Byzantine Synods called their opponents "Maximians." Understandably, given the opposition of the theologians of Constantinople to the Orthodoxy of Maximos and John Damascene in the seventh and eighth centuries, Maximos's theology only begins to be well known in Byzantium after the final collapse of iconoclasm; he was well known, for example, to Photios (patriarch of Constantinople 858–67, 877–86). Thereafter his influence continued, and he was read, not just by the learned, but was the favourite reading of Irene Doukaina, the wife of Emperor Alexios Komnenos—to the astonishment of her daughter, the historian Anna Komnena. He was an important influence on Gregory Palamas, and cited a great deal in the course of the Palamite controversy. In the great ascetic anthology, compiled by Nikodimos of the Holy Mountain and Makarios of Corinth and published in 1782, the *Philokalia of the Holy Ascetics*, which was to be so fruitful for the revival of Orthodox theology in the nineteenth and twentieth centuries, Maximos is allotted more space than any other writer, even Gregory Palamas. The twentieth century has seen a revival in the scholarly fortunes of St Maximos, with his importance being grasped and proclaimed not only by Orthodox scholars, but even more so by Roman Catholic scholars, notably Hans Urs von Balthasar and Dom Polycarp Sherwood, and also by the Lutheran scholar, Lars Thunberg.

References

van Esbroeck, M.-J. 1986. *Corpus Scriptorum Christianorum Orientalium 478, Scriptores Iberici*, 21. Louvain.

Quaestiones ad Thalassium, ed. C. Laga and C. Steel, Corpus Christianorum Series Graeca *7 & 22*. Brepols: Turnhout, 1980 and 1990.

Sherwood, P. 1952. *An Annotated Date-List of the Works of Maximus the Confessor.* (Studia Anselmiana, 30.) Rome: Orbis Catholicus, Herder.

Origen (*c*.185–254)

Alastair H. B. Logan

I. Life

Origen (*Horigeneēs*, meaning son of the Egyptian god Horus), one of the giants of early Christianity, is a figure about whom we know much more than most because of two—rather eulogistic—writings about him, the first by the pioneer church historian Eusebius of Caesarea (*c*.260–339 CE), particularly Book VI of his *Ecclesiastical History*, based on Origen's letters and on the recollections of people who had known him. The second is the encomium written to him by a pupil of his, usually identified as Gregory Thaumaturgus, ("Wonder Worker") (*c*.213–*c*.270 CE), the apostle of Cappadocia, who converted Macrina, grandmother of the Cappadocian theologians Basil of Caesarea and his brother Gregory of Nyssa. Origen was born in around 185 CE, probably in Alexandria, into what seems a well-off Christian family, the eldest of seven sons. His father, called Leonides by Eusebius, was beheaded at Alexandria in the persecution of Septimius Severus around 202, when Origen was about 16. According to Eusebius, Origen's father had been very anxious that, besides undergoing the normal educational curriculum, he should study the Bible, requiring him every day to learn passages by heart and repeat them aloud. Origen did this with alacrity, looking for something beyond the natural, literal sense, worrying his father with questions about the underlying meaning.

Whatever the truth of Eusebius's account, clearly the Bible was central to Origen from an early age.

Martyrdom was also an early passion: Eusebius tells us that, even before the arrest and execution of his father, Origen had a longing for martyrdom, and was only dissuaded, first, by his mother's appeal and then later (made even more determined by his father's arrest), by her hiding his clothes. He did, however, write to his father in prison urging him not to change his mind on account of his family. But the event must have profoundly affected Origen who boldly and openly continued to support the martyrs. With the family driven into destitution by the confiscation of the father's property, Origen was taken into the household of a very wealthy and distinguished Christian lady, to ensure his education was completed. However, she was the devotee of a certain Paul, Antiochene by birth, whom Eusebius calls "a notorious heretic," and whom the lady had adopted as her son. What kind of heretic Paul was we do not know, but in the light of Origen's later writings and concerns, he might have been a Valentinian. Eusebius assures us that despite living with him and despite his popularity, Origen never joined him in prayer, keeping from his earliest years the church's rule of faith, and, in his own words, "loathing" all heretical teachings.

On finishing his education he opened a school teaching Greek literature to help support himself. When a further bout of persecution beginning around

The Student's Companion to the Theologians, First Edition. Edited by Ian S. Markham.
© 2013 Blackwell Publishing Ltd. Published 2013 by Blackwell Publishing Ltd.

206 drove out the Christian leaders and teachers, including Clement of Alexandria (*c*.150–*c*.215 CE), leaving no one to instruct catechumens, and on being approached by some pagan enquirers, Origen voluntarily took over such instruction, a move later sanctioned by bishop Demetrius. Some of these early pupils were to distinguish themselves as martyrs, openly and fearlessly supported by Origen who had to move house often to escape arrest, while others became church leaders, such as Heraclas. But Origen soon felt unable to continue both activities; he ceased his teaching of literature, feeling it to be incompatible with his catechetical activity, selling his cherished library of classics to make himself financially independent. He devoted himself to a life of self-denial, taking Christ's sayings very seriously, instructing catechumens by day and studying scripture by night. This period clearly laid the foundations of his profound knowledge of scripture. Eusebius even relates that Origen took the saying in Matt. 19:12 about some being eunuchs for the sake of the kingdom of God literally, despite his later condemnation of such an interpretation.

We should also include in this period Origen's debt to the person and writings of Clement, who seems to have been among those responsible for catechetical instruction at Alexandria before him. Although he does not mention him, other evidence and his own writings attest his influence on him, particularly as regards working out the proper relation of Greek philosophy to Christianity, countering Gnostic heresy by defending the church's tradition, and developing a form of allegorical interpretation of scripture. As regards the latter, it was probably via Clement that Origen discovered the works of Philo of Alexandria (*c*.20 BCE–*c*.50 CE), the liberal Diaspora Jew influenced by Middle Platonism who applied Stoic allegorical interpretation to the LXX of the Pentateuch. Indeed we may well owe the survival of Philo's voluminous writings to Origen's copies in his later library in Caesarea. Origen's study of scripture and the consequent variants he found in the Greek versions he collected drove him to study the original Hebrew, enlisting the aid of a Jewish convert, probably from Palestine, who helped him learn the language and introduced him to Jewish exegetical traditions. This led him to produce his massive *Hexapla*, a word-for-word

comparison of the Septuagint with the Hebrew Bible and other Greek translations in six columns: the original Hebrew, a Greek transliteration, the more literal translations of Aquila, Symmachus, and Theodotion, then the Septuagint with critical marks denoting differences (additions, omissions, divergences) from the Hebrew.

Eusebius says that about this time (*c*.215?) Origen made the first of his four trips abroad, visiting Rome, anxious, as he said himself in one of his writings, to see the ancient Roman church, though some scholars have seen a different motivation, namely to find a more congenial place to teach, free of the critical scrutiny of Demetrius. En route, at Nicopolis near Actium in Greece, he discovered a fifth Greek version of the Psalms to add to the four he had already recorded. While in Rome he seems to have attended the lectures of the learned presbyter, Hippolytus, opponent of lax discipline, scourge of heretics, and defender of the reality and distinction of Father and Son versus the modalism of Noetus and Sabellius. However, he returned to Alexandria and to instructing the catechumens. But he soon realized he could not combine such elementary instruction with his advanced study of scripture, so he divided his pupils into two groups, allotting those needing catechetical instruction to Heraclas, his learned pupil (later to succeed Demetrius as bishop), while taking the more advanced himself.

But, as he says himself, this attracted some heretics to his classes, men trained in Greek philosophy, which forced him to tackle not only the ideas of the heretics but also the philosophical notions often underlying them. Here he claimed to be following not only the Stoic Pantaenus, Clement's teacher, but also Heraclas, who had already been a student of an unnamed teacher of Greek philosophy for five years, before Origen began attending his classes as well. That teacher is usually identified as the eclectic philosopher Ammonius Saccas, since the Neoplatonist Porphyry of Tyre (*c*.234–304 CE), who met Origen in his old age, relates that he became a pupil of Ammonius, later teacher of Plotinus (*c*.205–70 CE), founder of Neoplatonism and Porphyry's teacher. Ammonius left no writings behind but must have been an outstanding teacher with two such pupils. Under him Origen seems to have immersed himself in writings of the

Platonic and Pythagorean schools, and gained such a mastery of Greek philosophy that he even attracted a pagan audience to his Christian school. Eusebius notes his curriculum: after first teaching the elementary subjects—geometry, arithmetic etc.—he proceeded to study the systems of the philosophers, examining and criticizing the various schools, all as a sound basis for going on to the final goal, the study of scripture. Interestingly, Porphyry suggests that Stoic writers were the source of Origen's allegorical interpretation of that scripture. The fruits of such study resulted in Origen's classic *Peri Archōn* (*De Principiis*/*On First Principles*), embracing the first principles both of philosophy and of the Christian rule of faith, written about 229. It deals with the doctrines of God, of Son and Spirit, of rational beings, and of the material world, as well as with how properly to interpret scripture, filling in gaps in the church's rule of faith and seeking to present a rational and organic whole. In a new and significant development, Origen was encouraged to produce written commentaries on scripture by his wealthy friend Ambrose, whom he had won over from Valentinianism and who supplied him with shorthand writers and copyists. This helps to account for the enormous output of Origen and its wide dissemination.

About this time, letters came to Demetrius and the governor of Egypt from the governor of Arabia asking them to send Origen to consult with him. Events in Alexandria also led him to travel to Palestine in around 230, welcomed by Alexander, bishop of Jerusalem, who invited him, although a layman, to expound scripture in church. However, Demetrius soon summoned him home, where Ambrose urged him to write a commentary on John which would answer that of the Valentinian Heracleon. It was at this point that he received an invitation from the emperor's mother, Julia Mammaea, when staying at Antioch in 231, to come and expound his theological views to her. She even sent a bodyguard to fetch him and he stayed some months. Finally, Eusebius mentions the need to sort out an issue involving the church in Greece, which resulted in Origen travelling there via Caesarea in Palestine. The Greek issue more likely involved his desire to exchange Alexandria and Demetrius for the attractions of Athens, the center of Greek philosophy, with the intention of setting up a

Christian school there. During his brief stay in Caesarea the bishop, Theoctistus, ordained him presbyter, evidently to regularize his position. He then continued to Athens where he stayed for a year or more, completing his *Commentary on Ezekiel* and beginning his famous and influential one on the Song of Songs. However, his ordination outraged his bishop, who felt it was totally out of order, if not uncanonical, also bringing up the issue of his self-mutilation. He wrote to the bishop of Rome, Pontianus, complaining of the conduct of Theoctistus and Alexander and citing Origen's castration and claim in his *Dialogue with Candidus*, another Valentinian, that even the Devil might be saved. Pontianus replied in the name of the Church of Rome agreeing with Demetrius. However, Origen defended himself against the charges in a long autobiographical letter to Alexander, one of Eusebius's key sources, as did the two Palestinian bishops in a letter to Pontianus. They held a council of bishops from Palestine, Arabia, Phoenicia, and Greece which claimed that once Origen had ceased to live in Alexandria he had freed himself of Demetrius's jurisdiction and that his ordination by other bishops was thus perfectly valid. When Demetrius died, in 233, his successor Heraclas, despite having been a pupil of Origen, proved no less hostile. Origen decided to leave Greece in 234 and settle in Caesarea, where he would be welcome.

At Caesarea Origen preached regularly at eucharistic services, instructed the crowds of pupils that flocked to him and, reunited with Ambrose and his copyists, continued to publish. He completed several major commentaries that he had begun in Alexandria (Genesis, Isaiah, John) as well as a treatise on prayer and a key work of apologetic, the *Against Celsus* of 248 (Chadwick, 1953), both at the instigation of Ambrose. The latter work was a careful and comprehensive reply to the acute criticisms of Celsus, a Platonist philosopher, in his *True Doctrine* composed around 180. Origen seems to have been enlisted as an expert in several local theological disputes, debating with bishop Beryllus of Bostra in Arabia and others whose heretical views he sought to correct. A precious and revealing record of such debates with a bishop Heraclides and others was discovered in a quarry at Tura near Cairo in 1941. His teaching style and personal impact are graphically depicted in the *Address* to him between 238 and 245 of a certain Theodore, whom Eusebius identifies as Gregory Thaumaturgus, mentioned above. Gregory and his brother Athenodore had been travelling to Berytus to attend the famous law school there, but came across Origen in Caesarea, were captivated by the man and his teaching and abandoned their career plans, staying on as his pupils for eight years. His course of instruction, whose goal was the study of scripture, moved from teaching by Socratic conversations to think philosophically and dialectically, to instruction in the physical sciences and then in ethics as both an intellectual system and a way of life. Philosophy was thus treated as a preparation for theology, and Origen finally turned to the reading and study of scripture with his pupils.

It was probably after Gregory reluctantly left that Origen felt free to embark on a further visit to Athens. We hear from one of the few surviving letters that he also spent some weeks in Nicomedia and he was invited to Caesarea in Cappadocia by its bishop, Firmilian, a great admirer. He wrote his *Commentary on Matthew* in 25 books and, under the growing threat of persecution, his treatise in eight books against Celsus, as well as carrying on correspondence with bishops such as Fabian of Rome and Christian scholars like Julius Africanus, even writing a letter to the emperor Philip and one to his wife, Severa. But on the death of Philip his successor, Decius, was led to initiate the first official persecution of the Christians, which inevitably involved Origen. He was chained up and tortured in a dark cell, his legs stretched to the fourth hole in the stocks, threatened with fire and further tortures. But he resisted and survived, the judge, says Eusebius, trying by might and main to avoid sentencing him to execution. He related his own sufferings and never ceased to encourage others undergoing persecution by messages and letters of help and comfort. However, by now in his seventieth year and worn out by his sufferings, he died and was buried in Tyre in around 254.

II.   Writings

We have already noted some of his writings, which Epiphanius claimed amounted to 6,000 in total. In all that he did Origen claimed to be a theologian of

scripture, seeking its true understanding, and thus his pioneering text-critical and hermeneutical achievements, summed up in his *Hexapla* and sheer range of biblical commentaries, homilies, and *scholia*, as well as his treatment of hermeneutics in Book 4 of the *Peri Archōn*, cannot be overlooked. Nevertheless his most theologically significant works are quite limited in number, although we find profound insights throughout the rest. The former include, of course, the *Peri Archōn*, but also his Commentaries on Genesis, John, Matthew, and Romans, his apologetic *Against Celsus* and his little dogmatic treatise on prayer. We might also cite his *Dialogue with Heraclides*. However, the issue of the reliability of what remains of Origen, much of whose writings were destroyed after the attack on him by the emperor Justinian in 543 and the condemnation of Origenism by the Fifth Ecumenical Council meeting in Constantinople in 553, constitutes a significant problem. It is at its most acute in the case of the *Peri Archōn*, which survives complete only in a Latin version made by Rufinus of Aquileia (*c*.345–410) in the late 390s, in which Rufinus consciously omitted or amended what he felt was either inconsistent with Origen's statements elsewhere or heretical, believing it to have been tampered with. Rufinus also translated other works by Origen, which often survive only in his version, as well as the first book of Pamphilus's and Eusebius's six-book defense of Origen. Jerome (*c*.342–420), who had in his youth been a fervent admirer of Origen, translating some of his commentaries and incorporating their ideas, was led, under the influence of Epiphanius of Salamis, to denounce him and his views and cite the Greek original of contentious passages of the *Peri Archōn* in what he claimed was a literal translation. However, recent study of Rufinus's approach has tended to redress the balance: although his version loses something of the philosophical sophistication of the original and he has omitted Origen's views on the Trinity which seemed heterodox, he gives us a faithful picture of Origen's cosmology and eschatology. Two lengthy fragments of the original Greek survive in the *Philocalia*, an anthology of Origen's views on biblical interpretation and free will (but silent over creation and eschatology), traditionally ascribed to Basil of Caesarea (*c*.330–79) and Gregory of Nazianzus (*c*.330–90) as well as other fragments from the later condemnations. These, frequently taken out of context, were incorporated into the main text in G. W. Butterworth's fine 1936 translation, following Koetschau's use of them alongside Rufinus's renderings, perhaps tending to give a rather tendentious and outdated picture, not in line with modern scholarship as represented by recent French (1976, 1978–84) and German (1992) versions.

The picture presented by *Peri Archōn* can also be checked and complemented by utilizing works such as the *Commentary on John* and *Against Celsus*, products of his maturity, both of which survive in Greek and suggest a fair degree of consistency in his thinking on God, Christ, and the world.

III. Theology

Before we consider Origen's theology we should first deal with the vexed question of his relation to pagan, and particularly Platonic, philosophy. Porphyry, in his comments on Origen in his treatise *Against the Christians*, preserved by Eusebius, remarks that Origen, a hearer of Ammonius, the most proficient philosopher of his day, and much indebted to him, was as a Greek, educated in Greek learning, who drove headlong into barbarian recklessness (i.e., Christianity), hawking his literary skill. Thus while his manner of life was Christian and contrary to the law, in his opinions about material things and the divine he played the Greek and introduced Greek ideas into foreign fables. He goes on to mention his continual immersion in the works of Plato and of famous Middle Platonists and Neo-Pythagoreans such as Numenius, Cronius, Apollophanes, Longinus, Moderatus, and Nicomachus. Origen clearly had a very good knowledge and mastery of the various strands of the Greek philosophical tradition of his own time, which he used in his teaching, whose final goal, we should never forget, was the interpretation of scripture. But was he, as his condemnations in 543 and 553 hinted, and the traditional view has tended to suggest, a Platonist, if a critical one? Did he derive his views of a transcendent, incorporeal God and of the Trinity of three hypostases, of the demiurgic Word, of the pre-existent rational souls, their "fall" into bodies through free will and their salvation,

from the prevailing Middle Platonism of his time and place?

Mark Edwards has recently subjected this traditional view to a powerful critique (2002). He argues, with reference to Origen's doctrines of God and the soul and in his interpretation of scripture, that he developed an autonomous philosophy based on scripture and his own reflections, designed to answer the teachings of the philosophical schools. Although condemned for supposedly teaching Platonizing tenets such as an incorporeal realm of rational beings or souls which cooled and were trapped in material bodies of varying grossness, the creation of the visible world by a demiurgic intelligence (*Nous dēmiourgos*) rather than the Word, the transmigration of souls from higher to lower states, the perfect spherical shape of the ethereal resurrected body of the Lord, the destruction of the material body in the future judgment, and the final restoration of all things (*apokatastasis*) in which the end will be as the beginning, Origen was not guilty. According to Edwards (2002, 160f.), Origen rejected the Platonic ideas of a realm of incorporeal entities; he taught a finite, not an infinite, God who, if transcending mind, can be known particularly through the revelation of his Son, the eternal Word. More provocatively, Edwards argues that Origen, although allowing that all rational creatures were originally incorporeal, nowhere in his extant works expressly speaks of a fall of the soul from heaven; passages commonly supposed to apply to the previous existence of the soul can as plausibly apply to the soul's actions in the present life. The purpose of embodiment is not punishment but exercise in virtue, to complete the image of God by the purposely withheld likeness; the final goal is not the deliverance of the soul from the body but the subsuming of both soul and body in spirit. Moreover Origen did not teach that souls passed from one body to another, if allowing that they may fall or rise in the scale of virtue to become more bestial or angelic. Edwards's attempt to show that in many passages cited to demonstrate pagan philosophical influence a biblical and traditional Christian view is the more likely basis, is generally persuasive, if his defense fails to account entirely satisfactorily for the logic of Origen's system. Nevertheless, despite the ancient and modern criticism that Origen was too blinded by alien philosophy, he takes his place in the long and honorable tradition of Christian theologians who have made selective and critical use of contemporary philosophy to articulate and defend their theological views.

Origen bases his theology, as expressed particularly in the *Peri Archōn*, firmly in the church's rule of faith, which he summarizes in his preface. Against Gnostics and Marcionites this taught one God, both just and good, who created the universe out of nothing, the God of Old and New Testaments. It taught a belief in Jesus Christ as generated from the Father before every creature, who made all things and while being God was really incarnate, really suffered and died, and was truly raised from the dead. It associated the Holy Spirit, whose status was unclear, in honor and dignity with Father and Son, teaching its role in inspiring the prophets and apostles. It further taught the reality of the soul and the appropriate reward for its deeds— eternal life and blessedness or eternal fire and torture—and the resurrection of the body. Souls according to the rule possess free will and choice and are involved in a struggle with the Devil and his angels, yet not subject to necessity. The world is not eternal but was made at a certain time and will be destroyed because of its corruption. Finally, scripture was written by the Holy Spirit and has a hidden sense. This rule provides the basis for his own investigations, as gifted with wisdom and knowledge through the grace of the Holy Spirit, into topics not explored by the apostles, such as whether the Holy Spirit was begotten or not; whether the soul comes into existence at conception or has an earlier beginning; who the Devil and his angels are and how they came to exist; what pre-existed this world or will exist after it; and whether God is corporeal or not.

Origen then proceeds to deal with God the Father in terms of scripture, rejecting any anthropomorphic interpretations: God is incomprehensible and immeasurable, a simple intellectual existence, altogether monad, or indeed henad, a mind, the source of all intellectual being or mind. Indeed, echoing Plato, he can speak of him in his late work *Against Celsus* as beyond being and mind, simple, invisible, incorporeal. But, contrary to the appeal of Platonists like Celsus to human approaches in terms of synthesis (the *via eminentiae*), analogy (the *via analogiae*), or abstraction (the *via negativa*), Origen insists human nature is unable to know

him unless helped by him, revealing himself by grace to the pure in heart through his image, the Son or Word. God cannot be known via nature or by the senses, which apply only to what is visible, but only through the soul or mind, made in the image of God. God is immutable, and the passages in scripture that speak of him as suffering he admits should be interpreted metaphorically. He is omnipotent in the sense that he cannot do what is impossible or inconceivable. More strikingly, he is finite, creating a finite number of rational beings since, if he were infinite, he could not know himself, and if his creations were infinite he could not control them.

In a striking term which seems peculiar to Origen, owing more to John's Prologue than to contemporary Middle Platonism, God the Father is alone *autotheos*; he alone is ingenerate (*agennētos*), called by Christ "the only true God" (John 17:3). And because he cannot be omnipotent without the existence of subjects over whom to exercise his power, God out of his own goodness created a limited number of rational beings. Furthermore, since God is unalterable and unchangeable, there cannot have been a time when these beings did not exist; God created them in the beginning and thus it would seem they are co-eternal with him. However, Origen denies that God's creatures were unbegotten and co-eternal with him: his solution seems to lie in his understanding of "in the beginning." For him the beginning of Gen. 1:1 and John 1:1 is God's eternal Wisdom and Word, in whom the creation always existed in form and outline. Thus he interprets Prov. 8:22 LXX to refer to Wisdom, created at the beginning of the ways, as fashioning beforehand and containing in herself the species and causes of all creation. Wisdom, of course is identified with the Son as his primary epithet; the Son is God's wisdom existing as a concrete hypostasis. Further, since God can never have been without his wisdom, the Son eternally exists, being eternally generated so that there never was when the Son did not exist. Origen finds scriptural support for this concept in the language of Col. 1:15, Heb. 1:3, and Wisd. Sol. 7:25f.: the Son is the image of the invisible God, the express image of his substance, the brightness of the eternal light.

Origen is led to insist on the spiritual character of the Son's begetting by and being the image of the Father: he compares it with an act of will begotten by the mind, rejecting ideas of emanation, abscission, or separation. The Son is the invisible, incorporeal image of the invisible God. He is the link between the unity of the Father and the multiplicity of the created order, representing a plurality of aspects (*epinoiai*), some relating to his eternal being (Wisdom, Word, Truth, Life), others to his incarnate state (Door, Way, Resurrection). Further, the Son is inferior to the Father, logically if not temporally: he is God, but not God in himself (*autotheos*); indeed Origen can dub him a "second God." He is an image of God's goodness, but not goodness itself. Indeed, although he stresses the unity and similarity of Father and Son, his approach would seem to rule out the use of the term "consubstantial" (*homoousios*) to describe the relation of Son to Father, since the term only properly applies to corporeal entities, although there is some—disputed—evidence that Origen may have used that term.

This brings us to Origen's doctrine of the Holy Spirit and the Trinity. He notes that if some acquaintance with the doctrines of Father and Son or Word can be found in Greek philosophy, that is not the case with the Holy Spirit, whose personal character, existence, and activity are known solely through the revelation of scripture. He claims that there is nothing in scripture that would warrant calling the Spirit a created being; rather the Spirit is the most honorable of all the beings brought into existence through the Word, superior in rank to all the beings originated by the Father through the Son. The Spirit is the source of our knowledge of God and of our sanctification. It seems to have been Origen who, to counter Modalism, introduced the term *hypostasis* to apply to the eternally distinct reality and subsistence of each of the three. Talking of the Father and the Son in *Against Celsus* he argues that the Son is other in subsistence than the Father and that they are two things (*pragmata*) in hypostasis but one in unanimity, harmony, and identity of will, while in criticizing modalist ideas in his *Dialogue with Heraclides*, he is happy to speak of the two as two Gods in one sense, while one in another, namely in terms of power. Each has a particular activity and ministry: God the Father, as source of divinity, imparts being to everything; the Son, as less than the Father, is superior to the rational creatures which partake in him as Word; while the Spirit, who is still less and owes both his subsistence and

characteristics to the Son, dwells in the saints. What is more, Origen in his treatise on prayer insists that prayer is properly due only to the Father, to whom Christ himself prayed; prayer to Christ is offered by him to the Father. Thus, despite the valiant attempts of Edwards to argue that Origen does not present a subordinationist Trinity, one cannot avoid deducing it from what he says as entirely consonant with mainstream tradition seeking to maintain monotheism, and more importantly as deduced from his interpretation of scripture.

As regards Origen's doctrine of creation, this too is governed by his concerns to maintain the unchangeability of God and counter both the Gnostic question about what God was doing before he created the world and their appeal to the existence of evil and diversity in it. God the Father, who is good, righteous, and omnipotent, created through his Word a limited number of incorporeal rational beings (*logika*) possessing free choice, all alike and equal, which then fell away in varying degrees from their imitation of God and were clothed in various kinds of bodies, angelic, human, and demonic, depending on their character and actions. It was from these varied beings that God formed this world. Although their archetypes are eternal, existing in God's Wisdom, they are created, hence mutable. However, this approach requires that Origen at least consider the possibility of other, earlier worlds and lives to explain the status of rational beings in this world. In line with his experimental approach where he feels the rule of faith is unclear, he speculates that these rational beings or minds (*nous*) could have cooled in their descent or falling away from God and become souls, but that they through amendment and correction can again become minds. He is further led to speculate on the possibility of transmigration of souls from angels, humans, and demons to animals, although he repudiates that view both in the *Peri Archōn* and in *Against Celsus*.

He appeals to biblical texts, especially enigmatic ones about the prince of Tyre and fallen angelic figures, to suggest that one of the rational beings or intelligences, the Devil, since he possessed free will, chose to resist God and was rejected. All the other powers fell with him, apart from one, destined to be the soul of Jesus. Such a pre-cosmic Fall explains not only the diversity found in the cosmos, but also the universality of human sin, for which he finds support both in scripture and from the church's practice of baptizing infants. Adam's sin is allegorized as the sin of all humanity through their free will, and their "coats of skin" symbolize human mortality and frailty. However, if he does seem to teach that all were present in the loins of Adam, yet each individual grows to imitate Adam and is mysteriously guilty of the transgression which led to their expulsion from Paradise. Here again the principle of freedom, the linchpin of Origen's entire theology, is paramount. However, he does not see the body as evil in itself, or the principle of evil, but rather the consequence of diversity in the rational creatures and vehicle of purification: punishment for him is always remedial. Evil is always the result of the free choice of rational creatures, turned by God to good, to correction and healing.

Origen's doctrine of Christ fits in very well to this overall picture of God and his creation of rational beings. He begins his treatment in the *Peri Archōn* by identifying two natures in Christ: one divine, in that he is the only-begotten Son of the Father; the other human, taken at the incarnation. As we have seen, his divine titles include Wisdom and Word, as drawn from scripture, which Origen proceeds to expound and interpret as confirming the Son's eternal existence with and relation to the Father. When he comes later on to deal with the incarnation he speaks of his belief in the incomprehensible mystery of how the very Word and Wisdom of God existed in the compass of "that man who appeared in Judaea," and of "how the wisdom of God can have entered a woman's womb and been born as a little child and cried like children." He solves this supreme mystery and paradox in the most ingenious way by recourse to his idea of the rational creatures (*logika*). While all fell away from loving participation in God's Word through a weaker degree of love or for other reasons, one did not—that destined to be the soul of Christ. Possessing like all the rest the ability to choose either good or evil, it chose to cling to the Word "from the beginning of creation" and ever after in an inseparable and indissoluble union. Origen suggests the analogy of iron heated in a fire and goes on to argue that, in this manner, that soul which, like a piece of iron in the fire, was for ever placed in the Word and the Wisdom, for ever in God, is God in all its acts, feelings, and thoughts, coming

by its ceaseless kindling to possess unchangeability through its unity with the Word. This seems to exclude Edwards's claim that these passages refer not to the pre-existence of the soul of Christ, but to its creation just prior to the incarnation.

While carefully distinguishing the two natures, one divine and one human, suggesting that John's Gospel was more concerned with the former and the other three Gospels with the latter, and insisting on the reality of the human in its temptation and sufferings and its genuine growth, even involving Jesus' lack of knowledge, Origen insists on their unity in what he is the first to dub "the God-man." Although he does allot some of Jesus' sayings to the human nature and others to the divine, nevertheless, because of the indissoluble unity of the God-man, he also develops the concept of the interchange of properties (*communicatio idiomatum*), which was to become a characteristic of Alexandrian christology ever after, appealing to the way that the whole of scripture refers to the divine nature in human terms and the human in divine terms. But he insists versus Celsus that the incarnation cannot have involved any change in the being of the divine Word, who remains the Word in his essential being, merely adapting himself to the character and capacity of the individual who receives him, raising him till eventually he or she can behold him in what Origen calls his primary form. Thus Origen allows the possibility of Jesus having various outward forms of appearance. Although this might seem perilously close to the Gnostic view of the heavenly Christ descending through the various planetary spheres in disguise, taking on an appearance appropriate to each one, Origen's version is profoundly incarnational and pedagogical: Christ as the perfect teacher adapts himself to the perspective, capability, and situation of the person whom he encounters.

More worryingly, if he admits Christ's two distinct natures and the genuineness of the human as a result of the incarnation, he does affirm that Jesus' mortal body and human soul, by virtue of its unity and commixture with the Word, has become divine, and thus that the quality of that mortal body was changed by divine providence to a heavenly and divine quality. However, the process of deification only really seems to begin with the resurrection, if prefigured by the Transfiguration. This brings us to Origen's view of salvation, which he very much sees in terms of Christ's life, death, and resurrection as the perfect pattern for ours. The Word is our teacher, law giver, and model, but in seeking to be true to scripture, Origen adds to this exemplary model the ideas of the defeat of the Devil and of the powers of darkness that threaten us, of ransom, and even of vicarious substitution or propitiatory sacrifice. Kelly (2006, 186) claims that, despite the apparent inconsistency and complexity of Origen's views on redemption, they can to some extent be harmonized; if the sacrifice theme seems not to fit, Origen accepted its basis in scripture, if not necessarily for the more elite Christian. Even his distinctive view of the resurrection and the superior spiritual resurrection body as a symbolic way of talking about the continuation of a seminal principle is, he would claim, supported by Paul in 1 Cor. 15.

Finally, his distinctive eschatology, governed by the principle that the end is always like the beginning, is dominated by the scriptural theme of *apokatastasis* (Acts 3:21), the restoration of all things to their original unity, developed again by appeal to Paul in 1 Cor. 15. As Trigg points out (1998, 31), the logic of his system suggests that all rational beings will return to their original unity with God, and this implies for Origen not only a process of purification after death but also the existence of worlds before and after this one and the possibility that even devils will be saved. Thus Origen's key themes of providence and free will supply the basis for his distinctive protology and eschatology, as also for the later doctrine of Purgatory.

Origen's theology and practice are all of a piece: his life and career reflect his search for knowledge of and union with God, revealed by grace, found by searching the Scriptures, the goal of all study and prayer. Thus underlying everything—his theology, his ascetic spirituality, his hermeneutics, his educational theory and practice—is the idea of spiritual progress, set against the background of opponents and critics, inside and outside the church, as he battles with literalists and heretics. Perhaps the most significant of the latter for Origen's whole theological approach and innovations were the Valentinians. Their grand theological scheme threatened the Catholic doctrines of God, Christ, and salvation, and offered a very attractive solution to the fundamental question of theodicy. Thus Origen's championing of providence,

grace, and free will, and his concept of spiritual progress can be seen to counter Valentinian dualism and determinism and their division of humanity into three fixed categories: spiritual ("saved by nature"), psychic (Catholics capable through effort of an intermediate level of salvation only), and material (damned by nature). For Origen the free will and choice of rational creatures explained the evil and diversity of a world created by a good and loving God, and salvation did not involve a fixed determinate status, but rather allowed progress through various stages, bodily, psychic, and spiritual.

Origen's speculative, experimental approach in the *Peri Archōn*, based squarely on scripture and the church's "rule of faith" and seeking to answer the many and various challenges he faced, while perfectly mainstream in his own time, nevertheless was later to spark fierce resistance and condemnation. His allegorical approach to scripture was criticized and his views about the eternity of creation, the pre-existence of souls, and the spiritual nature of the resurrection body were attacked at the beginning and end of the fourth century. Furthermore he was regarded as the spiritual ancestor of Arius and "Arianism." Then, as now, he split theological opinion in East and West. Some were profoundly influenced, such as Athanasius and the Cappadocians, and a significant branch of monks in Egypt led by Evagrius Ponticus (346–99 CE), as well as Westerners resident in the East like Jerome and Rufinus, who later fell out over Origen's orthodoxy. From being a keen partisan Jerome, under the influence of Epiphanius and his virulent campaign from 393 on, turned totally against Origen's theological views, if remaining profoundly influenced by his biblical interpretation, which had a lasting effect on the West. Rufinus, as we have seen, translated a considerable amount of Origen into Latin, tidying up passages of the *Peri Archōn* which he thought had been interpolated.

However, the official condemnations of Origen did not occur until the sixth century, prompted by criticism of Origenist monks in Palestine, followers of Evagrius (Crouzel, 1999). The emperor Justinian (527–65 CE) issued an edict in 543 against monks in Jerusalem spreading supposed views of Origen, mainly arising from the *Peri Archōn*. The nine anathemas condemn the pre-existence of souls as minds cooling and falling into bodies as a punishment; the pre-existence of the soul of Christ; the formation of Christ's body in Mary's womb and later union with the Word; the assimilation of the Word to the angels; resurrected bodies as spherical; the sun, moon, and stars as animate and rational; future crucifixions of Christ for the devils; the finite character of God's power in creating rational beings co-eternal with him; and the limited temporal punishment and future restitution of the wicked. Of those which do seem to correspond with Origen's views, what he had presented tentatively as a speculation and often contradicted elsewhere is set forth as a bald dogmatic statement. And as Crouzel points out (1999, 314–15), the doctrines condemned by the Fifth Ecumenical Council of 553 are those of the Origenist monks, rather than Origen himself, named last in a list of heretics in canon 11.

IV.   Significance

Origen stands alongside St Augustine as one of the greatest and most influential theologians of the early church who, despite official condemnations, had a profound effect on both East and West right across the spectrum of theology. He was first and foremost a student of the Bible, textual critic and biblical interpreter par excellence, pioneer of hermeneutics, profound preacher and homilist. Stalwart foe of challenging heretics like the Valentinians, he was the author of the first Catholic systematic theology, the *Peri Archōn*, laying down a most profound view of God, who can be known only by grace as he reveals himself. He provided the basis of the later orthodox doctrine of the Trinity set out in the Creed of Constantinople (381), presenting a view of Christ which, if ultimately judged unsatisfactory, did at least preserve both his divinity and full humanity, offering an attractive theodicy that combined a beneficent, gracious God with human freedom, with a universalist eschatological perspective which sees divine punishment as entirely remedial, and offered a basis for the future doctrine of Purgatory. He was a doughty defender of the role of reason in theology against fideists, able to utilize—and criticize—the highest insights of pagan learning while developing his own uniquely Christian philosophy, defending and demonstrating in his person the intellectual respectability and moral seriousness of Christianity against pagan sneers. With his dynamic understanding of the Christian life as a spiritual progress, he has profoundly influenced monasticism and spirituality, Eastern and Western. Not surprisingly, he has attracted significant defenders, such as Erasmus in the Reformation era and in recent times French Roman Catholics such as de Henri de Lubac, Jean Daniélou, and Henri Crouzel, and English Anglicans like Henry Chadwick and Richard Hanson.

References

Butterworth, G. W. [1936] 1966. *Origen: On First Principles*. New York: Harper & Row.

Chadwick, Henry. 1953, 1965. *Origen: Contra Celsum*. Cambridge: Cambridge University Press.

Crouzel, Henri. 1999. "Les condamnations subies par Origène et sa doctrine." In *Origeniana Septima*, ed. W. A. Bienert and U. Kühneweg. Leeuven: University Press/Peeters, pp. 311–15.

Edwards, Mark J. 2002. *Origen against Plato*. Aldershot, UK: Ashgate.

Kelly, J. N. D. 2006. *Early Christian Doctrines*, 5th ed. London: Continuum.

Trigg, Joseph W. 1998. *Origen* (The Early Church Fathers). London and New York: Routledge.

The Apostle Paul

Efrain Agosto

I. The Apostle Paul in His Immediate Context

Besides Jesus of Nazareth, the Apostle Paul is no doubt the single most important figure in the foundations of earliest Christianity. In fact, some historians and theologians of earliest Christianity suggest that Paul, rightly or wrongly, created Christianity above and beyond what Jesus himself intended it to be (Bultmann, 1952). Bultmann, for one, taught how Paul took the religion of Jewish piety and spiritual renewal in the life and ministry of Jesus, and turned it into a call for transformation in a decisive turn toward Jesus as the Christ in the life of the individual believer. This famous anthropological perspective of Pauline theology did not proceed without challenge, even by Bultmann's own students (Käsemann, 1969), but the disconnect between the Jesus of history and the Christ of faith in the thought of the Apostle Paul was firmly established. The fact that Paul himself rarely cites a Jesus saying or writes much about the life and times of Jesus of Nazareth, but rather concentrates on his death, resurrection, and soon return (Gr. *parousia*), is evidence enough that Paul moved the Jesus movement within two decades of its founding away from concerns about the historical Jesus to his theological meaning. Decades later, the gospel writers revived concern for the living, breathing Jesus and his teachings and sayings in their original context. By then,

however, even these sayings, stories, and teachings had been affected by four decades of theologizing by the earliest believers in the "oral tradition," including Paul.

However, who was Paul, and why was he so influential, not only in today's Christian theological reflection, but in the earliest years of the movement? Much has been made of Paul's multiculturalism. He was a product of "three worlds"—Judaism, Hellenism, and the Roman imperial order (Wallace and Williams, 1998). Paul himself writes about how he excelled in the Judaism of his day, particularly as a Pharisee, perhaps the most law-observant Jewish group in the first century (cf. Phil. 3:4–6; Gal. 1:13–14). Yet, as a Hellenistic Jew, one raised not in Palestine but in the Greco-Roman Jewish Diaspora—specifically in the Greek city of Tarsus in the Roman province of Cilicia—Paul sought to interpret the Christian message, founded in the towns and villages of the Roman-controlled Jewish state by a wandering charismatic preacher and healer, a carpenter by trade, Jesus of Nazareth, for a wider community of Jews who spoke Greek, not Aramaic like Jesus and his first followers, and who lived in the cities of the Roman empire, not the villages of one of the empire's smaller, but most volatile territories. Given this wider cultural and linguistic trajectory, which began with Jews but soon included Gentiles and before long a theology for why Gentiles should be included, it is not surprising

The Student's Companion to the Theologians, First Edition. Edited by Ian S. Markham.
© 2013 Blackwell Publishing Ltd. Published 2013 by Blackwell Publishing Ltd.

that Paul indeed took the Christian message, which he called "the truth of the Gospel" (Gal. 2:14), beyond Jerusalem, where the movement had its start with the immediate first followers of Jesus, all the way to Rome, according to the record of Paul's travels in the Book of Acts and Paul's own intentions (Rom. 15:23–29), and every major Roman imperial urban center in between.

Moreover, Paul accomplished this mission in a relatively short time. Most chronologies date Paul's "conversion" around 34 CE, dating backwards from the beginning of his independent missionary enterprise in Asia Minor and Greece in the early 50s CE (Jewett, 1979; see Gal. 1:13–2:10), during which time he founded churches in Thessalonica, Philippi, Corinth, and Ephesus, among others. Each of these represents major urban centers of the Roman Empire. Paul's missionary strategy and, therefore, in part his theology, is based on establishing gospel-believing communities in these urban centers and letting his converts spread the word about Jesus Christ to outlying communities beyond these imperial cities (Meeks, 1983). By the late 50s CE Paul is writing to the Roman churches that he plans to visit them in order that they might support his next missionary journey—to Roman territories in Spain (Rom. 15:23–29). He did not establish churches in Rome and did not expect to stay long with them, but rather use them, as he did with churches in Antioch and later Ephesus, as a launching pad for ministry in Spain. This explains, in part, why Paul writes such an extensive explanation of his gospel message in his Letter to the Romans. These are churches that do not know him, but from which he needs financial support, and thus he will explain at length the nature of his preaching, that is, his theology. However, Romans is not the only letter that contains statements of Pauline theology. His letters, to which we will turn next, are the sources for understanding Paul's theology, although none of them, not even Romans, is a complete compendium of Paul's thought in the way a modern theology is often constructed. In the end, Paul did not get to Rome as a free man, as he had planned, but rather, according to Acts, as a prisoner of the Empire. Extra-biblical tradition indicates that Paul was executed sometime in the mid-60s in Rome, perhaps under the rule of the Emperor Nero.

II.   The Letters of Paul as Sources for Understanding His Theology

In the New Testament there are 13 letters ascribed to the Apostle Paul, written in the epistolary style and structure of the day to congregations founded by Paul in order to solve local pastoral issues. Paul uses theological themes and motifs, informed by the Jewish Scriptures, which were available to him in Greek translation (the "Septuagint" or LXX, which dated from c.300 BCE), in order to address behavioral, ethical, and theological issues confronting his congregations. However, some of these letters are considered by scholars to be written in the Apostle's name after his death. In fact, some of the theological themes, or the language the author uses to describe them, do shift in these so-called "Deutero-Pauline" or "Paulinist" letters. They are based on theological themes and approaches introduced by Paul in his earlier letters, but now filtered through a decade or two (or more) of church development, at a time after the Apostle's life and ministry. His immediate followers and spiritual descendents continued the ministerial and theological trajectories that Paul began. These Deutero-Pauline letters include 2 Thessalonians, Colossians, Ephesians, 1–2 Timothy, and Titus. Many scholars read these letters as the "interpreters of Paul" (Roetzel, 1998) and thus prefer that discussion about Pauline theology should be limited to the uncontested letters of Paul, which include Romans, 1 and 2 Corinthians, Galatians, Philippians, and Philemon.

Yet, these letters, like the Deutero-Paulines, must not be understood as compendia of Pauline thought. In essence, they are, in the language of the influential Pauline scholar J. Christiaan Beker (1980), "contingent" documents written in the heat of pastoral crises to which Paul must reply with every resource available to him, including knowledge of the social context to which he is writing, knowledge of the rhetorical devices that would best help him construct a persuasive argument, and the theological convictions that drive his missionary zeal on behalf of the gospel of Jesus Christ. Thus each letter, while having some "coherent" (Beker), basic understanding of the gospel teaching that Paul believes in and teaches, focuses that teaching in a way that makes sense for the particular situation and set of issues about which he is writing to that particular congregation at that particular moment in time.

Thus, for example, in his congregation at Thessalonica, a newly established community suffers from persecution at the hands of their fellow compatriots because of their newfound faith in Christ (1 Thess. 1:2–10). Since several of their members have died, quite possibly because of such persecution, and their surviving fellow believers and family members worry about their future—since Christ had yet to return as Paul promised that he would—Paul must introduce them to his teaching about the bodily resurrection of the dead in Christ (1 Thess. 4:13–18) as a way of assuaging their fears. Thus Paul employs the theological theme of eschatology—what God will do in the final days—in order to "comfort" a grieving community (4:18; 5:11).

Theology in the service of pastoral care is an ongoing modus operandi of the Apostle Paul. J. C. Beker argues that the eschatological "triumph of God" (1980, 1990) lies at the heart of Paul's "coherent" theology. However, other scholars put their emphasis on other Pauline themes in their search for the "center" of Paul's theology (Porter, 2006).

For example, in the Corinthian correspondence, especially 1 Corinthians, Paul puts an emphasis on the cross of Christ as the fundamental teaching of the gospel he preaches: "When I came to you, brothers and sisters, I did not come proclaiming the mystery of God to you in lofty words or wisdom. For I decided to know nothing among you except Jesus Christ and him crucified" (1 Cor. 2:1–2, in the NRSV, which will be the translation used in the citations throughout this essay). Why this focus on the cross of Christ in 1 Corinthians? Many leaders in the Corinthian community were using the gospel message and the gospel community as a source of pride and self-enhancement to the detriment of less well-to-do believers (1:26–31). Paul needs to remind them that the source of their faith is not a glorified Lord, like an emperor, but rather a crucified Christ, who in fact was executed on an imperial cross. Believers should live their lives in "cruciformity" (Gorman, 2001), modeled after the cross of Christ, not in a spirit of triumphalism. Thus Paul will often cite the hardships he has confronted in his ministry (Fitzgerald, 1988) to

demonstrate that the nature of his leadership conforms to the servant model of Jesus and not the expectations of imperial power (Agosto, 2005). A theology of the cross is fundamental to such Pauline teaching.

If "cross theology" (a crucified Lord) and eschatology (a "returning Lord") are fundamental to Paul's "pastoral" theology with his congregations, many scholars would argue that Martin Luther's Reformation focus on Paul's teaching of "justification by faith" must also stand at the core of Pauline theology. In fact, this language of "justification" is limited essentially to two of Paul's letters, Romans and Galatians. In Galatians, Paul defends the nature of his gospel preaching to a majority non-Jewish audience—Gentiles—as a so-called "law-free gospel." Gentiles should not be expected to fulfill circumcision rites and dietary laws in order to become members of the family of God, because, Paul writes, "We ourselves are Jews by birth and not Gentile sinners [invoking the language of his opponents]; yet we know that a person is justified not by the works of the law, but through faith in Jesus Christ. And we have come to believe in Christ Jesus so that we might be justified by faith in Christ and not by doing the works of the law, because no one will be justified by the works of the law" (Gal. 2:15–16). In Romans, after a long argument showing the need for divine intervention to eradicate the universal sin of all humans since the law only demonstrates the reality of sin (1:18–3:20), Paul concludes that "justification"—declaration of righteous status before a righteous God—can only take place by means of the faithfulness of Christ:

> But now, apart from law, the righteousness of God has been disclosed, and is attested by the law and the prophets, the righteousness of God through faith in Jesus Christ for all who believe. For there is no distinction since all have sinned and fall short of the glory of God, they are now justified by his grace as a gift, through the redemption that is in Christ Jesus. (Rom. 3:21–24)

Later, Paul details all the benefits one receives once justified in Christ, including peace with God, access to God's grace, and reconciliation (Rom. 5:1–11). These texts and others in Romans and Galatians convinced Luther that he needed to reform his theology, and the rest is religious history.

There can be no doubt that "justification by faith" is a fundamental teaching in Paul's theology. There is some question, however, in Pauline theological scholarship as to whether the faith that justifies belongs to Christ or to the believer. The debate rests with the interpretation of the Greek phrase *pistis Christou*—"faith of or in Christ"—meaning the faith that Christ exhibited (Hays, 1983) or the believer's faith in Christ (Dunn, 1990, in response to Hays). Traditionally, ever since Luther, the latter has been the understanding—believers must put their faith in Christ in order to be justified. However, if one were to follow Reformation logic, this reliance on the faith of the believer to acquire justification sounds like another dimension of human effort to achieve the righteousness of God, which Paul seems to reject: "no one will be justified by the works of the law" (Gal. 2:16b). Of course, the question arises about what Paul means by "the law." Does he simply mean the law given to Moses to which all Jews were expected to adhere, or does he mean any human effort to please God? If the latter, broader understanding is the case, which seems to be supported by Paul's discussion of Jewish law and universal human conscience, whether Jew or Gentile, in Rom. 2:1–29, then it stands to reason that it is the faithfulness of Christ in obeying God even to the point of death that secures justification for all those who would put their trust in God through Christ. Thus, the cross of Christ makes possible justification—an act of divine declaration making one righteous before God (Harrell, 2006, 75–77).

Nonetheless, the fact remains that "justification"—a term from the world of Roman jurisprudence—is a metaphor for Paul's theologizing about what God has done in Christ that has particular relevance for the conflictive situations in both the Galatian and Roman churches. In Galatians, a Gentile Christian majority has their faith questioned by a Jewish Christian minority and thus the language of law and justification helps Paul correct the undermining of Gentile faith by Jewish Christian believers. Faithfulness to God on the part of Christ has made possible a declaration of justice for all persons—Jew and Gentile—and this has been in the works by God ever since Abraham was promised to be a blessing for "all the nations" (Gal. 3:6–9). In contrast, in Romans, a Gentile Christian majority is undermining the role of the people Israel in God's salvation plan. Thus Paul once again invokes the language of justification, this time to show that all persons, Jew and Gentile, need divine intervention because of sin, but at the same time God's plan of salvation has been carried out through the people Israel, both in terms of the Hebrew prophets who foretold a "day of the Lord" and in terms of the Jewish Messiah whom God sent to the whole world, Jesus, "the Christ." Repeatedly in Romans, Paul writes that justification has been made available "to the Jew first and also to the Greek." This chronological order of justification sets the Roman Gentile Christians straight as to the respect due to the people Israel. For the Gentile believers have been "grafted in" to the "olive tree" that is Israel (Rom. 11:17–24). In the same way, they could be "cut off" from the olive tree if they are not careful about undermining the faith and justification—righteous declaration—of their Jewish brothers and sisters.

Thus once again, a major theological motif in at least two of Paul's letters—justification by faith—rather than standing alone as an abstract theological concept becomes a source of pastoral theology for communities in conflict. In fact, Elsa Tamez (1993) argues that justification is one metaphor among several that Paul utilizes to exercise theological reflection with his communities in moments of conflict and division in ways that will bring about "the amnesty of grace." In 2 Corinthians, the theme of reconciliation echoes this "justification"—the righting of wrongs between two parties. After a series of missteps that have led to a breaking of the relationship between apostle and congregation, Paul sends an envoy, his close associate Titus, to carry out a ministry of reconciliation—a balancing of relationship between two parties, as two sides of an accounting ledger are reconciled to each other in the world of commerce. Titus is successful (2 Cor. 2:12–13; 7:5–16) and Paul and the Corinthians are reconciled. Thus Paul describes what God has done in Christ for the world in terms of reconciliation: "All this is from God, who reconciled us to himself through Christ, and has given us the ministry of reconciliation; that is, in Christ God was reconciling the world to himself, not counting their trespasses against them, and entrusting the message of reconciliation to us" (2 Cor. 5:18–19). Not only is this passage a description of the gospel message Paul preached and taught—God was reconciling the world to Godself through Christ—but it echoes the language of justification—declaring right, through Christ, that which was in wrong relationship to God. The passage also bears testimony to Paul's missionary theology as well—having been reconciled with God, believers should go out to spread a message of reconciliation to others. Once again, a theological theme in Paul has both its coherent essence—divine intervention on behalf of humanity through Christ—and its contingent setting: Having been reconciled with the Corinthians, Paul uses the motif to promote the gospel message and do pastoral theology with his community.

III. Overall Theological Issues in Paul

Having surveyed some of the theological themes that dominate the discourse in several of Paul's letters in a way that shows that his theology is couched in terms of pastoral outreach and appropriate, relevant metaphoric language, what other overall themes has scholarship discussed with regard to Paul and his theology? Certainly, christology in terms of the cross of Christ and his relationship to God dominates the theological discourse about Paul and his teaching about the meaning of Christ. While no firm consensus has been reached about whether Paul believed that Christ was God, certainly by the time we read the letters of Paul's followers in Colossians and Ephesians, we are closer to a "high Christology," in which the resurrected Lord, whom Paul extols in his uncontested letters, such as in Phil. 2:5–11, the famous Christ hymn, has become almost equal with God (Harrell, 2006, 63–67).

Paul's connection to Judaism and the law is another major theme that transcends his letters. As noted, Paul has a harsh word to say about the role of the law in the life of the believer's relationship to God—"For all who rely on the works of the law are under a curse" (Gal. 3:10). Yet in Romans, Paul has a positive word to say about the law's role in showing us our sinfulness: "What then should we say? That the law is sin? By no means! Yet, if it had not been for the law I would not have known sin" (Rom. 7:7a). Later in the chapter, he concludes, "So the law is holy, and the commandment

is holy and just and good" (7:12). Sin is the problem, a point he wants to make most explicit in his letter to the Roman churches. Thus, E. P. Sanders (1977), for one, argued that we need to be careful about suggesting that Paul was trying to undermine the Judaism of his day as a legalistic, self-righteous religion. Rather, for Paul, Judaism's "covenantal nomism"—religion of the law in covenant with God and God's promises—always meant to include non-Jews in the new community that God was now forming in Christ. This theological conviction motivated Paul's polemic with some of his Jewish Christian opponents. An expanded covenantal theology was what drove Paul's argumentation and theologizing in his letters.

What about ethics? What drives Paul in his ethical exhortations in his letters? (Harrell, 2006, 80–3). J. Paul Sampley writes that Paul had an "interim ethic" (Sampley, 1991). Paul exhorts his communities toward holiness, justice, and being "children of light" instead of "children of darkness" (1 Thess. 5:1–11), in light of the soon return of Christ, the second epoch-changing event in history after the first coming of Christ. Thus Sampley posits "walking between the times" as the fundamental image for Pauline ethics. However, how is one empowered to do the right thing in anticipation of the return of the Lord? Here Paul's theology of the Spirit, "God's empowering presence" (Fee, 1994), comes into play in a major way throughout his letters. Invariably the presence of God through God's Spirit helps the believer live an ethical, holy life: "Live by the Spirit and do not gratify the desires of the flesh … Now the works of the flesh are obvious: fornication, impurity, licentiousness, [etc.] … By contrast, the fruit of the Spirit is love, joy, peace, patience, kindness, [etc.]" (Gal. 5:16, 19, 22).

IV. Conclusion

In short, to invoke theological themes in modern terms, Paul's theological thought includes reflection on christology (the nature and role of Christ, including reflection on his death and resurrection), Soteriology (including images of salvation, justification, and reconciliation), Pneumatology (the role of the Spirit in the believer's life between the first and second coming of Christ), Ethics ("walking" in holiness "between the times"), and Eschatology (the return of Christ and the attending apocalyptic expectation and judgment), among others. However, the critical point to emphasize in understanding Pauline theology is that "Paul's thinking emerged through conversations with his congregations" (Roetzel, 1999, 93). It is not accurate to discuss Pauline theology "as a fixed entity or as a systematic achievement" (Roetzel, 1999, 93). Rather, Paul composed letters, not fixed theology, in response to the pastoral needs of his congregations. He "interpreted and reinterpreted the gospel story for settings as diverse as life itself" (Roetzel, 1999, 94).

Nonetheless, Paul did have some fundamental "presuppositions" to guide his congregational theology (see Roetzel, 1999, 94–97). The God he served was the God of Israel, whose covenant with Israel was now extended to the entire world through participation in Christ. In Christ, a community of believers is established wherever Christ is proclaimed and believed in; Paul called these *ekklesiae*— "assemblies"—and he spent an entire career forming these communities, nurturing them, exhorting them, and correcting them through letters, envoys, and visits. It was in that missionary activity that he forged a "praxis theology"—what Roetzel (1999, 133–4) calls "theologizing"—in anticipation of the soon return of Christ. Thus, J. Christiaan Beker was right to describe Paul's eschatology in terms of the ultimate "triumph of God"; although perhaps not the only "essence of Paul's thought" (Beker, 1990), it was certainly at the core.

References

Agosto, Efrain. 2005. *Servant Leadership: Jesus and Paul.* St. Louis: Chalice Press.

Beker, J. Christiaan. 1980. *Paul the Apostle: The Triumph of God in Life and Thought.* Philadelphia: Fortress Press.

Beker, J. Christiaan. 1990. *The Triumph of God: The Essence of Paul's Thought.* Minneapolis: Fortress Press.

Bultmann, Rudolph. 1952. *Theology of the New Testament,* vol. 1. London: SCM.

Dunn, James D. G. 1990. *Jesus, Paul and the Law.* London: SPCK.

Fee, Gordon D. 1994. *God's Empowering Presence: The Holy Spirit in the Letters of Paul.* Peabody, MA: Hendrickson Publishers.

Fitzgerald, John T. 1988. *Cracks in an Earthen Vessel: An Examination of the Catalogue of Hardships in the Corinthian Correspondence.* Society of Biblical Literature Dissertation Series. Atlanta, GA: Scholars Press.

Gorman, Michael J. 2001. *Cruciformity: Paul's Narrative Spirituality of the Cross.* Grand Rapids, MI: Eerdmans.

Harrell, David G. 2006. *An Introduction to the Study of Paul,* 2nd ed. London and New York: T&T Clark.

Hays, Richard B. 1983. *The Faith of Jesus Christ: An Investigation of the Narrative Substructure of Galatians 3: 1–4:11.* Chico: Scholars Press.

Jewett, Robert A. 1979. *A Chronology of Paul's Life.* Philadelphia: Fortress Press.

Käsemann, Ernst. 1969. *Paulinische Perspektiven.* Tübingen, Germany: Mohr.

Meeks, Wayne. 1983. *First Urban Christians: The Social World of the Apostle Paul.* New Haven, CT: Yale University Press.

Porter, Stanley E. 2006. "Is There a Center to Paul's Theology? An Introduction to the Study of Paul and His Theology." In *Paul and His Theology,* ed. Stanley E. Porter. Leiden/Boston: Brill, pp. 1–19.

Roetzel, Calvin. 1998. *The Letters of Paul: Conversations in Context.,* 4th ed. Louisville, KY: Westminster John Knox Press.

Roetzel, Calvin J. 1999. *Paul: The Man and the Myth.* Minneapolis: Fortress Press.

Sampley, J. Paul. 1991. *Walking Between the Times: Paul's Moral Reasoning.* Minneapolis: Fortress Press.

Sampley, J. Paul and Krodel, Gerhard, eds. 1993. *The Deutero-Pauline Letters: Ephesians, Colossians, 2 Thessalonians, 1–2 Timothy, Titus.* Minneapolis: Fortress Press.

Sanders, E. P. 1977. *Paul and Palestinian Judaism: A Comparison of Patterns of Religion.* Philadelphia: Fortress Press.

Tamez, Elsa. 1993. *The Amnesty of Grace: Justification by Faith from a Latin American Perspective.* Nashville, TN: Abingdon Press.

Wallace, Richard and Williams, Wynne. 1998. *The Three Worlds of Paul of Tarsus.* New York: Routledge Press.

The Synoptic Evangelists: Mark, Matthew, and Luke

Leslie Houlden

I. Introduction

It may seem odd to readers of this book to include the three Synoptic Evangelists in a companion of theologians. Yes, of course their Gospels include pieces of theology (think, for example, of Matthew 11:25–30, or of the titles they use for Jesus), but from a conventional point of view, their books do not seem to be works of theology. They are narratives, not pieces of abstract thought. They tell what Jesus did and taught. Though these three Gospels overlap and, we believe, the last two both used Mark as their basic source, they all have their underlying format and concern in common: to tell the story of Jesus, his life, death, and resurrection. Of course they differ in the way they tell that story, but is that not because they choose to make use of different items of information, one knowing what the others do not or selecting what they choose to ignore?

Two modifications should be made to this picture. First, it assumes that theology can only be presented in abstract terms. True, that is of course how it has chiefly been done over most of the Christian period, though there have also been poetry, music, painting, and sculpture as ways of presenting theological ideas and theological sensibility. But, as the last sentence indicates, the broadly philosophical framework which has been the dominant medium for theology since the second century does not have the field wholly to itself.

Let us say that theology can also be stated verbally in narrative form: story can convey ideas and form minds. Second, the conventional way in which the Gospels have been taken has assumed that their writers were little more than channels by which Jesus' words and deeds came into written form. It did not strike people that their writers might have had minds of their own, ideas they wished to propagate, pictures they wished to paint: in other words, they might have been theological thinkers with something to say, using narrative as their natural medium. If that were so, then the selection of material and the way it was arranged and expressed would bear the stamp of a creative mind in each case, and the differences between the Gospels should be understood as the result of the different minds responsible for them. Of course the Gospel of John has always functioned as an exception to the picture just expounded: here one had Jesus himself speaking theologically, being his own theologian, one might say; and the evangelist filled out his words in recognizable theological terms, abstract in style. In John, then, the stories from Jesus' life seemed to be mere vehicles carrying the theology—which was what chiefly mattered. In reality, much of John's theological repute and usefulness in theology came from the fact that his terminology happened to coincide sufficiently with the idioms that early Christian thinkers found congenial (even if not always in the same key as that of the writer of the Fourth Gospel itself!).

The Student's Companion to the Theologians, First Edition. Edited by Ian S. Markham.
© 2013 Blackwell Publishing Ltd. Published 2013 by Blackwell Publishing Ltd.

Of course the dominant common use of the Gospels still treats them as if they were direct reproductions of Jesus' words and deeds, with the four evangelists as mere conduits. People say: "Jesus said …" or "Remember when Jesus fed the five thousand …," as if there had been tape recordings or televized pictures of his life. No, it cannot be so. Between the doing of Jesus' deeds and the speaking of his words there was a process lasting some 40 to 60 years before the writing down took place. During that time, words and picturings passed from mind to mind, each contributing somewhat to what was heard and understood. (And of course we modern readers, bringing our minds to bear, also contribute, reading and seeing as we can read and see.) All reading is therefore a process of development and tradition, however "fixed" the medium may seem to be, there printed on the page. And at the start of the process visible to us comes the mind of the writer—first of Mark, then of Matthew, Luke, and John. Visibly, Matthew and Luke, using Mark, modify and amplify what he wrote, each in terms of his own way of "seeing" and "believing in" Jesus: each painting his own portrait.

While it is true that this way of "reading" the Gospels remains rare in their ordinary use, in churches as elsewhere, it is necessary—and highly creative—for the reader or hearer. What is more, it does justice to the writer concerned: you might say that the least tribute we can rightly pay him is to try and "hear" his voice, understand his meaning, see his picture.

This way of reading the Gospels has come to be seen as desirable only gradually over the last century or so. That Mark came first among the Gospels was itself only propounded less than a couple of centuries ago and even then only gradually accepted as the truth of the matter. It is less than half a century since books have come to be written that set out to show us "the mind" of Mark, Matthew, and Luke; so that we can see with their eyes and (at long last, one might say!) grasp what they sought to communicate.

In the articles that follow, we shall attempt to give a brief account of what we may think to be the "gospel"—the saving message concerning Jesus—as our three writers meant us to see and hear it. Of course we shall be doing it in modern terms, far from their own, but at least we shall be making the attempt. And of course we cannot be sure we are "getting

them right," for we ourselves contribute to our own "seeing"; and moreover it is impossible for us to be sure we have a true picture of the circumstances for which they wrote and in which they were first read. One thing we can be fairly sure of is this: that they were written for oral performance. Nobody sat and read them as we read books, silently and individually. They were written to be read to a group. What is more, we can be pretty sure they were written to be read to Christian groups or congregations, perhaps relatively small in size. It may be the case, odd as it seems to us, that they were written to be read out as a whole, at a sitting—at least that is quite likely to be so for Mark, the shortest of the three. That means that connections of word and theme, lost to the modern hearer or reader, were obvious and illuminating— they worked their magic, conveyed their sense. Modern readers are "deaf" to such connections, not only because we hear or read only brief sections, but also because we do not have the training to "hear" as pre-literate communities often could. And even our education does not help: in the period of the composition of the Gospels, rhetoric, the art of persuasive speech, was a staple of such education as was available, even from early stages—and people picked up ways of "hearing" that are quite lost now. So we have to read alertly, if we are to get the point of what is being given to us.

II.   Mark

We begin by making sure we know exactly what we are discussing. The Gospel of Mark is a brief book about whose origins we know nothing reliable. There were later legends about them but none of them carry conviction. However, we can make a few intelligent guesses. This writing will have come to birth in an early Christian community somewhere in the Roman Empire, perhaps in Rome itself but more likely in the Eastern regions—let us say in Syria. It is probable that it was a community with Jewish elements but also Gentiles who had been admitted on fairly liberal terms, of the sort favored and established by Paul the Apostle. The evidence is that Mark shows Jesus as being free-minded about the observance of the sabbath (2:23–3:6) and about food restrictions (7:19), both central to orthodox Jewish life. Also, Mark is the only gospel writer to make significant use of the word "gospel" (or good news) to mean the Christian message, that which Jesus preached and his followers now continue. It is a word otherwise rare in early Christian writings—except that it is common in Paul's letters: it looks as if it was brought in by him to sum up what Jesus stood for. True, when Mark used it on the lips of Jesus, its central content, the death and resurrection of Jesus, still lay ahead. Still, it is interesting that Mark makes use of it so frequently as his summing-up word for the truth that is now preached.

We do not know what sources Mark may have had at his disposal, but we may assume that he had a stock of stories about Jesus and some elements of his teaching. But sources only take one so far. The question is what is then to be done with them and how might they be amplified, arranged, and presented. Here the mind of Mark himself, of course formed also by the needs of those Christians around him, comes into play. It is that mind that is our chief concern—rather than, for example, whether this or that story about Jesus is historically accurate in setting and content, in a modern historian's terms, or not precisely as it stands: for that we have no independent evidence at all and may as well fix our minds on what we do have, i.e., this book of Mark. It is brief, and a good exercise is to sit down and read it as a whole, to see what kind of impression it makes. But there is just one more preliminary point: older translations and editions of the Bible show Mark's Gospel ending at 16:20. Newer ones are more cautious and bring it to an end at 16:8. This is almost certainly correct; but it creates a difficulty—that which led to the adding, as early as the second century, of the other twelve verses. It is the mind that made this change that is our chief concern—rather than, for example, this or that story or theory about the production of those longer endings in the second century. The problem created by the original ending, at v.8, was that it left matters in much too enigmatic a state and there was a crying need to give us a clear and positive ending: Jesus has been raised, we are told in the words of a mysterious young man to three women at the tomb, but Jesus makes no appearance to back up the message (such as we have in the other Gospels) and the women are said to depart in silence and terror. It is, we are likely to feel, a very unsatisfying conclusion. But perhaps that is exactly what Mark meant for us—and it points us to aspects of his outlook that are at first sight both uncongenial and hard to understand.

This difficulty gets worse! For if we read the book as a whole, its dominant impression may well be that Jesus' career is firmly directed to his ignominious death and is in any case mysterious, hard to grasp the sense of. Neither of these features fits well with his purpose being to bring "good news" from God or with Christian preaching as ecstatically cheerful. He preaches the message of the "kingdom" or rule of God, but, as chapter 13 indicates, at his death it remains in the future by strictly temporal criteria—and to the naked eye it is in ruins. So the message seems to be deeply serious and challenging—and permanently so, despite the hint of new life right at the end: "he goes before you to Galilee; there you will see him." It is as if this promise is not meant to obliterate from our minds the ghastly horror of his life as directed to his death. And we should note that that death, which has the lion's share of the space in this little book, is put before our eyes long before it actually comes on the scene directly: see 3:6, for example (as well as direct prophecies by Jesus, e.g., 8:31). See also perhaps the addition to the quote from Psalm 2:7 ("Thou art my Son") in the baptism story, 1:11, of the word "beloved." Mark writes for a scripturally (i.e., Old Testament) literate audience, and they are to recognize here the use of that word in the Greek version of the searing and well-known story in Genesis 22 of the near-sacrifice of Abraham's only and late-born son, Isaac, the fragile thread by which God's saving purpose hangs. Jesus is just such a one. Everything hangs upon his death for God. Yet even that, when it comes, is made hard for us: "My God, my God, why hast thou forsaken me?," cries Jesus from the cross (15:34): yet still his death evokes the faith of the centurion, his executioner, first fruits of the mission to Gentiles that was soon to come. However hard it may seem, it is Jesus' death that is productive of faith and nothing must distract our attention from it. It is not surprising that some modern writers feel that Mark is just the Gospel for our turbulent and difficult times, when faith in God is produced cheaply by some Christians, while many people find it beyond credibility. It seems that Mark stared the issue in the face.

There is another strange impression that a reading of Mark may make upon us, and it is not wholly out of tune with the emphasis on Jesus' death that we have been discussing. If you identify the groups of people who appear through the course of the book, it seems that they are all either opponents of Jesus or else ambiguous and fragile in their attachment to him. This is obviously so with the Pharisees and scribes and other Jewish groups; their opposition appears first in 2:1–12, puts Jesus' death on the agenda as early as 3:6, and continues to the end. It is pretty solidly so too with Jesus' family. We have no trace of Mary, mother of Jesus, as an example and beacon for Christians here, except perhaps (and still ambiguously) in the final scenes (15:40, 47; 16:1), where she may be, allusively indeed, referred to—if you compare the list of Mary's sons with that in 6:3. And in the direct appearances of the family, they reject Jesus or treat him poorly: 3:21–22, 31–35; 6:1–6. No hint of Christmas devotion and warmth in this book! This may of course point to the effects of the difficulties in the early church, amply attested in Paul's career (see Galatians 1–2), between the old guard of Jesus' family in charge of the church at Jerusalem and the Gentile Christian communities developed by Paul's mission. Whether it reflects historical reality in Jesus' life is less clear, though the prominence of James, the brother of Jesus, in that early period of the church speaks against it. Perhaps this feature of Mark is indeed what we would call literary, but might better be called theological—part of a depiction of Jesus' lone confronting of human sin on all sides: in face of that, he stands alone as all forces range against him.

Usually enigmatic, then, is the depiction of Jesus' disciples. They are indeed called and respond with alacrity (1:16–20; 3:13–18; 6:7–12). But their comprehension and fidelity remain deeply flawed. Peter's confession in 8:29 immediately turns sour and is shown even to be diabolical as he refuses to accept the core of Jesus' calling (8:31–33). See also 8:14–21. The depth of their failure comes in the crisis of the passion, as the intimacy of the Last Supper is followed immediately by the treachery of Judas, the abandonment of Jesus by all (14:50), and the denials by Peter. In other words, these are pupils (disciples) who fail to learn, followers who give up. All the same there is at the end a clear chink of light: "go tell his disciples and Peter that he goes before you to Galilee; there you will see him." As restoration is promised, we note that there is no hint here that Judas is excluded. Is it not pure Pauline theology: that Jesus comes to save all sinners by his sacrificial death, with none excluded? We are saved by no achievement of our own, but only by God's gift.

By contrast with this painting of the big groups as fallible, some to the point of treachery, the small characters, who appear only once, are, without exception, on the right side—they are the successes of the kingdom of God, samples of the future bliss. We think of those healed, those fed, those raised from death, the children embraced; and chiefly perhaps the woman who anoints Jesus on the eve of his suffering, 14:3–9, who is praised beyond all. Yet there is mercy: the virtuous man who still cannot take Jesus' command to renounce his wealth, is alone said to receive Jesus' love (10:17–22).

Mark's theology tells us of a God, made present in Jesus, who is above all out for our restoration, but who will dispel all our false loves and prides, and even go to death to banish them. And all the same, we can be saved, but always by the skin of our teeth. Such is the timely theology of Mark. Doubtless his way of telling his stories and picturing Jesus owes much to his doctrine and to his arranging of his material. But if Jesus were not in truth as radical and outrageous as Mark tells us he was, is he likely to have been done to death? Doubtless, other views about Jesus' emphases and teachings were possible right from the start: any leader of this kind is seen through all sorts of different eyes, now as then, and people partly see in those they follow reflections of their own prejudices and preferences. In that sense, we must choose among the interpreters who are the only links we have. Mark had the first go: what of those who received him and then made their own contributions?

III.   Matthew

If you believe that Matthew used the Gospel of Mark and then wrote his longer book, adding much new material, the first question that arises is, why would he do such a thing? The most obvious answer is that he knew other things about Jesus and wanted to amplify

Mark's undeniably brief account. No doubt this would be for the use of his church, which presumably was accustomed to Mark but could profit from a greater range of material for its edification and for the good of its Christian life.

A reading of Matthew suggests that though this is indeed along the right lines, it does not tell all. We soon realize that Matthew was a different kind of person from Mark. In the first place, he was plainly a man steeped in the Jewish Scriptures and skilled in the techniques of their interpretation, as practiced among Jews in his day. It is reasonable to suppose that the addition of the words about a "scribe instructed for the kingdom of heaven," part of what he added to Mark's chapter of parables (4), is his own signature or self-description—a proud definition of his sense of his own particular role as a scribe dedicated now to the cause of Jesus—of the kingdom of heaven (13:52). Certainly he is careful to include scriptural passages at every turn, giving them a new interpretation in the light of Jesus, who he was and what he did. So we have a concentration of passages brought into service to make us see who exactly Jesus was: see chapters 1 to 2. Then at various points in the Gospel, we have a passage to back up, even validate, every aspect of Jesus' activity: for example, his teaching in parables (13:35), his healings (8:17), and his failure to win more support (13:14–15). In other words, Jesus' whole life and work is in fulfillment of scripture, just as he is, in his own person, accredited by his (surely far from unique!) descent from the line of Abraham and David (1:1–17)— a passage rarely attractive to modern readers, but vital to Matthew, part of his manifesto for Jesus, validating his messianic role. That is all central to Matthew's discipleship.

It is also central to Matthew's understanding of Jesus that he taught no straying from the observance of the law that was at the heart of Jewish faith and practice. In this he was, as we have seen, at variance with Mark; so radically different that we may wonder that he had any time for Mark's book. Perhaps he needed such a writing for his church's life and there was at that stage no alternative—until he himself provided it. Anyway, he certainly amended Mark to suit his own views in this matter: how far he was thereby closer to Jesus himself it is impossible to say and much depends on how far we see his alterations

and additions to Mark as his own work and how far he is drawing on traditions known to him that were closer to the historical reality. At all events, he was discontented with Mark's radicalism in this respect: the dismissal of food rules in Mark 7:19 is simply omitted; the sabbath dispensations in Mark are retained but argued for in a credible rabbinic way, and justified by Jesus' messianic status—he keeps Mark's statement that Jesus is "lord of the Sabbath" (2:28; cf. Matt. 12:8), while dropping the more radical Marcan words (2:27) that the sabbath was made for man, not man for the sabbath. Similarly, Matthew is dissatisfied with the looseness of Mark's exclusive focus on the two commands to love God and to love one's neighbor, with the conclusion: "There is no other commandment greater than these" (12:31); so he substitutes: "On these two commandments depend all the law and the prophets" (22:40). No get-out here! Matthew is here consistent with Jesus' teaching on this subject as presented in the Sermon on the Mount (5:17–20; see also 23:2). For Matthew's Christians, the old law remains in force and Paul's mission to Gentiles and his battles have passed him by—or probably infuriated him. It comes to this: that the criticism to be leveled at the Jewish teachers is chiefly that they are lax in their actual practice of the law they profess (23:3) and they fail to pursue its radical implications, as it points to total perfection (5:21–48). Jesus is then the teacher of a "greater righteousness" (5:20).

Matthew is also more friendly or reverential toward the disciples than Mark: they are indeed sometimes blunderers, but fundamentally on the right side, true disciples of Jesus, whatever encouragement they might sometimes need. So it is made clear that they win through the failures of the passion of Jesus, and are ratified in their great role, for all time (28:16–20): canonization is well on the way. And Judas alone is brought to pay for his sin (27:3–10), in accord with the principle stated in 16:27: "the Son of Man … will repay every man for what he has done." Matthew here lacks both the depth of the human moral crisis depicted in Mark and the radical nature of the grace available: he is a moralist who believes in the principle of retribution as an exact science!

Now one might feel that in these ways Matthew does not quite show himself to be a theologian as we have come to understand the term: he is more the moralist and the scriptural exegete. Yet there is implicit in his writing a profound and rounded theology of both the continuity of God's purposes, from start to finish, and the assurance of their completion (note the stress on the coming judgment and the end of the present age: chapters 24–25). There is also, of course, no hesitation in his depiction of Jesus as the central figure in the fulfillment of God's purposes: he is undoubtedly Messiah and therefore the bringer of the kingdom of heaven, now in embryo but in full force at the end of things. In these emphases, despite and indeed because of his total allegiance to Jesus, Matthew remains a Jew in his picture of reality, his sense of the purpose of human life and destiny, and his thoroughly scriptural belief about the ways God makes himself known. It is no wonder, however, that, as time went on, Matthew was not so much a source for Christian doctrinal reflection, as it blossomed along a more philosophical line, as for attitudes to morality—though few took seriously his attachment to the whole of the Jewish law—and for the rooting of Christianity in the Old Testament (as the Scriptures of Israel soon came to be seen). Nevertheless, there is in Matthew, as we have indicated, an implicit theology—of continuity and obedience—that his book has helped to fortify down the ages. There is also an undoubted reliance on the Christian community (he alone among the evangelists uses the term "church" for the Christian community as a whole, 16:18); so in that sense, he, along with Paul, may be seen as father of ecclesiology, doctrine concerning the church. Much has flowed from that teaching down the centuries, for both good and ill.

There is, however, a more serious issue involved in Matthew's ethical teaching. There has always been a tension, even a contradiction, in Christian life and policy between an emphasis on God's gracious love for all his people and his endless capacity to forgive us when we fail, on the one hand, and, as we see it, a more strictly judicial approach to us, with punishment as part of God's nature, alongside reward for those who have earned it. There is no trace in such an outlook of sophistication with regard to the relative roles of divine grace on the one hand and human will or decision making on the other. It is taken for granted that one earns what one receives and one is capable of achieving what one wills to achieve, just as one can

choose to give oneself to wicked disobedience to the known commands of God. All this is held without sophistication: no trace of psychological probing or social allowance-making. As was suggested above, the legacy of Matthew in this respect has frequently permeated practical Christian life, with its rules and counsels, its sense of future judgment and of rewards and punishments. In this as in other ways, Matthew's down-to-earth human straightforwardness, his moral simplicity, has been perhaps his most important bequest—alongside, of course, the moral teaching which provides a vision of what we might aspire to. "Stick and carrot" would be the banal way of putting it. There is, however, what many would now feel to be an excessively vivid and almost glad sense of the dreadful character of the punishments in store for the faithless and wicked. Matthew's is the gospel that gives us the threat of "wailing and gnashing of teeth" (just one reference elsewhere, Luke 13:28, perhaps itself derived from Matthew), fueling much modern complaint against the cruelty in Jesus' teaching. In this context, useful as he proved to perplexed and discipline-prone church authorities, Matthew may be seen as an obstacle to the free flow of the essential simplicities of the gospel and to a better theological understanding of the character of God and of his generous purposes for the world.

Matthew's picture of that world was of course, from our point of view, absurdly narrow. Even for his time, he shows little sense of much beyond the world of Judaism in which he had been reared, and then prospered. Then there had come his valiant decision, for whatever reason, to throw himself in with "the kingdom of heaven" and its Lord, bringing with it new and more demanding ideals, together with the joyful gift of his peace and "rest": in 11:28–30, we get a vision of a Matthew who knew of grace and joy, even though it seems he could scarcely give it free access to his mind. But the only time that he really shows any live awareness of the human race as a whole comes in 25:31–46, the judgment of it at the end of things, when all is done, not by grace but on grounds of achievement or performance—and (depending on how the parable is understood) especially in terms of how one has reacted to the needs of Christian missionaries in their courageous lives (the "little ones," "my brethren" would most naturally be taken in this way). Matthew was not a man of broad experience or vision (most of his more routine references to Gentiles are disparaging), and yet he has given us the testimony to a courageous move made from Israel of old to "the Church," with Jesus, the Messiah, at its head. And if usefulness is any criterion, his book has proved to be of infinite serviceability to Christians down the ages, often for their profit, but sometimes for the blunting of their spiritual and moral sensibilities and their sense of God's overwhelming love.

IV.   Luke

If our emphasis in this article is on "narrative" as a mode of expressing theology, then Luke stands out as the most thoroughgoing example. He is above all a teller of the story. It is essential from the start to recognize that his vision was unlike that of his fellow evangelists in that he took a wider view of the world and of history: he wrote not just the Gospel, which is our primary concern, but also the Acts of the Apostles; and the two books have to be taken together if we are to grasp his picture of things. In fact he is so much the teller of a historical story that, at first sight, it seems hard to justify his being seen as a theological writer in any intelligible sense of the word. But, like so many of his time, his historical interest is expressed in the context of a sense of God's purpose for the world and of course of the Christian message whose servant he is. His doctrine is expressed, however, only minimally in abstract terms, but comes to us through his way of selecting and arranging his narrative. It is none the less real for that.

So we must begin by getting a sense of his view of the time and of the world in which he was set and in which God was active in furthering his purpose. More than his earlier fellow evangelists, he has a lively sense of history as a whole and of the human race as a whole; so that in his genealogy he traces Jesus' ancestry not simply to Abraham, the Jewish originator (as Matthew did), but to Adam, first of the human race (3:38). Paul—Luke's "father" in terms of inspiration, though only rarely of idiom and style—had perceived Jesus in such terms, but more theologically: Jesus was the second Adam who had reversed the terrible legacy of the first Adam; he was in other words no less than a second founder of a renewed human race (Romans

5:12–17; 1 Cor. 15:22). Luke, we may say, has expressed this doctrine in narrative terms, insofar as "story" allows it to be done. But for Luke this Adamic, humanity-wide factor is not simply a matter of origins and their renewal, it is a matter of geography. He is acutely aware of the extent of the Roman Empire, in particular of the Mediterranean world, in which Palestine, though vital, is but a single part and Rome is its hub. So no wonder Luke sets out to show how the message of Jesus and the truth concerning him has made its way, through all kinds of heroic deeds done and travails endured, from Palestine to Rome itself, with Paul as its leading agent. In that sense, his two volumes tell a single story: the first part making use of the writings of Mark and perhaps Matthew too; the second telling the story first of the establishing of the church in Palestine and neighboring lands, a body that was, despite all hindrances and hesitations, capable of spawning the grand missions of Paul and his friends in Asia Minor and Greece—and then Paul's arrival, albeit as prisoner, like Jesus himself, in Rome. In telling this story, Luke's optimism never fails. Jesus' death turns out to be not a tragedy but the basis for his resurrection with all its marvellous developments—first the invigorating of the church in Jerusalem, and then the inspiring of that church to undertake movements to new populations, whether Samaritans or, in due course, Jews and Gentiles in the Palestine/Syria area itself, or finally Gentiles in city after city. It is a success story from end to end, whatever the apparent tragedies on the way. And so, we may understand, it will continue until the end of time. Despite all the setbacks and failures, it is not going too far to say that Luke has been broadly justified, in ways that he could never have foreseen. He is therefore first of all a theologian of history and a theologian of the church in history—not in a deeply sophisticated way, but implicitly. God is the lord of the world, we can take that for granted; and his purpose of love and goodness will be achieved, first by way of Israel, but now by way of the church that has inherited its mantle and its saving mission. This is established from Jesus' birth onwards: see the vision of Simeon on encountering the child Jesus in Luke 2:28–32.

So Jesus is not only the climax and furtherer of God's saving purpose for Israel, as experienced over long ages, but his agent for his whole creation. It is true that this width of perspective was by no means lacking in much of Israel's own sense of the divine plan for the world, though it was generally seen in terms of a rallying to Israel itself of the rest of humanity—Israel as beacon or point of gathering for the rest. But in the vision of both Paul and, in his own different idiom, Luke, this is seen in more relaxed terms, with a greater readiness to hold chiefly to the fundamentals of the God–human relationship and a greater tolerance of human diversity. In their perspective, Jesus had brought a fresh capacity to home in on the basic features of the purpose of God and his capacity to engage with people in their difference and in their variety of hopes and aspirations.

In this wide sense of both time and space, Luke must place both Jesus and then the church, the Christian movement whose growth he has witnessed with such satisfaction. His picture of Jesus is of course central to his vision. Not that he is speculative or original in any way in his perception of his person or the essence of his mission. He is content to use inherited terms, all Jewish in origin, when it comes to filling out his purpose. Jesus is messiah, son of God, son of man, lord: and it is, for the most part, hard to detect much Lucan originality in the use of any of them—they are simply terms of honor, and their older, Jewish scriptural senses do not seem to have impinged greatly upon his mind. And there is no speculation of a more theoretical kind that goes beyond them. You can even find an undue literalism in some of his words. At the end of his genealogy, we learn that, in the distant days of origins, Jesus was "son of Seth, son of Adam, son of God"—without any sense of moving from one register to another (3:38). It is neither commented on nor elaborated, here or elsewhere. It seems not to occur to him that "son of God" takes us into a different register from what has gone before; but of course his Annunciation story, 1:26–35, has put the birth of Jesus in terms that seem to see heaven and earth, God and humans, in such a continuum, that we should scarcely be surprised. To us it seems a primitive kind of theology, answering none of our natural questions. Special though Jesus is certainly seen to be in the manner of his conception, Luke does not see it as breaking continuities beyond recognition: the element of the divine action reminds us of Hannah in 1 Samuel 1–2, and Joseph is still, for Luke, Jesus' father (2:41, 48). In that

sense, therefore, Jesus is certainly one of us, however special his mission. Moreover, "son of God" is itself not a specialized term, unique to Jesus in some metaphysical way: in 20:36, he can happily use it to refer to angels, as if it simply implies "belonging specially to the other world." On the other hand, even with regard to Jesus himself, at his death, he can positively avoid the term: where, in Mark, the centurion said of Jesus at his dying, "Truly this was the son of God," and we should surely (despite doubt) take it as a confession of Christian faith, Luke writes instead: "Truly this was a righteous (or innocent) man." Now it is true that in the Wisdom of Solomon, a fairly new writing at this time, there is an equating of the two terms, "son of God" and "righteous one" (as if to say that God is "father" notably to those who are obedient to his laws), and Luke may have found his own expression more plausible on the lips of a Gentile officer; but still, on any showing, Luke is not being theological in any radically sophisticated sense—unless of course one thinks that one could say nothing higher of Jesus than that he was a splendid instance of God's human creative purpose, so much so that he received a key role in its working out.

No, it seems we must acquit Luke of sophistication where theological concepts are concerned. There is, however, one clear exception to this generality. It is in the sphere of what we now call social and moral theology. Here Luke is relentless in his insistence on certain plain moral lessons for which Jesus is both exemplar and teacher.

Luke took the step of moving the story of Jesus' unfruitful visit to his home town of Nazareth from some way down the narrative (Mark 6:1–6; Matt. 13:53–58) to the very start of Jesus' public work. Not just that, but he expands it, so that we are given Jesus' sermon, or rather his scripture reading, from Isaiah 61—which he then proceeds to endorse enthusiastically: "Today this scripture has been fulfilled in your hearing." All it tells us of Jesus' status is that he has been "anointed" by God, that is, authorized and empowered as "messiah." And his mission is social and ethical—he will preach good news to the poor, give release to captives, sight to the blind, and liberty to the oppressed—all in the context of proclaiming God's time of renewal ("the acceptable year of the Lord"—a year of jubilee when wrongs can be righted and a new start given). The "performance" of Jesus is greeted with rapture and wonder.

The rest of the Gospel shows Jesus working out this program in detail and with persistence. In Luke, story after story elaborates the social teaching given here in essence. We think of Jesus' insistence on the evil of wealth (16:19–31; 19:1–10) and the duty to relieve poverty (6:20–26); the duty to be open-hearted even in cases of awkwardness and when it could scarcely be demanded (10:25–37). All this because it is demanded by God's deepest character and purpose, as exemplified in the father who, in his love, forgets rejection and welcomes his returning son (15:11–32).

This plain statement of God's character and desire for the willing response of his people puts other possibilities of life in the shade, and we are a long way from the world of Matthew where life well pleasing to God consists in obedience to the law that he has given. Luke sees duty differently: in terms less of a moral injunction than a lifestyle where generosity of heart rules and love is without qualification the key to God's law. In a sense, Luke's social theology is as simple as could be. How does he see it as being possibly practical? The secret is to live in fellowship with Jesus—and Luke's many meal-scenes (e.g., 7:36–50; 22:14–38) are occasions not only of sharing company, with all the benefit that that implies, but also of teaching, where Jesus imparts his clearest principles—of love and generosity of heart. The Emmaus meal indicates that what began in his lifetime is to continue in the life of his followers (24:13–35).

A strange feature of Luke's work is that when it comes to Acts, which in so many ways is simply volume two of a single tale, continuing the narrative into the life of the church, there is scarcely a sign of this ethic—apart, that is, from the sharing of property that takes place in the early Jerusalem community. This is surprising. Perhaps we are to suppose that the lesson has been well and truly imparted, and we can be trusted to assume that the life of the churches that Paul and others established will be instructed and organized along these lines. All the same, it is a puzzle that such a major concern is simply dropped. The nearest we get is the sense that Paul the missionary is himself the recipient of welcome and hospitality as he visits the communities that have been established around the Mediterranean. But even this cannot be said to be emphasized. No, the theological concern of Acts is overwhelmingly with the universal scope of God's purpose in and through Jesus, worked out now in practical terms in ever-spreading circles around the Mediterranean, until Paul arrives in Rome as a prisoner, shades of Jesus himself, yet still preaches to the end of the book, "openly and unhindered." So perhaps we should say that a final and dominant theological concern of Luke is a doctrine of mission. Again, it is not argued about or conceptualized, but it is worked out in practice—and the mission is both essential and unstoppable. It was foreseen in the stories of Jesus' birth and early life—where Simeon said he was to be a light to the Gentiles—and rehearsed, we might say, in the mission of Jesus to Israel, where he laid down, in word and deed, the key features of God's world as it should be.

There is certainly implicit here a doctrine of the church. It focuses chiefly on the necessity of unity among Christians. The setting which Luke had experienced before he wrote his book was one of looming schism—between the churches loyal to the Jerusalem church, with its Jewish (Matthew-style) sense of the Christian message and the mission of Jesus, and the Gentile churches that were the fruit of the missions of Paul and his associates. Luke takes all pains to show how in essence this schism had been arrested by the agreement described in Acts 15. It seems likely that this alleged solution proved optimistic—and by Luke's time of writing the Jerusalem church had in any case gone from sight in the wake of the sack of Jerusalem by the Romans in 70 CE. Still, Luke hopes to preserve the sense of the church's dual heritage, Jewish and Gentile in composition and with Judaism and its Scriptures as part of its endowment—both essential to a grasp of God's age-long purposes.

If theology is the mind's way of making sense of belief about God, then all this is surely genuine theology; but it is given to us more by way of examples, instances, historical episodes, than by abstract words—the latter indeed are conspicuous by their absence. But through all Luke's writing the divine purpose made known and worked out in Jesus and those who follow him shines forth unmistakably. It is theology at its most down-to-earth, embedded in history and society. It is a living warning that theology that works by abstraction is full of risks, and open to much falsehood internally generated by the human mind.

Tertullian (Quintus Septimius Florens Tertullianus) (*c.*155–*c.*225)

D. H. Williams

Despite being the most prolific and theologically accomplished man of his age, very little is known for certain about Tertullian. From his few autobiographical references, we gather that he grew in a pagan household (*On Repentance* 1.1), admits to an adulterous affair earlier in life (i.e., a mistress, like many Roman men such as Augustine) (*On the Resurrection of the Flesh* 59.3), received a good education in Greek and Latin literature, philosophy, and, in particular, rhetoric (*Against the Valentinians* 8.3). It is also apparent that he was married, having written two open letters to his wife. The exact circumstances of his conversion to Christianity are unclear. Possibly, his decision was inspired by observing Christian martyrs boldly face death in the arena (*Apologeticum* 50.15; *Ad scapulam* 5.4); he may have been captivated by the conviction and courageousness of Christian martyrs he had witnessed. Indeed, one of the most moving passages in all his corpus is his address to those Christians who were recently thrown into prison for their witness. He writes encouragingly of their condition,

> It is full of darkness, but you yourselves are light; it has bars, but God has made you free; unpleasant odors are there, but you are an aroma of sweetness; the judge is daily awaited, but you shall judge the judges; sadness may be there for him who sighs after the world's enjoyments … but the leg does not feel the chain when the mind is in heaven. Where your heart shall be, there shall also be your treasure. (*To the Martyrs* 2)

From other sources we learn he lived in the North African city of Carthage (in present-day Tunisia) and that he began writing in 196/7 CE, continuing throughout the first two decades of the third century. There is the faintest suggestion that he was in Rome for a time (*On the Dress of Women* I. 7; Eusebius, *Eccl. Hist.* II. 2, 4). Apart from what can be gleaned from Tertullian's own comments, we have only a few passing references to him in subsequent years. Interestingly, Cyprian of Carthage never mentions him, though an oft-used remark by Jerome declares that Cyprian always referred to Tertullian as "the master." We have no way of vindicating Jerome on this score. Nevertheless, Cyprian may have relied on Tertullian's instruction on prayer and baptism. Lactantius, another African, writing at the end of the third century, briefly mentions Tertullian's *Apology* (*Divine Inst.* V. 4) and his knowledge of a vast amount of literature. Lactantius claims, however, that Tertullian was not so skilled in eloquence: "He was not polished and very obscure" (*Divine Inst.* V. 1). Eusebius of Caesarea quotes several times from a Greek translation of the *Apology* (*Eccles. Hist.* II. 4; 25, 4; III. 20, 9; 33, 3; V. 5, 5), which is the only work he cites. Not for 50 years do we hear Tertullian's name uttered again, this time by

The Student's Companion to the Theologians, First Edition. Edited by Ian S. Markham.

Hilary of Poitiers, who admits to a reticence in drawing on Tertullian's works (specifically his work on prayer) because "the subsequent error of the man has detracted from the authority of his commendable writings" (*On Matthew* V. 1). We may say with confidence that Hilary's view was widely shared and accounts for the scarcity of our information about him. The nature of the "error" refers to Tertullian's adoption in his later years of a pneumatic-purist movement called Montanism (see below). Nevertheless, Tertullian's theological constructions and metaphors are drawn upon, namelessly, by nearly every Latin thinker who wrote on the subjects of the Trinity or christology or the human soul.

The earliest sketch we possess about his life and writings comes from Jerome, who writes almost two centuries later (*On Famous Men* 53), stating that he was a man "of impetuous temperament," and lived during the rule of two Roman emperors: Septimius Severus (193–211) and Antoninus Caracalla (211–17). Both points can be substantiated. Tertullian's first and best-known literary effort was his *Apologeticum*, which he produced in response to the persecutions of Christians during the reign of Severus. He went on to write at least 30 other works on a host of issues during a 20-year period. Throughout these writings, especially the polemical, he often expressed himself in a convoluted style of Latin, heavily imbued with satire and irony that was effective in berating his opponents. But Tertullian was more than a clever debater. His intellectual brilliance will advance the sophistication of Latin theology as no other writer had done or will do until Augustine.

Jerome misidentifies Tertullian as a priest, a presbyter in Carthage. Tertullian was a layman, as he himself mentions three times in his extant works; he was certainly married (having written two open letters to his wife), and probably lived in Carthage all his life. Jerome also confuses Tertullian with a Roman jurist living about the same time also named Tertullianus. While the Christian Tertullian reveals an impressive knowledge of Roman law and history, there is no need to ascribe a specialized understanding of jurisprudence beyond the extensive rhetorical education he had obviously received.

Jerome too laments that an otherwise impressive career was cut short by Tertullian's lapse into "the teaching of Montanus," or what the adherents called the "New Prophecy." Indeed, the only works that Jerome lists of Tertullian's whole corpus are those he wrote in defense of Montanist practices, which might say something about how Tertullian's memory had come down to the fourth century. Finally, Jerome relates that Tertullian lived to an old age, for which there is no disputing evidence.

I.   His Literary Works

Historic Christianity is much indebted to Tertullian, who provided us with the fundamental articulation of the doctrines of the Trinity, of christology, of anthropology; and of Christian practice such as baptism, prayer, and righteous suffering in the face of persecution. Nearly all his works were written in response to the immediate needs and challenges facing Christians, which addressed critical matters involving apologetics, doctrine, polemics, morality, and liturgy. He certainly saw himself as a defender of orthodox Catholicism against pagan religion, against Marcionism, and against various gnostic groups. There are also devotional essays on prayer, baptism, penitence, and martyrdom, as well as small treatises, many from his pro-Montanist period, on what constitutes appropriate Christian practice (monogamy, chastity, veiling of unmarried women, etc.).

The two significant apologetic works that come from the early period (197–206) are *Ad nationes* and the *Apologeticum*. In these works he responds to pagan accusers, defending Christianity, and exhorting the pagans to become Christians. Other works of this period include: *Ad martyras* (an exhortation to those facing persecution), *Adversus Iudaeos* (which addresses controversial points between Jews and Christians) (the first eight chapters of this work are indisputably Tertullian's); *De testimonio animae* (the soul's testimony of God's existence). A number of moral treatises were written at this time: *De spectaculis* (against Christians' participation in games); *De oratione* (on prayer); *De patientia* (on the patient Christ); *De paenitentia* (on the sacraments preceding baptism); *De cultu faminarum* (on women's modesty); *Ad uxorem* (against second marriages); *De baptismo* (on baptism). In *De praescriptione haereticorum* Tertullian outlines a general method of refuting a heretical argument, and argues that only the church has the right to interpret the scripture. This prior point of order (*praescriptio*) must be proved before one can claim biblical authority for one's arguments. It is here where Tertullian's rhetorical skills are quite evident. In *Adversus Hermogenem* he defends creation against the teaching of the eternality of matter.

Doctrinal works written between *c.*207 and 212 show the great erudition and creativity of Tertullian. Writings of this period include his massive *Against Marcion* (who advocated the separation of the Gospel from the Old Testament), as well as a number of treatises against Gnostics, *Adversus Valentinianos* (anti-gnostic); *De anima* (on the soul); *On the Flesh of Christ* (on the incarnation); *On the Resurrection of the Dead* (on the second coming and resurrection). The moral and practical works of this period show Montanist leanings in their emphasis on asceticism and stringent church discipline: *De exhortatione castitatis* (against second marriages); *De virginibus velandis* (where he exhorts virgins to cover their heads in public for reason of keeping modesty intact); *De corona* (agues that Christians should not serve in the army); *Scorpiace* (on the value of martyrdom); *Ad Scapulam* (to the proconsul of Africa who attempted to persecute Christians). The date of *De idolatria* (written against idolatry) has been disputed.

Tertullian's writings of the last period of his literary activity (212–22) demonstrate Montanist tendencies more explicitly, and oppose the Roman church: *De fuga in persecutione* (where he argues against attempting to escape persecution); *Adversus Praxean* (on the Trinity against the "patripassianism" (or what modern scholars call Modalism of Praxeas); *De monogamia* (against second marriage, this time more rigorously than in the two earlier works on the subject); *De ieiunio adversus Psychicos* (a defense of fasting, against the Catholic Church's laxity). Finally, in *De pudicitia* he argues that only "spiritual men" (apostles and prophets), and not the church, can pardon certain serious sins.

II.   The New Prophecy

A mid-second-century movement that called itself "the New Prophecy" emerged from the province of Phrygia in western Asian Minor and rapidly spread to major cities in the Roman Empire. The movement, called by its opponents the Cataphrygians or Montanists, claimed that the Holy Spirit—called the "Paraclete" following John's Gospel—had only recently been revealed in its fullness through the new prophecies of an otherwise unknown prophet named Montanus and two women prophetesses, Priscilla and Maximilla. Their message was not anti-orthodox in a strictly doctrinal sense, but the very nature of their self-professed prophetic authority, by which they advocated a stricter and purer Christian ethic, challenged other types of authority in the church. The question at hand was whether episcopal and spiritual authority must coincide. Since Ignatius of Antioch, the answer was usually in the affirmative, but the reasons were dubious. Advocates of Montanism claimed the answer was yes and no, leaving open the reality of spiritual authority outside of the catholic institution. It was not long, therefore, before Montanism was deemed to be a threat to the stability of the church, and condemned. By the time Tertullian began to accept the prophecies as divinely inspired (*c.*206/7), the "New Prophecy" had a significant following in Carthage. Its condemnation was partly because of its challenge to church authority: obedience to the Paraclete's prophecies would necessarily be in conflict with the obedience to the bishop. And even the manner in which the Montanists entered a type of ecstatic state for making prophetic utterances caused concern among many. But Tertullian sided with the movement's ideals, which resonated with his admiration of martyrdom, strict ecclesiastical discipline, and the ascetic lifestyle. Most of all, the work of the Spirit in his own time offered a way of appealing to an authority that gave further certitude to Christian claims. At the same time, he was increasingly dissatisfied with the laxity of the Roman clergy with respect to church discipline, in particular, their willingness to forgive serious sins and allow second marriages on specious grounds. The undertones of disagreement with catholics increased throughout his later writings to the point of open conflict.

Nothing is known of Tertullian's life after he wrote *On Chastity* (*c.*217–22), a work that fiercely condemned the catholic bishop, presumably of Carthage, of leading the church into apostasy. It remains unclear whether Tertullian's support of Montanism went beyond defending it while remaining within Catholicism—or whether it led him to make a break with the church, as Augustine asserted. There are no contemporary witnesses to substantiate this claim. And although Augustine (*On Heresies* 86) wrote that Tertullian formed a splinter group of his own apart from the Montanists in Carthage, Augustine's sources for this claim are dubious and may have nothing to do with Tertullian himself. It is just as plausible, if not more so, to suggest that inauguration of a new work of the Spirit convinced Tertullian to seek the realization of Montanist ethical ideals within catholic circles. Just as he had acted as an apologist for Christianity against Roman belligerence, he now became an apologist for the New Prophecy. It is unfortunate that one of Tertullian's works, *On Ecstasy*, almost certainly written in his later years as a Montanist, does not survive. He probably advocated the prophetic state of past and present prophets in order to preach to "worldly" catholics. Because of his attachment to Montanism, Tertullian was never canonized as were most patristic theologians, and his works were officially condemned by a sixth-century *Gelasian Decree*. Of course, none of this prevented subsequent Latin writers from drawing liberally on his writings, even if they did so with rare mention of his name.

III.   Tradition

The way of truth was found in the tradition which was originally laid down by Christ, who delivered it to the apostles, who, in turn, handed it over it to the churches (*Apol.* 19 and 47). In *Against Marcion*, Tertullian claims Paul went up to Jerusalem after his conversion to compare the "Rule of his Gospel" with that of the other apostles (V. 3, 1). That same "Rule has come down [to us] from the beginning of the Gospel" (*Against Praxeas* 2). It is the link between the apostolic past and the present; it refers to the original message of the apostles, going back to revelation itself, and to the message proclaimed by the churches of his day.

This tradition, which Tertullian understood as having a divine character, was summarized in the "rule of faith" (*regula fidei*). It was both the distillation of scripture and set the boundaries guarding Christians from biblical misinterpretation. For Tertullian, the faith of the church, or tradition, is established by the rule (*On the Prescription* 14). As such, the rule and tradition were used as synonymous terms.

More than any other patristic writer, Tertullian quotes the rule of faith in *On the Veiling of Virgins* 1, *Against Praxeas* 2, and *On the Prescription of Heretics* 13 and 36. There are also smaller, more particularized, segments of the rule which Tertullian mentions in passing, such as *On Prescription* 37, *Against Praxeas* 30, and *Against Marcion* IV. 4. It is evident that the rule was never fixed in a single or master version, but was variable in its form and adaptable to the given didactic or polemical circumstances at hand. The three lengthy citations of the rule found in Tertullian's surviving corpus possess few exact verbal similarities, vary in length, and whose content is clearly accommodating three distinct situations. At the same time, however, all three versions exhibit a basic shared structure which reflects a common basis. His most descriptive use of the rule is in *Against Praxeas* 2:

> You must know that which prescribes the belief that there is one only God, and that He is none other than the Creator of the world, who produced all things out of nothing through His own Word, first of all things sent forth; that this Word is called His Son, and under the name of God, was seen variously by the patriarchs, heard always in the prophets, at last brought down by the Spirit and Power of the Father into the Virgin Mary, was made flesh in her womb, and, being born of her, went forth as Jesus Christ; thenceforth He preached the new law and the new promise of the kingdom of heaven, worked miracles; having been crucified, He rose again on the third day; having ascended into heaven, He sat at the right hand of the Father; sent the vicarious power of the Holy Spirit who leads the faithful; will come with glory to take the saints to the enjoyment of everlasting life and the heavenly promises, and to condemn the wicked to everlasting fire, after a resurrection of both classes has been effected, together with the restoration of the flesh. This rule, as it will be proved, was taught by Christ …

Gnostic teachers, like Valentinus, Basilides, and Marcion, were busy proliferating a gospel tradition based on a gnostic hermeneutic of scripture; in effect, another structure of authority allegedly based on divine revelation. Because scriptural interpretation was so often at issue between catholics (or "mainline"

Christians) and various forms of gnosticism, it became clear to Tertullian that any appeal to the Bible alone for maintaining pure doctrine was impossible. Tertullian therefore addresses himself to the problem of authority. For we must not be surprised, he says, that heresies utilize scriptural support for their positions. The stated purpose in *On the Prescription of Heretics* is to decide the question, "Who are the rightful owners of Scripture?" In order to answer the question, Tertullian declares that

> we must not appeal to Scripture … one point should be decided first, namely, who holds the faith to which the Bible belongs, and from whom, through whom, when and to whom was the teaching delivered by which men became Christians? For only where the true Christian teaching and faith are evident, will be the true Scriptures, the true interpretations, and all the true Christian traditions be found. (*On Prescription of Heretics* 19)

His statement is not meant to presume that he favored the authority of tradition over that of scripture, as some have contended. Neither Tertullian nor any of his peers would have imagined that the rule could operate completely independently of scripture, any more than scripture could act without the rule and the church. The issue is rather one of context. When one examines their texts, one finds that the relationship between the authority of scripture and that of tradition exchange the primal position, depending on what issues are at stake.

IV. Scripture

Tertullian had a profound familiarity with the Bible, both Old and New Testament. Almost every chapter of his writings contains an abundance of scriptural quotations and allusions. Because of this prolific use of scripture, historians are able to deduce which books were regarded as divinely inspired. By the late second century, recognition of what we now deem to be the canon of scripture, particularly the New Testament, was not complete. Translations of the Bible were also problematic. In Tertullian's time, several Latin versions of both Testaments were circulating, all of inferior quality in style and textual accuracy. These Latin versions of the Old Testament were themselves translations not from the Hebrew, but from a fairly literal translation of the Greek Septuagint. Moreover, the Latin New Testament had an obscure origin and was subject to frequent revision, which resulted in the proliferation of editions.

Scripture for Tertullian, nevertheless, was the indisputable witness of the apostles' preaching and testimony. It was the repository of divine truth, revealing a uniform agreement among its authors about the particulars of the church's rule of faith (*Against Marcion* IV. 2). It was on this basis that he refuted his opponents, "If it is not in Scripture, let him fear the woe that was meant for all those who add or take away" (*Against Hermogenes* 22). In scripture, one found full divine authority. The truthfulness of any doctrine or any part of tradition depended on its support from biblical evidence, as Tertullian declared against Praxeas (*c.*29): "Let it be enough to say that Christ, the Son of God, died, and this only because it is so written."

When it comes to Tertullian's method of interpretation, it is highly doubtful that he was conscious of a particular exegetical technique. Since his primary objective in scriptural usage was certitude, he tells readers to seek the plain and literal meaning of a text wherever possible. Curiosity and inquiry into dark or obscure passages is fraught with danger for the faithful believer. Nevertheless, if one must seek to understand the meaning of difficult texts, he will be kept from gross error by always adhering to the "marrow of Scripture" (*Scorpiace* 12). In other words, one will stay within orthodox parameters by following the overall scope or purport of scripture, which is preserved in the rule of the church's faith.

If we were to look into the motivation for his approach to the Bible, we would find that his exegesis was formulated in response largely to gnostic biblical interpretations, which were usually governed by mytho-poetic narratives about creation or redemption. Tertullian seemed comfortable using typology, by which he often interpreted the prophetic books of the Old Testament, but he frowned on frequent recourse to figurative exegesis, which he associated with the obscure fabrications of heretics, who stated "one thing in words, another in meaning, as is the case with allegories, with parables, and with riddles" (*Scorpiace* 11). Thus, Tertullian argues that the truth is concise and simple. In order to achieve clarity, the reader should begin with passages that are unambiguous in their meaning since "uncertain statements should be determined by certain ones, and obscure ones by such as are clear and plain" (*On the Resurrection of the Flesh* 21). Even when he was thoroughly immersed in Montanism, Tertullian observes the same principle in not taking parables as sources of doctrine. Rather, one should use doctrine as the norm for interpreting the parables (*On Chastity* 9).

V. Doctrinal Foundations

As a sure means of finding the truth, Tertullian looked to norms for preserving the apostolic faith and church in his day. Where should one turn to find these? Certainly God had provided a means for assurance. For the Christian God was *deus verus* (the true God), and those who find Him find the fullness of truth. Christ as True God was revealed in the flesh in order to lead humanity *in agnitionem veritatis* (to a knowledge of the truth) (*Apology* XXI. 30). Despite the fact that he was well learned in philosophy and literature, Tertullian took a dim view of any human reasoning when it was used independent of scripture and the church, since it was too often abused by pagan philosophers and found in the ideas of heretics. There was no doubt in his mind that the only sure ground for truth was to be found in divine revelation. But when one is looking to secure this truth through some tangible means, where should one look?

Should one turn to the succession of pastors in the churches, many of whom could trace a lineage several generations back to the apostles? Like his predecessors, Tertullian thought a demonstrable continuity of a shared faith within the churches offered strong testimony of apostolicity. At no point in his literary career, however, did he perceive the office of clergy as an automatic guarantee of orthodoxy, though he regarded the office as an authoritative one. The more involved with the New Prophecy Tertullian became the less credence he gave to this argument. By the end of his life, he was convinced that church leadership (not the church) had fallen away from faithful teaching regarding Christian practice as defined in this new age of the Spirit. Still, despite his quarrels with the local clergy, Tertullian will never claim that true doctrine can be divorced from the context of the church.

Tertullian attempts to formulate the doctrine of the Trinity rooted in the Bible in *Adversus Praxean*. This is a response to Praxeas's "modalistic" unitarianism of the nature of God. He is the first to use the words *trinitas* (the Trinity), *persona* (person), and *substantia* (substance) as technical terms in reference to the relation of God the Father, Christ, and the Holy Spirit. He will be the first to speak about the Godhead as three and one, as a single substance in three persons, although he uses *substantia* in at least three ways: in reference to what God is, to each of the persons of the Trinity, and to the divine and human natures of Christ (see *Adversus Praxean* 12.3, 6; *De pudicitia* 2, 21, 23). In framing a terminology for articulating God as the One and Many, Tertullian pioneered a Latin theological vocabulary that continued to inform Western thinkers into the Middle Ages.

Tertullian's contribution to christology is his teaching about the two substances and one person in Christ (*Adversus Praxean* 27.11). Occasionally (for instance in *Adversus Hermogenem* 4), he speaks of the Son as subordinate or *second* to the Father, which was not meant as a subordinationism, as later theology will think of it. Reflecting the state of christology during his epoch, Tertullian taught that the Son was the Logos of the Father, having been begotten at the event of Genesis 1:2: "And God said, 'Let there be light.'"

In the areas of eschatology and anthropology he stresses bodily resurrection against gnostic and docetic teachings of his time. His works offer a glimpse into Christian ritual, sacramental practices, and ethical concerns of his era.

With respect to Tertullian's relation to philosophy, some scholars suggest that he rejected philosophy in principle, and argued for the impossibility of grasping Christian truth rationally. Symptomatic of Tertullian's anti-philosophical view is his oft-repeated remark, "What does Jerusalem have to do with Athens?" (*De praescr.* 7). But his statement—another example of rhetorical posturing—should be taken with a grain of salt. Certainly philosophical ideas, especially drawn from Stoicism, were used no less in his own construction of theology. Other scholars (J.-C. Fredouille, R. Braun, J. Moingt) point out that, first, Tertullian opposed not philosophy or reason as such, but rather those elements in philosophy which were utilized by heretics; second, he followed an earlier tradition of scolding philosophy; and, finally, he himself used philosophical categories in developing his theology. Although Tertullian's linguistic and literary contribution is original in many ways, he is also now seen as a follower of earlier tradition (particularly Irenaeus). In sum, Tertullian draws on earlier literary tradition, both pagan and Christian. Yet he has made a significant original contribution in seeking to harmonize elements of pagan culture (philosophy, rhetoric, language) with Christianity. In light of recent research, Tertullian has been viewed as attempting to reconcile Christianity and surrounding culture rather than to promote their utter irreconcilability.

VI. Manuscripts

The extant manuscripts of Tertullian's works present an inconsistent and spotty record of preservation. Unlike the works of Hilary of Poitiers, Ambrose, or Augustine, Tertullian's written legacy does not come down to us through antiquity. Most manuscripts are late, dating from the fifteenth century or after. Several manuscripts that date from the ninth to the eleventh century contain only *Apologeticum*, and one from the eighth century contains *Against the Jews*. The first cluster of Tertullian's writings appears in the ninth-century Codex Agobardinus, now classified at the Bibliothèque Nationale as Codex Latinus 1622. Fortunately, a table of contents is listed at the front of the manuscript, since it has suffered damage and not all the texts survive, or they have been fragmented. The list is as follows (not in its original order): *To the Nations*, books I and II, *On the Prescription of Heretics*, *Concerning the Scorpion*, *On the Testimony of the Soul*, *Concerning the Crown [of the Martyrs]*, *Concerning the Games*, *On Idolatry*, *On the Origin of the Soul* (or, *On the Soul*), *On Prayer*, *Concerning Women's Attire*, I and II, *To [his] Wife* I and II, *Concerning an Exhortation for Chastity*, *Concerning the Flesh of Christ*, *Concerning Penitence*, *Concerning Patience*, *Concerning the Veiling of Virgins*, *On the Hope of the Faithful*, *Concerning Paradise*, *Concerning the Flesh and the Soul*, *On the Soul's Submission*, *Concerning the Superstition of the Age*. The last five works have been utterly lost to history. Only *Concerning Paradise* and *On the Hope of the Faithful* can be truly be attributed to Tertullian since he himself mentions having written them (*Against Marcion* V. 12 and III. 24 respectively). Surprisingly, there is no attestation for his anti-heretical writings, *Against Marcion*, *Against Praxeas*, *Against the Valentinians*, and *Against Hermogenes*, until the eleventh century, though they find frequent mention in subsequent manuscripts. Among other lost works that Tertullian provides witness to are: *On the Fates* (in *On the Soul* 20), a refutation of Apelles, a Marcionite (in *Concerning the Flesh of Christ* 8), and perhaps *On Ecstasy*, a treatise defending the New Prophecy. It seems that *Apologeticum* and *Concerning Baptism* were translated into Greek by the late third century, and that Tertullian himself wrote *Concerning the Shows* in Greek, as well as another work refuting heretical baptism.

References

Barnes, T. D. 1985. *Tertullian: A Historical and Literary Study*, rev. ed. Oxford: Clarendon Press.

Braun, René. 1977. *Deus Christianorum: recherches sur le vocabulaire doctrinal de Tertullien*, 2nd ed. Paris: Études augustiniennes.

Countryman, L. William. 1982. "Tertullian and the *Regula Fidei*," *The Second Century* 2: 221–6.

Daly, C. B. 1993. *Tertullian the Puritan and His Influence*. Dublin: Four Courts.

Daniélou, J. 1977. *The Origins of Latin Christianity*, trans. J. A. Baker. Philadelphia.

Fredouille, J. C. 1972. *Tertullien et la conversion de la culture antique*. Paris.

Klein, R. 1968. *Tertullianus und das römische Reich*. Heidelberg.

Labhardt, A. 1950. "Tertullien et la philosophie ou la recherche d'une 'position pure'," *Museum Helveticum* 7: 159–80.

Moingt, J. 1966–9. *Theologie Trinitaire de Tertullien Histoire, Doctrine, Méthodes*, 4 vols. Paris.

Osborne, E. 1977. *Tertullian: First Theologian of the West* Cambridge: Cambridge University Press.

Powell, D. 1975. "Tertullianists and Cataphrygians," *Vigiliae Christianae* 29: 33–54.

Rankin, D. 1955. *Tertullian and the Church*. Cambridge: Cambridge University Press.

Sider, R. D. 1982. "Approaches to Tertullian: a Study of Recent Scholarship," *Second Century* 2: 228–60.

Trevett, C. 1996. "Tertullian and the Church," *Journal of Theological Studies* 47: 668–71.

Waszink, J. H. 1979. "Tertullian's Principles and Methods of Exegesis." In *Early Christian Literature and the Classical Intellectual Tradition*, ed. W. R. Schoedel and R. L. Wilken. Paris: Edition Beauchesne, pp. 17–31.

Modern Critical Editions

A list of Tertullian's works is found in E. Dekkers, *Clavis Patrum Latinorum*, 3rd ed. (Brepols: Turnhout, 1995), pp. 1–36.

The critical editions include five series and collected editions:

1. *Patrologiae Cursus Completus, Series Latina,* 217 vols., ed. J.-P. Migne (Paris, 1844–64: PL 1–2).
2. F. Oehler, Q.S.F. Tertulliani opera omnia. Editio maior, vols. 1–3. Leipzig, 1851–54. Editio minor (Leipzig, 1854).
3. *Corpus Scriptorum Ecclesiasticorum Latinorum* (CSEL): A. Reifferscheid-G. Wissowa, CSEL 20 (1890); A. Kroymann, CSEL 47 (1939); H. Hoppe, CSEL 69 (1939); A. Kroymann, CSEL 70 (1942); V. Bulhart and J.W.Ph. Borleffs, CSEL 76 (1957).
4. *Corpus Christianorum, Series Latina* (CCSL): Tertullian, *Opera,* 2 vols., ed. Dom Eligius Dekkers. CCSL 1–2 (Turnholt: Brepols, 1953–4). This is a reprint of Kroymann's text in CSEL, with many revisions by Dekkers.
5. *Sources Chrétiennes* (Paris: Les Éditions du Cerf) 35, 46, 173, 216, 217, 273, 280, 281, 310, 316, 319, 332, 343, 365, 368, 394, 395, 399, 424, 439, 456.

Translations

Collections

P. Holmes and S. Thelwall, *Anti-Nicene Christian Library* (ANL) 7, 11, 15, 18. *Anti-Nicene Christian Library.* Edinburgh, 1864–.

Tertullian. In vols. 3–4 of *The Anti-Nicene Fathers*, ed. Alexander Roberts and James Donaldson, 1885–7, 10 vols. Repr. Peabody, MS: Hendrickson, 1994.

Individual works

Among translations of individual works into English the editions and translations by Ernest Evans should be noted: *Adversus Praxean* (London: SPCK, 1948); *De Oratione* (London: SPCK, 1953); *De carne Christi* (London: SPCK, 1956); *De resurrectione carnis* (London: SPCK, 1960); *De baptismo* (London: SPCK, 1964); *Adversus Marcionem,* 2 vols. (OECT: 1972).

Other translations of individual works:

The Apology, trans. E. J. Daly; *On the Soul*, trans. E. A. Quain (Fathers of the Church 10; Thomas P. Halton, ed.; Catholic University of America Press, 1950); *On the Prescription of the Heretics*, trans. S. L. Greenslade (*The Library of Christian Classics V: Early Latin Theology* (1956), 31); *Tertullian: The Treatise against Hermogenes*, trans. J. H. Washink (Ancient Christian Writers 24; 1956).

Middle Ages

Peter Abelard (1079–1142)

Joanne Maguire Robinson

Pierre Pallet, born in 1079 CE to parents of the minor nobility at La Pallet, Brittany, became the Peter Abelard best known in our day as the elicit lover of Heloise. Yet Abelard generated far more than scandal in his day: he was a highly accomplished teacher, logician, and theologian who straddled monastic and academic worlds to an extent unprecedented in his time. Abelard was perhaps the first thinker in the Christian West to separate thinking about God from experiencing God, and in doing so he set the stage for the more systematic methods of scholasticism. Abelard posited that human beings could understand something about God through reason and logic without direct experience. This willingness to apply dialectic (logic) to matters of faith was questioned by more traditional theologians of his day. Abelard was twice brought up on formal charges of heresy, twice condemned, and once (briefly) excommunicated from the church.

Abelard dedicated his life to scholarship and the church and in doing so renounced both a potential knighthood and an inheritance. In his youth he studied philosophy and logic under some of the brightest lights of his day: Roscelin (with whom he studied in the 1090s), William of Champeaux (who was his master beginning around 1100), and Anselm of Laon (his teacher around 1113). Abelard spent minimal time working under each of these men and was confident enough of his own ideas to establish schools in direct competition with his former tutors. The course of his professional life shows that Abelard rarely shrank from conflict with any opponent, whether teacher, student, or peer.

His peripatetic teaching life certainly allowed contact with many students, some of whom became influential in the church hierarchy. He established a school for logic at Melun in 1102 but moved shortly thereafter to Corbeil. He taught briefly at Notre Dame before reopening the school at Melun, moving shortly thereafter to Mont Ste Genevieve. He held a teaching post at Notre Dame again between 1114 and 1117. He seems to have retired from teaching after being appointed Abbot of St Gildas-de-Rhuys (c.1126–8), but he taught again in Paris during the 1130s until about 1140. He experienced tremendous conflict with the monks of St Gildas, who were not interested in his ideas about discipline and who, according to Abelard, conspired to kill him. He eventually sought solitude by establishing a private oratory that came to be known as "The Paraclete." He died at Cluny on April 21, 1142.

Abelard's tumultuous professional life was no match for the intrigue of his personal life. Indeed, many of those who have heard of Abelard know more about his relationship with Heloise than about his intellectual career. Sometime in 1115, Abelard began an affair with the niece of Fulbert, a canon of Notre Dame. By 1117, she was pregnant with their only child,

The Student's Companion to the Theologians, First Edition. Edited by Ian S. Markham.
© 2013 Blackwell Publishing Ltd. Published 2013 by Blackwell Publishing Ltd.

Astrolabe. Abelard sent Heloise to live with his family and married Heloise in secret after the birth, likely fearing for his status in the church in the wake of a public marriage. Heloise objected to the marriage in principle, disliking the notion of losing her status as a lover by becoming a wife. Fulbert, out of concern for his family's reputation, refused to keep the marriage a secret. His anger at the couple led Abelard to send Heloise for refuge to the convent of Argenteuil. Her uncle interpreted this as Abelard dispensing with his responsibility to Heloise and he promptly had Abelard castrated. After this humiliation, Abelard entered the monastery at St Denis and encouraged Heloise to join him in monastic life by becoming a nun.

Heloise eventually became the abbess of a community at the Paraclete, where the lovers were originally buried together. After several moves, their remains were finally interred in the Père Lachaise Cemetery in Paris. Much work has been done on their correspondence, and their story has become part of the mythic legacy of romantic love in the West. Yet their relationship seems also to have been a meeting of minds, as scholars uncover evidence that the well-read Heloise was a significant intellectual influence on Abelard.

Abelard studied widely and his work shows inspiration from Plato, Aristotle, Porphyry, Boethius, and John Scotus Eriugena. His writings in philosophy and theology survive alongside his more practical literary work. Unfortunately, much of what survives is fragmentary. His literary corpus comprises an epistolary autobiography, *Historia calamitatum* (*The Story of My Misfortunes*), written *c*.1132; a number of hymns and lyrics; seven letters to Heloise; and a poem dedicated to his son. Within these works we get a good sense of his historical context, his personal difficulties, and his ideas about monastic life and ethics.

Most of Abelard's extant writings are broadly philosophical, with particular focus on logic, theology, and ethics. His *Logica "ingredientibus"* (*Logic for Beginners*) is an unfinished series of commentaries on ancient works in logic. The *Tractatus de intellectibus* (*A Treatise on Understandings*) explores the nature of human cognition. Abelard also wrote two influential works on ethics: *Scito te ipsum* (*Know Yourself*), which explores sin, the human will, and human actions, and *Collationes* (*Comparisons*) which contains dialogues

between a philosopher and a Christian and a philosopher and a Jew.

Abelard spent much of his later life working out his theological ideas in light of his earlier work in philosophy. The structure of his *Sic et non* (*Yes and No*) was adopted by Thomas Aquinas and became part of the method of scholastic inquiry found in Peter Lombard's influential *Sentences*. Abelard also produced a commentary on Romans (*Commentaria in Epistolam Pauli ad Romanos*), which was used to support his condemnation at Sens in 1141. His *Theologia* (*Theology*) focused on explicating his ideas on the Trinity, and it was used as the basis for an early condemnation at the Council of Soissons in 1121. He tried to placate church authorities with several revisions, but the work was again condemned at the Council of Sens in 1140/1141. His accusers, Bernard of Clairvaux chief among them, accused him of various heresies, including Arianism, Pelagianism, and Nestorianism as well as Sabellianism, exemplarism, and tritheism. An overview of his thought sheds some light on these accusations.

Abelard's ideas about the Trinity, the atonement, and original sin and human volition caused much debate among his contemporaries. Abelard was a challenger of systems and ideas, and he freely entered the medieval debate over universals. Abelard's answer to the problem of universals was based in what has been labeled "conceptualism" or "sermonism." (Abelard changed emphases throughout his life on this issue, leading some to label him a "moderate realist" or even a "nominalist.") Abelard's view is something of a middle way between "extreme realists" (such as his teacher William of Champeaux) who argue that all like things share an objective nature independent of human thought or perception, and nominalists (such as Roscelin) who argue that only particulars are real. For Abelard, universals do not exist in an objective sense, but the words used to describe them have real and consistent meaning and thus function as universals. These concepts are the way human beings label likenesses among particular things (as, for instance, Plato and Socrates are both "men"). Moreover, these universals are not only the result of abstraction from concrete particulars; they also exist in God's mind as the templates with which he creates concrete particulars.

Abelard could recognize the Christian God in Plato's *Timaeus*, which, in his view, anticipated the Trinity. Although he did not dismiss biblical revelation by any means, he held that some Greek philosophers were, in effect, proto-Christians. This point of view and his ideas about the Trinity did not sit well with some of his contemporaries. Abelard was determined to explain how the three persons of the Trinity could be identical and distinct and yet one, and his eventual solution to this was twofold. He argued for the shared essence (sameness in substance) of the persons coexisting with differences in property. According to this view, each person of the Trinity possesses properties particular to each: for instance, God has the property of power, Jesus Christ has the property of wisdom, and the Holy Spirit has the property of love. Despite these different properties, all three share an essential God-likeness. Abelard believed he had elucidated objective truths about the Trinity and not simply explained the way humans, with limited reason, have come to understand it. Not surprisingly, Abelard's adversaries accused him of tritheism and of making God a mere abstraction.

Abelard's "moral theory" of the atonement was also the object of controversy. Dominant theories of the atonement in the tradition involved a ransom to the Devil or the payment of debt to God. Abelard dismissed the idea that the Devil has any control over humanity after the Fall; he even went so far as to argue that human beings inherit liability to punishment for Adam's fall but do not inherit the guilt. Consequently, human beings are not helpless captives of original sin and can, with the help of grace, do good. This was what Jesus showed in his death on the cross, a death that did not result in objective salvation for humanity. Nevertheless, the passion can have a strong psychological impact on any individual willing to see it as the perfect display of love. The atonement is thus an example for human beings, through which people can learn to act out of love (*caritas*) rather than fear.

This perspective on the atonement is related to Abelard's practical ethics. Abelard places intention at the center of moral responsibility. One is only culpable for an act one does with intent and knowledge. This premise led Abelard to argue that even those who persecuted Jesus were not responsible for their actions because they were ignorant of what they were doing. To judge people on their actions alone is absurd, as deeds by themselves are morally indifferent. Love (*caritas*) leads us to act rightly out of the proper intention. Although Abelard did not completely dismiss the power of grace in aiding human beings, he insisted that an individual's conscience should be the supreme guide in ethical decision making. According to Abelard's logic, Bernard argued, we accomplish our own redemption through our own human response, and he thus accused Abelard of Pelagianism.

For a thinker who wrote so much and taught so many, Abelard's influence is hard to pin down. His ideas and methods can be found in the writings John of Salisbury, Thomas Aquinas, Peter Lombard, and Gilbert de la Porrée. He certainly helped shift theological inquiry from "faith seeking understanding" to a more skeptical and systematic method of wrestling with questions of faith. Some scholars see his influence as primarily methodological, while others consider him a philosophical genius. His scuffles with the church likely blunted the impact he might have had if he had developed a more conservative and less provocative perspective. He did challenge the boundaries of theological inquiry of his time and thereby set the stage for far-reaching change.

St Anselm of Canterbury (1033–1109)

Travis E. Ables

I. Life

Biography

There are two main sources available for information on Anselm's life: his letters, and a biography by his friend and student Eadmer (Eadmer, 1962; Anselm, 1990–4; for biographies see Vaughn, 1987 and Southern, 1990). Anselm was born in 1033 in Aosta, in Italy. At the age of 23 he left home and traveled itinerantly in Burgundy, finally entering the monastery at Bec in Normandy as a student in 1059. The following year, he became a monk, and in 1063 succeeded Lanfranc as the prior and master of the school. In 1078, the abbot of Bec, Herluin, died, and Anselm became abbot in his stead. He held this position until his appointment as Archbishop of Canterbury, in 1093.

It was at Bec that he entered his first fruitful period of writing, though this did not begin until about 1076, when he was already past the age of 40. Anselm's corpus is not large; his main writings are comprised of 11 treatises, a short volume of prayers and meditations, and a moderate body of correspondence (for his main works, see the edition of Davies and Evans in Anselm, 1998, or Hopkins and Richardson in Anselm, 2000; the critical Latin edition of his works is Anselm, 1938–68; for his prayers, see Anselm, 1973; the translation used here will be that of Davies and Evans, unless otherwise noted). Consequently, an unusually systematic and consistent viewpoint emerges in his writings, even if there is a notable shift from the meditative, even mystical, perspective of the early works, to the ordered and sober tone of the later ones. Nevertheless, his thought remains largely constant across this oeuvre. His first work, the *Monologion*, appeared in 1076, and is followed by the *Proslogion* in 1077 or 1078; both focus on similar themes, i.e., the defense of the existence of God and the explication of God's nature, and were written, so Anselm claims, at the behest of the brethren at Bec. An exchange with a monk by the name of Gaunilo followed, who wrote a treatise, "On Behalf of the Fool," contesting Anselm's claim that only the "fool" (of Psalm 13) would dispute the necessity of the existence of God. While still at Bec, between 1080 and 1086, Anselm wrote what he called his "three treatises which pertain to the study of Sacred Scripture"—*On Truth*, *On Free Will*, and *On the Fall of the Devil*. The works are closely reasoned analyses of the respective subjects, centering around the theological significance of the uprightness (*rectitudo*) of the will and its fall into sin.

Anselm's archbishopric in Canterbury was far from placid; in fact, he seems to have spent the majority of his time in exile. A series of disagreements with William II, and then Henry I, compelled him to travel to Rome twice to seek the pope's adjudication. It is far from clear that Anselm was an ideal administrator, lacking the politic nature and diplomatic *savoir faire* that the position required in the early Middle Ages.

The Student's Companion to the Theologians, First Edition. Edited by Ian S. Markham.
© 2013 Blackwell Publishing Ltd. Published 2013 by Blackwell Publishing Ltd.

Indeed, according to Eadmer, Anselm resisted both the position of abbot at Bec and the seat at Canterbury, finally acquiescing only at the pleas of the monks at Bec and the bishops of England, respectively. Nonetheless, he continued to write in addition to his episcopal duties. The treatise *On the Incarnation of the Word*, written around 1093, attacked the position of Roscelin, a canon in France, who taught a quasi-tritheistic Trinitarian theology; Anselm showed the heretical results of this position, and clarified the manner in which orthodox Catholic teaching confessed the distinction and substantial unity of the Trinitarian persons. A few years later, Anselm's first self-imposed exile, instigated by a dispute with King William, found him abroad between 1097 and 1100, during which time he finished his famous work, *Why God Became Human* (*Cur deus homo*) in the Italian Alps, which had been begun several years earlier. The book, a rational exploration of the necessity of the incarnation for humanity's salvation, was followed by the writing of Anselm's important work, *On the Procession of the Holy Spirit*. The pope had requested Anselm's refutation of the arguments of representatives of the Greek church at the Council of Bari on the question of the *filioque*; the response was a rigorous elucidation of the logic of the Western position of the procession of the Spirit from the Father and the Son. Also while in exile, Anselm produced the *Meditation on Human Redemption*, a kind of devotional précis of *Cur deus homo*, as well as the text *On the Virgin Conception and Original Sin*. This latter is significant both as an extension of the reasoning of the three early treatises on free will, justice, and sin, and as an alternate but complementary account to *Cur deus homo* of the assumption of human nature by the Son of God.

In 1100, William died, and Anselm returned to Canterbury, but problems arose once again. At this point, controversy over investiture by monarchs (the right of the king to confer the episcopal ring and staff upon the bishop) was at a peak, and Anselm's refusal to accede to Henry I's claim to this right, and his loyalty to Pope Paschal II, resulted in another exile and journey to Rome, between 1103 and 1106. It was not until 1107 that Henry acquiesced and Anselm returned to Canterbury, now well into his seventies and frail. While in exile, in 1104, he had completed his *Prayers and Meditations*, the bulk of which were written between 1170 and 1180. He wrote one final work, *De*

concordia, or *On the Compatibility of God's Foreknowledge, Predestination, and Grace with Human Freedom*, dealing further with the themes of free will and grace first sounded in *On Free Will*. He died on April 21, 1109, and was canonized in 1494.

Influences

Anselm is sometimes described as "Augustine *redivivus*"; and while his indebtedness to the great bishop of Hippo can be overestimated, it certainly is the case that Augustine constitutes the first and primary influence upon Anselm's philosophical and theological thinking. To a certain point, this is tautologous; the thought of Augustine pervaded the theological discussions of the Middle Ages in the West, and the terms of many of the fundamental problems of scholastic theology were set by Augustine. Part of the genius of Anselm, however, was to appropriate and recast Augustinian themes in his own dialectical idiom such that they became wholly his own.

Augustine's influence is generally more suggested than named in Anselm, for he rarely references sources or authorities, though in *Monologion* and again in *On the Incarnation of the Word*, Anselm explicitly references the *De trinitate* of "blessed Augustine" as the authority by which his Trinitarian speculations should be judged (see Van Fleteren, 2002). But conceptually, several of the classic "Anselmian" tropes derive, in fact, from Augustine. For example, the slogan of *Proslogion*, *fides quaerens intellectum*, as well as the basic intent of the ontological argument, is echoed from Augustine's *On Free Will*, and the general idea of "faith seeking understanding" is scattered throughout the latter's oeuvre. Further, the explication of the Trinitarian processions according to the so-called "psychological analogies" of the second half of Augustine's *De trinitate* is the basis of Anselm's Trinitarian argument in *Monologion*; the emphasis Anselm places on the problem of grace and free will, as well as his idea of original sin, all derive directly from Augustine's thought, though Anselm significantly modifies both; the importance of the fall of the angels in determining the number of the elect in *Cur deus homo* draws upon *City of God*; and the notion of evil as privation is shared by the theologians. At a more fundamental level, to the extent that Anselm's thought is influenced by Neoplatonism, this is almost certainly mediated by Augustine's own complicated reception of Plotinian and Platonist thought, very few works of Plato being translated into Latin at the time. Although the extent of Anselm's debt to Neoplatonism is debated (see Henry, 1967; Schmitt, 1969; Hopkins, 1972, 30–2; Rogers, 1997; Matthews, 2004), the form of exemplarism that shapes the argument of *Monologion*, the strong emphasis on the simplicity and immutability of God, and the illuminationist tendencies of his epistemology likely are Augustinian in provenance.

Of a few secondary influences, most important is Boethius (died *c*.525), especially as a translator of Aristotle. Anselm's philosophical work *De grammatico* is heavily shaped by Aristotle's *Categories* via Boethius, and as Hopkins notes (1972, 28), the basic logical forms and syllogisms employed by Anselm and his contemporaries are likewise mediated by Boethius. It is possible that some of the Platonic resonances noted above owe their origin to Anselm's study of Boethius, as well; it is disputed to what extent Anselm knew the work of Pseudo-Dionysius and John Scotus Erigena. In general, it seems Boethius was more influential methodologically, rather than in terms of content, as is consistently the case throughout the Middle Ages. Finally, Gregory the Great (540–604) likely can be credited with the shape of some of Anselm's mystical tendencies (see esp. Stolz, 1935) inasmuch as the mystical ascent motif shapes the structure of *Proslogion* and particularly the *Prayers*; but again, the precise degree of Anselm's acquaintance with Gregory is uncertain (he does reference the latter's *Moralia* in letters 23 and 25), and, in any case, the theme of the mystical ascent was already well established in Western Christian thought.

II.   Method

If Anselm has been called "Augustine *redivivus*," he is also regularly labeled the "father of scholasticism." This somewhat paradoxical assessment of his importance has the advantage of highlighting just how significant a figure he is in the history of Western theology; nonetheless it also makes it easy to overlook the significance of his theological method as it was located at the turn of the twelfth century. To get a better sense of Anselm's uniqueness as well as the

legacy he bequeathed to the Middle Ages, it is necessary to examine more closely what is meant by his rubric, *fides quaerens intellectum*, as it relates to his oft-repeated maxim of proceeding "by reason alone" (*sola ratione*).

As G. R. Evans notes (Evans, 1980, 1993), in Anselm's era the distinction between philosophy and theology was not only far different from the standards of even the next century, but the term "theology" itself did not have the connotations that have come to be attributed to it; instead, Anselm and his contemporaries were far more likely to speak in terms of *studium sacrae scripturae* (the study of Holy Scripture). *Theologia* was customarily understood to refer to the study of God's own nature, rather than the systematic exposition and inquiry into the teaching of the Catholic faith. The distinction, which Aquinas would codify, more regularly drawn since Augustine, was between those truths of the faith that could be known to pagans by reason alone (e.g., the existence of God), and those given only in Christian revelation (the Trinity, the deity of Christ)—the truths of God as creator vs. God as redeemer. Further, there was increasing argument on the use of "dialectic"—most generally, the philosophy of Aristotle as it was known at the time—in the analysis of the Catholic faith (Gilson, 1955, 129, 615, n.41 has a helpful historical survey). On the one hand, Anselm resisted the idea that reason precedes faith, as if one could believe on the basis of philosophical reason; on the other, he opposed the monks who argued that secular reasoning had no place in understanding matters of faith. In fact, Lanfranc himself was decidedly uncomfortable with Anselm's method of *sola ratione*, eschewing as it did quotation of scripture or the fathers.

Moderate as it therefore was, Anselm's method was nonetheless significant: for his bold move was to investigate the truths of Christian doctrine, the truths of God as redeemer, on the basis of reason alone without consideration of revelation. Faith was presupposed, but this did not prohibit the use of reason without the specific data of scripture and tradition. As he states in *On the Incarnation of the Word* (6), apropos of *Monologion* and *Proslogion*, "I composed these works especially to show that compelling arguments apart from the authority of Scripture can establish things that we by faith hold about the divine nature and the divine persons." Hence, when he states in *Monologion* 1 that a rational person could persuade themselves of the truths of belief in the supreme nature by reason alone, he intends this to be understood, as he explains in the *prooemium* to *Proslogion*, as a "meditation on the meaning of faith from the point of view of one seeking, through silent reasoning within himself, things he knows not." The *Monologion*, then, is intended to demonstrate the nature of God as supreme good apart from the authority of scripture (see Viola, 1996).

The process is comparable in *Cur deus homo*, where Anselm seeks to demonstrate the rational necessity of the incarnation, but bracketing all knowledge of Christ and inquiring solely by "unavoidable logical steps." Anselm names two purposes in the "Commendation" to Pope Urban: to "confute [the] unwisdom" of unbelievers, and to nourish the hearts of the faithful by showing the basic reasonableness of the Christian faith. He is careful to say, however, that he does not intend believers to arrive at faith by reason, but at the same time, he understands rational understanding to stand "midway between faith and revelation." Hence, the procedure of *sola ratione* has the purpose both of apologetic and of edification; Anselm is using the tools of philosophical dialectic to explain the rational basis of the faith and demonstrate its cogency. His purpose in *Proslogion* is similar, though in contrast to the "chain of arguments" that he used in *Monologion*, that second work was intended to demonstrate the existence of God by a single proof in itself. Yet the so-called ontological argument of the *Proslogion* is difficult to interpret; for while it takes the form of a logical argument that purports to prove the necessity of the existence of God based on the very meaning of the term "God," it also is located in a treatise written as a prayer, so that the author prays "let me find You in loving You; let me love You in finding You ... I do not seek to understand so that I may believe; but I believe so that I may understand" (*Proslogion* 1; cf. Schufreider, 1994).

The question has often been asked, then: does Anselm seek to prove the truths of the Christian faith by virtue of a kind of "natural theology," or does he presuppose faith? The dilemma itself is anachronistic, and Anselm likely would have refused, or failed to understand, the question altogether. It is important to remember that most of his writings (e.g., the *Three treatises*, *On the Procession of the Holy Spirit*, or *De concordia*) are discussions of problems presented in Christian teaching, like free will and grace or the procession of the Holy Spirit, the truth of which is assumed as given in the deposit of faith. Anselm's innovative move is to examine and resolve these problems, not by exposition of scripture or citation of the fathers, but by the resources of reason and philosophy: *sola ratione* is a tool, then, that he uses to show the inherent coherence of the Christian faith in the logical analysis of its teachings. Thus he can simultaneously pray for illumination in *Proslogion*, and claim he has demonstrated God's existence by a single rational argument; indeed, as the final chapter (26) of that treatise shows, the knowledge of God this kind of rational meditation is meant to serve has as its purpose the love of God and rejoicing in God, as an anticipation of the beatific vision itself (see McCord Adams, 2004).

Anselm's method as "faith seeking understanding" is therefore the rational exploration and demonstration of the truth of the teachings of scripture, using philosophical tools to prove and explicate truth without reliance upon authority. But there is an additional dimension of the maxim *sola ratione* that is important to consider, and it is embodied in the small work *De veritate* (*On Truth*), which Anselm highly valued (he references it regularly in other works), but is often overlooked. This concerns the coincidence of truth, justice, and the divine goodness; truth is rightness, or rectitude (*rectitudo*; see Pouchet, 1964), and insofar as something, whether a proposition, a thought, the will, or an action, is true, it is in accord with and participates in the Supreme Truth, which is identical with God (see esp. *On Truth* 7). Thus, the very notion of truth requires a transcendental Truth; and thus insofar as reason functions rightly, it already participates in divine truth. For Anselm's method to function by reason alone, then, from the beginning presupposes reason's capacity to participate in God, and therefore to operate in intimate relationship with faith.

III. Theology

God

A consideration of Anselm's theology begins with the complementary treatises *Monologion* and *Proslogion*, and the question of the demonstration of the existence of God that is central to both of them. *Monologion* takes as its point of departure a simple question: whether, given the profusion of good things evident to the senses in the world, there is "some one thing through which all good things whatsoever are good?" (1). The answer is self-evident, and it follows that this supreme being is the exemplar and ground of all goods, for all goods must necessarily have a supreme good in whom those goods participate. From this basic Platonic point it follows by definition that such a supreme being must be simple, self-existent, and immutable: whatever is predicated of its essence is one and the same thing in it such that, for example, for it to be just is the same as for it to be justice itself (16, 17). The premise commits Anselm to arguing from the idea of particular goods to this highest good, for every created good participates in the idea of that good that is identical to the nature of the highest being that is the sum of all goods. The result of this demonstration is that this substance "must be whatever in every respect it is better to be than not to be. For this substance alone is that than which nothing at all is better" (15, Hopkins and Richardson translation). As such, strictly speaking the Supreme Being alone exists without qualification, insofar as all other substances exist derivatively by participation in it, and it necessarily exists immutably and eternally (28).

This point is important for understanding the transition to the proof of *Proslogion*; while *Monologion* demonstrates the existence of God, it does not do so to Anselm's satisfaction, since it demonstrates the divinity on the basis of the various created perfections. In *Proslogion*, however, he deploys the logic of a being that "it is better to be than not to be" to develop a proof of the existence of God that relies on nothing but the very *concept* of the deity itself—that "by itself would suffice to prove that God really exists" (*Proslogion*, preface). Instead of understanding the deity as the perfection of any given created good and the sum of all such perfections, Anselm focuses on the very idea implied in perfection itself: if God is, by definition, something than which nothing greater can be conceived, it necessarily follows that God exists. For, argues Anselm, insofar as one understands the idea of something than which nothing greater can be conceived, one must see that it cannot exist in the mind alone. For to exist in reality is greater than to

exist in the mind. Thus a being that exists solely in the mind cannot be something than which nothing greater can be conceived, for one can always conceive it of existing; therefore it *must* exist.

This, in brief, is the so-called "ontological argument" of ch. 2 of *Proslogion* (for some standard studies, see Anselm, 1965; La Croix, 1972; Campbell, 1976). Ch. 3 enlarges upon the argument briefly, asserting that if this being exists thusly, it "so truly exists that it cannot be even thought not to exist." That is, not only is God's existence logically demonstrable, but it is necessary: to conceive of the non-existence of God is incoherent, and hence only the "fool" could deny it. So the understanding of God as the being than which nothing greater can be conceived, an understanding which is analytic with the very meaning of the signifier "God," already accomplishes *in nuce* what it took nearly the entire treatise of *Monologion* to do: i.e., to demonstrate the existence *and* nature of God. For if God is this being, existing through Godself alone, then God is "whatever it is better to be than not to be" (5). This formulation had already appeared in *Monologion* 15, but Anselm had not grasped there that this idea in itself was enough to show the divinity's logical necessity. This is the *unum argumentum* of *Proslogion*; therefore, the rest of the text need merely explicate just what it might be to be this maximally perfect being: spirit, omnipotent, merciful and just, eternal, limitless, and simple.

This is a short overview of Anselm's quest for a rational demonstration of the existence of God, his first and perhaps chief claim to fame in the tradition. But he also made a significant contribution to Trinitarian theology. As with the above arguments, Anselm's importance lies not in contributing a significantly new doctrinal model or theory, but rather in his careful explication of the inner logic of the Western tradition of Trinitarian doctrine, received largely from Augustine. It was a major task of *Monologion* to explicate the triunity of the Godhead in the course of the argument, and the demonstration of the nature of the Trinity takes up the entire second half of the treatise. Beginning from the notion of the Supreme Spirit's "verbalization" or "expression" (*locutio*), Anselm develops a generally Augustinian understanding of the Trinity as memory, understanding, and love, each consubstantial with the other. The Son's procession as

Word (*verbum*) is particularly important, however, for the shape of the treatise insofar as he understands the Word alone to truly exist, and created things to exist through and according to the Word—Trinitarian theology is therefore central to the exemplarism of the treatise that grounds the relationship between creation and the divine as a relationship of created good to supreme good. Indeed, it is precisely insofar as the rational mind is the image and mirror of the supreme being (66, 67) that illumination by the Word in the mind brings self-knowledge and knowledge of God into intimate relation. But this is also, for Anselm, a pneumatological question, for the rational creature was made to love the supreme being as well; hence, just as God knows and loves Godself in God's subsistence as Word and Spirit, so the human creature knows and loves God by their own participation in God's *ratio* and *amor*.

In *Monologion* Anselm had followed the Augustinian dictum that the names of Father, Son, and Spirit were relational terms that thereby establish the plurality of the subsistences in the one divine person; he also states that whatever is essential to the Supreme Nature besuits each person perfectly such that they are not plural but one—the Father's goodness is identical to the Son's goodness insofar as they possess the one divine goodness consubstantially, for example—but that the Son's begetting and Spirit's procession are proper to them alone. This logic was expanded in two important later works, *On the Incarnation of the Word* and *On the Procession of the Holy Spirit*. In the former, Anselm controverts the teaching of Roscelin, who maintained that the Trinitarian persons were three "things" (*res*) in the same way that three angels are three things, for if they were not, the incarnation of the Son would have necessitated that of the Father and Spirit. Anselm shows Roscelin's basic equivocation: the persons are *distinct* though not *different* "things" with respect to their distinguishing properties (i.e., their processions) but one thing with respect to the one divine nature. In short: they are three in terms of relation (what is proper to the persons), and one in terms of substance (what is common to the divinity). *De processione* then takes up the same reasoning in defense of Western filioquism. The basic thesis of the text, which became axiomatic for Latin Trinitarianism, is that any predication of God signifies

the one being of God, the common nature of the deity, except for what is said of the opposition of relations. Thus, God necessarily exists from God in each procession as whole from whole, for the simplicity of the deity admits of no parts. Therefore, when the Son is begotten from the Father, he is begotten from the whole God, and likewise with the Spirit, excepting only the opposition of relation—that is, the Son proceeds from the whole God, except for his relation to the Spirit, and vice versa. Hence, either the Son must proceed from the Spirit along with the Father, or the Spirit must proceed from Father and Son. But since there is no opposition of relation by which the Son proceeds from the Spirit, we must understand the converse: the *filioque*. Therefore, there is one God, a Father from whom Son and Spirit originate: a Son who is begotten from the Father and with the Father breathes out the Spirit, and a Spirit who proceeds from Father and Son. Everything else that can be spoken of the deity must be spoken in common of all three as one God.

Christology

If the demonstration of the existence and nature of God *sola ratione* in *Monologion* and *Proslogion* constitutes the first contribution of Anselm to the Western theological tradition, the second, of at least equal importance, is the satisfaction theory attributed to the text *Cur deus homo*. Unlike in the former texts, however, Anselm contributes more than a logical examination and explication of theological themes received from the tradition; instead he proffers a substantive doctrinal model for understanding the incarnation of the Son of God and its salvific effects.

Cur deus homo is a protracted defense of the dignity of God's means of salvation in Christ, and the strict logical necessity of the fact that it took the form that it did. While many of Anselm's works (e.g., *De processione*) wield reason solely as a means of explicating the intrinsic rationality of the received faith, *Cur deus homo* explicitly sets out to prove that the incarnation is in fact logically necessary (see Root, 1987; Campbell, 1999) on its own terms—in fact, Anselm proposes to proceed as if Christ had never appeared (on the *Christo remoto*, see McIntyre, 1954; Campbell, 2002). Similar to the end of *Monologion*, the major purpose of the text is to show that rational human nature was created for happiness, has fallen from the means of acquiring that happiness through sin, and requires the incarnation of the God-man to attain that lost immortality. In essence, the central claim is simple: concerning the price for humanity's redemption, no one *can* pay it except God, but no one *should* pay it except a human being—therefore, the exigency of a God-man (II.6).

The problematic of *Cur deus homo* revolves around how it is indeed "fitting" for God to humble Godself in the birth and death of the Son such that God's honor is not denigrated, and the order of creation is upheld (see McCord Adams, 1999). Central to both of these considerations is the nature of the necessity at play in the fact that salvation took place in the manner that it did. That is, if it is necessary that God redeem the human race in the way God did, does this impose an external constraint upon the deity—surely an absurdity? For the first question that presents in the consideration is why God did not forgive sin out of mercy alone, rather than requiring repayment of the debt of sin—a repayment only Christ could render. Sin, for Anselm, is failure to uphold *rectitudo* of will—the failure to will the good for its own sake, that is, to will in accordance with God's will (I.11). To fail to pay this debt to God is to sin, and the problem of sin is not merely, as Anselm is often interpreted to be saying, that it is a slight upon God's honor, a personal affront to God; rather, sin by failing to uphold *rectitudo* is a disruption of the goodness and beauty of God's creation (I.15)—it is disorder, and such disorder cannot be merely forgiven, but must be put right (I.12). God's honor is maintained in punishing sinners, but God's basic purpose in creation is not, and it is this purpose that provides both the necessity of redemption through Jesus Christ and the condition for the satisfaction of God's honor; necessity is thus identical to God's will by which the blessed are to enjoy the Heavenly City in the contemplation of God. Because for God to fail to fulfill God's own created purpose would be the ultimate disruption of the *ordo* of the universe God must act to redeem humanity in order to accomplish God's own purposes.

Humanity cannot redeem itself, for it has lost its freedom as a result of the Fall and the transmission of original sin. Humanity took from God what God willed to do with that nature—its beatification—and

was therefore corrupted entirely. There is no human act that can justify a human being. Further, total obedience and rectitude is already owed to God as a matter of course, so no human act could suffice to merit redemption anyhow; humanity is in a double bind, therefore. But it is fitting that humanity be redeemed by a human being, even as it fell by a human being: "nothing could be more just," says Anselm's interlocutor, but "nothing could be more impossible" (I.23). This, then, is the exigency of the incarnation. Humanity is saved through Christ, who is both human, and therefore capable of paying satisfaction for humanity's sin, but is also divine, and therefore not subject to the penalty for sin that encompasses the entire human race. The birth of Christ from the race of Adam establishes the necessary condition of the redemption of that race; Christ renders the obedience to God that God requires of the human race, but because he does not sin he is not subject to the obligation to die; that he dies willingly nonetheless suffices to satisfy God's honor (II.10). And because his life is given gratuitously, that is, because it is a death willingly undergone not by penalty but as that which is fitting to satisfy God's honor, it suffices to outweigh all the sins of humanity. The reward for the Son's obedience is then given to humanity, for there is nothing the Father has that the Son does not already have, and it would be "unfitting" for the Son's obedience not to be rewarded. Hence, the result of Christ's work is the redemption of the human race.

It is important to distinguish Anselm's account from later theories of satisfaction, features of which tend to be read back into *Cur deus homo*. Two are particularly notable (on the following, see Burns, 1975). First, Anselm's is not a theory of substitutionary atonement. In fact, though *Cur deus homo* is regularly treated as an "objective" theory of atonement vis-à-vis "subjective" theories such as the so-called moral influence theory of Abelard, in fact it is in the latter's *Commentary on Romans* (as well as in Hugh of St Victor) that the death of Christ comes to stand in for the punishment for human sin. For Anselm, Christ's death is not a payment of the penalty of sin, but precisely a gratuitous offering of a death not required of him. Second, there is little notion of "merit" in Anselm's account in the sense of Christ earning a debt owed to him by God; this is a later theory of Duns Scotus.

Indeed, for Scotus, the death of Christ in accepting the passion yields a finite amount of merit adequate only for the forgiveness of the sins of the elect. In Anselm's theory the emphasis is laid on God's upholding of the beauty and order of God's creation by the offering of a good, the willing death of the one who did not owe it, that infinitely outstrips the evil of human sin; thus, God's honor in upholding the *rectitudo* of creation is maintained, and God's purpose for creation is fulfilled. The overarching rubric of the reason why God became a human, therefore, is that it is fitting within this *ordo*, a fittingness that touches even upon the aesthetic as the motor of necessity by which God always acts according to God's good purposes (cf. Vanderjagt, 1999; Hogg, 2004).

Anthropology

The final significant area of theological reflection Anselm engaged in finds him once more in Augustinian territory: the relationship of free will and grace, along with the concomitant concerns of original sin and election. But though Anselm picks up the problem from the bishop of Hippo, his conceptualizations are rather different. In *On Truth* Anselm locates truth in the will, insofar as truth is understood as *rectitudo* in accordance with the Supreme Truth, who just as *rectitudo* is identical with justice. The will has rectitude in willing what it ought, and this is justice: willing what is upright for its own sake. There is a close parallel here to the function of reason in Anselm's notion *sola ratione*, which we could likewise gloss as "thinking what is upright for its own sake": a created faculty of the human being approximates to its divine exemplar insofar as it participates in that exemplar by rightly adhering to the idea itself to which it is oriented. In other words, the human will functions rightly insofar as it adheres to justice, understood as *rectitudo*, by willing what is upright just because it *is* upright, which uprightness itself is identical to God.

This basic insight then provides a problem: why do humans will what they ought not? Anselm wrestles with a dilemma: on the one hand, the rational nature by definition always has free will insofar as it is able to preserve rectitude of will. On the other hand, it is also the case that Adam (and Satan) by subjecting themselves to sin deprived themselves of the ability to use

this freedom without grace (*On Free Will* 3). Hence, the rational nature is both slave to sin and unable to regain its rectitude without grace, and yet it always has free choice (10). Anselm resolves this by arguing that a person is enslaved insofar as they cannot regain lost *rectitudo* by their own efforts, yet this inability does not affect their present ability to keep uprightness (11). He interprets the Augustinian notion of a powerlessness not to sin not in the latter's sense of an inability to choose anything but sin, but rather in the inability to return to rectitude; the present capacity of freedom of will to choose rectitude—this capability not even God can take from a will (8).

In fairly radical distinction—even retreat—from Augustine, then, the effect of original sin does not corrupt the will such that it can only indulge in sinful appetites; rather, the soul's injustice is in its failure to control itself with respect to the appetites of the flesh (*On the Virgin Conception and Original Sin* 4). It is debt, not corruption, that is the inheritance of Adam's sin that is passed on in reproduction (10). God redeems by granting favor that remits the debt owed for past sins, but does not energize the will through the action of grace: grace assists natural free will by giving it back again the *rectitudo* that it then keeps by its native capacity for free will (*De concordia* 3). That is, while Anselm has a notion of co-operative grace, he has largely lost the fundamental Augustinian insight concerning *operative* grace.

IV.   Significance

Father of scholasticism

Calling Anselm the "father of scholasticism" is, like any such epoch-making status assigned by later generations, as much a distortion of his importance as it is appreciation. That this is the case is evident insofar as, in the tension of the times between the theology of the schools and the monasteries, Anselm is clearly aligned with the monastery. Further, it is at least arguable that scholasticism as a historically definable method was defined externally by the production of commentaries on Lombard's *Sentences*, and by the writing of theological summas, which traditions both postdate Anselm. Further, Anselm's direct influence on his immediate successors is debated, and remarkably little study has been devoted to the question (Evans, 1980 is the standard work). Research had generally focused upon the reception history of certain texts, especially the *Proslogion* and *Cur deus homo*. Less regularly, the question of Anselm's maxim *fides quaerens intellectum* is taken to be a definitive articulation of theology's relationship to philosophy and secular learning, though the interpretation of the formula shifts with exigencies of each given age. But it is more difficult to assess what Anselm's contemporaries and the classic scholastics made of his particular articulation of the relationship of faith and reason in light of the massive shifts in the understanding of theological rationality of the age, especially as the philosophy of Aristotle, and Jewish and Muslim Aristotelian scholars, came to set the agenda in the following centuries.

Nevertheless, we can say that at this early stage of formation of what would be viewed as the "medieval synthesis," Anselm was in basic agreement with Abelard and the dialecticians on the point that Aristotelian logic provided a means of carrying out theological reasoning with rigor and clarity, and their method is similar: the use of the resource of *sola ratione* to analyze and defend sacred doctrine. The difference lies in the capacity of that reason, which for Abelard was capable in itself of demonstrating the truths of faith, whereas for Anselm faith and reason were never independent of one another, and reason was always the tool of a faith seeking to understand. He represents the unity of the two faculties in a way that would quickly become difficult to maintain. This debate would be carried out throughout the Middle Ages; but Anselm clearly represents the position that would place reason in the service of faith.

Mysticism

As Gilson notes (1955, 139), Anselm's thought has a certain ambivalence: containing all the rigor and speculative thought of a philosopher and the exactitude of the later scholastics, it is also suffused with a "religious feeling which sometimes borders of mysticism." The *Proslogion* alone shows just how true this is: a kind of eleventh-century précis of the *Confessions*, it plainly follows the pattern of the mystical ascent that defined Western mystical theology from

Augustine to Eckhart and beyond (cf. esp. Schufreider, 1994; Turner, 1995; McMahon, 2006). His was an important work in synthesizing the ascent as fully integral with the quest of *fides quaerens intellectum*; thus his thinking would have an important influence on thinkers who bridged the distinction between mysticism and scholasticism, such as Bonaventure or Richard of St Victor. Further, his *Prayers and Meditations* quickly circulated and provided an important influence on medieval devotion (Anselm, 1973). The spirituality of the age was showing an increased devotion to Mary, and a compassionate identification with the humanity of Christ; Anselm's focus on Christ's obedience to God and solidarity with humanity in suffering, evident in his prayers, the *Meditation on Human Redemption*, as well as throughout *Cur deus homo* (Fulton, 2002, 170–92), was an important factor in the later mystical devotion to the humanity of Jesus.

The ontological argument and its reception

The ontological argument has had a life all its own (cf. Hartshorne, 1965; Plantinga, 1965; Hick and McGill, 1967). Appropriated by Bonaventure, it was strongly criticized by Thomas Aquinas. The general logic of the argument is central to Descartes' *Meditations on First Philosophy*, for the first thing the Cartesian subject is certain of, subsequent to its own being as *cogito*, is the idea of God, a being whose essence necessarily includes the idea of existence. It was Kant, who bestowed the appellation "ontological" on Anselm's argument, who also gave it its most renowned riposte: existence, he argued, is not a real predicate, and therefore it is meaningless to argue that it is greater to have existence than not to have it—a refutation of the key premise of the argument (see Viola, 2002).

The argument has had a lively career in modern analytic philosophy; it has been a regular interpretation since Hartshorne and Norman Malcolm (Plantinga, 1965, 123–59) to distinguish between the arguments of *Proslogion* 2 and 3, with the second offering a proof of the necessity of the existence of God that remains viable. Since Karl Barth's famous study on Anselm (1960), contemporary theologians have regularly taken up the question of the merits and status of Anselm's argument, and there has been a demonstrable trend among both theologians and philosophers to understand the function of the argument, and the method of *sola ratione* itself, as grounded in the life and experience of faith: the argument is a mode of reflection *posterior* to faith and the basis of its presuppositions, for such interpreters.

Atonement theory

Although Anselm's proposal in *Cur deus homo* has never been taken up in its entirety, it nonetheless provided the framework and categories that would be the starting point of much subsequent theorization on the work of Christ (see Robson, 1996). As Burns shows (1975, 304), three categories emerged as important in the medieval discussion: satisfaction for sin, substitution for its punishment, and restoration of the human race. Anselm's treatise only truly provides for the first, and even then his notion of satisfaction as an exigency of God's wounded honor and the restoration of the created *ordo* gradually became aligned with Abelard's notion of substitution so that the penal overtones of the latter became predominant in Protestant theorizations of the work of Christ. Although the precise nature of satisfaction became a lively topic of debate following Anselm, the meaning of the term remained polyvalent; the Council of Trent, for example, incorporated the term into Catholic dogma, but did not definitively specify in what satisfaction consisted. Nevertheless, Anselm *did* provide a notable advance beyond the discussions of the incarnation and atonement in the fathers, which tended to focus on general models of ransom to the devil, and on the *christus victor* pattern. Further, his basic formula that only God *can*, but only a human being *should* make satisfaction for sin was enormously influential.

References

Anselm. 1938–68. *Anselmi opera omnia*, 6 vols., ed. F. S. Schmitt. Rome and Edinburgh.

Anselm. 1965. *St. Anselm's* Proslogion, trans. with introduction and commentary by M. J. Charlesworth. Oxford: Clarendon Press.

Anselm. 1973. *The Prayers and Meditations of St. Anselm*, trans. with an introduction by Benedicta Ward. New York: Penguin Books.

Anselm. 1990–4. *The Letters of Saint Anselm of Canterbury*, 3 vols., trans. and annotated by Walter Fröhlich. Kalamazoo, MI: Cistercian Publications.

Anselm. 1998. *Anselm of Canterbury: The Major Works*, ed. Brian Davies and G. R. Evans. New York: Oxford University Press.

Anselm. 2000. *Complete Philosophical and Theological Treatises of Anselm of Canterbury*, trans. Jasper Hopkins and Herbert Richardson. Minneapolis: Arthur J. Banning Press.

Barth, Karl. 1960. *Anselm:* fides quaerens intellectum, trans. Ian W. Robertson. London: SCM Press Ltd.

Burns, J. Patout. 1975. "The Concept of Satisfaction in Medieval Redemption Theory," *Theological Studies* 36 (June): 285–304.

Campbell, Richard. 1976. *From Belief to Understanding: A Study of Anselm's* Proslogion Argument *on the Existence of God*. Canberra: The Australian National University.

Campbell, Richard. 1999. "The Nature of Theological Necessity." In *Cur deus homo: atti del congresso Anselmiano internazionale*, ed. Paul Gilbert, Helmut Kohlenberger, and Elmar Salmann. Rome: Centro Studi S. Anselmo, pp. 421–35.

Campbell, Richard. 2002. "*Fides quaerens intellectum—deo remoto.*" In *Saint Anselm—A Thinker for Yesterday and Today*, ed. Coloman Viola and Frederick Van Fleteren. Lewiston, NY: Edwin Mellen Press, pp. 176–81.

Davies, Brian and Leftow, Brian, eds. 2004. *The Cambridge Companion to Anselm*. New York: Cambridge University Press.

Eadmer. 1962. *The Life of St. Anselm, Archbishop of Canterbury*, ed. R. W. Southern. New York: Thomas Nelson and Sons Ltd.

Evans, G. R. 1980. *Anselm and a New Generation*. New York: Oxford University Press.

Evans, G. R. 1993. *Philosophy and Theology in the Middle Ages*. New York: Routledge.

Fulton, Rachel. 2002. *From Judgment to Passion: Devotion to Christ and the Virgin Mary, 800–1200*. New York: Columbia University Press.

Gilbert, Paul, Kohlenberger, Helmut, and Salmann, Elmar, eds. 1999. *Cur deus homo: atti del congresso Anselmiano internazionale*. Rome: Centro Studi S. Anselmo.

Gilson, Etienne. 1955. *History of Christian Philosophy in the Middle Ages*. New York: Random House.

Hartshorne, Charles. 1965. *Anselm's Discovery: A Re-examination of the Ontological Proof for God's Existence*. La Salle , IL: Open Court Publishing Company.

Henry, Desmond Paul. 1967. *The Logic of Saint Anselm*. New York: Oxford University Press.

Hick, John and McGill, Arthur C., eds. 1967. *The Many-faced Argument: Recent Studies on the Ontological Argument for the Existence of God*. New York: The Macmillan Company.

Hogg, David S. 2004. *Anselm of Canterbury: The Beauty of Theology*. Burlington, VT: Ashgate Publishing Company.

Hopkins, Jasper. 1972. *A Companion to the Study of St. Anselm*. Minneapolis: University of Minnesota Press.

La Croix, Richard R. 1972. Proslogion *II and III: A Third Interpretation of Anselm's Argument*. Leiden: E. J. Brill.

Luscombe, D. E., and Evans, G. R., eds. 1996. *Anselm: Aosta, Bec and Canterbury*. Sheffield: Sheffield Academic Press.

Matthews, Gareth. 2004. "Anselm, Augustine, and Platonism." In *The Cambridge Companion to Anselm*, ed. Brian Davies and Brian Leftow. New York: Cambridge University Press, pp. 61–83.

McCord Adams, Marilyn. 1999. "Elegant Necessity, Prayerful Disputation: Method in *Cur deus homo*." In *Cur deus homo: atti del congresso Anselmiano internazionale*, ed. Paul Gilbert, Helmut Kohlenberger, and Elmar Salmann. Rome: Centro Studi S. Anselmo, pp. 367–96.

McCord Adams, Marilyn. 2004. "Anselm on Faith and Reason." In *The Cambridge Companion to Anselm*, ed. Brian Davies and Brian Leftow. New York: Cambridge University Press, pp. 32–60.

McIntyre, John. 1954. *St. Anselm and His Critics: A Re-interpretation of the* Cur deus homo. Edinburgh: Oliver and Boyd.

McMahon, Robert. 2006. *Understanding the Medieval Meditative Ascent: Augustine, Anselm, Boethius, and Dante*. Washington, DC: Catholic University of America Press.

Plantinga, Alvin, ed. 1965. *The Ontological Argument: From St. Anselm to Contemporary Philosophers*. New York: Anchor Books.

Pouchet, Robert. 1964. *La rectitudo chez Saint Anselme: un itinéraire Augustinien de l'ame à Dieu*. Paris: Études Augustiniennes.

Robson, Michael. 1996. "The Impact of the *Cur deus homo* on the Early Franciscan School." In *Anselm: Aosta, Bec and Canterbury*, ed. D. E. Luscombe and G. R. Evans. Sheffield: Sheffield Academic Press, pp. 334–47.

Rogers, Katherin A. 1997. *The Neoplatonic Metaphysics and Epistemology of Anselm of Canterbury*. Lewiston, NY: Edwin Mellen Press.

Root, Michael. 1987. "Necessity and Unfittingness in Anselm's *Cur deus homo*," *Scottish Journal of Theology* 40(2): 211–30.

Schmitt, F. S. 1969. "Anselm und der (Neu-) Platonismus." In *Analecta Anselmiana*, ed. F. S. Schmitt. Frankfurt.

Schufreider, Gregory. 1994. *Confessions of a Rational Mystic: Anselm's Early Writings*. West Lafayette, IN: Purdue University Press.

Southern, R. W. 1990. *Saint Anselm: A Portrait in a Landscape*. New York: Cambridge University Press.

Stolz, Anselm. 1935. "Das *Proslogion* des hl. Anselm," *Revue Bénédictine* 47: 331–47.

Turner, Denys. 1995. *The Darkness of God: Negativity in Christian Mysticism*. New York: Cambridge University Press.

Van Fleteren, Frederick. 2002. "The Influence of Augustine's *De trinitate* on Anselm's *Monologion*." In *Saint Anselm—A Thinker for Yesterday and Today*, ed. Coloman Viola and Frederick Van Fleteren. Lewiston, NY: Edwin Mellen Press, pp. 411–43.

Vanderjagt, Arjo. 1999. "*Propter utilitatem et rationis pulchritudinem amabilis*. The Aesthetics of Anselm's *Cur deus homo*." In *Cur deus homo: atti del congresso Anselmiano internazionale*, ed. Paul Gilbert, Helmut Kohlenberger, and Elmar Salmann. Rome: Centro Studi S. Anselmo, pp. 717–30.

Vaughn, Sally N. 1987. *Anselm of Bec and Robert of Meulan: The Innocence of the Dove and the Wisdom of the Serpent*. Berkeley: University of California Press.

Viola, Coloman Etienne. 1996. "Authority and Reason in Saint Anselm's Life and Thought." In *Anselm: Aosta, Bec and Canterbury*, ed. D. E. Luscombe and G. R. Evans. Sheffield: Sheffield Academic Press, pp. 172–208.

Viola, Coloman Etienne. 2002. "Saint Anselme est-il le père de l'argument ontologique? Le *Proslogion* confronté à Kant." In *Saint Anselm—A Thinker for Yesterday and Today*, ed. Coloman Viola and Frederick Van Fleteren. Lewiston, NY: Edwin Mellen Press, pp. 67–149.

Viola, Coloman, and Frederick Van Fleteren, eds. 2002. *Saint Anselm—A Thinker for Yesterday and Today*. Lewiston, NY: Edwin Mellen Press.

Thomas Aquinas, OP (*c.*1224–74)

Minlib Dallh, OP

I. Life

Thomas Aquinas or Thomas of Aquino was born in the family castle at Roccasecca in 1224/5 near the town of Aquino in southern Italy. His father, Landulf, was a minor nobleman and his mother a descendant from Norman and Neapolitan gentry. Thomas's family was deeply involved in the complex and shifting politics of the day that opposed the Holy Roman Emperor against the pope (O'Meara, 1997).

Thomas was a Roman Catholic priest in the Dominican Order (Order of Preachers, OP). Philosopher and theologian in the scholastic tradition, Aquinas is held in the Roman Catholic Church as one of the greatest doctors of the church and the model teacher for those studying for the priesthood. Aquinas's subtle and delicate assimilation of Aristotle in both philosophy and theology had experienced favor and disfavor.

Thomas's biography is simple. He traveled very little—only between Italy, France, and Germany. Besides his time at the Roman Curia in Rome, he spent most of his life at the universities of Paris and Naples, where he preached, wrote, and lectured.

Thomas lived at a crucial cultural moment when the advent of Aristotelian philosophy coincided with the establishment of universities—Naples, Salamanca, Cologne, and Paris. Paris became the center of Western Christendom's higher education. This period of the High Middle Ages witnessed the study and integration of new sciences from ancient Greek works and the burgeoning of a new Gothic art of building and decorating churches. Chenu, the French Dominican medievalist, described the cultural age which would shape Aquinas's life in these terms:

> It is not irrelevant that in the days of Saint Louis and Frederick II, Saint Thomas should arrive at Paris at a time:
> - When, in a new society just entering upon a communal era, it was in the corporate university body that intellectual eagerness and curiosity were concentrated and which was to introduce Aristotle and ancient reason to Christian thought,
> - When the cathedral of Notre Dame of Paris was being completed and the Romance of the Rose written,
> - When Europe was entering on a new era in which it would cease to be a theocratic entity,
> - When the Muslims were hemming in the Western world by their military success and seducing it by their science and philosophy
> - When, finally, merchants and missionaries were pushing their way into the region of Cathay and discovering the world's dimensions and the variety of its civilizations. (Chenu, 1950)

Nevertheless, it is crucial to note that once Aquinas's theology was equated with orthodoxy or accepted as the official theology of the Catholic Church, hagiography took precedent over historicity. Thus, Aquinas was proclaimed as the *Doctor Angelicus* or the *Doctor Univeralis*.

The Student's Companion to the Theologians, First Edition. Edited by Ian S. Markham.
© 2013 Blackwell Publishing Ltd. Published 2013 by Blackwell Publishing Ltd.

Chenu noted that these flattering posthumous images of Aquinas were historical and doctrinal mistakes:

> These triumphant images hide two episodes: the double condemnation of 1270 and 1277 after Thomas's death. Deliberately, the disciples of Thomas hid these two painful episodes of his legacy as payback against history. In order to understand Aquinas's life and work, readers must on the one hand, free themselves from the triumphant and victorious Aquinas of the school of Thomism, and on the other hand abandon the devotional images in which St Thomas was presented as an abstracted, solitary person, which contemplative and intellectual life removed him from the conflicts and squabbles of his century. (Chenu, 1950)

Hence, Thomas Aquinas did not live to see Thomism triumph. Two historical features describe Thomas best: an intellectual genius and a striking spiritual freedom. He had a curious and relentless mind that searched for Truth, dissented with the status quo, and called into question the modus vivendi obtained for centuries. He embodied to the best of his abilities the Dominican motto of "search for Truth."

II.   Early Education

In 1230, at the age of five, Aquinas's father Landulf sent his son (as an oblate) to the powerful Benedictine Abbey of Monte Cassino for basic education. Landulf had hoped that eventually Aquinas would replace his uncle Landulf Sinnibaldo as the lordly abbot of an influential monastery. Monte Cassino was a well-regarded and richly endowed monastery. It was an astute move which was congruent with the social milieu and cultural climate of the feudal system (Chenu, 1950).

At the Benedictine Abbey, Aquinas acquired the rudiments of the contemplative life and learned to recite the Psalms. This early monastic immersion must have instilled in Aquinas a love for contemplation and an understanding of theology as essentially as an elucidation of sacred scriptures. "The impact of the monastic life in that great and ancient institution—communal order in graced tranquility, education joined to liturgy—must have impressed the young Thomas" (O'Meara, 1997).

The Dominican model of *contemplari aliis tradere* (to share the fruit of one's contemplation) touched a core

in the young Thomas when he arrived in Naples. The seeds of contemplation sown in Monte Cassino and Thomas's own disposition toward the life of the mind were nurtured by the Friar Preachers' dedication to search for Truth. Such an environment fostered Thomas's radical spiritual freedom and produced a towering theological, philosophical, and mystical figure in Western Christianity.

In 1239, after nine years with the Benedictines, Thomas was compelled to depart because Frederick II sent troops to occupy Monte Cassino after yet another papal excommunication (O'Meara, 1997). He was eventually sent to Naples. At the University of Naples, he enrolled in what we would call undergraduate studies in philosophy. There, the young Thomas was first introduced to the metaphysics of Aristotle under Peter of Ireland. O'Meara described Thomas's new abode:

> The Neapolitan university, with its faculties in arts, ecclesiastical and civil law, medicine, and theology, reflected the atmosphere of Frederick's court at Palermo where Latin, Muslim and Jewish scholars exchanged ideas, where Arab astronomy and Greek medicine met, and where the texts of Aristotle and his Arab commentators were being discussed and translated into Latin. (O'Meara, 1997)

At the University of Naples, Thomas encountered a new world of ideas in the thought of Aristotle and a new way of religious life in the Dominican Order. Unlike the monastery, where the monks gave themselves to manual work and prayer, the Dominican friars strove to find a balance between contemplative and active life. Their life was intellectual as well as meditative (Torrell, 2005).

The young Thomas turned his back on the monastic and feudal world. He determined the direction of his future against his family expectations; his choice to join the mendicant Dominican Order and not the prestigious Benedictine monastery (against his family's wishes) was counter-cultural. He entered a new religious order (founded 1216) rich in ideas and opportunities but without social status, and he entered it only 27 years after the order began. Chenu wrote:

> Thomas broke totally with the established regime (of feudalism and monasticism) and conquered for himself a

spiritual and intellectual freedom, the institutional freedom of the Order of Preachers as well as its liberty for religion ... Thomas was the audacious and balanced master of the cultural and intellectual strategy which created a civilization. (Chenu, 1950)

Furthermore, Thomas's interest in Aristotelian philosophy and his decision to join the Dominican Order spoke a great deal about the kind of person he was. Robert Barron wrote: "Thomas combined in his person the two great radicalities of his day: Aristotelianism and Gospel simplicity. As an Aristotelian radical, he was opting for this world, for science, for reason, for the beauty of the senses, and as a Gospel radical, he was opting for the life of the spirit, for trust, for deep faith and love of God" (Barron, 1996).

It is not surprising that a dramatic story is told about Thomas's family's attempt to reverse his decision to join the Dominicans. According to most biographers (Chenu, Torrell, O'Meara), Thomas's decision deeply unnerved and disappointed his parents. Hence, when Thomas was on his way to Paris to start his formal Dominican studies, he was kidnapped and forced to return to his family castle at Roccasecca. His parents and siblings tried to persuade him to abandon his idealism and join a more respectable religious order. Thomas stood firm against enticements and temptations that were placed before him. Finally, his family gave in and Thomas was allowed to continue his Dominican studies (Chenu, 1950).

III.   Thomas and Aristotelian Philosophy

Once Aquinas joined the Dominican Order, he was sent to Paris for his formal studies in 1244. By that time, Dominican friars were already associated with university theology and with the intellectual freedom to pursue new ideas. They were in Naples, Oxford, Bologna, and Paris. Paris was the undisputed intellectual capital of Christendom. According to Chenu, the rise of universities in Europe had a crucial influence on Aquinas's theological and philosophical life, but also on the entire Christendom.

Even though certain works of Aristotle were known to the Western world, he was considered dangerous to the faith. The Aristotelian metaphysics seemed incompatible with basic Christian beliefs concerning the immortality of the soul, creation, and the transcendence of God. The Aristotelian worldview was revolutionary and in contrast to the existing Neoplatonic Augustinian worldview.

Many Neoplatonic theologians sought to exclude Aristotelian philosophy. Hence Aristotle was banned in Christendom and repeatedly condemned by several popes. In Aquinas's day, reading and studying Aristotle was deemed consorting with the enemy. One can only imagine how it felt for Thomas and his Dominican professor Albert the Great to engage Aristotelian philosophy in the *studium* of Cologne and at the University of Paris. Aquinas had "*une sacre audace*" and a remarkable confidence to dare render Aristotelian philosophy intelligible to Christian faith—or better put, to render Christian faith intelligible through Aristotelian philosophy.

More than a philosophy, Aristotle was a challenge to Christians' "*imago mundi.*" The Neoplatonic philosophy of St Augustine and Pseudo-Dionysius were undermined. No wonder St Bonaventure, the Franciscan, and Thomas would have long debates at the University of Paris. They embodied two competing approaches to make intelligible their understanding of humanity and the religious order of things. With Aristotle, the whole order of Christian thought was at risk. How could Aquinas introduce into Christendom Aristotelian realism and the intelligibility of all things? (Chenu, 1960). Church teachings and Aristotelian philosophy seemed at odds.

The genius of Thomas enabled him to offer a systematic theology of Christian doctrines based on Aristotelian philosophy. Aquinas used Aristotle's formal logic. He reasoned in terms of actuality and potentiality, of material, formal, efficient, and final causes. He regarded intellectual contemplation as the supreme goal of human striving. He distinguished the material from the immaterial, the temporal from the eternal, and the body from the soul (Barron, 1996).

IV.   University Studies

Aquinas's contemplative and intellectual life found fertile ground in the universities as well as in the Dominican Order. One could say that the fate of medieval Christian thought found its causes and effects in the universities. The rise of universities shaped thirteenth-century European philosophy and theology.

The University of Paris was the Mecca of dialecticians, where Neoplatonic ideas, Aristotle's manuscripts, Arab commentaries, and texts of medical theorists lay side by side (O'Meara, 1997). The University of Paris gave rise to the scholastic methodology called the *disputatio*. It was in that context that Aquinas headed to Paris in 1244 (Torrell, 2005).

In Paris, Aquinas met Albert the Great (1200–80) who was a *magister*. He lectured in Paris and later in Cologne on the theological text of the time, the *Sentences* of Peter Lombard (d.1164). Albert would become Aquinas's providential guide and mentor. In 1248, the Dominicans founded in Cologne a Dominican school of theology and philosophy, a *studium*. Aquinas moved with Albert to Cologne and became his assistant for four years. Albert undertook the revolutionary step of lecturing on the writings of Pseudo-Dionysius and Aristotle's *Ethics*. He furthered the genius of Thomas and inspired the young friar to grasp the breadth of Aristotelian philosophy.

Once the House of Studies in Cologne was established, Albert the Great was appointed to teach philosophy and theology. Under his careful guidance, Aquinas pursued the study of Aristotelian philosophy. During his experiences in the Cologne years, Aquinas furthered his studies in multiple directions. His mind was extended to Neoplatonic Augustine and Pseudo-Dionysius as well as the thoughts of Ibn Sina (Avicenna), Ibn Rush (Averroes), and Moses Maimonides. In Cologne, Aquinas took note and wrote down most of Albert's lectures. After Cologne, Aquinas seemed ready to teach and write. O'Meara (1997) has laid out Thomas's academic itinerary thus:

1252–6 Bachelor of the Sentences at Paris
1256–9 Master in Theology at Paris (I)
1259–68 Period in Italy
    Naples (1259–61)
    Orvieto (1261–5)
    Rome (1265–7)
    Viterbo (1267–8)
1268–72 Master in Theology at Paris (II)
1272–3 Teaching and Writing in Naples.

V. Teacher and Writer

Albert suggested to the head of the Dominicans in Paris that Aquinas be assigned to Paris, in spite of his youth and the turbulent situation of the mendicants at the University of Paris. Thus, in 1252, Aquinas returned to Paris to begin his "postgraduate" studies in theology. For four years, Aquinas studied the Scriptures and the standard theological textbooks, mainly the *Sentences* of Peter Lombard. These *Sentences* were various patristic quotations that the author had gathered around major theological themes. Aquinas studied but also lectured on the *Sentences* and the Bible. Some biographers suggest that he opened new questions and resolved past issues in a clear and original manner (Chenu, 1950; Torrell, 1996; O'Meara, 1997).

At this time Thomas developed suitable theology and philosophy deeply rooted in his understanding of grace and nature. He was captured by the diversity of nature and grace, and admired the wonder of creation. Thomas was the foremost proponent of natural theology. He did not oppose nature and grace but saw clearly the relationship between grace and nature. He arrived at the conclusion that "grace builds on nature."

In 1256, Aquinas became master of theology and began to lecture in Paris. It is possible he first started lecturing as a novice-master in Cologne under the tutorship of Albert (O'Meara, 1997). His first lectures were on the prophets Jeremiah and Isaiah. At the University of Paris, his responsibilities as a master of theology were different.

First, he had to preach. He elucidated the Scriptures for the benefit of his students. The goals of preaching were not only to satisfy the curiosity of the mind (food for the mind) but above all for the conversation or salvation of souls in a pure Dominican tradition.

Second, his task consisted of writing biblical commentaries. His main task was not to lecture in philosophy or metaphysics or even systematic theology, but rather to illumine and explain the Scriptures. Thus, among Aquinas's works are his biblical commentaries, notably on Pauline epistles, the Psalms, Job, and the Gospels of John and Matthew. Finally, a *magister* dealt with problematic and unresolved issues of the time. He had to raise and respond to emerging questions (Barron, 1996).

The major forum for this theological exercise was the event called the *quaestio disputata*, a disputed question. A disputed question took place in public, the *magister* presiding over a large group of students and faculty. In a lively exchange, the master entertained questions and objections from the floor, responded to the best of his ability, and, finally, resolved the question at hand. The best-known work of Aquinas, The *Summa Theologiae*, or summary of theology, is the best example of this medieval methodology. This method might seem dry to the modern mind, but behind the scholarly pages the readers meet Aquinas the exegete (biblical commentaries) and the preacher (homiletics).

Thomas's biographers seem to agree that he was the most respected master of the *quaestio disputata* form at the University of Paris. These *quaestiones disputatae* included *De veritate* (On Truth), *De potentia* (On the Power of God in the Creation and Conservation of Things), *De malo* (On Evil), *De spiritualibus creaturis* (On Spiritual Creatures), and *De anima* (On the Soul) (Torrell, 2005).

Aquinas excelled in this scholastic method and disputed far more often than any other of his colleagues or Dominican brothers. He resolved pointed questions with a striking originality and intelligence. He showed that the student (Thomas) had outgrown the master (Albert). During this time, Aquinas wrote extensively on biblical commentaries, disputed questions, and a massive work on Aristotle.

In the middle of 1260, Aquinas began his most famous work, *Summa Theologiae*. The work is structured according to the way that leads from God to the world (*exitus*) and the way that leads the world back to God (*reditus*). The two paths are united in Jesus Christ, the Way. Jesus Christ is at the center of Aquinas's theology—the cornerstone and the summit and not an afterthought. Arguably, only St Augustine's writings have had equal influence on the theological thought of Western Christianity.

Besides *Summa Theologiae*, Aquinas wrote commentaries on Peter Lombard's *Sentences*. In philosophy, he wrote *On Being and Essence* and the *Principles of Nature* and a commentary on Boethius entitled *On the Trinity and De hebdomadibus*. Later, he wrote the *Summa contra gentiles*, another commentary on Aristotle, *On the Soul*, and finally some polemical works, such as *On the Eternity of the World* and *On There Being Only One Intellect*.

VI. Thomas the Intellectual Mystic

"Reginald, I cannot go on … All that I have written seems to me like so much straw compared to what has been revealed to me."

History and legend has it that Thomas uttered these eloquent words after undergoing a religious or mystical experience. On December 6, 1273, Thomas was celebrating Mass in the presence of his friend, Reginald. Something extraordinary took place that morning. Afterward, Thomas broke the routine that had been his for the previous 20 years. For the rest of his life, he hung up his instruments of writing. When Reginald, his *socius*, urged him to continue, Thomas replied very simply that he could not. The younger man persisted until Thomas declared the words given above.

This phrase summarized Thomas the theologian and the mystic. Ultimately, he had understood that God is beyond all images and analogies. Some other writers speculate that he might have suffered a stroke, or a psychological breakdown. In any event, the simple fact of his remarkable silence remained a mystery. Keeping in mind that Aquinas wrote thousands of pages about God, his abrupt silence was an emphatic insight into who God is.

Besides being an intellectual genius, Aquinas was also a contemplative. A careful reading of Thomas's homilies, disputations, and lectures reveal his mystical passion, his ascetic response to God. This intelligent mystical intuition suffused all that Aquinas taught and wrote. Any account of the life and spirituality of Aquinas would be incomplete without an awareness of the ultimate mystical experience at the end of his life.

Unfortunately, Aquinas scholars had overlooked Aquinas the mystic, thus missing a crucial element of Dominican spirituality: *contemplari aliis tradere*. Aquinas's contemplative and intellectual life was a marvelous example of this intelligent intuition of St Dominic of Guzman, the founder of the Dominican Order.

VII. Modern Influence

Thomas pursued Truth wherever he might find it. It meant taking seriously Aristotle the pagan and Ibn

Rush (Averroes) the Arab. Aquinas did not leave behind a gospel to recite and memorize but a methodology to emulate, which is an audacious, clear

spiritual and scholarly freedom in search of Truth. Aquinas's legacy is not a deposit or the revealed word of God but a style to seize upon.

References

Barron, Robert. 1996. *Thomas Aquinas: Spirituality Master.* New York: Crossroad.

Chenu, Marie Dominique. 1950. *Introduction à l'étude de saint Thomas d'Aquin.* Paris: Librairie Philosophique J. Vrin.

Chenu, Marie Dominique. 1964. *Toward Understanding St. Thomas.* Chicago: Regnery.

O'Meara, Thomas F., OP. 1997. *Thomas Aquinas, Theologian.* South Bend, IN: University of Notre Dame Press.

Torrell, Jean Pierre. 1993. *Initiation á Saint Thomas d'Aquinas*: Paris: Editions Cerf. (English translation, Saint Thomas Aquinas, vol.1: *The Person and His Work*, by Robert Royal, Washington: Catholic University of America, Press 1996.)

Torrell, Jean Pierre. 1996. *Saint Thomas d'Aquin, maître spirituel: initiation*, vol. 2. Fribourg: Editions Cerf.

Torrell, Jean Pierre. 2005. *Aquinas's Summa: Background, Structure, and Reception.* Washington, DC: Catholic University of America Press.

Weisheipl, James A. 1974. *Thomas D'Aquinas: His Life, Thought and Work.* Washington: Catholic University of America Press.

Bernard of Clairvaux (1090–1153)

Joanne Maguire Robinson

Bernard of Clairvaux was born in 1090 CE in the family castle at Fontaines-les-Dijons in Burgundy. His pious mother especially encouraged her third son in his pursuit of the religious life instead of a military career. Although he initially sought retreat from the world, Bernard became a remarkably worldly monk: he was advisor to popes, a leader at several key councils, a tireless preacher, the leader of a thriving monastic reform, a politician, and one of the most prominent mystics of the Christian tradition.

Bernard's early education was certainly solid, although he was never the pupil of a master. He did not learn dialectic (logic) formally, nor did he receive formal training in exegesis or classical philosophy. Bernard could best be considered a student of scripture, and his writing is suffused with quotations and allusions to both the Hebrew Bible and the New Testament. His extraordinary literary style and elegant Latin earned him the fitting nickname of *Doctor Mellifluus*. Bernard is known to have written about 330 sermons, approximately 500 letters, and 13 treatises on various topics.

Bernard began his career in 1113 at Citeaux, a Cistercian monastery founded in 1098 with the goal of adhering closely to the rule of St Benedict. Bernard joined the then-struggling monastery with 30 other noblemen, including several of his brothers, thereby helping to ensure Citeaux's future. Bernard was chosen to establish a new monastery a few years later in a remote, forbidding place called *Valle d'Absinthe* ("Valley of Bitterness"). Under Bernard's leadership it became the "Valley of Light" (Clairvaux) both literally and metaphorically. The early years of his monastic profession were harsh and Bernard became quite ill from his severe ascetic practices. Illness troubled him for the rest of his life. Bernard served as abbot of Clairvaux for 38 years until his death in 1153 at the age of 63. He personally oversaw the foundation of more than 60 other houses out of Clairvaux, including several foundations for women.

Despite his role as abbot of a settled community, Bernard traveled extensively. He played a key role in healing the papal schism begun in 1130 and was a strong voice at the Lateran Council of 1139. He traveled several times to Rome to intervene in disputes and spent time as papal envoy and as recruiter for the Second Crusade. Bernard was chosen by Pope Eugenius III to preach the Second Crusade in 1146; the crusade was an utter failure and Bernard's reputation suffered somewhat in its wake. He was instrumental in establishing the Knights Templar and assisted in stopping pogroms in the Rhineland in 1146. Bernard, fundamentally conservative in his theology, challenged the teachings of Peter Abelard on the Trinity, whom he helped to condemn at the Council of Soissons (1121) and Sens (1140). He also engaged in confrontations with Gilbert of Poitiers and Arnold of Brescia. He helped launch a mission

The Student's Companion to the Theologians, First Edition. Edited by Ian S. Markham.
© 2013 Blackwell Publishing Ltd. Published 2013 by Blackwell Publishing Ltd.

against heresy in Languedoc, focusing in particular on Henry of Lausanne (*fl.* 1116–40) and his followers. Bernard was, in short, a charismatic leader who did not shy away from letting his opinion be known.

The focus of a Cistercian monk's day was the *lectio divina*, the deliberate, contemplative, and reflective reading of texts. For Bernard as for his contemporaries, the meanings of scriptural texts could be uncovered with sufficient study. During Bernard's life this approach was changing. The traditional *lectio divina* was being supplemented (and eventually supplanted) by reading scripture in light of grammar, rhetoric, and logic. Bernard was alarmed by this incursion of the liberal arts into the province of faith, and he was particularly wary of subjecting what he considered to be scriptural truth to logic. In faith Bernard found certainty; in logic he found a threat to faith. Human reason, for Bernard, was quite limited. God could not be known through reason; God could only be known through love. The Christian life should focus on attaining salvation and finding union with God. As a traditional theologian, Bernard urged his followers to read scripture with acceptance rather than argument.

Bernard's writings attest to this conservative approach to scriptural exegesis mixed with a focus on the affective love and experience of human beings. His first major work is his *De Gradibus Humilitatis et Superbiae* (*Concerning the Steps of Humility and Pride*), written in the early or mid-1120s. As its name suggests, this treatise describes 12 degrees of spiritual progress, beginning with pride and ending in true humility. Bernard's *De gratia et libero arbitrio* (*Grace and Free Choice*), c.1128, laid out traditional Augustinian doctrine on issues of grace and free will. In Bernard's rather traditional theological anthropology, human beings were created in the image and likeness of God. The Fall destroyed the likeness but the image remains, however fragmented and hidden. The result is that human beings can no longer avoid sin without the help of grace. Human beings have, in a way, two identities: they are at once wretched and exalted. Those who live proper, humble Christian lives will experience the restoration of the image and likeness in heaven, while contemplatives can have a fleeting glimpse of this union during life. This is possible because Jesus took on flesh in a supreme act of humil-

ity. Bernard adheres to the traditional formula by positing that God became human so that humans could become God.

Humility is also central to his *De Diligendo Deo* (*On Loving God*), penned sometime between 1126 and 1141. Here we encounter Bernard's most extended consideration of love and the potential mutuality of love between creature and Creator. Bernard describes four degrees of love: to love oneself for one's own sake; to love God for the sake of oneself; to love God for God's sake; and to love oneself completely for God's sake. This last stage can only be reached rarely and briefly, after sometimes excruciating periods of absence and longing. In this mystical state, one completely overcomes the self and regains one's precreational union with God. By loving oneself for God's sake, one is manifesting true love for God, without limit. God created his creatures out of love, and they return to him through love by way of complete humility.

Like many medieval theologians, Bernard describes human life as a return from exile from God. He liberally uses metaphors of exile, pilgrimage, and ladders (up and down) to illustrate that dynamic. Ultimately, very few can attain brief union of wills (*unitas spiritus*) with God, because only the few can attain the deep self-knowledge required to reach that point. Those with true self-knowledge of their wretchedness possess true humility. With that humility, the creature can re-establish a proper relationship with the Creator through the traditional threefold stages of asceticism, illumination, and union.

Bernard's 86 sermons on the Song of Songs are strongly allegorical and mystical, focusing less on intellectual explanation than on making the Scriptures relevant to human experience. "Experience" as used in this context is communal, liturgical, and scriptural as well as individual. Jesus Christ is central to Bernard's thought as the perfect image of God in human flesh and thus the "Bridegroom" to the human "Bride." The metaphors Bernard uses for the human relation to God are by turn bridal, spousal, and maternal, and many are suffused with erotic overtones. He refers to both Jesus and abbot as "mother," nurturing and feeding "children" of faith. This focus on carnality can seem surprising in a tradition so negative toward the human body, but for Bernard love for the body of

Jesus is the essential starting point on the path back to God. The incarnation makes it possible for humans to attain divine status. The journey must always begin with the bodily Christ and one must learn how to love Christ both spiritually and carnally. One first loves Christ carnally; then one loves the spirit carnally; then one loves the flesh in spiritual way; and finally one loves the spirit spiritually. This path requires a mix of intellect and love.

Bernard's acceptance of the carnality of humanity leads naturally into his often erotic expression of mystical union. The love of the self for the sake of God is reached only by starting on the most basic level with love of self as an embodied creature. He also describes passionate, even violent, erotic love as he depicts the creature longing for union with the Creator. In one of his more memorable analogies, Bernard describes the approach to God as three kisses given to Jesus: first, the kiss of the feet (representing conversion and commitment to a life without sin); second, the kiss of the hands (showing progress through a life of repentance); and then the kiss of the mouth (indicating mystical union).

Bernard also wrote several works unrelated to mysticism, such as treatises justifying the condemnation of those he considered heretics; advice to candidates for priesthood and to monks on monastic life;

encouragement to those in military life; treatises on church governance; and numerous hymns. He gave guidance to Pope Eugenius III in his *De Consideratione* (*On Consideration*) of 1148. This work argues that the Pope should cede power to the secular ruler when appropriate. Many of his liturgical writings focus on the infant Jesus or extol the virtues of the Virgin Mary, both in her role as mother and as a star to whom travelers look for guidance.

Bernard of Clairvaux's influence is widespread and lasting. He was canonized by the Roman Catholic Church in 1174 and declared a Doctor of the Church in 1830. Pope Pius XII honored the 800th anniversary of Bernard's death in a 1953 encyclical that refers to him as "the Last of the Fathers." He appears as the wise spiritual guide in Dante's *Paradiso*. The influence of his thought can be found in monastic reform movements during and after his life; in Gregorian chant and Gothic art; and in the flourishing of mystical theology after his death. To say that Bernard was a pivotal and powerful figure in his day diminishes his far-ranging influence. Although Bernard was neither an original thinker nor a systematizer, his exquisitely beautiful Latin, his insights into the role of experience in spiritual life, and his tireless work on behalf of doctrinal orthodoxy have inspired many.

Bonaventure (c.1217–74)

Philip McCosker

Set against the background of all the ecumenical ventures of the twentieth century between the Roman Catholic church and the various Protestant, and other, denominations of Christianity, as well as recent increased interest in fuller, catholic, views of the theological discipline and its subject matter (including topics such as nature and grace, the sacraments, theological interpretation of scripture, deification, theologies of the Christian life, the spiritual senses—seen for instance in the activities and publications of the Radical Orthodoxy movement in the UK and beyond, and the Centre for Catholic and Evangelical Theology founded by Carl Braaten and Robert Jenson), the theology of Bonaventure offers a powerful mediating synthesis. His is a strongly christocentric and Trinitarian theology soaked in scripture, which would make him an attractive dialogue partner from the Catholic tradition for Protestant theologians captivated by the christological concentration of Karl Barth, for instance. This may explain his significant impact on the theology of Hans Urs von Balthasar. Bonaventure differs clearly in this and other respects from the dialogue partner usually chosen as a representative of the Catholic tradition, Thomas Aquinas, whose christology and theology of the Christian life are arguably less obvious. Bonaventure also presents an exemplary theology of creation and all that the Catholic tradition may expect from that. His theology may then help theological traditions until now resolutely opposed to each other realize they have more in common than they previously realized. An example of this is the way (Joseph Ratzinger's *Habilitationsschrift* supervisor) Gottlieb Söhngen's work on analogy in Bonaventure, and particularly its christological and Trinitarian anchoring, was able to influence the presentation of the doctrine of the analogy of being by Hans Urs von Balthasar to Karl Barth, who thought himself diametrically opposed to it (see Söhngen, 1935; von Balthasar, 1992b). Beyond this possible ecumenical trajectory, there are many topics of contemporary theological interest which Bonaventure could contribute to. These include the spiritual senses (on which see the classic treatment of Rahner, 1933, abridged in Rahner, 1979, and now the compendious study of Tedoldi, 1999), christological apophaticisms (see Turner, 2004, 52–62), integrations of theology and spirituality, the theology of the saints (see von Balthasar, 1992a with Nussberger, 2007, as well as Léthel, 1993 and Thompson, 1987). The time is ripe for informed study of Bonaventure, as more and more of his works are becoming available in modern and reliable translations.

I. Life

The man who was to become a saint and doctor of the universal church was probably born in 1217, as Giovanni di Fidanza in the little hilltop town of

The Student's Companion to the Theologians, First Edition. Edited by Ian S. Markham.
© 2013 Blackwell Publishing Ltd. Published 2013 by Blackwell Publishing Ltd.

Bagnoregio in Lazio, not far from Orvieto, surrounded by dramatic countryside, some 90 miles north of Rome. This was not long after the Fourth Lateran Council of 1215 had taken place and instituted its thorough program of pastoral and ecclesiastical renewal. Indeed, renewal in various forms marked the period in which Giovanni was to live.

Very little is known about Giovanni's early life. No contemporary biographical works survive: the earliest biography we have dates from the fifteenth century. Bonaventure himself tells us in his *Legenda maior* that he suffered a serious illness while a child and that it was thanks to the prayers of his mother to Francis of Assisi that he was cured (see Cousins, 1978, 182). This clearly marked him profoundly and contributed to the central place the Franciscan founder and his theology was to play in Bonaventure's own life and thought. It is probable that the young Giovanni received his early education from the Franciscans in Bagnoregio as a *puer oblatus* (boy oblate).

As a teenager (1234–5) he went to Paris to pursue studies in the faculty of arts. There he came under the strong influence of Alexander of Hales (*c.*1185–1245), a fact significant for the evaluation of Bonaventure's view of the relationship between philosophy and theology. Here in Paris three more or less contemporary movements of renewal affected the young Italian's life and studies. Paris itself was undergoing something of a renaissance under Louis IX, both physical and intellectual. The city was the birthplace of the new educational structure, the university. Education through the Middle Ages had taken place in cathedral schools or monasteries. Following a dispute, in 1200 Philip II granted a group of scholars a charter and privileges under the bishop of Paris and a chancellor, giving them their own semi-autonomous juridical status. Soon afterwards similar moves were made in Oxford and then in Cambridge. It was at this new structure that Giovanni came to study in Paris. At the same time in Paris a newly translated body of philosophical literature was making itself known to the scholarly community, namely the works of Aristotle. With the exception of his logical writings, which had been available because of the translation by Boethius, Aristotle's works had been unknown until this time. They were to know a period of great dissemination and study from now on, far greater in fact than ever before, even in the period

immediately after Aristotle's death. Alexander of Hales was one of Aristotle's main champions in this period and can be shown to have read all of his works. A major question in Bonaventurian scholarship in the twentieth century concerned the role philosophy played in his theology, and specifically the way Aristotle's philosophy is received in that theology (for a useful summary see LaNave, 2005, 14–26, as well as the fuller conspectus of views in Quinn, 1973, 841–96, the full exposition of the evidence in Bougerol, 1989b, and the recent discussion in Speer, 1997).

Likewise in Paris he joined the Franciscan Order, either in 1238 or in 1242, took the name Bonaventure, and made his novitiate there. The order had its very recent roots in the famous incident in which a young ex-soldier, Francesco Bernardone, of Assisi, heard a crucifix speaking to him in the church of San Damiano. The voice said "Francis, go and repair my church which, as you see, is falling down" (Moorman, 1968, 6). Francis decided to follow Christ as closely as he could, and soon gathered a group of like-minded men around him. In 1209 they sought the approval of Innocent III and formed the first of the mendicant orders which held no property in common but relied instead on alms and their own manual labor. The hallmarks of Francis's newly founded brotherhood were humility, simplicity, poverty, and prayer. Bonaventure himself tells that he was attracted to the order because he thought its life and growth were like a representation of the early Christian community (see Hayes, 1994, 39). The order and its ideals clearly appealed within its context because it saw extremely rapid expansion. In 1226, the year of Francis's death, the order is estimated to have had 5,000 members and by 1256 there were already 49 friaries in England (see Cullen, 2006, 6), far away from the order's native Italy. The newly created order, along with the Dominicans who were founded soon after, was an excellent vehicle for the pastoral reforms desired and mandated by Lateran IV.

Like all bachelors of arts, Bonaventure was required to comment on the *Sentences* of Peter Lombard. The latter work was the standard theological textbook of the time, since it had been finalized by Peter in 1155–7. One might say that the *Sentences* constituted the beginning of the modern discipline of systematic theology, organized as they were to set alongside each other differing opinions on theological topics from the tradition and then to reconcile them in something approaching a systematic vision. The *Sentences* remained a standard theological textbook until Cajetan started using the *Summa Theologiae* of Thomas Aquinas almost three centuries later. For this reason they are an extremely important source for the theology of the period, and it is regrettable that the work has not been greatly studied, not helped by the fact that it has never been translated into English (for more see Rosemann, 2007; there is an ongoing effort on the internet to complete an English translation of the *Sentences*, see Bugnolo, ongoing). Bonaventure's commentary on Lombard's text was written in 1254 and was his first major work (Bonaventure, 1881–1902, I–IV). It is likely that Bonaventure received his *licentia docendi* (license to teach) that same year. After a delay both he and Thomas Aquinas took up their chairs in the same university in 1257. Three months later Bonaventure was elected minister general of the Franciscan Order, thus beginning the second major phase of his adult life.

Upon his election Bonaventure faced a number of difficulties within the order: rapid expansion led to turbulent times. Most pressingly, his predecessor, John of Parma, was being tried for heresy, having come under the influence of the works of Joachim of Fiore which argued that the third age of Christianity was soon to come, the age of the Holy Spirit, which would liberate Christians from ecclesiastical structures and strictures and lead them to the life of true Christian freedom. Joachimite ideas had a strong impact on the new Franciscan Order and threatened to divide the community. In due course Bonaventure's christologically centered theology of history, which charted a middle course between Joachim's most radical ideas and Aquinas's total rejection of his work, presented the order with a reconciling solution (on which see Ratzinger, 1971 and McGinn, 1978). Here, as so often, we see Bonaventure opting for a reconciling middle position, embracing, as far as he could, opposing trajectories. This is a tendency which can be explained by his paradoxical christology and his theology of the Trinity. This paradoxicality—or coincidence of opposites—in Bonaventure's thought has been explored by Cousins (1978b), arousing comment and critique to which he has responded (1981). I have explored paradox in Bonaventure's works, alongside

other authors, in a different way (McCosker, 2008), focusing on the role of different kinds of opposites in various christological models of paradox.

Another difficulty that Bonaventure had to face concerned poverty. A controversy was stirred up in Paris, spearheaded by William of St Amour who argued that this new Franciscan stress on the mendicant way of poverty was undesirable, even evil. Bonaventure's response came in his *Disputed Questions on Evangelical Perfection* (Bonaventure, 2008), and followed the earlier reply of Thomas Aquinas. Nevertheless, despite these vigorous replies, and the condemnation of William's position by Alexander IV in 1256, the issue divided the Franciscan Order between those who took a strict view against all property, and those who advocated some leniency, for instance in the case of friars undertaking studies who needed books. Bonaventure's response was to set the order's charism of poverty within the overarching context of Christian humility and charity, arguing that poverty is a tool which helps one avoid *cupiditas*, greed or covetousness, and instead to practice *caritas*, charity or love.

In 1265 Bonaventure was invited to become the Archbishop of York, but declined the post. Later, in 1273, he was made a cardinal and asked again to take up a bishopric, this time the see of Albano, in the hills just south of Rome. He accepted, and consequently resigned his generalate. His last significant action was to make several contributions to the Second Council of Lyon in 1274, the main goal of which was reunification with the Eastern churches. For a short time that goal was achieved and a joint creed agreed on. Bonaventure did not live to see that agreement eventually fall apart. It had been forced upon the Eastern church by Emperor Michael VIII Palæologos for political reasons to gain the support of the pope and avoid attack on his empire; the union was resisted by the clergy of the Eastern churches and consequently did not last. Bonaventure died during the council (Thomas Aquinas had died on his way to it) and his funeral was celebrated by Gregory X and attended by the Western and Eastern council fathers in Lyon, where he was also buried. He was canonized in 1432 by Sixtus IV, a fellow Franciscan, and then declared a Doctor of the Church by Sixtus V in 1558. He is traditionally given the title *Doctor Seraphicus*, the seraphic doctor. His feast day falls on July 15, the anniversary of his death. Although his work had an immediate following, it was soon eclipsed by the theology of his confrère John Duns Scotus. Studies of his thought have revived since the publication of a critical edition of his works on the threshold of the twentieth century (Bonaventure, 1881–1902), and Étienne Gilson's groundbreaking study (Gilson, 1965).

II. Works

Bonaventure left a vast body of works, some of which have already been mentioned. The longest and earliest of these was his *Commentary on the Sentences of Peter Lombard*, which takes up four volumes of the 10-volume critical edition of his works (on the deficiencies of this edition see Hamesse, 1997). Besides that, he wrote a number of scriptural commentaries on Ecclesiastes (Bonaventure, 2005), Wisdom, Luke (Bonaventure, 2003, 2004), and John (Bonaventure, 2007b). He also wrote a number of disputed questions, on Evangelical Poverty (Bonaventure, 2008), on the Knowledge of Christ (Bonaventure, 1992), and on the mystery of the Trinity (Bonaventure, 2000). During his generalate he produced a number of "collations," on the Ten Commandments, on the Seven Gifts of the Holy Spirit (Bonaventure, 2007a), and on the Six Days of Creation (Bonaventure, 1970). Two very significant works are his *Breviloquium*, or "summary" (Bonaventure, 1963), something of a Bonaventurian *summa* (celebrated by Marie-Dominique Chenu as containing the most attractive writing on scriptural interpretation of the thirteenth century: Chenu, 1957, 54, and as revealing "a power of total synthesis never seen again" by Henri de Lubac; see de Lubac 1959–64, I/1, 425), and his *On Retracing the Arts to Theology* (Bonaventure, 1966, 13–32), which, as its title suggests, situates all branches of knowledge in relation to theology. In addition to these more academically oriented works, Bonaventure left a total of 569 sermons in the critical edition (for a significant sample in translation, including the important sermon *Unus est magister noster Christus*, see Hayes, 1974b), and a number of works focused on the theology of the Christian life, the most influential of which is his work on *The Journey of the Mind into God* (translated in Cousins, 1978, 51–116) which describes the stages passed through by the Christian on the way to union with God. He also wrote a life of St Francis, which became the official biography for the order and had to be found in every friary. It is a theological interpretation of the life of Francis and as such is highly important for the interpretation of Bonaventure's theology (on this see LaNave, 2005, 122–45). Amongst his other works with this focus the most important are *The Threefold Way* (now translated in Coughlin, 2006, 81–133), and *The Tree of Life* (translated in Cousins, 1978a, 117–75).

III. Theology

Bonaventure's theology is resolutely Trinitarian and christocentric: christocentric because Trinitarian and Trinitarian because christocentric—the two are not in competition. It shuns the exclusively rationalistic approach to theology which was being developed by some of his contemporaries in the new universities, but was careful to give philosophy a relative autonomy within his theological vision. Bonaventure significantly insisted on the interrelation of theology and what we would now call spirituality, thought, and life. For him, as for the ancient philosophers (as Pierre Hadot, 1981, has reminded us), philosophy goes together with a way of life. Thus in Bonaventure's vision, knowledge, or *scientia* (difficult to encapsulate in English), needs holiness to reach wisdom, its goal (this three-part integration of knowledge and action is most insightfully and thoroughly addressed in LaNave, 2005). The structures of his theology, which did not change radically over the course of his life, can be said to be designed to integrate these aspects. This makes him especially attractive in today's theological climate, ever more aware as we are of the fragmentation which the once unified discipline of theology underwent several centuries ago. Although it is hard to date the infamous divorce between theology and spirituality, most would now agree it has taken place (see, for instance, von Balthasar, 1989 and Verdeyen, 2003). Two particular ways in which Bonaventure effects this reintegration are in his christology and, connectedly, his strong dependence on the figure of Francis of Assisi.

Largely reflecting one of its main influences, that of the Pseudo-Dionsysius (on which influence see the important study of Bougerol, 1989c, as well as Beierwaltes, 1997), Bonaventure's theology can be said to be *circular*, or perhaps better, *spiralling* (for if simply circular, history and ultimately creation would be of no account). That is to say that it considers reality in the light of God as source and goal of creation, as well as the means of attaining that goal (on the motif of the circle in Bonaventure see Hellman, 2001, 16–18). This is clearly related to the Dionysian and Proclean *mone* (rest), *proodos* (procession), and *epistrophe* (return), or more simply the *exitus* and *reditus* familiar from more or less Neoplatonic theologies. So Bonaventure describes the task of his theological metaphysics as "the study of all beings in terms of ideal principles, retracing all things to one first cause from which they proceed, that is, to God as origin, end, and exemplar" (*On Retracing the Arts* 4: Bonaventure, 1966, 18). We should notice here that all is defined from the point of view of God. Bonaventure's support for the important doctrine of *creatio ex nihilo* (creation out of nothing), as well as his related rejection of the arguments for the eternity of the world, clearly underpin this radically contingent view of creaturely reality (see for instance *Breviloquium* II.1: Bonaventure, 1963, 69).

It is Christ who is at the center of this theological vision, and is the motor of its dynamic movement. "Such is the metaphysical Center that leads us back, and this is the sum total of our metaphysics: concerned with emanation, exemplarity, and consummation, that is, illumination through spiritual radiations and return to the Supreme Being. And in this you will be a true metaphysician" (*Collations on the Six Days*, I.17: Bonaventure, 1970, 10). Bonaventure has an extremely nuanced christology of Christ as middle and center. By contrast with contemporary discussions of theological "middleness," both in John Milbank's account of Henri de Lubac's understanding of the relation of nature and grace (Milbank, 2005), and William Desmond's "metaxological" thought, which focuses on God as *between* theology and philosophy (Desmond, 2008), Bonaventure has a christologically determined account of middleness, which links up Trinitarian theology and his theology of the Christian life (see Milbank, 2005; Desmond, 2008; for a critique of Milbank see McCosker, 2006, and for

more on middleness see McCosker, 2008, ch. 2). Most often Bonaventure expresses his view of Christ as middle in paradoxical conjunctions of human and divine attributes. Thus at the apophatic summit of his masterpiece describing the ascent of the Christian to God, *The Journey of the Mind into God*, the pilgrim on the journey, having considered the traces (*vestigia*), images (*imagines*), and similitudes (*similitudines*) of God to be found both outside ourselves in his creation and within ourselves in ourselves, thus following the Augustinian movement inward and upward, is now on the threshold of the *transitus*, or passing over, to God. It is at this point that the pilgrim contemplates

> Christ the Son of God, who is the image of the invisible God by nature, our humanity so wonderfully exalted, so ineffably united, when at the same time it sees united the first and the last, the highest and the lowest, the circumference and the center, the Alpha and the Omega, the caused and the cause, the Creator and the creature, that is, the book written within and without, it now reaches something perfect. (*Journey of the Mind into God*, VI.7: Cousins, 1978a, 108–9)

It is in this important work, moreover, that one finds Bonaventure's synthesis of Augustinian and Dionysian mysticism (on which see Murphy, 1993; Turner, 1994).

If Christ is at the middle or center of Bonaventure's theology, it finds its source and goal in God the Father. Bonaventure, recalling the emphasis in much Greek patristic theology on the Father as "well" of the Trinity (for instance in Gregory of Nyssa, Basil of Caesarea, and Pseudo-Dionysius, but also more widely: see Widdicombe, 2000), emphasized the person of the Father as the *fontalis plenitudo*, or overflowing/fontal fullness of the Trinity (see Kvame, 1999):

> …the Philosopher … states that the more primary causes are, the greater power they have, and that the first cause has greater influence and that the cause that is absolutely first has an influence in every respect … where there is an order of person, primacy in the first person is the reason for the production of the other persons. And since innascibility signifies primacy, it follows that it signifies fountain-fulness [*fontalem plenitudinem*] in relation to the production of the persons. (*Commentary on the Sentences* I, d. 27, p. 1, q. 2, translated in Cousins, 1978b, 103)

This is linked to his adoption of the Dionysian principle that the good is self-diffusive (*bonum diffusivum sui*) and therefore depends on Dionysius's metaphysics of the good (see Delio, 1999), which he modifies with Richard of St Victor's Trinitarian theology of personal love. God as the Good is perfectly self-diffusive. Paradoxically Bonaventure also stressed the innascibility of the Father (see Bonaventure, 2000, 260–6, as well as Hayes' useful comments at 41–3; the entirety of Hayes' introduction, 13–103 is extremely valuable). It is the paradoxical conjunction, indeed the identification of the Father's fontality *and* innascibility which gives him primacy in the Trinity (on this theme see Durand, 2006, which is developed in Durand, 2008).

Bonaventure's Trinitarian theology is often given a bad press, mainly for stereotypically scholastic-sounding descriptions such as this: "Sacred doctrine contributes to the right understanding of this faith by teaching that there are, within the Godhead, two modes of emanation, three hypostases, four relations, and five concepts; and yet in all only three personal properties" (*Breviloquium* III.1; Bonaventure, 1963, 38). Henri de Lubac is not alone in finding such lists and classifications "tiresome" (see Falque, 2001, 5). However, on the whole Bonaventure's Trinitarian vision is dynamic and very attractive for its emphasis on the interpretative categories it frequently uses: expression, communication, and love (and here Bonaventure draws on Augustine and Richard of St Victor: see Bonaventure, 2000, 13–24). It is for this reason that Christopher Cullen has written of his "semiotic metaphysics" (see Cullen, 2006, 25, 77, 129, as well as Cullen, 2000). This focus on the sign character of all that is produced by God, whether *ad intra* within the Trinity in the eternal generation of the Son, or *ad extra* in the creation of the world, enables us to see that all point back to their source, their examplars in the mind of God. Bonaventure depends heavily on Augustine for this theme of exemplarism (the classic treatment is that of Bissen, 1929, but see now Cullen, 2006, 71–7), as well as his related use of the Augustinian epistemology of illumination (on which, see, for instance, Hayes, 1994, 91–3). These are important ways of linking God and his perfect expression of himself in the Word, to the Word's expression in creation, and Christ the

medium of creation's return to God (the classic treatment remains that of Gerken, 1970, and now Hayes, 1978). These interlocking contours of Bonaventure's theology do not fit together out of bare, rigid, necessity; rather, for Bonaventure the criterion is that of *convenientia*, fittingness—another important topic in the study of his thought (see Hayes, 1974a). It is fittingness which drives Bonaventure's circular view of theology: "What more suitable act of wisdom than to bring the universe to full perfection by uniting the First and the last: the Word of God, origin of all things, and the human creature, last to be made?" (*Breviloquium*, IV.2: Bonaventure, 1963, 144).

Not surprisingly, scripture is a supreme source for Bonaventure's theology, indeed at times he seems to identify the two: "Holy Scripture, which is called theology" (*Breviloquium*, Prologue: Bonaventure, 1963: 1, see also *Breviloquium* I.2. For a recent controversy on this identification see, with its references, Falque, 2002). But, given his emphasis on Christ as the center of all our knowledge, scripture is also central for *all* knowledge. "The whole body of our knowledge, therefore, must rest in the knowledge of sacred Scripture, most of all in its anagogical sense by which any light is retraced to God from whom it had come forth. And so the circle is closed at this point, the six-fold series completed, and there is rest" (*On Retracing the Arts* I.7: Bonaventure, 1966, 21). For Bonaventure, then, theology does not operate in its own disciplinary ghetto, alongside other disciplines, but rather it relates to all possible subject matter and relates substantively to all subjects. Consonant with Bonaventure's overall theological vision, he sees our reading of scripture as not simply an intellectual or literary exercise, but rather one that begins in faith and prayer, and is ordered to action: "And that we may attain this fruit and end rightly, by the straight road of Scripture itself, we must begin at the beginning. That is, we must reach out in a spirit of pure faith to the Father of Lights, and kneeling in our hearts, ask Him to give us, through his Son and in the Holy Spirit, the true knowledge of Jesus Christ, and together with knowledge, love for him" (*Breviloquium*, Prologue: Bonaventure, 1963, 4). The fruit of such activity is the fullness of eternal happiness.

References

von Balthasar, Hans Urs. 1984. "Bonaventure." In von Balthasar, *Glory of the Lord: A Theological Aesthetics. Volume II: Studies in Theological Style: Clerical Styles*, trans. Andrew Louth, Francis McDonagh, and Brian McNeil. San Francisco: Ignatius, pp. 260–362.

von Balthasar, Hans Urs. 1989. "Theology and Sanctity." In von Balthasar, *Explorations in Theology. I: The Word Made Flesh*. San Francisco: Ignatius, pp. 181–209.

von Balthasar, Hans Urs. 1992a. *Two Sisters in the Spirit: Thérèse of Lisieux & Elizabeth of the Trinity*, trans. Donald Nichol, Anne E. Englund, and Dennis Martin. San Francisco: Ignatius.

von Balthasar, Hans Urs. 1992b. *The Theology of Karl Barth*, trans. Edward Oakes. San Francisco: Ignatius.

Beierwaltes, Werner. 1997. "Dionysius und Bonaventura." In *Denys l'Aréopagite et sa Posterité en Orient et en Occident: Actes du Colloque International, Paris, 21–24 septembre 1994*, ed. Ysabel de Andia. Paris: Institut d'Études Augustiniennes, pp. 487–99.

Bissen, Jean Marie. 1929. *L'exemplarisme divin selon saint Bonaventure*. Paris: Vrin.

Bonaventure. 1881–1902. *Doctoris Seraphici S. Bonaventurae S. R. E. Episcopi Cardinalis Opera Omnia iussu et auctoritate R.mi P. Bernardini a Portu Romatino totius Ordinis Minorum S. P. Francisci Ministri Generalis*. Quarrachi: Typographia Collegii S. Bonaventurae. 11 vols.

Bonaventure. 1963. *The Works of Bonaventure II: The Breviloquium*, trans. José de Vinck. Paterson, NJ: St Anthony Guild Press.

Bonaventure. 1966. *The Works of Bonaventure III: Opuscula Second Series*, trans. José de Vinck. Paterson, NJ: St Anthony Guild Press.

Bonaventure. 1970. *The Works of Bonaventure V: Collations on the Six Days*, trans. José de Vinck. Paterson, NJ: St Anthony Guild Press.

Bonaventure. 1990. *Le Christ maître: édition, traduction et commentaire du sermon universitaire "Unus est magister noster Christus"*, ed. and trans. Goulven Madec. Paris: Vrin.

Bonaventure. 1992. *Disputed Questions on the Knowledge of Christ*, ed. and trans. Zachary Hayes. Saint Bonaventure, NY: Franciscan Institute.

Bonaventure. 2000. *Disputed Questions on the Mystery of the Trinity*, ed. and trans. Zachary Hayes. Saint Bonaventure, NY: Franciscan Institute.

Bonaventure. 2002. *Les sentences: Questions sur Dieu. Commentaire du premier livre des Sentences de Pierre Lombard*, ed. and trans. Marc Ozilou. Paris: Presses Universitaires de France.

Bonaventure. 2003. *St. Bonaventure's Commentary on the Gospel of Luke, Chapters 9–16*, ed. and trans. Robert J. Karris. Saint Bonaventure, NY: Franciscan Institute.

Bonaventure. 2004. *St. Bonaventure's Commentary on the Gospel of Luke, Chapters 17–24*, ed. and trans. Robert J. Karris. Saint Bonaventure, NY: Franciscan Institute.

Bonaventure. 2005. *Commentary on Ecclesiastes*, ed. and trans. Campion Murray and Robert J. Karris. Saint Bonaventure, NY: Franciscan Institute.

Bonaventure. 2007a. *Collations on the Seven Gifts of the Holy Spirit*, ed. and trans. Zachary Hayes and Robert J. Karris. Saint Bonaventure, NY: Franciscan Institute.

Bonaventure. 2007b. *Commentary on the Gospel of John*, ed. and trans. Robert J. Karris. Saint Bonaventure, NY: Franciscan Institute.

Bonaventure. 2008a. *Disputed Questions on Evangelical Perfection*, ed. and trans. Robert J. Karris and Thomas Reist. Saint Bonaventure, NY: Franciscan Institute.

Bonaventure. 2008b. *The Sunday Sermons of St Bonaventure*, ed. and trans. Timothy J. Johnson. Saint Bonaventure, NY: Franciscan Institute.

Bougerol, J. Guy. 1964. *Introduction to the Works of Bonaventure*, trans. José de Vinck. Paterson, NJ: St Anthony Guild Press.

Bougerol, J. Guy. 1989a. *Saint Bonaventure: Études sur les sources de sa pensée*. Northampton: Variorum.

Bougerol, J. Guy. 1989b. "Dossier pour l'étude des rapports entre saint Bonaventure et Aristote." In Bougerol, *Saint Bonaventure: Études sur les sources de sa pensée*. Northampton: Variorum, pp. 135–222.

Bougerol, J. Guy. 1989c. "Saint Bonaventure et le Pseudo-Denys l'Aréopagite." In Bougerol, *Saint Bonaventure: Études sur les sources de sa pensée*. Northampton: Variorum, pp. 33–123.

Bugnolo, Alexis, ed. Ongoing. "Translation of Peter Lombard's *Sentences*." Online: http://www.franciscan-archive.org/lombardus/I-Sent.html

Chenu, Marie-Dominique. 1957. *La théologie comme science au XIIe siècle*, 3rd ed. Paris: Vrin.

Coughlin, F. Edward, ed. 2006. *Works of St. Bonaventure X: Writings on the Spiritual Life*. Saint Bonaventure, NY: Franciscan Institute.

Cousins, Ewert, ed. and trans. 1978a. *Bonaventure: The Soul's Journey into God, The Tree of Life, The Life of St. Francis*. New York: Paulist.

Cousins, Ewert. 1978b. *Bonaventure and the Coincidence of Opposites*. Chicago: Franciscan Herald.

Cousins, Ewert. 1981. "Bonaventure and the Coincidence of Opposites: A Response to Critics," *Theological Studies* 42(2): 277–90.

Cousins, Ewert. 1997. "Bonaventure's Christology: A Resource for the Third Millennium." In *That Others May Know and Love: Essays in Honor of Zachary Hayes, OFM: Franciscan, Educator, Scholar*, ed. Michael F. Cusato and F. Edward Coughlin. Saint Bonaventure, NY: Franciscan Institute, pp. 211–35.

Cullen, Christopher M. 2000. "The Semiotic Metaphysics of Saint Bonaventure." Unpublished PhD dissertation. Washington: Catholic University of America.

Cullen, Christopher M. 2006. *Bonaventure*. Oxford: Oxford University Press.

Delio, Ilia. 1998. *Crucified Love: Bonaventure's Mysticism of the Crucified Christ*. Quincy, IL: Franciscan Press.

Delio, Ilia. 1999. "Bonaventure's Metaphysics of the Good," *Theological Studies* 60: 228–46.

Delio, Ilia. 2007a. "Theology, Metaphysics and the Centrality of Christ," *Theological Studies* 68: 254–73.

Delio, Ilia. 2007b. "Christology from Within," *Heythrop Journal* 48: 438–57.

Desmond, William. 2008. *God and the Between*. Oxford: Blackwell.

Durand, Emmanuel. 2006. "L'innascibilité et les relations du Père, sous le signe de sa primauté, dans la théologie trinitaire de Bonaventure," *Revue Thomiste* 106(4): 531–63.

Durand, Emmanuel. 2008. *Le Père, Alpha et Oméga de la vie trinitaire*. Paris: Cerf.

Falque, Emmanuel. 2000. *Saint Bonaventure et l'entrée de Dieu en théologie: La somme théologique du Breviloquium (Prologue et première partie)*. Paris: Vrin.

Falque, Emmanuel. 2001. "The Phenomenological Art of *Perscrutatio* in the *Proemium* of St. Bonaventure's *Commentary on the Sentences*," *Medieval Philosophy and Theology* 10: 1–22.

Falque, Emmanuel. 2002. "Le contresens du mot *theologia* chez Bonaventure: Réponse au frère Henry Donneaud," *Revue thomiste* 102: 215–24.

Gerken, Alexander. 1970. *Theologie des Wortes: Das Verhältnis von Schöpfung und Inkarnation bei Bonaventura*. Düsseldorf: Patmos.

Gilson, Étienne. 1965. *The Philosophy of St. Bonaventure*, trans. Dom Illtyd Trethowan and Frank J. Sheed. Paterson, NJ: St Anthony Guild Press.

Hadot, Pierre. 1981. *Exercices spirituels et philosophie antique*. Paris: Études augustiniennes.

Hamesse, Jacqueline. 1997. "Évaluation critique des éditions de Quarrachi-Grottaferrata. À propos des *Opera Omnia* de saint Bonaventure." In *Editori di Quaracchi 100 anni dopo: bilancio e prospettive*, ed. Alvaro Cacciotti and Barbara Faes de Mottoni. Rome: Edizioni Antonianum, pp. 41–58.

Hayes, Zachary. 1974a. "The Meaning of *Convenientia* in the Metaphysics of St. Bonaventure," *Franciscan Studies* 34: 74–100.

Hayes, Zachary, ed. 1974b. *What Manner of Man: Sermons on Christ by St. Bonaventure*. Chicago: Franciscan Herald.

Hayes, Zachary. 1978. "Christology and Metaphysics in the Thought of Bonaventure." In *Celebrating the Medieval Heritage: A Colloquy on the Thought of Aquinas and Bonaventure*, ed. David Tracy. *Journal of Religion* Supplement, 58. Chicago: University of Chicago Press, pp. 82–96.

Hayes, Zachary. 1981. *The Hidden Centre: Spirituality and Speculative Christology in St. Bonaventure*. New York: Paulist.

Hayes, Zachary. 1994. "Bonaventure: Mystery of the Triune God." In *The History of Franciscan Theology*, ed. Kenan B. Osborne. Saint Bonaventure, NY: Franciscan Institute, pp. 39–125.

Hellmann, J. A. Wayne. 2001. *Divine and Created Order in Bonaventure's Theology*, ed. and trans. J. M. Hammond. Saint Bonaventure, NY: Franciscan Institute.

Houser, R. E. 1999. "Bonaventure's Three-Fold Way to God." In *Medieval Masters: Essays in Memory of Msgr. E. A. Synan*, ed. R. E. Houser. Houston, TX: Center for Thomistic Studies, pp. 91–145.

Hughes, Kevin L. 2002. "Eschatological Union: The Mystical Dimension of History in Joachim of Fiore, Bonaventure, and Peter Olivi," *Collectanea Franciscana* 72(1): 105–43.

Hughes, Kevin L. 2003. "Remember Bonaventure? (Onto) Theology and Ecstasy," *Modern Theology* 19(4): 529–45.

Hughes, Kevin L. 2004. "The Crossing of Hope, or Apophatic Eschatology." In *The Future of Hope: Christian Tradition Amid Modernity and Postmodernity*, ed. Miroslav Volf and William Katerberg. Grand Rapids, MI: Eerdmans, pp. 101–24.

Hughes, Kevin L. 2005. "St. Bonaventure's *Collationes in Hexaëmeron*: Fractured Sermons and Protreptic Discourse," *Franciscan Studies* 63: 101–24.

Kuntz, Paul G. 1987. "The Hierarchical Vision of St. Bonaventure." In *Jacob's Ladder and the Great Chain of Being*, ed. Marion Leathers Kuntz and Paul Grimley Kuntz. New York: Peter Lang, pp. 83–100.

Kvame, Janet C. 1999. "The *fontalis plenitudo* in Bonaventure as a Symbol for his Metaphysics." Unpublished doctoral dissertation. New York: Fordham University.

LaNave, Gregory. 2005. *Through Holiness to Wisdom: The Nature of Theology according to St. Bonaventure*. Rome: Istituto Storico dei Cappucini.

Léthel, François-Marie. 1993. *Théologie de l'Amour de Jésus: Ecrits sur la théologie des saints*. Venasque: Éditions du Carmel.

De Lubac, Henri. 1959–64. *Exégèse médiévale: les quatres sens de l'écriture*. Paris: Aubier.

McCosker, Philip. 2006. "Middle Muddle?" *Reviews in Religion and Theology* 13: 362–70.

McCosker, Philip. 2008. "Parsing Paradox, Analysing 'And': Christological Configurations of Theological Paradox in some Mystical Theologies." Unpublished PhD thesis. Cambridge: University of Cambridge.

McElrath, Damian, ed. 1980. *Franciscan Christology: Selected Texts, Translations and Introductory Essays.* Saint Bonaventure, NY. Franciscan Institute.

McGinn, Bernard. 1978. "The Significance of Bonaventure's Theology of History." In *Celebrating the Medieval Heritage: A Colloquy on the Thought of Aquinas and Bonaventure*, ed. David Tracy. *Journal of Religion* Supplement, 58. Chicago: University of Chicago Press, pp. 65–81.

Milbank, John. 2005. *The Suspended Middle: Henri de Lubac and the Debate concerning the Supernatural.* Grand Rapids, MI: Eerdmans.

Moorman, John. 1968. *A History of the Franciscan Order: From Its Origins to the Year 1517.* Oxford: Clarendon.

Murphy, Anthony. 1993. "Bonaventure's Synthesis of Augustinian and Dionysian Mysticism: A New Look at the Problem of the One and the Many," *Collectanea Franciscana* 63(3–4): 385–98.

Noone, Timothy B. 1999. "The Franciscans and Epistemology: Reflections on the Roles of Bonaventure and Scotus." In *Medieval Masters: Essays in Memory of Msgr. E. A. Synan*, ed. R. E. Houser. Houston, TX: Center for Thomistic Studies, pp. 63–90.

Nussberger, Danielle. 2007. "The Saint as Wellspring: Hans Urs von Balthasar's Hermeneutic of the Saint in a Christological and Trinitarian Key." Unpublished PhD dissertation. University of Notre Dame.

Quinn, John F. 1973. *The Historical Constitution of St. Bonaventure's Philosophy.* Toronto: Pontifical Institute of Medieval Studies.

Rahner, Karl. 1933. "La doctrine des 'sens spirituels' au Moyen Age, en particulier chez saint Bonaventure," *Revue d'ascétique et de mystique* 14: 263–99.

Rahner, Karl. 1979. "The Doctrine of the 'Spiritual Senses' in the Middle Ages." In *Theological Investigations. Volume XVI: Experience of the Spirit, Source of Theology*, trans. David Morland OSB. London: Darton, Longman & Todd, pp. 104–34.

Ratzinger, Joseph. 1971. *The Theology of History in St. Bonaventure*, trans. Zachary Hayes. Chicago: Franciscan Herald Press.

Rosemann, Philipp W. 2007. *The Story of a Great Medieval Book: Peter Lombard's Sentences.* Orchard Park, NY: Broadview.

Schmaus, Michael. 1973. "Neuplatonische Elemente im Trinitätsdenken des Itinerariums Bonaventuras." In *S. Bonaventura 1274–1974*, ed. Jacques Guy Bougerol et al. Grottaferrata: Collegio S. Bonaventura 2, pp. 45–69.

Söhngen, Gottlieb. 1935. "Bonaventura als Klassiker der analogia fidei," *Wissenschaft und Weisheit* 2(2): 97–111.

Speer, Andreas. 1993. "The Certainty and Scope of Knowledge: Bonaventure's *Disputed Questions on the Knowledge of Christ*," *Medieval Philosophy and Theology* 3: 35–61.

Speer, Andreas. 1997. "Bonaventure and the Question of a Medieval Philosophy," *Medieval Philosophy and Theology* 6: 25–46.

Tavard, Georges. 1954. *Transiency and Permanence: The Nature of Theology according to St Bonaventure.* Saint Bonaventure, NY: Franciscan Institute.

Tedoldi, Fabio Massimo. 1999. *La dottrina dei cinque sensi spirituali in san Bonaventura.* Rome: Antonianum.

Thompson, William M. 1987. *Fire and Light: The Saints and Theology. On Consulting the Saints, Mystics, and Martyrs in Theology.* New York: Paulist.

Turner, Denys. 1994. "Hierarchy Interiorised: Bonaventure's *Itinerarium mentis in Deum*." In Turner, *The Darkness of God: Negativity and Christian Mysticism.* Cambridge: Cambridge University Press, pp. 102–34.

Turner, Denys. 2004. *Faith, Reason and the Existence of God.* Cambridge: Cambridge University Press.

Verdeyen, Paul. 2003. "La séparation entre théologie et spiritualité: Origine, conséquences et dépassement de ce divorce." In *Theology and Conversation: Towards a Relational Theology*, eds J. Haers and P. de Mey. Leuven: Leuven University Press, pp. 675–88.

Widdicombe, Peter. 2000. *The Fatherhood of God from Origen to Athanasius*, rev. ed. Oxford: Clarendon.

Duns Scotus (*c.*1266–1308)

Richard Cross

I.   Background

Duns Scotus was born *c.*1266 in the small town of Duns, just north of the border between England and Scotland, and sometime early in his life became a Franciscan friar, a decision that had important educational consequences. For, unlike the other key intellectual order in the middle ages—the Dominicans—the Franciscans did not tie their teachings statutorily to the thought of just one theologian (Aquinas, in the case of late thirteenth-century Dominicans), and thus did not suffer from the kind of stifling of theological originality that arguably prevented the Dominicans from producing further world-class theologians. By inference from the place of his ordination in 1291—Northampton—we learn that Scotus was studying at Oxford by that date, and he remained in Oxford until at least 1301, initially producing various sets of questions on works of Aristotle while undertaking his theological study.

In the last couple of years of the thirteenth century Scotus started lecturing on Peter Lombard's *Sentences*, a necessary step for someone with the degree of Bachelor of Theology to hold that of Master of Theology. These early lectures are known as the *Lectura*, and Scotus began revising them for publication in 1300—resulting in his massive but unfinished *Ordinatio*. We know that Scotus was in Paris, lecturing on the *Sentences* again, during the academic year 1302–3, in order to qualify as Master of Theology in the pre-eminent of the two great medieval

theological centers. These lectures survive in student notes or reports—the so-called *Reportatio parisiensis*. Some elements of the discussion from these lectures are reflected in later portions of the *Ordinatio*, though there is considerable doubt as to the precise chronology of the various revisions. Scotus became Master of Theology at Paris in 1305, and produced one set of magisterial *quodlibetal questions*: disputed questions on topics suggested by anyone present at disputations in Advent or Lent held by a master in theology, and doubtless reflective of what the audience wished to quiz the presiding master on. The Franciscan authorities moved Scotus to Cologne in 1307, where he died in the following year: traditionally, the date of his death is November 8, the day on which the church now observes his feast day following his beatification in 1993. Scotus was known from very soon after his death as the "subtle doctor," and his sometimes difficult work represents a powerful attempt to make full use of the tools of philosophy in the analysis of Christian theology.

II.   Christocentrism and the Immaculate Conception

Scotus is most famous today for two theological claims that, while not original to him, were nevertheless defended by him far more rigorously than by previous theologians. The first of these claims is that

The Student's Companion to the Theologians, First Edition. Edited by Ian S. Markham.
© 2013 Blackwell Publishing Ltd. Published 2013 by Blackwell Publishing Ltd.

Mary was conceived without original sin: the Immaculate Conception; the second, that God's intention in creating the world was to become incarnate, and thus that God would have become incarnate even if there were no human sin. Earlier theologians argued for these claims on the grounds that the two envisaged states of affairs are better than their opposites, and thus that these states of affairs obtain, since God acts in the most fitting way. Scotus's defense of the two claims is very different from this. In favor of the Immaculate Conception, Scotus starts with two presumably scriptural claims: that Christ is the most perfect mediator, and that Mary is the recipient of this most perfect form of mediation (doubtless he is thinking of Luke 1:28). He argues as follows:

> The most perfect mediator had the most perfect possible act of mediating with respect to some person for whom he mediated. Therefore Christ had the most perfect degree of mediation possible with respect to some person with respect to whom he was mediator. But he had no higher degree of mediation than he had with respect to Mary. Therefore [he had the most perfect act of mediating with respect to Mary]. But this would not be unless he merited for her to be preserved from original sin. (*Ordinatio* III, d. 3, q. 1, nn. 17–18: Duns Scotus, 1950–, vol. 9: 174–5)

The basic gist is that the most perfect form of mediation requires that such mediation brings about that someone is not offended by someone else in the first place: and this is precisely the situation in the case of Mary's preservation from original sin (*Ordinatio* III, d. 3, q. 1, n. 20: Duns Scotus, 1950–, vol. 9: 176). Scotus is thinking mathematically here. For we are weighing goods, and *ceteris paribus* it is better for someone not to be offended at all than it is for him to be offended and then placated. Assume that goods can be measured against each other. On the standard mediation model, an offense of value $-n$ is balanced out by a gift of value $+n$ (or more). In the case of the prevention of an offense, a gift of value $+n$ (or more) prevents the offense of value $-n$. So in the latter case, the offense is zero (since it is prevented in the first place). So the overall amount of good in this second case is $+n$ greater than it is in the former case. So the more perfect kind of mediation is that which allows for the prevention of an offense. And since mediation is

exhaustively divided into pre- and post-offense, it seems that the most perfect kind of mediation is that which brings about the prevention of the offense.

Scotus's defense of christocentrism is rigorously deductive, though likewise made on the basis of revealed data: that Christ is God incarnate, for example. Basically, Scotus appeals to two reasonably secure philosophical claims about motivation: namely, that one wills the end before the means, and that (ideally) one wills better things before one wills less good things. Given this, it is clear, first, that God wills the goal for human existence— salvation and the beatific vision—"before" he wills or permits any other human activity. (I place "before" in scare-quotes, because Scotus, as we shall see, believes God to be immutable, and he holds that any immutable thing is timeless [see Cross, 2005, 121–3]. So the order invoked here is merely logical or explanatory.) On the first principle, salvation is willed prior to any divine permission of human sin (*Ordinatio* III, d. 7, q. 3, n. 61: Duns Scotus, 1950–, vol. 9: 287). The second principle entails that the predestination of Christ's soul to glory, being a greater good than the predestination of any other soul to glory, is willed prior to the predestination of any other soul. Thus God's decision to predestine Christ's soul to glory is antecedent to the decision to predestine any other soul, and is therefore antecedent to God's foreknowledge of any human action, or his permission of any human sin (*Ordinatio* III, d. 7, q. 3, nn. 61–66: Duns Scotus, 1950–, vol. 9: 287–8). How do we know that the predestination of Christ's soul is a greater good than the predestination of any other soul? Merely on the basis of revelation. And how do we know that the predestination of Christ's soul is made on the basis of God's being incarnate in Christ? Again, merely on the basis of revelation:

> The grace which is given to the soul of Christ seems to be so great that it is owed to no soul other than to the assumed, according to the verse in John [1:14], "We have seen his glory, glory as of the only-begotten of the Father, full of grace and truth," because [it is] glory which is not suited to a nature other than as united in this way (and perhaps no nature could have such great grace unless it were united, or at least should not have such great grace unless it were united); if therefore such great grace is given that something not united to the Word should not have, it follows that the nature is united prior to its possession of grace. (*Lectura* III, d. 2, q. 2, n. 94: Duns Scotus, 1950–, vol. 20: 106)

As Scotus reads the Gospel, God has given unique grace to Christ, grace that pertains to the "only-begotten of the Father." Given that God has decided to give this unique grace to Christ's human nature, it follows that God willed the predestination of this nature prior to his decision to predestine any other human being. And the conclusion is that this grace presupposes the incarnation—in other words, that the union is a necessary condition for this grace. We learn from revelation that no other soul should have such great grace. Thus, we discover by a complex inference from revealed data that God's intention in creating the universe was to become incarnate.

III.   Theological Language

Clearly, all of this presupposes that God's motivation—his decision-making "process"—maps quite closely onto the human models that we are familiar with. Scotus is notorious in some circles today for holding that there are some human concepts that apply as much to God as to creatures—and thus that such "mapping" is unproblematically justifiable. Scotus calls such concepts "univocal," and believes that they are required for any sound theological argumentation (*Ordinatio* I, d. 3, p. 1, qq. 1–2, n. 26: Duns Scotus, 1950–, vol. 3: 18). The idea is that, if we are to be able to reason deductively in theology, then the words we use need to have exactly the same senses or meanings throughout our argument. Since, in the world of medieval Aristotelianism, the meanings of words are concepts, we need to be able to employ univocal concepts in our theological deductions. Furthermore, theological tradition is, Scotus believes, firmly in favor of our being able to argue deductively in such contexts:

> Unless being implies one simple concept, theology will simply perish. For theologians prove that the divine Word proceeds and is begotten by way of intellect, and the Holy Spirit proceeds by way of will. But if intellect and will were found in us and in God equivocally, there would be no evidence at all that, since a word is begotten in us in such and such a fashion, it is so in God—and likewise with regard to love in us—because then intellect and will in these two cases would be of a wholly different kind. (*Lectura* I, d. 3, p. 1, qq. 1–2, n. 113: Duns Scotus, 1950–, vol. 16: 266–7)

Put in more medieval terms, theology is a science, and Aristotelian sciences consist of ordered series of deductive arguments. Since syllogistic argument requires univocity—that our words have the same meanings in premise and conclusion—the scientific nature of theology similarly requires univocity. The alternative view—classically found in Aquinas—agrees that the meanings of words are concepts, and that there can be concepts applicable to both God and creatures. But Aquinas includes within the notion of the "same" concept various different *rationes*—and these different *rationes*, somehow related to each other, mean that the words we use of God and creatures, since they necessarily involve different *rationes*, are at best analogous (*Summa Theologiae* I, q. 13, aa. 3 and 5: Aquinas, 1952–6, vol. 1.1: 66a, 67b–68a). But without a theory of just how these *rationes* relate, and just what the meanings of words signifying one and the same concept under different *rationes* are, Aquinas's analogy will turn out to be insufficient as a basis for theological deduction—at least, according to Scotus's critique.

This does not mean that he rejects the notion of analogy—merely that he gives a new account of what analogous concepts might be. Specifically, he thinks that analogous concepts are concepts that included something univocal, along with something else as well. For example, the concepts *infinite being*, proper to God, and *finite being*, proper to creatures, count as analogous. If the concepts did not include something that was the same in each concept, then how could they be anything other than wholly equivocal (*Ordinatio* I, d. 3, p. 1, qq. 1–2, n. 26: Duns Scotus, 1950–, vol. 3: 18)?

IV.   Divine Infinity and the Formal Distinction

The claim that some of the same concepts apply equally to God and creatures is what Heidegger labeled "ontotheology." In modern interpretation, this ties in with a view of metaphysics, and philosophy more generally, as something in principle independent of theology. Ontotheology is often criticized for entailing idolatry. But whatever else we make of Scotus's theory, this is clearly an unfair criticism. Univocity does not *ipso facto* entail misidentifying

God, and it does not commit those who uphold it to a belief that there is something real that is somehow greater than God—perhaps Being, or something like that. The only claim is that there is a concept (e.g., *being*) that includes in its scope both God and creatures. But concepts are not things in the world; they are merely ways of thinking about the world. Holding that God is a being does not preclude holding that he is very much more besides. Scotus basically talks about this "very much more" in terms of divine infinity: God is in all respects limitless, and as well as having all great-making properties he has those properties limitlessly. Scotus invites us to picture all this on the lines of the mathematical infinite:

> If we were to understand there to be, among beings, something actually infinite in entity, that should be understood proportionately to the imagined actual infinite in quantity, such that that being is said to be infinite that cannot be exceeded in entity by anything, and that truly will have the feature of a whole, and of something perfect: whole, for although the whole actually infinite in quantity lacks none of its parts, or no part of such a quantity, nevertheless each part is outside the other, and thus the whole is from imperfect things. But a being infinite in entity has nothing entitative "outside" in this way, for its totality does not depend on things imperfect in entity: for it is whole in such a way that it has no extrinsic part (for then it would not be totally whole). So although the actually infinite could be perfect in quantity—for it is lacking nothing of the quantity, according to itself—nevertheless each part is lacking some of the quantity, namely, that which is in another [part]: neither is it perfect in this way [i.e., quantitatively] unless each [part] of it is imperfect. But an infinite being is perfect in such a way that neither it nor any of its [parts] lacks anything. (*Quodlibetum* 5, n. 3: Duns Scotus, 1639, vol. 12: 118)

The idea is that both God and each divine attribute are *intensively* infinite—much as would be a quality increased to an infinite degree. This infinity counts as a *mode* of God and of each divine attribute; not adding further content to the attribute, but intensifying it limitlessly.

Scotus's account of the univocal nature of religious language entails a further very distinctive Scotist claim, one that he makes use of both when discussing the divine attributes and when expanding on God's

Trinitarian nature. This is the so-called "formal distinction." Roughly, two entities are formally distinct when they exist inseparably within one and the same thing. A paradigm case would be the distinct essential properties of any one substance: rationality and animality in a human being, for example. What it is to be animal does not encompass what it is to be rational, or vice versa: nevertheless, we should not want to think of my rationality and animality as like two things tied together by some kind of real relation. Scotus holds that this kind of distinction can be found in God too—for example, between the various divine attributes. The argument is that the terms that we predicate of both God and creatures must include reference to univocal concepts. But the concept of (for example) wisdom does not encompass the concept of (for example) goodness, since one can be realized quite independently of the other. So wisdom and goodness—wherever realized—must always be somehow distinct; not really distinct in God, since the criterion for real distinction is separability, and God's wisdom and goodness are inseparable. So these attributes must be formally distinct, and joined to each other by some kind of non-relational tie, one that Scotus labels "real identity" (understandably enough, since he denies that the attributes could be really distinct or separable) (see e.g., *Ordinatio* I, d. 8, p. 1, q. 4, nn. 192–3: Duns Scotus, 1950–, vol. 4: 261–2).

V.   The Metaphysics of the Trinity

Scotus makes use of his formal distinction as a way to solve certain problems in Trinitarian theology too. The principal difficulty is that, according to many of Scotus's predecessors, divine simplicity entails that the personal properties that distinguish the persons from each other—the relations of paternity, filiation, and passive spiration—cannot be anything over and above the divine essence. This means that each person is identical with the divine essence, which in turn seems to entail that each person is identical with each other person—and thus that modalism is true. Scotus uses the formal distinction to block the first claim here. The personal properties are entities over and above the divine essence, and it is not the case that each person is identical with the divine essence (other than in the very weak sense of necessarily including that essence) (see *Ordinatio* I, d. 2, p. 2, qq. 1–4, nn. 388–408: Duns Scotus, 1950–, vol. 2: 349–58). Scotus believes that, even given this distinction, he is not committed to tritheism. For there to be three Gods, there would need to be three divine essences—much as there is a sense in which, according to Scotus, there being (for example) two or more human beings entails that there are two or more human natures—yours and mine, for example. Unlike the case of human nature, the divine essence is numerically identical in the three persons (see *Ordinatio* I, d. 2, p. 2, qq. 1–4, nn. 376–89: Duns Scotus, 1950–, vol. 2: 344–9).

In line with this, Scotus prefers Richard of St Victor's characterization of persons as *incommunicable* to Boethius's characterization of persons as *individuals*. The divine essence is indivisible (= individual), but nevertheless communicable to—shared by—the three divine persons. Persons are in every sense unshareable: they cannot be features of anything else. Individuality does not capture this most distinctive aspect of personhood, since according to Scotus, all attributes or features, whether shared or not, are individual (see Cross, 2005, 158–63).

Scotus is notable for a further innovation in Trinitarian theology, though one that he came to abandon in the last couple of years of his life: namely that divine simplicity and unicity do not require that the divine personal properties are *relations*. Scotus does not see how positing non-relational properties would make each divine person any more composite than positing relations does; neither does he see that positing such properties would entail that each person has a distinct divine nature (on this, see Cross, 2005, 195–202). What sort of thing would such a non-relational property be? Scotus holds in general that created substances are individuated by something that he sometimes called a "haecceity" (a "thisness")—a property that is unique to the particular and not possibly shared by any other particular (see *Ordinatio* II, d. 3, p. 1, qq. 5–6, nn. 168–88: Duns Scotus, 1950–, vol. 7: 474–84). The thought is that a divine person could be so distinguished from any other divine person too. The divine essence is also a "this"—but it is so through its status as infinite, and does not require anything other than this mode to distinguish it from anything else (there cannot be more than one infinite being) (*Ordinatio* I,

d. 8, p. 1, q. 3, n. 149: Duns Scotus, 1950–, vol. 4: 227). The entities that particularize the divine persons—much as the relations between them—are not themselves infinite in this way. If they were, then they would be further divine essences—something precluded by the doctrine of divine unicity. Scotus's theory of the individuation of created substances is nevertheless quite new, and a theory particularly associated with him.

Even though Scotus abandoned the hypothesis that divine persons could be individuated by haecceities, his entertaining it in the first place shows that he is not committed to a standard Anselmian argument in favor of the *filioque*—the belief that the Holy Spirit proceeds from the Father and Son jointly. The standard argument is that divine persons are distinguished by relations of origin, such that (for example) there could be no distinction between the Son and the Spirit unless it were the case that the Son had a role in producing the Spirit (see Anselm, *De processione spritus sancti* 1: Anselm, 1946–61, vol. 2: 180–5). Scotus holds instead that what distinguishes the Son and the Spirit is that they proceed from the Father in different ways—the Son by a production from intellect, and the Spirit by a production from will (Cross, 2005, 190–5). Scotus means the "from intellect" and "from will" claims quite literally here ("not metaphorically," as he strikingly states: *Ordinatio* I, d. 13, q. un., n. 23: Duns Scotus, 1950–, vol. 5: 75), and he uses this as a premise in an argument to show from first principles—without reference to revelation—that God must be a Trinity of persons. But this proof itself depends on a prior proof that there is a God at all, and I return to it after examining Scotus's proof for God's existence.

VI.   God's Existence

Scotus argues that there is a God, and just one God, in three different ways, ways that he bases on a tradition that comes from Aristotle and is mediated through the proof offered by Henry of Ghent. According to Henry, it is possible to argue that there is some first cause of, some final goal of, and something more perfect than, all created substances, and Scotus uses these three ways to argue that there is a God, and just one God. Since, according to Aristotle, any syllogistic proof requires premises that are necessary rather than merely contingent, Scotus, adopting Henry's insights, claims that we can argue for God's existence by presupposing three necessary premises: first, that some producible nature exists (*De primo principio* 3, n. 1: Duns Scotus, 1982, 43); secondly, that some nature able to be directed to a goal exists (*De primo principio* 3, n. 8: Duns Scotus, 1982, 59); thirdly, that some nature able to be exceeded in perfection exists (*De primo principio* 3, n. 9: Duns Scotus, 1982, 61). When talking of "natures" here, Scotus is not talking about particulars, but about the kinds that particulars can exemplify. So his claim is that such natures can be exemplified in the real world. Scotus understands the modalities here—the "can"— to be parasitic on the constitution of the real world: if there "is" a *being producible*, for example, this is because the following two conditions are satisfied: *being producible* is internally coherent and its exemplification compatible with the world as constituted. Given this understanding, the three premises immediately imply that some nature able to produce exists (*De primo principio* 3, n. 1: Duns Scotus, 1982, 43); that some nature able to be a goal of activity exists (*De primo principio* 3, n. 8: Duns Scotus, 1982, 59); and that some nature able to exceed in perfection exists (*De primo principio* 3, n. 9: Duns Scotus, 1982, 61). According to Scotus, the property of *being producible*, for example, is correlative to the property of *being able to produce*: the existence of the one property requires the existence of the other. Scotus has not made any claims about individuals in the world; his point is merely that the causal constitution of the actual world is not such as to block the existence of causes of, goals of, and things more perfect than, other things.

Scotus argues at considerable length for the impossibility of an infinite regress of causes, at least in cases where the causal relations are transitive ("essentially ordered," as Scotus puts it). He argues as follows: "The totality of essentially ordered causes is caused: therefore by some cause that does not belong to the totality (for then it would be its own cause), for the whole totality of dependent things depends, and on no member of the totality" (*De primo principio* 3, n. 3: Duns Scotus, 1982, 47). The first cause of any essentially ordered causal series is not itself a part of that series. Every member of an essentially ordered series is dependent; by removing the first member from the series in this way, Scotus can ensure that, since every member of the series is dependent, the whole series is, and thus requires some first cause.

Given the impossibility of an infinite causal series, Scotus argues that the possibility of a first producer entails that some simply first nature able to produce exists (*De primo principio* 3, n. 2: Duns Scotus, 1982, 45). Scotus goes on to argue for an existential conclusion: that something simply first, able to produce, exists. He does this by subscribing to what we might call the actuality principle: "Nothing can not-be unless something positively or privatively incompossible with it can be" (*De primo principio* 3, n. 6: Duns Scotus, 1982, 53). What the actuality principle means, in effect, is that it is non-existence, rather than existence, that requires explaining: actuality is in every sense primary, and a nature is actual—is exemplified—unless something in the actual world prevents it. Putting it crudely, if there is nothing about the causal constitution of the actual world that prevents something from existing, then that thing exists. If something can be, at some time it is, and this is because its possibility is precisely the result of the causal constitution of the actual world. If there is nothing incompatible with the existence of a first being, then that being exists.

Scotus is aware that none of this entails that there is just *one* exemplification of these various attributes. To show this, he appeals to the claim that any exemplification of the relevant attributes must be *infinite*. There cannot be two perfect infinite minds, for how would such minds know each other? If directly, then each would be dependent on the other, and thus not wholly perfect. If by means of a representation, then each would understand itself better than it understands the other mind, and thus would not have wholly perfect knowledge of the other (*De primo principio* 4, n. 38: Duns Scotus, 1982, 149).

This last argument presupposes that the first being has knowledge. Why should we accept this? Scotus's reasoning begins from the thought that the universe appears to be contingent, and to include events that occur contingently—i.e., events that do not have to occur. The contingent events that Scotus has in mind are particularly the results of human free will. If there is genuine contingency, then the first cause too must be able to cause contingently. But Scotus, in common with his broadly Aristotelian age, holds that there are no random events: "There is no principle of acting contingently other than will, or something requiring the will, for everything else acts by the necessity of nature, and thus not contingently" (*De primo principio* 4, n. 5: Duns Scotus, 1982, 83). But voluntary activity requires that there are goals of activity that are known, and thus requires a mind (*De primo principio* 4, n. 5: Duns Scotus, 1982, 83).

VII.   The Proof for the Trinity

In addition to arguing that God has intellect and will, Scotus believes that it is possible to show that God is immutable. The infinite cannot gain or lose attributes, since then it would not be infinite (*Ordinatio* I, d. 8, p. 1, q. 1, n. 17: Duns Scotus, 1950–, vol. 4: 160). So God cannot be the subject of accidental properties— changeable and inherent properties (*De primo principio* 4, n. 33: Duns Scotus, 1982, 139). This conclusion— along with the claim that the one God has intellect and will—is used by Scotus to argue for the existence of a Trinity of divine persons. His argument does not make use of any revealed premises, and thus constitutes an argument for the Trinity independent of any specifically Christian assumptions. He reasons that intellect produces acts of cognition. So, on the assumption that God's intellect is relevantly similar to other intellects (something compatible with Scotus's univocity theory), God's intellect produces such acts. And God's intellect must produce an act that has his own essence as its object, and will thus be (like the essence) infinite (*Ordinatio* I, d. 2, p. 2, qq. 1–4, n. 222: Duns Scotus, 1950–, vol. 2: 260–1). But God cannot be the recipient of any accident—so what is produced cannot inhere in God. And there is only one infinite being, so what is produced cannot be distinct from God:

> Intellect … is by some act of its productive of an end term equal to it, viz. infinite ([proved] from the preceding question). But nothing produces itself (*De Trinitate* 1, c.1); therefore what is produced by an act of the intellect, is distinguished in some way from the producer. But it is not distinguished essentially, because the divine essence, and any essential perfection intrinsic to it, is indistinguishable ([proved] from the question on the unity of God); therefore the product is distinguished personally from the producer. There is therefore some person produced by an act of intellect. The same is argued about the thing produced by an act of will. (*Ordinatio* I, d. 2, p. 2, qq. 1–4, nn. 355–356: Duns Scotus, 1950–, vol. 2: 336)

Scotus here refers to Augustine, *De Trinitate* (Augustine, 1968, vol. 1: 28), but he need not, since he believes himself elsewhere to have shown that self-production is impossible (*De primo principio*, 2, n. 1: Duns Scotus, 1982, 15). God is a subsistent being, so, given that there is a divine production, a subsistent being—a divine person—produces another such person. And the same holds for God's will. Things with will necessarily produce acts of love or desire, and things with perfect wills produce acts somehow equal to them. God's perfect will is productive of such an act, and thus of something infinite that is not other than the divine essence—and thus, another divine person (*Ordinatio* I, d. 10, qu. un., n. 9: Duns Scotus, 1950–, vol. 4: 342).

Why just two such produced persons? Scotus, as we have seen, believes that God has intellect and will. He holds that there are only two kinds of production—necessary and free—and he holds further that all free productions involve some kind of will or desire. So knowledge—as a necessary product—and will—as involving some other kind of production (necessitating some kind of *goal* or something *desired*)—represent these two kinds of production in God. So the primary divine person produces things equal to himself in these two ways (*Ordinatio* I, d. 2, p. 2, qq. 1–4, n. 300: Duns Scotus 1950–, vol. 2: 305). So why only two such equal products? Scotus claims that unless there were some intrinsic block on further productions, then there would be infinitely many products of the relevant kind. But it is impossible (in Scotus's Aristotelian universe, much as in ours) for there to be infinitely many beings. So there must be an intrinsic block on there being more than one production of the relevant kind (*Quodlibetum* 2, n. 17: Duns Scotus, 1639, vol. 12: 52). This yields just two productions in God.

Of course, the other famous medieval argument for the Trinity of persons in God is found in Richard of St Victor: that God is love (and this requires the production of a lover), and that the best kind of love is mutual, a love which has a third thing as a mutual object of love. Scotus holds that the love that each divine person has for the divine essence cannot be excelled—and thus that it does not require any further mutual love between the divine persons (*Ordinatio* I, d. 12, q. 1, n. 33: Duns Scotus, 1950–, vol. 5: 42–3— though see the correction to this text proposed in

Cross, 2005, 218). So Scotus rejects Richard's argument, and replaces it with his own.

Scotus's account of the Trinity has a direct bearing on his rejection of the Anselmian argument for the *filioque*. Son and Spirit are distinguished not by their relations, but on the way in which they are produced—by intellect and will, respectively. So Anselm's defense of the *filioque* is not open to Scotus. Scotus defends the *filioque* by a wholly different strategy. He holds that all power in the Trinity is to be ascribed to the persons in virtue of their possession of the divine essence. Since, in the logical or causal order, Father and Son possess the divine essence prior to the production of the Spirit, and since the Son is produced "prior" to the Spirit, it cannot be the case that the Father produces the Spirit without the Son also doing so (*Ordinatio* I, d. 11, q. 1, nn. 11–12: Duns Scotus, 1950–, vol. 5: 4). Why suppose that the production of the Son is prior to that of the Spirit? Scotus could appeal to the tradition here, but he is interested in providing some kind of a priori argument in favor of the Trinity, so instead he offers a reason that he believes should appeal to all. Given that (as he believes himself to have shown) there are productions in God from intellect and will, he argues that, necessarily, productions from intellect precede those from will: nothing can be desired unless it is first known (*De primo principio* 4, n. 5: Duns Scotus, 1982, 83). So the production of the Son must be "prior" to that of the Spirit.

VIII.   God's Knowledge and Will, Ethics, and Human Freedom

Scotus's claim, noted above, that God is wholly unconditioned—not subject to accidents, and thus not subject to anything external to himself—has a direct bearing on Scotus's view of God's knowledge of the created order. For God's knowledge cannot be determined by things external to himself, a claim that Scotus takes to be sufficient against the standard view that God knows future contingents by somehow timelessly "seeing" them (*Reportatio* IA, d. 38, qq. 1–2, n. 24: Söder, 1999, 230). Rather, Scotus holds, God knows contingent facts about things external to himself simply by willing them (*Reportatio* IA, d. 38, qq. 1–2, n. 37: Söder, 1999, 233–4). This, of course, would

raise a huge problem for any thinker who believes that human beings are free in the sense that, in any given situation, they could do other than they do. And Scotus is the first theologian or philosopher not only to believe that this is the case, but to offer an account of how it might be the case. Crucial in Scotus's development of his account of freedom is a new conception of what philosophers call modality—concepts of possibility, contingency, and necessity. Basically, in this context Scotus replaces older, Aristotelian notions of possibility—according to which, for something to be possible, it must at some time be actual—with a new notion according to which the possible is that which does not entail a logical contradiction (*Ordinatio* I, d. 2, p. 2, qu. 1–4, n. 196: Duns Scotus, 1950–, vol. 2: 249). Thus, something is contingent if its non-existence does not entail a logical contradiction: "I do not here call contingent everything that is neither necessary nor everlasting, but that whose opposite could have happened when this did. For this reason I did not say 'something is contingent,' but 'something is caused contingently'" (*Ordinatio* I, d. 2, p. 1, qu. 1–2, n. 86: Duns Scotus, 1950–, vol. 2: 178).

The significance of the simultaneity claim is that contingency—and modality in general—is "understood to involve a consideration of several alternative states of affairs with respect to the same time" (Knuuttila, 1982: 353). The contrast with the older, Aristotelian, accounts of modality, is that, on the older account, modalities are understood fundamentally as expressing temporal facts about the real world: whatever is possible is at some time actual, and the necessary is the everlasting. (Compare Scotus's "actuality principle" mentioned in section V above—his development of the new account is not consistently revealed in his various arguments.) Commentators sometimes call this account of modality "diachronic," and contrast it with Scotus's new "synchronic" modalities. Scotus uses this synchronic account of modality in his development of a new notion of freedom. According to this account, a free power is "not determined of itself, but can cause this act or the opposite act, and act or not act" in the selfsame circumstances (*Quaestiones super libros Metaphysicorum* IX, qu.15, n. 22: Duns Scotus 1997–2006, vol. 4: 680–1). These features entail, for Scotus, that a free power can "determine itself" in both ways (that is, both to act rather than not act, and to act in one way rather than another) (*Quaestiones super libros Metaphysicorum* IX, qu.15, n. 32: Duns Scotus, 1997–2006, 4: 683), and that it does this on the basis of its "unlimited actuality" (such that it is not, or need not be, in passive potency to any causal activity external to it) (*Quaestiones super libros Metaphysicorum* IX, qu.15, n. 31: Duns Scotus, 1997–2006, vol. 4: 683). This account of freedom requires the notion of synchronic contingency (considering alternative states of affairs with respect to the same time), since it requires the notion of real alternatives at one and the same time. But why suppose we are free in this way? Scotus's argument is introspective: we experience that, when we do *a*, we could have done not-*a*, or refrained from acting altogether (*Quaestiones super libros Metaphysicorum* IX, qu.15, n. 30: Duns Scotus, 1997–2006, vol. 4: 682–3).

Scotus finds it hard to reconcile his belief in human freedom with his belief in God's omniscience. Scotus reasons that, given that God knows the future by determining it, and that human beings are self-determining free agents, it must be the case that a free creaturely action has two causes which are jointly necessary and sufficient: God and the creature. The way that Scotus sees it, God's action is not causally prior to the creature's; rather, the two causes are both immediately necessary for the effect. As Scotus puts it, "In one instant of nature … the two efficient causes cause a common effect, such that neither causes without the other" (*Ordinatio* II, dd. 34–7, qq. 1–5, n. 145: Duns Scotus, 1950–, vol. 8: 429–30). But this account does not tell us *how* the theory could be true—and presumably it is not intended to. On the face of it, the account remains problematic: in order for God to know the future in the manner Scotus describes, his choice must be not merely necessary for the outcome of a creaturely choice: it must be sufficient. And if the creature's free choice is necessary for the outcome, God's cannot be sufficient for it.

Scotus's belief in God's wholly unconditioned nature affects Scotus's account of ethics too. Scotus holds that everything that God causes externally is caused contingently. Part of his reason for this has to do with his seeing God as the only ultimate goal of activity. God, as necessary of himself, is wholly independent. This, his act of love for himself, thus depends on nothing other than himself, having nothing other than himself as a necessary condition. So God does not require anything else, and his willing of everything else is thus contingent. Thus, every external causal activity of God's is contingent (*De primo principio* 4, n. 9: Duns Scotus, 1982, 91). Scotus understands this in the strongest way possible. He supposes not only that the fact of divine external activity is contingent; he supposes that there are no constraints other than logical on what God can do. So Scotus believes that whatever God wills for creatures, with the exception of commands and prohibitions that have God as their object, is just or right in virtue of being willed by God. God is a sufficient source of moral goodness by commanding and prohibiting, and with the exception of commands and prohibitions related to creatures' dealings with God, God's choices are unrestricted:

> Whatever God knows prior to the act of his will, he knows necessarily and naturally, such that there is no contingency to opposites. In God there is no practical knowledge, since if before the act of his will his intellect were to understand something as "to be done" or "to be produced," the will would either will this necessarily, or not necessarily. If necessarily, then it would be necessitated to producing the act; if not necessarily, then it would will against the dictate of the intellect, and thus be bad (since that dictate cannot but be right). (*Lectura* I, d. 39, qq. 1–5, n. 43: Duns Scotus, 1950–, vol. 17: 492)

If, prior to any act of his will, there were any obligations placed on God (if God had "practical knowledge") with regard to the actions he directs toward creatures, then either God would be bound to will them, or he would not be so bound. In the first case God would fail to be free with regard to his creature-directed actions. And this would make his actions dependent on the natures of creatures, which in turn would mean that God failed to be wholly unconditioned—such that he could not be affected by anything external to him. In the second case, God could will against some of his obligations—and this would make him bad. But, just as (for the medievals) it is impossible for God to be affected by anything external to himself, so it is impossible for him to act badly. So there cannot be any obligations placed on God—with regard to the actions he directs toward creatures—prior to any act of his will. The way Scotus sets up the disjunction—lack of freedom vs. (moral) badness—entails that there are no restrictions on how God can behave to his creatures in relation to these creature-directed actions, and thus that he can command creatures as he will, at least with regard to their behavior toward each other. If God were to do so, he would still be just, of course; the whole point of the discussion is to preserve divine justice. With regard to Godward aspects of creatures' moral duties, however, the case is rather different: God's nature is an automatic source of moral obligation, and the inference from God's nature to God alone being such that he should be loved as God is logically necessary. So in this case a factual claim straightforwardly entails an evaluative one, as on standard natural law theories; hence the commands of the first table of the decalogue "belong to natural law, taking law of nature strictly" (*Ordinatio* III, d. 37, q. un., n. 6: Duns Scotus, 1639, vol. 7: 645).

References

Anselm. 1946–61. *Opera Omnia*, ed. Franciscus Salesius Schmitt. 6 vols. Edinburgh: Thomas Nelson and Sons.

Aquinas, Thomas and Petrus, Marc. S. 1967. *Thomae Aquinatis Liber de veritate catholicae fidei contra errores infidelium, qui dicitur Summa contra gentiles.* Turin and Rome: Marietti, 3 vols.

Augustine, Saint, Bishop of Hippo. 1968. *De Trinitate.* Turnholti: Brepolis.

Cross, Richard. 2005. *Duns Scotus on God.* Ashgate Studies in the History of Philosophical Theology. Aldershot and Burlington, VT.

Duns Scotus. 1639. *Opera Omnia*, ed. Luke Wadding. 12 vols. Lyon.

Duns Scotus. 1950–. *Opera Omnia*, ed. C. Bali and others. Rome: Typis Polyglottis Vaticanis.

Duns Scotus. 1982. *A Treatise on God as First Principle*, 2nd ed., ed. Allan B. Wolter. Chicago, IL: Franciscan Herald Press.

Knuuttila, Simo. 1982. *Modalities in Medieval Philosophy.* Topics in Medieval Philosophy. London and New York: Routledge.

Söder, Joachim Roland. 1999. *Kontingenz und Wissen: De Lehre von den future contingentia bei Johannes Duns Scotus.* Beiträge zur Geschichte der Philosophie und Theologie des Mittelalters, Neue Folge. 49. Münster: Aschendorf.

Julian of Norwich (1342–c.1416)

Kevin Magill

Our modest starting point is a young woman who lived in mid-fourteenth-century Norwich and described having a visionary experience centered on the crucified Christ. Julian of Norwich, as she is now known to us, had already lived 30 years before this visionary encounter. The remainder of her life was dedicated to understanding the vision's meaning. Despite the private nature of the experience and the complex spiritual teaching it contained, Julian was convinced that the vision was not meant for her alone. Understanding Julian's significance as a theologian, therefore, requires full recognition of her place and role in the religious community. Julian has too often been categorized as an author, mystic, or recluse without further analysis of these labels in their medieval context. This article will situate Julian in her historical and cultural context. In so doing a fresh picture of Julian and her theological activity emerges.

Details of Julian's life are not easy to determine. It is generally agreed that "Julian" was named after St Julian's church in Norwich where she lived a substantial part of her life as a church anchoress. She received a vision or "showing" of God's love on May 13, 1373, though it is not clear whether she had taken up the solitary life before this date or that her desire for the anchoritic life was a response to the vision. There is no extant text composed in Julian's hand, yet there is a consensus amongst Julian scholars that she authored short and long responses to the vision, constructing, in the process, an organic theological system.

In the 25 chapters of the short manuscript account, the scribal introduction identifies a devout woman named Julian who was a recluse at Norwich and still alive in 1413 (Reynolds and Holloway, 2001, 711). The longer version containing 86 chapters records 16 "showings" revealed to a "simple unlearned person" (Reynolds and Holloway, 2001, 143, 147). Both short and long versions state that Julian was 30½ years old when she received the vision, an age that gives her an approximate birth date of December 1342.

Remaining evidence for Julian's identity can be pieced together from several bequests or wills that name "Julian" as an anchorite and resident at St Julian's church in Norwich. The first bequest of two shillings was made by Roger Reed the rector of St Coslany, Norwich, dated March 20, 1393/4 to "Julian ankorite" (Colledge and Walsh, 1978, 33). The last known bequest was made in 1429 by Robert Baxter, who left three shillings and four pence to the anchorite in the churchyard of St Julian's church in Conisford. If Robert Baxter's bequest was left to the Julian that is our concern, when alive, the anchoress would have been in her late 80s. The precise date of Julian's death is not known.

Julian of Norwich's popularity as a figure of scholarly debate began its modern life with Grace Warrack's (1901) critical edition of a version of the long text.

The Student's Companion to the Theologians, First Edition. Edited by Ian S. Markham.
© 2013 Blackwell Publishing Ltd. Published 2013 by Blackwell Publishing Ltd.

Warrack's publication, allied to a growing interest in Christian medieval literature at the turn of the twentieth century, brought Julian's profound spiritual insight to the notice of academics and practitioners alike. The long text is commonly referred to by its editorial title *Revelation(s) of Divine Love*, a shortening of the title given by the Benedictine Serenus Cressy who published the first printed edition in 1670 (Cressy, 1670). The title of *Showings* designating manuscripts attributed to Julian is due, in large part, to Colledge and Walsh's (1978) critical edition of the short text and Paris manuscript version of the longer text. *Showing of Love*, the title used in this article, was chosen by Reynolds and Holloway (2001) to publish a much-needed complete set of Julian manuscripts in both Middle and Modern English.

Despite references to Julian's skill as a writer in academic literature, the surviving eight manuscripts of the Julian corpus are all scribal productions, not original works. The earliest, the Amherst manuscript or short text, dates approximately to 1413–50, 40 years at best after Julian's vision, with the later versions of the long text copied between 1650 and 1795/6. The exemplar *Showing of Love* text from which the later copies were made has never been discovered.

Julian does not fit the category of author neatly. If Julian did write the text of *Showing of Love*, it is unlikely that she relied solely on the transmission of the vision in a textual form. In practical terms, the activity of writing was challenging enough in the Middle Ages. The earliest paper documents did not appear in England until 1296–1303, in the form of correspondence between Italy and Edward I's bankers. The earliest paper records made in England were from major seaports, a place where paper could be imported. There are extant seaport registers from King's Lynn in 1307 and another from Lyme Regis dating to 1309. As Clanchy notes, summarizing the limited resources for medieval writers of the early fourteenth century, "The most significant fact about paper in England in the period up to 1307 is that it was scarcely known" (Clanchy, 1993, 120). Paper did not begin to replace the use of parchment until the fifteenth century. The shift was brought about on economic grounds, with a quire of paper (25 sheets) providing eight times as many leaves as parchment of equivalent cost. The private act of writing by an

anchoress like Julian, not renowned for personal possessions or great wealth, is not easy to imagine. The scarcity of paper alone would have meant that her writing project relied on acquiring a ready supply of expensive parchment. The materials for Julian to write *Showing of Love* would have been difficult to come by and very costly.

Dictation was the most proficient way of committing words to writing in the Middle Ages. Following Clanchy again:

> "Reading and dictating" were ordinarily coupled together, not "reading and writing"; the skill of writing a letter in proper form was the "art of dictation" (*ars dictaminis*), a branch of rhetoric. Writing was distinguished from composition because putting pen to parchment was an art in itself. Even when an author declares that he is writing something, he may in fact be using the term metaphorically. (Clanchy, 1993, 125–6)

Julian's narrative style is often in a spoken voice, and frequently in dialogic form. Speech anticipates the immediacy of an audience in the way that writing does not. In the thirteenth century, St Francis complained of the spiritually empty book-learning of monks. In his "Seventh Admonition," Francis laments, "They have been killed by the letter, who want only to know words in order to be reckoned wiser than other men" (Brooke, 1975, 126). In medieval treatises, charters, and contracts the written word alone was considered inadequate. The seal for a charter, for example, would be considered more than a method of authentication for its medieval audience. The seal was a tangible object signifying the wishes of the donor. Some seals were disproportionately large compared to the written document they accompanied, which is evidence that visual impact of such objects held sway over the presence of text. John of Salisbury famously remarked: "Fundamentally letters are shapes indicating voices. Hence they represent things which they bring to mind through the windows of the eyes. Frequently they speak voicelessly the utterances of the absent" (Camille, 1985, 31). In the Middle Ages, the visual and oral still retained considerable influence in the textual world.

Julian does not identify her authority to communicate the vision with the act of writing, but in her ability to share its teaching. The Amherst manuscript, for example, records Julian's plea:

> Because of the Showing I am not good, but only if I love God better, and so may, and so should, each one who sees it and hears it with good will and intent. And so is my desire—that it should be for every such man the same profit as I desired for myself. Thereto was I moved by God the first time I saw it, for since we are all one, the Showing is common to all. (Reynolds and Holloway, 2001, 725)

This utilitarian ideal distinguishes Julian's transmission of her vision from other female visionaries that celebrate the act of writing. For instance, the first page of Mechthild of Magdeburg's (d.1285) *Flowing Light of the Godhead* reads:

> This book is to be joyfully welcomed, for God Himself speaks in it ... The book proclaims Me alone and shows forth My holiness with praise ... This book is called The Flowing Light of the Godhead. Ah! Lord God! Who has written this book? I in my weakness have written it, because I dared not hide the gift that is in it. (Petroff, 1986, 23)

Mechthild's self-effacing reference to her "weakness" is a common literary device rather than a genuine inferiority complex. Julian too uses a "humility topos" to introduce her audience to what she was shown, yet the emphasis is less on Julian the author than the potential spiritual benefit for her audience. Julian first reminds her audience, "God forbid that you should say or take it so, that I am a teacher ... For I am a woman, unlettered, feeble and frail" (Reynolds and Holloway, 2001, 727). To overcome any self-doubt, Julian reasserts the wider significance of the vision:

> But I know well this that I say—I have it on the Showing of Him who is Sovereign Teacher—and truly charity urgeth me to tell you of it, for I would that God were known and my even-Christians helped ... Because I am a woman should I therefore believe that I ought not to tell you about the goodness of God. (Reynolds and Holloway, 2001, 727)

Julian is concerned less with her ability to articulate what she was shown than the audience's ability to access sovereign teaching. She is confident that where her own efforts at presenting the complexities of the vision are lacking, Christ, the true teacher, will gently instruct the community. Julian's ability to step back from her identity as an author is reflected in the various modes of communication that feature in *Showing of Love*. Julian mixes her commentary on the vision with simple descriptions of what she was shown and words spoken to her. She does not attempt to interpret all the sights she was shown or the words spoken. Befitting her pastoral role as a church anchoress, she offers her version of what was shown to comfort and counsel.

Julian's audience was responsive to methods of communication that had the greatest immediacy, methods which mirror Julian's stark confrontation with the crucified Christ of her vision. Julian wanted to be a first-hand witness to the crucifixion so that she may suffer for love as Christ suffered on the cross. Julian's descriptions of Christ's "plenteous bleeding" and "pellets" of brown, thick blood cascading from under the crown of thorns are the words of a witness not a literary device. Furthermore, it was an image of suffering that Julian's contemporaries could reimagine for themselves, using a vast repository of images, lyrics, and plays that focused on Christ's humanity. As Gail McMurray Gibson notes, with specific reference to devotional practices in fifteenth-century East Anglia, religious art and devotion centered round an "incarnational aesthetic" that had communal rather than private significance (Gibson, 1989, 12). In the figure of St Francis and the Franciscan meditative tradition that developed in the fourteenth and fifteenth centuries, devotion to Christ's bodily life, his physical and emotional suffering, created a blueprint for Christian living (see Depres, 1989). In the late Middle Ages, Christ's suffering human body, not the Godhead, presented an accessible depiction of God and humankind's relatedness.

Having emphasized that the vision she was shown does not guarantee her sanctity, Julian states: "I do not say this to those who are wise for they know it well. But I say it to you who are simple, for ease and comfort, for we are all one in love. For truly it was not showed to me that God loves me better than the least soul that is in grace" (Reynolds and Holloway, 2001, 177). Julian retains the oral trope of "saying" to convey meaning throughout *Showing of Love*. Julian

speaks to uneducated Christians to offer them comfort. It is important when reading *Showing of Love* to
remain sensitive to the spoken word. Julian does not
say that she is writing for these simple Christians. The
spoken voice in the text is a deliberate reference to
the most commonplace form of communication
between Julian and the world outside her anchorhold.

Accessibility and absence of privileged access to
the vision are points that Julian refers to repeatedly.
Having been shown the three modes of God's teaching in the vision (bodily sight, ghostly [spiritual] sight,
and words formed in her understanding), Julian
reminds her audience, "In all this I was much stirred
in charity to my fellow-Christians, that they might all
see and know the same as I saw; and I would that it
were a comfort to them" (Reynolds and Holloway,
2001, 727). The vision is profitable to all Christians.
Julian's role in the community and the place of her
vision in her fulfillment of that role is central. By presenting a vision for the edification of the Christian
community, Julian contributes something distinctive
to existing studies of Christian mystical texts. Few
Julian scholars, if any, have provided a sustained treatment of the didactic potential of Julian's vision. Both
Julian's solitary life as a church anchoress and the
psychological model for understanding mystical
phenomena as private, mental events have acted as
persistent deterrents.

In the early Christian tradition the hermit and
anchorite were synonymous. To be termed a hermit
or anchorite meant to withdraw, a meaning derived
from the Greek (*anachōrein*) "to go away" to the desert
(*eremus*), from which the word hermit (*eremita*) is
derived. As the tradition developed into the Middle
Ages, the desert of the early eremitic tradition was
symbolized by the anchorite's cell or anchorhold,
usually close to or attached to a church. What seems
beyond question is the requirement for the anchorite
to live in solitude, before God alone. It seems less
likely that an anchoress like Julian should be active
within the community, and yet throughout *Showing of
Love* she is insistent that the vision's meaning must be
communicated.

The odds were against Julian. The author of the
Ancrene Wisse, an anonymous though highly influential thirteenth-century guide for anchoresses, offers
straightforward advice on the possibility of an

anchoress instructing others. The scene depicts a
caricatured version of the anchoress as a gossip who
speaks too much when she should be listening:

> Someone, perhaps, is so learned or so wise in speaking
> that she wants him who sits and speaks with her to know
> it, and pays him back word for word. And she who
> should be an anchoress becomes a teacher, and teaches
> him who has come to teach her. She wants to be recog-
> nized and known at once for her talk among the wise.
> Known she is—because on account of the very things
> for which she expects to be held wise, he understands
> she is a fool, since she hunts for praise and catches blame;
> for at the very least, when he has gone away, he will
> say, "This anchoress talks a lot." (Savage and Watson,
> 1991, 72–3)

The *Wisse*'s author warns against the anchoress being
regarded a fool for seeking attention—a disposition at
odds with a life of solitude. To live a life of solitude,
the anchoress's speech must be controlled and the
community's access to the anchoress must be limited.
After all, a requiem mass was performed during an
anchoress's enclosure ceremony to symbolize her new
status as dead to the world.

The picture that *Ancrene Wisse* paints is a bleak one
and perhaps not altogether accurate. The *Wisse*'s
author is not describing the behavior of anchoresses
who gossip; he is set against any interaction between
the anchoress and the outside world even when
directed to legitimate, pastoral ends. In support of
Julian's identity as an anchoress who instructs, Anneke
B. Mulder-Bakker has identified a number of anchoresses and recluses named as educators (Mulder-Bakker,
1995). Hildegard of Bingen, who had a reputation for
great learning, was instructed by her aunt and fellow
recluse Jutta of Sponheim; Eve of Liège and Juliana of
Cornillon, Marie D'Oignies and the anchoress
Hedwig are further examples of mutual instruction
and edification amongst pairs of female solitaries.
Mulder-Bakker's initial findings question whether the
form of instruction anchoresses and recluses engaged
in was always a private matter or had a broader, communal significance. She asks:

> Should we further imagine these schools as a kind of
> internal school, like those which monasteries and con-
> vents used to have, where young novices were trained by

older monks or nuns to learn the profession? This is how we usually tend to interpret the evidence, the old recluse transmitting her knowledge to her servant and subsequent successor. Or is it better to understand the anchorage as an external school, a cultural and educational centre for the faithful in the town? (Mulder-Bakker, 1995, 247)

Margery Kempe's description of her visit to Julian's anchoress's cell is an explicit example of communication between a so-called solitary and a member of the lay religious community. It is interesting that Margery at no stage considers her visit to be unusual. According to Margery's version of events, Julian is an acknowledged expert in discerning the efficacy of visionary experiences. The method of Julian's counsel is a combination of technical advice and pastoral care. Julian tells Margery that her weeping is authorized by St Paul and St Jerome as more torment to the devil than the pains of hell. Julian then prays that Margery be granted perseverance and patience. In a typical example of Julian's pastoral voice, she tells Margery: "Set all your trust in God and fear not the language of the world, for the more spite, shame and reproof that you have in the world the more merit you have in the sight of God. Patience is necessary for you in that shall you keep your soul" (Staley, 1996, 54, my translation).

Several passages in *Showing of Love* are devoted to nurturing patience in an effort to counteract sloth (impatience), despair, and doubtful fear. The exemplar for the development of patience is Christ of the passion, who suffered for love. Thus Margery is counseled to be patient, suffering as Christ suffered the pains of the crucifixion: "Most meekly our Lord showed the patience that he had in his hard Passion. And also the joy and the liking that we have of that Passion for love. And this he showed in example so that we should gladly and easily bear our pains" (Reynolds and Holloway, 2001, 450).

Julian counsels Margery, who constantly feared she was in danger of being deceived in her visions, on the necessity of patience and the constancy of Christ's love. Julian listens and then offers instruction on the necessity for patience as an expression of love, for which the example she should follow is Christ who suffered for love alone.

The educative potential of love is found in many places in the anchoritic guides of the medieval period.

In Chapter 87 of the *Scale of Perfection*, for example, the Augustinian canon Walter Hilton deals with the question of the soul's relation to its beloved object. He states:

> For what is man but his thoughts and loves? These make a man only good or bad. As much as thou love thy God and thine even Christians and knowest Him, so much is thy soul; and if thou little love Him, little is thy soul; and if thou would think what thou love, look whereupon thou think; for there thy love is, there is thine eye. (Bestul, 2000, 211–12, my translation)

According to Julian's contemporary, Hilton, where the anchoress's affections are directed toward God and her even-Christians, as the soul's object of love, the soul is both knowing and virtuous. The reverse is the case where the soul has little or no love for God and her even-Christians. The eye of love must be turned to immediate objects, such as one's fellow Christians. In this respect, Hilton advises that the anchoress should turn from her private prayer and devotion, because she will see God in the people that will seek her out for advice and guidance.

Love has several expressions in *Showing of Love*. Love is the unity of Christians, the meaning of the visionary sequence as a whole, and God's true nature. It is also the concept that underpins Julian's desire for her fellow Christians to profit from the vision as she profits. Divine love admits no partiality, and it draws Julian into relationship with her fellow Christians, who are loved as one, not as individuals. The lesson of divine love is instantiated in how relationships with others are conducted:

> For in this oneness of charity is the life of all mankind that shall be saved. For God is all that is good, and God has made all that is made and God loves all that He has made. So if any man or woman withdraw his love from any of his fellow-Christians, he loves right nought, for he loves not at all. (Reynolds and Holloway, 2001, 725)

Julian's lesson in divine love is learned through her love of her fellow Christians. Julian of Norwich was an anchoress who invested personally in her relationship with the community. The expression of Julian's religious life was outward not inward, public rather than private, seeking out God in a life of faith which she shared with the Christian community.

References

Bestul, T., ed. 2000. *The Scale of Perfection*. Kalamazoo, MI: Medieval Institute Publications.

Brooke, R. 1975. *The Coming of the Friars*. London: Allen & Unwin.

Camille, M. 1985. "Seeing and Reading: Some Visual Implications of Medieval Literacy and Illiteracy," *Art History* 8: 26–49.

Clanchy, M. 1993. *From Memory to Written Record: England 1066–1307*, 2nd ed. Oxford: Blackwell.

Colledge, E. and Walsh, J., eds. 1978. *A Book of Showings to the Anchoress Julian of Norwich*, 2 parts. Toronto: Pontifical Institute of Mediaeval Studies.

Cressy, S., ed. 1670. *XVI Revelations of Divine Love, Shewed to a Devout Servant of God, called Mother Julian*. S.I., London.

Despres, D. 1989. *Ghostly Sights: Visual Meditation in Late-Medieval Literature*. Norman, OK: Pilgrim Books.

Gibson, G. 1989. *The Theater of Devotion: East Anglian Drama and Society in the Late Middle Ages*. Chicago: University of Chicago Press.

Mulder-Bakker, Anneke B. 1995. *Sanctity and Motherhood: Essays on Holy Mothers in the Middle Ages*. New York: Garland.

Petroff, E., ed. 1986. *Medieval Women's Visionary Literature*. New York and Oxford: Oxford University Press.

Reynolds, A. and Holloway, J., eds. 2001. *Showing of Love: Extant Texts and Translation*. Tavarnuzze, Firenze: Sismel.

Savage, A. and Watson, N., trans. 1991. *Anchoritic Spirituality: Ancrene Wisse and Associated Works*. Classics of Western Spirituality. New York: Paulist Press.

Staley, L., ed. 1996. *The Book of Margery Kempe*. Kalamazoo, MI: Medieval Institute.

Warrack, G. 1901. *The Revelations of Divine Love/recorded by Julian anchoress at Norwich*. London: Methuen.

William Ockham (*c.*1280–*c.*1349)

J. Elton Smith, Jr.

William of Ockham, sometimes spelled Occam, was born in the mid-1280s most likely in the hamlet of that name not far from London. Ockham is important both as theologian and philosopher. Today, his political works are perhaps of greater interest to many historians than his more strictly theological ones, as the political works contain teachings which point the way toward a separation of the political realm from the religious, though Ockham's intent was that the two realms should always co-operate. It is impossible to separate Ockham's theology from his philosophy, or his politics from either. Ockham had joined the Franciscans as early as 1301, perhaps somewhat earlier, and most likely at the order's house in London. He became a sub-deacon in 1306, moving to Oxford around 1309 where he studied, first, subjects in the arts and then, from 1310 to 1315, theology with the Franciscans at their Oxford house.

Ockham's academic career followed the normal path of the time, including the requirement of copious study of Peter Lombard's *Sentences*, as well as preparation and delivery of lectures on scripture. By 1321 Ockham had risen to the level of a Master of Theology, but he never received appointment to a chair of theology at Oxford, due in part to political factors and the determined enmity of John Lutterell, the chancellor of the university. One of Ockham's nicknames, *venerabilis inceptor*, stems from this failure to achieve a chair of theology, which left him an "inceptor" or

venerable "beginner" in rank in the academic world. As many have pointed out, the nickname has sometimes mistakenly been taken to mean originator or beginner of the philosophical school of nominalism, sometimes referred to as terminism. Another nickname by which he is known, and which aims to communicate the mistaken suggestion sometimes associated with the first nickname, is *Princeps nominalium*, the prince or founder of nominalism. However, even here it is important to note that others before Ockham suggested some of the concepts associated with nominalism. For Ockham, nominalism was a reference to the names, or terms, of individual things. The names of particulars in essence referred only to those particular things, and not to any universal reality. The name of a particular thing functioned as a signifier of that thing and referred to no universal reality beyond the particular.

Lombard's *Sentences*, a work from the twelfth century in four sections, was the reigning theological textbook of the Middle Ages until Thomas Aquinas's *Summa Theologiae* took its place. Anyone studying theology in a formal way in this period inevitably encountered the theology of Lombard, and Ockham's treatment of Lombard's first volume was called the *Ordinatio*, which he completed in the early 1320s. This is the book by Ockham which yields massive amounts of detail about what Ockham thought about theology and philosophy, and the work shows evidence of

The Student's Companion to the Theologians, First Edition. Edited by Ian S. Markham.

careful revision by Ockham himself. The *Ordinatio* was properly about the doctrine of God, who God is, and what the nature and attributes of God are. The book which followed naturally in sequence from the *Ordinatio* was the *Reportatio*, and it was an extension of comment on the remaining three books of Lombard's *Sentences*, based on lectures by Ockham on Lombard. These lectures dealt with Ockham's considerations of Lombard's views of creation and the fall of human-kind, and how God brought about a plan to save humankind from its sinfulness, ending with the con-summation or accomplishment of divine redemption in the fullness of time. There are some technical ques-tions of manuscript evidence which reflect at least some questions of subsequent editing in the *Reportatio*. Anyone who wished to study theology at university was required to master Lombard in the most careful way, and Ockham's treatment of Lombard is a good example of this practice.

Another work by Ockham, also from the 1320s, was the *Quodlibeta septem*. It included questions on a wide-ranging array of subjects, in which the scholastic debate or disputation provided a framework for seek-ing truth. Though there were other works of a theo-logical nature, perhaps the most notable was *Tractatus de praedestinatione et de praescientia Dei et de tuturis contingentibus*, in which Ockham explored how God knows what God knows, and whether God can know things that are contingencies in the future, and how all of these problems relate to the question of God's fore-ordination or predestination of events. Ockham's major philosophical work on logic was his *Summa logicae*, which was composed before 1324.

No stranger to controversy, Ockham soon achieved unfavorable notice by university authorities, particu-larly Oxford's chancellor, John Lutterell. Eventually Ockham came to the negative attention of Pope John XXII, partly at the hand of Lutterell, who was a devoted follower of Thomas Aquinas. Lutterell so hounded Ockham that Ockham, even though aca-demically qualified, was prevented by the chancellor from gaining a chair of theology at Oxford. Lutterell himself came into conflict with much of the univer-sity and was eventually removed as chancellor, in about 1322, but even this did not prevent him the next year from personally advocating Ockham's con-demnation by the Pope at Avignon. In about 1324

Ockham was made to appear before an official papal inquiry there, a protracted procedure that took several years. During this time, it is likely that he lived in the Franciscan house in Avignon, in community, and not under official censure or suffering from any loss of freedom, as long as he remained within the city. Notwithstanding the propriety of interpreting a body of work within its own context, the Pope's advisors secured the issuing of negative judgments regarding 51 of Ockham's particular theses. These theses were culled from Ockham's own commentary on Lombard's *Sentences*. However, these negative judgments did not follow on to the formal, juridical condemnation of the works themselves.

Another source of personal irritation to Pope John XXII was Ockham's insistence on the strict Franciscan view of what constituted authentic apostolic poverty. However, Ockham did not turn to this controversy during the first few years of his sojourn in Avignon. The head of the Franciscans, Michael Cesena, advo-cated strongly the purist view, a position which called for not only the rejection of personal ownership of property, but even communal ownership of property. Ockham was asked by Cesena to research the matter of apostolic poverty, and ended by siding decisively with Cesena, but not all Franciscans were persuaded to adopt the stricter view. This dispute over poverty was in its own way as bitter as that between Thomists and the emerging nominalists.

Ockham became a close advisor of Cesena, even fleeing from Avignon with him in 1328. Ockham received a sentence of excommunication that year, as well. As they left Avignon, Michael Cesena and Ockham took with them the official seal of the Franciscans, which gave them a strong claim as bearers of the authentic teaching of their order. Ockham eventually became the keeper of the order's seal, after Michael of Cesena's death in 1342. Strict Franciscans, or those who embraced Michael's and Ockham's pur-ist views of apostolic poverty, saw Ockham as the new leader of the order.

According to perhaps less reliable sources, it was seven years later, in 1349, that Ockham died, but at any rate the last few years of his life were even more politically and personally precarious than before, due to the death of his protector Louis of Bavaria in 1347. There have been suggestions that Ockham had become reconciled to the church, meaning a lifting of his sentence of excommunication, but this does not find support in the best historical sources. Louis's death was a severe blow, as the Holy Roman Emperor had received Ockham under his personal sponsorship. The relationship between Louis and Ockham had certainly been mutually beneficial, as Ockham and Louis both had bitterly protested the Pope's prerogatives and, from their perspective, lack of true biblical piety. Perhaps the most important thing about their relationship was that it had enabled Ockham to carry on with his writing in Munich, under Louis's guarantee of support and safety.

Ockham was a purist in arguing for a return to a clearer, simpler teaching on what it meant to give up all for Christ and to follow Christ as a disciple. He had become so disenchanted by what he saw as papal abuses regarding material wealth that he took the controversial and impolitic step of judging the Pope to be heretical. According to Ockham, papal heresy involved necessarily an immediate abandonment of the papal office. Therefore, if the Pope were in fact a heretic, then he was no Pope, and obedience to him was not only unnecessary but sinful. In this dispute Ockham seems to have confused doctrine with piety, again exhibiting the purist's tendency to push the implications of doctrine toward more radical conclusions than the institutional church was able to accept. After Ockham's flight from Avignon in 1328, also the year of his excommunication, he had enjoyed for almost the next two decades the secular protection of Louis of Bavaria, the Holy Roman Emperor. This patronage and protection provides a context for understanding Ockham's strident condemnations of abuses of authority by the Pope and also the basis of Ockham's theoretical and academic support for the right of secular authorities to wield their own power separate from the power of the church. Ockham's continued excoriation of the Pope led to the decision of the remainder of the Franciscans to expel him from their ranks in 1331.

Ockham's thought about the relationship between secular and ecclesiastical power has been rightly linked to the major medieval challenge to papal authority. In essence, then, Ockham's political contributions were very much "occasional," brought about by the crucible of his experience of conflict. Therefore his politics are seen by some as not fundamental to his thought as a whole but rather as "incidental," or an expression of his personal struggles to come to terms with what he saw around him in the administration of the church and what he thought the church should be. In this sense, his politics are an almost reverse image of his epistemology. In his epistemology, Ockham sought to show things as they were, not as "they should be," but in his political ethics the reverse was true.

Conciliarism, as a theoretical and systematic approach to how power should be granted, exercised, and checked within the church, came into its own in the 1300s and 1400s. This movement was based less on a pyramidal view of polity and more on the idea that the church should be governed with the sharing of power between high church dignitaries. It was argued that this was more of a biblical paradigm of governance, based on early apostolic experience in the church, and that the papal system as known in the high Middle Ages had actually introduced and concentrated much more authority into the chair of St Peter than had originally been intended. Interestingly, the Eastern Orthodox experience of conciliarism, in which the Patriarch of Constantinople was primus inter pares, was perhaps philosophically more in accord with what Ockham seemed to be arguing for in the West. Naturally, advocates of conciliarism found allies among secular political rulers eager to chip away at the authority of the pope; and, as well, popes found it necessary to oppose conciliarism vigorously as an infringement on the divine prerogative of the church and her pope.

Still, it is important to note that Ockham clearly recognized the legitimacy of more than one source of power and authority in the world. There was the power which came from God, a power which was rightly exercised within the church. There was also the power which existed in government, sometimes called secular power, though one must not read into this term the antagonism which it often implies today toward religiously based power. Ockham thought that religious or spiritual power and secular or political power should be in support of each other, as they both worked toward the same goal, which was good order in society. Therefore both spiritual power and secular power found their origin in God. The limits placed on spiritual power flowed from the obligation to prevent its abuse. This was why Ockham was able to justify his opposition to Pope John XXII. This pope's abuse of power, in Ockham's estimation, justified rejection of his claim to exercise spiritual power in any legitimate way.

A similar argument is present in what Ockham called secular or political power. When a ruler abused his power in society, the people had a right, even an obligation, to oppose this misuse of power. This obligation extended even to the drastic step of rebellion. Revolt, though never a good thing in itself, was justifiable if a ruler so violated natural law as to have departed from the basic nature of what a ruler is: someone who protects and provides for the people. If a ruler deserted these crucial and fundamental functions by being rapacious, not just somewhat less than effective as a ruler, then the people could rightly overthrow him. Seeds of later political philosophy and the right to revolt against unjust power are found in Ockham's political thought. Theorists such as Jean Bodin and John Locke formulated concepts related to ideas already found in Ockham. Of interest as well is Ockham's position that a single civil government throughout the earth was preferable to many civil governments, each with its own limited territory to govern. This view may rightly be seen as quite far ahead of contemporary political thought of this period. Again, even in this political view, the principle of economy comes to the fore for Ockham.

Ockham's political works included his *Opus nonagenta dierum*, from about 1332, and entitled such because it was supposedly written in about 90 days, in which he castigates Pope John XXII over his purportedly erroneous teaching on what was the nature of true apostolic poverty. Yet John XXII was not the only pope to be condemned as heretical at the hand of Ockham, for he also rejected Benedict XII and Clement VI as true popes. Other political works included *Dialogus super dignitate papali et regia* from the 1330s in which he explored how church and state were different from each other and had different powers and how they should coexist in the world. *Octo questiones de potestate papae* from about 1340 argued that the secular ruler rightly has temporal authority intentionally given to him by God and that the pope should not have or exercise this type of power.

Breviloquium de principatu tyrannico from the beginning of the 1340s and *Tractatus de imperatorum et pontificum potestate* from around 1347 continued Ockham's arguments against papal power in the secular realm and his support for a rightful existence and exercise of secular power outside the control of the church.

At least on the surface something hard to reconcile in Ockham's politics and philosophy is his understanding that something is right because God commands it—what is sometimes called positivism—rather than something being right solely because it is inherently right. However, the problem is not so acute when one remembers that Ockham also taught that God would never command anything that was wrong. However, a "trickle-down" theory does not derive from this, since popes and secular rulers could and did command things which were clearly wrong, in Ockham's estimation. Positivism in God was one thing, but positivism in fallible people was not acceptable to him, no matter how lofty might be the position that a person occupied. In this regard, then, Ockham was moving the basis of social ethics out of theology and clearly into philosophy, in this case, political philosophy. Nonetheless, it must be remembered that Ockham's personal experience of abusive power at the hands of the Pope had a formative and powerful influence on his political thought.

The political questions over secular versus religious power were clearly a large part of Ockham's controversial reputation. It is impossible to separate them fully from questions of philosophy and theology. Nonetheless, the primary intellectual reason for Ockham's controversial reputation and his condemnation by the church was something deeper: his radical unsettling of the elaborate marriage between Aristotelian philosophy and Christian theology which had been so carefully synthesized by Thomas Aquinas.

Ockham believed that the intellectual frame of scholasticism was in need of radical revision. And Ockham's thought provided a basis for this revision. However, Ockham's conclusions were more than a mere adjustment to the balance between philosophy and theology. Instead, his thought provided a basis for splitting philosophy away from theology. This was problematic for many in the church's leadership because it opened the question of whether the church's fund of truth was able to tolerate the existence of truth from another source which was not as clearly subject to the church's control. This split had revolutionary implications, opening the way to modern philosophical thought, the "via moderna" or "the modern way," in opposition to Aquinas's "via antiqua" or "ancient way." Also of radical importance were the implications of Ockham's philosophical approach for modern science, in which the inductive method of experimentation displaces the deductive method. Though it is false to suggest an easy dichotomy between "science" and "religion," as is evidenced by the existence of scientists among the clergy of the church, still the intellectual bases and presuppositions of how one arrives at truth were profoundly challenged by Ockham's work.

The most enduring piece of Ockham's philosophical contributions has to do with the field of logic, particularly causation. Ockham's thought has even entered the common vocabulary in the well-known phrase "Ockham's Razor," which exhorts searching first for the explanation of any particular phenomenon with a simpler explanation rather than a more complex one. Here one sees the coincidence of both logic and the subfield of causation in his thought.

Yet there are many other important ways in which Ockham enriched philosophical thought, such as his work on the problem of particulars and universals. The high medieval theological and philosophical tradition of the church favored the concept of universals as underlying all expressions of particulars. This involved no denial that particulars existed. Rather, it was thought that a given particular instance of an object was made possible because a universal of that object already existed. To argue such was to deduce the existence of the particular from the universal, but Ockham wanted to start instead with the particular object. He did not find it necessary, however, to argue that the universal existed because a particular object did exist. Rather, it was simply enough to say that the individual object existed. Such a position, which did not necessarily have to involve the denial of universals, when taken on its face, was infuriating to the church and to the received scholastic philosophy of the period. What Ockham was saying was that, in terms of philosophical methodology, the existence of a particular did not require the existence of a universal. This is clearly different from saying that universals did not exist at all,

but it is easy to see how Ockham's philosophical focus on the particular could be taken that way.

Theology was accepted by Ockham as capable of showing truths which could not be demonstrated through philosophy. What Ockham was insisting upon was that this other source of truth (theology) was not itself philosophy. Theology, on the other hand, was perfectly free to argue for the existence of universals, but this was from a premise of faith, based on divine revelation. Nonetheless, Ockham rejected the idea that theology could establish the truth of something which was demonstrated through the use of philosophical method to be untrue. In other words, if a proposition could be proven to be false by philosophical method based on reason, no reliance on theology could make any false statement true. Something was either false or true. For Ockham, it was essential to recognize that God would not, indeed could not, will two mutually exclusive things to be true. This has sometimes been called the principle of non-contradiction. However, non-contradiction as a principle by no means explains all things, for Ockham also recognized that, of some things, their truth or falsehood was not currently known.

An example of the interplay between theology and philosophy in Ockham's teaching is seen in Ockham's acceptance of the foundational Christian doctrine of the Trinity, one God in three Persons, though he could not establish the truth of this doctrine by use of philosophical method. In other words, Ockham was able to accept the doctrine of the Trinity as true because he accepted that theology was also a legitimate source of truth. Therefore, Ockham accepted the fact that theology could put a brake on where philosophy, on its own, might lead. This is seen in that Ockham's general philosophical method, a preference for the reduction of the number of beings whenever possible, was not applicable to the doctrine of the Trinity. Of course this begs the question whether in philosophy "persons" equates with the term "beings."

One way to summarize the conflict between Ockham and the church is to say that their respective methodologies of how one arrived at truth aroused mutual suspicion. Ironically, this conflict was not necessary for either side, but the hostility of life in the church and society, clouded by personalities and power struggles for authority and precedence between the pope and secular rulers, made the likelihood of keeping theology and philosophy together within one "house" impossible. Thus was engendered the antagonism so long noted by many between faith and reason, an antagonism which reached much greater intensity during the Enlightenment and led much later to various attempts subsequently to reunite the two, such as the romantic project of Schleiermacher.

In addition, Ockham engendered fear among very traditional church authorities by his insistence, from a philosophical perspective, that the truth of an individual proposition had to be based on observation. Here it is critical to remember that Ockham allowed for the truth of a proposition to be maintained solely by means of theology, but, again, such was not philosophy. For many in the Catholic Church, this divorce of philosophy and theology led to a loss in coherence of worldview, but this was not a necessary result. Nonetheless, for Ockham, the experience of truth by the individual in terms of philosophy was grounded itself in the individual's experience. This naturally shifted the locus of authority away from what the church said to what the individual perceived. Even if one could assume that two individuals would experience the truth of a given thing to be the same truth in every way, the locus of deciding what was true and what was not true had been irrevocably shifted, in Ockham's schema, from an institution to the individual. This is perhaps the crux of why Ockham got into so much trouble with the Catholic Church, and also why some see him as a forerunner of Protestantism, if one understands by Protestantism to mean in part theological skepticism.

As the sources of authority within Protestantism became less clearly defined over time, traditional devotees of Catholicism might argue that the seeds of subjectivism which they detect within Protestantism were sown by Ockham's exaltation of philosophical method over theological method as guided by a church with magisterial teaching authority. However, even a representative of a church claiming magisterial teaching authority has still to interpret what the teaching of that faith is, and then again one is bogged down in the question of experience—in this case, how does one experience in one's own understanding the meaning of the teaching of the Catholic Church? Ultimately, it seems impossible to get away from Ockham's problem of individual experience and what

one interprets truth to be, though it is at least somewhat minimized within Catholicism, though by no means eliminated.

A related problem for Ockham's philosophy is how one can be certain of anything, other than some limited propositional truths in logic. Again, here it is necessary to remember that Ockham did hold that certain theological truths could be maintained with certainty, such as the doctrine of the Trinity, but only as theology and not as philosophy, and this was again troubling to the institutional church, which sought to hold together theology and philosophy as mutually co-operative guides to truth. In a theological sense, Catholic teaching was trustworthy as true, even in its minute particulars, but this was not demonstrable from philosophy. Philosophy could give one the likelihood that something was true, but not the certainty (other than some propositions in logic). Ockham has sometimes been called, for this reason, a fideist when it comes to theological truth. In other words, one should believe something because scripture or the church says that point is true, but not because it can be demonstrated through philosophy that such a concept is in fact true.

Against this backdrop, Ockham's ideas have been taken farther than he intended by rationalistic skeptics who were unwilling to accept his premise of faith. For these skeptics, Christianity is largely unacceptable because it is a "self-authenticating system." A system based on faith ultimately asks "who," while a system based on philosophy ultimately asks "how." The question of reliability of knowledge is related to this difference between the "who" and "how" questions. For the theologian, any possibility of certainty is ultimately grounded in faith, but for the person operating on philosophical method or scientific method (who could happen also to be a person of faith), reliability and certainty are less attainable and lie more in the realm of probabilities of truth. For Ockham, the idea of God as free and omnipotent is without question essential for God to be God. Ockham had felt constrained to oppose the concept that within the mind of God there were certain ideas which necessitated the way in which God had had to act. Such a concept made God subject to the ideas, rather than these ideas being subject to God. For Ockham, the creation of the world was not required or necessary, but was the result of God's free will and choice to create it.

Nothing about the world was in and of itself necessary. The world could have been very different from how it is, had God willed it to be that way.

Part of the context of Ockham's emphasis on the freedom of God is found in his rejection of the Averroist philosophical school, which had been condemned by the church in the 1270s for holding that God was bound by certain ideas which limited what God could do in the world. Ockham thought that God's absolute freedom (excepting of course non-contradiction) included the ability of God to be the direct cause of events in the world, rather than solely working through secondary causes. This view set Ockham at odds with the medieval philosophical tradition, which placed more emphasis on secondary causes. Ockham, however, did not hold that God could not work through secondary causation, but that he was not forced to do so. God's power in the world could be seen through ordinary ways in which it was manifested, the *potentia ordinata*, which would be more normally expected or predictable based on human experience, but God's power could also be expressed directly through the *potentia absoluta*, in which God might choose to cause an effect in the world in a direct way which departed from expected ordinary means of acting. However, though God could certainly depart from ordinary means into more direct means of causation, Ockham still stressed that God was not a God of whimsy or caprice.

Ockham accepted that one singular could cause an effect on another singular in the world of finite objects, but that a causal relationship was limited to those two singulars. One could not extrapolate from one singular's effects on another singular that a general principle of cause and effect would always be present, even in seemingly similar cases. For this reason, some have noted a similarity between Ockham and Hume regarding causal relations or their predictability. Nonetheless, Ockham's focus on finite singulars and the immediate, sensory intuition of them helped pave the way for the growth of the scientific method and a shift away from abstraction and universals. Ockham was so focused on the finite singular object that he saw the essence of such a singular as being no different from the fact of that singular's existence. In other words, the singular could not exist apart from its essence. Ockham saw no philosophical way to prove

that the existence of any particular singular was due to the existence of God, but Ockham, as a matter of belief, clearly thought that faith could tell us that God had created a singular.

Ockham rejected the notion that God had any inherent limits, other than the constraint of non-contradiction. In other words, God was free to do things as God wished, and God had not been in any way forced to accomplish them in a certain way. Thus God was truly free. Nonetheless, Ockham did not think that the omnipotence of God was subject to proof by philosophical method, though he did think that theology required belief in such a doctrine of omnipotence. Similarly, God could not be philosophically demonstrated to be the only god, though again Christian theology called for assent to this proposition, an assent which Ockham gave willingly as a theologian but could not grant as a philosopher. Ockham also thought that God was omniscient, but that this could be held only by faith and not as a position which could be maintained through philosophical method. Still, Ockham did not think that philosophy called necessarily for the existence of more than one god. Again, here Ockham fell back upon faith as a guide to truth; faith based on the premise of revelation, however, and not on logic.

It is easy to misunderstand Ockham's philosophical rejection of universals. As stated above, Ockham recognized that theology had every right to argue for the existence of universals, but this would be a prerogative arising from theology and not from philosophy. However, some have argued persuasively that Ockham did not reject the possibility of all universals in philosophy, but simply rejected the ways in which his predecessors and contemporaries in philosophy had argued for the existence of universals. Nonetheless, Ockham's perception as one who rejected universals was due to the principle of economy, often called "Ockham's Razor." As alluded to earlier, if a phenomenon could be explained with one step, then why posit the existence of several? This principle has been phrased in several ways, but one rendering is: "Do not multiply where fewer may suffice." To do so would be to engage in superfluity. Economy, also known as parsimony of beings, was Ockham's guiding principle.

Ockham therefore wished to do away with what he viewed as an unnecessary multiplicity of "beings," which amounted to a preference for simplicity in ontology. However, if one assumes that in terms of philosophical method Ockham generally did not believe that universals existed, it does not follow from this that Ockham argued that there were no such things as commonly accepted categories to which objects could be assigned through observation by the senses or by experimentation. Nonetheless, even within such categories, each member within the category had its own particularities which made it different from all others within the category, even if the differences were subtle. For instance, Ockham would argue that there was no such thing as a universal of "fruit," and he had no difficulty in accepting that there were different particular categories of fruit, such as apples, figs, pears, etc. In addition, within the finer category of figs, individual types of figs existed as well, but as particulars (not universals), even though there were categories of these various types of figs. Further, each individual fig within each sub-category of figs existed as its own object and exhibited its own characteristics and traits, capable of distinct description based on observable things such as appearance, size, ripeness, smell, taste, feel, etc. It is crucial to note that those who disagreed with Ockham's "parsimony" in the number of beings which existed obviously thought of their own estimation of the proper number of beings as not in any way excessive. Thus, it was never a question of others' insistence on extra, unnecessary beings versus Ockham's insistence on only necessary beings. Instead, it was a disagreement over which beings were in fact necessary.

Ockham clearly accepted that a truth could be revealed and was therefore to be accepted. Ockham's sources of revealed truth included scripture as well as the teaching of the Catholic Church. Ockham's acceptance of revelation is sometimes downplayed or distorted by those who wish to force Ockham into their own artificial image of him as heroic trailblazer who was throwing aside the "confining shackles of faith." But one can argue, indeed, that Ockham's commitment to logic and reason was an expression of his faith. Not to use every possible source of truth from reason would be to dishonor the God who had made all things. Not to follow where reason led was to sin against the God who gave human beings the capacity to exercise reason, unless that path of reason led one

to deny some aspect of revealed truth. It is a misunderstanding to think that Ockham saw as truth only those things which could be apprehended by the senses through observation. Having said this, Ockham did not go on to say, as Thomists would, that one must accept the existence of an idea as universal. Ockham therefore stressed that the essence of an object was the nature only of that object. For instance, each particular elm tree, though it shared similarities with other elm trees, would not participate in the universal idea of "elm tree-ness." Instead, each elm tree had its own particular nature. Again, it is important to note that Ockham was not denying that there were observable similarities between discrete elm trees, but that he was denying that these observable similarities constituted a universal idea or concept, which was "real." This was a clear break with the Thomist tradition.

Ockham's importance lies in part in his modification of philosophical methodology. Rather than beginning with the concept or idea as that which is "real," Ockham instead begins with the discrete object. For Ockham, what matters is what an object is in itself, rather than thinking about how any particular object is a manifestation of a universal reality. Ockham therefore endeavors to explain how a thing is, not how it should be. This endeavor places a premium on the use of the human mind, on logic and reason. This shift in focus blew apart the methodological world of how people thought about *scientia* or knowledge. Ockham opposed the high medieval system known as "realism." He has been called a nominalist, but many historians of philosophy argue that he is better called a "conceptualist." Though Ockham opposed "realism," his work has led to a redefinition of the idea of what is "real." But what is more real: a universal or a particular? Because of his focus on the individual object which can be apprehended by the senses, Ockham planted the seeds which changed the prevailing concept of what it meant to call something real. For most "moderns" or "post-moderns," metaphysics has become insubstantial while science has become the new, observable reality. In this sense, then, Ockham could be rightly viewed by inheritors of the *via moderna* as much more of a realist than those whose philosophical teaching he opposed, even though an earlier meaning of the term "realism" was claimed by and for those who believed that universals were real.

Conclusion

The historical context of Ockham's life was complex. His thought was necessarily affected by his experience of conflict in the university, within the Franciscans, and with the pope. The interplay of politics and religion, both within and without his order as well as the broader church and Europe itself, provided a set of contexts from which he could not emerge unaffected. Modern theories of what would become an expanded vision of the role of civil government and a subsequent curtailing of religious authority were emerging in this tumultuous period.

Ockham's philosophy cannot be understood apart from his theology. Ockham, though formally excommunicated, still very much understood himself to be a Christian theologian. The dual premises of faith and reason not only informed but were essential to Ockham's thought. Ockham is above all complex. Subtlety is required in both understanding and interpreting his thought. It is wrong to see Ockham as a sole initiator of modern scientific method, though he helped prepare an intellectual context within which it would flourish. His philosophical approach was clearly inductive as opposed to deductive.

However, it is wrong to see in Ockham someone who was an absolute enemy of the medieval philosophical tradition of Aquinas, though he was its major critic and his work stimulated new ways of thinking about problems important to Aquinas. It is also incorrect to see in Ockham the sole champion of philosophical reductionism in the face of other philosophers who sought for some needless multiplicity of entities. Instead Ockham simply had a different way of thinking about which beings were necessary in and of themselves, and what it meant for beings to be in relationality with each other. Relationality was itself not an entity for Ockham, but more of something incidental. Ockham differed from his fellow Franciscan John Duns Scotus in that Ockham saw no place for formal distinctions. It was this type of reductionism which Ockham favored, not any reductionism which required elimination of anything which was truly necessary. Also, it is incorrect to see in Ockham all the seeds of modern secular political philosophy, though his thought contributed to the emergence of representative government.

Ockham's legacy has been much more that of a philosopher, but by this judgment one must not neglect the truth that throughout his life he remained also a theologian. He has been seen by some historical theologians as preparing a path for Martin Luther and thus the break with the Catholic Church and the unfolding of the Protestant Reformation. Luther's teaching of two spheres, the spiritual and the civil, one for the church and the other for the state, certainly finds precursors in Ockham's political thought. Ockham, though excommunicated, still believed himself to be a faithful Christian, who sought the best for the church, trying to help steer it toward his vision of apostolic simplicity and purity. Some works once attributed to Ockham have been proved spurious. Among these are the *Tractatus logicae minor* as well as the brief *Elementarium*. Scholars have debated the date of his death. One tradition has Ockham's death in 1347, but another view holds it to be two years later in 1349. Munich seems, though, to have been the place of his death, and its cause may have been bubonic plague. Though some sympathetic followers of his have argued otherwise, Ockham's excommunication, which dated from 1328, was never revoked, and he appears to have died unreconciled to the church.

References

Adams, Marilyn McCord. 1987. *William Ockham*. Notre Dame, IN: University of Notre Dame Press.

Boehner, Philotheus. 1976. *Philosophical Writings: A Selection, William of Ockham*. Indianapolis: Bobbs-Merrill Company.

Courtenay, William J. 1999. "The Academic and Intellectual Worlds of Ockham." In *The Cambridge Companion to Ockham*, ed. Paul Vincent Spade. Cambridge: Cambridge University Press.

Fairweather, Eugene R., ed. 1970. *A Scholastic Miscellany: Anselm to Ockham*. New York: Macmillan Company.

Freddoso, Alfred J. 1999. "Ockham on Faith and Reason." In *The Cambridge Companion to Ockham*, ed. Paul Vincent Spade. Cambridge: Cambridge University Press.

Kilcullen, John. 1999. "The Political Writings." In *The Cambridge Companion to Ockham*, ed. Paul Vincent Spade. Cambridge: Cambridge University Press.

Klocker, Harry. 1992. *William of Ockham and the Divine Freedom*. Milwaukee, WI: Marquette University Press.

Spade, Paul Vincent. 1999. "Ockham's Nominalist Metaphysics: Some Main Themes." In Spade, ed., *The Cambridge Companion to Ockham*. Cambridge: Cambridge University Press.

Stumpf, Samuel Enoch. 1966. *Socrates to Sartre: A History of Philosophy*. New York: McGraw-Hill.

Reformation Period

John Calvin (1509–64)

Mary E. Coleman

I. Introduction

John Calvin was born at Noyon in Picardy, France on July 10, 1509, and died at Geneva, May 27, 1564. Although trained as a lawyer as well as a theologian and never ordained, he is considered by many to be the foremost theologian to emerge from the Reformation period. It would be hard to overestimate his importance to the reformed churches of the succeeding centuries. However, while he was such an important theologian it is equally important to remember that he was also a caring teacher and an effective pastor. His concerns with these last two aspects may, in part, undergird his lasting importance to contemporary reformed churches.

His family was part of the French middle class. For many years of his childhood his father served as attorney for the local bishop, practicing both civil and canon law, although the relationship ended in a serious dispute which caused his father's eventual excommunication. However, while the relationship lasted it provided financial support for Calvin's extensive and prolonged studies in Paris. When Calvin was quite young his father had purchased the freedom of the city of Noyon, indicating both his ambitions for his family and his prosperity. Calvin was the fourth of six children, raised in a devout family; he associated as a youth with the aristocratic families of his community and developed the tastes and manners of this elite.

At age 14 he went to Paris to study and prepare himself for a career in theology.

Intending to study for a career in theology, he had earned a master of arts degree during his first 11 years of study in Paris. However, as a result of his father's dispute with the bishop, his father required Calvin to discontinue his work in theology and instead study law. Accordingly, Calvin moved to Orleans, at the time the site of the best faculty of law in France. He also spent time in additional study of law at Bourges and Paris. This allowed him to compete his doctorate and licentiate in three years (Jones, 2005). Shortly after his father's death in 1531, Calvin returned to his first interest, theology.

Calvin's scholarship was not limited just to his impressive facility with the Greek, Hebrew, and Latin languages but also extended to a broad familiarity with the classical authors and philosophers. Calvin's deep reading of Aristotle, Plato, Seneca, and Cicero among others was critical to his ability to set scripture within an appropriate Greco-Roman context (Zachman, 2006).

In 1533 he was forced to leave Paris as a result of his involvement with his friend Nicholas Cop, rector of the University of Paris, who had delivered an address which included, with approbation, some of Luther's ideas. The authorities of Paris, both civil and ecclesiastical, were not pleased by the tumult which followed the discussion of the ideas nor, needless to say, with those who introduced these then radical ideas.

The Student's Companion to the Theologians, First Edition. Edited by Ian S. Markham.
© 2013 Blackwell Publishing Ltd. Published 2013 by Blackwell Publishing Ltd.

In the summer of 1536 Calvin visited Geneva, intending only a short stay, as this was a detour on his way to Strasbourg. He was urged to stay so strongly by the reformer Guillaume Farel that he was to remain there for the rest of his life, with the exception of a brief period of exile to Strasbourg (1538–41). In fact, Farel, a former colleague in Paris who had been working very hard to convince the indifferent residents of Geneva to reform, seems to have threatened Calvin with the anger of God if Calvin did not do his duty, as Farel saw it, and work with him to reform the city. Calvin's relationship with Geneva was never as peaceful as the three-year exile to Strasbourg demonstrates, but he seems to have been able to regard the strains of his life there as part of his calling from God. In any case he continued to be a prolific writer and compassionate teacher.

Calvin was never a leading member of an established academic institution once he left Paris, but his influence was all the more significant because of the public position he held in Geneva. In 1537, as requested by the Consistory, he wrote a church ordinance, *Articles concernant l'organisation de l'Eglise*, which was to define the practice of the evangelical church in Geneva and to be a model for many others to follow. This plan prescribed the celebration of the Lord's Supper at a minimum of once a month. Most significantly for further church development, it required the exclusion of those unworthy of the celebration. He also included a catechism—one of three he was to be responsible for, and a confession of faith. All the citizens of Geneva were required to take an oath to abide by this form of church polity. The ramifications of this oath taking were to contribute to his banishment from the city, but after three years he was called back and remained a most significant force in the definition of the reformed church polity for Geneva and those influenced by its example.

With the establishment of the Geneva Academy— later the University of Geneva—in 1559, Calvin's influence over the scholars of Europe took on an added importance. With his direction of this institution he was able to set an important part of the agenda for reform in the churches of France, the Netherlands, Scotland, and Scandinavia.

II.   Key Influences

During his first period of study in Paris, Calvin had been influenced by several teachers, including Cordier of the Collège de la Marche, who were followers of a christocentric spirituality often referred to as the *devotion moderna*. He was also exposed to the thought of Martin Luther through the tutelage of Melchior Wolmar, a scholar and teacher of New Testament Greek (Hillerbrand, 1996).

During Calvin's second period of study in Paris, in the early 1530s, he was a part of the newly founded Collège Royal. While there he was greatly influenced by the work of Erasmus and Faber Stapulensis. Their humanistic teaching and work was much in contrast to the arch-conservative Faculty of Theology of Paris (Sorbonne), which at the time was allied with the Inquisition. Because of the break in his theological studies Calvin seems to have been much less influenced by the more traditional scholasticism found in many of the theological colleges of Paris.

Additionally, because of the ties with the minor aristocracy which Calvin had developed in his youth, as well as his personal attainments, he was welcomed into the largely humanistic court circles of the king, Francis I.

Aside from the influences of his teachers and those of the court, Calvin was undoubtedly influenced by the difficulties attendant on the death and burial of his excommunicate father in 1531. Obtaining permission for a Christian burial in this circumstance was highly problematic and may have reinforced his concerns for his relationship with the church as much as his only slightly later incident with the powers of the Inquisition related to Nicholas Cop's equally problematic speech. Although the new theological teaching of Luther and Jacques Lefevre d'Etaples were well known in Paris during his early student days, it appears that it was not until several years later, when he had become friends with reform-minded individuals both at the court and in the intellectual circles of Paris, that he began to even consider the switch to the reformed faith.

In 1532, Calvin published a commentary to Seneca's *On Clemency*. This was his first book; while clearly demonstrating his mastery of classical subjects, it did not bring him any particular notice. At this point in his career he was one among a number of promising theologians. His gift for biblical languages was apparent but he had not yet demonstrated the power of this gift as he would later in his commentaries on the Bible.

In 1536, the first edition of Calvin's *Institutes of the Christian Religion* was published in Basle. The *Institutes* was originally written in the beautiful and elegant Latin so favored by humanist scholars. In 1539, while he was in exile in Strasbourg, he had the leisure to complete an expanded version in Latin as well as one in French. The *Institutes* would continue to be revised and expanded several more times over the course of Calvin's life.

Calvin's biblical commentaries on all but a very few of the books of the Bible were published over many years. The Commentary on Romans, the first, was published in 1540; the latest, Joshua (1564) and Ezekiel, chapters 1–20 (1565), were published after Calvin's death. The Commentaries were translated into English soon after they were published (1581). They were also translated immediately into French and somewhat later into Dutch and German. Calvin's Commentaries have profoundly influenced the churches of the Reformed tradition. The Commentaries fill 45 volumes in English: 30 on the Old Testament, 15 on the New Testament (in the series of the Calvin Translation Society). His attitude to scripture and the principles which guided him are nowhere stated in the Epistle Dedicatory to his first commentary:

> Such veneration we ought indeed to entertain for the Word of God, that we ought not to pervert it in the least degree by varying expositions; for its majesty is diminished, I know not how much, especially when not expounded with great discretion and with great sobriety. And if it be deemed a great wickedness to contaminate any thing that is dedicated to God, he surely cannot be endured, who, with impure, or even with unprepared hands, will handle that very thing, which of all things is the most sacred on earth. It is therefore an audacity, closely allied to a sacrilege, rashly to turn Scripture in any way we please, and to indulge our fancies as in sport; which has been done by many in former times.

The *Harmony of Exodus–Deuteronomy* (four volumes in English) and the *Harmony of the Gospels* (three volumes) deserve special mention as major works of organization, both of narrative and of topics. They are, in fact, convincing evidence of Calvin's grasp of scripture as a whole and in detail. Calvin comments with the conviction that any passage of scripture he may examine contains a Word of God full of God's wisdom, applicable to the condition of his hearers and readers in one respect or another. This conviction enables him to respond to the Bible with a vitality and intelligence. Most of the Old Testament Commentaries were first delivered as lectures. Calvin spoke slowly and quietly, so that his words could be recorded fairly accurately by his students and more exactly by his secretaries. Afterward he went over what had been taken down, corrected it, and allowed it to be published with proper dedications to friends and persons of importance in England and elsewhere.

It is important to remember that these lectures were delivered at the Academy, which educated the children of Geneva, and attracted many students of theology from France, England, Scotland, and Holland. Some of the major Protestant theologians of the day were trained there. Calvin commented on the up-building of these people and the churches they came from and were to return to.

He always began his lectures with the prayer, "May the Lord grant that we study the heavenly mysteries of his wisdom, making true progress in religion to his glory and our upbuilding." The closing prayer was longer, and in it Calvin laid before the Lord the special needs of the faithful as the scripture just studied had revealed them. In general, the Old Testament Commentaries were delivered as lectures, and the New Testament Commentaries were dictated at home.

Calvin's refusal to be diverted from his main purpose—to open the Scriptures to the eyes of both the learned and the unlearned—is clear also in his use of classical and early Christian literature. The list of classical references is a long one. Cicero appears most often (16 times in the Pentateuch Harmony alone); but there are quotations from all the better-known Latin authors (Horace, Juvenal, Seneca, Terence, Cato, Quintilian, Virgil, Plautus, Suetonius, Tacitus, Livy, Pliny), and from the Greek authors (Homer, Euripides, Xenophon, Ovid, Aristophanes, Epicurus, Plutarch, and Aesop). He quotes Plato and Aristotle with respect. He admires Plato's wisdom and piety, but objects to certain aspects of his work, most notably his "angelology." He quotes Aristotle on the distinction between anger and hatred (from "The Second Book on Rhetoric"), and refers with approval to his saying that the tongue should be an image of the understanding. In the field of law, he speaks of Portius's law, Flavian law, the laws of Sempronius, and Valerius's law. Sometimes it is not possible to tell whether Calvin is depending on his own memory of a passage, or on a collection of quotations such as the *Adagies* of Erasmus. Calvin was admired by his friends and feared by his enemies as a most learned man. But his erudition is not allowed to compromise his presentation of the meaning as he saw it and his communication with his hearers and readers.

This is also true of his use of ancient Christian literature. It is obvious that Calvin had an extensive and masterly knowledge of Augustine, Jerome, and Chrysostom. He depended upon the latter two, as well as on Josephus, for his knowledge of biblical times and places. He makes reference also to Tertullian and Cyprian; to Irenaeus and Origen; to Cyril of Jerusalem, Epiphanius, Basil, Gregory Nazianzen, Hilary, Lactantius, and Ambrose of Milan; to Eusebius and Socrates, the historians; to Pope Leo I, Gregory the Great, and Bernard of Clairvaux. The Fathers are consulted for help in understanding scripture; they do not interfere with his exposition of it.

Calvin published his Commentaries to give his readers insight into the Word of God and to point out its relevance to their own life and situation. To this end he cultivated accuracy, brevity, and lucidity. Every important point of Calvin's theology is discussed, and is often more briefly and clearly and persuasively presented, in the direct statements of the Commentaries than in the sustained and more technical arguments of the *Institutes*.

An understanding of the technical thrust of Calvin's theology is perhaps best developed through a careful reading of his *Institutes*, in any or all of its many editions. In it he discusses all of the themes that he will discuss in his other works, whether of biblical commentary, sermons, or even his polemical writings. Indeed the 1559 version of the *Institutes* was, until late in the current century, the standard work to which seemingly all Calvin scholars referred when attempting to understand his theological positions (Zachman, 2006).

Fundamental to his theology is his understanding, shared with Luther, that salvation is by grace alone through faith. Beyond this, Calvin seems to have understood both the Old and New Testaments to contain the same message of redemption. He normally approached his work in theology through these themes rather than through an often more common approach of specific theological topics. To him the relationship between God and man is the base of theological discussion. He agrees with St Augustine that man is created for communion with God and that fulfillment is found by resting in God. For Calvin *knowledge* of God seems to be used synonymously with the concept of *faith*.

This interchangeability of terms seems to lead Calvin to a sense of trust and worship of the goodness of God as well to an appreciation of the bounty or blessings of God. Thus for Calvin "the creation of all good things in the world for the benefit and enjoyment of humans is not, therefore, an end in itself, but was rather the way God initially reveals to humankind that God is the author and the fountain of every good thing" (Zachman, 2006).

It is from the gratitude for this bounty that Calvin is able to develop some of his most beautifully sustaining concepts for the people of God. What later generations may have interpreted as the sternness of Calvin, on closer reading of his work rather seems to suggest a profound and boundless gratitude for the goodness of God which requires much of those who would wish a closeness with God. This sense of gratitude is reflected in many of his pastoral writings, particularly those that seek to instruct parents as to the rearing of children in a faithful home.

Calvin is clear that while all things were originally created by God in a perfect state, the Fall has changed all perfection of Creation; thus his concern with redemption. Human beings are bound by their sinful nature. They must depend on God. Therefore, the only virtues they may claim are humility, sobriety, and an openness to learning about God. Calvin makes a distinction between those who he considers unlearned (that is, those who did not have a knowledge of Greek, Hebrew, and Latin), and those who are learned; he tried many methods to reach both audiences as effectively as he could. As Zachman (2006) explains it, "Calvin envisioned the church as a school in which all Christians act as both students and teachers, under the instruction of the Holy Spirit, the author of Scripture."

For Calvin this concept of the church as a place of learning about the nature of God meant that he spent a good deal of his time in Geneva trying to understand and then explain to the members of the church just how this process of learning could proceed. For this reason Calvin, who had produced his first book for the most learned persons in the European academic community, turned to creating the rest of his writings for the edification of those least learned in the community of the church. His Commentaries on most of the books of the Bible, his sermons, and the revisions of his *Institutes* were all designed to make the reading of the Scriptures more meaningful to the "unlearned." Calvin sought to teach following the humanistic model.

It is clear that Calvin expected parents to attend the Sunday catechism service, to instruct their children at home, as well as to attend sermons and to read scripture to and with their children and servants. Because of this shared role, all members of the church needed to have available to them the tools for study. One of the most effective tools for use was the content of the sermons. Calvin routinely used this medium to convey his understanding of the application to daily use of the lessons of the Scriptures. A good example

would be the plurality of ways Calvin used his series of sermons on Ephesians to this purpose.

Calvin envisions the world as a beautiful garment for God, meant to reveal in some limited way the glory of God. It is therefore not to be neglected or scorned in any way. It is interesting to note the way Calvin uses images of the world as well as the most important image of Jesus Christ to convey to the church a sense of the reality of God. It is a false dualism to assume that Calvin's insistence on the removal of images from churches meant that he did not use images to fire the imagination of the church to a better understanding of the characteristics of God. However, he maintained that the images developed in words were more efficacious in producing a sense of the reality of God in his listeners and readers than those which could be created by painted images, statues, or stained glass windows.

No discussion of Calvin's influence on the tumultuous events of the sixteenth century can be complete without remarking on the pastoral concern evident in all his writing. Although he was a brilliant theologian, well versed in the refinements of disputation and rhetoric, he deemed it his duty to God to make the knowledge of God accessible to as many of the faithful as he could. His entire adult life was spent in the effort to make what he could discern of God available to all the faithful.

References

Hillerbrand, Hans J., ed. 1996. *The Oxford Encyclopedia of the Reformation*. New York: Oxford University Press.

Jones, Lindsay, ed. 2005. *Encyclopedia of Religion*, 2nd ed. Detroit: Macmillan Reference USA.

Zachman, Randall C. 2006. *John Calvin as Teacher, Pastor and Theologian: The Shape of His Writings and Thought*. Grand Rapids, MI: Baker Academic.

Richard Hooker (1554–1600)

Martyn Percy

Reading the works of Richard Hooker is not unlike trying to simultaneously study the writings of Shakespeare and Kant. It may (eventually) turn out to be a very rewarding experience, but it would require the full concentration of any scholar. And yet he is well known and well read by many Roman Catholics, scholars of rhetoric, historians, and political scientists. Indeed, it is not an overstatement to suggest that it is virtually impossible to understand the Anglican Church without having some grasp of Hooker, and specifically the *Laws of Ecclesiastical Polity*. Yet he is rarely read by general readers, although often alluded to. Why is this so?

Part of the answer must lie in the density of his language, which to the unsuspecting reader will appear forbidding at first sight. Hooker wrote prose that was remarkable for its clarity, grace, and modernity: it was stately, dignified, and rhythmic. Although a polemicist, he is first and foremost a theologian, and he adopts an extraordinary range of tone in the presentation of his arguments. He is sometimes ironic and sarcastic, although not usually in relation to his Puritan opponents, whom he treats with respect. As an advocate, he adopts a number of personae: teacher, critic, wise expounder (maxims), respectful student (of the fathers and philosophers), fellow Christian, cleric, and moderate nationalist.

Analysis of his writing reveals a person who understood the power of rhetoric and how to construct it for his own argument. There are short sentences—"little daggers," as Cicero called them—which are invariably telling. Yet the more normative style of Hooker is long sentences. Book 1 of *The Laws* has a sentence of 267 words; even the average number is 42. In Book 5 of *The Laws*, there is a sentence that exceeds 500 words. Despite the density of the work, Hooker's prose is one of nobility and power as he tries to win over his readers to a new kind of "ecclesial intelligence."

C. S. Lewis described Hooker's writings as *architectonic*, built up into a huge and carefully constructed edifice: it is hard to quote well from such a work. In the *Laws of Ecclesiastical Polity*, we meet a writer who belongs to a kind of early English empiricism. These "Laws" were never to be imposed uncritically or literalistically, but were rather "discovered" and "fashioned," as though sculpting from the finest materials. Hooker's legacy is the presentation of Anglicanism as a kind of system or craft, inculcating beauty, truth, politics, persuasion, logic, worship, tradition, faith, reason, and feeling. And all of this is in the service of God, for the shaping of the church and for the good of society.

I. Hooker's Life and Context

Hooker was born in Heavitree, Exeter in 1554. He grew up as a child of the emerging "Elizabethan settlement" and became committed to it. But it was a fragile

The Student's Companion to the Theologians, First Edition. Edited by Ian S. Markham.
© 2013 Blackwell Publishing Ltd. Published 2013 by Blackwell Publishing Ltd.

covenant. On the one hand, there was the opposition of Catholics, perhaps epitomized by John Jewel (1522–71), Bishop of Salisbury, who argued for a church based firmly on Catholic truth, claiming a continuity with the undivided church of the early centuries (*Apologia Pro Ecclesia Anglicana*, 1562). Then there were Puritans, posing an array of threats clustered around congregationalism, literalism (in reading scripture), and the dismantling of socio-ecclesial order. In his eight volumes of the *Laws of Ecclesiastical Polity*, Hooker was to defend the church against the will of the Puritan reformers, a body of people so named not because of their actual moral purity, but because they sought to "purify" and ultimately purge the church of much of its tradition.

Hooker was ordained a priest in 1582, aged 28. He is colorfully portrayed by Izaak Walton, his biographer, as a man of reticence and modesty. From 1568 until 1584, Hooker was at Corpus Christi, Oxford, first as a student and then as a Fellow. Walton describes Hooker's time at Oxford in glowing terms:

> [He] had by a constant unwearied diligence attained unto a perfection in all the learned languages; by the help of which, an excellent tutor, and his unintermitted studies, he had made the subtlety of all the arts easy and familiar to him, and useful for the discovery of such learning as lay hid from common searchers; so that by these added to his great reason, and his industry added to both, he did not only know more of causes and effects; but what he knew, he knew better than other men. (Walton, 1997, 1: 14)

Walton adds that in four years, Hooker missed the college chapel prayers only twice. He further reports that in his studies, Hooker enriched his

> quiet and capacious soul with the precious learning of the philosophers, casuists, and schoolmen; and with them, the foundation and reason of all laws, both sacred and civil … And as he was diligent in these, so he seemed restless in searching the scope and intention of God's Spirit revealed to mankind in the sacred scripture … And the good man would often say, that "God abhors confusion as contrary to his nature;" and as often say, that "the scripture was not writ to beget disputations and pride, and opposition to government; but moderation, charity and humility, obedience to authority, and peace to mankind: of which virtues," he would as often say "no man did ever repent himself upon his death-bed." (Walton, 1997, 1: 18–19)

In March 1585 Hooker was appointed as Master of the Temple for the Inns of Court in London. It was a fraught appointment (following the death of Dr Richard Alvey, a noted Puritan), with the leading candidate for the post being Walter Travers. Elizabeth's Chancellor, Lord Burghley, strongly supported the candidature of Travers; but it was sunk by a sharp missive fired by Whitgift, Archbishop of Canterbury, who wrote to the Queen describing Travers as "an earnest seeker after innovation." Whitgift's own first choice was too sick to take the post. Hooker was Whitgift's second, and the Queen appointed him.

The description applied to Travers was coded language, which indicated him to be a Puritan. A continental reformation based on Luther's prescription that the church should not perpetuate any practice to which scripture was demonstrably opposed was now fused to a new conviction that nothing at all should be done unless provable from scripture. It was a tide of opinion which swept through the Elizabethan church, making the borders with continental Protestantism indistinct, questioning the identity of the church.

It was this form of Puritanism that Hooker was to set his face against. Yet Hooker was to encounter considerable opposition. Travers was a radical reformer. Worse, for Hooker, he was also a lecturer and preacher at the Temple. After a sermon by Hooker, Travers appealed to the Privy Council (sometime in 1590), accusing Hooker of claiming God to be merciful to Romanists, who might place more emphasis on works rather than justification by faith.

It was probably to escape the worst exertions of such controversies that Hooker sought to leave the Mastership for a return to parish ministry. Yet he also wished to devote a great proportion of his time in the parish to take part in that controversy by writing *The Laws of Ecclesiastical Polity*. From 1591 to 1595 he was Rector of Boscombe, Subdean of Salisbury, and a Prebend of Netheravon. It is from there that Books 1 to 4 were published in 1593.

In 1595 Hooker moved to Bishopsbourne, near Canterbury, where Book 5 was published in 1597. Books 6 to 8 were completed (probably only partially) before Hooker's death on November 2, 1600. But some manuscripts were then subsequently lost, and the *Laws* as we now have them are later constructions based on some notes and earlier drafts. Books 6 and 8 were not published until 1648, and Book 7 in 1662, the year of the Restoration.

The notion of "ecclesial polity" that Hooker developed is one of the richest treasures to have emerged from the Anglican Church. It suggests both form, a system of government, and process; how governing is done. It is suggestive of policy (yet more basic), elucidating the grounds on which policy may be made, and, more widely, pointing to the means by which policy is carried out.

The aims of *The Laws of Ecclesiastical Polity* are clear: to defend "the present state of the Church of God established among us." Hooker's work is an apologia for an ecclesiology that is faithful to both the Catholic and Reformed traditions, and yet cannot be owned by either of these extremes. Hooker therefore writes against congregationally centered Puritanism, as much as against a kind of hierarchical magesterium.

Although he reserves much of his formal theological refutation of Puritanism and the defense of episcopacy for Books 6 and 7 of *The Laws*, the very tenor of the Preface suggests this agenda—namely the dangers of "biblicism"—is on his mind from the very beginning:

> … The Church of Christ is a body mystical. A body cannot stand unless the parts thereof be proportionable. Let it therefore be required at both parts, at the hands of the clergy, to be in meanness of state like the Apostles; at the hand of the laity, to be as they were who lived under the Apostles: and in this reformation there will be, though little wisdom, yet some indifferency.
>
> But your reformation which are of the clergy (if yet it displeases you not that I should say that ye are of the clergy) seemeth to aim at a broader mark. Ye think that he which will perfectly reform must bring the form of church-discipline unto the state which then it was at. A thing neither possible, nor certain, nor absolutely convenient.
>
> Concerning the first, what was used in the Apostles' times, the Scripture fully declareth not; so that making their times the rule and canon of church-polity, ye make a rule, which being not possible to be fully known, is as impossible to be kept.
>
> Again, sith the latter even of the Apostles' own times had that which in the former was not thought upon; in this general proposing of the Apostolical times, there is no certainty which should be followed: especially seeing that ye give us great cause to doubt how far ye allow these times. (Hooker, 1990, Pref. IV.3–4)

Overall, the Preface—nine "chapters," in actual fact—engages with great wit and tenacity against the

Puritan claim that church life should be based only on what is demonstrably proven by scriptural precedent. This endeavor, argues Hooker, is wrongly conceived and impossible to carry out. Moreover, Hooker is anxious to refute these "spiritual credentials"—even though he considers them erroneous—for he detects behind them the hand of separatism; and behind that, socially subversive implications for Elizabethan society.

II.   Summary

To what extent have these books mattered to others? They sold slowly during Hooker's lifetime. Whitgift, to whom they were dedicated, clearly read them. Pope Clement VIII was a devotee. *The Laws* were studied by Charles I who enjoined his son to do likewise. Indeed they were hugely influential on the development of Anglican thought in the Caroline period with Laud, Lancelot Andrews, John Donne, Bishop Cosin, and Jeremy Taylor finding Hooker to ecclesiology what Crammer was to liturgy.

Hooker would doubtless be surprised by the longevity of his writings. Yet in a typical passage, he adopts a characteristic modesty that would grace any theology:

> Dangerous it were for the feeble brain of man to wade far into the doings of the Most High; whom although to know be life, and joy to make mention of his name; yet our soundest knowledge is to know that we know him not as indeed he is, neither can know him; and our safest eloquence concerning him is our silence, when we confess without confession that his glory is inexplicable, his greatness above our capacity and reach. He is above, and we upon earth; therefore it behoveth our words to be wary and few. (Hooker, 1990, Book 1. II.2)

The eighteenth century was a quieter one for the reputation of the *Laws*, with no fresh publications between 1723 and 1793. Yet modern interest in Hooker was to receive fresh impetus from a superbly annotated edition of the *Laws* edited by John Keble between 1836 and 1841. Other editions soon followed. Richard Church and Francis Paget revised the Keble edition in 1888, and Everyman produced a popular version of Books 1–5 in 1907. The twentieth century eventually saw a complete Folger Library edition published in the USA.

References

Hooker, Richard. 1990. *Of the Laws of Ecclesiastical Polity*, ed. A. S. McGrade, Raymond Geuss, and Quentin Skinner. Cambridge: Cambridge University Press.

Hooker, Richard, and Secor, Philip Bruce. 2003. *Richard Hooker on Anglican Faith and Worship: Of the Laws of Ecclesiatical Polity*, Book, V, modern ed. London: SPCK.

Walton, Izaak. 1997. *The Lives of Doctor John Donne, Sir Henry Wotton, Mr. Richard Hooker, Mr. George Herbert and Doctor Robert Sanderson*. Aldershot: Ashgate Publishing.

Martin Luther (1483–1546)

Christy Lohr

Martin Luther is considered by many to be the father of the Reformation. Yet, it was not ultimately his intention to spark such a seismic wave of reform. In his writings, sermons, and classroom lectures Luther was primarily concerned with working out an understanding of salvation that made sense in light of revelation in scripture and that meshed with church teaching. When he felt that these two elements—scripture and works of men—did not align, he deferred to the Word of God. Church doctrine and practice, after all, were designed by fallible humans, but the Word of God stood fast.

His deep concern for the state of the Catholic Church of the late Middle Ages compelled him to take a stand against what he perceived as the corruption, abuse of authority, and misrepresentation of scripture. Three central principles constituted the foundation of Luther's Reformation theology: belief that scripture, not church teaching or doctrine, is the sole authority; doctrine of justification by faith alone not through human works; concept of a priesthood of all believers. In the process of articulating his concerns with the state of the church and seeking a message of salvation, he outlined a theological movement that shaped the global face of Christianity and continues 500 years later.

Born November 10, 1483 in Eisleben, Germany, Luther was named for St Martin on whose feast day he was baptized. Hans Luther, a stern, inflexible man known for his harshness, was a copper miner of little means who placed a premium on his son's education but who also instilled a sense of piety in his children. Luther's childhood is rumored to have been joyless. Hans dreamed of seeing his son become a lawyer, and to that end, Martin was sent off to the University of Erfurt in 1501. Four years later he began a master's degree focused on the study of law. In the legal discipline he acquired the critical thinking and debate skills that would later serve him well. After completion of his courses, Luther turned his attention to the areas of philosophy and theology. While returning to school from a visit home one stormy night in 1505, Luther was frightened by lightening and fell to the ground. Terrified for his life, he swore an oath to St Anne that if he survived the storm he would leave the field of law and devote himself to the priesthood. In July of that year, he took monastic vows with the Augustinian friars in Erfurt. His father was not overjoyed about this.

In 1510 Luther was sent to Rome on church business. This being his first trip to the seat of his church he took advantage of the opportunity for reflection and pilgrimage. He was disturbed by the lack of piety he witnessed around him in the holy city, however, and returned to Erfurt with a troubled heart. The seeds of disillusionment with the mother church had been sown.

Soon thereafter, Luther was transferred to Wittenberg, where in 1512 he earned a doctorate and took on a university professorship in biblical studies.

The Student's Companion to the Theologians, First Edition. Edited by Ian S. Markham.
© 2013 Blackwell Publishing Ltd. Published 2013 by Blackwell Publishing Ltd.

In Wittenberg Luther also assumed the position of preacher at the town church. It was through his lectures at the university and his sermons delivered in the community that Luther worked out much of his theology over the following decade. For example, his lectures on the book of Galatians provided the testing ground for his thinking on law and gospel. Similarly, lectures on the book of Romans formed the basis for his theology of justification by faith that formed the backbone of Reformation theology. Luther was an accomplished linguist who enjoyed interpreting texts from their origins. His readings of Old Testament texts from their original Hebrew allowed him unique insight into the words of the scripture and formed the basis of many of his written works.

In 1517 Johann Tetzel, a Dominican monk, gained permission to sell indulgences near Wittenberg. Proceeds from the sale of these indulgences were going toward funding Pope Leo X's construction of St Peter's Basilica in Rome as well as the debt that Archbishop Albrecht of Mainz incurred while gaining three sees and his office. Indulgences granted the purchaser absolution of sins and a remission of time in purgatory for oneself or a loved one. Priests who refused to grant absolution to the holder of an official indulgence were threatened with excommunication. Luther's difficulty with the indulgence issue was that it gave practitioners, many of whom were poor and uneducated, the impression that they could buy their way out of sinfulness without confession, contrition, or repentance. He believed that in order to be granted absolution from sins, a person needed to come to confession with a sincerely penitent spirit. One must deeply desire forgiveness to the point that he would learn from his past actions and strive not to repeat them and buy his way out of guilt.

Frederick the Wise, Elector of Saxony, was also opposed to Tetzel's sale of indulgences, and had prohibited their sale in his lands. Yet, Tetzel had permission to peddle them nearby in areas under the jurisdiction of Archbishop Albrecht and in parts of Brandenburg. Believing that this habit of financing papal projects and local bishops through such sales was a disgrace and a means of taking advantage of uninformed believers, Luther protested the arrival of Tetzel. On October 31, 1517 he posted his *Ninety-Five Theses* against the practice on the door of Wittenberg's Castle church as a means of sparking a lively discussion of the issue among his colleagues. This was a natural place to post topics for debate such as Luther's disputation on the efficacy of indulgences. Yet, the act of hammering these statements has become the popular defining moment of his perceived rebellion. (More rebellious, however, was his burning of the papal bull three years later in 1520. This would mark his official break with the Church of Rome.) The posting of the *Ninety-Five Theses* was the first event that really gained notoriety for this rather obscure monk and teacher in a small college town.

It is ironic that no one responded to Luther's invitation to debate the topic formally in Wittenberg, yet debate on the topic took place elsewhere and in other forms for many years to come. Wide dissemination of the *Ninety-Five Theses* in Latin and German forced Luther to clarify his position on his statements against indulgences. Many saw his actions as an attack on papal authority. Tetzel felt the effect of Luther's challenge in the coffers and launched a campaign to have Luther stopped and reprimanded. Pope Leo X initially saw the issue as a mere squabble between two rival orders—Dominicans and Augustinians—that he did not want to get involved in. Pressure from other sources and accusations of heresy against Luther, however, forced his hand. The Pope ordered John Staupitz, Luther's superior in the Augustinian Order, to silence the young monk. In the hopes of offering a challenging corrective from his peers and fellow monastics, Staupitz invited Luther to speak at the regular gathering of Augustinians in Heidelberg. Unrelenting, the Dominicans continued to press for disciplinary action. The Pope issued a citation for Luther to appear in Rome. By this time, Frederick the Wise was enjoying the attention Luther brought to his university. Wanting to keep his famous scholar and preacher in Wittenberg, he intervened. Frederick persuaded Cardinal Cajetan, head of the Dominican Order, to have the citation replaced with an interview between Luther and the Cardinal at the Diet of Augsburg in 1518. Despite Cajetan's attempts, he could not get Luther to recant. During the course of the next year the Pope was distracted from the issue of this recalcitrant priest by the death of Emperor Maximilian and the election of Charles I of Spain as Emperor Charles V.

Meanwhile, Luther felt himself attacked from various angles. John Eck challenged Luther and his

Wittenberg colleague Andreas Bodenstein von Karlstadt to a debate on papal authority in the summer of 1519 in Leipzig. This debate saw Luther clarify his assertions that the papal office was one humanly, not divinely, appointed and that church councils could and did err. Here Luther voiced his belief that scripture was the ultimate authority for Christians. Following this, in the spring of 1520, the Pope appointed Eck and Cajetan to a commission examining Luther's works. They pinpointed 41 theological mistakes in Luther's writings which were misleading to readers. Condemning these, Leo issued a precursor to excommunication, the papal bull *Exsurge Domine* on June 15, 1520. This commanded Luther to recant his heresies within 60 days of the bull's publication in Germany and called on all Christians to reject his preachings, as well.

Luther waited until the end of the 60-day grace period and in December he responded by burning a copy of the canon law and a number of Catholic books that he deemed erroneous in their support of papal authority. He also threw the papal bull into the fire. While the nailing of the *Ninety-Five Theses* on the door in Wittenberg marked the start of the altercation, this action marked Luther's recognition that an official break with Rome and the mother church was imminent. Two publications emerged in which Luther attempted to defend himself against the attack from Rome: *Defense and Explanation of All the Articles* and *Why the Books of the Pope and His Disciples Were Burned*. In these he relied on the authority of the Scriptures, not the pope or man-made doctrines, to support his claims.

In 1520 Luther also published three of his most famous works that spelled out his positions on various themes central to the Reformation. Under the protection of Fredrick III of Saxony, Luther also was free to flesh out the particulars of his case against Rome during this time. These were *The Address to the German Nobility*, *The Babylonian Captivity of the Church*, and *The Freedom of a Christian*. The first tract boldly called for a complete reform of the church. Here Luther challenged the authority of the pope over government leaders. He rejected the teaching that the pope was the ultimate interpreter of scripture. He accused the Roman Curia of corruption, and he developed his concept of the priesthood of all believers. In *The Babylonian Captivity of the Church* he disparaged the

sacramental practices of the church, claiming that current hierarchy kept control over all Christians. Reduction of the sacraments from seven to two and reinterpretation of the events of the Eucharist were key developments of the Reformation.

The Freedom of a Christian spelled out Luther's beliefs on the simultaneous enslavement and freedom of the human will. "A Christian is a perfectly free lord of all, subject to none. A Christian is a perfectly dutiful servant of all, subject to all" (LW [*Luther's Works*] 31: 344). Humans are freed from sin thanks to God's living grace; yet, they are enslaved to love of neighbor by this same act.

This master–slave dichotomy that he gets from Paul is crucial to understanding Luther's theology and its divergence from traditional Catholic teaching. For Luther this was a question of absolutes. Humans are absolutely sinful. This is why they have the law—to help them follow specific guidelines that lead away from sinfulness. Yet, in Christ and through baptism humans are also absolutely saints. Redemption is whole and complete. For Luther, a person quite literally dies and is reborn through the waters of baptism, yet both people remain: the sinful is still present but it is also in the presence of the saintly. Luther referred to this as *simul justus et peccator*, simultaneously sinful and justified. In traditional Catholic understanding, when a person acted sinfully he or she could have sins removed or mediated through confession and absolution. Inevitably, however, sinful action would return. The individual would slide back into sin. In Luther's understanding, the person never "backslides" because the person is never free from sin. While this sounds shocking at first, it is not when one remembers that the person is also simultaneously redeemed. One is always sinful and always forgiven thanks to the love of Christ. This is a sticky paradox with which Luther came to terms: Christians are just as fully free as they are enslaved. The Christian is simultaneously given inner freedom from sin and death through Christ but also must live a life in service to his or her neighbor.

Luther wrote *The Freedom of a Christian* in a non-confrontational tone and sent it to Leo X, accompanied by a letter explaining that Luther did not intend to attack the Pope personally. This was a final attempt at reconciliation to which Leo did not respond. Rather, in response to Luther's previous inflammatory tracts, the pope issued an edict of excommunication, *Decet Pontificem*, on January 3, 1521.

The Freedom of a Christian sparked a debate with an influential philosopher and contemporary of Luther, Erasmus of Rotterdam. Suggesting that a human does not have the power to choose or deny salvation, Erasmus challenged the ideas Luther put forward in the tract. Luther argued that the human will is bound in matters of salvation and that this is a good thing. Since mankind does not have the self-control to govern itself appropriately, an unbound will would surely and perpetually run amok and miss the opportunity to know Christ. The tipping point in the debate was Erasmus's inability to differentiate between God's law and gospel—a distinction central to Luther's theology.

In April of that year, Luther was called to Worms to stand trial for his heresies before the imperial diet. This was done, rather than excommunicating him directly from Rome's edict, in part because of Frederick's influence. Charles V offered Luther one last opportunity to publicly recant his allegedly fallacious statements and granted him safe conduct to Worms. Many were opposed to this. Luther's friends were worried that he would suffer the same fate as previous reformers, such as John Huss who was burned at the stake. His enemies in Rome did not want to give this recalcitrant heretic an audience or public platform. An audience before the emperor at the Diet of Worms, after all, would only add to his celebrity. Charles, however, was willing to offer Luther an interview as a favor to Frederick the Wise and as a means of fulfilling every legal step to excommunication.

Luther believed that the trip to Worms would mean his death because he did not see how he could recant and still remain true to the Word of God. He saw the imperial summons as a flimsy cover for the completion of Rome's work. Luther understood himself to be a lowly servant of God, like so many prophets and leaders before him who challenged a hierarchy engorged and delusional from its own power. He could not in good faith place the word of man above the Word of God. He could not recognize the authority of the pope above that of the scripture. He could not betray the gospel for his personal safety.

At Worms Luther was asked to confirm that books presented were, indeed, written by him. He was also asked whether he would like to recant anything in them. At the first question, he quickly replied that they were his writings. At the second, he asked for additional time to consider his response carefully. He was granted a day to deliberate about it, provided that his final response was to be made orally and not in writing.

When he went before the diet in April of 1521, he considered his writings in three categories. First, there were those which were meant for instruction of Christian men and women. Of these even the authorities in Rome had admitted that they held some merit. Since even his attackers acknowledged the solvency of these works, Luther did not feel it appropriate to recant them. Secondly, there were his books that brought to light the ways in which the papal misuse of doctrinal statements had taken property from and wreaked havoc on the lives of innocent Christians. Luther claimed that were he to recant these writings it would only give the papacy more power to continue these malevolent practices unabated. Thirdly, there were his books that attacked individuals who perpetuated the tyranny of authority. For him to recant these, Luther felt, would also add fuel to the fire of the oppressors. He admitted his lowly state as a mere sinful human and invited anyone to outline from within scriptural reasoning the mistakes present in his works. He would be willing to recant the writings which could be proven to be scripturally erroneous. When asked for a simpler, more direct answer, Luther famously responded:

> Unless I am convinced by the testimony of the Scriptures or by clear reason (for I do not trust either in the pope or in councils alone, since it is well known that they have often erred and contradicted themselves), I am bound by the Scriptures I have quoted and my conscience is captive to the Word of God. I cannot and I will not retract anything, since it is neither safe nor right to go against conscience.
>
> I cannot do otherwise, here I stand, may God help me, Amen. (LW 32: 112–13)

With this, the decision was final.

Luther's response before the Diet of Worms is important in light of his theology. A key point of the Reformation was recognition of the Bible as the Christian's sole authority. This encouraged believers not to endorse or uphold teachings or doctrine that were not supported biblically. For the church in Rome, which was solidly built on a clearly defined hierarchy that gave authoritative voice to men hold-ing ecclesiastical offices, this concept had the potential to be devastating.

Luther was excommunicated, but the emperor had promised him safe conduct to and from the meeting. Fearing for Luther's life, however, Frederick had him abducted on the way back to Wittenberg.

Luther was taken to the Wartburg Castle at Eisenach where he was hidden away until the controversy had calmed a bit. At first Luther resisted this, but soon he welcomed the opportunity to devote himself to scrip-tural study and reflection. He spent the next few years translating the New Testament into German and composing tracts to offer his views on events taking place beyond the walls of his isolation. The translation project was a labor of love that allowed Luther to combine his affection for language with his love of scripture. This lifelong project of making the Scriptures accessible to everyone, completed in 1534, had a huge impact on biblical understanding and translation for centuries to come.

Luther's translation affected in large part the words and linguistic nuances of the German language. Additionally, Luther was a talented hymn writer whose songs communicated salient theological points while rousing a person's spirit. Perhaps his most famous hymn is "Ein' Feste Berg" or "A Mighty Fortress Is Our God." While in the Wartburg, Luther also translated the Mass into German. This also marked a relevant aspect of Luther's theology. By translating the New Testament and the Mass into the language of the people, Luther gave the common person the gift of reading scripture and understanding the liturgy for himself. This was a remarkable breakthrough for the German populace, many of whom had never under-stood the words of the Mass or read scripture for themselves. It represents Luther's commitment to the priesthood of all believers, a theological point that emphasized the equal ability of all people, not only the priesthood, to establish a relationship with God.

The priesthood of believers was a fundamental principle of the Reformation. It attempted to break down the hierarchy between the people and the priest. It claimed that through baptism all believers have equal status before God. It removed a necessary intercessor for prayers and confession. It also held all people accountable for witness—sharing the Word,

pastoral care—loving one's neighbor, and forgiveness. Thus, corporate confession became a marker of "Lutheran" worship, and the role of lay people in the operation of the church was emphasized. This concept of the priesthood of all believers put the authority to forgive sins in the hands of the believer. It did away with individual confession and increased the account-ability of individuals to seek and understand the availability of forgiveness.

From his early days as a priest, Luther struggled with feelings of shamefulness in front of God. He saw God as an angry judge before whom he would never be worthy of redemption. Constantly questioning his motivation for doing good works or even seeking absolution in the Eucharist, Luther was wracked with anxiety, uncertainty of his righteousness, and a fear of death. He felt that he could never live up to the expectations placed on him. In struggling with this and studying the writings of Paul, he was led to an understanding and distinction of law and gospel.

The law is spelled out clearly in scripture. It pro-vides God's rules for right living, God's expectations for human behavior. Humans simply have to follow these precepts and honor and glorify God. Unfor-tunately, however, this is not so simple. Humans are constantly falling short of fulfilling the law. It was widely known from the early days of Judaism when Moses received the Ten Commandments that there was no way that a person could follow all of the laws spelled out in scripture. To attempt to do so would be utterly defeating. Yet, religious observers were expected to try to keep the law. If one did not suc-ceed, then one was considered to be sinful. Happily for the sinful person—and everyone is a sinful person—the law is only half of the story. Gospel is the other side of law that offers a corrective. Gospel is right-eousness, which marks all humanity as children of God. This good news of redemption is given to all through Jesus Christ. So, regardless of mankind's many failed attempts to maintain the law, those who seek repentance for their false actions and false gods receive the good news: the gospel of salvation.

Luther's theology was evangelical. In other words, proclamation of the Word of God was fundamental. Thus, the teaching and preaching positions in Wittenberg were fundamental to him. He strongly believed that the preaching office was crucial to God's plan for humanity. God's Word was available for all to hear. It was a foundational source for instructing people how to live. Yet, many Christians in the sixteenth century were illiterate, or at the very least could not read the Scriptures written in Latin, Greek, or Hebrew. Therefore, the transmission of the word through the preaching arts was an essential link in the communication of God's message. The good news of the gospel, delivered by a skilled preacher, gives people the Word. The Word gives people faith. And it is through faith that people attain salvation.

Remembering his focus on the priesthood of all believers, Luther also appreciated that anyone could preach the Word. One does not need to be ordained as a priest to share the gospel. All believers have this ability.

This ability to share the Word also ties into Luther's emphasis on all believers knowing the word. Christian education in the congregation was a primary focus for Luther. Thus, he developed teaching tools to assist local pastors in Christian formation, particularly among children and ordinary parishioners. The *Large and Small Catechisms* were printed in 1529 and became widely disseminated. Both were eventually incorporated into the body of Lutheran confessions. They are still used to instruct young people and new members today.

Luther read all scripture with an eye toward Christ; everything was understood in relation to Christ and his suffering on the cross. This led to his theology of the cross that maintained the paradox of God crucified in Christ. To Luther it was beyond human logic and reason to comprehend God voluntarily assuming the mantle of humanity. It was even more ridiculous to think of God hanging on a cross and dying. Yet this is exactly what happened. And, Luther believed, it was knowledge of this event that should keep Christians from merely trying to imitate Christ in their daily lives, a theology advocated by the church in the Middle Ages. No one in his right mind would want to join Christ in his suffering. Yet it is this lowly image of a man, broken in spirit with his life slipping away, that is the most liberating for Christians. It is in the suffering of the cross that Christians become justified. It is through this act that they know unequivocally of God's love. It is through this inconceivable event that they receive the beauty of salvation. The theology that arises from this concept looks for God in the unlikely and hidden places. It elevates the downtrodden and exalts the oppressed. In many ways it is a backward or negative theology that lifts up the lowly. It demands a theology of humility in which one seeks conformity with Christ. This conformity does not boast of good works, however. Instead it focuses on self-sacrifice and meekness.

Luther imagined the way justification and redemption worked to be like that of a courtroom in which God is the judge. Humans stand in front of God, aware of their total depravity and inability to do anything to earn merit. They come before God as a defendant and are found guilty. But when time comes for sentencing, the punishment does not match the crime because humankind is completely acquitted. God judges but does not punish. Christ stands in as a substitutionary defendant. Through faith in Christ, one is justified. In this justification, not only is a person wiped clean of sin, but he or she is also renewed. Faith leads to justification and justification renews the soul and breeds good works. These works are not done out of fear of retribution or to win favor, rather they are the grateful heart's response to the gift of grace. Luther based much of his doctrine of justification by faith on his reading of the book of Romans.

Luther had a different perspective on the sacraments than his fellow Catholics. He understood sacraments to be outward signs of an inward grace. They were acts that Christ instituted. In this way they were commanded by God and offered a promise of grace. They had a material as well as spiritual element. He considered baptism and Eucharist to be the only legitimate sacraments, thus reducing the number of sacraments from seven to two. The sacraments carried a function of forgiveness and required faith to be effective.

He introduced the concept of real presence in the Eucharist that was slightly different from the Catholic understanding of transubstantiation. Luther maintained the doctrine of consubstantiation, which understood the body and blood of Christ to be fully present in the eucharistic hosts of bread and wine. At the same time, the elements of bread and wine did not physically change as a result of this presence. In this way, God comes to the sinner during communion where Christ and all the saints are met.

Luther's thoughts on church and society garnered much attention and were built on the distinction between the kingdom of God and secular authority in daily life. This is commonly referred to as his doctrine of two kingdoms. During Luther's exile in the Wartburg in the early years of the Reformation movement tensions grew between peasants and the ruling authorities. Violence broke out against priests and churches that he could not condone. In his 1523 treatise *Temporal Authority* he spelled out the distinction between religious and secular authority and how believers should respond to both. Temporal authority was instituted to address evil-doers and should be obeyed unless it demanded wrong action on the part of the Christian. The government has a divine function but is to rule in the best interest of the subject and not for vainglory. It should not undermine the gospel or compel the Christian to behave against his or her conscience. The Christian has an obligation to participate fully in just government systems and even the church does not lie outside the bounds of temporal authority. Luther advocated this in direct opposition to the popular position of the church that considered itself to be the supreme authority on earth. When the Peasants' Revolts took place from 1524 to 1525, Luther condemned the violence of the people who used his writings and theology of equality to justify their attacks on government authorities and princes. He admonished the violence and implored the princes to treat the peasants with leniency. Many questioned his clear allegiance to the ruling authorities after that.

Juxtaposed to the two kingdoms, Luther also had a concept of three estates. These were temporal authority, priestly estate, and the estate of marriage. These estates were vocations that pleased God. They were ways in which a person could be involved in society and fill an important contributing role.

One of the reforms that Luther instituted was that of a married priesthood. This grew in large part from his rejection of celibacy for those who had taken religious vows. Luther's belief was that this type of forced celibacy was unnatural, ran counter to human impulses, and caused one to sin. Luther and his fellow reformers viewed marriage as a divine estate, a vocation. God calls people to live out their baptisms in marriage and it requires the same lifelong commitment as other covenants. Marriage sanctifies sexual relations, which Luther viewed as blessed in proper, monogamous relationships. It creates families, which

are the building blocks of society. It also mirrors the relationship between God and God's church.

Many priests who left the Catholic Church to join Luther's reform movement took wives. Luther, himself, married in 1525. Katherine von Bora was a Cistercian nun in Saxony who escaped the convent with eight other nuns in 1523. They sought refuge in Wittenberg where Luther found husbands for most of them. Katherine, however, had her eye on the founder of the movement and, rumor has it, let him know in no uncertain terms that only he would she marry. Reluctant at first, Luther eventually consented. He later would unabashedly proclaim his love for Katie.

Katie Luther had her own impact on the reformation movement, as the Luther household she managed was often the seat of hospitality and decision making. She supervised the family's funds and maintained a small farm to augment Luther's salary. Of their six children, four survived to adulthood. The Luther household became a model for Protestantism. In the same way, clergy families who lived in a nearby parsonage would often become the center of a church's life.

No modern summary of Luther's theology would be complete without reference to his relationship to non-Christians, particularly the Jews. Like any marginalized minority group, the Jews of the sixteenth century had no voice, no rights, and few opportunities. They were understood to have been the killers of Christ and bringers of the plague. In a word, they were despised and discriminated against.

Reflecting what he saw as the moral decline of his day, Luther used his writings on Judaism to call for reform in the lives of his fellow Christians. He did this first in *That Jesus Christ Was Born a Jew*, written in 1523. In this he highlighted the medieval mistreatment of Jews, claiming, "If the apostles, who also were Jews, had dealt with us Gentiles as we Gentiles deal with the Jews, there would never have been a Christian among the Gentiles. Since they dealt with us Gentiles in such brotherly fashion, we in our turn ought to treat the Jews in a brotherly manner" (LW 45:200). Using this "Golden Rule" type of logic, Luther implied that his neighbors should behave in a more *Christian* manner toward their Jewish neighbors.

Because of this, at one point early in his career, Martin Luther was considered by some to have been an advocate for Jews. During a time when racism was rampant across Europe, his early writings caused Luther to be seen as one of the less anti-Jewish reformers. His opponents criticized what they saw as a pro-Jewish sentiment expressed in *That Jesus Christ Was Born a Jew*. This treatise was written in response to accusations that Luther believed Jesus was born from Abraham's seed, thus questioning Luther's commitment to the virgin birth.

Following this publication, he received both applause and criticism for taking a gentle approach to a population considered a blight on society. In this discourse he advanced the premise that Jews hold a special place in creation because God's original covenant was made with them. Their kinship with Jesus also gave them high rank. Luther wrote: "When we are inclined to boast of our position we should remember that we are but Gentiles, while the Jews are of the lineage of Christ. We are aliens and in-laws; they are blood relatives, cousins, and brothers of our Lord. Therefore, if one is to boast of flesh and blood, the Jews are actually nearer to Christ than we are." (LW 45:20) This treatise is often used to "proof-text" a pro-Jewish sentiment in the young Luther and is contrasted to his hostile statements decades later.

Luther was convinced that once the abuses of the church were cleaned up and they had the opportunity to hear the Word of God truly preached, the Jews would see the beauty of Christianity. Despite his ultimate aims at their conversion, the Jewish community considered Luther an appreciative scholar and colleague. Because he was an advocate for the study of Hebrew, a number of rabbis and Talmudic scholars respected him and considered him an ally.

Yet, Luther's advocacy of Hebrew scholarship was laden with his own christological agenda. He believed that reading the books of the Old Testament in Hebrew showed how the Hebrew texts, from the beginning, pointed to the coming of Christ. This concept marked the introduction to his *On the Last Words of David*:

> If we do not apply all diligence to interpret the Hebrew Bible, wherever that is feasible, in the direction of the New Testament, in opposition to the interpretation of the rabbis, it would be better to keep the old translation (which, after all, retains, thanks to the New Testament, most of the good elements) than to have so many translations just because a few passages presumably have a different reading or are still not understood. (LW 15:270)

His later treatise, *On the Jews and Their Lies*, confronts the Jews in a much more hostile way than his earlier tract. In this Luther urges fellow Christians to cling more firmly to their beliefs in Christ in light of the fact of the Jews' failure to convert and see the glory of God, as well as their continued denial of Christ as the Messiah. Luther calls for Jews' synagogues and houses to be burned to the ground, their books to be confiscated, and safe conduct be denied them. These writings were used in modern times to justify the injustices perpetuated by anti-Semitic regimes.

Luther had similarly hostile things to say against the Turks who were a political threat with the advancing armies of the Ottoman sultan, Suleiman the Great. He walked a similar line of appreciation and disdain for Islam as he did with Judaism. He saw it as a religion that blatantly promoted works righteousness. At the same time, he applauded the Turks' cleanliness, modesty, and moderation. He perceived the imminent Turkish invasion to be God's condemnation of a country gone astray. His writings on the Turks were not as well publicized as those against the Jews, however, and were not used as widely to justify violence against Muslims.

With heart problems, digestive discomfort, and kidney stones, Luther's health began to weaken him in the 1540s. During this same period, Katie suffered a miscarriage and his daughter, Magdalena, died. These things combined to cast Luther into depression. In early 1546 he returned to Eisleben with his sons to deal with a property issue. He died there on February 18, 1546, and was returned to Wittenberg for burial at the Castle church. The reforms he set into motion, however, lived on after him.

Martin Luther was prolific. A talented hymn writer, Bible translator, thoughtful pastor, and scholarly theologian, he cared deeply that the message offered by the church be one that was biblically based, available to all people, and that communicated the grace and love of God. The fact that his reforms have endured until today proves that his was a message whose time had come.

Reference

Luther, Martin. 2002. *Luther's Works*, ed. J. J. Pelikan, H. C. Oswald, and H. T. Lehmann. Philadelphia: Fortress Press, and St Louis: Concordia Publishing House. [CD-ROM]

Philip Melanchthon (1497–1560)

Christy Lohr

Whereas Martin Luther is thought of as the author of the Reformation, Philip Melanchthon is easily said to be its translator. Friend and colleague of Luther at Wittenberg, Melanchthon was a powerful influence on the movement's shape and dissemination. While Luther was noted for his fiery temper and vocal proclamations, Melanchthon was a quieter teacher and theologian. He is largely responsible for drafting the documents that codified belief in the evangelical doctrine, including the *Augsburg Confession* (1530) and his later *Apology to the Augsburg Confession* (1531). Elements of the *Augsburg Confession* made their way into foundational documents of other Reformation and Protestant traditions. While Luther was the Reformation's primary preacher, Melanchthon was its primary teacher. His *Loci Communes Rerum Theologicarum* (1521 and revised in later editions) is considered the first Lutheran systematic theology, to which Luther himself gave high praise by saying that it should be canonized.

Melanchthon was born Philip Schwartzerdt on February 16, 1497 in Bretton, Germany. His father George, an armorer for Philip the Upright, elector of Palatinate, named his son after his employer. After his father's death in 1508, Philip's mother sent him to Pforzheim where he was enrolled in a Latin school. Well-known humanist John Reuchlin was a relative of the Schwartzerdts and he took an interest in young Philip, who was proving to be quite an able scholar.

Reuchlin gave the boy a Greek grammar book inscribed with the Hellenized version of his family name ("black earth"), and Philip referred to himself as "Melanchthon" ever after. He enrolled in the University of Heidelberg and earned a Bachelor of Arts degree. Despite having completed the necessary requirements, he was denied an advanced degree due to his young age. Because of this, he moved to the University of Tubingen for his master's degree, where he also taught. At Reuchlin's suggestion, Frederick the Wise, elector of Saxony, invited Melanchthon in 1518 to join the faculty of his university in Wittenberg as professor of Greek. He remained on the staff there until his death in 1560.

Melanchthon was a committed layperson who never took ordination vows, yet his influence on the developing Reformation movement was great. During his first years at Wittenberg he earned a Bachelor of Theology degree under the tutelage of Martin Luther. After this, he began teaching in the theological faculty. He maintained his position in the humanities department as well, and introduced logic and rhetoric into the study of philosophy.

Melanchthon affirmed the authority of scripture and introduced New Testament Greek texts into his humanities courses. His commentaries on biblical books are among the corpus of his works. He also wrote on moral disciplines, sciences, and Greek poetry and literature. His textbooks on grammar, Latin, Greek,

The Student's Companion to the Theologians, First Edition. Edited by Ian S. Markham.
© 2013 Blackwell Publishing Ltd. Published 2013 by Blackwell Publishing Ltd.

and rhetoric were used widely. Melanchthon was also influential in improving the German school system.

In keeping with a central tenet of the Reformation, Melanchthon firmly subscribed to the doctrine of justification by faith through grace. This was outlined most expressly in his *Loci Communes* (1521), which drew heavily on Paul's epistles to the Romans and held that the faithful person's sinfulness was wiped away through the grace of God. This grace is made known through Christ and the Scriptures. This concept relates back to the key Reformation concept of law and gospel. God gives the law that humans perpetually fail to keep. God also gives the gospel that proclaims the good news of forgiveness of sins and salvation through Christ. God's law is written on the hearts of humankind. When a person receives the grace of God, his or her natural response is to live according to God's law.

Melanchthon's understanding of law grew in large part from his training in classical Greek philosophy and natural law. This holds that the universe has been ordered by God in a way that allows humankind to attain knowledge of God. This law is written on people's hearts and allows them self-awareness of their sinful natures. The Ten Commandments outline the law that humankind already knows naturally. Melanchthon attempted to reconcile an understanding of free will that moved away from determinism with the concept of justification by faith in which he firmly believed. Humans, after all, were not forced into salvation against their wills, as determinism would imply.

The question of a person's free will and ability to follow God's design for his or her life became a sticking point for Melanchthon and several of his Reformation colleagues. Having been trained in philosophy, Melanchthon was criticized by many as being a humanist. He had written from a humanist perspective before moving to Wittenberg and coming under Luther's influence. In his university days he had gained recognition from Erasmus for his insights and works. Humanists believed that all people had the ability to behave morally and that a universal understanding of the good was inherent to humankind, a concept that could easily devolve into a belief in humankind's ability to attain righteousness through meritorious works. Melanchthon was accused of attempting to synergize humanistic philosophy with

evangelical ideals. He rejected these accusations and defended himself against such attacks in a way that kept the peace with Luther but eventually broke off relations with his early mentor Reuchlin.

A measure of humanism was accepted by all of the early Lutheran reformers, however. Humanism encouraged a return to the primary sources of information. For Luther and Melanchthon, who both encouraged interpreting the Bible in its original Greek and Hebrew, this was a key philosophy. Additionally, humanist thinking also allowed Melanchthon to introduce classical learning and rhetoric into his teaching. He took this learning style beyond the walls of Wittenberg University and was applauded for instituting German school reform at the high school level. Melanchthon was a primary shaper of educational systems as well as religious thought. He established a pedagogical model that traveled as far as England and was employed during the reign of Queen Elizabeth I.

Melanchthon also received criticism for what appeared to be his changing understanding of the Lord's Supper. In early writings, he clearly aligned himself with Luther's thinking on transubstantiation. In later writings, however, his interpretation shifted somewhat to imply a more symbolic understanding of Christ's presence in the Eucharist. This reduced the real presence of Christ's body and blood in the bread and wine, which Luther criticized as being too close to the understanding of Protestant theologian Ulrich Zwingli. The tensions with Luther over this issue were never insurmountable, but they affected the relationship between the two Wittenberg theologians in the years before Luther's death.

In the years after Luther's death, when Emperor Charles V attempted to reunite the Catholic Church divided by Luther's reforms under the Augsburg interim, Melanchthon struggled to keep the evangelical theology intact. Yet he was harshly criticized by many Lutherans of the day for yielding too much and allowing the reinstatement of Catholic rites that were not part of essential church doctrine. This allowance of indifferent or non-essential practices and beliefs, termed *adiaphoria*, was acceptable by many theologians. Many others, however, felt that the allowance of such practices would reintroduce false doctrines that they had worked so hard to overcome. The debate on this issue continued after Melanchthon's death until it was settled in the *Formula of Concord* in 1577, but the damage done to Melanchthon's credibility as he tried to broker an agreement that would give Lutherans freedom to practice in "Catholic lands" would last for a century or more.

Melanchthon was a primary representative of the expanding movement from the moment he joined the theology faculty in Wittenberg, but especially in the mid-1500s following the death of Luther. He was committed to maintaining open dialogue with the Catholic Church as well as Protestant leaders. In this way, Melanchthon was an early advocate of ecumenical interaction. The Peace of Augsburg in 1955, five years before Melanchthon's death, was signed between Charles V and the princes of the Smalcald League— those German princes embracing the practice of Lutheranism in their territories and forming a layer of protection for the emerging movement. This formally recognized the presence of two official religious institutions: Roman Catholicism and Lutheranism.

A key concern for Melanchthon was clarity in theology. He insisted that doctrine and commentaries should clarify and illuminate positions of faith. Thus, he attempted to spell out teachings on key issues such as justification and Eucharist. As confusion or controversy arose over his writings, Melanchthon would answer these with revisions and clarifying comments. He also altered documents as his own thinking progressed. Doing this with the *Augsburg Confession*, presented at the Diet of Augsburg in 1530, garnered criticism against Melanchthon. His reworked versions of the *Augsburg Confession* carried the label *Variata*. He also made multiple revisions to his early work *Loci Communes* throughout his life. In these he clarified his position on free will so as to remove deterministic language, and clarified his approach to philosophy.

More recent Lutheran scholarship has reclaimed an appreciation for Melanchthon and the contributions he made to the early Reformation. Trapped under various charges of being untrue to the theology of Luther that sparked the movement, Melanchthon remained committed to his core beliefs and held firm as a stalwart champion of reform. An advocate for church unity and co-operation, he also lobbied for peaceful resolutions to doctrinal disagreements. For centuries Philip Melanchthon was largely overshadowed by a primary focus on the works and life of his colleague, friend, and mentor, Martin Luther. As someone who was equally as prolific in his writing and teaching as Luther was, however, Melanchthon made his own lasting contribution to the tradition.

The Reformation

Mary E. Coleman

I. Introduction

"The Reformation" is the term usually used by historians to describe the extraordinary events of the sixteenth century which profoundly affected the Western Christian church. Many of the ideas which came to be accepted in this century of upheavals are still part of the definition of certain Western Christian churches and in some cases serve to delineate their place within the modern Christian church. In fact there are those who still refer to "the Reformed churches" to denote those denominations such as Anglicans, Baptists, Calvinists, Lutherans, Presbyterians, and the many others who developed out of this turmoil.

There were certain ideas common to all these reform movements: an emphasis on biblical revival and the translation of the Word of God into the vernacular; an improvement in the intellectual and moral standards of the clergy; emphasis on the sovereignty of God; insistence that faith and the Scriptures are at the center of the Christian message; and a return to what were considered to be early church practices. In the very early decades of this movement the intention was to reform from within the church. It quickly became evident that for a variety of reasons this might not be possible.

There were also non-religious influences of importance to the Reformation, most notable of which was the recent invention, and spreading use, of the printing press. This enabled many of the ideas related to social and economic reforms, grounded in the revival of classical learning in the Renaissance, to have a significant influence not just among the scholarly elite but the middling classes as well. Additionally, in some of the geographical areas most affected by the Reformation, political conflict contributed a measure of instability that allowed and encouraged the ideas of the Reformation to flourish and make a lasting impact.

II. Historical Background

Although historians often date the Reformation from the furor that developed once Luther had posted his *Ninety-Five Theses* (October 31, 1517), in reality, the beginnings of the Reformation are now conceded by many historians to be somewhat earlier. Influential theologians and clerics had begun reacting to what they perceived as excesses of the church at least a century before Luther's action.

One fact that all historians will agree to is that the church was at the center of late medieval European society. While many histories of the period will refer to the "Roman Catholic church" or the "Protestant church," it is important to remember that the people of the sixteenth century would not have thought in those terms. To them, there was "the Church." One was either a part of it or not … and the vast majority

The Student's Companion to the Theologians, First Edition. Edited by Ian S. Markham.
© 2013 Blackwell Publishing Ltd. Published 2013 by Blackwell Publishing Ltd.

of people considered themselves to be sons and daughters of the church. It was not until late in the century, once people began to feel that there might be no way to integrate the reforms so ardently sought by Calvin, Luther, Zwingli, and their followers, that the terms "Catholic," "Protestant," or "Reformed" came into use.

Whether one looked at the calendar with its cycle of holy days, feasts, and festivals or the organization of towns and cities in parishes, one saw the church. Education was usually controlled by the church: both what would be studied and who could study in any formal setting. For the most part education was to be used for the administration of the church. The term "cleric," which has come to mean in modern times those who serve the church as ministers or pastors, is very much related to the term "clerk" as originally applied to those men who were specifically educated by the church to perform both sorts of tasks. The church had a separate legal system with its own courts, and laws specific to those courts; often these were in conflict with civil authority. While the ethical structure of all of lay life was defined by the church, its primary role was as mediator of salvation and arbiter of eternal truth.

Significantly, many of those social services we now consider the duty of the modern state—medical care for the indigent, or financial support for the disabled, and other social services—had until that time been organized and administered primarily by the church either through parishes or through church-sponsored monastic foundations. But that was beginning to change. Political entities, particularly the municipal councils of the free cities of the German territories were beginning to assume responsibility for education and the care of the poor and sick, and to supervise public morality.

Generally, by the fifteenth century the church provided a sense of stability and structure to the general populace and for the most part received its support and respect. As in all times and places there were areas of tension, but for the vast majority of the laity the church was woven into the fabric of life without question. The many church festivals provided entertainment as well as economic opportunity (at the trade fairs which were often a part of these events), and pilgrimages to the many local shrines constituted not only a manifestation of popular piety but were often the equivalent of modern-day package tours. The rising prosperity of the non-elite classes allowed them the opportunity to travel throughout Europe. Later, this ease of movement would contribute to the spread of Reformation ideas.

III.   Issues Common to the Reformation Movements

As mentioned above, certain concepts were shared by almost all the reformers. Perhaps the most important was that both faith and scripture should be at the center of the Christian message. Because of the importance of the Scriptures to the laity, translation of the Word of God into the vernacular became paramount. To a laity who, for the most part, had not had the ability to read the Scriptures for themselves—since they were usually in Latin, or in some cases Greek for the New Testament, and thus unavailable to all but those with training in these languages—the importance of having access to translations in the vernacular cannot be underestimated. Although there had been earlier efforts to translate the Bible into English, most notably by John Wyclif in the late fourteenth century, William Tyndale (1494–1536), working with Martin Luther, published his complete version in 1525. The complete Bible in German, translated by Martin Luther, was first printed 1534. Portions of the translation had been appearing throughout the 1520s. At virtually the same time, Jacques Lefèvre d'Étaples (c.1450–1536) was working on a translation of the New Testament into French, which was published in 1530.

Within the next few decades almost all other European languages had a version of the Scriptures available, often in relatively inexpensive popular editions. Many of these editions had marginal notes to help guide the laity in their study of the text. The 1560 Geneva Bible, with commentary, was the result of the work of English exiles living in Geneva. The commentary was significantly influenced by the writings of John Calvin.

Although it is difficult to know just what the effective literacy rates were during this period, the evidence of the steadily increasing sales of all types of religiously related printed materials suggests that during this period many more of the laity were interested in being able to read the Scriptures for themselves. In many household inventories, if there were any books listed at all, they would be a copy of the Bible, a Psalter, or a commentary on the Bible.

Just as the translation of the Scriptures provided a means for the laity to educate itself as to the contents of the Scriptures, the recognition of many churchmen of the previous century that the education of the lower clergy was deficient was highlighted by the increasing familiarity of the laity with the Bible. It was no longer sufficient for the clergy to be able to say a few prayers in Latin or to recite the Mass by rote. The laity began to require a more learned clergy. Although some of the clergy responded to these demands by claiming authority to act as they chose by right of their ordination, many responded by learning to preach and to teach in more biblically based ways.

A low educational standard was not the only issue of concern for the parish clergy during this century. Some of these clergymen had dubious reputations in their personal lives. It was not uncommon for some to fail to abide by their vows of chastity or poverty. Late medieval and early modern popular literature is full of caricatures of a very much less than saintly clergy. By the late fifteenth and early sixteenth century, these offenses, along with the offense felt by having a church hierarchy seemingly more concerned with temporal power and wealth and less concerned with the abuses of the lower orders of clergy and the needs of the laity, added to the perceived need for reform. Particularly in the German states, but in other countries as well, it was the norm for all members of the upper levels of the church hierarchy to be members of elite landowning families. The hierarchy of the church was inextricably intertwined by birth and interests with the aristocracy of Europe.

Another main concern of the reformers was to place the emphasis on the sovereignty of God above any possible concern for the sovereignty of the church or individual members of the church hierarchy. The forms and dogmas of the church were to be aligned with the will of God as expressed in the Scriptures. As reforming theologians re-examined the Scriptures for precedents regarding the governing of the church, they tended to regard as unjustified by the authority of the Bible many of the accretions to the power and authority of the Western Christian church. Therefore, they began to question which elements were essential and which aspects were merely customary or traditional. The doctrine of the priesthood of all believers, developed in the course of the early years of the reform, and the importance placed on preaching the Word of God with the hope that it would lead to an educated clergy, and the later institution of decentralized church communities were part of an attempt to be better able to prevent abuse of ecclesiastical privilege.

Finally and most importantly, the reformers desired to place faith rather than form at the center of Christian worship. Although there were differences among the reformers, particularly after the middle of the sixteenth century, regarding just what were the essentials, they were agreed that personal faith and piety should be grounded in the practices to be found in the Scriptures. A significant effort was made to seek out and emulate the practices of the early church. Where there was uncertainty or seemingly contradictory practices, there were the grounds for disagreements among the reformers. The traditional sacraments of the Western Christian church—baptism, confirmation, confession, communion, marriage, extreme unction, and ordination or holy orders—were all reconsidered. For some reformers, there were only two recognized sacraments, baptism and communion, because these were clearly seen to be instituted by God and recorded in the Scriptures. Many other reformers wanted to retain certain of the others because there was good reason to believe that these were implied by the actions of Jesus as described in the Scriptures.

IV. Major Reformation Figures

Although they were born much earlier than the sixteenth century, many historians consider John Huss and (slightly later) Erasmus of Rotterdam to be significant precursors to the Reformation. John Huss (Jan Hus) was born in Bohemia (now part of the Czech Republic) in about 1371. After receiving a master's degree from Charles University in Prague in

1396, he became a professor of theology in 1398, was ordained a priest 1400, and was made rector of the University in 1402. Responding to the crisis of authority in the church, Huss began to denounce various church abuses in his sermons. His disputes with authority did not concern basic theological issues, but rather matters of church discipline and practice. The most significant was that he taught that the office of the pope did not exist by divine command, but was established by the church that things might be done in an orderly fashion. Given the time, the Church Council, having just succeeded in uniting Western Christendom under a single pope after years of chaos, was not about to have the authority of that pope questioned; it found Huss guilty of heresy, and burned him at the stake on July 6, 1415.

After Luther published his *Ninety-Five Theses*, cartoons and graffiti appeared implying that Luther was the spiritual heir of John Huss. When Luther encountered the pope's representative, Johannes Eck, in a crucial debate, Eck sidestepped the questions of indulgences and justification by faith, and instead asked Luther whether the church had been right to condemn Huss. Luther said that Huss had been unjustly condemned and the whole question of the authority of popes and councils was raised anew.

Desiderius Erasmus (1466–1536), the Dutch humanist, was born at Rotterdam. The six years he spent in a monastery may have contributed to his lifelong enmity toward monks and monasteries. After taking priestly orders he traveled and lived in both France and England. In 1519 he published his *Colloquia*, usually regarded as his masterpiece. The incisiveness with which he treats the abuses of the church prepared people's minds for the subsequent work of Martin Luther.

In his work, including the annotated New Testament and his edition on St Jerome (in nine folio volumes), he attempted to introduce a more rational conception of Christian doctrine, and to eliminate the pedantic methods of the scholastic theologians. While he did not support Luther's opinions on reform, his work certainly made an effective preliminary to it. Perhaps in an attempt to distance himself from the many Lutheran controversies, he produced a long list of editions of classical and patristic writers. However, he continued to be embroiled in controver-

sies, including those with Ulrich von Hutten, Luther, and the Sorbonne. The controversies did not lessen his fame or influence in Europe.

John (Jean) Calvin (1509–64) was born in France and raised in a traditional church family. His father was an administrator for the local bishop. Although the new theological teaching of Luther and Jacques Lefevre d'Etaples were well known in Paris during his student days, it was not until later when he had become friends with reform-minded individuals that he began to consider changing to the reformed faith. At the behest of his father he studied law rather than theology. But by 1533 Calvin had made the decision to convert. For the next few years, while living in various places outside France, he studied, preached, and worked on the *Institutes of the Christian Religion*. He had planned only a brief trip to Geneva in 1536, but after being invited by a local reformer to stay in the city, he did so. Except for a three-year period as a pastor to French refugees in Strasbourg (1538–41), he was to live in Geneva until his death. During that time he was busy lecturing, preaching, and writing commentaries, treatises, and various editions of the *Institutes*. Calvin shared with Zwingli a belief that only those practices firmly rooted in scripture were to be considered valid for believing Christians.

Martin Luther (1483–1546) was a graduate of the University of Erfurt, studied philosophy and theology, and, having received his master's degree in 1505, entered an Augustinian monastery there. Ordained a priest in 1507, Luther was sent to the newly founded (1502) University of Wittenberg to teach philosophy and to continue his theological studies. In late 1513 he received his doctorate and was made a member of the theology faculty. He held highly responsible administrative positions as well as teaching. During the next few years, struggles with his personal faith caused him to begin to develop what has become known as his doctrine of "justification by faith." It was at this juncture that he was confronted by the abuse of indulgences. He did not disagree with the basic doctrine so much as the misunderstanding of what indulgences were, as understood by the laity. His experiences as a priest suggested that they were very problematic. So he posted his *Ninety-Five Theses* on October 31, 1517 as a way of beginning a discussion on what to do about this question. The reaction was not at all what he expected. Johann Eck, a brilliant theological scholar, seemed to find a whiff of the Hussite heresy in them and his reputation was such that Luther was in for a long and contentious engagement with the hierarchy of the church. By 1521, he found himself excommunicate and an outlaw.

As a result of this extended and personally painful process, Luther, the monk who had wished to discuss reforms within the church, was to become a revolutionary outside the church. And it was during this time that Luther began to write and publish in German rather than the Latin of the academy. His style of writing was often confrontational and the fact that he wrote in the vernacular made him a powerful voice to the people. Whether writing on the impossibility of monastic orders or the need for a revision in the sacraments, Luther did not hesitate to call into question many of the basic foundations of the Roman Church. He often wrote in a coarse and disrespectful manner, particularly when engaged in controversy with his academic peers. But he did appeal to the common people and to their personal concerns regarding piety and, ultimately, their salvation.

Ulrich Zwingli (1484–1531), the leader of the Swiss reformation party, was based in the city-state of Zurich. He was much influenced by the humanism of Erasmus. Very popular in Zurich for his opposition to Swiss mercenary service in foreign wars and his attacks on indulgences, he was a critic of indulgences, as was Luther. Zwingli had risen through the ranks of the church. In 1519 he was appointed "People's Priest," the most powerful ecclesiastical position in the city. However, he agreed with the ideas of Luther's reform program. In 1523, the city adopted Zwingli's basic ecclesiastical reforms. Zwingli's theology and morality were based on a single principle: if the Old or New Testament did not say something explicitly and literally, then no Christian should believe or practice it … thus his critique of indulgences. Zwingli tried to build perhaps the most strictly Christian society, in religious, social, and moral terms. He disagreed with Luther over major doctrinal issues, the most important of which was the nature of the Eucharist. Luther, according to church tradition, believed that the bread and wine of the Eucharist was spiritually transformed into the body and blood of Christ, while Zwingli believed that the Eucharist only *symbolized* the body and blood of Christ.

V. Progress of Reform in Some Specific Countries

In all of the countries where reform ideas were contested there is to be found a general sequence of events. A theological discussion begins, normally related to concerns regarding perceived abuses in either the doctrine or the discipline of the church. The initial intention is usually to reform within the context of the Western Christian church. The purpose is to acquire legal recognition for these proposed reforms. In many of the countries there were legal proclamations of the changes: in France, the Edict of Nantes (1598); in Poland, the Confederation of Warsaw (1573); and in Scotland, an act of Parliament (1560). Additionally, in all the countries the course of the debate regarding the reforms was greatly influenced by the political situation. Whether the reformers met with success or failure was very often determined not by the force or appeal of their theological arguments but by the political reality of the territory. This is made clear by the fact that as much as all the reform movements shared a deep commitment to the primacy of scripture and the renewal of piety, there was also a concomitant concern with the uses and abuses of authority, particularly in regard to the claims for authority that emanated from the pope in Rome.

In the German states, historians generally consider the beginning of the Reformation to be the date in 1517 when Luther posted his *Ninety-Five Theses* (October 31) on the door of the Castle church in Wittenberg. This posting was within the tradition of academic disputations of the age and might have been considered unremarkable, except that Luther also sent a copy of the *Theses* with a letter of explanation to the archbishop. The archbishop in turn referred it to his councilors and to the theologians at the University of Mainz, who declared the substance of the *Theses* to be heretical. In the *Theses* he had undertaken a particularly probing and detailed analysis of the theology underlying the sale of indulgences. Indulgences had had a fairly long history within the church, but Luther was writing in response to a particularly egregious instance of the sale of indulgences, which had been authorized by the pope in Rome in order to pay for a singularly expensive building project. Unfortunately for Luther, he had chosen to question this practice at a time when it was most important to both the papacy and the archbishop that the sale of indulgences not be hindered by a close examination of the practice. The reaction by those authorities was quick and strong. Luther's academic disputation rapidly became a public trial involving much more than the theology faculty of his own university. After three years of ecclesiastical procedural process, Luther was excommunicated in 1521. During this time his message was for a deepened spirituality among the laity, allied with some fairly mild criticism of the clergy. Three months after his excommunication the diet issued the Edict of Worms declaring him a political outlaw.

The effect of the edict was clearly not what was intended. Luther disappeared. Some of his supporters thought he was dead, but he was, in fact, preparing himself for his next steps. In the interim, his supporters took up the issue of what a deepened lay spirituality would mean. The discussion was carried on in a number of popular pamphlets directed toward the laity. The ideas that were emphasized in these short, easily read works were related to personal piety rather than theological dogma. Some of the key ideas were encapsulated in phrases like "works righteousness," "the pure word of God," and, fatefully, the "declaration that the papacy was the seat of the antichrist" (Jones, 2005). The importance of the pamphlets lay in the fact that the reformers chose to discuss these issues in everyday language, not as part of an academic discourse, but as part of a conversation with the laity. They put the people and their needs from the church at the very center of the discussion. Even more telling, the reformers addressed a multitude of social and political concerns as well as strictly religious ones.

The politico-social ideas were important to the spread of the Reformation ideas. The cities of Germany and Switzerland, the first areas affected by the reformers, were the centers of literacy as well as economic and political power. Furthermore, they were the traditional locales of conflict between the authority and economic clout of the church as well as of the laity. It was usual for the councils of the cities to be the seat of secular power and as such they were often the sites of challenges to the ecclesiastical order of the community. For the next three decades

(1530–60) the impact of the reformers would reverberate through the deliberations of these councils. From the Diet of Speyer (1529), where what would be termed the Catholic forces managed to field a bare majority intent on enforcing the Edit of Worms, to the meeting of the Diet of Augsburg (1530), called by Charles V in order to complete the resolution of the controversy, the issues continued to be related to the status of the sacraments, authority (not just papal authority) within the hierarchy, and the question of justification by faith. The Augsburg diet was unable to obtain an acceptable compromise. Because of Charles's distraction caused by the need to respond militarily to the Turkish invasion of his territory, it would another decade and more before serious attempts were made to resolve the theological conflict. By that time the reformers had been able to firmly establish the revised practices in much of Germany. In 1555 the Peace of Augsburg formally recognized the concept of "Cuius region, eius religio," which is to say, each territory's ruler had the right to decide whether to follow the reforms of Luther (i.e., Lutheranism) or to retain the traditional practices of the church (i.e., Catholicism)—not only for himself but for the people of his territory.

Many Reformation scholars, while recognizing the international impact of the Lutheran controversy in the German states, will emphasize the forces within France which were well in advance of the reform ideas. The work of Jacques Lefèvre d'Étaples, related to his translation of the New Testament, is thought by some to anticipate Luther's ideas. Yet most would agree that the turmoil in Germany helped with the widespread dissemination of these ideas (Jones, 2005). Later, Calvin's work would come to have a significant place in the thought of the French in regard to reforms. As in Germany, the political situation greatly affected the course of the search for reforms. Until the middle of the century the official position of the monarchy was to suppress the reforms and the reformers. After the *affaire placard* of 1534, Francis I saw to it that his government pursued a policy of persecution of the reformers, allied with censorship of non-orthodox printed materials. His successor, Henry II, continued this policy, issuing the Edict of Chateaubriand in 1551.

By the early 1560s some French reformers, emboldened by Calvin's doctrine of the right of resistance to rulers who did not fulfill their duty, asserted their rights as members of the nobility to oppose the king when they thought he violated the law. These assertions were a result of the untimely death of Henry II in 1559 and the need for regency rule during the minority of Francis II. Cardinal Guise had taken control and the Bourbon family resisted. The reformers anticipated a more welcoming response to their concerns from the Bourbons than from the Cardinal. By 1598 the Edict of Nantes ended the struggle. The reformers were granted the right of freedom of religion, but France remained officially allied with the church headed by the pope in Rome.

In England there had been a significant party of reformers from the mid-fourteenth century, including Lollards and later humanists. However, Henry VIII was a staunch supporter of the church during the early part of his reign and the reformers were not able to have much effect on actual church discipline or doctrine. All of this changed when, as a result of his difficulties in securing approval from the church for a divorce from his first wife, Henry declared that the king was the supreme head of the English Church and appropriated church property. In 1549 the Book of Common Prayer, which employed some elements of Reformation doctrine, was published. Much of the reform was reversed under the short reign (1553–8) of his daughter of this first marriage, Mary. When the daughter of his second marriage, Elizabeth I, took the throne on the death of her sister, she once again reverted to a more reformed church polity. Elizabeth was not a particularly avid supporter of reforms proposed by some of that party, but the legitimacy of her claims to the monarchy rested on her acceptance of the separation of the English church from that of the church in Rome. In Scotland, although the reigning monarch Mary (1542–67) was a supporter of the church, she was too weak a political force to exert her preference. Under the influence of Calvin and the dynamic leadership of John Knox, a reformed church titled the Presbyterian Church of Scotland was established in 1560.

The course of reform in Bohemia, Poland, Scandinavia, and Switzerland followed the general outline stated above. Bohemia had a long tradition of interest in reform dating at least as far back as John Hus. Poland, Scandinavia, and Switzerland shared many of the concerns of Germany, but in Switzerland the influence of Zwingli caused the reforms to take a decidedly different form. In a like manner, the influence of the thought of Calvin was to interact with that of Luther to shape the character of each of the uniquely "Lutheran" national churches in Scandinavia.

VI. Historiography of the Terms "Reformation" and "Counter-Reformation"

As indicated above, the terms used during the sixteenth and early seventeenth century for the reform movements and the participants in them were, in many cases, much different from those we would use today. We can see with the benefit of historical vision that these movements all shared a model which use scripture as the primary authority and the early church as a model (Hillerbrand, 1996). In addition, all the movements rejected the authority of the papacy and with it many of the traditional beliefs and practices of the church, to one degree or another. In many cases they attempted to establish a new church for the community; in some cases, but rarely, they were content with allowing multiple polities to exist.

In the study of the phenomena of the Reformation, scholars recognize that over the course of the sixteenth century both "reformation" and "reform" became confessionalized. One of the earliest of the confessions was recognized as "Lutheran" as opposed to what would be termed "Catholic"—Catholic with a large "C" to differentiate it from the concept of "catholic" meaning universal church. Additional confessions would develop out of the ongoing debate as to what "reformed" truly meant. Many of these confessions would follow the ideas developed by a leader of the movement such as Calvin or Zwingli. In time these confessions would be referred to collectively as the *Reformed* confessions.

It was not until the eighteenth century that historians, most notably Leopold van Ranke (1795–1886), began to use the term "Reformation" to refer this specific era of European history. At this point it took on a larger meaning, including not just the theological, spiritual and church-related concerns of the age, as it had formerly been used by the Lutheran historian Veit Ludwig von Seckendorf (1626–92), but also to denote the social and political factors more common to the study of history.

It was not until the mid-twentieth century that both Catholic and Protestant historians began to use the term. By then Catholic historians had begun to move away from using the term "Age of Schism" to refer to the religious events of sixteenth-century Europe. In general, secular as well as religious historians now employ the term "Reformation" to include cultural, political, social, as well as religious aspects of the century.

The term "Counter-Reformation" also has an evolving sense and usage. The term was first used in the mid-seventeenth century. It referred to the various attempts of the secular authority to return to traditional Catholic doctrine and practice. Catholic historians tended to reject this use of the term and by the mid-twentieth century were using the term to designate both those efforts of return but also the continuing efforts, dating from the medieval era, to reform ecclesiastical practices. As might be expected, both of these terms continue to evolve with regard to the events and practices to be included and also to the time frame considered.

References

Hillerbrand, Hans J., ed. 1996. *The Oxford Encyclopedia of the Reformation*. New York: Oxford University Press.

Jones, Lindsay, ed. 2005. *Encyclopedia of Religion*, 2nd ed. Detroit: Macmillan Reference USA.

Teresa of Ávila (1515–82)

Siobhán Garrigan

Teresa de Cepeda y Ahumada, who in later life signed herself Teresa de Jesús, and whom we know today as Teresa of Ávila, was born on March 24, 1515. She arrived into a large, loving household headed by her merchant father and her noblewoman mother. They lived in a fine residence with courtyard gardens inside the huge walls of the city of Ávila and were deeply respected in the local community, despite her father's opposition to his neighbors' habit of keeping of slaves. Like the daughters of many wealthy families in Castile, Teresa was taught to read and write (Spanish, but not Latin) and was influenced greatly by the reading material available in the family home. Her mother's collection of what might be termed "light" reading was dominated by tales of the chivalrous deeds of the knights at court and this provided Teresa with her early "damsel" narratives, the acting-out of which resulted in her being boarded in an Augustinian convent by her father from the age of 16 to 18. Her father's collection of devotional and theological books laid the foundations for Teresa's subsequent turn to the religious life, which culminated in her entering a Carmelite convent against her father's wishes at the age of 20 and staying there, apart from treatment for illness or when she was traveling to start up new convents, for the rest of her life. The story of Teresa of Ávila is, then, the story of a nun.

Convents were an enormously important part of the fabric of Spanish society in the sixteenth century, in which gender roles were highly delineated: once a woman reached 15 or so she was expected to marry. If she did not marry, or if she could not marry (for example because she had no dowry), of if she was deemed otherwise troublesome, then she was expected to enter a convent. Inside the convent, life closely mimicked the hierarchies that conditioned all aspects of Castillian life outside the convent: nuns who came from poor families occupied tiny unfurnished cells and performed hard labor, while nuns from noble families had well-furnished suites and spent much of their day entertaining guests. The understanding of "honor" and how it dictates who defers to whom in such a society was a constant guiding ethic, and one that Teresa came to question on theological grounds: by seeing God as being alone worthy of honor, the deference supposedly meant to be accorded from one human being to another was cast as misplaced, if not heretical, God being the only being worthy of honor.

Already, then, in this example of her view of "honor" and her challenge to others to rethink it, we are confronted with the tight weave of ecclesial obedience, reforming drive, theological reflection, and personal testimony that are the complicated hallmark of Teresa's writing. The tricky thing about writing about Teresa as a theologian is that we tend to be trained to discern "the theology" of a theologian and to give some account of their life and times by way of historical context. Teresa defies such a method

The Student's Companion to the Theologians, First Edition. Edited by Ian S. Markham.
© 2013 Blackwell Publishing Ltd. Published 2013 by Blackwell Publishing Ltd.

because her theology is inextricably woven with her biography, by which I mean not the details of her life and times, but her spiritual autobiography: her own narrative account of her relationship with God. As such, Teresa's theological method might be thought to have much in common with that of feminist, womanist, *mujerista*, and other emancipative women's theologies of recent decades, which hold as a central tenet the insistence on one's own experiences as the primary site for the doing of theology. But already we are in trouble, for Teresa was not a feminist in the contemporary sense, and she was keen that her "experiences" not be understood to be in any way primary in her account of her faith. So begins the deeply complex and highly nuanced trail of grasping the theology of Teresa of Ávila in the twenty-first century.

Teresa was a mystical theologian, which means not just that we think of her as a theologian with "mystical" sensibilities (someone who felt extraordinary moments of connection with God and who had visions of Christ throughout her life), but that we are probably best guided in our interpretations of her by understanding her within the specific genre of theological discourse that is known as "mystical theology." Mystical theology is that strand of Christian thinking, built on Platonic principles, that credits direct communication between God and a believer as a significant source of knowledge of God. The mystical theologian gains her knowledge of God not from sustained study of sacred texts (like biblical theologians), nor through the development of speculative argument (systematic or doctrinal theologians), but directly from God. Teresa is adamant that she is making no claim to be a "*letrado*" (a "lettered" sort of theologian, meaning one who could read Latin and engage in discourse about God) and she subtly places herself instead in that lineage of theologians whose knowledge of God was given to them by God, not acquired by their own efforts through study.

So when Teresa says, of seeking God in prayer, that, "All one need do is go into solitude and look at Him within oneself, and not turn away from so good a Guest but with great humility speak to Him as to a father" (*Way of Perfection*, 28: 2), we detect the influence of Augustine on her thought, Augustine's *Confessions* being one of the foundational texts for subsequent mystical theologians. And when, in her *Life*, she sets out a four-part typography of "ascent" (chapters 10–13), we witness her internalization of the classic works of mystical theology by Pseudo-Denys, the central motif of which was tracing the ascent of the soul to God in contemplation. Then, when Teresa identifies the first of those four stages as involving "recollection," we also hear echoes of Osuna and the popular Franciscan discipline of prayer that he is credited with developing in the sixteenth century. While steeped in the stream of medieval mystical theology, Osuna's emphasis on *recogimiento* (recollection) was nevertheless a significant development, both as a method for prayer and as a notion of mystical awareness. Teresa's work, however, although exhibiting Osuna's influence, can also be seen to be correcting its perceived errors, many of its followers (especially its female followers) having been publicly decried in one form or another.

The business of correcting errors was no small matter in Teresa's life and work. Like a double-edged sword, her writing strove both to correct errors in her own and others' perception of her prayer/ministry and to correct errors in the various mystical theologies that were circulating at the time. As such, it reads as both an exceedingly modest (often self-deprecating) account of her thought, which she ardently desires to be in line with the thinking of ecclesial authorities, and, simultaneously, a stringent articulation of the joys of mystical union: thus, "Teresa artfully addresses her discourse to an actual dual audience of confessor and nuns" (Weber, 1990, 86). This was post-Trent Spain and the Inquisition was at the height of its powers of investigation, censorship, and, when it found error, condemnation. All that Teresa did and said, therefore, from her living in community, to her founding of a convent, to her reform of the order, to her spiritual counsel to other nuns, to her writings through the latter part of her life, all of it was done under the scrutiny of both the Inquisition and Spanish high society, which was not shy about informing the Inquisition of its gossip. Confessors and nuns alike were, then, part of a network of watchers: all were watched and watching.

Teresa was especially keen to avoid being seen as an "*alumbrada*" (women who claimed "illumination" by the Holy Spirit for the interpretation of scripture, but were not necessarily cloistered or otherwise obedient to the church), and if she was to be seen as an "*espiritualada*" (which she would prefer not to be, but because of her "spiritual" insights inevitably was), then she wanted it to be with very significant clarifications. Her intentional rebuffs of such potential misperception were overt; but there was also present in her life the covert habit of making sure she was not seen as a "*converso*" (convert). The Inquisition in Teresa's Spain might have had its hands full with supposedly heretical theologians, but it is important to remember that the Inquisition had come to Spain in the first place to make sure that families like Teresa's—Jewish, forced to convert to Christianity—were in fact behaving in a fully Christian way. Teresa would probably not have come under direct scrutiny for this particular aspect of her identity—by his own father's public penance and by marrying a woman of aristocratic birth, her father seems to have secured for his family the perception that they were fully Christian—but it is a very significant aspect of her identity, anti-Semitism being a searing facet of her social context, and thus a part of the general panoply of attacks that Teresa was constantly seeking to prevent.

Just as Teresa did not let the heavy cast of potential and actual critics looking over her shoulder impede her from doing the work she felt called to do, so must we not let this business of the correction of errors and the hefty rhetoric it produces in her writings impede us from grasping the extraordinary freshness and insight of Teresa's theology. Teresa's writings, like the life they describe, are a prolonged meditation on the nature of the incarnation. Specifically, Teresa understood God in Christ Jesus, through the power of the Holy Spirit, to be utterly accessible to mortals and, moreover, wanting nothing more than that we would turn to God and realize our union with God. It is true that Teresa meditated hard on the mystery of the Trinity and had a faithfully Augustinian conceptualization of it, but it is in the conclusions she draws about the incarnational aspects of the Trinity that we find what is distinctive in Teresa's thought. In her most mature book she wrote:

> When the soul is brought into that dwelling place, the Most Blessed Trinity, all three Persons, through an intellectual vision, is revealed to it through a certain representation of the truth. ... the soul understands as a most profound truth that all three Persons are one substance and one power and one knowledge and one God alone. ... Here all three Persons communicate themselves to the soul, speak to it, and explain those words of the Lord in the Gospel: that He and the Father and the Holy

Spirit will come to dwell with the soul that loves Him and keeps His commandments. (*Interior Castle*:VII.1.6)

For Teresa, God is accessible not merely as a creator awaiting the return of her creation, but as the one who can and does draw us into utter union with her: "... whether the experience comes in one way or another, the Lord joins the soul to Himself" (*Interior Castle*:VII.1.5).

Union with God is the key to Teresa's understanding of both the incarnation and our relationship to it. The destination of the "Way of Perfection," just like the apex of the spiral of rooms that compose the "Interior Castle," is not apprehension of the divine, but *union with* the divine. Such union is not something we can accomplish through our own effort, although we do have to create the conditions in which to become aware of it; rather, God makes it happen in us. It is a gift, and one that she recognized as not necessarily given to all, as an earthly experience of altered mood, rapture, or vision, even as it manifested in these ways in her own case. What mattered about such rapturous moments for Teresa was not the sensation of them but that they led to good works ("an increase in virtue"). For Teresa, this was the main criterion for judging that God (and not the devil, or self-delusion) must have been the source of the union because all things genuinely from God, she believed, produce an increase of virtue in their effects. Her understanding of union with the divine has as its premise the notion that God is constantly revealing herself, her will, and her work in the world. And this was a risky notion to elaborate at a time when the Roman Church was imposing the idea that it, and it alone, was the mediator of whatever revelation God might be performing in history.

Union was both the content of her theology (human beings in their purest state are one with God) and a method by which human beings could do theology (although she would not have called her work "doing theology"). While she acknowledged that rapturous union was a gift, and that it was not given to all human beings, it was the state in which she came to know God more fully, and she had ssssdifficulty understanding how others might also gain their knowledge of God, even as she insisted her way was but one way. A modern word for this "union" might be symbiosis. "Union" to our ears connotes the idea that we are "united," that our is-ness is made part of God's is-ness through God's grace; this might come close to what Teresa is saying but it misses a vital ingredient and that is the sense that "symbiosis" conveys: that we are made of the same stuff as God, that humans are part of the biotic being that is God, even as God is also eternally different from and greater than human beings.

What does this have to do with the incarnation? Well, it is in the distinction that it is not that we get to glimpse God in this awareness of union; it is, rather, that we become profoundly aware of our one-ness-of-being with God. It is important here to make explicit what Teresa was not claiming, as well as what she was. It would be easy, for example, to deduce that Teresa was somehow claiming that human beings are on a par with Christ, but she was not making any such claim. Rather, she encourages us to empathize as strongly as possible with Jesus, especially in his suffer-ing, so that we might see our own relation to God through him; and, conversely, so that God can work to love in the world through us, just as she did in Christ. The crux of Teresa's incarnational insight is that God is accessible, meaning God is *directly* acces-sible to any and all of her creatures. Moreover, God is accessible through totally ordinary activities: prayer, Teresa says, should be simply "an intimate conversa-tion between friends"—a chat, if you like.

Somehow, Teresa managed to navigate this territory in such a way as to make her claim and not be condemned by the Inquisition whose job it was to ensure that access to God was sought exclusively through the clerically administered rites of the church. Her main help in doing this was her complete devotion to the Eucharist. Not only did this indicate to her watchers her faithfulness to the church's sacerdotal identity, but it (literally) fed her sense that God desires that we know his utter accessibility—why else would he have given us this way of being fully present to us, of inviting us to come into his presence, on a daily basis? In one of the passages in which her rhetoric is directly addressed to Christ, she asks: "Well, what father could there be, Lord, who having given us his son, and a son like this who receives such treatment, would con-sent that he remain among us every day to suffer? Certainly no father, Lord, but Yours" (*Way* 33.3).

When Teresa here refers to Jesus remaining among us every day, she is speaking of the daily celebration of the Eucharist (which she calls the Blessed Sacrament): she understands God to give Christ every single day, to take on our broken humanity again and again through the sacrament's representation of the cross and resurrection. The Eucharist thus served as both a re-enactment of Jesus' cross and resurrection, with all its atoning grace—a daily reminder of the fact that God takes on our suffering in this world—and, simultaneously, as a "medicine" for our mortal ills. It is with the latter in mind that she argues against the mores of the time for frequent reception of the host: "Certainly I think that if we were to approach the most Blessed Sacrament with great faith and love, once would be enough to leave us rich. How much richer from approaching so many times as we do" (*Song of Songs* 3.13).

One cannot understand this view of our union in Christ with God without understanding the place of the Eucharist in Teresa's life in particular and in medi-eval religious life in general. It was for Teresa, as it was for many others at this time and of this faith, the primary location of encounter with God in the world. God, in Christ, was thought to be actually physically—"substantially"—present in the host. Also, the celebration of the Eucharist was understood as a sacrificial offering: a re-enactment (although that is too weak a word) of Christ's suffering, death, and resurrection—and all the atoning power medieval people understood this sequence to confer—every single time it was offered. Common theology had it that one only received communion once or twice a year because such presence, on the one hand, and such atoning power, on the other, made it too rich to ingest more often—like taking strong medicine, perhaps. However, Teresa longs for the Eucharist (just as she longs for union with God in prayer) and is given per-mission by one of the wiser of her spiritual directors to receive it on a regular basis.

However, when it comes to the incarnation, she makes a distinction between our meeting God in Christ in the Eucharist and the knowledge of God that comes of union: union produces a "certitude remaining in the soul that only God can place there," about which she warns: "Don't be mistaken by think-ing that this certitude has to do with a corporal form, as in the case of the bodily presence of our Lord Jesus Christ in the Most Blessed Sacrament even though we do not see Him. Here the matter isn't like that; it concerns only the divinity" (*Interior Castle* V.1.10 and 11). In union, we are momentarily united with pure divinity without, as we might say today, the mediatory signifier, whereas in the Eucharist, we meet the divine-incarnate through the indispensable corporeal sign. Teresa's incarnational point is common to her approach to both: in both, God comes among us: "He gives from what He has, which is what His Son had in this life. He cannot grant a higher favour" (*Castle* V.2.12.). However, it is important to note the distinction Teresa is making: mental prayer is an "intellectual" union where the Eucharist is a "corporal" one; our challenge is to understand such a distinction in contemporary terms, given that such categories are not current in our ways of thinking today.

Teresa was advocating mental prayer at a time at when it was specifically discouraged by ecclesial authorities that were keen to impose vocal prayer. Mental prayer was the practice of contemplation: turning the mind to God and being open to God's presence in the space thus opened up. Vocal prayer was the recitation of prayers authorized for devotional practices by the Roman Catholic Church (such as the "Our Father" and the "Hail Mary") and the prescription of this style of prayer at the expense of all others was one way in which the Tridentine church was trying to establish absolute control over people's spiritual lives. Teresa herself was adept at vocal prayer and her extraordinary, line-by-line, theological meditations on the "Our Father" manifest her mature internalization of the prayer and demonstrate how utterly she incorporated the prayers of the church into her own prayer life. At the same time, the mere recitation of such prayer forms was not enough for her and she saw no reason not to also contemplate in her prayer, and to develop the habit of mental prayer, as had so many in the tradition of mystical theology before her. Besides, she refused to see the distinction that the Inquisitors saw: "But I tell you that surely I don't know how mental prayer can be separated from vocal prayer if the vocal prayer is to be recited well with an understanding of whom we are speaking to" (*Way* 24: 6).

As time went on, her writings advocated more and more strongly for contemplation. Contemplation, in Teresa's view, is both a simple and a complicated thing: simple in that it involves just coming before God in

prayer and talking directly to her, not needing to be perfect before doing so, but rather bringing all that one is, awkwardly before God and letting her do the rest ("we have no part to play in bringing it about no matter how much effort we put forth"); complicated in that, being human, all sorts of distractions and delusions make doing such a simple thing in actual fact quite difficult. It would be a mistake, however, to interpret Teresa's many how-to advices on mental prayer as being just about sitting in a bare room with your eyes closed. On the contrary, she believed that books were extremely helpful as an aid for prayer, and part of the reason she herself started writing in the first place was so that her nuns would have the sorts of reading material that she felt so vital to prayer. Although Teresa always says that she is only writing because she has been told to do so (implying by church authorities, although it is debatable whether this was the case), she also tells us in her first book, her *Life*, that she found getting going in prayer almost impossible without a book to help her focus her mind, and in her later work she admits that she is writing as "teaching" for her nuns because she wants them to have the literature they need to do their main work, which she understood to be prayer. The reason they were lacking in such was that the church, through the second half of her life, had been gradually undermining the production of materials in the vernacular that had been such an important influence on Teresa's young life. This movement culminated in the *Valdez Index of Prohibited Books* in 1559, a church–state edict against the owning or reading of nearly all devotional and theological books in the vernacular. Thousands of books previously used for prayer and devotion had to be destroyed and because only books in Latin, about dogma, were allowed, women (who were not allowed to study Latin or dogma) were squeezed out as authors.

Simply reciting prayers was not going to provide the prayer power that Teresa envisaged as being needed to counter the evils of the world. And make no mistake, Teresa's campaign for mental prayer was not fueled by the hope that her nuns would have wonderful personal life-enriching experiences; on the contrary, its goal was outward. Teresa's ardent desire for communities of women grounded in mature and fervent practices of mental prayer did not have an aesthetic or psychological goal or purpose; rather, she believed that such prayer was a vital force for good in the world, a conduit through which God's work could be accomplished on earth. Prayer accomplished this by obliterating opportunities for the devil to do his work—by the self-knowledge mental prayer inculcated in the individual, and by the increase in love it wrought in communities. Teresa's method of prayer was in a sense a "grass roots" movement, in that it was based on the idea that if enough individuals and enough small communities put things right in their own lives, the whole world could change. Modern readers may be surprised that while describing this power-to-change, Teresa makes so very many references to the devil; this is because, like her contemporaries, she saw the devil as a very real and active force in daily life, whose determination to sabotage individuals' efforts at prayer was one of his main ways of ensuring the persistence of evil in the world.

Prayer was also the means by which Teresa thought her nuns could participate (lead, even) in the missionary endeavors of the church of the day. Teresa supported these so completely that we might dare to characterize her as a missionary theologian. Teresa's notion that women might not be able to travel but could nonetheless play a role in the missions, through prayer, was a bold one. But it was not just through prayer that we see Teresa the missioner. In her establishment of many new convents, each run according to a renovated Carmelite rule, we can perhaps detect in microcosm the colonizing drive that was so much a characteristic of Spain in her day. We remember nationalist colonizing efforts with such criticism that it is hard to remember also, as we must if we are to understand Teresa's theology, that she ardently believed that were the colonizers not to baptize the whole of the earth, all those souls would be condemned eternally to hell. It was, for her, as for her Christian contemporaries, an urgent matter, a matter of life and death, of literally saving the world, as well as a compassionate and self-sacrificing effort on the part of the missioners. She absolutely did not see, as we do, that such missions often served imperial economic purposes and caused absolute and horrific harm to so many of the peoples of South America and elsewhere. Spreading the true Word, whether through reform of religious life in Spain, or through the baptizing of lost

souls in South America, was an act of Christian witness, not colonial self-serving, in Teresa's mind.

Her missionary ethic also provided the lens through which she prayed about Martin Luther and his followers. She thought Luther to be utterly mistaken, even as it is highly unlikely she ever read anything he had written, and she saw the work of her nuns' prayer as helping to rid the world of what she saw as his scourge. History casts such an opinion as acutely ironic, given the similarities we now see between the two theologians. They shared, "a profound hostility to scholastic theology in itself; a reverence for the tradition of passive abandonment to God in 'mystical' prayer; a suspicion of externals, both the busy habits of piety and the attempt to secure God's favour by amassing a record of virtuous deeds; and a confidence in the possibility of hidden, interior, transformation by grace" (Williams, 1991, 37).

They were also both, of course, ecclesial reformers—people of intense faith, raised in the Western Christian church who, in desiring their beloved church communities to become more truly faithful, to return to the way of life to which they were originally called, led a campaign of measures to improve things. Like Luther, Teresa's reforming passion stemmed not from managerial efficiency or strategic improvement as values in themselves, but from the acute theological insight that came to her through her prayer. It is for this reason that she is increasingly recognized as being part of a "reformation" and not the "counter-reformation" in Christian history. In Teresa's case, the object of her reforming concern was the lifestyle of those living in religious orders. She felt that the Carmelite communities had become lax in their observance of the rule upon which their common life had been founded, and the changes she made in the 17 convents that she started before she died set about correcting the error of what had become standard ecclesial practice.

Perhaps the most radical characteristic of Teresa's convents was that they were not endowed. The norm at the time was that a convent could only be created if a wealthy benefactor put up a large sum of money to underwrite the venture. Teresa perceived this system as having led to all sorts of abuses (such as the benefactor making too many social or prayer requests of the nuns, or nuns who were friends of the benefactor living in relative luxury while nuns from less well-connected families suffered malnutrition) and so she insisted that each of her convents be free of endowment, so that the "poverty" to which they vowed themselves as Carmelites (a mendicant order) could be fully embraced and so that the community in which they were situated knew that the nuns were there to serve all, and not just some, of its people. Her nuns wore wooden or leather sandals instead of shoes (hence the name "discalced" Carmelites); they wore habits that Teresa designed to indicate a greater separation from the world and a simple life; and she insisted on far more disciplined practices of silence, prayer, and rigorous spiritual direction as the daily rhythm of community life.

It is in her very practical instructions about the details of community life that we gain perhaps the most insight into Teresa's theology, because it is a staggeringly communitarian theology. "[W]hat the first eighteen or so chapters of the *Way* show us is that in fact the radical exposure to God's will involved in praying seriously is not separable from the structure of the life in which such exposure is made possible" (Williams, 1991, 113). This is easy for the modern reader to miss, because so much of Teresa's writing is about the journey of the soul to God, and we find it almost impossible to conceive of the soul except as a radically individual thing. However, it is vital to understand that the journey of the soul is impossible without the precondition of daily chores, constant self-examination of one's mood in relation to others, attendance at Mass, arguments with one's sisters, common meal-taking, mental prayer, seriousness about one's duties to family and friends, care for one's health, and so forth. God meets our souls in no other context than these, the round of mental and physical activities that comprise day-to-day life in community. Should we fall into isolation, she warns, we will become depressed and it will be very hard to encounter God. Should we neglect our duties, we fall away from the vital connection to God that responsibility affords in our lives. And should we neglect our friendships, or engage in unhealthy friendships, we fall into spiritual danger.

Friendship is one of the most important components of Teresa's vision of community life and one of the most compelling images in her theology. Reacting against the large convents that were becoming the norm, she mandates that her reformed communities should be small, with a maximum of 13 people, in order to facilitate friendship between each and every member. This stemmed from her understanding that community life is impossible if people are merely putting up with one another; on the contrary, for community to exist, its members have to actually love one another, care for one another, and share the trials and joys of day-to-day life with one another. Such a vision accords with her sense that community life is the "living book" that God gives us as the mechanism by which we can come to know God in this world; and it also accords with her belief, born of experience, that strained human relationships are the most profound obstacle to relationship with God.

Teresa had a remarkable number of close and complex relationships in her lifetime, the correspondence from which is some of the most interesting literature in the theological library. Some of her most intense friendships were with other people whom we remember as spiritual leaders and theologians in the church, especially John of the Cross and Jerónimo Gracián. But she also had intimate and long friendships with people whose names are not always known to us, and her writings display the very developed degree to which she had reflected upon these. Consequently, Teresa can give extremely practical and specific advice about what to avoid and what to cultivate in friendships. For example, she argues hard against "excessive love" in friendships (by which means just being too attached to another single individual) because of its effect on the individual—"it takes away the strength of will to be totally occupied in loving God"—and because of its effect on the community: "It gives rise to the following: failing to love equally all the others; feeling sorry about any affront to the friend; desiring possessions so as to give her gifts; looking for time to speak with her, and often so as to tell her that you hold her dear and other trifling things rather than about your love for God. For these great friendships are seldom directed toward helping one love God more" (*Way* 4: 6).

A certain play between the themes of interpersonal friendship and human–divine friendship permeates much of Teresa's theology. Mental prayer is "friendship with God" and Teresa speaks about and to God with the same ease and intensity that she speaks about and to her mortal friends. She relied on her human friends to help her interpret her friendship with God, and she relied on her friendship with God to make sense of the web of desires she felt regarding other people. She sees mental prayer not as "cultivating" friendship with God, but as allowing the soul to participate in the friendship that God so earnestly desires to have with it and the concomitant love God so wholly desires to thereby create among people. For Teresa, God is the "One who with so much love wanted to be their friend and proved it by deeds" (*Castle* IV 3:10)—and she warns that those who fall away from the discipline of mental prayer greatly endanger themselves precisely because it is this desire on God's part, this friendship with God, that they are refusing. Her own experiences—God's "deeds" in her life—had convinced her that nothing could be worse in life, nothing could separate us more from others or ourselves, than to have fallen out with God.

I have deliberately left mention of Teresa's "experiences" until the end. Her levitations, locutions, premonitions, visions of Christ (and corresponding intense sensations of pain or ecstasy), and her recurring encounter with a cherub who pierces her heart with a golden spear are what Teresa is often known for. They are also what cause commentators nowadays to speculate about Teresa's mental health: Was she anorexic? Were her visions the product of mania? Was she bipolar? And so on. I have delayed mention of such phenomena, and the questions they raise, in order to relativize their importance because Teresa's behavior is deemed so strange in today's world that a focus upon it can undermine, obscure, or even distort the theological insights that also need to be noted. In summary, "the distinctiveness and contemporary relevance of mediaeval mysticism lies precisely in its rejection of 'mystical experience,' and locates the mystical firmly within the grasp of the ordinary and the every day" (Turner, 1995, i), and so our inclination to focus upon her "experiences" as if they were unusual or phenomenal needs to be undercut by an attentiveness to her context, on the one hand, and her constructive theological conclusions, on the other. Teresa herself was keen to point out to those who tried to make strange her experiences, that she was not encountering or inventing anything new: everything she professes accords with orthodox accounts of the record of Christian revelation. Unlike

other women mystics who claimed to have been given new revelation for the church, for Teresa, "a locution bears the credentials of being from God if it accords with the teachings of Sacred Scripture"—by which she meant, the teachings of the church.

However, her experiences were exceptional even for her own day, and they were a hugely important source of insight and inspiration for Teresa. In later life she worried that the intense fervors experienced by her nuns during mental prayer could mimic or even bring on illness and, not being one to romanticize illness, this caused her considerable distress. Teresa was aware that illness could undo human beings, even as, in her own case, she had always plumbed its depths for the reassurance of God's presence and God's word that she also believed could be found there. From her first long period of devastating illness in her early twenties to her last, which took her out of this world on October 4, 1582 at the convent at Alba de Tormes, in sickness and in health, her life-work was, in effect, a protracted meditation on the insight that God meets us in our suffering.

The little girl whose parents immersed her in stories of the lives of the saints, who as a seven-year-old ran away with one of her brothers hoping to be martyred by the Moors and thus become a saint, (she only reached just outside the city walls before her uncle spotted them and brought them home), grew up to be a nun who lived a life of such extraordinary saintliness that she was canonized less than 40 years after her death, which is to say, remarkably quickly, especially for someone upon whom the Inquisition had kept such a close eye. Canonization is a political business; it values some things while ignoring others. At the time of her beatification Teresa was, like so many other female saints of the period, praised for her "purity, passivity and social-withdrawal," proving the success of her self-presentation as possessing the two vital virtues (for women) of "humility and obedience" (Ahlgren, 1996, 23). And where she was recognized as having contributed something of theological value, it was emphasized that this was because God enabled her to transcend her gender, only men being thought capable of intellectual endeavors.

In our times, Teresa's theological insight, her political acumen, her sheer tenacity (she successfully petitioned King Philip to persuade the Inquisition to stop persecuting John of the Cross!), her self-awareness, her vision of community life as the realm of God in microcosm, her love of the church, her realism about human relationships, and perhaps mostly her sense of the close friendship offered by God, all inform our sense of her as a saint, a person whose life and witness point to God in our world. In 1969 the Roman Catholic magisterium named her one of its "Doctors of the Church," the first woman so named. It is most important, then, when we turn to Teresa for her theology that we remain conscious of this central fact: she was a woman. With thinly veiled disgust for the misogyny of the church of her own day she wrote the following; one can only speculate as to what she might say on learning that at the turn of the twenty-first century she remains one of only three women named "Doctors" by her Church:

When you walked on this earth, Lord, you did not despise women; rather you always helped them and showed great compassion towards them. And you found as much love and more faith in them than you did in men … Is it not enough, Lord, that the world has intimidated us so that we may not do anything worthwhile for you in public or dare to speak some truths that we lament over in secret, without your also failing to hear our just petition? I do not believe, Lord, that this could be true of your goodness and justice, for you are a just judge and not like those of the world. Since the world's judges are sons of Adam and all of them men, there is no virtue in women that they do not hold suspect … when I see what the times are like, I feel it is not right to repel spirits which are virtuous and brave, even though they be the spirits of women. (From the *Way*, in du Boulay, 1991, 143)

References

Ahlgren, Gillian T. W. 1996. *Teresa of Avila and the Politics of Sanctity*. Ithaca, NY: Cornell University Press.

du Boulay, Shirley. 1991. *Teresa of Avila*. London: Hodder and Stoughton.

Teresa of Avila, *Life*, *The Way of Perfection*, *Meditations on the Song of Songs*, and *The Interior Castle*, all quoted from the translation by Otilio Rodriguez and Kieran Kavanaugh. 1980. *The Collected Works of St. Teresa of Avila*, vols. I–III. Washington DC: ICS Publications.

Turner, Denys. 1995. *The Darkness of God: Negativity in Christian Mysticism*. Cambridge: Cambridge University Press.

Weber, Alison. 1990. *Teresa of Avila and the Rhetoric of Femininity*. Princeton, NJ: Princeton University Press.

Williams, Rowan. 1991. *Teresa of Avila*. London: Continuum.

Enlightenment and Modern Period

Donald Baillie (1887–1954)

George Newlands

I. The Early Years

Donald Baillie was born on November 5, 1887, 18 months after his brother John, also to become a distinguished theologian. From Inverness Royal Academy, Donald went on to a First in philosophy at Edinburgh and an assistantship in the philosophy department. He studied theology in Edinburgh, Marburg, and Heidelberg, and after a brief period with the YMCA in France, was inducted at the parish of Bervie in 1918.

The Bervie period saw the publication of Schleiermacher's *The Christian Faith in Outline* in 1922. When the full *Christian Faith* was published in translation in 1927, the first 32 paragraphs were translated by Donald. In 1920 he had published an article in *The Expositor* entitled "What Is the Theology of Experience?" based on Schleiermacher and critical of James and Russell.

In 1923 he moved to St John's, Cupar, and thence to Kilmacolm and eventually to St Andrews University. Throughout his life people testified to Donald's sense of humor and his great capacity for building friendships. He was said to be a man with no enemies.

II. Faith in God

The year 1927 saw the publication of *Faith in God and Its Christian Consummation*, based on Kerr Lectures delivered in Glasgow. The book was concerned, like all Donald's work, with the relation between faith and experience. Faith, experience, and practice are integrally related. The book was of first-rate quality, but the thesis about the relation between faith and morality was very controversial, then and now. After much criticism, his basic argument has become more popular again in recent writing. It can be said that Donald's name was not well known until the appearance of *God Was in Christ* 20 years later.

Part I sets out from a chapter on faith, authority, and reason. Faith is not dependent on custom, authority, or suggestion. It is not dependent, either, on reason or philosophy. On the contrary, it is now seen that philosophy is dependent on faith. Faith is "reason's highest exercise." It is often held that faith is based upon religious experience (Schleiermacher)—but belief and religious experience are the same thing; or that faith is based on an empirical psychological investigation of the religious experience of mankind (James)—but this is not faith's own testimony. Empirical psychology has a real though limited value in assessing belief. There is a revolt against experience in Brunner and Barth, which is of some value if not overdone.

The will to believe is impossible. Faith has to be waited for as a gift from God. But James has taught us that faith is somehow conditioned by the will. The next chapter covers faith and moral conviction. The way out of doubt to faith is by the moral consciousness. If morality means anything, it ultimately means God. Good men have an unconscious

The Student's Companion to the Theologians, First Edition. Edited by Ian S. Markham.
© 2013 Blackwell Publishing Ltd. Published 2013 by Blackwell Publishing Ltd.

faith—this is the religious a priori. Tyrell and others are adduced in parallel: "True spiritual religion is a development, not of magical religion, but of the moral life." Morality without religion is meaningless.

The last section of Part I is entitled "Faith and the Knowledge of God." This chapter deals with objections that the account given is too irrational—religion in fact arises from fear; but that is not true. Religion is more than morality, but not separate from morality.

Part II is entitled explicitly "Christian Faith." How is faith related to history? "The historical fact of Jesus becomes certain to us in kindling our faith in God." This is faith in God through Jesus Christ. "The object of Christian faith is neither God apart from Christ, nor God and Christ, but God in Christ."

We come to "Faith and the Gospel of Jesus." There is much recent concern with faith healing. In fact "suffering, nobly borne, has a peculiarly refining influence on character." It can be accepted in faith as part of "the mysterious discipline of pain" (p. 290). "Thus the cross of Christ became for all time the supreme example of God's paradox." He ends with these lines, which in many ways encapsulate his whole understanding of the Christian life:

We must be neither too impatient of antinomy nor too tolerant of it, if we are to advance to a clearer understanding of the deep Christian secret. Yet it is not altogether by thinking the matter out, but by living it out in daily Christian faith and love, that we shall arrive at a deeper insight in which the paradox will be less acute. And a book about hope cannot end better than upon this note of hope and expectation (p. 308).

In 1930 Donald left Cupar and moved to moved to Kilmacolm. In 1934 he became Professor of Systematic Theology in the University of St Andrews. Though he had done academic work, he had not worked in an academic context before. This pattern was not untypical before the advent of the modern career structure of lecturer to professor; the scholar/minister brought his parish experience to academic life and the education of the ministers of the future.

III.   A Preaching Ministry

Much of Donald's literary legacy consists of unpublished sermons—often models of theological refinement and literary art. Donald had political views, notably on the need for social justice, in relation to the miners' strike. But the sermons are concerned largely with individual faith and morality. Though Donald knew Niebuhr, there is little on the complexity of the modern industrial world, the grey areas of *Moral Man and Immoral Society*. His world was largely that of the small town and the university in delightful rural settings. From St Andrews he was often at Swanwick, at Student Christian Movement (SCM) conferences. He was involved in much discussion with student groups—this in some ways was his great strength.

IV.   The Later 1930s

The year 1935 saw him in Germany, leaving St Andrews on July 31 on a nostalgic journey via Cologne to Marburg, during which he appears, as we shall see later, to have attempted to liaise with members of the Confessing church and to find out what was going on. On July 26 there is a letter from Rudolf Bultmann, thanking him for his hospitality in St Andrews and looking forward to seeing him in Marburg. There is a postcard from Marburg on August 7. By August 9 Donald is writing from the Hospiz St Michael, Wilhelmstrasse 34, Berlin. He has come from Marburg and a stay with the Bultmanns. Of the Bultmanns he writes that "he and his wife were kindness itself" and contributes a poem to their visitors' book: Bultmann arranged for him to meet Von Soden, Hermelink, and Frank, who was Paul Natorp's successor. "It is somewhat thrilling to be in Berlin, and I'm looking forward to exploring it—seeing such legendary places as Unter den Linden, and the Brandenburger Tor and the Tiergarten." On September 19, replying to a letter from John written from Hohenschwangau, he mentions a service in the Old Catholic Church in Heidelberg: "But at several points the priest had to pause for quite a time owing to the deafening noise made by brownshirts marching outside … He was about as pro-Nazi as anybody I met in Germany." He adds: "I hope you are enjoying Munich, Nuremberg, Wurzburg and Brussels."

The year 1936 was to be eventful. In the 1930s he was much involved in SCM work in Scotland and England. He travelled to Marseilles, and represented the church at the Geneva celebrations of the Reformation and at the Faith and Order Committee in Lausanne. On May 8 he has a conversation in Lausanne with Tillich. Tillich thinks the Germans very pro-Nazi. Donald is not so sure, from conversations in Berlin, Marburg, and Munich. Writing on May 26 from Lausanne, he says that the Nazis are acceptable to some in Germany because they saved Germany from communism. "I was thinking last night that it is extraordinarily difficult for anyone living on the Continent just now to be other than pessimistic." By September 12 he is writing from St Andrews: "I think I am very much the better of my five and a half months away from Scotland … I'm much interested to hear that you visited Niemoeller in Dahlem. I've read more than a third of Barth's Word of God in English. It really is a terrible book."

In 1938 Donald was again on the Continent. A postcard from Berlin on August 27 comments: "Last night at Frau N's house. Lunch today at home of As [mussen]. I've learned a very great deal about things." In a note from Karlsruhe on the 29th he says that he had spent a fortnight in 1910 "bei Fraulein Zeiss" in Jena. "I am now more convinced that criticism and discontent are far more widespread and acute than ever." He then he travels to Geneva, spends a few days in Heidelberg and is back home on September 6. On the 10th he writes: "I have on my mantelpiece a beautiful photo of Niemoeller that his wife gave me." On March 18 he had written to John about, "Non Aryans who are hoping to come to Edinburgh."

V. 1939–54

Donald and John remained very close, not least on social issues. On November 18, 1941 he reminds John of the need to stress more of the social challenge of the gospel than he has done to date. On May 12, 1943 he made a broadcast in German on "Die Hoffnung des Evangeliums," in a very eirenic tone. This continues—Donald to John, November 12, 1944: "It seems to me that public utterances are getting foolisher than ever about 'what to do with Germany' and with hardly a voice raised against them, except that of the Bishop of Chichester (who has perhaps spoilt his chances of succeeding at Canterbury by his brave utterances)."

In 1946 Donald was chairman of the Communion and Intercommunion section of the preparatory committee for Amsterdam. He was prepared to speak when necessary in the General Assembly of the Church of Scotland. On May 26, 1946 he seconded an amendment to a motion by his friend Nevile Davidson to limit the spread of the atom bomb: "To have any bombs already made dismantled … would have an immense effect on international affairs." The motion was defeated.

The year 1948 brought his masterly *God Was in Christ*. The American response was very positive. There is a good review in *Time* of August 23, 1948. On October 20 James McCord wrote to Scribners (with a view to an American edition) that, "In every respect I believe that it is the most significant book in the field of christology, at least for a decade."

Pit Van Dusen called it, "incomparably the most satisfactory interpretation of the person of Christ published in this century" (in *Christianity and Crisis*, December 25, 1950). *God Was in Christ* was completed in July 1947, but includes material from 1942 and reflects a theme on which Donald had been working for many years before. It was beautifully and clearly written. And for many people it struck just the right note in christology. It defended historical criticism. It preserved the mystery of the incarnation in the tradition, under the banner of paradox.

The first section of chapter 1, on the end of Docetism, firmly settles for the centrality of Jesus' full humanity. The case is substantiated in the next chapter. But more is necessary. Why a christology? (chapter 3). "We shall never do justice to the love of God if we leave out the supreme paradox of the Incarnation … A true Christology will tell us not simply that God is like Christ, but that God was in Christ" (pp. 65f.). Christology is a check on modern misinterpretations of history.

Chapter 4 offers a critique of christologies— anhypostasia, kenosis, leadership, and lordship. We might wonder if he would have found in Rahner a view of kenosis very similar to his own outlook— God is the one for whom to be is to give oneself away to others—but that was not then available. His own favored concept was of course paradox (chapter 5). We have seen that he had spoken of paradox years earlier. The fundamental paradox in Christian life is

"Not I, but the grace of God" (p. 122): this is a reflection of the incarnate Christ. A toned-down christology is absurd. "It must be all or nothing—all or nothing on both the human and the divine side" (p. 132). This was the vision which Donald pursued, sometimes painfully but always unswervingly, in his own life.

Chapter 6 develops the Godward side of incarnation, in a chapter on incarnation and Trinity. A succinct discussion of Barth and Hodgson leads to reappraisal. Experience of grace is experience of God, Father, Son, and Spirit. Trinity is central to faith and devotion. But Christian experience is not neutral. It is rooted in the framework of sin, forgiveness, and reconciliation, hence atonement (chapter 7). People may lack a sense of sin, yet suffer from all sorts of mental complexes. They are looking for acceptance, by themselves and others. In addition, our actions often hurt others. Reconciliation in depth is costly—hence the cross, and (the next chapter) the Lamb of God. The death of Jesus shows the essential nature of God's love. Atonement is both objective and subjective. Atonement renders the incarnation comprehensible to us, through the forgiveness of our sins. A short epilogue on the body of Christ stresses the importance of Christian community: a society of sinners forgiven becomes the nucleus of a new humanity.

Karl Barth was to raise a question about a central area of the book in his *Church Dogmatics* (KD 4.2.60, (1955) = CD 4.2.55–6):

> As he sees it, a text like Gal. 2.20, "Nevertheless I live; yet not I, but Christ liveth in me," is not merely a statement about the being of the apostle or the Christian, but it offers a *schema* for the knowledge of Jesus Christ himself ... And somewhere along this way the question will always arise whether the relationship between the *unio hypostatica* and the *unio mystica* may not be reversed; whether it is better reversed, whether the *unio mystica* is not to be understood as the true and basic phenomenon ... and the *unio hypostatica* as the secondary ... the representation or mythological copy of the religious happening as it takes place in us.

From Barth's perspective this was the Achilles heel of religious neo-Protestantism yet again. But Baillie too had reservations about aspects of mysticism, and might perhaps have responded that the faith-creating presence of God is as objective as anything in the created order, while the Chalcedonian formula is as much a cultural construction as it is a revealed blueprint of the divine nature. All our concepts remain limited eschatological suggestions, as Barth once famously put it.

The year 1950 brought the publication of *David Cairns: An Autobiography*. The "Memoir" contributed by Donald in some ways echoes his own life. The great man had serious doubts and imperfect health: "Again I have a vivid snapshot of myself standing beneath a flaring gas-jet in my bedroom in Lonsdale Terrace, absolutely dismayed ... I remember how cold the starlight seemed on those winter nights" (pp. 10–11).

VI.   Theology of the Sacraments

This book (1957) is the posthumously published course of Moore Lectures delivered in San Anselmo, California in 1952. The introductory chapter explores "Sacrament, Nature and Grace." Today there is a rediscovery of biblical theology, and it would be good to have a rediscovery of the sacraments. The word is important. But ours is a sacramental universe, and sacraments operate through human faith. We then come to "The Sacraments and Sacred History." What can we say of the dominical institution of the sacraments? They go back "right into the life and ministry of Jesus." There is a continuity between the incarnation and the sacraments. They also have an eschatological reference, pointing forward to the Kingdom.

We come to "The Sacrament of Baptism." There is a connection between the ministry of Jesus and a baptismal rite of repentance and cleansing and initiation (1957, 77). In baptism children are brought into a new environment. God's initiative precedes our faith (89).

Chapter 4, "The Real Presence," goes back again to the Highland communion season. "The most objective and penetrating kind of presence that God can give us is through faith." The feast is a memorial feast but it is also more. The fifth chapter deals with "The Eucharistic Offering." All our worship is an offering to God, in which we offer ourselves, but "we can only make an offering in union with Christ's eternal sacrifice" (116). This involves the whole church. "May it not be that both the doctrine of the Real Presence and the doctrine of the eucharistic offering, begin to come right and to take their true shape when they are controlled by the idea of the sacrament as a corporate act of the one body of Christ?" (124). In dealing with the sacraments he starts out, as often, from human nature and human experience. On the Trinity, too, he affirms that, "the main truth is that the doctrine is based on history and experience."

Something should be said here of John's biographical essay on Donald at the beginning of the *Theology of the Sacraments*. A main theme of the essay is that "Donald especially was from an early age haunted with religious doubts. The strain on his spirit was acute. His only confidante was his mother" (15). Stress and depression often reappeared. He suffered from chronic asthma. "He would put to himself and to me the question as to whether the extreme bodily lassitude was the cause or the result, or merely the accompaniment, of the darkness of soul" (21). The other side of all this was his charm and generosity, the "gentleness, wit and piety" of which his pupils were so often to speak, the "I yet not I" of the paradox of grace which he so profoundly instantiated in his own person. Donald would appear to have been one of those highly talented individuals for whom great achievement is linked inexorably with suffering. The deep shadow of the Calvinist culture in which he was brought up was perhaps a burden that alternately stimulated and crushed his creativity.

VII.   What Is the Church?

Donald's commitment to ecumenical causes was deep, but it was not uncritical. At the General Assembly of 1953 Donald presented the report of the Inter-Church Relations Committee. He stressed that the ecumenical movement was increasingly important, though still in its infancy. The task of the church regarding refugees (an old concern of Donald's) was still very important. There was a need for more study of christology and ecclesiology, "because it was by going deeper that the Christian churches came nearer to each other in Christ."

Donald Baillie died in October, 1954. C. B. Ketcham, an American graduate student, wrote in a letter: "We came expecting to be impressed, but we were overawed. We came expecting to be friends, but we were loved. Great men and great scholars may come to St Mary's College, but no man can ever take his place in our hearts" (Baillie Papers, University of Edinburgh).

The German translation of *God Was in Christ* appeared in 1954. Rudolf Bultmann wrote to John on December 27, 1954: "Es ist das bedeutenste Buch unserere Zeit ueber das Thema der Christologie. Zu dieser Interpretation, das ich in meiner Terminologie also 'existentiale' bezeichnen moechte, fuehle ich mich tief mit ihm verbunden und reich gefoerdert" (It is the most significant book of our time on the subject of Christology. I feel myself deeply identified with and richly encouraged by this interpretation, which I might call in my terminology "existential.")

VIII.   The Sermons

Donald gained a reputation for being an outstanding preacher, yet he never published his own sermons. His sermons, rather like Newman's, tended to be concerned for the individual in concern for other individuals. *To Whom Shall We Go?* was published in Edinburgh in 1955. *Out of Nazareth* appeared in 1958. Another area to which Donald gave much attention was prayer. This dimension lent a stability and a catholicity to his work which was a source of theological freedom.

IX.   Conclusion

Taking as a whole the testimony of written and oral evidence, it would seem that if twentieth-century Presbyterians could be saints, Donald Baillie came about as close as anyone to that category. He seems to have been universally liked and respected, loved by many. His friendship was hugely valued by those who knew him best. He was modest, genuinely humble, intellectually brilliant. He was imaginative—perhaps sometimes too much so for his own good. He was certainly a man of flesh and blood, sometimes frustrated, angry about what he regarded as unfair practices, with distinctive theological and political views. He struggled against debilitating illness for most of his life. He devoted himself to others—to his mother, to his congregations, to his students—in ways which might not always have been in his own best interest. His published work was neither voluminous nor encyclopedic in its range, nor even always strikingly original. It was always perceptive, judicious, creative. It represented an open Christian faith which sought inclusivity and hospitality, which recognized weakness and suffering for what they are, and pointed to faith and love as ways of coping with any circumstances.

References

Baillie, Donald. 1927. *Faith in God and Its Christian Consummation*. Edinburgh: T&T Clark.

Baillie, Donald. 1948. *God Was in Christ*. London: Faber and Faber.

Baillie, Donald. 1955. *To Whom Shall We Go?* Edinburgh: Saint Andrews Press.

Baillie, Donald. 1957. *Theology of the Sacraments*. London: Faber.

Baillie, Donald. 1958. *Out of Nazareth*. Edinburgh: Saint Andrews Press.

Cairns, David. 1950. *David Cairns: An Autobiography*. London: SCM Press.

John Baillie (1886–1960)

George Newlands

John Baillie, theologian and Church of Scotland minister, was born on March 26, 1886 in the Free Church manse at Gairloch, Scotland, the eldest of the three sons of John Baillie, Free Church of Scotland minister, and his wife, Annie Macpherson. John and his brother Donald were among the most distinguished Scottish theologians of the modern era. Although Baillie later recalled "a rigorously Calvinistic upbringing," mainly by his mother, who was soon widowed, there were also liberal strands in Free Church culture and a huge respect for learning, which drove the brothers through brilliant academic careers at Inverness Royal Academy and at the University of Edinburgh, both graduating with firsts in philosophy and distinction in divinity. John Baillie spent the summer terms of 1909 and 1911 at the universities of Jena and Marburg, respectively. For a short time assistants in the philosophy department, the brothers spent time in the YMCA in France during World War I.

In April 1919 Baillie married Florence Jewel Fowler and moved to Auburn Theological Seminary in New York State; he was ordained in the Presbyterian church there in 1920. Their only child, Ian Fowler Baillie, was born in 1921. *The Roots of Religion in the Human Soul* appeared in 1926 and *The Interpretation of Religion* in 1929. These books reflected wide cultural and theological experience from the manse in Gairloch to American society—the latter's poetry and politics, the polarization of church politics in the fundamentalist

debate, as well as participation in conferences on the social gospel in the early 1920s. Baillie moved in 1927 to Emmanuel College, Toronto, in the newly formed United Church of Canada. His wife was suffering from tuberculosis during much of the 1920s, and was in sanatoria between 1923 and 1930.

In 1930 he moved back to the Union Theological Seminary in New York, then arguably the world's greatest theological seminary. It provided a forum for theology where, along with Henry Sloane Coffin, Reinhold Niebuhr, and Pitney Van Dusen, he was to have a major impact on Western theology for the next two decades. Though Baillie returned to Edinburgh in 1934, the four men exerted huge influence on the new World Council of Churches. They agreed on a *via media* between extreme liberalism on the one hand, and a narrow Barthianism on the other. Baillie was professor of divinity at Edinburgh University from 1934 to 1956. He also served as Principal of New College, Edinburgh, and dean of the faculty of divinity (1950–6).

We shall now look at John's writings in the 1920s.

The Roots of Religion in the Human Soul (1926)

The preface mentions the influence of the volume *The Army and Religion*, edited by D. S. Cairns and E. S. Talbot. The soldiers' charge against the church

The Student's Companion to the Theologians, First Edition. Edited by Ian S. Markham.
© 2013 Blackwell Publishing Ltd. Published 2013 by Blackwell Publishing Ltd.

was that: "There is a lack of reality about the religion of the Christian Church, and a conspicuous unrelatedness to the real problems of human life" (p. 12). Baillie offers appreciation of Schleiermacher. There is no mention yet of Barth. Something is happening to religion: something new, something momentous.

Men in war faced enormous horror. They were thrown back upon the roots of their being and there was in consequence "a most remarkable and hardly-to-be-exaggerated sense for reality and for the difference between reality and sham." The average man admires moral virtues—deeds not belief. "They were living Christianity without realising it" (p. 31). Philosophical speculation offers no consensus. Religion is too vital to be an academic speculation.

Religion is more than morality. Pringle-Pattison is quoted: "the worship of the ideal conceived as the eternally real." Here is trust in eternal goodness. The essence of Kant is explored (p. 125). Religious faith as "trust in the promise of the moral law." The importance of both Schleiermacher and Kant is stressed. "It is now impossible to mention any religion that is regarded by the historians as a unit clearly separable from the rest of world-religion" (p. 141). As for Christianity, "it is just religion itself, religion at its best and widest."

Chapter 5 is devoted to "How Faith Arises in the Soul." First, there is a sense of duty—"To believe in God is, at least in its beginnings, hardly more than a deeper way of believing in duty" (p. 221). Moral argument for God has some value. Man finds God in his values (p. 240). If we love one another, God dwelleth in us. Incarnation is the ultimate clue. One great strength of this book was its freshness. It communicated a sense of urgency, of approach to a number of the major concerns of the audience to which it was addressed: the aftermath of the war, the alienation of millions, the need for radicalism, for a return to roots and for new growth.

The Interpretation of Religion (1929)

This book, completed in Toronto in 1928, is much more substantial and magisterial. The work is divided into two parts: the method and the inquiry.

We begin with "What Theology Is," in four sections: theological science defined, the problem of theological science, the parallel nature of the ethical problem (significantly), and the nature of theological criticism. Theology may be defined as the science of religion. There is need of a rapprochement between the dogmatic textbook and the general science of religion (p. 67). Religion has to be studied in its own light.

Naturalism is not enough, he says. "Our best clue to the understanding of the rise of religion in the racial soul is our knowledge of how 'I' arises in our own souls" (p. 171). We turn to theological intuitionism and the "religious a priori" (pp. 235f.). We come then to religion as grounded in our consciousness of value. Kant is again central. There is everywhere an integral connection between religion and the moral life, and the relation of value to reality (p.317). "The central affirmation of faith may accordingly be expressed by saying that the inner core of reality must be continuous with the moral consciousness" (p. 325).

Religions can only be tested from within. They are true or false "in accordance with the extent to which they are true to their own central principle" (p. 406). As for Jesus, "he had made discovery of a new moral value—and he applied it to his faith in God" (p. 440). The principle of it is best summed up in the New Testament word *agape*, which means brotherly love (p. 440). He had discovered it in the life of the family (p. 441). The centre is in the cross of Christ.

The final chapter is devoted to the "Idea of Revelation." To our human activity there has always seemed to correspond a divine activity of grace (p. 448). The concept of revelation has developed from earliest times. If we would know what God is like, it is to a man that we must turn—"the man Christ Jesus" (p. 467). Love is not merely an outward mark and symbol of his presence, but is his very self in action in our world. And in the soul of the man of Nazareth, and in his life and death, wherein our world's highest values are embodied and love for us made perfect, it was no mere dim-descried shadow of an otherwise masked and inscrutable God that we saw and knew but, as his church has always believed, very God of very God (p. 470).

The Place of Jesus Christ in Modern Christianity

In the 1929 christology, *The Place of Jesus Christ in Modern Christianity*, there are some very radical strands. Baillie confesses to sharing personally a perplexity about traditional christology: "What we cannot help feeling is that, at least in the forms in which it has often been presented to us, it contains an element of something very like *mythology*." We find it both inadequate and yet somehow reflecting deep truth. Despite our perplexity about the tradition, in our day there is "such a rediscovery of the spirit of the man Jesus as has hardly been made in all the Christian generations." This influences international relations, social teaching, personal psychology, and religious dialogue.

He then turns to the Christian fellowship as a potential source of illumination. This was a koinonia of *agape*. It includes brotherhood, and it includes God's love for us. God is a God who delights in fellowship. Where did this spirit of love come from? Paul's understanding of the character of God is stressed. "No reader of the Gospel narratives can fail to see that Jesus was a teacher first and foremost." But he was more than a teacher. His life and death, his *story* was important. We then come to faith's assessments of God in Christ. "In the spirit of his life it has found not merely an ideal for humanity, but also the self-disclosure of deity." Faith is concerned not only with man's search for God but also with God's search for man.

We turn in chapter 7 to "Some Unsatisfying Interpretations." This includes a critique of Chalcedon. There are problems too with a formula such as "Jesus is God." "The Christian gospel is rather that we must revise our old conception of deity in the light of the new predicate of Christlikeness" (p. 147). The consequences are spelled out in a reconsideration of atonement.

We come to "Some Final Clarifications." This includes the doctrine of the Trinity. "This Trinitarian mould, however radically it had in the end to be changed in order to adapt itself to its new filling, was not a thing newly spun by Christianity out of its own peculiar substance, but rather a thing which it found ready to hand in Hellenistic philosophy" (p. 186).

Later dogmatic developments were not especially fruitful. Are we able to make exclusive claims about Jesus Christ? "Surely the only properly inclusive definition of Christianity is that it is the religion of all those who love God with their heart and soul and mind and strength, and their neighbours as themselves" (p. 211).

The theme of the presence of God to faith was central to the three books that followed Baillie's first publications: *And the Life Everlasting* (1933), *Our Knowledge of God* (1939), and *Invitation to Pilgrimage* (1942). An emphasis on spirituality was manifested in *A Diary of Private Prayer* (1936), which sold tens of thousands of copies; it was a devotional work combining honest self-examination with concentration on God's reconciling grace.

Our Knowledge of God (1939)

This book centers on a narrower compass than *The Interpretation of Religion*. It does not argue for, but assumes the centrality of religion, and indeed of faith: "Not one of us has been left alone by God." All Christians would agree on this. But when he goes on to say that, "We can live in forgetfulness of Him, but not with peace of mind," John is clear that his own early memories "are already heavy with 'the numinous' " (p. 4). "I was somehow aware that my parents lived under the same kind of authority as that which, through them, was communicated to me" (p. 5). Here is a more exclusive stress on the religious a priori than 10 years earlier in *Interpretation*. This may be partly an echo of his new, more church-centered setting, partly an awareness of the shadow of Barth, partly an unease with humanist perspectives under the threat of war. Ultimate reality calls for more than respect for a law, as in Kant. However, it is the witness of experience that only "in, with and under" other presences "is the divine presence ever vouchsafed to us" (p. 178). The immediacy of God's presence is a mediated immediacy (p. 190): "The knowledge of God first came to me in the form of an awareness that I was not my own, but one under authority" (p. 182). The presence is mediated, but it is a reality. "We are never more truly ourselves than when we do nothing but what is done by the spirit of God in us" (p. 234).

We would not be seeking God if we had not already found him. Awareness of the divine love brings gratitude. Our spiritual life is always a life of dependence on God (p. 258).

Invitation to Pilgrimage (1942)

This book is a version of the Glasgow Alexander Robertson Lectures. The first chapter is entitled "The Fork in the Road," which turns out to be the choice between belief and unbelief. Baillie explores seeking and finding, realism and romanticism. A section on "Thinking and Believing" appeals to Maritain. Rationalism overreaches itself; we come to unreason. "It is obvious that the appearance of certain extreme anti-Liberal movements in theology has closely synchronized with the appearance of the extreme anti-liberal movements in politics. The two are plainly products of the same spirit of the age." John quotes *Mein Kampf* here, and adds: "Much as I have learned from the theologians of the Barthian school … they distress me because their language bears too suspicious a resemblance to the language of the totalitarian propagandists whom nevertheless many of them most staunchly and gallantly oppose" (p. 33). He adds: "There is only one good reason for believing, and that is the perception of the inherent truth of the gospel itself." "Dogmatic theology should not be taught thus dogmatically."

A new chapter examines obedience to parents, and the pros and cons of morals without religion. He commends Demant. He insists (chapter 7) that the challenge and the promise of the gospel mean good news. The last chapter, "Invitation to Church," considers again the Hitler *Jugend*, and quotes Niebuhr on "synthetic barbarianism." What of the Church (p. 129)? "In a broken and shattered world it still retains something of the character of a universal community … It can transcend our human relativities only because its obedience is to the absolute and eternal God." The book was well received, and some have seen it as John's best. Though short, it related Christian theology directly to the current national crisis, and was written in an imaginative and thoroughly accessible style.

A wider social and political concern was demonstrated, during his moderatorial year in the Church of Scotland in 1943, with the preparation for the general assembly of the report of the special commission for the interpretation of God's will in the present crisis. The report, published in 1946 as *God's Will for Church and Nation*, combined critique of the Nazis with a program for social reconstruction after the war, a program echoed in the Beveridge reports. The report recognized the difficulty in applying Christian principles in society, and took the route of "middle axioms," which should "exhibit the relevance of the ruling principles to the particular field of action in which guidance is needed" (p. 45). It argued that, "Economic power must be made objectively responsible to the community as a whole" (ibid., 156). The result is "the clear declaration that the common interest demands a far greater measure of public control of capital resources and means of production than our tradition has in the past envisaged" (p. 157, from 1944.) The report reflected awareness of the German church struggle, numerous Church of England and ecumenical gatherings, and also the work of the Moot, an influential forum that met in Oxford and London. As well as J. H. Oldham, its founder, participants included such influential writers and theologians as Eric Fenn, H. A. Hodges, Karl Mannheim, Walter Moberley, Alec Vidler, T. S. Eliot, H. H. Farmer, Donald Mackinnon, and John Middleton Murry. In 1952 Baillie became one of the presidents of the World Council of Churches.

Baillie's death precluded the delivery of his Gifford Lectures, but they were published posthumously as *The Sense of the Presence of God* (1962). They provided a masterly synthesis of his life's work. In them he displayed a characteristic combination of an appeal to experience with an exploration of rational grounds for belief in God. Knowledge seems to imply certitude, he argued, but often does not go beyond probabilities. Our knowledge of the realities is primary, and our knowledge of truths concerning them secondary. Moral convictions are central to human life, and "Our total experience of reality presents itself to us as a single experience" (p. 50). Baillie also discussed procedures for verification and falsification, and argued that, "A faith that is consistent with everything possible is not a faith in anything actual" (ibid., 71), stressing that the ultimate refutation of doubts was theological and incarnational. Faith was "an awareness of the divine presence itself, however hidden behind the veils of sense" (ibid., 89). Baillie argued that, "In the widest sense of the term all language may be said to be symbolic" (ibid., 113), but admitted that not all theological statements were analogical. Despite being known in, with, and under other realities, there is a certain directness in apprehension of God. Love of God is always related to love of neighbor, and beyond this to a new humanity. Baillie thought that it was important not to confuse dogmas with the primary perceptions of faith, and also raised the wider issue of "Faith and the Faiths." What does it mean to speak of salvation in a name? he asked. While there was an awareness of God in "the pagan religions," the way of Christ was decisive. In Baillie's view, scientific and religious accounts of the world complemented one another. What others may see as coincidence, Christians will read as providential. Furthermore, gratitude was "not only the dominant note of Christian piety, but equally the dominant motive of Christian action in the world" (ibid., 236). Propositions were necessary but not sufficient, as faith depended on trust. We have to do with "a God whose living and active presence among us can be perceived by faith in a large variety of human contexts and situations" (ibid., 61).

Baillie's theology, like that of his brother, remained resolutely liberal and evangelical. Sympathetic critics of each other's work and sensitive to theology in context, they could deploy arguments from various theological traditions when this seemed right. They deplored exclusivism and dogmatic narrowness. Baillie's "strongly independent mind made him resistant to passing fashions, while his irenic spirit preferred to discover underlying unities rather than sharpen distinctions into conflicts" (DSCHT, 50). He has been characterized as steering a middle course between American fundamentalists and modernists. A Companion of Honour from 1957, Baillie received numerous honorary doctorates, and at his death was widely regarded as the doyen of Scottish theologians. He died in Edinburgh in 1960.

What may be learned from the Baillies for the future? Both John and Donald Baillie were concerned to do theology in context, and to look to the future. They would not have been interested in a repristination of their own detailed arguments, which were fashioned for their time. Their work would appear to point to a theology which is both resolutely liberal and resolutely evangelical. This would mean resistance to an easy assimilation with the prevailing culture, in the name of the vulnerable Christ who is the judge of all the exploitation which is common in church and state. This would also mean resistance to a complacent retreat to the calm of paradise the blessed, in a church and theological framework in which all answers are known in advance, and all nonconformists excluded. Secular totalitarianism was not to be met with Christian totalitarianism.

References

Baillie, John. 1926. *The Roots of Religion in the Human Soul.* New York: George H. Doran.

Baillie, John. 1928. *The Interpretation of Religion.* New York: Scribner.

Baillie, John. 1930. *The Place of Jesus Christ in Modern Christianity.* New York: Scribner.

Baillie, John. 1939. *Our Knowledge of God.* New York: Scribner.

Baillie, John. 1942. *Invitation to Pilgrimage.* New York: Scribner.

Baillie, John. 1962. *The Sense of the Presence of God.* New York: Scribner.

DSCHT (*Dictionary of Scottish Church History and Theology*). 1993. Ed. Nigel M. de S. Cameron. Edinburgh: T&T Clark.

Fergusson, D., ed. 1993. *Christ, Church, and Society: Essays on John Baillie and Donald Baillie.*

Newlands, George. 2002. *John and Donald Baillie: Transatlantic Theology.* Oxford: Peter Lang.

Karl Barth (1886–1968)

Stephen H. Webb

Writing about Karl Barth is like writing about theology itself, because he shaped every theological issue he touched, and he grabbed them all with vigor and gusto. Even those who have never read him or think they know why they do not like him acknowledge him as one of the greatest theologians of the modern (or indeed, any) period. His career was mired in controversy, though the attempt to demarcate its trajectory and its various stages is itself a controversial enterprise. His writings are so voluminous and intense that they are hard to digest as a whole, and the secondary literature about him is even more enormous—and growing every day. Perhaps most significantly, he reinvigorated the theology of liberal Protestantism, which had become moribund by the beginning of the twentieth century. How he did that, how he changed as he did so, and what he left as his theological legacy are questions still very much open to debate.

Barth's reputation has always been more daunting and intimidating that he deserves. He was a great writer, capable of infusing the most obscure intellectual debates with passion and integrity. John Updike, one of America's greatest novelists, paid him a supremely literary compliment by having the main character of *Roger's Version*, a seminary professor, affectionately and attentively describe Barth's prose: "the superb iron of Barth's paragraphs, his magnificent seamless integrity and energy in this realm of prose—the specifically

Christian—usually conspicuous for intellectual limpness and dishonesty … it caresses and probes every crevice of the unknowable" (Updike, 1986, 41–2). Barth blended technical precision with a capacious sense of irony about the human condition and thus the limits of theological explanation. He was an unmatched prose stylist who could simultaneously alienate his audience by the sheer weight of his convictions and seduce them with the childlike simplicity of his faith.

Although he is sometimes called "a theologian's theologian," he is more accurately understood as a theologian of and for the church, even if the level of theological literacy in most churches makes him hard to read. Nevertheless, he remains a favorite author of pastors seeking strength to face the pulpit on a weekly basis. Oddly, Barth has been stereotyped as a narrow-minded biblicist, even though his interpretation of the authority of the Bible never found favor with conservative and evangelical Christians. Barth never founded a school either, even though the adjectival form of his name is often used polemically to indicate disapproval or even contempt. Some of his most devoted followers have lost sight of Barth's rhetorical power by submersing his thought in the narrow confines of scholastic debates over the minutiae of his development. Others have tried to recruit him for the very kind of liberal political agenda that he spent so much time fighting. Nonetheless,

The Student's Companion to the Theologians, First Edition. Edited by Ian S. Markham.
© 2013 Blackwell Publishing Ltd. Published 2013 by Blackwell Publishing Ltd.

there is plenty of Barth to appropriate, and the more he is used (and misused), the longer is the shadow he casts across the religious landscape.

Barth was born in Basle, Switzerland, in 1886. His father, Fritz, was a Swiss Reformed minister and New Testament scholar, and he was raised in Bern, where his father taught. He studied theology at Bern, Berlin, Tübingen, and Marburg universities, although he never earned a doctorate. He married Nelly Hoffman in 1913, with whom he had five children. In Berlin he took a course from the great liberal historian Adolf von Harnack, and discovered the work of Friedrich Schleiermacher. In Marburg he studied under the Kantian idealist Wilhelm Herrmann, who was one of the most influential theologians in Germany. Harnack found the essence of religion in a universal morality severed from the traditional creeds, while Herrmann sought the identity of Jesus in the spiritual experience of the Christian community. Barth absorbed these teachings but would soon turn against them with a vehemence that the last great generation of liberal theologians never understood.

After his studies, Barth entered the parish ministry. He spent over 10 years preaching and baptizing, first in Geneva and then in Safenwil, where he struggled to become an exemplary modern Christian. Safenwil was a small, Swiss agricultural village undergoing the pains of industrialization, and Barth threw himself into the study of trade unions, factory legislation, and economics. He advocated a form of Christian socialism as much as a way to awaken the workers to the drama of Christian faith as to solve the problem of rapid social dislocation. He argued that true socialism was something very different from leftist dreams based on Marxist ideology. What drew him to socialism was its power to break through ordinary social conventions. Barth was interested in the way socialism functioned analogously to the coming Kingdom of God. Socialist agitation expressed some of the power of the proclamation of the gospel that liberal Protestantism had been in the process of repressing. Barth was afraid that Christianity had become such an integral part of Western culture that people could no longer recognize just how radical it was. Debates continue about both the depth and the ongoing significance of Barth's early infatuation with radical politics and economics.

The secondary literature is also full of debates about precisely how, when, and why Barth turned against liberal theology. Barth worked in Safenwil during the outbreak of World War I, and he shared his anxiety about the war with his good friend Eduard Thurneysen. According to one version of Barth's departure from liberal theology, he was shocked by the number of his liberal teachers who signed the "Declaration of German Intellectuals," which was issued on August 1, 1914, the day the war began. It called for loyalty to the Kaiser and was published in a leading Christian journal. Barth was disillusioned and drew the conclusion that Christianity had become too closely identified with nationalism and patriotism. Christians had fallen into the habit of equating their spiritual lives with their social and cultural experiences. While the support of the liberal theologians for the war makes for dramatic storytelling, it was not the sole catalyst for Barth's transformation. Nevertheless, it was a jarring symptom of a problem that Barth devoted his life to trying to understand. How can Christianity be saved from its debilitating entanglement in the Western culture—a culture to which it had given birth, but which had since turned its back on its theological origins?

Out of his wartime experience, Barth began seeking a new foundation for theology. He developed not only a new theology, but a new way of writing theology. He decided that analyzing the mistakes of liberalism was not enough. Instead, those mistakes needed to be uprooted with a rhetoric that would be powerful enough to do justice to the gospel. The gospel needs to be proclaimed with the same heightened urgency that the socialists were putting into their economic and political schemes. The task of the theologian was to sound the alarm that theology had lost its way. The solution was to speak the gospel truth to the very theologians who had turned faith into a tepid reflection of cultural and moral conventions.

The result was Barth's shattering commentary on the Epistle to the Romans. He published the first edition of this commentary in 1919 and the second in 1922. It is the second edition that is the most famous, though scholars continue to debate the relationship between the two. The second edition is more radical in its language and more negative in its attitude about the possibility of positive theological knowledge about

God. In this commentary, Barth turned to a cast of colorful thinkers for support: Franz Overbeck, the friend of Friedrich Nietzsche, who argued that Christianity stands as a contradiction to this world; Ludwig Feuerbach, a German philosopher who suspected that religion is little more than a social projection of the unresolved frustrations and unmet desires of a society's collective subconscious; Fyodor Dostoevsky, the Russian novelist whose story of the Grand Inquisitor doubted that Jesus Christ would be recognized by his own church if he were to return today; and most of all, Søren Kierkegaard, who emphasized "the infinite qualitative distinction" between time and eternity. Barth melded this set of figures into his own unique style.

It might seem that Barth had invented the first fully articulate version of an existential theology, even though the group of thinkers associated with Kierkegaard and Nietzsche were not yet called by that name. Barth was way ahead of others when he met the social chaos of post-World War I Germany with his own announcement of the crisis of Christianity. Kierkegaard and Nietzsche were still fresh voices on the cultural scene, and Barth took up their cause with an explosive urgency. His commentary, however, was more radical than the proto-existentialism of Kierkegaard and company. He argued that the crisis facing Europe was not that of individual indecision or despair. It also was not directly caused by the Great War. Instead, it was a crisis brought about by God. The only crisis worth thinking about is the eternal crisis that eternity causes by threatening to break into time; and the Bible, far from resolving this crisis, only intensifies it.

Far from being an abstract metaphysical lament on the impossibility of knowing the divine, Barth's Romans commentary was actually a close reading of that book of the Bible. Barth read Paul, however, as an intimate companion, not a distant historical figure. For Barth, the Bible speaks to us directly, but it does not speak any language of consolation or explanation that we already know. It breaks through our expectations with promises and demands that defy the understanding. Only when we submit to God's judgment do we put ourselves on the path of theological understanding. God's speech to us in the Bible is, in fact, the essence of the crisis that faces every individual at every point of their existence.

To talk about this crisis, Barth relied on a hyperbolic prose that forced religious language into a continuously emergency mode. He also adopted an ironic tone, because he recognized that by declaring a religious crisis, he easily could sound as though he were trying to pass himself off as a prophet or, worse, a theologian satisfied with his own certainty about the state of the world. Theology, Barth argued, cannot be satisfied with anything, neither its conception of God, which always falls short, nor its valiant attempts to shore up the ruins of Christian faith in the midst of the spiritual ravages of modernity. The more theologians try to reassure Christians that their faith is still relevant to the modern world, the more their compromises with modernity only betray the faith. And the more they try to persuade skeptics that God truly exists, the more they betray God by reducing the divine to an effortlessly consumable human artifact.

Critics accused Barth of exaggerating the sorry state of liberal theology and the corrosive conditions of modernity, but that was just the point. His commentary on Romans was a call for a theological revolution that threatened the self-understanding of liberal optimism and rationality. Barth, for example, called God the "wholly other," by which he meant that God is more different from us than any kind of otherness we might experience in our daily intercourse with other people. God, in fact, is not God!, Barth insisted. The God we think we know is the No-God, by which Barth meant the God who says "no" to all of our attempts at theological understanding. The church too comes in for a verbal lashing from Barth. The church is the greatest sign of unbelief in the world because the church is where people go to find the God they think they already know. The church should be a place where we sacrifice our ideas about God like idols that need to be destroyed. Instead, we go to be comforted with the idea that God is little more than the summation of all of our most idiosyncratic hopes and longings. Religion is thus little more than the strenuous efforts people make as they try to come to terms with their lack of faith. Religion is humanity's efforts to put God in a box. Barth's analysis of the church, it should be pointed out, is not sociological. He is not saying that some churches fail to adequately proclaim the gospel, while others do a good job. He is saying that all churches fail of necessity. It follows that theology must be written as a form of that failure. It must incorporate its own destruction into what little truth it has to express. Theology must be ironic because God is ironic. God reveals himself, after all, only in the cross, where nothing is what it seems and all of our expectations about who God is are left in ruins.

As exciting as this is, the rhetoric of the Romans commentary could not be sustained, and Barth soon realized that his own persuasive power was an egotistical trap. Followers took his program and turned it into a school, sometimes called dialectical theology or neo-orthodoxy. He had erected yet another monument to the human spirit in his attempt to level the religious landscape to make possible a proper view of the divine. His assault on theology could easily become yet another theological option, with the tropes of hyperbole and irony becoming predictable and banal. This indeed is the risk that many radical theologians cheerfully embrace, even though they end up falling far short of Barth's own masterpiece of crisis theology. The nature of Barth's departure from his crisis period, however, is as hotly debated as the impact of his early commitment to socialism and his break with liberalism. A start can be made by saying that Barth rediscovered the richness of the theological tradition and the importance of the church as the place where that richness is preserved and reinvested.

What is not the case is that Barth became a stodgy conservative after the wild days of his Romans period. Barth continued to write with rich irony and much humor. He knew that theology was a limited discipline, but he also knew that theology could be confident in its objectivity as a science because theology is a responsive, not creative discipline. He continued to think that Christians had gone too far in compromising with Western culture, but he now decided that his radical rejection of theological knowledge was itself an aspect of that compromise. Wallowing in despair, in other words, is itself one of the options that Western culture forces upon the Christian in the modern period. Barth decided that he did not want to limit Christian freedom by accepting the modernist narrative of religious history. Christianity has its own history of the world, and it is a history that encompasses the modern period, not vice versa.

Throughout the 1920s, during the economic, social, and cultural crises of the Weimar Republic, Barth began looking for a new theological path. He once again was working against the direction most theologians were going. This time, however, many of them were going in the direction that they thought he had established. Barth made a preliminary attempt to write a Christian dogmatics that he later judged to be a false start. He also wrote a very important book on Anselm of Canterbury, arguing that the motto of "faith seeking understanding" means that theology does not have to rely on philosophy or culture to justify itself. Understanding is an internal moment to faith, and faith has its own rational coherence.

While Barth was sharpening these insights, the Nazis were on the move. In an astounding act of hermeneutical insight, Barth realized that the Nazi ideology was formally similar to liberal theology. This might seem like a perverse argument, but Barth saw how the Nazis tried to discover religious truth in social experience. In the case of the Nazis, this religious truth was pagan to the core, and the social experience was mired in social Darwinism and racism, so that its violent mythology had nothing in common with Christianity. Nevertheless, both liberal Protestantism and Nazism looked to collective experience to validate their spiritual insights. Both reduced God to a projection of social hopes and human needs. Barth was thus well prepared to become a vigorous opponent of the Nazi regime, especially its efforts to turn Protestant churches into a German church in order to legitimate its racist ideology. In opposition to the so-called German Christians, Barth and others formed the Confessing church. At their first Synod, in May of 1934 in Barmen, Barth wrote what became known as the Barmen Declaration. This statement declared that only an absolute loyalty to the sovereignty of the Word of God in Jesus Christ can combat the idolatry of the German Christians, who subordinated the church to Nazi racism. Throughout his career Barth defended a divine command theory of morality, and in this declaration he made it very clear that Christians who obey God's command cannot be commanded to turn race or nationality into a substitute for the divine.

Barth was certain that liberal theology had ruined itself by trying to find God in the depths of human nature, rather than realizing that true humanity can only be found in Jesus Christ. That is why Barth pronounced his famous "Nein!" against the efforts of some of his previous collaborators to ground revelation in anthropology. Barth had little use for natural theology, which is the attempt to find traces of God or confirmations of divine revelation in patterns of human experience. Barth's dealings with Nazi Germany and the German Christians only confirmed in his mind the dangers of substituting the immanence for the transcendence of God. When God is collapsed into the realm of the human, the human is elevated to the status of the divine. Nazi racism, which made the fictitious Aryan race the bearer of world history and glory, is only the most disastrous result of this theological mistake. Barth would later admit that there is a human component to the divine, but that component is Jesus Christ, not some generic definition or abstract speculation about the essence of humanity.

In 1935, Barth refused to pledge his allegiance to Hitler, as was required by German law of civil employees, and he was dismissed from Bonn University, where he had been teaching. He returned to his native Basle, where he would live until his death in 1968. During these years he wrote extensively and spent most of his labor on his magnum opus, the *Church Dogmatics*. Scholars again debate about the subtle changes Barth underwent as he worked his way through the basics of the Christian faith, and there have been many attempts to try to summarize the principal themes and ideas of the *Church Dogmatics*. The problem is that the *Church Dogmatics* is hardly a retreat from the rhetoric Barth had mastered in his battles with liberalism. True, Barth embraced a new shift toward objectivity that was evident in the arts in the late 1920s, just as he had created a theological style worthy of expressionism in the early 1920s. Nonetheless, he continued to think of theology in ironic terms, and he applied a hyperbolic sword to polemical engagements with his critics. What changed is that he learned how to listen to the past before engaging the present. What remained consistent was his commitment to liberating theology from its captivity to momentary cultural concerns. He did this not just to put theology on a firmer footing but, more fundamentally, to free

theology to listen to the ever new and always unchanging Word of God. In the Romans commentary, Barth was concerned to protect the otherness of God from the encroachments of any theology that would imprison faith in rationality or morality. In the *Church Dogmatics*, Barth was dedicated to shaping a theological discourse that would allow God to be the One who loves in freedom. In his later work, Barth was less anxious to dispel the influence of disciplines that are foreign to theology. He opened his work to a joyous spirit that accepts insights wherever they originate, as long as they do not become methodological drags on the sovereignty of God.

The *Church Dogmatics*, then, remains as hard to summarize as the commentary on Romans. It is organized in four "volumes," each of which is divided into two to four large books. Volume I, which treats the Word of God, for example, is divided into Volume I/1, which is about the three forms of the Word of God (preached, written, and revealed), while Volume I/2 goes into more detail about the incarnation as the origin and source of these three forms. Volume II is on the doctrine of God, III is on the doctrine of Creation, and IV is on the doctrine of reconciliation. He was working on the last part of Volume IV at his death.

Reading any of these volumes, even by experts, is bound to result in surprises and delights, as well as provocations and complications that are completely unexpected. Barth could write about animals, for example, in a way that anticipates much of the animal theology movement. His views on the complementarities of the genders continue to be both insightful and controversial. His emphases on God's freedom, the goodness of creation, and the nothingness of evil are still the subject of much debate, as is his subordination of theology to the church, which has given rise to much Barthian suspicion about the role and function of theology in colleges and universities. One example of Barth's creativity is his radical revision of the doctrine of election. For Barth, God elected himself, in a way, as the basis of choosing first Israel and then the church to embody God's love. That is, God elected himself in Jesus Christ to suffer and die on our behalf. Barth stopped short of universal salvation, but he intimated that the consequence of his doctrine of election means that God elected every human being in the election of Christ.

Some liberal-minded theologians used to accuse Barth of being too narrow, too biblicist, too disengaged from philosophy, and too lacking in critical resources. Little of that is heard these days, and for good reason. Barth can and should be criticized for any of his arguments, but his positions are always deeply informed by current events, critically related to contrasting theologies, and decisively shaped by a close reading of the Bible that nonetheless acknowledges the bulk of historical scholarship.

To end with one last example of the debates in the secondary scholarship, Barth's politics, after his early flirtation with socialism, were not easy to pin down. This was intentional. He wanted to free the Word of God to speak anew to the changing circumstances of the modern world. Nevertheless, near the end of his career he was accused of returning to the spirit of his early socialist leanings in a way that was naïve and narrow. Throughout the Cold War, Barth did not just refuse to take sides between the Soviet Union and the United States, a position that might be explained as a natural outgrowth of his Swiss background; he actually discouraged active criticism of communism in the Eastern Bloc. In 1958 he wrote a letter to Protestant pastors in East Germany encouraging them to give their loyalty to the communist regime (Burleigh, 2007, 442). For a theologian with such an international reputation, his refusal to condemn communism was as puzzling as it was, in some circles, thought to be profound.

References

Barth, Karl. 1936–75. *Church Dogmatics [Kirchliche Dogmatik]*, trans. T. H. L. Parker, W. B. Johnston, Harold Knight, and J. L. M. Haire; ed. G. W. Bromiley and G. T. Thomson. Edinburgh: T&T Clark.

Barth, Karl. [1947] 1949. *Dogmatics in Outline*, trans. G. T. Thomson. New York: Philosophical Library.

Barth, Karl. [1956] 1960. "The Humanity of God," in *The Humanity of God*, trans. John Newman Thomas. Atlanta: John Knox Press, pp. 37–65.

Barth, Karl. [1935] 1962. *Credo*. With a foreword by Robert McAfee Brown. New York: Charles Scribner's Sons.

Barth, Karl. [1933] 1968. *The Epistle to the Romans*, trans. Edwyn C. Hoskyns from the 6th German ed. [*Römerbrief*]. London, Oxford, and New York: Oxford University Press.

Barth, Karl. 1993. *The Holy Spirit and the Christian Life: The Theological Basis of Ethics*, trans. R. Birch Hoyle with a foreword by Robin W. Lovin. [1st English ed. London: F. Muller, 1938]. Louisville, KY: Westminster/John Knox Press.

Barth, Karl. 2006. *On Religion*, trans. Garrett Green. New York: T&T Clark.

Burleigh, Michael. 2007. *Sacred Causes: The Clash of Religion and Politics from the Great War to the War on Terror*. San Francisco: HarperCollins.

Hunsinger, George. 1991. *How to Read Karl Barth: The Shape of his Theology*. New York and Oxford: Oxford University Press.

Jehle, Frank. *Ever Against the Stream: The Politics of Karl Barth, 1906–1968*, trans. Richard and Martha Burnett. Grand Rapids, MI: Eerdmans.

Jenson, Robert W. 1997. "Karl Barth." In *The Modern Theologians: An Introduction to Christian Theology in the Twentieth Century*, ed. David Ford. Cambridge: Blackwell.

Torrance, Thomas F. 1995. "The Ground and Grammar of Theology" [1980]. In The Christian Theology Reader, ed. *Alister McGrath*. Oxford and Cambridge, MA: Blackwell, pp. 85–8.

Von Balthasar, Hans Urs, and Oakes, Edward T. 1992. *The Theology of Karl Barth: Exposition and Interpretation*. San Francisco: Ignatius Press.

Webb, Stephen H. 1991. *Re-Figuring Theology: The Rhetoric of Karl Barth*. Albany: SUNY Press.

Webb, Stephen H. 1997. "Review of Bruce L. McCormack, *Karl Barth's Critically Realistic Dialectical Theology*," *Journal of Religion* 77 (April): 308–9.

Webb, Stephen H. 2001. "Review of Timothy Gorringe, *Karl Barth: Against Hegemony*," *Anglican Theological Review* 83(4): 901–2.

Webb, Stephen H. 2006. "Review of William G. Rusch, ed., *Karl Barth, the Church, and the Churches*," *Reviews in Religion and Theology* 13(3) (July): 379–82.

Webster, John. 2005. *Barth's Earlier Theology*. New York: T&T Clark International.

Updike, John. 1986. *Roger's Version*. New York: Fawcett Crest.

Emil Brunner (1889–1966)

Christian Collins Winn

One of the most influential theologians of the twentieth century, Emil Brunner has experienced something of an eclipse in recent decades. Though his contemporary and sometime theological antagonist Karl Barth (1886–1968) continues to generate interest and influence—as does the work of Paul Tillich (1886–1965), Rudolph Bultmann (1884–1976), and Dietrich Bonhoeffer (1906–45)—Brunner's theological influence has waned considerably since his death in 1966.

I. Life

Brunner was born on December 23, 1889 in Winterthur in the canton of Zurich. Brunner's family, though Swiss Reformed, was deeply influenced by the moderate Pietism of the Württemberger's Johann Christoph (1805–80) and Christoph Friedrich Blumhardt (1842–1919), whose eschatology would later influence a number of prominent twentieth-century theologians, including Karl Barth. Brunner began his theological studies in 1908 at the University of Zurich, later studying for a time at the University of Berlin. He returned to Zurich to pursue doctoral studies with, among others, Leonard Ragaz (1868–1945) the famous Swiss Religious Socialist. He completed his doctorate in 1912, later publishing his dissertation, *The Symbolic in Religious Knowledge* (1914), in which he dealt with questions of religious epistemology. The work shows

the influence of Schleiermacher, Kant, Husserl, and Bergson. In this early work, Brunner can already be seen attempting to correct the perceived mistakes in varying options (in this case, the "objectivism" of Protestant scholasticism and the "idealism" of Hegelianism) while offering a constructive alternative. This scholarly conceit would mark much of his later work and has led many to describe Brunner's work as an attempt at *via media* (McKim, 1997).

Brunner was ordained in the Swiss Reformed Church and had a short stint as an interim pastor in Switzerland (September 1912 to Easter 1913) before teaching French in England from 1913 to 1914. With the outbreak of World War I, Brunner returned home to serve in the Swiss army. Brunner also served as assistant pastor under the guidance of Hermann Kutter (1863–1931) in the Neumünster in Zurich. In 1916 he was called to pastor a small church in the mountain village of Obstalden in the canton of Glarus. There he met and married Margrit Lautenburg, niece of Hermann Kutter, with whom he had four sons.

In 1919–20, Brunner took a leave of absence from his pastorate to study at Union Theological Seminary in New York City. Upon return he wrote *Experience, Knowledge and Faith*, a critique of modern philosophical epistemologies, which was subsequently published in 1921. This work was followed by the longer and more critical work, *Die Mystik und das Wort*, published in 1924. Both works won Brunner an appointment

The Student's Companion to the Theologians, First Edition. Edited by Ian S. Markham.

to the Chair in Systematic and Practical Theology at the University of Zurich in 1924, a position that he held till 1955. These works reveal significant continuities and discontinuities with his earlier dissertation.

Both works are concerned with epistemological questions; both offer substantial critiques of specific theological and philosophical traditions; and in both works Brunner can be found attempting to offer an alternative to the "half-truths" of modern philosophy and theology as he understood them. All of these concerns and characteristics, in one form or another, reveal formal continuities with Brunner's 1914 dissertation. The major element of discontinuity occurs on the material level and can be found above all in Brunner's scathing attack on Schleiermacher and his theological epigone, an attack that is most clearly seen in *Die Mystik und das Wort*. Brunner's basic thesis was that modern idealist philosophy and its theological appropriation by Schleiermacher had identified human self-consciousness with "consciousness of God"—a precognitive intuition of the absolute dependence of all things on the divine—such that there was no longer any need for a mediator between humanity and God. According to Brunner, by this identification, revelation or "knowledge of God" no longer occurred objectively or even subjectively as rightly understood, but "mystically" and immediately, thus leading to the possibility that knowledge of God was merely humanity's knowledge of itself and its own ability to transcend itself. In the nineteenth century, atheist philosopher and theologian Ludwig Feuerbach (1804–72) had argued this very thesis as a demonstration that "theological knowledge" was nothing other than humanity's own knowledge of itself alienated and projected onto an otherworldly realm.

According to Brunner, Schleiermacher's construal of the relation between human self-consciousness and the so-called "consciousness of God" was a betrayal that threatened to undermine theological knowledge altogether. Behind this criticism was Brunner's newly formed conviction that in the "event of revelation" (more on this below) the community and the individual are confronted by a reality and a Word which is radically "other" than humanity. Contra Schleiermacher, and in accord with his interpretation of the Reformers Luther and Calvin, Brunner argued that knowledge of God is radically distinct from

human self-consciousness and that because of our finitude and sinful condition, humanity's relationship to God is one of discontinuity rather than continuity. Contra Feuerbach, the radical otherness of revelation, which was implied in the discontinuity of relation between God and humanity, was in fact a sign that the knowledge and experience gained in faith were not projections of human consciousness or "wish fulfillment," but rather a real Word of judgment and grace. The key sources of Brunner's new conviction were the dialectical theology of Karl Barth, the religious philosophy of Søren Kierkegaard (1813–55), and the emerging "I–Thou" philosophy of Ferdinand Ebner (1882–1931) and Martin Buber (1878–1965). These three influences worked together to set Brunner on a theological trajectory that he would follow from the late 1910s till his death in 1966.

In 1927, Brunner published *The Philosophy of Religion from the Standpoint of Protestant Theology* and *The Mediator*, both of which show the continuing influence of Barth, Kierkegaard, and Ebner/Buber. The publication of these two texts elevated Brunner onto the international stage and it was during this period that Brunner's extensive travels began. From 1927 to 1955, Brunner embarked on numerous lecture tours across Europe, North America, and Asia. In 1938–9 he served as a visiting professor at Princeton Theological Seminary, and in 1947 he gave the prestigious Gifford Lectures at the University of St Andrews in Scotland, which were later published in two volumes as *Christianity and Civilization* (1948–9). The climax of Brunner's international service was his two-year appointment at the International Christian University in Tokyo from 1953 to 1955.

In the 1930s and 1940s, Brunner's works were more widely read than any of his theological contemporaries, including Barth, Bultmann, and Tillich. This state of affairs was due in part to his extensive travels, but was also the result of his own enormous literary output and the variety of issues, themes, and topics to which Brunner brought his considerable talents. His works were especially prized because of his ability to deal creatively with traditional problems, while also bringing clarity to difficult themes through an elegant prose. In the 1930s alone he published *The Word and the World* (1931), *The Divine Imperative* (1932), *Nature and Grace* (1934), *Man in*

Revolt (1937), *The Church and the Oxford Group* (1937), and *The Divine–Human Encounter* (1938), which was later rewritten and published as *Truth as Encounter* (1963), as well as numerous shorter published volumes and essays. These works were followed by a multi-volume Christian Dogmatics—*Revelation and Reason* (1941), *The Christian Doctrine of God* (1950), *The Christian Doctrine of Creation and Redemption* (1952), and *The Christian Doctrine of the Church, Faith and Consummation* (1962)—substantial volumes on social ethics, and a number of volumes and essays on topics ranging from ecumenical theology and ecclesiology to eschatology and missiology.

Brunner's theological influence began to wane in the 1950s. Upon his return from Tokyo in 1955, Brunner suffered a cerebral hemorrhage. Though he experienced some impairment from this event, he remained reasonably healthy for several more years. He died on April 6, 1966.

II.   Theology

"Truth as encounter"

Though his theology was wide ranging in scope and intention, Brunner's early interest in religious episte-mology, his self-proclaimed attempt to find a "third way" between liberalism and orthodoxy, and his con-cern to articulate the Christian faith to the modern world produced his most distinctive contribution to modern theology: "truth as encounter." In his concern with epistemology and the doctrine of revelation, Brunner shows himself a child of the modern age.

"Truth as encounter" is Brunner's description of the "event of revelation" and refers to three simulta-neous and mutually constitutive elements: (1) the *objective* event of God's revelation in Jesus Christ; (2) the *subjective* event of human reception of God's rev-elation in the Holy Spirit and faith; and (3) the *truth criterion* or *self-authentication* of the simultaneous objective-subjective event of revelation.

In contradistinction to Protestant liberalism, Brunner argued that revelation does not originate with humanity, but with God: "Revelation is a divine action; it is a movement which does not proceed *from* man, but one which comes *to* him" (Brunner,

1946, 32). For Brunner, the objective event of God's revelation—God's making known his ultimate intentions toward the cosmos and humanity—is above all to be identified with Jesus Christ, knowl-edge of whom is given to us in the Holy Spirit. This means, however, that the act of revelation and the knowledge given therein is not so much a knowledge *about* God, as it is a personal encounter *with* God: "It thus becomes unmistakably clear that what God wills to give us cannot really be given in words, but only in manifestation: Jesus Christ, God himself *in persona* is the real gift. The Word of God in its ultimate meaning is thus precisely not 'a word from God,' but God in person, God himself speaking, himself present, Immanuel" (Brunner, 1964, 132). The objective knowledge given in the event of revelation is content rich, but as a relational knowledge rather than a knowledge of cold facts. In contradistinction to various forms of Protestant orthodoxy, therefore, Brunner argued that the objective event of revelation is not so much about God's conveying "propositions" as it was an encounter with the living God known under the name Jesus Christ.

Constitutive of the objective act of God's revelation in and as Jesus Christ is the "subjective" moment of faith in the one who receives revelation: "Revelation is a transitive event which proceeds from God and ends in man, a light ray with these two poles" (Brunner, 1946, 33). Revelation is not just the objective event of God's self-revealing; rather it is the encounter of the self-revealing God and the one to whom that God speaks, i.e., believing humanity. Faith, for Brunner, is the subsequent event in which humanity is encountered by the living God and surrenders to the One by whom it is addressed. Thus, for Brunner, God's self-disclosure and the human act of faith are co-ordinate and mutually constitutive aspects of the single reality of revelation. To be sure, God's address precedes humanity's reception. But there is no event of divine address that does not assume the *telos* of human reception.

An important qualification for Brunner in his understanding of revelation was that the encounter in which God "makes himself accessible to me" (Brunner, 1964, 114), does not occur mystically, but through the objective media of scripture as it is actualized by the Holy Spirit. It is as the Spirit takes up the human witness of scripture and speaks it into the heart that the event of God's revelation occurs and our reconciliation with God is disclosed. "The *testimonium spiritus sancti* and the clarity of God's word are one and the same thing" (Brunner, 1937, 151). For Brunner, this qualification avoids both objectivism and subjectivism because in the event of revelation God speaks about himself through the media of human witness: "The Bible is human testimony about God, but through this human factor God bears witness to Himself" (Brunner, 1937, 155). Thus, revelation is *God's* speech about Himself, but it is so *through* the objective media of historical human witness. God speaks, but that speech is the "living history" of the life, death, and resurrection of Jesus Christ as it is portrayed in scripture.

Brunner developed his understanding of the event of revelation in dialogue with the categories of Ferdinand Ebner and Martin Buber's "I–Thou" philosophy. The event of revelation–faith is a personal encounter between an "I" and a "Thou." In God's self-revelation in Jesus Christ, humanity is addressed by the Person of God. In the faithful hearing of humanity the responsiveness and responsibility of humanity is both disclosed and actualized as humanity surrenders itself to the God who speaks to humanity as "Thou." In this way, the event of revelation–faith is understood as having the character of knowledge and the character of fellowship.

Unlike other acts of knowledge, Brunner was especially concerned to show that the knowledge given in revelation was different in kind. It was not an "I–It" knowledge, but an "I–Thou" knowledge. As noted above, the content of the knowledge of God was not a detached set of "facts" or "propositions." Rather, the knowledge of God given in revelation *is* the relationship established by God and humanity as actualized in the event of Jesus Christ. Thus, one does not "have" this knowledge, so much as one finds oneself "in" it. "This truth cannot be *held*, or possessed. Its nature is, rather, such that it takes possession of us, 'lays hold of us' " (Brunner, 1964, 28). In this way, the "truth" criterion of revelation is not something external to revelation. Rather, in the event of revelation, in the address of the divine "Thou" to the human "I," the truthfulness of Jesus Christ is revealed precisely because in that knowledge: (1) our humanity is reaffirmed and regrounded in the divine address that reveals to us

our responsiveness and responsibility, i.e., our full humanity; (2) our fellowship with God is re-established as the antithesis of sin is revealed to be overcome in Jesus Christ; and (3) both of these cognitive "truths" *become* existentially transformative as our relation with God in revelation and faith is understood as an ongoing personal fellowship of encounter.

III.   Anthropology, Eristics, and Social Ethics

Brunner considered theological anthropology the "cardinal point of his theology" (Kegley, 1962, 331). When seen in light of the above discussion the theological justification for this emphasis is not difficult to surmise. Brunner's concern with the doctrine of humanity was intimately connected to his concern to do justice to the existential pole of the revelational event. It was this concern that also fueled his interest in "eristics" and social ethics. "Eristics" (literally, "to debate") is often misunderstood by interpreters as Brunner's way of describing apologetics. Brunner, however, conceived of "eristics" as a critique of modern philosophical and ideological conceptions for the purpose of showing the internal contradictions and non-scientific character of modern thought. Thus, "eristics" was an offensive engagement with the contemporary intellectual milieu with a missional aim, rather than an attempt to "defend the faith."

The missional aim of "eristics" was to free unbelieving humanity from the various delusions it had constructed about itself, and thereby to prepare it to hear the decisive Word of revelation. It was a missional strategy whereby modern humanity's obsessive concern about itself could be used in service to the gospel. Or, put differently, "the question 'What is God?' may be regarded as unanswerable or out of date, or uninteresting, but no one would say the same about the question: 'What is Man?' " (Brunner, 1952, 46). "Eristic" critique was above all concerned to show that the various philosophical and ideological anthropologies, by their mere existence, reveal that humanity longs to be addressed about its own purpose and responsibility. This longing to be addressed is the "point of contact" that revelation seeks, and the work of "eristics" is to clear away the philosophical and ideological attempts to answer that question so that the address of God can be heard.

Likewise, Brunner's extensive writings on social ethics were also fueled by a missional impulse. In his important work *The Divine Imperative* (1932), Brunner developed a theological ethics that sought to integrate the dynamic "ethics of divine command" of Barth with the more traditional categories of "the orders of creation." In the former, God's address to the individual and the community is what sets the individual and community in motion, rather than the strictures of conscience or natural law. In the latter, the assumption is that there are structures built into creation—marriage, family, and state—"given by God to provide an ordered framework for God's basic will for humanity, which is community" (Hart, 2001, 118). The *telos* of the "command ethics" is the transformation of the status quo, which has been distorted by sin. Conversely, within the framework offered by "the orders of creation," the actions of the community and the individual are fundamentally conservative in that the given structures of society are not to be rejected, but transformed. Brunner's integration of the two ethical conceptions was to argue that though there are general structures in creation given by God, they are distorted by sin. A true Christian ethics will identify those structures, and under the impetus of the divine command, work to transform them by co-operating with God's work of reclamation.

The missional strategy is evident primarily in his development and deployment of the "orders of creation." These are general structures within creation (i.e., marriage, family, and state), shared by both Christian and non-Christian, and are thus an evidence of God's gracious presence in the created world. Though Brunner argued that these structures were fundamentally distorted and in need of the transformative action fueled by God's gracious address and humanity's obedient action, nonetheless, their presence constitutes another "point of contact" that the theologian or "eristician" can call to the attention of the non-believer.

References

Brunner, Emil. 1937. *The Philosophy of Religion from the Standpoint of Protestant Theology*, trans. A. J. D. Farrer and Bertram Lee Woolf. New York: Charles Scribners Sons.

IV.   Significance

Brunner's theology was marked by the desire to do justice to the twin poles of God and humanity. The theme "truth as encounter," Brunner's most significant and enduring theological contribution, seeks to do just that by arguing that the initial divine address ssalways-already presupposes a subsequent human response. Brunner's use of the "I–Thou" philosophy of Ferdinand Ebner and Martin Buber is also an outstanding example of how theology can be enriched through dialogue with the insights of other disciplines.

Brunner's significance is also associated with his role in mediating the new theological direction initiated by Karl Barth to the English-speaking world. During the 1930s and 1940s it was to Brunner that most turned to understand the new trajectories and proposals being developed among the so-called "dialectical theologians." Brunner was also tirelessly involved in ecumenical discussions, participating in study sessions for both "Faith and Order" and "Life and Work" from 1930 to 1955. His ecumenical temperament can also be adduced by his multiple attempts to find a middle way between "orthodoxy" and "liberalism" in his theological construction.

Aside from the theme "truth as encounter," however, Brunner's ongoing theological significance is difficult to gauge. The reception of Brunner's conception of "eristics" and "natural theology" suffered from the historical entanglement in the infamous Barth–Brunner debate over the publication of Brunner's *Nature and Grace* (1934), during the height of the "German Christian Movement." Brunner's social ethics, developed using the ill-fated concept of "the orders of creation"—a concept originally coined by Friedrich Gogarten (1887–1967) and later appropriated by Nazi propagandists—fared even worse. It may be that assessing Brunner's theological importance will always suffer due to his proximity to the twentieth century's greatest theological luminary, Karl Barth.

Brunner, Emil. 1946. *Revelation and Reason: The Christian Doctrine of Faith and Knowledge*, trans. Olive Wyon. Philadelphia: The Westminster Press.
Brunner, Emil. 1952. *The Christian Doctrine of Creation and Redemption*, trans. Olive Wyon. Philadelphia: The Westminster Press.

Brunner, Emil. 1964. *Truth as Encounter: A New Edition*, trans. Amandus W. Loos. Philadelphia: The Westminster Press.

Hart, John W. 2001. *Karl Barth vs. Emil Brunner: The Formation and Dissolution of a Theological Alliance, 1916–1936*. New York: Peter Lang.

Kegley, Charles W., ed. 1962. *The Theology of Emil Brunner*. New York: The MacMillan Company.

McKim, Mark G. 1997. "Brunner the Ecumenist: Emil Brunner As a *Vox Media* of Protestant Theology," *Calvin Theological Journal* 32(1): 91–104.

John Nelson Darby (1800–1882)

Ian S. Markham

I. Introduction

It was J. Gordon Melton who wrote of J. N. Darby: "Probably no Christian thinker in the last 200 years has so affected the way in which English-speaking Christians view the faith, and yet has received so little recognition of his contribution as John Nelson Darby" (Melton, 1999, 107). It is the theology of Darby that lies behind the astonishing success of the *Left Behind* series. This series of books tells the story of the "end times": starting with the rapture, it documents the rise of the Antichrist and the final battle between Israel and the other nations. These books, co-written by Tim LaHaye and Jerry Jenkins, are bestsellers that have captured the imaginations and informed the theological worldview of millions of Americans. Indeed one could make the claim that Darby is the single most influential theologian on modern American fundamentalist theology.

II. Locating the Life

Darby was born on November 18, 1800 in Westminster, London. Perhaps because of his Irish background, he studied at Trinity College, Dublin. He distinguished himself as a scholar, receiving prizes, especially in classics. Although he trained as a lawyer, his passion

was the church and in 1826 he was ordained a priest in the Church of Ireland. Initially, he was seen as a High Churchman (Rowdon, 1967, 46).

His move away from the Church of Ireland was gradual. It perhaps starts with the rather unwise decision of Archbishop Magee of Dublin in 1827 to require converts from the Roman Catholic Church to take the oath of allegiance to the English crown. This was a decision taken when significant numbers of Catholics were converting. The result, explains Darby, was "ruinous." He goes on to explain that this decision "stopped the deliverance from Popery of masses, perhaps of all Ireland" (Darby in Coad, 1968, 27). He felt that this requirement on the Irish was making the church a slave of the state. This was the start of a journey. Slowly, Darby came to believe that Anglicanism had lost sight of the simplicity of scripture. Christendom, Darby began to think, was not really the church. So in 1828, he resigned his curacy and wrote his first pamphlet, which was entitled "Considerations of the Nature and Unity of the Church of Christ." Darby started to meet with others who were unhappy with the major church options; however, for several years he kept his options open. Even in 1834, he was still tenuously connected with the Church of Ireland. However, it was also in 1834 that a new journal was published out of Plymouth, England. This journal did not simply reproduce Darby's pamphlet, but was also advocating a distinctive

The Student's Companion to the Theologians, First Edition. Edited by Ian S. Markham.
© 2013 Blackwell Publishing Ltd. Published 2013 by Blackwell Publishing Ltd.

position outside the Anglican churches. For Darby, unity could only be built on Christ. Given this, a schism with the Anglican churches was essential.

Congregations formed rapidly. And Darby was slowly emerging as a major force in the movement. Starting in Plymouth, congregations formed throughout the West Country, Hereford, Bristol, as well as Oxford. Darby then started working overseas. One of his earliest trips was to Geneva in 1837. A second one in 1839 was part of a four-month stay on the Continent, where he linked with sympathizers and developed congregations. His travel continued for the rest of Darby's life.

Inevitably differences would emerge in the movement. Disagreements arose over infant baptism: some in the movement wanted to affirm "believers' baptism," while Darby continued to affirm "infant baptism." However, the major disagreement was ecclesiological. Darby had a deep fear of "heresy"; he believed that a heresy could capture a congregation and then spread, with deep and tragic consequences. For Darby, doctrinal differences could not be tolerated. Those who wanted a sense of autonomy for a particular congregation were problematic. The movement finally divided and split, with Darby insisting on uniformity of belief across the various assemblies.

It is clear that Darby had a significant presence. This was despite his appearance. His attire was often shabby; his appearance slightly disorientating; yet his impact was dramatic. F. Roy Coad summarizes the results of Darby's labors when he writes:

> His energy was prodigious, and his gifts scarcely less so. When he died, he left behind him some fifteen hundred churches—in Britain and on the Continent, in North America and the West Indies, in New Zealand and Australia—who looked to him as their founder or their guide. His writings fill over forty volumes, and include comments and controversy over most of the great ecclesiastical events occurring during his long lifetime. In addition to a five volume *Synopsis of the Books of the Bible*, his individual commentaries cover the larger part of the Bible. His linguistic gifts were of no mean order, and he translated the whole Bible not only into English ... but also into French and German, and the New Testament into Italian. His travels were world-wide. (Coad, 1968, 106)

III. Theology

Darby is best known for dispensationalism. Dispensationalism is a structure designed to explain the relationships between the two testaments. This age-old conundrum was solved, argued Darby, by identifying different dispensations in which God relates differently with humanity. In addition, the promises made to Israel in the Old Testament will be literally fulfilled.

For Darby there are seven dispensations. These are the dispensations of innocence (up until the Fall), conscience (from Adam to Noah), government (from Noah to Abraham), patriarchal rule (Abraham to Moses), Mosaic Law (from Moses to Christ), grace (from Christ to today), and the thousand-year rule that will be ushered in at the end of the age.

The two most important are the dispensation of law and the dispensation of the church. A deep interest for Darby was eschatology (the end of the age) and the way in which this dispensation would come to an end. Darby argued that a close reading of scripture suggests that the Second Coming of Jesus would be divided into two distinctive phases. The first was the rapture (when those who are born again in Christ rise and meet him in the skies); and the second was the visible return, which will usher in the thousand-year rule on earth. In between these two stages, Darby believed that there would be seven years' tribulation, during which the Antichrist would rise to prominence. During the period the Jewish people would be subject to attack from the other nations of the world.

This, in a thumbnail sketch, is the eschatology which has its roots in Darby's dispensationalism. Although dispensationalism has increasingly been challenged by evangelical scholars, the eschatology remains as popular as ever. The problems with dispensationalism are well known: it does sound a little odd to insist that technically the Lord's Prayer was never intended for the dispensation of the church (come to that neither was the Sermon on the Mount) since this was a teaching for an age when the Messiah had been accepted and recognized (see Barr, 1981). As for the eschatology, it has generated a veritable industry examining the "signs of the times" and seeking to identify how close the Second Coming is.

Any survey of the theology of Darby needs to describe his strict teaching around separation from the world. Darby taught the importance of withdrawing from evil (see Callahan, 1996). The key text is 2 Timothy 2:19: "The Lord knows those that are his; and, Let everyone who names the name of the Lord withdraw from iniquity" (as translated by J. N. Darby). The so-called Exclusive Brethren take this text very literally. One cannot eat with those who are outside the sect; one cannot watch television, listen to the radio, or use the internet. All contact with the outside world is kept to a minimum. Darby's teaching contained the seed for the extreme expression of it currently practiced today.

References

Barr, James. 1981. *Fundamentalism*. London: SCM Press.

Callahan, James Patrick. 1996. *Primitivist Piety: The Ecclesiology of the Early Plymouth Brethren*. Lanham, MD: Scarecrow Press.

IV.   Significance

Darby's impact on Christianity has been major. He simultaneously created a theology that holds the popular imagination and was popularized very effectively in the margins of the Schofield Bible, and, at the same time, created a secret denomination. Interestingly, it is not that he is studied today (save by historians of theology who are curious to see where the rapture eschatology comes from). Yet he has done sufficient to merit an entry in the *Companion to the Theologians*.

Coad, F. Roy. 1968. *A History of the Brethren Movement*. Exeter: Paternoster Press.

Melton, J. Gordon. 1999. *The Encyclopedia of American Religions*, 6th ed. Detroit and London: Gale Research 1999.

Rowdon, Harold. 1967. *The Origins of the Brethren, 1825–1850*. London: Pickering and Inglis.

Georges Vasilievich Florovsky (1893–1979)

Augustine Casiday

I. Summary

G. V. Florovsky was a Russian Orthodox priest and theologian. He pursued his career outside of Russia—first in Eastern Europe, then Paris, and eventually the United States. He was the intellectual architect of the "Neo-Patristic Synthesis," which is at present the predominant idiom of Orthodox theology in the West and which has successfully promoted *ressourcement* in the Orthodox world. Additionally, Florovsky was for over 30 years deeply involved in the modern ecumenical movement at local, national, and international levels, among other things serving as a founding member of the World Council of Churches (WCC). Florovsky did not shy away from taking controversial positions and from clashing with other major theologians. For example, he worked out his synthesis in confrontation with another major mode of Orthodox theology, "Russian religious philosophy," which in recent years has experienced something of a revival. As regards his contributions to the ecumenical movement, in many ways they have been left behind over the decades. In both cases, however, his influence is tremendous and it may be hoped that, if his legacy is treated with the kind of care and scrutiny that was his own ideal in theological and historical research, his contributions will continue to enrich Christian theology generally.

II. Life

Georges Vasilievich Florovsky was the fifth child of Klavdia Georgievna Popruzhenko (1863–1933) and Vasili Antonovich Florovsky (1852–1928), born in Elizavetgrad, Russia, on August 28, 1893. His parents had made their home in Odessa previously and, though they lived in Elizavetgrad for a decade, Odessa was very much the family home. They returned there soon after Georges's birth. Both of Florovsky's grandfathers were priests: his paternal grandfather, in a tiny village near Novgorod; his maternal grandfather, in Odessa, where he was professor of Hebrew and Greek in the theological seminary. Florovky's father was headmaster of ecclesiastical schools and later in life became dean of Odessa Cathedral. His mother was a cultured and literate person from an academically inclined family. Breadth of intellectual activity was characteristic of the household. All of the Florovsky children (with the exception of Maria, who died in infancy in Elizavetgrad) were well educated. The eldest, Vasilii (1881–1924), trained as a physician. He was the only member of the family to remain in Russia after the Bolshevik Revolution. He was also the only one of Florovsky's siblings not to pursue an academic career: Klavdia (1883–1963) was a talented linguist and medievalist who studied throughout Western Europe, and Antonii (1884–1968) became professor of Russian history in Prague's renowned Charles University.

The Student's Companion to the Theologians, First Edition. Edited by Ian S. Markham.
© 2013 Blackwell Publishing Ltd. Published 2013 by Blackwell Publishing Ltd.

Florovsky's intellectual formation appears to have been rather more grounded in practical disciplines than were those of many eminent Russians born a generation earlier. His formal education was regularly interrupted by his poor health, but he was a bookish child and began amassing his vast erudition from an early age. In 1902, he registered at the Fifth State Gymnasium in Odessa. He completed the course of study with distinction in 1911, and that autumn he registered as a student in the university in Odessa. There he chiefly studied philosophy, but one of his professors was a committed positivist and insisted that Florovsky familiarize himself with experimental physiological psychology—which resulted in an early publication, supported by Pavlov (Florovsky, 1917). He was awarded a university diploma in 1916. Whilst preparing for the examinations leading to a master's degree (1917–19), he taught philosophy and history of philosophy locally. After completing the examinations (1919), he became a *privatdozent* in the university. But shortly thereafter, he left Russia with his father, mother, and sister as a direct result of the social and political turbulence that followed in the wake of the Revolution.

The family first relocated to Sofia, Bulgaria. There, in late 1921, Florovsky met Xenia Ivanovna Simonovna as she and her sister were traveling to Prague. In December of that year, Florovsky accepted a scholarship offered through the Czechoslovakian Academic Commission of the Committee to Provide for the Education of Russian Studies. He undertook a dissertation on the historical philosophy of A. I. Herzen (1812–70). While in Prague, Florovsky again met Xenia and the two were married that April. Meanwhile, President Thomas G. Masaryk's initiative, "Action Russe" (Riha, 1958), which was funding Florovsky's scholarship, began attracting to Prague a large number of intellectuals whom the Bolsheviks expelled from Soviet Russia. Soon, Florovsky found himself in the midst of a vibrant community of highly educated Russians (Raeff, 1990, 47–72). Out of this community developed the Russian Law Faculty, which existed from 1922 to 1928, under the aegis of Charles University. After completing and defending his dissertation, Florovsky was made *privatdozent* in the Russian Law Faculty, where his colleagues included P. B. Struve, N. O. Lossky, and Fr Sergii

Bulgakov (see the photographic guide to the faculty in 1927, reprinted in Blane, 1993), all of whom had serious interests in the philosophical pursuit of religious questions.

During this time, a synod of Russian bishops formed at Sremsi Karlovci, Serbia, to provide direction for the religious life of Russian Orthodox Christians in Western Europe. Relations between the religious communities in the West were not always cordial and local problems were compounded by developments within Soviet Russia and irreconcilable differences amongst the emigrants about how to respond to them. Three distinct groups formed within the Russian diaspora (see Raeff, 1990, 118–55): those who remained under the jurisdiction of Moscow; those who belonged to the Karlovci Synod, subsequently known as the Russian Orthodox Church Abroad (ROCA); and those who sought to be taken into the jurisdiction of the Church of Constantinople as the Exarchate of Parishes of Russian Tradition in Western Europe, under the direction of Metropolitan Evlogii (Georgievskii). The Exarchate was—and is—based in Paris and in 1925 its members founded a major center for higher education: the Institut de théologie Saint Serge. Florovsky's colleague from Prague, Sergii Bulgakov, was dean and he recruited Florovsky to join the faculty in 1926, encouraging him to study the fathers to prepare himself to teach patristic theology. In 1932, Evlogii ordained Florovsky to the priesthood as an assistant to Fr Sergii Chetverikov in the chapel of the Russian Christian Student Movement.

The Russian Christian Student Movement was from its inception in contact with other Christian organizations, being supported by the International YMCA and the Christian Student Movement under the leadership of Dr John R. Mott, a prominent Methodist. The Russian Christian Student Movement joined with the British Christian Student Movement in 1928 to found the Fellowship of St Alban and St Sergius, an explicitly ecumenical organization. Florovsky attended the annual meetings of the Fellowship from its beginning and the contacts that he made there resulted in regular invitations to lecture at theological colleges and religious establishments throughout the United Kingdom. These travels and lectures laid the foundation for Florovsky's long and productive ecumenical engagement (as when he participated in the Second Faith and Order Conference in Edinburgh, 1937) and led to his eventual participation as a founding member of the World Council of Churches. In France, Florovsky participated in an ecumenical colloquium organized by Berdaiev and attended by Maritain, Marcel, Gilson, Boegner, Monod, Vysheslavtsev, and Lot-Borodine among others. This group met for about a decade, until the mid-1930s, when it ended after fierce arguments between the conservative Maritain and the liberal Berdaiev.

Such debates were by no means limited to interconfessional meetings. In the mid-1930s, an intense debate arose around Bulgakov's teachings about the figure of Sophia, or divine Wisdom (Lialine, 1936; Lossky, 1936; Cioran, 1977, 247–72; Nichols, 1992; Blane, 1993, 65–8; R. Williams, 1999, 172–81; Valliere, 2000, 287–9; Geffert, 2005; Klimoff, 2005). In emphasizing the Wisdom of God, Bulgakov was part of a rapidly forming tradition that requires some introduction (for background, see Rosenthal, 1996; Valliere, 1996). The proximal source for this tradition was a man known and admired by Bulgakov: Vladimir Soloviev (1853–1900), an enigmatic visionary in whose philosophical, theological, and literary writings Sophia plays a prominent role (Cioran, 1977; Kornblatt, 1991; Pyman, 1994, 226–42). Taking as his point of departure much older, if largely inchoate, Slavic traditions (Ammann, 1938), Soloviev expressed in fluid poetry an intense yearning for the Wisdom of God, the "Eternal Feminine," who appeared to him in a vision three times: "Near, far off, not here, not there / In realms of mystic reveries, / In a world invisible to mortal eyes, / In a world neither of laughter nor of tears, // There it was, goddess, that I first / Recognized you one misty night …" (Soloviev, 1996, 19). Sophia enables the conjunction of divinity and humanity, and as such is central to an important series of lectures by Soloviev (Soloviev, 1948). The second major figure in Russian Sophiology was Pavel Florensky (1882–1937), a polymath whose chief writing contains an extensive treatment of Sophia (Florensky, 1997, 231–83), which he held back when submitting the work to the Moscow Theological Academy. The creative scope, intellectual audacity, and pace of development of early experiments in Sophiology are exceptional.

Bulgakov was personally devoted to Soloviev's memory (Klimoff, 2005, 73) and was a friend of Florensky. Bulgakov felt prophetically charged to proclaim Sophia himself (ibid., 68, n.6): "God has chosen me, a weak and unworthy man, to be a witness to the Divine Sophia and to her revelation." He contributed greatly through his own writings to the domestication—even the attempted indigenization—of Sophia into Orthodox dogmatic theology that would go well beyond the eclectic, frankly syncretistic and deeply personal writings of his predecessors. It would be inaccurate to depict Sophiology as a characteristic preoccupation of Russian religious theologians at large, but it is fair to say that interest in the topic (contributing directly to its evolution) found a natural and accommodating home in Russian religious philosophy. Florovsky devotes considerable attention in *Ways of Russian Theology* to criticizing that tradition as a whole, and Sophiology in particular. The book was published in 1937, when controversy over Sophia was raging in the Russian theological community. The theological issues at stake were important—particularly as they illuminate Florovsky's theology—but we shall reserve treatment of them for the moment and consider instead the social circumstances.

Like Florovsky, Bulgakov belonged to the Exarchate and taught in its academic institution, but in 1935 condemnations of his theology were independently issued by the Moscow Patriarchate and ROCA. The political and personal circumstances were fraught, and only aggravated the situation as mutual recriminations began to fly (Klimoff, 2005, 82–5). Evlogii empanelled a theological committee to evaluate Bulgakov's teachings and offer a response. Naturally, he turned for theological expertise to the faculty at Saint Serge. As we have noted, Florovsky was by this time already established as a strong critic of the "sophiological" tradition. But he was also on friendly terms with Bulgakov and owed much of his career development to him, so he was understandably reluctant to participate, but Evlogii obliged him to (Blane, 1993, 66). Although Florovsky was candid in corresponding with friends about the events, in public he maintained studied silence, to the great exasperation of Chetverikov who constantly petitioned Florovsky to take an active part in formulating a response (Klimoff, 2005).

The commission produced two reports (Geffert, 2005; see also Blane, 1993, 65–8, and Klimoff, 2005), both of which rejected the condemnations while duly noting that some points in Bulgakov's teachings may be understandably disquieting. But there is a striking difference in tone between them. The majority report vindicates Bulgakov at length, whereas the minority report (drafted by Chetverikov and endorsed by Florovsky) expresses much more concern at Bulgakov's teaching:

> It is true that Fr Bulgakov attempts to establish or confirm his teaching by arguments from tradition. Nevertheless in his teaching on Sophia the Wisdom of God his references to tradition cannot be recognised as satisfactory. … The attempt to mitigate this cleavage of opinion between Fr Bulgakov and the main stream of the teaching of the Fathers, by reference to another opinion in patristic literature, cannot be regarded as convincing. (Geffert, 2005, 63)

In a letter sent to Florovsky, a shrewd contemporaneous observer assessed the factions within Evlogii's theological committee in this way: "They divide into those whose sincere purpose is to vindicate sound theology, and those whose equally sincere purpose is to defend Fr Sergius" (quoted by Klimoff, 2005, 91).

Long after the events, Florovsky reported that on the basis of these reports a *retractio* was requested and duly received from Bulgakov (see Blane, 1993, 67), though no documentary evidence in support of this recollection has been found (thus Klimoff, 2005, 94). Furthermore, even while Evlogii's committee conducted its work—and for years thereafter, if we may judge from Alexander Schmemann's memoirs of his student days at Saint Serge, near the end of Bulgakov's career (ibid., 81)—Bulgakov continued to advocate his Sophiacentric theology, even bringing out a book that summarizes his position (Bulgakov, 1937) in the same year that Florovsky's *Ways of Russian Theology* appeared. Bulgakov survived the ordeal, secure in Evlogii's patronage and at Saint Serge. By contrast, despite his efforts to stand aloof from the processes, Florovsky's reputation suffered very badly because of his involvement: he was even flatly accused of intrigue against Bulgakov in hopes of taking control of Saint Serge (see Klimoff, 2005, 85–6, 97). The vitriol that

made Florovsky's position in Paris untenable was fueled by the resentment that others felt by proxy for Bulgakov, despite the fact that Bulgakov and Florovsky's personal relationship seems not to have been damaged by the events. Further, the frosty reception that Florovsky's magisterial *Ways of Russian Theology* received from the Russian community in the West upon its publication indicates that Florovsky was at odds with the zeitgeist (Berdiaev, 1937; Schmemann, 1952–3, 8; Blane, 1993, 52–3). Florovsky increasingly availed himself of the opportunity to study and to lecture abroad, spending much time especially in England.

In 1948, Florovsky accepted an invitation to join the faculty of the St Vladimir's Orthodox Theological Seminary in New York. The seminary had recently been formed and was in a period of transition. Florovsky became the seminary's second dean in 1950 and set a course for the fledgling institution that has largely been followed, despite some tumult (Meyendorff et al., 1988). His vision was for Anglophone education that would enable the Orthodox to present the truth of their legacy in America and the West. As he said in an address shortly before taking up the post,

> Orthodoxy is not a thing which can be kept simply by inertia. No tradition can survive unless it is continued in a creative effort. The message of Christ is eternal and always the same, but it must be reinterpreted again and again so as to become a challenge to every new generation … We have not simply to keep the legacy of the past, we have to do everything we can in order to present it to others as a living thing … (Blane, 1993, 93)

To that end, he recruited to St Vladimir's from Paris two talented young scholars each of whom would eventually become dean of the seminary: the liturgiologist Alexander Schmemann (1921–83) and the Byzantinist John Meyendorff (1929–92). Despite some considerable successes, Florovsky's administrative style provoked hostility, as when, for example, he attempted to make the study of Greek mandatory. This and related difficulties ultimately led to his dismissal at the end of the 1954–5 academic year (Blane, 1993, 110–12). He lectured for a year at Holy Cross Greek Orthodox Seminary during the next year, and in 1956 he was appointed as Lecturer in Eastern Church History in the Divinity School at Harvard. He taught there (and occasionally in the College's program in Slavic Studies) until he reached 70 years of age, at which point he faced compulsory retirement. In recognition of his work, he was made professor emeritus.

The Florovskys then moved to Princeton, where from 1964 to 1972 he was appointed annually by the university to teach seminars in Slavic literature, Russian history, and patristic theology. At the end of this period, Florovsky was nearly 80 years old and so could not be reappointed. However, they were not able to afford retirement, so his friends arranged additional funding to supplement his pension and savings; Florovsky arranged to sell off his personal library—estimated at no fewer than 16,000 volumes—to Princeton University's library (see Blane, 1993, 202 n.184); and Princeton Theological Seminary provided him a stipend and the title Visiting Lecturer in Church History in exchange for continued teaching. Xenia, his wife of 55 years, died on November 5, 1977; Florovsky himself died in Princeton, New Jersey, on August 11, 1979.

During this long and varied career, Florovsky wrote prolifically. His bibliography includes approximately 400 items (Blane, 1993, 341–401), many of which were collected into a 14-volume series (Florovsky, 1972–1989). (According to Blane [1993, 209 n.28], Florovsky only approved of the first two volumes in this series and expressed grave concerns at editorial changes in Vol. 3, going so far as to have his lawyer write to the publisher; the subsequent volumes were not subject to Florovsky's review because they appeared posthumously.) He was awarded honorary doctorates by the University of St Andrews (1937), Boston University (1950), Salonika University (1959—as part of the celebrations for the sixth centenary of the death of St Gregory Palamas), Notre Dame University (1966), St Vladimir's Orthodox Theological Seminary (1968), Yale University (1973), and Princeton University (1974). He was elected into the Academy of Athens, the American Academy of Arts and Sciences, and the Belgian Académie des Sciences Religieuses (1965), and was a corresponding fellowship of the British Academy (1976). During his lifetime, three *Festschriften* were dedicated to him (Neiman and Schatkin, 1973; Blane and Bird, 1974;

Blane, 1975). He maintained an international profile in ecumenical engagements (Visser 't Hooft, 1979), attending Faith and Order Conferences for the WCC (Edinburgh, 1937; Lund, 1952) and, as a member of the Central Committee and Executive Committee of the WCC, the Amsterdam Assembly (1948), the Evanston Assembly (1954), and the New Dehli Assembly (1964), after which he stepped down from the Central Committee and the Executive Committee. He also attended the Uppsala Assembly (1968). He attended the International Byzantine Conference in Munich (1958) and two meetings of the International Conference on Patristic Studies (Oxford, 1959/1963). His most prominent former student is John Zizioulas, Metropolitan of Pergamon, who has carried forward and developed Florovsky's work on personhood and his characteristic emphasis on the liturgical roots of Christian theology (though this to anticipate our next section). And while he taught at Princeton Theological Seminary, his classes were attended by Gebre Medhin Wolde Yohannes, now known as Abune Paulos, patriarch of the Ethiopian Orthodox Tewahedo Church (1992–present), and one of the eight presidents of the World Council of Churches (2006–present).

III.   Theological Legacy

Across his vast corpus of writings, many themes emerge (see Schultze, 1941, 1942, 1946; Künkel, 1991; G. Williams, 1993) but two are particularly important: the "Neo-Patristic Synthesis" and ecumenism, both of which are rooted in his emphasis on orthodox christology. In brief, the Neo-Patristic Synthesis describes a method for rediscovering and reinterpreting traditional Christianity in the modern period; ecumenism is the frame of reference in which Florovsky presented this rediscovered, reinterpreted tradition; christological orthodoxy is the meaning of the tradition as well as the basis for ecumenism and the criteria for evaluating theological developments (cf. Künkel, 1982, 74–100). An excellent but concise example of these three themes in situ is found in a homiletic essay in which he asserts the contemporary relevance of Chalcedonian christology as a response to the tragedy of the human condition and describes some of the dangers of falling short of an orthodox confession of faith (Florovsky, 1972, 9–16). But it is worth while to take the major themes of his work in turn.

Neo-Patristic Synthesis

Florovsky's call for a creative appropriation of historical Christian belief was worked out through the process of critically studying the history of Russian theology (Florovsky, 1979, 1987a). What he found was a "breach" between theology and the ecclesiastical experience of prayer (Florovsky, 1979, 134), the consequences of which are seen in a "rupture and divergence" between intellect and instinct (Florovsky, 1987a, 57–8). The experience of this rupture was felt by many intelligent and devout people, but most of the responses served only to compound the problem—whether by introducing into Russian Orthodoxy alien habits of thought and so generating "pseudomorphoses" (Florovsky, 1979, 72), or through cultivating false nostalgia in "confessionalism of custom and routine" (ibid., 87) contributing to sectarianism (ibid., 97–8), or else promoting irresponsibility and capriciousness under the guise of freedom (Florovsky, 1987a, 241), or even encouraging "an exodus from history" (ibid., 221) through breaking from the traditional Byzantine Greek heritage of Russian Orthodoxy. Florovsky's response is otherwise (cf. Florovsky, 1979, xvii–xviii), based as it is on a conscientious, even "ascetic" (Florovsky, 1987a, 161, 289), entry into the historical experience of Christianity in all its specificity, which includes first and foremost the experience of Christian worship (cf. ibid., 293). Significantly, Florovsky regarded the liturgical books of the church as the first theological texts he read (Blane, 1993, 25, 153) and would come to criticize other projects for preferring esoteric imagery to the panoply of orthodox liturgical poetry (Florovsky, 1987a, 85–6). Because he identified the breach between theology and prayer as the underlying cause of these problems, his strategy for a viable contemporary theology was through an integration of worship and understanding in the classical Byzantine mode with all that that implies in terms of self-discipline, charity, and ascetic humility.

Because of the importance of Byzantium in his theological vision, Florovsky's project is often called "Christian Hellenism"—though he also endorsed a more descriptive title: the "Neo-Patristic Synthesis" (Künkel, 1991, 261–76; G. Williams 1993; Horuzhy, 2000). Rowan Williams has rightly said of Florovsky's work that it "is not a closed system, but a programme for positive contemporary theological exploration" (in Mascall and Williams, 1980, 72; cf. Blane, 1993, 155). It is arguably the highpoint of what one commentator has called "the Russian Oxford Movement" (Tyszkiewicz, 1938, 292). Although the project as a whole has been criticized for its perceived conservatism and inability to address itself to contemporary intellectual life (see Valliere, 2000, 1–7 and 343–403, who draws heavily from Bulgakov [1937] 2006), it is clear that as Florovsky conceived it the project is no justification for retrograde nationalism, mechanical repetitiveness, or saccharine nostalgia. To the contrary, according to Florovsky, it

> should be more than just a collection of Patristic sayings or statements. It must be a *synthesis*, a creative reassessment of those insights which were granted to the Holy Men of old. It must be *Patristic*, faithful to the spirit and vision of the Fathers, *ad mentem Patrum*. Yet, it must also be *Neo*-Patristic, since it is to be addressed to the new age, with its own problems and queries. (Blane, 1993, 154)

The synthesis is necessarily a dynamic engagement with the modern world and, as such, it belies attempts to trivialize it by comparison with the intellectually adventurous schemes of some of Florovsky's older contemporaries. That his project can sustain creative reinterpretation of historical material is abundantly clear from the work of his former student, John Zizioulas, who has for decades systematically explored the Greek Christian heritage (especially the writings of the Cappadocian fathers and of Maximus Confessor) in conversation with modern theology. Some prominent Orthodox patrologists are outspokenly critical of Zizioulas's theological project (for an evaluation, see Brown, 2007), but in any case Zizioulas's writings represent an organic continuation of Florovsky's research program.

The difference between the "Synthesis" and Russian religious philosophy is neatly illustrated by the Sophia controversy. In contrast to free play with traditional themes found in Florensky's (thus,

Florovsky, 1987a, 276–81) and in Soloviev's writings (ibid., 57–8, 80–1, 85–6), who found in Sophia a quasi-personal disclosure of the Divine Essence, Florovsky insisted that the authentic tradition of Orthodoxy identifies Sophia *as Christ* (Florovsky, 1975, 131–5). This claim has been contested (e.g., Zander, 1956), but several subsequent scholars corroborate it (Meyendorff, 1987; Fiene, 1989). Another area of difference between the Synthesis and Russian religious philosophy is in the theological concept of the "person": Florovsky's ideas were developed in conversation with traditional Orthodox literature (see Künkel, 1982, 120–40; 1991, 337–97), whereas Bulgakov's ideas (see Gallaher and Kukota, 2005) were freely adapted and revised with tenuous references to traditional categories. These contrasts point to two basic values of the Neo-Patristic Synthesis.

First, it insists that the past must be taken seriously and rejects carelessness about the past (whether that is to the benefit of the reputation of the past, or to its detriment)—and it does so in a genuinely critical way by learning from conversation with philosophers of history (cf. Florovsky, 1974, 31–65). Florovsky made his point quite bluntly in a letter to Bulgakov, criticizing Soloviev and Bulgakov himself for being influenced by him:

> I believe that in your case, too, Solov'ev long hindered you in your search for the main thing [sc., the church's doctrine of Sophia]. For the road to discovering it lies through Christology, not through Trinitology [*sic*], since only with Jesus Christ did the worship of the trinity become a reality. *The point here is that only in history, in the realm of historical experience, are we capable of understanding the creaturehood of creation.* (Cited by Klimoff, 2005, 75; emphasis added)

Soloviev and, by implication, Bulgakov have basically identified a serious problem (cf. Florovsky, 1987a, 57–8, 80–1), but their response is methodologically unsound and theologically flawed. Florovsky criticizes not creative engagement with the present, but catastrophic discontinuity with the past and the attempt to fill in the gaps with extrinsic ideas. Continuous development, proved by the touchstone of historical experience, is well within the remit of the Neo-Patristic Synthesis. Second, the deeper roots of Florovsky's synthesis (as compared to the various

syntheses attempted by representatives of the "Russian school") give the Neo-Patristic Synthesis a less culturally over-specified basis for interacting with other Christians—and a broader basis for interacting with Christians whose approach to faith is informed by history. Since that difference points us toward Florovsky's ecumenical work, we will delay consideration of it for now.

To borrow from Florovsky's appraisal of a contemporary innovation, his ideal is not a "return" or "reversion" to the past, but "a brave encounter with the advancing future" (Florovsky, 1987a, 283; likewise, see Florovsky, 1979, 42). Florovsky was as sensitive as Soloviev to the awful temptation for Orthodox Christians that traditionalism poses and would have sympathized with Soloviev's cautionary tale about the Antichrist beguiling Easterners away from Christ by offering them instead a "World Museum of Christian Archaeology …, with the aim of collecting, studying, and preserving all relics of church antiquity, especially of the Eastern Church" (Soloviev, 2000, 280). As Florovsky states (1987a, 292): "What is necessary is not a return to a naive primitivism but entry into history and the acquisition of its ecumenical and catholic traditions." The reference to ecumenical traditions is not incidental: the program will enable theologians "to get beyond the modern theological disputes, to recover the true 'catholic mind,' which would embrace the whole of the historical experience of the Church in its pilgrimage through the ages" (Florovsky, 1972, 58). The ecumenical implications of Florovsky's thinking, captured neatly in his idea of "ecumenism in time," bring us to his contributions to ecumenical theology.

Ecumenism

Like many Russian theologians over the last century and a half, Florovsky was preoccupied with the meaning of the church's "catholicity" (on Florovsky's ecclesiology, see Lelouvier, 1968; Chamberas, 1973; Salis Amaral, 2003; Nikolaev, 2005). Looking to Vincent of Lérins's famous saying, "what has been believed everywhere, always, by everyone," Florovsky (1972, 51–4) found it thought-provoking but inadequate. What Florovsky saw in the church's catholicity was first and foremost unity that derives from the fact that the church's "very being consists in reuniting separated and divided mankind" (ibid., 39). This reunion can occur within the church precisely because "Christ conquered the world. This victory consists in His having created His own Church. In the midst of the vanity and poverty, of the weakness and suffering of human history, He laid the foundations of a 'new being.' The Church is Christ's work on earth; it is the image and abode of His blessed Presence in the world" (ibid., 37). Florovsky understood Christ's Presence as an abiding presence, a historical feature of a church that exists in time. This understanding helps explain why he regarded Christian tradition as being so important to Christian theology (Florovsky 1972, 73–92, 123–5; ibid., 105–20, 127)—and it also helps explain why he regarded the multiplicity of churches as a tragedy: Christ is one, but unity among Christ's flock has been disrupted (Florovsky, 1989c, 28–33). As we noted above, Florovsky dedicated years of effort to ecumenical collaboration aimed at redressing that problem. Even though he vindicated the church's right to be involved in society, he was always wary of encroaching social activism insofar as it tends to distract from the main business of addressing differences in belief and doctrine (Florovsky, 1974, 131–42; see also Blane, 1993, 135–7). To use Florovsky's terms, "ecumenism in space" must be complemented by "ecumenism in time":

> No agreement that fails to do justice to the age-long process of Christian thinking and devotion can have a lasting value. The time itself must be redeemed and reintegrated. "Others have labored, and you have entered into their labors." It is but fair to say that we have not yet entered deeply enough into the labours of the preceding generations, of our fathers and forefathers in God. We are too much imprisoned in our own age. (Florovsky, 1989c, 32; see also Chamberas, 1973, 424–5)

That final sentiment recurs throughout Florovsky's writings. It is an earnest warning of the dangers that encompass those who are innocent of (or misinformed about) the past and, as such, are unable to understand the present and act appropriately.

Florovsky's *Ways of Russian Theology* is a massive testament to the possibility, even likelihood, of Orthodox succumbing to those dangers. Likewise, Florovsky is candid in evaluating the discrepancy between the holy calling of Orthodoxy and the human response to it:

> This does not mean that everything in the past or present state of the Orthodox Church is to be equated with the truth of God. Many things are obviously changeable; indeed many things need improvement. The true Church is not yet the perfect Church … The Church of Christ has to grow and be built up in history. Yet the whole and the full truth has been already given and entrusted to the Church. (Florovsky, 1952, 204–5)

Accordingly, Florovsky asserted (1989c, 160–4)—often to the intense frustration of others—that the role of the Orthodox Church in the World Council of Churches is to bear witness. However, the Orthodox Church bears witness, not to itself, but to Christ. The charge is awesome, entailing accountability before God, and as such it prompts stirrings of humility rather than pride. But since "the whole and the full truth" is a gift from God, it also prompts hopefulness and charity, even in the face of deep failures and entrenched problems.

With regard to the Christian West, Florovsky calls for a moratorium on the "old 'polemical theology'" that "has long ago lost its inner connection with reality"; what is needed instead as a response to the "western religious tragedy," he urges, is for it to "be reendured and relieved, precisely as one's own, and its potential catharsis must be demonstrated in the fullness of the experience of the Church and patristic tradition." He continues: "In this newly sought Orthodox synthesis, the centuries-old experience of the Catholic West must be studied and diagnosed by Orthodox theology with greater care and sympathy than has been the case up to now" (Florovsky, 1987a, 302–3). Further comments indicate that this co-suffering will link the Orthodox with the Christian West as a whole, not merely with the Church of Rome, in a movement of fraternal love.

In his ecumenical work, Florovsky's method of historical theology enables us to conjecture how this sympathetic entry into the West might bring about reconciliation (though not necessarily what form such reconciliation will take, since we are dealing here with a program, not a formula). While recognizing disruption and discontinuity as serious—even tragic—events that have shaped the circumstances of Russian theology, Florovsky accepts that Christ abode, abides, and will abide in the church and therefore has hope that the shortcomings of the past can be put right through entering into historically conditioned experience and so facing the present with creativity and courage. If this program is accepted, and the parameters are expanded from post-Kievan Russian Christian history to incorporate Christian history as a whole, then Florovsky's mode of historical theology can suggest a mode of ecumenical theology that will identify the mistakes of the past and rectify them as far as possible, doing all things to realize the truth of God in the perfection of the church.

IV. Conclusion

Although Florovsky's searching critique of his own theological heritage led to accusations that he stood apart, thundering down judgment upon it (Berdiaev, 1937), he was securely imbedded in the culture of twentieth-century Russian Orthodox Christianity (thus, Horuzhy, 2000). Areas of substantial agreement include Florovsky's emphasis on personal freedom (see Raeff, 1993, 255–7; G. Williams, 1993, 292–3), on which account he may be compared to Berdiaev (Spinka, 1950; Vallon, 1960); his lifelong attempt to articulate an authentically Orthodox theology that was not constrained by outmoded polemics, on which account he may be compared to Bulgakov (see Schultze, 1941); and his efforts to revivify the Russian Orthodox faith through a return to the sources so as to fortify it for its ecumenical role, on which account he may be compared to Soloviev (cf. Tyszkiewicz, 1938, 291–2, with its possible allusion to d'Herbigny, 1911). Florovsky was hardly averse to adapting ideas from other quarters, as morphological similarities between Florovsky's theological method and Heidegger's philosophical method indicate (see Horuzhy, 2000, 316–19). It is sometimes difficult to perceive these deep similarities because of the violent confrontations in which Florovsky was involved. But even in those confrontations, we can see that Florovsky was motivated to oppose a particular development (e.g. Bulgakov's Sophiology) out of commitment to a common belief (in this case, emphasis on personal freedom: see Mascall and Williams, 1980, 72), despite the fact that what he was opposing had itself been motivated by another common belief (i.e., the modern articulation of Orthodox theology).

More problematic than some perceived haughtiness with respect to Russian tradition is the overly schematic character of Florovsky's claims about history. We have already considered the importance he attributes to popular religions in Russia (Florovsky, 1987a, 293: "Faith is kept indivisible in the depths and innermost recesses of church experiences"; cf. his criticism of Berdyaev at Florovsky, 1950, 306). The positive content of this faith, cherished by anonymous generations, is unspecified—and this makes his implicit confidence in continuity in popular worship difficult to accept (cf. Raeff, 1993, 363). It is not clear that Florovsky meant to imply that the faith is somehow inscrutable and mysterious in principle, but in any case accounts of Russian Orthodoxy as lived and practiced in various eras are now available (see Fedotov, 1946; Kivelsen and Greene, 2003) and they give a lively impression of ages that are important to, but missing from, Florovsky's narrative. Leaving this material unaccounted for, even though as the bearer of continuity it is crucial to his argument, is a serious deficiency in Florovsky's work. Even his unsentimental account of the social situation of the priestly class and its effects of their children (Florovsky, 1987, 263–4), which offsets somewhat the problem, reads more like familial anecdote than the result of historical research. These shortcomings can be regarded as fallow ground for the further application of Florovsky's theological program. On a related note, a recent evaluation of Florovsky's ecumenical work (Petersen, 1996) identifies potential in that work for solutions to such problems as environmental degradation (ibid., 232–4), churches and mission (ibid., 234–8), and personhood (ibid., 238–42). There are, to be sure, specific claims in his writings—e.g., about Origen's intellectual responsibility for iconoclasm (Florovsky, 1974, 101–19)—which scholarship has disproved or else rendered otiose (see Casiday, 2004, 36–8). But on the whole the particulars of Florovsky's detailed work are not as significant as the method and principles of theological research that he articulated, which outline a process of creativity that honors the past and engages with the present whilst looking for the future.

References

Ammann, A. M. 1938. "Darstellung und Deutung der Sophia in vorpetriniscen Russland," *Orientalia Christiana Periodica* 4: 120–56.

Berdiaev, N. 1937. "Ortodoksiia a chelovechnost," *Put'* 53: 53–65.

Blane, Andrew, ed. 1975. *The Religious World of Russian Culture*. The Hague: Mouton.

Blane, Andrew, ed. 1993. *Georges Florovsky: Russian Intellectual, Orthodox Churchman*. Crestwood, NY: SVS Press.

Blane, Andrew. 1993. "A Sketch of the Life of Georges Florovsky." In Blane, 1993, pp. 11–217.

Blane, Andrew and Bird, Thomas E., eds. 1974. *The Ecumenical World of Orthodox Civilization*. The Hague: Mouton.

Brown, Alan. 2007. "On the Criticism of *Being as Communion* in Anglophone Orthodox Theology." In *The Theology of John Zizioulas: Personhood and the Church*, ed. D. Knight. Aldershot: Ashgate, pp. 35–78.

Bulgakov, S. [1936] 2006. "Dogma e Dogmatica." In *Lo spirituale della cultura*, trans. Maria Campatelli. Rome: Lipa, pp. 127–144. Original publication: 1936. "Dogma i Dogmat." In *Zhivoe Predanie. Pravoslavie v sovremennosti. Pravoslavnaja mysl'* 3: 9–24.

Bulgakov, S. 1937. *The Wisdom of God*. London: Williams and Norgate.

Casiday, A. 2004. "Christ, the Icon of the Father, in Evagrian Theology." In *Il Monachesimo tra Eredità e Aperture*, Studia Anselmiana 140, ed. M. Bielawski and D. Hombergen. Rome: Sant'Anselmo, pp. 31–60.

Chamb000ras, Peter. 1973. "Some Aspects of the Ecclesiology of Father Georges Vasilevich Florovsky." In Neiman and Schatkin, 1973, pp. 421–36.

Cioran, Samuel D. 1977. *Vladimir Solov'ev and the Knighthood of the Divine Sophia*. Waterloo, ON: Wilfred Laurier University Press.

d'Herbigny, Maurice. 1911. *Une Newman russe: Vladimir Soloviev (1853–1900)*. Paris: Beauchesne.

Fedotov, G. P. 1946. *The Russian Religious Mind*, vol. I. Cambridge, MA: Harvard University Press.

Fiene, Donald M. 1989. "What Is the Appearance of Divine Sophia?" *Slavic Review* 41: 449–6.

Florensky, Pavel. 1997. *The Pillar and Ground of Truth*, trans. B. Jakim. Princeton, NJ: Princeton University Press.

Florovsky, Georges. 1917. "On the Mechanism of Reflex Salivary Secretion," *Bulletin de l'Académie Impériale des Sciences* 6(2): 119–37 and plates I–IV.

Florovsky, Georges. 1950. "Review of *Introduction to Berdyaev* by Clarke and *Nicolas Berdyaev* by Spinka," *Church History* 19: 305–6.

Florovsky, Georges. 1952. "Confessional Loyalty in the Ecumenical Movement." In *Intercommunion*, ed. D. Baillie and J. Marsh. London: SCM, pp. 196–205.

Florovsky, Georges. 1972–89. *The Collected Works*, 14 vols., ed. R. S. Haugh.

Florovsky, Georges. 1972. *Volume 1: Bible, Church, Tradition*. Belmont, MA: Nordland.

Florovsky, Georges. 1974. *Volume 2: Christianity and Culture*. Belmont, MA: Nordland.

Florovsky, Georges. 1975. *Volume 4: Aspects of Church History*. Belmont, MA: Nordland

Florovsky, Georges. 1976. *Volume 3: Creation and Redemption*. Belmont, MA: Nordland.

Florovsky, Georges. 1979. *Volume 5: Ways of Russian Theology, Part I*. Belmont, MA· Nordland.

Florovsky, Georges. 1987a. *Volume 6: Ways of Russian Theology, Part II*. Vaduz, Liechtenstein: Büchvertriebsanstalt.

Florovsky, Georges. 1987b. *Volume 7: Eastern Fathers of the Fourth Century*. Vaduz, Liechtenstein: Büchvertriebsanstalt.

Florovsky, Georges. 1987c. *Volume 8: Byzantine Fathers of the Fifth Century*. Vaduz, Liechtenstein: Büchvertriebsanstalt.

Florovsky, Georges. 1987d. *Volume 9: Byzantine Fathers of the Sixth to Eight Centuries*. Vaduz, Liechtenstein: Büchvertriebsanstalt.

Florovsky, Georges. 1987e. *Volume 10: Byzantine Ascetic and Spiritual Fathers*. Vaduz, Liechtenstein: Büchvertriebsanstalt.

Florovsky, Georges. 1989a. *Volume 11: Theology and Literature*. Vaduz, Liechtenstein: Büchvertriebsanstalt.

Florovsky, Georges. 1989b. *Volume 12: Philosophy*. Vaduz, Liechtenstein: Büchvertriebsanstalt.

Florovsky, Georges. 1989c. *Volume 13: Ecumenism I: A Doctrinal Approach*. Vaduz, Liechtenstein: Büchvertriebsanstalt.

Florovsky, Georges. 1989d. *Volume 14: Ecumenism II: An Historical Approach*. Vaduz, Liechtenstein: Büchvertriebsanstalt.

Gallaher, A. B. and Kukota, Irina. 2005. "Protopresbyter Sergii Bulgakov: Hypostasis and Hypostaticity: Scholia to *The Unfading Light*," *St Vladimir's Theological Quarterly* 49: 5–46.

Geffert, Bryn. 2005. "The Charges of Heresy against Sergii Bulgakov," *St Vladimir's Theological Quarterly* 49: 47–66.

Horuzhy, S. S. 2000. "Neo-Patristic Synthesis and Russian Philosophy," *St Vladimir's Theological Quarterly* 44: 309–28.

Kivelsen, V. A. and Greene, R. H., eds. 2003. *Orthodox Russia. Belief and Practice under the Tsars*. University Park, PA: Pennsylvania State University Press.

Klimoff, Alexis. 2005. "Georges Florovsky and the Sophiological Controversy," *St Vladimir's Theological Quarterly* 49: 67–100.

Kornblatt, J. D. 1991. "Solov'ev's Androgynous Sophia and the Jewish Kabbalah," *Slavic Review* 50: 487–96.

Kornblatt, J. D. and Gustafson, R. F., eds. 1996. *Russian Religious Thought*. Madison, WI: University of Wisconsin Press.

Künkel, Christoph. 1982. "Man's Creation and Salvation according to George V. Florovsky." MA thesis, Department of Theology, University of Durham, Durham.

Künkel, Christoph. 1991. *Totus Christus: Die Theologie Georges V. Florovskys*. Gottingen: Vandenhoeck & Ruprecht.

Lelouvier, Yves-Noël. 1968. *Perspectives russes sur l'Eglise: Un théologien contemporain*. Paris: Centurion.

Lialine, C. 1936. "Le Débat Sophiologique," *Irénikon* 13: 168–205, 328–9, 704–5.

Lossky, Vladimir. 1936. *Spor o Sofii*. Paris: YMCA Press.

Mascall, E. L. and Williams, R. 1980. "George Florovsky (1893–1979)," *Sobornost* 2: 69–72.

Meyendorff, J. 1987. "Wisdom-Sophia: Contrasting Approaches to a Complex Theme," *Dumbarton Oaks Papers* 41: 391–401.

Meyendorff, J. et al., eds. 1988. *A Legacy of Excellence*. Crestwood, NY: SVS Press.

Neiman, D. and Schatkin, M. A., eds. 1973. *The Heritage of the Early Church: Essays in Honor of Georges Vasilievich Florovsky*. Rome: Pont. Institutum Studiorum Orientalium.

Nichols, Aidan. 1992. "Bulgakov and Sophiology," *Sobornost* 13: 17–31.

Nikolaev, Sergei V. 2005. "Spiritual Unity: The Role of Religious Authority in the Disputes between Sergii Bulgakov and Georges Florovsky Concerning Intercommunion," *St Vladimir's Theological Quarterly* 49: 101–24.

Petersen, Rodney L. 1996. "Local Ecumenism and the Neo-Patristic Synthesis of Father Georges Florovsky," *Greek Orthodox Theological Review* 41: 217–42.

Pyman, Avril. 1994. *A History of Russian Symbolism*. Cambridge: Cambridge University Press.

Raeff, Marc. 1990. *Russia Abroad: A Cultural History of the Russian Emigration, 1919–1939*. New York: Oxford University Press.

Raeff, Marc. 1993. "Enticements and Rifts: Georges Florovsky as Russian Intellectual Historian." In Blane, 1993, pp. 219–86.

Riha, T. 1958. "Russian Émigré Scholars in Prague after World War I," *The Slavic and East European Journal* 2: 22–6.

Rosenthal, Bernice. 1996. "The Nature and Function of Sophia in Sergei Bulgakov's Prerevolutionary Thought." In Kornblatt and Gustafson, 1996, pp. 154–75.

Salis Amaral, Miguel de. 2003. *Dos visions ortodoxas de la Iglesia: Bulgakov y Florovsky*. Pamplona: EUNSA.

Schememann, Alexander. 1952–3. "Roll of Honor," *St Vladimir's Seminary Quarterly* 1: 5–11.

Schultze, Bernhard. 1941. "Problemi di teologia presso gli ortodossi, I," *Orientalia christiana periodica* 7: 149–205.

Schultze, Bernhard. 1942. "Problemi di teologia presso gli ortodossi, II," *Orientalia christiana periodica* 8: 144–82.

Schultze, Bernhard. 1946. "La nuova soteriologia russa, II," *Orientalia christiana periodica* 12: 130–76.

Soloviev, Vladimir. 1948. *Lectures on Godmanhood*. London: Dennis Dobson. [N.B. The author's surname is transliterated in this case as "Solovyev".]

Soloviev, Vladimir. 1996. *Vladimir Solovyov's Poems of Sophia*, trans. B. Jakim and L. Magnus. N.p.: Variable Press.

Soloviev, Vladimir. 2000. "A Brief Tale about the Antichrist." In *Politics, Laws, and Morality*, ed. and trans. V. Wozniuk. New Haven, CT: Yale University Press, pp. 264–89.

Spinka, M. 1950. *Nicolas Berdyaev: Captive of Freedom*. Philadelphia: Westminster.

Tyszkiewicz, S. 1938. "Compte-rendu: R.P. Georges Florovksy," *Puti Russkago Bogosloviia*. *Orientalia Christiana Periodica* 4: 288–91.

Valliere, P. 1996. "Sophiology as the Dialogue of Orthodoxy with Modern Civilization." In Kornblatt and Gustafson, 1996, pp. 176–92.

Valliere, P. 2000. *Modern Russian Theology*. Edinburgh: T&T Clark.

Vallon, M. A. 1960. *An Apostle of Freedom: Life and Teachings of Nicolas Berdyaev*. New York: Philosophical Library.

Visser 't Hooft, Willem. 1979. "Fr. Georges Florovsky's Role in the Formation of the WCC," *St Vladimir's Theological Quarterly* 23: 135–8.

Williams, George H. 1965. "Georges Vasilievich Florovsky: His American Career (1948–1965)," *Greek Orthodox Theological Review* 11: 7–107.

Williams, George H. 1982. "Faculty of Divinity-Memorial Minute: Georges Florovsky," *Harvard University Gazette* 78(5): 5, 11.

Williams, George H. 1993. "The Neo-Patristic Synthesis of Georges Florovsky." In Blane, 1993, pp. 287–340.

Williams, Rowan. 1999. *Sergii Bulgakov: Towards a Russian Political Theology*. Edinburgh: T&T Clark.

Zander, Lev. 1956. "Die Weisheit Gottes im russischen Glauben und Denken," *Kerygma und Dogma* 2: 33–6, 40–6.

Georg Wilhelm Friedrich Hegel (1770–1831)

Craig A. Phillips

I. Biography

The Hegel family first settled in Württemberg during the sixteenth century when Protestant refugees fled from the Austrian territory of Ferdinand II to the duchy of Württemberg in southern Germany. Many of Hegel's ancestors and descendants served as church pastors and deacons.

Georg Wilhelm Friedrich Hegel was born in Stuttgart on August 27, 1770. His father, Georg Ludwig Hegel, who had studied law at Tübingen, served as a revenue officer and later as an expeditionary councilor in the duchy of Württemberg (Wiedmann, 1968, 9). His father and his mother, Maria Magdalena Louisa Fromm, were married in 1769. They had six children; only three survived into adulthood. Hegel had two younger siblings: a sister, Christiane Luise, and a brother, Georg Ludwig. Christiane never married, choosing after her mother's death to care for her father. She died a short time after Hegel. His brother became an officer in the service of Napoleon and was killed during the campaign in Russia.

Hegel began his schooling in Stuttgart at the age of three in the German School. At the age of five he enrolled at the Latin School. Before he began his classes at the Latin School, Hegel's mother, who was quite educated for a woman of her time, taught him the first declension and vocabulary in Latin in preparation for his studies. In 1777 Hegel began his education at the Gymnasium in Stuttgart where the curriculum focused primarily on Greek and Roman classics.

The most traumatic event in Hegel's early childhood was the death of his mother, who died of an abdominal infection when Hegel was only 11 years old. Hegel was deeply attached to his mother and her death was a strain on his relationship with his father.

Hegel excelled in his studies and in 1788 he was sent on a ducal scholarship to the Theological Seminary at the University of Tübingen. At Tübingen Hegel established significant friendships with his fellow students, the poet Friedrich Hölderlin (1770–1843) and the philosopher Friedrich Schelling (1775–1854). He and his classmates shared an interest in Rousseau and an enthusiasm for the ideals of the French Revolution. As a tribute to the Revolution, one Sunday morning in 1791 Hegel and a few of his classmates planted a liberty tree in a field outside of town. Hegel matured in a time of enormous political, social, artistic, and religious change. The egalitarian political aspirations of the revolutions in America and in France gave impetus to democratic social aspirations throughout Europe. Hegel and his classmates keenly observed these developments and they served as an important inspiration to Hegel in his studies and earliest writings.

The final certificate given to him by his teachers at Tübingen upon completion of his examinations

The Student's Companion to the Theologians, First Edition. Edited by Ian S. Markham.
© 2013 Blackwell Publishing Ltd. Published 2013 by Blackwell Publishing Ltd.

read: "He did not neglect his theological studies and worked zealously at sacred oratory [but] in his delivery he was seen to be no great orator. Not ignorant of philology, he devoted much labor to philosophy" (Wiedmann, 1968, 23).

Upon graduation from the theological seminary Hegel did not go into the ordained ministry. In 1793 he became a private tutor to a wealthy family in Bern until 1797 when, at the urging of his friend Hölderlin, he moved to Frankfurt to take a similar position. These positions allowed Hegel time for writing and study. When Hegel's father died in 1799, leaving Hegel a small inheritance, Hegel wrote to Schelling in Jena asking for his assistance in making academic connections at the University of Jena. In 1801, with Schelling's help, Hegel accepted a position as an unsalaried lecturer (*Privatdozent*) in Jena. His first published work in that year examined the "Difference between Fichte's and Schelling's Systems of Philosophy," which led many to the conclusion that Hegel was a disciple of Schelling. Together Hegel and Schelling founded the *Critical Journal of Philosophy* to which Hegel contributed many articles. In the meantime, Hegel was quietly at work developing his own philosophical system. The first book in which Hegel announced the outline and shape of his own philosophical system, *Die Phenomenologie des Geistes*, was published in 1807. (Because of the meaning of the German word *Geist*, this book can be translated as *The Phenomenology of Spirit* [Hegel, 1977] or *The Phenomenology of Mind* [Hegel, 1967].) Many philosophers consider this to be Hegel's greatest work.

The Battle of Jena, which took place on October 14, 1806, effectively closed the University of Jena; Hegel as a result was forced to look for work elsewhere. From 1807 to 1808 he worked as the editor of the *Bamberger Zeitung*. In 1808 Hegel became the rector of a Gymnasium in Nuremberg, a position he held until 1816.

Hegel had four children. A son, the result of an affair between Hegel and his landlord's wife during the time he lived in Jena, was born in 1807. In 1811, at the age of 41, Hegel married the 20-year-old Maria von Tucher of Nuremberg. They had three children: a girl who died in childhood, and two boys.

Between 1812 and 1816 Hegel published the three volumes of his *Science of Logic* (*Die Wissenschaft der Logik*). In 1816 Hegel received offers to teach from three universities: Erlangen, Heidelberg, and Berlin. He accepted the offer from Heidelberg. In 1817 Hegel published *The Encyclopedia of the Philosophical Sciences in Outline* (*Die Encyklopädie der philosophischen Wissenschaften im Grundrisse*, 2nd. ed 1827, 3rd ed. 1830). This work outlined the three major divisions of his philosophical system: a logic, philosophy of nature, and philosophy of spirit. In 1818 Hegel was offered the chair that J. G. Fichte had held in Berlin. Hegel rose to the height of his fame during the time he was in Berlin. There he published his lectures on the Philosophy of Religion, Aesthetics and the History of Philosophy, and his Philosophy of History. Significant political and social unrest followed the 1819 assassination of the conservative German playwright August Freidrich von Kotzebue, who had served the Russian Tsar. In response to this, Hegel published his *Outline of a Philosophy of Right* (*Grundlinien der Philosophie des Rechts*) in 1821. In this work Hegel proposed a philosophy of the state that he hoped would provide the ground for a stable political and social order. In 1830 he became the rector of the University of Berlin. Only a year later, on November 14, 1831, Hegel died during an outbreak of cholera.

II. Reading and Interpreting Hegel

Hegel's philosophical prose is dense and often difficult to follow. The vocabulary as well as the abstractness and complexity of his writings make the explication of his philosophical work difficult and sometimes frustrating. Hegel's colleague at the University of Berlin, Arthur Schopenhauer, once wrote that "the greatest effrontery in serving up sheer nonsense, in scrabbling together senseless and maddening webs of words, such as had previously been heard only in madhouses, finally appeared in Hegel. It became the instrument of the most ponderous and general mystification that has ever existed, with a result that will seem incredible to posterity, and be a lasting monument to German stupidity" (Houlgate, 2005, 1; Schopenhauer, 1969, xxiv, 429). In his reflection on Schopenhauer's "tirades" concerning Hegel's "bombast," Theodor Adorno observed that, "In the realm of great philosophy Hegel is no doubt the only one with whom at times one literally does not know and cannot conclusively determine what is being talked about, and with whom there is no guarantee that such a judgment is even possible" (Adorno, 1994, 87). In spite of the obvious difficulty in reading and understanding Hegel's writings, with attentive reading, the depth of Hegel's philosophical insight and ability become apparent, even if the meaning at times remains elusive.

III.   Hegel: The Philosopher of Freedom

Hegel's early theological writings were most heavily influenced by his classical studies as a youth and by the moral and philosophical writings of Immanuel Kant (1724–1804).

In his treatise "What is Enlightenment" (1789) Kant announced that the time for Enlightenment had come, that it was time to remove the shackles that encumbered the free use of reason. It was time to challenge all authority, particularly if that authority was not based on rational principles or ideas. In this treatise Kant proclaimed his bold motto of Enlightenment: "*Sapere Aude!* Have the courage to use your own intelligence!" (Friedrich, 1949, 132). The free use of reason, Kant maintained, is only possible if the public is given its "freedom" by their "rulers" and "self-appointed guardians" (ibid., 133–4). This free, public use of reason, free from any and all heteronomous influences, alone could foster the conditions needed for the establishment of a truly enlightened social order. As people engage their free thought, Kant reasoned, they "gradually become more capable of acting in freedom" (ibid., 139).

Hegel can be described best as a philosopher of freedom. Hegel maintained that freedom was not the fulfillment of personal desires or whims, as it is often misunderstood, but rather was a rare condition that allowed people to live rationally and self-consciously in community with others. In his philosophical writings Hegel tended to focus his attention not on the individual human person, or on the particular consciousness of the individual person but on a collective notion of social consciousness that he felt was necessary if persons were to live in a freely and rationally

organized community or state. History, for Hegel, is the story of the growth and maturation of freedom and rationality. Hegel argued that reason matures and develops in a dialectical process of growth and development and that freedom grows concomitantly with it. In the process of its own maturation, reason eventually comes to a kind of self-knowledge of itself as free, that is, free from all external or heteronomous influences. The subject in this story of growth and development is not the individual human subject but rather the "task" of development is "performed by the universal individual," which might be described as a kind of collective consciousness, or universal subject (Hegel, 1977, §28: 16).

The free consent of the governed was required for the formation and preservation of the modern state that was beginning to emerge in parts of Europe and which had already begun to emerge in the newly formed republic of the United States of America. At times the concepts of "freedom" and "reason" seem to be synonymous terms in Hegel's writings. Hegel's understanding that freedom can only be worked out in the ongoing process of human history is central to all of his writings.

IV.   Hegel's Early Theological Writings

At the time of his death many of Hegel's early theological writings remained unpublished. In 1907 Herman Nohl published an edited collection of these manuscripts with sectional headings under the title *Hegels theologische Jugendschriften* (Nohl, 1907; Hegel, 1948, vi).

Between 1795 and 1796, while living in Bern, Hegel wrote the first two parts of a treatise entitled "The Positivity of the Christian Religion." Around 1800, after Hegel had moved to Frankfurt, he completed the third part of this work. In this treatise Hegel was extremely critical of the Christian tradition and church. Hegel contrasted the "non-positive religions" of antiquity, which cherished and nurtured human freedom and dignity, with the "positive religion" of Christianity, which was destructive and oppressive. A "positive faith," Hegel wrote, "is a system of religious propositions which are true for us because they are presented to us by an authority which we cannot flout." They are "often said to be objective truths" yet "what is required of them is that they should now become subjective truths, truths for us" (Lukács, 1976, 18). Positivity, then, refers to the heteronomous authority that acts externally on a subject thereby restricting his or her free moral autonomy.

Hegel asserted that Jesus and his teachings were the origin of this positivity within the Christian religion. Jesus, he argued, always addressed himself to the individual and not to society as a whole. Reflecting on the story of Jesus' encounter with the rich young man in which Jesus advised the man that if he wished to be perfect he needed to sell all that he had and give it to the poor, Hegel observed: "This image of perfection, which Christ proposes contains the proof that his teachings were concerned primarily with the education and perfection of the individual man and they make it very clear how little such teachings are capable of being extended to society as a whole" (Lukács, 1976, 62–3).

Up until 1797 Hegel was strongly under the influence of Kant. The change in Hegel's philosophical and theological perspective after 1797 is visible when one compares what Hegel wrote after 1797 with what he had written prior to it. In Frankfurt, most likely between 1798 and 1799, Hegel wrote a treatise to which Nohl gave the title "The Spirit of Christianity and Its Fate." In this work Judaism replaced Christianity as the focus of Hegel's criticism. He now criticized Judaism for its positivity primarily because of its understanding of the utter transcendence of God and its insistence on moral obedience to the law (Hodgson, 1997, 58). At the same time Hegel had become more critical of Kantian ethics and its requirement of absolute obedience to a positive moral law. He now understood Kant's ethical system, centered on the moral duty of the individual, to be one more example of the positivity he had identified within Judaism. Hegel found a reconciliation between the Greek religion of beauty and Kantian moralism in the person of Jesus and in his message of love (Hegel, 1948, 10–11).

This treatise also gives evidence of one more change in Hegel's interpretation of Kant after 1797. Where Kant tended to be more interested in the formal principles of ethics, Hegel was more interested

in their social content. As a result Hegel asserted that the moral laws derived by Kant's method were not grounded in concrete human communities and practices but rather tended to function as supra-historical, positive principles. Hegel argued, moreover, that moral imperatives (or duties) were already part of a social whole that is always in the process of change and development. Moral imperatives as a result are never isolated from their historical and social context. They are part of the dialectical process by which they interact, negate, destroy, and re-emerge in a form different than that from which they began. Hegel's hope, then, was for the development of moral laws that led to genuine freedom within human history.

Hegel's early theological writings on the whole are unremarkable. If Hegel had written on these topics alone, his work most likely would have been forgotten or ignored by future generations. It was the philosophical work that followed Hegel's early theological writings, particularly *The Phenomenology of Spirit*, and the subsequent further development and explication of his own philosophical system, that cemented Hegel's later reputation as a brilliant philosopher. The most important use of Hegel's early theological writings is to help interpreters of Hegel see how the seeds of Hegel's system were first planted in them, but they are not much help when it comes to understanding the comprehensive philosophical system Hegel was to develop in his later philosophical and political writings.

V. The Beginning of Hegel's System: The Recasting of Kantian Critical Philosophy

In Hegel's first published philosophical work, "The Difference between Fichte's and Schelling's Systems of Philosophy," he began to formulate his own philosophical system. Because the work of both Fichte and Schelling consisted of philosophical responses to key questions first raised by Kant, it is important to examine how Hegel responded to those key questions and look at the suggestions he offers for their philosophical clarification or resolution.

Kant's critical philosophy first and foremost was a challenge to dogmatic metaphysics. Kant set limits on the capacity of human reason to gain knowledge of the realm of noumenal ideas. This epistemological assumption of Kant effectively questioned the ability of finite human beings to have any real knowledge of the realm of the infinite. In his three critiques, *The Critique of Pure Reason*, *The Critique of Practical Reason*, and *The Critique of Judgment*, Kant focused his attention respectively on the three transcendentals of truth, good, and beauty. The three critiques focused in turn on metaphysics, ethics, and aesthetics. Where phenomenal objects are physical and material, and therefore available to human empirical experience and verification, noumenal ideas, Kant argued, are metaphysical and therefore unavailable to direct empirical experience and verification.

In *The Critique of Judgment* Kant offered the hope that communal aesthetic judgments about works of art might open the possibility of a limited knowledge of noumenal things. This idea, however, was not fully developed and as a result was more suggestive than it was a fully worked-out solution.

Kant's critical philosophy announced an epistemological separation between the finite (sensory experience) and the infinite (God and the realm of ideas). The epistemological limitations Kant placed on noumenal ideas did not deter subsequent philosophers from attempting to gain knowledge of them. It led rather to the emergence of a variety of approaches broadly grouped under the category of "Romanticism." If a unified knowledge of phenomenal and noumenal things was denied to them by the putative limitations Kant placed on the scope of human reason, then, following the lead Kant had offered in *The Critique of Judgment*, Romantic philosophers including Friedrich Schiller focused their attention on emotion, feelings, or works of art as a way to gain access to noumenal ideas and to reconnect the infinite with the finite.

In *The Critique of Pure Reason* Kant argued that human beings experience the world through a framework of categories. Our sensory experience is never unmediated or given to us in a pure state but comes to us through these categories. We experience the world around us, in other words, through a framework of categories that are themselves the preconditions for all thought. They allow us to see the world

available to us through the knowledge produced by thought but that knowledge does not allow us to know things as they are in themselves. It is impossible for us to know the object of knowledge in itself, what Kant called the "thing in itself" (*das Ding an sich*).

Hegel could not accept this basic Kantian assumption that the objects of knowledge could never be known in and of themselves. In response to Kant, Hegel argued that the categories do not separate us from the objects of knowledge, or increase our distance from them, because the things in themselves are the very preconditions that allow us to gain genuine knowledge of things as they are. The categories make genuine knowledge possible because human thought and the reality thought seeks to discover are integrally connected, and, in the final analysis, are one and the same thing. Where Kant sundered the connection between rational thought and reality, Hegel on the other hand focused his attention on the fundamental continuity between thought and reality, arguing that "the True is the whole" (Hegel, 1977, §20: 11).

Hegel also had a different understanding of the transcendental nature of the categories than Kant did. For Kant the categories, the preconditions for all thought, were fixed and immutable. They provide a permanent transcendental framework that undergirded all human knowledge. Hegel, on the other hand, understood the categories to be historically conditioned and capable of evolutionary change and advancement. These categories, he maintained, were capable of change and development, depending on their environment, historical location, or the stage of the culture from which they emerged. The categories, in other words, were not static as in Kant's critical philosophy, but rather they participated in the same dialectical process of growth and development that was outlined throughout all of Hegel's philosophical method.

Hegel's philosophy must be interpreted against the dual background of Kantian critical philosophy and German Romanticism. More than anything else Hegel sought the reunification of the finite with the infinite. His writings are all part of a system of philosophical thought that sought to consolidate all human understanding under one comprehensive philosophical approach or system. This concern with the connection between the finite and the infinite gives

Hegel's philosophical writings a theological cast. While Hegel was not a theologian in the traditional sense, he claimed always that his method of speculative philosophy shared the same goal as that of Christian theological discourse, replacing the pictorial language of theology with the rational language of philosophy.

VI. Hegel's Logic

The heart of Hegel's philosophical system rests in his dialectical logic. Because this method of thought is central to all of Hegel's work, it is instructive to discuss this in brief before examining Hegel's other philosophical writings. Logic, in the sense Hegel uses the term, refers to the dynamic motion of thought. Philosophical thought requires a rigor that allows the questioning of every idea, every postulate, or every assumption. Hegel's logic is triadic in structure. The dialectical process is intended by Hegel to describe the working of the mind (or thought) and to describe how the mind comes to real, genuine knowledge or "science" (from the Latin *scientia* meaning "knowledge").

In his *Science of Logic* (*Die Wissenschaft der Logik*), published in three parts in 1812, 1813, and 1816 and later revised after his death, Hegel began with the dialectical tension in thought between being and nothing which at first appear to be opposite ideas or thoughts. When the mind attempts to think of being, pure in itself, that is, in its complete abstractness, the mind can only think of nothing. In the same way, when the mind attempts to think about nothing, it necessarily thinks of something. Holding both of these ideas simultaneously in thought leads to the realization that each idea is at once both something and nothing. This dialectical tension, Hegel argued, leads consciousness to the further realization that the two ideas are brought together with a new idea that is born out of the tension between the two ideas, namely that of "becoming." In other words, the positing of an idea, contradicted by its opposite, leads to the positing of a new idea which will in turn be contradicted in a similar process. This process continues, Hegel maintained, until consciousness came to genuine philosophical knowledge, or "science."

One of the central assumptions of Hegel's dialectical logic is that every perspective has truth in it, but that truth is only partial and not a fully developed truth. The struggle within consciousness between two opposite ideas leads to the destruction of the first idea and its replacement by a wider, more comprehensive idea brought into possibility by the inherent tension in dialectical thinking. The tension between the original thesis and its antithesis, according to Hegel's logic, leads to what he calls a sublation (*Aufhebung*) of the two ideas. Hegel plays with two possible German meanings of this word because it can refer to both the "destruction" of the idea or its "preservation" in a new form. Thus sublation is not a synthesis of the two ideas but rather a new idea that has reached a (potentially) higher state of consciousness.

VII. *The Phenomenology of Spirit*

In 1807, just as Napoleon and his troops began fighting on the outskirts of Jena, Hegel sent the manuscript of first major work of philosophy, *The Phenomenology of Spirit*, to his publisher. This was to become Hegel's most famous work.

Hegel begins *The Phenomenology of Spirit* heralding a new birth of freedom brought into being as reason is allowed to illuminate the whole world. Hegel writes:

> It is not difficult to see that ours is a birth-time and a period of transition to a new era. Spirit has broken with the world it has hitherto inhabited and imagined, and is of a mind to submerge it in the past, and in the labour of its own transformation. Spirit is indeed never at rest but always engaged in moving forward. ... The Spirit in its formation matures slowly and quietly into its new shape, dissolving bit by bit the structure of its previous world, whose tottering state is only hinted at by isolated symptoms. ... The gradual crumbling that left unaltered the face of the whole is cut short by a sunburst which, in one flash, illuminates the features of the new world. (Hegel, 1977, §11: 6–7)

Although Hegel later wrote other introductions to his philosophical system, *The Phenomenology of Spirit* was the first and most enduring introduction to his system of philosophical thought. In this work he also began to develop the method of dialectical logic that came to full flower in his later writings on logic.

Hegel's philosophy is often called "Idealist" because Hegel asserted that Mind or Spirit (*Geist*) was the ultimate reality. Hegel understood all of reality to be the progressive unfolding or manifestation of "Absolute Spirit" (or "Mind") within human history. This was achieved within a dialectical process in which mind or spirit, through the process of alienation and negation, arrives at an ever-higher unity, until it attains a complete knowledge of itself. Human history, for Hegel, is the site in which the absolute becomes conscious of itself and in which it moves toward full self-consciousness. Noumenal Absolute Spirit, therefore, is always in the process of being revealed within the phenomenal, physical, and material world.

Hegel's concept of Absolute Spirit is taken from the Greek concept of the *logos*—the rational principle that pervades the cosmos—and from the Christian understanding of the incarnate Logos and its involvement within the course of human history in the person of Jesus (Jay, 1984, 54). Absolute Spirit for Hegel then is both the creator and a created, and, as such, is the unifying ground of all being. This concept of Absolute Spirit is most accurately described as panentheistic, that is, that the divine is in all things and unifies all things but ultimately is greater than all things. Where Kant understood the realm of Nature (the phenomenal realm) to be in opposition to the realm of Spirit, or Mind (the noumenal realm), Hegel by contrast asserted that nature could only be understood as the emanation of Spirit. Absolute Spirit, for Hegel, is at the same time both transcendent and immanent to creation. For that reason there can be no real separation between the noumenal and phenomenal or the spiritual and physical. Hegel's understanding of Absolute Spirit is similar to Spinoza's idea of God, but is much more of a dynamic concept than the more static conception of God outlined in Spinoza's writings.

The Phenomenology of Spirit tells the story of the growth and maturation of Absolute Spirit. The story of the dynamic journey of Absolute Spirit that Hegel narrates parallels the genre of the *Bildungsroman*; it is the story of the social and moral formation of a subject, namely "Absolute Spirit," who moves from "a subjective totality" at the beginning of its journey to an "objective totality" at its end (Jay, 1984, 55). In *The Phenomenology of Spirit*, Hegel outlined "the series of configurations which consciousness goes through" along the "road" to genuine human knowledge or science. It is "the detailed history of the education of consciousness itself to the standpoint of Science" (Hegel, 1977, §78: 50). Hegel writes:

> *History* is a *conscious*, self-*mediating* process—Spirit emptied out into Time; but this externalization, this kenosis, is equally an externalization of itself; the negative is the negative of itself. This Becoming presents a slow-moving succession of Spirits, a gallery of images, each of which, endowed with all the riches of Spirit, moves thus slowly just because the Self has to penetrate and digest this entire wealth of its substance. As its fulfillment consists in perfectly *knowing* what *it is*, in knowing its substance … (Hegel, 1977, §808: 492)

Hegel continues: "The *goal*, Absolute Knowing, or Spirit that knows itself as Spirit, has for its path the recollection" of all previous embodiments of Spirit, in all stages of its dialectical development and growth (Hegel, 1977, §808: 493). *The Phenomenology of Spirit*, then, is the study of these moments in the growth and development of Spirit (or Mind) as it comes to self-consciousness. Each of the successive moments in the progressive journey of Absolute Spirit gives the philosopher a view of objectivity, as if it were frozen in time, for philosophical examination and consideration. Along the way the dualisms prevalent in Kant's critical philosophy—between the infinite and the finite, the moral ought and the empirical is, the noumenal world of ideas and the phenomenal world of experience, and the object of thought and the thing in itself—are shown to be illusory. Only a vision of a larger philosophical totality could adequately address the antinomies and contradictions of the Kantian system, and, at the same time, provide the framework for them to be overcome. At the end of this philosophical journey the difference between subjective knowledge and objective truth is destroyed. The sublation of these two ideas at that moment shows that each necessarily involves the other, so that knowledge and truth become one.

VIII. Hegel's Philosophy of Religion

Hegel's system is redolent with the language of Christian theology. Although Hegel decided not to go into the ordained ministry, he had spent many years in the theological seminary at Tübingen studying theology and was fully conversant with the form and manner of its discourse. This is evident in Hegel's reference to the "kenosis" of Absolute Spirit into human history (Hegel, 1977, §808: 492) in philosophical language. Hegel directly borrowed the biblical imagery of the kenosis, or self-emptying, of the divine Logos into human history in the incarnation of the Logos into the form of a human person, Jesus (Phil. 2:7). In the concluding paragraphs of *The Phenomenology of Spirit*, Hegel called the dialectical journey of Absolute Spirit there described, a speculative Good Friday, the "Calvary of absolute spirit" (Hegel, 1977, §808: 493). The parallels between the journey of Absolute Spirit and the Christian story of redemption can hardly be missed. The movement of Spirit into the world parallels the incarnation of the divine Word of God; the negation of Spirit and the process by which it is opposed by its dialectical opposite parallels the crucifixion and death of the Son of God; and the positing of a new stage in the life of Spirit after its own destruction and sublation (*Aufhebung*) parallels the resurrection of Jesus from the dead to new life. Where the Christian story is understood to have happened only once in history, the journey of Absolute Spirit that Hegel narrated happens again and again until Spirit arrives at its goal.

Hegel's philosophy of history cross-pollinates, as it were, his philosophy of religion. In the philosophical story Hegel narrates, the religion of God the Father (the religion of Judaism) is negated in the dialectical processes of incarnation and crucifixion in which the "Mediator," the Son of God, is killed. In the language of dialectical thought this represents the moment in which "God Himself is dead" (Hegel, 1977, §785: 476). The sublation of this dialectical process leads to resurrection and the arrival of a conceptual Pentecost, in which the life of the Spirit of God now brings a new age of freedom (Hegel, 1977, §787: 477–8). In this process, the religion of Judaism

and its particularism is overcome and its content, in a fully rationalized understanding of Christianity, is now made universal.

Throughout his writings Hegel recast the Christian story of salvation history in the guise of speculative philosophy. Hegel always claimed to be a devout Lutheran and asserted that the traditional language of faith and his speculative, conceptual, reinterpretation of that language for the purposes of his idealist philosophy had the same goal and purpose. Each offered a distinctive perspective to the same story (Mattes, 2000, 250).

In his writings on religion Hegel distinguished between the pictorial language of religious faith and its uncritical representations (*Vorstellungen*) and the, more philosophically rigorous use of the concept (*Begriff*). Philosophy is understood to be a higher, more critical and conceptual version of the less critical representational language of ordinary religious faith. At the same time Hegel maintained that his speculative philosophy was entirely coherent with a Christian understanding of the Trinity.

Philosophers and theologians differ on Hegel's pronouncement that religion and philosophy share the same task, and on the overall success of his attempts to reconcile the two disciplines. On the one hand, J. D. Findlay argues that Hegel is understood best as a Christian theologian. "The Christian God is essentially redemptive, and Hegel's philosophy is essentially a philosophy or redemption of a self-alienation that returns to itself in victory. If Hegel was nothing better, he was at least a great Christian theologian" (Hegel, 1977, xxvii). Robert Solomon, on the other hand, argues that Hegel is a "humanistic atheist" and that "Hegel is not a Christian and his philosophy is only a pretence of Christian apologetics" (Solomon, 1983, 614, 580–639).

For the philosopher, Hegel's concept of Absolute Spirit is easily recognizable as a philosophical idea of God stripped of the defining characteristics of the God professed in the Christian faith. For the practicing Christian, however, Hegel's description of the three moments of Absolute Spirit in the following example: "There are thus three distinct moments: essence, being-for-self which is otherness of essence and for which essence is, and being-for-self, or the knowledge of itself in the 'other'" (Hegel, 1977,

§770: 465), would hardly be recognized as an ortho-dox interpretation of the Trinity. His interpretation of the Father as the essence, the Son, or the divine Logos, as the creator of the realm of nature, and the Spirit as the ground of self-consciousness is certainly a more heterodox than orthodox interpretation of Christian faith.

IX. Hegel's *Lectures on the Philosophy of Religion*

In 1821 Hegel gave his first *Lectures on the Philosophy of Religion* (*Vorlesungen über die Philosophie der Religion*). These lectures were repeated in 1824, 1827, and 1831. Hegel wrote and rewrote these lectures, giving schol-ars ample material with which to investigate his changing views on religion in the last ten years of his life (Hodgson, 2005, 6).

In the *Lectures on the Philosophy of Religion*, Hegel interpreted religion as a form of rational thought or "thinking," and not first and foremost as a feeling (*Gefühl*) that one has. Hegel wrote:

> In religion, I am myself the *relation* of the two sides as thus determined. I who think, who am that which lifts myself up, the active Universal, and Ego, the immediate subject, are one and the same "I." ... The *relation* of these two sides which are so sharply opposed—the absolutely finite consciousness and being on the one hand, and the infinite on the other—exists in religion for me. In think-ing I lift myself up to the Absolute above all that is finite, and am infinite consciousness, while I am at the same time finite consciousness, and indeed am such in accord-ance with my whole empirical character. ... I am, and it is *in myself* and for myself that this conflict and this con-ciliation take place. (Hegel, 1962, I: 63–4)

The two "sides" of the finite and the infinite exist within the self or the "I." The dialectical tension between the finite and the infinite and the need for its resolution—central to Hegel's philosophical project—is resolved by the act of the thinking subject.

Hegel's *Lectures on the Philosophy of Religion* is shaped partly in response to the work of his colleague at the University of Berlin, Friedrich D. E. Schleiermacher. In response to the epistemological limitations placed by Kant on the capacity of reason to fathom noumenal ideas, most particularly what can be known of God, Schleiermacher proposed a solution shaped by the Moravian Pietism in which he was raised and by the discourses of German Romanticism. To find a resolution to the Kantian separation of faith and rea-son Schleiermacher rejected Enlightenment rationality and turned to feeling and emotion. (This, as noted above, is not the rational approach that Hegel had taken to resolve this same problem.) In *The Christian Faith*, Schleiermacher proposed that the essence of religion was found in the "feeling of absolute depend-ence" on something greater than oneself, namely God. "To feel oneself absolutely dependent and to be conscious of being in relation with God are one and the same thing; and the reason is that absolute depend-ence is the fundamental relation which must include all others in itself. This ... includes the God-consciousness in the self-consciousness in such a way that ... the two cannot be separated from each other" (Schleiermacher, 1928, 17). When the religious sub-ject has the feeling of absolute dependence within consciousness, this feeling of the contingent creature of his or her own absolute dependence on God, Schleiermacher argued, connects that person to the ultimate causality, which is God (Schleiermacher, 1928, 13–18, 131–3, 198).

Hegel believed that Schleiermacher's reliance on religious experience was overly subjective and could not unite the competing claims of religious feeling that would arise in any group of people. Appeal to one's own feeling, Hegel argued, "breaks off the con-tinuity between us," whereas in rational discourse "we meet one another on the soil of universal ration-ality" (James, 2007, 96). Hegel did not, however, reject feeling outright but understood it to be foun-dational for all religious experience. Feeling is but one aspect of a balanced view of religious discourse and experience. In the *Lectures on the Philosophy of Religion* Hegel argued that religion moves from feel-ing (*Gefühl*) through representation (*Vorstellungen*) and then to the concept (*Begriff*). In other words, reli-gious faith is founded upon a religious experience or feeling of the presence or activity of God in one's life. As one reflects on this foundational religious experi-ence one begins to use the pictorial language of reli-gious faith, referring for example in the case of

Christian faith to God as "Father" or to Jesus as the "Son of God." For Hegel one final step must take place before religion can claim the status of "science": the representational language of faith needs to be replaced by a thoroughgoing rational reflection on this faith so that this experience becomes universal, that is, fully open to rational, conceptual reflection and public discussion. Near the end of his lectures on religion, Hegel wrote that "the goal of philosophy is the cognition of truth—the cognition of God because God is the absolute truth." The task of philosophy, he continued, is "to show forth the rational content of religion [*die Vernunft der Religion*]" (Hegel, 1987, 3: 246–7; Hodgson, 2005, 15). This is accomplished within philosophical discourse by transforming the metaphorical, symbolic, and representational language of religion into the scientific, conceptual, and rational language of philosophical thought. Theology thus is transformed into "the intellectual science of God" (Hegel, 1985, 2: 252; Hodgson, 2005, 15). This transformation was the overall goal of Hegel's philosophical investigation of religion.

With all the attention that Hegel devoted to religion, it is difficult to maintain with Solomon and other such interpreters that Hegel was an atheist and that he hid this fact by the difficulty and obfuscation of his writings. In his final years, during which he taught at the University of Berlin, Hegel returned again and again to his *Lectures on the Philosophy of Religion*. The lectures reveal a Hegel who is deeply interested and passionately committed to the scientific, rational study of religion.

X. Hegel's Legacy

Hegel had an important influence on twentieth-century philosophy and theology, perhaps an even greater influence than he had on the philosophy of his own century, which after his death was dominated by the interests and agendas of neo-Kantian philosophy. Hegel's influence and legacy is evident in Marxist, Existentialist, and Deconstructionist thought, in the works of a diverse group of philosophers including Søren Kierkegaard, Karl Marx, Georgy Lukács, Jean-Paul Sartre, Martin Heidegger, and Jacques Derrida. Hegel's dialectical interpretation of the Christian doctrine of God in Trinity finds a central place in the theological writings of Wolfhart Pannenberg, Jürgen Moltmann, and Eberhard Jüngel. The legacy of Hegel's concern for a new birth of freedom for all people is found in the political struggles for freedom all over the earth (Tönsing, 1995) and in a wide variety of political movements and theologies of human liberation.

References

Adorno, Theodor W. 1994. *Hegel*, trans. Shierry Weber Nicholson. Cambridge, MA: MIT Press.

Friedrich, Carl J., ed. 1949. "What is Enlightenment." In *The Philosophy of Kant: Immanuel Kant's Moral and Political Writings*. New York: Modern Library, pp. 132–9.

Hegel, Georg Wilhelm Friedrich. 1948. *Early Theological Writings*, trans. T. M. Knox. Chicago: University of Chicago Press.

Hegel, Georg Wilhelm Friedrich. [1832, 1840] 1962. *Lectures on the Philosophy of Religion*, trans. E. B. Speirs and J. Burdon Sanderson. New York: The Humanities Press, Inc.

Hegel, Georg Wilhelm Friedrich. [1827] 1984, 1985, 1987. *Lectures on the Philosophy of Religion*, ed. Peter C. Hodgson; trans. R. F. Brown, P. C. Hodgson, J. M. Stewart, with the assistance of H. S. Harris. 3 vols. Berkeley: University of California Press.

Hegel, Georg Wilhelm Friedrich. 1967. *The Phenomenology of Mind*, trans. J. B. Baille. New York: Harper Torchbooks.

Hegel, Georg Wilhelm Friedrich. 1977. *Phenomenology of Spirit*, trans. A. V. Miller. Oxford: Oxford University Press.

Hodgson, Peter C. 1997. *G. W. F. Hegel: Theologian of the Spirit*. Minneapolis, MN: Augsburg Fortress.

Hodgson, Peter C. 2005. *Hegel and Christian Theology*. Oxford: Oxford University Press.

Houlgate, Stephen. 2005. *An Introduction to Hegel*. Oxford: Blackwell Publishing.

James, David. 2007. *Hegel: A Guide for the Perplexed*. New York: Continuum.

Jay, Martin. 1984. *Marxism and Totality: The Adventures of a Concept from Lukács to Habermas*. Berkeley: University of California Press.

Lukács, Georg. 1976. *The Young Hegel*, trans. Rodney Livingstone. Cambridge, MA: MIT Press.

Mattes, Mark C. 2000. "Hegel's Lutheran Claim," *Lutheran Quarterly* XIV: 249–79.

Nohl, Herman. 1907. *Hegels theologische Jugendschriften.* Tübingen.

Schleiermacher, Friedrich D. E. [1830] 1928. *The Christian Faith*, trans. H. R Mackintosh and J. S. Stewart. Edinburgh: T&T Clark.

Schopenhauer, Arthur. 1969. *The World as Will and Representation*. E. F. J. Payne. New York: Dover Publications.

Solomon, Robert C. 1983. *In the Spirit of Hegel: A Study of G. W. F. Hegel's Phenomenology of Spirit.* New York: Oxford University Press.

Tönsing, Detlev. 1995. "The Importance of Hegel for Contemporary Theology," *Journal of Theology for Southern Africa* 90: 56–66.

Wiedmann, Franz. 1968. *Hegel: An Illustrated Biography*, trans. Joachim Neugroschel. New York: Pegasus.

Immanuel Kant (1724–1804)

Medi Ann Volpe

Immanuel Kant was born on April 22, 1724, in Königsburg, East Prussia. His mother, Anna, influenced him greatly, instilling in him principles of right and wrong during his earliest years. She died when Kant was 13, and during his difficult teenage years Kant probably felt the loss acutely. Kant entered university in 1740, but did not complete his master's thesis and dissertation until 1755, having spent several years as a private tutor in the interim. About the time he finished his dissertation, Kant returned to the university as a teacher. During his teaching years, Kant's attention shifted from the aspects of scientific and philosophical inquiry that formed the subject matter of his thesis, dissertation, and *habilitationsschrift* (professorial thesis). For several years, Kant published nothing. Then, in 1781, he published the *Critique of Pure Reason*, which centers on the conditions of possibility for all human knowledge. With the first *Critique* Kant began the project of critical philosophy for which he is most widely known.

The *Critique of Pure Reason* details the epistemology central to Kant's critical philosophy, which continues to influence theories of knowledge. For Kant, human understanding itself is endowed with 12 categories that allow the knowing subject to organize data collected through the senses according to quantity, quality, relation, and modality. Kant argues that each individual possesses these transcendental concepts that make the production of knowledge possible. The knowing subject is thus universal—everyone possesses the *same* transcendental concepts—and the laws governing human knowledge are likewise universal.

In his second volume of critical philosophy, the *Critique of Practical Reason*, Kant turns to the foundation of ethics. His moral philosophy centers on the categorical imperative, Kant's moral law. The categorical imperative rules out any action (including a verbal action like lying) that one cannot simultaneously will as a universal law. For example, a lie only has the desired effect if it is believed, and so depends upon a moral universe in which people are expected to tell the truth. If lying were the accepted practice, a lie would not have the desired effect; thus one should not lie. At the same time, as is rarely emphasized in discussions of Kant's ethics, the categorical imperative has a *positive* application. To continue with the above example, the categorical imperative demands truth telling as a way of life. For Kant, the categorical imperative not only prohibits immoral action, but promotes moral action as the duty of every individual. Kant's third *Critique*, the *Critique of Judgment*, offers sustained reflection on the possibility of something like a law governing aesthetic judgments. Kant again aims for universality, in this case developing a framework for universal recognition of the beautiful; the third *Critique* has not, however, had the same impact on theology as the first two.

The Student's Companion to the Theologians, First Edition. Edited by Ian S. Markham.
© 2013 Blackwell Publishing Ltd. Published 2013 by Blackwell Publishing Ltd.

Kant's critical philosophy affects the history and practice of theology in two ways. First, the laws governing human knowing do not allow knowledge of God. Given that we know by the combination of sense data with the categories of the understanding, and that we cannot have sense data regarding God, knowledge of God is ruled out of court. We may postulate the existence of God, but—since God does not have an "appearance" in the world—nothing whatsoever can be predicated of God. Moreover, since God is outside the categories of the understanding, it is impossible for the human mind to produce any knowledge of God. Kant's anthropology portrays humans as not fit for knowledge of God. In particular, the notion that human beings are created for participation in and reflection of God, common especially in late ancient theology, finds no place in Kant's consideration of human nature. Second, Kant's approach to ethics and to biblical interpretation reflects these epistemological and anthropological principles. Kantian ethics center on a sense of duty that is universal and binding for every human being. Because humans' relationship to God has no place in this system, Kant relies on a transcendental ethic that allows no contingency. To return to the example of lying: faced with the same case study, Rahab's lie to protect the Israelite spies, Augustine and Kant agree that the lie was nevertheless wrong. For Augustine, however, the "wrong" lie, which was a *sin*, is overcome by God's redemption. For Kant, while there is room for moral improvement, redemption has no place: duty is the highest human achievement.

Kant's own "theology" follows from his ethics. In spite of his negative assessment of religious practice in his day, Kant saw in Jesus a perfect model of the moral individual. For Kant, Jesus offers us an example of what duty requires and demonstrates our ability to do it. In *Religion within the Limits of Reason Alone*, Kant examines the biblical portrayal of Jesus, especially as the Bible presents Jesus as the Son of God. The "savior" in Kant's *Religion* is the moral archetype, the Son of God image. This image matches our a priori image of the moral paragon that derives from reason, not scripture. Kant interprets that which in Christian scripture speaks of Christ as describing perfected humanity. Kant's notion of the possibility of human perfection comes from reason, which presents to human beings the idea

of moral perfection. Thus Kant describes the moral archetype as *The Personified Idea of the Good Principle*, an idea that saves by demonstrating that it is indeed possible to do what duty requires. Personified as the Son of God, this idea itself is the object of faith of a particular sort: belief in the moral perfectibility of humanity, which is necessary for the adoption of perfection as our end. Like transcendental freedom, the moral perfectibility of humanity is an idea that only has objective reality in the realm of practical reason. In acting as though the idea is real, human beings can make it so. Kant explains that the faith he describes does not require an object of experience; even if no person emerges to represent this idea, the image of morally perfect humanity would yet exist in our reason. We would see that we ought to conform to such an image. And if we ought, Kant reasons, we can. Our faith, then, is in virtue—that moral progress which leads us to moral perfection. The example stands as proof that our freedom makes doing what duty requires possible. The Son of God image in *Religion Within the Limits of Reason Alone* shows us our duty, and the recognition of our duty fuels the resolution to do it.

Kant finds, however, that human action is never adequate to duty, which he portrays in the *Religion* as a holy law. Human imperfection is persistent and "natural" evil cannot be overcome. Therefore Kant developed a form of justification that would solve the difficulty of our ineradicable imperfection. A person makes the transition from evil to good by a conversion of sorts: one puts aside the old person and puts on the new. Kant argues that this is a single act, throughout which the good principle is present. The good principle endures suffering (pain caused by the immoral disposition) and even death (of the old person). So, Kant finds, the person changed is both the same (physically) as the old and yet (morally) entirely new, deserving of punishment in the former and not in the latter disposition. The suffering of the "new man" provides a "surplus" that Kant sees as the analogue to Christian grace. But this grace has nothing whatsoever to do with the death of an actual Christ. Rather, Kant draws an analogy between the good principle, which is present in every individual, and the Son of God described in the Bible. Jesus is the good principle, personified: he represents, in a concrete form, the moral principle that allows each person to distinguish right from wrong. It is the suffering that one endures after having adopted the new, moral disposition which is reckoned as justificatory. The "Son of God" is the moral principle—in fact, the new person—which "suffers" so that the person may be "saved."

In the wake of Kant's deconstruction of traditional Christian doctrine and interpretation of scripture, theologians have generally found it necessary to reckon with his philosophy in some way. Schleiermacher and Barth provide two clear examples of the way in which this has been done. Schleiermacher avoids the problem of knowledge of God by claiming that experience of God is possible outside the categories of the understanding. The evidence of God's existence and of human need for God derives from each individual's feeling of absolute dependence, rather than from knowledge of God. Christian doctrine ultimately rests on this experience, which Schleiermacher takes to be universal. Thus, knowledge of God that might conform to Kantian standards is not necessary for Christian faith. Barth assumes that Kant is right about the production of knowledge, and concludes that God can be known only if God is a thing in the world like other things. Barth's theology of revelation allows human beings involvement with God, though this involvement depends upon God's initiative. Human beings cannot reach God, but God's revelation through God's Word allows human beings to hear the judgment against them and also to receive the grace that overcomes that judgment. Barth's *Church Dogmatics* shows the whole of Christian doctrine as grounded in the incarnation and the scripture that attests to it. Barth and Schleiermacher offer just two examples of the way in which Kant's philosophy, especially his epistemology, shaped modern theology. The shift to a "non-foundationalist" approach in postmodern theology may finally represent a break from Kant, but even as it does so it gestures toward the search for foundations that characterized his philosophy.

References

Allison, Henry. 1983. *Kant's Transcendental Idealism*. Yale.

Allison, Henry. 1990. *Kant's Theory of Freedom*. Cambridge.

Guyer, Paul, ed. 1992. *The Cambridge Companion to Kant*. Cambridge.

Korsgaard, Christine. 1996. *Creating the Kingdom of Ends*. Cambridge.

Kuehn, Manfred. 2001. *Kant: A Biography*. Cambridge.

Søren Kierkegaard (1813–55)

Craig A. Phillips

I. Biography

Søren Aabye Kierkegaard was born in Copenhagen on May 5, 1813. He was a writer who gained wide popularity long after his death. "In a real sense," as Alec Vidler observed, Kierkegaard "belongs to the twentieth rather than to the nineteenth century." As he wrote and published his works in Danish, they did not reach a wider European audience until after World War I. But in his own time, in his native Denmark, he did make "a great, if baffling, impact" (Vidler, 1971, 201). Because the content of his philosophical and religious writings was deeply personal and often autobiographical, it is necessary to understand something about his life before examining his writings.

Kierkegaard's father, Michael Pedersen Kierkegaard, was born to a poor farming family in Jutland where as a child he worked as a shepherd (Vidler, 1971, 202). When he was 12 he began working for his uncle in a shop in Copenhagen and by the age of 40 he had amassed a sizeable fortune in the hosiery business. The elder Kierkegaard was so successful that he was able to retire. After his first wife died childless in 1796, he married his housekeeper who gave birth to seven children. Kierkegaard's father was a dour, puritanical, melancholic, and deeply guilt-ridden man who traced many of the misfortunes in his life, including the death of several of his children in childhood, to a day when as a child he had stood on a cliff

and cursed God, and to the fact that he had married his second wife when she was already four months pregnant with their first child. His deep melancholy was a trait that was passed on to his youngest and favorite child, Søren.

Kierkegaard spent much of his unhappy childhood in Copenhagen, often in seclusion and quiet introspection. As an older youth he studied theology at the University of Copenhagen, but by his own admission often spent his time in idleness, pursuing pleasure. His father died in 1838 at the age of 83, leaving Kierkegaard a home in Copenhagen and an inheritance that paid for his schooling, allowed him to support himself as an independent scholar after graduation, and also paid for the publication of a few of his early writings.

In 1840 Kierkegaard was engaged to Regine Olsen but, feeling that marriage was impossible for a man of his disposition and melancholy, he broke off the engagement less than a year later in 1841. Throughout his life he questioned whether he had made the right decision and his writings suggest that he continued to love her for the rest of his life.

In 1841 Kierkegaard graduated with the degree of Magister Artium, having completed his dissertation on "The Concept of Irony with Continual Reference to Socrates." This work contains many of the themes that will be found in Kierkegaard's later writings particularly subjectivity, inwardness, and irony. Upon graduation he decided not to go into the ordained

The Student's Companion to the Theologians, First Edition. Edited by Ian S. Markham.
© 2013 Blackwell Publishing Ltd. Published 2013 by Blackwell Publishing Ltd.

ministry in the Lutheran state church of Denmark, something his father before his death had asked Kierkegaard to consider. From 1843 with the publication of his first book *Either-Or, A Fragment of Life* until his death, Kierkegaard worked as an independent scholar and religious writer.

In 1846 Peder Ludvig Møller published a critical review of Kierkegaard's *Stages on Life's Way*. Kierkegaard responded to the review by attacking Møller and by revealing that Møller was a contributor to the satirical Danish newspaper *The Corsair (Den Corsaren)*. This revelation proved damaging to Møller's career. When Kierkegaard challenged the newspaper to satirize him, it began a relentless attack on his person, voice, appearance, habits, mannerisms, and dress that lasted for months. Scholars continue to debate how much the "Corsair Affair," as it is called, influenced the form, content, and tone of Kierkegaard's subsequent writings.

In 1854 Bishop Mynster, who had been a close friend of Kierkegaard's father, died. Shortly afterwards Kierkegaard began openly to criticize the state church of Denmark. When Kierkegaard's former theology professor Hans Martensen, the leading Danish Hegelian scholar and theologian of his day (1808–84), in his funeral sermon introduced Bishop Mynster into "the holy chain of truth-witnesses that stretches through the ages from the days of the Apostles," this provided the impetus for Kierkegaard to begin a public critique of the church (*KW* [*Kierkegaard's Writings*] XIV, 12). He waited a few months and then began to engage in unrelenting written attacks on the established Danish church, its clergy, and on Christendom in general.

In the midst of his continued attacks against the established church, on October 2, 1855, Kierkegaard collapsed on the street in Copenhagen. He died on November 11, 1855.

II.   Kierkegaard's Anti-Hegelianism

Kierkegaard completed his dissertation in 1841, 10 years after the death of Georg Wilhelm Friedrich Hegel. He studied theology with Hans Martensen and was well acquainted with Hegel's philosophical and theological writings. Hegel's political, philosophical,

and theological writings had an enormous influence on European philosophy and theology throughout Kierkegaard's life. Kierkegaard's writings gain a particular cogency when they are interpreted against the prevailing Hegelian philosophy of his day.

Kierkegaard's critique of Hegelian philosophy focused on the following points: Hegel's logic and his method of dialectical thought, his all-encompassing philosophical system and the disappearance of the individual subject within that larger system, the tendency toward pantheism in Hegel's thought, and the tendency to identify the Christian state with the Kingdom of God.

In Hegel's model of dialectical thinking the opposition of two conflicting ideas resulted in the emergence of a new idea, while at the same time the original opposing ideas were preserved alongside the new idea. Kierkegaard noted that the preservation of ideas inherent in Hegel's dialectical logic resulted in a view of the world that could best be described as *both/and*, and one in which the status quo is inevitably preserved. When Hegel's dialectical logic was applied to art, politics, and religion, it resulted in a cultural and political conservatism that quickly identified the state as the sole repository of freedom and identified the established church with the Kingdom of God.

Kierkegaard, by contrast, saw irreconcilable contradictions in political philosophy and religious discourse that he felt could not be resolved by the mechanics of dialectical thought. As a result, Kierkegaard championed what he called the *either/or* in place of the Hegelian *both/and*. This is seen in Kierkegaard's valorization of the paradox, in which two ideas find no dialectical resolution but remain in tension. The unresolved tension within the paradox offered new perspectives that in the closed system of Hegel might have disappeared or been ignored.

For Hegel "the true is the whole" and the whole is always greater than the sum of its parts. For Kierkegaard, on the other hand, the true often was to be found, not in a larger collective Idea but rather within the individual and private self. In Hegel's system the individual self is but one part of a larger collective mind or consciousness that is more important than the individual consciousness of particular persons. The importance Kierkegaard placed on the individual subject who endeavors to live faithfully in relation both to God and to other human beings is perhaps his most important contribution to the philosophical and theological thought of his day.

III.   Characteristics of Kierkegaard's Writings

It is difficult for the first-time reader to find his or her way through Kierkegaard's philosophical and religious writings. This is no fault of the reader. The difficulty is intentional on Kierkegaard's part.

One of the most distinctive elements in Kierkegaard's writings is that they were published both under his own name and under a variety of pseudonyms. The use of pseudonymous authors was a literary device that allowed Kierkegaard to propound differing points of view, often within the same book. This device allowed Kierkegaard to express himself in voices that may or may not have been his own, while never giving the reader the evidence needed to distinguish between their views and his own. Sometimes the observations of the pseudonymous authors reflect biographical elements within Kierkegaard's own life but it is a mistake to identify the ironic, even sarcastic, voices of the pseudonymous writers with Kierkegaard's own authorial voice. Experienced readers of Kierkegaard learn that one must not work too hard to reconcile the voices of his different narrators but rather must respect their diversity and differences.

"The task" of reading and understanding his writings, Kierkegaard once observed in his *Journal*, "must be made difficult, for only the difficult inspires the noble-hearted" (*JP* [*Journals and Papers*] I, 656). Commenting on the structure of *Stages on Life's Way*, Kierkegaard wrote, "Thus it is left to the reader to put it all together by himself, if he so pleases, but nothing is done for the reader's comfort" (*KW* XII.1, 298). He also admitted that he gave the "whole enterprise the appearance of choice and caprice" (*JP* V, 5891). Similarly, the pseudonymous author Johannes Climacus declared that his task was "to make difficulties everywhere" (*KW* XII.1, 187). Kierkegaard described his "role" as "the joint role of being the secretary and, quite ironically, the dialectically reduplicated author of the author or the authors" (*KW* XII.1, 627).

The dual authorship of his writings—those published under his own name and those published under the name of a variety of pseudonymous authors—with its accompanying complexity of voices presents the greatest challenge to the interpreter of Kierkegaard. Kierkegaard intended to create this complexity and confusion for his readers. To understand Kierkegaard it is helpful, therefore, to start with the few signposts to the writings that he gave his readers, particularly those found in his retrospective comments about his own writings.

IV.   Kierkegaard's Writings

Kierkegaard's published works comprise 38 works in two parallel series of pseudonymous works and signed works (Hong and Hong, 1978, ix). The "authorship regarded as a totality," Kierkegaard wrote, "is religious from first to last (*KW* XIII, 495). "The first-division of the books is esthetic writing; the last division of books is exclusively religious writing—between these lies *Concluding Unscientific Postscript* as the *turning point*" (*KW* XIII, 523).

In a footnote to *The Point of View for my Work as an Author*, written in 1848 but published posthumously in 1859, Kierkegaard identified the books he included in each division of his writings:

> First division (esthetic writing): *Either/Or, Fear and Trembling, Repetition, The Concept of Anxiety, Prefaces, Philosophical Fragments, Stages on Life's Way*—together with eighteen upbuilding discourses, which came out successively. Second division: *Concluding Unscientific Postscript*. Third division (only religious writing): *Upbuilding Discourses in Various Spirits, Works of Love, Christian Discourses*—together with a little esthetic article: *The Crisis in the Life of an Actress*. (*KW* XIII, 521)

Kierkegaard's first series of pseudonymous writings began in 1843 with the publication of *Either/Or* and ended in 1845 with the publishing of *Stages on Life's Way*. Eighteen signed works, published serially in six volumes, paralleled the writings of the pseudonymous authorship. Kierkegaard published nine discourses in 1843 in sets of two, three, and four discourses and another nine in 1844 according to the same pattern (Hong and Hong, 1978, 84). Where the pseudonymous works focused primarily on the esthetic / ethical themes, the 18 signed discourses focused on the ethical / religious, or on what Kierkegaard called "religiousness."

Concluding Unscientific Postscript was intended to mark the movement away from the all-encompassing Hegelian system that tended to overshadow the private reflections of the individual subject. Where Kierkegaard's first authorship focused primarily on issues raised by the philosophical and theological writing of G. W. F. Hegel, the "second authorship" from 1846 to 1853 focused its attention primarily on the shortcomings and failures of Christendom.

The pseudonymous works that paralleled the "third division" of Kierkegaard's writings included *Sickness unto Death* and *Practice in Christianity*. They were published under the name of the pseudonym Anti-Climacus. (Johannes Climacus had been the name of the pseudonymous author of *Philosophical Fragments*, *Johannes Climacus*, and *Concluding Unscientific Postscript*.) Kierkegaard explained that where Climacus said "that he himself is not a Christian, one seems to be able to detect in Anti-Climacus that he considers himself to be a Christian on an extraordinarily high level ... I would place myself higher than Johannes Climacus, lower than Anti-Climacus" (Hong and Hong 1978, 350; *JP* VI, 6433).

Kierkegaard described the authorship somewhat enigmatically as a movement "*from* 'the poet,' from the esthetic—*from* 'the philosopher,' from the speculative —*to* the indication of the most inward qualification of the essentially Christian; **from** the pseudonymous *Either/Or*, **through** the *Concluding Postscript*, with *my name as editor*, **to** *Discourses of the Communion on Fridays* ..." The purpose of the whole authorship is "to *make aware* of the religious, the essentially Christian—but 'without authority'" (*KW* XIII, 494). "From the very beginning," Kierkegaard continued, "I have enjoined and repeated unchanged that I was 'without authority.' I regard myself rather as a *reader* of the books, not as the author" (*KW* XIII, 501).

Kierkegaard developed two particular forms for use in his signed works, "reflections," translated by some as "deliberations," and "upbuilding discourses." Each of the "upbuilding discourses" was addressed to that "single individual whom I with joy and gratitude call

my reader" (*KW* V, 79). He called them "discourses" to distinguish them from sermons, because the author, he wrote, "not being an ordained member of the clergy, does not have the authority to preach" (Hong and Hong, 1978, 84). The purpose of a "reflection" (or "deliberation") is different. Its purpose is "to provoke" and "sharpen thought." "Reflections," as Kierkegaard noted in an 1847 journal entry, "ought to be a 'gadfly'; therefore the tone ought to be quite different from that of edifying discourse, which rests in mood, but reflections ought in good sense to be impatient, high-spirited in mood. Irony is necessary here and the even more significant ingredient of the comic" (Kierkegaard [1847] 1962, 12). The Socratic tone of these reflections is intended for the education of the reader and for his or her self-examination and increase of self-knowledge (ibid., 13).

Kierkegaard's writings can be read as a kind of philosophical and theological therapy. They have two simultaneous audiences: Kierkegaard himself—the autobiographical—and his "dear reader" whom he hopes to address with a message that will bring about a transformation. His task on the largest scale is to introduce Christianity to Christendom, that is, to address the cogency and force of the gospel message of Jesus that had been occluded by the established church and adapted to comfortable bourgeois Danish life. Kierkegaard's signed authorship in particular was not addressed to "cultured despisers of religion" as the 1799 addresses of Friedrich Schleiermacher were, but rather to the comfortable, often self-satisfied, practitioners of the Christian faith in Kierkegaard's own native Denmark. In his philosophical and theological reflections Kierkegaard was a Socratic gadfly seeking to awaken self-knowledge, repentance, and the conversion of his reader to a self-reflective life and a more genuine Christian faith.

In the "Conclusion" to *The Point of View for my Work as an Author* Kierkegaard allowed the "poet who will usher me to the place among those who have suffered for an idea" to offer a retrospective evaluation of his life:

> Yet also here in the world he found what he sought: "that single individual"; if no one else was that, he himself was and became that more and more. It was the cause of Christianity that he served; from childhood his life

was wonderfully fitted for that. Thus he completed the task of reflection—to cast Christianity, becoming a Christian, wholly and fully into reflection. (*KW* XIII, 582)

V. Kierkegaard's Legacy

As mentioned earlier, Kierkegaard's writings remained in relative obscurity outside of his native Demark until the early years of the twentieth century, when his work began to be translated into German. The emphasis he placed on human subjectivity, particularly on the subjectivity of the individual, spoke to a generation whose mass political movements subsumed individual consciousness within the collective.

Kierkegaard's writings exerted a strong influence on the dialogical hermeneutics of Martin Buber and the dialectical theology of Karl Barth, particularly his discussion of the radical otherness of God (Vidler, 1974, 215).

Kierkegaard has often been called the "Father of Existentialism." His account of individual existence greatly influenced both the existentialism of Martin Heidegger and the atheistic existentialism of Jean-Paul Sartre. Both Heidegger and Sartre rejected the religious elements of Kierkegaard's writings while preserving the earlier, more philosophical, esthetic elements. Kierkegaard's reflections on anxiety, despair, individual choice, and the human search for meaning were central to the existentialist writings of the twentieth century.

References

Hong, Howard V. and Hong, Edna H. eds. 1978. *The Essential Kierkegaard*. Princeton, NJ: Princeton University Press.

Kierkegaard, Søren. 1978–2000. *Kierkegaard's Writings*, I–XXVI. Princeton, NJ: Princeton University Press. (Abbreviated as *KW*.)

Kierkegaard, Søren. 1901–6. *Søren Kierkegaards samlede Vœrker*, I–XIV. Copenhagen: Gyldendal.

Kierkegaard, Søren. 1967–78. *Søren Kierkegaard's Journals and Papers*, I–VII. Bloomington: University of Indiana Press. (Abbreviated as *JP*.)

Kierkegaard, Søren [1847] 1962. *Works of Love: Some Christian Reflections in the Form of Discourses*, trans. Howard and Edna Hong. New York: Harper and Row.

Vidler, Alec R. 1971. *The Church in an Age of Revolution, 1789 to the Present Day*, The Pelican History of the Church, Vol. 5. London: Penguin Books.

C. S. (Clive Staples) Lewis (1898–1963)

Molly F. James

I.   Introduction and Biography

C. S. Lewis might be rather surprised to find himself in a companion to the theologians. He did not consider himself a theologian. He was a writer, a scholar, and a Christian apologist, but he did not believe he was truly qualified to be an expert in matters of theology. Although he did not consider himself a theologian, one cannot deny the theological content of his work. Lewis was perhaps most well known and beloved for his popular writings including *The Chronicles of Narnia*, *The Great Divorce*, and *A Grief Observed*. Yet his writings on Christianity have been widely read, especially his classic apologetic work *Mere Christianity*. Lewis has been described by one of his biographers as "the most popular and influential Christian apologist of our time" (Cunningham, 1967).

Lewis was born in Belfast on November 29, 1898, and he was raised in the Anglican tradition. Lewis was younger of two sons. His father was the son of a Welsh farmer and his mother the daughter of a minister. Both his parents were well educated: his father was a lawyer, and his mother had a bachelor's degree. His mother died of cancer in 1908 and shortly after this, Lewis followed his brother to school in England. With the exception of a brief return to Belfast for one year of schooling, England would become Lewis's home. In 1916 he entered University College at Oxford. He served briefly in the British Army during World War I,

returning to his studies at the end of the war in 1918. After graduation he served as a tutor, and then, in 1925, he was appointed as a professor of English at Magdalen College at Oxford. He held this post for 29 years before taking up a post as a literature professor at Cambridge University in 1955.

Throughout his life, Lewis was very close to his brother. They lived together for many years after his brother retired from military service in 1932. Lewis lived most of his life as a quiet bachelor. In 1955, however, he married an American, Joy Davidman, in a civil ceremony to provide her with British citizenship. A Church of England ceremony was also performed in Joy's hospital room later that year when she was thought to be dying of cancer. What had begun as a marriage of practicality blossomed into one of love. Joy recovered for a short time, but eventually succumbed to the disease in 1960. The pain of this loss is closely documented in Lewis's *A Grief Observed*. Lewis himself died only three years later on November 22, 1963.

II.   Theology

Lewis was not always a man of faith. He was an atheist as a teenager, but as a young man found himself increasingly aware of God's presence in his life. He was not happy to become a believer. He writes of his

The Student's Companion to the Theologians, First Edition. Edited by Ian S. Markham.
© 2013 Blackwell Publishing Ltd. Published 2013 by Blackwell Publishing Ltd.

conversion in *Surprised by Joy*: "In the Trinity Term of 1929 I gave in, and admitted that God was God, and knelt and prayed: perhaps, that night, the most dejected and reluctant convert in all England" (Lewis, 1955, 221).

This conversion became the foundation for a large body of writing that deals with theological themes. Lewis does not set forth in any of his writings a systematic theology. He did not see this as his role. Lewis saw his role as a "translator," putting Christian doctrine into language the average person could understand (Christiansen, 1979, 22). "It was only when theologians, or any other professionals, strayed from their specific fields of competence into the realm of general philosophy that he felt he had something worthwhile to offer" (ibid., 39). Additionally, Lewis does not believe that Christianity lends itself to a systematic theology. "We may observe that the teaching of Our Lord Himself, in which there is no imperfection, is not given to us in that cut-and-dried, fool-proof, systematic fashion we might have expected or desired. He wrote no book. We have only reported sayings, most of them uttered in answer to questions, shaped in some degree by their context. And when we have collected them all we cannot reduce them to a system" (Lewis, 1960, 95). Yet there is still much theology to be gleaned from his writings and from those who wrote about him.

When Lewis became a Christian he returned to the Anglican tradition of his youth, and in many ways his theology embodies important tenets of Anglicanism. The Anglican tradition is perhaps best known for its *via media*, for its desire to navigate a "middle way" between extremes. Anglicans are comfortable living with questions, comfortable with gray areas, comfortable holding two seemingly conflicting truths simultaneously. Lewis too was willing to "live in tension with two conflicting points of view" (Christiansen, 1979, 81). Lewis also embodies the Anglican view of "real presence" in the Eucharist, a middle way between the Roman Catholic belief in transubstantiation and the liberal Protestant view that the bread and wine are mere symbols. In his view on scripture, Lewis also falls in the middle. He does not believe the Bible to be inerrant, nor is he willing to take it as mere story. Even if the story of the Fall in Genesis is a myth that does not detract in any way

from its truth. Yet Lewis would not let the Gospels be classified as merely educational stories from the minds of the evangelists. He believed that the evidence in favor of the historicity of the New Testament was convincing (Christiansen, 1979, 35). He felt that if one were to deny the reality of the Gospel miracles or the resurrection then one was leaving the Christian faith (ibid., 40). The true reality of Christ's birth, life, death, and resurrection were essential elements of the Christian tradition that could not be ignored or discarded.

Lewis was not particularly concerned with developing a systematic understanding of the atonement or other elements of Christian doctrine. He believed that experiencing one's faith was more important than fully understanding it. Regarding the Eucharist, he reminds us that the command of Christ is "Take, eat" and not "Take, understand" (Christiansen, 1979, 30). Regarding the atonement, Lewis wrote:

> Of course, you can express this in all sorts of different ways. You can say that Christ died for our sins. You may say that the Father has forgiven us because Christ has done for us what we ought to have done. You may say that we are washed in the blood of the Lamb. You may say that Christ has defeated death. They are all true. If any of them do not appeal to you, leave it alone and get on with the formula that does. And, whatever you do, do not start quarrelling with other people because they have a different formula from yours. (Lewis, 1960, 93)

Although Lewis emphasized the importance of the experience, he also realized the importance of theological discussion. Lewis is perhaps most recognized in theological circles for his argument for the existence of God. This argument is set forth in *Mere Christianity*, but has been excerpted in theological textbooks. Lewis uses morality as a basis for arguing for the existing of God. He writes: "Think of a country where people were admired for running away in battle, or where a man felt proud of double-crossing all the people who had been kindest to him. You might just as well try to imagine a country where two and two made five" (Lewis, 1952, 5). He also argues that the law is something that is outside of humanity, and not something merely created or made up by humans (ibid., 16). He comes to the conclusion that points to the existence of God:

> All I have got to is a Something which is directing the universe, and which appears in me as a law urging me to do right … I think we have to assume it is more like a mind than it is like anything else we know—because after all the only other thing we know is matter and you can hardly imagine a bit of matter giving instructions. (Ibid., 20)

Although Lewis was able to make a strong argument for the existence of God, he also acknowledges that theology is only a map, it is not "the real thing." Theology is different from having a personal experience of God. Theology is "the science of God," and it has value in its own right. Theology is how one learns about God. For Christians, theology is the study of Christian doctrines. There is more to becoming a Christian than just feeling religious. As Lewis notes, "you will not get eternal life by simply feeling the presence of God in flowers or music. Neither will you get anywhere by looking at maps without going to sea. Nor will you be very safe if you go to sea without a map" (Lewis, 1952, 119–20).

Lewis also tackles the challenging relationship of God and Time. Over the centuries many theologians have debated whether God is in time, outside of time, or somehow both in and out of time simultaneously. Lewis comes down on the side of God being outside of time. According to Lewis there is an eternal "now" for God, and only humans have a sense of past, present, and future. This means that God does know what we are going to do tomorrow, but we must also remember that it is not "tomorrow" for God, it is now. Lewis offers the analogy that if time is a line on paper, God is the sheet of paper (Lewis, 1952, 132–3).

Lewis even ventures into discussion of the Trinity. He speaks of the Trinity in the traditional language of "persons." He speaks of the parental relationship between the Father and the Son, and of the Holy Spirit as that which "grows out of the joint life of the Father and the Son." As with the rest of Lewis's theological discussions, the Trinity is not something that is just meant to be an abstract subject debated by learned minds, it is to be lived. "The whole dance, or drama, or pattern of this three-Personal life is to be played out in each one of us; or (putting it the other way round) each one of us has got to enter that pattern, take his place in that dance. There is no other way to the happiness for which we were made" (Lewis, 1952, 136–7).

III.   Conclusion

Lewis's discussion of the Trinity is perhaps emblematic of Lewis's mode of theological discussion. Lewis strives to make theology and Christianity readable and approachable to the average person. Given that his books have sold millions of copies, one can certainly say his writing is approachable. Yet whether he was truly engaging in theological inquiry and discussion is a matter of debate. Some might say that Lewis's influential status merits his inclusion in a companion to the theologians. In his *A History of Christianity in the United States and Canada*, Mark Noll puts Lewis's influence on a par with that of Alfred North Whitehead and states that their influence on "laity and clergy from many denominations" has been even greater than that of Karl Rahner or Hans Kung (1992, 522). That is august company for a literary professor. Yet others might say he is a fraud. He was a scholar and novelist who wrote on theological themes, and if we used that criterion then almost any science fiction writer or popular novelist could merit the title "theologian." As noted above, Lewis himself might agree with his critics; he did not want to be considered a theologian. Yet his texts are full of theology, and they are full of an important aspect of theology: practicality. Lewis reminds us that theology gains real meaning when it is lived out. Is theology truly theology if it does not engage in dialogue with scholars of other disciplines? Is it truly theology if it stays in theoretical form? Lewis reminds us that the heart of the Christian faith is effectual; it changes people's lives. To be a Christian theologian, then, is to be engaged in the study of that process of change. It is to study what God in Christ has done and how that truth has been, is being, and will be lived out in the lives of people all over the world. If this is what it means to be a "theologian," C. S. Lewis is certainly worthy of the title.

References

Christiansen, Michael. 1979. *C. S. Lewis on Scripture*. London: Hodder & Stoughton.

Cunningham, Richard. 1967. *C. S. Lewis: Defender of the Faith*. Philadelphia: Westminster Press.

Lewis, C. S. 1952. *Mere Christianity*. New York: Scribner.

Lewis, C. S. 1955. *Surprised by Joy: The Shape of My Early Life*. New York: Harcourt & Brace.

Lewis, C. S. 1960. *Reflections on the Psalms*. London: Fontana Press.

Noll, Mark A. 1992. *A History of Christianity in the United States and Canada*. Grand Rapids: Eerdmans.

Peterson, Michael, Hasker, William, Reichenbach, Bruce, and Basinger, David, eds. 2001. *Philosophy of Religion: Selected Readings*. New York: Oxford University Press.

John Henry Newman (1801–90)

Christopher L. Webber

A deeply divisive yet influential figure in his own time—and still today—John Henry Newman is remembered primarily for his leadership in what is variously known as the Tractarian or Oxford Movement in the Church of England and for his subsequent conversion to Roman Catholicism. Newman was not primarily a theologian and his most popular writings are his parochial sermons, published in eight volumes, and his autobiography, *Apologia Pro Sua Vita*. He also contributed many of the 90 Oxford tracts, wrote a significant study of Arius, and published important essays on the development of doctrine and the theory of a liberal education.

I. Background

Because the bulk of Newman's writing was directly occasioned by events in the changing world around him, it is important to sketch in the nature of those events. Early nineteenth-century England was a society in dramatic transition from an agricultural to an industrial, urban society and from a unitary society with an established church to a pluralistic community in which ecclesiastical conformity would no longer be a requirement of public life. To accommodate a society in which Christians of evangelical and Roman Catholic churches played an ever-increasing part, the government began to remove disabilities dating to the Restoration (1662) and to reshape the established church itself where, as in Ireland, the structure of dioceses and allocation of resources had come to reflect another age.

Such a transformation inevitably engendered opposition. The memory of the violent French Revolution was still vivid in England and a new French revolution with more bloodshed had only recently occurred when Newman's first tract was published in 1834. England, also, after nearly 50 years under Tory (Conservative) government had seen a more liberal (Whig) government come to office and the established powers, in particular those within the church, feared the possibility of still more radical and violent change. The increasingly prominent and vocal middle class and laboring people, on the other hand, felt a growing frustration with their continuing exclusion from involvement in their own government. It was when the Tory Party itself suggested changes to accommodate this demand, and the bishops of the established church provided the votes needed to defeat those proposals, that violence did break out. In Bristol crowds broke into the jail and set fire to the Bishop's palace. Elsewhere bishops had to be protected from the mobs.

The Oxford Movement was primarily a conservative reaction to these forces of change. The underlying issues were far from academic or narrowly ecclesiastical. The event that triggered the movement

The Student's Companion to the Theologians, First Edition. Edited by Ian S. Markham.
© 2013 Blackwell Publishing Ltd. Published 2013 by Blackwell Publishing Ltd.

was the government's reformation of the Irish church, eliminating a number of dioceses and redirecting the church's income. Whether such changes were appropriate was never seriously argued by Newman and his Oxford University colleagues. It was the notion that the government could create or eliminate bishops and dioceses without reference to the church's own leadership that struck them as unacceptable. The Tractarians (as they came to be known) rejected the notion that the state had authority to restructure the church whatever the need. They asked, not unreasonably, how a secular government could govern an established church. After a few inconclusive meetings, Newman, with little reference to his colleagues, launched a series of tracts intended to reclaim the heritage of the Church of England as the catholic church in England, a church which claimed apostolic foundation and was a more authentic expression of the Christian faith than could be found in the Roman or evangelical systems.

In the early nineteenth century, the Church of England was no longer in reality the church of a great many English people. Through all the changes since the Reformation and in spite of vigorous persecution at certain times, a core of Roman Catholic adherents had survived, sometimes tolerated and sometimes persecuted. As a result of the Catholic Relief Acts of 1778, 1791, and 1829 Roman Catholics were able again to practice their faith openly and to serve in Parliament. Their numbers were then rapidly augmented by the immigration of Irish peasants fleeing the potato famine (1845–9) and seeking jobs in English factories. The Vatican, treating England as a mission field, established a system of Apostolic Vicariates to minister to these diverse populations, employing both educated and aristocratic priests of the surviving Roman population in England and other priests, often poorly educated, who were brought from Ireland.

Completely separate from the Roman Catholic population but sharing some of the same concerns were Presbyterian, Baptist, Independent, and Methodist congregations. These were both the dissenters who had not accepted the established church of the Elizabethan settlement as adequately reformed, and also the new ranks of Methodists, followers of John Wesley, who remained for the most part not yet

fully separated from the established church. Though they had their own meeting places and ministers, they often worshiped at times not in conflict with the services of the local parish church and would come together to the evening service.

A religious census made in 1850 surprised people with specific information showing what current religious affiliation and practices were: on a given Sunday over five million individuals had attended Church of England services and just under five million, divided almost equally between Methodists on the one hand and Baptists and Independents on the other, had attended services of those churches. Less than half a million were thought to have attended Roman Catholic services.

Many contemporary observers looked at the Tractarian movement against this background and in the context of its demands for freedom from the state and saw the possibility of another new church being formed. Such a church might have emerged in semi-separation like the Methodists or become an independent body like the Episcopal Churches in Scotland and the United States. Newman and others of the Tractarian leadership saw such disestablishment as a very real possibility. But Newman's vision was always in terms of catholicity and wholeness: ideally, that the Church of England could once again present itself as the catholic church in that country or that the Church of Rome, for all its failures, might somehow fulfill that vision. When he left the Church of England, a few hundred other clergy followed him and a certain number of lay people, but the established church was not greatly shaken. It was Pusey, Keble, and those who stayed in the Church of England who made an enduring impact on Anglicanism and helped create a church more deeply aware of its catholic heritage.

Newman's career

Born into a very middle-class family in London, Newman learned something of Christian faith from a Calvinist viewpoint from his mother and underwent a "conversion" at the age of 15, which he always considered a critical turning point in his life. This conversion took place under the influence of one of his schoolteachers, Walter Mayer, an evangelical Christian, and of his reading. It is characteristic of

Newman that he could, on the one hand, consistently look back to this moment as foundational and that his teaching, especially in his sermons, always reflected an evangelical orientation, while on the other hand, he moved from an evangelical abhorrence of the pope and papacy through his Oxford years in which he continued to denounce the papacy while becoming an advocate of Anglican catholicism, to a final period of his life in which he became the most famous convert of his day to papal catholicism. There is a remarkable consistency underlying a life that seemed on the surface to be one of radical change, moving from one pole of Christian faith to another.

Newman himself wrote:

> From the age of fifteen, dogma has been the fundamental principle of my religion: I know no other religion; I cannot enter into the idea of any other sort of religion; religion, as a mere sentiment, is to me a dream and a mockery. As well can there be filial love without the fact of a father, as devotion without the fact of a Supreme Being. What I held in 1816, I held in 1833, and I hold in 1864. Please God, I shall hold it to the end. (*Apologia*, p. 45)

As a child of an unimportant family and the product of an education that did not include such elite schools as Harrow and Eton, Newman arrived at Oxford in 1817 as somewhat of an outsider. Pushing himself too hard to succeed, he failed to obtain honors but put himself forward nonetheless a year later, in 1822, for a position as a Fellow of Oriel College. This time he succeeded against all expectation but then found himself again in the position of an outsider, part of a very small and exclusive academic institution and feeling like a duckling among swans. A senior Fellow, Richard Whately, afterwards Archbishop of Dublin, took it upon himself to draw Newman out and succeeded brilliantly. With Whately's guidance, Newman found that he could not only hold his own in his new world but even exercise leadership.

It was in 1829 that Newman discovered his ability to shape political events. Prime Minister Robert Peel, a Tory (Conservative), had moved legislation to remove some of the disabilities under which Roman Catholics in England had suffered since the Reformation. Peel understood that times had changed and that it was no longer realistic to exclude substantial numbers of

citizens from the privileges of citizenship. Newman reacted negatively more by instinct than principle. He had no fixed position on Roman Catholic emancipation but he felt the proposal was evidence of what he called "indifferentism" in religion, a falling away from the deep commitment that had been central to his life since his conversion. When Peel stood for re-election from Oxford, Newman worked hard to rally the opposition and succeeded in defeating Peel. It was an experience which would shape his response to Keble's Assize sermon four years later and the beginning of the Oxford Movement.

At almost the same time, Newman discovered a deep and abiding interest in patristic studies. It was a natural area of study for a young Anglican theologian since Anglicans had always appealed for authority to the undivided church and to the first ecumenical councils. Newman focused his scholarly attention on Arius and the Arian controversy of the fourth century. At first, Newman found in this study corroboration of the Anglican position, but in the end he began to see himself and the English Church as being in the position that the heretics were in during the early centuries of the Christian era.

From 1833 when the first tract was published until the last tract was published in 1841, Newman led a public debate on the nature of the church, arguing always that the Church of England was a catholic church that had inherited its episcopal character in direct historic succession from the apostles and therefore could not properly subject itself to a secular government. Although the question was raised immediately whether the logical outcome of Newman's line of argument was not submission to the Church of Rome, Newman himself strenuously resisted such an idea for many years. He pointed to what he considered to be the abuses of Roman devotional and political development but never made any first-hand examination of the existing Roman Catholic Church itself until he had become a member of it. It has been suggested that Newman at last became a Roman Catholic because so many of his followers had done so that he was in danger of finding himself without a "support group" unless he followed them. In September, 1843, Newman preached his last sermon as an Anglican and resigned his position as Vicar of St Mary's Church.

Newman was formally received into the Roman Catholic Church in October, 1845, but there had been no preparation on either side for this change and for some time, arguably for the remainder of his life, the Roman Church was not quite sure what to do with this famous convert. Newman had already given up his position within the Church of England and he never attained a position of influence within the Roman Church. In 1848 he was summoned to Rome, ordained as a priest of the Roman Catholic Church, and sent back to Birmingham to establish an Oratory or study center. In 1852 he was sent to Ireland to establish a university, but there were too many obstacles to be overcome and Newman returned to Birmingham and remained there until his death in 1890. He was named a cardinal of the church in 1879 but no new authority came with the title. It was rather like an honorary degree, a recognition of past achievement.

II. Newman's Theology

In both phases of his life, Anglican and Roman, Newman's influence was exercised primarily through his eloquent writing and preaching. In these, though they are in large part deeply involved in the particular issues of his day, he sometimes reflects a surprising sensitivity to the larger changes taking place in human and societal self-understanding that were expressed somewhat later in the insights of both Darwin and Freud.

Newman's writings may be divided into three areas: the homiletical, aimed at the ordinary church member; the theological, analyzing especially the controversies of the early church; and the prophetic, calling the church to deal with new issues ranging from an expanded role for the laity to freedom of theological inquiry. The first group made Newman popular and the third group had the enduring significance; the second group, the specifically theological writings, are important today primarily for the light they throw on Newman's own thought and the theological controversies of his time.

Newman, in the end, was an influential figure but not a leader. Although he set out to create a national debate through the tracts and to reshape the Church of England, he never created a political structure within or beside the church to advance his goals. And although Newman was a persuasive writer, he was not an original or systematic theologian. His sermons are his best-known writing and these were often devotional or polemical. Deeply conservative in some ways, Newman looked for authority in an appeal to antiquity and scorned those who would either dismiss or commend religion as a matter of private judgment. Yet he was ahead of his time in calling for a larger role for laity in the church, in recognizing the need for a new approach to the Bible, in analyzing the function of language in a scientific world, and in his analysis of the relationship between the claims of science and those of religion. In his lectures on *The Idea of a University* (1852) he contended that the contemporary Christian must be in full conversation with the best thought of the times. In the end, it may be Newman's analysis of the nature of knowledge and the use of language that is most relevant to the twenty-first century.

III. The Arians of the Fourth Century

The traditional Anglican appeal to the early church brought patristic studies to Newman's attention early in his Oxford career and he found such studies extremely congenial, setting out to read through all the writings of the early Christian theologians. He then focused his attention on Arius, the most significant of those condemned by the first Councils. The resultant volume, *The Arians of the Fourth Century* (1833), is not so much a systematic study of Arius as it is of the early church and the development of doctrine, an issue that would continue to interest Newman.

Although Newman would later attempt to apply the standards of the early church to the church of his own day, it is also true that he tends to apply the standards of his own day to the early church. He speaks, for example, of Arius's "attack on the Catholic doctrine" and consistently refers to Arius as "the heresiarch." But when Arius wrote, the Catholic doctrine of the incarnation had yet to be defined and Arius's voice was simply one of many attempting to gain acceptance for a particular understanding of the nature of Christ. That Arius was a heretic could be asserted after the Council of Nicaea had issued its doctrinal statements but by then Arius was 70 years old and the controversy had been going on for many years. Indeed, although Arius could legitimately be termed a heretic after the Council of Nicaea, the issue was still far from settled and Arius accepted the decrees of Nicaea just before his death at the age of 80. Rowan Williams seems to go too far in saying that Newman's argument in his study of Arianism is "built up on a foundation of complacent bigotry and historical fantasy" (Williams, 2002, 5). Newman was working within the culture of his own day and the sort of objective scholarship that is valued now was unknown. Nevertheless, it must be recognized that Newman came at his study of Arius with a definite agenda and that was to ground the ideas of the early Oxford Movement in the teaching of the early Christian church. Newman looked at the Athanasian party and saw the Tractarians; he looked at the Arians and saw evangelicals. It was because of that methodology that Newman, in a later critical passage, could say, "I looked at the Donatists and I saw myself." Newman never meant to imply that his theology was that of the Donatists; rather, he saw them as a group standing apart from the mainstream of Christian teaching and saw himself, as an Anglican, in that same position and realized that he was no longer comfortable there.

IV.   The Sermons

In his own time and still today, Newman's reputation rests largely on his sermons. It was through his sermons, drawing a growing audience of Oxford students, that Newman first began to attract attention to himself and his ideas. Frequently praised for their eloquent use of the English language, they sold well when first published and continued to provide Newman with an important source of income even after he resigned his positions in the Church of England.

The first eight volumes of sermons were published as *Parochial and Plain Sermons* and the title is accurate. The sermons were preached at St Mary's Church, Oxford, and, for sermons of that era especially, they are indeed relatively plain and straightforward. The

opening paragraph usually indicates clearly what Newman plans to do in the sermon and a large part of what follows often discusses the background for his text. Often half or more of the sermon will be used to provide an analysis of the biblical text and this part of the sermon is ordinarily not significantly different from an essay. It provides useful information but makes no direct appeal to the hearer. The final section of the sermon is where Newman is likeliest to speak directly to his listeners and exhort them to consider and change their way of living. Yet even here the appeal is often very low key: "May He give you grace so to hear what has been said, as you will wish to have heard, when life is over; to hear in a practical way, with a desire to profit by it, to learn God's will, and to do it."

Perhaps the most surprising aspect of Newman's sermons is that, in an era when the tracts had made his name widely known and highly controversial, they not only make no direct reference to the controversy but make very little effort to advance the doctrines for which elsewhere he was contending. Indeed, the sermons for the most part fail to reflect a catholic view of Christian doctrine at all but might well have been preached by someone of the evangelical school. The usual theme is the hearer's way of life and there are frequent references to the "dreadful day of judgment" which all human beings will ultimately face. There is a remarkably consistent emphasis on human sinfulness and the need for repentance. These characteristics remain typical of all Newman's non-polemical sermons both before and after his affiliation with Rome. In editing the successive volumes of sermons, Newman paid no attention to chronology and, although studies have now been done to date the sermons so that they could be arranged in sequence, there is no reason to do so. Newman is quite correct in his implicit recognition that there is no significant development in his thought and method over the years. Whatever changes Newman may have made in his ecclesiastical allegiance, it would seem that at a very basic level Newman himself did not change. He continued throughout his life to proclaim a simple message, appealing to his hearers and readers to change their lives through a deeper personal commitment to Christian faith.

Nor do the sermons vary significantly whatever the text or season being observed. Even in a Christmas or

Easter sermon, when joy and celebration might appropriately have been the dominant emphasis, the reminders of human sin are always very present. Thus in a Christmas sermon, Newman says:

> It is a day of joy: it is good to be joyful—it is wrong to be otherwise. For one day we may put off the burden of our polluted consciences, and rejoice in the perfections of our Saviour Christ, without thinking of ourselves, without thinking of our own miserable uncleanness; but contemplating His glory … (*Sermons*, VIII, 254)

and in an Easter sermon:

> Glorious, indeed, will be the spring time of the Resurrection, when all that seemed dry and withered will bud forth and blossom. … Who would miss being of that company? Wretched men they will then appear, who now for a season enjoy the pleasures of sin. Wretched, who follow their own selfish will, instead of walking by faith, who are now idle, instead of trying to serve God, who are set upon the world's vanities, or who scoff at religion, or who allow themselves in known sin, who live in anger, or malice, or pride, or covetousness, who do not continually strive to become better and holier, who are afraid to profess themselves Christians and take up their cross and follow Christ. (*Sermons*, II, 280–1)

Conversely, there is very little about the sacraments or the church or the nature of the catholic faith. There is a marked difference, however, between the eight volumes of the *Parochial and Plain Sermons*, which were preached to the congregation of St Mary's Church, Oxford, when Newman was the vicar, and the other volumes of sermons. The latter, whether preached at Oxford while he was still an Anglican, or at Birmingham, or elsewhere after he became a Roman Catholic, tend to be far more theological or polemical. They were often preached on special occasions such as the opening of the Oratory.

V.   The Oxford Tracts

The Oxford Tracts, so closely associated with Newman's name, were indeed his creation and reflect his developing search for an ecclesiastical home in

which he could be completely comfortable. Newman had met with others who shared his concerns about the government's emerging effort to reshape the relationship between church and state but Newman began to write and distribute tracts before any agreement had been made to do so or any organization created to sponsor them.

The first tract was a simple and straightforward appeal in less than 2,000 words to the apostolic authority of the church. Later tracts had become more books than tracts and the famous Tract 90 that ended the series was a substantial volume of 30,000 words. Apart from Tract 90, the most important tracts are probably those published as Tracts 38 and 41 under the title *Via Media*, and republished after his conversion under the title *Lectures on the Prophetical Office of the Church*. The original title would lead a reader to expect a definition of the Anglican middle way but what Newman provides is sketchy in the extreme. He writes that, "The glory of the English Church is, that it has taken the VIA MEDIA, as it has been called. It lies *between* the (so called) Reformers and the Romanists" (Tract 38, p. 37). Yet what follows in the form of a dialogue between "Clericus" and "Laicus" is not an expansion and interpretation of the title so much as an argument that the nineteenth-century church had gone beyond the intentions of the sixteenth-century church to identify itself in many ways with the teaching of Luther and Calvin. The fundamental question Newman engages is not so much the content of the *via media* as its location: nearer to the Continental Reformers than to Rome. Indeed, Newman argues that Calvin in many ways was more catholic than the nineteenth-century Church of England. Nor does the essay seem to envision the *via media* as a positive attempt to hold fast to the central teachings of the ancient and undivided church, rejecting the errors of both Rome and the Continental Reformers, but rather as a position drawing something from both sides but having no specific character of its own. Newman points to elements in the Prayer Book such as the reading of the Daily Office and the observance of saints' days and fasting that have fallen into disuse and discusses other aspects of the Prayer Book like the Athanasian Creed and teaching of regeneration in baptism that were widely questioned. All this indicates to "Clericus" (Newman) that the

Church of England had strayed from the middle road marked out by the sixteenth-century reformers.

In discussing the *via media*, Newman suggests that change must inevitably take place in any church over a period of a few hundred years. Earlier, in discussing Arian teaching, Newman had observed the process of development in the early church, development both in heretical teaching and in a fuller statement of the orthodox faith. Now, he had talked about development since the Reformation. But is development unavoidable, and what principles underlie it, and how can one distinguish valid developments from invalid?

These were questions to which Newman would give his full attention later in his *Essay on the Development of Christian Doctrine*.

Tract 90

Newman said that *Tract 90* was an attempt to hold others in the Church of England, but it might also be seen as a last effort on Newman's part to talk himself out of becoming a Roman Catholic. The Church of England had always required candidates for ordination to profess allegiance to the "39 Articles," a series of brief statements concerning basic Christian beliefs and issues that had divided the sixteenth-century church. Although intended to be broadly inclusive, they had usually been taken as a protestant manifesto and a condemnation of Roman Catholic positions. Now, however, Newman argued that it was possible to hold all the teaching of the 39 Articles while at the same time receiving the decrees of the Council of Trent that summarized the teaching required of Roman Catholics. Newman suggested, in effect, that one could be a member of the Church of England while accepting the entire teaching of the Roman Catholic Church. The tract aroused a violent reaction within the Church of England and may have increased the pressure Newman felt to abandon his effort to remain within its fold.

Essay on the Development of Christian Doctrine

The essay on the *via media* together with *Tract 90*, however, inevitably led to another and more important statement in Newman's *Essay on the Development of Christian Doctrine*. Newman had earlier issued a tract (*On the Mode of Conducting the Controversy with Rome*; Tract 71; 1836) in which he discussed several Roman Catholic teachings (purgatory, invocation of saints, et al.) that he held to be inconsistent with scripture and the teaching of the early church. Now, in writing about development, Newman justified these doctrines and practices as inevitable and proper developments of Christian doctrine.

Newman's theological method is, perhaps, nowhere so clear as in this essay. Newman was an intuitive theologian, using his theological investigations to elucidate the truth he had already grasped. It was after Newman's study of primitive Christianity led him to decide that Roman Catholicism represented the true continuation of the apostolic church that he set out to write this essay, and it was before he had finished writing it that he took the inevitable step of submitting himself to Roman authority.

Newman's intuitive conclusion "that modern Catholicism is nothing else but simply the legitimate growth and complement, that is, the natural and necessary development, of the doctrine of the early church" led him to seek to provide a logical set of criteria for this conclusion. If, as he believed, genuine development was implicit in the original revelation and was a logical unfolding of its implications, there ought to be guidelines with which to differentiate between the genuine and the false, the orthodox and the heretical. Newman listed seven "notes of genuine development" and summarized them as follows:

> The point to be ascertained is the unity and identity of the idea with itself through all stages of its development from first to last, and these are seven tokens that it may rightly be accounted one and the same all along. To guarantee its own substantial unity, it must be seen to be one in type, one in its system of principles, one in its unitive power towards externals, one in its logical consecutiveness, one in the witness of its early phases to its later, one in the protection which its later extend to its earlier, and one in its union of vigour with continuance, that is, in its tenacity. (*An Essay on the Development of Christian Doctrine*, p. 206)

The difficulty with this set of criteria, of course, is that it can be seen as identifying what should be with what is. Newman admits that there have been times in the church's history when it has wandered rather far from its proper course and he compares it to a human life in which the individual falls asleep and awakes refreshed. But for the person living in a particular time of corruption, it may be difficult to believe that all is well and that a new age will find the church renewed in vigor and possessed of new insights. It is also of little assistance to one questioning the authenticity of a new development in church life to be offered a set of criteria that can be used to assess it properly only after several centuries.

Yet by raising the question of development, Newman had, again intuitively, focused attention on an issue of critical importance over the next century and more of the church's life. The rapidly changing society of the industrial age had provided human beings with an intense awareness of historical change and development. Fifteen years later Darwin would publish his theory of evolutionary development, but the term "evolution" was already being used. Christian theologians were acquiring a new sense of the church's own history and development as archaeologists began to provide a new wealth of information about the Bible and the early church and as ancient documents were discovered to provide a clearer picture of the church's early history and growth. Newman's particular criteria would not serve very well to deal with this information explosion, but the fact that such issues had been raised within an institution that had seen itself as unchanging through the ages provided an enormous service to that church. It is often said that Newman was the theologian who prepared the way for the Second Vatican Council and its dramatic reappraisal of the church's life and mission.

The Idea of a University

Newman was always his own man. Although in form he "submitted to Rome," he was, as much in the Roman Church as in the English, one who thought for himself. Nowhere is this clearer than in Newman's lectures on *The Idea of a University* (1852). The idea of a Roman Catholic university in Ireland with Newman at the head had been put forward in 1851 and the Pope himself had endorsed it. Newman went to Dublin the next year and gave the series of lectures published under the title *The Idea of a University*. But

as time went on it became increasingly clear that Newman's concept of the project was not at all that of the Irish bishops who distrusted the idea of an educated laity in general and the notion of entrusting leadership to an Englishman and recent convert in particular. By the time Newman actually went to Dublin and settled into the work of creating a university, he knew himself that his vision could not be fulfilled. He returned to Birmingham in 1857 and resigned his position not long afterwards.

The lectures on *The Idea of a University* remain, however, important landmarks not only in Newman's own life but in the development of educational theory. The years in which Newman wrestled with the idea of creating a new university centered on a specific vision were years in which the great English universities of Oxford and Cambridge were being radically transformed. In 1845, when Newman left the Church of England, Oxford was still an institution of the church. The heads of the various colleges were all clergy and so were most of the Fellows. Sciences were not an important part of the curriculum; the great advances in biology, geology, and chemistry that had taken place in the first half of the century were largely unrecognized in the nation's most distinguished institution of higher learning. Over the next five years a radical transformation, summed up as "secularization," took place; the sciences found their place in the curriculum, and laymen and non-Anglicans assumed important roles in university affairs.

Newman, who saw himself as an opponent of "liberalism" throughout his life, set forth in his lectures a vision of what can only be called a "liberal education." Even at the Oxford of his student days, Newman had learned the importance of free inquiry. Religion was, to his mind, that which tied together the various fields of study, but all those fields must be open to the inquiring mind. Liberalism, in Newman's definition, was not a political question. It was "the mistake of subjecting to human judgment those revealed doctrines which are in their nature beyond and independent of it, and of claiming to determine on intrinsic grounds the truth and value of propositions which rest for their reception simply on the external authority of the Divine Word" (*Apologia*, p. 493). It had to do with rationalism on the one hand and sentimentalism on the other. Newman believed that there were revealed truths, clear and certain, on which faith could rest. But this confidence enabled him to champion intellectual freedom and a "liberal" education since it would inevitably defeat the claims of mere human reason and purely emotional sentiment.

In laying out his idea of the role of a university and the goal of education, Newman found himself more truly than ever in the position that he had abandoned, the *via media*. On the one hand, he rejected the idea that education is simply the acquisition of scientific knowledge and, on the other, that it cannot be open to all inquiry. But what he urged on his hearers most eloquently was the need to face without fear every aspect of the society around the university:

> Proscribe, I do not merely say particular authors, particular works, particular passages, but Secular Literature as such; cut out from your class-books all broad manifestations of the natural man; and these manifestations are waiting for your pupil's benefit at the very doors of your lecture-room in living and breathing substance. They will meet him there in all the charm of novelty, and all the fascination of genius or of amiableness. Today a pupil, tomorrow a member of the great world; today confined to the lives of the Saints, tomorrow thrown upon Babel—thrown on Babel without the honest indulgence of wit and humour and imagination having ever been permitted to him, without any fastidiousness of taste wrought into him, without any rule given him for discriminating "the precious from the vile," beauty from sin, the truth from the sophistry of nature, what is innocent from what is poison. You have refused him the masters of human thought, who would in some sense have educated him, because of their incidental corruption; you have shut up from him those whose thoughts strike home, to our hearts, whose words are proverbs, whose names are indigenous to all the world, who are the standard of the mother tongue, and the pride and boast of their countrymen, Homer, Ariosto, Cervantes, Shakespeare, because the old Adam smelt rank in them; and for what have you reserved him? You have given him a "liberty unto" the multitudinous blasphemy of his day; you have made him free of its newspapers, its reviews, its magazines, its novels, its controversial pamphlets, of its Parliamentary debates, its law proceedings, its platform speeches, its songs, its drama, its theatre, of its enveloping, stifling atmosphere of death. You have succeeded but in this—in making the world his University.
> (*Idea of a University*, pp. 218–19)

Newman's idea of education was, of course, deeply connected to his doctrine of development. A church or university closed off from the world would have no way to test its teaching or any need to develop it; the truths inherent in its founding revelation would never need to be explored and enlarged upon. In his doctrine of development, Newman had noted the way in which the church's teaching had most often evolved and unfolded in response to heresy. So it is precisely in an atmosphere of open inquiry that the church can thrive and heresy be detected and defeated. The Roman Church of Newman's day and for a century afterwards still had a Censor of Books to determine what volumes the faithful could safely read. Newman's *Idea of a University* was remarkable in its valuation of free inquiry.

An Essay in Aid of a Grammar of Assent

Newman's last major work, *An Essay in Aid of a Grammar of Assent* (1870), was a final attempt to explain himself to himself. He had been converted to Christianity at a young age and had spent much of his life trying to persuade others to be faithful. But what was it that led some to accept the faith and others to remain indifferent? Clearly it was not an intellectual matter since some Christians were not well educated and some well-educated people were not Christians. By the middle of the nineteenth century, experimental science was beginning to assume the central place in human thought that it would increasingly occupy in the following century. What could Newman say to those who rejected any statements that were "unscientific"?

By the middle of the twentieth century, the dominant school of philosophy was "Logical Positivism," which maintained that only mathematical, logical, and scientific statements are literally meaningful, or have truth values. Newman had been there already and argued that to reduce human knowledge to that which is provable in scientific terms is to reduce humanity. He had always been aware of the element of mystery and the inadequacy of formulas. Human beings, he argued, have the ability to arrive at certainty by using memories, probabilities, associations, testimonies, and impressions, in order to reason and conclude and believe spontaneously with success, but without the aid of explicit analysis:

> I am what I am or I am nothing. I cannot think, reflect, or judge about my being, without starting from the very point which I aim at concluding. My ideas are all assumptions, and I am ever moving in a circle. I cannot avoid being sufficient for myself, for I cannot make myself anything else, and to change me is to destroy me. If I do not use myself, I have no other self to use. My only business is to ascertain what I am, in order to put it to use. It is enough for the proof of the value and authority of any function which I possess, to be able to pronounce that it is natural. What I have to ascertain is the laws under which I live. (*Grammar of Assent*, p. 346)

The scientific worldview seems to some to give us stronger grounds for belief, but Newman argues that it does so only by ruling out much of the equipment God gave us with which to understand the universe. I may know the boiling point of water but I know nothing of the meaning of life. Such an approach impoverishes human life and has no lasting value.

So Newman, who had always acted intuitively, not only justified himself to himself but marked out a way forward for human beings in society. The development of doctrine is not a science but it enlists the fullness of human capacities to think, to sense, to reflect, and to conclude. Facing the particular issues of his small, even parochial, world, Newman was among the first to grapple with the very large issues that the world would face in the next century as it attempted to find a way to be human in a world of machines.

References

Bouyer, Louis, 1986. *Newman's Vision of Faith: A Theology for Times of General Apostasy*. San Francisco: Ignatius Press.

Chadwick, Owen. 1966. *The Victorian Church*. New York: Oxford University Press.

Hutton, Richard H. 1891. *Cardinal Newman*, London: Methuen and Co.

Ker, Ian. 1993. *Newman and the Fullness of Christianity*. Edinburgh: T&T Clark.

Meynell, Wilfrid. 1907. *Cardinal Newman*. London: Burns and Oates.

Moody, John. 1945. *John Henry Newman*. New York: Sheed and Ward.

Mozley, Anne, ed. 1903. *Letters and Correspondence of John Henry Newman During His Life in the English Church with a Brief Autobiography*. London: Longmans, Green, & Co.

Newsome, David. [1966] 1993. *The Parting of Friends*. Grand Rapids, MI: Eerdmans.

O'Connell, Marvin R. 1969. *The Oxford Conspirators: A History of the Oxford Movement 1833–1845*. New York: Macmillan.

O'Faolain, Sean. 1952. *Newman's Way*. New York: Devain-Adair Company.

Turner, Frank. 2002. *John Henry Newman: The Challenge to Evangelical Religion*. New Haven, CT: Yale University Press.

Williams, Rowan. [1987] 2002. *Arius: Heresy and Tradition*, Grand Rapids, MI: Eerdmans.

Books by John Henry Newman (showing date of firstpublication and re-publication)

Arians of the Fourth Century (1833; 1871)

Tracts for the Times (1833–41)

On the Prophetical Office of the Church (1837; 1877) (*Via Media*, vol. 1)

Lectures on Justification (1838; 1874)

Parochial and Plain Sermons:
  Volume I (1834; 1869)
  Volume II (1835; 1869)
  Volume III (1836; 1869)
  Volume IV (1839; 1869)
  Volume V (1840; 1869)
  Volume VI (1842; 1869)
  Volume VII (1842; 1869)
  Volume VIII (1843; 1869)

Select Treatises of St. Athanasius, editor (1842, 1844)

Lives of the English Saints, editor (1843–4)

Via Media, vol. 2 (various; 1883)

Essays on Miracles (1826, 1843; 1870)

Oxford University Sermons (1843; 1871)

Sermons on Subjects of the Day (1843; 1869)

Development of Christian Doctrine (1845; 1878)

Retractation of Anti-Catholic Statements (1845; 1883)

Loss and Gain (1848; 1874)

Faith and Prejudice and Other Sermons (various)

Discourses to Mixed Congregations (1849)

Difficulties of Anglicans (1850)

Present Position of Catholics in England (1851)

The Idea of a University (1852 and 1858; 1873)

Cathedra Sempiterna (1852)

Callista (1855; 1888)

The Rambler, editor (1859–60) with *On Consulting the Faithful* (1859)

Apologia Pro Sua Vita (1865)

Letter to Dr Pusey (1865) (*Anglican Difficulties*, vol. 2)

The Dream of Gerontius (1865)

An Essay in Aid of a Grammar of Assent (1870)

Sermons Preached on Various Occasions (various; 1874)

Letter to the Duke of Norfolk (1875) (*Anglican Difficulties*, vol. 2)

Five Letters (1875)

Sermon Notes, 1849–78

Meditations and Devotions

Select Treatises of St. Athanasius, editor (1881; 1887)

    Volume 1: *Translations*

    Volume 2: *Appendix of Illustrations*

On the Inspiration of Scripture (1884)

Development of Religious Error (1885)

Other miscellaneous works

Addresses to Cardinal Newman and His Replies (with Biglietto Speech) (1879)

Discussions and Arguments (various; 1872)

Essays Critical and Historical (various; 1871)

    Volume 1

    Volume 2

Historical Sketches (various; 1872)

    Volume 1

    Volume 2 (with *Church of the Fathers*)

    Volume 3

Historical Tracts of St. Athanasius, editor (1843)

Prefaces

    Froude's Remains (1838)

    Hymni Ecclesiae (1838)

    Library of Fathers (various)

    Catena Aurea (1841)

    Church and Empires (1873)

    Notes of Visit to the Russian Church (1882)

Tracts Theological and Ecclesiastical (various; 1871)

Verses on Various Occasions (various; 1867)

Reinhold Niebuhr (1892–1971)

Matthew Berke

I. Overview

Preacher, teacher, author, and activist, Reinhold Niebuhr emerged from a small German-immigrant denomination to become a leading light of the American Protestant establishment and a "public intellectual" who explained the deeper meaning of current events to secular elites as well as believers. In a career spanning five decades, from the teens to the sixties, Niebuhr argued that biblical religion is relevant to the great issues of politics and public life: for its idealism, which can be harnessed to the cause of progressive change, but also for its wisdom about the dark side of human nature and the limits and perplexities of seeking justice in a fallen world.

Niebuhr served 13 years as a parish minister in Detroit (1915–28) and 32 as a professor of Christian Ethics at Union Theological Seminary in New York (1928–60). Throughout, he was a popular speaker on the college lecture circuit. He wrote thousands of articles and nearly two dozen books, including classic works of theology and social ethics such as *Leaves from the Notebook of a Tamed Cynic* (1929), *Moral Man and Immoral Society* (1932), *Beyond Tragedy* (1937), *The Nature and Destiny of Man* (two volumes, 1941/1943), *The Children of Light and the Children of Darkness* (1944), *The Irony of American History* (1952), and *Christian Realism and Political Problems* (1953). In both his religious and his political thought he was a leading liberal and a leading critic of liberalism.

Niebuhr's theology rehabilitated classic doctrines of sin and atonement in modern terms. But he rejected modern illusions about human perfectibility and inevitable progress, citing man's perennial capacity for evil as well as good—especially evil mixed in with good. Self-giving, self-sacrificing love is the true law of human existence, Niebuhr said, but egoistic self-assertion remains a constant temptation, a false but tangible consolation for man's anxiety over mortality and the apparent meaninglessness of life. Earnest ethical striving can improve conduct, but only up to a point, because human beings have an endless capacity for rationalizing their selfishness; even their altruistic projects are often tainted by self-righteousness and a hidden will-to-power. For Niebuhr the ultimate moral and religious problem is the sinfulness that men practice even when they try to do good. In the end he affirmed the Reformation principle that people become "justified" (i.e., made right with God) through divine forgiveness rather than by their own merit.

Niebuhr's social and political theory, known as "Christian realism," stressed the inevitability of conflict in history, but also the possibility of meaningful ethical action. Contrary to the Social Gospel movement that inspired his career, Niebuhr came to believe that a "rough justice" or "tolerable harmony" in society is best achieved not through "moral suasion" but by a balance of power. He urged idealists and reformers to accept power as a necessary instrument of justice,

The Student's Companion to the Theologians, First Edition. Edited by Ian S. Markham.
© 2013 Blackwell Publishing Ltd. Published 2013 by Blackwell Publishing Ltd.

albeit a morally hazardous one that needs to be supplemented by prudence and magnanimity. He viewed all causes and ideologies as ambiguous and potential vehicles for self-aggrandizement. Love, though unattainable, is politically relevant because it holds all achievements under ultimate judgment, preventing complacency and inspiring people to seek the best approximations of justice that circumstances permit. Like Abraham Lincoln, whom he admired, Niebuhr held that even imperfect men and nations are called to historically significant tasks, and that they must act according to their best lights, trusting that God will complete their fragmentary achievements, and pardon their excesses, in a realm beyond history.

Niebuhr worked out his ideas largely in response to the crises of the twentieth century: war, economic breakdown, class struggle, totalitarianism, nuclear stalemate. Though he passed through a Marxist phase in the early 1930s, by the 1940s he retroactively endorsed Franklin D. Roosevelt's New Deal, which had, he believed, vindicated liberal democracy as the best means for arbitrating society's inevitable conflicts of interest. Along with many other Depression-era intellectuals, Niebuhr moved from the radical left to "the vital center" (as Arthur M. Schlesinger Jr. later called it). He defended the postwar "liberal consensus" on democratic pluralism, the mixed economy, the welfare state, and the full range of civil and personal freedoms. He brought to that consensus a unique dimension of depth, arguing that democracy, with its blending of altruistic cooperation and pluralistic competition, is a permanently valid form of social organization, rooted in the ethical ambiguity of human nature: "Man's capacity for justice makes democracy possible," Niebuhr declared (1944, xiii), "but man's inclination to injustice makes democracy necessary."

In foreign affairs he jettisoned his youthful pacifism to become an advocate of intervention against Nazi Germany. He helped prepare the churches for the moral challenges of war, and chided religious and secular isolationists for the false innocence of neutrality; better, he said, to dirty one's hands in responsible engagement than to permit "the triumph of an intolerable tyranny" (1957, 272). He described modern totalitarian movements as idolatrous political religions that had rushed in to fill a spiritual void at the center of Western civilization. During the 1940s and

1950s he defended America's Cold War policies of containment and deterrence. The democracies of America and the West, though flawed, had a right, indeed a duty, to resist Soviet aggression and subversion, he argued. As a co-founder of Americans for Democratic Action in 1947, he brought strong liberal bona fides to the anti-communist cause. He worried that the nation might shirk its duty altogether or, alternatively, that it might adopt a dangerous chauvinism.

In his prime Niebuhr was regarded by many as a prophetic figure, a man for all seasons brimming with energy and good humor, eager to assume the practical responsibilities of the hour, yet reflective about historical and theological purposes that transcend conscious human striving. By mid-century, according to Richard Wightman Fox, "he stood alongside such figures as Margaret Mead and Walter Lippmann as a cultural sage of broad stature" (Fox, 1995, 496). *Time* magazine, in its March 8, 1948 cover story, confirmed his status as America's pre-eminent theologian. Every seminarian knew the commandment to "Love thy Niebuhr" (a young Martin Luther King Jr. regarded him as indispensable); even secular intellectuals thought his sober idealism well suited to an era of shattered illusions (one quipped that there should be an organization called Atheists for Niebuhr). In literary and diplomatic circles the adjective "Niebuhrian" suggested attentiveness to life's contradictions, paradoxes, and ironies—a tragic sense that the world cannot be perfected but also a solemn, almost stoic, duty to improve it as much as possible.

II. Career

He was born Karl Paul Reinhold Niebuhr on June 21, 1892 in Wright City, Missouri. In 1902, his family moved to Lincoln, Illinois. His father, Gustav, was a German-immigrant pastor; his American-born mother, Lydia, a pastor's daughter. He had an older brother Walter, an older sister Hulda, and a younger brother, Helmut. (Helmut, as H. Richard Niebuhr, would become a prominent theologian in his own right and an important influence on Reinhold's spiritual and intellectual development.) The family belonged to the German Evangelical Synod of North

America, an immigrant church whose doctrines borrowed from Luther and Calvin. (The Synod lost its distinct identity in a series of ecclesiastical mergers that began in 1934 and culminated in the United Church of Christ in 1957.)

Reinhold, the favored son, knew from an early age that he would follow his father's example and enter the ministry. Despite a mediocre education at denominational institutions, his intellectual formation benefited from at least one exceptional teacher, Samuel Press, and, above all, from his father. Each man, in his own way, combined personal piety with intellectual freedom—a balancing that Niebuhr would struggle to maintain in his own life and thought. A scholarship enabled him to attend Yale Divinity School where he earned a BD (1914) and an MA (1915), before financial problems forced an end to his studies.

In 1915 Niebuhr accepted an assignment to Bethel Evangelical Church, a Synod parish in Detroit. In addition to fulfilling his pastoral duties, he became involved in various social justice issues, especially the trade union movement, which was struggling to win a toehold in the automobile industry. Niebuhr was appalled by the plight of factory workers: inadequate wages, long hours, seasonal layoffs, dangerous conditions, and almost no safety net of pensions, medical benefits, or unemployment insurance. As a disciple of the Social Gospel—a movement that blended Protestant idealism and progressive reform—he criticized the modern church for emphasizing personal rectitude but failing to offer its witness regarding social injustice. At the same time he tried to balance the need to speak prophetically against the potential corruption of self-righteousness. *The Christian Century* under Charles Clayton Morrison provided the main outlet for Niebuhr's commentary and analysis, though his writings appeared in a variety of religious and secular publications. Through the financial and organizational assistance of Sherwood Eddy, national secretary of the YMCA, he traveled extensively, preaching and lecturing at seminaries and colleges on the social responsibility of religion.

In 1928 Niebuhr, with Eddy's help, moved to New York to teach Christian Ethics at Union Theological Seminary, an interdenominational institution. He would hold that position until retiring in 1960. Three years into his tenure at Union, he married Ursula

Keppel-Compton, a young Englishwoman who had been one of his students. The couple had two children: a son, Christopher, and a daughter, Elisabeth.

For a quarter-century, until he was finally slowed down by a stroke in 1952, Niebuhr maintained an extremely busy schedule, his life a whirl of sermons, lectures, committees, conferences, and consultations. He made two unsuccessful runs for political office on the Socialist ticket (for the state senate in 1930 and the US House of Representatives in 1932). He was a leading member of the Fellowship of Reconciliation, a Christian pacifist group formed after World War I, but left it in the 1930s to become a leading anti-pacifist advocate of collective security. He was active in labor and political organizations, and advised agencies as diverse as the World Council of Churches, UNESCO, and the US State Department. He wrote constantly, especially for small journals that he edited such as *World Tomorrow*, *Radical Religion*, and *Christianity and Crisis*; he was also a frequent contributor to *The Christian Century*, *The Nation*, *The New Republic*, *The New Leader*, and other journals, newspapers, and magazines too numerous to mention. Niebuhr's Gifford Lectures, delivered at the University of Edinburgh in 1939, formed the basis for his two-volume masterpiece *The Nature and Destiny of Man* (1941/1943). In addition to promoting Christian ecumenism, Niebuhr also contributed significantly to Christian–Jewish relations: he was a strong defender of the State of Israel, and the first major churchman to call for ceasing efforts to convert the Jews (1958, chapter 7). In 1964 he was awarded the Presidential Medal of Freedom, the nation's highest civilian honor.

III.   Theology and Politics

Though his theology has frequently been described as "neo-orthodox," Niebuhr himself rejected the label—largely because of its association with Karl Barth, whose thought he regarded as fundamentalist and obscurantist. Nevertheless, the word itself, freed from such associations, nicely captures the peculiar blending of new and old in Niebuhr. On the one hand, he clearly belongs to the liberal Protestant tradition that stretches back to the German idealist thinkers of the eighteenth and nineteenth centuries. Consistent with such "liberalism," the starting point and touchstone of his analysis tends to be universal human experience rather than holy writ or church authority—the biblical worldview, for Niebuhr, is validated principally by its ability to make sense of the perplexities of life and history, whereas alternative worldviews are unable to comprehend or reconcile the contradictory elements of human existence (1949, chapter X). Niebuhr also borrowed heavily from more recent schools, such as existentialism (mainly Kierkegaard) and pragmatism (mainly William James), and took account of all forms of non-orthodox learning, including modern biblical criticism. At the same time, his analysis was thoroughly interwoven with scripture and classic theology (especially St Paul, St Augustine, and the Protestant Reformers), and his substantive conclusions were frequently orthodox or traditional.

A close reading of Niebuhr's mature thought must inevitably begin with the paradox of human existence. For Niebuhr, man (the now-dated generic is ubiquitous in his writings) exists "at the juncture of nature and spirit" (1941, 17). He is "a child of nature, subject to its vicissitudes, compelled by its necessities, driven by its impulses, and confined within the brevity of years which nature permits"; at the same time he is "a transcendent spirit who stands outside of nature, life, himself, his reason, and his world" (1941, 3). Though conditioned by genetic, environmental, and cultural factors, man has some latitude to rise above his circumstances, to envision new possibilities, to change his ideas, institutions, and customs—in short, to make history.

Transcendent freedom, then, is the source of human creativity and greatness, but it is also a source of misery, for when man attains self-consciousness he recognizes his weakness, contingency, and insignificance in the vastness of time and space. At some level, he is always mindful that he is dust that returns to dust, and that all his hopes and endeavors stand before an "abyss of meaninglessness" (1941, 182). Intimations of mortality shadow his days, occasionally breaking through, if only vaguely, to the conscious level, inducing a sense of crisis that Kierkegaard described as "anxiety."

This existential anxiety becomes an occasion of sin whenever it tempts man to dominate and exploit others in order to gain a feeling of mastery over his own fate. But his aggression "arouses fears and enmities,"

and he finds himself caught in a "vicious circle" of conflict. Ironically, and tragically, the attempt to gain security on the level of nature produces heightened insecurity on the level of history, in the form of injustice, anarchy, and war (1941, 192).

Man's will-to-power is rooted in the natural will-to-live, Niebuhr explained, but its expansiveness derives from his spiritual insecurity. Likewise with a second large category of sin, "sensuality," meaning any form of egotism in which man seeks not to dominate the world but to lose himself in one of its vitalities or processes, whether sex, gluttony, drunkenness, or materialistic extravagance. In both sensuality and pride, a natural impulse or faculty, good in itself, is corrupted into excess by spiritual anxiety rather than physical need: "Man is mortal. That is his fate. Man pretends not to be mortal. That is his sin" (1937, 28).

The "ideal possibility," Niebuhr said, is that "faith in the ultimate security of God's love" will "overcome all the immediate insecurities of nature and history" (1941, 183), for in faith "man understands himself in his finiteness, realizes the guilt of his efforts to escape his insufficiency and dependence, and lays hold upon a power beyond himself which both completes his incompleteness and purges him of his false and vain efforts at self-completion" (1943, 57). God's self-giving, self-sacrificing love for man attains its most perfect expression in the life of Jesus Christ, particularly in the crucifixion, in which God takes upon himself the punishment that would otherwise be visited on a sinful humanity.

This divine love (or *agape*) then becomes the model for human relations (cf. Jesus' summary of the commandments in Matthew 22:37–40, i.e., to love God wholeheartedly and to love your neighbor as yourself). The "law of love," Niebuhr said, is partly an act of obedience and gratitude to God, but it is also a truth inscribed on the heart as the fulfillment of humanity's essential, or better, nature. Man is a naturally gregarious creature, but the principle that perfects both his social nature and his individual spirit is loving engagement in the lives of others. In the peak experiences by which they define their lives, Niebuhr said, people recognize the validity of the gospel paradox: "He that findeth his life shall lose it: and he that loseth his life for my sake shall find it" (Matt. 10:39; cited 1941, 251 and *passim*). Happiness, in other words, is not so much an object to be pursued and attained as it is the by-product of a morally responsible life.

Niebuhr sometimes distinguished between "sacrificial love," the ideal in its purest form, and "mutual love," which involves genuine fellow-feeling and concern but also seeks reciprocity (1943, chapter III, and *passim*). Mutual love, he said, is the highest ethical standard that political life can aspire to, but it draws its inspiration and sustenance from the ultimate ideal of sacrificial love.

Despite its validation in life and logic, love is never "a simple possibility" for man. Even approximations and derivatives of love, embodied in various rules of justice, are hard to maintain. Human beings, however much they prefer altruism to egotism in principle, still succumb to their sinful impulse. Living in constant tension (*justus et peccator simul*, as Luther put it—simultaneously righteous and sinful), they rationalize the selfishness they cannot or will not control. Such pretensions of righteousness are intended to deceive the self as well as others. Niebuhr, following Hume, saw reason as a two-edged sword: on the one hand, a critical perspective for reining in selfishness; on the other hand, a valuable aid for making it respectable.

Thus at every level of intellectual, spiritual, and ethical advance, there is at least some measure of hypocrisy and pretension. Indeed, hypocrisy is a vice that seems to *increase* with the development of reason and conscience. Those who understand life's moral and spiritual requirements, and who even fulfill them in significant measure, are the ones who are most easily tempted to overestimate their virtue and thereby transmute it into vice. They treat their virtue as a license to judge and lord over others, especially those who disagree with them or resist their idealistic projects. This phenomenon occurs in political as well as personal life: in one generation, the self-righteous zealots are religious persecutors, in another, idealistic reformers or revolutionaries. In either case, the moral and spiritual pride of "good" people is often more dangerous, subtle, and intractable than the gross selfishness of ordinary sinners.

Niebuhr explained this curious facet of moral life through the concept of "original sin." While denying the literal reality of Adam and Eve's fall as recounted in Genesis, he insisted that the human condition is nevertheless one of fallenness. Original sin, as he used the term, essentially meant that after all factors of environment, culture, and psychology have been taken into account, there is a mysterious, and ineradicable, inclination to selfishness at the center of human personality. He equated original sin, or fallenness, with imperfect faith and estrangement from God (1941, 252, 253): "The anxiety of freedom leads to sin only if the prior sin of unbelief is assumed." For "[i]f man knew, loved, and obeyed God as the author and end of his existence, a proper limit would be set for his desires including the natural impulse of survival." Though the ultimate source of this fallenness is left unclear, its ethical and psychological substance is summarized, for Niebuhr (1941, 272, 278), in a passage from St Paul (Rom. 7:18–19): "I can will what is right, but I cannot do it. For I do not do the good I want, but the evil I do not want is what I do."

Because the egoistic inclination is a permanent reality of history, infecting (to some degree at least) even man's moral and spiritual achievements, only divine mercy can make him "justified," i.e., right with God. Accordingly, Niebuhr's christology focused more on the cross than on the moral example of Jesus. The Gospels, in his view, reveal not so much an attainable standard as an *un*attainable one that man is nonetheless responsible for. The resulting tension should induce a kind of despair: "the godly sorrow" that "worketh repentance to salvation," as St Paul put it (2 Cor. 7:10). Only when man turns to God with a contrite spirit and a broken heart is he finally able to receive divine grace and forgiveness. In that sense, Niebuhr affirmed the classic Reformation doctrine of "justification by faith"—though with a certain flexibility that allowed for the salvation of non-Christians through hidden forms of grace (1943, 109–10 fn.).

Niebuhr stressed that grace and forgiveness provide not just ultimate salvation but also an ethical payoff in this world. By reducing the anxiety that leads to sin and pretension, grace is a source of power as well as pardon, "a miracle which the self could not have accomplished" on its own (1943, 115). Put in the more secular idiom of his later writings, and borrowing from psychologist Erik Erikson, the experience of being loved and forgiven instills a sense of "basic trust" that allows people to be more giving and less grasping (1965, 109). He insisted, however, that man never attains ethical perfection, and that he is most free, and does his best, when he recognizes the limitations of his moral freedom. If, on the other hand, the knowledge and experience of grace leads man to think he is perfect, righteousness is betrayed into *self-righteousness*; such moral and spiritual pride is, in certain respects, the ultimate sin because it corrupts the highest good.

Niebuhr contrasted his account of sin's persistence and guile with the unwarranted optimism of modern culture. For all their variety and difference, he said, modern schools are united by their "easy conscience" and their rejection of original sin (1941, 93). In the modern liberal view, Niebuhr said, man is seen as an essentially benign being—if not perfect now, perfectible in the long run through education, moral exhortation, and social reform. Niebuhr, while favoring practical programs of melioration, warned against the "perfectionist" illusion that sin can be reasoned or reformed out of history. Bad ideas and institutions, he argued, may aggravate and give specific form to sin, but the underlying tendency to evil lies within the human self. Niebuhr applied this line of criticism not just against secular thought but also against modern, liberal strains of Christianity that denied the importance of original sin and human fallenness. (He described such Christianity as "Pelagian" or "semi-Pelagain," a reference to the early church writer Pelagius, b.354, who took a similar approach.)

Despite his emphasis on original sin, Niebuhr always held that man, even in his fallen state, retains a significant measure of "original righteousness" (1941, chapter X). He agreed with Pascal that without some core of blessedness, man would be incapable of knowing that he is a sinner at all.

For Niebuhr, love and justice come closest to fulfillment within small homogeneous groups, like the family. In such contexts, people know and understand one another, sympathetic feelings have an opportunity to flow, and the relative needs and abilities of all are appreciated. Morality and altruism, though hardly inevitable, have at least a chance to prevail in some measure.

Between large social collectivities or groups, such as nations, races, and socio-economic classes, however, there is relatively little appreciation of the needs and claims of others, the consequences of injustice are often unseen, and the complicated laws and institutions through which injustice is perpetuated are dimly understood. Modern commerce, Niebuhr frequently observed, has aggravated the impersonality of group relations by expanding human interdependence without providing the loyalties, habits, or institutions that might make these new relations bearable. Given the obstacles to normal moral sentiments, Niebuhr explained, relations *between* groups exhibit greater selfishness and hypocrisy than relations *within* groups. A prophetic minority within every group often rises above collective selfishness and hypocrisy, but it does not usually sway the majority.

In addition to their moral inertia, groups also possess a capacity for active malice. Individuals who feel personally powerless and insignificant find they can exercise their will-to-power through the group, participating vicariously in its "power, majesty, and pseudo-immortality" (1941, 212). Their devotion to a group or cause beyond themselves is a genuine moral achievement, but it has the ironic effect of exhausting their limited capacity for altruism and sharpening differences among groups, especially nations. In this "ethical paradox of patriotism," as Niebuhr called it (1932, 91), altruistic self-loss and aggressive will-to-power merge into a single commitment. Such collective egoism reached its most egregious form in modern totalitarianism, he argued. Fascism and Nazism expressed this tendency in openly cynical and tribal terms, while Soviet communism did so beneath a universalist veneer. Only a transcendent God, holding all earthly powers and majesties in derision, is capable of shattering such idolatry and pretension, he concluded.

In any event, man's inability to conform his collective behavior to his personal ideals is "one of the tragedies of the human spirit": "As individuals, men believe that they ought to love and serve each other and establish justice between each other. As racial, economic, and national groups they take for themselves whatever their power can command" (1932, 9). Thus, relations between groups will "always be predominantly political rather than ethical, that is, they will be determined by the proportion of power which each group possesses at least as much as by any rational and moral appraisal of the comparative needs and claims of each group" (1932, xxiii). On this point Niebuhr rebuked naïve idealists for adding to the "moral and political confusion of our day": "They do not recognize that when collective power, whether in the form of imperialism or class domination, exploits weakness, it can never be dislodged unless power is raised against it. If conscience and reason can be insinuated into the resulting struggle they can only qualify but not abolish it" (1932, xii–xiii).

This view, given full elaboration in Niebuhr's aptly titled *Moral Man and Immoral Society*, went against the whole thrust of liberal Protestant reformism, which had sought to preach and persuade society into righteousness (as if a large, diverse nation could be charmed into the harmony of a small, homogeneous Midwestern town). By accepting power and coercion—in extreme cases, even violence—as legitimate political tools in the quest for justice, Niebuhr alienated many old friends, including Sherwood Eddy and Charles Clayton Morrison.

His Christian realism embraced St Augustine's dictum that the peace and justice of this world is always an uneasy armistice of contending factions (1943, 273; 1953, 126). The practical question for Niebuhr in the 1930s was how such an armistice could be accomplished in America and other industrial democracies. Liberal democracy, in the grip of a shortsighted capitalist oligarchy, seemed to him incapable of meaningful reform. On the other hand, he feared that a socialist or communist order uniting political and economic power in a central government would quickly become a dictatorship, and probably a cruel, vindictive one. Most of all, he worried about a future of endless anarchy and civil war. He vacillated between reform and revolution.

In the end, historical events, processed through his growing theological awareness, revealed to Niebuhr a way out of the crisis of the 1930s. The postwar liberal consensus that he ultimately endorsed was not the ideal of any party or faction or class, but rather, a kind of providential stalemate that was skillfully worked into a settlement by the national political leadership and ratified by a pragmatic, non-ideological electorate. Though initially disdainful of Roosevelt as an opportunist, by the end of the decade Niebuhr had come to appreciate his internationalism in the face of isolationist opposition. Domestically, the New Deal had made society both more stable *and* more just by empowering industrial laborers to defend their

interests within the system; more broadly, it had expanded the jurisdiction of modern constitutional democracy to the economic realm, proving that it was a system capable of incorporating interests other than those of the middle classes that had given it birth. The administration's commitment to human freedom and Western values, overriding elite preferences, demonstrated to him that democratic government is not simply the executive committee of the ruling class, as the Marxists of the day had been arguing.

After World War II, Niebuhr called for a foreign policy commensurate with America's great, and recently acquired, power. He dismissed the clamor for world government as a naïve illusion (1953, chapter 2). The international system is inherently anarchic, he said; it desperately requires a leading, or hegemonic, nation to provide some rudimentary order so that over time it can, perhaps, build up the institutions, loyalties, and "organic" ties of genuine community. In the meantime, exercising such hegemonic power was a moral imperative, Niebuhr said, even if it lacked the legal and ethical clarity of liberal social contract theory and American constitutionalism. He warned against the twin perils of dereliction on the one hand, hubris on the other.

A moderate critic of communism in his socialist period, Niebuhr, during the Cold War, became increasingly harsh in his statements about both Marxism and the Soviet Union. He continued to regard Marxist realism about power and ideological false consciousness as superior to liberal "sentimentality," but such virtue was vitiated by its cynicism. Marxism, he said, had completely misunderstood the problem of ethics, falsely supposing that exploitation and domination derive solely from private property rather than from factors inherent in human nature and the human condition. It then grants unchecked power to a party that has, if not formal ownership of property, total control over the means of production. Monopolies of power always lead to injustice, but they are particularly dangerous when aggravated by self-righteous fury and "monstrous" pretensions of social "omnipotence and omniscience," indeed of "playing God to history" (1953, 39, 40). In pursuit of an illusory utopia, Niebuhr said, communist rule destroys the agencies and institutions that provide real protection for real people in a fallen world.

Communism, a "demonic" secular religion, had "distilled injustice and cruelty out of its original promise of a higher justice." It transforms social idealism into "the nightmare of a coercive community" and brings forth "every possible evil fruit and corrupting every virtue" (1952, 1, 3, 14–15).

He tempered such criticism by observing that liberal democratic civilization was implicated in the terrible class conflict of the age. Having tolerated extreme inequality during its laissez-faire period, it had enabled Marxism to gain a measure of plausibility. Many of Marxism's errors, moreover, were really our own liberal, bourgeois errors in aggravated form: philosophical materialism and naturalism; worship of science and technology; faith in human power and wisdom rather than providence as the guiding force of history; confidence in the perfectibility of man and society. The case for resisting communism—like Lincoln's defense of union and emancipation over secession and slavery—depended not on America and the West being blameless, but on the duty that even sinful men and societies have to make responsible choices between relativities of good and evil.

Niebuhr rejected not just Marxist utopianism but the whole progressive thrust of modern thought since the Renaissance and Enlightenment. There is no immanent force within history gradually replacing evil and anarchy with goodness and order, he insisted. There is historical progress in the sense of growing knowledge and increased technical mastery over physical nature, but such capabilities are inevitably used for evil as well as good. The cycle of pride and fall is re-enacted in every age; not only will wars and rumors of war persist into the indefinite future, but they will occur against a background of enhanced potencies and perils. Every age, Niebuhr argued, has characteristic virtues and vices, and later epochs do not necessarily incorporate the benefits of earlier ones. Only the Kingdom of God, a divine achievement coming "at the end of history," can gather all the good that has been accomplished and purge all the evil.

And yet, as many observers have suggested, Niebuhr did not advance a pure biblical view of history; rather, he sought to reconcile the hopeful activism of modern thought with the sober sense of limits found in Augustinian-Reformation Christianity. For Niebuhr, the unchanging element throughout history is man's responsibility to do his best within the concrete circumstances of his own era, balancing ideals against necessities and forgiving others as he hopes to be forgiven.

IV. Legacy

As with other great thinkers, Niebuhr's rise to prominence was due partly to the timeless cogency of his arguments and partly to the fact that he spoke to the perceived needs of his age, bringing coherence to its seemingly chaotic events and validating the hard choices that intellectuals and political leaders felt they had to make. However, as the postwar consensus began to break down in the 1960s, Niebuhr's stature declined. In the years immediately before his death in 1971, and in the decades after, the polarization of American culture and politics further reduced his natural constituency. In religion, his neo-orthodox theology came to be seen as too neo- for some and too orthodox for others. Likewise in politics, religious activists whose path Niebuhr pioneered began to accuse him of abandoning radical hope, while neo-conservatives whose worldview he helped shape often felt uneasy with his residual liberalism.

Despite his appealing mixture of traditional faith and intellectual sophistication, Niebuhr's discussions of scripture in terms of "myth" and "symbol" troubled many readers. His famous—and problematic—dictum that we should "take Biblical symbols seriously but not literally" (1943, 50) opened the door to suggestions that he himself took them only in a psychologically, but not religiously, serious way. Stanley Hauerwas, in his 2001 study *With the Grain of the Universe*, has developed such criticism into a comprehensive indictment of Niebuhr as a closet humanist who cloaked anthropological and psychological arguments in Christian language.

In fact Niebuhr did insist on *religious*, and not merely psychological or humanistic, realities behind biblical symbols. The situation is complex, however. He accepted the resurrection as a genuine event, for example, but rejected the empty tomb; embraced the metaphysical mystery of human fallenness but rejected the historical Fall of Adam and Eve; and so on. Though he applied the word "myth" to theological narratives whose content defies ordinary human comprehension and language, he later repudiated this semantic gambit (in Kegley, 1956, 515): "The word has subjective and skeptical connotations. I am sorry I ever used it, particularly since the project for 'demythologizing' the Bible has been undertaken and bids fair to reduce Biblical revelation to eternally valid truths without any existential encounter between God and man."

Such statements have enabled Niebuhr's defenders to affirm his basic faithfulness, even while challenging specific theological formulations and compromises. Gabriel Fackre (2002, 25) has attributed Niebuhr's anti-literalism, in part at least, to intellectual modesty, pointing to his argument (1943, 294, 298) that "a decent measure of restraint" must be exercised in describing the "furniture of heaven and the temperature of hell," while at the same time, "it is equally important not to confuse restraint with uncertainty about the validity of hope that 'when he shall appear, we shall be like him; for we shall see him as he is' (1 John 3:2)." Fackre added: "He elaborates further on the mysteries of our resurrection in poignant 1967 remarks on his approaching death. Niebuhr's minimalist description of our final destiny might not be sufficient for the concluding chapter of a textbook in systematic theology, but it is outrageous to deny that this ethicist and unsystematic theologian did not hold to core Biblical testimony about the world to come."

Politically, Niebuhr has become almost anathema among the religious and seminary left, despite his role in making radical perspectives respectable within establishment religion. As mainstream liberalism moved ever leftward—at elite seminaries as in the general political culture—Niebuhr's older progressive style was superseded by more ambitious theologies of liberation. Niebuhr was criticized for having abandoned socialism and supported America's Cold War policies. Indeed, reviewing his early thought in light of its later development, it became clear that even in his leftist phase he never regarded the poor and the oppressed as an unambiguous force of social redemption. The poor might, in the moment of their victimhood, possess a "provisional" moral advantage over the privileged, but once they asserted themselves, they and their leaders (especially the leaders) were as likely to oppress as their erstwhile oppressors. Niebuhr's mature Christian realism simply confirmed that the search for justice, to the very end of history, will be a process of balancing will against will and adjusting interest to interest—not a storming of heaven by the righteous.

On the political center-right Niebuhr has been ignored rather than vilified. At one time, perhaps, neo-conservatives cited him as a thinker who anticipated their own arguments on pluralism, gradualism, limited government, and a strong foreign policy. Yet his influence waned over time, particularly as many of these arguments could be drawn from other sources without having to deal with Christian realism's constant self-criticism.

In both religion and politics Niebuhr remains difficult to categorize. His theology neither conforms to, nor seeks to conform, to the doctrines of any particular church. His political thought, though influencing both liberalism and conservatism, has no obvious home in either of the major parties. Though some commentators have opined that a Niebuhr revival is exactly what we need in a post-9/11 world (Brooks, 2002; Elie, 2007), none has arisen or appears imminent. The only institution that *has* self-consciously founded itself on Niebuhrian principle is Alcoholics Anonymous, which, in 1950, chose as its motto a slightly altered version of his "Serenity Prayer." That prayer, in its original form (Sifton, 2003, 7), reads: "God, give us grace to accept with serenity the things that cannot be changed, courage to change the things that should be changed, and the wisdom to distinguish the one from the other."

References

Books by Reinhold Niebuhr (a short list)

Niebuhr, Reinhold. 1929. *Leaves From the Notebook of a Tamed Cynic*. New York: Willett, Clark and Company (reprinted by Westminster/John Knox Press, 1991).

Niebuhr, Reinhold. 1932. *Moral Man and Immoral Society*. New York: Scribner's.

Niebuhr, Reinhold. 1937. *Beyond Tragedy*. New York: Scribner's.

Niebuhr, Reinhold. 1941. *The Nature and Destiny of Man* (Vol. 1). New York: Scribner's.

Niebuhr, Reinhold. 1943. *The Nature and Destiny of Man* (Vol. 2). New York: Scribner's.

Niebuhr, Reinhold. 1944. *The Children of Light and the Children of Darkness*. New York: Scribner's.

Niebuhr, Reinhold. 1949. *Faith and History: A Comparison of Christian and Modern Views of History*. New York: Scribner's.

Niebuhr, Reinhold. 1952. *The Irony of American History*. New York: Scribner's.

Niebuhr, Reinhold. 1953. *Christian Realism and Political Problems*. New York: Scribner's.

Niebuhr, Reinhold. 1957. *Love and Justice*, ed. D. B. Robertson. Philadelphia: Westminster (reprinted by Peter Smith Publishers, 1976).

Niebuhr, Reinhold. 1958. *Pious and Secular America*. New York: Scribner's.

Niebuhr, Reinhold. 1965. *Man's Nature and His Communities*. New York: Scribner's.

Niebuhr, Reinhold. 1974. *Justice and Mercy*, ed. Ursula M. Niebuhr. New York: Harper & Row.

Niebuhr, Reinhold. 1984. "Intellectual Autobiography," in *Reinhold Niebuhr: His Religious, Social, and Political Thought*, ed. Charles W. Kegley. New York: Pilgrim Press (an updated version of the volume co-edited with Robert W. Bretall and published in 1956).

Books and articles about Niebuhr

Bingham, June. 1961. *Courage to Change: An Introduction to the Life and Thought of Reinhold Niebuhr*. New York: Scribners.

Brooks, David. 2002. "A Man on a Gray Horse," *The Atlantic Monthly* (September).

Durkin, Kenneth. 1989. *Reinhold Niebuhr*. Harrisburg, PA: Morehead.

Elie, Paul. 2007. "A Man for All Reasons," *The Atlantic* (November).

Fackre, Gabriel. 2002. "Was Reinhold Niebuhr a Christian?" *First Things* (October): 25–7.

Fox, Richard Wightman. 1985. *Reinhold Niebuhr: A Biography*. New York: Pantheon.

Fox, Richard. 1995. "Niebuhr, [Karl Paul] Reinhold." In *A Companion to American Thought*, ed. Richard Wightman Fox and James T. Kloppenberg. Oxford and Cambridge, MA: Blackwell.

Hauerwas, Stanley. 2001. *With the Grain of the Universe: The Church's Witness and Natural Theology*. Grand Rapids, MI: Brazos Press.

Kegley, Charles W., ed. 1984. *Reinhold Niebuhr: His Religious, Social, and Political Thought*. New York: Pilgrim Press (an updated version of the volume co-edited with Robert W. Bretall and published in 1956).

Lasch, Christopher. 1991. *The True and Only Heaven: Progress and Its Critics*. New York: Norton.

McCann, Dennis P. 1981. *Christian Realism and Liberation Theology*. Maryknoll, NY: Orbis.

Meyer, Donald B. 1960. *The Protestant Search for Political Realism, 1919–1941*. Berkeley: University of California Press.

Oakes, Edward T. 1998. "Original Sin: A Disputation," *First Things* (November).

Sifton, Elisabeth. 2003. *The Serenity Prayer*. New York and London: Norton.

Friedrich Daniel Ernst Schleiermacher (1768–1834)

Ian S. Markham

Schleiermacher has been described as the Father of Modern Theology. He is the probably the greatest theologian of the modern period. Heavily influenced by Immanuel Kant (1768–1834), Schleiermacher made two key assumptions. First, the classical arguments for the existence of God are unhelpful. Schleiermacher writes:

> [N]o obligation would arise for the system of doctrine to prove the existence of God; that would be an entirely superfluous task. For since in the Christian Church the God-consciousness should be developed in youth, proofs, even if youth were capable of understanding them, could only produce an objective consciousness, which is not the aim here, nor would it in any way generate piety. … Dogmatics must therefore presuppose intuitive certainty or faith; and thus, as far as the God-consciousness in general is concerned, what it has to do is not to effect its recognition but to explicate its content. (Schleiermacher, 1999, 136)

To defend faith, argued Schleiermacher, we need to move away from reasons and stress instead "experience." This is what produces piety and faith. Second, Schleiermacher assumes the Kantian account of knowledge. For Kant, we do not know how things really are in reality. This is inaccessible because any attempted description of the world is a result of an experience being interpreted by the mind. Our mind-interpreted sense of reality is the limit of human knowledge—what Kant called the phenomenal world. So for Schleiermacher, the universal awareness of God (our sense of dependence on God) is the heart of religion. Doctrine is a result of reflection and interpretation of this basic experience. Schleiermacher claims that, "[t]his account of the origins of dogmatic propositions, as having arisen solely out of logically ordered reflection upon the immediate utterances of the religious self-consciousness, finds its confirmation in the whole of history" (Schleiermacher, 1999, 81). He believes that experience, interpreted in community, makes sense of the whole history of religion, including the Scriptures. Out of these two assumptions, Schleiermacher created an entirely distinctive approach to Christian theology, which has been very influential.

I. Life

Schleiermacher was born into a family who were part of the Moravian Brethren in Breslau in southeastern Saxony. Both his grandfather and father were ordained. The deep piety of the Moravian Brethren stayed with Schleiermacher all his life. His education was rich and demanding—along with an impressive range of languages and a intense training in mathematics, there was a through training in scripture. He attended seminary at Barby, where he joined a secret group which

The Student's Companion to the Theologians, First Edition. Edited by Ian S. Markham.
© 2013 Blackwell Publishing Ltd. Published 2013 by Blackwell Publishing Ltd.

read Kant and Goethe. Slowly he decided that some of the tenets of his upbringing were no longer justified by the text of the Bible (for example, the vicarious atonement) and he wrote to his father to let him know of his skepticism. Yet even in his doubts, his sense of religion stayed with him. Schleiermacher writes, "Religion helped me when I began to examine the ancestral faith and to purify my heart of the rubble of primitive times. It remained with me when God and immortality disappeared before my doubting eyes" (Schleiermacher, 1996, 8). This quest for a religion beyond doctrine is the underlying characteristic of Schleiermacher's entire project.

Schleiermacher moved from Barby to the University of Halle. In 1790, he passed his exams in theology. He became a tutor for an affluent family in Schlbitten, East Prussia. It was while working with the family that he had a brief meeting with Immanuel Kant who was at Königsberg at this time. This meeting anticipates a lifetime of conversation between the works of Kant and the theology of Schleiermacher. Kant's philosophy is discussed in an essay that Schleiermacher writes. He publishes a book of sermons; and he serves as a chaplain to the Charity hospital in Berlin. As events move on and "deism" becomes more popular, Schleiermacher decides that the time is right for a written contribution. So when Schleiermacher was 29 and celebrating his birthday, his friends urged him to write a book, which became *On Religion: Speeches to Its Cultured Despisers*. This was published in 1799. It is a text that anticipates all the major themes of Schleiermacher's theology.

From 1809 to 1834, Schleiermacher served as the professor of theology at the University of Berlin and as the preacher at the Holy Trinity Church in Berlin. This gave him some space for curriculum development; it was while in Berlin he got married. In 1821–2, Schleiermacher wrote the book that would make him famous. This was *The Christian Faith*. Schleiermacher died on February 6, 1834.

II. *On Religion*

Schleiermacher's achievement is to rethink radically the nature and task of theology. Instead of a turgid exposition of biblical texts or the crude, yet skeptical,

rationalism of the deists, Schleiermacher advocates a religion of feeling. The genius of *On Religion: Speeches to Its Cultured Despisers* is that those most alienated from official forms of religion are closest to it. Schleiermacher shares the concerns of the cultural elites that official forms are misguided, but he wants them to recognize their own religious intuitions. So he writes:

> I entreat you to become familiar with this concept: intuition of the universe. It is the hinge of my own speech; it is the highest and most universal formula of religion on the basis of which you should be able to find every place in religion, from which you may determine its essence and its limits. ... The universe exists in uninterrupted activity and reveals itself to us every moment. Every form that it brings forth, every being to which it gives separate existence according to the fullness of life, every occurrence that spills forth from its rich, ever-fruitful womb, is an action of the same upon us. (Schleiermacher, 1996, 24–5)

Religion is beyond the institution, the Bible, and doctrine. For Schleiermacher, one finds religion within; it is an encounter with the universe. It is our sense of dependency.

It is interesting to note how Jesus is almost absent in this book. Indeed, when Schleiermacher asks the question, "what is revelation?," he gives the following answer: "Every original and new intuition of the universe is one, and yet all individuals must know best what is original and new for them. And if something of what was original in them is still new for you, then there revelation is also one for you, and I advise you to ponder it well" (Schleiermacher, 1996, 49). This poses the obvious question: In what sense can religion be Christian? It is an issue that he does discuss in the third speech of *On Religion*, but a full response had to wait for his major work *The Christian Faith*.

III. *The Christian Faith*

The Christian Faith is a masterpiece. At the start of section III of Chapter I, Schleiermacher provides a definition of Christianity: "Christianity is a monotheistic faith, belonging to the teleological type of religion, and is essentially distinguished from other such faiths by the fact that in it everything is related to the redemption accomplished by Jesus of Nazareth" (Schleiermacher, 1999, 52). The primary characteristic of Christianity, for Schleiermacher, is that it is a religion of redemption. This means that it is a life-transforming experience, which moves us from evil and from "God-forgetfulness to God-consciousness, so that the latter awareness predominates in all the states and activities of life" (Clements, 1987, 40). So Schleiermacher's conviction that religion is an experience of the infinite is given a particular form in Christianity, where it is an experience of redemption. The emphasis here is on "experience"—here the influence of Romanticism can be seen—with, in the case of Christianity, redemption being primary. So one should not see Christianity as a belief in miracles of the Bible; instead it is engagement with the transformative power of redemption through Jesus.

The location of this redemption for Schleiermacher is interesting. It is the life that is important. As Terence Tice puts it:

> In itself his death made bear [sic] redemptive overtones, as it were, but it is not a necessary component of redemption for the religious consciousness of Christians. Thus, although many incipient theories of his "atonement" by death appear in the New Testament, Schleiermacher does not derive any theory of atonement from them. Essential for faith is the nature of the relationship between Christ and God. As the original, ideal, complete, or perfect human being in this respect, he is thereby rightly said to have a fully developed God-consciousness and to be wholly without sin. (Tice, 2006, 37)

It is the christology (the view of Christ) that is important for Schleiermacher. Jesus has the perfect God-consciousness; he had the perfect sense of God—the infinite. Jesus radiated this to the disciples, who then formed the community of the church, in which all Christians now participate. Schleiermacher saw the church as the vehicle through which the perfect God-consciousness is "communicated" to our imperfect God-consciousness.

All of this means that Schleiermacher has an unconventional account of sin. Sin is not a matter of breaking rules, but is the impediment to our intimate experience of God. Catherine Kelsey explains: "Sin is not a thing in itself that a rule can identify. Sin is an absence of relationship with God and any diminishment of our relationship with God, however that might occur" (Kelsey, 2003, 59). In other words, it is as we develop our sense of the redemption modeled by Jesus that we start seeing what sin is. Or to put it in more traditional language, our sense of grace is prior to our sense of sin.

So the account of God being assumed here is one that transcends nature yet is experienced through our sense of ourselves within nature. This almost panentheistic (a belief that God and world are identified together, but God is greater than the world) account of God enables Schleiermacher to provide an account of the relationship of God to the world in such a way that took Isaac Newton's discoveries seriously. As the modern scientific view took shape, there was a widespread sense that the options were limited: on the one hand, we had the deism of the rationalists which put God several steps removed from our lives and experience; and on the other hand, we had the God of traditionalists who wanted to postulate an interfering God in a big machine. Schleiermacher suggests the following: "The religious self-consciousness, by means of which we place all that affects or influences us in absolute dependence on God, coincides entirely with the view that all such things are conditioned and determined by the interdependence of Nature" (Schleiermacher, 1999, 170). And at the start of the next section: "It can never be necessary in the interest of religion so to interpret a fact that its dependence on God absolutely excludes its being conditioned by the system of Nature" (Schleiermacher, 1999, 178).

So we have the following picture: it is true that nature is an elaborate integrated system. It is also true, explains Schleiermacher, that in the unity of nature we have a sense of our "absolute dependence on God." These two should not be seen in opposition to each other. One does not exclude the other. In fact the scientific story reinforces the sense of our God which transcends, flows through, and underpins all nature.

Schleiermacher then would consider arguments between science and religion deeply misguided. He would also oppose any "god of the gaps" theology (this or that aspect of the natural processes needs a particular action by God to help it be). Instead, one has the religious experience partly made possible by our sense of what nature is like.

It is clear that Schleiermacher is a theologian who, at the time he lived, challenged all the conventional aspects of Christianity. It is an approach to Christianity that starts in a different place. Although Jesus, christology, and redemption are central, other aspects of Christianity seem virtually absent. The doctrine of the Trinity is a good example. Schleiermacher suspected that traditional accounts of the Trinity are too dependent on Athanasius, when Sabellius should be taken more seriously. He places the Trinity at the end of *The Christian Faith*, which has confused commentators. Is it the climax of his systematic theology or an addendum that is really incidental to his system?

Francis Schüssler Fiorenza confronts this question explicitly in an exceptionally fine essay, in which he defends Schleiermacher. The position of the Trinity in *The Christian Faith* is neither indicative of neglect or excessive overemphasis. Instead, the doctrine of the Trinity emerges out of Schleiermacher's account of God. In a traditional systematic theology, one might expect an account of God to be offered at the start, followed by exploration of the divine attributes, but instead a description of God is infused throughout the book. Then Schüssler Fiorenza writes:

> The concluding doctrine of the Trinity, then, articulates this explicitly Christian consciousness of God. The attributes of God, spread throughout the *Christian Faith*, culminates in the Christian consciousness of God as wisdom and love. The Trinity follows then not as an appendix but as a "conclusion" ... that explicates this specifically Christian consciousness of God.
>
> A parallel exists between the understanding of God and the divine attributes and the understanding of the Trinity. Just as the experience of the divine causality in various modulations leads to the consciousness of the diverse attributes of the one God, so too does the Christian experience of the being of God in Christ and in the church lead to an understanding of God as triune. It is the distinctively Christian experience of the divine causality that experiences and understands God not as power, but primarily as love. ... The consciousness of God as love perfected in wisdom is the heart of the Christian faith, whereas the consciousness of God as

power is an abstraction from the Christian experience of God as love. (Francis Schüssler Fiorenza in Mariña, 2005, 176)

The important point here is that the doctrine of the Trinity is an authentic part of the system. However, the details of the account do contrast markedly with traditional Christianity. Tice summarizes thus:

> God is indeed triune in God's fulfillment of the one eternal decree of redemption; but Christ was not preexistent, unless this simply means intended in the mind of God; Christ did not have two natures but possessed a perfect God-consciousness; and Christ did not become God. The Holy Spirit, conceived as the common spirit of the church, is the same thing as "Christ in us," the same thing as Christ's continuing presence in and through the church after Jesus' death. (Tice, 2006, 42)

This discussion of the Trinity captures the Schleiermacher project clearly. For Schleiermacher, modernity has forced us to radically rethink our account of the faith. Instead of grounding faith in traditional doctrines (and defending those doctrines with increasingly implausible arguments), we relocate the place of faith into our experience of the infinite God, mediated in and through a "God-consciousness" that is best developed and expressed in Jesus, which is then communicated to us through the church. Around this core experience, doctrine then becomes "accounts of the Christian religious affections set forth in speech" (Schleiermacher, 1999, 76). It is essential, explains Schleiermacher, that "the doctrines in all their forms have their ultimate ground so exclusively in the emotions of the religious self-consciousness, that where these do not exist the doctrines cannot arise" (Schleiermacher, 1999, 78). This means that doctrine must always connect with the core experience of redemption: if it fails to do so, then the ideas expressed in those doctrines are no longer helpful.

IV. Significance

When one reads Schleiermacher, one is aware that this is an exceptional mind at work. The project of rethinking the faith in the light of science and modernity meant that he became the inspiration for all forms of revisionist theologies (see Markham in Webster, 2007). From David Tracy to Robert Neville, the basic approach to theology was shaped by Schleiermacher. All liberal theology owes a massive debt to him.

Modern talk about "spirituality" rather than "religion," which pervades many of the mainline denominations in Europe and America, has its roots in the thought of Schleiermacher. He is responsible for disentangling the doctrine, which becomes a construct, from experience. In so doing he opened up the option of a spirituality that is not religious.

Schleiermacher should also receive credit for a more sympathetic attitude to other religious traditions. Keith Ward points out that the Schleiermacherian picture of theology opens up the dialogue with other faith traditions. Ward writes:

> When it comes to describing what is apprehended, one must use concepts drawn from the culturally available stock, and at this point Schleiermacher elaborates the idea, present in various embryonic ways in Spinoza, Kant, and Schelling, of one supreme reality expressing itself in an infinite variety of forms, and being apprehensible in and through these forms, when they are apprehended by the religious sense. … Schleiermacher was right to see, in his early work, that both these understandings open the field of possible revelation beyond the confines of the Christian tradition. … [I]t seems rather unlikely that the infinite would only disclose its nature in one way and within one cultural tradition. (Ward in Jobling and Markham, 2000, 65)

Indeed Schleiermacher does not simply open up a charitable approach to religious diversity, but also feeds a strong sense of the historical and cultural nature of religious development. Looking at religion through the eyes of Schleiermacher makes one aware of the human nature of religious discourse.

It is this last point that makes some of Schleiermacher's critics very nervous. In terms of methodology, Schleiermacher offers an approach that contrasts markedly with the approach of Karl Barth. When Karl Barth was a student, he was deeply impressed by Schleiermacher. But after World War I,

Barth believed that Schleiermacher was deeply corrupting. He writes:

> Until better instructed, I can see no way from Schleiermacher or from his contemporary epigones, to the chroniclers, prophets, and wise ones of Israel, to those who narrate the story of the life, death, and resurrection of Jesus Christ, to the word of the apostles—no way to the God of Abraham, Isaac, and Jacob and the Father of Jesus Christ, no way to the great tradition of the Christian church. For the present I can see nothing here but a choice. And for me there can be no question as to how that choice is to be made. (Barth, 1982, 271f.)

For Karl Barth, Schleiermacher's theological approach is deeply misguided. Ultimately, it is an approach which offers little more than a pious agnosticism. For Barth, we are either going to construct our theology from the "anthropological horizon" and project a guess into the skies or we are going to ground our theology in a definitive disclosure—a revealing—of the Eternal Word in the life, death, and resurrection of Jesus. Schleiermacher's approach is the former; Barth's approach is the latter.

Schleiermacher would retort that Barth's place is no longer available. The Enlightenment has meant that humanity has lost its innocence: we cannot return to premodern assumptions that there is a secure definitive location of revelation. Barth believes that the Enlightenment can be interpreted and accommodated differently.

This issue is absolutely critical in the debate over theological method. Much depends on one's attitude to Kant. Is knowledge of the way things really are utterly unobtainable? There is now a growing consensus that wants to challenge the Kantian parameters of modernity. If we can "know" in science, then perhaps we can "know" in metaphysics as well. The mood is changing. Seen in this light, Schleiermacher looks increasingly problematic. If Schleiermacher's assumptions can be challenged, then there is no obligation to confine one's theology to the realm of anthropology.

No theological student can avoid an encounter with Schleiermacher. He poses all the right questions and provides deeply provocative and interesting answers.

References

Barth, Karl. 1982. *The Theology of Schleiermacher. Lectures at Göttingen 1923–24*. Edinburgh: T&T Clark and Grand Rapids, MI: Eerdmans.

Clements, Keith. 1987. *Friedrich Schleiermacher: Pioneer of Modern Theology*. London: Collins.

Jobling, J'annine and Markham, Ian, eds. 2000. *Theological Liberalism: Creative and Critical*. London: SPCK.

Kelsey, Catherine L. 2003. *Thinking about Christ with Schleiermacher*. Louisville, KY: Westminster John Knox.

Mariña, Jacqueline. 2005. *The Cambridge Companion to Friedrich Schleiermacher*. Cambridge: Cambridge University Press.

Schleiermacher, Friedrich. 1996. *On Religion: Speeches to Its Cultured Despisers*, ed. Richard Crouter, 2nd ed. Cambridge: Cambridge University Press.

Schleiermacher, Friedrich. 1999. *The Christian Faith*, ed. H. R. MacKintosh and J. S. Stewart. London and New York: T&T Clark.

Tice, Terrence. 2006. *Schleiermacher*. Nashville, TN: Abingdon Press.

Webster, John, Tanner, Kathryn, and Torrance, Iain, eds. 2007. *The Oxford Handbook of Systematic Theology*. Oxford: Oxford University Press.

Gottfried Thomasius (1802–75)

David R. Law

I. Background

Gottfried Thomasius's contemporaries ranked him among the leading theologians of the day and rated his *Christi Person und Werk* (Christ's Person and Work) as one of the most outstanding products of nineteenth-century Lutheran theology ("Gedächtnis," 1875a, 115; Stählin, 1887, 35, 44). It was above all Thomasius's contribution to *kenotic christology* that established him as a major theologian.

The noun "kenosis" and the adjective "kenotic" are derived from the use of the term *ekenōsen* in Phil. 2:7, where we read of "Christ Jesus, who, though he was in the form of God, did not regard equality with God as something to be exploited, but *emptied himself* [*heauton ekenōsen*], taking the form of a servant, being born in human likeness." On the basis of the use of the term *ekenōsen* in this text, "kenosis" has come to be used as shorthand for a series of issues arising from the claim that Christ is both truly divine and truly human. How can divinity and humanity coexist in the one, united person of Christ without undermining the integrity of either nature? "Kenotic christologies" are those christologies which attempt to address this problem by arguing that Christ "emptied" himself of some aspect of his divine nature in order to become a human being.

Both Thomasius's admirers and critics acknowledge that Thomasius advances a particularly rigorous form of kenotic christology. Loofs describes part two of Thomasius's *Christi Person und Werk* as "the masterpiece of the modern theory of kenosis" (Loofs, 1901, 248) and comments that Thomasius "gave the doctrine its scientific formulation" (Loofs, 1914, 686). Mackintosh describes Thomasius's christology "as the classic form of the Kenotic theory" (Mackintosh, 1927, 267), while Welch regards Thomasius as kenotic christology's "most important defender" (Welch, 1965, 9, n.11).

Although Thomasius's influence and that of kenotic christology in general gave way in Germany in the 1880s to Ritschlianism, kenotic christology enjoyed a second flowering in Britain between *c*.1880 and 1930, where elements of Thomasius's thought were either taken up or reacted against by Charles Gore, A. M. Fairbairn, H. R. Mackintosh, Frank Weston, and others. In recent years there has been a renewed interest in kenotic christology (see, for example, Evans, 2006). Any current attempt to formulate a coherent and viable kenotic christology will need to return to Thomasius's work, above all to his *Christi Person und Werk*, for, as Welch comments, in Thomasius's theology one sees "more clearly than anywhere else, the theory's presuppositions and possibilities" (Welch, 1965, 9, n. 11).

II. Life and Works

Gottfried Thomasius was born on July 26, 1802 in Egenhausen, Germany, but spent most of his youth in Ehingen, where his father was pastor (Zezschwitz,

The Student's Companion to the Theologians, First Edition. Edited by Ian S. Markham.

1875, 6). In 1821 Thomasius began his theological studies at the Protestant Theology Faculty at the University of Erlangen (Stählin, 1887, 36), before continuing his studies at the Universities of Halle and Berlin ("Briefe," 1875b, 113). After Thomasius completed his studies in August 1825 ("Briefe," 1875b, 126), he spent the next 17 years in parish ministry. He continued to do theological research, focusing above all on patristics and the history of dogma (Stählin, 1887, 39), and embarked on a thorough investigation of the theology of Origen. This led in 1837 to the publication of his *Origenes. Ein Beytrag zur Dogmengeschichte des dritten Jahrhunderts* (Origen. A Contribution to the History of Dogma in the Third Century). During his ministry Thomasius was also appointed to teach religion at Nuremberg Grammar School, which led in 1842 to the publication of his *Grundlinien zum Religionsunterricht an den mittleren und oberen Klassen gelehrter Schulen* (Guidelines for Religious Education in the Middle and Upper Classes of Grammar Schools), a work which enjoyed a wide readership both in and outside Bavaria (Stählin, 1887, 40).

On March 11, 1842 Thomasius was appointed professor of dogmatics at the University of Erlangen (Stählin, 1887, 40). In this year he was also appointed university preacher, a post he would hold until 1872 (ibid., 53). During the 30 years he occupied the chair of dogmatics, Thomasius brought out several significant works of dogmatic theology. In 1844 he published a treatise entitled *De controversia Hofmanniana* (On the Hofmann Controversy), which according to Stählin resulted in Thomasius gaining a seat and voting rights on the university senate (ibid., 44). The next year he published a major article in the *Zeitschrift für Protestantismus und Kirche* (Journal for Protestantism and Church), entitled "Ein Beitrag zur kirchlichen Christologie" (A Contribution to Ecclesial Christology). This was Thomasius's first venture into kenotic christology and laid the foundation for his later, more substantial work.

Thomasius's kenotic christology arose out of his response to the threat he believed to be posed to Lutheran orthodoxy by contemporary theological and philosophical developments (Thomasius, 1845a, 3). David Strauss in the second part of his *Die Christliche Glaubenslehre* (The Christian Doctrine of Faith) and F. C. Baur in his *Die christliche Lehre von der Dreieinigkeit und Menschwerdung Gottes* (The Christian Doctrine of the Trinity and the Incarnation of God) had attempted to undermine the doctrine that Christ is truly divine and truly human. I. A. Dorner, too, had raised objections to orthodox Christology in his *Entwicklungsgeschichte der Lehre von der Person Christi* (History of the Development of the Doctrine of the Person of Christ). Indeed, for Thomasius Dorner's critique was the more disturbing, for the latter did not share the destructive tendencies of other critics of orthodox christology, but was striving to construct a Christian theology. For Thomasius, meeting these challenges meant returning to the roots of the christology of the Lutheran Church, namely, to the Chalcedonian Definition that Christ is truly human and truly divine and that these two natures are united in his one person. Lutheran christology was, according to Thomasius, a deepening and refinement of the Chalcedonian Definition. To attack Chalcedon, then, was to attack the roots of Lutheranism itself.

For Thomasius the criticisms of Lutheran theology applied only to the *forms* in which Lutheran doctrines had been expressed, not to the contents of the doctrines themselves. The problem was merely that these doctrines were underdeveloped and in their current forms lent themselves to contemporary criticism. The task, then, was not to abandon the core doctrines of Lutheranism and look for new ways of doing theology, but was rather to unfold as fully as possible the resources and deep insights contained in those doctrines. In the case of christology this meant deepening the notion of kenosis (Thomasius, 1845a, 107). In "Beitrag" Thomasius argued that the tensions within Lutheran christology could be resolved only by reformulating the doctrine of the person of Christ in terms of a self-limitation of the Logos.

Thomasius's article provoked considerable debate. As Matthias Schneckenburger, one of the first critics of Thomasius's christology put it, Thomasius's work "has ignited a denominational controversy which has driven men who had otherwise been personal friends into considerable mutual exasperation" (Schneckenburger, 1846, 1848). Schneckenburger, as well as I. A. Dorner and J. H. A. Ebrard, the other early critics of the theology of "Beitrag," attacked Thomasius's christology for allegedly being incompatible with Lutheran orthodoxy, being based on a dubious analogy between the incarnate Logos and the divine spirit that dwells in all human beings, and undermining the doctrines of the Trinity and divine immutability. Further criticisms were leveled at Thomasius's treatment of the *communicatio idiomatum* (communication of attributes) and alleged inconsistencies in his treatment of kenosis as self-limitation.

The publication of "Beitrag" was followed in 1845–6 by *Dogmatis de obedientia Christi activa historia et progressiones inde a confessione Augustana ad formulam usque concordiae, particula prima, altera et tertia* (Of the Dogma of the Obedience of Christ. Its Practical History and Advances from the Augsburg Confession up to the Formula of Concord, parts one, two, and three). In 1848 Thomasius published *Das Bekenntniss der evangelisch-lutherischen Kirche in der Konsequenz seines Prinzips* (The Confession of the Evangelical-Lutheran Church in the Consequence of Its Principle), a historical study and defense of the Augsburg Confession and the Formula of Concord.

The criticisms of Schneckenburger, Dorner, and others led Thomasius to rethink the kenotic christology of "Beitrag" and to reflect more deeply on the Trinitarian and anthropological consequences of his christology. His first attempts at meeting his critics' arguments took the form of articles. In 1845 and 1846 he published two "replies" in the *Zeitschrift für Protestantismus und Kirche* (Thomasius, 1845b, 1846), which were followed in 1850 by another "Beitrag zur kirchlichen Christologie" (Thomasius, 1850a) as well as an article on Christ's work (Thomasius, 1850b), both published in the same volume of the *Zeitschrift für Protestantismus und Kirche*. His most sustained and significant attempt to develop a Lutheran christology capable of meeting contemporary criticism, however, was his *Christi Person und Werk*.

The first edition of *Christi Person und Werk* appeared between 1853 and 1861. Because of the criticism leveled at the early volumes of the first edition, Thomasius began revisions for the second edition before all three volumes of the first edition had appeared. The second edition was published between 1856 and 1863. A third and abridged edition, edited after Thomasius's death by F. J. Winter, was published between 1886 and 1888, but it is the second edition that is regarded as the mature and authoritative statement of Thomasius's kenotic christology.

During his writing and publication of the first two editions of *Christi Person und Werk* Thomasius brought out in 1857 a work entitled *Das Bekenntniss der lutherischen Kirche von der Versöhnung und die Versöhnungslehre D. Chr. K. von Hofmanns* [The Confession of the Lutheran Church concerning Reconciliation and Dr. C. K. von Hofmann's Doctrine of Reconciliation] and published his sermons of 1852–60 in five collections. In 1861 these were published as a single volume together with some other sermons, and were organized according to the church year (Stählin, 1887, 54). In 1860 there appeared his *Praktische Auslegung des Briefes Pauli an die Kolosser* (Exegesis of Paul's Letter to the Colossians), which was followed in 1867 by *Das Wiedererwachen des evangelischen Lebens in der lutherischen Kirche Bayerns* (The Reawakening of Evangelical Life in the Lutheran Church of Bavaria), a work which dealt with the history of the Lutheran Church in Bavaria between 1800 and 1840, focusing especially on the revivalist movement. Thomasius's final work was his *Die christliche Dogmengeschichte als Entwicklungsgeschichte des kirchlichen Lehrbegriffs*. The first volume of this work appeared in 1874 and dealt with the development of dogma in the early church. The second volume, which dealt with the history of dogma in the Middle Ages and the Reformation, was not published until after Thomasius's death.

Thomasius died on January 24, 1875.

III.   Thomasius's Theology

The doctrine of God

1.   God as absolute personality

The believer experiences his/her relationship with God as a personal relationship, namely as the "relationship between I and Thou" (Thomasius, 1856, 12). It is thus appropriate to describe God in terms of personality. This conception of God as personal, however, must be qualified if it is not to be misunderstood, for God is a qualitatively different form of personality from all other persons, for God is "absolute causality and unconditionedness" (Thomasius, 1856, 12; cf. 1850a, 2–3). Consequently, if we are to speak of God in terms of personality, then we must describe him as "absolute personality" (Thomasius, 1856, 12; cf. 1850a, 2–3).

God's absolute personality comprises three "determinations of essence" (*Wesensbestimmtheiten*) (Thomasius, 1856, 52), namely: (1) "absolute self-determination [*Selbstbestimmung*]" or "will"; (2) "self-consciousness"; and (3) "being" or "absolute life." The reasoning that leads Thomasius to posit these three determinations of essence within the absolute personality of God is as follows.

The absolute personality must be understood as "absolute self-determination, or, since self-determination is will, as absolute will" (Thomasius, 1856, 19), because nothing determines what God is. God alone wills what God is, therefore essence and will are one and the same thing in God. God is what he wills, and wills what he is. Consequently, the will of God can be understood as the "essence" or "root" of absolute personality. Furthermore, if God is absolute self-determination or will, then he must also be characterized by self-consciousness, for a consciousless will would simply not be a will. Thomasius thus concludes that, "Self-determination is *eo ipso* self-consciousness" (Thomasius, 1856, 19). The third essential determination of God as absolute personality is "being" or "absolute life" (Thomasius, 1856, 19). All three determinations of essence can be grouped together under the concept of "Spirit."

2. *The divine attributes*

For Thomasius attributes do not belong to the essence of God, but rather arise from the distinctions within the divine essence: "Attributes are in general nothing other than the modalities of a thing in relation to other beings" (Thomasius, 1856, 48). Consequently, "there are attributes only in so far as there are relations; but there are relations only where there are distinctions" (Thomasius, 1856, 52). The divine attributes can thus be categorized according to the types of relations from which they arise. This allows Thomasius to distinguish between two basic kinds of attribute, namely, immanent and relative attributes.

(A) THE IMMANENT ATTRIBUTES

Thomasius defines immanent attributes as "the immanent determinations of absolute personality in relation to itself" (Thomasius, 1856, 48). There are two types of immanent attribute, namely those that issue forth from the internal relations between the three distinctions of absolute self-determination or will, self-consciousness, and being or absolute life within the absolute personality of God, and those that arise from the internal Trinitarian relations.

(i) *The immanent attributes of absolute personality.* The immanent attributes that arise from the internal relations within the absolute personality of God are "absolute power or freedom," "absolute intelligence," and "absolute blessedness" (Thomasius, 1856, 54). Absolute power is not the same as omnipotence, which is a relative attribute by means of which God acts upon the world, but is, as Welch succinctly puts it, "the unconditioned power of will over itself, thus wholly in the service of will" (Welch, 1965, 68–9, n.11). Similarly, Thomasius argues that absolute intelligence is not identical with omniscience, but is rather "the utterly unconditioned and perfect knowledge of God" (Thomasius, 1856, 54). Finally, absolute blessedness is God's possession within himself of the fullness of perfect life and his consciousness of this possession (Thomasius, 1856, 54).

(ii) *The immanent attributes of the Trinity.* In thinking through the immanent attributes of the Trinity Thomasius takes as his starting point the determinateness of the Christian consciousness of God. The characteristic feature of this Christian consciousness of God is the experience of God's love through the mediation of Christ in the Holy Spirit (Thomasius, 1856, 57–60). In other words, Thomasius takes as his starting point the Christian's experience of the economic Trinity and then traces this experience back to its source in the immanent Trinity, which must be posited as "the necessary presuppositions of our relationship with God" (Thomasius, 1856, 68).

The experience of God as Trinity needs to be united with the Christian experience of God as absolute personality. Thomasius argues that the divine absolute personality is ontologically prior to the Trinitarian persons. Indeed, it is his claim that the immanent Trinity has the absolute personality as its "presupposition" (Thomasius, 1856, 109). This distinction between absolute personality and the Trinity allows Thomasius to address the problem of the unity and distinctness of the Trinitarian persons by enabling him to show how the divine hypostases are derived from the absolute personality. He does this by focusing on "absolute will." The Trinitarian hypostases, he argues, are not mere "modalities" of the divine essence, but are "acts of the absolute will" (Thomasius, 1856, 105). This means that the hypostases are "distinct, independent persons in the one absolute personality" (Thomasius, 1856, 106; cf. 1857a, 293), between whom "an I–Thou relationship, a mutual willing, knowing, and living is enacted" (Thomasius, 1856, 69). The absolute personality brings forth out of itself the Trinitarian persons by means of acts of will and preserves its unity by the fact that the hypostases are all acts of the one absolute will of the absolute personality.

This distinction between absolute personality and the Trinitarian persons allows Thomasius to address the problem of the relation between the Trinitarian persons. We saw earlier that in absolute personality essence and will are one and the same: God is what he wills. This allows Thomasius to conceive of how the Son can possess a certain "conditionedness" (Thomasius, 1856, 105, 110; 1857a, 203, 294) over against the Father. Thomasius writes: "the will of the Father is the content of the hypostasis of the Son … While the Father wills the Son, the Son wills himself as willed by the Father, consequently he wills himself not for his own sake but in order to devote himself to the Father" (Thomasius, 1856, 108–9; cf. 1857a, 49–50, 203–4). This means, Thomasius points out, that the Son sustains a relationship of "dependence" on the Father (Thomasius, 1856, 110, 124; 1857a, 294). The Holy Spirit, on the other hand, is "the objective unity of the mutual willing" of both the Father and the Son (Thomasius, 1856, 109). Thomasius concedes that this means that the Father possesses a certain degree of precedence over the other two persons, by virtue of the Father's sustaining "a relationship of origination …, because which the first person is the ground of the other two" (Thomasius, 1856, 106). In support of this view Thomasius points out that in scripture the Father has "a certain priority" (Thomasius, 1856, 136; 1857a, 294).

The absolute personality's will to express itself in Trinitarian terms has consequences for the attributes of the absolute personality, namely absolute power, intelligence, and blessedness. These are now defined in Trinitarian terms and thereby receive "a richer, more concrete content: they become holiness, truth, and love" (Thomasius, 1856, 137, cf. 43). This is an unequal Trinity, however, for "love" is not only an attribute but also the factor which binds the three attributes together into a unity (Thomasius, 1856, 138). Despite this overarching role of love, however, Thomasius refuses to identify love with the divine essence, because this would reduce divine holiness and wrath merely to forms of love, which would undermine the doctrine of reconciliation (Thomasius, 1856, 154–5). Rather confusingly, Thomasius adds absolute power to the three attributes of holiness, truth, and love in part two of *Christi Person und Werk*, despite the fact that in part one he has defined absolute power as one of the attributes of absolute personality.

These three (or four) attributes of holiness, truth, and love (and absolute power) are essential to the Godhead. Without them God cannot be God. Consequently, they cannot be divested without God ceasing to be God.

(B)   THE RELATIVE ATTRIBUTES

God is the Lord of creation (Thomasius, 1856, 208–9), who creates, sustains, and acts in the world. God does not need the world, for as God he is sufficient unto himself. He acts toward the world not out of compulsion but out of freely given love. As Thomasius puts it, God's creation and sustaining of the world are "an act of divine freedom,… an act not of necessity, but of the free love of God" (Thomasius, 1856, 207).

God acts in the world by the exercise of his relative attributes, namely omnipresence, omnipotence, and omniscience, which, as Thomasius puts it, are the means by which "the immanence of God operates in and on the world" (Thomasius, 1856, 208). These attributes are relative, firstly, because they arise from the *relation* God sustains to the world, and secondly, because they do not belong essentially to the absolute personality of God. If the relative attributes belonged to absolute personality, Thomasius argues, it would mean that God needed the world. Thomasius's point can be most clearly seen in the case of omnipotence. Omnipotence requires a world upon which it can be exercised. Power cannot be exercised in a vacuum, but needs an object upon which it can exert itself. Consequently, if omnipotence were an immanent attribute, i.e., an attribute that belonged to the very essence of the divine absolute personality, then God's independence from the world would be endangered, for he would need the world in order to be able to exercise the attribute of omnipotence (Thomasius, 1856, 52). The distinction between immanent and relative attributes is thus necessary to avoid the conclusion that God is dependent upon the world (Thomasius, 1857a, 242, cf. 546).

The incarnation

Armed with this understanding of the doctrine of God, Thomasius turns in Part Two of *Christi Person und Werk* to a consideration of the doctrine of the incarnation.

1. The presuppositions of the incarnation

(A) THE EMPIRICAL JUSTIFICATION OF THE DOCTRINE OF THE INCARNATION

For Thomasius the starting point for dogmatic theology is the Christian experience of redemption. This applies pre-eminently to christology, where our starting point must be Christians' present communion with God mediated to them through the living, personal Christ, a communion in which the believer participates experientially through faith in Christ (Thomasius, 1857a, 4, 7). This present experience of communion with God points both forwards and backwards. It points forwards because it looks ahead to a future consummation in the transfiguration of the world. It points backwards because it looks "backwards to the fact of the historical appearance and redemptive activity of Christ in the flesh" (Thomasius, 1857a, 7). That is, the Christian's experience of justification points back to an original saving event which has made the Christian's present experience of justification possible. The Christian's experience of salvation thus compels him/her to posit the existence of a historical savior who brought about the present experience of communion with God. As Thomasius puts it, the person of the historical Christ is the "postulate of our communion with God" (Thomasius, 1857a, 143). This postulate of a historical savior is corroborated and confirmed by the Gospels, which provide us with a historical portrayal of the historical Christ (Thomasius, 1857a, 143).

(B) THE TWO-NATURES DOCTRINE

The postulate of a historical savior on the basis of the Christian's present experience of communion compels us to accept the two-natures doctrine. That we as Christians stand in communion with God presupposes that Christ, who mediates this communion to us, is "personally one" with both human beings and with God (Thomasius, 1857a, 8). Christ must be divine because only divinity is capable of wiping away sin and restoring communion between God and sinful humanity. Christ must be human because only as a human being can his restoration of communion with God be a historical reality for human beings. To perform the mediating office of establishing communion between God and sinful human beings it is thus crucial that Christ is both truly divine and truly human. To act as mediator, then, Christ must be a human being just as much as he is God. In short, he must be a divine-human person.

(C) THE HYPOSTATIC UNION

For Christ to act as a mediator it is necessary not only that he be both fully divine and fully human, but also that these two natures are united in *one* person. If the two natures are not united in the one person of Christ but exist alongside each other, as it were, then Christ is no longer divine-human, but is divided into divine *and* human elements (Thomasius, 1857a, 11). The characteristics of the two respective natures would then "belong only either to the one or to the other side, but not simultaneously to both—and thereby their inmost nerve is severed" (Thomasius, 1857a, 11). With regard to Christ's divine nature this would mean that "what we really and personally have in him is then always merely the divine side of his being; what we receive from him is always merely divine influences or communications" (Thomasius, 1857a, 12). Thomasius's point seems to be that if the divine nature is not united with the human nature, there can be no sanctification of the human nature. The attributes of the divine nature are *not* communicated to the human nature. At best we can speak only of an inspiration of the human nature or, as Thomasius puts it, "merely divine influences or communications." In short, without the concept of the hypostatic union of the two natures there can be no genuine incarnation and therefore no redemption of human nature. The hypostatic union of the two natures of divinity and humanity in the one person of

Christ is thus essential for the mediation to human beings of communion with God. Thomasius concludes that, "on every side it is the most profound practical interests that compel us to conceive of the person of the mediator as a living unity, as a unitary ego, as one divine-human person" (Thomasius, 1857a, 12).

Through reflection on the present Christian experience of redemption, then, we arrive at the classical doctrine of the person of Christ, and thereby confirm the Christian conviction that "the human being Jesus Christ is God" (Thomasius, 1857a, 12).

2.   *The act of incarnation: Kenosis as self-limitation*

Having shown the possibility of the divine Logos's assumption of human nature, Thomasius's next task is to show how a union of the two natures of divinity and humanity was able to come about without compromising the integrity of either nature. It is in order to address this problem that Thomasius turns to the notion of kenosis.

To grasp the incarnation not merely as an abstract relationship between divinity and humanity, but as a real, historical reality, it is necessary to posit the notion of the *self-limitation* of divinity in the incarnate Son of God. The necessity of affirming that the Logos underwent self-limitation in order to become a human being is evident from the intolerable christological consequences that result if we do not affirm the self-limitation of the Son of God in incarnate form. If there is no limitation, then the Son continues to be omniscient and exercise universal governance during his earthly existence. This leads to what are for Thomasius two unacceptable conclusions. Firstly, refusal to accept the Son of God's self-limitation means that

> there is here a twofold mode of being, a double life, a doubled consciousness; the Logos is or continues always to have something which is not taken up into his historical appearance, which is not also that of the human being Jesus—and this seems to destroy the unity of the person, the identity of the ego; there thus occurs no living and complete penetration of both sides, no genuine being-human of God. (Thomasius, 1857a, 142)

Secondly, refusal to accept the self-limitation of the Son of God means that no sense can be made of Christ's genuinely human experiences, the reality of which is clearly manifest in the New Testament witness. The

only way around these problems, Thomasius claims, is "to posit the incarnation itself precisely in the fact that he, the eternal Son of God, the second person of the Godhead, surrendered himself to the form of a circumscribed human existence, and in doing so gave himself up to the limitation of a temporal-spatial existence, under the conditions of a human development, to the limits of concrete historical being" (Thomasius, 1857a, 143).

But what is the nature and extent of the limitation that the Logos undergoes on becoming incarnate? "It is certainly not," Thomasius emphasizes, "a divesting of what is essential to divinity in order to be God, but is rather a divesting of the divine mode of being for the sake of the human, creaturely form of existence, and *eo ipso* a renunciation of the divine glory which he had from the beginning with the Father and which he exercised in his governance and rule over the world" (Thomasius, 1857a, 143). Nor does the incarnation entail the surrender of the divine ego. It is rather, Thomasius emphasizes, "a divesting of a higher form of existence, a surrender of a God-like relationship for the sake of a humanly limited and conditioned one" (Thomasius, 1857a, 146).

The kenosis involves two actions. Firstly, it involves the Logos divesting himself of the relative attributes so that he can live a genuinely human life. On becoming incarnate the Logos freely gives up the attributes of omnipotence, omniscience, and omnipresence (Thomasius, 1857a, 241–2). Secondly, the kenosis involves the incarnate expression of the essential attributes of absolute power, holiness, truth, and love, in a form consistent with human existence. Let us look at each of these actions in more detail.

(A)   THE DIVESTING OF THE RELATIVE ATTRIBUTES

On becoming incarnate the Logos gave up the attributes of omnipotence, omniscience, and omnipresence, which he had exercised during his pre-existent state, in order to live a genuinely human existence.

The Logos's laying aside of omnipotence meant that he was genuinely unable to exercise unrestricted divine power for the duration of the incarnation. Christ "did not actively rule the world at the same time that he walked on earth as man, suffered and died." Nor, Thomasius emphasizes, was it "as if he were at the same time actually ruling over and governing the universe in a hidden way" (Thomasius, 1857a, 238). The miracles are no argument against this, for according to Thomasius Christ did not perform miracles by means of his own power, but had this power granted to him by the Father (Thomasius, 1857a, 238). Christ, then, "was not an omnipotent human being" (Thomasius, 1857a, 238).

The Logos also laid aside his omniscience on becoming incarnate. Like all human beings Christ's knowledge developed and matured during his earthly life according to his human capacity. The argument for the renunciation of omniscience is not refuted by the gospel witness to moments of unusual insight on Christ's part, however, for Christ's knowledge, Thomasius argues, "is comparable to the prophetic insight, not to that intuitive divine insight before which past and future lie there like an open present" (Thomasius, 1857a, 238–9). Christ, then, "was not an omniscient human being" (Thomasius, 1857a, 239).

The third of the relative attributes divested by the incarnate Logos is omnipresence. For Thomasius,

> the assumption that he existed during this stage outside the limitation of space manifestly destroys the truth of his entire historical existence; for such a mode of existence would contradict not only the natural restriction and conditionedness of the earthly material body, but also utterly contradicts the condition of the spiritual-corporeal human nature as it is at present determined in everyone. No, the corporeal existence of the Redeemer was restricted to the arena of his redemptive activity; his wandering from place to place, his coming and going, was a truly local behavior. (Thomasius, 1857a, 239)

In order to have lived a genuinely human life, the Logos must have renounced the attribute of omnipresence on becoming incarnate. Christ, then, was not an omnipresent human being.

(B) THE REVELATION OF THE ESSENTIAL ATTRIBUTES

Although kenosis entails the laying aside of omnipotence, omniscience, and omnipresence, it does not involving giving up anything essential to the divine nature, and even in the incarnate state the Logos "lacks nothing which is essential for God to be God" (Thomasius, 1857a, 242). This is because the Logos renounces only the *relative* attributes, but continues to possess in incarnate form the *immanent* attributes of absolute power, holiness, truth, and love that belong to the divine essence. Indeed, for Thomasius one of

the purposes of the incarnation is the revelation of the divine attributes in the person of the incarnate Christ. For Thomasius, the immanent attributes "shine through his entire self-witness and shed over his life in the flesh that heavenly radiance which beams forth bright and clear from the midst of his poverty and lowliness" (Thomasius, 1857a, 237). Thus absolute power manifests itself "as the freedom of self-determination, as the mighty will completely his own" (Thomasius, 1857a, 237), while absolute truth manifests itself in Christ "as the clear knowledge of the divine concerning itself, more precisely as the knowledge of the incarnate one concerning his own essence and the will of the Father" (Thomasius, 1857a, 237).

Kenosis, then, is the Son's laying aside of the relative attributes, while retaining the *immanent* attributes. Because the relative attributes are not essential to the Godhead, since they pertain not to the internal relations within the Godhead, but to the Godhead's external relations to the universe, they can be surrendered by the Logos without loss of divinity. Consequently, even in the reduced and limited form the Logos assumes on becoming incarnate, he still retains the immanent attributes and consequently remains fully divine.

3. *The Trinitarian consequences of the incarnation*

For Thomasius the kenosis of the Son does not undermine the Trinity, because the kenosis is an expression of the united will of the three persons. Consequently, *all three persons* participate in the incarnation (Thomasius, 1857a, 49, 292). Thomasius develops his argument by focusing on what unites the three persons. This point of unity is "being and will." Once we have grasped this, we can move away from the misleading notion of the three persons as three static substances, which would be very difficult to conceive of in unity with each other. Such a static notion needs to be replaced by a dynamic notion of the divine persons centered on the notion of the will (Thomasius, 1857a, 292–3). The basis of unity of the three persons is that they proceed from the one united will of the absolute personality of God. The Trinitarian persons are, as it were, a secondary layer of divine self-differentiation brought forth from the will of absolute personality (Thomasius, 1857a, 293).

Armed with this understanding of the Trinitarian relations, Thomasius argues, we can now go on to address the issue of the impact of the Son's kenosis on the Trinity. The first question Thomasius addresses is: "Why, if one person of the Trinity becomes a human being, do the others not thereby also become human by virtue of their essential unity with that person?" (Thomasius, 1857a, 293). As Thomasius understands it, the problem is "how then could one person of the divine Triad have entered into humanity, in order from then on to exist in a human way, without either the other two persons also having become a human being or the incarnate one having retired from the consortium of the Trinity" (Thomasius, 1857a, 292)? Thomasius admits that these problems may be intensified by his version of kenotic christology (Thomasius, 1857a, 292).

Thomasius addresses this problem by pointing to the *hypostatische Eigenthümlichkeit* of the Son, a phrase which Welch helpfully translates as "hypostatic specificity" (Welch, 1965, 82). Thomasius writes: "For as the Father wills and knows himself eternally as the ground of himself, so it is the hypostatic specificity of the Son to be willed by the Father as his other ego, and to will and know himself as conditioned by him" (Thomasius, 1857a, 294). That is, there is a mutuality between the Father and the Son that is grounded in the inner-Trinitarian relations. This mutuality is centered on the will. The Father wills the Son and the Son wills himself to be willed by the Father. This mutual and complementary relationship of willing and being willed continues in the earthly existence of the incarnate Logos, but now acquires "a temporal-historical form in which the Father constantly wills and knows himself as the conditioning one in relation to the Son, while the Son wills and knows himself as the one conditioned by the Father" (Thomasius, 1857a, 294). It would not be possible for this relationship of mutual willing to be reversed, however. Although Father and Son exist in a relationship of complementary willing, the Father cannot become the one who is willed, nor can he for this very reason be the Trinitarian person who became incarnate. Nor can the Son will the Father, for this would reverse their roles and thereby deny the Son's "hypostatic specificity." Both persons remain true to what is specific and distinctive to their hypostasis.

The second question Thomasius addresses is whether his kenotic christology does not result in the modification of the inner-Trinitarian relations. Thomasius concedes that this is indeed the case. This modification takes place through the Son's taking up of humanity

into the life of the Trinity, the result of which is that, "The immanent life-movement of the three persons has from now on become to a certain extent a divine-human one" (Thomasius, 1857a, 295). Although this seems to imply that the Godhead itself has undergone a transformation, Thomasius claims that "this appearance vanishes when we consider that although the incarnation is a temporal-historical fact, it rests on a pre-temporal, i.e., extra-temporal, decision of the eternal God, and consequently is the content of his eternal intuition, of his eternal willing and thinking" (Thomasius, 1857a, 296). That is, the decision that the Son's relationship with the other Trinitarian persons should be mediated through the human nature assumed by the Logos was made in the state of pre-existence that preceded the incarnation. Because the united will of the Trinitarian persons has co-eternally willed the incarnation, the incarnation is not a break with divine nature but an expression of it.

The third question that Thomasius feels he needs to address is the significance of Christ's life history for the inner-Trinitarian relations. The life of Jesus does not result in an undermining of the Trinitarian relations, because the historical events of the life of the incarnate Logos reflect the relations that exist between the Trinitarian persons. Thomasius writes: "The eternal generation of the Son from the Father becomes the temporal birth into humanity; the immanent devotion of the Son to the Father takes the form of the historical subordination to the Father" (Thomasius, 1857a, 297). Indeed, the subordination of the Son is so radical that he is prepared to allow it to intensify to the point where it becomes *dissimilarity* between himself and the Father. Thomasius comments: "the subordination proceeds to the point of dissimilarity to him; the humiliation extends to the depths of human limitation, to the human pain of death, to the night of God-forsakenness and of the grave. The Christ surrenders himself, his divine-human life, in order though such self-surrender to be transfigured into God-like glory" (Thomasius, 1857a, 294). Thomasius seems to be arguing that even the most extreme experiences undergone by the incarnate Son, namely, suffering, God-forsakenness, and death, do not disrupt the Trinitarian relations. This is because these experiences are the expression of the Son's subordination to the Father's will, a subordination which the Son is prepared to follow even to the point where he becomes dissimilar to the Father. This dissimilarity, however, does not indicate a rupture in the inner-Trinitarian relations but is rather the deepest expression of the pre-existent will of the Son to subordinate himself to the Father for the duration of the incarnation.

A further reason Thomasius cites for the kenosis not disrupting the inner-Trinitarian relations is that the incarnation of the Son is the continuation of the limitation that God has imposed upon himself through his creation of the world. In creating the world and laying down the laws of nature, God has imparted to the world a "relative independence." Similarly, his creation of human beings with free personalities also constitutes a self-limitation on the part of God with regard to human beings (Thomasius, 1856, 208, 255, 268, 458; II: 553). Indeed, "without a self-limitation of God there would be no history of humankind" (Thomasius, 1850a, 5 n.). The self-limitation that God imposes upon himself through the incarnation is thus in continuity with the limitation he has imposed upon himself through the act of creating the world.

Just as the Son's relations with the other persons of the Trinity are not interrupted by the incarnation, so too does the Son's relation to the world suffer no interruption when he becomes a human being. On the contrary, for Thomasius the incarnation is a continuation and a deepening of the Son's role as agent and sustainer of creation. The impression that the Son is no longer sustaining the world "is an appearance that attaches only to the external consideration of this relation; viewed more deeply, the world-redeeming activity is *the center of the sustaining and ruling of the world*" (*Christi Person und Werk* II: 300). Christ's redemption of the world is not an action limited to the incarnation, but is embedded in the divine will from the very beginning. Indeed, it is an expression of God's sustaining activity, for redemption is necessary to restore the world to its proper condition. God continued to sustain the world despite human sin because of his intention to restore the world through Christ. Thomasius seems to be saying: we should not start with the Son's cosmic functions and worry about how kenosis seems to undermine these functions. We should start with kenosis as an *expression* of those functions.

From these considerations it becomes clear that the incarnation was not an interruption of the Son's cosmic powers, but rather their continuation at a deeper level. Indeed, it is the incarnation that forms the center and meaning of God's world governance.

IV. Thomasius's Achievement

Thomasius's kenotic christology was a rigorous and sustained attempt to defend the Chalcedonian Definition's affirmation that Christ is both truly human and truly divine. The weakness of previous christologies was that their emphasis on Christ's divinity often threatened to undermine the reality of his humanity. To Thomasius the only way of remaining true to the Chalcedonian Definition, while simultaneously doing justice to Christ's humanity, was by accepting that the eternal Logos underwent a genuine self-limitation in order to become incarnate. Thomasius believed that this solution was supported both by scripture and by the inner dynamic of church doctrine. His predecessors, however, had merely touched upon or hinted at this solution. Thomasius is arguably the first to develop a thoroughgoing and rigorously thought-out kenotic christology.

There are, however, some significant problems with Thomasius's christology. His doctrine of God has been criticized for conflating the absolute personality of God, which is supposed to precede the Trinity, with one of the Trinitarian persons, namely, the Father. This was pointed out by Gess, who asks whether Thomasius "alternates between two ways of viewing the Trinity which are in fact essentially different from each other. On the one hand, he understands the Father as the source of the Godhead, and conceives of the First Person as the ground of the other two … On the other hand, he speaks of the One absolute personality which determines itself in a threefold way as Father, Son, and Spirit" (Gess, 1856, 197).

This conflation of absolute personality with the Father results in Thomasius lapsing into subordinationism (Stählin, 1887, 51; Breidert, 1977, 72–3). Despite affirming the unity of the Trinitarian persons Thomasius is forced at certain points in his argument to posit a clear hierarchy among the three persons. The Father has "hypostatic priority" and wills the Son. The Son appears to be subordinate, for he is that which is willed by the Father. The Father seems thus to be purely active, whereas the Son's activity is limited and seems to consist only in willing to be willed by the Father. Thus whereas in volume one of *Christi Person und Werk* the three persons seem to be equal in status, at certain points in his argument in volume two Thomasius resorts to a subordinationist view of the Trinity in order to ward off the criticism that his kenotic christology has introduced a modification in the Trinitarian relations.

There is also a problem with Thomasius's distinction between "determinations of essence" and "attributes." Firstly, the distinction between determinations of essence and divine attributes seems highly artificial, a fact which is made apparent by the fact that Thomasius himself does not always consistently apply it. In some passages in volume one, for example, he treats determinations of essence and attributes as identical, whereas at other points in his argument he distinguishes between them (Breidert, 1977, 69, n. 116).

Secondly, Thomasius's derivation of divine attributes from distinctions within the absolute personality of God as well as his distinction between the absolute personality of God and the Trinitarian persons arguably leads him into a form of Sabellianism. The Trinitarian persons seem to be only expressions or manifestations of the absolute personality.

It is furthermore difficult to see how Thomasius can argue that the immanent attributes of absolute power, intelligence, and blessedness arise from the internal *relations* of the divine absolute personality. Thomasius's description of these attributes consists in unfolding the *activity* of the respective "essential determination." Thus absolute power is the activity in which absolute self-determination and will manifest themselves. Absolute intelligence is the perfect knowledge that results from God's possession of absolute self-consciousness. Absolute blessedness is the fullness and perfection of life which God enjoys by virtue of his being absolute being and life. The difference between the absolute essential determinations and the immanent attributes appears simply to be that the absolute essential determinations refer to *states* of absolute personality, whereas the imma-

nent attributes refer to activities that can be carried out by virtue of these states. It is difficult to see how the immanent relations result from the difference between the essential determinations within the divine absolute personality, as Thomasius would have us believe.

There are also significant problems with Thomasius's distinction between immanent and relative attributes. Stählin regards Thomasius's "strange distinction" between immanent and relative attributes "not as the strength, but as the weakness of Thomasius's doctrine" (Stählin, 1887, 48). Dawe further comments:

> the traditional Christian doctrine of God had always held that there was nothing unessential in the divine nature. God's being is full actuality. This means there is nothing unessential in God that can be sloughed off. God is a unity, not a compound of parts—some essential, some unessential. There remains a basic incongruity between Thomasius's conception of kenosis and the doctrine of God to which he was trying to relate it. This was an incongruity that no amount of speculative ingenuity could overcome. (Dawe, 1963, 99–100)

Thomasius himself hints that the divine attributes cannot be separated in the way he suggests in *Christi Person und Werk* when he states that the relative attributes are related to the immanent attributes in the way appearance and outward action are related to the essence which acts in them (Thomasius, 1857a, 546). Arguably, the relative attributes must necessarily be in some way contained in the immanent attributes.

Despite these problems, however, Thomasius's kenotic christology remains a major achievement. At a time when the Chalcedonian Definition was being challenged by the development of historical criticism, the rise of psychology and the development of notions of personality, and increasing awareness of the humanness of Jesus, he provided a sustained and rigorous defense of the fundamental—and to my mind indispensable—truth of the Christian faith that Christ is truly human and truly divine.

References

1875a. "Zum Gedächtnis an Thomasius," *Zeitschrift für Protestantismus und Kirche* 69: 113–17.

1875b. "Briefe aus der Universitätszeit des seligen Thomasius," *Zeitschrift für Protestantismus und Kirche* 70: 113–27.

Baur, Ferdinand Christian. 1841. *Die christliche Lehre von der Dreieinigkeit und Menschwerdung Gottes in ihrer geschichtlichen Entwicklung.* Tübingen: C. F. Osiander.

Breidert, Martin. 1977. *Die kenotische Christologie des 19. Jahrhunderts.* Gütersloh: Gütersloher Verlagshaus Mohn.

Dawe, Donald G. 1963. *The Form of a Servant. A Historical Analysis of the Kenosis Motif.* Philadelphia: Westminster Press.

Dorner, I. A. 1839. *Entwicklungsgeschichte der Lehre von der Person Christi von den ältesten Zeiten bis auf die neueste.* Stuttgart: Liesching. ET: *History of the Development of the Person of Christ*, trans. William Lindsay Alexander and D. W. Simon. Edinburgh: T&T Clark, 1861–3.

Evans, C. Stephen, ed. 2006. *Exploring Kenotic Christology.* Oxford. Oxford University Press.

Gess, Wolfgang Friedrich. 1856. *Die Lehre von der Person Christi entwickelt aus dem Selbstbewusstsein Christi und aus dem Zeugnisse der Apostel.* Basle: Bahnmeiers Buchhandlung.

Loofs, Friedrich. 1901. "Kenosis." In *Realencyclopädie für protestantische Theologie*, 3rd ed., vol. 10, pp. 246–63.

Loofs, Friedrich. 1914. "Kenosis." In *Encyclopaedia of Religion and Ethics*, vol. 7, ed. James Hastings with the assistance of John A. Selbie and other scholars. Edinburgh: T&T Clark, pp. 680–7.

Mackintosh, H. R. 1927. *The Doctrine of the Person of Jesus Christ.* Edinburgh: T&T Clark.

Schneckenburger, Matthias. 1846. Rezension von G. Thomasius, "Ein Beitrag zur kirchlichen Christologie," *Literarischer Anzeiger für die christliche Theologie und Wissenschaft überhaupt*, ed. F. A. Tholuck.

Stählin, Adolf von. 1887. *Löhe, Thomasius, Harleβ. Drei Lebens- und Geschichtsbilder.* Leipzig: J. J. Hinrichs'sche Buchhandlung, pp. 33–58. Originally published in *Realencyclopädie für protestantische Theologie*, 2nd ed., vol. 15, pp. 623–35.

Strauss, David Friedrich. 1840–1. *Die christliche Glaubenslehre in ihrer Entwicklung und im Kampfe mit der modernen Wissenschaft dargestellt*, 2 vols. Tübingen and Stuttgart: C. F. Osiander and F. H. Köhler.

Thomasius, Gottfried. 1837. *Origenes. Ein Beytrag zur Dogmengeschichte des dritten Jahrhunderts.* Nuremberg: Schrag.

Thomasius, Gottfried. 1842. *Grundlinien zum Religionsunterricht an den mittleren und oberen Klassen gelehrter Schulen.* Nuremberg: August Recknagel.

Thomasius, Gottfried. 1844. *De controversia Hofmanniana.* Erlangen: Recknagel.

Thomasius, Gottfried. 1845a. "Ein Beitrag zur kirchlichen Christologie," *Zeitschrift für Protestantismus und Kirche* 9: 1–30, 65–110, 218–58.

Thomasius, Gottfried. 1845b. "Erwiederung," *Zeitschrift für Protestantismus und Kirche* 9: 345–56.

Thomasius, Gottfried 1845c–6. *Dogmatis de obedientia Christi activa historia et progressiones inde a confessione Augustana ad formulam usque concordiae, particula prima, altera et tertia.* Erlangen.

Thomasius, Gottfried. 1846. "Erwiederung," *Zeitschrift für Protestantismus und Kirche* 11: 284–93.

Thomasius, Gottfried. 1848. *Das Bekenntniss der evangelisch-lutherischen Kirche in der Konsequenz seines Princips.* Nuremberg: August Recknagel.

Thomasius, Gottfried. 1850a. "Ein Beitrag zur kirchlichen Christologie," *Zeitschrift für Protestantismus und Kirche* 19: 1–42.

Thomasius, Gottfried. 1850b. "Christi Werk," *Zeitschrift für Protestantismus und Kirche* 19: 279–316.

Thomasius, Gottfried. 1856. *Christi Person und Werk. Darstellung der evangelisch-lutherischen Dogmatik vom Mittelpunkte der Christologie aus*, 2nd ed., vol. 1: *Die Voraussetzungen der Christologie.* Erlangen: Theodor Bläsing.

Thomasius, Gottfried. 1857a. *Christi Person und Werk. Darstellung der evangelisch-lutherischen Dogmatik vom Mittelpunkte der Christologie aus*, 2nd ed., vol. 2: *Die Person des Mittlers.* Erlangen: Theodor Bläsing.

Thomasius, Gottfried. 1857b. *Das Bekenntnis der lutherischen Kirche von der Versöhnung und die Versöhnungslehre D. Chr. K. von Hofmanns.* Erlangen: Bläsing.

Thomasius, Gottfried. 1860. *Praktische Auslegung des Briefes Pauli an die Kolosser* Erlangen: Deichert.

Thomasius, Gottfried. 1862. *Christi Person und Werk. Darstellung der evangelisch-lutherischen Dogmatik vom Mittelpunkte der Christologie aus*, 2nd ed., vol. 3, part 1: *Das Werk des Mittlers.* Erlangen: Theodor Bläsing.

Thomasius, Gottfried. 1863. *Christi Person und Werk. Darstellung der evangelisch-lutherischen Dogmatik vom Mittelpunkte der Christologie aus*, 2nd ed., vol. 3, part 2: *Das Werk des Mittlers.* Erlangen: Theodor Bläsing.

Thomasius, Gottfried. 1867. *Das Wiedererwachen des evangelischen Lebens in der lutherischen Kirche Bayerns.* Erlangen: Andreas Deichert.

Thomasius, Gottfried. 1874. *Die christliche Dogmengeschichte als Entwicklungsgeschichte des kirchlichen Lehrbegriffs*, vol. I: *Die Dogmengeschichte der alten Kirche.* Erlangen: Deichert.

Thomasius, Gottfried. 1876. *Die christliche Dogmengeschichte als Entwicklungsgeschichte des kirchlichen Lehrbegriffs*; vol. II: *Die Dogmengeschichte des Mittelalters und der Reformationszeit.* Erlangen: Deichert.

Welch, Claude. 1965. *God and Incarnation in Mid-Nineteenth Century German Theology.* New York: Oxford University Press.

Zezschwitz, Carl Adolf Gerhard von. 1875. *Gedächtnisrede auf Dr. Gottfried Thomasius.* Erlangen: Andreas Deichert.

Paul Tillich (1886–1965)

Kelton Cobb

I. Biography

Paul Tillich, the son of a Lutheran pastor, was born in Prussia, in Starzeddel (Starosiedle), about 80 miles southeast of Berlin, a small town now in Poland. He spent his early years in this region of Prussia, including three years at a *Gymnasium* in Königsberg, the hometown of Immanuel Kant. He moved to Berlin with his family in 1901, and then attended university in Berlin, Tübingen, and Halle. He earned two doctoral degrees—the first in philosophy (1910), with a dissertation on the concept of the history of religions in Friedrich Schelling's philosophy; the second in theology (1911), with a dissertation on the place of mysticism and guilt consciousness in Schelling's philosophy. A year later he was ordained a minister in the *Evangelischen Kirche*, and was called to a church in a working-class neighborhood of Berlin, which he served for two years.

In September of 1914, he got married, and within a month, with the outbreak of World War I, he volunteered for military duty and found himself at the western front as an army chaplain. He served for the duration of the war, more than four years, most of it at the front lines, in the trenches and under fire. He counseled officers and foot soldiers, hauled the wounded to field hospitals, did what he could to bolster morale, preached and held worship services, comforted the wounded and dying, dug graves, officiated at burials,

suffered several breakdowns, read Nietzsche, Marx, and Freud, and grew disillusioned with the liberal theology in which he had been trained, and with traditional notions of a personal God who attended to our collective and individual lives. He returned to Berlin after the war, to a broken marriage and divorce.

His experiences of class injustices during the war had drawn him toward socialism, and in Berlin he fell in with a like-minded group of intellectuals, many of them Jewish, who identified themselves as the "*kairos* circle"—so named by Tillich, from the New Testament word *kairos*, which describes a moment when the eternal breaks into and shakes up the ordinary flow of time. Like many other Germans after the war, they were disillusioned with the Kaiser, capitalism, the class system, bourgeois satisfactions, and the established church—each of which had colluded in the misguided and humiliating war. In place of the old order they contemplated a "religious socialism" that offered correctives from the biblical prophetic witness to the Bolshevik movements that were erupting across Germany and Russia. They were particularly astute at warning of the dangers of a naïve utopianism that tainted socialism with a demand for justice so uncompromising that its adherents would inevitably succumb to disappointment, and then to either violence or passivity.

It was in the company of this circle of friends that Tillich, through the early 1920s, was awakened to the

The Student's Companion to the Theologians, First Edition. Edited by Ian S. Markham.
© 2013 Blackwell Publishing Ltd. Published 2013 by Blackwell Publishing Ltd.

power of visual arts, and particularly Expressionism, as well as the avant-garde poetry, theater, and café culture that flourished during the Weimar period. To make ends meet, he taught as a *Privatdozent* at the University of Berlin and wrote articles for various journals. In 1924, he married Hannah Werner, an artist, and soon afterward accepted an invitation to join the faculty at the University of Marburg, indeed to fill the position of the newly retired Rudolf Otto, with whom Tillich developed a friendship, and alongside Rudolf Bultmann and Martin Heidegger, who had themselves only recently begun teaching at Marburg. It was during the brief time he was there—three semesters—that he prepared for publication his first popular book, *The Religious Situation*, which became a success across Germany, and was the book by which Tillich was introduced to the English-speaking world when it was published in New York (in 1932), translated by H. Richard Niebuhr, who also wrote the preface.

In 1925, Tillich was lured to the Dresden Institute of Technology, which was in the process of establishing a humanities department; he was offered a full professorship in religious studies. Four years later he moved to Frankfurt, appointed to a university chair in philosophy and sociology that had just been opened by the premature death of Max Scheler. It was in this role that Tillich taught and developed many of his ideas about social ethics, the meaning of history, and political theory. He taught at Frankfurt for four years, during which time he supervised the dissertation of Theodor Adorno, and was instrumental, with Adorno, Max Horkheimer, and Leo Lowenthal, in establishing the Frankfurt Institute for Social Research in 1930—the birthplace of what has come to be known as the "Frankfurt School," or "Critical Theory."

In connection with this circle of friends, Tillich grew increasingly politically involved, resisting the rising tide of National Socialism. He helped launch a popular magazine that promoted the alternative politics of the Social Democratic Party and wrote an animated anti-Nazi tract, *The Socialist Decision* (which was immediately banned). In 1932, following orchestrated, violent attacks on left-wing and Jewish students by Nazi students and storm troopers at the university, Tillich spoke publicly in defense of the students who had been attacked, and called for the expulsion of the Nazi students. Several months later, Hitler seized total

control of the government, brownshirts occupied the university, and Tillich's name appeared in the newspaper on a list of enemies of the state. He was suspended from the faculty, and by the fall of 1933, at the urging of his wife and friends and with an offer of a small salary and lodgings from Union Theological Seminary in New York, Tillich left Germany and emigrated with his family to the United States, where he would remain for the rest of his life. To cover his salary for the first year, and recognizing the danger he was in, every member of the Union faculty voluntarily surrendered five percent of his own salary.

His early years in New York were spent learning English, adjusting to seminary culture in the States, developing friendships with his Union colleagues—Reinhold Niebuhr, in particular—and organizing other recently arrived German refugees into a network of social support for each other and those who followed them—most of them professionals, many of them Jews, who had lost much in their passage. Tillich served as chairman of this group for 15 years, scaring up jobs and apartments, twisting the arms of college admissions officers, and consoling those who were haunted by what they had left behind. Among the refugees were friends of Tillich's from the original *kairos* circle in Berlin and the principal members of the Frankfurt School. He became a US citizen in 1940, and, after the United States entered World War II, Tillich secretly contracted with the Voice of America to write radio addresses that were broadcast into Germany, appealing to his homeland, and particularly to Christians there, to face the anti-Semitism and atrocities which were occurring around them and to resist the Nazi regime.

With the end of the war, Tillich's reputation in America accelerated. Having taught at Union for 15 years, many of his former students were scattered across the country in academic and ecclesial positions and carried his influence with them. Between 1948 and 1952 he published *The Protestant Era*, *The Shaking of the Foundations*, the first volume of *Systematic Theology*, and *The Courage to Be*. *The Courage to Be* became a bestseller, tuning in as it did to a mood among many in America who were ready to hear the angst that arose from what had been witnessed during the years of war articulated and analyzed with consummate skill. With this book, Tillich introduced many in the

United States to religious existentialism. It was his installment on the genre of "speeches to the cultured despisers of religion" that had been invented by Friedrich Schleiermacher 150 years earlier.

In 1955, Tillich retired from Union and accepted an invitation to become a distinguished University Professor at Harvard, where he taught for seven years, following which he was appointed to a chair at the Divinity School at the University of Chicago, where he taught until his death in 1965. During this final decade he completed the second two volumes of his *Systematic Theology*, traveled and lectured extensively, and became a widely regarded public figure. He is recognized today as one of a handful of the most influential Protestant thinkers of the twentieth century.

II.   What Is Theology?

Soon after the end of World War I, in the spring of 1919, Tillich gave a lecture to the Kant Society in Berlin. The lecture, "On the Idea of a Theology of Culture," introduced an approach and themes that were to become a charter for Tillich's work in the years ahead. In it, he distinguished between "theology of the church," which consists of the interpretation of materials found in the overt religious sphere (scriptures, doctrines, church architecture, symbols, and rituals of worship), and "theology of culture," which consists of searching for manifestations of religious "substance" within the other spheres of culture (science, art, morality, politics, economy). For much of his career, he pursued these two theologies independently. His early book, *The Religious Situation*, exemplifies his theology of culture, taking a look at cutting-edge movements in science (Bergsonian vitalism), art (Van Gogh and Munch, Rilke and Stefan George), politics (democratic socialism), and ethics (the emancipation of women and Nietzschean critiques of bourgeois mores). Between the lines of these various revolts, he spies a paradoxical blend of simple, unadorned, sober-eyed acceptance of things as they are together with faith in the transcendent depth of reality that shines through them—what he called "belief-ful realism." Much of Tillich's work has this aim in mind—to discover in places we least expect the rumblings of the

Unconditioned, from which we rightfully derive our passion for life. It is toward this end that Tillich wrote so much about art and architecture, politics and philosophy, music, literature, and nature.

He frequently invoked theology of culture with the formula: "Religion is the substance of culture and culture is the form of religion." Without reference to the ground of being, culture lacks depth and the inexhaustibility of being that it requires to sustain itself. Religion "is the life-blood, the inner power, the ultimate meaning of all life. The 'sacred' or the 'holy' inflames, imbues, inspires, all reality and all aspects of existence" (1957b, 43). But on the other side, organized religion relies upon all forms of cultural expression—such as language, music, art, philosophy, architecture, ritual, ethics, and technology (writing, printing presses, telecommunications). Without these cultural forms, religion "cannot express itself even in a meaningful silence" (1963, 249).

But Tillich was also a "theologian of the church," and held himself accountable to the whole sweep of church theology—the writings of scripture, the church fathers, the medieval scholastics and mystics, the Reformers, Pietists, Schleiermacher, and the streams of religious idealism that flowed through Fichte, Schelling, and Hegel. While it is clear that Tillich first sketched out his systematic theology in lectures he gave while teaching at Marburg in 1924, it is from his fully formed *Systematic Theology*, completed between 1950 and 1963, that we can best understand his distinctive approach to church theology.

For Tillich, Christian theology is necessarily apologetic. It cannot simply proclaim a revelation which it has received. Theology must be a reasoned defense of the credibility of inherited Christian symbols, myths, and doctrines in light of widely held categories of knowledge and experience—categories which evolve over time. A credible apologetic, or "systematic," theology must, according to Tillich, "satisfy two basic needs: the statement of the truth of the Christian message and the interpretation of this truth for every new generation" (1951, 3). The means by which this is best achieved, Tillich proposed, is through the "method of correlation." The theologian's task in its simplest terms is to correlate situation and message. By "situation," Tillich has in mind the present cultural situation, or "the totality of human creative self-interpretation in a particular period" (1951, 4), which the theologian must ascertain by examining the most cogent theories and events in the science, art, ethics, politics, economics, architecture—all realms of culture—that prevail in his or her time. By "message" he has in mind the vast treasury of symbols, myths, institutions, and ideas in which Christianity has embodied its ultimate concern—which is Jesus who has been recognized as the Christ. The message is "contained in the Bible, but it is not identical with the Bible" (1951, 4). The entire scope of biblical and church history constitutes the treasury from which theology can legitimately draw. It is the theologian's task to organize the totality of the human creative self-interpretation of a particular time in relation to the answer given by the Christian message.

Sometimes Tillich described the correlation in terms of "question" and "answer," to indicate that human questions are answered by the Christian message. This has misled some of his critics, who charge that his method of correlation lacks reciprocity between its poles. But Tillich was clear that the method is reciprocal to the extent that in the creative act of interpreting the situation through the inherited symbols, the symbols themselves are reinterpreted, disclosing latent and even new meanings. Thus, in practice, the method of correlation reanimates the symbols and their power to make sense of human existence.

The importance of *system* to Tillich deserves comment. In the minds of many people, the very notion of systematic thinking implies an iron cage, a routinizing of living, graceful forces. Given how disposed Tillich is to speaking of God as the ground and abyss of being, and his unending celebration of ecstatic moments of losing oneself in a state of mind that is beyond reason, it seems ironic that he argued so strenuously for theology that is systematic. But that is precisely what he did. In the opening sentences of the first volume of *Systematic Theology*, he wrote: "It has always been impossible for me to think theologically in any other than a systematic way. The smallest problem, if taken seriously and radically, drove me to all other problems and to the anticipation of a whole in which they could find their solution" (1951, vii). One can hear in these words not only his apologetic thrust, but an existential angst that drove it. With his "belief-ful realism," Tillich was realistic about the fragmentation of human expe-

rience, but trusted that between and beneath the fragments was an encompassing reality that was worth inquiring after. Building a system out of the available materials (situation and message) was the very exercise that allowed him to gain a more intimate knowledge of the meaning and limits of finitude, creating the conditions that allowed him to peer beyond, through its gaps and doorways, and lay eyes on the infinite.

Furthermore, the fact that his systematic inclinations led him to adopt the method of correlation put him in good Reformed company. As Tillich points out, John Calvin launched his *Institutes* with the claim that all sound wisdom consists of two parts: the knowledge of God and the knowledge of ourselves. One knowledge cannot be had without the other. In Calvin's estimation, which is not far from Tillich's, the experience of human misery gives us the existential basis for our understanding of God's glory (1951, 63).

How does a theologian sort, systematically, through the contents of the Christian faith in order to determine how its message answers the quandaries of human existence? Tillich offers a very disciplined response, reflecting first on the disposition of the theologian to the object that is being investigated, then on the sources, medium, and norm from and through which the contents of the faith are determined.

The theologian must have everything at stake in the act of doing theology. Theology is not a detached science. The one engaged in it must inhabit what Tillich calls "the theological circle," by which he means having faith in the unconditioned reality into which one is inquiring, and having a stake in the life of the church—its symbols, traditions, and activities. The reality of God, the absolute object of the inquiry, must be an existential matter of being or not being for the theologian; it must be his or her "ultimate concern." An ultimate concern is the axis around which one's life rotates; it is the source from which all of one's other cares and concerns derive their meaning and relative value. Without this *disposition* toward God, the inquirer may be investigating similar metaphysical realities, but as a philosopher, not as a theologian.

The *sources* that theology relies upon for its knowledge of God are the Bible and the Christian tradition. The Bible is primary because "it contains the original witness of those who participated in the revealing events" (1951, 35). The Christian tradition picks up where the Bible left off, serving as a record of the continuing reception of the revelation to which scripture first attests, and knowledge of this history rightfully serves as a source to guide our understanding of what we read in the Bible.

The *medium* through which we receive the contents of faith is experience. Experience is *not* an independently productive source of the Christian message; it is the medium through which the sources of the scriptural witness and church history are apprehended, interpreted, and presented in a transformed way by the theologian. The contribution of experience is thus derivative. But as the medium, the influence of experience on the theology that is presented is enormous. Experience conditions what is made of the sources as each new tier of the tradition is laid down to become the record of revelation's continuing reception for the next generation.

Finally, the *norm* of theology for Tillich is Jesus as the Christ. But because what it means to identify Jesus as the Christ has not been a stable designation over the centuries, the exact meaning of this norm has evolved. In the early church, in Tillich's estimation, to speak of Jesus as the Christ was to stress the power of resurrection that Jesus initiated, and resurrection of the dead was the central norm of theology. In the medieval and Reformation era, that Jesus was the Christ meant atonement for sinners and reconciliation with God, which, in turn, became the norm for measuring the truthfulness of theological claims. During the Enlightenment, that Jesus was the Christ meant that he was a complete, autonomous, and exemplary human being, and the credibility of any theological claim was found in the extent to which it fostered the development of a similar personality among those who claimed it. In the twentieth century, the norm, according to Tillich, is that in Jesus as the Christ the New Being has been manifest. The gold standard for theological sources, experiences, and claims, then, is the extent to which they recognize that in spite of our estrangement from God and our alienation from each other and from nature, a new era has entered history, ushering in processes by which all that is separated will move toward reunion.

III.   Revelation

For Tillich, revelation is the answer to the question of reason. Reason, in its barest terms, is the process by which knowing subjects are united to knowable objects in both active and passive ways. The human consciousness is equipped with mechanisms and filters for apprehending the world around itself, and this world and everything within it is constituted by certain structures that can be both apprehended and transformed by knowing subjects who act upon it. But this union of subject and object is always incomplete, and there is a depth of being, what Kant had called the noumena, that remains out of reach. It remains out of reach, but persists in beckoning the subject to know it in its fullness. This unclosable gap between the desire of the subject to know and the unreachable depth of being of the object is evidence of our estrangement from the world around us. The impasse we reach with every frustrated effort to know the other in its fullness is what compels and disposes us to be receptive to revelation.

Having framed the "question" in this way, Tillich defines revelation as mystery, ecstasy, and miracle. It is *mystery* in the sense that it reveals, or unveils, some of the hiddenness of being that our ordinary powers of reason could not. It is *ecstasy* in that revelation occurs as an event of "numinous astonishment" in which the normal subject–object structure of experience is momentarily transcended, and one's consciousness is overwhelmed by "ontic shock," or, put differently, by the Holy, which is simultaneously terrifying and fascinating. Revelation is a *miracle* in the way that when it occurs, something is given to us that we could not have acquired through the exercise of the normal processes of reason, and one's own consciousness and the depth of reality are knitted together in a new and unforgettable manner. Tillich describes this miracle as a "sign-event," in the sense that when revelation occurs the mystery of being has been pointed to in some tangible, shareable way.

The quintessential miracle in Christian theology is Jesus who is the Christ, the word made flesh, a sign-event given through sheer grace. While Tillich offers the sacramental assurance that "there is no reality, thing, or event which cannot become the bearer of the mystery of being," and delineates how the natural world, human history and personalities, and the lowly word—human language—have been vehicles of revelation, he maintains that Jesus as the Christ must serve as the criterion by which the validity of what is revealed in these other things is determined. To this end, he refers to Christ as the "original revelation," and the history of the church and its proclamation, along with these other bearers of revelation, as "dependent revelation." Dependent mediums of revelation have no inherent revelatory power; their capacity to reveal is participatory and derivative—effective to the extent that it draws upon and enlarges what happened in the miracle of the Christ-event.

One of Tillich's most influential contributions to our understanding of revelation has been his account of the language of revelation, and particularly the religious symbol. Over time, he attributed these characteristics to religious symbols:

1. The material of religious symbols is borrowed from finite reality, e.g., natural phenomena, words, a historical figure or event, the plot of a story, etc.
2. Like signs, religious symbols point beyond themselves.
3. They participate in that to which they point.
4. They open up levels of reality otherwise closed to us.
5. They disclose dimensions of the human spirit otherwise hidden.
6. They cannot be intentionally contrived, but must emerge spontaneously.
7. Like living beings, they mature and die.
8. They have both integrating and disintegrating powers.

IV.   Doctrine of God

It is the question of the finitude of being to which the doctrine of God is the answer. After completing an existentialist-informed analysis of human finitude and the ontological structures of being, Tillich speculates what this implies about God, who is the ground of being. To understand his doctrine of God, then, it is necessary to begin with Tillich's analysis of human

finitude. As finite beings, we humans are conscious of being suspended along three polarities, which involve us in certain disruptive anxieties.

First, we are suspended between *individualization and participation*. We are created as individual beings, and, furthermore, estranged as individuals as a consequence of the Fall. But it is only through participating in community with others that we can become "centered and complete selves." It is in receiving training and affirmation from others, as well as in resisting others, that we become individuated persons. With this necessity of participation, however, we run the risk of being subsumed in the collective.

Second, we spend our lives attempting to balance *dynamics and form*. Dynamism is the unformed power and potentiality of what we might become; form is the structure that gives shape to this potentiality, requiring it to express itself in this way and not in other ways. With too much form, the vitality of dynamism is diminished and our creative capacities trail off. But with too little form, potentiality remains just that—unrealized capacity that never becomes anything.

Third, we exist in a tension between *freedom and destiny*. Destiny is the term that covers all the givenness of life—one's natural endowments, cultural matrix, and moment in history. Freedom has to do with the ability to transcend the given. What is given through destiny is actually the basis of our freedom—without genes, gender, mother tongue, cultural parameters, and historical circumstances, there is no person to commit a free act. But without freedom, all is determined and destiny smothers its makers.

These three polarities characterize all beings. They constitute what Tillich calls the ontological structures of being. Within each polarity, being defies non-being—being asserts itself to rise out of non-being and resists dissolving back into non-being. There is both a struggle and an interdependency between being and non-being in the realm of finite beings. Tillich uses this paradox as the aporia out of which to reflect on the doctrine of God.

God, he explains, is being-itself. This means that God is not a being, but the ground of being, the power inherent in everything, the power of being whereby being resists non-being. It is for this reason that Tillich famously said that God does not exist. To exist is to be subject to the categories of finitude (space, time, causality, and substance). To imagine God as subject to these categories, even to do so in superlative terms, e.g., to say that God is the "highest being"—the most perfect or the most powerful—is a denial of God, who is infinite (*not*-finite) and unconditioned (not dependent upon the realm of causality).

Tillich distinguishes within his conception of God as the ground of being the features of God as "abyss" and "Logos." As abyss, God is the inexhaustible well out of which all of being flows; as Logos, God is the order and structure which this undifferentiated being adopts in order to make distinctions and meaning possible. This parsing of the ground of being into abyss and Logos is how Tillich distinguishes the Father and Son in his treatment of the Trinity.

"There is," Tillich claims in very Kierkegaardian fashion, "no proportion or gradation between the finite and the infinite. There is an absolute break, an infinite 'jump.' On the other hand," he continues as an heir to both St Thomas and Schleiermacher, "everything finite participates in being–itself and in its infinity. Otherwise it would not have the power of being" (1951, 237).

It is on the basis of this last assertion—namely, everything finite participates in being–itself—that Tillich determines it is possible to speak about God. While it is true that God does not exist, this is not a denial, Tillich insists, of the "actuality" or "reality" of God. God is being–itself, the very power of being, and we humans, who exist and thereby participate in being, can make use of the Thomistic tool of the *analogia entis* by first reflecting on our own beingness, on the structure and dynamism of our finitude, and use this to point toward God who is the ground of this structure. We can, in other words, reflect on what is required for us to be (in an ontological sense) and reach certain conclusions about God who has supplied what was required. This means, as with Schleiermacher, that theology is reflection upon our sense of absolute dependence. Its most refined and dogmatic claims are descriptions of qualities of our relation to God, and not direct assertions about divine aseity. Therefore, to say that "God is good" is to say that God is the ground of all finite good; to say that "God is living" is to say that God is the ground of life; etc.

After all of his warnings about how improper it is to speak of God as a being, then, Tillich concedes that using symbols drawn from our experience as beings does guide us to speak about the ground of being in instructive ways, in ways that attune us to the reality of God. With this he undertakes an inventory of God's attributes under three headings—God as living, creating, and related.

As *living*, God can be spoken of as containing the three polarities of being. With respect to the *polarity of individualization and participation*, God is transcendent and immanent, transcending everything yet "participating in every life as its ground and aim" (1951, 245). Regarding the *polarity of dynamics and form*, in God we find that sheer power is bound to goodness, that God is an active going out (into creation, into incarnation, into history) and a returning to (God will remain God, constant to God's own purposes). In terms of the *polarity of freedom and destiny*, God is free but not arbitrary. From this polarity we derive an appreciation for how God conforms to what has been set in motion, to the contingencies in creation which themselves evolve over time. These become the conditions (destiny) to which God freely submits God's freedom.

As *creating*, God originates, sustains, and directs creation. This is Tillich's way of retrieving the wisdom of traditional doctrines of creation, preservation, and providence. Indeed, the biblical account of creation *ex nihilo* is at the heart of Tillich's ontology, securing in Christian theology the reminder that to be a creature is to have been snatched out of non-being and to bear that "heritage" and be haunted by it. This helps us to make some sense of the ever-threatening, existential shock of non-being. In sustaining creation, God is the ground of being both in "giving the power of being to everything that has being," and in ensuring the continuity of the structures of reality, "the regular and calculable in things" (1951, 262). And by affirming that God directs creation we learn something of God's love, which is manifest in the assurance that creation has purpose and *telos*—which, ultimately, is for all things to be reunited with God.

Under the heading of God as *related*, Tillich reflects on many of the remaining traditional attributes of God that have to do with ways that humans sense the bearing of God upon our lives—divine holiness, majesty and glory, omnipotence, omnipresence, omniscience and eternality, love, justice, wrath, grace, lord, and father—and how each of these might be best understood.

V.   Anthropology

Tillich conceptualizes the human condition as a movement from essence to existence. The human being is *essentially* "finite freedom"—a being with enormous potentiality that is limited only by the categories of finitude (space, time, causality, and substance). All beings are limited by the categories, but only humans are aware it—and this rises in the consciousness as anxiety. Anxiety is the awareness that these limits imply non-being, that we are hedged about by non-being, and that any move we make out of our potentiality into actuality is a tragic choice, i.e., a choice that in actualizing one possibility cuts off the myriad unchosen possibilities and expels them to non-being.

The other feature of essential humanity is that we live suspended along the three ontological polarities (individualization and participation, dynamics and form, freedom and destiny). To live in these three polarities without any distortions which favor or err in either direction is what it means to be essentially human. Living perfectly suspended midway on each polarity is what constitutes the healthy structure of the human being in its finite freedom.

But there are no essential human beings. The human condition is to move from this essential state into existence, from potentiality to actuality, to make the tragic choice, to succumb to the anxieties which estrange us from our essential selves and from the ground of being (God). This is how Tillich understands the Fall of Adam and Eve, who succumbed to the temptations of the serpent to deny their finitude ("You shall be as gods"), and made the tragic choice to leave behind the "dreaming innocence" and state of non-actualized potentiality that constituted life in the garden. In their act of disobedience to God, they made the irreversible choice to actualize their freedom by selecting some of their potentialities and rejecting others, and in so doing became selves. This was simultaneously an achievement and a tragic loss—the choice to become a self was at the same time a choice to lose intimate communion with God, which is what occurred in their expulsion from the garden. In order to become selves and to enter history, which is the realm of tragic and irreversible choices, Adam and Eve had to choose to be estranged from God—the source and meaning of their lives.

This transition from essence to existence is what is meant by the doctrine of original sin. It is also what it means to be human. The myth of the Fall tells us what every human being has undergone—as both the milieu into which we've been born (original sin as a universal fact) and the freely made decisions of every self for which we bear personal guilt (sin as an individual act). We have all willed possibilities that have made us who we are but at the same time have alienated us from the ground of our being. This haunts us because we cannot forget that we belong to God, and that in our estrangement from the ground of being and from our essential selves we risk the eventual dissolution of the essential structures of our own being. And this points toward the culminating paradox of the human condition: While estrangement has the power to destroy us, both the possibility of becoming a self *and* the conditions necessary for us to freely return God's love—not as dreaming innocents but as selves who can choose to do otherwise—require it. Returning God's love is the opposite of estrangement; it rolls back estrangement and is precisely the possibility that has been initiated into the world through the New Being of Jesus as the Christ.

VI.   Christology

For Tillich, the appearance of Jesus as the Christ inaugurated a new eon for humanity, indeed, for the cosmos. He is very Pauline in his christology—"So if anyone is in Christ, there is a new creation: everything old has passed away; see, everything has become new!" (2 Cor. 5:17). In our estrangement, creation was succumbing to the threat of non-being. The cross and resurrection restored the ontological integrity of reality, reversing its disintegration, inaugurating a new state of things. Thus the Christ is the inaugural event of New Being.

Initially the disciples, when Jesus was still among them, came to believe that he was "the Christ," the one who would bring about a new state of things. As Tillich describes it, "Christianity was born not with Jesus, but in the moment in which one of his followers was driven to say of him, 'Thou art the Christ' " (1957a, 97). When he went to his death on the cross, this expectation was crushed. But instead of abandoning their hopes, the disciples' horizon was opened up and they came to recognize the cosmic significance of the revelation of which Jesus was the bearer. This is the meaning, Tillich claims, of the resurrection. In the resurrection, Jesus, who had just come to a miserable end on the cross, is restored to the dignity of the Christ in their understanding, and the range of his power to effect a transformation of the cosmos is expanded far beyond the hopes they had nurtured during his ministry among them. Tillich calls this the "restitution theory" of the resurrection, to distinguish it from physical, spiritual, and psychological theories.

In the "essential God-manhood" of Jesus as the Christ, which is Tillich's reinterpretation of the doctrine of the incarnation, Tillich held that the New Being manifest in Jesus testified to a reunion of being with God, a reconciliation of being with the ground of being that was already underway. In Jesus, "essential manhood has appeared under the conditions of existence without being conquered by them" (1957a, 94). That it had happened in an individual human life was key. The redemptive work of God had manifested itself in this one personal life such that Jesus, who was not "a divine-human automaton," but shared our finite freedom and experienced "serious temptation, real struggle, and tragic involvement in the ambiguities of life" (1957a, 135), did not succumb to the offer of divine knowledge and power, but refused them if it meant having them without God (Tillich compares Adam's compliance to the serpent with Jesus' defiance of the devil in the wilderness). In Jesus there was no estrangement, but only undistorted "unity with God." To borrow Schleiermacher's expression, in Jesus we behold a continuous, unimpeded God-consciousness.

This union with God stood up to its acid test on the cross. As hopes were lodged in Jesus by the disciples and by widening circles of followers, Jesus, Tillich points out, turned his face toward Jerusalem—toward his arrest and execution. This was a scandal to those who were coming to believe in him and expecting him to triumph over their oppressors, but it was a necessary turn of events if he was to be an effective bearer of the New Being. Jesus of Nazareth had to be sacrificed for the sake of Jesus as the Christ. The particular in this one man was crucified in order to maintain his transparency to the mystery he came to reveal. For Tillich, the cross is the quintessential symbol intended to train the Christians to stop short of absolutizing any reality that is less than God. This is what makes the cross the greatest treasure among all Christian symbols.

The cross was the necessary prelude to the resurrection, which is the event that confirms that the New Being that appeared in Jesus had not been conquered by the conditions of existence. It is this completed picture of Jesus as the Christ, crucified and resurrected, that awakens in his followers and in subsequent generations the faith that God is love and has not left the created world to its own devices. The salvation that enters the world through Christ as the New Being is the message that God is reuniting that which is estranged.

VII. Spirit

For Tillich, the "Spirit of God" is the symbol for the presence of the divine life within creaturely life, the symbol for what theology calls divine immanence. When he turns to this topic in the *Systematic Theology*, he first gives an account of the ways in which human beings negotiate their lives along the three polarities, and how, in the end, even the most agile attempts to do so arrive at certain ambiguities. It is in the midst of our struggles to overcome these ambiguities that the theological symbol of the Spirit of God offers answers.

We attempt to negotiate the polarity of *individualization and participation* through the activity of self-integration, striving for centeredness between the two poles. This is done in a circular fashion: "Every living being is … a process of going out and returning to itself as long as it lives. It takes in elements of the encountered reality and assimilates them to its own centered whole, or it rejects them if assimilation is impossible" (1963, 35). If this ceases to happen—either because the self refuses to venture out from its center (in which case one is never changed or enlarged), or because the self ventures out in so many directions that it loses its way back (in which case one forfeits an identity)—the self disintegrates. Completing the circle, venturing out and returning to reintegrate the self, is a moral act. The ambiguity in this process is that while one must venture out, every venturing out risks that the self who returns may be a betrayal of the self who initially set out, and that is unavoidable.

The polarity of *dynamics and form* is negotiated in the experience of self-creativity. Through the use of language and tools, humans are constantly drawing newly encountered forces into order and under their control. This is a creative expansion of the human world that we call culture. The ambiguity here is that our forms can never fully do justice to the powers of life that we encounter. We cannot live in chaos, and therefore language and technology are indispensable in the necessary task of extending the range of human order. But it is inescapable that, in the process, realities with their own integrity will be transformed or distorted into things which are granted only utilitarian value.

Negotiating the polarity of *freedom and destiny* involves the experience of self-transcendence. Here we are always pressing against the limits of finitude, testing their resistance and givenness, aspiring to push them out and make more room for the exercise of freedom. This is the life process that gives rise to religion. Through it, we are constantly renegotiating the realms of the profane and the sacred by reaching out beyond our small and familiar precincts to mysteries beyond, inviting them into our world. The ambiguity here is that while religion is the unsurpassable expression of our efforts to be in relation to the sacred, religion is also the most effective way to profanize the sacred, to diminish it within religious words, images, and rituals, to bring the sacred under our thumbs.

The ambiguities reached through each of these human activities (morality, culture, and religion) make us receptive, Tillich argues, to manifestations of the Spiritual Presence of God. The distortions that inevitably occur as we try to proceed with life under the gravitational pull of the polarities suggest to us that we cannot negotiate them effectively relying entirely on our own devices (autonomy), nor by acquiescing without a struggle to solutions those in authority impose upon us (heteronomy). To achieve the balance necessary to live in response to the polarities, we do well to recognize that every struggle to be a self or to generate and maintain vital moral, cultural, and religious institutions is driven by ultimate concern. Some ultimate concerns are less than ultimate, and will consequently become destructive. As we engage in each of these activities it is important to be guided by an ultimate concern that is genuinely ultimate—the unconditional, holy ground of being, which is not a strange source and measure, nor of our own making, but the innermost law of our being. This is what Tillich called "theonomy"; those cultural creations that direct attention to the depth that inspired and sustains them are theonomous, and derive purpose from their participation in the Spiritual Presence.

VIII. Church

Tillich offered two particularly trenchant contributions to how we can think about the institutional church. The first is his pairing up of the terms "Protestant principle" and "Catholic substance," primarily as a way to reflect on the sacraments, but also more generally as a way to think about the church as a bearer of the sacred. The Protestant insight has been to invoke the prophetic veto of graven images as a reminder that sacraments and other religious symbols must point beyond themselves to divine realities, and that if they lose their transparency, we will idolatrously confuse God with creaturely realities. But Tillich was equally adamant that while the holy is present everywhere as the ground of being, we are most effectively trained to see it when we are reminded to look for it in special places and materials and rituals. These two insights are mutually corrective, he claimed, and ought to be upheld by both Protestants and Catholics.

The second contribution is his revision Augustine's distinction between the invisible and visible churches. Tillich preferred the terms "latent and manifest spiritual communities," in order to capture his experience, following World War I, of how Berliners, disillusioned with a state church that had over-identified with the German war aims, began associating outside the church in a variety of communities. He cites "youth alliances, friendship groups, educational, artistic, and political movements" (1963, 153)—what we would today call voluntary associations or cells of civil society—as illustrations of the latent spiritual community. Having participated in some of these, he vouched for "how much latent Church there is in them," given that within them he had experienced firsthand "the quest for the eternal and the unconditioned, and absolute devotion to justice and love; a hope which is more than any Utopia; an appreciation of Christian values; and a most delicate apprehension of the ideological misuse of Christianity in the Church and State" (1936, 48).

And, although he commented in 1931 that "it often seemed to me as if the latent Church, which I found in these groups, were a truer church than the organized Churches" (1936, 48), after further reflection and given his subsequent experience of how some of these groups succumbed willingly to Nazism, he concluded many years later that while genuine faith and love were present in these communities, they finally lacked something necessary that is found within the manifest church. What they lacked was the "ultimate criterion" of the Christ who goes to the cross so as not to block the vision of the faithful who strain to see God *through* him; the criterion, that is, of the necessary self-negation of all true religious symbols (1963, 154). Because these latent church communities lacked this self-negating principle, they did not, in the end, resist absolutizing the goods that originally brought them together.

IX.   Reception and Influence

Tillich stands as one of the most influential theologians of the twentieth century, and one can expect his influence to continue. Many of his books remain in print and much of the vocabulary he invented or refined (ultimate concern, religious symbols, the ground and abyss of being, the demonic, God beyond God, *kairos*) permeates the fields of theological and religious studies and beyond.

He had critics during his lifetime, pre-eminently Karl Barth. Barth was suspicious of any attempt at apologetic theology, and bristled at the notion of a correlation between our questions and God's answers. For Barth, theology must remind us that God is the one who questions us. The two also had a long public debate over natural theology, and while neither of them agreed that natural theology was possible, Tillich insisted that human beings do have a "point of contact" within the structure of their consciousness that is receptive to God, while Barth rejected this, insisting that the very idea of it denies the ugly ditch between the finite and the infinite, and that, instead, our ability to hear the Word of God is entirely dependent upon the divine initiative in any given moment,

and not on some capacity of which we are in possession. The post-liberal heirs of Barth (e.g., George Lindbeck, Stanley Hauerwas, William Placher) have sustained this suspicion. Hauerwas once described Tillich's theology of culture as "hard to distinguish from journalism." It must be said that Tillich has had a strong if ambivalent effect on many who have read him. Many find that he invites them into a world charged with religious electricity, in which the Unconditioned hums beneath every surface; others experience his writings as a transit station on the way to losing faith—at first excited by the prospect of the God beyond God, but then concluding that there's not much of a community there, and little tangible guidance about how to live.

But Tillich's positive reception and continuing influence is best understood by considering two trajectories that have their point of origin in his thought.

Theology of culture

Tillich's student, Langdon Gilkey, was the most adept theologian of culture to follow Tillich, capable of discerning the religious substance operating below the surface of multiple cultural forms (science, art, the professions, nature, politics), but others have carried this analysis on in specific fields, such as literature (Nathan Scott, Robert Detweiler, Ralph Wood), art (John and Jane Dillenberger, Margaret Miles), political economy (Max Stackhouse, Ronald Stone, Robert H. Nelson, Robert Bellah), music (Martha Bayles, Jon Michael Spencer), and popular culture (David Jasper, Catherine Albanese, Clive Marsh, Kelton Cobb, Gordon Lynch).

Method of correlation

Tillich, of course, claimed that theologians had been using this method since the church fathers, and that he was just drawing attention to it, giving it a more disciplined shape. Theologians who have since incorporated the method into their own work, conscientiously following Tillich, include David Tracy, Karl Rahner, John Macquarrie, and Peter Hodgson. Less obvious is the role Tillich has played in the emergence of identity theologies—black theology, feminist theology, Latin American liberation theology, minjung theology, womanist theology, mujerista theology.

These are fundamentally correlation theologies, making the experience of a particular community the constitutive element in determining how traditional doctrines are constructively re-examined. And while Tillich will often come under fire in these treatments as representative of the male-dominated, eurocentric theology that must be dismantled, his method and many of his central ideas (ecstatic revelation, God as Being-Itself, the operation of religious symbols, the New Being, the demonic, the courage to be) are heavily pilfered. His contribution to the study of theology is so wide, it seems, that nearly half a century after his last book was finished, you can't get around it, and so deep, you can't get under it.

References

Tillich, Paul. [1919] 1969. "On the Idea of a Theology of Culture." In *What Is Religion?* trans. James L. Adams. New York: Harper & Row.

Tillich, Paul. [1926] 1932, 1956. *The Religious Situation*, trans. H. Richard Niebuhr. New York: Meridian Books.

Tillich, Paul. [1932] 1977. *The Socialist Decision*, trans. Franklin Sherman. New York: Harper & Row.

Tillich, Paul. 1936. *The Interpretation of History*. New York: Charles Scribner's Sons.

Tillich, Paul. 1948. *The Shaking of the Foundations*. New York: Charles Scribner's Sons.

Tillich, Paul. 1951. *Systematic Theology*. Vol. I. Chicago: University of Chicago Press.

Tillich, Paul. 1957a. *Systematic Theology*. Vol. II. Chicago: University of Chicago Press.

Tillich, Paul. 1957b. *The Protestant Era*. Chicago: University of Chicago Press.

Tillich, Paul. 1963. *Systematic Theology*. Vol. III. Chicago: University of Chicago Press.

Tillich, Paul. 1998. *Against the Third Reich: Paul Tillich's Wartime Radio Broadcasts into Nazi Germany*, ed. Ronald H. Stone and Matthew Lon Weaver. Louisville, KY: Westminster John Knox Press.

B. B. Warfield (1851–1921)

Ian S. Markham

A key influence on reformed Presbyterian theology in the United States was Benjamin B. Warfield. Warfield is also indicative of the dramatic influence that Princeton Theological Seminary had on American theology. Mark Noll writes of Warfield that "at the end of the nineteenth and the beginning of the twentieth centuries, Benjamin Brekinridge Warfield was the most widely known American advocate of confessional Calvinism" (Noll in Elwell, 1993, 26). At a time of dramatic change, Warfield sought to defend the key classical themes of reformed theology, for example, the inerrancy of scripture and the sinfulness of humanity.

I. Life

Warfield was born in 1851 near Lexington in Kentucky. On his mother's side, there was a strong Presbyterian commitment; his grandfather, for example, was a Presbyterian preacher. On his father's side, there was a solid Puritan influence. William Warfield was part of the Puritan migration to avoid English persecution.

Warfield was educated at the College of New Jersey (which later became Princeton University). This was the start of a connection that would endure throughout his life. He returned to Princeton for Seminary in 1873, where he was heavily influenced by Charles Hodge; he graduated and married Annie Kinkead in 1876. His postgraduate studies were in Germany.

Here he worked with Ernst Luthardt (1823–1902) and Franz Delitzsch (1813–90).

In 1879, he was ordained into the Presbyterian Church. Although he did some supply work in congregation and served briefly as an assistant pastor, he discovered his passion as a professor at the Western Theological Seminary (which is now known as Pittsburg Theological Seminary). His position was in New Testament Language and Literature. It was here that he developed his reputation as a great instructor and formidable intellect.

Therefore it was not surprising that he moved back to Princeton Seminary in 1887. He took the Charles Hodge Chair of Exegetical, Didactic, and Polemic Theology. He stayed in Princeton for the rest of his life.

II. Theology

Warfield is deeply admired for his capacity to resist the liberal trends in the academy. For Warfield, the core Christian commitments are essential. In this respect, he was typical of the Princeton of this period. He combined his core commitment with a capacity to be shaped by contemporary philosophy and accommodate certain scientific discoveries. On philosophy, he appreciated the work of Thomas Reid and identified with the "common sense" school. On science, he believed that Darwinian evolution could be accommodated.

The Student's Companion to the Theologians, First Edition. Edited by Ian S. Markham.
© 2013 Blackwell Publishing Ltd. Published 2013 by Blackwell Publishing Ltd.

Working within these parameters, the key themes of his theology were a robust articulation and defense of inerrancy and classical reformed systematics. On inerrancy, he insisted that this was the historic position of the Christian church. Warfield's significance was that he formulated a careful response to modern views of scripture. This was not simply a repetition of older views, but a carefully formulated precise rearticulation, which took into account the new debates and arguments. So, for example, he outlines the power of the Bible in its use—a text that in the end had to be printed, translated, and read—and a book that can bind diverse cultures around the world. So Warfield writes:

> We approach here the greatest achievement of the Bible as the people's book. Because it is pre-eminently the book of the people, it is the greatest unifying force in the world, binding all the peoples together as the people of the book. Consider how the Bible, as it becomes the book of people after people, assimilates the peoples to one another in modes of expression, thought, conception, feeling, until they are virtually moulded into one people, of common mind and heart. The Bible comes to a new people; this alien book—how alien it is to those who first come to know it!—is first received, then assimilated, and in the end, having become its heart's treasure, assimilates it to itself. (Warfield, 1970, 20)

This is typical Warfield. He brings together an anthropological and cultural argument for scripture, which makes his writing very distinctive.

His most sustained writing on inerrancy occurs when the Presbyterian Church wanted to revise the Westminster Confession during the period 1889 to 1894. He confronts his opponents directly: the phrase "Scripture says," he argues, is intended to mean "God says"; inspiration is not dictation, but *concursus* ("a joint product of divine and human activities, both of which penetrate them at every point"; Warfield, 1929, 547); and the lack of the original autographs does not make inerrancy incoherent.

In systematics, he was a careful exegete of the Bible. He was the main opponent of dispensationalism as it swept America. The theology of John Nelson Darby and C. I. Schofield was packed full of "faulty exegesis, questionable theological construction, and errors on the work of the Holy Spirit" (Noll in Elwell, 1993,

32). Warfield, in contrast, read the text of scripture with enormous care.

On evolution, he was a pioneer in seeing that it was compatible with biblical inerrancy. In fact, Warfield believed a Calvinist account of creation could help accommodate evolution. He argued that God built into the creation the mechanisms that would enable humanity to emerge and guided the process by God's providence. In this respect, it would be very misguided to characterize Warfield as a fundamentalist.

Warfield's theology was not grounded in experience (unlike his teacher Charles Hodge); for Warfield there were real reasons for faith and therefore there was an apologetic emphasis to his work. Right reason, argued Warfield, should be able to discern the truth of Christianity, which is the "one revealed religion" (Warfield, 1927, 23).

Warfield time and time again returns to Calvin. He marvels at Calvin's achievement. It was Calvin's use of the Bible that Warfield so admired. Warfield writes: "Calvin introduced a new exegesis—the modern exegesis; and he is justly called, therefore, as Diestel, for example calls him, 'the creator of genuine exegesis.' Accordingly, his commentaries alone, of those of his age, remain in use today, and continue to be appealed to by the most scientific of modern expositors" (Warfield, 1970, 397). Warfield made John Calvin available to the twentieth-century American church.

III. Significance

As a teacher at a major American seminary, his influence was considerable. Countless ministers were shaped by his worldview. However, Warfield had an additional vehicle for the dissemination of his view. He was the editor of the *Princeton Review* from 1889 to 1921. As we have seen, he saw himself as properly "conservative," believing, for example, that the attempt to revise the Westminster Confession was deeply misguided. He was constantly pushing back against the liberalizing trends in the church and in theological education.

He was the primary voice in defending Calvinist theology. He opposed views of humanity that suggested perfectionism; he feared for a culture where anything old had to be rejected or revised. He saw the potential of German higher criticism to radically destabilize the traditional view of scripture. Therefore he continues to be read and admired by many evangelical and fundamentalist scholars.

References

Elwell, Walter A. 1993. *Handbook of Evangelical Theologians.* Grand Rapids, MI: Baker Books.

Warfield, B. B. 1927. *Works of Benjamin B. Warfield.* Oxford: Oxford University Press (repr. Grand Rapids, MI: Baker, 1981).

Warfield, B. B. 1929. *Works of Benjamin B. Warfield.* Oxford: Oxford University Press.

Warfield, B. B. 1970. *Selected Shorter Writings of Benjamin B. Warfield,* ed. John E. Meeter. Nutley, NJ: Presbyterian and Reformed.

Twentieth Century to Present

Hans Urs von Balthasar (1905–88)

Mark McIntosh

Few such major theologians of the modern era have understood their tasks as broadly as Hans Urs von Balthasar (1905–88). Theology in the more academic sense was for him always a collateral enterprise, something he developed in service to his work as a spiritual director, publisher, and leader of a religious community. Von Balthasar chose never to hold an academic teaching position in spite of numerous prestigious invitations over many years.

From the time of his youth he had an enormous love for music and literature, and his doctoral training was in the field of German literary studies. In 1928 he completed his dissertation at the University of Zürich, examining the changing interpretation of human destiny in German literature and philosophy. The following year, after a profound sense of calling during an Ignatian retreat, von Balthasar entered the Jesuit novitiate. After the wide-ranging and interdisciplinary nature of his doctoral work, he found the academic neo-scholasticism of his Jesuit training to be fairly constricting. The theologian-in-making took refuge during this period in a massive revision and extension of his dissertation, later published in three volumes (1937–9) as *The Apocalypse of the German Soul*. This critique of German idealism and its more ominous tendencies was presciently aware of its times; the final volume bore the subtitle *The Divinization of Death*.

As the war began, von Balthasar chose to take up work as a student chaplain in Basle. He had been exposed during his Jesuit training to the efforts of French Roman Catholics to recover and reappropriate the patristic sources of Christianity. Now he began a similar though even broader task which was to become a lifetime's publishing work, an almost continuous project of translating, editing, and anthologizing Europe's cultural heritage and its Christian roots. Until his death, von Balthasar remained involved in various series of such publications, always seeking to make available to the present the best of the great tradition in literature, drama, poetry, philosophy, and religious thought. Especially notable in this area are his translations of the poets and dramatists Péguy and Claudel and his lengthy books on such novelists and writers as Georges Bernanos and Reinhold Schneider. The more overtly theological side of this task of exploration and recovery was manifested in his translations and original books on Origen, Gregory of Nyssa, and Maximus the Confessor. Central ideas from each of these thinkers developed into crucial insights in von Balthasar's later work.

During the 1940s a close theological friendship and discussion began to develop between von Balthasar and Karl Barth, fostered perhaps by their mutual love of Mozart. Barth's christocentric impulses were abidingly fruitful in von Balthasar's thought, and while neither thinker converted the other (and von Balthasar was famous for effecting conversions), their respective theologies are perhaps more reciprocally illuminating

The Student's Companion to the Theologians, First Edition. Edited by Ian S. Markham.
© 2013 Blackwell Publishing Ltd. Published 2013 by Blackwell Publishing Ltd.

when studied together than any other pair of twentieth-century theologians. Another encounter, undoubtedly the most significant of von Balthasar's life, also began in this period, namely his spiritual partnership with Adrienne von Speyr, one of the first woman physicians in Switzerland. Her conversion and subsequent baptism by von Balthasar in 1940 was widely noted. Thereafter von Balthasar's role as her spiritual director led him deeply into a life-transforming mission. Her spiritual gifts were authentic and overwhelming in von Balthasar's eyes, and together they founded a religious community and a publishing house as vehicles for sharing and mediating von Speyr's spiritual insights. Von Balthasar spent countless hours recording Adrienne's dictations, eventuating in some 60 volumes of her work. In 1950 von Balthasar took the painful step of leaving the Society of Jesus in order to continue this theological mission with von Speyr. Part of the difficulty stemmed from the Society's concern that it would not be able adequately to support the Community of St John which von Balthasar and Adrienne von Speyr had founded. This community was to remain at the center of his life's work. An institute for laypersons who continued to hold regular secular jobs, the Community is a place of spiritual formation and contemplative mission. Many of the most central themes of von Balthasar's theology are crystalized in von Speyr's thought and in the Community's objectives, which were designed to give concrete form to those insights: in particular one notes the christological vision of obedience to mission, the silent but often costly readiness to allow the gospel to become luminous in the world by means of the vehicle of one's own life. Von Balthasar's brief, potent, and lyrical work *The Heart of the World* provides a vital introductory glimpse into the mutual theological vision that continued to shape his life and work long after von Speyr's death in 1967.

The remaining 20 years of von Balthasar's life continued to be hectic and overwhelmingly busy with lectures, retreats, endless correspondence, work for the publishing house and the Community, and a debilitating series of illnesses. Amazingly, it was during this period that his greatest theological work was written: the 15-volume trilogy in which theology is orchestrated according to the three transcendentals of the beautiful (*The Glory of the Lord*), the good

(*Theo-Drama*), and the true (*Theo-Logic*). The Dominican Cornelius Ernst once wrote that "theology is an encounter of Church and world in which the meaning of the gospel becomes articulate as an illumination of the world." This would be a valuable way of understanding von Balthasar's great project. In each "panel" of the triptych, the writer is concerned to show how the most fundamental patterns and structures of human culture are purified, redirected, and consummated in God, how the world is illuminated precisely as it is taken up into a lived exposition of the gospel.

So, in *The Glory of the Lord*, von Balthasar examines the processes of human esthetic perception in order to lead the reader to an awareness of the enrapturing power of Being; and this is made concrete, visible, and actually achieved in the living, dying, and rising of Christ: the visible form (the Beautiful) of the concrete universal (Being), which can only be perceived in the world we have made as the One who is despised and crucified. Similarly, in *Theo-Drama*, the dramatic structures of human life are exposed to illuminate the real goal and purpose of human freedom, as that becomes enacted precisely in terms of the infinite self-giving of God (the Good) in Christ. Finally in *Theo-Logic*, von Balthasar analyzes the ways in which human understanding and the apprehension of truth are embraced within and transformed by God's speaking and self-understanding (the Truth) in Christ and the Holy Spirit. Or, in his own most lapidary formulation: "A being *appears*, it has an epiphany: in that it is beautiful and makes us marvel. In appearing it *gives* itself, it delivers itself to us: it is good. And in giving itself up, it *speaks* itself, it unveils itself: it is true (in itself, but in the other to which it reveals itself)" (von Balthasar, 1993, 116).

In the later years of his life von Balthasar relterated an abiding theme in his work, the intrinsic connection between theology and holiness. In interpretations of mystical figures such as Thérèse of Lisieux and Elizabeth of Dijon, in a variety of theological analyses of prayer, and in the context of countless retreat presentations and brief essays, von Balthasar stressed the inherently objective, social, and theological significance of Christian spirituality. In an important later work, *The Christian State of Life* (*Christlicher Stand*, 1977; English translation 1983), essentially a theological explication of the theme of vocation, von Balthasar draws on years of work with the *Spiritual Exercises* of Ignatius to free the self from a Cartesian incommunicado and a Kantian disjunction between consciousness and reality. For von Balthasar the unity of the self with the world is guaranteed by the radically relational structure of human selfhood. In his view, human personhood and identity come to fulfillment precisely as the person is called forth into a communal mission in the world—a movement, even an *ekstasis*, that is itself grounded in the trinitarian processions that constitute the Divine Persons. The differences between this perspective and the transcendental analysis of human subjectivity that plays so important a role in the thought of Karl Rahner sometimes led to disagreements between the two sons of Ignatius.

One of von Balthasar's most astute commentators has remarked that "for all their mutual esteem," Rahner and von Balthasar "never understood each other at a really deep level. Rahner's starting point was Kant and scholasticism, while von Balthasar's was Goethe and the Fathers" (Henrici, 1991, 38). This also helps to explain von Balthasar's concern that theology not understand its present task as necessarily falling into either a grim retreat to bureaucratic pronouncements (he had already argued vigorously against such a trajectory in 1952 with *Razing the Bastions*) or else an overly optimistic accommodation to modernity's most basic tendencies (an option he criticized very sharply in 1966 with *The Moment of Christian Witness*). Instead von Balthasar was tireless in advocating a confident missionary engagement with the world. He frequently approached this task by employing a Goethe-like genealogical taxonomy of cultural forms and ideas, showing how the Christian pattern of life and thought intersected and swept up human history into an utterly unforeseen yet overwhelmingly apt fulfillment. It is significant for contemporary theology that by adopting this approach von Balthasar offers a phenomenological, cultural, even political alternative to the kind of universalizing metaphysical claims about which postmodern thought has begun to raise many important questions.

Hans Urs von Balthasar died on June 26, 1988, as he was preparing to celebrate daily Mass. Two days later he was to have been elevated as a cardinal.

Theological Habits of Mind

Certain key motifs can be found throughout von Balthasar's thought and a brief survey of them may prove a useful tool in navigating his theology. Generally speaking, these are habits of von Balthasar's theological mind and they tend to shape his approach to most questions, but they should only be taken as pointers toward what is always a lively and flexible approach to theology.

The ever greater

This theme, drawn from von Balthasar's study of Gregory of Nyssa and his Ignatian spiritual heritage, emphasizes the infinity of God's trinitarian life. Because God is an eternal activity of self-giving among the Divine Persons, reality and being are best understood in terms of event and act rather than essence. The eventful character of being is therefore always in motion. Creation, revelation, the incarnation, are all extensions in time of the ever greater trinitarian activity of self-giving love. What takes place in Christ, for example, is not simply the figural representation of something that is always already everywhere true anyway, so that once having grasped the meaning of the (symbolic) historical event, one might no longer need an actual event in time (Kant). On the contrary, for von Balthasar the kenosis of Golgotha is grounded in the eternal mutual kenosis of the Divine Persons, and as such has a new, eventful significance even for God; it is a particular, actual unfolding of the infinite possibilities inherent in the trinitarian relationality.

Inclusivity

Since all particular beings are created within the activity of the ever greater trinitarian life, all realities and especially all forms of human relationality are never simply overcome or transcended but can become apt expressions of the divine relationality. Creaturely forms such as culture, language, social solidarity are all natural conversation partners with theology. The ultimate significance of cosmic life and human personhood become apparent as creaturely existence is drawn not into a completed, static divine silence that negates the creaturely, but precisely as the creaturely is included within the divine trinitarian super-expressivity which is the mutual life of the Divine Persons. In this way the creaturely becomes more alive, more itself, by being embraced and included as an element, a "part of speech," within the "speaking" that is God's own life.

The objectivity of form

Human understanding of God is not primarily a correlate of innate human insight or a supposed transcendental quality to human knowing and willing. Rather is it the response to the concrete and objectively present forms of God's self-disclosure. Von Balthasar is uniformly suspicious of any reading of human interiority that might tend to isolate it from the other and especially to ignore the power of objective form to shape and even enrapture the knower. The process of human understanding is therefore irreducibly relational and social. Thus both contemplation and action in the world are forms of attentiveness to Christ; they are not the search for an inner truth but the means of interiorizing and apprehending by personal interpretation the public truth of God's work in the cosmos. Hence for von Balthasar human growth and knowledge emerge as one places oneself at the disposal of the other, above all in loving obedience to Christ. The objectivity of the divine self-disclosure is not less objective for being unfolded and interpreted organically in the life of believers.

Calling and mission

Von Balthasar understands the call to participation in the divine life as fundamental to creaturely existence. Central to his theology is his vision of the trinitarian Persons as constituted precisely by their relational processions. And the particular processions of the Word and Spirit include but are not reducible to their missions in time and human history. For von Balthasar this is what it means to be a person, to be in relational self-giving with the other. And human personhood is itself most consummately achieved as every individual participates uniquely in the trinitarian mission of the Word made flesh. Jesus comes to a full recognition and enactment of his personal identity as God's Beloved as he is drawn to respond to the Father's love by radical availability for the human other. In this sense von

Balthasar sees the ever greater call of the human other as the sign and beckoning of the divine Other, and it is by faithful response to this calling that human beings become who they are created to be. This becomes most clearly enacted as the church fulfills its mission as the Body of Christ, the *Spiel-raum*, the playing space or stage upon which every human life discovers its true meaning and fulfillment through participation in the mission of Christ. Through the process of discerning and following one's call within the mission of the eternal Word, every human person makes the crucial transition from mere role-playing to authentic personhood; and at the same time the meaning of the trinitarian missions becomes luminous in concrete lives of human persons. The openings here for dialogue with various forms of phenomenological thought, perhaps that of Levinas in particular, are very intriguing.

Plurality and synthesis

Von Balthasar certainly believes that theology is not simply a reflection upon states of human self-transcendence nor propositional speculation about divine truths. The infinite fruitfulness of the trinitarian life means that theology is always drawn beyond itself into the mystery of God's own life. Because of the infinitely new and unfolding expressions of self-giving in the Trinity, the creaturely apprehension of trinitarian fecundity is quite naturally plural and variously concrete. The participations of the saints and mystics in the interior mystery of Christ are not to be overlooked in the task of theology. Theology's goal is not to reduce this plurality of silence by a process of rational abstraction but rather to render all the concrete forms translucent to their ever greater and ever ungraspable synthesis in God. Rational coherence is not the only "logic" for theology, which must always point toward a multidimensional and pluralistic synthesis of faith and action, form and content, truth and obedience, all converging in the primordial concreteness and self-giving of the trinitarian life.

The Trinitarian Ground of Being

By now it will be clear how entirely von Balthasar's trinitarian vision permeates his thought. His trinitarian theology is, however, rooted in his understanding of

Christ; it is not speculative but an attempt to take seriously the historical events of Jesus's ministry, death, and resurrection for our understanding of God. He regularly criticizes what he sees as gnosticizing tendencies in theology that make so much of the eternal heavenly reality that the historical events of Jesus's life seem only pale reflections (e.g., von Balthasar, 1990a, 34 and 94).

Von Balthasar analyzes the radical self-giving of Jesus to his neighbors and so finally to God, and he sees this kenosis as both freely given and constitutive of Jesus's identity. It is the momentum that seems to carry him through his whole ministry and reaches consummation on the cross and the realized public form of that self-bestowal in the resurrection and Pentecost. Drawing importantly on his study of Maximus and on his Ignatian concept of mission, von Balthasar arrives at a crucial sequence of conclusions: the personal identity of Jesus is given in and with his mission, his mission is defined by a radical relationality and self-giving toward the other, the ultimacy of this self-giving is nothing less than the expression in human history of God's trinitarian relationality. Jesus's life, death, and resurrection become the interpretive key to understanding both who he is (doctrine of the incarnation) and what the condition for the possibility of his appearing is (doctrine of the Trinity).

First the incarnation, Von Balthasar adopts a strongly Chalcedonian christology, emphasizing that the union of the divine and human in Christ is not according to the order of nature or essence (as though the divine "essence" were simply another kind of essence that had somehow to be filtered into the human version of it). Rather, the union of divine and human in Christ is according to the order of person. Jesus is a fully human being with all the psychological and biological characteristics consistent with humanity, but the identity that he enacts (the personhood that constitutes *who* he is) is realized in the concrete shape of his mission. And this mission is to be the Word of God, to enter completely into what is most other than the Father and speak the divine love even there, something that can only be accomplished by bearing the fearful separation of the creature from God and resting in utter solidarity with those who have come to be most alienated from God (descent into hell). Doing this is who Jesus is, and it is a personal identity so radically in relationship to the Father

that the earliest Christians were, in von Balthasar's view, quite justified in coming to understand Jesus' identity, his personhood, as nothing less than the enactment in time of a divine pattern of existence. By the time of the Cappadocians, this perception, which had been aroused by Christ, has been further specified: "God" is no longer captive to a divine essence, but is recognized as being an infinitely living event of personal self-giving. In other words, the vulnerable human obedience and love which the church has met in Christ comes to be understood as the speaking in time of an aspect, a Person, of God.

Von Balthasar's interpretation of christology highlights what he takes to be the most remarkable feature of the early Church's experience, namely that the only conceivable condition for the possibility of what has happened in Jesus is itself God's own life. Nevertheless, von Balthasar is keen to avoid any hint that Christianity's new understanding of God thus subjects God to a new kind of necessity: "Even if it is true that the coming to light of the inner-trinitarian mystery in the dispensation of salvation lets us see something of the law of the immanent Trinity, it is nevertheless impossible to deduce from the inner law that this going-forth [of the incarnation] was necessary" (von Balthasar, 1990a, 215). So just as Jesus freely chooses to give himself away to the other, the divine ground of this self-giving must be understood as super-eminently a free act. The divine act of existence is, in von Balthasar's view, constrained by no putative laws of "divine essence" but rather the divine essence is itself the eternally constituted event of the free, mutual self-giving of the Divine Persons. God is "free to do what he will with his own nature. That is, he can surrender himself; as Father, he can share his Godhead with the Son. ... In generating the Son, the Father does not 'lose' himself to someone else in order thereby to 'regain' himself: for he *is always* himself by giving himself. ... (Without grasping this there is no escape from the machinery of Hegelian dialectic)" (von Balthasar, 1990b, 256).

It is precisely this divine self-bestowal, this "othering" which is God's life, and it is also this that makes possible a created other, and even the possibility that creatures may share in the divine life without losing their creaturely reality and freedom: there is room within the event of God's "othering" (trinitarian) life for the creature's own kind of otherness. In fact, von Balthasar argues that it is precisely the divine delight in the trinitarian communion of Persons that assures the distinctness of the Persons and a respect for their mutual otherness: "Something like infinite 'duration' and infinite 'space' must be attributed to the acts of reciprocal love so that the life of the *communio*, of fellowship, can develop" (von Balthasar, 1990b, 257). This holding open a place for the genuinely other in God is not some kind of cosmic individualism but exists precisely for the sake of a real event of love, an eternal overcoming and delighting in infinite otherness. This is the very basis of the divine life and, in von Balthasar's view, it is this "room" for otherness, expectation, and fulfillment in God that grounds genuine creaturely participation—as an other in the Other—in the trinitarian *perichoresis*.

Here, then, we can see the basis for the union of the divine and human in the eternal Person of the Word. If the basis for union were simply divine essence per se Jesus's human existence would inevitably slide toward an absorption into the divine, to the loss of his real humanity. By contrast von Balthasar suggests that Christ's radical and perfectly human self-giving has made it possible for the church to recognize, as the ground of Jesus's existence, an infinite self-giving in God. This is a self-giving so free, so constitutive of life that it can only be understood as "personal," as having a hypostatic existence quite beyond the inexorable requirements of any essence or nature. Jesus' humanity is "personalized" and enters into life according to the particular pattern of divine self-giving which we call the Word or Son of God.

Indeed von Balthasar argues that as the church comes to participate more and more profoundly in Jesus's mission, a deeper and deeper apprehension of the inner trinitarian life becomes possible. There is this unmistakable reciprocal motion in Balthasar's thought: the historical impact of Jesus opens up within the church a sensibility for what God's life must really be, and the more this life is participated in, the more its patterns and fruitfulness are recognized, in the form of Christ, as the very ground of all creaturely existence. In his early study of Gregory of Nyssa (1942; von Balthasar, 1995), von Balthasar had already noted the Cappadocian's significant break with Origen in stressing the infinity and incomprehensibility of God.

And what most struck von Balthasar about Gregory's conception of the divine infinity was its complete rootedness in God's triunity. God's infinity does not lie, in other words, in an absolute divine essence lying somehow beyond the historical missions of the Word and Spirit. Rather, the radical incomprehensibility of God is itself an aspect of the infinitely mysterious and fruitful self-bestowal of the trinitarian Persons.

Von Balthasar sees this new apprehension of God as emerging in the church's encounter with Christ. The concrete actuality of the cross, especially, confronts the usual religious and metaphysical aspirations of humankind, arresting humanity's ever ascending inner quest for God as the purest form of an imagined common being. The crucifixion jolts humanity out of this natural religious quest; Instead, von Balthasar sees the church's life being constituted by the ever new event of the radical personal freedom of Christ, and by the ground of Christ's freedom in the free decision of the divine Persons to exist and to exist precisely by a mutual self-giving. This opens for the church an awareness of reality beyond nature/essence, namely the radical freedom of the Divine Persons' mutual bestowal of existence: the act of existing comes to be seen as a new thing, an event that is not simply another necessary manifestation of nature but something that is ontologically ecstatic, personal, free, and yet irreducibly social and relational. It is this new awareness that, in von Balthasar's view, has even now still to be completely unfolded in the church's life and thought:

> This is the immense revelation that has been granted to us by the Incarnation: God is Life. Most certainly he had appeared to us, from the time our desire had its first awakening, as that Ocean of Being that our thought would never be in a position to capture. ... we believed that becoming and Being were opposites. ... Through the Incarnation we learn that all the unsatisfied movement of becoming is itself only repose and fixity when compared to that immense movement of love inside God: Being is a Super-Becoming. (von Balthasar, 1995, 153)

The implications of this insight from his early patristic studies would continue to be worked out throughout the Balthasarian aeuvre. Not only does the infinite vivacity of this *trinitarian* "giving place" to the other make room for a real *creaturely* freedom and becoming, it would also become for von Balthasar the condition for the possibility of the incarnation and redemption. The complete abandonment of the Divine Persons one to another in love and freedom represents a divine form of "powerlessness" which includes within itself all possible earthly manifestations:

> We shall never know how to express the abyss-like depths of the Father's self-giving, that Father who, in an eternal "super-kenosis", makes himself "destitute" of all that he is and can be so as to bring forth a consubstantial divinity, the Son. Everything that can be thought and imagined where God is concerned is, in advance, included and transcended in this self-destitution which constitutes the person of the Father, and, at the same time, those of the Son and the Spirit. God as the "gulf" [Eckhart: *Un-Grund*] of absolute Love contains in advance, eternally, all the modalities of love, of compassion, and even of a "separation" motivated by love and founded on the infinite distinction between the hypostases—modalities which may manifest themselves in the course of a history of salvation involving sinful humankind. (von Balthasar, 1990a, viii–ix)

Several points need unfolding in this very important passage. It is clear that for von Balthasar the divine reliability, or, to use the older terminology, the divine immutability, is grounded not in some unchanging divine essence (which would need to be kept pristinely secure from the variability of earthly life) but in the activity of the trinitarian processions of self-giving love. This makes it possible for von Balthasar to conceive of the deepest possible interaction of God in Christ with the suffering and transformation of the world. The sinful brokenness of the world and its alienation from God is capable of being embraced within the ever greater relationality of the Divine Persons. The infinity of mutual trinitarian self-abandonment is an eternally ecstatic giving of love, but when this same pattern of "othering" is enacted within the fragmented life of *our* world it takes the form of the dereliction of Golgotha and, in the resurrection, the declaration by the Spirit of the superabundance of the divine loving. "God, then, has no need to 'change' when he makes a reality of the wonders of his charity. ... All the contingent 'abasements' of God in the economy of salvation are forever included and outstripped in the eternal event of Love" (von Balthasar, 1990a, ix).

So von Balthasar does not accept anything like a Process account of divine reality. God does not in any way need the universe in order to become more completely God through some process of temporal development. And yet, for all that, von Balthasar is able to envisage a real "becoming" in the ever more of the trinitarian relational life, and this fruitfulness can include the participation of the creatures in the historical missions of the Word and Spirit. But how, exactly, can von Balthasar hold that these creaturely participations are non-necessary to God and yet also represent a real gift with real significance in the unfolding of the Trinity?

We have already noted how von Balthasar learned from Gregory of Nyssa a new conception of divine perfection which is not a philosophical vision of static being but a christologically-centered apprehension of God's infinite vivacity, a "super-becoming" which is the ever greater unfolding of the mysterious personal event of love. This is especially significant because it highlights the central role played by trinitarian personhood in von Balthasar's thought, not only as the explanation of the ever more in God's life, but as the ground and basis for all human personhood. In other words, God is God precisely in the mystery of personal loving, always full of yet more surprise, expectation, and richness in the unfolding of the personal relations by which God's reality as Love is constituted. Quoting, significantly, from the work of Adrienne von Speyr, von Balthasar writes:

> We can say that, if human love is enlivened by the element of surprise, something analogous to it cannot be excluded from the divine love. It is as if the Son born of the Father "from the outset surpasses the Father's wildest expectations". God loves despite his omniscience, constantly allowing himself to be surpassed and surprised by the Beloved. (von Balthasar, 1998, 79)

The more the Divine Persons abandon themselves to one another, the more they unfold and delight in the mutual giving. There is no end to the giving away, because the act of this divine giving is itself not constrained by a prior divine essence but is purely the free personal decision of the Divine Persons to exist in no other way than by giving place to the other. Perhaps the simplest analysis of this complex of ideas in von Balthasar lies in his conviction that what is principally revealed in Christ is Love itself, divine life as the freely chosen loving of one another by the Divine Persons. The pure gratuity of this personal love grounds both the divine existence and also the non-necessary existence of the universe. But this personal freedom also means that there is "room" in God's life for an infinite unfolding of "gifts" as the modes by which the Divine Persons *are* eternally by being *for* one another. There is a kind of blissful playfulness in von Balthasar's conception the Divine Persons' infinite mutual expectations and fulfillments. God's activity in creation and redemption can be seen as utterly gratuitous, but thereby also of real significance in the mutual divine delighting of the trinitarian Persons: "the inner participation of creatures in the life of the Trinity becomes an internal gift from each Divine Person to the Other" (von Balthasar, 1998, 507).

In a sense we could say that the universe is, in von Balthasar's view, God's way of dramatizing God's love for God. The wonderfully various and freely existing life of creatures is a particular mode of trinitarian delighting and self-giving. And this is nowhere more so than when in Christ the reconciliation of the world to God becomes itself an endlessly costly and cherishable self-offering of God:

> It is not a pale image of heavenly truth that is acted out on earth; it is the heavenly reality itself, translated into earthly language. When the Servant here below falls to the ground tired and spent from the burden of his day's labor, when his head touches the earth to adore his God, this poor gesture captures in itself all of the uncreated Son's homage before his Father's throne. And the gesture forever adds to this eternal perfection the laborious, painful, inconspicuous, lusterless perfection of a human being's humility. (von Balthasar, 1979, 50)

The inclusion of humanity in the trinitarian self-giving is not necessary to God, nor does it complete God in some way, yet because we are talking about God not in terms of a fixed divine essence but as the event of triune love there is a sense in which creaturely participation in triune life "adds" something to God: it is a new expression of the continually unfolding desire of the Persons to be *for* One Another. Consider an analogy. If someone gives her beloved a gift, this does not exactly mean they have more love than before, but it *is* a significant expression of their love and a new manifestation of their ever unfolding

relationship. "Infinite richness is rich in freedom and can enrich others (and hence itself) in ways that are ever new; all the more so, since absolute richness lies precisely in the gratuitousness of giving, which presupposes a will to be 'poor', both so that it may receive and so that it may expropriate itself" (von Balthasar, 1998, 509). In von Balthasar's view we catch a glimpse of this poverty of the Divine Persons, this divine desire to live completely from and for the Other, in the poverty and helplessness of Bethlehem and Calvary. And for that reason the only authentic revelation of God's trinitarian self-abandonment for the Other must take place in a way that elicits this pattern of existence in creaturely terms. That is why the divine self-communication takes the form of vulnerability, in order to awaken a corresponding love within the creaturely life; in this way God's self-giving life is "spoken" and becomes incarnate as Jesus, precisely as humanity is drawn forth into an answering self-giving love. This human participation in God's life is a real event of God's self-communication and self-sharing. It is a concrete unfolding in time of the infinite possibility of love among the Divine Persons, expressed as the rescuing embrace of the creature's lost existence.

Holiness and Truth

The ever more of the trinitarian richness has of course very definite implications for anthropology, the work of theology, and the human journey towards the truth. If the divine existence and unity are not simply a necessary given, but rather, in von Balthasar's view, the eternally delighted achieving of the Divine Persons' self-giving, then humankind created in the divine image is going to bear the trace of a similar momentum toward the other. Furthermore, the process by which the human community comes to understand something of God's life and to move toward an ever greater apprehension of truth is also going to be marked by a profoundly concrete and existential calling, a lived availability for truth. The world will come to understand the truth of reality only as it "is able to take the divine things it has received from God, together with the gift of being created, and return them to God as a divine gift" (von Balthasar, 1998,

521). In this sense von Balthasar's anthropology and epistemology are markedly "eucharistic," shaped and fulfilled by participation in the historical self-giving of the Word to the Father in their Spirit. Far from thinking that knowledge and faith are separate, let alone opposed, faculties of human life, von Balthasar is convinced that worldly knowledge comes to its own proper fulfillment in faith. The broken and isolated shards of the world's being are rendered luminous in their true meaning as they are assembled by faith in the light of God's absolute self-giving in Christ, as they are made once more into an offering, a participation in the divine dialogue.

We noted above how for von Balthasar every human being comes to the fullness of life not in a solipsistic way but exactly by means of availability and obedience to the call of the other. This mission and obedience awakens a human being from sheer biological persistence into the freedom and ever greater mystery of true personhood, in direct created analogy to the constitutive mutual self-giving of the Divine Persons. While there is a receptivity to the other inherent in being for the other, there is also a sense of worth and dignity, of having been entrusted with that which is unfathomably significant to God. There is an awakening of mobility, strength, and personal freedom as one's commitment to mission begins to turn into the discovery of one's authentic personhood and identity.

For example, in his treatment of Thérèse of Lisieux, von Balthasar explicates her active self-surrender in terms of this new growth in freedom and authority: "The result is something far removed from passivity which slackly waits on the turn of events, or resignation which bows its head in advance to whatever is to come. Her attitude remains intensely active; she is ready to plunge into the fray. ... Surrender, *abandon*, is a human act, the highest of human acts since it passes over into the omnipotence of God" (von Balthasar, 1954, 242). Importantly, obedience for von Balthasar must always be characterized by freedom and love, and apart from these it degenerates into dangerous forms of oppression. Love alone makes obedience authentic, for it transforms what might have been merely an external obligation or demand into a free choice, because the desire of the beloved becomes also the desire of the lover.

This growing access of personal freedom and responsibility reflects the spiritual transition that von Balthasar likens to the shift from mere role-playing to mission, from an artificial kind of play-acting to a new apprehension of one's true identity and authenticity. And for von Balthasar this transition is possible, as human beings are aroused by the calling of the Word, by the concrete participation in the mission of Jesus. Obedience to this mission is no alien passivity because it is in the image of the Word (i.e., the Word's relationality to the Divine Other) that every human being is created. Thus the individual awakening into personhood has begun to sense that the Word is "the truth of me and about me; the word which reveals me and gives me to myself. For we have been created in this word, and so it contains our entire truth, the whole concept of each of us, a concept so unimaginably great and beatific that we would never have thought it possible" (von Balthasar, 1986, 26).

Already we can see here important implications for von Balthasar's understanding of truth. Humankind in its creaturely nature is accustomed to knowing things that are graspable, items of finite nature. When this tendency comes into play with respect to the Truth, who is ultimately the free, personal God, then conceptual knowledge is indistinguishable from idolatry – all the more sinister for being so metaphysically refined. Human knowing of the divine, then, is most authentically apophatic and is far more appropriately undertaken in terms of continuing personal conversion and obedience to the call of God. And because the mission into which God calls the human is its own truth and freedom as a person, human knowledge of God is most likely to be apprehended not in terms of objective knowledge of certain truths about "something" but in terms of a developing sense of one's own personal identity in God. The human being's personhood, discovered in mission, is itself the language by which God speaks to him or her.

In a real sense the entire theological aesthetics (*Glory of the Lord*) is an analysis of the event whereby the truth of divine existence shows itself in the veiling of earthly form; in this process the human only comes to know the truth as it enraptures the knower and arouses interiorly a new way of living. This is a knowing of truth by means of a following in which the knower is literally "in-formed" by the truth, recognizing it through the apophasis of one's own life of discipleship. The final segment of von Balthasar's trilogy, *Theo-Logic*, begins by considering the habits by which humankind knows truth and the kinds of truths humans know, observing how the truth-knowing capacities of the world are ripe for transfiguration. This is only possible, however, if the convertibility of beauty, goodness, and truth with being itself is kept in mind. "The reduction of a knowledge of the truth to a purely theoretical kind of evidence from which all living, personal, and ethical decisions have been carefully excluded entails such a palpable narrowing of the field of truth that it is already thereby robbed of its universality" (von Balthasar, 2000, 18). But (in *Theo-Logic* II) human patterns of knowing are reintegrated with all three transcendental determinants of being, for they are taken up and transfigured in the incarnation of the Logos. Human speaking and acting become in Christ the vocabulary within which the divine Word can come to expression in the words of a human life. And finally (in vol. III) the pneumatological process is explored, by which God the Spirit arouses the human spirit toward the personal journey into truth by participation in the mission of Christ.

The point in all this is that just as absolute truth is, in God, not a static thing, but an unfolding event of triune personal giving, so human apprehension of truth can only be something that "takes place" in the personal self-sharing of a faithful life. So the pursuit of truth draws one into an ever deeper personal encounter with God and yet arouses all the more wonder at the divine mystery:

> Where there is genuine personal love between two people, there is simultaneous growth in intimacy and in

respect for the other person's freedom. So God cannot be simply the "Wholly Other" (and hence the Unknowable), but neither can the "revealed religion" become "religion unveiled", transmuted into some kind of absolute information about God. (von Balthasar, 1990b, 120)

The simultaneity of ever greater intimacy with ever greater mystery that marks personal knowing is a vital characteristic of truth. This self-surrendering quality of absolute truth is, in von Balthasar's view, indispensable to the world's own freedom and wholeness. For if worldly knowledge is cut off from the habit of self-giving love that is intrinsic to faith then it tends always to become a dominating utilitarian "knowledge." In such cases knowledge becomes merely manipulable, productive, and "the springs and forces of love immanent in the world are overpowered and suffocated." The result is "a world in which power and the profit-margin are the sole criteria, where the disinterested, the useless, the purposeless is despised, persecuted and in the end exterminated" (von Balthasar, 1968, 115). For the sake of the world, the world's own tendencies to reductive and impersonal knowledge need to be immersed in the habit of self-giving love. The inter-personal, trinitarian, ground of truth means that knowing and understanding always include personal involvement and transformation, delight in the illimitable richness of life, and reverence for the humility and availability to the other that mark authentic participation in truth.

Perhaps in this sense von Balthasar may be said to provide a measure for the adequacy and intelligibility of his own theological work: it is true insofar as it awakens in his readers real wonder, and real delight in expropriating oneself for the sake of understanding and loving the other.

References

Works by Hans Urs von Balthasar

1951. *Karl Barth. Darstellung und Deutung seiner Theologie*, Einsiedeln: Johannes Verlag. (*The Theology of Karl Barth: Exposition and Interpretation*, trans. E. T. Oakes, SJ, Communio Books. San Francisco, CA: Ignatius Press, 1992.) (Perhaps von Balthasar's best known work, a controversial and illuminating reading of his greatest Protestant interlocutor.)

1954. *Thérèse of Lisieux: The Story of a Mission*, trans. D. Nichols. New York: Sheed and Ward. (Originally published as *Thérèse von Lisieux: Geschichte einer Sendung.* 1950; reprinted with *Elisabeth von Dijon und ihre geistliche Sendung* [1952], in *Schwestern im Geist*. Einstedeln: Johannes Verlag, 1970; English translation, 1992.) (With the work on Elizabeth, this is a prime example of von Balthasar's concern to rediscover the objective ecclesial and theological patterns disclosed in the supposedly "subjective" realm of the saints and mystics.)

1968. *Love Alone: The Way of Revelation*. London: Sheed & Ward. (Originally published as *Glaubhaft is nur Liebe*. Einsiedeln: Johannes Verlag, 1963.) (Though highly compressed, this is an excellent preliminary survey of the entire range of the trilogy; it could be complemented by the author's *Epilogue* (English translation, 1992), written as he concluded the last of the trilogy.)

1979. *Heart of the World*, trans. E. S. Leiva. San Francisco, CA: Ignatius Press. (Originally published as *Das Herz der Welt*. Zurich: Arche, 1945.) (A lyrical meditation on the incarnation and redemption, capturing already much of von Balthasar's sense of the drama and polgnancy of the history of salvation. For an excellent introduction to this work, see the essay by A. Louth in Riches 1986.)

1982. *The Glory of the Lord: A Theological Aesthetics*, vol. I, *Seeing the Form*, trans. E. Leiva-Merikakis. Edinburgh: T&T Clark. See also vols. II–VII. San Francisco, CA: Ignatius Press, 1984–91. (Originally published as *Herrlichkeit, Eine theologische Ästhetik*, vols. I; II.1, II.2; III/1.1, III/1.2, III/2.1, III/2.2. Einsiedeln: Johannes Verlag, 1961–84.) (The first segment of the trilogy, according to the transcendental of beauty, containing a vast array of Old and New Testament Interpretations as well as studies of major Balthasarian conversation partners and fascinating reflections on the relations between aesthetics, metaphysics, and theology.)

1983. *The Christian State of Life*, trans. Sister Mary Frances McCarthy. San Francisco, CA: Ignatius Press. (Originally published as *Christlicher Stand*. Einsiedeln: Johannes Verlag. 1977.) (A reading of central themes in the *Spiritual Exercises* of Ignatius of Loyola; an important elucidation of the spiritual underpinnings of much Balthasarian theology.)

1986. *Prayer*, trans. G. Harrison. San Francisco, CA: Ignatius Press. (Originally published as *Das Betrachtende Gebet*. Einsiedeln: Johannes Verlag, 1955.) (A theological study of contemplation written for members of the various religious groups founded by von Balthasar; exemplifies the integration of theology and spirituality in his thought.)

1990a. *Mysterium Paschale*, trans. A. Nichols, OP. Edinburgh: T.&T. Clark. (Originally published as *Theologie der drei Tage*. Einsiedeln: Benziger, 1969.) (A polyphonous interpretation of the events of Holy Week and Easter in which the integrity of Christ's mission and the church's life is explored from within.)

1990b. *Theo-Drama: Theological Dramatic Theory*, vol. II, *The Dramatic Personae: Man in God*, trans. G. Harrison. San Francisco, CA: Ignatius Press. See also *Theo-Drama*, vols. I–IV. San Francisco, CA: Ignatius Press, 1988–94. (Originally published as *Theodramatik*, vols I; II.1, II.2; III; IV. Einsiedeln: Johannes Verlag, 1973–83.) (The *Theo-Drama* was regarded by von Balthasar as the most important part of the trilogy and contains his sustained treatments of anthropology, christology, soteriology, ecclesiology, trinitarian thought, and eschatology.)

1993. "Retrospective 1998," in *My Work: In Retrospect*, Communio Books. San Francisco, CA: Ignatius Press. (Originally published as *Mein Werk—Durchblick*. Einsiedeln: Johannes Verlag, 1990.) (Useful collection of essays by von Balthasar, attempting at five different points in his life to offer a synopsis of his concerns and work.)

1995. *Presence and Thought: An Essay on the Religious Philosophy of Gregory of Nyssa*, trans. Mark Sebanc. Communio Books, San Francisco, CA: Ignatius Press. (Originally published as *Présence et pensée: Essai sur la philosophie religieuse de Grégoire de Nysse*. Paris: Beauchesne, 1942.) (A fascinating early glimpse of crucial themes.)

1998. *Theo-Drama: Theological Dramatic Theory*, vol. V, *The Last Act*, trans. Graham Harrison. San Francisco. CA: Ignatius Press. (See 1990b above.)

2000. *Theo-Logic*, vol. 1: *The Truth of the World*, trans. A. J. Walker. San Francisco, CA: Ignatious Press. Originally published as *Theologik*, vol. I, *Wahrheit der Welt*. Einsiedeln: Johannes Verlag. See also vols. II and III. Einsiedeln: Johannes Verlag, 1985–7. (The final segment of von Balthasar's trilogy, according to the transcendental of truth; the second volume comprises a christological interpretation of truth, and the third a pneumatology.)

2003. *Cosmic Liturgy: The Universe According to Maximus the Confessor*, trans. B. E. Daley. San Francisco, CA: Ignatius Press. (Originally published 1941, as *Kosmische Liturgie: Höhe und Krise des griechischen Weltbilds bei Maximus Confessor*. Freiburg: Herder.) (Perhaps, as a single volume, one of von Balthasar's greatest works; crucial christological and trinitarian insights carefully revised in the later 3rd edition, and centrally significant throughout his work.)

Secondary literature

de Schrijver, G. 1983. *Le Merveilleux Accord de l'homme et de Dieu, Étude de l'analogie de l'être chez Hans Urs von Balthasar*. Leuven: Leuven University Press.

Gawronski, R. 1995. *Word and Silence: Hans Urs von Balthasar and the Spiritual Encounter between East and West*. Edinburgh: T&T Clark.

Heinz, H.-P. 1979. *Der Gott des Je-mehr: der christologische Ansatz Hans Urs von Balthasar*. Berne: Herbert Lang.

Henricl, P. SJ. 1991. "Hans Urs von Balthasar: a Sketch of His Life." In *Hans Urs von Balthasar: His Life and Work*, ed. D. L. Schindler. Communio Books. San Francisco, CA: Ignatius Press.

Krenski, Rudolf. 1990. *Passio Caritatis: trinitarische Passiologie im Werk Hans Urs von Balthasars*. Einsiedeln: Johannes Verlag.

Lochbrunner, M. 1981. *Analogia Caritatis*. Freiburg im Briesgau: Herder.

McIntosh, M. A. 1996. *Christology from Within: Spirituality and the Incarnation in Hans Urs von Balthasar*, Notre Dame, IN: University of Notre Dame Press.

Oakes, E. T. 1994. *Pattern of Redemption: The Theology of Hans Urs von Balthasar*. New York: Continuum.

O'Donnell, J. 1992. *Hans Urs von Balthasar*. Collegeville, MN: Liturgical Press.

O'Hanlon, G. F. 1990. *The Immutability of God in the Theology of Hans Urs von Balthasar*. Cambridge: Cambridge University Press.

Riches, J, ed. 1986. *The Analogy of Beauty: The Theology of Hans Urs von Balthasar*. Edinburgh: T&T Clark. (See especially Rowan Williams, "Balthasar and Rahner.")

Scola, A. 1995. *Hans urs von Balthasar: A Theological Style*. Grand Rapids, MI: William B. Eerdmans.

Serge Laugier de Beaurecueil (1917–2005)

Minlib Dallh, OP

I. Introduction

Serge Laugier de Beaurecueil, OP was a Dominican friar (French Province) in the Roman Catholic Church. Beaurecueil was for the Dominican Order of Preachers what Bede Griffiths, OSB (1906–93) was for the Benedictine Order. Both Serge and Bede were admirable examples of inter-faith dialogue. In his case, Serge learned through a different faith tradition (Islam) how to better live his own tradition (Roman Catholic), without syncretism or compromise. In his last book, *Je crois en l'étoile du matin* (2005), Serge states:

> I met Someone, the living God, who "seduced" me, to speak like Jeremiah. I do not believe at all in ideologies, but I believe in Jesus of Nazareth. I do not believe at all in morals, but I believe in the Holy Spirit, guiding my steps from within. I do not believe that I "possess" the Truth and that I could, from the heights of my superior stand, hand it down. I wish, only, with others, often by and through them, step by step, day by day, to move toward the Truth, in order that she possesses me. At times, no matter how dark is our night, I believe with all my being, for them (others) and for me, in the radiant morning star.

Serge's spiritual path exemplified an encounter between two religious traditions: Islam and Christianity; two cultures and civilizations: Persian-Arabic and Western European, without clash or the negation of the other. After years of intense struggle and hard work, Beaurecueil became a world-renowned scholar on Abdullah Ansari of Herat (1006–95). One could say that Ansari seduced the French Dominican priest to settle in Afghanistan for 20 years. Like Louis Massignon's (1883–1962) love relationship with the works of the great Sufi martyr Husayn B. Mansur al-Hallaj (d.922), Beaurecueil's mystical path blossomed when he entered into conversation with the mystical writings of Abudullah Ansari of Herat (Afghanistan). Serge's encounter with Ansari's work transcended history and theology.

Khwanja Abudullah Ansari was an erudite hanbalite Sufi who lived in the eleventh-century Abbasid dynasty. Born in Herat in 1006, Ansari is one of the most celebrated Persian poets and Sufis. His poems are an intimate dialogue of the soul with God in the form of a monologue. His treatises and poems are among the best of Persian Sufi poetry.

Therefore, in the footsteps of Massignon, George C. Anawai, OP (d.1994), Charles de Foucauld (1858–1916), and many others, Serge walked the path of an authentic Christian mystic in the land of Islam. Serge was one of those

> who live in a way least thought of by others, the way chosen by [Jesus of Nazareth], to make headway against all the power and wisdom of the world. It is a difficult and rare virtue, to mean what we say, to love without deceit, to think no evil, to bear no grudge, to be free from selfishness, to be innocent and straightforward …

The Student's Companion to the Theologians, First Edition. Edited by Ian S. Markham.

simple-hearted. They take everything in good part which happens to them, and make the best of everyone. (John Henry Cardinal Newman in his homily on the Feast of St Bartholomew)

The Arab and Islamic world of Beaurecueil was as complex and difficult then as it is today. On theological and anthropological grounds, he had to grapple with Amin Maalouf's questions in his book *Les Identités Meurtrières*: What is the meaning of our collective need of belonging, be it cultural, religious or national? Why does this genuine and legitimate desire often lead to the fear and negation of the other? (Maalouf, 2001).

An honest historical consciousness would suggest that false essentialisms, the dangerous rhetoric of either/or and simplistic answers to complex historical and religious situations are the common sources of the fear and negation of the other. But, as Richard Bernstein puts it, "the basic condition for all understanding requires one to test and risk one's convictions and prejudgments in and through an encounter with what is radically 'other' and alien" (Bernstein, 1992). Thus, Beaurecueil's meeting with Ansari was a genuine encounter with "what is radically other and alien" on the most difficult ground, namely, religious beliefs and faith traditions.

II. Life, Study, and Work

Brother Serge Laugier de Beaurecueil was born on August 20, 1917 and died in Paris on March 2, 2005. He was the son of a cavalry officer, and the second child of three. After early schooling and secondary education at l'Ecole de Gerson and at Lycée de Janson de Sailly in Paris, he passed his baccalaureate in philosophy with Arabic as a third language. In 1935, Serge joined the Dominican province of France. His choice to become a friar preacher opened the doors to years of scholarship in Islamic studies. First he learned Arabic and then Persian.

He was sent to Le Saulchoir, the Dominican studium of the time, for theology and philosophy. There, he met Marie Dominique Chenu, who was the students' master of Le Saulchoir. At the studium, Chenu's intelligent intuition prompted him to ask a number of Dominican brothers to engage in a serious

study of Islam and Muslim societies. Chenu wanted the brethren to study Islam as a way of salvation and not as some oddity.

Four years later, in 1939, World War II started and Serge interrupted his studies at Le Saulchoir. He was called to accomplish his military service in the city of Jounieh in Lebanon (at that time, Lebanon was a French protectorate). He stayed in the service until the end of the war. In June 1940, he was discharged from military service and re-entered Le Saulchoir in order to complete his studies.

Toward the end of his theological studies, Serge enrolled at l'Ecole nationale des langues orientales in Paris to continue his studies of Arabic. There he met the great French orientalist Louis Massignon, who would have a decisive influence on him. According to Merigoux, OP, Serge completed his doctorate in theology at Le Saulchoir and obtained a diploma at the Ecole nationale de langues orientales in Paris and a licentiate in Islamic studies and Arabic at the time of his priesthood ordination (Merigoux, 2005).

In 1943, Serge was ordained Roman Catholic priest in the Order of Preachers by Cardinal Suhard. Around Serge's ordination year, George Anawati, OP (d.1994) and Jacques Jomier, OP (1917–) moved to Cairo (Egypt) in order to establish a Dominican center for Islamic studies and Muslim societies. The idea of establishing a Dominican center for the study of Islam was put forward in 1938 by the Dominican Order in conversation with the Holy See. Thus, Beaurecueil, Anawati, and Jomier were the founding members of the IDEO, the Dominican Institute of Oriental Studies in Cairo.

Serge arrived in Cairo in 1946 to join Anawati and Jomier and started his studies on Islam and Muslim societies. He stayed in Cairo for 17 years. At the IDEO, he oriented his research toward Sufism, the mystical tradition of Islam. First, he worked for the IFAO, the French Institute of Oriental Archeology in Cairo, and then became a full member of the IDEO.

Serge kept in mind the advice of Chenu, "do not study doctrines, but the people who conceived them in their context and time. Otherwise, one runs the risk of not understanding doctrines at all" (Merigoux, 2005). Therefore, in 1953–4, Serge published in the IFAO a commentary on Ansari's *The Book of Stages*. Later in 1963, he published a critical edition of the same book. He pursued his study of Ansari and wrote many articles. In 1963, on the ninth-century lunar anniversary of Ansari's death, the Afghanistan government invited Serge, in gratitude for his work and interest in Ansari, to come to Kabul for a big celebration. On his return, he published *Manuscrits d'Afghanistan* (IFAO, 1964).

In 1971, he obtained his PhD from the prestigious University of the Sorbonne for his work on Ansari (see MIDEO, 1972, 11: 291–300). After his doctorate, he moved to Kabul and stayed there until the Russian invasion in 1981. First, he was invited to come to Kabul and teach at the university; he was awarded the chair of professor in Islamic mysticism. However, the plight and misery of children on the street would change his career.

He abandoned his professorship to open a house for street children. He dedicated his life to their care. He became their teacher, advisor, and mentor. The number of children, who belonged to many tribes, soon reached 25. At the same time, he got a job as a French teacher and academic advisor at the Lycée Francais Esteqlal of Kabul.

In the midst of a Muslim community, Serge lived his life as a Dominican friar and priest. He was the only Catholic priest in the country. He shared this unique experience of a Dominican friar among Muslims in two books: *Nous avons partagé le pain et le sel* (Cerf, 1965) and *Prêtre des non-Chrétiens* (Cerf, 1968).

In *Nous avons partagé le pain et le sel*, Serge recounts the act of thanksgiving (Eucharist) in the midst of a dire social milieu. The book describes an intimate and familiar gesture, breaking bread and sharing salt, with poor Afghan children. He draws us into the infinite horizon of Afghan people's hospitality. He notes,

> When I broke bread and shared salt the first time with Ghaffar, it was in a little room next to the chapel where I consecrated the Eucharist. I celebrated Eucharist in Eastern rites. The same bread was shared to seal our friendship and we became the body of Christ. Ghaffar did not understand I knew it … But, the mystery was there, independent of whether or not we understood. (Beaurecueil, 1965, 38)

Unfortunately, Serge left Afghanistan in a dramatic manner in 1983. First, he went to Brussels where he was a prior of the Dominican priory for three years. Then, he moved to the Annunciation's Priory in Paris. It was in Paris that Serge compiled a memoir of his experiences with Afghan street children. He published *Un Chretien en Afghanistan* in 1985 and *Mes enfants de Kaboul* in 1992. However, Ansari's work and thought never left him. In 1985, he published *Ansari: Chemin de Dieu. trois traites spirituels* and in 1988, *Cris de coeur.*

Beaurecueil's departure from Afghanistan was very painful. He grew to love not only the work of his beloved master Ansari but the complexity of the land and its people. Afghanistan was for Serge what Florence was for Dante. The desert landscape of Herat, the shrine of Ansari and the crowd of visitors, were part of him. Several times, he went for retreat and conversation with the Khwanja at the shrine in Herat. Naturally, Brussels and Paris did not fill the emptiness he felt and the agony he endured.

Finally, he found in Paris, at the hospital Saint-Fargeau, a way of pursuing his ministry to help children. His experience of the house of care for street children in Kabul served him well and kept the memory of Afghan children and Lycée Esteqlal close to his heart.

Fortunately, in Kabul one of the boys who had lived with Serge opened a house of hospitality for street children in the footsteps of Serge. One can only imagine how Serge felt and how he cherished his pupil's accomplishment. He had the great joy of visiting Kabul in 2003, in the company of the French television program *Envoyé Special* featuring Serge and entitled "A Priest in Kabul." It was an emotional and awe-filled experience.

Serge returned to the Dominican Institute for Oriental Studies in Cairo to give lectures and seminars on Ansari. He died in 2005. He gave his ultimate lecture, "L'Amour de Dieu chez Ansari," in 2004. His intimate knowledge of Islam through Sufism and Muslim societies, via his care for the street children of Kabul, gave Serge unparalleled insight and awareness of Islamic societies. His experience in Bayreuth, Cairo, and above all in Kabul as a Dominican friar among Muslims is a bold testimony of inter-faith dialogue.

Beaurecueil's life is a finger pointing to Christian–Muslim dialogue. Ultimately, his mystical path embodied the possibilities and vulnerabilities of what it means to take inter-faith dialogue seriously.

References

Amin, Maalouf. 2001. *Les identités meurtrières*. Paris: Grasset & Fasquelle.

Anṣārī al-Harawī, ʿAbd Allāh ibn Muḥammad, and Beaurecueil, Serge de. 1985.*Chemin de Dieu: trois traités spirituels*. Paris: Actes Sud.

Anṣārī al-Harawī, ʿAbd Allāh ibn Muḥammad, and Beaurecueil, Serge de. 1988. *Cris du cœur – Munâjât*. La Bibliothéque de l'Islam. Paris: Sindbad.

Beaurecueil, Serge de Laugier. 1965. *Nous avons partagé le pain et le sel*. Paris: Cerf.

Beaurecueil, Serge de. 1965. *Khwādja ʿAbdullāh Anṣārī (396–481H./1006–1089); mystique hanbalite*. Beyrouth: Impr. catholique.

Beaurecueil, Serge de Laugier. 1968. *Prêtre des non-Chrétiens*. Paris: Cerf.

Beaurecueil, Serge de Laugier. 1985. *Un Chretien en Afghanistan*. Foi vivante, 209. Paris: Editions du Cerf.

Beaurecueil, Serge de Laugier. 1988. *Cris de coeur*.

Beaurecueil, Serge de Laugier. 1992. *Mes enfants de Kaboul*. Foi vivante, 295. Paris: Éd du Cerf.

Beaurecueil, Serge de Laugier. 1992. *Chronique d'un témoin privilégie: lettres d'Afghanistan*, III, 1981–1983. L'IMPASSE and Ceredaf.

Beaurecueil, Serge de Laugier. 2005. *Je crois en l'etoile du matin*. Paris: Cerf.

Bernstein, Richard J. 1992. *The New Constellation: The Ethical—Political Horizon of Modernity/Postmodernity*. Cambridge, MA: The MIT Press.

Articles by Serge Laugier de Beaurecueil

In MIDEO, the annual collection of articles from the IDEO, he published a number of articles:

"Anṣārī: Référence bibliques de l'itinéraire spirituel chez Ansari," MIDEO, 1: 9–38.

"Place du prochain dans la vie spirituelle d'Ansari," MIDEO, 2: 5–70.

"Identification des commentaires anonymes des 'Manazil al sa'irin,' " MIDEO 2: 312.

"Lacunes de l'édition des commentaires de 'Abd al –Mo'ti sur les 'Manazil,' " MIDEO, 2: 314–20.

"Esquisse d'une biographie de Ansari," MIDEO, 4: 94–140; 5: 45–114; 6: 37–402, tranduction en Persan, 7, I: n 223.

"Le retour a Dieu (*tawba*), éléments essentiel de la conversion selon Ansari—et ses commentaires," MIDEO, 6: 55–122.

"L'aspiration (*raghba*), rectification de l'espérance, selon Ansari—et ses commentaires," MIDEO, 7: 1–20.

"Neuvième centenaire de la mort d'Ansari (1962)," MIDEO, 7: 219–35.

"Les festivités, publications, dont La pensée d'Ansari," MIDEO, 7: 230–3.

"Dix-sept années d'études," MIDEO, 7: 234 s.

"Khwuja—(CR, GCA)," MIDEO, 8: 253 ss, "Jami et Ansari," 8: 401–6.

"Structure du 'Livre des Etapes,' " MIDEO, 11: 77–125.

"Présentation d'Ansari," MIDEO, 11: 291–300.

"Afghanistan, Voyage d'étude," MIDEO, 2: 388.

"Catalogue des messages," MIDEO, 3: 75–206.

"Publications de la société d'histoire d'Ansari," MIDEO, 7: 236–40.

"Jésus par un écrivain persan contemporain (Shin Parto)," MIDEO, 2: 310–12.

"Psaumes : Introduction a 'quinze psaumes traduits en arabe,' " MIDEO, 4: 1–3; 23–26; Ps. 1a 25; 5: I, 45 n., Ps. 26–50, 6: I s, 53 s.

"Le millénaire lunaire de la naissance de Khwaja 'Abdollah Ansari Harawi' (I 136 H), avec liste des publications," MIDEO, 13: 305–14.

"Introduction a Conseils … de méthodologie," MIDEO, 7: 241.

With George C. Anawati: "Une preuve de l'existence de Dieu chez Ghazali et St Thomas," MIDEO, 3: 207–58.

Weda, vingt ans, cellule 5, Kaboul: Lattes, 1991.

Weda Padari, vingt ans cellule 5 Kaboul: Latte, 1997.

Black Theology

Ian S. Markham

For any white person living in America there is a deep puzzle at the heart of the American experience. Almost all the settlers were Christians. The Founding Fathers recognized the importance of God in the Declaration of Independence and spoke about the equality of humanity. Yet it is a country that, for a whole host of reasons, perpetrated the evil of slavery against black people and continued to tolerate the evil of institutional and legally entrenched segregation until the late 1960s.

The racism of America is an export from Europe. It was the European powers that created the trade in slavery; it was the European settlers who brought a theology of superiority that was indifferent to the non-white. The words of James Cone summarize this history with brutal clarity:

> How do we account for such a long history of white theological blindness to racism and its brutal impact on the lives of African people? Is it because white theologians do not know about the tortured history of the Atlantic slave trade, which according to the British historian Basil Davidson, "cost Africa at least fifty million souls"? Have they forgotten about the unspeakable crimes of colonialism? Author Eduardo Galeano claims that 150 years of Spanish and Portuguese colonization in Central and South America reduced the indigenous population from 90 million to 3.3 million. During the twenty-three-year reign of terror of King Leopold II of Belgium in the Congo (1885–1908), scholarly estimates suggest that approximately 10 million Congolese

> met unnatural deaths—"fully half of the territory's population." The tentacles of white supremacy have stretched around the globe. No people of color have been able to escape its cultural, political, and economic domination. Two hundred forty-four years of slavery and one hundred years of legal segregation, augmented by a reign of white terror that lynched more than five thousand blacks, defined the meaning of America as "white over black." White supremacy shaped the social, political, economic, cultural, and religious ethos in the churches, the academy, and the broader society. (Cone, 2003, 131–2)

It is important to remember the sheer extent of the suffering that these figures hide. Slavery was a cruel and wicked trade. Perhaps we need a witness to remind us of the suffering. This description from a slave on a Portuguese ship is typical:

> The stench of the hold while we were on the coast was so intolerably loathsome that it was dangerous to remain there for any time, and some of us had been permitted to stay on the deck for the fresh air; but now that the whole ship's cargo were confined together, it became absolutely pestilential. The closeness of the place, and the heat of the climate, added to the number in the ship, which was so crowded that each had scarcely room to turn himself, almost suffocated us. This produced constant perspirations, so that the air soon became unfit for respiration … This wretched situation was again aggravated by the galling of the chains, now become

The Student's Companion to the Theologians, First Edition. Edited by Ian S. Markham.
© 2013 Blackwell Publishing Ltd. Published 2013 by Blackwell Publishing Ltd.

insupportable; and the filth of the tubs, into which the children often fell, and were almost suffocated. The shrieks of the women, and the groans of the dying, rendered a scene of horror almost inconceivable. (Equiano in Thomas, 1997, 412)

While we might feel able to distance ourselves from the crimes of the 1730s, the recent past is much harder to handle. This is just one of thousands of stories from the civil rights campaign. This particular one dates from the summer of 1963 and Mrs. Hamer is recollecting the case of a young girl who had been arrested at a voter registration workshop:

June Johnson, a fifteen-year-old black teenager who had attended the voter registration workshop, was the next person led by Mrs. Hamer's cell in this grim parade of tortured bodies. "The blood was runnin' down in her face, and they put her in another cell." In the booking room, whence Johnson was coming, the sheriff had pulled the young girl aside for his own personal whipping. He asked her whether she was a member of the NAACP [National Association for the Advancement of Colored People]. She told him yes. Then he hit her on the cheek and chin, and when she raised her arms to protect herself, he hit her on the stomach. He continued to ask her questions about the NAACP—"who runs that thing?" "do you know Martin Luther King?" Soon the four men in the room—the sheriff, the chief of police, the highway patrolman, and another white man—threw Johnson onto the floor, beat her, and stomped on her body in concert. The men ripped Johnson's dress and tore her slip off; blood soaked her tattered clothes. (Marsh, 1997, 19)

For many of us today, this is so obviously wrong and incompatible with the Christian gospel that there seems to be little more that needs to be said on the topic. Indeed with the abolition of slavery and then the passing of the Civil Rights Act of 1964, many assume that these injustices have been rectified. However, this is untrue for several reasons. Although there has been progress, the problems of racism and the oppression of African Americans continue to the present day. There are more blacks than whites in poverty; there is a disproportionate number of blacks over whites in prison and on death row. The political right argues that the problem is

the behavior of the African American community; they point, for example, to the higher number of single mothers. The solution, they argue, is a revival of the Protestant work ethic. Cornel West is right when he writes:

Conservative behaviorists talk about values and attitudes as if political and economic structures hardly exist. They rarely, if ever, examine the innumerable cases in which black people do act on the Protestant ethic and still remain at the bottom of the social ladder. Instead, they highlight the few instances in which blacks ascend to the top, as if such success is available to all blacks, regardless of circumstances. Such a vulgar rendition of Horatio Alger in blackface may serve as a source of inspiration to some—a kind of model for those already on the right track. But it cannot serve as a substitute for serious historical and social analysis of the predicaments of and prospects for all black people, especially the grossly disadvantaged ones. (West, 1994, 21)

Every white person knows that West is right. We know it just isn't true to say that "if a black person decides to work hard, then they will succeed." We know it is false because we know too many white people, often very respectable, who are still racist. And we know that when a black person complains that they still find white society racist, it is true. Even those of us who pride ourselves that we are progressive on such issues have sat with our "friends" and heard and tolerated (for fear of creating "an atmosphere") the critical remark, the racist joke, and the criticism of "mixed marriages." And if we are honest we suspect that there are cab drivers who prefer to find a white passenger or employers who prefer someone "familiar" or promotion boards that decide they don't want white people reporting to a black manager (of course this will not be the explicit justification). West complains about the propensity of many to see "black people as a 'problem people'" (West, 1994, 5). The truth is that the problem people are the white people who are still quietly racist (almost politely racist) even though they know about the evils of slavery and segregation. Somehow it has not got through how evil racism is. Those who question this quiet middle-class racism are accused of "political correctness" or being "humorless." It is as if these intelligent nice racists have forgotten how many lives were killed and damaged through racism.

And as with feminism, Christianity often provided the justification for a racist worldview. Although it seems obvious to many that Christianity and racism are incompatible, many do not see it. Black theology is not simply for the African American, but also a vitally important challenge for any theology.

There are six aspects of black theology that any theology must learn from. But before developing these, it is worth clarifying the precise meaning of black theology. James Cone explains that the term "black theology" is a merger of the insights of Malcolm X and Martin Luther King. He writes, "The word 'Black' in the phrase was defined by the life and teaching of Malcolm X—culturally and politically embodied in the Black Power movement. The term 'theology' was influenced by the life and teaching of Martin Luther King, Jr.—religiously and politically embodied in the Black Church and civil rights movement" (Cone, 1993, 1). For many historians, Malcolm X and Martin Luther King are viewed as opposites: Malcolm X is depicted as the militant (and some allege a "black racist") and Martin Luther King is the moderate. For most theologians involved in black theology there is a growing consensus that this reading is wrong. Malcolm X provides a stronger analysis of the extent of the racism, while Martin Luther King remains the great theologian who detected the Christian obligation on this matter. James Cone explains:

> Martin and Malcolm embodied in their lives and work the African American struggle for identity in a society that is not sure what to do with us. There is a little bit of Martin and Malcolm in all African-Americans … We should not listen to Martin's "I Have a Dream" speech without also listening to Malcolm's answer in his "Message to the Grass Roots." "While King was having a dream," Malcolm said, "the rest of us Negroes are having a nightmare." Without confronting the American nightmare that Malcolm bore witness to, we will never be able to create the beloved community articulated so well by Martin King. (Cone, 2005, 106)

The important point is that any theology must confront the militancy of Malcolm as well as the vision of Martin.

The first aspect is methodological. The sources central to black theology are entirely compatible with the sources that shaped the mainstream Christian tradition. In a working paper prepared by the Kelly Miller Smith Institute at Vanderbilt University, black theology is described as (1) story, (2) story of our faith in God, (3) story of our faith-understanding and our freedom struggle, (4) biblical, and (5) contextual (Kelly Miller Smith Institute in Cone and Wilmore, 1993, 165). There is a strong claim, implicit in this list, to see black theology as the authentic theology of the Christian tradition. Along with the liberation theologians, black theology believes that the Bible is about liberation from oppression. Therefore the Bible belongs to the African American community. Gayraud S. Wilmore is broader when he suggests that there are three sources for black theology. The first is the existing black community, "where the tradition of Black folk religion is still extant and continues to stand over against the institutional church" (Wilmore in Cone and Wilmore, 1993a, 133). The second is "the writings and addresses of the Black preachers and public men of the past" (Wilmore in Cone and Wilmore, 1993a, 134). These are people like Nat Turner, Richard Allen, and Martin Delany. And the third source is "the traditional religions of Africa, the way those religions encountered and assimilated, or were assimilated by, Christianity, and the process by which African theologians are seeking to make the Christian faith indigenous and relevant to Africa today" (Wilmore in Cone and Wilmore, 1993a, 136).

Black theology is grounded in the Bible and takes seriously the combination of experience (the story of oppression) and the insights that can be derived from the "non-Christian" traditions that shaped the African American story.

The second aspect is the insight that the gospel is about liberation. Thanks to the Latin American Liberation theologians, this is now accepted by many Christians. The pietistic gospel about individual salvation and the eternal destiny of the soul does not convey the message of the prophets and the teaching of Jesus. Instead, if we read the Bible through the eyes of those who suffer, we see more clearly that God cares about injustice, oppression, and poverty, and obliges us to work for the liberation of those suffering. The theme of liberation is one of the earliest themes of black theology.

Back in 1969, the statement by the National Committee of Black Churchmen says:

> Black Theology is a theology of black liberation. It seeks to plumb the black condition in the light of God's revelation in Jesus Christ, so that the black community can see that the gospel is commensurate with the achievement of black humanity. Black theology is a theology of "blackness." It is the affirmation of black humanity that emancipates black people from white racism, thus providing authentic freedom for both white and black people. (National Committee of Churchmen in Cone and Wilmore, 1993a)

The gospel must mean a changed world, in which the curse of racism no longer destroys and dehumanizes the black person.

The third aspect is the centrality of "self-love." Cornel West has made this a central theme of his work. There is a crisis of nihilism: men and women are giving up hope. West explains that this nihilism takes the form of a "profound sense of psychological depression, personal worthlessness, and social despair so widespread in Black America" (West, 1994, 20). And the appropriate response is a conversion. West writes:

> New models of collective black leadership must promote a version of this politics ... [T]here is always a chance for conversion—a chance for people to believe that there is hope for the future and a meaning to struggle ... Nihilism is not overcome by arguments or analyses; it is tamed by love and care. Any disease of the soul must be conquered by a turning of one's own soul. This turning is done through one's own affirmation of one's worth—an affirmation fueled by the concern of others. A love ethic must be at the center of a politics of conversion. (West, 1994, 29)

One aspect of Christianity that can be deeply problematic to an oppressed people is the idea that "love involves selflessness" or even "love is self-giving." The danger here is that one starts to believe that the Christian duty is to be constantly available to the oppressor and, as an act of love, to tolerate the abuse. When in 1 John we find the expression, "we love God because God first loved us," we find a more appropriate model of love. To love others, one needs a self to love with. "Love you neighbor as yourself" carries

the same self-affirmation. We need to start loving ourselves before we have any chance of loving anyone else. For an oppressed people, this is especially true. Imagine what it is like to be ignored, stared at for daring to walk into a predominately white restaurant, or passed over for promotion. When society does not provide the affirmation, indeed does the opposite, it is vitally important that the person finds the resources for "self-love."

The fourth aspect is the stress on a "contextual theology." The located nature of theology is often recognized theoretically but ignored when it comes to preaching and teaching. How do we think of Christ when we are preaching? Many churches take the white Christ of European Christianity. This is both wrong historically and wrong theologically. Historically, Albert Cleage is right in at least this respect when he writes: "Jesus was a nonwhite leader of a nonwhite people struggling for national liberation against the rule of a white nation" (Cleage in Cone and Wilmore, 1993a, 101). Theologically it is wrong because, as Matthew 25 teaches us, we find Christ in the oppressed. And black people are oppressed in America. James Cone makes the point thus:

> [W]hether whites want to hear it or not, *Christ is black, baby*, with all of the features which are so detestable to white society. ... If the Church is a continuation of the Incarnation, and if the Church and Christ are where the oppressed are, then Christ and his Church must identify totally with the oppressed to the extent that they too suffer for the same reasons persons are enslaved ... Therefore Christ is black because he is oppressed, and oppressed because he is black. (Cone in Cone and Wilmore, 1993a, 70–1)

Christ becomes black in America because that is where the oppression is. In the same way that we should contextualize our christology, so we should contextualize our understanding of God. It is important to listen to a critique from the perspective of black theology. Theodore Walker, Jr. has reflected on the relationship between the two. He picks up the criticism that process theology often talks of God's love as unconditional, indiscriminate, and universal. The difficulty with this is that black theology needs to think of God not as on everyone's side but as on the side of the poor. But, as Walker goes on to show, if God experiences the damaging impact of oppression on the personhood of both the oppressed and the oppressor (and every act of cruelty to another person destroys the character and well-being of the oppressor), then God must be working for liberation of the oppressed (Walker in Cone and Wilmore, 1993b, 35–52).

The fifth aspect is the impact on our view of suffering, theodicy, and justice. It was William R. Jones who asked the question in a brilliant essay: Is God a white racist? He provides a critique of three theologians: Joseph Washington, James Cone, and Albert Cleage. He examines their implicit theodicies. Washington builds on the suffering servant theme and suggests that in much the same way as the Jewish people were called to witness to "one God," the blacks are called to "witness to the one humanity of the one God" (Jones in Cone and Wilmore, 1993b, 144). And as the Jews suffered for their calling, so the blacks will suffer. Jones disagrees strongly with the implication that this suffering might be in perpetuity. Similarly, Cone makes the black people an "oppressed people" with whom God identifies. However, the difficulty with this, explains Jones, is that it is not obvious that liberation will come: yet surely God would want to bring such liberation about? As for Cleage, he overcomes the accusation that God is a racist by making God and Jesus both non-white; this God allows the oppression and suffering because it is "deserved punishment": all suffering in the universe is a response to earlier cosmic sins. Jones correctly identifies the difficulty with this explanation, namely the extent of black suffering and the comparative lack of white suffering.

This is a challenging article for several reasons. First, our standard treatments of theodicy tend to be very undifferentiated. We talk of "natural suffering" (earthquakes, illness etc.), and "moral evil" (acts of violence and war against each other). Jones is forcing us to admit that there is "group suffering." Moral evil would work as a category if each group in the world had a virtually equivalent number of individuals who suffer and who do not suffer. However, the truth is that power in history has privileged certain groups. And with the advent of modernity, white Europeans have been especially privileged. If we are going to talk about an active God in human history, then we do need to provide some explanation for the uneven experience of different groups in respect to suffering.

The final aspect is the emergence of "womanist" theology. Kelly Delanine Brown Douglas writes:

> Black women in the United States have given voice to a new theological perspective: womanist. Although the meaning of the term "womanist" originated with Alice Walker's interpretation of the Black cultural expression, "You acting womanish," it goes beyond her words. It points to the richness and complexity of being Black and female in a society that tends to devalue both Blackness and womanhood. (Brown Douglas in Cone and Wilmore, 1993b, 290)

It is undoubtedly true that the experience of the double oppression has been especially challenging. The experience of this double oppression opens up contrasting ways of understanding the nature of oppression and therefore of the processes necessary for liberation.

As a white theologian writing this article, it is important for me to conclude by examining the demands that are necessary in terms of repentance. James H. Cone writes:

> Is there any hope for the white church? Hope is dependent upon whether it will ask from the depths of its being with God: "What must I do to be saved?" ... It must own that it has been and is a racist institution whose primary purpose is the perpetuation of white supremacy. But it is not enough to be sorry or to admit wrong. To repent involves change in one's whole being. In the Christian perspective, it means conversion ... For the white churches this means a radical reorientation of their style in the world towards blacks. It means that they must change sides, giving up all claims to lofty neutrality ... A racist pattern has been set, and the Church has been a contributor to the pattern. Now it must break that pattern by placing its life at stake. (Cone in Cone and Wilmore, 1993a, 78–9)

This is challenge we have a duty to attend to. The explicit racist arguments of Sam Bowers (Imperial Wizard of the White Knights of Ku Klux Klan and suspected of "orchestrating at least nine murders, seventy-five bombings of black churches, and three hundred assaults, bombings, and beatings" [Marsh, 1997, 89], between 1964 and 1967) have been, on the whole, disowned by the white church. His capacity to link the civil rights movement with godless communism represents a particular brand of American paranoia. Other Western nations were much more nuanced in their evaluation of Marxism and communism. His passion for neo-Nazi literature and the novels of Thomas Dixon (who portrayed the black man as a sexual degenerate) provided a pseudo-scientific and non-Christian justification for racial purity. Christianity, ironically, provided the apocalyptic framework in which Bowers saw himself with a mission to save the world and to engage in this war against the forces of darkness with any means possible. This statement is typical of the cosmic dualism underpinning his worldview:

> We Knights are working day and night to preserve Law and Order here in Mississippi, in the only way it can be preserved: by strict segregation of the races, and the control of the social structure in the hands of the Christian, Anglo-Saxon White men, the only race on earth that can build and maintain just and stable governments. We are deadly serious about this business … Take heed, atheists and mongrels, we will not travel your path to a Leninist Hell, but we will buy YOU a ticket to the Eternal if you insist. Take your choice, SEGREGATION, TRANQUILLITY AND JUSTICE, OR BI-RACISM, CHAOS AND DEATH. (Bowers in Marsh, 1997, 70)

Although almost all church leaders would repudiate, unequivocally, this worldview, the church still needs to confront the climate that permitted this distorted worldview to flourish. Charles Marsh sets out the theology of such a church in his critique of Douglas Hudgins (Hudgins was a Southern Baptist Minister in Mississippi through the 1950s and 1960s). This theology was a combination of a focus on personal conversion and sanctification that made civil rights irrelevant coupled with a residual sympathy for white supremacy. Marsh explains,

> As the shepherd of First Baptist's highly influential congregation, Hudgins preached a gospel of individual salvation and personal orderliness, construing civil rights activism as not only a defilement of social purity but even more as simply irrelevant to the proclamation of Jesus Christ as God. The cross of Christ, Hudgins explained at the conclusion of a sermon in late 1964, has nothing to do with social movements or realities beyond the church; it's a matter of individual salvation. (Marsh, 1997, 89)

A theology of neglect was a convenient device to preserve power and maintain oppression. It is so simple to insist that Christianity is confined to the redemption of the soul that leaves a body crying out for food and justice. It is such a betrayal of the biblical witness that it defies belief that exponents of such theology had read their Bible with any real attention. A partial explanation, explains Marsh, is the impact of residual doctrines of racial superiority. So Marsh writes:

> In 1912 the Home Mission Board of the Southern Baptist Convention—the agency in charge of religious instructions for minorities and the poor—called on white Christians to help blacks reach their full potential as a separate race, for in so doing, the report stated, "we shall save Anglo-Saxon supremacy." Far less charitable was the writer of an article in Mississippi's *Baptist Record*, who argued that God intended for the white race to rule supreme over blacks, because "a race whose mentality averages on borderline idiocy" is quite obviously bereft of any divine blessing … White supremacy was the "divine law," intoned the *Laurel Leader Call*, "enacted for the defense of society and civilization." (Marsh, 1997, 93)

If this doesn't move a reader to a state of rage, then we are in a state of sin. And this is the reason why continuing white racism must be actively resisted and challenged by the white church. It should be the theme of our preaching. It must be named and confronted. The residual impact of such arguments should be forbidden. The jokes that hide implicit racist assumptions should be condemned as evil. These arguments have shaped behavior and theology and in so doing led to death and suffering on a vast scale. Zero-tolerance is our only way forward.

The latest device to evade the task of repentance is the charge of "political correctness." Apparently, with these injunctions to forbid racism from our churches, we are simply being "politically correct." But the logic of accepting the charge is to make an intelligent discussion of social problems impossible. We must not evade the challenge of repentance. Those who want to be "politically incorrect" often want to be racist. They do not want to recognize the crime that has been committed and the remorse we need to show.

Although explicit sympathy with "white superiority" has in fact largely disappeared, the pietist gospel that insists that social justice is not part of the message continues to flourish. It is important to note that there are evangelicals who recognize that an acceptance of the authority of the Bible entails an acceptance that Christ should be Lord of all aspects of our lives, including the political and social (Sider, 1977). Most Christian theologies recognize that a gospel indifferent to social justice is a betrayal of the tradition we have inherited. The assimilation of the political dimensions of the gospel is an imperative for us all.

References

Cleage, Albert B. Jr. 1993. "The Black Messiah." In James H. Cone and Gayraud S. Wilmore, *Black Theology. A Documentary History, Volume 1*, p. 101.

Cone, James H. 1993. "Introduction" to James H. Cone and Gayraud S. Wilmore, *Black Theology. A Documentary History, Volume 2*.

Cone, James H. 2005. *Risks of Faith: The Emergence of a Black Theology of Liberation, 1968–1998*. Boston, MA: Beacon Press.

Cone, James H. and Wilmore, Gayraud S. 1993a. *Black Theology. A Documentary History, Volume 1: 1966–1979*. Maryknoll, NY: Orbis Books.

Cone, James H. and Wilmore, Gayraud S. 1993b. *Black Theology. A Documentary History, Volume 2: 1980–1992*. Maryknoll, NY: Orbis Books.

Equiano, Olaudah. *Equiano's Travels*, 2 vols., ed. Paul Edwards (New York, 1967) as cited in Hugh Thomas. 1997. *The Slave Trade: The History of the Atlantic Slave Trade 1440–1870*. London: Picador, p. 412.

Kelly Miller Smith Institute. 1993. "What Does It Mean to be Black and Christian?" In James H. Cone and Gayraud S. Wilmore, *Black Theology. A Documentary History, Volume 2*.

Marsh, Charles. 1997. *God's Long Summer. Stories of Faith and Civil Rights*. Princeton, NJ: Princeton University Press.

National Committee of Black Churchmen. June 13, 1969. Statement as reproduced in James Cone and Gayraud S. Wilmore, eds., *Black Theology. A Documentary History, Volume 1*.

Sider, Ronald. 1977. *Rich Christians in an Age of Hunger*. London: Hodder and Stoughton.

West, Cornel. 1994. *Race Matters*. New York: Vintage Books.

Wilmore, Gayraud S. 1993. "Black Power, Black People, Theological Renewal." In James H. Cone and Gayraud S. Wilmore, *Black Theology A Documentary History, Volume 1*.

Dietrich Bonhoeffer (1906–45)

John W. de Gruchy

Dietrich Bonhoeffer is probably better known beyond the confines of the church than any other twentieth-century Christian theologian. Two reasons immediately come to mind. The first is his participation in the German conspiracy to assassinate Hitler and his subsequent murder at the hands of the Gestapo. The second is the extent to which his fragmentary theological reflections published posthumously in his *Letters and Papers from Prison* have attracted attention. Within the broader sphere of ecumenical Christianity Bonhoeffer has achieved unofficial canonization as a result of his role in the church struggle against Nazism and his martyrdom (Slane, 2004). Several documentary films have been produced on his life,[1] his poetry has been set to music,[2] and he is the subject of an opera.[3] Few theologians, if any, have attracted such attention. Yet his status as a latter-day Protestant saint has not been uncontested.

Indicative of the controversy over Bonhoeffer was the bizarre declaration by the German government in August 1996 that he was no longer regarded as a traitor. This might say more about Germany's legal conservatism than about Bonhoeffer's status. But it also reminds us that the reception of Bonhoeffer in his native land has by no means always been positive. Some who applaud his role in resisting Nazi ideology during the church struggle (*Kirchenkampf*) draw back from approving his participation in the plot to assassinate Hitler. Reservations have also been expressed about his theology especially as reflected in the *Letters and Papers from Prison*. As many blame Bonhoeffer for the ills besetting modern theology as praise him for helping them to remain Christian in a "world come of age." Yet, however one might assess him or interpret his legacy, it is difficult to ignore him. There is as much scholarly and popular interest in his life and work today as ever before (see de Gruchy, 1997, 1999; Haynes, 2004). Indicative of this phenomenon is the recent completion of the new critical edition of his works published in 16 volumes and their translation into English (see Floyd, 1999) and other languages.

Bonhoeffer's theological development cannot be understood apart from the context within which he lived and worked. Indeed, it might be said of Bonhoeffer more than any other theologian of the twentieth century that his theology and biography are intrinsically related. This does not mean that his theology cannot be critically evaluated on other grounds, but that it can hardly be understood apart from his life. Hence the need for a brief biographical sketch (see Bethge, 1999) before we examine Bonhoeffer's theology.

A Fragmentary yet Fulfilled Life

Dietrich was one of eight children born in Breslau in 1906 moments before his twin sister Sabine. His parents came from a long and distinguished line of

The Student's Companion to the Theologians, First Edition. Edited by Ian S. Markham.
© 2013 Blackwell Publishing Ltd. Published 2013 by Blackwell Publishing Ltd.

scholars, theologians, and civic leaders. The family moved to Berlin when Dietrich's father became professor of psychiatry at Berlin University in 1912, and it was this city with its rich cultural heritage, intellectual life, and political activity which became Bonhoeffer's cherished home. The Bonhoeffer family was not overtly religious and seldom attended church. Nonetheless, the twins were influenced by the piety of their Moravian nanny and the less overt piety of their mother. Family hymn singing was a regular and popular event around the piano, reflecting as much the musical talent of the family as it did their Christian heritage. Few who witnessed Dietrich's childhood in the secure and comfortable surroundings of Berlin's upper-class suburbs or the family holiday home in Friedrichsbrunn prior to 1914 could have anticipated how insecure his life was to become. The death of his second eldest brother Walter on the war front in 1918 shattered the tranquility of the home and deeply affected the whole family. By then Dietrich was already sensing a call to become a theologian, not least because he wanted to prove that he could succeed in a different career to those chosen by his brothers. But his choice was much to the chagrin of his father for whom such a vocation was a waste of his youngest son's undoubted talents.

Having started his theological studies at the University of Tubingen, Bonhoeffer proceeded to the University of Berlin where, at the age of 21, he obtained his doctor's degree. His dissertation, *Sanctorum Communio*, was an unprecedented attempt to integrate theology and sociological theory in the development of an ecclesiology grounded in revelation yet rooted in reality. Deeply influenced by Karl Barth's critique of liberal theology yet sensitive to the expectations of his more liberal and neo-Hegelian teachers and, above all, eagerly seeking ways to make Christian faith socially concrete, Bonhoeffer propounded the thesis that "Christ exists as church-community."[4] The "theology of sociality" which characterizes this early work was developed further in his *Habilitation* published in 1931 as *Act and Being* (1996a). Although *Sanctorum Communio* and *Act and Being* have often been neglected by those who have been interested in Bonhoeffer's role in the church struggle or his theology in prison, they laid the foundations for much of what was to follow (Green, 1999).

Already during his early student days Bonhoeffer was eager to travel and experience different cultures, something that remained important for him throughout his life. A visit to Rome while he was still studying in Heidelberg led him to focus his attention on the church as a living community in which Christ is present. After he had completed his studies in Berlin he spent a year working as an assistant pastor in a German-speaking church in Barcelona, Spain (see Bonhoeffer, 2002). This gave him a fresh perspective on the bourgeois character of so much Protestant Christianity, something reinforced when he returned to Berlin as an assistant lecturer. Then in 1930/1 he was a visiting student fellow at Union Theological Seminary in New York (see Bonhoeffer, 2008). While he was not impressed by mainline North American theology or preaching, he came to appreciate the concern of his teachers in relating faith and social witness. He also became aware of the racism that permeated American society. This was reinforced through his involvement in the black Abyssinian Baptist church in Harlem. Moreover, as a result of his friendship and discussions with another visiting student, the French pastor Jean Lasserre, Bonhoeffer was challenged to read the Sermon on the Mount more existentially. This was an essential step in his becoming not just a theologian but, as he later recalled, also a Christian for whom the Bible was far more than a doctrinal or homiletic source book.

Bonhoeffer continued his work at the university after his return to Berlin (see Bonhoeffer, *Berlin 1933*, forthcoming). He also became a pastor in a working-class parish of the city where he had particular responsibility for the children of the poor and unemployed. This latter experience reinforced his sensitivity to the alienation of the working class from the church. Meanwhile his lectures, which conveyed his own deepening commitment to the message of scripture, soon gained an enthusiastic following. Notable amongst them were those on "Creation and Sin," later published as *Creation and Fall*, in which Bonhoeffer demonstrated his ability to interpret the Bible (in this case Genesis 1–3) in a way which spoke directly to his time and context (Bonhoeffer, 1997). But it was those on "Christology," subsequently reconstructed from students' notes (Bonhoeffer, *Berlin 1933*, forthcoming), which became pivotal for understanding the development and shape of his theology from then on.

The Germany to which Bonhoeffer returned was in crisis. The ill-fated Weimar Republic was in a state of collapse. Adolf Hitler came to power in 1933 and the National Socialist era of totalitarian horror began. Bonhoeffer publicly challenged the claims of absolute authority associated with the "Führer-principle" from the outset.[5] Indeed, even before Hitler's election he was anticipating confrontation with the state. His essay on "The Church and the 'Jewish Question,'" published in 1932, clearly expressed the need to resist the state if it failed to fulfill its proper role. In a celebrated passage he declared:

> There are three possible ways in which the church can act towards the state: in the first place it can ask the state whether its actions are legitimate … Secondly, it can aid the victims of state action … The third possibility is not just to bandage the victims under the wheel, but to put a stake in the wheel itself. Such action would be direct political action, and it is only possible and desirable when the church sees the state fail in its function of creating law and order. (Bonhoeffer, 1977, 225)

Bonhoeffer's attention was dominated, however, by the attempt of the Nazi "German Christians" to take over control of the Evangelical Church (Lutheran and Reformed) and make it subservient to Nazi ideology. Though there were others who agreed with his outspoken position, Bonhoeffer was disappointed by the tendency to compromise on the issues. So during 1933 he accepted an invitation to serve two German congregations in London (see Bonhoeffer, 2007). In his absence German church opposition to Nazism began to gather momentum and in May 1934 the first Confessing Synod of the Evangelical Church was held at Barmen. This act of defiance against the official *Reichskirche* launched the Confessing Church. The Barmen Declaration, largely drafted by Barth, unequivocally affirmed the Lordship of Jesus Christ over against the ideological claims of Nazism, though it did not speak out on the "Jewish Question." Bonhoeffer, who was in constant contact with the situation in Germany, became an advocate of the Confessing Church within British circles and took a leading role in seeking to isolate the Nazi Christians from the ecumenical church. His papers and addresses of this period, most notably that on "The Confessing Church and the Ecumenical Movement," demonstrate the clarity of his thought and the incisive way in which he brought theology to bear on the critical issues of the day (Bonhoeffer, 1977, 326ff.).

By 1935 Bonhoeffer was back in Germany as the director of a seminary for ordinands in the Confessing Church located in the remote Baltic village of Finkenwalde. In a remarkable experiment in German Protestant theological formation, Bonhoeffer introduced his students to the unaccustomed discipline of community life centered on Bible study, worship, and prayer. Bonhoeffer and his students also participated fully in the life and witness of the Confessing Church congregations in the vicinity. Amongst the first intake of students was Eberhard Bethge, who soon became a close friend and confident of Bonhoeffer's. During the next 10 years, until Bonhoeffer's death, their friendship flourished both through personal contact and then, during Bonhoeffer's imprisonment, through correspondence. Bethge would later become the custodian of Bonhoeffer's legacy, editing his works and writing his biography (see de Gruchy, 2005).

While at Finkenwalde, Bonhoeffer was in regular touch with events taking place in Berlin. Increasingly under the surveillance of the Gestapo, he was eventually forbidden to teach or preach in Berlin. It was during this period that Bonhoeffer wrote several expositions of biblical texts and themes, including his famous book on *Discipleship*.[6] The Gestapo closed the seminary in 1937, but it continued to function underground for several more months. Bonhoeffer's little but profound book on the nature of Christianity community, *Life Together*, was written at this time, and summed up what he had set out to achieve at Finkenwalde (Bonhoeffer, 1996b). But perhaps the most significant happening as this phase of his life drew to an end was his surprising engagement to Maria von Wedemeyer, a love story that cannot be told here. Yet it is one which, in hindsight, had considerable influence on Bonhoeffer's closing years and the way in which he began to rethink his theology in prison (Bonhoeffer and von Wedemeyer, 1994).

In 1939 Bonhoeffer, unwilling to be drafted into the army, had the opportunity to go into exile in New York. After one agonizing month there he decided that he had to return to share in the fate of a Germany on the brink of war. Soon after, he joined the conspiracy against Hitler. Several of the leaders of the assassination plot were members of the wider Bonhoeffer family circle and some were in high positions within government and the military. Bonhoeffer himself was made a member of the German Military Intelligence (*Abwehr*), which, ironically, was the center of the conspiracy. Although the Gestapo suspected something was amiss, he was able to use his position to help Jews escape to Switzerland. On a visit to Sweden he also sought, through the mediation of his long-time friend Bishop George Bell of Chichester, to gain the support of Winston Churchill and President Roosevelt for the work of the resistance. It was also during this period that Bonhoeffer began work on a book on ethics. But apart from spending some quality time in the Benedictine monastery in Ettal working on this project, the posthumously published *Ethics*, though substantial, was never completed (see Bonhoeffer, 2005). Despite this, the *Ethics* remains one of the most important sources for understanding both Bonhoeffer's more mature theology and Christian moral responsibility.

Bonhoeffer was arrested by the Gestapo in April 1943 on suspicion of aiding Jews to escape, and placed in Tegel prison in Berlin. Thus began the final episode of his life that is so well documented in his *Letters and Papers from Prison*. Tragically, the attempt to assassinate the Führer on July 20, 1944 failed, and shortly after this all the conspirators were arrested. Information soon came to light implicating Bonhoeffer in the conspiracy. He was then moved from Tegel prison to the Gestapo prison in Berlin; later to the concentration camp in Buchenwald; and finally to Flossenburg, where he was executed on April 9, 1945 just a few days before the camp was liberated by the Allies. A year before, on February 20, 1944, Bonhoeffer wrote a letter to his parents in which he reflected on the fragmentary character of life as he and his generation were experiencing it in comparison with that of his parents and previous generations. Their lives, he wrote, was probably "why we feel especially strongly how unfinished and fragmentary our lives are."

Christ the Centre

Many would regard Bonhoeffer's lectures on *Christology* given in Berlin in 1933 as the pivotal text in his theological development. For that reason we will begin our exploration of his theology with these lectures, then take a step back to consider some of the foundations of his thought in his earlier dissertations *Sanctorum Communio* and *Act and Being*, before giving our attention to the theology of the *Ethics* and his letters and papers from prison.

Christology, Bonhoeffer told his students, is not an attempt to answer the question "how" the eternal Word of God could have become a human being, but to discover "who" this Word is for us today.[7] The mystery of the incarnation is beyond the grasp of human reason, but in the proclamation of Jesus Christ as the crucified "Word made flesh" God addresses us with an immediacy that demands not just the response of the intellect but of the whole person. Christology has to do with this proclamation and its claims. This presupposes the classical affirmation of the Council of Chalcedon (451) that Jesus Christ is "truly God and truly human." Chalcedon thus sets the parameters for Bonhoeffer's christology even though it does not answer the contemporary and contextual question, "who is Jesus Christ, for us today?". In seeking to answer this question, Bonhoeffer adopts Martin Luther's "theology of the cross" (*theologia crucis*), insisting that the primary question in christology is "about the concealment of the God-Man in his humiliation" (Bonhoeffer, 1978a, 54). In Jesus Christ God freely places himself at the service of humanity and the world "for me" and "for us" (*pro me* and *pro nobis*), whether in the cradle or on the cross, whether on the eucharistic altar or in the proclamation of the gospel. It is in and through God's humiliation in Christ that we are redeemed and brought into community. This has far-reaching consequences for what it means to be the church. For it "is with this humiliated one that the church goes its own way of humiliation … There is here no law or principle which the church has to follow, but simply a fact—put bluntly, it is God's way with the church" (Bonhoeffer, 1978b, 113). Where Christ goes, there the church must follow.

The question "*who* is Jesus Christ" leads directly to the question "*where* is Jesus Christ?" Christ, says Bonhoeffer, is at the center of reality. In other words, christology does not have to do with a Christ confined to religion or the church, but with God's presence at the center of the life of the world. Christ is the center of human existence, the center of history and the state, and the center between God and nature. To speak of Christ in this way does, of course, open up the danger of triumphalism on the part of the church, yet that goes directly contrary to Bonhoeffer's intention. For Christ exists at the center as the "humiliated one." This means that he exists at the center in solidarity with humanity in all its pain and suffering, acting vicariously and redemptively on behalf of the world. If the church is to follow Christ it must be engaged as a community in solidarity with those who are its victims. It is in this way, says Bonhoeffer, that Christ both challenges the false messianic pretensions of those who exalt in power, and affirms the true messianic hopes of those who long for God's salvation.

Those familiar with the fragments of Bonhoeffer's prison theology will recognize the extent to which so much is already anticipated in these lectures on christology. But in order to trace the other main trajectories in Bonhoeffer's theological development we now need to take a step back and consider his first two academic treatises, *Sanctorum Communio* and *Act and Being*. For while it is true that *Christology* is the pivotal text in his theological development, it is equally true that some of the main concepts which recur and gave shape to Bonhoeffer's theology during the church struggle and later in his *Ethics* and prison reflections, are already in embryonic form in his dissertations.

A Theology of Sociality

There is a qualitative difference between Bonhoeffer's lively and existentially demanding lectures on christology and the densely packed academic dissertations *Sanctorum Communio* (1927) and *Act and Being* (1930/1). The difference can be explained by reference to Bonhoeffer's own personal journey and the historical crisis facing the church in the year of Hitler's triumph. Bonhoeffer was not trying to impress his academic mentors in order to become part of the theologians' guild; he was concerned about the awesome challenge facing those who wish to follow the "humiliated Christ" at the center of history gone wrong. Yet, despite the differences between the christology lectures and the dissertations, there are some important continuities that have often been overlooked.

Both *Sanctorum Communio* and *Act and Being* reach their climax with the declaration that "Christ exists as church-community." This shows not only Bonhoeffer's early interest in ecclesiology but how, from the outset, Bonhoeffer's theology was grounded in a social understanding of human existence interpreted in the light of God's revelation in Jesus Christ. Bonhoeffer's theology is, from beginning to end, a theology of sociality (Green, 1999). Christ is undeniably *pro me*, yet this existential relationship is always located within a broader framework, for my identity as a human person is inseparable from "the other," and especially the ethical demands which "the other" makes upon me. Bonhoeffer's language reminds one of Martin Buber's *I and Thou*, yet the personalism he affirms is more ethical in character, with "the other" providing the boundary to my existence in such a way that only in responding to him or her do I truly become a person. The fundamental human problem is that "in Adam" community has been destroyed through the alienation of "the other"; it has become "a community of sinners" (*peccatorum communio*).

Bonhoeffer was aware of the dangers of a communalism that denies the place or rights of the person, subjugating him or her to false authority and domination. But he was equally aware of the dangers of a rampant individualism that made the "self" the center. Both were evidence of humanity "in Adam." Only in the "body of Christ" was it possible for the human person to be truly a person in relation to "the other," only through Christ's vicarious action is human community restored. The vicarious or representative character (*Stellvertretung*) of Christ's death and resurrection is the "life-principle of the new humanity" (Bonhoeffer, 1998, 147). "God" writes the young Bonhoeffer, "established the reality of the church, of humanity pardoned in Jesus Christ—not religion, but revelation, not a *religious community, but church*. This is what the reality of Jesus Christ means" (Bonhoeffer, 1998, 153). And yet Bonhoeffer refuses to reduce the church to an event that has no historical reality. After all, his intention was to relate a theology of revelation to social philosophy and thereby to the empirical existence of the church. So he goes on to say: "yet there is a necessary connection between revelation and religion as well as between religious community and the church" (ibid.) The church is not a voluntary society of atomistic individuals but the empirical form of this "new humanity" that Christ has brought into being and of which he is the center: "Christ exists as church-community."

Act and Being, undoubtedly Bonhoeffer's most difficult book, continues his explorations in theological sociality and anthropology, only now in terms of epistemology. Both transcendentalism, with its emphasis on the "act" that breaks into human consciousness from beyond, and ontological systems that posit the continuity of the human self and "being-in-itself," are problematic. The first, as represented by the early Barth (the Barth known to Bonhoeffer), disallows any continuity between the divine and the human and therefore any way whereby human reason can grasp hold of revelation. The second, variously represented by phenomenology, liberal Protestantism's emphasis on religious experience, confessional orthodoxy, or Roman Catholicism (the doctrine of *analogia entis* or "analogy of being"), stresses the continuity between the divine and the human, but in doing so revelation becomes captive to human experience, reason, the confessionalism, or the church understood as institution. But, as Bonhoeffer sets out the problem and the way in which he will address it, "the meaning of 'the being of God in revelation' must be interpreted theologically, including how it is known, how faith as act, and revelation as being, are related to one another and, correspondingly, *how human beings stand in light of revelation*" (Bonhoeffer, 1996a, 27f.). Bonhoeffer seeks to resolve the problem by reference to the freedom of God *for* rather than *from* humanity. The truth of the Christian gospel is that God has freely chosen to become a human being in Jesus Christ, and therefore, while remaining "truly God" has fully bound himself to us. God, in Jesus Christ, has become available for us. This brings Bonhoeffer, in conclusion, back to the sociality of his earlier dissertation, for it is within the church-community that Christ exists as the one who is God *for* us. In Christ, understood in this way, humanity is set free from guilt and sin, the true self is restored, and genuine human community is established.

As we previously noted, prior to his 1933 Berlin lectures on christology, Bonhoeffer taught a course on "Creation and Sin," published as *Creation and Fall*. In many respects, these earlier lectures provide the link

between the central theme of his two dissertations, his christology and his theological ethics (Bonhoeffer, 1997, 9ff.). We may balk at Bonhoeffer's christological interpretation of the Old Testament, but at a time when Nazism demanded the rejection of everything Jewish from the life of the church and nation, Bonhoeffer's strong affirmation of the Hebrew scriptures as Christian was a firm counter to any anti-Semitic Marcionism. Later, in prison, Bonhoeffer preferred to read the New Testament in the light of the Old, but now his intention was different—and for good reason. Throughout the history of the church, the downplaying of the Old Testament invariably has led to a Gnostic separation of creation and redemption, and therefore to a dualism which kept body and spirit apart. Such "thinking in two spheres," as he described it in his *Ethics*, meant that the church no longer took any responsibility for the life of the world and nature, and therefore also eschewed any political responsibility (Bonhoeffer, 2005, 57–62). This was directly related to the Lutheran (but not Luther's) doctrine of the orders of creation which, on the basis of the creation story, gave autonomy to the nation (*das Volk*), the state, the family, and culture. This meant, as some distinguished theologians of the time argued in sympathy with the Nazis, that these were independent of God's revelation in Jesus Christ, and therefore outside the mandate of church responsibility and witness. Over against this, Bonhoeffer argued that in the light of Christ these "orders" are for the sake of preserving human life; they do not have the autonomy or authority to develop their own norms and values independent of God's revelation in Jesus Christ. Later, in his *Ethics*, Bonhoeffer revisited this issue, taking his position one step further away from any possible support for autonomous spheres of morality by speaking of God's mandates, for this spoke more clearly of God's demands upon us in Jesus Christ rather than as something inherent within creation (Bonhoeffer, 2005, 388–408).

At the heart of Bonhoeffer's theological exposition of *Creation and Fall* is his christological interpretation of the meaning of the "image of God" or *imago Dei*. In continuity with his argument in *Act and Being*, Bonhoeffer rejects the notion that this refers to some inherent quality of being which relates the human and divine, just as he rejects any liberal idea that gives autonomy to the human subject. Against the Catholic doctrine of the *analogia entis*, then, he speaks of an *analogia relationis*, or an analogy of relationships. Once again Bonhoeffer's early "theology of sociality" is apparent, but only now more clearly rooted in scripture, more decisively christological, and more immediately related to the existential and historical demands of his context. God creates human beings to rule over creation, but their freedom requires responsibility or deputyship (*Stellvertretung*). Sin is the abnegation of such responsibility. Redemption is the recovery of being truly free "for others," and therefore responsible for the world.

Confessing Christ Here and Now

All the theological building blocks were now in place that were to guide Bonhoeffer's involvement and reflection in the fateful church struggle (*Kirchenkampf*) against Nazism. What remained was the need to speak out clearly and in the most concrete way possible about the meaning of Jesus Christ as Lord against the absolute claims of Nazi ideology. But for Bonhoeffer the corollary to confessing Christ was a confessing church. In a sermon on Peter's confession at Caesarea Philippi (Matt. 16:13–18) preached at the time of the church elections in July 1933, Bonhoeffer asked the searching question: where is the church which is built on the rock against which "the powers of death shall not prevail"? His unequivocal answer was that the true church of Jesus Christ is the church that confessed him faithfully. "Church stay a church! But church confess, confess, confess!" he exhorted. And then went on to declare: "The Confessing Church is the eternal church because Christ protects her" (Bonhoeffer, 1977, 217).

It is beyond the scope of this essay to discuss the many essays and papers that Bonhoeffer wrote or delivered during the church struggle period. Virtually all the themes we have already mentioned so far find expression in some form as he takes up the cudgels on behalf of the Confessing Church, the ecumenical search for peace or, however haltingly at first, the Jewish victims of Nazi policy. Confessing Christ concretely meant, for Bonhoeffer, rejecting the compromises of the *Reichskirche*, which had become a "false church," and following Jesus Christ alone. This uncompromising message lay at the heart of his teaching at Finkenwalde. It also found powerful expression in his book on *Discipleship* that had been gestating in his heart and mind ever since his encounter with Jean Lasserre at Union Theological Seminary in New York.

Discipleship (2001) is divided into two parts, the first being an exposition of the Sermon on the Mount, the second being an interpretation of Paul's theology of justification by faith and ecclesiology. Bonhoeffer undoubtedly wanted to demonstrate that following Jesus the suffering Messiah as described in the synoptic gospels was directly related to what St Paul taught about living by faith in Jesus Christ as Lord within the "body of Christ." In this way he was intent on countering the traditionally Lutheran tendency to separate "justification by faith alone" from costly discipleship. Such a separation, he argued, inevitably resulted in the cheapening of grace and the undermining of true evangelical faith and witness. This, Bonhoeffer believed, was at the heart of the problem of the evangelical church in Germany. "Like ravens," he wrote, "we have gathered around the carcass of cheap grace. From it we have imbibed the poison which has killed the following of Jesus among us … Luther's teachings are quoted everywhere, but twisted from their truth into self-delusion" (Bonhoeffer, 2001, 53). The truth is, "*only the believers obey*, and *only the obedient believe*" (ibid., 63). Believing in the doctrine of "justification by faith alone" was never intended as a substitute for discipleship; on the contrary, without taking the step of obedience through following Christ, faith is not a reality. "Discipleship is commitment to Christ. Because Christ exists, he must be followed. An idea about Christ, a doctrinal system, a general religious recognition of grace or forgiveness of sins does not require discipleship (ibid., 59). "Whenever Christ calls us, his call leads us to death" (ibid., 87).

That Bonhoeffer practiced what he proclaimed in *Discipleship* is self-evident, and that he sought to ensure the spiritual formation of his students along the same pattern is equally clear from *Life Together*. This remarkable interpretation of Christian community also brought together many of the key themes in Bonhoeffer's earlier theology, notably those of *Sanctorum Communio*. But now Bonhoeffer weaved them into a more explicitly biblical form and practically related them to the daily life of a church-community intent upon following Christ in the midst of a hostile world. The christological foundation of Christian community is also evident from the outset. "Christian community means community through Jesus Christ and in Jesus Christ. There is no Christian community that is more than this and none that is less than this ... We belong to one another only through and in Jesus Christ" (Bonhoeffer, 1996b, 31). Such a community is not an ideal to be sought and implemented by like-minded individuals, but a divine reality, a gift, which God brings into being through his Word. Those who turn to *Life Together* for guidance in building community along more "humanistic" or "group therapy" lines soon discover that they have entered a very different ethos. "In the spiritual community the Word of God alone rules; in the emotional, self-centred community the individual who is equipped with exceptional powers, experience, and magical, suggestive abilities rules along with the Word ... In the one, all power, honor, and rule are surrendered to the Holy Spirit; in the other, power and personal spheres of influence are sought and cultivated" (ibid., 40). Bonhoeffer was fully aware of the strength of his own personality and therefore of the danger in building the "community of brothers" at Finkenwalde around himself. Only Christ could be the true foundation of Christian community, and such community can only be sustained by the Word and the Spirit.

The Ethics of Free Responsibility

Even though Bonhoeffer was not impressed by the theology he encountered during his year of study at Union Theological Seminary, he soon acknowledged the particular importance which American theologians gave to social ethics and the social witness of the church. Ten years later, after his second, but very brief sojourn in New York, Bonhoeffer had a sense that American theology was improving under the influence of neo-orthodoxy, and he commented with appreciation on the work of his former teacher and now his colleague, Reinhold Niebuhr. Yet, he still felt that even Niebuhr's theology lacked an adequate christology. "In American theology," he wrote,

"Christianity is still essentially religion and ethics. But because of this, the person and work of Jesus Christ must, for theology, sink into the background and in the long run remain misunderstood, because it is not recognised as the sole ground of radical judgement and radical forgiveness" (Bonhoeffer, 1977, 115). For Bonhoeffer any notion that Christian ethics, whether personal or social, was a separate discipline with its own norms and methods was alien to his way of doing theology and what it means to confess Jesus Christ in the midst of the world. With this in mind we turn to his *Ethics*.

From Bonhoeffer's perspective, the history of the West from its conversion to Christianity until the Enlightenment could be understood as one in which Christ was shaping the values and norms of society. This inheritance was now squandered (Bonhoeffer, *Ethics*, 130–3). The West had become hostile to Christ, as was blatantly shown in the Nazi persecution of the Jews. Whereas previously Christians knew what God required even if they failed to do it, ethics had now become a matter of finding out what is good on the basis of reason and then trying to apply such moral principles to life in the world. However, the fundamental point of departure for Christian ethics, and therefore for the reconstruction of Western society, Bonhoeffer insisted, was not the question "how can I be good?" or "how can I do something good?" but rather "what is the will of God?" (ibid., 47). For Bonhoeffer this leads directly to the reality of God's revelation in Jesus Christ as the point of departure for Christian ethics, which is quite distinct from philosophical ethics. Yet it is not simply an ethics for the believer or the church, for the revelation of God in Jesus Christ irrevocably brings together the reality of God and the world. It is therefore impossible to experience the reality of God apart from the reality of the world. Any separation of Christian ethics from public life is untenable. Such "thinking in two spheres" falsely assumes that there are areas of life outside the Lordship of Jesus Christ.

By insisting that the will of God is to be discovered in God's revelation in Jesus Christ, Bonhoeffer also rejects any attempt to base Christian ethics on the "orders of creation" or on "natural law," though he does begin to express interest in the latter as his *Ethics* unfolds, relating it to his discussion of the divine mandates. But even so,

Christian ethics is not a matter of applying certain moral principles to life in the world. "God did not become an idea, a principle, a program, a universally valid belief, or a law. God became human" (ibid., 99). In other words, the starting point for Christian ethics is the incarnation or, put differently, Christ taking form in the world:

> The church's concern is not religion, but the form of Christ and its taking form among a band of people. If we let ourselves stray even the least bit from this perspective, we fall unavoidably into those programs of ethical and religious world-formation from which we have departed. (Bonhoeffer, *Ethics*, 97)

At one level, Christian ethics is fairly straightforward for it requires that we love God and our neighbor. The difficulty arises in boundary situations where the only choices facing one are morally murky. Moral dilemmas abounded in Nazi Germany, where the traditionally Christian and upright bourgeoisie had capitulated to state immorality. Questions concerning the right to life were made far more problematic because of the program to rid society of people who did not measure up to the Nazi model of Aryan purity and health. Even the question of telling the truth was problematic, for how could one do so if it meant that the life of a Jewish friend or neighbor was threatened? And, of course, Bonhoeffer was now part of the German conspiracy. Was it really legitimate to kill Hitler given the fact that it meant reneging on the oath of loyalty to the Führer which all German officers had taken; that it ran counter to everything treasured within patriotic German tradition; and, above all, that it meant disobeying the sixth commandment? This is the background to Bonhoeffer's discussion of "The Structure of Responsible Life" which lies at the heart of his *Ethics* (ibid., 257–88).

Christian ethics on the boundary, Bonhoeffer argued, required taking the risk of concrete decision. It might be wrong to lie, but that might be the more responsible action than "telling the truth"; it might be wrong to commit murder, but it was morally irresponsible not to assassinate Hitler. Not to take such a moral risk, not to engage in such an act of "free responsibility," would, on the basis of the conspirators' analysis of the situation, lead to many more deaths and increasing devastation. Yet, in taking such a step it

was necessary for the conspirators to acknowledge that they were also stepping beyond the boundaries of important and cherished moral norms, and therefore incurring guilt. "Those who act responsibly take on guilt—which is inescapable for any responsible person—place this guilt on themselves, not on someone else, they stand up for it and take responsibility for it" (ibid., 282). Such a person is wholly dependent upon God's grace. "Those who act out of free responsibility are justified before others by dire necessity; before themselves they are acquitted by their conscience, but before God they hope only for grace" (ibid., 282–3). In the end, then, Christian ethics is about the formation of men and women who will act rightly and justly precisely because the incarnate, crucified, and risen One has shaped their lives.

Christianity in a World Come of Age

Bonhoeffer did not complete his *Ethics*. Instead he found himself in prison where his thoughts began to move in new and unexpected directions even though many of his key prison insights are anticipated in his earlier writings. We cannot explore all of Bonhoeffer's insights as these found expression in his letters to his parents, his fiancée, and especially to his close friend Eberhard Bethge, or in his remarkable poetry. This is a pity for there is so much else that is of interest and significance than just his more controversial comments on Christianity in a "world come of age." Yet it is undoubtedly these latter reflections, starting with those in a letter to Bethge on April 30, 1944, that have attracted most attention (Bonhoeffer [1953] forthcoming). Of course, all that we have is fragmentary in form, for Bonhoeffer was engaged in sharing his thoughts with his close friend and not expecting them to be published, at least not in that form. Yet it is helpful to recall that Bonhoeffer was also engaged in writing a book related to his reflections, and even though all that remains of that project is a tentative outline, this does provide a coherent framework within which to locate his thought. Bonhoeffer had three chapters in mind (Bonhoeffer, 1971, 380ff.). The first, a "Stocktaking of Christianity," would examine the state of Christianity in a "world come of age"; the second, on "The Real Meaning of Christian Faith," would provide a "non-religious interpretation of Christianity"; and the third would discuss the consequences which the preceding discussion would have for the church.

As we might now expect, the point of departure for Bonhoeffer's reflections was a christological question. "What is bothering me incessantly," he wrote to Bethge, "is the question what Christianity really is, or indeed who Christ really is, for us today." Yet this question, which weaves his theological development together, now opens up fresh possibilities. Bonhoeffer is no longer primarily concerned about confessing Christ as Lord against Nazi idolatry, nor is he struggling to come to terms with the moral dilemmas of the conspiracy. What is at issue as he reflects on the state of Christianity in anticipation of the postwar period is the fundamental change in the worldview and consciousness of the West that has come about as a result of the Enlightenment, the French Revolution, and the rise of modern science. In the past, Christian proclamation had assumed a human "religious a priori," even claiming to be the true religion, but in the meantime the world had become increasingly "religionless." The nineteenth-century critique of religion as a human construction, along with Barth's own contention that God's revelation in Jesus Christ was a judgment on all religion, had to be taken seriously. But this was not just a theoretical or philosophical matter. Bonhoeffer was deeply concerned about the fact that both the working class and his secular compatriots in the conspiracy were estranged from both Christianity and the church, not least because of their well-founded suspicion of religion. Hence the question: "How can Christ become the Lord of the religionless as well?" And, as always for Bonhoeffer, this christological question immediately raised the further questions: "What do a church, a community, a sermon, a liturgy, a Christian life mean in a religionless world?" (Bonhoeffer, 1971, 279f.)

The phrase "world come of age" relates, of course, to the historical process of secularization in the West. Borrowed from Immanuel Kant and Wilhelm Dilthey, it does not mean that the world has become a more moral place but that it has undergone a fundamental reorientation. With regard to religion, this has meant the withdrawal of Christianity from public life into the private sphere. God himself has been pushed out onto the boundaries of life and become the God of individual piety, bourgeois privilege, and a ghetto church. In fact, God has been reduced to a *deus ex machina* who is only called upon when everything else has failed. This might be the God of religion, the God affirmed by the pious and rejected by the "religionless," but it is not the God of the Bible. Rather than trying to fit God into the gaps of our experience, Bonhoeffer would "like to speak of God not on the boundaries but at the centre, not in weakness but in strength; and therefore not in death and guilt but in the life and goodness of people" (ibid., 282). Indeed, "God would have us know that we must live as people who manage our lives without him" (ibid., 360). The transcendence of God has to do with God's presence "in the midst of our life," not some epistemological theory. Thus, what "is above this world is, in the gospel, intended to exist *for* this world." By this Bonhoeffer does not mean a return to the anthropocentric approach of liberal, mystical, pietistic, or ethical theology, "but in the biblical sense of the creation and of the incarnation, crucifixion, and resurrection of Jesus Christ" (ibid., 286).

Bonhoeffer's celebrated description of Jesus as the one who "is there only for others" is therefore not reductionist; it refers to our experience of transcendence (ibid., 381) from the perspective of the cross, and that means from the perspective of the victims of society. The God revealed in Jesus Christ is the God who "lets himself be pushed out of the world on to the cross. He is weak and powerless in the world, and that is precisely the way, the only way, in which he is with us and helps us." The God of the Bible is not the god of religion, but the "suffering God." That, Bonhoeffer declares, "will probably be the starting-point for our 'secular interpretation'" (ibid., 361)—an interpretation undoubtedly influenced by Bonhoeffer's whole life experience, whether in the black ghettos of New York, the slums of Berlin, or more recently in his identification with the plight of the Jews in Nazi Germany. As he told his fellow conspirators shortly before his arrest, "We have learnt to see the great events of world history from below, from the perspective of the outcast, the suspects, the maltreated, the powerless, the oppressed, the reviled—in short, from the perspective of those who suffer (ibid., 17).

The consequences of this for the church and for Christian life in the world are far-reaching. Indeed, the words just quoted, perhaps more than any others from Bonhoeffer's whole legacy, have had a remarkable influence on the shaping of theologies of liberation around the world. For what is at stake in Bonhoeffer's "non-religious" interpretation is not apologetics or hermeneutics, but a fundamental reorientation or *metanoia* which leads to an identification with Christ in his sufferings (ibid., 361) and therefore to a different way of being the church-community in the world. If Jesus exists only for others, so too the church must not seek its own self-preservation but be "open to the world" and in solidarity with others. This does not mean that the church must surrender its own identity, for that would simply be another example of "cheap grace," or a confusion of the penultimate and the ultimate. It is necessary for the church to recover the "discipline of the secret" (*disciplina arcanum*), whereby the mysteries of the faith are protected from profanation (ibid., 286). Prayer, worship, the sacraments, and the creed, remain at the heart of the life of the church, but they must not be thrust upon the world in some triumphalist manner. In sum, as Bonhoeffer wrote from prison on the occasion of Dietrich Bethge's baptism, "All Christian thinking, speaking, and organizing must be born anew out of [this] prayer and action." He continued:

It is not for us to prophesy the day (though the day will come) when men will once more be called so to utter the word of God that the world will be changed and renewed by it. It will be a new language, perhaps quite non-religious, but liberating and redeeming—as was Jesus' language; it will shock people and yet overcome them by its power; it will be the language of a new righteousness and truth, proclaiming God's peace with men and the coming of his kingdom. (Bonhoeffer, "Thoughts on the Day of the Baptism of Dietrich Wilhelm Rüdiger Bethge," 1971, 300)

Notes

1. For example, *Hitler and the Pastor—the Dietrich Bonhoeffer Story*, the Dietrich Bonhoeffer Film Project, New York.
2. The *Bonhoeffer-Triptychon*, by Herman Berlinski, Heinz Werner Zimmermann, and Robert M. Helmschrott, was first performed at Union Theological Seminary in New York by the Dresden Chamber Choir under the direction of Hans-Christoph Rademann, August, 12, 1992.
3. *Bonhoeffer*, composed by Ann K. Gebur, premiered at Pennsylvania State University, October 1999.
4. This is the new translation of "Christus als Gemeinde existierend" in Bonhoeffer (1998).
5. See Bonhoeffer's broadcast on "The Leadership Principle," which the German authorities cut off soon after he began. See Bonhoeffer (1977, 190ff.).
6. Previously translated in English as *Cost of Discipleship*. Dietrich Bonhoeffer, *Discipleship*, trans. Barbara Green and Reinhard Krauss. Dietrich Bonhoeffer Works, General Editor: Wayne W. Floyd; volume editors: Geffrey B. Kelly and John D. Godsey, vol. 4 (Minneapolis: Fortress, 2001).
7. English translations are from Bonhoeffer, *Christ the Centre* (1978a).

References

Bethge, Eberhard. 1999. *Dietrich Bonhoeffer*, ed. Victoria Barnett, rev. ed. Minneapolis: Fortress Press. (This is the standard account but there are several other outstanding biographies.)

Bonhoeffer, D. [1953] Forthcoming. *Letters and Papers from Prison*, volume 8 of *Dietrich Bonhoeffer Works in English*. Minneapolis: Fortress Press. (A new critical and much expanded English edition.)

Bonhoeffer, D. 1965. *Ethics*. New York: Macmillan.

Bonhoeffer, D. 1971. *Letters and Papers from Prison*, trans. Eberhard Bethge. London: SCM.

Bonhoeffer, D. 1977. *No Rusty Swords: Letters Lectures and Notes 1928–1936*, Collected Works of Dietrich Bonhoeffer, vol. 1. London: Collins.

Bonhoeffer, D. 1978a. *Christ the Centre*. New York: Harper & Co.

Bonhoeffer, D. 1978b. *Christology*, trans. E. H. Robertson. London: Collins.

Bonhoeffer, D. 1996a. *Act and Being: Transcendental Philosophy and Ontology in Systematic Theology*, Dietrich Bonhoeffer Works, vol. 2. Minneapolis: Fortress Press.

Bonhoeffer, D. 1996b. *Life Together: Prayerbook of the Bible*, trans. Daniel W. Bloesch and James H. Burtness. *Dietrich Bonhoeffer Works*, vol. 5. Minneapolis: Fortress Press.

Bonhoeffer, D. 1997. *Creation and Fall: A Theological Exposition of Genesis 1–3*. Dietrich Bonhoeffer Works, vol. 3. Minneapolis: Fortress Press.

Bonhoeffer, D. 1998. *Sanctorum Communio: A Theological Study of the Sociology of the Church*, trans. Reinhard Krauss and Nancy Lukens. Dietrich Bonhoeffer Works, vol. 1. Minneapolis: Fortress Press.

Bonhoeffer, D. 2001. *Discipleship*, trans. Barbara Green and Reinhard Krauss. Dietrich Bonhoeffer Works, General Editor: Wayne W. Floyd; volume editors: Geffrey B. Kelly and John D. Godsey, vol. 4. Minneapolis: Fortress.

Bonhoeffer, D. 2002. *The Young Bonhoeffer: 1918–1927*, trans. Mary C. Nebelsick with Douglas W. Stott. Dietrich Bonhoeffer Works, General Editor: Wayne W. Floyd Jr. and Clifford J. Green; volume editors: Paul Duane Matheny and Marshall Johnson, vol. 9. Minneapolis: Fortress Press.

Bonhoeffer, D. 2005. *Ethics*, trans. Charles C. West and Douglas W. Stott Reinhard Krauss. Dietrich Bonhoeffer Works, General Editor: Wayne W. Whitson; volume editor: Clifford J. Green, vol. 6. Minneapolis: Fortress.

Bonhoeffer, D. 2007. *London 1933–1935*, trans. Isabel Best. Dietrich Bonhoeffer Works, General Editor: Victoria J. Barnett; volume editor: Keith Clements, vol. 13. Minneapolis: Fortress Press.

Bonhoeffer, D. 2008. *Barcelona, Berlin, New York 1928–1931*, trans. Douglas W. Stott. Dietrich Bonhoeffer Works, General Editor: Victoria J. Barnett; volume editor: Clifford J. Green, vol. 10. Minneapolis: Fortress Press.

Bonhoeffer, D. Forthcoming. *Berlin 1933*, trans. Isabel Best and David Higgins; supplementary material trans. Douglas W. Stott; ed. Larry L. Rasmussen. Minneapolis: Fortress Press.

Bonhoeffer, D. Forthcoming. *Letters and Papers from Prison*, trans. Lisa E. Dahil Isabel Best and Nancy Lukens. Dietrich Bonhoeffer Works, General Editor: Victoria J. Barnett; volume editor: John W. de Gruchy, vol. 8. Minneapolis: Fortress Press.

Bonhoeffer, D. and von Wedemeyer, Maria. 1994. *Love Letters from Cell 92*. London: HarperCollins.

Green, Clifford. 1999. *Bonhoeffer: Theology of Sociality*. Grand Rapids, MI: Eerdmans.

de Gruchy, John W. 1997. "Bonhoeffer. Apartheid, and Beyond: The Reception of Bonhoeffer in South Africa." In *Bonhoeffer for a New Day: Theology in a Time of Transition*, ed. John W. de Gruchy. Grand Rapids, MI: Eerdmans.

de Gruchy John W., ed. 1999. *The Cambridge Companion to Dietrich Bonhoeffer*. Cambridge: Cambridge University Press.

de Gruchy, John W. 2005. *Daring, Trusting Spirit: Bonhoeffer's Friend Eberhard Bethge*. London: SCM.

Floyd, Wayne Whitson, Jr. 1999. "Bonhoeffer's Literary Legacy." In *Cambridge Companion to Dietrich Bonhoeffer*, ed. John W. de Gruchy. Cambridge: Cambridge University Press.

Haynes, Stephen R. 2004. *The Bonhoeffer Phenomenon*. Minneapolis: Fortress.

Slane, Craig J. 2004. *Bonhoeffer as Martyr*. Grand Rapids, MI: Brazos.

James Cone (1938–)

Joseph Constant

Black liberation theology has a history that can be traced back over 400 years in history. Despite its roots steeped in the work of Richard Allen, and the historical work of W. E. B. Dubois and Frederick Douglass, it was not until the late 1960s that a formal doctrine of theology was posited by James Cone. Cone once stated that, "Every theologian must take what he believes to be the central theme of the biblical message and relate that theme to his historical situation" (Cone, 1970). Drawing upon his upbringing in segregated Arkansas, the oppression of blacks in America, and the disconnect that Cone felt from the traditional church, Cone joined with other pastors in calling for a Black Power movement. This movement was a challenge to recognize that white men had significant power with no principles and blacks suffered from too many principles without any power. Cone argued for the liberation of blacks, the poor, and the oppressed, believing that this was the revelation of Jesus Christ. This revelation of Jesus Christ became the foundation of Cone's black liberation theology.

Drawing upon the Civil Rights movements of the 1950s and 1960s, Cone connected the black struggle for justice in the United States with the gospel of Jesus Christ. Building upon a 400-year history of oppression and slavery, Cone wanted to identify his place in the church, connecting his understanding of the biblical message and faith with the experience of black America. Cone condemned the theology of the white church, which was largely tied to patriotism and excused the oppression of black America as an act ordained by God. Cone argued that the black theology was a Christian theology, built upon a gospel that raises up an oppressed community and that is centered on Jesus Christ (Cone, 1970).

Born and raised in Arkansas in 1938, Cone was raised by working-class parents. His father was a woodcutter who fought to ensure his family did not succumb to the dehumanizing white–black relationships. He resisted the Arkansas social structure that asked for the black woman to be the maid for the white family, for the black man to labor day in and day out in the factory. These were all structures Cone's father chose to fight against. He went so far as to sue the Board of Education, arguing that separate was not equal when it came to education. While James's father provided him with the tenets of black power, it was his mother who served as the religious leader of the family, requiring Cone's father to attend church before she would even marry him. Mrs. Cone believed religion was the source of identity and survival and it was God that recognized them as children of God.

James Cone lived amongst segregation and poverty, growing up in a town of 1,200 people, 800 of whom were white and 400 of whom were black. Cone described the dichotomy of his childhood, surrounded by a white population which believed that blacks were amongst them solely to serve, and yet active in

The Student's Companion to the Theologians, First Edition. Edited by Ian S. Markham.

the African Methodist Episcopal Church, filled with sermons, prayers, and music about the well-being of its black membership. Segregated schools, movie theaters, and restaurants, and violence and political and economic inequality were the images that filled Cone's childhood. Even his church was not safe from the threat of disruption and violence. Cone's childhood was filled with the realities of white injustice and yet it was also fed by the word of God, a faith that sustained him amongst the injustice. And as Cone grew up, he saw the leadership of the church, the clergy who stepped forward to speak out against and protest the oppression, struggling for justice in the name of the gospel. It was this leadership from the church that inspired Cone's own career.

After obtaining his BA from Philander Smith College, Cone's interest in religion and faith drew him to Garret Theological Seminary, a seminary of the United Methodist Church in Evanston, Illinois. Cone later received his PhD in history and literature of religion in 1965 at Northwestern University. He married Rosa Hampton, and had four children. Cone began his teaching career at Philander Smith College, and then continued at Adrian College in Michigan before being called to Union Theological Seminary in New York City, in 1969, where he serves as the Charles A. Briggs Professor of Systematic Theology.

Throughout his career Cone has been a prolific writer; his works include *Black Theology and Black Power* (1969), which defined his conversion journey into black theology, reconciling black power with Christianity. Cone strongly believed that one must understand their identity to sustain oneself in society. He wanted to define a religious identity that could serve black America, and identified God with the struggle of black people and the ultimate liberation of the oppressed through the life, death, and resurrection of Jesus Christ. *Black Theology and Black Power* was the first scholarly publication on black theology. Using his own experience of growing up in racially segregated Arkansas, Cone was eager to embrace a Christian faith in which Jesus Christ was the center and savior. However, the European Christian tradition which he saw in both the black churches and the white almost led him to leave his faith. His identification of Jesus as the savior of the poor, the one who embraced the oppressed, led to the development of a black liberation theology. Following publication of *Black Theology and Black Power*, Cone was invited to present his theology at the National Conference of Black Churchmen (NCBC) and make a statement on black theology. He believes that NCBC was the organizational and political implementation of his theological perspective.

Cone continued developing this theological perspective with *A Black Theology of Liberation* (1970), which defined theology as the "study of the being of God in the world in light of the existential situation of an oppressed community, relating the forces of liberation to the essence of the gospel, which is Jesus Christ" (Cone, 1970). Cone explores key church doctrines through the eyes of impoverished blacks.

Cone's writing and theology was not entirely well received. His critics crossed a broad spectrum of races and theologians, some believing Cone's writing was too exclusive and others believing he was not exclusive enough (Cone, 1982). Further, there was resistance to Cone's assertion that true faith came from oppression, or, as Cone asserted, "There can be no theology of the Gospel that does not arrive from an oppressed community (Cone, 1970). But some of Cone's greatest criticism came from Charles Long, Professor at University of Chicago, and Carleton Lee, Professor at Western Michigan University, who questioned whether Cone's theology was black theology or white theology that was "painted black."

In Cone's next two books, *The Spirituals and the Blues* (1972) and *God of the Oppressed* (1975), Cone responded to his critics. In *The Spirituals and the Blues*, Cone addressed the question of whether his black theology should be based on scripture rather than a text based solely on the experience of African Americans. For Cone's critics, scripture is the text used by white colonial powers to oppress black Africans; a theology based upon the scripture was viewed as unacceptable. Cone responded by broadening his theology to examine the sacred and religious dimensions of the musical experience of blacks. In this context, he argues that the blues are very spiritual in the sense that they highlight the essential God-given humanity of black people as they struggle to deal with the stresses of day-to-day living.

Returning to the roots of his initial inspiration, in 1991 Cone wrote *Martin and Malcolm and America:*

A Dream or a Nightmare. Cone compares the thoughts and philosophies of both leaders, their impact on the African American struggle, and how each leader understood their view of the best way of achieving justice in America. Cone argues that that both Malcolm X and Martin Luther King Jr. shared the same vision for African Americans—that is, freedom—but that they differed on the best way to achieve and live out that sense of freedom. King favored integration and advocated that African Americans emphasize their American identity. On the other hand, Malcolm believed that the only way to achieve freedom is for

African Americans to underline their African identity and origin. Cone's own beliefs reflect the precepts of both Malcolm X and Martin Luther King. Cone's beliefs are based in justice and blackness—the Christian principles of Dr King and the black consciousness of Malcolm X.

Cone's black theology has impacted the discussion and perceptions of theology. His work has been translated and examined internationally since it is viewed as a theology of hope for the oppressed. Much of the growth of liberation theology in Latin America and Asia can be traced to the influence of Cone.

References

Cone, James H. 1969. *Black Theology and Black Power.* New York: Seabury Press.

Cone, James H. 1970. *A Black Theology of Liberation.* Philadelphia: Lippincott & Co.

Cone, James H. 1972. *The Spirituals and the Blues.* New York: Orbis Books.

Cone, James H. 1975. *God of the Oppressed.* New York: Seabury Press.

Cone, James H. 1982. *My Soul Looks Back.* Nashville: Abingdon Press.

Cone, James H. 1991. *Martin and Malcolm and America: A Dream or a Nightmare.* New York: Orbis Books.

Hornden, William. 1971. "Dialogue on Black Theology," *The Christian Century.*

Murphy, Larry G., Melton, J. Gordon, and Ward, Gary L. 1993. *Encyclopedia of African American Religions.* New York and London: Garland Publishing, Inc.

Satya. 2004. *Malcolm and Martin: Still Teachers of Resistance: The Satya Interview with James H. Cone.* Available from www.satyamag.com

Austin Farrer (1904–68)

Brian Hebblethwaite

Austin Marsden Farrer was a philosophical and biblical theologian. Educated at St Paul's School, London and Balliol College, Oxford, Farrer trained for the priesthood at Cuddesdon and was ordained deacon in 1928 and priest in 1929. After serving a curacy at All Saints, Dewsbury in the diocese of Wakefield, he returned to Oxford in 1931 as chaplain and tutor in theology and philosophy at St Edmund Hall. During these next years he paid a number of visits to Germany and acquired a critical acquaintance with German theology. In Oxford, at this time, he also met his future wife, Katharine Newton, then studying Litterae Humaniores at St Anne's.

In 1935 Farrer moved to Trinity College as chaplain and tutor. Two years later he and Katherine were married in the church at Ashwell of which her father was rector. In the same year Farrer was elected Fellow of Trinity, where he remained until 1960. During the 1940s and 1950s Farrer was a leading light in the "Metaphysicals," a group of high Anglican philosophers and theologians that included Eric Mascall, Basil Mitchell, and John Lucas, who met regularly to discuss—and oppose—the anti-metaphysical bias of the current Oxford philosophy. In 1960 Farrer became Warden of Keble College. He died in office there in 1968.

The way in which Farrer combined, in life as in thought, philosophical acuity, theological perspicuity, and spiritual insight greatly impressed and moved his pupils and hearers throughout his teaching and preaching career, and has continued to impress and move the readers of his books ever since. He is widely regarded as one of the greatest Anglican theologians of the twentieth century.

Farrer's acute metaphysical mind was evident in his first major work, *Finite and Infinite* (1943), in which he argued, against positivist criticism, for a theistic metaphysic being implicit in the analysis of human subjectivity and agency. Farrer acknowledged the limited scope of this substantial monograph. Rational theology, he says, leads us to "the knowledge of existent perfection conceived through the analogy of spirit, and the knowledge that this Being is the creator of all finite existence. But that is all … [N]o sound reason for a belief in Providence is deducible from these premises." By the time he came to issue the second edition of *Finite and Infinite* in 1959 we find these words added to the Preface: "unless a general and sovereign Providence makes sense, the link is cut between life and creationist belief, and the investigation of that belief appears superfluous." In order to discover whether the God of rational theology acts in the world by providence or grace, he concludes, "we must turn to the field of particular 'contingent' events, and see whether he habitually so acts, or whether in one or more revealing events he has given the promise of so acting." In the light of this, it is not surprising to find the topic of divine providence coming to occupy more and more of Farrer's attention.

The Student's Companion to the Theologians, First Edition. Edited by Ian S. Markham.
© 2013 Blackwell Publishing Ltd. Published 2013 by Blackwell Publishing Ltd.

Nevertheless, a theistic metaphysic is a necessary, if not a sufficient, condition of belief in providence, and Farrer remained committed to *Finite and Infinite*'s argument for such a metaphysic. His actual doctrine of God, however, underwent significant development.

Between the first and second editions of *Finite and Infinite* Farrer was preoccupied with two topics in particular: revelation and will. His Bampton Lectures, *The Glass of Vision* (1948), is primarily about revelation and "the form of divine truth in the human mind." Farrer's treatment here of the way in which divine revelation is conveyed through the core biblical images forms the bridge between his philosophical theology and his biblical theology. His biblical work bore fruit in four books on the New Testament: *A Rebirth of Images* (1949), *A Study in St Mark* (1951), *St Matthew and St Mark* (1954), and *The Revelation of St John the Divine* (1964). The understanding of typology that underlies these books is set out in an article in *The Expository Times* for 1955/56 in which he shows how New Testament authors saw key figures and incidents in the Old Testament as types prefiguring the story of Jesus Christ and bringing out its revelatory significance.

Farrer's Gifford Lectures, *The Freedom of the Will* (1958a) constitutes an outstanding philosophical refutation of determinism and defense of human action, volition, and creativity. Its theological import, however, only emerges toward the end, where Farrer admits that theology has its own version of the determinist problem, namely the paradox of creative and creaturely wills.

This sets the scene for his later treatment of divine providence, that is, of divine action in and through the action and interaction of creatures, in the four, more popular, works of his final decade: *Love Almighty and Ills Unlimited* (1961), *Saving Belief* (1964), *A Science of God?* (1966), and *Faith and Speculation* (1967). A key motif in these books is that of "double agency," as he calls the interrelation of God's action and that of creatures. According to Farrer, divine providence makes the creature make itself by drawing together the various threads of evolution, history, and individual life, without faking or forcing the natural or human story, in order to further God's purposes.

The theme of divine providence is, of course, inseparable from the problem of evil that forms such a massive stumbling block for any serious theistic belief. Farrer's attempt to show why the created universe is so vulnerable to evil and suffering centers on the idea that God's rooting and grounding his personal creatures in a physical, evolving universe and letting the human world make itself precisely in and through the processes of evolution and history are the necessary conditions for the formation of finite persons. Only when thus formed, with their own being and nature, can they be drawn into relation with their Maker and eventually immortalized.

Farrer's last book, *Faith and Speculation*, also presents a revised theology of God, modeled on the analogy of personal interaction. And it is fascinating to observe how Farrer had moved from the basically Thomist position of *Finite and Infinite* to a much more dynamic theistic metaphysic. The theistic position reached here is certainly "voluntarist." God is defined as "Unconditioned Will." By contrast with the world's—and our—unexplained and conditioned existence, its—and our—ultimate explanation is to be found in "the God who is all he wills to be, and wills to be all he is: for his act is himself, and his act is free." By itself, this definition may seem far from perspicuous. But Farrer has already made it clear that God is to be thought of, in wholly personal and spiritual terms, as free, incorporeal, unconditioned Spirit.

The most interesting aspect of Farrer's development is his recognition that the traditional conception of God's eternity as timelessness cannot be sustained. Farrer suggests that, if God is to be thought of in personal terms as active and interactive will, there must, within God's own reality, be something *analogous* to the temporal form that characterizes ours. So, while he does not attempt to apply temporal categories univocally to God and the world (as process theology appears to do), he does suppose there to be, within God's "prior actuality," a primordial temporality analogous to our temporality.

Farrer's work on the doctrines of the Creed also repays close study. The main source here is *Saving Belief*, although his articles, sermons, and devotional writings, all informed by his acute philosophical mind, are equally illuminating. There are five volumes of sermons (four published posthumously): *Said or Sung* (1960), *A Celebration of Faith* (1970), *The Brink of Mystery* (1976), *The End of Man* (1973), and *Words for Life* (1993); two posthumous collections of occasional pieces, *Reflective Faith* (1972) and *Interpretation and Belief* (1976); and three devotional books, *The Crown of the Year* (1952), *Lord I Believe* (1958b), and *The Triple Victory* (1965). Sifting through all this material, one sees Farrer combining spiritual insight and rational reflection in order to bring out the meaning of Christian doctrine, and its import for life and discipleship.

One example is his treatment of soteriology. Farrer refuses to drive a wedge between God's attitude and God's action. Justification is of a piece with sanctification. Precisely because God is God, his forgiveness *is* his act of reconciliation. To quote Farrer's beautiful summing up: "What, then, did God do for his people's redemption? He came amongst them, bringing his Kingdom, and he let events take their course. He set the divine life in human neighbourhood. Men discovered it in struggling with it and were captured by it in crucifying it."

A second example is Farrer's treatment of eschatology. On the resurrection of Jesus Christ and its relation both to God's providential work in history and to the ultimate destiny of all God's personal creatures, he writes:

> The Resurrection is not a miracle like any other. It is a unique manifestation within this world of the transition God makes for us out of this way of being into another. But no one who believes that God remakes the life of the dead in a new and glorified fashion supposes that he forces or violates their natures in thus fulfilling and transforming them.

Farrer also writes eloquently of heaven: There are two worlds, the old and the new creations of God. The two worlds are our universe, the place of God's natural creatures, and Christ's heaven, the place of God's glorified creatures. The former does not contain the latter, but the latter embraces the former. For spirit touches spirit, and from his heaven, freed from the limitations of physical being, Christ already draws us into his presence. Our union with God in Christ will be fulfilled beyond death, where we will see him face to face.

The question arises whether Farrer was a universalist, that is, a believer in the ultimate salvation of all. He confessed that the fate of ultimate impenitence was a mystery into which he was reluctant to look. On the other hand, he refused to rule out universalism or conditional immortality—the view that life after death is restricted to those who have responded positively to the love of God. He had no such reservations, however, in rejecting the idea of a personal devil. His arguments to this effect, in brief, are these: in the first place, to attribute either human wickedness or natural disaster to the devil's agency simply diverts attention from our own responsibility and from our own understanding of the world of nature. Secondly, it makes no theological sense to suppose that God not only preserves in being forever an irredeemable fallen creature but also allows that creature to wreak havoc in the world. So, for Farrer, talk of the devil is figurative talk. "Lucifer expresses our sin, he does not explain it." One further point against literal acceptance of the demonology characteristic of pre-scientific cultures should be emphasized. Farrer was quite clear that there is no parallel at all between belief in Satan and belief in the Creator. There are no metaphysical arguments for postulating a supernatural source of evil comparable to the metaphysical arguments for postulating God.

Thus we come back to the irreplaceable role, for Farrer's whole position in philosophical theology, of the theistic metaphysic argued for in his first book, *Finite and Infinite*.

References

Books by Farrer

Farrer, A. M. [1943] 1959. *Finite and Infinite*. London: Dacre Press.

Farrer, A. M. 1948. *The Glass of Vision*. London: Dacre Press.

Farrer, A. M. 1949. *A Rebirth of Images. The Making of St John's Apocalypse*. London: Dacre Press.

Farrer, A. M. 1951. *A Study in St Mark*. London: Dacre Press.

Farrer, A. M. 1952. *The Crown of the Year. Weekly Paragraphs for the Holy Sacrament*. London: Dacre Press.

Farrer, A. M. 1954. *St Matthew and St Mark*. London: Dacre Press.

Farrer, A. M. 1958a. *The Freedom of the Will*. London: A. & C. Black.

Farrer, A. M. 1958b. *Lord I Believe. Suggestions for Turning the Creed into Prayer*. London: Faith Press.

Farrer, A. M. 1960. *Said or Sung. An Arrangement of Homily and Verse*. London: Faith Press.

Farrer, A. M. 1961. *Love Almighty and Ills Unlimited*. New York: Doubleday (1962, London: Collins).

Farrer, A. M. 1964. *The Revelation of St. John the Divine*. Oxford: Clarendon Press.

Farrer, A. M. 1964. *Saving Belief. A Discussion of Essentials*. London: Hodder & Stoughton.

Farrer, A. M. 1965. *The Triple Victory. Christ's Temptations According to St Matthew*. London: Faith Press.

Farrer, A. M. 1966. *A Science of God?* London: Geoffrey Bles.

Farrer, A. M. 1967. *Faith and Speculation*. London: A. & C. Black.

Farrer, A. M. 1970. *A Celebration of Faith*. London: Hodder & Stoughton.

Farrer, A. M. 1972. *Reflective Faith. Essays in Philosophical Theology*. London: SPCK.

Farrer, A. M. 1973. *The End of Man*. London: SPCK.

Farrer, A. M. 1976a. *Interpretation and Belief*. London: SPCK.

Farrer, A. M. 1976b. *The Brink of Mystery*. London: SPCK.

Farrer, A. M. 1993. *Words for Life*. London: SPCK.

Other books

Conti, Charles. 1995. *Metaphysical Personalism*. Oxford: Oxford University Press.

Curtis, Philip 1985. *A Hawk among Sparrows: A Biography of Austin Farrer*. London: SPCK.

Eaton, J. C. 1980. *The Logic of Theism: An Analysis of the Thought of Austin Farrer*. Lanham, MD: University Press of America.

Eaton, Jeffrey C. and Loades, Ann, eds. 1983. *For God and Clarity: New Essays in Honor of Austin Farrer*. Allison Park, PA: Pickwick Publications.

Hebblethwaite, Brian. 2007. *The Philosophical Theology of Austin Farrer*. Leuven: Peeters.

Hebblethwaite, Brian and Henderson, Edward, eds. 1990. *Divine Action. Essays Inspired by the Philosophical Theology of Austin Farrer*. Edinburgh: T&T Clark Ltd.

Hedley, Douglas and Hebblethwaite, Brian, eds. 2006. *The Human Person in God's World. Studies to Commemorate the Austin Farrer Centenary*. London: SCM Press.

Hefling, Charles C. 1979. *Jacob's Ladder. Theology and Spirituality in the Thought of Austin Farrer*. Cambridge, MA: Cowley Publications.

Hein, David and Henderson, Edward Hugh. 2004. *Captured by the Crucified. The Practical Theology of Austin Farrer*. New York and London: T&T Clark International.

Loades, Ann and McLain, Michael, eds. 1992. *Hermeneutics, the Bible and Literary Criticism*. New York: St Martin's Press.

McLain, Michael F. and Richardson, W. Mark. 1999. *Human and Divine Agency. Anglican, Catholic and Lutheran Perspectives*. Lanham, MD: University Press of America.

Hans Frei (1922–88)

Medi Ann Volpe

Hans Frei was born in Germany in 1922, but lived for most of his life in the United States. Fearing for his safety in the 1930s, Frei's parents sent him to school in England; shortly thereafter, he moved with them to the USA. Frei's early life thus consisted of a series of national and cultural displacements. Eventually, Frei landed at Yale as a student, and returned as a professor of theology, where he taught until his death in 1988. His name is frequently associated with the "Yale School." The term is something of a misnomer: Frei's theological style influenced many, including his colleague George Lindbeck, but his approach to theology never stood still long enough to form the basis for a school. Postliberal theology—Lindbeck's term for the "Yale" approach—attempts to preserve the truth of classical Christian doctrine in a way that neither repeats past formulations verbatim nor translates them into contemporary, extra-ecclesial idiom. While the style itself owes much to Frei's own method, no single theologian or movement bears Frei's mantle: his influence is at once more profound and more diffuse than the idea that "Yale School" suggests.

Frei's sudden and unexpected death in 1988 left behind several unfinished academic projects. Thus, the two monographs he published during his lifetime, *The Eclipse of Biblical Narrative* (1974) and *The Identity of Jesus Christ* (1975), do not tell the whole story of Frei's theology. Frei completed his Yale doctoral dissertation, "The Doctrine of Revelation in the Thought of Karl Barth, 1909–1922: The Nature of Barth's Break with Liberalism," in 1956, but he never published it. Likewise, the many lectures Frei delivered in the intervening years display the theological ideas he was developing, but these mostly remain unpublished. Although two books have appeared since Frei's death, the history of modern christology (1700–1950) on which he was working in the mid-1980s remains unfinished.

Frei's theology cannot be separated from the figures that influenced him or from those whose theology he shaped. First and most obviously, Barth played a key role in Frei's theological development: Frei began his theological thinking in a critical engagement with Barth, which in many ways set the course for his own project. In contrast to Frei's work on Barth, Frei's negotiation of the space between Strauss and Schleiermacher led him to investigate the origin and development of "liberal" theology. Frei's final assessment of Schleiermacher has only recently been fully appreciated: in drafting his typology (see below), Frei came to see Barth and Schleiermacher as much closer methodologically than the typology might initially suggest. The apparent shift in Frei's appreciation of Schleiermacher leads to the question of a turning point, or a milestone, that might differentiate "early" from "later" theology. Such a clear distinction is not to be found. What Frei sees in Schleiermacher's theology that draws him closer to Barth stems from the ongoing

The Student's Companion to the Theologians, First Edition. Edited by Ian S. Markham.
© 2013 Blackwell Publishing Ltd. Published 2013 by Blackwell Publishing Ltd.

development of Frei's interpretation of philosophy and (or versus) Christianity. Thus, Frei's later descriptions of Schleiermacher would better be described as reflecting the growth of his theology toward the "generous" orthodoxy that drew him to the Episcopal Church in the late 1940s.

Frei's engagement with Barth cannot be considered apart from his years as a student of H. Richard Niebuhr, who drew him to Yale Divinity School and supervised his doctoral dissertation. Two intertwined themes in Frei's overall theological project bear the marks of his inheritance from Barth and Niebuhr: his portrait of Jesus and his approach to theological method. Frei's insistence on understanding the place of Jesus within the Christian community represents a creative synthesis of Barth's christology and Niebuhr's method. Frei takes a step forward, to be sure, but he steps *from* Barth and Niebuhr to create his characteristic approach to theological construction. The uniqueness of Jesus Christ and his place *within* the community of faith cannot be separated from Frei's theological practice: understanding Jesus takes place within the community of faith, whose interpretation relies on a decision about the significance of Jesus that transcends the text itself. Frei builds his method, insofar as we can call it "method," as he engages the material with which he works: it is always eclectic and pragmatic.

The two monographs Frei published in the middle of his career, *The Eclipse of Biblical Narrative* and *The Identity of Jesus Christ*, offer a snapshot of his thinking to the mid-1970s and suggest the direction of his work into the mid-1980s. The content of these two volumes represents Frei's detailed research; the construction of theological argument in each is equally significant. In *The Eclipse of Biblical Narrative* Frei argued that the loss of the sense of narrative continuity in the Bible, and the connection of that story with the people of God, from the calling of Abraham to the present-day church, deprives the Christian community of a crucial interpretive framework for biblical interpretation. The substitution of general hermeneutical theories for a literal-sense consensus, he suggested, will not do. Frei followed up this argument later with "The Literal Sense: Does It Stretch or Will It Break?" Only a "literal sense" that arises out of a community's reading of the scripture will stretch, Frei

argued; hermeneutical theories—whether traditional historical-critical or postmodern deconstruction— "break" the text by asking of it questions it should not be made to answer. (This essay has also been edited and republished by Kathryn Tanner; see below.)

In *The Identity of Jesus Christ*, Frei shifted the question concerning Jesus' resurrection from the historical-critical setting to an ecclesial one. While he does not suggest that the historicity of the resurrection is totally unimportant, he does say that the question of historicity is not the one with which Christians ought to be most concerned. Jesus' identity is given through the texts, which attest to his resurrection: the resurrection, in turn, is true in these texts and for the church in which their authority is central. The texts and the community provide the proper arena for considering Jesus' death and resurrection. The reader might well ask, upon finishing Frei's book, whether he believed that Jesus was *really* raised. Yes, Frei might say, but that answer only makes sense within a community for which Jesus' resurrection is the basis for a way of life. Taken together, Frei's two monographs reveal a theological methodology focused on the indispensability of internal language in second-order analysis of Christian faith and practice. No study of Christianity that operates from the perspective of an outsider will be able to assess the truth of its proclamation. The influence of Barth, however mediated by Frei's Yale context, is unmistakable.

Frei's own influence in the field is difficult to calculate, not least because for the last decade or so of his life, he gave lectures and continued his work without publishing much at all. Interpersonal relationships, especially with students and colleagues, thus form the central avenue for his influence during these years. Evidence of his influence is clear, however, in the work of colleague George Lindbeck and students Kathryn Tanner and William Placher, who (together with George Hunsinger) have edited and published some of Frei's work in progress. The first to appear, *Types of Christian Theology* (1992), sets out Frei's typology of Christian theological methodology. The five types are ordered according to the relationship between first-order Christian proclamation and the second-order framework the theologian uses to analyze the ordinary language of Christian faith. Frei measured the relationship between first-order language (or internal description) and second-order interpretation (or external description) by the extent to which Christian theologians appropriated secular, philosophical models in their analysis. On one end of the spectrum (Type One), Frei set theology done as a philosophical discipline within the academy. On this end of the scale, the first-order proclamation tends to disappear into the philosophical analysis. For Frei, Gordon Kaufman represented this type of theology. At the other end, Frei identified a type of theology that eschewed the use of any external categories of analysis; theologians like D. Z. Phillips argued that a general theory of religion falsely portrayed Christianity as one instance of the genus "religion." Thus only the internal language of the Christian community should be used in interpretation. Frei's own approach hovered near the middle: like Barth (and also, it has been argued more recently, like Schleiermacher), Frei made use of philosophy where it suited the subject matter, but never allowed it to displace the language of proclamation.

The essays collected in *Theology and Narrative* (1993), while not as clearly focused as the material in *Types*, offer the reader a glimpse of Frei's own vision of his theological project, in terms of both content and method. The essays reveal a theologian who cared deeply about the practice of theology in a time of uncertainty about its place and its future. The volume is significant particularly for what it adds to Frei's published works: a paper in which Frei reflects on Barth's theology following his death in 1968, a discussion of Barth and Schleiermacher, and essays that return to themes in and questions raised by his two monographs. Importantly, the book clarifies Frei's position with respect to postliberalism. Frei exemplifies much of what is best about postliberalism, but transcends it. Although Frei may have inspired Lindbeck's proposal for a way of doing theology, he cannot be described as a "postliberal" theologian. Book-length treatments of Frei's theology have only just begun to appear, and his influence is sure to continue into future generations.

References

Books by Hans Frei

1974. *The Eclipse of Biblical Narrative: A Study in Eighteenth and Nineteenth Century Hermeneutics*. New Haven: Yale University Press.

1975. *The Identity of Jesus Christ*, ed. George Hunsinger and William Placher: Eugene, OR: Wipf & Stock Publishers.

1992. *Types of Christian Theology*, ed. George Hunsinger and William Placher. New Haven, CT: Yale University Press.

1993. *Theology and Narrative: Selected Essays*. Oxford: Oxford University Press.

Secondary sources

DeHart, Paul. 2006. *The Trial of the Witnesses: The Rise and Decline of Postliberal Theology*. Oxford and Malden, MA: Blackwell.

Higton, M. A. 2004. *Christ, Providence and History: Hans W. Frei's Public Theology*. London and New York: T&T Clark.

Colin Gunton (1941–2003)

Clive Marsh

Colin Gunton was one of the most significant voices in British systematic theology in the final three decades of the twentieth century. He grew up in Nottingham, England, studied classics and then theology at Oxford, undertaking doctoral studies under Robert Jenson, John Marsh, and John Macquarrie. His thesis on the doctrine of God in Charles Hartshorne and Karl Barth, completed in 1973, was published as *Becoming and Being* in 1978 (Gunton, 2001a). By then he had married (1966), begun to lecture in the philosophy of religion at King's College London (1969), and become a minister in the United Reformed Church (1972). He was an associate minister at Brentwood URC from 1975 until his death in 2003, became Professor of Christian Doctrine at King's College London in 1984, and served as convenor of the United Reformed Church's Doctrine and Worship Committee when it produced its new *Service Book* (1989). The meshing of academic and church commitments was crucial to who he was and what he understood theology to be. In 1988 he cofounded the Research Institute in Systematic Theology at King's with Christoph Schwoebel. Along with their supervision of many postgraduates at the department of theology and religious studies at King's, the Institute contributed to fostering a new confidence in the study of doctrine and systematic theology in Britain. In particular, it promoted fresh attention to the doctrines of the Trinity and creation,

doctrines which, along with christology, the atonement and revelation (Gunton, 1997, 1988, 1995) came to prominence in Gunton's own work. Gunton gave the Bampton Lectures in 1992 (Gunton, 1993) and the Warfield Lectures in 1993 (Gunton, 1995). He also played a key role in the UK-based Society for the Study of Theology (of which he was Secretary 1977–87 and President 1993–4), which turned its attention toward constructive approaches to doctrinal themes throughout the 1980s and 1990s. A recipient of a number of honorary doctorates (London, Aberdeen, and Oxford), he was made a fellow of King's College posthumously.

Gunton's own theological position may best be described as a robust orthodoxy. Though he resisted any easy ascription of the label "Barthian" it was clearly from Barth that he derived many of his emphases. The resurgence of systematic interest in the doctrine of the Trinity is in part due to Barth. Both Barth and Gunton worked at a creative rediscovery of the doctrine of the Trinity for their own time and place based on their participation within a living tradition of Reformed theology and spirituality (Gunton, 2007b). Other conversation partners proved crucial too. Irenaeus's use of the metaphor of the Son and the Spirit as the "two hands" of God the Father is a prominent motif in his work. Augustine and Calvin also appear regularly, though Edward Irving, Thomas Torrance, and his erstwhile London

The Student's Companion to the Theologians, First Edition. Edited by Ian S. Markham.
© 2013 Blackwell Publishing Ltd. Published 2013 by Blackwell Publishing Ltd.

colleague, the Greek Orthodox theologian John Zizioulas, also feature extensively in his work. Characteristic of Gunton's position is his attempt to define an appropriate understanding of the notion of "person" in the doctrine of the Trinity, given the primacy of the relational within Trinitarian theology. He resisted what he regarded as lazy ways of reasserting the Trinity, and relationality in theology. Too much prior attention to human relationships prevented appropriate attention to the otherness of God and to the primacy of God's Trinitarian life as the context and stimulus for an adequate understanding of humanity. Against this background Gunton was fiercely critical of many Enlightenment-inspired trends in modern theology. Whilst welcoming the use of rigorous, rational, critical thought in theology, he regarded as "red herrings" the many attempts to begin from human experience (be that inner, "religious" experience, or the political commitments of various forms of liberation theology). He thus felt able to dismiss liberal and liberationist alike in the name of a revelation-focused, critically rigorous orthodoxy.

His theology was profoundly church-related. Whilst committed to the academy and the place of theology as a discipline within it, he sought to assist the church toward a new critical self-understanding of its place and role in society (Gunton and Hardy, 1989). He could not be a detached academic. Gunton will not be understood as a person or as a thinker without reference to his preaching. Alongside many academic books and essays, two books of sermons have appeared to date (Gunton, 2001b, 2007a). Both the content and intent of his theology, and the way he lived, bear witness to his conviction that "Christianity is gospel before it is theology" (Gunton, 2003, 2007b, 29).

Gunton might have been able to receive more than he realized from some of the modern movements he criticized. The liberalism he opposed was sometimes more critically traditional than he acknowledged. Liberationists want as much as he did to let Christian theology live, rather than simply be thought, or thought about. His legacy, however, remains his participation in the late twentieth-century movement to reconnect critical, orthodox Christian theology with the church as a community with both divine and human dimensions.

References

Gunton, C. E. 1988. *The Actuality of Atonement: A Study of Metaphor, Rationality and the Christian Tradition*. Edinburgh: T&T Clark.

Gunton, C. E. 1993. *The One, the Three and the Many: God, Creation and the Culture of Modernity*. Cambridge: Cambridge University Press.

Gunton, C. E. 1995. *A Brief Theology of Revelation*. Edinburgh: T&T Clark.

Gunton, C. E. [1983] 1997. *Yesterday and Today: A Study of Continuities in Christology*. London: SPCK.

Gunton, C. E. [1978] 2001a. *Becoming and Being: The Doctrine of God in Charles Hartshorne and Karl Barth*. London: SCM Press.

Gunton, C. E. 2001b. *Theology through Preaching: Sermons for Brentwood*. Edinburgh and New York: T&T Clark.

Gunton, C. E. [1991] 2003a. *The Promise of Trinitarian Theology*. London and New York: T&T Clark.

Gunton, C. E. 2003b. *Father, Son and Holy Spirit: Toward a Fully Trinitarian Theology*. London and New York: T&T Clark.

Gunton, C. E. 2007a. *The Theologian as Preacher: Further Sermons from Colin Gunton*. London and New York: T&T Clark.

Gunton, C. E. 2007b. *The Barth Lectures*, ed. Paul Brazier. London and New York: T&T Clark.

Gunton, C. E. and Daniel W. Hardy, eds. 1989. *On Being the Church: Essays on the Christian Community*. Edinburgh: T&T Clark.

Gustavo Gutiérrez (1928–)

Ian S. Markham

Gustavo Gutiérrez is a theological giant. He has been an influence on a whole range of theologies (black, feminist, gay); and perhaps the majority of theologians working in British and American universities have been shaped by Gutiérrez's theology.

I. Life

Gutiérrez was born into a poor family in Lima, Peru, in 1928. From the ages of 12 to 15, he was incapacitated by an illness that meant that he spent considerable time in bed: this led to his voracious appetite for reading, which created the option of an academic trajectory.

At university, he started out on a medical degree, intending to be a psychiatrist. However, his growing sense of call to the priesthood made him move across to theology. His bishop spotted his academic potential and sent him to some of the finest universities in the world to further his education. From 1951 to 1959, he studied in Belgium, France, and Rome; he collected a master's degree from the University of Louvain. In 1959, he was ordained to the priesthood and started teaching at the Pontifical Catholic University of Peru.

He rose to prominence and started serving as the theological advisor to the Roman Catholic bishops of Latin America. Gutiérrez provided many of the arguments and position papers for the Second General Meeting of the Latin American Episcopate at Medellí, Colombia, in 1968. Here, some of the themes that proved central to his theology emerged: God was not neutral in the "class" war—instead the God of the Bible was on the side of the poor; we should be working for the reign of God to be visible on earth now; and we should build on the theological themes and insights emerging from Vatican II (1962–5).

Throughout his life, Gutiérrez managed to weave a commitment to actual ministry in Peru with an international profile and reputation as theologian. His best-known book is his first, *A Theology of Liberation* (1973), but he has also written on the book of Job and a major study of Bartolomé de la Casas—the Dominican friar who worked closely with indigenous people of Latin America.

II. Theology

For Gutiérrez's critics, he is seen as the theologian who combined Marxism with Christianity, at a time when Marxism was increasingly discredited. This ignores the reality that Gutiérrez starts with scripture—with the God revealed in the text. In many ways, he is a theologically conservative theologian. James B. Nicholoff is exactly right when he writes, "It is easy to see why some critics, Christian and non-Christian alike, find Gutiérrez overly 'traditional'. Yet there is no

The Student's Companion to the Theologians, First Edition. Edited by Ian S. Markham.
© 2013 Blackwell Publishing Ltd. Published 2013 by Blackwell Publishing Ltd.

way to understand his thought (or his life) apart from his appropriation of the Word of God" (Nicholoff, 1996, 6). For Gutiérrez, we are required to read scripture within the context of the actual lived ecclesial community. The result is a realization that a major theme of scripture is "God's preferential option for the poor." In a world of exploitation, where structures emerge that create the chasm between the rich and the poor, God is not neutral. Gutiérrez did learn from Marx that the task of theology is not simply to critique the world, but to change it. And this change must involve those who are most oppressed. Gutiérrez insists that the "process of liberation requires the active participation of the oppressed" (Gutiérrez, 1974, 84). The assumption here is that the text is read differently by those looking at it through the eyes of struggle and oppression. When the Bible is read from the vantage point of affluence, one might not notice the cries of the slaves for release from Egypt and the God who hears those cries. One might not notice a Jesus who is constantly requiring those who are rich "to go and sell everything they have and give it to the poor." The poor of Latin America do not find the Western gospel message of individual souls requiring redemption, leading to eternal life in heaven, provided all sexual sin is kept under control. So Gutiérrez advocated the creation of base communities where Christians work for liberation in a setting that constantly reminds them what the gospel is all about.

Gutiérrez recognizes that all people are located in history. And he learns from Marx that history can be read from the vantage point either of those who are privileged or of those who are oppressed. A key aspect of the "theology of liberation" is the obligation to read history from the perspective of the poor. The meaning of liberation here needs to be seen on a variety of contrasting levels. One aspect is the external liberation from injustice and socio-economic conditions that are oppressive. For Gutiérrez, there is an immediate, political dimension to the gospel: it is intended to transform society. Another aspect is internal liberation—injustice creates an internal insecurity and set of conflicts, from which we can be liberated. An additional aspect is the freedom from sin made possible in Christ; we are invited to participate in a different way of being as a result of the liberation.

Along with a reading of history from the perspective of the poor, there is also a theological reading. Gutiérrez recognizes in the life of the poor the very life of God's love and redemptive power. The love of God is located within the life of the poor.

So we have a distinctive theological method (theology should start with praxis and scripture should be read from the vantage point of the poor) and a distinctive account of liberation, which incorporates the political and social dimensions of living. In this mix, we have a distinctive view of sin. Gutiérrez makes much of the witness of scripture that sees sin in political and social ways. The Western preoccupation with individual sin (especially sexual) makes it too easy for those who are rich not to be challenged. For Gutiérrez sin has a political and corporate dimension. When a rich Western Christian participates in society, there are countless structural connections with oppression. This is a dimension of sin that needs to be recognized.

Thus far this account of Gutiérrez's thought has stressed the biblical roots and the theoretical input from Marx. Another important source is Roman Catholic social teaching, especially as seen through the perspective of Vatican II. However, Gutiérrez's views have provoked some criticism from the Roman Curia. In 1984, Cardinal Ratzinger (now Pope Benedict XVI) set out some of the key difficulties that the Vatican had with Gutiérrez's theology, when he wrote:

> Let us recall the fact that atheism and the denial of the human person, his liberty and rights, are at the core of the Marxist theory. This theory, then, contains errors which directly threaten the truths of the faith regarding the eternal destiny of individual persons. Moreover, to attempt to integrate into theology an analysis whose criterion of interpretation depends on this atheistic conception is to involve oneself in terrible contradictions. What is more, this misunderstanding of the spiritual nature of the person leads to a total subordination of the person to the collectivity, and thus to the denial of the principles of a social and political life which is in keeping with human dignity. (Ratzinger, 1984)

In a similar vein, Pope John Paul II in 1990 worried that liberation theology was too ideological in a narrow way. In a sermon, Pope John Paul II explained:

When the world begins to notice the clear failures of certain ideologies and systems, it seems all the more incomprehensible that certain sons of the Church in these lands—prompted at times by the desire to find quick solutions—persist in presenting as viable certain models whose failure is patent in other places in the world.

You, as priests, cannot be involved in activities which belong to the lay faithful, while through your service to the Church community you are called to cooperate with them by helping them study Church teachings …

… Be careful, then, not to accept nor allow a Vision of human life as conflict nor ideologies which propose class hatred and violence to be instilled in you; this includes those which try to hide under theological writings. (John Paul II, 'Option for the Poor' sermon in Mexico, 1990)

The key objections are the reductionist tendency to identify the gospel and salvation with the political and the use of Marxist theory within the analysis.

Are these criticisms justified? Gutiérrez replies to these criticisms in 1986 in *The Truth Shall Make You Free*. He makes it clear that he is opposed to the atheism and historical determinism of Marxism. However, he does want to recognize that the historical sensitivity, the effect of unjust economic relations on the shape of a theology, and the need to change the world are insights that he learned from Marx. Many of these insights, while perhaps articulated with particular clarity by Marx, are now part of the furniture of our postmodern self-understanding. There is a sense in which Gutiérrez no longer needs Marxism: the key themes of his theology are, in many ways, traditional Christianity.

III.   Significance

There is no question that Gutiérrez is the most influential of all the liberation theologians. He demonstrated a tangible link between theology and politics that is so easily overlooked and ignored. As Rebecca Chopp and Ethna Regan put it: "Gutiérrez has uncovered, for many of us, the presuppositions of power, dominance, and injustice in our basic theological beliefs" (Chopp and Regan in Ford and Muers, 2005, 477).

Primarily, however, it is a recovery of major themes grounded in the witness of scripture. Scripture does talk about a political and social transformation of society; scripture does envisage slaves in Egypt really being liberated by the Promised Land; scripture does talk about social sin; scripture does call on those who are rich to recognize the demands of the kingdom of God and live differently; and scripture does invite us to identify with those who are excluded by oppression.

Liberation theologies, in general, and Gustavo Gutiérrez, in particular, have been misused when they became tools of an unthinking skeptical theology of a left-leaning politics, which has so infected many mainline seminaries in the United States. In many ways, Gutiérrez offers a traditional and richly orthodox theology. John Macquarrie, when reflecting on the work of the Jesuit liberation theologian Jon Sobrino, writes:

> The christology presented in this book, though it has radical political implications, remains theologically in the orthodox tradition. This is typical of liberation theologians in general. A few years ago I heard Dr. Sobrino declare at a symposium in the United States, "No liberation theologian known to me has ever denied the divinity of Christ." (Macquarrie, 2002, 411)

It is odd how liberation theology has become part of a package, which is often deeply revisionist and therefore non-incarnational and non-Trinitarian. In reality the purpose of this theology is to feed on the disclosure of God in the Word to confront the church with the reality of that message.

References

Ford, David, and Muers, Rachel. 2005. *The Modern Theologians: An Introduction to Christian Theology since 1918*. The Great Theologians. Malden, MA: Blackwell Pub.

Gutiérrez, G. 1973. *A Theology of Liberation: History, Politics, and Salvation*. Maryknoll, NY: Orbis Books.

Gutiérrez, G. 1986. *The Truth Shall Make You Free: Confrontations*. Maryknoll, NY: Orbis Books.

John Paul II. 1990. 'Option for the Poor' sermon given in Mexico. See Vatican website: www.vatican.va

Macquarrie, John. 2002. *Twentieth-Century Religious Thought*. Harrisburg, PA: Trinity Press International.

Nickoloff, James B., ed. 1996. *Gustavo Gutiérrez: Essential Writings*. Minneapolis: Fortress Press.

Ratzinger, Joseph. 1984. *Instruction on Certain Aspects of the "Theology of Liberation"*, as found at: http://www.vatican.va/roman_curia/congregations/cfaith/documents/rc_con_cfaith_doc_19840806_theology-liberation_en.html

Stanley Hauerwas (1940–)

Samuel Wells

Stanley Hauerwas is one of the most influential theologians writing in the United States today. In this article I set out to identify the main aspects of his career, demonstrate the inner dynamic guiding his work, assess the key theological and philosophical movements that have been channeled through him, and gauge the significance of his achievement for theology and ethics in the years to come.

I.   Career

Hauerwas's range of publications is so extensive, diverse, and overlapping that it defies summary and discourages even a simple list. His preferred form of discourse has been the lecture or essay, often grouped together in a volume with other essays on converging themes. He often acknowledges that he is not the best person to offer a summary or overview of his own work. Instead the best way to paint an overall picture of his project is to gain an understanding of the key environments in which his work has emerged and the conversation partners and disputants who have shaped his thinking.

The first significant context is Texas, where Stanley Martin Hauerwas was born, on July 24, 1940, in Pleasant Grove, and where he spent the first 21 years of his life. His mother had emerged from deep poverty. His father was a bricklayer, and growing up

Stanley learned to lay brick. This artisan background with its profound awareness of poverty would later flavor his distaste for the pretensions of the academy, and inform a colorful tongue that would gain him a reputation for unsettling the refined ears of the pious. But more importantly, the disciplines of becoming a careful craftsperson became the lens through which he would come to perceive the foundations of ethics. He and his family attended worship at his local Methodist Church. His undergraduate years were spent at Southwestern University, then a Methodist-affiliated regional liberal arts college in Georgetown, Texas, close to the state capital Austin. Here he came under the influence of his most significant teacher, John N. Score, longtime professor of religion and philosophy, 1955–95. Hauerwas developed the habits of voracious and eclectic—one might say comprehensive—reading that were to mark him out from almost all his academic peers throughout his career.

The next important environment is Yale, where Hauerwas studied for his BD, MA, MPhil, and PhD. The academic culture of Yale in the 1960s was one that later came to be famous as the cradle of the "new Yale theology" associated with Hans Frei and George Lindbeck. However, Hauerwas's interests at this stage were more analytical and philosophical. While it is widely imagined that students at Yale in these years read little besides Karl Barth, Hauerwas's key influences were Aristotle, Thomas Aquinas, R. G. Collingwood,

The Student's Companion to the Theologians, First Edition. Edited by Ian S. Markham.
© 2013 Blackwell Publishing Ltd. Published 2013 by Blackwell Publishing Ltd.

and Ludwig Wittgenstein. Significant voices were Julian Hartt, Paul Holmer, James Gustafson, and Gustafson's mentor H. Richard Niebuhr, and these influences were important to the shaping of Hauerwas's emerging career. Yet Hauerwas continued to read very widely and it is illuminating to note that a significant portion of his dissertation was given over to a discussion of Rudolf Bultmann. The 1960s were a notoriously turbulent time, and issues of protest, revolution, and the situation ethics debate are visible in Hauerwas's early published work. A stand about race was responsible for Hauerwas being asked to leave his first appointment at Augustana College, an historic Lutheran university in Rock Island, Illinois, in 1969.

The third major culture in which Hauerwas deepened and clarified his perceptions was Notre Dame, a Roman Catholic university in South Bend, Indiana. Here Hauerwas was again an outsider, not so much this time because of his class or place of birth (he has always regarded Texans as a race apart) but because he was a Protestant. While at Notre Dame he published the four books that made his name as a leading voice in the so-called "recovery of virtue" and the emergence of narrative as a theme in Christian ethics— *Vision and Virtue* (1974), *Character and the Christian Life* (1975), *Truthfulness and Tragedy* (1977), and *A Community of Character* (1981). At Notre Dame he discovered the place of worship and the communion of saints, and began to understand the significance of the church for ethics; but he also spent time with people with disabilities, and, perhaps most significant of all, met, befriended, and came under the influence of his fellow faculty member, the Mennonite theologian John Howard Yoder. A key dialogue partner was David Burrell, who demonstrated a way to harmonize the theology of Thomas Aquinas with the philosophy of Wittgenstein, and with whom Hauerwas co-authored the seminal essay that introduces *Truthfulness and Tragedy*. Hauerwas's crowning achievement at Notre Dame was *The Peaceable Kingdom* (1983), a book that begins to articulate an ethic of christological pacifism.

The fourth and longest episode in Hauerwas's career began with his move in 1984 to Duke, a university in central North Carolina with historic ties to Methodism and a Methodist-affiliated divinity school. Here the significance of his early and continuing experience as a Methodist became more significant;

by now he had become one of the most prominent and talked-about theologians in the United States and his work diversified, with publications of popular polemical works, notably *Resident Aliens* (with William H. Willimon, 1989), which sold around 150,000 copies and made him (in the limited and somewhat two-dimensional world of church celebrity) famous. The combative nature of his style is disclosed by the titles of some of his books from this period, such as *Against the Nations* (1985), *After Christendom* (1991), and *Dispatches from the Front* (1994). This reputation for polemic has tended to divert attention from some of his subtler work on health, disability, and theodicy, found in books such as *Suffering Presence* (1986) and *Naming the Silences* (1990). Meanwhile his dialogues and essays on practical and theoretical ethical themes continued in works such as *In Good Company* (1995) and *Sanctify them in the Truth* (1998); his characteristic method of theology in dialogue with a host of conversation partners is best represented by *Wilderness Wanderings* (1997). During this period Hauerwas settled on the occasional essay as his preferred method of doing theology; his church has always been a pilgrim church—with no safe place to lay its head. Neither his church nor his theology can take refuge in any secure transcendent superstructure. This period increasingly marks his transition from an ethicist to being more explicitly a theologian. His profoundly theological and devotional *Cross-Shattered Christ* (2004) is, for example, a very long way from his more formal work at Notre Dame.

Perhaps the high-water mark of this period is found in two works. *With the Grain of the Universe* (2001) constitutes the Gifford Lectures delivered in St Andrews, Scotland, in 2001, and represents the most sustained theological treatise of his career, demonstrating his debt to Karl Barth and his determination to ground his polemics in profound theological and philosophical commitments; and *The Blackwell Companion to Christian Ethics* (2004, edited with Samuel Wells) is an ambitious attempt to shape the discipline of ethics around the Eucharist, with contributions from a host of theological conversation partners, many of whom were once Hauerwas's students—thus demonstrating his far-reaching influence and his distinctive, infectious way of doing theology through dialogue and friendship. By 2007

Hauerwas had directed more PhD dissertations than any other faculty member at Duke University—a fact that underlines the degree of his influence and his preferred method of extending it.

II.   Inner Dynamic

While it is well known that Hauerwas's early membership of and participation in the Methodist Church was not one that was rigorously theologically informed, and that he has spent more time in recent years worshiping in an Episcopal congregation than in Methodist ones, I suggest that the inner dynamic running through his career is one that is intrinsic to Methodism, and one of which he became aware as early as his undergraduate days.

There is a long-standing tension in Methodism about the central characteristic of the movement as it looks back to the life and ministry of John Wesley. For many, the defining moment is Wesley's Aldersgate experience in 1738, when, at the age of 34, he recalls this moment of listening to a reading of Luther's preface to Romans: "While the leader was describing the change which God works in the heart through faith in Christ, I felt my heart strangely warmed. I felt I did trust in Christ alone for salvation; and an assurance was given me that He had taken away my sins, even mine, and saved me from the law of sin and death" (The Journal of John Wesley, May 24, 1738). The way Methodism spread in the United States, particularly during the Second Great Awakening (1790–1830) with its pattern of camp meetings and revivalism— with its emphasis on a moment of personal conversion— became widely associated with Methodist identity. Hauerwas frequently alludes to the revivalist Sunday evening Methodist meetings of his youth, suggesting, not entirely in jest, that he became a theologian because he "couldn't get saved."

However, once detached from this particular American reception, Methodism appears to many to be more rooted in a sustained and disciplined quest for holiness, through regular meetings, scripture study and exposition, worship, and a personal pursuit of perfection inspired by the Holy Spirit. This may be a minority perspective in historic and contemporary American Methodism, but it is one that represents the

key to the ethics of Stanley Hauerwas. For Hauerwas perceived the correspondence between the flaws he saw in revivalist Methodism—the ephemeral, self-absorbed nature of the conversion experience, the lack of connection to historic tradition or wider church practice, the vulnerability to become captive to whatever prevailing ideologies dominated the notion of Christianity in each era—and the flaws he saw in conventional approaches to ethics.

The situation ethics debate focused both the weaknesses in contemporary Protestant Christianity and the tendencies of conventional ethics. On the one hand, Joseph Fletcher's proposal that love should be the guiding influence in ethics failed to appreciate that love—like faith—was anything but a self-authenticating quality. The ensuing discourse demonstrated just how much love needed the concrete activities of people and communities over time to spare it from the manipulations and deceptions of self-serving fantasy. On the other hand, Fletcher's notion of the "situation" as the center of ethics begged huge questions about the identity of the agents in question, the circumstances and purposes that had brought them into this dilemma, and the other considerations and commitments in their lives that gave such a quandary some context.

The problem in both Methodism and conventional ethics was an over-concentration on the moment—of conversion or of ethical decision—to the neglect of everything else. It is that everything else to which Hauerwas has devoted his career. In the first place it meant the character of the agent making the decision; his original doctoral work considered how a correct appreciation of character preserved the notion of the "agent" from either determinism or a disembodied limbo of perpetual choice. But examination of character brought him into conversation with those interested in what became known as virtue ethics, and thus opened the way to a classical and medieval account of what constituted the good life. Virtue led to an interest in habits and traditions, those largely non-cerebral vehicles of good practice over time; and this in turn underwrote Hauerwas's interest in people with developmental disabilities, as agents who could embody habits and traditions even though they might not be able to articulate a decision or name a moment of conversion. Narrative arose as a category that could preserve the unity of the self through all its accumulated environments and decisions over time.

But the crucial transformation came in the early 1980s when Hauerwas began to articulate the narrative of Jesus as the definitive narrative, the virtues disclosed by this narrative as the key virtues, and the prominence of peace amongst those virtues and in that narrative. The church came to be more prominent as that community which preserved the story, embodied it in discipleship, and celebrated it in worship. And thus Hauerwas came to write increasingly about those communities and those practices that either did or did not make virtuous lives conceivable and liveable, hence his interest in democracy, the university, the novel, papal encyclicals, and the legacy of the theologians that had shaped his youth.

One consistent strand in Hauerwas's work is his relentless struggle to identify what it might mean for Christianity to be true. Whereas for many scholars and lay people this is a question of searching for and upholding proofs that are free of contingent embodiments, for Hauerwas this has never been of interest. For Hauerwas, to say something is true is to say that it *matters*, personally, communally, contingently, and only in this sense metaphysically and ultimately. Hence his work in ethics and his occasional essay style are congruent with his desire to discover and demonstrate where and how theology and Christian convictions genuinely *matter*. This is most explicitly the case in his work on those with developmental disabilities: theology matters here because the logic of liberal democracy and broadly utilitarian ethics would be simply to eradicate developmental disability. The electricity in Hauerwas's writing, and much of its polemical force, is generated by the meeting of this search for truth and its existential significance in lives such as those of the developmentally disabled. This is why the role of witness becomes crucial in Hauerwas's theology. A witness does not constitute the center of the universe—unlike the Enlightenment subject or the modern liberal self—but a witness does live a life that is meaningless unless Christian convictions are true. This is the life Hauerwas most admires. Hauerwas is known as an ethicist, but for him ethics has become no more than the branch of theology in which the notion that truth needs to *matter* is most explicit.

If Hauerwas's interests seem to lie more in the evangelical commitments of tight-knit communities, the Catholic commitments of practical discernment over the centuries, and the radical commitments of those looking to re-envision theology, philosophy, and politics along the contours of peace, then that is because his understanding of Methodism is that it was in its inception and still should remain an evangelical, catholic, and radical renewal movement within Anglicanism in particular and the world church in general. When he is challenged about where his version of the church exists and what its ecclesial justification is, he is as baffled as John Wesley was to explain himself ecclesially. It was the wrong question for Wesley—and it is the wrong question for Hauerwas. The extent to which Hauerwas has become alienated from contemporary Methodism in the United States perhaps represents the degree to which contemporary Methodism has departed from those foundational qualities and aspirations—of holiness and perfection—which Hauerwas regards as its core.

III. Key Theological and Philosophical Debates

Thus Hauerwas made a decisive break with conventional deontological and consequential approaches, both of which see the moment of decision as the principal subject matter of ethics. He made this break at the outset of his career and it has shaped almost all of his subsequent commitments. But, if not in decision, where instead does the subject matter of ethics lie? Hauerwas has given a number of answers to this question, and I shall review the most significant ones here. His style is invariably to offer critique by bringing forward a perspective or tradition that has been wrongfully neglected, and identifying such a tradition with a particular author—often an author who is recovering an older tradition. Thus in what follows I shall identify both the contemporary dialogue partners and the older traditions each represents.

Hauerwas's first, but least abiding, answer to the question is "vision." His essay "The Significance of Vision," in *Vision and Virtue*, enters into discussion with Iris Murdoch and Simone Weil, in a tradition going back to Plato. For Murdoch, we act in the world that we see, and thus the center of ethics is that act of loving attention in which we learn to see things aright. This has implications for formation, since coming to be called a Christian means allowing one's vision to be shaped according to a new perspective—to see through a new set of lenses. Yet Murdoch's point is that seeing is not simply a passive process, but an active engagement with a person, context, or issue. In the end Hauerwas moves away from Murdoch, largely because her work is too much indebted to Plato rather than to Hauerwas's habitual guide Aristotle; Hauerwas in due course is looking for more concrete ways in which good practice is habituated in persons and communities than Murdoch is able to offer. What remains consistent in Hauerwas's thought is the vital importance of description in ethics. This leads him to explore the role of the moral imagination, which takes him in different modes to narrative, to the novel, and to worship. All of these significant aspects of Hauerwas's work are rooted in his initial exploration of vision and thus were inspired by Iris Murdoch.

Hauerwas's second answer to the question is that ethics resides fundamentally in character, what he initially (in *Character and the Christian Life*) calls "the form of our self-agency," and in the virtues that contribute to good character. In *Vision and Virtue* he says, "Our character is our deliberate disposition to use a certain range of reasons for our actions rather than others (such a range is usually what is meant by moral vision), for it is by having reasons and forming our actions accordingly that our character is at once revealed and modelled" (59). While such arguments arose in perceiving the shortcomings of analytic philosophy, the conclusions reached associated Hauerwas with the moral philosopher Alasdair MacIntyre and a tradition stretching back through Thomas Aquinas to Aristotle. It is MacIntyre who perhaps more than anyone else (besides perhaps Michel Foucault) made fashionable an intellectual style that rests on retelling a historical narrative in such a way that the fault lines in contemporary philosophy reflect moves made many centuries ago, and thus that the limb is so badly set that it needs to be broken again in order to heal. This style has been influential on John Milbank and many imitators. Hauerwas has been attracted by such historical

approaches, but in his characteristic way has never wholeheartedly practiced the method or endorsed its results. MacIntyre's *Three Rival Versions of Moral Enquiry* (1990), building on his earlier *After Virtue* (1981), sets out three philosophical options—the encyclopedia of the Enlightenment, the nihilism of Nietzsche, and the virtue tradition of Aristotle and Thomas Aquinas. These options were by no means new to Hauerwas, and there is little that MacIntyre says about virtue that is not articulated or assumed in Hauerwas's early work, but what *After Virtue* and MacIntyre's subsequent works brought to Hauerwas was that style of tracing intellectual and social history as having a living impact on contemporary assumptions. Prior to this Hauerwas largely adopts a literary style more in the tradition of analytic philosophers such as G. E. M. Anscombe—for example in her influential 1958 essay "Modern Moral Philosophy," where significant ethical movements are arrayed without an overarching narrative.

It is perhaps as much due to Hauerwas as to anyone else that virtue ethics are now invariably set alongside deontological and consequential ethics as a third approach (or in some cases an afterthought) to ethics. But Hauerwas would not see things that way. For him, deontological and consequential ethics have more in common than is generally supposed, and agree more significantly than they differ. This is because both assume that the moment of decision is crucial, and regard the character and history of the protagonists as at best secondary or at worst irrelevant. Much of Hauerwas's writing about issues such as medicine is devoted to pointing out that medicine can never hope to resolve questions that highlight dilemmas of care if it restricts itself to decisionist (i.e., deontological and consequentialist) ethical approaches. Yet opening itself out to questions of virtue and character means medicine needs to discuss the formation and significance of moral communities—a discussion that modern liberal democracy is reluctant to have, because it is so heavily weighted toward creating and assuming individual freedom. And this is the root of Hauerwas's relentless criticism of what he rather broadly calls "liberalism"—by which he means those forces in society that, in the name of individual freedom, dismantle the resources by which morality can be the shaping of character in community, and thus turn ethics in particular and life in general into a series of insoluble dilemmas made up of arguments and agents that not only cannot be reconciled but cannot even find a vocabulary with which to interact.

While Hauerwas largely leaves behind debates about virtue in general, he remains interested in the virtues in particular, as his book *Christians Among the Virtues* (1997, with Charles Pinches) shows. Here Hauerwas is very much in sympathy with readings of Thomas Aquinas that make explicit the latter's theological commitments. Whereas Aquinas is often read as providing a philosophical and ethical substructure that can exist independently of theological assumptions, Hauerwas (along with Milbank and a number of other contemporary theologians) utterly rejects such a view. The virtues—justice, prudence, courage, and temperance as much as faith, hope, and love—are discovered in the context of life in community, made explicit in worship, and embodied in the practices of disciplined discipleship. They are not simply a shortcut to an alternative ethical theory.

The place where character, the virtues, and vision all converge is narrative, as Hauerwas saw from the very beginning (in *Vision and Virtue* he has an essay entitled "The Self as Story"). "Narrative" is a confusing term in theology and ethics, and so its significance for Hauerwas needs explaining with care. Until the mid-1980s Hauerwas works with several different notions of narrative. The first concerns the contingent, created character of the self. Simply to ask, in the moment, "What should I do?," may well miss the more far-reaching "Who (or what) am I?," and thus the more obviously narrative-based, "How have I come to be here?" The second associates narrative with the ability to thread together separate events and realities in one's life: an individual who can do this has established an identity; a community that can do this has established a tradition. Conventional ethics try to study the self outside such a narrative setting, and thus miss most if not all of what "matters" about the self. These two claims about narrative are formal ones, which characterize ethics in general. The third claim, which eventually becomes dominant in Hauerwas's thinking, is about Christian ethics in particular. The heart of revelation is the story of the covenant with Israel, its recapitulation first in the life, death, and resurrection of Jesus, and over again in the history of the church. Narrative is thus the shape of the Christian life which seeks to conform to the character of God's salvation.

This transition from the first two senses of narrative to the third really marks the transition from Alasdair MacIntyre to John Howard Yoder as Hauerwas's key conversation partner and the emergence of non-violence rather than character or virtue as the conceptual key to Christian ethics. Thereafter Hauerwas's notion of virtue dovetails behind his non-violence. No longer is the virtue of Aristotle normative, because Aristotelian virtue is that of the soldier, presupposing violence. Now Hauerwas's virtue is more explicitly that of Thomas Aquinas, for whom not the soldier but the martyr (or witness) is the fullest expression. Yoder has no interest in narrative as a formal category. Instead he demonstrates, particularly in his work *The Politics of Jesus* (1972), that the narrative of Jesus, especially the pattern of going voluntarily to the cross as the non-violent path between establishment conformity and revolutionary zealotry, and then being raised from death, constitutes the definitive template for the disciple and the church. It is this notion of narrative (even though narrative is a word Yoder seldom uses) that becomes central to Hauerwas's understanding of the foundation of Christian ethics.

One significant element that arises in Hauerwas's work at just the point where he makes this transition from the more formal claims of MacIntyre to the more particular approach of Yoder is his understanding of the church. While there is a definitive character to Hauerwas's notion of the Christian story, focusing on Jesus' passion, death, and resurrection, there is no such definitive character to his notion of church. Church is a community that through disciplined practices of worship, catechesis, mutual correction, study, witness, and service becomes a school for virtue—a community where people come to take the right things for granted, where they are shaped to walk the paths that make for peace. Hauerwas's notion of the church has been a frequent flashpoint both in his critics' exasperation with him and in his bewilderment in how to respond to them. He has been criticized, on the one hand, for advocating a church that does not exist and, on the other hand, for overemphasizing the distinction between church and world in such a way that implies sectarianism.

In response to those who maintain that Hauerwas's church does not exist he simply points to all the examples of where, on the contrary, it does. Lying behind this criticism are two levels of misunderstanding. One is the assumption made by many of Hauerwas's critics that the diversity among the denominations of the contemporary church is a given, and the task of the theologian is to identify and advocate for the one perceived to be the right (or at least the best) one. Here it is important to remember that Hauerwas has always been and remains a relentless critic of his own denomination. He regards Methodism as a renewal movement within Christianity as a whole, not a fixed denomination to remain as a permanent archetype. The church in general has no such fixed quality in Hauerwas's writing. He wastes little time on speculating about the best denomination to join (although he makes no secret of his admiration for the Mennonite heritage), because to do so underwrites what he sees as liberal assumptions that discipleship is essentially about choice. In this sense Hauerwas may be described as having a lay rather than a clerical perspective on the American church, for he sees not the ponderous judicatories or the laboring denominations but the reality of lived lay discipleship. The second level of misunderstanding concerns the nature of Christian ethics. Hauerwas has a radical notion of the enterprise that regards the real battle as fought in the moral imagination. He sees his role not as soberly identifying the least bad options for a moderately enhanced future but as provoking the imagination of Christians and the church to enter a world made possible by the purposes of the Father, the action of Christ, and the ministry of the Holy Spirit—a realm beyond the comprehension of the "world"—including most of the church. If some of his recommendations seem ambitious, that is inherent in the style of one whose task is to provoke the imagination.

In response to those who regard him as sectarian Hauerwas consistently, and with increasing exasperation, questions what he regards as the Troeltschian stranglehold on social ethics. Ernst Troeltsch's great work *The Social Teaching of the Christian Churches* (1912) categorized three modes of interaction between Christians and society: church-type, sect-type, and mystical-type. Troeltsch had an underlying agenda concerning his anxiety over the future of Western civilization and he organized his argument to show how only the church-type of interaction could serve this goal. Thus to say that Hauerwas's ethics look like Troeltsch's sect-type is not to deliver a knockout blow to Hauerwas's project but merely to endorse Troeltsch's underlying agenda, an agenda that Hauerwas identifies in the work of Troeltsch's successors, notably Reinhold Niebuhr. A similar set of assumptions from which Hauerwas is often criticized are those outlined by H. Richard Niebuhr in his influential book *Christ and Culture* (1951). Here Niebuhr offers a fivefold typology designed to support his preferred mode of social interaction, "Christ the transformer of culture." Again Hauerwas does not dispute that he falls foul of Niebuhr's model, but he relentlessly questions why Niebuhr's profoundly flawed model is regarded as so definitive. Why, asks Hauerwas, is it universally assumed that the principal role of the church is to underwrite the functioning and assumptions of modern Western liberal democracies?

As his crucial work *With the Grain of the Universe* makes clear, underlying this Yoderian turn in Hauerwas's theology is the figure of Karl Barth. *With the Grain of the Universe* is the pinnacle of Hauerwas's theological achievement because it not only crystallizes his criticism of conventional ethics but shows how dazzlingly ambitious is Hauerwas's alternative. Reinhold Niebuhr, the *éminence grise* of twentieth-century American social ethics, is mercilessly dismantled and his assumptions ruthlessly exposed. "For Niebuhr, God is nothing more than the name of our need to believe that life has an ultimate unity that transcends the world's chaos and makes possible what order we can achieve in this life" (Hauerwas, 2001, 131). "Justification by faith is loosed from its Christological context and made a truth to underwrite a generalized version of humility in order to make Christians trusted players in the liberal game of tolerance" (ibid., 136). Niebuhr became "the theologian of a domesticated god capable of doing no more than providing comfort to the anxious conscience of the bourgeoisie" (ibid., 138). Thus theology became ethics, and ethics became about sustaining liberal social orders in a Stoic fashion. This is methodological atheism.

What Karl Barth realized, Hauerwas argues, is that the central issue was Ludwig Feuerbach's claim that

God was no more than a projection of human value. The *Church Dogmatics* constitute "Barth's attempt to overturn epistemology and overcome metaphysics" (ibid., 190). The key question is always "Who is God?" (*not* the natural theologian's question, "How do we know God?"). The answer to the first question, that God has chosen never to be except to be for us in Christ, also answers the second question—but no answer that begins with the second question can answer the first question. Natural theology risks domesticating truth: for Barth, the greater danger is not that humans may misunderstand and reject the gospel, but that they may possess it and render it innocuous (ibid., 198n53). Through the *Church Dogmatics*, Barth seeks to train Christians to be faithful witnesses, disciplining them in their habits of speech and in what he calls "the necessary, thrilling and beautiful tasks which are fruitful for the Church and for the world" (ibid., quoted 179). Only thus can they gain a *theological* metaphysics, and see the universe as it truly is. In conclusion, Hauerwas takes up the most pressing question of the natural theologian—"but is it *true*?" Barth's rejection of non-theological standards of rational justification seems to jeopardize appeal to truth. Hauerwas, with Barth (but more strongly), states that witness is the only justification. If what was to be defended was only deism, this would not be so; but while arguments from first principles can reach a disembodied first cause, they can never reach the Trinitarian God of Jesus Christ: only witnesses can. Thus Barth provides the key that weaves together Yoder's appeal to Jesus and MacIntyre's identification of virtue with a satisfying return to Murdoch's conception of vision—for theology begins when God's transformation of all things in the cross and resurrection is identified as the hermeneutical key to the universe—the one truly natural thing.

IV. Significance

Stanley Hauerwas's theological project is still a work in progress and it is much too soon to assess his theological legacy. There is no doubt that his name is and will continue to be widely linked with such movements as the recovery of virtue in ethics, the emergence of narrative theology and ethics, the distinctiveness of Christian ethics, the strand of theology known as postliberal, and perhaps more latterly the relationship between liturgy and ethics. He tends to avoid identifying directly with such trends, fearing the oversimplification and superficiality which tend to accompany such associations. Nonetheless it is possible to anticipate his significance by perceiving his key role in three perspectives.

The first concerns where Hauerwas belongs among the small group of figures in contemporary theology whose work is widely perceived to be of lasting significance. Here we may briefly locate Hauerwas in relation to five other contemporary figures: Alasdair MacIntyre, Jeffrey Stout, Oliver O'Donovan, John Milbank, and John Howard Yoder. For MacIntyre, as we have seen, the ethical quest remains principally a philosophical, and thus universal one. While Hauerwas would share with him a sense of a trajectory that goes back through Thomas Aquinas to Aristotle, Hauerwas would search in vain in MacIntyre for a detailed sense of the significance of the church or a specific articulation of the ethical template offered by Jesus. Nonetheless, MacIntyre's shadow is so long in contemporary philosophy that Hauerwas's legacy will in many circles be seen through the lens of virtue and narrative. For Jeffrey Stout the question is how civil society can be upheld and enriched in such a way that enhances democracy while cherishing tradition. He applauds the aspects of Hauerwas that are still influenced by MacIntyre—what are sometimes, somewhat misleadingly, known as communitarian commitments—but objects to the particularity and apparent sectarianism that emerges under Yoder's influence. Nonetheless the debate between Stout and Hauerwas is likely to be one of the most abiding tests of the latter's legacy. For Oliver O'Donovan the task is to identify and articulate the distinctively political character of Christianity and the uniquely Christian character of politics. O'Donovan has little time for the perspective of the Radical Reformation and practically ignores Yoder: he perceives strong continuities between the politics of today and those of medieval Europe, and his dialogue partners come largely from the great tradition of political theology, from Augustine to Calvin. For all Hauerwas's immense appreciation for O'Donovan, O'Donovan's imperviousness to the stories in the two paragraphs that follow this one makes his and Hauerwas's perspectives somewhat incommensurable. Like O'Donovan, John Milbank has his sights set on the philosophical imagination of the academy—and society—as a whole. By contrast Hauerwas tends to see such ambitions as Constantinian in the way they privilege society over discipleship and thus tend to make the church invisible. The key difference between Milbank and Hauerwas is their choice of dialogue partners. The Continental European philosophers of the last generation are vastly more significant for Milbank than for Hauerwas. There are other differences. Milbank takes the art of reconstructing a historical narrative to a level to which Hauerwas does not aspire. Milbank has exhibited a level of disdain for other disciplines that Hauerwas has reserved only for other theologians. But both Milbank and Hauerwas seem likely to be remembered for restoring theology's confidence and articulating an unapologetic theological voice in the contemporary academy. Finally, John Howard Yoder and Stanley Hauerwas are in each other's debt in broadly equal measure. While a troublesome theologian to the other four figures here briefly examined, and one whose Radical Reformation perspective makes it hard to receive the whole of church history as a gift, Yoder brought to Hauerwas many of the latter's most radical theological moves. Meanwhile, one of Hauerwas's most obvious legacies is to have brought the work of Yoder to a wider audience.

The second perspective is the story of Christian social ethics in America. One can tell this story in four generations. First comes Walter Rauschenbusch and the social gospel movement in the early decades of the twentieth century. Here was a broad and somewhat uncritical identification between the social program of Jesus and the potential human and industrial relations of America. Next comes Reinhold Niebuhr with a wholesale critique of the social gospel, largely shaped around a renewed and profound awareness of the significance of sin. The two Niebuhrs between them set the agenda of Christian ethics in twentieth-century America, and all subsequent contributors have had to adapt to the reality they had articulated. The third generation is that of figures such as Paul Ramsey and James Gustafson, scholars whose constructive work both reflects the assumptions of their forebears and begins to adapt to a world that

no longer shares the assumptions of a broad Christian (in fact, largely liberal Protestant) benevolence. In this story Stanley Hauerwas emerges as a leading, if not *the* leading, figure in a fourth generation that includes James McClendon and John Howard Yoder. This generation pointed out that, in Hauerwas's words, the subject of Christian ethics in America has never been the church: it has always been America. America was taken to be the society that Troeltsch had posited, the body that Christian ethics was designed to serve. Thus Hauerwas is prominent among a generation of those in theological ethics who castigated their forebears for making the church invisible in Christian ethics, and for constantly replacing the church with America. Though it is not significant in his early work, the church is crucial to Hauerwas's theological ethics because it becomes the political, social, and (most importantly) imaginative alternative to enable people to enter the world of discipleship inspired and empowered by the definitive figure of Jesus.

The third perspective is the story of the church and academy in twentieth-century America. Here Hauerwas's significance is more debatable, but perhaps even more significant than in relation to ethics alone. One can tell a story in which what we might call "universal" ethics was once dominant. This was a period when most of the major institutions in America were in the grip of a liberal Protestant elite, when women had a largely hidden social role, and when African Americans were in many cases excluded from walking the corridors of power and privilege. It seemed that one could write about the nature and destiny of "man," and not acknowledge or even realize how narrow that notion of "man" in fact was. The subsequent period (loosely known today as "the sixties") both gradually and in some cases dramatically broke or blew apart the narrowness of that "man" that had been taken to be an unquestioned universal. We could call the style of ethics that identifies with this period "subversive," because its principal objective is to critique and correct the "universal" project, particularly through the now privileged perspective of those formerly ignored or excluded on such grounds as gender, race, and class. Hauerwas's achievement, along with but perhaps unmatched by others, has been to describe a third approach that we may call "ecclesial" ethics. While universal ethics sees itself as ethics for anyone and subversive ethics sees itself as ethics for the excluded, ecclesial ethics simply sees itself as ethics for the church. Hauerwas endorses much of the critique that subversive ethics makes of universal ethics. Many of his critics overlook this, and thus often speak of him as allying with or opening the door to conservative religious, social, or political movements. This criticism is verging on the absurd— as Hauerwas reminds his critics, no such conservative movements claim him. But Hauerwas also adeptly points out how many assumptions subversive ethics

tends to share with universal ethics—and furthermore he is concerned with a positive program of shaping people of character through disciplined communal practices centered on performing and embodying the one apparently particular but in fact truly universal story—a positive agenda that is not always forthcoming from subversive ethics. It is perhaps in imagining, describing, and inspiring such a way to do ethics and be the church beyond conventional liberal–conservative divisions that his greatest significance may come to lie.

References

Barth, Karl, Bromiley, Geoffrey William, and Torrance, Thomas F. 2004. *Church Dogmatics*. London: T&T Clark International.

Hauerwas, Stanley. 1974/1981. *Vision and Virtue: Essays in Christian Ethical Reflection*. Notre Dame, IN: University of Notre Dame Press.

Hauerwas, Stanley. 1975/1985. *Character and the Christian Life: A Study in Theological Ethics*. San Antonio, TX: Trinity University Press.

Hauerwas, Stanley. 1977. *Truthfulness and Tragedy: Further Investigations in Christian Ethics* (with Richard Bondi and David Burrell). Notre Dame, IN: University of Notre Dame Press.

Hauerwas, Stanley. 1981. *A Community of Character: Toward a Constructive Christian Social Ethic*. Notre Dame, IN: University of Notre Dame Press.

Hauerwas, Stanley. 1983. *The Peaceable Kingdom: A Primer in Christian Ethics*. London: SCM.

Hauerwas, Stanley. 1985. *Against the Nations: War and Survival in a Liberal Society*. Minneapolis: Winston Seabury Press.

Hauerwas, Stanley. 1986. *Suffering Presence: Theological Reflections on Medicine, the Mentally Handicapped, and the Church*. Edinburgh: T&T Clark.

Hauerwas, Stanley. 1989. *Resident Aliens: Life in the Christian Colony* (with William H. Willimon). Nashville, TN: Abingdon Press.

Hauerwas, Stanley. 1990. *Naming the Silences: God, Medicine, and the Problem of Suffering*. Grand Rapids, MI: Eerdmans.

Hauerwas, Stanley. 1991. *After Christendom: How the Church Is to Behave if Freedom, Justice, and a Christian Nation Are Bad Ideas*. Nashville, TN: Abingdon Press.

Hauerwas, Stanley. 1994. *Dispatches from the Front: Theological Engagements with the Secular*. Durham, NC: Duke University Press.

Hauerwas, Stanley. 1995. *In Good Company: The Church as Polis*. Notre Dame, IN: University of Notre Dame Press.

Hauerwas, Stanley. 1997. *Wilderness Wanderings: Probing Twentieth-Century Theology and Philosophy*. Boulder, CO: Westview.

Hauerwas, Stanley. 1998. *Sanctify Them in the Truth: Holiness Exemplified*. Edinburgh: T&T Clark.

Hauerwas, Stanley. 2001. *With the Grain of the Universe: The Church's Witness and Natural Theology*. Grand Rapids, MI: Brazos.

Hauerwas, Stanley. 2004a. *Cross-Shattered Christ*. Grand Rapids, MI: Brazos.

Hauerwas, Stanley, ed. 2004b. *The Blackwell Companion to Christian Ethics*, edited with Samuel Wells. Oxford: Blackwell.

Hauerwas, Stanley and Pinches, Charles Robert. 1997. *Christians Among the Virtues: Theological Conversations with Ancient and Modern Ethics*. Notre Dame, IN: University of Notre Dame Press.

MacIntyre, Alasdair. 1981/1984. *After Virtue: A Study in Moral Theory*. London: Duckworth.

MacIntyre, Alasdair. 1990. *Three Rival Versions of Moral Enquiry*. London: Duckworth.

Niebuhr, H. Richard. 1951. *Christ and Culture*. New York: Harper and Row.

Troeltsh, Ernst. 1912/1992. *The Social Teaching of the Christian Churches*. Louisville: Westminster/John Knox.

Wesley, John. 1974. *Journal*. Chicago: Moody.

Yoder, John Howard. 1972/1994. *The Politics of Jesus: Vicit Agnus Noster*. Grand Rapids, MI: Eerdmans.

John Hick (1922–2012)

David Cheetham

I. Introduction

If one were to glance through any text in the philosophy of religion that has been published in the past few decades it is highly likely that one would find John Hick's name mentioned somewhere. It is a tribute to the lucidity and relevance of his work that he remains one of the most popular and frequently cited thinkers in the field, and his particular views have become "landmarks" which other scholars feel obliged to either build upon or demolish before proceeding to advance their own positions. Moreover, a survey of his work will show that he has not just focused on one particular area within his chosen field. Rather, Hick has made substantial contributions to just about every aspect within philosophy of religion. Thus, terms like "experiencing-as," "epistemic distance," "eschatological verification," "soul-making," "the 'replica' theory," "many lives in many worlds," "the Real" have been woven into the very fabric of contemporary religious philosophical thought.

In work that extends over almost half a century it is hardly surprising that his stance on a variety of theological topics has shifted and changed. It is commonplace for thinkers to expand their intellectual borders or change their minds during the course of their careers. Thus, in the earlier part of his career it would have seemed accurate to describe him as a fairly orthodox philosophical theologian preoccupied with making sense of the Christian faith. His first two books, *Faith and Knowledge* (1957) and *Evil and the God of Love* (1966) appear to inhabit largely a Christian worldview. However, as we proceed chronologically through Hick's output, for example *Death and Eternal Life* (1976), *The Myth of God Incarnate* (1977), and *An Interpretation of Religion* (1989), we see the broadening out of his worldview and an embracing of a pluralistic outlook. Such changes have not involved the wholesale discarding of what might be called the foundational aspects of his thought—his view of religious belief in the context of "experiencing-as," the Irenaean intuition of a soul-making universe, and the affirmation of a life beyond death have remained. Instead, he has sought to adjust his thinking within certain limits in order to accommodate his pluralism. The most important example of this is the way Hick refers to the divine. In earlier days he was content to use the term "God" in the Christian theistic sense; but in his later work he adopts "the Real" as his preferred term, which he thinks is more "transcategorial." This raises an interesting methodological question as to how we should treat Hick's overall output. Perhaps his various works can be considered as discrete contributions to particular topics—religious epistemology, evil, life after death, pluralism—that are not intended to be part of an overall Hickian *system*. Thus, a conservative Christian student interested in the problem of evil may gain much from reading *Evil and the God of Love*

The Student's Companion to the Theologians, First Edition. Edited by Ian S. Markham.
© 2013 Blackwell Publishing Ltd. Published 2013 by Blackwell Publishing Ltd.

without worrying too much about what Hick has said elsewhere about religious pluralism. However, Hick's approach in all his works has been to gain the best possible understanding of a given topic in terms of its relatedness to the *whole*, so it seems problematic to argue that we might consider his works in isolation from one another. Consequently, given the expansion of his thinking, it can be suggested that with every new publication he may have advanced too far beyond his earlier work, even canceling it out. Gerard Loughlin, a critic of Hick, draws attention to this (see Loughlin, 1990). Thus, the views in Hick's earlier books that were worked out from within a fairly "orthodox" Christian framework have been filtered through his later pluralistic hypothesis and rendered "mythological." The question is whether or not they have actually become unrecognizable when viewed in the light of these later shifts in his thinking.

Alternatively, because he has retained some common themes, we might argue that there is an essential unity to his work. This is pointed out by Chris Sinkinson, who suggests that this unity can be found in his epistemology (see Sinkinson, 2001). For example, Hick's early emphasis on the voluntary nature of religious experiencing (first expressed in *Faith and Knowledge*) was actually the seedbed for his final arrival at his pluralistic perspective. Provocatively, Sinkinson suggests that Hick's work has never in fact been "Christian" because its prior loyalties have always been to an Enlightenment or Kantian philosophical tradition. Such loyalty finally finds full expression at the end of Hick's career in the form of a pluralistic hypothesis that draws a Kantian-style distinction between the Real *in itself* and the Real *as it is perceived*.

Of course, these are two sides of the same coin. So, Hick's work is indeed unified by his basic epistemological commitments, but difficulties have also emerged as a result of his philosophical and theological development. Hick has subtly repositioned his earlier work into a mythological framework and it is possible that the result is too sophisticated or abstract to have real meaning. Nevertheless, it would be wrong for us to conclude that the earlier work is irrelevant. He is able to argue that this work has value—for example, he would see his Irenaean theodicy (even in the form it takes in *Evil and the God of Love*) as a helpful "true myth" when it comes to making sense of evil and

suffering. His pluralistic hypothesis does not seek to cancel out first-order religious discourse. Rather, it is a second-order meta-theory about that first-order discourse.

II. Life

John Hick was born in Scarborough on January 20, 1922. His first academic studies were in law at Hull University (then University College, Hull), and it was during this time that he was converted to Christianity. His early Christian experience "was Calvinistic orthodoxy of an extremely conservative kind" (Hick, 1993a, 139). From Hull he went to Edinburgh University in 1940 to study philosophy. However, it was not long until his studies were interrupted by the war, during which he served in the Friends' Ambulance Unit. He returned to Edinburgh to resume his philosophical studies and graduated in 1948 with a First. During this time his initial fundamentalist fervor had begun to wane. He was unimpressed with what he has described as "a lack of intellectual integrity in fundamentalist circles, in that any potentially unsettling questions were regularly suppressed rather than faced" (1993a, 139).

Hick decided to proceed to Oriel College, Oxford University to research for a doctorate in the philosophy of religion. He undertook this research under the supervision of the philosopher H. H. Price (whose work he was later to refer to in his studies on the possibility of disembodied minds). The thesis that emerged from this time was to become his first book, *Faith and Knowledge*.

In 1956, Hick moved to America to take up his first academic position at Cornell University. Three years later he took up another position at Princeton Theological Seminary and it was here that Hick's career as a controversial theological figure began. Already a minister in the English Presbyterian Church, he wished to transfer to the American Church. However, his orthodox views had "slipped" somewhat and he felt unable to confess such things as the literal six-day creation, predestination, the verbal inerrancy of the Bible, and the Virgin Birth. This led to controversy, and the issue was only finally settled in Hick's favor when it reached the national Assembly.

After seven years of teaching in America, Hick returned to Britain in 1963 and took up a lectureship in the philosophy of religion at Cambridge University. It was here that he developed his now famous Irenaean theodicy (influenced by the early church father Irenaeus), and published what is widely reckoned to be one of the definitive works on the problem of evil, *Evil and the God of Love*.

In recognition of some of these outstanding early achievements, Hick was appointed to the H. G. Wood Professorship at the University of Birmingham in 1967. Birmingham is one of the most multicultural cities in Europe and the experience of living and working in this city was to shape the future orientation of Hick's philosophical theology (or, more accurately, philosophy of religions). During the early 1970s he was to become involved in community relations projects. This was a turbulent time in British immigration politics, and some of Hick's colleagues in these projects were physically attacked. In such eventful times, he found himself working in partnership with Muslims, Jews, Hindus, and Sikhs, and this began to affect his religious and philosophical outlook. He writes that, "it was not so much new thoughts as new experiences that drew me, as a philosopher, into issues of religious pluralism, and as a Christian into inter-faith dialogue" (1993a, 141). In 1973, Hick published *God and the Universe of Faiths*, in which he argued that there needed to be a revolution in religious and theological thinking that saw all religions as equally valid. Further to this, and largely as a result of his Birmingham experiences, Hick felt drawn to investigate the different religious traditions more deeply, and he made a number of study visits to India and Sri Lanka. The result was another major work in which Hick explored the different religious accounts concerning the future/afterlife, *Death and Eternal Life*.

The ideas that Hick had been developing on the question of religious pluralism meant that whole areas within Christian theology had to be re-examined. With his next book (which he edited) he brought together a series of contributors who, in their various different ways, challenged one of those areas—the traditional views of Christ. *The Myth of God Incarnate* was destined to be one of Hick's most controversial projects.

Hick returned to America in 1982 to take up the Danforth Chair in the Philosophy of Religion at Claremont Graduate School in California. It was here that he developed and extended his thinking, which resulted in the Gifford Lectures of 1986 and the publication of what many estimate to be his tour de force: *An Interpretation of Religion*. He retired in 1993 and returned to Birmingham as a Fellow of the Institute for Advanced Research in Arts and Social Sciences at the University of Birmingham. Nevertheless, during his "retirement" his thinking has developed, particularly about the nature of religion in light of the critiques of scientific humanism and the fact of religious diversity. Thus, he has published further works, including *The Fifth Dimension* (1999) and *The New Frontier of Religion and Science* (2006). In the latter work, he challenges a strictly materialistic outlook and casts doubt on purely naturalistic assumptions about the brain. On the contrary, he thinks that we should take seriously non-physical as well as physical reality. In fact, it is a spiritual or mystical outlook that can unite humanity around the globe.

III. Key Themes and Contributions

Experiencing-as

Experience is an important starting point for Hick. This being the case, we might characterize his basic philosophical orientation as empiricist in that there is an emphasis throughout his work on the evidence of the senses and experience. Moreover, as an interesting corollary, we cannot, thinks Hick, divide into neat compartments our various beliefs; all beliefs are in some way connected or affected by our total experience. So, the experience of God does not arrive as something separate from the rest of our environment. It is not a "pure" or direct knowledge, but is mediated through other objects.

Another way of speaking about this comprehensive experience is what Hick calls "significance." He explains significance in the following: "By significance, I mean that fundamental and all-pervasive characteristic of our conscious experience which *de facto* constitutes for us the experience of a 'world' and not of a mere empty void or churning chaos" (1966, 98).

This experience of a "world," or seeing a significance in things, also says something about our interpretative freedom. This is not to imply that the "real" world changes at our interpretative whim. Hick is not advocating solipsism (the belief that the world is wholly a creation of our minds). Rather, the world enters our consciousness through an interpretative filter. Thus, an atheist and a believer inhabit the same world, but this world appears different to them; that is, it has a different significance for each.

Hick characterizes *all* experience as "experiencing-as." Here he has borrowed and developed the concept of "seeing-as" put forward by the modern philosopher Ludwig Wittgenstein (1889–1951). Wittgenstein pointed out that it is possible to see the same thing differently. He made reference to "picture-puzzles," such as a picture which, depending on how you looked at it, was either a duck or a rabbit. That is, it is perfectly possible to see the picture in two different but equally legitimate ways—as a duck or a rabbit. Hick extends the somewhat mono-dimensional idea of seeing-as to "experiencing-as." Furthermore, he wants to say that "experiencing-as" is not just something that occurs in special puzzle cases (like being confronted by a "duck–rabbit" picture), but it refers to all our seeing and experiencing; that is, it is something far more all-embracing or, as we have said, significant.

According to Hick, the amount of freedom we have in respect to interpreting our world varies in proportion to the sphere in which we are operating. There are different degrees of freedom in interpretation. For example, our interpretative freedom is most restricted (or involuntary) at the level of everyday sense experiences. We may choose to interpret a bus speeding toward us as an illusory creation of our imagination, but the bus will tend to ignore such mental sophistry and assert its reality! Thus, Hick notes that for us the significance of the physical world is that it is something objective whose "laws we must learn, and toward which we have continually to relate ourselves aright if we are to survive" (1966, 107). At the level of inter-personal relationships and morality our freedom is less restricted. However, it is still closely connected to the most basic kinds of sense perception and interpretation just mentioned because such things take place within the natural environment. That is, our moral experience does not take place in an abstracted

world, but within our physical world. Hick writes that the "world of moral significance is, so to speak, superimposed upon the world, so that relating ourselves to the moral world is not distinct from the business of relating ourselves to the natural world but is rather a particular manner of so doing" (1966, 107). And finally, there is religious experience, which is yet another layer of interpretation. At this level there is great freedom to interpret the world in many different ways; that is, we might say that seeing or perceiving religious significance (or none) is "a voluntary act of interpretation" (1966, 123). The advantage that Hick obtains in this epistemological construction is that religious experience is not separated out from, but made continuous with, the interpretative nature of human experiencing in general. However, the disadvantage is that the sense of something "definitive" or normative being received through revelation—which characterizes more propositional models of revelation—is lost in his scheme.

Consistent with all this, Hick argues (from a philosophical-explanatory perspective) that the world is religiously ambiguous in that neither the arguments for a religious nor those for a naturalistic interpretation of it are conclusive. Nevertheless, although he wishes to stress the nature of religious beliefs as involving personal experience, he also argues for their cognitive (or realist) status as "fact-asserting." That is, contra non-cognitivists, religious beliefs are not just vacuous poetry or edifying moral narratives, they also make factual statements about the world and reality. Even so, Hick adds the important caveat that he does not adhere to the sort of naïve realism that might seek to advocate a crude literalism; rather, he prefers a *critical realism* that maintains that the real world enters the consciousness through our interpretative experience. However, a commitment to a "realist" understanding of religious statements means that there is a challenge to say what actual difference such statements make to our experience of the world. Put simply, if the statement "God exists" is meant to refer to a reality independent of our minds, then one should expect to demonstrate that the statement *is the case* or, at least, suggest how one might go about doing so. Hick's notable response to this challenge is to look at things eschatologically. He argues that the future fulfillment of religious expectations will constitute an *eschatological verification* of religious statements and thus render them "factually" meaningful. However, here again there may be advantages and disadvantages. Hick may have succeeded when it comes to formally defending religious statements as fact-asserting, but do his proposals for an eschatological resolution mean that religious certainties in the present become redescribed as *provisional*? Thus, does Hick's theory fail to take seriously religious commitment in the here and now? Not necessarily. Hick argues that as a philosopher of religion he is engaged in a second-order explanatory activity rather than a first-order confessional one. Thus, for example, his eschatological verification model is offered not as an actual description of people's religious attitudes, but more as a "theoretical" defense against a philosophical (verificationist) challenge.

Soul-making

The eschatological theme in Hick's thinking crops up in other areas too. He regards purely naturalistic pictures as pessimistic, and argues that the cosmic optimism present in the majority of religious expectations should point to a life after death. Such optimism is the basis of Hick's treatment of the problem of evil and suffering in Christian theology. *Evil and the God of Love* contains his definitive historical survey of Christian approaches to the problem of evil together with his own distinctive Irenaean response. Irenaeus (130–202 CE) distinguished two stages in the human story. First of all, humanity has been created in the "image of God" (*imago dei*). This is indicative of the potential of humanity. However, the destiny of human beings is to become like God (*similitudo dei*). The outworking of the process from the first of these stages to the second is a long, arduous struggle. Here, evil and suffering are understood as remedial rather than punitive. That is, sufferings are divine utilities toward helping us reach *similitudo dei*.

Hick's theodicy is a contemporary reading of these basic ideas. He argues that the responsibility for the existence of evil cannot be successfully placed on the shoulders of created beings; instead one must admit that, ultimately, God is responsible for the way the world is. Thus, theodicy should not look back to an error made by humanity (i.e., a *fall*) but be forward looking (eschatological) and seek to justify the God of

Love by a limitlessly good outcome in the future. From the beginning, human beings have been placed into a religiously ambiguous world full of suffering and challenge, and they will eventually emerge from life's journey as perfected souls. However, a single earthly lifetime is not sufficient for the soul-making process to be completed. This means that our earthly lives must be extended into the afterlife where there will be further opportunities for development in another challenging world. Moreover, in order for Hick's eschatological resolution to work, he argues for the universal salvation of all human beings. If God is ultimately responsible, then it is crucial that the soul-making process is *conclusive* and that there is no dualism (e.g., heaven and hell) perpetuated.

Broadening the perspective, Hick has approached the issues from what might be called an Irenaean and a Copernican standpoint. This means, firstly, that he is committed to an evolutionary account of human existence and progression; and, secondly (analogous to the astronomical revolution brought about by Copernicus) that he is committed to seeing all religions, including Christianity, as revolving around Ultimate Reality (rather than religions revolving around Christianity). Given these basic starting points, Hick has sought to investigate the possibilities for a global theology of death that draws on all the available evidence with regard to the future life. He is committed to the idea that the different religions point toward "a common conception of human destiny" (1976, 34). Moreover, he favors the framework of many lives rather than one continuous life because of the shape that it gives to personal development. This is something he has characterized as "many lives in many worlds": that is, successive lives—each bounded by their own deaths—which provide a meaningful structure and challenge for the making of souls. His work on this largely appears in *Death and Eternal Life* and constitutes an impressive synthesis of Eastern and Western conceptions of the afterlife. Criticisms have focused on Hick's methodology. So, for example, is a methodology that seems to adopt, in the words of one critic, a "deliberate eclecticism" (Penelhum, 1979, 152) a valid approach? And, is it realistic to handle the religions as data on a universal playing field rather than as self-contained or tradition-specific units?

What appeals about Hick's soul-making universe is the fact that it seems to steer away from tyrannical and juridical pictures of an omni-perfect God who exacts punishments for evil. Instead, it portrays God as very much a personal (even "parental") Being who wishes to authentically interact with human beings. The effect of this is that it seems to bring God more into the world of the sufferer; that is, God accepts ultimate responsibility for evil and is perceived to work within the process to bring all people into a limitlessly good outcome for their lives. However, critics have sought to focus upon the sheer amount of evil in the world and the fact that it seems to exceed the requirements of a soul-making world. Or else, there is a refusal to accept that evil and suffering can be justified by good consequences in the future. Moreover, it is possible that authentic human freedom and the promise of universal salvation are two notions that are not easy bedfellows. Perhaps, if human freedom is upheld there must be the possibility of some people deciding to remain at variance to the divine will? However, in assessing the validity of some of these complaints much depends on the value-judgments of the assessors themselves. The Irenaean theodicy is the work of a philosopher of religion. However, it is also an insightful attempt to understand the human condition and its purpose. It is not presented as an algebraic philosophical treatise that is content with a Pyrrhic victory. Rather, it seeks to consider human life as it is actually experienced and felt.

The Metaphor of God Incarnate

In 1977, Hick edited a controversial book called *The Myth of God Incarnate*. This book provoked a tremendous reaction at the time of its publication, and it may be one of his most well-known books. More than a decade later he published another book, *The Metaphor of God Incarnate* (1993), which provides a more extended treatment of his thinking.

There are roughly three areas that are of interest to Hick: the first concerns what the historical Jesus actually said and claimed; the second addresses the logical problems associated with "literal-metaphysical" approaches; and the third concerns the implications of the existence of other religions.

Hick thinks that the historical Jesus did not claim to be God. Such claims express the developing theology of the early church rather than the words of Jesus himself. Even if Hick is correct in this assumption (which is questionable), he is not using it to argue that the Christian faith is one big hoax. Instead, he thinks that Jesus was an exceptional man who exhibited such a spirit-filled life that "a close encounter with Jesus in first-century Palestine would be a conversion experience" (1993b, 38). Furthermore, because Jesus was so open to the presence of God, "the divine creativity flowed through his hands in bodily healing and was present in his personal impact upon people, with challenging and re-creating power" (1993b, 38). It is this picture of an historical Jesus completely filled with the Spirit of God, or agape, that Hick is impressed with. The metaphysical doctrines relating to Jesus' two natures (divine and human) owe themselves more to the later influences of Greek philosophy on the church's thinking than to the actual Jesus of history. Thus, in adopting an "inspiration" christology (referring to Jesus' intensely inspired relationship with God), Hick thinks that we are getting back to a more authentic picture of things. Moreover, he thinks that such a picture is not in conflict with much recent New Testament criticism, and it is more helpful in light of religious pluralism.

Secondly, can we make sense of the doctrine of the incarnation as traditionally understood? Hick thinks not. This is because it is impossible to explain coherently the actual meaning behind the notion that an individual is both fully divine and fully human. For example, how can a finite man embody or contain infinite qualities? How can an omniscient being also express ignorance about something, or an all-powerful being be vulnerable and weak? In short, arguing in Greek fashion about Jesus being of one "substance" with God only leads us into numerous insoluble conundrums that, despite immense intellectual effort over the centuries, have never been satisfyingly resolved. It is a mistake, thinks Hick, to approach the meaning of incarnation using "literal-metaphysical" rather than metaphorical or mythological modes of discourse. The whole idea of an individual being both fully divine and fully human at the same time is rather like trying to visualize a square circle; that is, it is a ludicrous proposition. Moreover, such descriptions of "substance"

are static, immovable conceptions which are preoccupied with abstract metaphysical questions of Being.

Nevertheless, one criticism is that Hick is tending to
define the problem in ways that create a deliberately
constricted atmosphere. For example, the "square circle" complaint deals with the matter as if it were a case
of a simple geometrical contradiction. It is precisely this
kind of approach that the theologian Maurice Wiles,
for example, expresses reservations about. Wiles comments that: "It is much harder to plot the borderline
between sense and nonsense in talking about the mystery of God" (Wiles, 1979, 7). If this is the case, then
perhaps the language of incarnation should not necessarily be taken to imply clear-cut, humanly comprehensible distinctions. Nevertheless, to make these kinds
of points is actually to fall into Hick's hands. For it is
precisely an admission of the inadequacy of the "literal-
metaphysical" language that leads Hick to recommend
his mythological approach! However, he hasn't really
shown why the choice is between the language of substance in Greek philosophy, on the one hand, and the
complete mythologization of the incarnation, on the
other. Instead there could be an appeal to mystery
(something which is a frank admission by innumerable
theologians throughout history), which nonetheless
upholds the metaphysical sense as important.

As well as finding difficulties with the classical substance christologies, Hick is also unimpressed by other
interpretations such as the idea of divine kenosis
(self-emptying). He thinks that the idea of kenosis
or self-emptying serves as a "vivid metaphor" of the
divine love, but one should not seek to turn a good
metaphor into "bad metaphysics" (Hick, 1993b, 78).
Hick prefers a more fluid and non-metaphysical view
of incarnation; and furthermore a view which he feels
that human beings living in the contemporary world
can connect with. So instead of speaking the outdated
metaphysical language of Chalcedon we might instead
portray Jesus as an outstanding individual who "incarnated," in a metaphorical sense, the divine, and inspires
us to realize our potential to be fully spirit-filled.
Thus, in doing God's will, God was acting through
Jesus; Jesus exemplified the life led in openness to
God, and he finitely incarnated the infinite agape love
of God. Jesus embodied these things to such an extent
that people who came into contact with him sensed
the presence of God.

The third problem of asserting the incarnation in
its traditional form (i.e., the pre-existent divine Son
descending from heaven to atone for the sins of the
world and then returning to the eternal Trinity) is that
it implies the superiority of the Christian faith above
other faiths. This is incompatible with the pluralistic
picture that Hick wishes to present of Christianity
being just one salvific religion amongst many. Hick is
recommending that the development of Christian
doctrine (and christology in particular) be undertaken
not just within its own community, but with reference
to the existence (and teachings) of the world religions.
However, this raises important methodological questions: Is Hick correct in seeking to reform the
Christian tradition according to *extra*-traditional
factors—that is, is a proper methodology one which
seeks to develop a christology as an *intra-textual* exercise (i.e., internal to the Christian tradition)—or
should one take a liberal approach and consider
Christian doctrines in light of non-Christian insights
and influences? These questions reflect a perennial
debate in theology generally and so it is unlikely that
they will be fully resolved. However, the success of
Hick's theological reconstructions will depend to a
large extent on how well they can be accepted by
those within the Christian tradition; otherwise he is
really just speaking for himself. This depends on
Christians being able to feel that his theological
method is *faithful* as well as being exploratory.

Religious pluralism

Hick's pluralistic hypothesis is presented as a *meta-
theory* (intended as a second-order philosophical exercise); it is an explanation of religious pluralism. This
means that he is not actually trying to construct a
"global" religion or seeking to bulldoze religions into
the image of a "first-order" pluralistic tradition.

Hick observes that "people of other faiths are not
on average noticeably better human beings than
Christians, but nor on the other hand are they on
average noticeably worse human beings" (Hick, 1995,
13). Further to this, he makes the point that if there is
some kind of soteriological parity between different
religions (that is, if a Buddhist monk seems to be as
"spiritually" or ethically advanced as a Christian
monk), then can we so easily draw a stark distinction

between "saved" and "lost," to use Christian parlance? Maybe there is a kind of Barthian reason for some people being in the light and others in darkness. Alternatively, if the rule is "By their fruits you shall know them," then can we honestly say, asks Hick, that fruits such as generosity, kindness, non-violence, gentleness, selflessness, and so on, are not present in abundance in all faiths? And if these practical expressions of faith are seen, in their own way, as human responses to some sort of higher reality, then is it not likely that such examples (being so similar) should be seen as equally veridical responses to that higher reality?

Hick proposes that there should be a "Copernican" revolution in theology. He argues that Christians must "shift from the dogma that Christianity is at the centre to the realization that it is God who is at the centre, and that all religions ... serve and revolve around him" (Hick, 1973, 131). Here, he is still using "personal" references to the divine, but later, in 1989, Hick published *An Interpretation of Religion*, where the nature of the divine was elevated far beyond personal or impersonal terms. That is, Hick in his later writings refers to the Transcendent as "the Real," which he sees as transcategorial. One critic, Gavin D'Costa, has said that Hick has traveled from christocentrism (his pre-Copernican days) to Theocentrism and, finally, to Realocentrism (see D'Costa, 1991).

Hick's theory is complex, and it is a mistake for critics to focus on one aspect of his thinking and pursue it as if it is the only thing that he has to say on the matter. Firstly, consistent with his views on "experiencing-as," Hick sees religions as culturally conditioned, soterio-pragmatic systems which provide meaningful narratives and forms of life that lead to a transformation of the self (as defined by that particular system). Thus, there is a focus on the practice of religion and its transformative effect on the adherents rather than on metaphysical beliefs or doctrines. Nevertheless, if we left it at this we might conclude that Hick was committed to some kind of anti-realist account of religious life: that is, the view that although religious discourse and practice bestows meaning and effects beneficial transformation, it does not correspond with something "out there" (e.g., an actually existing God). However, Hick is committed to the idea of an actually existing ultimate referent. So, even though he believes that the various religions are

culturally constructed systems, he nonetheless believes that there is an ontologically real higher reality to which these different systems refer. These two aspects are held together in Hick's hypothesis, and much critical discussion has centered on the coherence of him being able to do so.

In order to address this issue, Hick has incorporated a Kantian-influenced epistemology into his pluralistic hypothesis. Kant drew the distinction between the perceived world (phenomena), and the world as it is (noumena). Applying this model to our knowledge about a higher or transcendent reality, Hick draws the distinction between the "noumenal" Real and the "phenomenal" Real. That is, there is the noumenal Real (higher reality)—which is beyond human conception—and then there are the various phenomenological conceptions/apprehensions of the Real evidenced in the world's wide variety of religious experience. He writes that the "great world faiths embody different perceptions and conceptions of, and correspondingly different responses to, the Real" (Hick, 2004, 376); and again they "constitute different ways in which the same ultimate Reality has impinged upon human life" (Hick, 2004, 373). Thus, to clarify Hick's view further, religion is a mix of culturally conditioned responses to a higher reality and the universal impingement of the Real. Hick uses the word "impinged" because he is trying to capture a sense of the Real's activity (rather than passivity) in human religion without using loaded terms such as "revelation" which would favor one religion's discourse above another. However, it is also important to remember that the Real's activity should not be understood according to our human comprehension. The noumenal Real, or the Real in itself, is beyond our comprehension, so concepts like activity or non-activity are transcended. Furthermore, because Hick's Real occupies a place beyond the various religious descriptions of it (it/him/her), it is no longer valid to apply literal predicates to it.

It may seem impossible to conceive of something holding together incompatible things within itself. So, for example, how can the Real in itself be both personal and impersonal? As we have just said, the Real in itself transcends the distinction between impersonality and personality; thus the seeming contradiction of both these characteristics being present in the same thing occurs not in the Real in itself but in the human comprehension of the Real. However, some critics have questioned Hick's apparent agnosticism on these issues and feel that he has to come down on the side of personality or impersonality.

Such ambiguity with regard to the noumenal Real reveals Hick's intention to affirm differences between religions rather than cause all religions to conform to a homogenizing agenda. Although Hick postulates an ultimate referent called "the Real," he does not wish to say anything concrete about it. If he chose to indicate that it was either personal or impersonal he would effectively be insisting that one religious claim about reality was more valid than another (e.g., either Christian theism or Buddhist atheism). Instead, he remains deliberately silent on this issue so as to render his hypothesis as comprehensive as possible. Moreover, being a "second-order" philosophical explanatory (meta) theory means that he seems to be intending his pluralistic hypothesis to have a somewhat "ghostly" character. That is, Hick is not endorsing the convergence of religions into a new pluralistic religion (designed by him). Rather his view of religions is "complementary": he intends people to see the different religions as rich, legitimate, and effective responses to the Real, each of which contains within itself well developed appropriate myths which can transform their followers. People should therefore stay in whatever religion they have "received" or embraced; but they might also acknowledge the validity of the paths sincerely followed by others, and those other paths can contain insights or practices that could complement their own.

So, the various religious responses to the Real are not concrete pictures of the Real in itself, but they are nevertheless legitimate and valid responses to it. That is, under Hick's pluralistic system, various religious propositions from the wide spectrum of beliefs become mythologically true rather than being literally true. This, it would seem, is how Hick circumvents the problem of incompatible truth claims. That is, by saying that religious truth claims are mythologically true of the Real in itself, he has cushioned or softened the incompatibilities that would perhaps be insuperable if one asserted that such truth claims were literally true of the Real in itself. Things appear to be incompatible from the phenomenal level, but they are

not at the noumenal level. For Hick, the value of myth lies in its utility toward creating the appropriate attitude to the Real, and the impetus to grow away from ego-centeredness toward Reality-centeredness.

Questions might be asked about the success of Hick's hypothesis in a postmodern intellectual climate. Hick's religious pluralism goes against the grain by seeking to be comprehensive rather than tradition-specific. It is a liberal rather than conservative vision. However, to some extent, criticism of Hick's hypothesis from this angle will only reflect current theological fads and allegiances. Nevertheless, a basic concern might be that Hick's theory appears to adopt a neutral stance. From a postmodern perspective (with its emphasis on many different "truths" rather than one overall truth), this is impossible; we cannot help being bound within our own modes of discourse. Even without the postmodern critique, the claim to neutrality seems an imperialistic imposition made all the worse because it is a position denied to the religions themselves. In response to this, Hick does not claim to stand in superior judgment over the religious landscape. His criteria (like salvation/liberation) are drawn from the religions themselves. However, his hypothesis does seem to contain a certain claim to neutrality because, as we have seen, he has characterized it as a second-order philosophical exercise, a meta-theory which reflects on religious diversity and offers an explanation of the data. Such a characterization might lead to further questions about the religious effectiveness of his hypothesis. That is, how are we meant to *use* a hypothesis that is characterized as a meta-theory? Can a meta-theory change people in their attitudes toward other religions (and their own)? Furthermore, is a "pluralistic" hypothesis the most effective way of creating dialogue and discussion between faiths, or are there other more tradition-specific constructions that might be equally or *more* effective? It seems clear that Hick's pluralistic hypothesis, despite its second-order status, has implications for the way that religions describe themselves. Moreover, it is possible that conservatives in all religions will feel that Hick's views inevitably entail an unacceptable reinterpretation, or discarding, of important doctrines (for example, the incarnation for Christians, or the finality of the Qur'an for Muslims). It becomes clear that Hick is presenting a significant challenge to the self-understanding of religions. Whatever our views on Hick's proposals, it seems clear that his pluralism will continue to be a major reference point in the debate about theology and other religions.

IV. General Assessment

Hick's work has a provocative quality. It is very difficult to present an account of his thinking without offering some kind of engagement with it. Moreover, it is this quality that will ensure that his work continues to have an important role in the philosophy of religion. Hick's clarity of style is such that his work is accessible to a wide audience and this will extend his importance beyond a purely academic arena. Nevertheless, the future success of Hick's work will largely depend on the future of religious liberalism. Whilst powerful intellectual forces are persuading many toward postmodern or postliberal interpretations, Hick is committed to a liberal vision that extends itself beyond "tradition-specific" boundaries. Being a liberal, he borrows from many different disciplines: scientific, psychological, sociological, historical, philosophical and so on, and from all the major world faiths as well. His is a universal vision not content to stay within a carefully staked-out Christian discourse, but open to the whole world of religious experience. Additionally, his work seems to treat religious experience, including revelatory experience, as raw data in a journey toward truth. Thus, for Hick, truth results from a cumulative amassing of data and experience. It does not arrive like a bolt of lightening.

Some might argue that this desire by Hick to be comprehensive and universal in scope is indicative of a truly sincere religious quest. That is, in the best religious style, Hick has sought to find an answer to all

that there is. Indeed, we have seen that this is his preferred perspective: one that sees religious faith as a free interpretation and experience of the world rather than the committed adherence to a definitive revelatory intervention. Others will see these same characteristics as the actual weaknesses in Hick's approach. He has "cast off" from his Christian moorings and is adrift in a sea of different faiths and philosophies.

In 1991, Hick wrote that he was in sympathy with a theological movement "which is theologically liberal, and yet conservative in its basic affirmation of the reality of God and of human immortality ..." (Hick, 1991, 104). That is, his vision is one which is open to a vast range of religious possibilities; however, he is also committed to a critically realist conception of religious language. But is it possible to be both of these things? Indeed, can it be maintained that his later views about "the Real" are so empty of content that it is possible that he has undermined and weakened the case for critical realism? Moreover, have his theological advances meant that he can no longer use the kind of arguments that he employed in his earlier work? For example, can he still speak of a God of Love and the *value* of a soul-making universe in light of his transcategorial Real? His own theological journeying means that he has rarely sought to speak for a particular religious community or denomination. However, this being the case, where is his theological constituency? Perhaps he is a spokesperson for liberals in all religions or for those who embrace some sort of "interfaith" religious persuasion? Hick does not speak for those whose positions are already fixed; rather he will appeal to those who prefer to continue traveling.

Finally, one thing is clear: Hick's work has always addressed questions that *interest* people: What does my religious talk mean? Why do we suffer? Shall I live after death? What about other religions? Perhaps his most significant contribution is that his questions (and his pursuit of answers) seem to make *religious sense*.

References

D'Costa, G. 1991. "John Hick and Religious Pluralism: Yet Another Revolution." In *Problems in the Philosophy of Religion*, ed. H. Hewitt. London: Macmillan.

Hick, J. [1957] 1966. *Faith and Knowledge*. London: Macmillan.

Hick, J., ed. 1977. *The Myth of God Incarnate*. London: SCM Press.

Hick, J. [1966] 1978. *Evil and the God of Love*. New York: Harper & Row.

Hick, J. [1976] 1985. *Death and Eternal Life*. London: Macmillan.

Hick, J. [1973] 1988. *God and the Universe of Faiths*. London: Macmillan.

Hick, J. 1991. "Reply to P. Badham and L. Stafford Betty." In *Problems in the Philosophy of Religion*, ed. H. Hewitt. London: Macmillan.

Hick, J. 1993a. *Disputed Questions in Theology and the Philosophy of Religion*. London: Macmillan.

Hick, J. 1993b. *The Metaphor of God Incarnate*. London: SCM Press.

Hick, J. 1995. *The Rainbow of Faiths*. London: SCM Press.

Hick, J. 1999. *The Fifth Dimension*. Oxford: Oneworld.

Hick, J. [1989] 2004. *An Interpretation of Religion*: London: Macmillan.

Hick, J. 2006. *The New Frontier of Religion and Science: Religious Experience, Neuroscience and the Transcendent*. London: Palgrave.

Loughlin, G. 1990. "Prefacing Pluralism: John Hick and the Mastery of Religion," *Modern Theology* 7.

Penelhum, T. 1979. "Review and Critique of *Death and Eternal Life*," *Canadian Journal of Philosophy* 9.

Sinkinson, C. 2001. *The Universe of Faiths: A Critical Study of John Hick's Religious Pluralism*. Carlisle: Paternoster Press.

Wiles, M. 1979. "A Survey of Issues in the *Myth* Debate." In *Incarnation and Myth: The Debate Continued*, ed. M. Goulder. London: SCM Press.

Elizabeth A. Johnson, CSJ (1941–)

J'annine Jobling

Elizabeth A. Johnson, CSJ is an eminent Roman Catholic theologian and church worker, currently a Distinguished Professor at Fordham University in New York. She is typically described as a "feminist theologian." Certainly, a keen awareness of the significance of gender and sexism permeates her work. However, this is within the context of an inclusive emphasis on justice and anti-oppression, aimed at establishing a genuinely mutual community. While especially concerned with the position of women, she is aware that oppressions are interlocking—whether on the basis of sex, ethnicity, economic location, geography, or any other factor. She brings this perspective to bear on a wide range of issues. She writes on, for example, the question of religious language and how one should most appropriately talk about God; the problem of suffering in light of God's relationship with the world; the Holy Spirit; the communion of saints; Mariology; the dialogue between science and religion; and ecology.

Johnson is a former president of both the Catholic Theological Society of America and the American Theological Society. She has a strong presence in the life of the church. This includes acting as a consultant to the Catholic Bishops' Committee on Women in Church and Society, as well as contributing to fora, initiatives, and committees across a range of other areas (for example, Lutheran–Catholic dialogue, the dialogue between science and religion, interreligious dialogue, and American Catholicism). She is a frequent public lecturer.

Johnson is a contextual theologian, deeply committed to engagement with this-world and its issues. As such, biography and theology are for her intertwined. Her life has shaped her perspectives, and provides some of the compass points for her scholarship. She was born in Brooklyn, New York, on December 6, 1941. In 1959, she began her undergraduate study of theology with the Congregation of St Joseph, Brentwood, New York; completed an MA at Manhattan College in 1971; and was awarded her doctorate in 1981 by The Catholic University of America. Before her academic career, she taught religion and science in Catholic schools. During her studies, she was deeply influenced by Thomas Aquinas, a lasting legacy in her work. She describes her own intellectual autobiography as including the following (Johnson, 1999):

- Vatican II documents, in particular *Gaudium et Spes*;
- post-Vatican II biblical scholarship;
- the death of God theology in America;
- European theology, both Catholic and Protestant (she cites in particular the work of Rahner, Metz, and Schillebeeckx on the one hand, and Barth, Bonhoeffer, and Pannenberg on the other);
- Latin American liberation theology (including its interpretation in South African contexts also);

The Student's Companion to the Theologians, First Edition. Edited by Ian S. Markham.
© 2013 Blackwell Publishing Ltd. Published 2013 by Blackwell Publishing Ltd.

- the multiple voices of feminist theology, which includes womanist, mujerista, Asian-American and Third World expressions;
- other intellectual trajectories in the fields of comparative theology, ecotheology, and postmodernism.

As can be seen from the above, Johnson's theology is one of encounter with contemporary movements and ideas, and the specificity of the modern world; she takes seriously the experiential basis of theology, especially with regard to those whose experiences have traditionally been marginalized or excluded in the conduct of theology, notably women. A feature of Johnson's work, however, is that she places these emerging perspectives in on-going conversation with traditional texts, teachings, and symbols; she does not dismiss the latter, but seeks to approach them afresh. In receiving the Jerome Award from the Catholic Library Association in 2004, she stated that she does not "reject the good, nourishing insights that generations of male theologians have labored to bring forth"; nevertheless, for the church of today and tomorrow, this is not in itself enough.

Spiritually, she locates the summer of 1965 as a key turning point (Johnson, 2003b). It was then that she pondered whether or not to take the final vows in her religious order, the Sisters of St Joseph. She was concerned that her own world-affirming and world-embracing spirituality would not be wholly comfortable in a religious order restricting involvement with the world. The draft of *Gaudium et Spes* convinced her that the two would not be incompatible, from its opening words onward: "The joys and the hopes, the griefs and the anxieties of the people of this age, especially those who are poor or in any way afflicted, these too are the joys and hopes, the griefs and anxieties of the followers of Christ." She has continued to hold fast to the vision of *Gaudium et Spes* and Vatican II despite subsequent ecclesiastical counter-trends.

In 1990, she examined new waves in christological understanding within middle and late twentieth-century Catholicism; her wide-ranging study incorporated a renewed emphasis on Jesus' humanity, the impact of biblical scholarship on understandings of Jesus' historical context, the impact of liberation, ecological, and feminist theologies, and relations with other religious traditions. She argued that christology, of all church doctrines, was the one most used in the oppression of women. Basically, this is because the maleness of Jesus is elevated from historical contingency, and part of his personal particularity, to ontological necessity and a universal principle. This reinforces the notions that God is only properly represented as male, and that male human beings are paradigmatic of what it is to be human. She points out to the contrary that the Jewish scriptures do image God in female form, as mother, midwife, nurse, mother bird; and that Jesus also employed female images in his preaching and parables. The reign of God is likened to the yeast a woman kneads into dough; God's search for the sinner is likened to a woman seeking a lost coin. Jesus was also identified with Sophia, a feminine personification of the Wisdom of God. Furthermore, Jesus' preaching and ministry was inclusive of women, who formed part of his discipleship circle. Divisions are transcended in the unity of the body of Christ (see Gal. 3:28).

The maleness of Christ is often cited as a reason for a male priesthood; Johnson supports the ordination of women within the Catholic Church, arguing that this is an act of responsible dissent within the context of assent to both the gospel of Jesus Christ and church traditions (1996). She points out that church tradition does develop in light of new moral and critical insights and cultural change—for example, it was once held that married couples should take no pleasure in sex, that slavery was allowable, that historical-critical analysis of the Bible should not be permitted. An act of conscience and integrity, such dissent involves rigorous self-scrutiny as to motivation—which should spring from a deep conviction of the truth, be respectful of the leadership office in the church and the consciences of others, and sensitive to possible harm to community values.

Her reflections on the significance of how we image God are continued in *She Who Is: The Mystery of God in Feminist Theological Discourse* (1992). This book was to have a significant impact in the theological world. It won a number of awards (Grawemeyer Award in Religion, University of Louisville, Kentucky; Crossroad Publishers Women's Studies Award; Catholic Press Association Book Award, Academic Books category; Choice: Outstanding Academic Books).

Here, she argues that male and female images of God are equally appropriate, and neither is adequate. The transcendent God transcends gender, and both male and female are images of the God who created them and may be used to represent the divine. She highlights aspects of the tradition that do evoke God in feminine terms, as Spirit, as Sophia, as Mother. She also undermines tendencies to interpret Father–Son–Spirit in subordinationist fashion by reversing this pattern, and beginning her triune theology with the Spirit. For Johnson, talk about God is always analogical, and always begins with experience of God's mystery; what is important is that it does "characterize the living God mediated through Scripture, tradition, and present faith experience, for example, divine liberation action or self-involving love for the world" (1992, 7). For Johnson, language more expressive of women's lives and experiences is required, recognizing that "being female is an excellence" (242).

Her 1998 book, *Friends of God and Prophets: Toward Inclusive Community* is a companion volume to *Truly Our Sister: A Theology of Mary in the Communion of Saints* (2003a). The first of these works is a call to a revised model of sainthood, emphasizing the call to holiness as community-oriented—an all-inclusive community of friends, moreover, stretching across time to incorporate the living, dead, and unborn. These are companions in a cloud of witnesses, an "egalitarian community of grace … all seekers of the divine, in a circle around the eucharistic table, the body of Christ which encompasses the earth itself" (1998, 262). This restores the potential for christomorphic identity and holiness to the whole community, rather than restricting it to a bureaucratized elite largely comprised of men. Their narrated stories, past and present, become a "verbal sacrament" of the work of the Spirit (1998, 175). This lays the groundwork for her quest to revision Mary in a way that is "theologically sound, ecumenically fruitful, spiritually empowering, ethically challenging and socially liberating" (2003a, 3). This is achieved through locating Mary within the communion of saints as defined above, as a "real" woman, not a perfect woman "[c]ocooned in a bubble of privileges, her very humanity … bleached of blood and guts" (2003a, 108). *Friends of God and Prophets* was awarded the American Academy of Religion Award of Excellence in the Study of Religion, Constructive Category, 1999. *Truly Our Sister* was awarded in 2004 the Outstanding Book Award, College Theology Society and the Catholic Press Association Book Award. *Truly Our Sister* formed the basis for her 2004 book, *Dangerous Memories: A Mosaic of Mary in Scripture*.

Her most recent book, *Quest for the Living God: Mapping Frontiers in the Theology of God* (2007), continues her fascination with God as triune. Johnson does not like the possible linguistic inference that God as "Trinity" represents three separate entities; she believes that to speak of God as "Triune" instead captures more fully the unity as well as threefold nature of the Christian God. She also wishes to reaffirm the centrality and dynamism of the role of the Spirit in a relational theology. Here she considers the doctrine of God in relation to recent currents in theological thought, many of which should by now seem familiar aspects of Johnson's work: transcendental, political, liberation, feminist, black, Hispanic, interreligious, and ecological.

Johnson is a prolific writer and has produced numerous essays and articles. Also worthy of note is the text of her 1993 Madeleva Lecture in Spirituality at St Mary's College, Notre Dame, Indiana, published as *Women, Earth, and Creator Spirit*. This is an expression of Johnson's deep interest in ecological matters, and intertwines feminist, theological, biblical, and ecological insights; a model of kinship with the earth is proposed with an emphasis on Creator Spirit. Another significant work is her 2002 edited collection on *The Church Women Want*, to which the Catholic Press Association awarded first place in Gender Studies.

Johnson's contribution to theology has been of great significance. Her work is characterized by a constructive creativity, sourced in the wellspring of her own spirituality. She is committed to engaging both contemporary culture and church traditions. Her work has been translated into a number of languages, including Dutch, French, German, Indonesian, Italian, Korean, Lithuanian, Polish, Portuguese, and Spanish. Her innovative theologies are not universally appreciated, however; there are those who find, for example, that her proposals to rethink how we speak of God are simply too radical and comprise an untenable breach with the church. But Johnson lays emphasis on the living God, and for her this is connected with a living and developing tradition; revelation is relational and dynamic.

The array of honors and awards bestowed upon her testify to her standing within academic and religious contexts. She has received 12 honorary doctorates: from St Mary's College, Notre Dame, IN, 1994; Maryknoll School of Theology, NY, 1995; Catholic Theological Union, Chicago, IL, 1996; Siena College, Loudonville, NY, 1998; Le Moyne College, Syracuse, NY, 1999; St Joseph College, Brooklyn, NY, 2001; College, Riverdale, NY, 2002; School of Theology in Berkeley, CA, 2003; College of New Rochelle, NY, 2004; Villanova University, 2005; St Joseph's College, West Hartford, CT, 2006; St Paul University, Ottawa, 2008.

Besides those granted for her books, as noted above, other awards include: *U.S. Catholic* Award, 1994; Teaching Award, Fordham University Graduate School of Arts and Sciences, 1998; Sacred Universe Award (from environmental group SpiritEarth), 1999; University Medal, Siena Heights University, Adrian, MI, 1999; Loyola Mellon Award in the Humanities, Loyola University Chicago, 2000; Elizabeth Seton Medal in Theology, Mount St Joseph College, Cincinnati, 2000; Woman of Wisdom Award, College of St Catherine, St Paul, MN, 2003; Fordham *Sapientia et Doctrina* Lecturer and Medalist, 2003; John Courtney Murray Award, Catholic Theological Society of America, 2004; Jerome Award, Catholic Library Association, 2004; Monika Hellwig Award for Promoting the Intellectual Life of Catholics, Association of Catholic Colleges and Universities, 2006; Yves Congar Award in Theology, Barry University, 2008; Myser Award for Promoting Catholic Identity, College of St Catherine, St Paul, MN, 2008.

References

Gaudium et Spes (Pastoral Constitution on the Church in the Modern World). Vatican Council II, 1965.

Johnson, Elizabeth A. 1990. *Consider Jesus: Waves of Renewal in Christology*. New York: Crossroad.

Johnson, Elizabeth A. 1992. *She Who Is: The Mystery of God in Feminist Theological Discourse*. New York: Crossroad.

Johnson, Elizabeth A. 1993. *Women, Earth, and Creator Spirit*. New York: Paulist Press.

Johnson, Elizabeth A. 1996. "Disputed Questions: Authority, Priesthood, Women," *Commonweal* 123 (January 26): 8–10.

Johnson, Elizabeth A. 1998. *Friends of God and Prophets: A Feminist Theological Reading of the Communion of Saints*. New York: Continuum.

Johnson, Elizabeth A. 1999. "Forging Theology: A Conversation with Colleagues." In *Things New and Old: Essays on the Theology of Elizabeth A. Johnson*, ed. Phyllis Zagano and Terence W. Tilley. New York: Crossroad, pp. 91–123.

Johnson, Elizabeth A., ed. 2002. *The Church Women Want: Catholic Women in Dialogue*. New York: Paulist Press.

Johnson, Elizabeth A. 2003a. *Truly Our Sister: A Theology of Mary in the Communion of Saints*. New York: Continuum.

Johnson, Elizabeth A. 2003b. "Worth A Life." In *Vatican II: Forty Personal Stories*, ed. William Madges and Michael Daley. Mystic, CT: Twenty-Third Publications, pp. 200–4.

Johnson, Elizabeth A. 2004. *Dangerous Memories: A Mosaic of Mary in Scripture*. New York: Continuum.

Johnson, Elizabeth A. 2007. *Quest for the Living God: Mapping Frontiers in the Theology of God*. New York: Continuum.

Martin Luther King, Jr. (1929–68)

Cynthia Stewart

Martin Luther King, Jr. was born in relative obscurity, a son of the parsonage to his father the Reverend Martin Luther King, Sr. and his mother, Alberta, on January 15, 1929 in Atlanta, Georgia. His biography (nobelprize.org: 1964) reflects the fact that he "was born Michael Luther King, Jr., but later had his name changed to Martin." Historians place him as the second of three children—Willie Christine, his older sister, was born two years before him and his younger brother, Alfred Daniel, was born two years after him.

Following in the footsteps of his grandfather, "the Reverend A. D. Williams, pastor of Ebenezer Baptist church and a founder of Atlanta's NAACP, and … Martin Luther King, Sr., who succeeded Williams as Ebenezer's pastor," (King, 2007), Martin Jr. answered the call to ministry and first became pastor at the age of 24 (King, 2007, 24) when appointed pastor of the Dexter Avenue Baptist Church in Montgomery, Alabama.

The year before accepting the pastorate at Dexter Avenue he married Coretta Scott and this union yielded four children: Yolanda Denise, Martin Luther King III, Dexter, and Bernice Albertine. The year after he began his career as pastor, he graduated with a PhD in systematic theology in 1955.

I. Theology

One wonders if Martin Jr.'s sermons gave pellucid indication of his theology, and the questions still arise as to whether his social theologies were so vividly portrayed or expressed in the footprints of his life or in the speeches he made along life's way.

His was, comparatively speaking, both in number of years and quality, a life worth living twice over; but his theology stands out clearly almost five decades later, as one that may well be described as upholding all aspects of Christian teaching by way of non-violence and passive resistance. This is perhaps his primary theological theme. Passive resistance in and of itself seems to be an oxymoron, but it ably expresses Martin's theology.

King went on to study at Crozer Theological Seminary in Pennsylvania, having graduated from Morehouse College in Atlanta. He then moved on to "Boston University, where he deepened his understanding of theological scholarship and explored Mahatma Gandhi's nonviolent strategy for social change" (King, 2007). It was at Boston Univeristy that he earned a PhD.

The Student's Companion to the Theologians, First Edition. Edited by Ian S. Markham.
© 2013 Blackwell Publishing Ltd. Published 2013 by Blackwell Publishing Ltd.

According to Paris (1993), initially Martin's position was as follows:

> It was the Sermon on the Mount, rather than a doctrine of passive resistance, that initially inspired the Negroes of Montgomery to dignified social action. It was Jesus of Nazareth that stirred the Negroes to protest with the creative weapon of love. As the days unfolded, however, the inspiration of Mahatma Gandhi began to exert its influence. I had come to see early that the Christian doctrine of love operating through the Gandhian method of nonviolence was one of the most potent weapons available to the Negro in his struggle for freedom … Nonviolent resistance (or Passive Resistance) had emerged as the technique of the movement, while love stood as the regulating idea. In other words, Christ furnished the spirit and motivation while Gandhi furnished the method.

Many have through the ages sought to emulate Jesus' behavior and portray his teaching. There is every indication that King Jr. found his supreme example initially in non-violence, which gradually elevated to passive resistance. A cursory look at the Bible substantiates Jesus' non-violence/passive resistance after which King fashioned his movement. Probably most well known are Jesus' words as recorded in Matthew 5:39 (NIV), "But I tell you, Do not resist an evil person. If someone strikes you on the right cheek, turn to him the other also." It takes a special kind of human being to turn the other cheek—Christian or minister, one has to first truly believe in one's heart before it can really be manifested in one's life, especially in the context of oppression and abuse. Martin Luther King, Jr. was one such because of his belief that as a man and a Christian he was called to transcend hatred and vilification, as Jesus did.

For many admirers of King, the parallels between the life of Jesus and the life of Martin Luther King are striking. In the same way that Jesus met hatred and harsh and uncouth behavior with love and kindness, so did King. In the same way that Jesus was ultimately killed for this witness, so was King. Indeed one could make the case that, like Jesus, King knew that his journey could end in an untimely death.

Portions of his "I Have a Dream" speech, especially from the perspective of hindsight, are claimed to be prophetic words which speak to the fact that he knew that if he continued along the road of passive resistance, death awaited him sooner than later. This was well exemplified in his speech on April 3, 1968 entitled "I've Been to the Mountaintop," where he said:

> Well, I don't know what will happen now. We've got some difficult days ahead. But it doesn't matter with me now. Because I've been to the mountain top. And I don't mind. Like anybody, I would like to live a long life. Longevity has its place. But I'm not concerned about that now. I just want to do God's will. And He's allowed me to go up to the mountain. And I've looked over. And I've seen the Promised Land. I may not get there with you. But I want you to know tonight, that we, as a people, will get to the promised land. And I'm happy, tonight. I'm not worried about anything. I'm not fearing any man. Mine eyes have seen the glory of the coming of the Lord.

Stewart Burns states that "King in his early years saw violence as a way to gain his objective … in fact he even carried a gun" (Burns, 2004). So this willingness to die for a non-violent witness was a result of a deepening meditation on the life of Jesus. However, it was also accompanied by a great admiration for the Hindu witness of Mahatma Gandhi: King weaves together the commitment to non-violence seen in Gandhi with a christology that recognizes that Jesus was in an occupied country, and provides a method which is more than just non-violent; it is also world changing. It is this world-changing aspect of King's theology that makes it important to recognize that this is a theology of passive resistance rather than non-violence, since merely the play of words indicates an underlying layer of resistance that called for a core of action.

In James Cone's masterpiece *Martin & Malcolm & America: A Dream or a Nightmare*, the theology of passive resistance is central. He wrote:

> For Martin, nonviolence did not mean passivity or doing nothing, as so many critics have suggested. His philosophy was nonviolent *direct action*. And no one was more actively involved in the struggle for justice than Martin. Indeed Malcolm and the Black Muslims were often criticized for talking loud but doing nothing. Not so with Martin. He put his *body* on the line and risked his life for what he believed in. Whatever critique one might make against him, he cannot be justly criticized for not acting or for not being involved. Martin's philosophy of nonviolence was strongly influenced by Jesus and Gandhi, with the former providing the religious motive that was persuasive in the Negro religious community

and with the latter providing the practical method that was effective in the South. Martin often said that "Christ furnished the spirit and motivation, while Gandhi furnished the method." Contrary to Malcolm, who contended that nonviolence disarmed the oppressed, Martin claimed that it disarmed the oppressor. "It weakens his morale" and "exposes his defenses. And at the same time it works on his conscience. And he just doesn't know what to do," Martin told an audience of Negroes. "Now I can assure you," he continued, "that if we rose up in violence in the South, our opponents would *really* know what to do, because they know how to operate on this level." They are experts on violence. "They control all the forces of violence." But nonviolence confounds the oppressor. "If he beats you, you develop the power to accept it without retaliating. If he doesn't beat you, fine. If he throws you in jail in the process, you go on in there and transform the jail from a dungeon of shame to a haven of freedom and human dignity. Even if he tries to kill you, you develop the quiet courage of dying if necessary without killing." The oppressor ends up frustrated. "This," King said, "is the power of nonviolence." Nonviolence, therefore, was not a sign of weakness or of a lack of courage. Quite the contrary. *King* believed that only the strong and courageous person could be nonviolent. He advised persons not to get involved in the civil rights struggle unless they had the strength. (Cone, 1991)

The project of changing America through passive resistance to oppression was national. So it was not built on the foundation of freedom for the oppressed in the south only, but rather for blacks in all America (Cone, 1991). Cone and others verbalize the fact that as King grew in his understanding of God and sought to reflect the same, his efforts were to have his movement exemplify agape love rather than justice, for certainly if God met humanity with justice rather than love the question must be, where would we all be? But the emphasis seems to be in the fact that when people rise to the level of agape love, they can move beyond their own prejudices and discriminations and love one another because of God's love for us, and it was this evolution of thought which really moved King toward passive resistance.

It is interesting to track the progress of the growth and development of Martin's theology through the eyes of those around him, especially since it was inextricably tied to their daily lives and the political environments in which they found themselves. James

Washington (Washington, 1992) explains that the Greek word for love, *agape*, caught the significance of Martin's theology of non-violence/passive resistance; for, according to him, when one begins to love on this level one begins to love people not because they are likable, or because they do things that are attractive, but because God loves them, and thus we are able to love the person who did the evil deeds while hating only the deed that the person did. According to Washington, King posits that this is the type of love that stands at the center of the movement.

This too is supported by Paris, who states that "over and over again King reminded his followers that agape was for the strong and courageous not for the weak and the cowardly. In spite of persecution or even death itself agape works diligently and untiringly for the realization of the community" (Paris, 1993). Peter Paris has come to some of the same conclusions, for it is his theory that:

> Throughout his writings he (Martin Luther King, Jr.) constantly viewed the method of nonviolence (passive resistance) as commensurate with the principle of love. In fact, he understood nonviolence (passive resistance) as the vehicle or form that love should assume in the struggle of the oppressed against their oppressors. Chronologically and theologically, the priority of love is made abundantly clear.

Charles E. Silberman (1964) addressed this matter too, no doubt pitting the black Muslim groups against Dr King's movement. Silberman noted that the Muslims played upon the natural human trait or desire for vengeance and the promise of the same:

> The weakness of Reverend Martin Luther King's movement (theology)—In the opinion of some psychologists, it's fatal flaw—is that it asks more of Negroes than any but a handful of men can ever give. For Dr. King is asking Negroes not just to forego violence, not just to forgo hatred; he is demanding that they actually love their oppressors. It is doubtful whether the masses of any oppressed group can sublimate their bitterness and resentment to that extent—particularly not Negro Americans who are acculturated enough to acquire the white Southern tradition of aggression and violence. (Silberman, 1964)

Notwithstanding, King did ask it of his followers and set out to show them how to achieve the same.

II. Key Influences of King's Theology of Love and Passive Resistance

These themes of passive resistance and the link between agape and non-violence were developed gradually. In an article in the *Christian Century*, "How My Mind Has Changed," King draws an analogy between Kant's moment of illumination provoked by the reading of Hume (Hume challenged Kant's dogmatic slumber) and his own liberal theology being shattered. According to James Washington, King would say he became so enamored of the insights of liberalism that he almost fell into the trap of believing in the natural goodness of humanity and the natural power of human reason. But this optimistic theology of humanity and the affirmation of liberal reason would not work in the movement of non-violence or passive resistance.

It is Washington's view that King began to question some of the theories that had been associated with so-called liberal theology. It was the writings of theologians such as Reinhold Niebuhr, Kierkegaard, Tillich, Nietzsche, Jaspers, Heidegger, and Sartre that got King's attention but could not convince him to become a disciple. Whereas these thinkers challenged King particularly with the concept of neo-orthodoxy, he never could accept the "wholly other," and felt it stressed an uncritical biblical approach. Although King mastered all this education in systematic theology and philosophy, he realized that back in Atlanta their social ills still festered and so his thoughts moved toward social ethics.

Paris supports this by underscoring King's search for a "methodology that would provide firm ground for the biblical understanding of a God of history, who is creator and savior, that is true. Christianity affirms that at the heart of reality is a Heart, a loving Father who works through history for the salvation of his children" (Paris, 1993).

So when and how did he solemnize his thinking about turning the other cheek? Washington attributes this to the work Martin did while in seminary as he sought to give serious thought to eliminating social evil and became immersed in the social gospel. It is reported that he read the work by Walter Rauschenbusch entitled *Christianity and Social Crisis*. King felt Rauschenbusch's thinking was the closest to giving American Protestantism a sense of social responsibility. It was after reading such works as Rauschenbusch that King reportedly turned to accept the social gospel of "loving your enemy and turning the other cheek."

It was here that King would learn more about the teaching of Mahatma Gandhi, and as a matter of fact, he became fascinated with Gandhi's campaign of non-violence/passive resistance. In Gandhi, King would find himself and his theology of non-violence. Here King would rediscover—or perhaps for the first time discover—the true meaning of agape love. As a result of this he went on to say that the Christian doctrine of love, operating through the Gandhian methods of non-violence, was one of the most potent weapons available to oppressed people.

According to James Cone (Cone, 1991), "King became convinced … that Passive Resistance/ non-violence were the best method for achieving integration …" King had heard of Gandhi's non-violent/passive resistance movement in India and felt that Gandhi was a spiritual leader and a man worthy of emulation. He was also deeply moved by lectures/sermons from A. J. Muste and Mordecai Johnson on the life of Gandhi. King's theology is further defined in what Cone refers to as the second point of King's idea of the American dream, as he began to analyze thoroughly the connection between what he dubbed the triple evils of racism, poverty, and militarism of policies of the US government. Key here was that King knew that if blacks were to be accepted and gain full constitutional rights it could not come by violence and hate but by passive resistance and love.

King began to notice a relationship between Gandhi's non-violence methods and Christian teachings. He saw that Gandhi had advocated the power of love as being the same as the power of soul or truth, and that pure love is one and the same with complete non-violence, being the absence of ill will against anyone. This pure love, says Phillips (1998), can be found in King's faith; it is this faith of "agape love that seeks nothing in return." This is the theology that helped him to develop a movement of non-violence or passive resistance.

King's theology is reflected in his total being, his mannerisms, his speeches, his sermons. According to

Phillips (1998) his life was set in a violent society yet he rose above violence to reach a spirituality that supported soul, or, as Gandhi would say, "truth force" or "love force." Again, this soul or spiritual force comes from both Jesus and Gandhi after whom he fashioned his movement, said Stewart Burns (2004).

Meanwhile, it is Dyson's (2000) view that King played a unique role in the black freedom struggle. He was above all its most popular, then most misunderstood, and finally, its most prophetic symbol, a man whose willingness to burn bridges in order to bring justice is nearly unparalleled in American history. His faith (and religious foundation) gave King the will not to settle for less than full equality for blacks and the poor. The method to attain these goals? Passive resistance and non-violence.

The use of passive resistance/non-violence by King was a means to coerce social change. In short, King wanted to force America to live up to its constitutional promise of life, liberty, and the pursuit of happiness (Dyson, 2000). He thought the way to gain the moral support of whites was to do all the things that they believed, such as getting a good education. He mastered all these things and still he and blacks were not accepted. It is Dyson's position that "King's hunger to find the best weapon of resistance was fed by his theology, a simmering gumbo of neo-orthodoxy, the social gospel, evangelical piety, liberalism and above all, radical Black Christianity. King saw this in what he called the "beloved community." Speaking in like manner, Linda Thomas (2004) points out that "King's prophetic voice bespoke God's intolerance of structural poverty in a world filled with enough resources for all creation."

It seems that the consensus of opinion, one substantiated by the clips, films, and horror stories of those days, kept King on his knees in dealing with the suffering of his people, and brought him closer to God.

The six principles King developed for his passive resistance/non-violence movement and published in his book *Stride Toward Freedom* are outlined by Maddox:

First, passive resistance/nonviolence is a way of life for courageous people; second, passive resistance/nonviolence means seeking friendship and understanding among those who are different from you; third, passive resistance/ nonviolence defeats injustice not people; fourth, passive resistance/nonviolence holds that suffering can educate and transform people and societies; fifth, passive resistance/ nonviolence chooses loving solutions, not hateful ones; and sixth, passive resistance/nonviolence means the entire universe embraces justice. (Maddox, 2008)

Passive resistance is a way of life for courageous people because, as King so often said, agape love is not a weak, passive love but one that demands action, including loving one's enemies and those that are totally different from you. It takes a person who has moved to living on a higher plane to achieve this. If King were alive today, what would he say about the reversal of so many aspects of progress for blacks in America and about the wars in which America is currently involved? This must perforce include the depths to which his own people have sunk, some claiming they are searching for a place to belong—drugs, gang membership, an epidemic of initiations of the most dastardly kind, and black-on-black crime, to name but a few.

His theology of passive resistance/non-violence extended to the suffering of Vietnamese children, which led him to condemn the Vietnam war as immoral. Indeed, according to Cone, he said, "America is the greatest purveyor of violence in the world today" (Cone, 1991). This led some Third World leaders also to posit a stance of passive resistance as they too fought for acceptance, justice, and equality for their people. This connection to the use of the symbolism of Exodus depicts God's action in history.

III. Theological Summary

Paris (1933) provides a discussion of King's theological and political understandings, the theological aspects of which may be summarized as follows:

- The major theme of all of Dr King's speeches and writings deals with God, an outgrowth of which are subjects such as love, non-violence, justice, human dignity, reconciliation, freedom and ethics.
- He believed in a God whose character is personality and who relates to persons in love, grace, and mercy in the midst of immediate experience.
- King employed the insights of philosophy, social science, literature, and general historical experience

but usually only when it supported some particular biblical understanding. A Christian and preacher from a young age, it is not surprising that his theological position is deeply rooted in the biblical tradition.

- Knowledge of God is gained only by knowing Jesus in faith.
- God is in control of history, guiding it to its true end, and further, any apparent victories of evil over good are illusory.
- Humankind is in nature but at the same time above nature because man is a spirit being and spirit is the realm of humankind's freedom, being made in the image of God.
- Humanity is not ignorant of its sin, because God speaks through conscience and inner voice.
- God's will is that all humans should acknowledge His divine parenthood and its consequent kinship.
- Passive resistance/non-violence is commensurate with the principle of love.
- Love could be a powerful and effective force for constructive social change and be a massive non-violent resistance to evil in social action.
- The end of love is community and non-violence facilitates that goal.
- For Martin Luther King, Jr., love had one meaning—Christian agape, which expresses the nature of God.
- All people are related to one another, because God is the parent of all.
- Since humans are made in the image of God and for communion with God and others, all efforts to destroy that image and to disrupt that communion are antithetical to God's will and are the essence of human evil.
- When love resists evil it does so for the sake of the desire for restoration of community.
- The cross of Christ symbolized, for King, suffering and victory. Christ, the personification of agape, suffered an ignominious death because he dared to live consistently the life of love. In that event history witnesses the sacrificial element implied by love. Love is no guarantor against persecution and suffering. Christ died praying for his executioners, thereby manifesting the community his life and mission exemplified.

- Love is the supreme religious and ethical principle that aims at the restoration of community between people and God and between person and person.
- Humanity must co-operate with God in eradicating evil from the world.
- God supported those who combated evil only when they acted in love.
- King's God-centered ethic is that humanity's ultimate loyalty ought to be to God and not to any human-made construct.
- Those who know the will of God ought to oppose evil whenever it is the will of God.

One cannot examine, even cursorily, the theology of Dr Martin Luther King, Jr. and not come face to face with the fact that the crux of his belief was wrapped up and tied up in his core understanding and belief in agape love—loving in spite of! He is said to have often quoted I John 4:7–8, 12: "Let us love one another; for love comes from God and everyone that loveth is born of God and knoweth God. Whoever does not love does not know God, because God is love … If we love one another, God lives in us, and his love is made complete in us." It is this core belief that love does not delight in evil, does not envy, does not boast or keep any record of wrongdoing that caused King to hold fast to passive resistance as a method of fighting back against a system that brought the pain and hurt that apartheid did to blacks in America.

As Maddox opines, King's theme song "We shall overcome" is a song of faith in the unseen (Maddox, 2008). Critics have claimed this song to be too much "pie in the sky" religion, yet, since it came into being, it has not yet failed in its purpose of bringing hope to believers, not even at 9/11 and after.

Freedom and peace in a land of racism, a land of hatred, a land of sexism, a land of prejudice and discrimination are in the hands of the Creator and King believed that if he was a faithful leader he could lead the black and poor peoples of America to the Promised Land of freedom by using the method of both Jesus and Gandhi, that of non-violence or passive resistance. Many industries have now been created in several countries that the trickle down serves as an opiate that make passive resistance or non-violence seem a mere lofty dream and not a part of daily living. It is very easy to imagine that King was simply an idealist.

However, King's message is the same now as it was when he was alive: evil may seem to triumph over right, but with passive resistance and agape love, and because of the Gandhis and Kings and others who have effectively embraced a life of passive resistance, it is not so—there is hope!

References

Books

Burns, Stewart. 2004. *To The Mountaintop: Martin Luther King Jr's Sacred Mission to Save America 1955–1968*. New York: Harper San Francisco.

Cone, James H. 1991. *Martin & Malcolm & America: A Dream or a Nightmare*. Maryknoll, NY: Orbis Books.

Dyson, Michael Eric. 2000. *I May Not Get There With You: the True Martin Luther King, Jr.* New York: The Free Press.

Echols, James, ed. 2004. *I Have A Dream: Martin Luther King Jr. and the Future of Multicultural America*. Minneapolis: Fortress Press.

Holy Bible. New International Version.

Maddox, Odinga Lawrence. 2008. "Martin Luther King, Jr." White Plains, New York (unpublished paper).

Paris, Peter J. 1993. *Black Religious Leaders: Conflict in Unity*. Louisville, KY: Westminster/John Knox Press.

Phillips, Donald T. 1998. *Martin Luther King, Jr. on Leadership: Inspiration and Wisdom for Challenging Times*. New York: Warner Business Books.

Silberman, Charles E. 1964. *Crisis in Black and White*. New York: Random House.

Thomas, Linda E. 2004. *Living Stones in the Household of God: The Legacy and Future of Black Theology*. Minneapolis, MN: Fortress Press.

Washington, James M. 1992. *Martin Luther King, Jr. I have A Dream: Writing and Speeches*. San Francisco: Harper.

Websites

nobelprize.org. Martin Luther Jr. The Nobel Peace Prize 1964.

King, Martin Luther (2007) http://www.stanford.edu/group/King/about _king/biography of Martin Luther King, Jr.

Liberal Theology

R. John Elford

"Liberalism" is here understood as the right to reserve and amend judgment in the face of evidence and to respect others who do the same, particularly when they come to different conclusions. A liberal is thus a person who is ever open-minded and at the same time generous toward the different opinions of others, with the proviso, only, that they are similarly open-minded. Even to those that are not, the liberal is expected to show a genuine charity. Alec Vidler captures the spirit of liberal theology when he writes:

> Here the word "liberal" denotes not a creed or a set of philosophical assumptions or an 'ism, but a frame of mind, a quality of character, which it is easier no doubt to discern than to define. A liberal-minded man is free from narrow prejudices, generous in his judgment of others, open-minded, especially to the reception of new ideas or proposals for reform. Liberal is the opposite not of conservative, but of fanatical or bigoted or intransigent. It points to the *esprit large* and away from the *idée fixe*. (Vidler, 1957, 21–2)

In general, theologians who are liberal hold the view that there is no such thing as an original Grand Narrative of Christianity that contains a once-and-for-all revealed faith in a form which is applicable to changing circumstances for all time without ever changing itself. Different expressions of the Grand Narrative view can be found throughout Christian theologies and churches. This is the conservative position. For some conservatives, it is a gospel which is revealed; for others it is a message about Jesus; and for others it is revealed in and preserved through the sacraments. What these views have in common is a belief in a given repository, the acceptance of which is the very condition of faith itself. Intellectual or other difficulties with such acceptance are seen as hurdles to true believing which must be put aside. They are never allowed to become the means of testing the adequacy or otherwise of the Grand Narrative itself. It simply has to be accepted against all the odds. Indeed, often the greater the odds appear, the greater the faith which overcomes them in this way is considered to be.

At its most absurd, this view turns faith into the acceptance of impossible things and firmness of faith into the sheer perversity of ever seeing the need to question them. Popular, or contemporary, philosophies and forms of wisdom are invariably eschewed as being inevitably passé. One example is the way in which so-called "postmodernism" is dismissed on th grounds that if that can be shown to be false (which of course it arguably can be), then the Grand Narrative *must* be true. Amazing though all this seems, it is a widespread and often seemingly theologically and ecclesiastically sophisticated manifestation of Christian orthodoxy for the simple reason that it is invariably represented by powerful establishments. These do all they can to offer certainty in matters of faith and

The Student's Companion to the Theologians, First Edition. Edited by Ian S. Markham.
© 2013 Blackwell Publishing Ltd. Published 2013 by Blackwell Publishing Ltd.

religion as a comfort to the insecure and confused. The lack of the shortage of the latter can, furthermore, create the impression that the Grand Narrative conservatisms are popular; perhaps even the most popular forms of religion around.

Against all this, liberal theologians see no tenet of belief or faith as being critically "off limits." Everything has to yield to the ever-inquiring mind as life's circumstances and knowledge changes.

Understood in this general sense, liberalism can be found throughout Christian history including the New Testament. There, for example, successive writers faced ever-changing circumstances and developed received wisdom in order to communicate the faith to different people at different times. Mark's narrative was first, but it was targeted at a specific audience and even this was soon overcome by changing events that required the narrative to be reworked. That is precisely what the subsequent gospel writers did and what, in fact, Christian theologians have been doing ever since. The history of Western Christianity can be read in the same way. As circumstances changed, particularly when they changed dramatically, visible paradigm shifts occurred as the understanding of faith was kept in the mainstream of Western thought and culture (Elford, 1999, Ch. 12).

Against such a general background, this article will show, however, that the encounter with modern theological liberalism began at the end of the eighteenth century following the challenge to received philosophical wisdom by the Scottish philosopher David Hume and the German philosopher Immanuel Kant. This interpretation of the origin of modern theological liberalism is, therefore, basically that partially set out by H. R. Mackintosh in *Types of Modern Theology*, first published in 1937 (Mackintosh, 1964).

The continuing dynamic of modern theological liberalism will be here deliberately traced through British and American writers to contrast with the German and European Continental ones written about by Mackintosh. Others would, no doubt, give reasons for selecting yet different illustrations of this broad and often complex liberal tradition. After discussion of these examples, including contemporary ones, we will conclude by extrapolating from them the themes and emphases which, however loosely, bind them together.

The liberalism here referred to is, therefore, noticeably Northern European and, for that reason, it also has roots in the post-European Enlightenment philosophies of thinkers such as Thomas Hobbes, John Locke, and Jean-Jacques Rousseau. Whilst the extent to which any writer such as these might be considered liberal in the light of our opening definition may be questioned, they all stood for an open-mindedness toward social, political, and philosophical reform which clearly puts them in the liberal tradition. Central to this was a growing belief in the inviolability of human agency and of its power when freed from the shackles of convention. Karl Marx, for example, wrote forcefully about this in his pre-1848 philosophy, stressing that what human beings had made they could also change. In these and other ways, the roots of modern theological liberalism are clearly to be found in the widespread reforming zeal of the eighteenth-century Enlightenment.

For all these reasons, it is not possible to identify liberal codes as such, or even over-much agreement among so-called liberals on specific, theological, philosophical, political, or economic issues. It is, therefore, an "ism" of mood rather than content which values the agency of the individual before the trammels of convention. From this simple but powerful idea there flowed a widespread creativity which nurtured individual freedoms of both thought and action. Respect for such is still the stuff of the liberal outlook. This is what makes it often unpredictable and always dynamic. For these reasons, it is seldom at ease with the establishment and invariably at odds with all forms of institutionalized self-interest. Modern theological liberalism, as we shall see, draws deeply on, and clearly reflects, so many of these origins.

Theological liberals are seldom to be found in identifiable and discrete groups. Such liberal political parties or churches as have and do exist represent a numerically small and not always most influential part of wider liberal forces. These, rather, are to be found among liberals who remain part of wider philosophical thinking and social organizations. This very diffuseness which so frustrates definition is, however, an important part of the overall complex phenomenon of liberal attitudes and activities.

This is part of its very strength since it enables the liberal spirit often to act as a means of reconciliation between those of different views, providing, of course, they can at the same time aspire to the liberal virtues. This, as we shall see, gives theological liberalism an exciting agenda in the twenty-first century.

Liberalism is constantly being challenged by those who offer certainties, which are ever sought by more than enough people for whom fixed points and secure tenets have an enduring allure. This constant interaction of the liberal traditions with more conservative ones is self-evident in theology and the life of the churches more generally. Indeed, as we shall see in passing, it has been the source of controversy in area after area as traditions have had to come to terms with modernity in all its forms.

The Challenge of Hume and Kant

The German philosopher Immanuel Kant once wrote that the Scottish philosopher David Hume had awoken him from his dogmatic slumbers by showing "the nullity of all pretensions of reason to advance beyond the empirical" (Kant, 1964, 607). What Hume had essentially done was to question the integrity of one of the most central claims of philosophy, i.e., that we can actually know about things. Even the most fundamental form of knowledge—self-knowledge—is challenged. When, Hume argues, we reflect upon ourselves we can only observe fleeting impressions, none of which last long enough or relate to each other enough for us to construct self-knowledge. Ideas, such as that of "the self," which lie behind fleeting impressions are therefore fainter still. He did not deny the existence of the self as such, but he emphatically did deny that we can have anything like a satisfactory knowledge of it. Similarly, Hume denied that we can have a philosophically satisfactory knowledge of causation. That too, he claimed, exists only in the mind. In these ways, Hume laid the philosophical axe to bear on the unreflective philosophical rationalism of the eighteenth century. At the same time he severed the influential and comfortable marriage between that rationalism and theology. The central truths of religion could no longer be presupposed to be rationally self-evident in the way that Archdeacon

Paley and others had claimed without demur. Hume did write *Dialogues Concerning Natural Religion*, but at his personal request they were not published until 1779, after his death in 1776. These do not attack religion as such; what they do is to show that the traditional apologetic rational arguments for religious truth are unacceptable: to show, that is, that the centuries-old alliance between religion and reason was a sham which did neither justice. In his famous essay "Essay on Miracles," for example, he claimed that in none of the records of them is there sufficient evidence for belief in their truth (Hume, 1902, 127). More positively and hauntingly, in the *Dialogues*, whilst not making his own position explicit, Hume points to the acceptability of an older classic understanding of religion which respects that the *via negativa* is so often the only and the more profound way to proceed. With seeming approval, Hume, through the voice of Philo in the *Dialogues*, argues that

> no absurdity ought ever to be assented to with regard to any subject. A total suspense of judgement is here our only reasonable resource. And if every attack, as is commonly observed, and no defence, among theologians, is successful; how complete must be *his* victory, who remains always, with all mankind, on the offensive, and has himself no fixed station or abiding city, which he is ever, on any occasion, obliged to defend. (Hume, 1947, 186)

Here and throughout, Hume essays the notion of the ideologically "baggage free" mind and at the same time explores its infinite possibilities. All this caused much reaction, with the result that Hume effectively set the agenda for the subsequent critical discussion of religion. Henceforth, if it were to survive with any sort of intellectual integrity, new grounds for it would have to be found.

As if all this were not enough, it prompted an even greater attack on the rational justifications for religion by Immanuel Kant. Just as Hume challenged the very basis of knowledge, Kant pressed the point that we can never know things-in-themselves. Where Hume had seemingly at least destroyed epistemology (the study of knowledge), Kant went further and destroyed ontology (the study of being) by claiming that we can never have knowledge of things-in-themselves. All attempts to achieve this have ended in failure (Kant, 1964, 22).

This led him famously to criticize the five rational arguments for the existence of God. The first three he criticized because they were all premised on the notion of causation. The other two, Kant criticized because they were premised on the notion of God's necessary existence (ibid., 495). Such existence, he argues, is inconceivable because existence itself is unintelligible to us. Indeed, Kant, with the use of the irony that is so common in his writing and which made him such a popular lecturer (from whence all his writings were derived), claimed that "existence" cannot be used as a predicate of anything let alone God.

Whilst embracing and pressing further Hume's criticisms of rational religion, Kant profoundly realized (as of course Hume had also done) that such skepticism left everything to be desired from the point of view of making the most of human life. More than Hume, he did much to reconstruct both religion and morality in ways which avoided his own strictures. This is why Kant remains so influential in the post-Enlightenment study of religion and why the term "post-Kantian" is still used in its description.

Whilst there were in the immediate aftermath of all this—and still are—those who held that the old truths of religion were rationally defensible, there were also many who could see why they were not. If the liberal mind, as we have described it, was still to find truth in religion, new ways of justifying that would have to be found.

The Beginning of the Modern Liberal Theological Response

As we have seen briefly in passing, both Hume and, more explicitly, Kant wrote extensively on how the integrity of religion could be reconstructed in the face of their own criticisms. Indeed, Kant did that equally for morality and at the same time showed how it required religion for its own integrity. By common consent, however, the first great attempt to reconstruct religion after Hume and Kant was that made by Friedrich Schleiermacher (1768–1834). He was a polymath who at various stages of his academic career had taught most theological subjects. His first major work, *Speeches on Religion to Its Cultured Despisers* (1799),

paved the way for a new anthropocentrism in theology. The starting point of this, for Schleiermacher, was human piety, the stuff of religious experience. Under the influence of the then increasingly popular Romantics, Schleiermacher set out to ennoble the human quest for the infinite. Accordingly, religion was to be approached not as a grand rational theory (which could be despised) but as a living experience of the infinite. So understood, it requires room for passion and emotion before it requires rational construction. At the time, this became what we would now call a "paradigm shift" in theology and it paved the way for others to follow so effectively that it set the tone of nineteenth-century protestant theology. In the twentieth century it was to be attacked, particularly by Karl Barth, for this very reason.

Schleiermacher's mature and most influential work is *The Christian Faith*, 1821. This is a systematic exposition in the sense that it is orderly, coherent and for him definitive of his views on religion. It had the lasting effect of making what he thought easily and unambiguously available. For this reason it is sometimes contrasted with Kant's equally magisterial three *Critiques*, which were all subject to constant revision, thereby often causing not a little confusion in their overall interpretation. Here again, the datum of religion is taken to be the living experience of faith in the religious life, a piety which facilitated feeling, knowing, and doing in what he called combined states (Schleiermacher, 1928, 11). Of this he famously wrote: "the self-identical essence of piety, is this: the consciousness of being absolutely dependent, or, which is the same thing, of being in relation with God" (ibid., 12). This dependence is characterized by a freedom which comes from the reciprocity of the relationship of the religious believer with the Other, with God (ibid., 14), what he calls "the really original signification of that word" (ibid., 16). Such doctrines as can be constructed from this, or which may be necessary for its explication, are nothing other than the verbalization of fundamental religious experiences. He calls these "accounts of the Christian religious affections set forth in speech" (ibid., 76) and adds that they can be interpreted as such throughout Christian history from the earliest times. For Schleiermacher, everything else about the Christian faith follows from these fundamentals; all intellectual activity, preaching, and ecclesiology. None of these things, he claimed, could ever make sense unless they were grounded in the fact of religious experience. We will see below that he was followed in all this by the eventually even more influential American writer, William James.

Schleiermacher is clearly a liberal thinker in the light of our working definition of what that means. He takes as proven the Humean and Kantian criticisms of rationally constructed views of religion and amends his judgment accordingly. He therefore bases his understanding of religion on something which is not susceptible of such criticism: religious experience. All else makes sense if and only if it remains grounded in this living tradition of religious believing and acting. Modern liberal Protestant theology can be interpreted as a dialogue with such seemingly simple beginnings. They were influential because they also reflected the nascent anthropological self-confidence of the early nineteenth century, which was becoming evident in other areas of human understanding: in, for example, biological scientific and evolutionary thinking in general. If one of the abiding hallmarks of the liberal mind is that of maintaining integrity with the best of given human understanding at any time, then Schleiermacher achieved it in great measure. He did not reduce religion to human experience as others were, perhaps under his influence, to do. He, rather, defended the otherness of God as well as the mystical means whereby the knowledge of God is apprehended. The redemptive activity of Christ is also approached by him in this way (ibid., 429). Schleiermacher addresses the powerful "otherness" of religion in a manner which is effectively impervious to the received criticisms of religion which were so much an inspiration for his writing as he did. That he also does this, as we have seen, with such systematic clarity is more than enough explanation of his being widely dubbed the Father of Modern Theology, or, more explicitly for our purpose, of modern liberal theology.

The story of what follows could and has been well related in many different ways. We will trace one of them through selected influential thinkers. We will then conclude by identifying issues which are now at the top of the liberal theological agenda and by summarizing the import of this theological tradition.

The Bampton Lectures have been delivered annually in Oxford since 1780 and were often the center of attention and controversy. Those of 1858 proved no

exception. They created a controversy which equaled and perhaps eclipsed in column inches those of the better-known Darwinian controversy of the period. Its protagonists were the then Bampton Lecturer Henry Mansel and F. D Maurice, Professor of Theology at the newly created King's College in London, who published *What Is Revelation?* and *Strictures on the Bampton Lectures of 1858* as instant replies.

Henry Mansel, then theology Tutor in St John's College Oxford and later (1868) Dean of St Paul's Cathedral, was arguably one of the first English-speaking popular writers to respond to the strictures of Kant and others which, as we have seen, so inspired Schleiermacher and others elsewhere. This also set him in the liberal tradition of theology, though some of his arguments, as we shall see, would scarce be entertained by latter-day exponents of the same tradition.

The Lectures were entitled *The Limits of Religious Thought Examined* (Mansel, 1859). Their style is readily accessible in the sense that they reflect rather than parade their author's wide reading in Continental European, idealistic, and Scottish, empirical, philosophy, the latter principally from the works of Sir William Hamilton. Here was a Bampton Lecturer profoundly steeped in the philosophical life and times of those he addressed. This, again, is why we can locate him principally in what we are describing as the liberal tradition.

Mansel's theology can be approached briefly under four headings: the limits of thought, belief in God, revelation, and analogy. After Hamilton, human thought, he held, is limited to finite objects. What can be conceived is bound by experience; therefore human thought cannot transcend possible finite experience. Philosophy, here understood, is confined to the expression of consciousness. Mansel argues that whether the human knowledge of God is given in the form of knowledge, or of feeling, or of practical impulse, it can only be given as a form of consciousness which is subject to the conditions under which consciousness is alone possible. In other words, there is no special way of knowing God. What is infinite can only become known if it becomes finite since the infinite, which is beyond human consciousness, is unknowable. This is what Mansel means by the limits of thought in relation to the knowledge of God. The conception of a rational theology is, therefore, a contradiction in terms, an oxymoron. Rather in the manner of Schleiermacher, he preferred what he called a philosophy of religion from the human side. In this he identifies three sources of the knowledge of God: the moral and intellectual consciousness, the constitution and course of nature, and the proper evidences (of revelation). When held in balance these three sources of divine knowledge enable the affirmation of divine truth, by experience, and the avoidance of fanaticism, by rational circumspection.

On belief in God, Mansel insists that we cannot know anything about the manner of God's existence, only *that* God does so. Although he agreed with the Kantian strictures against the classical arguments for the existence of God, Mansel nevertheless protested "against the pernicious extent to which the reaction to the use of reason in theology has in too many instances been carried" (1859, 75). Very similarly to Schleiermacher, Mansel talks about a "feeling of dependence" (ibid., 75) upon God in which a sense of moral obligation enables us to assume intuitively the existence of a moral deity. Purely at the level of natural reflection, this is what enables belief in God. This is not the same thing as a *knowledge of* God and can be sustained in the absence of that knowledge. (This, as we will briefly see, is what so enraged F. D. Maurice.) Indeed, Mansel did respond to other criticisms of this view and developed his views on analogical discourse about God in reply. Talk of God as "a person" or as "infinite," two logically contradictory terms, is, therefore, only analogous talk. Without undue justification, Mansel assumes that the God of which we are so able to speak is identical with the God on whom we intuitively depend. By the same token, as we shall see, he also assumed that it is the same God as the God revealed in Jesus Christ. At this point it is difficult not to come to the conclusion that Mansel is claiming too much for natural theology. However, he replies to such criticism by adding that such knowledge of God is not speculative knowledge; it is, rather, "regulative" in the sense that it does not "serve to satisfy the reason, but to guide the conduct" (ibid., 100). Here again the influence of Kant is close at hand. Mansel's use of the word "regulative" is clearly indebted to the Kantian idea of the "regulative ideal." For all practical purposes, therefore, knowledge that is speculatively inadequate or even unintelligible might well be regulatively sufficient when it is considered only to be analogous knowledge.

As we have seen, Mansel's theology of revelation is based on the presupposition *that* God exists. "Revelation," he writes, "represents the infinite God under finite symbols" (ibid., 21). In revealing Godself in Jesus, God does not reveal that self as it actually is but only through the limited finite capacities of God's creatures. Without this adaptation, revelation would have no practical effect since it would be unintelligible. Revelation cannot, therefore, answer our speculative questions concerning the nature of the infinite God. Its whole purpose, according to Mansel, is to "regulate" human conduct. Mansel contrasts the Bible with what he calls "mythologies of human invention." Its strength lies in the fact that it is fully sufficient for the purpose of inculcating in human beings a reverent agnosticism which is compatible with the limitations of human thought, whilst at the same time it regulates human life in relation to the God who cannot be fully comprehended. Mansel talks often about the "evidences" of revelation. These are the facts of its promulgation and the effects it has subsequently produced among human beings. The miracles are such evidences and they can be accepted as truly evidential because of the central miracle of the resurrection. His point on miracles is clear; any detraction from their supernatural character or from their importance as historical facts would result in the overthrow of Christianity.

Mansel's view of our knowledge of God as being analogical knowledge has already been referred to in passing.

Again, Mansel exemplifies the spirit of liberalism in the sense that he is responding to the intellectual strictures of his age whilst, at the same time, showing how the Christian faith can be sustained. In the ensuing controversy he again exemplified the liberal spirit by responding meticulously to his critics and modifying his views as and whenever he thought their criticisms required. Like many of his contemporaries he was a prolific pamphleteer, so we can trace the processes by which some of this occurred. His chief critic, F. D. Maurice, remained implacably opposed, mainly on the ground that if we do not know God as God is in Godself then we do not know God at all.

Many of Mansel's presuppositions about miracles and about the nature of the biblical text would not be necessarily shared by those who would consider themselves latter-day liberals, for the simple reason that biblical criticism and understanding has moved on beyond what could have been imagined in the middle of the nineteenth century. Today our knowledge of the texts, of their purposes and historical setting, is immensely detailed and our judgments about what they can and cannot purport has to be suitably amended. However, all that effectively illustrates is that such knowledge inexorably moves on and all we can ever do is to make the best of whatever is available to us at the time.

Mansel's Kantian-derived notion of "regulative truth" embraces a wider theory of truth in religion than he explored. He was satisfied that such truth was found in the evidences of revelation, which is why, as we have seen, he wrote so extensively upon it and defended it from criticisms. However, there is yet another way of approaching truth in religion which is not at all so dependent on the truth claims of revelation and it focuses on "regulative truth" alone. Could it be that religious truth claims can be verified by looking at the adequacy, or otherwise, of religiously regulated conduct? Whilst Mansel was among those who paved the way for doing this, he had no reason for doing so himself. That task was to be taken up influentially elsewhere, in North America, by William James and others—the so-called pragmatic philosophers.

As a psychologist as well as a philosopher, William James initially approached religion as a social phenomenon after the manner of James Frazer in *The Golden Bough*. Another influence was that of his extensive reading in British empiricism along with the writings of C. S. Peirce, who is generally recognized as the founder of modern American philosophical pragmatism. Peirce variously claimed that the purpose of thinking at all was to produce patterns of habit and action. On this view, thought and action are so closely intertwined that there could not, literally, be a difference of thought of any consequence if it did not also result in a difference of action. James was later to make much of this simple, but profound point. In a discussion of "What Pragmatism Means" James wrote with characteristic clarity and eloquence:

> It is astonishing to see how many philosophical disputes collapse into insignificance the moment you subject them to the simple test of tracing a concrete consequence. There can *be* no difference anywhere that doesn't *make* a difference elsewhere—no difference in abstract truth that doesn't express itself in a difference in concrete fact and in conduct consequent upon that fact,

imposed by somebody, somehow, somewhere and somewhen. The whole function of philosophy ought to be to find out what definite difference it will make to you and to me, at definite instants of our life, if this world-formula or that world-formula be the true one. (James, 1917, 201–2)

This led James and others to a radical view about the truth claims of religion. They were to be sought not in abstract formulae and metaphysical speculation, but, rather, in looking at whether or not religious beliefs and practices made any difference for the better in ordinary lives. In other words, the religious life was to be judged exclusively by its results (James, 1904, 21). Everything was to be eschewed except the study of "personal religion pure and simple" (ibid., 29). This is just what James set out to do in his Gifford Lectures of 1901–2, published as *The Varieties of Religious Experience: A Study in Human Nature*, published in 1904. This was followed in 1907 by *Pragmatism, a New Name for Some Old Ways of Thinking* (James, 1907).

James held that religion was about how we "accept the universe" (James, 1904, 41): if we do this with the cheerfulness of the saints then we are able to acquire through religious feeling a whole new sphere or power which can be found nowhere else but in religion (ibid., 48). This, he claimed, could now be understood in a healthy-minded way in contrast to the old hell-fire views of religion which were anything but. The word James used to describe this is "saintliness." "The saintly character," he writes, "is the character for which spiritual emotions are the habitual centre of the personal energy; and there is a certain composite photograph of universal saintliness, the same in all religions, of which the features can easily be traced" (ibid., 271). It is this which adds positive and discernible value to life's ordinary experiences. In this way, God becomes real in the effects God makes to ordinary life. This is the real, discernible, and even measurable stuff of the religious life.

The popular pragmatic defense of religion as expounded by William James was, as we have briefly seen, rooted in his wide reading and communicated lucidly and even, through his lectures on which his writing are based, entertainingly. It was and remains enormously influential, not least in the way it inspired others to essay in different ways what difference religion made to life's ordinary experiences. Reinhold

Niebuhr's writing on "political realism" can be interpreted in this way. His own Gifford Lectures for 1939, however, are critical of James's metaphysical skepticism and for this reason they are often described as being "postliberal" (Neibuhr, 1941, vol. 1: 77–8).

Niebuhr focuses on the Christian doctrine of man and on the way in which that can be used to compare other such doctrines unfavorably. However, the tone, at least, of Niebuhr's writing echoes that of James in the sense that he tests the Christian doctrine of man in a practical way by considering the relative merits of its relation to political realities in comparison with other views. Postliberal writing which is, in turn, still discernibly influenced by Niebuhr, maintains this respect for political and economic realities along with different ways of interpreting the metaphysical import of religion. Indeed, this has been a central issue in the recent past in the UK in the discussion of the writings of Don Cupitt.

In *Christ and the Hiddenness of God*, Cupitt takes up the discussion about the nature and status of our knowledge of God more or less where Mansel had left it. Speculative theology, he argues, is seemingly impossible for three reasons: it has no object, the nature of its object is obscure, or its method is wrong. Commenting on the second, Cupitt acknowledges, after Kant, that,

> Theology may … be objectively impossible in that God, being absolute, cannot as such enter into the relation to a knower which theology's possibility would require. This extreme view was taken by Mansel—on a strict interpretation of his teaching—who held that speculative theology is not merely contingently impossible because of what we are, but that it is logically impossible because of what God is. (Cupitt, 1971, 29–30)

This book concludes with the Mansellian suggestion that our knowledge of God is vindicated in the way Christ's resurrection brought about the possibility of "knowing" him in the life of the church. Any attempts to go further than this by speaking about the absolute nature of God anthropomorphically are doomed to failure. In later works, Cupitt explores why it is that the possibility of such a failure should and can be avoided. In *Taking Leave of God*, he stresses that religion is essentially "inner clarity and simplicity" (Cupitt, 1980, 101) and adds that God "must be quite

indeterminable, for if God were to become in any way determinate he would restrict the freedom which is the essence of spirituality" (ibid., 107). So understood, God is not to be treated as a "substance" knowable independently of the religious life (ibid., 164). What God is must be internalized in the spiritual life. Cupitt later, in *The New Christian Ethics*, explored the implication of the, still Mansellian, view of God in its application to morality and came to similar conclusions. Any form of two-world metaphysical dualism is eschewed in favor of a theology of redemption in which value is created in the here and now in what he describes as an ethics of self-realization. He concludes by claiming that religion can only achieve this "after we have come to accept a thoroughly anthropological and symbolist interpretation of its rites and teachings" (ibid.). In subsequent debate of Cupitt's work his position became known by the unfortunate term "non-realism," to contrast it, presumably, with the claims made variously by others to the effect that religious experience cannot make sense unless it is premised on "realist" assumptions about our knowledge of God. Defenders and detractors of these terms have been and still are in an often-heated debate which is at least reminiscent of that between Mansel and Maurice a century and a half ago. The battle, so to speak, for the soul of religion is still being fought in the same field. Its contestants are still those on the one side who want to find the truths of religion by what we are describing as liberal means, and those on the other who still insist that religion cannot make sense or even exist unless it affirms in whatever way, the preconditions of the old metaphysical certainties. Academics and ecclesiastics alike are to be found so arraigned.

Contrary to what many writers on secularization supposed as recently as the 1960s, the phenomenon of religion is still, therefore, center stage. It has not, as they forecast it would, slipped into irrelevant obscurity. Some forms of organized religion are, of course, showing signs of doing that, but that is juxtaposed by widespread "spirituality," whatever that catch-all term might actually mean in this survey or that of public attitudes.

The terrorist attacks on North America of September 11, 2001 became a focus for this in at least two ways. People turned to, even organized, religion for solace in surprising numbers and a public debate was prompted about whether religion is a force for good or evil. Those believing the latter have pointed to religion as a reason for social division and civil unrest as well as claiming that it is an all-too-ready source of fanaticism. Clearly some types of religion are capable of at least exacerbating such things and wherever this can be shown to be the case they must be judged accordingly and even harshly. We will return to this in the conclusion. But, it must still be asked, can religion, in general, yet be a force for good and, in particular, for social cohesion? For this to happen at all, particular religions will have to find ways of defending their own claims as not being in competition with, and over and against, the claims of others. Even this simple requirement might well prove too much for many of them as they fall back on old retrenchments and defenses of difference. There are now, however, important signs that an alternative is emerging and, if it is, then it will have the potential to become the major encounter of liberalism with theology in the new century and even millennium.

The widespread human desire for such an alternative approach to religion is, it can be speculated, driven centrally by two things: the desires for world peace and preservation of the environment. We no longer live in a world where human conflict can be tolerated, for whatever reason, or where the earth's resources can be squandered without thought of the morrow. These are powerful realizations which have been taken up in the work of a seminal twentieth-century writer on religion, Wilfred Cantwell Smith. He writes, "Unless men can learn to understand and to be loyal to each other across religious frontiers, unless we can build a world in which people of profoundly different faiths can live and work together, then the prospects for our planet's future are not bright" (Smith, 1978, 9). After September 11 it is ever more important to turn again to his work.

In *The Meaning and End of Religion*, Cantwell Smith addresses the fundamental phenomenological question of religion and religious faith: namely, what is it? He asks this of the "rich panorama of man's religious life over the centuries" (ibid., 4) and realizes that finding an answer to these questions poses an enormous task. He claims that even understanding one's own religion now depends upon finding these answers.

Smith claims that the Christian notion of *ecclesia* introduced a new notion into the way religion manifested itself in society. By this means, it became a discrete community system which had the immediate effect of defining those who were within and without it. The preservation and development of the community *ecclesiology* became a new focus that did not exist in older forms of loose religious associations and syncretisms. From this came the notion that there were right and wrong ways to worship God. Of this he writes, "This clear-cut choice superseding the previous unselfconscious coexistence of numerous patterns of worship and numerous objects of worship was for the Christian first not an intellectualist problem to be conceptualised but a dramatic existential one" (ibid., 26). In other words, it tangibly affected the way the new communities behaved socially. No longer could there be any casual participation in other religious rites. Religion now bound the religious by separating them from all else. "The new notion of boundaries is beginning to take shape: a *religio* of one set of people, clearly and radically distinct from the *religiones* of outsiders" (ibid., 27). From now on, this new understanding of religion was to become so successful that it defined the religious activities and attitudes of others. The willingness to die for the truth not just so conceived, but so socially organized, became the cause of martyrdom. Similarly, laments over apostasy became commonplace. And so on. Little wonder, on further reflection, that these *ecclesia* would ever fragment from within as disagreement arose and inevitable further separations came into existence. Bigger wonder, perhaps, that religious groups such as Christian ones have not fragmented more than they have done over two millennia. And, no wonder, that it is so difficult to bring them together in ecumenical movements.

Another and far later development, according to Smith, further exacerbated all this. That was understanding "religion" as a noun. He observes that this is a comparatively recent historical phenomenon, of some 200 years, which has been exported by the West. Prior to that, religion was understood as an adjective attached to persons, rather than as entity in itself (ibid., 20). He calls for the redress of this on the ground that it separates and juxtaposes religions to such an extent that they become defined by their differences in ways that, in turn, make those differences a necessity. This is then exacerbated beyond measure whenever one or other of the discrete religions claims to be the "true" one. Such claims, of course, are common among even people who would think themselves to be reasonable. They are, however, here clearly beyond the bounds of ordinary reason if only in the sense that no individual or group of individuals could possibly have access to the unimaginable range of information which alone could justify the claim. So understood, the claim that one's own religion over and against that of another is *the*, or the *more*, true one is nothing short of a breathtaking arrogance which at once prohibits those making it from availing themselves of true piety, even that in their own tradition. (This is what Smith means by claiming that understanding the religions of others is now a pre-requisite of understanding one's own.) In this way "religion" has, therefore, become "an enemy of piety" (ibid., 19) and no progress will be made unless the term is abolished.

According to this view, what defines religion is what separates it from all else, particularly from other religions. Monotheism could clearly only survive in such a system by those in its discrete parts believing that their version was the only true one. The one thing which should, therefore, bind them together is robbed of its power to do so. Without the restoration of that power the future is a bleak one, given, as we have observed in passing, the effective failure of the practically still effete official ecumenical movements. None of this is to say, of course, that individual religious people cannot and have not done far better in managing their relationships with those of other religions. This, in fact, is often the source of the grace by which religion is redeemed whenever people place sharing their common humanity before their institutional loyalties, or at least, come to find ways of living with the discrepancy.

Nothing less than a world theology can ever effectively begin to put any of this right—a sort of theology, that is, which might have existed before the roots of Christian separatism were laid in the foundations of Israel three millennia ago. The Christian *ecclesiology* we have criticized could never have come about as it did were it not for its prefiguring in the social arrangements of Israel. Of course, whether the desired new world theology has ever been prefigured we will never know, for the simple reason that, in Western culture at least, our real knowledge of religious pre-history is so colored by what we have seen may well be the lasting defects of the Judaeo-Christian tradition.

In the last decade or so, the need for a global ethic has been widely recognized and written upon. Hans Kung has been foremost in this and he remains confident that progress can be made toward the creating of globally common value systems which elicit the assent and support of otherwise discrete value systems (Kung, 1993). It remains to be seen how effective any of this actually can be and there is much to be done in the exploration of that. More widely for our discussion, however, it might be asked whether such a global ethic can be realized unless it can be created in the context of a global theology. Here, as we have seen, there is even more to be done. Will we ever be able to get it back (if it ever existed in the first place, that is)? And, what effect would its emergence have on the institutions of religion that would be struggling to produce it? Could they really be reformed in ways which would put the combined yield of religion(s) (whatever that is) to the wider benefit of the human race? Finding answers to some of these awesome questions must now be at the top of the liberal theological agenda. Only here, or in some such place, could the *will* to make progress be found. It cannot, clearly, come from religious extremists, and even conservatively minded religious people are more hindered in this cause than they are generally willing to recognize.

A literature of a world theology scarcely exists. Cantwell Smith, again, published *Towards a World Theology* in 1981. Following his earlier work, he seeks to discover what an understanding of the salvation history of the whole human race would be like. That, in fact, is what a global theology would be. It clearly has to be *theo-* and not *Christo-centric*. That alone would exclude many Christians from offering their labors, for reasons we have briefly considered. Many such are now to be found recognizing and even extolling the virtues of pluralism, but that simply reinforces old ways of thinking that are so much the cause of the problem. Pluralism is invariably proffered as a virtue and a too-ready one at that. The "dialogue" it purportedly facilitates is seldom anything that is really worthy of such a description, though it is to be infinitely preferred to an otherwise total lack of communication. Nothing short of a new monotheism will ever suffice—a new way, that is, of relating the total human experience of spiritual realities to conform to the awesome reality of the one God. If human religious history in general, and Judaeo-Christian religious history in particular, has taken wrong—and fundamentally wrong—turns, can it ever be so redirected? The hope *must* be that it can. A weak reason for this is because attempts to synthesize new religions, such as theosophy, have singularly failed. The strong reason must be that humankind's total religious experience has so much to benefit from following such a wider theological reconstruction. In its turn, that reconstruction will better place all the religions to serve others in pursuit of the good.

We have briefly considered how theological liberalism has manifested itself in strands of English-speaking theology since the end of the eighteenth century. We have also now considered something of the breathtaking scale of its contemporary and worldwide agenda. In conclusion, we will now extrapolate and summarize some of the themes we have touched upon.

Christians began the debate about the relationship of their faith with culture in the New Testament. Indeed, the clash with Neronian culture was probably the main reason for the first gospel, St Mark, coming into existence. The ever-changing world in which Christians then continually found themselves clearly required and prompted the writing of the other gospels, the letters of St Paul, and the other literature in the New Testament. In page after page, the external world impinges upon what we have already briefly considered to be the variously enclosed earliest Christian communities. In other words, the Christ and culture dichotomy, so much a feature of Christian history, was endemic to Christianity from its very beginning. The classic modern essay on this which indicates, at least, that Christ is best understood as the "transformer" of culture (understood as "whatever man imposes upon the natural"), suffers from the lack of recognition that the "Christ" of the New Testament is itself a cultural construct based on the historical Jesus (Niebuhr, 1951, 190ff.).

Much modern New Testament scholarship since Richard Niebuhr wrote has been in discussion of that. Many issues remain unresolved, though recent scholarship had brought to the fore the strangeness of Jesus and pointed to the radical nature of his teaching. The problem of the relationship of Christianity to culture remains as effectively unresolved as it ever was, proba-

bly for the same reasons that it ever was. Whilst many Christians, in the Niebuhrian terminology, want to see the Christ as the "transformer" of culture, we have seen why that will not do. The ongoing dialogue between the Christian tradition and the ever-renewing modernity of culture requires more subtlety in its understanding. Liberal theology provides the nurture for this.

A main reason why it does this is because it is, so called, "baggage-free." It invariably approaches new challenges with an open-mindedness which does not rule out any possible solutions to cultural problems from the beginning or in principle. This is clear, at least, in the way liberal theology engages with the myriad debates caused by the rapid development of the sciences and their technologies. Those in the life sciences are to the fore in this. Clearly, huge benefits to human well-being have already come from them and will continue to do so, if, at the same time, we can obviate their dis-benefits. Religions are scarce able to engage in these debates if they limit themselves to posturing from the sidelines. Nothing less than their active engagement is required if their insights are to be brought to bear where they are most needed in the wider pursuit of harnessing technology in the service of human welfare. The respect for evidence, which we have seen is so much a feature of the liberal theological traditions, serves them well in these debates. This inculcates humility toward the ever-expanding human knowledge of the natural world. It also increases the likelihood of religion playing a definitive part in the fulfillment of the potential of the natural order, not to say its very survival. Nowhere, perhaps, is the demand for liberal humility greater than in the need to get religions to recognize that the natural order is finite and, therefore, literally time-limited. So much Christian and wider religious debate about the natural order has been bedevilled by sloganizing and posturing, which has obscured the real evidences that cry out for discussion.

This engagement of liberal theology with culture requires and generates visible creative and sustaining energy. In area after area of public life liberal theologians have been welcomed into secular discussion once it has been recognized that they are willing to respect evidences and the general rules of discussion along with everyone else. Just one illustration of this can be found in the way liberal theologians have and do engage in the debates about the nuclear technologies, particularly those about nuclear weapons. Whilst some theologians identified with this group or that—the pacifists, the unilateralists, or multilateralists—others wanted to eschew these, for them, unrealistic options, and work with others to find possible solutions to, say, the nuclear arms race, which could become a reality. All this demands huge creative energy and hard work, often in the face of opposition from fellow theologians. In area after area of public debate, the liberal theological traditions can be seen to have sustained this.

Liberal theologies which facilitate the sustained and energetic reconciliation of this kind between religion and culture have yet more potential. It is that of further reconciling religious extremists in their own traditions as well as helping to bring about reconciliation with members of other religious traditions. Indeed, theological liberals can often be found to have closer sympathies with liberals of other religious traditions than they do with members of their own with whom they would more naturally be expected to identify. This happens at all levels of religious interaction, within denominations and traditions as well as between them. The potential for good of such liberal alliances is obvious, and nowhere more so than in areas where religions are, rightly or wrongly, perceived to be the cause of social division, unrest, and particularly conflict. Northern Ireland and the Middle East are just two areas where some reconciliation of like-minded liberals on all sides has been achieved but where the need for progress is still pressing.

The agenda of all this contains more than enough opportunity for liberal theologians to present, so to speak, the apology for religion in a secular word, and nowhere more so than where, as we have seen, religion is held responsible for its many unrests. This apology is not self-justifying. It is rather an apology which emerges from the effective strength of the engagement of religion with the world's ills. This is most evident whenever, in ways we have briefly considered, religious believers and theologians work alongside all people of good will in whatever cause. What possible better way could ever be found for enabling others to see the wisdom of the religious traditions in action?

Theological liberalism also enables the discernment of good and bad reasons for being religious. It does this, as we have seen, by taking credible criticisms of religion seriously. This, alone, is invariably more than enough to put it at odds with religious establishments, which will brook no criticism at all and in so doing often achieve little more that the repetition of pedantry. In stark contrast, the liberal reaction keeps open the possibility that there are understandings of religion which survive even radical criticism and which remain important. We have seen some of the ways in which this has been achieved by exemplars of this tradition in the recent past. There may well be—and are for some, of course—criticisms of religion which even theological liberalism cannot answer. That freedom of choice will always remain. For some, it will make any sort of religious belief or practice impossible. For others, it might invite a hovering on the edge of religion. This is a well-recognized phenomenon in Christianity. So-called "God-fearers" are those who cannot walk away but at the same time are reluctant to commit themselves. From the liberal point of view this is to be respected and even encouraged. At the very least it enables the recognition that people can avail themselves of the insights and purposes of religion without having to ignore their reserved judgments about it. Some religions enable this recognition more easily than others. Some versions of Christianity, for example, have very clear ideas about who is and who is not "in the fold." Indeed, it may well be the case that Christianity, more than other religions, has created traditions in which truths are to be embraced only from the inside. If this is so, then Christianity at least is a religion with an infinite capacity to create social division. That it has done this historically to a considerable extent in European history alone, is obvious. Sadly, it still does so in communities that remain defined largely by religious allegiance. The so-called "ecumenical" movements that seek to address these issues have, at official levels at least, such little success because, as we have seen, they invariably do not address these more fundamental issues. Indeed, much of the thankfully improved relations between religious denominations have either come directly from secular sources or indirectly from secular influences on religious behavior. The overall point here is that theological liberalism is particularly able to recognize, articulate, and evaluate the nature and purpose of religion in these sensitive areas.

References

Cupitt, D. 1971. *Christ and the Hiddenness of God*. London: Lutterworth.

Cupitt, D. 1980. *Taking Leave of God*. London: SCM Press.

Cupitt, D. 1988. *The New Christian Ethics*. London: SCM Press.

Elford, R. John. 1999. *The Pastoral Nature of Theology*. London: Cassell.

Hume, David. 1902. *Enquiries Concerning the Human Understanding*, 2nd ed. Oxford: Clarendon.

Hume, David. 1947. *Dialogues Concerning Natural Religion*. New York: Bobbs-Merrill.

James, W. 1904. *The Varieties of Religious Experience: A Study in Human Nature*. London: Longmans.

James, W. 1907. *Pragmatism, a New Name for Some Old Ways of Thinking*. London: Longmans.

James, W. 1917. *Selected Papers in Philosophy*. London: J. M. Dent.

Kant, I. 1964. *Critique of Pure Reason*, trans. N. K. Smith. London: Macmillan, second impression.

Kung, H. 1993. *A Global Ethic: The Declaration of the Parliament of the World's Religions*. London: SCM Press.

Mackintosh, H. R. 1964. *Types of Modern Theology*. London and Glasgow: Fontana Library.

Mansel, H. L. 1859. *The Limits of Religious Thought Examined*. London: John Murray.

Niebuhr, R. 1941. *The Nature and Destiny of Man*. London: Nisbet.

Niebuhr, H. Richard. 1951. *Christ and Culture*. New York: Harper.

Schleiermacher, F. 1928. *The Christian Faith*. Edinburgh: T&T Clark.

Smith, Wilfred Cantwell. 1978. *The Meaning and End of Religion*. London: SPCK.

Smith, Wilfred Cantwell 1981. *Towards a World Theology*. London: Macmillan.

Vidler, A. R. 1957. *Essays in Liberality*. London: SCM Press.

George Lindbeck (1923–)

Stephen H. Webb

George Lindbeck is a distinguished Lutheran theologian with a long and varied career. Perhaps the key to his work dates back to his service as one of the 60 "delegated observers" at the Second Vatican Council from 1962 through 1965. He was a young untenured faculty member at Yale (where he would retire, in 1993, as the Pitkin Professor of Historical Theology), with the requisite language skills the Lutheran World Federation needed for someone to take on this daunting task. At the end of the Council, Lindbeck was optimistic about what it had accomplished and expected a smooth implementation of its directives. More specifically, he thought that agreement about the doctrinal differences that emerged in the conflicts of the sixteenth century would be decisive in paving the way for ecclesial dialogue and reunion. He was, of course, disappointed in this, and his experience over the ensuing confusions about the meaning of Vatican II shaped his commitment to developing a truly ecumenical theological method (Weigel, 1994).

Lindbeck's grasp of the cultural diversity of Christianity began long before Vatican II. He was born in China in 1923, the son of Lutheran missionaries. The year before Pearl Harbor he turned 17 and left China for Gustavus Adolphus College in Minnesota. As a sickly child, he experienced China mostly through books and in his imagination, and he was especially captivated by the buried ruins of Luoyang, China's ancient capital city (Lindbeck,

2006). At first he was struck by the contrast between Luoyang's majestic past and its shabby present state. Then he began to observe continuities in Chinese history and culture. He became convinced that culture shapes individuals more than individuals shape culture. He also became impressed with the way cultures with strong textual traditions can maintain continuity through thousands of years of social upheaval and political transformation. These insights are at the bottom of his cultural-linguistic theory of religion, which is his most influential contribution to the study of theology.

Lindbeck introduced the cultural-linguistic theory of religion in *The Nature of Doctrine* (1984), which was the most debated book on theological method in the 1980s. Key to his approach is the idea that becoming part of a religious tradition is analogous to learning how to speak a particular language. The best way to learn a new language is not to start with its grammar. The grammatical rules can be picked up along the way. The best way to learn a language, in fact, is to be surrounded by people who speak it. Studying grammar can help, but the successful mastery of a language results in the internalization of grammatical rules. If you have to look up the grammar, then that is a sure sign that you have not learned the language yet. This does not mean that grammar is unimportant. No language can evolve without a set of grammatical rules and principles, and written languages become

The Student's Companion to the Theologians, First Edition. Edited by Ian S. Markham.
© 2013 Blackwell Publishing Ltd. Published 2013 by Blackwell Publishing Ltd.

more complex by means of debates about the nature and limits of those rules. Of course, most speakers of a given language are competent in their use of it without being able to articulate its grammatical rules. Indeed, many of the best speakers of a language can perform its nuances exceptionally well without knowing how it works. Nonetheless, grammar exists, and its scrutiny is helpful in solving linguistic conundrums.

What does this have to do with religion? For Lindbeck, doctrine plays a role in religion that is similar to the role grammar plays in language. Theologians thus function like grammarians in their oversight of the proper explication of doctrinal rules. Doctrinal statements, for Lindbeck, do not refer directly to reality, and they do not have any metaphysical significance beyond their capacity to regulate the proper use of religious language. Doctrines, to employ one of his favorite distinctions, are a species of second-order language, and thus they are subordinate to the first order of language of prayer, testimony, Bible reading, preaching, and so forth. Lindbeck developed this approach to doctrine in order to understand how first-order religious language can change while second-order rules remain the same, as well as to understand how doctrines themselves can develop as the process of making explicit the linguistic usages of the faithful. Doctrines are only as strong as the social bonds they reflect. The idea is that the truth of doctrines is not located in a once-and-for-all propositional form or in their subjective appropriation within an individual's inner experience but in the function they serve in helping to constitute an ongoing linguistic community.

Perhaps the most controversial aspect of Lindbeck's theory is the way he defined it in opposition to two alternatives. He contrasted the cultural-linguistic theory of religion with what he called the experiential-expressivist theory, which defines religion according to its personal effects and subjective origins; and the propositional theory, which treats religious doctrines as truth statements that can be extracted from their cultural context. Many theologians thought these categories were too broad or unfairly employed. Critics also disparaged the cultural-linguistic theory for making religious truth relative to culture and, consequently, demoting the task of the theologian from

systematic, constructive, and metaphysical thinker to the more mundane job of a sociological observer of linguistic usage. Indeed, since most speakers of a language feel no obligation to know its grammatical rules—which is especially true given the rapid pace of linguistic change in modern languages and the assumption that grammatical rules are heuristic, flexible, and dispensable—it is hard not to think that Lindbeck's proposal effectively marginalizes theologians as fussy guardians of obscure and incidental laws that can be broken without any significant consequences.

Two corollaries of Lindbeck's theory pertain to the meaning of conversion and the nature of the church. Becoming a Christian, for Lindbeck, is not matter of examining and accepting a set of Christian beliefs. Instead, it is a matter of becoming a skilled speaker of Christian discourse. That discourse is maintained and reproduced by the church, just as any language lives only in communal usage. For Lindbeck, the church is like Israel in its cultural specificity. He does not mean that the church is a New Israel that supersedes the old. On the contrary, the church, for Lindbeck, is an enlargement of Israel. The church is constituted, just as was Israel, by all the customs, manners, rituals, norms, and habits that make sharing a language possible. The church is not something radically different from Israel, as if Israel were constituted by law, and the church by something subjective called faith.

Nearly 25 years after its publication, Lindbeck's work can now be placed in its own cultural-linguistic time and place. Shaped by the expectations of Vatican II, he wrote for an audience that still thought that doctrinal differences could be overcome through ecumenical dialogue, rather than through co-operation in the struggle for social justice. In retrospect, Lindbeck's work marks the end of the deluge of books about theological method that swamped the 1960s and 1970s. Theology was in such a state of disarray in these decades that the best theological minds undertook the hopeful quest for a method that could keep theologians talking to each other. That disarray has settled into various camps and factions today, but it has also led to a revival in traditional, dogmatic theology that treats Christian beliefs as truth claims worthy of the most serious philosophical investigation. From this perspective, Lindbeck's program of limiting the role of theologian to that of the referee of a sporting event (keeping, enforcing, and elaborating on the rules of the game being played) appears to be a final plea for significance on the part of a generation of theologians who could not find their doctrinal voices.

Probably Lindbeck's most lasting influence is on the theological movement known as postliberalism. This is a term that he popularized in *The Nature of Doctrine*, but its precise meaning has led to interminable debates. Associated with Yale Divinity School, postliberalism never became a systematic school, in part because Lindbeck's own work was easily interpreted in contrary ways. The rhetoric of this school, if it can be called that, was always directed at liberal theology, or what is sometimes called theological revisionism, which postliberals typically collapse into Lindbeck's category of experiential-expressivism. While liberals were their target, postliberals never took the step of becoming conservative in their theological outlook. This is

probably why their movement never coalesced into a proper school and why its long-term impact is so minimal. The "post" of postliberalism was never adequately defined, and one might wonder how much distance Lindbeck really wanted to open up between his theological program and the liberalism of the 1960s and 1970s. Lindbeck's goal has always been to deepen mutual understanding by overcoming intellectual barriers, rather than to strengthen existing communities by tightening doctrinal standards. Although his ecumenism differed from liberals who wanted to promulgate consensus on the basis of social justice issues, his emphasis on the proper use of religious language and his rejection of realistic or objective theories of truth made his theology as pragmatic and moralistic as the liberals he rejected. Some of his students have gone off in different directions, like Kathryn Tanner, who has developed a more subtle theory of culture, and Bruce Marshall, who has worked on a more robust theory of theological truth.

References

DeHart, Paul J. 2006. *The Trial of Witnesses: The Rise and Decline of Postliberal Theology*. Oxford: Blackwell Publishing.

Lindbeck, George. 1984. *The Nature of Doctrine: Religion and Theology in a Postliberal Age*. Philadelphia: The Westminster Press.

Lindbeck, George. 2002. *The Church in a Postliberal Age*, ed. James J. Buckley. Grand Rapids, MI: Eerdmans.

Lindbeck, George. 2006. "Performing the Faith: An Interview with George Lindbeck," *Christian Century* (November 28): 28–35.

Marshall, Bruce. 2000. *Trinity and Truth*. Cambridge: Cambridge University Press.

Tanner, Kathryn. 1997. *Theories of Culture: A New Agenda for Theology*. Minneapolis: Fortress Press.

Weigel, George. 1994. "Reviewing Vatican II: An Interview with George Lindbeck," *First Things* (December 1994): 44–50.

Donald MacKinnon (1913–94)

Brian Hebblethwaite

Donald MacKenzie MacKinnon, moral philosopher and philosopher of religion, was born in Oban, Argyll. He went, as a scholar, to Winchester College, from which a further scholarship took him to New College, Oxford, where he read Litterae Humaniores and Theology, graduating in 1935. His first academic appointment was as assistant in Moral Philosophy to Professor A. E. Taylor at Edinburgh University. During this time he met his future wife, Lois Dryer, daughter of a Church of Scotland minister. They married in 1939 and the marriage lasted until MacKinnon's death. He himself had become a High Episcopalian, but she remained a Presbyterian, and this ecumenical partnership was reflected in MacKinnon's work and concerns throughout his life.

In 1937, MacKinnon was appointed Fellow and Tutor in Philosophy at Keble College, Oxford, where he soon established a formidable reputation as teacher and eccentric. The regard in which he was already held by fellow Oxford philosophers is evident from his being invited by J. L. Austin and Isaiah Berlin, along with Stuart Hampshire of All Souls, to join the informal group which they had formed the previous academic year for regular philosophical discussion.

MacKinnon held the Wilde Lectureship in Natural and Comparative Religion during his last two years in Oxford. In 1947 he moved to Aberdeen as Regius Professor of Moral Philosophy.

After 13 years in Aberdeen, MacKinnon was appointed Norris-Hulse Professor of Divinity in the University of Cambridge, and Fellow of Corpus Christi College. Until his retirement in 1978, he was one of the leading figures, nationally and internationally, in the fields of philosophy of religion, philosophical theology, and ethics. His lectures, his writings, and his supervision of graduate students had a profound effect on generations of scholars and teachers in these subjects.

The MacKinnons had retained a cottage in Argyll during their sojourns south of the border, but on his retirement, they moved back to Aberdeen.

MacKinnon's influence stemmed more from his lectures, seminars, and occasional writings—and from his powerful personality—than from his relatively few published monographs. Apart from two early short theology books, *God the Living and the True* and *The Church of God*, there were only two substantial monographs, *A Study in Ethical Theory* (1957), coming out of his years in the Aberdeen chair, and *The Problem of Metaphysics* (1974), a much reduced version of his 1965/66 Gifford Lectures. The former is still important for its thoughtful comparison and contrast of utilitarian and Kantian moral philosophy, and especially for its chapter on the ethical writings of Bishop Butler. The latter gives some idea of MacKinnon's profound reflections on the themes of parable and tragedy as windows into the transcendent. It is a noteworthy fact that of all the named

The Student's Companion to the Theologians, First Edition. Edited by Ian S. Markham.

lecture series that MacKinnon gave—the Wildes at Oxford, the Stantons at Cambridge, the Giffords at Edinburgh, the Prideauxs at Exeter, the Riddells at Newcastle, and, after his retirement, the Boutwoods back in Cambridge—only the last of these (just two lectures) and the Giffords (in reduced form) found their way into print. One-off lectures, such as his Cambridge inaugural, "Borderlands of Theology," his Gore Memorial Lecture in Westminster Abbey, "Kenosis and Establishment," and his Martin Wight Memorial Lecture at the LSE, "Power Politics and Religious Faith," were published and can be found, among many others, in his four volumes of collected papers, *Borderlands of Theology* (1968), *The Stripping of the Altars* (1969), *Explorations in Theology 5* (1979), and *Themes in Theology: the Three-Fold Cord* (1987). Indeed it is in these four volumes that the heart of MacKinnon's deep and tortuous wrestlings with such subjects as substance, christology, evil, nuclear warfare, Kant, ecumenism, time and space, tragedy—and many more—can be found. Several of the pieces in these books originated as broadcast talks, notably "The Inexpressibility of God"—his reflections on Schoenberg's opera, *Moses and Aaron*. We also find a number of the papers he gave, annually for a time, at the Rome Colloquium on philosophy of religion, an international forum, initiated by Enrico Castelli, of which MacKinnon was a prominent member.

MacKinnon was a polymath. His reading (in several languages) in ancient and modern philosophy, in theology and church history, in political theory and current affairs, and in literature and biography, was prodigious. But it is virtually impossible to summarize his views. He founded no school. His colleagues and pupils simply learned from him how to ponder and probe a whole range of metaphysical, theological, and ethical issues relentlessly, without evasion, and in depth. Moreover, his reflections took place not just at the theoretical level, with reference to his favorite philosophers (Aristotle, Kant, Collingwood), but with a wealth of particular examples, from literature (Sophocles, Shakespeare, Conrad), from history (the Albigensian Crusades, Lenin, the Holocaust), and from the daily newspaper. Mention should also be made of his profound sense of humor and of the way in which, with sometimes caustic wit, he would

protractedly gnaw over some instance of human folly like a dog with a bone.

There were two Festschriften published in MacKinnon's honor: Hebblethwaite and Sutherland (1982) and Surin (1989). The latter came out of a conference on his work held, in his presence, in Cambridge. Public recognition was marked by his election to a Fellowship of the British Academy in 1978 and to a Fellowship of the Royal Society of Edinburgh in 1984. Something of the deeply impressive nature of the man and his contribution was captured in a memorial tribute by his friend George Steiner given in Cambridge in May 1994 (Steiner, 1995).

Three areas of MacKinnon's work may now be explored in a little more detail. First, his ecumenical concerns. It was typical that, in preparing his first book, *God the Living and the True*, he consulted both the Presbyterian Barthian scholar T. F. Torrance, and also the Roman Catholic Dominican Fr Gervase Mathew. His lifelong friendship with Torrance and the many conversations they had over such subjects as natural theology and christology are reflected in the remarkable essay on "The Relation of the Doctrines of the Incarnation and the Trinity" that he contributed to Torrance's Festschrift (reprinted in MacKinnon, 1987). In his early years, MacKinnon was actively engaged in ecumenical conferences. He participated in the 1937 Life and Work Conference in Oxford and in the 1952 preparatory meeting in Bossey for the Evanston World Council of Churches Assembly. At Bossey he encountered the great Swiss theologian Karl Barth, in person, and made such an impression on him that, in later years, allegedly, Barth's reaction to mention of MacKinnon's name was to exclaim "Das ist ein Mensch!" Some of his later reflections on ecumenical matters, not least his remarks on Anglican arrogance (he was himself an Anglican), may be found in *The Stripping of the Altars*.

If the Protestant Karl Barth was one major figure with whose thought MacKinnon wrestled, the Roman Catholic Hans Urs von Balthasar was another, as we see from his essay, "Masters in Israel III: Hans Urs von Balthasar," reprinted as a foreword to Balthasar's *Engagement with God* (1975), and from his essay on Balthasar's christology in Riches (1986).

These last two references bring us to the second—indeed the main—area of MacKinnon's work:

metaphysics and theology. Mention has been made of the Gifford Lectures and their treatment of our apprehension of the transcendent through parable and tragedy. But if there is a persistent metaphysical stance that can be attributed to MacKinnon, it is a dogged realism in both philosophy and theology. In philosophy, this may be seen in two essays (in MacKinnon, 1979) on the conflict between realism and idealism, the first being his 1976 presidential address to the Aristotelian Society, the second based on a paper to the Rome colloquium the following year. Conscious as he was of the contribution of the knowing mind to what we know—he was, after all, very much preoccupied with Kant—he remained convinced that, in experience and thought alike, we have to face up to what we *find* to be the case. The theological bearing of this conflict may be seen in many of his essays, for example in a 1984 article (reprinted in MacKinnon, 1987) on "Some Aspects of the Treatment of Christianity by the British Idealists." What worried MacKinnon most were the deterministic implications of the Idealists' holistic view of history. Christianity, he was convinced, cannot dispense with the particularity and objectivity—and contingency—of the incarnation. Thus it is that we find him resolutely opposed to subjectivism in theology. Three examples may be cited on this recurring theme: the essay " 'Substance' in Christology—a Cross-bench View" in Sykes and Clayton (1972), the essay "Subjective and Objective Conceptions of Atonement" in Healey (1966), and the fascinating exchange with his Cambridge colleague, Professor Geoffrey Lampe, *The Resurrection* (Lampe and MacKinnon, 1966). A quotation from the last of these will indicate MacKinnon's stance: "I must admit that my readiness to use objectivist language more freely than he [Lampe] does may have its roots (at least in part) in an eagerness, in questions of general epistemology, to endorse the views of those who emphasize the element of *discovery* in coming to know, and the authority of brute *fact* in the refutation of hypotheses."

The third area of MacKinnon's work was that of political and personal ethics. *A Study in Ethical Theory* has already been mentioned, as has the Wight Memorial Lecture on "Power Politics and Religious Faith." Another example of his searching work on political ethics is "Law, Change and Revolution: Some

Reflections on the Concept of *raison d'état*," given first in Rome and later to the Society for the Study of Theology, of which he had become President. The practical nature of MacKinnon's concerns is exemplified by the volume he edited, *Christian Faith and Communist Faith* (1953). The work came out of a series of discussions, initiated by Bishop George Bell, on Christian reactions to the sweep of Marxist-Leninist dogma across the world. It was also exemplified by his membership of the Labour Party and his support for the Campaign for Nuclear Disarmament. His preoccupation with the latter issue is evident from the Boutwood Lectures (reprinted in MacKinnon, 1987) and also from the lecture on "Ethical Problems of Nuclear Warfare," with which he began the Cambridge Divinity Faculty Open Lectures in 1962. These hugely popular lectures, entitled *God, Sex and War*, were published the following year (MacKinnon's own lecture was reprinted in MacKinnon, 1968). The year 1963 saw an even more influential series of Open Lectures, *Objections to Christian Belief*, to which MacKinnon contributed on "Moral Objections" (Vidler, 1963). These Open Lectures, like his broadcast talks, illustrate MacKinnon's ability to hold the attention of non-specialist audiences on matters of deep concern. One example, from "Moral Objections," will show how MacKinnon faced up, with the utmost seriousness, to criticisms of Christian belief. Having insisted that the Christian claim about Jesus "stands or falls by the truth or falsity of certain statements relating to matters of historical fact," he goes on to say that

> Christians must realize that the crucial importance of this issue for their faith raises grave doubts in their critics' minds concerning the honesty with which they will approach it … Christians give weight, and must give weight to belief that certain events have actually happened; how far does this make them prejudiced and narrow and unwilling to open their minds to uncertainties concerning particular strands of human history? This objection is a moral objection in that it urges that faith, as the Christian understands it, is incompatible with a proper intellectual objectivity.

Such honest and open self-criticism was typical of MacKinnon's contribution to the philosophy of religion.

References

Balthasar, Hans Urs von. 1975. *Engagement with God.* London: SPCK.

Healey, F. G., ed. 1966. *Prospect for Theology: Essays in Honour of H. H. Farmer.* Welwyn: James Nisbet and Company Limited.

Hebblethwaite, Brian and Sutherland, Stewart, eds. 1982. *The Philosophical Frontiers of Christian Theology.* Cambridge: Cambridge University Press.

Lampe, G. W. H. and MacKinnon, D. M. 1966. *The Resurrection. A Dialogue between Two Cambridge Professors in a Secular Age.* London: A. R. Mowbray & Co Ltd.

MacKinnon, D. M. 1940a. *God the Living and the True.* Westminster: Dacre Press.

MacKinnon, D. M. 1940b. *The Church of God.* Westminster: Dacre Press.

MacKinnon, D. M., ed. 1953. *Christian Faith and Communist Faith. A Series of Studies by Members of the Anglican Communion.* London: Macmillan & Co Ltd.

MacKinnon, D. M. 1957. *A Study in Ethical Theory.* London: Adam & Charles Black.

MacKinnon, D. M., ed. 1963. *God, Sex and War.* Glasgow: Collins. The Fontana Library.

MacKinnon, D. M. 1968. *Borderlands of Theology and Other Essays.* London: Lutterworth Press.

MacKinnon, D. M. 1969. *The Stripping of the Altars.* Glasgow: Collins, The Fontana Library.

MacKinnon, D. M. 1974. *The Problem of Metaphysics.* Cambridge: Cambridge University Press.

MacKinnon, D. M. 1979. *Explorations in Theology 5.* London: SCM Press Ltd.

MacKinnon, D. M. 1987. *Themes in Theology: The Three-Fold Cord. Essays in Philosophy, Politics and Theology.* Edinburgh: T&T Clark Ltd.

Riches, John, ed. 1986. *The Analogy of Beauty. The Theology of Hans Urs von Balthasar.* Edinburgh: T&T Clark Ltd.

Steiner, George. 1995. "Tribute to Donald MacKinnon," *Theology* XCVIII: 2–8.

Surin, Kenneth, ed. 1989. *Christ, Ethics and Tragedy. Essays in Honour of Donald MacKinnon.* Cambridge: Cambridge University Press.

Sykes, S. W. and Clayton, J. P., eds. 1972. *Christ, Faith and History. Cambridge Studies in Christology.* Cambridge: Cambridge University Press.

Vidler A. R., ed. 1963. *Objections to Christian Belief.* London: Constable.

John Milbank (1952–)

Medi Ann Volpe and Lewis Ayres

John Milbank is a British Anglican theologian who is currently Professor in Religion, Politics and Ethics and head of the Centre of Philosophy and Theology at the University of Nottingham. He studied at the Universities of Oxford and Cambridge, at the latter being taught by Rowan Williams, with whom he continues to be in conversation, and whose influence persists in his work. After earning his PhD on the thought of Giambattista Vico from the University of Birmingham, Milbank taught at the Universities of Lancaster and Cambridge before accepting a chair in Philosophical Theology at the University of Virginia. He returned to the UK in 2005.

Milbank's first major work, *Theology and Social Theory*, was published in 1989 while he was at Lancaster. *The Word Made Strange* (1997) follows up the argument of the previous volume with a proposal about the nature of theology that it embodies as much as it argues. *Truth in Aquinas* (with Catherine Pickstock), *Being Reconciled*, and *The Suspended Middle* have outlined further dimensions of his project. The "project" is still clearly in progress: Milbank's current method of engaging in great depth secular philosophers and cultural theorists (most recently Slavoj Žižek), attempting to reveal the necessity of a turn toward the theological (as he understands it), means that we still await an extended overall account of how Milbank articulates the Christian doctrinal vision.

Milbank is one of the founders of the "radical orthodoxy" movement centered in the UK, and its main theorist. With Catherine Pickstock (who was Milbank's student at Cambridge and now holds a position there) and Graham Ward (University of Manchester), Milbank co-edited *Radical Orthodoxy* in 1999, a collection of essays that sketch the themes of the project. Radical orthodoxy became the subject of debate in the United States particularly clearly following its "launch" at the American Academy of Religion/Society of Biblical Literature annual meeting in 1999. The hallmarks of radical orthodoxy are: (1) an understanding of theology's central task as that of retrieving the truth of what is seen as the patristic and medieval Christian synthesis in the context of late and postmodernity and against post-Enlightenment secular reason that exalts the purely natural; (2) the development of a specifically Christian metaphysics that reflects classical Christian cosmology and cosmogony, while engaging its contemporary critics; (3) an emphasis on the sufficiency of Christian theology to address the social and political questions of the day without sacrificing its theological character; and (4) criticism of modern and postmodern philosophy and theology that grants any ontological purchase to evil.

Over the past two decades Milbank has developed a narrative of Christian history that is also found in many other self-identifying radically orthodox thinkers

The Student's Companion to the Theologians, First Edition. Edited by Ian S. Markham.
© 2013 Blackwell Publishing Ltd. Published 2013 by Blackwell Publishing Ltd.

(though it is noticeably less significant for Graham Ward). In this narrative, the influence of the non-Christian Platonic tradition on Christian thought during the patristic and medieval periods was a largely positive one; Christian adaptation of Platonic themes (not simple adoption) enabled Christians to offer a metaphysic of participation in the inexhaustible Good and an understanding of Christian thought as fulfilling all the demands of ancient philosophy. Thomas Aquinas is read in this narrative (at least in Milbank's works subsequent to *Theology and Social Theory*) in the light of that scholarship which sees his thought as still inherently Platonist (the increasing significance of Platonic themes since 1989 may be in part owing to Milbank's conversation with Catherine Pickstock). The emergence of Scotist thought, late medieval nominalism, and early modern commentators on Thomas led to the demise of this vision and the willingness of Christians to envisage a sphere of the purely "natural" set in relation to the divine. For Milbank, then, much of the Enlightenment stems from the loss of the classical Christian vision during the period between Scotus and the Reformation. This story of a decline in Christian thought is mirrored by a story of ecclesiological decline. The gradual emergence of the centralized Roman Church and the subsequent Reformed ecclesial bodies represents a decline from earlier more federative models (it is no accident that in his politics as widely understood Milbank owes much to nineteenth-century Christian federative socialist thinkers).

Milbank's narrative identifies an alternative tradition of moderns who recognize the sterility of Enlightenment secularism and modern Christian thought, seen for example in his holding up of Hamann and Jacobi over against Kant. Milbank sees his own recovery of earlier tradition as also a reinterpretation of it; in the introduction to *Radical Orthodoxy* he holds out the possibility of a recovery that will not again fall victim to that which wreaked havoc on the medieval vision. The character of Milbank's reinterpretation of patristic and medieval Christianity may be seen in two emphases of his work. First, he argues that we must shape our accounts of the nature of reality as gift and as a sharing in the divine life by reading with what he terms "the extremists": reading Aquinas via Eckhart, for example. Milbank has developed this aspect of his thought via a wide-ranging engagement with modern accounts of gift across the fields of social anthropology and philosophy. Second, Milbank seeks to develop material from patristic and medieval Christian thought that he sees as pointing toward Christianity as an "active reception" of that which we receive as gift: our cultural production should be our form of Christian living. In this light Milbank is concerned to promote the revival of a Christian culture that does not set itself apart from the world, but rather reinvents and restores human culture (and in this he perhaps differs most clearly from his friend Stanley Hauerwas).

A central theme in Milbank's appropriation of Augustine is his proposal of an "ontology of peace" as the basis for a Christian meta-narrative. Milbank argues that while ancient and modern secularist philosophies suppose an original struggle between good and evil, the Christian narrative presupposes God's being as the foundation of the world. This ontological peace is not, Milbank suggests, an antitype of modern hegemony in which difference is denied, but—because God is Trinity—is the perfect, eternal difference-in-unity. The ontology of peace also implies a different account of the moral life than that suggested by deontological ethics, or any ethical system that views self-sacrifice as concomitant with virtue. Instead, Milbank proposes, the Christian acts from the principle of plenitude: participation in God means that the very life of the Christian comes from God, and so, in a sense, cannot be taken or given away. The resurrection ensures that even the ultimate sacrifice—death—is not final: the one who lays down her life receives it back from the One who has the power to take it up again.

These general positions find a more personal ethical complement in his essay "The Force of Identity." Here Milbank employs Gregory of Nyssa to argue that Christian existence depends on an understanding of human life as truly meaningful only as it is seen as participation in the life of God. Milbank introduces the term "active reception" as a name for Christian life as lived from and toward God, and defines "active" by appealing to Gregory's account of the passions. On Milbank's reading, the apparent passivity of ecstasy is actually the activity of the pure soul. The soul is created for participation in divine love, and the active soul pursues the union with God that is its destiny. The passions, in this scheme, effectively shut down the soul:

the soul subject to the passions, though it might seem active, really *fails* to act according to its nature. The soul that fails to receive divine joy is the passive soul, and the active soul is defined by receptivity. The essay as a whole argues that Gregory's account of Christian life should shape our own vision of Christian faith and practice. Here Milbank attends to Gregory as a fourth-century theologian and is careful not to assume points of agreement that take Gregory's thought out of that context, yet he does not approach Gregory as an historian (and indeed historians would probably not agree to every point in his discussion of Gregory), but as a constructive theologian whose interest is to articulate Christian doctrine faithfully in the present.

References

Milbank, John. 1990. *Theology and Social Theory: Beyond Secular Reason*. Oxford: Blackwell.

Milbank, John. 1997. *The Word Made Strange: Theology, Language, Culture*. Cambridge, MA: Blackwell Publishers.

Milbank, John. 2003. *Being Reconciled: Ontology and Pardon*. Radical Orthodoxy series. London: Routledge.

Milbank, John. 2005. *The Suspended Middle: Henri De Lubac and the Debate Concerning the Supernatural*. Grand Rapids, MI: Eerdmans.

Milbank, John, and Pickstock, Catherine. 2000. *Truth in Aquinas*. London: Routledge.

Milbank, John, Pickstock, Catherine, and Ward, Graham. 1999. *Radical Orthodoxy: A New Theology*. London: Routledge.

Jürgen Moltmann (1926–)

Ryan A. Neal

Jürgen Moltmann is one of the most widely published and influential theologians of the postwar period. Concerned with issues relevant to both Western and non-Western worlds, Moltmann ventures into doctrines relevant to Protestant, Catholic, and Orthodox theology. This article examines Moltmann through three areas of interest: (1) generative experiences and influences; (2) major themes of his theology; and (3) significance.

I. Life

Born April 8, 1926 in Hamburg, Germany, Moltmann grew up in a secular "enlightened" family, wishing to study science and mathematics, viewing Einstein, Planck, and Heisenberg as "heroes" (Moltmann, 1980, 7; Moltmann, 1997, 3). His focus changed dramatically during his experience as a prisoner of war: after surrendering in February 1945, he spent the next three years as a prisoner of war in three locales: Mass Camp 2226 in Zedelgam, Belgium; Labour Camp 22 in Kilmarnock, Scotland; and finally in Norton Camp near Nottingham, England (Moltmann, 1997, 3; Moltmann, 1980, 7). These proved to be formative years. As a soldier his reading material consisted of the works of Nietzsche as well as Goethe's poems and *Faust*. As a POW, an American military chaplain gave him a copy of the New Testament and the Psalms. His entrée into studying theology and scripture began in Norton Camp, where the YMCA supplied a theological library and brought in speakers. He heard lectures on ethics, theology, and history; he was taught Hebrew and New Testament; he read Dietrich Bonhoeffer (*The Cost of Discipleship*), Anders Nygren (*Eros and Agape*), and Reinhold Niebuhr (*The Nature and Destiny of Man*). The Psalms of lament (especially Ps. 39) displaced Goethe as he discovered God, or perhaps more accurately, "[God] found me" (1997, 5).

Upon returning to West Germany (he was repatriated in April 1948) he pursued not mathematics and science, but rather theology at the University of Göttingen, where he was heavily influenced by three professors: Hans Joachim Iwand, Ernst Wolf, and Otto Weber (Moltmann, 2000, 87–91; Meeks, 1974, 19ff.). In 1952 he completed his exams, married Elisabeth Moltmann-Wendell (a feminist theologian in her own right), and moved to Berlin, where their attempts to move to East Germany were unsuccessful. The following year, after a brief stint as a chaplain (with the help of Otto Weber) he became pastor of the Evangelical Church of Bremen-Wasserhorst for the following five years. In 1957 he completed his *Habilitationschrift* at Göttingen under Weber, who convinced him to go to the Kirchliche Hochschule in Wuppertal in 1958, founded by the Confessing Church (where most notably Wolfhart Pannenberg

The Student's Companion to the Theologians, First Edition. Edited by Ian S. Markham.
© 2013 Blackwell Publishing Ltd. Published 2013 by Blackwell Publishing Ltd.

also taught). In 1963, he moved to Bonn University, and in 1967, again at Weber's urging, he moved to Tübingen University, where he was professor of systematic theology, until retiring as emeritus professor of theology in 1994.

II.   Context

Before proceeding to the key elements of Moltmann's project, the role of context needs to be emphasized. Context is crucial in determining his approach, presuppositions, questions, and conclusions. Here are three examples.

First, one needs to appreciate fully his context as a prisoner of war returning to the motherland after the Holocaust. His first moment of theological insight came in July 1943 in the form of two questions: "My God, where are you?" and "Why am I not dead too?," prompted by the Royal Air Force "fire storm" that devastated his hometown, killing 40,000 people, including his friend who died standing next to him (Moltmann, 1997, 2). His years-long experience of war, tragedy, and suffering, coupled with the subsequent collective guilt of Germany, are powerful generative influences on his understanding of the necessity of theology to speak about both hope and suffering (Moltmann, 2000, 4).

Second, in the 1950s Moltmann became convinced that Karl Barth had unfortunately "transposed eschatology into eternity" by positing redemption as a category of the future beyond history and outside time (1996, 13ff., 44–6). This was the initial impetus to go beyond the conclusions of the preceding generation and to investigate eschatology at the beginning of theology rather than at the end. His work constantly interacts with and advances beyond Barth. Other figures prove to be interesting dialogue partners (especially Rudolf Bultmann, Wolfhart Pannenberg, Karl Rahner, and Hans Urs von Balthasar), while still others provoke original insight (namely Ernst Bloch, Joachim of Fiore, and Isaac Luria), but from the outset he challenges some key Barthian claims: the nature, role, and importance of revelation, eschatology, soteriology, and the doctrine of God. If one does not understand this context, one will be ill equipped to understand fully Moltmann's project.

Third, although Moltmann is a white, male, German Protestant he is bound by neither creed nor confession. This gives him the theological flexibility and freedom to challenge typical answers and constructions. An awareness of his Reformed background might lead some to take for granted his presuppositions, doctrinal stances, or conclusions. When reading Moltmann, uninformed presuppositions will not do. Indeed, one can expect a surprise or two along the way as he tantalizingly lobs attacks on some unexpected thinkers and theological claims. Over time, one sees that a cycle of questions and answers may be the closest discernible modus operandi in his project. His writing (especially through the mid-1980s) has a restless quality. He seems intent on questioning widely held beliefs at virtually every turn, prepared to disabuse his readers of incorrect assumptions and beliefs, convinced that those that have come before him have invariably misunderstood the issues, asked the wrong questions, arrived at the wrong conclusions, or have combined these errors.

III.   Moltmann's Theology

For Moltmann, theology is "an adventure of ideas. It is an open, inviting path" (Moltmann, 2000, xv). This leads him to some unexpected places for sources and streams of thought. Convinced that theology has no clear boundaries, his interests lack typical confinement and restraint to only a few theological loci. Moltmann has been involved in many dialogues or reconciliation efforts: the Paulusgesellschaft, a society which brought together Christians and Marxists; Jewish–Christian dialogues; and ecumenical dialogues in the Faith and Order Commission of the World Council of Churches. Additionally, although it occupies relatively little explicit attention, his motivation for writing *The Trinity and the Kingdom* is a devotion to resolving the *filioque* dispute, believing that a newly formed doctrine of the Trinity goes "hand in hand" with "overcoming the ecclesiastical dispute" (Moltmann, 1981, 179). And at various times, his theology is in direct conversation with ecology, history and time, politics, and ethics. Related to this is his penchant for drawing on atypical sources for theological insight. For doctrinal sources he is unhindered by labels, citing heterodox, Orthodox, Catholic, Protestant, Jewish, and even atheist sources as they suit his needs (see the usage of Bloch and Luria, below).

Debate has ensued about the central doctrine in Moltmann's theology. A variety of candidates appear for this title. History, promise, Trinity, christology, messianic theology, theodicy, and praxis have each been heralded (see Wakefield, 2002, 295–316). While each of these is important, none is comprehensive; ultimately each fails in being too limiting, incapable of containing the diversity of themes across his entire career. The determining factor for Moltmann's theological judgments, regardless of time or topic, is hope. Only hope proves capacious enough to contain the exhaustive array of concerns across such an expansive output, now stretched beyond four decades (Neal, forthcoming).

IV. Writings

Moltmann's writings exhibit his wide-ranging interests. His programmatic works are best grouped into two series: the early trilogy and the "systematic contributions." The trilogy includes: *Theology of Hope* (1967), *The Crucified God* (1974), and *The Church in the Power of the Spirit* (1977). In each of these works he looks at theology from a particular angle: first, he approaches theology from the resurrection; second, from the angle of the cross; and the final book in the trilogy comes from an ecclesial vantage point, with a strong pneumatological emphasis. The second series comprises the six "systematic contributions to theology": *The Trinity and the Kingdom* (1981), *God in Creation* (1985), *The Way of Jesus Christ* (1990), *The Spirit of Life* (1992), *The Coming of God* (1996), and *Experiences in Theology* (2000). In the contributions, each text is devoted to one doctrine, made plain by the title, with one notable feature: his methodology appears at the end, rather than the beginning.

While these nine works are the core of his program, they are far less than half of his overall oeuvre. Beyond solitary journal articles, he has a long list of works that are collections of essays and papers, typically centered on one theme or doctrine. The most important of these include: *Religion, Revolution, and the Future* (1969), *The Experiment Hope* (1975), *Umkehr zur Zukunft*

(1977), *The Future of Creation* (1979), *Creating a Just Future* (1989), *History and the Triune God* (1991), *God for a Secular Society* (1999), and *In the End– the Beginning* (2004). (His autobiography, *A Broad Place*, is scheduled for release October 2007.)

V. Major Themes

There are numerous ways one could structure the key themes in Moltmann's project. He has steadfastly refused to approach theology as if organizing a table of contents, with a pre-set menu of how doctrines fit together and form a unified whole. Theology is much more fluid and interrelated than an outline or system can exhibit or allow. And yet still, there is a certain ordered progression to Moltmann's work, especially as his theology has matured. It is much simpler to understand a thinker when his or her views can be located in a text devoted to a specific topic. There are limitations to this procedure when approaching Moltmann's work, due principally to the fact that in his hands theological lines are present, but often blurred, akin to a watercolor painting. Indeed, topical isolationism is not viewed positively by Moltmann, so for the sake of flow and clarity, this section has been arranged along lines that exhibit the intertwining nature of theological topics: (1) resurrection and future; (2) crucifixion and Trinity; (3) the spirit of creation; (4) eschatology and divine indwelling; and (5) political theology and ethics. This arrangement allows readers to find salient information quickly, and also serves as a reminder of the theological interdependence and interconnectedness imprinted in Moltmann's project.

Resurrection and future

In his first programmatic work, *Theology of Hope* (1967), Moltmann makes it clear that the content of eschatology is not limited merely to "the last things." Eschatology is not theology's appendix, but rather its centerpiece. Eschatology is "the keynote, the daybreak colours of a new expected day which bathe everything in their light" (Moltmann, 1980, 11). Currently, this is an unexceptional premise; but theology has spanned quite a distance since the 1960s, thanks in part to Moltmann's efforts. As noted before, his desire to move beyond Barth was crucial, but to understand *Theology of Hope* fully, it is also important to keep in mind the influence of the Jewish atheist heterodox philosopher Ernst Bloch (see Adams, 2000). For better or worse, Bloch's three-volume magnum opus *The Principle of Hope* is an important antecedent to *Theology of Hope* (Moltmann, 1977b, 10), and influences Moltmann's understanding of the nature of hope and the future.

The importance of eschatology for Moltmann is located in the centrality of Jesus' resurrection and the future. The second paragraph of *Theology of Hope* opens up the issue at hand: "There is therefore only one problem in Christian theology … the problem of the future" (Moltmann, 1967, 16). Stated briefly, on Moltmann's reading, Greek metaphysics has radically and negatively influenced theological claims for far too long, most notably regarding the doctrine of God, especially related to God's nature as immutable, which rests on a faulty understanding of eternity related to divinity. In order to move beyond this problem, Moltmann concentrates on the importance of the resurrection.

In *Theology of Hope*, Moltmann has a positive view of the future compared with a negative view of the present. This view is the essence of the cross-resurrection dialectic at the beginning of his project, especially the first two works, *Theology of Hope* and *The Crucified God*. It is important to realize that the dialectic grounds his entire project (Neal, forthcoming), and while the dialectic expands over the years, focusing more on the dialectical identity of Jesus Christ, its importance here is that the cross equals death and the present, while the resurrection equals life and the future. In the act of the resurrection, then, God guarantees divine promises, opens up the future, while simultaneously contradicting present reality. Following Gerhard von Rad, Moltmann shows the Old Testament background to this understanding (1967, 142ff.), but to understand best how his view of the resurrection supplies his solution to the problem of the future, one must appreciate its context. Primarily, he rejects: (1) Pannenberg's view of the resurrection as historically verifiable (who follows Ernst Troeltsch's understanding of historical investigation as analogy) (1967, 112–20), and (2) Bultmann's perspective that the resurrection's importance can be equated with subjectivity (1967, 172–90).

For Moltmann, the resurrection is not only historically important, but rather eschatologically significant and necessitates not historical investigation for verification (which operates under the assumption that the resurrection is like any other event), but rather the eschaton. With greater force, he denounces equating the importance of the resurrection with an "existential moment" (à la Bultmann), reducing the relevance of theology to the subjective response of faith. This perspective fails because it divides theology from its proper historical grounding. In Jesus' resurrection, God has acted in a new way, to bring a new future into existence: "Easter is the historical origin and the continuing basis of the Christian faith, the Christian church, and the Christian hope" (Moltmann, 1975, 56).

These distinctions for understanding the resurrection led to an important feature of Moltmann's work. Beginning in 1966 (following Emil Brunner) Moltmann insists throughout his writings on distinguishing between two understandings of the future, a distinction which appropriately impinges on the essence of his project, but especially all that he says regarding resurrection, hope, and promise. The first term for future is *futurum*, which describes events that emerge from the past and continue through the present to the future. Essentially *futurum* is extrapolation, the future for which people can plan based on present experience and contingency. For Moltmann, this understanding of the future is unable to carry the weight of Christianity's hope for the future, because *futurum* can never be totally new. So, he distinguishes between what will be (extrapolation) from that which is coming (anticipation) by employing a set of terms that he views as functionally equivalent (*Zukunft*, *Adventus*, and *parousia*) to convey the future as new, as coming, and most importantly as unhindered by present possibilities. Rather than being determined by the past and limited by present possibilities, *Zukunft* has the power to establish the ontological priority of the future over against *futurum* (Moltmann, 1979b, 29).

Here is a prime example of context serving as impetus for theological discovery. Undoubtedly his postwar return to Germany influences the value he accords anticipation over against extrapolation. This is not merely semantics; it is theologically central, providing Moltmann an intelligible rationale to pronounce the true nature of the eschatological future.

Christian hope, in the face of Auschwitz, must rely on the future as anticipation as the category that can provide a new horizon. If the only future available is rooted in present possibilities, then death, fear, and resignation reign. Because of God's new act in the resurrection of Jesus, however, Christians are convinced that death does not reign, ultimately. Contextually, this framework has extraordinary power, authority, and resonance to rehabilitate an emphasis on the future in the postwar period. Indeed, in Europe and beyond, *Theology of Hope* placed Moltmann as the leader of the "school of hope." While the resurrection plays a crucial role in all his works, the other side of the dialectic must be expounded.

Crucifixion and Trinity

While the distinctive elements of Moltmann's views on the cross and Trinity warrant separate lengthy entries, here they are linked for clarity and relevance. It is important to understand that his views of the cross and the Trinity are intertwined and an alteration to one has ramifications on the other. Arguably, not since Luther has a theologian so forcibly and radically placed the cross at the center of the doctrine of God. Moltmann's theology of the cross will be summarized first and then special attention can be devoted to how this informs his doctrine of the Trinity.

In *The Crucified God* (1974), Moltmann turns to the cross as the criterion of Christianity: "the cross is the test of everything which deserves to be called Christian" (Moltmann, 1974, 230). For Moltmann, the cross, seemingly without contradiction, is also the criticism of Christianity, as he relentlessly shows how it is iconoclastic, dismantling inappropriate images of the divine. He insists that the cross necessitates a "revolution" in the concept of God, by devoting his attention to answering one question: "how can the death of Jesus be a *statement about God*?" (1974, 201; italics in original). Many threads come together in his second work, including his adoption of, and reaction to, critical theory and also his appreciation for Bonhoeffer, but primarily he is following Luther's concentration on the hiddenness of God (*Deus absconditus*) and relying heavily on Hegel's insistence that God is in need of the world (to be sure, Moltmann's view of Hegel is ambivalent, but he is greatly indebted to him). These threads are woven together as Moltmann sets out a bold picture:

> In Christ's God-forsakenness, God goes out of himself, is there, present, dies with a cry for God, by whom he feels forsaken. Where is God in what happens on Golgotha? He is *in* the dying Christ. To the question "why" there are many answers, and none of them adequate. More important is the question "where." And for that Christ himself is the answer. (1994, 38)

Moltmann rejects two intertwining and commonly held views that make his theology of the cross unique: divine impassibility and two-natures christology.

In Moltmann's view the cross mandates divine passibility. Grounded in analogy, impassibility is erroneous, funded by Greek metaphysics, and it removes God from active involvement in history. On Moltmann's reading, the apathy axiom can only be understood as a foreign imposition onto the doctrine of God, forcing one to rely on the philosophical restraints of apophatic theology instead of the revelatory narrative history of Jesus. (Note: as with Barth, the primary location of divine revelation is Jesus Christ as recorded in the biblical witness, but not the Bible itself.) In place of the traditional view he inserts his own axiomatic claim: a being who loves is open to suffering; a being who cannot suffer, cannot love. Overthrowing impassibility leads him to take another step away from tradition: rejecting two-natures christology. Moltmann fears that two-natures christology specifically requires a static separation of suffering from divinity, since Jesus' sufferings are thereby constrained to the human nature. This understanding is insufficient, Moltmann is convinced, because it prejudicially mutes the passion narratives of the true nature of Jesus' suffering, threatening christology with docetic tendencies (1974, 227).

While there is room for debate on whether Moltmann has given the tradition fair treatment or whether his axiom must reject two-natures christology, he operates under a key assumption: the particular informs his understanding of the universal. Accordingly, for Moltmann the historical activity of God in the life of Jesus governs one's view of the Trinity. This method necessitates prioritizing the economic over the immanent Trinity. Thus, a proper theology of cross, removed of the philosophical presupposition of impassibility, avoids merely allowing divine passibility; it elevates it to a constitutive element of God's experience. Passibility does not express weakness, but rather love, which is the true, essential nature of God. (Again, note the relevance of his context, living in Germany, post-Holocaust.) To press his point, Moltmann focuses on the Son's abandonment by his Father. Claiming that the Markan record of Jesus' cry points not to a recitation of Ps. 22 (and thus triumphant), but rather is a genuine cry of abandonment, Moltmann unyieldingly stresses divine abandonment, equating the incarnation of Jesus, especially the crucifixion, with the Trinitarian being of God. Indeed, he consistently maintains that the cross is rightly viewed as the theological shorthand for the doctrine of the Trinity (Moltmann, 1974, 246; Moltmann, 1981, 265).

Moltmann has found traditional Trinitarian thinking severely lacking because it has never provided an appropriate explanation for God as Trinity. The way past insufficient Trinitarianism is by altering linguistic and conceptual frameworks: over against depicting God using one absolute subject (or one supreme substance) and then moving to three persons, Moltmann insists on speaking of three persons in relationship. Related to this is his radical conclusion that monotheism is an inappropriate label to affix to the Christian doctrine of God, but rather the result of misplaced reductionism (Moltmann, 1981, 172ff.; 1986, 293–4; 2002, 112–22). A social understanding of the Trinity, not monotheism, is the proper interpretation for the doctrine of God, since Jesus' crucifixion is incoherent without a Trinitarian frame:

> The one divine life cannot be completed only by one subject or only by one person. Only the doctrine of the tri-unity of God is in the position to perceive the immense contradiction of the cross and to integrate it into the infinite life of God. Therefore the doctrine of the Trinity constitutes the sublation [*Aufhebung*] of that contradiction—"God is dead" and "God cannot die." (1979a, 175)

As is his custom, Moltmann diagnoses a problem in theology and offers a solution: "Only when we are capable of thinking in Persons, relations, and changes in the relations *together* does the idea of the Trinity

lose its usual static, rigid quality" (1981, 174). "Strict monotheism obliges us to think of God without Christ, and consequently to think of Christ without God as well" (1981, 131). Moltmann promotes perichoresis as the correct framework, informed by the biblical history of salvation, which tells the story of the Father, the Son, and the Spirit. God is not distant, beyond time, but rather involved and active (Moltmann, 1974, 249; 1981, 148–50).

To undermine assertions related to God's inability to interact with history, Moltmann looks to the biblical narrative (especially the cross) and Jewish authors to ground his argument (especially Abraham Heschel, Gershom Scholem, and Franz Rosenzweig; see Moltmann, 1981, 25–30). Because he prizes love over impassibility for God's nature, his model of perichoresis is central to both divine ontology and action. Additionally, he rejects the traditional single *taxis* of Father–Son–Spirit, since in his view perichoresis necessitates speech of God related to three persons as three subjects, each distinct but involved in the other (Moltmann, 1981, 174). This bold rethinking of divine attributes and relations leads him to rethink a variety of relationships. In the section following, the effects will be apparent on the necessity of creation.

The spirit of creation

Moltmann, when invited to present the prestigious Gifford Lectures, devoted his attention to creation (given 1984–5, University of Edinburgh; published as *God in Creation*, 1985). This emphasis on creation is a switch from his early work, where human history was the primary focus of reality and the primary referent for divine action (Moltmann, 1985, 31, 137–8). Moltmann's concern for creation is situated in his then-emerging awareness of the ecological crisis. Christianity, when rightly understood, does not advocate anthropomorphic escapism, but rather envisions the redemption of creation, which is one community of nature and humanity. Moltmann believes the scriptural assertion that the life-giving Spirit will be poured out "on all flesh" (Joel 2:28) encompasses not only human life but also all living things (1990, 258; 1996, xiii). His theology of creation includes his thoughts not merely on creation "in the beginning," but also on the present and future. He develops a doctrine of creation through a wide-ranging discussion: the Spirit's immanence, the *Shekinah*, the eschatological Sabbath, ecology, "creation as an open system," creation's consummation, the necessity of creation, and God's experience of creation as kenosis. While Moltmann puts a distinctive stamp on each of these, the last two issues will be commented upon.

In developing his understanding of creation, Moltmann overturned the traditional understanding of God's relationship to creating the world. While the tradition regards the divine act of creation as free, Moltmann thinks this is faulty and argues that God creates out of necessity because "it is impossible to conceive of a God who is not a creative God. A non-creative God would be incomplete compared with the God who is eternally creative" (1981, 106). This, he insists, does not mean that God is under duress or outer compulsion: "when we say that God created the world 'out of freedom', we must immediately add 'out of love' " (Moltmann, 1985, 75). Love, which was crucial for Moltmann's extensive reworking of the Trinity, is again used to rework the relationship between God and creation. This issue reappears below, in relation to the eschaton.

Whereas earlier Moltmann centrally located God's capacity for suffering in the abandonment of the Son, when referencing creation he begins to draw on the Old Testament understanding of *Shekinah*, to argue that God's suffering takes on many forms (1981, 28ff.). Moltmann asserts that divine self-humiliation occurs first in creation; the very act of creation is kenotic: "a self-limitation, a self-humiliation and a self-surrender of the Spirit" (1985, 102). Though it has strong pneumatological overtones, his argument relies heavily on Isaac Luria's mystical concept of *zimsum*, which, at its most elementary, depicts creation as first a withdrawal of God's space, which Moltmann employs as the first episode of divine kenosis. Though many disagree with this move, it is important to note for the present discussion that he subscribes to this Lurian vision because it allows him (1) to show that God is kenotic from the beginning of creation and (2) to situate creation's need of redemption. The importance of creation's redemption will become clear in the following section. Due to the Spirit's immanence, creation is God's home now, and in the eschaton the Trinity will fully dwell in the new creation.

Eschatology and divine indwelling

Throughout his career Moltmann has been exercised by the role of eschatology in Christian theology. Over 30 years after his first programmatic work, Moltmann issued his mature eschatology, *The Coming of God* (1996), for which he won the 2000 Louisville Grawemeyer Award in Religion (*Theology of Hope* is eschatological, but not eschatology proper). Two features of his eschatology merge together: universal salvation and divine indwelling. (For a helpful collection of essays on the key issues in Moltmann's eschatology, see Bauckham, 1999).

At a mere six words, Paul's prognostication "God will be all in all" (1 Cor. 15:28) is provocative. Its brevity belies its importance and is arguably the major scriptural source of Moltmann's eschatology. This verse makes two decisive claims on his eschatological vision: God is the subject and all will participate. Regarding the fate of humanity, the question which leads Moltmann to universalism is not primarily related to christology, soteriology, or anthropology, but rather is theocentric: "what does God lose in losing anyone?" (1996, 324). He rejects double predestination, whose only asset, in Moltmann's view, is its artistic symmetry (1996, 247). Regarding soteriology, "yes" and "no" are not symmetrical, but rather asymmetrical:

> In the divine Judgment all sinners, the wicked and the violent, the murderers and the children of Satan, the Devil and the fallen angels will be liberated and saved from their deadly perdition through transformation into their true, created being, because God remains true to himself, and does not give up what he has once created and affirmed, or allow it to be lost. (Moltmann, 1996, 255)

His doctrine of universalism has been unfolding for decades, and in *The Coming of God* he develops a more sustained and substantial recommendation for the salvation of all. Only two surprises appear in Moltmann's advancement of universalism: (1) (contra Barth) he pronounces it as dogmatic assertion, rather than as an eschatological hope; and (2) he includes Satan. The steps he takes to arrive at universalism are numerous, but the central points are the nature of eschatology coupled with God's nature as sociality and love (Moltmann, 1990, 337). God needs creation in the beginning and so God works to save creation at the consummation, so that God may indwell in the new creation. This understanding removes vestiges of an apocalyptic expectation of the last judgment where the judge simply enacts retaliation (Moltmann, 1999b). Eschatology is not a mere accounting of one's life, disclosing the accumulation of past events; rather it is open, unlimited by the past, and allows God to work anew. By fusing his understanding of the future to 1 Cor. 15″28 ("God will be all in all"), he concludes that when creation is "consummated through the indwelling of God, then the unlimited possibilities open to God will indwell the new creation and glorified [humanity] will be free to participate in the unlimited freedom of God" (1976, 130). A driving force in this understanding is panentheism, developed from the social Trinity and God's need for relationship: "all created beings are drawn into the mutual relationships of the divine life, and into the wide space of the God who is sociality" (1996, 336).

Because he has consistently tried to show how philosophical underpinnings have negatively influenced much of Christian theology, it is not surprising that Moltmann posits the coming God in contradistinction from the Greek pattern: "Zeus was, Zeus is, and Zeus will be: Zeus is eternal" (1996, 23; see also 1977b, 156; 1979, 25–7). Moltmann, here at least, looks to the biblical text to govern his ideas regarding time and divinity. Thus: "Grace to you and peace from him who is and who was and who is to come" (Rev. 1:4), is the proper description of the coming God. The last phrase provides the necessary correction; the future tense "who will be" is not asserted but instead the "ontological concept of eternity is broken through by the expression 'who is to come'" (Moltmann, 1979b, 26). Thus, his eschatology shows the ways in which his doctrine of God and creation cohere, both fueled by his insistence on the future as anticipation. The eschaton will bring about a new relationship between God and creation: the divine will fully indwell the new creation, with restored humanity participating in the divine life of the social Trinity.

Political theology and ethics

With Moltmann's early (and often) insistence that history, not eternity, is the central category for reality he overthrows dialectical theology's overriding stress on both eternity and eternal presence (see especially 1967, 37–94). This move beyond dialectical theology's stress on eternity is critical for understanding Moltmann's emphatic insistence on history's openness, fundamentally grounded in God's promises. These claims hang together: a promised temporal future (over against timeless eternity) leads to possibilities of transforming the present world (Moltmann, 1967, 18, 102ff., 328–31; 2000, 51). Such a view enables humanity to set out to change present circumstances in light of the promised future.

Moltmann's theology is emphatically political, which is to say that it insists on the validity of theological claims for contemporary issues in society. His view of the church's relationship with society clearly draws upon Bonhoeffer: Christianity is not a religion of "equilibrium and harmony but … of conflict and hope" (Moltmann, 1989, 96). The premise that he operates under is a revision of Karl Marx's eleventh thesis: "The theologian is not concerned merely to supply a different *interpretation* of the world, of history and of human nature, but to *transform* them in expectation of a divine transformation" (Moltmann, 1967, 84). By this he means, at the very least, that theology (when properly done) explains and engages reality, precisely because the present is inadequate, and needs correcting, improving, and transforming. This stems, of course, from his insistence on stressing the future as new. And while he grounds his views in the promised future, the prototype he uses to greatest effect is the crucifixion: "The crucified God is in fact a stateless and classless God. But that does not mean that he is an unpolitical [*sic*] God. He is the God of the poor, the oppressed and the humiliated" (1974, 329). This exhibits the application of the dialectic identity of Jesus as the crucified and resurrected one.

The best and most obvious example of Moltmann's call for the church to be a social critic stems from his own reflections on Germany's reaction to Hitler. The church can never be neutral, because the result is always the same: a collating of state and church interests. Christianity will find itself in fundamental "conflicts between the powers of the past and the forces of the future, between oppression and liberation" (Moltmann, 1977a, 83).

Moltmann's stress on active, political engagement is a thread running throughout his career. (Early on he argued for revolution, but this term was dropped.) This feature has given his work a vital contemporary texture. Christianity, when interpreted correctly, avoids a dualism seeking retreat. On his reading, salvation is not oriented to a reality "above," it has to do with this world. At its most extreme, the church has swerved too far and made salvation a flight from the present into the future or away from society. This, Moltmann insists, is insufficient. Whether the issue is nuclear weapons, war, the environment, minority rights, racism, or capitalism, the church needs to avoid simply interpreting reality, but must set out to change it.

Unfortunately, Moltmann's call for political engagement tends to get reduced to self-evidential references imploring Christians to change the status quo and to oppose oppression. Of course his comments are often correct, but too often they are extremely vague, and threaten to be inapplicable. There are seeds of great potential in developing the ethical application of his political theology, but many have been left undone. Indeed, the lacunae in Moltmann's oeuvre is a fully developed "ethics of hope" which he advertised early on but never completed (1977b, 13; 1979a, 189).

VI. Significance

Measured by his prodigious output, the commentators engaging his thought, and the numerous doctoral works devoted to his theology, Moltmann is one of the leading figures in contemporary theology in the post-Barthian period. Even among scholars who have engaged Moltmann's work, he remains a divisive figure (for a very helpful bibliography, see Wakefield, 2002). At one extreme are readers who dismiss his project fully, due perhaps to methodology, (in)consistency, or perceived lack of philosophical refinement. At the other extreme are readers who agree with virtually everything he writes, finding nothing objectionable, and thus who are unable to offer a helpful appraisal. Thus, scholarship (whether too dismissive or too generous) often fails to engage his work at the level of its fundamental premises, causing his defenders and accusers alike to miss or misunderstand his project's inner workings. This level of polarity is also due, it seems, to his methodology, which exhibits his penchant for variety and spontaneity.

VII. Methodological Variety

Moltmann equates the theologian to "Jacob, who wrestled all night with the angel of God and emerged from his encounter with a lame hip but also with a blessing" (1987, viii). One of his methodological presuppositions is the nature of theological development and outline. Indeed, if there is a method to his approach it is a refusal to be led by a pre-set method (recall that his methodology appeared as the final, not the first, volume in the "contributions"); he never intended a comprehensive theology, a multi-volume "systematics" wherein he authoritatively and conclusively said all that was necessary (Moltmann, 1981, xiii; 2000, xiv–xix). The explicit underlying basis of his refusal to promote a one-sided authoritative approach is his conviction that theology is likened to a conversation. (And yet, there is a good measure of conviction in his works, as he boldly pronounces judgment on key issues.) While this approach certainly has its detractors, Moltmann's influence will be in part gauged by the long-term acceptance or rejection of such a method.

Regarding the contextual features mentioned at the beginning, some will undoubtedly view them as unnecessary distractions from Moltmann's wider project. This would be a serious error. His context is interwoven into his program and losing sight of this fact promotes misreadings of his project. The manner of his response to these issues is revealing. Because Moltmann's work is strongly self-aware, a good bit of his writing is arguably more than "contextual," it is reactionary. This seems to be both positive and negative. It gives his writing energy, élan, and texture, but it might be off-putting to some, and furthermore, it may have led him to swerve too far in correcting theological claims (recall his rejection of the label monotheism for Christianity and his dogmatic universalism).

Near the beginning of this article the importance of theology as a questioning enterprise was emphasized. Questions (some rhetorical) are asked of his interlocutors and his readers alike. Some will welcome this feature; others will not. Such restless questioning ends up being, it seems, both a credit and deficit to his program. One's reaction to this feature may serve as a good indicator for how one will view Moltmann's writing as a whole: those applauding his unabashed criticisms of either specific doctrines or those espousing such doctrines will appreciate much of his work (if not his conclusions), while those disapproving (viewing it as audacity) may find his project lacking and his reinterpretations faulty.

It is notable that in the topics discussed above, Moltmann sets out to overthrow a set of presuppositions and truth claims regarding a doctrine and replace it with a properly conceived set. He intentionally reclaims the biblical narrative of the Israelites, the Apostles, and Jesus as instructional and determinative over against philosophy (whether Hellenism or German Idealism). Whether one finds persuasive the arguments and conclusions he makes, this feature heightens Moltmann's significance. Recovery of the testimony of God's faithfulness and activity in human history is sorely needed. Hopefully, his importance extends in depth and breadth as others join him in the task of Christian theology. His is one voice in a conversation. Regardless of whether one agrees with his project, his wide-ranging and bold approach to issues in search of truth, correct teaching, and application is commendable.

References

Primary

Moltmann, Jürgen. 1967. *Theology of Hope: On the Ground and the Implications of a Christian Eschatology*, trans. James. W. Leitch. London: SCM.

Moltmann, Jürgen. 1969. *Religion, Revolution, and the Future*, trans. M. Douglas Meeks. New York, NY: Scribner's.

Moltmann, Jürgen. 1974. *The Crucified God: The Cross of Christ as the Foundation and Criticism of Christian Theology*, trans. R. A. Wilson and John Bowden. London: SCM.

Moltmann, Jürgen. 1975. *The Experiment Hope*, ed. and trans. M. Douglas Meeks. London: SCM.

Moltmann, Jürgen. 1976. "Creation and Redemption," trans. R. W. A. McKinney. In *Creation, Christ and Culture: Studies in Honour of T. F. Torrance*, ed. Richard W. A. McKinney. Edinburgh: T&T Clark, pp. 119–34.

Moltmann, Jürgen. 1977a. *The Church in the Power of the Spirit: A Contribution to Messianic Ecclesiology*, trans. Margaret Kohl. London: SCM.

Moltmann, Jürgen. 1977b. *Umkehr zur Zukunft*. Gütersloher Taschenbücher Siebenstern, 154. München: Kaiser, 1970; Gütersloh: Gerd Mann, 2nd ed.

Moltmann, Jürgen. 1979a. "Antwort auf die Kritik an 'Der gekreuzigte Gott'." In *Diskussion über Jürgen Moltmanns Buch "Der gekreuzigte Gott"*, ed. Michael Welker. München: Kaiser, pp. 165–90.

Moltmann, Jürgen. 1979b. *The Future of Creation*, trans. Margaret Kohl. London: SCM.

Moltmann, Jürgen. 1980. *Experiences of God*, trans. Margaret Kohl. London: SCM.

Moltmann, Jürgen. 1981. *The Trinity and the Kingdom: The Doctrine of God*, trans. Margaret Kohl. London: SCM.

Moltmann, Jürgen. 1985. *God in Creation: A New Theology of Creation and the Spirit of God*, trans. Margaret Kohl. The Gifford Lectures 1984–85. London: SCM.

Moltmann, Jürgen 1986. "Trinitarier und Antitrinitarier," *Evangelische Theologie* 46: 293–4.

Moltmann, Jürgen. 1987. Foreword. In *Moltmann: Messianic Theology in the Making Moltmann*, ed. Richard Bauckham. Basingstoke: Marshall Pickering, pp. vii–x.

Moltmann, Jürgen 1989. *Creating a Just Future: The Politics of Peace and the Ethics of Creation in a Threatened World*, trans. John Bowden. London: SCM.

Moltmann, Jürgen. 1990. *The Way of Jesus Christ: Christology in Messianic Dimensions*, trans. Margaret Kohl. London: SCM.

Moltmann, Jürgen. 1991. *History and the Triune God: Contributions to Trinitarian Theology*, trans. John Bowden. London: SCM.

Moltmann, Jürgen. 1992. *The Spirit of Life: A Universal Affirmation*, trans. Margaret Kohl. Minneapolis, MN: Fortress.

Moltmann, Jürgen. 1994. *Jesus Christ for Today's World*, trans. Margaret Kohl. London: SCM.

Moltmann, Jürgen. 1996. *The Coming of God: Christian Eschatology*, trans. Margaret Kohl. Minneapolis, MN: Fortress.

Moltmann, Jürgen. 1997. *Source of Life: The Holy Spirit and the Theology of Life*, trans. Margaret Kohl. London: SCM.

Moltmann, Jürgen. 1999a. *God for a Secular Society: The Public Relevance of Theology*, trans. Margaret Kohl. Minneapolis, MN: Fortress.

Moltmann, Jürgen. 1999b. "The Logic of Hell," trans. Margaret Kohl. In *God Will Be All in All: The Eschatology of Jürgen Moltmann*, ed. Richard Bauckham. Edinburgh: T&T Clark, pp. 43–7.

Moltmann, Jürgen. 2000. *Experiences in Theology: Ways and Forms of Christian Theology*, trans. Margaret Kohl. Minneapolis, MN: Fortress.

Moltmann, Jürgen. 2002. "Kein Monotheismus gleicht dem anderen: Destruktion eines Untauglichen Begriffs," *Evangelische Theologie* 62: 112–22.

Moltmann, Jürgen. 2004. *In the End—the Beginning: The Life of Hope*, trans. Margaret Kohl. Minneapolis: Fortress.

Secondary

Adams, Nicholas. 2000. "Eschatology Sacred and Profane: The Effects of Philosophy on Theology in Pannenberg, Rahner and Moltmann," *International Journal of Systematic Theology* 2: 283–306.

Bauckham, Richard. 1987. *Moltmann: Messianic Theology in the Making*. Basingstoke: Marshall Pickering.

Bauckham, Richard, ed. 1999. *God Will Be All in All: The Eschatology of Jürgen Moltmann*. Edinburgh: T&T Clark.

Meeks, M. Douglas. 1974. *Origins of the Theology of Hope*. Philadelphia, PA: Fortress.

Neal, Ryan A. Forthcoming. *Theology as Hope: On the Ground and the Implications of Jürgen Moltmann's Doctrine of Hope*. Princeton Theological Monograph Series. Eugene, OR: Pickwick Press.

Wakefield, James. L. 2002. *Jürgen Moltmann: A Research Bibliography*. ATLA Bibliography Series. Lanham, MD: Scarecrow.

Richard John Neuhaus (1936–2009)

Stephen H. Webb

The career of Richard John Neuhaus has traced two trajectories that have been equally paradigmatic for many other theologians. First, he has journeyed from Protestantism to Roman Catholicism, and second, he has moved from the political left to the religious right. Others have taken these routes, of course, but with his vision of a vibrant and traditional form of American Christianity, Fr Neuhaus has aligned them into one well-trodden road. The journey to Rome, needless to say, is not identical with a departure from the left wing of the Democratic Party, but Fr Neuhaus makes these two moves seem like co-ordinated aspects of one seamless motion. His integration of the political (in its broadest sense) with the theological (in its deepest) has been so exemplary that pundits have called him the father of the "theocons," a purportedly new school of public-minded theology. The result is a remarkable body of work that is both representative of the social transformations of the latter half of the twentieth century and indicative of the theological possibilities of the new millennium.

Although Neuhaus's theological project has been badly interpreted as a case of nostalgia for theocracy (Linker, 2006), his politics are actually pretty moderate. Indeed, he is a liberal in the classical sense of that term. Neuhaus wants more freedom for religious expression, not a reactionary return to a putative Christian America. He wants Christians to be more active in shaping government policies because he believes that

Christianity, democracy, and capitalism are inextricably linked. These are the points he made in *The Naked Public Square* (1984), the book which cemented his shift to the right and guaranteed him a ranking in any list of the most influential American theologians of the past 50 years.

Perhaps surprisingly, given his willingness to acknowledge the role of patriotism in theology and his stature in American conservative circles, Neuhaus was born in Canada, in 1936. His father was a Lutheran minister, and after a period of rebellion at school and working at a gas station in Cisco, Texas, he decided to follow his father's vocation, eventually serving as pastor of St John the Evangelist, an underprivileged parish in Brooklyn. In New York City he became active in the civil rights and anti-Vietnam War movements, marching alongside Martin Luther King, Jr. He remained an activist throughout his career, but increasingly saw the restoration of theological orthodoxy as the most important foundation for political and social reform. He was received into the Roman Catholic Church in 1990 and one year later ordained a priest. Although this dramatic decision has served as a reference point for many other faith journeys, he has always insisted that he became Catholic only because he wanted to be more fully what he was as a Lutheran.

His journey toward the hierarchical continuity and structural stability of Rome was in some ways a culmination of his retreat from the political left.

The Student's Companion to the Theologians, First Edition. Edited by Ian S. Markham.
© 2013 Blackwell Publishing Ltd. Published 2013 by Blackwell Publishing Ltd.

Neuhaus grew disillusioned with the protest movement by 1971, when he published *In Defense of People*, a trenchant critique of the environmental movement. He thought that environmentalism was anti-democratic in its attempt to place political decisions in the hands of experts rather than the people, and anti-humanistic in its prioritizing of ecological systems over the needs of the human community. His criticisms of the way the affluent exercised a politics of choice without regard to the necessities of the poor was an effort to thwart the drift of liberalism away from its populist roots, but it fell on deaf ears. He was also appalled that liberals spoke of the survival of the earth, rather than truth and beauty, as the highest good. Morality, he declared, is humanity's most endangered renewable resource. His habitual readiness to protect the unprotected led him to become involved in the abortion debate, although here too he worked at first to convince liberals that they should side with the unborn. While *Roe v. Wade* (1973) put him on the path to a conservative radicalism, other issues were nearly as important. In 1975, for example, he was aghast that his friends who remained involved in leftist circles refused to sign a petition condemning human rights abuses by the communist government in Hanoi. By the end of that decade he had come to the conclusion that the revolutionary rhetoric of the 1960s had been a grand mistake.

His reaction to the hardening of liberal thought, however, was hardly reactionary. He briefly supported President Carter and continued to be a member of the Democratic Party. What he deplored was the reigning prejudice of secularism that people of faith have nothing from their faithfulness to contribute to public debates. To provide a forum for those contributions, he founded *First Things* in 1990, an ecumenical journal "whose purpose is to advance a religiously informed public philosophy for the ordering of society."

One of his most prophetic books is *Time Toward Home* (1975), written in the aftermath of the Vietnam War (Webb, 2004, 56–7, 60). This book sounded the alarm about the decline of the doctrine of providence in Christian reflections on history and politics. The doubts about America's role in the world hardened after Vietnam into the dogmas of the political and religious left. Left-leaning theologians did not reject the traditional American belief that God had

chosen America for great things in the world. Instead, they stood that belief on its head by arguing that God had chosen America for special punishment due to her arrogance, wealth, and imperial ambitions. This perversion of the traditional providential reading of American history became more common after 9/11, which many leftist theologians interpreted as God's just retribution for America's meddling in the Middle East and Afghanistan. In *Time Toward Home*, Neuhaus argued that identifying America with Babylon is hardly any better than identifying America with Israel. Neuhaus insisted that there is only one Israel, so that those who think America is uniquely chosen by God for a global mission are mistaken, yet America is no Babylon either. America, he declared, has done more good than harm in the world. Thus, any political theology that wants to keep ideology to a minimum must begin with that admission. More generally, and devastatingly, he appropriated the message of the leftist theologians who emphatically declared that redemption comes through our concrete historical situation. If so, Neuhaus rejoined, then our nationality is not irrelevant to the nature of God's salvific plan. One of Neuhaus's most controversial statements follows from this insight: "When I meet God, I expect to meet him as an American," just as when we are redeemed, "part of the American experience [will be] redeemed" (1975, 64, 56).

For Neuhaus, America is indeed a nation under God, but what that means demands careful theological attention. Neuhaus wrote the important declaration entitled "Christianity and Democracy" for the Washington-based Institute on Religion and Democracy in 1981 in order to combat those who insisted on a moral symmetry between the Soviet Union and the United States (reprinted in Neuhaus, 1996). In it he says that "under God" means "first of all, a nation under judgment." America is "the primary bearer of democratic possibility in the world today," which is why America is so crucial to any theology of providence today. "Because America is a large and influential part of God's creation, because America is the home of most of the heirs and of Israel of old, and because this is a land in which his church is vibrantly free to live and proclaim the Gospel to the world, we believe that America has a peculiar place in God's promises and purposes." Neuhaus has continued to deepen and nuance this point of view during the Presidency of George W. Bush. His many articles and essays in support of a closer association of Christian faithfulness at home and political freedom abroad has led President Bush to give him the nickname "Father Richard." Due to his influence in Republican circles, *Time* magazine named him one of the 25 most influential evangelicals in America for 2005.

Perhaps his most significant contribution to public affairs has been his influence on the institutional reconfiguration of the religious right. In the wake of the decline of the Moral Majority, Fr Neuhaus has worked hard through groups like "Evangelicals and Catholics Together" to create a broader religious consensus to replace the political influence of Protestant fundamentalism and the cultural influence of the declining Protestant mainline churches. His articles in *First Things*, which are easily accessible on the internet, continue to provoke, inspire, and inform.

References

Linker, Damon. 2006. *The Theocons: Secular America Under Siege*. New York: Doubleday.

Neuhaus, Richard John. 1971. *In Defense of People: Ecology and the Seduction of Radicalism*. New York: The Macmillan Company.

Neuhaus, Richard John. 1975. *Time Toward Home: The American Experience as Revelation*. New York: Crossroad.

Neuhaus, Richard John. 1984. *The Naked Public Square: Religion and Democracy in America*. Grand Rapids, MI: Eerdmans.

Neuhaus, Richard John. 1996. "Christianity and Democracy," *First Things* (October): 30–6.

Neuhaus, Richard John. 1999. *Appointment in Rome: The Church in America Awakening*. New York: Crossroad.

Neuhaus, Richard John. 2001. *Death on a Friday Afternoon: Meditations on the Last Words of Jesus from the Cross*. New York: Basic Books.

Neuhaus, Richard John. 2002. *The Chosen People in an Almost Chosen America: Jews and Judaism in America*. Grand Rapids, MI: Eerdmans.

Neuhaus, Richard John. 2003. *As I Lay Dying: Meditations Upon Returning*. New York: Basic Books.

Neuhaus, Richard John. 2007. *Catholic Matters: Confusion, Controversy, and the Splendor of Truth*. New York: Basic Books.

Webb, Stephen H. 2004. *American Providence: A Nation with a Mission*. New York: Continuum.

Webb, Stephen H. 2007. "The Dastardly Peril of Conservative Christianity: Review of Damon Linker, *The Theocons*," *Conversations in Religion & Theology* 5 (May): 65–72.

James Packer (1926–)

Ian S. Markham

James I. Packer was born in 1926 in Gloucester, England and currently lives in Canada. He has had a dramatic impact on American evangelical theology.

I. Life

Packer studied at Oxford University, achieving both his BA (1948) and PhD (1955). He became a priest in 1953 the Church of England, having studied at Wycliffe Hall in Oxford. He worked for a variety of institutions: for a short time he was at Oak Hill Theological College in London, then at Tyndale Hall, Bristol, and Latimer House, Oxford. In 1970, he was involved in the merger of Tyndale Hall, Bristol, Clifton College, and Dalton House-St Michael's. The result was Trinity College, Bristol, of which Packer served as the Associate Principal from 1971 to 1979.

It was during this time that Packer developed his international profile. In 1978, he was one of the organizers and subsequent signatory of the *Chicago Statement on Biblical Inerrancy*. So it was not surprising that he was persuaded in 1979 to move to Canada. He became the Sangwoo Youtong Chee Professor of Theology at Regent College, in Vancouver, a position he held until his retirement.

Throughout his life, he was very productive. It is estimated that he has sold over four million copies of his various books. And *Time* magazine identified Packer as one of the top 25 most influential evangelicals in the world. He was involved in the joint Catholic and Evangelical declaration organized by Richard John Neuhaus in 1994. For this ecumenical gesture, some evangelicals were deeply critical. This was not the first time he had provoked controversy for his ecumenism: in 1970, he contributed to a collection of essays with the Anglo-Catholic Eric Mascall. In 2008, Packer announced his departure from the Church of Canada over the issue of human sexuality. He joined the Anglican Network of Canada, which recognizes the authority of the primate from the Southern Cone.

II. Theology

Packer describes himself as a "Calvinist Anglican." His grounding is scripture. For him, this is unequivocal authority for all Christian doctrine. His involvement in the *Chicago Statement on Biblical Inerrancy* was important: inerrancy was located with the original autographs of scripture; it was not dependent on the authority of the church or tradition; and it extended to the entire corpus in all areas (including science, history, and morality).

The Student's Companion to the Theologians, First Edition. Edited by Ian S. Markham.
© 2013 Blackwell Publishing Ltd. Published 2013 by Blackwell Publishing Ltd.

He is best known for *Knowing God* (1973). The five principles at the start of this book are a good summary of Packer's theology. These are:

1. God has spoken to man, and the Bible is His Word, given to us to make us wise unto salvation.
2. God is Lord and King over His world; He rules all things for His own glory, displaying His perfections in all that He does, in order that men and angels may worship and adore Him.
3. God is Saviour, active in sovereign love through the Lord Jesus Christ to rescue believers from the guilt and power of sin, to adopt them as His sons, and to bless them accordingly.
4. God is Triune; there are within the Godhead three persons, the Father, the Son and the Holy Ghost; and the work of salvation is one in which all three act together, the Father purposing redemption, the Son securing it, and the Spirit applying it.
5. Godliness means responding to God's revelation in trust and obedience, faith and worship, prayer and praise, submission and service. Life must be seen and lived in the light of God's Word. This, and nothing else, is true religion. (Packer, 1973, 15–16)

In these five principles, we find classical reformed theology. A sovereign triune God, who saves, reveals, and compels a life-transforming response is at the heart of this theology. *Knowing God* was a book of genius: it is both accessible, yet erudite. For many Christians, this was theology at its most intelligible and applied. It was a theology that made a difference to living.

For Packer, knowing God was a practical work. His *Evangelism and the Sovereignty of God* (1961) was more theological: here he was pushing back on the criticism that the affirmation of God's sovereignty makes "evangelism" unimportant. For Packer, human decision and behavior remained important. Divine sovereignty provides the framework—the message, method, and motivation—but there is still room for the moment of decision.

All the members of the Trinity have been an important part of Packer's theology. In 1984, Packer wrote *Keep in Step with the Spirit*. A similar pattern can be found here as elsewhere: he wants to challenge popular misconceptions. So while it is true that the Holy Spirit provides power for living, performance in service, purity of value, and presentation for decision—all of these need to be seen together and other aspects need

to be added. This is the text where Packer engages most sympathetically with the charismatic movement.

While much of his theology was deliberately popular and accessible, his more overt scholarly contributions were in the areas of the Puritans. His largest book was called *A Quest for Godliness: the Puritan Vision of the Christian Life* (1990). Here Packer articulates his deep sympathy with the Puritans. And in a manner that is characteristic of his work, he organizes his work into six sections—the Puritans in Profile, the Puritans and the Bible, the Puritans and the Gospel, the Puritans and the Holy Spirit, the Puritan Christian Life, and the Puritan Ministry. Packer in this work shows his exceptional competence as a scholar.

III. Influence

Countless contemporary evangelical scholars consider James Packer a key influence on their thought. These evangelicals include the exceptionally prolific Alister McGrath, John R. W. Stott, and Mark Noll. Mark Noll, in particular, has found the theology of so much evangelicalism in the United States frustrating (because of the lack of historical sensitivity) and warmly welcomes the contribution of James Packer. Noll writes:

> Packer has exerted that influence by combining characteristics that have rarely been joined together in America. In a word, he is an *educated, Reformed, Anglican evangelical*, with each of the four ascriptions vital as a counterweight to the other three. As the history of Christianity in America has shown so often, any of these commitments by itself can easily become a threat to clarity of Christian thought and integrity of Christian activity. Together, at least as they have been conjoined in Packer's writing and speaking, they have been water to a parched and weary land. (Noll in Lewis and McGrath, 1996, 199)

For Noll, the popularity of James Packer is slightly puzzling. He is not always saying what his constituency wants, yet he is widely read anyway. Perhaps one way to explain this mystery is that everyone who writes about him remarks on the remarkable way he models the theology of his books. Given that so much of his impact has been through the lecture and the sermon, this might be the reason why he is widely read.

References

Elwell, Walter, ed. 1993. *Handbook of Evangelical Theologians.* Grand Rapids, MI: Baker Books.

Lewis, Donald and McGrath, Alister. 1996. *Doing Theology for the People of God: Studies in Honor of J. I. Packer.* Downers Grove, IL: IVP.

Packer, James. 1958. *"Fundamentalism" and the Word of God.* Grand Rapids, MI: Eerdmans.

Packer, James. 1961. *Evangelism and the Sovereignty of God.* Chicago: Inter-Varsity Press.

Packer, James. 1973. *Knowing God.* London: Hodder and Stoughton.

Packer, James. 1980. *Beyond the Battle for the Bible.* Westchester, IL: Cornerstone.

Packer, James. 1990. *A Quest for Godliness: The Puritan Vision of the Christian Life.* Wheaton, IL: Crossway.

Packer, J. I. 2005. *Keep in Step with the Spirit: Finding Fullness in Our Walk with God.* Grand Rapids, MI: Baker Books.

Wolfhart Pannenberg (1928–)

Nathan J. Hallanger

I. Background

Wolfhart Pannenberg was born in 1928 in the city of Stettin, once part of Germany but now part of Poland. As a boy Pannenberg moved with his family to Scheidenmuhl, and to the city of Aachen two years later. While in Aachen he grew increasingly interested in music, having begun piano lessons at the age of seven, writing his own music and listening to the local symphony orchestra. He moved to Berlin in 1942, though Pannenberg and other school-age children were soon sent out of the city for school because of Allied air attacks. The family home was destroyed by bombs in 1944, and Pannenberg moved in with relatives in Pomerania. While in the library searching for books about music, Pannenberg happened upon Friedrich Nietzsche's *The Birth of Tragedy from the Spirit of Music*, and soon he had read as much Nietzsche as he could find. In 1945 Pannenberg experienced an event that would change his life:

> On the sixth of January, while I was walking back home from school … an extraordinary event occurred in which I found myself absorbed in the light surrounding me. When I became aware again of my finite existence, I did not know what had happened but certainly knew that it was the most important event in my life; I spent many years afterwards to find out what it meant to me. (Pannenberg, 1988, 12)

Before he had time to reflect on this event, Pannenberg joined the German army. Though he was trained and prepared to be sent to the front, he was spared by a case of scabies and later taken prisoner by the British.

Returning home in 1945 after the war, Pannenberg continued his schooling. One of his teachers, who taught German literature, was a Christian who did not fit the picture of Christianity Pannenberg had read in the works of Nietzsche. Still curious about his experience of 1945 and intrigued by the degree to which his teacher enjoyed living as a Christian, in 1947 Pannenberg enrolled at Humboldt University to study philosophy and theology. Though his parents had left the church in the 1930s, Pannenberg soon felt fascinated with Christianity, and, as he put it, "I knew I was to be a theologian for the rest of my life" (1988, 13).

Pannenberg subsequently studied at Göttingen with Friedrich Gogarten and Nicolai Hartmann, and in Basle with Karl Barth and the philosopher Karl Jaspers. Returning to study at Heidelberg, he heard lectures from Gerhard von Rad and became interested in the role that history played in theology. Pannenberg and several other students formed a discussion group to explore the theological implications of history, a group that came to be known as the "Heidelberg Circle" or "Pannenberg Circle." Pannenberg finished his dissertation on the doctrine of predestination in Duns Scotus in 1953, and, after encouragement from Edmund Schlink, two years later completed a

The Student's Companion to the Theologians, First Edition. Edited by Ian S. Markham.
© 2013 Blackwell Publishing Ltd. Published 2013 by Blackwell Publishing Ltd.

Habilitationsschrift on the concept of analogy in medieval philosophy. That same year he was ordained a Lutheran minister in Heidelberg.

Pannenberg's teaching career began at Heidelberg, and continued in 1958 at Wuppertal. He briefly taught at the University of Mainz, and then moved to the University of Munich in 1968 where he taught for 25 years until his retirement.

Pannenberg's first major work, *Revelation as History* (1968), was a collection of essays which Pannenberg edited, introduced, and to which he contributed a chapter. The focus was a new interpretation of God's relationship to historical events, largely influenced by Pannenberg's thinking. Several years later Pannenberg published an extensive study of christology, *Jesus—God and Man*. As in his earlier work on revelation, Pannenberg focused on the question of history and its relationship to the meaning of Jesus Christ. He continued to publish a number of theological essays and shorter works on Christian ethics, religion, and politics, theological anthropology, and a wide range of topics of concern. In the early 1970s he published an extensive study on the status of theology's truth claims in relation to other forms of knowledge, particularly science (*Theology and the Philosophy of Science*, 1976). Pannenberg later explored the need for defending theology's truth claims in terms of anthropology (*Anthropology in Theological Perspective*, 1985). Pannenberg published the first of his three-volume *Systematic Theology* in 1991, with the second volume coming in 1993 and the final volume in 1998.

Throughout his career, Pannenberg has sought to explicate the contents of the Christian faith in a public and rational manner. The privatization and internalization of religious belief has been an unfortunate turn in theology and culture, he believes, because theology's impact is not simply on the individual believer. Rather, the implications for Christian theology and belief profoundly affect the entirety of creation. Christian theology that concerns only the privatized belief of individual believers fails to take account of the comprehensive nature of the Christian truth claims on the world; in fact, truth cannot be truth if does not make a claim on the whole of reality. For Pannenberg God is the all-determining reality, and thus theology must engage the world in all its richness and complexity in order to fully explicate what the impact of Jesus' life, death, and resurrection is on the created order. Pannenberg's numerous publications provide evidence of his own efforts at providing a rational exploration of the scope and meaning of the Christian message. Within that broader effort, a number of Pannenberg's particular contributions to theology have been widely influential, especially his writings on revelation and history, christology, and methodology.

II. Revelation and History

Early in his career, Pannenberg and some of his colleagues initiated discussions on the nature of revelation and history. For the previous generation of neo-orthodox scholars, revelation was a singular event in which the believer experienced a direct experience of God's self-revelation. This experience required the presence of God's grace given by the presence of the Holy Spirit for revelation to be recognized as such. Thus, the failure for some to experience revelation could be explained by the mysterious presence of the Holy Spirit—or lack thereof. Historical knowledge could not be revelation in the strict sense without these "eyes of faith." Pannenberg and his colleagues were dissatisfied with these notions of revelation and history, and met for late-night discussions to develop an alternative picture of the relationship between the two. The resulting essays were published in 1961 as *Offenbarung Als Geschichte* (the English translation *Revelation as History* was published in 1968). Here Pannenberg and his colleagues provided a distinctively new understanding of revelation.

For Pannenberg, the starting point is the distinction between direct revelation and indirect revelation. Using the model of direct communication and indirect communication, Pannenberg shows that direct revelation is unmediated revelation whose content is God himself. On the other hand, indirect revelation does not have God as the content directly. Rather, the individual events seen as God's revelation reveal partially who God is in God's self. Pannenberg makes clear, however, that no single act can be seen as God's complete revelation. In fact the tendency to view single actions as God's complete revelation could lead toward idolatry.

What, then, is the relationship between individual events of indirect revelation and the totality of revelation in history? How can individual acts as a partial revelation of God fit into the totality of history as the manifestation of the complete revelation of God? The totality of history is inaccessible to us, Pannenberg argues, and even if it were accessible, the totality would seem to undercut the importance ascribed to Jesus Christ (1968, 19).

Pannenberg's solution to this conundrum draws on the contributions of his biblical scholar colleagues in the "Pannenberg Circle." Two main points form the basis for Pannenberg's answer. First, Pannenberg argues that the history of Israel recorded in the Old Testament ratifies the view of God's revelation as a series of historical occurrences, each of which partially reveals something about Yahweh. In the New Testament, the Pauline literature confirms that the fate of Jesus also indirectly reveals God. For the second generation of New Testament witnesses, the revelation of God in Christ becomes a past event, but not merely a past event. The book of Hebrews reminds us that the focus of the past event of Christ is the future salvation of humanity. The future orientation of this past event affects "the present participation in salvation in the Spirit" (1968, 130).

Second, the indirectness of revelation also points to its consummation at the end of history. If God's revelation is not confined to a single activity, then the fullness of God's being can be comprehended only when the totality of the partial, indirect series of revelatory acts is in full view. The Old Testament again shows the accuracy of this view, Pannenberg believes, for it is only in looking back at the historical acts of God from their completion in the return to the land of Israel that one sees the totality of the acts of Yahweh. Jesus Christ provides a proleptic glimpse of the consummation of history, for God has pre-actualized it in the resurrection of the crucified Jesus.

Pannenberg contends that revelation is not only indirect in history but also accessible without any additional testimony of the Holy Spirit, as it were. Against an earlier generation of theologians who had described the need for outward revelation to be supplemented by a certain internal inspiration, Pannenberg argues that revelation that requires any such supplement is not true revelation. Revelation by its very definition must be recognized as such without any inward testimony of the Spirit. This assertion takes the form of a thesis: "In

distinction from special manifestations of the deity, the historical revelation is open to anyone who has eyes to see. It has a universal character" (Pannenberg, 1968, 135). For Pannenberg, there is a danger in thinking otherwise. Viewing historical revelation as requiring additional inspiration or insight transforms revelation into secret, gnostic knowledge, inaccessible to and unassailable by other natural knowledge. Yet Pannenberg is careful to note that being open to anyone with eyes to see does not reduce revelation to human projections or previous human knowledge obtained via the intellect. Revelation contains true knowledge of God and has "transforming power" (ibid., 137). Furthermore, such divinely revealed events "speak their own language, the language of facts" (ibid.). If this were not the case, "then the Christian truth is made into a truth for the in group, and the church becomes a Gnostic community" (ibid.). Such an outcome is unacceptable given the universality of revelation and the language of divine events.

From the perspective of proclamation, the implications of historical revelation's universality are even greater. One must assert the truth of the gospel message, Pannenberg maintains, or "one would have to cease being a theologian and a Christian. The proclamation must assert that the facts are reliable and that you can therefore place your faith, life, and future on them" (1968, 138). Anything less than the reliable truth of the Christian message is unworthy of one's ultimate trust.

Yet if "the facts are reliable," as Pannenberg says, it seems unclear why some do not see the truth of God's historical revelation. In other systems, the problem of the visibility of revelation, as it were, normally is settled by appealing to the internal testimony of the Spirit or an infusion of God's grace or some additional facet of God's presence. And the question of why God is present in some and absent in others is left to divine mystery. Pannenberg finds this method unsatisfactory. If it is to be universal, revelation must be open and available to all. Pannenberg's solution to the problem of persons who fail to see revelation in history is to suggest that such persons are not blind to revelation but have failed to see clearly:

> That these and other [divinely revealed] events are veiled from many men, indeed, from most men, does not mean that this truth is too high for them, so that their reason

must be supplemented by some other means of knowing. Rather, it means that they must use their reason in order to see correctly. (1968, 137)

Rationality is key to discerning and recognizing the facts of God's indirect revelation in history. The universal character of revelation means that it is in principle open to all. Still, the difficulty posed by the fact that God's acts are veiled from most will return in the discussion of theology and its relationship to the sciences.

In this early work on revelation, Pannenberg provides a brief look into the methodological concerns that have continued to influence his work. God's indirect revelation in history is universal in character and cannot be seen as secret gnostic knowledge. The truth of these historical occurrences is critical, for they are also the basis of faith. Furthermore, though doubt questions its sources, faith should be strengthened by the quest for knowledge and be provided "new insight into its own foundations" (1968, 157 n.15). "The process of knowledge in which faith firms up its foundation," Pannenberg reminds us, "is normally held in process by faith that is marked by an assurance that anticipates the results of understanding." This process "takes place in view of the anticipation of its results and receives its impulse from this" (ibid.). Elsewhere, Pannenberg emphasizes this aspect of knowledge as anticipatory: "I would rather like to use 'knowledge' as a rather open category, so we can say that we are aware in some sense of our human situation, of the incompleteness of our existence and therefore that we need a future fulfillment, and a directing of our lives toward the future destiny" (1972, 295). The character of historical revelation is analogous to the search for knowledge: both recognize that they are provisional and incomplete, and both anticipate their future completion and wholeness.

III. Christology

Pannenberg's influence as a theologian of significance was solidified with the appearance of his next major work, *Jesus—God and Man*. As with revelation, Pannenberg recasts christology with an eye toward a publicly accessible and therefore rational discussion of the nature and person of Jesus Christ. Pannenberg's

christology incorporates some elements rejected by many theologians of the early twentieth century, including questions about the historicity of Jesus' resurrection and its accessibility to critical-historical method. Yet as *Revelation as History* had suggested, history serves a key role for Pannenberg. *Jesus—God and Man* proved influential across the theological spectrum as conservatives applauded its affirmation of the historicity of the resurrection and liberals celebrated its emphasis on historical method and rationality.

Pannenberg signaled a turn to developing a christology "from below" in *Jesus—God and Man*. Rather than begin with a faith statement about the divinity of Christ (a christology "from above"), Pannenberg begins with the history of the man Jesus and explores what the events related to this historical person mean for Christian faith. There are several interrelated conclusions that Pannenberg develops related to christology, yet they all center on the event of Jesus' resurrection.

Biblical accounts of the empty tomb and of Jesus' resurrection appearances, Pannenberg argues, represent clear evidence of the fact of Jesus' resurrection. Here Pannenberg parts company with Rudolph Bultmann, who had demythologized the resurrection by arguing that Jesus was raised from the dead in the preaching of the kerygma. In his review of biblical scholarship, Pannenberg finds that the empty tomb and resurrection appearances developed independently and thus are mutual confirmations of Jesus truly being raised from the dead. In the context of the resurrection, Pannenberg once again insists that the historical evidence is open to rational scrutiny, and once examined will confirm the Christian narrative of Christ's life, death, and resurrection. Nothing outside the historical account is needed to confirm its truth.

The meaning of the resurrection for Pannenberg is twofold. First, the resurrection confirms what had been true about Jesus throughout his life, namely, that he is the Son of God. By raising Jesus from the dead, God has affirmed Jesus' relationship to God as his son. In Trinitarian terms, Jesus has become the Son of the Father. Second, Jesus' resurrection provides a proleptic glimpse of the future destiny of all humanity and of all creation. The instantiation of the Kingdom of God has arrived ahead of time in the resurrected Jesus and provided a foretaste of the New Creation. This Kingdom of God that Jesus had preached about was not merely an ethical community. Pannenberg believes that biblical scholarship shows that Jesus understood the Kingdom as a future reality and that the bringing about of the Kingdom of God will demonstrate that creation has been rooted in God's future all along.

Furthermore, in both cases the resurrection reveals something both future and present. The Kingdom of God is certainly a future reality, but not one disconnected from the present. God's promised resurrection of the dead is a future event, but not one severed from human nature in the present. The future destiny of creation and of humanity reveals their very nature.

IV.   Theology and Sciences

Theology and the Philosophy of Science is Pannenberg's engagement with contemporary philosophy of science (contemporary for the early to mid-1970s, at any rate) in a discussion about what constitutes a discipline as *wissenschaftlich*, as "scientific." This task requires mapping the complex landscape of both contemporary philosophy of science (*Wissenschaftstheorie*) and the implications of the philosophy of science for theology's self-understanding. Pannenberg's conclusions provide one rationale for placing theology in dialogue with the "scientific" disciplines of the university and represent a key move in his efforts to provide a coherent and rational explanation for the Christian faith.

Pannenberg offers a clear explanation why this discussion is necessary for theology: "The questioning of the scientific character of theology within theology itself is paralleled in recent discussion in philosophy of science by influential tendencies which seek to deny Christian theology any claim to scientific validity" (1976, 20). Thus there are two facets to the question of theology as a science, internal and external. An unfortunate consequence of efforts to provide unassailable foundations for theology has been the use of such efforts as proof of theology's non-scientific status. To begin reasserting theology's place among the sciences, Pannenberg analyzes both theology's internal structure and the philosophy of science. The wide acceptance of modern natural sciences' paradigmatic role in the quest for knowledge complicates this task. Indeed, because of their wide-reaching successes the natural sciences need no longer argue for their epistemological starting

point. The natural sciences are assumed to be a scientific endeavor that furthers knowledge and expands understanding, and as such have become in some sense gatekeepers to the font of knowledge. The question of how it is that we come to know seems to have a concrete answer in the method of the natural sciences.

Yet for Pannenberg the sciences do more than simply accumulate observational data that seem to be read off the natural world. He argues that for scientific hypotheses to be meaningful, they must be placed within the context of the world they attempt to describe. Part of that context includes metaphysics. Such metaphysical ideas that guide and inspire scientific inquiry are not accidents but help determine the validity of such inquiry. Consequently, Pannenberg believes that theology as metaphysics should not be excluded from discussions of the validity and truth of scientific claims, even if (and likely *when*) such scientific claims are made without explicit reference to their implicit metaphysical assumptions. The process of scientific discovery includes placing such discoveries in context to test for their validity in explaining the world, and as the widest possible context, theology has a role in the interpretive process of the sciences.

Having established the manner in which scientific analysis is hermeneutical, Pannenberg assesses the degree to which the process of meaning is scientific. Critics who deny the scientific status of hermeneutics argue that its logic is circular, beginning with a pre-understanding that enables real understanding, which is then potentially applicable to one's life situation. It would seem that the language of the hermeneutical circle has been taken to represent the logic of the process rather than as a heuristic tool for analyzing the process of meaning. Science, the critics continue, does not operate to explicate pre-understanding but to test hypotheses. However, as Pannenberg's argument attempts to show, meaning in the sciences as well as in hermeneutics depends upon the context of the whole, upon projecting a speculative vision of that whole and locating the particular within that whole. The components of understanding represent a means of testing hypotheses about the meaning of the whole.

Pannenberg next asks how is it that the process of meaning by which we understand the particular in relation to the whole reaches any approximation of truth? His answer involves the nature of the whole in which one's assertion of truth is located. Assertions are located within a context of meaning, and when that context of meaning is the totality of experience, there is nothing outside that totality to refute its truthfulness. "In the all-encompassing totality of meaning, therefore, meaning and truth coincide. To this extent it is an intrinsic part of the hermeneutical consideration of the composite meanings of linguistic utterances to investigate their truth" (1976, 220). Even assertions with a limited horizon place themselves in the context of a complete horizon of meaning and open themselves up to the question of their truth. And as an anticipation of truth "the proposition claims to be true while at the same time laying itself open to refutation" (ibid.).

Despite its unavoidably contested status, the vision of theology and the sciences put forth by Pannenberg represents a key move toward true dialogue. Because theology is scientific, theology need not simply alter its own formulations apologetically, but instead can pose questions to scientists in a manner that legitimizes the theological questions as scientific. Points of contention clearly exist, but because reality is essential future, one must live with the provisionality of any claim to the truth and test such claims by their coherence with the scientific disciplines and their implications for one's understanding of this as-yet unfinished reality.

As Pannenberg sees it, Christian theology's task is to confirm the explication of God's revelation in history in relation to all of known reality. In order to do so in a public way and engage the disciplines of the university, theology must adhere to criteria by which such disciplines are judged to be scientific. As Pannenberg points out, most disciplines do not take their scientific status as a given, but rather must continually re-examine the philosophical basis for its given area of expertise. In the contemporary period, however, the natural sciences have achieved such unrivaled triumphs in advancing human knowledge that for these fields such philosophical and methodological reflection appears unnecessary. The natural sciences have become paradigmatic for what it means to be a scientific discipline. But as Pannenberg contends, being scientific must be interpreted with greater precision when one recognizes theology and the sciences' shared basis in hermeneutics. Both disciplines develop scientific hypotheses that attempt to explain the one reality determined by God.

V.   Anthropology

With the publication of *Anthropology in Theological Perspective*, Pannenberg defended the notion that Christian theology had to be defended against the privatization of belief on the one hand and atheistic critiques of humanity on the other. The ground for these debates was the human person, so for theology to retain its hold on truth it was necessary to defend theological assertions by first challenging the assumptions about anthropology. In *Anthropology in Theological Perspective* Pannenberg argues that anthropology has unearthed a human desire for self-transcendence through openness to others and to the world. This innate "exocentricity" enables humanity to be open to the infinite, giving humans an essential religious sense that can be concretized by engagement with a living religious tradition.

In his earlier work Pannenberg points to the vital importance of exploring anthropology. "The most general foundations of systematic theology," he argues, "will therefore have to come from anthropology. Moreover, a theology broaches the anthropological phenomena with a view to their religious and theological implications" (1976, 422). Thus, Pannenberg's *Anthropology in Theological Perspective* is not meant as a full statement of theological anthropology (that occurs in the *Systematic Theology*, vol. II, Chapter 8); rather, the extensive volume is an exercise in "*fundamental-theological* anthropology." He restates his assertion from *Theology and the Philosophy of Science* that "human biology, psychology, cultural anthropology, or sociology" should be examined "with an eye to implications that may be relevant to religion and theology" (1985, 21).

Pannenberg's concern with anthropology is based on a number of intersecting concerns. Pannenberg describes how the history of theology has focused on the human person, particularly as the person is the concern of salvation. This concern is rooted as well in God's incarnation as a specific individual human person. Philosophy as well has placed the human person at the center of its study. As its history suggests, philosophical reflection begins by examining the human relationship to God.

Pannenberg traces how cultural trends influenced the growing importance of anthropological reflection, particularly "the privatization or at least segmentation of religion in modern society" (1985, 13). From the seventeenth century onward, Pannenberg observes, "a shared conception of the human person, human values, and human rights became the basis for social coexistence" (1985, 15). As a result, both theists and atheists ground their arguments about the viability of religious faith in anthropological arguments. If Christians fail to provide a legitimate basis for faith in anthropology, then they can no longer maintain a strong commitment to the truth of their message. Faith would no longer be the universal truth of God but the private preferences of individuals, and religion and theology merely would be seen as human projections and illusions. Accordingly, Pannenberg notes, "Theologians will be able to defend the truth precisely of their talk about God only if they first respond to the atheistic critique of religion on the terrain of anthropology" (1985, 16).

Pannenberg's response to the atheistic critique of religion aims to show the truth of the biblical message by explaining its fundamental coherence with contemporary scientific descriptions of human nature. Here Pannenberg describes the particularly religious nature of human beings in terms of the ability for self-transcendence and an attitude of openness toward the world (or "exocentricity"). This openness, Pannenberg continues, has given humanity the ability to perceive beyond the relationship between individual and object, to reach beyond the relation between self and other objects. There is a universal element to this perception, given in one's perceiving an individual object, and this process is unlimited. Pannenberg's conclusion is that the "exocentric structure of human living has therefore an openness that is not restricted to the things of this world" (1985, 68). Awareness of this structure provides a religious theme to one's existence and raises the question of that which underlies and supports one's life. He believes this shows that humanity has an innate religious sense, one that is abstract until made concrete by the experience of a living religious tradition. In fact, only after one has experienced a religious tradition does one retrospectively recognize that innate religious sense as an awareness of God.

VI.   Systematic Theology

Pannenberg's contributions to theology are brought to their final form in his three-volume *Systematic Theology*. Drawing together the threads of his earlier works on revelation, history, theological method, christology, anthropology, and numerous other subjects, Pannenberg weaves an eschatalogically oriented picture of a triune God who determines all of reality.

Key to his entire project is the nature of Pannenberg's method, the consummate statement of which occurs in the first volume of the *Systematic Theology*. Here, Pannenberg's focus is on the relationship between the question of truth and the task of systematic theology. He begins by describing the contemporary situation of the academic disciplines of Christian theology. With the development of the historical-critical method, the historical theological disciplines have viewed the documents of Christian history as works awaiting exposition and critical analysis. The result has been the shifting of the burden of defending the truth of these documents to dogmatics as systematic theology, both for itself and for all of theology. Only here is the question of the truth of the theological disciplines explored and defended.

Pannenberg then surveys the history of dogmatics— "the exposition and testing of dogmas" (1991–8, I: 16)—to show that dogmatics is concerned with both the content and the truth of dogma. Since the early eighteenth century, "systematic theology" has been used to describe the task of presenting Christian teaching in a consistent and coherent fashion. One of the tasks of systematic theology is to provide proofs and confirmations of these teachings. "The proof and confirmation," Pannenberg writes, "come chiefly by way of the form of systematic presentation itself as a connection between the various Christian doctrinal statements and also between these statements and whatever else is regarded as true" (1991–8, I: 19). Thus systematic theology includes as part of its task the discussion and defense of its truth; indeed, "these are not things we must add later to their systematic presentation" but are "linked to the systematic presentation itself" (ibid.).

The kind of truth that concerns systematic theology is "*truth as coherence*, as the mutual agreement of all that is true" (Pannenberg's italics, 1991–8, I: 19). This applies both internally and externally to the various theological parts of the system and to the relationship between the systematic articulation and other knowledge. In other words, Pannenberg's goal is to show how Christian doctrine is true because it has both inner coherence in its content and coherence with all truth. The question of truth is not a subset of the systematic task, or a later addition; rather, "inquiry into the truth of the content is linked to the systematic presentation itself" (ibid.). And the truth of Christian doctrine should not be assumed prior to the explication of the content of doctrine, as did the subjectivist theologies of Friedrich Schleiermacher and Karl Barth. (Pannenberg describes Karl Barth's theology as "subjectivist" because of his efforts to establish the truth of Christian doctrine prior to discussion of its content, and thus to rely on a faith as the basis of Christian truth claims; see 1991–8, I: 40–8.) Theology should be about the reality of God, which can only be accomplished by not assuming truth but by arguing for truth.

Additionally, Pannenberg applies his earlier work on theories of knowledge to his own systematic treatment of theology. Truth is not unchanging and static prior to the eschaton. Truth claims, including those made by the Christian faith, are hypotheses to be tested in light of their ability to explain reality. Still, the unfolding of the systematic treatment of Christian theology will show that the Christian message provides a viable explanation that coheres with what is known about the nature of reality and humanity's place within it.

VII. Conclusion

From his early contributions on the relationship between revelation and history, Wolfhart Pannenberg has continued to develop one of the most innovative and comprehensive theological visions of the late twentieth century. His renewed emphasis on the future orientation of the Christian message, combined with a desire to bring Christian theology into conversation with the scientific disciplines of the university, has led to a uniquely eschatological theology that engages anthropology, philosophy of science, critical-historical method, and the natural sciences in constructing a publicly accessible and rationally structured theology. His efforts have spawned a great deal of critical discussion on nearly all aspects of his theology. His theology shows his clear grasp of the history of Christian theology as well as contemporary developments in the social and natural sciences. His emphasis on rational and public discourse in theology has been heralded by some and derided by others. Yet there can be no doubt that Pannenberg has produced a theology that is encompassing in scope and ambitious in its aims.

Pannenberg has argued that the truth of Christian theology only will be known with certainty at the eschaton. That may be true of Pannenberg himself, for it will only be in retrospect that Pannenberg's true contribution to theology will be known. Indeed, critics have noted that if the future of theology lies in the proliferation of contextualized, occasional theologies that eschew attempts at universalizing truths, then Pannenberg may represent the last of an outmoded method of theology, one grounded in a classical tendency no longer relevant to a changing faith. If, on the other hand, the future of theology lies in a return to efforts at creating global, universalizing truth claims, then Pannenberg may prove prescient in his claim that truth cannot be truth if it remains only subjective.

References

Pannenberg, Wolfhart. 1972. "A Theological Conversation with Wolfhart Pannenberg," *Dialog* 11: 295.

Pannenberg, Wolfhart. 1976. *Theology and the Philosophy of Science*, trans. Francis McDonagh. Philadelphia: Westminster Press.

Pannenberg, Wolfhart. 1977. *Jesus—God and Man*, trans. Lewis L. Wilkins and Duane A. Priebe, 2nd ed. Philadelphia: Westminster Press.

Pannenberg, Wolfhart. 1985. *Anthropology in Theological Perspective*. Philadelphia: Westminster Press.

Pannenberg, Wolfhart. 1988. "An Autobiographical Sketch." In *The Theology of Wolfhart Pannenberg: Twelve American Critiques*, ed. Carl E. Braaten and Philip Clayton. Minneapolis, MN: Augsburg, pp. 11–18.

Pannenberg, Wolfhart. 1991–8. *Systematic Theology*, 3 vols., trans. Geoffrey Bromiley. Grand Rapids, MI: Eerdmans.

Pannenberg, Wolfhart, Rendtorff, Rolf, Rendtorff, Trutz and Wilkens, Ulrich. 1968. *Revelation as History*, trans. David Granskou. New York: Macmillan.

Grenz, Stanley. 2005. *Reason for Hope: The Systematic Theology of Wolfhart Pannenberg*. 2nd edn. Grand Rapids, MI: Eerdmans.

Charles Philip Price (1920–99)

Nancy C. James
(with contributions from John M. Graham)

I. Background

Charles P. Price, an American Protestant theologian, worked primarily in the areas of christology, liturgy, and social justice. Price connected his existentialist theology with bold social action, and he achieved a vast legacy in the area of social change both in the United States and throughout the global Anglican Communion. A group of Episcopal leaders wrote, "No single individual had a greater influence on the Episcopal Church in the latter part of the twentieth century" than did Charles Price (Forward, 2003, 7). His probing intellect achieved mastery in a wide variety of subjects including theology, mathematics, science, philosophy, and music. His depth of thought is widely respected in many differing arenas. Price created a systematic theology that plumbed the depths of *anamnesis* for both theology and liturgics. His theology also has ramifications for the areas of social justice and liberation theology.

Charles Philip Price was born in Pittsburgh, Pennsylvania. In 1941 he graduated from Harvard with a BA summa cum laude, with a concentration in mathematics. He then served in World War II on a Navy destroyer and briefly taught at the Naval Academy. After this experience, he carried a life-long belief about the vitality that can be achieved through duty and sacrifice.

Following his service in the military, Price attended Virginia Theological Seminary from 1946 to 1949. While attending VTS, his mentor became Dr Clifford Leland Stanley, who was an interpreter of Søren Kierkegaard. In 1949 Price received a BD and was ordained an Episcopal priest. In 1961 Price wrote about the philosophy of Kierkegaard in *Existentialism: Question or Answer?* He developed a life-long conviction that truth was inward.

Price attended Union Theological Seminary and received his ThD in 1962, with a concentration both in theology and Old Testament. He wrote his dissertation on "Remembering and Forgetting in the Old Testament and Its Bearing on the Early Christian Eucharist." At Union Theological Seminary, Price studied the systematic theology of Paul Tillich. Price returned to VTS where he became Assistant Professor of Systematic Theology and taught there from 1956 to 1963.

Then President of Harvard, Nathan Pusey, invited Price to become Preacher to Harvard University and Chair of the Board of Preachers. Price did this from 1963 to 1972. From 1967 to 1972 Price also taught in the position of Plummer Professor of Christian Morals at Harvard. Price's trademark was his expansive prophetic vision. He created an ecumenical and open church by inviting speakers from many faiths. Price declared that the Christian vision challenges oppressive social realities. He wrote, "One cannot live

The Student's Companion to the Theologians, First Edition. Edited by Ian S. Markham.
© 2013 Blackwell Publishing Ltd. Published 2013 by Blackwell Publishing Ltd.

seriously with an eschatological vision and not try to actualize it" (Price, 1975, 55).

After the assassination of President John F. Kennedy, Price preached an influential sermon on November 23, 1963, to an overflow crowd of over 2,000 people. Later his words were rebroadcast in the United States and to the armed forces overseas. He captured the sense of grief that many felt. "The rent in our social and political fabric signalized by this deed of horror is awesome to contemplate. Who can comprehend it? We only know that we have been maimed and violated. Our common life has been diminished, our joy darkened, our light tarnished. Words cannot restore them. Only courage will do that" (Price, 1964, 207–8).

Price's concern for social and political realities led him to work avidly for the civil rights movement. In 1964, he hosted a conference on civil rights at Harvard University. In January 1965 Price invited Dr Martin Luther King, Jr. to preach at Harvard. In April 1968 Price led a memorial service for Dr King and in the same month he welcomed Coretta Scott King to Harvard University.

After the death of Dr Martin Luther King, Jr., Price once again rose to prominence as he spoke truths about racial relationships. J. Anthony Lukas wrote about this:

> But it was Charles P. Price, preacher to the university, who pointed out a simple reality … nobody had dared to mention: virtually the entire throng in the church was white, for blacks were holding their own service on the steps outside. The separate services were "a mark of the estrangement between white man and black man that exists today," Price said. "We meet in sorrow and repentance for what we have done to create a situation and sustain such a gap that we cannot even mourn together." Then he led the congregation in singing, "We Shall Overcome." (Lukas, 1985, 10–11)

Price's lifelong passion for ecumenical, racial, and religious unity led him to bring many ecumenical speakers to Harvard. Price arranged Noble Lectures from the long-term secretary of the World Council of Churches, Dr Willem Adolph Visser't Hoofe. He also invited members of the Jewish, Roman Catholic, Protestant, and Greek Orthodox faiths to speak at Daily Prayers. Price arranged the first Sunday morning

Roman Catholic speaker, the Reverend John Courtney Murray, SJ, of Woodstock College.

In 1966, with the ongoing confrontations over the Vietnam War, Price asked Eugene McCarthy to speak at the Memorial Church. When students at Harvard University protested the war and were locked out of buildings, Price opened up the church as a base for traumatized students. The current Preacher at Harvard, Peter J. Gomes, writes that after this Price became, "one of the few establishment figures to whom people of conflicting opinions would listen" (Forward, 2003, 18).

Price also supported the feminist movement when he welcomed the first woman to preach at Harvard. In 1971, Professor Mary Daly preached her historic sermon titled, "Beyond God the Father." At the end of the sermon, Dr Daly led a walk-out from the church which became a cornerstone of the feminist movement. In 1975 Price published an article advocating for the ordination of women.

From 1972 until 1989 Price taught at VTS as William Meade Professor of Systematic Theology. He continued working for ecumenical relationships and actively explored more avenues for deeper unity among the world religions. The "Islam and the Modern Age Society" based in New Delhi, India, asked him to write a theology of the Christian faith for persons in all religions. In 1977, in response to this request, Price published his major book, *Principles of Christian Faith*.

Price's vast influence on religions included his participation in the Anglican–Roman Catholic Consultation/Dialogue Commission from 1977 onwards. Price also wrote a commentary for the "Concordat of Agreement" that allowed shared communion between the Lutheran and Episcopal Churches.

Price participated in the twentieth-century liturgical movement and served as Chairman of the Standing Liturgical Commission of the Episcopal Church of the General Convention. He wrote many portions of the 1979 Book of Common Prayer and theologically assessed other parts. Price stated that the two principles of flexibility and enrichment provided criteria for these controversial liturgical revisions. He stated that liturgical changes were needed to restore *anamnesis* (a Greek work usually translated as "remembrance") in the Greek form to the eucharistic prayer. Price also introduced more expressions of thanksgiving throughout the prayer book, as well as writing his own General Thanksgiving. He wrote an eloquent prayer for the incarcerated that included the phrase, "Constrain us to improve their lot" (1979, Book of Common Prayer, 826). Price co-operated with other denominations to produce the same contemporary form of the Lord's Prayer that allowed possibilities for ecumenical unity. In 1977 Price published *Introducing the Proposed Book of Common Prayer*. Following the successful completion of this project, he worked on the revision of the Episcopal hymnal.

In 1979 Dr Price's *Liturgy for Living* (co-authored with Louis Weil) shows the implications of worship for living a rich and faithful life. This has become a classic book in the Anglican Communion. In the 1994 Reinicker Lectures at VTS, Price articulated that in *anamnesis* the power of God's actions in history are immediately and existentially present to both the individual and the community.

As early as 1978, Price began to write about controversy and possible division in the Anglican Communion; he accurately predicted that the Anglican Communion was heading toward crisis. In 1995 he published his theological position to support the ordination and consecration of practicing homosexuals and lesbians. This support indirectly helped lead to the controversial 2003 consecration of the homosexual Bishop Gene Robinson of the diocese of New Hampshire. This consecration has harmed the ecumenical relationship between the Episcopal Church and the Roman Catholic Church. Price helped create the distinctive inclusive character of the Episcopal Church. The current division in the Episcopal Church can be traced in part to the Episcopal Church that Charles Price helped develop.

When, in 2001, the former President of Harvard University, Nathan Pusey, died, the *Harvard Gazette* ran a picture of Nathan Pusey on the steps of the Memorial Church talking to an animated Dr Martin Luther King, Jr. In the picture's background, Dr Charles Price stands quietly. This picture displays Price's stance in his work. He played an important role in the social changes of the twentieth century, while he thought deeply about how to allow history to unfold with maximum freedom for everyone. At the same time, he never drew attention to himself but only to his passionate quest for unity and peace. His effective work in the area of social justice can be seen in his visionary accomplishments at Harvard University, VTS, and in the global Anglican Communion.

In 1999 Charles P. Price died and was buried in the cemetery at VTS.

II.   Theology

In his earliest writings, Charles P. Price developed a distinctive theology influenced by the existentialist philosophy of Søren Kierkegaard, evangelical Protestantism, and the concept of remembering. Out of these three influences, Price developed his profound systematic theology. Price recognized existential human suffering, while *anamnesis* makes present the effects of the sacrifice and redemption of Jesus of Nazareth.

Price is most remembered for his work about *anamnesis*. He recognized a threefold significance to *anamnesis* or remembering: in its liturgical power, in its ecumenical connections, and in its potential growth for personal awareness.

First, Price analyzes the liturgical functions of remembering in the Hebrew Bible that influenced the Christian Eucharist. In the Eucharist, the liturgical idea of *anamnesis* contains three significant elements: offering, remembering, and giving thanks. *Anamnesis* is not a human capability but a liturgical possibility. Price writes:

> It is God who empowers this kind of remembering, and God does so, customarily and usually when a congregation gathers to worship. *Anamnesis* in this strong sense of the word is the gift of the Holy Spirit.
>
> In the cultic moment, the congregation finds itself in the presence of God "who inhabits eternity, whose name is Holy." All time is present to God in one eternal Here-and-Now. To that Here and Now we come. All the events of time, are, so to speak, accessible in that cultic moment. Now the fact is that human beings can't take them in all at once. We're finite. The weight of all that simultaneity would destroy us. The work of a congregation in that setting, granted the biblical model of worship, is to recite, or recall, its history. In that setting when Israel recites or recalls the mighty acts of God for its deliverance, as in those long historical psalms like the 105th or 106th, the community lives through the events again—culturally, liturgically, but powerfully and really.

So that, for example, when Israel gathered in Shechem for such recitals year by year, it could be said, "Not with our ancestors did the Lord make this covenant, but with all of us here alive today," having rehearsed or perhaps being about to rehearse the sacred story once more. In a Christian setting, when one comes either to baptism … or Eucharist and remembers, recalls, recites the work of Christ, the Spirit lifts us to the divine presence, to that "altar on high," where those events are accessible to us. Their effects are present to us.

Because of *anamnesis*, the mighty redemption of Jesus of Nazareth becomes accessible and "the cross and resurrection are present in their dread power" (Price, 1994, 10).

Secondly, Dr Price writes that the idea of *anamnesis* provides theological support for new ecumenical relationships. The theology of remembrance in the Eucharist had previously divided denominations at the time of the Reformation as theologians failed to agree on what remembrance means. Price saw new possibilities for union as *anamnesis* grounds the varying eucharistic theologies. Price states that Christian churches could agree that in the eucharistic *anamnesis*, all of God's actions in history are present and their effects accessible. This change helped build connections with the Roman Catholic Church since some of the post-Vatican II Roman Catholic rites had made the same change. One form of celebrating the Eucharist in the 1979 Book of Common Prayer can also be used in the Roman Catholic Church, as well as in a number of Protestant churches.

Thirdly, *anamnesis* also carries existential significance as the revelation of ultimate reality. In 1966 in a sermon at Harvard, Price said: "For the religion of the Old Testament and New Testament the meaning is communicated in an experience of liberation, a moment of deliverance, a time when somebody— some people—got through safe despite prior expectations. So profound is the experience in that moment that it is taken to be a disclosure of the underlying character of all reality" (Price, 1966, 2–3). He defined this experience of *anamnesis* later as "ultimate *reality*, the touchstone by which all other reality is to be measured" (Price, 1977, 37).

Price developed the existential significance of *anamnesis* when he applied psychoanalysis to remembrance, saying: "To remember an experience in the presence of one who accepts means to live through it again, to appropriate it afresh in a new and creative (rather than destructive) way, hence to become more completely one's self. In this 'uncommon' understanding of remembering something of the living power of the word in its Biblical sense has been reborn" (Price, 1963, 403). This became his life-long quest to elucidate the subtlety of thought surrounding *anamnesis* as well as apply this thought to liturgy, ecumenical connections, and human existence.

Price's second major theme was the redemption of Christ. Price uses Friedrich Schleiermacher's statement that in Christianity "everything is related to the redemption accomplished by Jesus of Nazareth" (Price, 1977, xiii). Price states that redemption is the central symbol for Jesus' work. This action of redemption by God in Jesus of Nazareth accomplishes a victory over death and evil. Price defines this as "the basic evangelical concern, sacrificial death of Jesus—the Grand Sacrifice, as it came to be called" (Price, 1994, 3). Price and Protestant theologian Jürgen Moltmann bear close resemblance in their ideas of the crucified Christ as the ultimate criterion for Christian life and theology.

Price said that the people writing the Bible used many symbols, such as victory, deliverance, salvation, justification, and so on, to describe the experience of redemption. Price says that this "language was enlisted with almost careless exuberance" (Price, 1977, 112) by the Christian community to capture the experience of release caused by redemption. This redemption accomplished by Jesus through the power of *anamnesis* is "one of release" (Price, 1977, 112).

This theology of liberation also carried ramifications for ethical thought. Price emphasizes the role of the redemptive Christ as pre-eminent over that of the Scriptures. Dr Price states that the incarnate Christ is the standard for scripture. Because of this relationship, only scriptures that fully reflect Christ's compassion and love are to be used as measures for Christian behavior.

Price explains this theology by stating that the ethics of the New Testament in the letters of Paul is based in Greek Stoicism. He writes: "St. Paul lays down the ethical duties of various classes of persons in a manner which suggest the customary Stoic morality of the day" (Price, 1977, 254). Price asserts that Christianity did not introduce a new ethical code but "it did bring a new criteria [*sic*]" of the risen Christ. On that basis,

Christians scrutinize existing social and political systems in order to make needed changes in society. One prominent example of this change is the ending of slavery. Price points out that other needed changes have been centuries in coming. He recognizes—and indeed lived through—some such experiences with his courageous stands for equality, and states that the "transformation does not often take place without pain and anguish" (Price, 1977, 256).

Price states that the Anglican Communion should be this place of tolerance and ethical change. The essence of Anglicanism lies in the Christian doctrine of the incarnation. Because of this primary doctrine, tolerance and diversity claim an important place in Anglican thought.

Price's theology about *anamnesis* remains his distinctive contribution. Much of Dr Price's legacy also lies in the area of increased possibilities for individuals and religious institutions. His theology opened doors for feminist theology as well as supporting the ordination of women in the Christian churches. Price is remembered as an active participant in the civil rights movement. His liturgical changes continue to shape the Anglican Communion. He taught hundreds of priests and bishops at Virginia Theological Seminary for service in the Anglican Communion, and he wrote hymns used widely in many Christian denominations.

Price's work is crucial in light of the current Anglican controversy over the consecration of Bishop Gene Robinson. His work includes incipient influences for liberation theology. Charles Philip Price influenced Anglican theology worldwide in his speaking, preaching, and theology; scholarship still remains to be done on the work of such an influential man.

References

Book of Common Prayer. 1979. New York: Church Publishing Incorporated.

Booty, John E. 1995. *Mission and Ministry: A History of Virginia Theological Seminary*. Harrisburg, PA: Morehouse Publishing.

Forward Publishing. 2003. *Each of Us Will Never Be the Same: Memories of Charles Philip Price*. Cincinnati, OH.

Lukas, J. Anthony. 1985. *Common Ground: A Turbulent Decade in the Lives of Three American Families*. New York: Alfred A. Knopf, pp. 10–11.

Price, Charles P. 1961. "Existentialism: Question or Answer?" In *Three Lectures by Albert T. Mollegen. One Lecture by Charles P. Price*. Albert T. Mollegen.

Price, Charles P. 1963. "Remembering and Forgetting in the Old Testament and Its Bearing on the Early Christian Eucharist." Dissertation.

Price, Charles P. 1964. "A Man Named John F. Kennedy: Sermons on His Assassination." In *Some Words for John F. Kennedy*, ed. Charles J. Stewart and Bruce Kendall. Glen Rock, NJ: Paulist Press, pp. 207–8.

Price, Charles P. 1966. "The Controversy," *Virginia Seminary Journal* XVIII (December): 1–6.

Price, Charles P. 1975. "The Argument from Theology." In *Women Priests? Yes Now!* ed. Canon Harold Wilson. Nutfield: Denham House Press.

Price, Charles P. 1977a. *Principles of Christian Faith*. New Delhi: Islam and the Modern Age Society.

Price, Charles P. 1977b. *Introducing the Proposed Book of Common Prayer*. New York: Seabury Press.

Price, Charles P. 1978. "The Identity and Viability of the Anglican Tradition." Lecture, School of Theology of the University of the South.

Price, Charles P. 1983. *Matter of Faith*. Wilton, CT: Morehouse-Barlow Co.

Price, Charles P. 1994. "New Life for Old: Christian Sacrifice. The 1994 Reinicker Lectures," *Virginia Seminary Journal XLVI* (December): 2–19.

Price, Charles P. 1995. "Sex, Homosexuality and Ordination," *Virginia Seminary Journal XLVIII* (August): 21–36.

Price, Charles P. and Weil, Louis. 1979. *Liturgy for Living*. Church's Teaching, vol. 5. New York: Seabury Press.

Process Theology

Shannon C. Ledbetter

It is generally agreed that the inspiration behind process theology is the brilliant mathematician A. N. Whitehead. Whitehead was born in 1861; his father was a Church of England minister, which may explain Whitehead's sympathies with religion throughout his life. His process thought (or, more accurately, his speculative philosophy of organism) developed while he worked in America. He moved to Harvard in 1924, when he was 63. Charles Hartshorne was Whitehead's disciple and he explicated extremely clearly the implications of Whiteheadian thought for religion. Process theology as a movement developed primarily around the so-called Chicago School—people such as Daniel Day Williams and John Cobb.

Process theology is not easy to summarize or understand. It is a distinctive metaphysics that contrasts markedly with traditional ways of understanding the world. A few preliminary comments are necessary. It is undoubtedly true that process thought is a positive engagement with the discovery of the evolutionary hypothesis of Charles Darwin. Pittenger notes, "The central conviction of American process-thought is that the evolutionary perspective must be taken with the utmost seriousness" (Pittenger, 1967, 98). In this respect there are similarities with the project (although not necessarily the conclusions) of Teilhard de Chardin. Charles Hartshorne claims, "I have never consciously not been an evolutionist" (Cobb and Gamwell, 1984, xii).

Whitehead wants to provide an alternative way of interpreting the world. The traditional interpretation tends to stress its static nature: we tend to think of the universe as made up of "facts" and "stuff." If we ask the question, "what is the basic unit of the universe?" we are likely to find ourselves talking about protons, neutrons, and electrons. Whitehead's task was to provide an entirely different terminology that has given us a language in which to think about the universe in a much more dynamic way.

Whitehead's understanding of the world is briefly analyzed:

1. The fundamental elements of reality are "actual entities." Whitehead writes, "How an actual entity becomes constitutes what the actual entity is: so that the two descriptions of an actual entity are not independent. Its 'being' is constituted by its 'becoming'. This is the 'principle of process'" (Whitehead, 1978, 31). Actual entities, sometimes described as actual occasions or occasions of experience, are moments of experience. The use of the word "experience" is in part analogical. On the one hand, the image suggests that experiences are neither isolated nor static—experiences need objects and receivers; on the other hand, Whitehead is not assuming that the experiences are "conscious." Instead, an actual entity is shaped by other entities to become an event and then

The Student's Companion to the Theologians, First Edition. Edited by Ian S. Markham.
© 2013 Blackwell Publishing Ltd. Published 2013 by Blackwell Publishing Ltd.

achieves uniqueness as a result of the interaction. Once an event, the actual entity will then shape other actual entities into new events. John Cobb likens this to (non-digital) movies, when he writes, "Time is not a single smooth flow, but comes into being in little droplets. A motion picture suggests an analogy: the picture appears to be a continuous flow, whereas in reality it is constituted by a series of distinct frames" (Cobb and Griffin, 1978, 14). Robert Mellert helpfully summarizes, "The concept of actual occasion is the central notion of Whiteheadian thought. Actual occasions, or 'drops of experience,' are the final real things of which the world is made, and there is no going behind them to find anything more real. … They are the only reasons for things. Outside of actual entities, there is nothing at all" (Mellert, 1975, 22).

2. To supplement "actual entities" the other fundamental objects in Whitehead's thought are "eternal objects." These are the colors, sounds, and scents that appear and disappear in different contexts. There is one critique worth mentioning regarding "eternal objects." Whitehead claims that eternal objects may only be associated with God: "in principle the kind of decision by which eternal objects become relevant for God is categorically impossible for all other actual entities." Cobb answers this by asserting, "Whitehead should not preclude in *principle* the possibility that a temporal occasion may have toward some eternal object the kind of relation God has toward all." This fine-tuning of Whitehead's philosophy allows the possibility of a "radical co-creativity" between humanity and God. In other words, it allows for the potential possibility that eternal objects may be effective without the express will of God alone.

3. The means of "actual entities" becoming moments of experience is "prehension". Whitehead defines prehensions as the concrete facts of relatedness and writes, "Every prehension consists of three factors: (a) the "subject" which is prehending, namely, the actual entity in which that prehension is a concrete element; (b) the "datum" (or object), which is prehended: (c) the "subjective form" which is how that subject prehends that datum." We will come to subjective form presently, but

staying with prehensions for a moment, Mellert explains them thus: "An emerging entity is similarly related to eternal objects and past actual entities in that these are the elements out of which the new entity is to become. Prehension, therefore, also indicates that the relatedness of these elements to the emerging actual entity is determinative because the related constitutes the entire data available to that entity in its process of becoming" (Mellert, 1975).

4. We rarely experience "actual entities" in isolation. They come to us as groups (nexus). Mellert again is helpful: "A nexus is a set of actual occasions experienced as related to each other. Sometimes it is called a society of occasions. The human body is a society of this type because the actual occasions of each part of the body are experienced as being spatially connected in the formation of a single body."

5. When an actual entity emerges at a particular moment in time and space, it has its own subjective aim (i.e., it wants to reach some focus or satisfaction). And the precise ways it interacts depends on its subjective form, "which is the particular mood or attitude by which the subject prehends a particular datum." Subjective forms include such things as consciousness, emotions, purposes, and aversions.

6. After each "actual entity" achieves its subjective aim, it perishes. However, it has of course contributed to the reality of subsequent entities that succeed it, which in turn, contribute to the whole.

7. This is what Whitehead means by "creativity." Mellert writes: "Because each actual occasion is its own unique synthesis of its past, each contributes its own actualization to the totality of reality. Each becomes part of the many, and adds itself to the complex environment that gives rise to a new occasion. The new occasion emerges by the unique way in which it objectifies, immortalizes and brings to a new unity the elements of its relevant past. When it achieves that satisfaction, it, too, perishes, clearing the way for the process to continue. … This is what Whitehead means by creativity. It is the ultimate principle by which the multiplicity of relevant data becomes one actual occasion, illustrating the fact that it is the nature

of things that the many enter into complex unity." Whitehead himself states: "Neither God, nor the World, reaches static completion. Both are in the grip of the ultimate metaphysical ground, the creative advance into novelty. Either of them, God and the World, is the instrument of novelty for the other."

The basic points of Whitehead's thought are as follows: Instead of thinking of the universe in a state of "givenness," think of it as in process or becoming. Instead of thinking of the world as made up of discrete separate blocks, think of it as radically interconnected. Instead of contrasting the world of becoming with a static and perfect world of being, think of each discrete element as becoming and temporal, each integrated into the whole.

It is also important to describe Whitehead's account of God, which involves the following components:

1. Whitehead's initial description of God seems to confine God to being the principle of limitation. So God sees all possibilities and makes available to the "actual entities" those possibilities that are necessary to its/their actualization. This ensures, argued Whitehead, the subsequent emergence of these actual entities. John Cobb describes the process thus: "Whitehead affirms substantial activity as the ultimate reality at the base of things. What this means is that the occurrence of events, the sheer fact that something happens, is not itself accidental and is not subject to explanation by anything beyond itself" (Cobb, 1966, 139).

2. If God's role is to envisage possibilities then God must be real, which means God must be "actual entity." Mellert explains, "[A]s an actual entity, he can be described in the same terms as every other actual entity. He is temporal; he prehends physically and conceptually; he has a subjective aim and seeks satisfaction. Furthermore, he is constantly increasing and is an integral part of the process of all reality. Although he is not perfect or ultimate in any absolute sense, he has a perfection and ultimacy relative to all other things." Now, there is some disagreement between followers of Whitehead here. At the very least Mellert would concede that there is of course one major differ-

ence with all other "actual entities," and that is that God does not perish. Rather, God exemplifies everlastingness (i.e., there was never a moment when God came into being and there is never a moment when God will cease to be). However, Charles Hartshorne does not want to envisage God as an actual entity; instead he sees God as a whole sequence of entities.

3. God operates in a dipolar way. God has a primordial nature and a consequent nature. The primordial nature is "the abstract side of God, or God 'alone with himself.' " God's primordial nature provides the means by which God appreciates all possibilities and provides the context in which certain possibilities are actualized. The consequent nature is God's actual relationship with physical reality. These two natures, bearing in mind Cobb's critique, allow for an incredibly interactive God where "wonderfully created, and yet more wonderfully restored" applies not only to God's creation, but to elements of God within God's creation, as Whitehead states:

> God's rôle is not the combat of productive force with productive force, of destructive force with destructive force; it lies in the present operation of the overpowering rationality of his conceptual harmonization. He does not create the world, he saves it: or more accurately, he is the poet of the world, with tender patience leading it by his vision of truth, beauty, and goodness.

John Cobb makes the implications for a process theologian's doctrine of God brilliantly clear. In his foreword to *Process Theology: An Introductory Exposition* (1976), Cobb describes five "Gods" that process theologians do not believe in. As these explanations illustrate precisely why process theology is so important, the passage is worth quoting in full:

1. God as Cosmic Moralist. At its worst this notion takes the form of the image of God as divine lawgiver and judge, who has proclaimed an arbitrary set of moral rules, who keeps records of offences, and who will punish offenders. In its more enlightened versions, the suggestion is retained that God's most fundamental concern is the development of moral attitudes. This makes primary for God what

is secondary for humane people, and limits the scope of intrinsic importance to human beings as the only beings capable of moral attitudes. Process theology denies the existence of this God.

2. God as the Unchanging and Passionless Absolute. This concept derives from the Greeks, who maintained that "perfection" entailed complete "immutability," or lack of change. The notion of "impassibility" stressed that deity must be completely unaffected by any other reality and must lack all passion or emotional response. The notion that deity is the "Absolute" has meant that God is not really related to the world. The world is really related to God, in that the relation to God is constitutive of the world—an adequate description of the world requires reference to its dependence on God—but even the fact that there is a world is not constitutive of the reality of God. God is wholly independent of the world: the God–world relation is purely external to God. These three terms—unchangeable, passionless, and absolute—finally say the same thing, that the world contributes nothing to God, and that God's influence upon the world is in no way conditioned by divine responsiveness to unforeseen, self-determining activates of us worldly beings. Process theology denies the existence of this God.

3. God as Controlling Power. This notion suggests that God determines every detail of the world. When a loved one dies prematurely, the question "Why?" is often asked instinctively, meaning "why did God choose to take this life at this time?" Also, when humanly destructive natural events such as hurricanes occur, legal jargon speaks of "acts of God". On the positive side, a woman may thank God for the rescue of her husband from a collapsed coal mine, while the husbands of a dozen other women are lost. But what kind of a God would this be who spares one while allowing the others to perish? Process theology denies the existence of this God.

4. God as Sanctioner of the Status Quo. This connotation characterizes a strong tendency in all religions. It is supported by the three previous notions. The notion of God as Cosmic Moralist has suggested that God is primarily interested in order. The notion of God as Unchangeable Absolute has suggested God's establishment of an unchangeable order for the world. And the notion of God as Controlling Power has suggested that the present order exists because God wills its existence. In that case, to be obedient to God is to preserve the status quo. Process Theology denies the existence of this God.

5. God as Male. The liberation movement among women has made us painfully aware how deeply our images of deity have been sexually one-sided. Not only have we regarded all three "persons" of the Trinity as male, but the tradition has reinforced these images with theological doctrines such as those noted above. God is totally active, controlling, and independent, and wholly lacking in receptiveness and responsiveness. Indeed, God seems to be the archetype of the dominant, inflexible, unemotional, completely independent (read "strong") male. Process theology denies the existence of this God. (Cobb, 1976, Foreword)

Charles Hartshorne

Whitehead's philosophy has traditionally been built on by utilizing the work of his disciples, Charles Hartshorne, John Cobb, and others. Primarily, scholars have chosen to provide a complex summary of Whitehead's contribution and then move on to make use of subsequent writings. So, our knowledge of Whitehead is primarily filtered through his followers. However, this in no way warps our understanding of Whitehead, but serves to clarify much of his complex theory. It may be argued that Whitehead's achievement was to create a paradigm shift, becoming himself caught between the folds of history, with his disciples emerging onto the other side. This shift in thinking brings us from talking of a God entirely separate from the universe, to talking of God embracing the universe; instead of stressing power and might, process thought stresses love; instead of defining perfection exclusively in terms of changelessness, process thought redefines it to include dynamic change. It is important to add, as with all traditions, that process theologians have addressed a range of questions on a range of issues. It is neither a monolithic tradition nor a simple one.

In the tradition of other process theologians, in this next section an account of God in three parts will be developed, drawing heavily on the work of Charles Hartshorne: First, the two great challenges Hartshorne believes are encroaching on our modern mindset: classical theism and humanism; second, the process answer to these challenges, which is panentheism or dipolar theism; third, the attributes of God as seen by process theology are listed. These include: perfection, a "social" God, creativity, power and knowledge and love.

Hartshorne is undoubtedly Whitehead's main disciple and leading advocate of a process account of God. Hartshorne contends that the two major options facing our age are classical theism and humanism. This is the great metaphysical battle, which on the whole classical theism is losing. Both, he argues, are problematic. Against classical theism, Hartshorne identifies all the major objections already cited previously in this article. He does not consider a timeless, immutable, and simple God adequate in respect of coherence, worship, and morality. The coherence problems include the whole relationship of God alongside a free and dynamic creation or a dynamic participation; the worship problems include the sense that a God who is not able to appreciate the worship of God's creatures is not worthy of worship; while the morality problems encompass the whole issue of a God who cannot empathize and envelop our suffering. Humanism, Hartshorne defines thus, "First, it implies that, except for the animals and for the speculative possibility of inhabitants upon other heavenly bodies, man is evidently alone in the universe, dependent for friendship upon his own kind. Second, it maintains that the recognition of this loneliness will aid rather than hinder the good life here upon earth." He has a range of arguments against this approach, including the notion of the growing importance of the state that was popular in the 1930s. Hartshorne expresses alarm about the danger that if there is nothing beyond God, then what is going to stop the nation state becoming "God"? So Hartshorne contends,

Without God as a real individual above man, what can each of us concretely realize as so great and definite that his individual and collective egoisms are humbled in its presence? Humanity? Surely this is too abstract and

formless an object to perform any such function. And surely there are none so blind as they who will not see that in fact it does not perform it! And what have recent times shown if not that humanism is a feeble bulwark against the collective egoism of state-and race-worship?

This creates a new model of God: this is dipolar theism or panentheism. Panentheism is probably the label that provokes most hostility. It sounds too "Hindu" for most Christian sensitivities. It is important to distinguish panentheism from pantheism. John Cobb is helpfully clear:

God's standpoint is all-inclusive, and so, in a sense, we are parts of God. But we are not parts of God in the sense that God is simply the sum total of the parts or that the parts are lacking in independence and self-determination. God and the creatures interact as separate entities, while God includes the standpoints of all of them in his omnispatial standpoint. In this sense God is everywhere, but he is not everything. The world does not exist outside God or apart from God, but the world is not God or simply part of God. The character of the world is influenced by God, but it is not determined by him, and the world in its turn contributes novelty and richness to the divine experience. … [I]t differs from much traditional theism insofar as the latter stresses the mutual externality of God and the world, with God conceived as occupying another, supernatural, sphere. It differs from pantheism when pantheism is understood to be the identification of God and the world. (Cobb, 1969, 79–80)

This panentheism is conceived of in a dipolar way, meaning that there are two poles to God, namely the abstract and the concrete. Hartshorne's development of Whitehead's distinction between the primordial and consequent natures of God is a logical progression: instead of thinking of God as either entirely changeless or entirely changing, think of God as encompassing both. Gragg writes: "The abstract aspect of God is his absolute, eternal, and necessary existence; and, as such, this aspect can be known by abstract metaphysical argument and logical proof. On the other hand, the concrete aspect of God is his dependent, related, and contingent actuality; and it, being entirely inaccessible to rational proof, can only be known by direct, empirical observation or 'encounter' " (Gragg, 1973, 83). God is radically consistent, yet at the same time is dynamically and creatively engaged with the world.

This concept of God combines a conviction that God is participating in all elements of creation, as well as taking within God's self those elements, but is also completely unique. God is totally superior in every aspect to all other beings. This is a dipolar understanding of God.

What are the attributes of this God? Hartshorne denies the traditional attributes of perfection associated with God and affirms the necessity of redefining perfection as an inclusion of change and feeling as positive traits and not imperfections. A dynamic deity is much more appropriate, and therefore, more "perfect", than a static one.

Starting with this non-traditional account of God, the literature describes attributes not normally considered divine. For example, this God is a "social God." God is not able to operate in isolation. Gragg explains: "Hartshorne's deity is an eminently social God who corresponds exactly with the social nature of all reality. Indeed, it is not incorrect to say that God is the love, or sympathy, or sociality of things. Since mind or awareness is the most relational of all entities, Hartshorne concludes that God as eminent mind is the supremely related, most dependent being of all." Indeed, this most certainly implies that there must have always been some material (or energy) for God to work with. God and the world are thereby linked together. The implications of this assertion have caused Christians to express concern at the loss of the doctrine, "*creatio ex nihilo.*" It is true that in the process view creation becomes an act of molding and shaping rather than a creation out of nothing. Pittenger writes:

> Creation, then, need not mean that first there was quite literally nothing at all and then a split-second later there was a world … It can and should mean that from the range of possibilities and by the use of the material which antecedent events have already moulded, God brings into existence something that as an emergent is genuinely new, yet is in continuity with what had gone before and with the total process of creative advance. The genuinely new is a configuration, a constellation, a focusing, in an entity with its initial aim, its potentialities, its capacity for decision, its opportunity to actualize and hence bring to fulfilment what God purposes—but with opportunity also, by the same capacity for decision, to fail to do this. The word "nothing" in this context need not signify some hypothetically absolute *nihil*, but

simply the absence of that particular occasion with its potentialities. (Pittenger, 1982, 70–1)

The next major attribute of God is God's creativity. Cobb explains:

> If sympathetic responsiveness is an essential aspect of Christian love, creative activity is no less essential. Whether it be considered a theme or a presupposition, the notion that God is active in the world, working to overcome evil and to create new things, is central to the Biblical tradition. To be in harmony with the God of Israel and of Jesus is to be involved in the struggle to overcome the various impediments to the fullness of life.

Hartshorne describes the process as a "growth in richness" that takes previously determined factors and, after their integration, *creates* an entirely new and unthought-of state which progresses forward in time. Logically, if this formula works in the present, for the future it would also be historical; a state had previously consisted of its own entities which had been *created* and *integrated* in a unique manner, and so on back through time. This process may be called a "multiplicity of iteration" (Ledbetter, 2002, 47). Hartshorne explains creativity thus: "And creativity is positive. It does not mean merely that what happens is *not* fully specified by the causal conditions and laws; it means that there is *more* definiteness in reality after a causal situation has produced its effect than before. This increase or *growth in richness of determinations* is not an absence of something, it is a positive presence … Growth is inherent in the very meaning of becoming, and a being is only a potential for becoming" (Hartshorne, 1970, 34–5).

The process theologian has systematically reconfigured and released humanity from the classical theistic account of God into a world of untold freedom and creativity. Creation is not simply waiting for its own culmination, but two important factors are at work. First, creation is very much active in the progression of creation and, second, God, God's self is progressing along with God's creation. The next important distinction is Cobb's designation of God as "a living person" rather than as "an actual entity." This is related to the first point in that God in a very real way participates with God's creation rather than being an interested bystander.

Here process theologians make a significant adjustment. We have a God embracing everything that is, luring everything to fulfill its "satisfaction," operating within temporal constraints: so what sort of power and knowledge can this sort of God have?

On power, the main theme is that God's ultimate power is the power to influence. Anna Case-Winters helpfully explains and contrasts Hartshorne's with Calvin's understanding. She writes:

> Calvin and Barth understood omnipotence to mean that world process—in general and in all its particulars—is actively and effectively brought into conformity with divine willing in a kind of unilateral determination. For Hartshorne, omnipotence does not entail unilateral divine determination. God is seen as influencing world process but not controlling it in such a way that it is made to conform to divine willing. (Case-Winters, 1990, 129)

For Hartshorne, God is the greatest and most significant power amongst many powers. Power in this context means the capacity "for self-creation as well as other-creation." If God is going to create actual entities, then God has allowed alternative power sources to coexist in the universe. God has the capacity both to affect and to be affected by the rest of creation. God has maximal power in that God has the choice of ultimate power over the other entities containing power. This, instead of being a reduction of the tradition, retains a commitment to the power of God without sacrificing the significance of the creation. This is a power that even the democratic principle can recognize.

The final attribute is knowledge. As discussed earlier, traditionally God, timelessly, has complete knowledge of time in its entirety. Our past, present, and future are all before God in a timeless instance. Hartshorne rejects this. Instead, God is also experiencing the duration of the universe within the totality of God. However, Hartshorne, in characteristic style, does not want to be decisive even on indecision: "it is fallacious to say that either God is finite or he is not finite. The real disjunction is, God is in all aspects finite, in no aspect finite, or in some aspects finite and in others not." Given God's vantage point, then, knowledge of all time in all permutations is not an option. God may be confined to complete powers of accurate prediction based on God's knowledge of the present. However, Hartshorne accepts that creation

involves the introduction of a radical freedom into the universe and with it the possibility of surprise and uncertainty.

Process Theology and Providence

One of the clearest accounts of providence from a process perspective is been provided by Norman Pittenger in *Picturing God*. Pittenger identifies six aspects of the way in which God works in the world. "These are (1) ordering, (2) initiating, (3) luring, (4) receiving, (5) responding, and (6) harmonizing" (Pittenger, 1982, 78).

Pittenger shares the traditional view that one of the primary roles for God is the "ordering" one. God is that which prevents chaos and sustains and enables everything that is to form the patterns in creation. Pittenger quotes Whitehead approvingly when he writes, "There is a 'ground-plan', a 'creative advance' in Whitehead's phrase, which is inescapable and by which both God and the world operate." God, in short, provides the cosmic framework for all creativity that then takes place.

The second aspect involves initiating. One interesting feature of Whitehead's philosophy is that God is always the source of the genuinely novel and original. For scientists generally it is a mystery how prior states can generate innovation and difference. The difficulty arises with the axiom that every event or entity must have a cause. Whitehead needs God to explain "originality," as may be seen in the following quotation: "God and the world introduce the note of interpretation. They embody the interpretation of the cosmological problem in terms of a fundamental metaphysical doctrine as to the quality of creative origination, namely, conceptual appetition and physical realization." Certainly Pittenger sees this as part of God's role: so God has a pivotal role in evolution (where we have endless examples of more complex entities coming from less sophisticated ones). Pittenger explains:

> Within the wider continuity, there is room for the emergence of what is genuinely new, although this does not come about through intrusive or interruptive entrance from outside. Rather, it comes about by introduction of an aim or objective such as shall result in a

modification of patterning; what went before now acquires different qualities or characteristics. Life emerges from inanimate existence; consciousness from living existence; self-awareness from conscious living existence. (Pittenger, 1982)

It is important to note that this model of the universe is not the mechanistic machine of Descartes and Newton, but is initiated by a God who pervades that which God has created and facilitates change in co-operation with God's universe.

The third aspect of God working in the world is "luring." This emerges out of Whitehead's "subjective aim" for each entity. This has already been described; however, just to make the link explicit, the idea here is that as each entity becomes so it is invited to reach its "satisfaction": this is the subjective aim. It is the act of invitation that is the act of luring. God is the one who lures, who pursues, in issuing the invitation. Pittenger again stresses that no coercion is used: "Force is not used, but great persuasion is exercised to accomplish this, largely through the lures which, by prehension or grasping from the other effective entities, can be brought to bear upon this or that given occasion." Pittenger describes the activity thus: "In the strange and bewildering complex of human willing and action, God moves through lure and attraction to bring the greatest good out of the confusion of human events."

The first three aspects all stress the creatorial role of God: God who provides the framework (ordering); God who enables innovation in creation and thereby enables the process of evolution (initiating); and God who persuades the created entities to realize their aims (luring). The next two stress God's own evolution in response to the creatorial activity within the universe.

The fourth aspect of God working in the world has God "receiving." The new manifestations brought about within the creation become integrated into the life of God. The "multiplicity of iterations" made possible by God's persuasion acting on the created entities is then received into the vastness of what may be considered God. The changes are contained within the mind of God and God's being and then influence each subsequent interface, thereby continuing the process of iteration. Arguments have been posed against God being surprised by the evolution

in creation. However, because of God's knowledge of each infinitesimal step, surprise is limited to progression of miniscule proportions. Human knowledge is greatly limited and the next step or manifestation may be surprising in the breadth of its progression, unlike God's, whose wide knowledge makes the element of surprise minimal.

The fifth aspect of God acting in the world is "responding." God is in constant conversation with the entirety of what God has made. This leads to the final aspect, which is "harmonizing." Harmonizing is what in traditional Christian language we would call the act of redemption: "The harmonization is made possible because in God's consequent aspect there is always a loving concern and care that 'nothing be lost which can be saved' and that all which can be 'saved' shall be used for the realization of the divine intention and the forwarding of the general over-all pattern which is basic in the cosmos as a whole."

Essential to God's nature is love. We know what God is like because God is revealed in Jesus. The love that Jesus represented—the call to justice for all those who are oppressed—captures the work of God in process theology. Pittenger quotes approvingly Whitehead's image of love traveling from heaven to earth. Whitehead writes: "The perfected actuality … is transformed into a reality in heaven, and the reality in heaven passes back into the world. By reason of this reciprocal relation, the love in the world passes into the love in heaven, and floods back into the world." Pittenger explains: "Here is an account of the world which follows from our taking Love divine and cosmic as the best model for God, which redeems existence as we know it from the threat of triviality, meaninglessness, and frustration, and which provides exactly that feeling of cosmic 'refreshment and companionship' which working religion both requires and expresses."

The God that process thought describes has the following components: a God who is inextricably linked to the world; a God who is enabling and shaping everything that is; a God who is intrinsically bound to love and desires to persuade, to lure, all of creation to loving ends; and finally, a God who takes and builds on the progressions which creation returns to God. Process theology deserves the credit for realizing perfection does not necessarily entail immutability; it does emphasize the link between God and the world; and it does assert the contingency of the future and the significance of human free will and love. Process theology is also a movement able to accommodate significant differences between its exponents (see Whitehead and Hartshorne, for example). Process thought in this way seems to mirror the actualities of existence with its multiplicity of diversity and ambiguities.

Alongside God, what sort of anthropology does process theology offer? Process theology emphasizes the locatedness of people (indeed the locatedness of all entities—all of creation remains a nexus of entities). Cobb's designation of God as a "living person" rather than Whitehead's "actual entity" is helpful. Each living person is born into the world as a result of the myriad of decisions that shape us. This is the material with which humanity must work and begin its own creative process. While the "multiplicity of iterations" may work together to produce a particular entity, feeling, or event, there is no ultimate determinism in process theology. Humanity is not wholly determined by the past. Genuine choice and radical free will, alongside other entities that together produce a future that cannot be controlled or predicted, govern the human story.

Process theology illuminates a God who has created the universe with genuine freedom within it; freedom for every created being, the highest expression of such freedom is human will. Each segment of the next phase of creation has an element of uncertainty: even God cannot be completely sure whether God's ultimate aim of love will triumph. Each human life, then, is constantly facing choices: "Am I to live for love or do I choose to frustrate love?"

The dilemma a person faces whether to further love's aims or to frustrate love needs to be explained more fully. The loving choice is rarely the only option available as a course of action. Perhaps in Nazi Germany there were such moments: "Do I disclose the whereabouts of my Jewish neighbors?" In most cases there are perhaps numerous courses of action that will open up loving possibilities. Thus a child could become a train driver or a baseball player or a nurse and all could be right. All could create numerous moments that would enhance love in its totality within the universe. The ability to frustrate love is of course different. These are conscious decisions to thwart loving possibilities.

The whole project of creation within process theology makes human beings "co-creators" with God. Humanity is in the business, with God, of furthering the ends of love, which, in the end, is God's will. As has already been noted, there may be at any one moment probably several good and legitimate ways of progressing love. In the same way, as there are many great stories an artist could depict, so there are many appropriate and worthwhile lives that can be lived. Yet the call of God does make a difference for each of our individual lives. It is the act of discernment that enables one to recognize that certain courses of action are not appropriate to the uniqueness of the individual. And, what may be considered the most important aspect of all, it remains a social obligation to ensure that all those around us are shaped by the same expectation of loving purpose that God has for each person. Process theology stresses the idea that a multitude of entities bring each subsequent entity into being. Each person is the result of a particular act of becoming and whose location begins as a result of numerous other decisions within creation, which have then been taken into the life of God, and then, finally, expressed themselves into a particular moment, only to continue the process ad infinitum.

Individual entities move to a given social entity and obligation almost imperceptibly. Process theology strongly rejects any doctrine of individualism, whether it is economic or political. All people are born into families, communities, and societal structures with a million and one connections already established and are finite creatures with particular links into the various structures (human and environmental) around us. Having been shaped by these social factors humanity will proceed to shape further social factors through the utilization of our gifts to the full. By "gifts" is meant those skills and talents that each person has been given and that are an integral part of their being.

In order to be followers of process theology, it is essential to make a full contribution to the demands of love. Love can be defined in one or both of the following ways. First, love may be acknowledged as God in God's self. Second, love may be lived and felt as the fulfillment and meaning to existence through the integral relations of God and God's creation. Love is wholeness; love is constructive; love is opening the world up to more loving possibilities. D. D. Williams in his classic *The Spirit and the Forms of Love* sets out a helpful history of the different accounts of love and then provides his philosophical critique of love in the light of the insights of process theology (Williams, 1968, 114–22). Williams suggests five categories as necessary for love. The first is individuality, and taking account of the other. This means that real people are needed who are willing to love the other in such a way that their identities are not crushed and their distinctiveness as people is recognized. The second is freedom. Although love often feels "fated" (i.e., there is nothing a person can do about the feeling that drives him or her), Williams wants to insist that freedom is important. Given our historical context we live in a world where the future is always unclear and contingent; "freedom in love" writes Williams, "consists in the way in which we accept, face, and interpret that risk." In addition, freedom also recognizes the freedom of the other, which can of course in love involve the possibility that the other will not love. The third is action and suffering. The action of giving in love to others will inevitably bring suffering. Williams writes, "It is one of the conditions of love that suffering enters into the texture and meaning of the relationship. It is by what is suffered as well as by what is given that love is recognised and its quality affirmed." The fourth is causality. This draws attention to the interconnectedness of love, and for Williams it links many of the other categories. So "causality in love involves not only the prehension of the past but response to possibilities in the future. Human freedom depends on real openness to the future … It is the requirement that for the reality of love human decisions must enter into the determination of the future." Fifth, love involves the impartial judgment in loving concern for the other. Love has to make many tricky decisions and this requires the capacity for impartial judgment. Williams writes: "The

settlement of claims in the light of an objective standard available to all is the meaning of equity, and equity is not the contradiction of love but one of the principles by which love respects the actualities of life. Without love we do fall below the standard of equity, and without forgiveness we miss the element in love which transcends purely rational justice."

Whitehead's critique of traditional Christian thought and a dismissal of the "hail the conquering hero" motif for God is the surface argument of process thought. However, love is at the heart of the process theologian, as exemplified by Whitehead's gentle and profound interpretation of God:

> There is, however, in the Galilean origin of Christianity yet another suggestion which does not fit very well with any of the three main strands of thought. It does not emphasize the ruling Caesar, or the ruthless moralist, or the unmoved mover. It dwells upon the tender elements in the world, which slowly and in quietness operate by love; and it finds purpose in the present immediacy of a kingdom not of this world. Love neither rules, nor is it unmoved; also it is a little oblivious to morals. It does not look to the future; for it finds its own reward in the immediate present. (Whitehead, 1978, 343)

The ever-changing flux of our world will create new and different situations quite naturally. Ultimately, it is God who remains in constant cognition of the minutiae of our universe, shaping each of our locations and granting us the capacity to create new skills, while everything we accomplish and feel is being taken into the life of God who is truth. God then returns to us all of those accomplishments and feelings perfected by God to create even more opportunities for love to triumph. Process theology provides an important insight into how the Creator and the created are interrelated and can move towards "the vision without which people perish" and to "become the change they wish to see in the world."

References

Augustine. 1984. *Concerning the City of God Against the Pagans*, trans. Henry Bettenson. London: Penguin Books.

Case-Winters, Anna. 1990. *God's Power: Traditional Understandings and Contemporary Challenges*. Westminster: John Knox.

Cobb, Jr., John B. 1966. *A Christian Natural Theology*. London: Lutterworth Press.

Cobb, John B. 1969. *God and the World*. Philadelphia: Westminster Press.

Cobb, Jr., John B. 1976. *Process Theology: An Introductory Exposition*. Philadelphia: Westminster Press.

Cobb, Jr., John B. and Gamwell, Franklin I., eds. 1984. *Conversations with Charles Hartshorne*. Chicago: University of Chicago Press.

Cobb, Jr., John B. and Griffin, D. R. 1976. *Process Theology: An Introductory Exposition*. Philadelphia: The Westminster Press.

Cobb, John B. and Griffin, David Ray. 1978. *Mind in Nature: Essays on the Interface of Science and Philosophy*. Washington, DC: University Press of America.

Gragg, Alan. 1973. *Charles Hartshorne*. Waco, TX: Word Books.

Hartshorne, Charles. 1970. *Creative Synthesis*. London: SCM Press.

Hartshorne, Charles. 1984. *Existence and Actuality: Conversations with Charles Hartshorne*. Chicago: University of Chicago Press.

Ledbetter, Shannon. 2002. "Vocation and Our Understanding of God." In *Modern Believing*, 2(4): 38–49.

Mellert, Robert B. 1975. *What Is Process Theology?* New York: Paulist Press.

Nash, Ronald, ed. 1987. *Process Theology*. Grand Rapids, MI: Baker Book House.

Pittenger, N. 1967. *God in Process*. London: SCM Press.

Pittenger, N. 1982. *Picturing God*. London: SCM Press.

Whitehead, A. N. 1978. *Process and Reality*, corrected edition, ed. D. R. Griffin and D. W. Sherburne. New York: The Free Press.

Williams, Daniel Day. 1968. *The Spirit and the Forms of Love*. New York: Harper and Row.

Karl Rahner (1904–84)

F. J. Michael McDermott

Born March 5, 1904 in Freiburg, Karl Rahner received a classical formation in a *Gymnasium* before following his brother Hugo into the Society of Jesus in 1922. After a two-year novitiate he was educated in Suarezian Thomism for philosophy (Feldkirch and Pullach) and theology (Valkenberg). He was ordained on July 23, 1932. All the while he was also studying the church fathers and St Thomas's own texts. Sent to Freiburg for a doctorate in history of philosophy, he fell under the influence of M. Heidegger and accepted basic insights from the transcendental Thomism of Maréchal and Rousselot—to such an extent that his mentor, Martin Honecker, refused to accept the doctoral thesis, *Spirit in the World* (1939), due to its alleged departure from St Thomas's thought. Rahner returned in 1936 to the theological faculty at the University of Innsbruck where he completed a theological doctorate on a patristic theme as well as other requirements for university teaching, and began lecturing in theology in 1937. After the Nazis closed the theological faculty and the Jesuit college in 1939, he went to Vienna's Pastoral Institute as a theological consultant. In that role he delivered a series of lectures in Salzburg, later published as *Hearers of the Word* (1941), a brilliant theological anthropology showing how man is naturally open to revelation. During the war's last year he was pastor in a Bavarian parish. After teaching theology at Pullach for three years, he returned in 1948 to the newly reopened theology faculty at Innsbruck,

remaining there until a call to replace Romano Guardini in Munich arrived in 1964. His main interest focused on grace and justification, but he also taught courses on creation and original sin, the theological virtues, and the sacraments of penance, anointing of the sick, and holy orders.

Although over the years his outspokenness had led to some limitations on speaking engagements as well as several rejections of written works by Jesuit censors, he enjoyed the support of his order and many in the church. When the Holy Office imposed a preliminary Roman censorship in 1962, his friends countered by having John XXIII appoint him a *peritus* for the upcoming Vatican Council. He also served as Cardinal König's special advisor. With the opening of Vatican II and his growing role in it the cloud over him dissipated. The council vindicated many of his positions, and he exercised a tremendous influence on postconciliar theology. From his countless talks, articles, sermons, spiritual reflections, and seminars, many were published in the 16 volumes of *Schriften zur Theologie* (1954–84: 23 volumes in English as *Theological Investigations*). From 1967 to 1971 he taught at Münster before returning in 1971 to Munich. There he published *Foundations of Christian Faith* (1976), which some consider his final speculative synthesis centered on christology, but it really presupposes *Spirit, Hearers,* and many articles. In 1981 he went back to Innsbruck, where death met him on March 30, 1984. His bibliography

The Student's Companion to the Theologians, First Edition. Edited by Ian S. Markham.
© 2013 Blackwell Publishing Ltd. Published 2013 by Blackwell Publishing Ltd.

is immense (cf. Pedley, 1984 for a partial bibliography) and his works were translated into many languages. Besides founding the series *Quaestiones Disputatae*, he also edited various lexicons, including the second edition of *Lexikon für Theologie und Kirche* (10 volumes) and *Sacramentum Mundi* (four volumes, six in English). On the whole his theology is marked by extraordinary flexibility and a firm rooting in Catholic dogmatic tradition, resulting doubtless from his wide reading in the fathers and his four editions of Denzinger's collection of magisterial pronouncements. Although he sometimes pushed the limits of flexibility in his interpretations of dogma and was outspoken in his criticism of church officials, he never denied any dogma of the church, to which Ignatian spirituality bound him (Fischer, 1974; Vorgrimler, 1986; Neufeld, 2004). Though he has been sharply criticized by some for being unthomistic and inadequately Catholic (Fabro, 1974; Vass, 1985), most theologians appreciate his enormous contributions to twentieth-century theology.

In theology Rahner early determined to overcome the sharp neo-scholastic distinctions between nature and grace, reason and faith, that apparently relegated revelation to the role of an external intrusion or addition to an already completed nature. Man's natural desire for the beatific vision, creatively exploited for Thomism by Rousselot, served to relativize the conceptual distinction between natural and supernatural, philosophy and theology. To ground his unified vision, in *Spirit* (1939) Rahner borrowed Heidegger's starting point: man as the question which opens an infinite horizon of being in its search for an answer. Unlike Heidegger, whose question was rooted in the feeling of concern swelling to anxiety, Rahner postulated a thematic question, an intellectual act that implies knowledge in its very quest to overcome confessed ignorance. This question arising from man's innermost depths reveals his internal constitution, which consists in an Augustinian thirst for truth and love, incapable of assuagement short of God. Interpreting radically the Thomistic axiom of being's convertibility with truth, Rahner identified being with luminous self-consciousness (*Sein ist Bei-sich-sein*). Thus the proportionate object of human knowing is double: self and the essence of a material reality. Presence-to-self paradoxically implies a certain distance from self. This alienation from self is grounded in the intellectual opacity and ontological non-being of matter. Unity and diversity of spirit and matter are reflected in the Thomistic understanding of soul as both the form of matter and the opposite of matter. Unlike the more static conceptual distinction of essential form from unintelligible matter, Rahner's spirit, primarily existential, involves a constant *Schwebe*, oscillation and tension, between itself and matter. The spirit's union with matter's opacity forces it to go outside itself in order to come back to itself to possess itself. Besides functioning as the principle of individuality, matter serves to place the incarnate spirit into relation with the material universe. Bodiliness implies limitation by other bodies, and limitation implies contact, and, therefore, continuity. Rahner even held later that the universe can be conceived as "the single body of multiple self-consciousnesses" (1976, 190). Thus the Cartesian problem of the bridge between subjective knowing and external reality has been overcome since external reality has already entered the subjective spirit's sphere of luminosity. The attempt to overcome matter's lack of intellectual luminosity, which finds manifestation in the question, propels the spirit beyond itself and everything finite toward the infinite horizon of being. No finite concept, judgment, or reality can satisfy the spiritual dynamism's quest for meaning. For once a limit is recognized, it is already intellectually surpassed. The intellectual movement is designated by the word *Vorgriff*, "a grasping beforehand"; it dynamically anticipates the final possession of the term of its movement. Very much in a participation schema, it reflects both the positivity and the negativity of the initial question: on the one hand, it possesses in part the term toward which it is attracted; on the other, it is not yet in full possession.

The term of the *Vorgriff* is variously identified. In *Spirit* incarnate spirit moves toward *esse commune*. Since man's knowing is expressed in a judgment, or *conversio ad phantasma*, which infrangibly links subject and predicate as categorical reality and transcendent horizon, man's knowledge of being always involves a reference to material being. This horizon of being known in judgment, an *esse* which oscillates between the material singular and infinite extension, is *esse commune*. Beyond the limitation of such knowledge and being is *esse absolutum*, God; yet insofar as God can be conceptualized, he can be located within the horizon.

For man also forms an analogous concept of being, which in its unity-plurality oscillates like the judgment between matter and God. Indeed the judgment of being can be conceptualized. Hence Rahner's dynamic, existential (ontological) categories can be expressed in more static (ontic) categories, and vice versa. This possibility of mutual translation of the two languages permitted him to uphold the permanent validity of traditional dogmatic statements, even when they can be improved and reformulated (Burke, 2002; McDermott, 1994, 1996, 2007).

Rahner developed a proof of God's existence in *Hearers* (1941 and 1963) from an analysis of man's basic judgment-question. The knowledge implicit in the question seeks a final ground beyond itself. Contrary to Sartre, the transcendent point of reference cannot be nothing; otherwise intelligibility is denied. Contrary to Heidegger, the spirit's unending transcending cannot itself be identified with being, for such a "finite infinity" would be recognized as finite and thereby transcended. The only alternative is the recognition of a God as pure Existence, capable of terminating man's fundamental desire. Since no concept of God, *qua* finite, can satisfy that desire, only God seen face-to-face suffices to render man intelligible to himself within God's infinite mystery. Thus Rahner explicated Thomas's doctrine of the natural desire for the beatific vision (McDermott, 1988).

The spirit's movement over the world to God grounds Rahner's doctrine of analogy. Since judgment transcends the concept in providing man's access to reality, philosophy does not start with a univocal concept which is stretched by the ways of negation and eminence to refer to God's infinity. Rather the analogous is prior to the univocal. Insofar as there is no objectivity except over the judging subject and the subject cannot be understood apart from his term, a net of mutually illuminating relations is established: the realities of this world cannot be understood without reference to the human subject, nor can the incarnate subject be understood without reference to the world and God; finally, God without reference to the world and incarnate subjects. Thus theology can be understood as anthropology, not in reducing God to man's measure à la Feuerbach but in opening man to God's infinite mystery. For man exists in dynamic relation to both God and world, the oscillating middle

between them. In this the basic structure of the judgment, or *conversio ad phantasma*, has been developed. The one act of judgment unites subject with predicate, categorical, i.e., material, reality with transcendental horizon, over the dynamic subject. Indeed sensation, abstraction, and judgment all occur in the same *conversio ad phantasma*. Insofar as sensation recognizes the perceived other as other, it is already transcending the limit constituting the otherness toward the unlimited horizon. Insofar as the sensible other stands under the infinite horizon of being, which knowing presupposes, it is recognized as limited; as such it does not exhaust the horizon and can be repeated indefinitely; this repeatability is the defining characteristic of the universal concept. In this way the ultimate unity of sensation, abstraction, and judgment corresponds to the ultimate unity in man of body, soul, and existence, which corresponds to the ontological unity in beings of matter, form, and existence. Because of its production in the *conversio ad phantasma*, Rahner's universal concept is not just pure, abstracted form; it always contains an implicit reference to the material singular. Thus the universal is always linked to the concrete instance and conceptualization's structure entirely parallels judgment's; indeed they are the same (McDermott, 1994, 1996; Burke, 2002). (Thomas similarly recognizes form's reference to "common matter": the form "man" must include some bodiliness if "man" is not to be equated with an angel.)

The dynamic, incarnate spirit also overcomes the neo-scholastic division of intellect and will, identified in terms of their formal object, the true and the good. As a desire, the intellect moves to the true as its good. Since the original judgment involves the necessary affirmation of a contingent, singular existent, the contingent is related to the horizon of being as its ground. Not having its own necessity, it depends for its existence upon God, the horizon, who has posited it freely. Since every human affirmation is responding to God's original, free positing, that response involves an answering love. Thus man's necessary knowledge contains a love, and, as the true and good are convertible— God terminates the intellectual drive as Truth and Goodness—intellect and will mutually influence each other. Hence the free decision "co-determines" knowledge and "the deepest truth is also the most free" (1963, 131). Since man is oriented beyond all limiting materiality to an infinite horizon as the term of his love, no finite object can compel the will's adhesion. Naturally this "freedom" does not consist of an arbitrary choice. Rather human freedom depends entirely upon God and the more one gives of oneself in responding to God's call, the closer one is united to God, man's true end, and the more one is oneself. Radical dependence on God and creaturely autonomy grow in the same proportion. Such freedom is not grounded in a neutral faculty, distanced from reality by the process of abstraction, but consists in a subject concretely engaged, deciding about and making itself, for or against God in every choice; it is the capacity for determining oneself before God definitively. Ultimately true freedom is liberated freedom (Rahner, 1976; McDermott, 1990).

Despite his strong emphasis on dynamic liberated freedom and explicit rejection of freedom as a neutral faculty, Rahner did not entirely exclude the neo-scholastic freedom of indifference. However well man's orientation to God, the infinite Good, explains the divine causality in effecting every human choice of finite goods, which participate in the infinite God, the fact that man can sin implies that he can distance himself from his natural orientation and pervert it. Were this choice between good and evil not possible, Rahner's theory of the fundamental option would be an illusion (cf. below). Furthermore, in christology, while maintaining Christ's beatific vision, Rahner justified his distinction of the beatific vision, non-conceptual or unthematic, from Jesus' gradual thematization of his unthematic knowledge on the ground that his human liberty required choices and limited knowledge in overcoming temptation (McDermott, 2007).

Lest the natural desire for the beatific vision seem an arrogant intrusion by man into God's intimacy and destroy the natural–supernatural distinction fundamental to Catholic theology, Rahner made provision for its preservation. While the spiritual dynamism's movement threatens to relativize conceptual abstractions, without concepts no distinction can be upheld, and without distinction no movement occurs. Rahner, as we saw, grounded universal abstractions in the spiritual dynamism itself. Hence concepts enjoy a certain validity and can serve the distinction between nature and grace. Although man is de facto oriented to grace and glory—there is only one supernatural order in

actuality—in a concreteness that does not allow for an adequate distinction between nature and grace, one might speak of a "remainder concept" of nature as that which would remain, if all supernatural elements were abstracted from man's existential state. This notion of nature, which cannot be definitively specified, might serve as the basis to which the supernatural is added. Yet corresponding with Rahner's oscillating analogy the dynamic correlate of the static concept is understood as the spirit's movement that asymptotically approaches God, "greeting Him, as it were, from afar" (1963, 102f.) On this nature, inadequately grasped in concepts, God bestows a supernatural existential, i.e., a concrete elevation in the existential order that does not mutate or destroy the nature in the essential order. Thus the spiritual nature's dynamism is de facto oriented to the God of grace. Henceforth man's dynamic nature is conceived as a *potentia obedientialis* actively opening itself to grace as its own surpassing culmination. Without this elevating addition the dynamic existential nature would be oriented to *esse commune* in a movement that constantly fails to attain its term. For man can never on his own overcome his own material infinity, his cloying frustrating bind to matter; without grace this natural movement would be "that empty and hollow infinity, that dark and in its doubt self-devouring infinity, that we ourselves are, the infinity of discontented finitude" (Rahner, 1956, 57; McDermott, 2007).

The intellectual-volitive dynamism spanning the natural–supernatural distinction functions as the axis around which Rahner's subsequent theology develops. In writing "theology is anthropology" he intended to open man to the infinite, grounding his mystery in the ever greater mystery of God. For if man has a natural desire for the supernatural, God desires to save all men, communicating himself in grace. Grace is primarily understood as the unmerited condescension whereby God becomes immediately present in the human soul, offering himself and effecting his own reception. This "coming close" of God effects in the soul sanctifying grace as its first created product, which in mutual causality also serves as the soul's ultimate disposition, elevating it to receive the divine indwelling—just as the *lumen gloriae* is the ultimate disposition for the beatific vision as well as its first effect. Surely the continuity between grace and its flowering in the intuitive vision of God allows each aspect of the mystery to illuminate the other. Since actual graces in scholastic theology are oriented to sanctifying grace, Rahner could subsume them also into the experience of uncreated grace; they no longer were necessary preparations for sanctifying grace, now offered continually to all—indeed constituting interiorly the human being—and after sanctifying grace's reception they might be explained as its subsequent effects in insight and actions. (Rahner also considered the first offer of grace to man "actual grace," apparently to preserve human freedom's co-operation; although the immediate presence of God to the soul does not allow freedom of indifference, but, like the beatific vision, renders man impeccable, Rahner knew that some "room" must be made between God and the soul to allow for grace's rejection as well as its reception.) While it might seem strange to speak of God as "coming close" to man in grace insofar as his infinity (or in scholastic language, "immensity") renders him omnipresent, the conceptual distinction between God and the world, presupposed in the doctrine of creation by efficient causality, allows God and man to be distinguished and juxtaposed metaphysically "previous" to their juncture in grace. Though from the dynamic perspective the unity of God and man is considered "ultimate," i.e., "the first and ultimate reality [*das Erste und das Letzte*]," from the more static conceptual perspective God alone is the "one distinct from all others" as "the absolute ground of all particular beings" (1976, 67, 70–2). The union of grace and glory is described in terms of "quasi-formal causality" in order to indicate both the similarity with formal causality in the immediacy of union and that God's immensity, even while informing the finite soul, cannot be restricted to it as a proportionate form but utterly transcends the soul it informs (Burke, 2002; McDermott, 2007).

This oscillation in perspective between the God–man unity and their distinction devolves from Rahner's awareness of the fundamental metaphysical conundrum of the One and the many. For Rahner as a Christian and a modern thinker God is infinite: hence creation cannot be outside him, yet creation must be distinct from him, its free cause. Concepts are necessary for distinguishing one reality from another. Rahner postulated an analogous concept of being oscillating between matter's non-being and God's

infinite *esse*. Hence God and the world can be conceptually juxtaposed and this separation allows efficient causality—an external causality—to describe the relation between them in creation. Yet a dynamic understanding transcends the difference toward unity. Rahner employed the natural existential dynamism to join natural and supernatural orders as well as God and man. Yet, given the gratuity of grace, he portrayed God as coming to man in his self-offer. If grace is accepted under the attraction of the Good, then God is imagined as present in and to the soul, informing it while transcending it. Actually God's natural immensity would seem to render redundant a separate presence in grace, but Thomistic theology always suffers this embarrassment. The tension is even greater for Rahner insofar as finite being is inherently self-conscious: God's immediate present to the soul means that the soul must be conscious of him, but this would entail equivalently the beatific vision, which Rahner wished to restrict to the incarnate Christ alone (McDermott, 2007).

Despite the direct presence of God offered to all men, Rahner did not deny the doctrine of original sin. He realized that Adam's sin had severely influenced his progeny. Since human freedom is constituted interiorly by its relation to the world which represents the concrete objectifications of other finite freedoms for good and for ill, the sins of others condition the exercise of every individual's freedom. One cannot entirely dispose of oneself in a free act since resistance is encountered within one's own nature. Concupiscence can be understood as the human dynamism preceding free choice as its conditions of possibility but also as the resistance offered to one's desire to dedicate oneself completely in a free choice. This can prevent a complete commitment to evil as much as impede a total dedication to God. The latter aspect is concupiscence in a strict theological sense, resulting from and inciting to sin. It is "natural" to man because of the distinction between person and nature which manifests itself most obviously in the tension between spirit and body, yet it is simultaneously "unnatural" insofar as it hinders man's concrete calling to live for eternity in union with God. If an oscillation of perspective marks Rahner's doctrine on concupiscence, a similar oscillation structures his understanding of original sin: on the one hand, due to Adam's sin man is marked by an "existential" as the lack of grace that should be present; on the other hand, grace is also offered freely to every man as his "existential" *propter Christum*. Because grace's presence cannot be adequately thematized, it is impossible for men to know with certitude whether or not they are in the state of grace (Rahner, 1954, 1967b, 1976).

On the theme of revelation Rahner's thought underwent a momentous shift. Previous to 1963 he propounded the traditional neo-scholastic interpretation whereby supernaturally revealed propositions (truths) are the material object of faith. To these correspond a subjectivity elevated by grace so as to be capable of perceiving the supernatural quality of its object and giving its assent. The *praeambula fidei*, i.e., the natural signs and arguments preparing the way for faith, would be recognized and properly interpreted in the assent itself. But, since faith as an infused supernatural virtue implies sanctifying grace, which is caused by uncreated grace's presence in the soul, and because the soul is present to itself, the soul must be immediately, though unthematically, aware of God's presence. Hence, God's self-communication in grace is equivalently his revelation, and man's acceptance of grace is faith. Consequently Rahner shifted the primacy from propositional revelation to "transcendental revelation." Since grace and revelation coincide in human subjectivity and God wishes all men to be saved (1 Tim. 2:4), his saving revelation must be offered interiorly to all. Christian faith does not depend upon indoctrination from without; the preacher should presume faith in his hearers, an unthematic faith which has to be led to complete christological and ecclesiological thematization. Fundamental theology's task consists then in demonstrating the correspondence of the explicit Christian message with man's interior experience of grace. Since dogmatic theology deals with the reality of God's self-revelation, it too is referred back to the subject's experience of grace. For "the entirety of the Christian message of faith is given in a transcendental experience" (1970, 122). Transcendental experience, however, is not ahistorical since the structure of human knowing involves always a reference to the phantasm, a sensible singular (Burke, 2002; McDermott, 2007).

The great mystery of the triune God in experienced in grace. Since there is no objectivity apart from subjectivity, the immanent Trinity is identical with the economic Trinity. Man's experience of God must correspond to who God is in himself. Indeed the missions are grounded in the processions. Since there is but a single existence and consciousness in God, the three persons are experienced as three *modes* of presence or subsistence: the Father as the incomprehensible ground and origin of the mystery of salvation, the Word as encountering man in concrete history, and the Holy Spirit as divinizing the inmost center of the individual. The two missions are conceived not as independent but as existing in mutual causality. While apparently the subjective starting point might render inconceivable a Trinity without reference to the world, the relative validity of concepts, which abstract from time and space, permit God to be thought without reference to the world. Thus the Trinitarian persons, considered in themselves, can be called modes of subsistence and, considered in the economy, can be called modes of presence, i.e., present to human subjects. The missions and the processions are also identified—the economic Trinity is the immanent Trinity—insofar as the immutable God decides to create and redeem the world. These two stages of the same decision, preserving the double gratuity of creation and grace, are not identical with God's eternal essence insofar as they produce contingent terms outside of God; creation does not emanate from God necessarily. Nonetheless, since these freely chosen acts are not accidental to God, they must belong to His essence, which is thereby placed into relation with the world and mankind. Thus, even in God the oscillation between unity and plurality has its place, reflecting the unity in diversity of concept and judgment (1967a, 1969).

A similar oscillation is found in Rahner's christology, which adopts various starting points, first from above, then from below. Noting first that plurality need not be an imperfection insofar as the Trinity involves diversity in unity, Rahner argued that a symbolic reality necessarily expresses itself in order to come to itself. So the human soul expresses itself in a body to realize itself. Likewise in the Trinity the Father knows himself in the Word and is who he is only in relation to the Word in the Holy Spirit. Then in deciding to express himself *ad extra*, he creates the world in order that he might reveal himself most adequately in the humanity of Christ. As the Word reflects the Father, so the Son expresses himself in Christ's humanity, and Christ's soul reveals itself through his body. All that Jesus did, suffered, and taught reflects the divinity and because of the unity in diversity of the symbol with the symbolized, even the Sacred Heart of Jesus can be accorded adoration. Corresponding to that movement from above is a movement from below in which Christ's human nature, seen within an evolutionary movement upward toward God, in recognized as a *potentia obedientialis* for the hypostatic union. Thus human nature desires the hypostatic union as well as the beatific vision. As an authentic human center of self-consciousness and freedom, Jesus' humanity freely responds to the grace offered. From the very beginning the humanity enjoys the beatific vision as a constitutive element of the hypostatic union. This unthematic vision, however, is not entirely conceptualized in Jesus' intellect. Hence growth in thematic knowledge occurs and crises of identity might arise. Rahner even allowed for a certain "error" about the imminent arrival of the parousia insofar as Jesus' intention to express God's immediate proximity—the truth intended—borrowed limited concepts from his culture to convey that truth in temporal terms. Consequently, despite maintaining the immediate vision of God in Jesus' humanity, Rahner attributed to Jesus also faith vis-à-vis the mystery of God. The movement from below culminates in the event of cross and resurrection, Jesus' perfect response to grace that is accepted by the Father. Thus this moment from below to perfect self-giving in death complements the movement from above which otherwise might have appeared to let the fact of the incarnation be the supreme revelation of God. In this way Rahner wished to maintain the eternal validity of all that Jesus did—as the ultimate revelation of God—while preserving the real significance of growth toward cross and resurrection. Thus time possesses a significance even for God who is said in his historical self-expression to "become on the other" while remaining immutable in himself. Insofar as we know God as he is and this involves God's relation to us in time, a type of becoming, reaching its culmination in Christ, exists in God, but insofar as God can be conceived as apart from the world he remains essentially immutable. This distinction between God in himself with his abstract "metaphysical" properties as Absolute Being and his

freely chosen behavior in the economy is rooted in God's transcendent freedom over the world, which allows him to enter the world and make history his own irrevocably in Jesus Christ (Sanna, 1970; Wong, 1984; Burke, 2002; McDermott, 1986, 2007).

Although Rahner held that God's will to save became irreversible and irrevocable with Christ, he also maintained—again oscillating between economic and metaphysical qualities—that God's love of the world has been constant; his wrath did not have to be transformed into love by what Christ accomplished in redemption. Love is the incarnation's reason. The incarnation–cross–resurrection constitute the manifestation of that love with a quasi-sacramental type of causality. Jesus redeems us not just by affecting all in the spiritual–material web of this world's interrelationships but primarily by being the highest member in the order of grace which is the cause of all others in that order, influencing the others by a type of final causality. Though Rahner admitted the metaphysical difficulty of grounding the necessity for the permanent mediation of Christ's humanity, he insisted on it, recalling that even the beatific vision does not immediately beatify the soul but employs the created *lumen gloriae* to mediate the soul's access to glory. This insistence on mediated immediacy preserves the initial structure of the judgment, the spirit's double reference to categorical, material realities and the infinite horizon (McDermott, 1986, 2007).

Grace finds its complete revelation at the resurrection. Since there is no objectivity without subjectivity, the resurrection includes believing witnesses. This event constitutes the church, which is the continuing manifestation of Christ's victorious grace in time. In members of the church the grace of Christ effects its symbolic presence until the end of time; otherwise Christ's definitive revelation would disappear from the earth and God's plan of salvation would be frustrated. Thus divine predestination guarantees the church permanence and infallibility, the capacity to define her belief. Scriptural inspiration is interpreted as the expression of the church's common belief which the church recognizes to be in accord with her own life of grace. The bishops and pope serve as ultimate instances of defining faith but always in relation to the people of God as two poles mutually conditioning each other. The magisterium functions not as an authority above revelation, but as an internal constituent of revelation itself, providing the ambient or tradition in which scripture is properly understood. Beyond scripture and tradition the event of grace–revelation–faith finds a "denser" expression in the sacraments. Since the church is interpreted as the primordial sacrament (*Ursakrament*), the sign making grace present in the world, the Eucharist serves as the central sacrament, the supreme actualization of the church's social, hierarchical, ministerial life of grace, to which all the other sacraments are oriented as their source and goal. It perdures as a visible sign of the Lord's love from Holy Thursday until the world's end. Because grace intends a corporeal expression, sacramental efficacy *ex opere operato* is conceived primarily in terms of final causality. "The sign effects grace insofar as grace effects the sacrament as *sign* of the occurrence of grace" (Rahner, 1961, 36). There is a double oscillation in this sacramental theory. On the one hand, though grace is given immediately to individuals, the church as a whole bears the reality of Christ's eschatological victory; the failure of individuals does not destroy the sacramental efficacy *ex opere operato*. This juncture to the social whole is to be expected since grace presupposes while penetrating and perfecting a nature that is corporeal and social. On the other hand, while grace effects the sacramental sign as its inherent finality, the sign itself refers in its finality back to God, the source of all being and grace. The same oscillation in a relation of mutual causality characterizes the original, existential judgment's unity in diversity of subject and predicate manifests itself in the relations between God and Christ's humanity and between God and the church sacraments. This is to be expected, given the fluid transition, unity in diversity, between grace and nature as well as between affirming subject and objective reality affirmed. While from one viewpoint the ultimate unity of God and world (*esse commune*) would let God "become on the other" and be influenced (or "caused") by the sacramental sign, from the other viewpoint the diversity of God (*esse absolutum*) and world maintained by conceptual distinction ensures God's utter transcendence of the world (Fields, 2000; Burke, 2002; McDermott, 2006, 2007).

The dynamic flexibility of Rahner's thought allowed him to answer major problems of conceptualist theology that identified supernatural revelation with propositions promulgated on authority. These propositions surpassing human insight hardly submitted to the development of dogma discovered by historical research. Similarly the necessity of explicit faith in propositional truths made it difficult to take seriously God's universal salvific will. For without faith there is no salvation (Heb. 11:6; Rom. 10:9–17). Rahner's notion of an unthematic faith permitted him to see dogmatic development as a series of explications of faith within various cultural and philosophical horizons. Though the defined pronouncements of the magisterium remain always true, authoritative, and inerrant, because of their inability to exhaust the infinite mystery to which they refer, they are capable of being reformulated according to the needs of diverse cultures and epochs. In 1970 Rahner defended papal (and ecclesial) infallibility against H. Küng, who denied that any finite statement might adequately grasp the divine mystery (Rahner, 1970a); yet later he admitted that opposed, even contradictory statements can be justified as true as long as, being finite, analogous expressions, they refer to the divine mystery. This obviously reduces the significance of infallibility insofar as every statement about God, except a deliberate lie, intends the truth and is thereby infallible. The church's mediation is likewise diminished in importance since God always offers to all men the grace of Christ as constituting their being human; those who accepted that grace without explicit awareness are anonymous Christians. Indeed, insofar as the anonymous grace finds expression in non-Christian religions, these can be considered means of leading men to God. Nonetheless, precisely because grace tends to its full expression and God's will should be sought in its fullness, all men are obliged to seek the fullness of truth and revelation in the Catholic Church (Burke, 2002; McDermott, 2007).

Though Rahner wrote little explicitly on ethics, he exercised great influence on recent developments. Since God is known and loved in relation to the world, the unity of love of God and of neighbor is so profound that neither can be found without the other, at least implicitly. Insofar as concepts are valid, he could uphold universal, or "absolute," norms, yet since objectivity is always related to a subject dynamically oriented to a transcendent God, God's will could be mediated directly in individual cases. All men are faced with a fundamental option, i.e., in making a choice to accept or reject God's love mediated through finite creatures, especially human beings. Because freedom's choice occurs at a depth beyond thematic awareness, it can happen that an atheist explicitly denying God is unthematically affirming him in his life, just as a confessing Christian may in the depths of his being be an atheist, denying God. Given the union of body and soul and, over the body, man's link with the universe, Rahner tended to emphasize the situatedness of all choices. Without denying the possibility of a fundamental option, he indicated how materiality prevents, short of death, the total giving of oneself to any single choice. Indeed, since God is the condition of possibility of all thinking and willing, implicitly affirmed in every judgment and choice, it is hard to explain how God can be refused freely by men. Nonetheless, since human freedom would be meaningless if man could not take a definitive stance to his life as a whole and to its ground, God, Rahner held that a fundamental option against God, though "a real, absolute contradiction" (1976, 106), was possible (McDermott, 1990, 2007).

The central nucleus of Rahner's thought consists in the flexible unity in diversity of subject and object, transcendental horizon and categorical reality, manifested in the initial question–judgment. Add the consequence of the natural–supernatural diversity in unity and one can find a very flexible intellectual instrument for making the Christian faith relevant to the modern age and answering some difficult questions about dogmatic development. Used by an intelligent, balanced theologian well grounded in the tradition and loyal to the church, Rahner's thought can illuminate many aspects of the Christian mystery. Its danger derives from its very flexibility: all dogmas can dissolve into the central, ineffable mystery which is reduced to the individual subject's experience of the infinite God. Historical mediation and inner-worldly objectivity can be excessively relativized. Ultimately there is no inherent reason why a particular pole of a tension is referred to another; much depends upon the theologian's subjective stance. To three diverse notions of nature (static correlate of the "remainder concept," intellectual-voluntary dynamism, and concretization of the past (*Verhältnis*, 334, 339–42; *Zum theologischen Begriff*, 393–5) may be added at least as

many notions of person (modes of presence and subsistence in Trinitarian theology, a self-conscious, free center of activity indistinguishable from an individual human nature, and the point of freedom with regard to the necessity of the past). A final reflection considers the same reality as person and nature, depending on the perspective taken: "God's self-expression (as content) is the man Jesus; the self-expression (as event) is the hypostatic union. Christology is the most radical anthropology (effected through God's free grace)" (1968, 952f.). Furthermore the relation between infinite and finite is not adequately clarified since a finite dynamism can never exhaust the infinite and a dynamism without the possibility of satisfaction is doomed to frustration (McDermott, 2007).

Out of Rahner's basic ontological-epistemological structure many postconciliar theologies have evolved. Insofar as nature and grace are dynamically amalgamated, a theology of secularity developed, refusing a dichotomy between sacred and secular and seeing grace at work in the secular realm. Insofar as nature is oriented to *esse commune* and can never fulfill its desire to see God, nature can be considered frustrated and senseless without grace. This explains why many Protestant theologians make use of Rahner's formulations without becoming Catholics and why Catholic theologians, consciously or not, uphold Protestant theses. While the basic Neoplatonic (Augustinian) thrust of Rahner's thought has encouraged ecumenical dialogue, the very imprecision or ambiguity of that thought must be overcome if final union is to be attained. Because will and intellect dynamically coalesce and the free decision "co-determines" knowledge, some theologians emphasize orthopraxis over orthodoxy and thus open the way to theologies of liberation without, unfortunately, providing intellectual norms for discerning the correctness of action. Because until the end he held on to the necessity of valid concepts, Rahner avoided extreme positions. Because he thought that ontic and ontological analyses could be translated into each other's terminology, he never explicitly denied any dogma of the Catholic Church, but he sought always to make dogma relevant to the experience of modern people. His flexibility of thought sometimes led him to reinterpret in novel ways traditional formulations. Due to his system's wide range and tremendous flexibility Rahner stands at the center of twentieth-century Christian theology. A student who masters Rahner's thought can easily dialogue with many other theologies and perceive the delicate balance that must be preserved in Catholic theology between the infinite God and man's finitude in being, knowing, and acting. For that fundamental tension finds recurrent expression in all areas of philosophy and theology.

References

Burke, Patrick. 2002. *Reinterpreting Rahner*. New York: Fordham University.

Fabro, Cornelio. 1974. *La Svolta antropologica di Karl Rahner*. Milan: Rusconi.

Fields, Stephen. 2000. *Being as Symbol*. Washington: Georgetown University.

Fischer, Klaus. 1974. *Der Mensch als Geheimnis*. Freiburg: Herder.

McDermott, John M. 1986. "The Christologies of Karl Rahner," *Gregorianum* 67: 87–123, 297–327.

McDermott, John M. 1988. "Rahner on Two Infinities: God and Matter," *International Philosophical Quarterly* 28: 439–57.

McDermott, John M. 1990. "Metaphysical Conundrums at the Root of Moral Disagreement," *Gregorianum* 71: 713–42.

McDermott, John M. 1994. "Dialectical Analogy: The Oscillating Center of Rahner's Thought," *Gregorianum* 75: 675–703.

McDermott, John M. 1996. "The Analogy of Knowing in Karl Rahner," *International Philosophical Quarterly* 26: 201–16.

McDermott, John M. 1999. "The Context of *Veritatis Splendor*." In *Prophecy and Diplomacy: The Moral Doctrine of John Paul II*, ed. John Conley and Joseph Koterski. New York: Fordham University, pp. 115–72.

McDermott, John M. 2006. "Vatican II and the Theologians on the Church as Sacrament," *Irish Theological Quarterly* 71: 143–78.

McDermott, John M. 2007. "Karl Rahner in Tradition: The One and the Many," *Fides Quaerens Intellectum* 3(2): 1–60.

Neufeld, Karl H. 2004. *Die Brüder Rahner*, 2nd ed. Freiburg: Herder.

Pedley, C. J. 1984. "An English Bibliographical Aid to Karl Rahner," *Heythrop Journal* 25: 319–65.

Rahner, Karl. 1939. *Geist in Welt*. Innsbruck: Rauch.

Rahner, Karl. 1941. *Hörer des Wortes*. Munich: Kösel-Pustet.

Rahner, Karl. 1954. "Zum theologischem Begriff der Konkuspiscenz." In *Schriften zur Theologie* 1: 377–414. Einsiedeln: Benziger.

Rahner, Karl. 1956. "Die ewige Bedeutung der Menschheit Jesu für unser Gottesverhältnis." In *Schriften zur Theologie* 3: 47–60. Einsiedeln: Benziger.

Rahner, Karl. 1960. "Zur Theologie des Symbols." In *Schriften zur Theologie* 4: 275–311. Einsiedeln: Benziger.

Rahner, Karl. 1961. *Kirche und Sakramente*. Freiburg: Herder.

Rahner, Karl. 1963. *Hörer des Wortes*, ed. Johannes B. Metz, 2nd ed. Munich: Kösel.

Rahner, Karl. 1967a. "Der dreifaltige Gott als transzendenter Urgrund der Heilsgeschichte." In *Mysterium Salutis*, ed. Johannes Feiner and Magnus Löhrer, 2: 317–401. Einsiedeln: Benziger.

Rahner, Karl. 1967b. "Erbsünde." In *Sacramentum Mundi*, ed. Karl Rahner and Alfons Darlap, 1: 1104–16. Freiburg: Herder.

Rahner, Karl. 1968. "Jesus Christus." In *Sacramentum Mundi*, ed. Karl Rahner and Alfons Darlap, 2: 922–54. Freiburg: Herder.

Rahner, Karl. 1969. "Trinität." In *Sacramentum Mundi*, ed. Karl Rahner and Alfons Darlap, 4: 1005–21. Freiburg: Herder.

Rahner, Karl. 1970a. "Kritik an Hans Küng," *Stimmen der Zeit* 186: 361–77.

Rahner, Karl. 1970b. "Überlegungen zur Methode der Theologie." In *Schriften zur Theologie*, 9: 79–126. Einsiedeln: Benziger.

Rahner, Karl. 1976. *Grundkurs des Glaubens*. Freiburg: Herder.

Sanna, Ignatio. 1970. *La cristologia antropologica di P. Karl Rahner*. Rome: Paoline.

Vass, George. 1985. *Understanding Karl Rahner*, 2 vols. London: Sheed and Ward.

Vorgrimler, Herbert. 1986. *Understanding Karl Rahner*, trans. John Bowden. New York: Crossroad.

Wong, Joseph. 1984. *Logos-Symbol in the Christology of K. Rahner*. Rome: Salesiano.

Rosemary Radford Ruether (1936–)

Medi Ann Volpe

Rosemary Radford Ruether is one of a handful of women whose impact on theology in the United States in the last 20 years would be hard to overestimate. Now the Carpenter Emerita Professor of Feminist Theology at Pacific School of Religion and the Graduate Theological Union, as well as the Georgia Harkness Emerita Professor of Applied Theology at Garrett Evangelical Theological Seminary, she is a visiting professor at Claremont Graduate University. Ruether prepared for her distinguished career in theology by studying philosophy, ancient history, classics, and patristics; she earned her PhD from Claremont Graduate School in 1965. Her dissertation, published as *Gregory of Nazianzus: Rhetor and Philosopher* (1969), argued that the theologian subordinated Christian theology to the demands of Greek philosophy: here one sees the beginning of Ruether's exploration of the tension between liberative Christian truth and the philosophical and traditional forms in which Christian theology developed. During her earliest years as a scholar, Ruether's interests included the question of women's ordination in the Roman Catholic Church, nuclear disarmament, the ecological crisis being hastened on by misuse of the earth, and black liberation theology (she reviewed James Cone's *Black Liberation Theology* and *Spirituals and the Blues*). In addition to her dissertation, during the 1970s she published numerous articles and several books in which she pursued this wide range of interests.

Ruether's background in ancient history and classics shaped what is perhaps her most widely read work, *Sexism and God-Talk: Toward a Feminist Theology*, originally published in 1983. Ruether's point of departure in her theological work—both in that volume and in her other projects—is a sense that something is wrong in Christian faith and practice. She takes into the study of theology the idea set forth in Betty Friedan's 1963 book, *The Feminine Mystique*. Friedan suggested that women were led to believe, falsely, that their fulfillment was to be found in caring for home and family. Ruether explores the question whether women's understanding of God, which often reinforced the patriarchal structures of church and society, is not based on false representations and mistakes about God handed down as tradition.

Ruether questions in a liberationist key the patriarchal practice of Christianity. Her concern for what promotes the full humanity of women is her guiding principle. Ruether's work thus focuses on extricating key Christian symbols from their patriarchal setting to reveal their liberative potential. Although Ruether observes that Christian practice has tended to perpetuate social structures of oppression, she acknowledges the persistent influence of Christian symbols. Instead of dismissing Christian faith, therefore, Ruether reinterprets its central doctrines, creating a new framework within which traditional symbols no longer serve patriarchy but point to its demise.

The Student's Companion to the Theologians, First Edition. Edited by Ian S. Markham.
© 2013 Blackwell Publishing Ltd. Published 2013 by Blackwell Publishing Ltd.

Ruether's *Sexism and God-Talk* offers a paradigmatic example of her work of reinterpretation.

In this foundational work, Ruether sifts through classical Christian doctrines in order to articulate the freeing word of the gospel clearly. For example, her reworked christology explores the question whether a male savior can save women. On the one hand, she answers clearly: no. If Jesus' maleness is normative, then women are excluded from the salvation he brings. That is, if only the male represents the fullness of human nature, then women—somehow less than fully human—are not included in the redeemed humanity signaled by Christ's resurrection. Ruether suggests, however, that the salient feature of the humanity of Jesus Christ is his social status, not his gender. Ruether proposes a christology in which Jesus symbolizes the marginalized and the oppressed—those whom God redeems through Christ.

Following *Sexism and God-Talk*, Ruether has continued to lead feminist theological discourse. Her *Women-Church: Theology and the Practice of Feminist Liturgical Communities* (1985) explores the implications of liberative Christian feminism for the shape of liturgy, while her introduction to Hildegard of Bingen, Mechthild of Madgeburg, and Julian of Norwich (*Visionary Women: Three Medieval Mystics*, 2001) suggests that the church has always recognized the potential for women's spiritual authority. Ruether's presentation of these three mystics locates them within local communities who enabled and preserved their work; the place of these women in the church's history attests to a tradition of recognizing women's capacity for holiness and prophetic gifts.

More recently, Ruether has published two major works of theological and historical import. Her *Goddesses and the Divine Feminine: A Western Religious History* (2005) traces the development of religious traditions, beginning with prehistory and continuing through ancient Hebrew, Gnostic, patristic and medieval religious symbol systems to Aztec-Christian and the Protestant millennial religious expressions. In this compendious study, Ruether engages the work of scholars in several disciplines, suggesting that there is greater depth and complexity to their feminine symbolism than has been recognized. In an equally significant volume, *Integrating Ecofeminism, Globalization, and World Religions (Nature's Meanings)* (2005), Ruether addresses the ideological implications of globalization, focusing on the intersection of ecology and religion with issues of race, class, and gender. Her research suggests that resistance to corporate global power forces open spaces within which we can imagine a world not subordinate to them, and looks to the positive contribution of ecofeminist spirituality and ethics in precisely this imaginative work.

Ruether's critical stance toward Christian tradition has not always been graciously received. Her position on the ordination of women in particular has put her at odds with the Vatican her entire career. Yet some of the criticisms of Ruether's work are not unjustified. From Ruether's earliest works one finds a tendency to attribute that which conceals the liberative potential in Christian symbols to the improper importation of external philosophical systems in the development of doctrine. Methodologically, then, the task of the liberation theologian is to pry loose the symbol from its philosophical-cultural lodging in patriarchy. This strategy, however, will not do: postmodern feminist theologians have here charted new territory that views the development of Christian theology differently. Nevertheless, Ruether, now in her fourth decade of leadership in feminist theology, continues to influence a younger generation of scholars whose work takes forward the questions she has raised throughout her career.

References

Hinton, Rosalind. 2003. "Contextualizing Rosemary," *Cross-Currents* 53: 600–3.

LaCugna, Catherine Mowry. 1993. *Freeing Theology: The Essentials of Theology in Feminist Perspective*. San Francisco: Harper San Francisco.

Ruether, Rosemary Radford. 1969. *Gregory of Nazianzus: Rhetor and Philosopher*. Oxford: Clarendon Press.

Ruether, Rosemary Radford. 1976. "What Is the Task of Theology?" *Christianity and Crisis* (May): 121–5.

Ruether, Rosemary Radford. 1983. *Sexism and God-Talk: Toward a Feminist Theology*. Boston: Beacon Press.

Ruether, Rosemary Radford. 1985. *Women-Church: Theology and Practice of Feminist Liturgical Communities.* San Francisco: Harper and Row.

Ruether, Rosemary Radford. 1998. *Women and Redemption: A Theological History.* Philadelphia: Fortress Press.

Ruether, Rosemary Radford. 2001. *Visionary Women: Three Medieval Mystics.* Minneapolis, MN: Fortress Press.

Ruether, Rosemary Radford. 2005a. *Goddesses and the Divine Feminine: A Western Religious History.* Berkeley: University of California Press.

Ruether, Rosemary Radford. 2005b. *Integrating Ecofeminism, Globalization, and World Religions. Nature's Meaning.* Lanham, MD: Rowman & Littlefield Publishers.

Thistlethwaite, Susan Brooks. 1993. "Beyond Dualisms: Rosemary Radford Ruether's New Woman/New Earth," *Christian Century* 110: 399–402.

Traina, Christina. 1993. "An Argument for Christian Ecofeminism," *Christian Century* 110: 399–402.

Elisabeth Schüssler Fiorenza (1938–)

Medi Ann Volpe

Elisabeth Schüssler Fiorenza is Krister Stendahl Professor of Divinity at Harvard Divinity School, where she teaches New Testament ethics and rhetoric, feminist theory, biblical interpretation, and theology. Although she was born in Romania in 1938, her family fled to Germany during World War II, and Schüssler Fiorenza was raised and educated in Germany. As a young woman desiring to become a theologian, Schüssler Fiorenza was the first woman to complete the course of study at the University of Würtzberg for those training to become Catholic priests. She continued her academic training in the Catholic Theological Faculty in Münster, where she studied New Testament and early Christianity. Her struggle for acceptance in a male-dominated field shaped Schüssler Fiorenza's interests and methodology. In her first scholarly works Schüssler Fiorenza began the program of teaching, research, and advocacy that has marked her career. The core of her academic project is the recovery of women's voices in the history of the church in a distinctively feminist-theological key.

Schüssler Fiorenza's early work focused on the book of Revelation, offering a political reading of the text. Rather than concentrating her analysis on the otherworldly dimension of the Apocalypse, she suggested that the text communicates a vision of a just world. The flavor of her rendering of this biblical material permeates her later work. In 1983, Schüssler Fiorenza published *In Memory of Her: A Feminist Theological Reconstruction of Christian Origins*. The themes of her earlier work are evident in this influential volume, which showcased the goals of her scholarship and set the stage for the books Schüssler Fiorenza has published since. With the publication of *In Memory of Her*, Schüssler Fiorenza's place in the development of feminist theology and feminist biblical interpretation became evident. She started her research from the basic assumption that women's agency in Christian ministry in the New Testament and the early church had not been recognized. She then argued that the place of women *then*, properly perceived, should open doors for women *now*. In *Memory of Her* proposes not simply an argument about women's place in the church's ministry and history, but a methodology that allows their history to be seen more clearly. This key text within Schüssler Fiorenza's overall project sketches its central task: a work of reconstruction that is feminist and historical, whose goal is to disrupt prevailing interpretive discourses.

Schüssler Fiorenza's methodology makes three basic moves. Her first step is to problematize the category "woman," drawing attention to the ways race, ethnicity, class, and religion contribute to the marginalization of all the oppressed—whether male or female. In so doing, Schüssler Fiorenza emphasizes the double jeopardy in which women of color find themselves,

The Student's Companion to the Theologians, First Edition. Edited by Ian S. Markham.
© 2013 Blackwell Publishing Ltd. Published 2013 by Blackwell Publishing Ltd.

and at the same time widens the scope of her analysis to include the problem of men's marginalization. Thus, instead of referring to the power structure that must be resisted as "patriarchal," Schüssler Fiorenza uses the term "kyriarchy" or "kyriocentric" to describe the socio-political configuration that true Christianity must resist.

Schüssler Fiorenza's second step focuses on historical-critical interpretation in biblical studies and the uses of history in systematic theology. Thus, for example, she questions biblical scholarship that claims to render the meaning of the text. She proposes a shift into a rhetorical space for interpretation that avoids any suggestion of a positivistic approach to biblical or historical texts, and questions reconstructive methods and models in biblical and theological scholarship. Schüssler Fiorenza emphasizes the shaping of the resources used by all scholars of the Bible and early Christianity (herself included) by centuries of interpretation and mediation by the church. Thus she seeks not to construct an accurate account of Christian beginnings (seeing such a project as questionable at best), but to persuade her audience to rethink Christian history. Rather than placing the burden of proof on the feminist scholar, who would be required to produce evidence for women's agency in early Christianity, Schüssler Fiorenza sets it squarely on the shoulders of those scholars who would deny women's role in the shaping of Christian belief and practice. She begins with unconventional assumptions that shape her methodology.

Schüssler Fiorenza's third methodological move centers her work on the project of liberation. She presupposes that Christian struggles and arguments for liberation originate long before Jesus' birth, and continue into the present toward the future. This belief stamps Schüssler Fiorenza's theological method: rather than looking for clues to the liberative message of the gospel, she begins from the perspective that Jesus' place is within the trajectory of liberation that commences with Israel and continues through the church after Jesus' death, resurrection, and ascension.

Yet the methodology at the heart of Schüssler Fiorenza's work is not immune to criticism. Challenges to her methodology come not only from the theological or biblical studies establishment, but also from scholars who share Schüssler Fiorenza's liberation focus. The assumptions with which she begins, it is argued, lead to her conclusions without requiring a specifically Christian framework for their development. In other words, although Jesus is important for Schüssler Fiorenza in the abstract, some critics claim that the arguments she makes for the liberation of all the marginalized could be made without reference to the New Testament or early church history. Still, those who share her passion for liberation affirm the basic direction of her work, and praise her achievement. There can be no denying the profound influence Schüssler Fiorenza has had on feminist biblical scholarship. Her radical starting point for biblical and theological research has helped to shape a generation of scholars who take women's place in the history of Christianity for granted in a way previously unthinkable.

References

Works by Elisabeth Schüssler Fiorenza

1972. *Priester für Gott; Studien zum Herrschafts und Priestermotiv in der Apokalypse.* Münster: Aschendorff.

1983. *In Memory of Her: A Feminist Reconstruction of Christian Origins.* New York: Crossroad.

1984. *Bread not Stone: The Challenge of Feminist Biblical Interpretation.* Boston: Beacon Press.

1991. *Revelation: Vision of a Just World.* Minneapolis: Fortress Press.

1992. *But She Said: Feminist Practices of Biblical Interpretation.* Boston: Beacon Press.

1994. *Jesus: Miriam's Child, Sophia's Prophet: Critical Issues in Feminist Christology.* New York: Continuum.

Substantial reviews

Castelli, Elizabeth. 1996. "Review of *But She Said: Feminist Practices of Biblical Interpretation* and *Jesus: Miriam's Child,*

Sophia's Prophet: Critical Issues in Feminist Christology," *Religious Studies Review* 22(4): 296–300.

D'Angelo, Mary Rose. 1996. "Review of *But She Said: Feminist Practices of Biblical Interpretation* and *Jesus: Miriam's Child, Sophia's Prophet: Critical Issues in Feminist Christology*," *Religious Studies Review* 22(4): 293–6.

Kraemer, Ross. 1985. "Review of *In Memory of Her: A Feminist Reconstruction of Christian Origins*," *Religious Studies Review* 11(1): 5–9.

West, Cornel. 1985. "Review of *In Memory of Her: A Feminist Reconstruction of Christian Origins*," *Religious Studies Review* 11(1): 1–5.

Dorothee Sölle (1929–2003)

Mary E. Coleman

Dorothee Sölle was a popular theological writer in the best sense. Her books were, for the most part, brief, readable, and not over-laden with scholarly apparatus. At the time of her death, she was one of Germany's most widely read writers on religious faith. At that time a spokesperson for the Protestant Church in Germany stated, "Up until the end of her life, Sölle championed the credibility of theology." "Her theological statements always had the character of courageous, perhaps perilous thought."

She began her studies in classical philosophy and philology and moved into theology while still an undergraduate. In her nearly 40-year career she wrote or co-wrote more than two dozen books. Most of her books were first written in German and then translated. While she never held a major academic post in the German university system, her work was well known and well regarded on both sides of the Atlantic. She can be described as a mystic as well as an academically trained theologian. While she identified herself as a feminist rather late in her career, she displayed a sensitivity to class and cultural issues which incorporated many feminist concerns from very early in her writing. She has aptly been described as a political theologian as well.

Dorothee Nipperdey was born in Cologne on September 30, 1929 to the family of a labor lawyer. She was the fourth of a family of five children. Her primary and secondary education in Cologne was interrupted during the war. Although her parents strongly opposed the Nazis in private, even going so far as to hide a Jewish woman in their home for a period of time (Pinnock, 2003), they did not oppose the government publicly.

After completing her undergraduate studies in Protestant theology and German in Göttingen in 1954, she married the Dutch painter Dietrich Sölle. She was an instructor of Religion and German at the Gymnasium for Girls for the next six years. During this period she gave birth to the first three of her four children, Martin (1956), Michaela (1957), and Caroline (1961). She also worked as a freelance writer on theological and literary topics for radio and periodicals. In 1962 she became an assistant at the Philosophical Institute of the Technical University of Aachen. In 1964 her marriage ended in divorce and she returned to Cologne to become the Director of Studies at the Institute of German Studies for the University of Cologne. In late 1968 she became involved in the Political Evensong events in Cologne. It was through this activity that she met her second husband Fubert Steffensky, a former Benedictine priest. They were married in 1969 and her fourth child Mirjam was born in 1970.

She earned her doctorate from the University of Cologne in 1971 with a dissertation on the relationship between theology and poetry entitled "Studies in the Structures of Bonaventura's Vigils." From 1972 to

The Student's Companion to the Theologians, First Edition. Edited by Ian S. Markham.
© 2013 Blackwell Publishing Ltd. Published 2013 by Blackwell Publishing Ltd.

1975 she was a Sessional Instructor at the University of Mainz. Having been awarded the Theodor-Heuss Medal in 1974, she was asked to join the faculty of Union Theological Seminary as Professor of Systematic Theology. She taught there from 1975 to 1987, spending half the year in New York and half with her family in Cologne during this time. Later in her career she was a visiting Professor at the University of Kassel (1987–8), the University of Basle (1991–2) and named Honorary Professor of the University of Hamburg (1994).

During the 1980s she became involved in many civil disobedience actions including protests outside American military installations in Germany. In 1988 she was found guilty of "attempting to provoke arrest." In a German obituary it was noted that she was "long seen as a model of faith-inspired political activism." As well as "[a]n independent spirit who irritated church authorities with her free interpretation of Christian tradition and leftist convictions," she was "a religious thinker for whom a Christian life, political commitment and theology were inseparable. A vocal pacifist, she demonstrated against the Vietnam War, the Cold War arms race and exploitation in the developing world." At times she was criticized by both Catholic and Protestant leaders as "unnuanced" and "naïve." Yet she remained convinced that her activism was necessary. "Church and state are perhaps separable, but the spirit of faith and politics are not," she once wrote.

Born into a Lutheran family, she remained a member of that church for her entire life. Sölle has written that she came to her religious faith independently, after a personal search for meaning in a nation heavily burdened by its past. "My faith comes from the German catastrophe, from Auschwitz," she has explained. In other contexts she has explained that she found her entrance into that search for a faith through studying Kierkegaard, Rudolf Bultmann, and Friedrich Gogarten (Ring, 2005). Another significant element of her theology was the influence of the medieval mystic Meister Eckhart. His involvement in the life of the people as well as his mystical qualities helped to shape her approach to a life of Christian activism.

Once when describing activism as an act of worship that is needed to make divine intention unfold, she stated: "From the mystics, I have learned that our love for God is as important as God's love for us … To embrace God means to embrace a process—a process

of love, a process of going forward, a process of infusing everything. Only with our partnership can that love become incarnate in our world every day."

Sölle was well known in the United States among academics as well as non-academics. In Germany she was considered to be a popular writer despite her academic background. It was not until late in her career that she came to be more appreciated by the German academy. Although her many books of both prose and poetry, as well as her articles, were clearly informed by her scholarship, for the most part they failed to conform to the expectations of the German academy and as such were devalued.

Dorothee Sölle was the author of more than 20 books, many, many articles, and much poetry during her 40-year career. Her first book was published in 1965 and her final book in 1999. The titles give a clear sense of the trajectory of her concerns. Sölle's books in English translation include *Theology for Skeptics: Reflections on God* (1968), *Beyond Mere Obedience* (1970), *Political Theology* (1974), *Suffering* (1975), *Revolutionary Patience* (1977), *Choosing Life* (1981), *The Arms Race Kills Even Without War* (1983), *Of War and Love* (1983), *To Work and to Love: A Theology of Creation* (1984), *Strength of the Weak: Toward a Christian Feminist Identity* (1984), *Window of Vulnerability* (1990), *On Earth as in Heaven: a Liberation Spirituality of Sharing* (1993), *Creative Disobedience* (1995), *The Silent Cry: Mysticism and Resistance* (1997), and *Against the Wind: Memoir of a Radical Christian* (1999).

Dorothee Sölle's theology was initially deeply christocentric. This aspect was to lessen in time as she shifted her focus to a more theocentric discourse. It would seem that this shift was necessary in order that she be able to include all the elements and people whom she felt it was necessary to include in any socially viable theology. To Sölle a real theology needed to be a useful theology—a political theology. She became more and more convinced over the course of her life of the imperative of the need to re-evaluate and reject any theology which could lead to the destruction of the plan, the undervaluing of certain groups of persons, or the belief that war could be of value. She saw her work as necessarily involved in reconciliation. Her concerns were to focus on areas of peace, justice, and the preservation of the whole creation. She was humble about her personal ability to effect those changes, but saw her efforts as a part of the efforts of all who wished to think of themselves as truly being responsible to God the creator.

Some excerpts from her writings are the best way to understand her particular artistic and theological sensibilities. In *Against Death* Sölle writes:

> I must die. But that is all that I will do for death. I will refuse all other requests to respect its officials or celebrate its banks as humanly friendly and its inventions as advances of science. I will resist all the other seductions to mild depression, socialized relationlessness and the secure knowledge of eventual victory. I must die but that is all I will do for death. I will laugh against death, tell stories how death was outwitted and how women expelled death from the country. I will sing and reclaim the land with every act.
>
> The dear God has many special friends and joys, childlikeness and serious responsibility, anger, delight in life and courage if one is unloved. Courage can be a professional risk. One can be stamped unscientific and excluded. The more this courage is shown, the more it will be a shining example.
>
> Giving and taking, attentiveness and suffering are the three aspects of love. Charity is a relation, not a virtue. From relations arise the net of life. When we give without calculating or take without shame, we become attached to this great net and make it more reliable.

In *Pain* Sölle explains:

> We know that we are never finished with love and always remain in its debt. That we always fall behind love is the messianic pain in the not-yet redeemed world. I would love to be the tree that lives in giving and receiving and is attentive to the earth and the sun. But pain separates me from these brothers and sisters … (Sölle, 2006, 49).

Loving your neighbor as yourself means being attentive, learning to give and take and not denying pain!:

> The problem is the contradiction between inward- and outward morality, of family and the working/business world, between private- and social spheres. This contradiction intensifies. Practicing giving and receiving is impossible for example for a mother who must educate children for competition.
>
> The fate of love in the middle class world is its reduction. Love is no longer able to meaningfully define relations between people and regulate them satisfactorily.

May one conclude that love that refuses to entrench itself in the family and join in renunciation on justice still has different future possibilities? Is the technocratic watchword that declares the deepest needs non-existent and manipulates them out of the world the only watchword? Or is a society conceivable that takes needs more seriously than earlier times because it seeks to realize giving and taking on a different economic base for all people? (Sölle, 2006, 55)

On Home includes the following: "Persons do not simply belong to the sphere of nature. Therefore the experience of homelessness is queued up. A harmless domesticated Christianity is a danger" (Sölle, 2006, 124).

Perhaps one of the strongest examples of her later work, *The Anesthetization of Life is the Enemy of Human Community*, spells out her concerns for all persons:

> This is the double face of apathy: denial and repression of one's own suffering and icy tolerance of the other's suffering. The strategies for avoiding suffering in our intimate relations are connected with the breath-taking tolerance with Awhich we watch the genocide of whole peoples. (Sölle, 2006, 33)

> The person is the political. The truth of this slogan from the women's movement was never so clear as in the problem of apathy, white middle-class apathy in the first rich world. Apathy with its dimensions of subjective paralysis, repression of suffering and objective incapacity for suffering may be a new psycho-social quality, similar to what the young Marx called "alienation." When sympathy is classified with crime and criminalized, what else can be expected of citizens? Apathy, technologically possible, publically desired and culturally affirmed apathy! (Sölle, 2006, 34)

> The state of permanent structural injustice that we enjoy has obvious consequences for our value system. We have reversed the relation of love and suffering and the order of precedence. Being and remaining free of suffering until death is certainly the highest accepted value. Health is the highest good, as everyone knows. Being alive, transcending the ego and being in communication and sympathy with all living things is subordinated to freedom from suffering. Apathetic freedom from suffering, privation, pain and involvement is promoted as the supreme value like smooth beauty, spotless cleanliness and the unbroken career that characterizes our lifestyle before other people. The goal of becoming capable of love and enabling justice is subordinated to the goal of getting away "good" and "intact." (Sölle, 2006, 36)

Grace is the reunification of life with itself, the reconciliation of oneself with oneself, the re-acceptance of what was rejected … (error-friendliness!). (Sölle, 2006, 40)

Her *Credo for the Earth* is uncompromising in its call:

I believe in God's good creation, the earth. This creation is holy, yesterday, today and tomorrow. Do not commodify it; it does not belong to you or any corporation. We don't own it like a thing that one buys, uses and throws away. It belongs to another.

We can know this from God, our mother. How can we speak of God without the flowers that praise God, without the wind and the water that tell of him in whispers? How can we praise God without learning protection from our mother?

The earth exists for everyone, not only for the rich. It is holy, every single leaf. The ocean, the land, the light and the darkness, being born and dying—all sing the song of the earth.

… as is her *On The 1999 Human Rights Congress in Nurnberg*:

New forms of slavery arise today before our eyes in the course of deregulation and globalization of the economy. The worst violations of human rights today are the consequences of the world economy. Boundless world trade is the new idol that dominates us.

Technical progress has produced a mega-machine that disfigures all nature and everything created. It believes in its second creation that should be better than the first. Joining this culture of apartheid and death with life will not be easy. ("What I believe", 1990)

The echoes of her life-long concern with the events of World War II are evident in this speech, "At a Peace Gathering":

We are not only 10,000, I say, we are more! The dead of the two wars are with us! A journalist asked me, how I could know this. I said: Haven't you seen them? Haven't you heard your grandmother moan? Do you dwell completely alone without once allowing the dead to drink with you? Do you really imagine that you are only you?

This brief prayer reminds the reader of her continuing attachment to the mystics: "Ask God daily for the gift of tears, I read with the mystics. Daily, may we be salt and shame, daily may we become free, O God."

And finally, from *A Letter to My Children*:

Organized religion is dialectical with its ifs and buts. Organized religion is Yes and No at once … I hope that you all become a little pious. Don't forget the best! That you praise God sometimes, not always since only gossips do this but sometimes when you are happy so that happiness entirely by itself flows into gratitude and you sing Hallelujah or the great Ohm of the Indian religion …

The straightforward thrust of her writing demonstrates why she might not have been welcomed by the establishment, but it also illustrates why and how her writing could have a profound effect not just on her students but on any who read her books. She was a popular theologian because she was able to make the connections between theology and everyday actions clear to so many people.

References

Borger, Renate. 2003. Address at the 2003 Ecumenical Church Day in Berlin. This is available on the web in translation at http://la.indymedia.org/news/2004/12/120480.php

Brower, David Ross. *Credo for the Earth*. San Francisco: One Heart Press, 2004.

Havel, Václav, and Wilson, Paul. 1991. "On Home," *New York Review of Books*. (Offprint), 2.

Klausner, Abraham J. 2002. *A Letter to My Children from the Edge of the Holocaust*. San Francisco: Holocaust Center of Northern California.

Pinnock, Sarah K., ed. 2003. *The Theology of Dorothee Soelle*. Harrisburg, PA: Trinity Press International.

Ring, Nancy C. 2005. "Dorothee Solle." In *Encyclopedia of Religion*, 2nd ed. Vol. 12, ed. Lindsay Jones. Detroit: Macmillan Reference USA, pp. 8511–12.

Sölle, Dorothee. 2006. *Essential Writings*, selected with an introduction by Dianne L. Oliver. Maryknoll, NY: Orbis Books.

Richard Swinburne (1934–)

Gary Chartier

Richard Granville Swinburne is a British philosopher who has pioneered the use of Bayesian probability calculus in the philosophy of religion; undertaken rigorous philosophical analyses—and, on occasion, reconstructions—of the central doctrines of Christianity; and carefully explored a wide range of problems in the philosophy of science, metaphysics, epistemology, ethics, and other areas of philosophy.

I. Biography

Swinburne studied at Charterhouse School and then at Exeter College, Oxford, where he earned first-class honors in Philosophy, Politics, and Economics (1957) before completing a BPhil in philosophy (1959) and a Diploma in Theology (1960; with distinction). He held a Fereday Fellowship at St John's College, Oxford, from 1958 to 1961 and a Leverhulme Research Fellowship in the History and Philosophy of Science at the University of Leeds from 1961 to 1963. A member of the philosophy faculty of the University of Hull from 1963 to 1972, he became Professor of Philosophy in the University of Keele in 1972. In 1985, he was elected Nolloth Professor of the Philosophy of the Christian Religion in the University of Oxford, retiring in 2002.

He has published 16 monographs, four edited books, and in excess of 120 scholarly articles. His teaching (including the supervision of some 25 doctoral students, primarily at Oxford) and scholarship have allowed him to exert a profound impact on the philosophy of religion. Elected a Fellow of the British Academy in 1992, he delivered the Wilde Lectures in Natural and Comparative Religion at Oxford from 1975 to 1978; the Gifford Lectures at the University of Aberdeen from 1982 to 1984; and the Aquinas Lecture at Marquette University in 1997. He has held visiting appointments at institutions including the University of Maryland, the University of Adelaide, the University of Rome, the Catholic University of Lublin, Syracuse University, Yale University, and the University of St Louis.

Swinburne trained as a Russian interpreter during his two years of national service before enrolling at Oxford. As chair of a committee of the Society of Christian Philosophers, he has been responsible for organizing three conferences involving Russian philosophers and theologians. He has lectured in Russia several times in Russian.

Early in his career, Swinburne considered taking orders in the Church of England. Though his academic work has extended well beyond the bounds of the philosophy of religion, he has consistently understood his scholarship as contributing to an integrated project in natural theology. In the mid-1990s, citing concerns related to doctrinal tendencies in the Church of England, he joined the Orthodox Church.

The Student's Companion to the Theologians, First Edition. Edited by Ian S. Markham.
© 2013 Blackwell Publishing Ltd. Published 2013 by Blackwell Publishing Ltd.

Swinburne's work can be divided into several broad categories (although, given the overlaps and intersections of the topics on which he has worked, the boundaries here are somewhat arbitrary). Early in his career, he established his credibility in metaphysics with *Space and Time* (2nd ed., 1981). *The Evolution of the Soul* (rev. ed., 1997) and *Personal Identity* (1984; co-authored with Sydney Shoemaker) focus on the philosophy of mind and related metaphysical questions. In epistemology and the philosophy of science, he has published *An Introduction to Confirmation Theory* (1973) and, more recently, *Epistemic Justification* (2001). In the philosophy of religion, he has authored *The Concept of Miracle* (1971), *The Coherence of Theism* (rev. ed., 1993), *The Existence of God* (2nd ed., 2004), *Faith and Reason* (2nd ed., 2005), and *Providence and the Problem of Evil* (1998). (*Is There a God?* [1996] discusses some of the issues considered in these books at a popular level. Reflecting his international profile, this book has been translated into languages including Dutch, Finnish, Hungarian, Polish, Portuguese, Russian, Italian, Turkish, Persian, Chinese, German, Amharic, and Romanian, with others, in languages including Czech and Korean, forthcoming.) On the border of theology and the philosophy of religion are *Responsibility and Atonement* (1989), *Revelation: From Metaphor to Analogy* (2nd ed., 2007), *The Christian God* (1994), and *The Resurrection of God Incarnate* (2003). (*Was Jesus God?* [2008] summarizes Swinburne's views on these matters for a popular audience.)

He has discussed foundational questions in meta-ethics in several articles (as well as in portions of *The Coherence of Theism*, *The Existence of God*, and *Responsibility and Atonement*) and some questions in applied ethics in articles, in *Responsibility and Atonement*, and in the second edition of *Revelation*. He has addressed issues related to logic, language, and the philosophy of science in various articles. His four edited books have focused on induction, Bayes's theorem, space, time, and miracle.

His work in philosophy that is not explicitly focused on religious questions provides the backdrop for his work in the philosophy of religion and the philosophy of Christian doctrine. Thus, for instance, his arguments regarding the soul, personal identity, and free will have informed his conclusions about evil, atonement, and divine action.

II. Principal Theological Arguments

While he recognizes that he has no remit, as a philosopher, to engage in detailed historical argument, Swinburne is convinced that the project of rational theology in which he is engaged is relevant to the assessment not only of general metaphysical theses like those about God and the soul, but also of the positive theological claims of the Christian church. Rejecting fideism, he maintains that rational argument can play a vital role in the Christian life. A priori rational considerations set the stage for our consideration of claims about the reality of God and God's action in the world, helping us to determine what is possible and what it is reasonable to expect. They also guide our assessment of a posteriori evidence (not, in itself, a matter, of course, for the philosopher or theologian).

In *The Concept of Miracle*, Swinburne defends the notion that miracles are conceivable and that we can responsibly claim, when appropriate evidence is available, that a miracle—a violation of a law of nature brought about by a personal divine act—has occurred. *The Coherence of Theism* develops and defends the internal consistency of a conception of God as a personal agent. Swinburne's position generally parallels that of many proponents of classical theism, but there are also noteworthy differences. For Swinburne, God is *metaphysically* necessary (in a sense he carefully develops) but not *logically* necessary. Thus, the ontological argument for God's reality is unsuccessful. In addition, God is everlasting, not timelessly eternal. And this means, in turn, that God lacks certain knowledge of future contingents.

In *The Existence of God*, widely regarded as his most important work, Swinburne defends the aptness of a probabilistic, a posteriori approach to assessing the question of the reality of God and deploys such an approach to defend the conclusion that there is God. This claim is a large-scale metaphysical hypothesis that can, he maintains, be assessed using the criteria we employ to evaluate other proposed large-scale metaphysical, scientific, and historical theories, notably including simplicity. He suggests that a range of considerations (including the order of nature, miracles, and the fine-tuning of the universe—with the balance tipped decisively by religious experience) render the judgment that there is God more probable than not. While his use of a cumulative case argument renders his position similar to that of his predecessor as Nolloth Professor, Basil Mitchell, Swinburne's approach is distinctive in virtue of the rigor of his arguments and their formalization using Bayesian probability calculus.

Faith and Reason offers a general account of the role of rational reflection in religious life. Belief on the basis of the testimony of others will be sufficient for some people all of the time, and for all people some of the time. But religious claims must be susceptible of rational scrutiny, and personal commitment must depend on the warranted judgment that religious claims are true. *Revelation: From Metaphor to Analogy* continues Swinburne's reflection on reason and authority in religion. Building on a general philosophical account of communication and meaning, he maintains that Christianity involves belief in a range of revealed truths and that belief that such truths have been revealed can be—and, in fact is—justified (paralleling in brief fashion his more detailed arguments elsewhere for a divine revelation centered on the life, death, and resurrection of Jesus). He also addresses the interpretation and application of putatively revealed truths, taking some disputed issues in Christian sexual ethics as examples.

Swinburne defends the view that the human mind or soul is an indivisible, immaterial substance, specially created by God, that is distinguishable from, though intimately related to, the body in *The Evolution of the Soul*. While *Evolution* is primarily an impressive essay in the philosophy of mind, it is relevant in several ways to Swinburne's work more explicitly concerned with religious questions. The idea that the soul is a special divine creation, that no law of nature determines which soul is connected with which body, paves the way for Swinburne's account of the incarnation. Substance dualism allows Swinburne to make sense of personal identity over time (also defended in *Personal Identity*), including the identity of persons before and after death, and so to make out the accounts of resurrection, heaven, and hell he wishes to defend. And his defense of libertarian free will provides the background for claims about, among other things, the appeal to creaturely freedom as an essential component of an adequate theodicy and the predication of responsibility for morally wrong choices.

Responsibility and Atonement develops an account of moral responsibility and reparation before proceeding to offer an integrated understanding of several related topics, including original sin, atonement, heaven, and hell. Swinburne defends a view of sin as pervasive (while denying the aptness of Calvinist talk about total depravity); argues for a satisfaction theory of atonement in accordance with which we identify with Jesus' representative reparation; and rejects hell as eternal torment, while defending the possibility of something like purgatory and considering a variety of possible fates for the irreparably impenitent, including annihilation and endless absorption in triviality.

The Christian God builds on a carefully crafted metaphysical account of personhood to defend several claims. These include the claim that there are strong a priori reasons to affirm a social conception of God's Trinity and the claim that the incarnation of the second person of the Trinity consisted in the acquisition of a human consciousness and body in addition to the second person's divine consciousness. On the view Swinburne articulates, the second person of the Trinity had human thoughts and performed human actions in the light of a genuinely human system of beliefs, as well as living the divine life of the second person. He also lays the groundwork for an assessment of the *historical* credibility of the claim that Jesus was God incarnate.

He continues this project in *The Resurrection of God Incarnate*. He maintains that it would be reasonable on a priori grounds to expect that God would become incarnate in and as a human person and would confirm that a divine incarnation had occurred with what Swinburne terms a "super-miracle." Relatively restrained judgments about the historical evidence, reached in light of the relevant a priori considerations, suggest that it is highly probable that the compound proposition *Jesus of Nazareth was God incarnate and God raised him from the dead* is true.

In *Providence and the Problem of Evil*, Swinburne advances a detailed defense of the goodness of God in the face of evil. He deploys the familiar free-will defense, which maintains that free creatures are responsible for many of the world's evils and that God has good reason not to interfere with the exercise of creaturely freedom. Also central to his argument is the claim that an orderly, predictable world, not always malleable to creaturely wishes, and capable of causing great harm, provides a necessary backdrop to free and rational creaturely action.

III.   Criticism

Given the lucidity and influence of Swinburne's arguments in the philosophy of religion and Christian doctrine, it is not surprising that he has been criticized from multiple quarters. Atheists like John Mackie have argued that he has simply failed to make out a persuasive probabilistic case for theism, while Richard Dawkins and others have attacked his account of the problem of evil as morally insensitive. Christian philosophical critics aligned with Alvin Plantinga's program of "Reformed epistemology" have questioned whether the probabilistic method Swinburne espouses is appropriate given the unswerving commitment that is arguably integral to Christian faith. Brian Hebblethwaite, among others, has questioned the moral persuasiveness of Swinburne's account of atonement. While Swinburne owes a substantial debt to Thomas Aquinas, some contemporary scholars in the Thomist tradition have questioned whether he takes seriously enough the ontic and epistemic gap between God and creation and the difficulties associated with employing human language to talk about God. Some atheist critics have objected to Swinburne's use of simplicity as a criterion for theory acceptance. Some have denied that practicing scientists do, in fact, appeal to this criterion, while others have denied that the hypothesis that there is God is actually simple in the relevant sense.

The effectiveness of Swinburne's cumulative case for theism (and more specifically for Christian belief)

can only be judged on the basis of more fine-grained analysis than is possible here. But he credibly defends the view that careful rational argument is useful and important in relation to religious questions, while granting that not everyone needs to believe on the basis of rational argument. (Plantinga, in turn, has acknowledged the success of a variety of rational arguments for religious conclusions, while doubting their necessity or centrality. So the dispute between Swinburne and the Reformed epistemologists may be more a matter of degree than it might initially seem to be.) Swinburne's account of religious language likely tracks the views of the ordinary religious believer more than that of the neo-Thomists, and he could reasonably maintain that the neo-Thomist view runs the risk of evacuating talk of God of all meaningful content. The plausibility of his arguments regarding atonement and theodicy will depend in part on the aptness and persuasiveness of moral judgments he defends on quite non-theological grounds. Whether or not his views of these matters finally carry the day, he has made his case for his positions with the same refusal to remain question-beggingly within the charmed circle of theological discourse that has characterized the rest of his work.

IV.   Assessment

Careful, precise, and responsive to the concerns and convictions of the ordinary person, Swinburne's contributions to rational theology exemplify the best English philosophical and theological scholarship. Whatever the final verdict on his particular arguments, he is rightly recognized for the power, clarity, and scope of his efforts to place Christian belief on a firm intellectual footing in a manner respectful of the best contemporary science and philosophy.

References

Swinburne, Richard. 1971. *The Concept of Miracle*. London: Macmillan.

Swinburne, Richard. 1973. *An Introduction to Confirmation Theory*. London: Methuen.

Swinburne, Richard. 1981. *Space and Time*, 2d ed. London: Macmillan.

Swinburne, Richard. 1989. *Responsibility and Atonement*. Oxford: Clarendon Press.

Swinburne, Richard. 1993. *The Coherence of Theism*, rev. ed. Oxford: Clarendon Press.

Swinburne, Richard. 1994. *The Christian God*. Oxford: Clarendon Press.

Swinburne, Richard. 1996. *Is There a God?* Oxford: Oxford University Press.

Swinburne, Richard. 1997. *The Evolution of the Soul*, rev. ed. Oxford: Clarendon Press.

Swinburne, Richard. 1998. *Providence and the Problem of Evil*. Oxford: Clarendon Press.

Swinburne, Richard. 2001. *Epistemic Justification*. Oxford: Clarendon Press.

Swinburne, Richard. 2003. *The Resurrection of God Incarnate*. Oxford: Clarendon Press.

Swinburne, Richard. 2004. *The Existence of God*, 2d ed Oxford: Clarendon Press.

Swinburne, Richard. 2005. *Faith and Reason*, 2d ed. Oxford: Clarendon Press.

Swinburne, Richard. 2007. *Revelation: From Metaphor to Analogy*, 2d ed. Oxford: Clarendon Press.

Swinburne, Richard. 2008. *Was Jesus God?* Oxford: Oxford University Press.

Swinburne, Richard and Shoemaker, Sydney. 1984. *Personal Identity*. Oxford: Blackwell.

Vatican II

F. J. Michael McDermott

The Second Vatican Council (October 11, 1962 to December 8, 1965) represents a watershed in Catholic theology, a change of theological perspective with major implications for the Catholic Church and all Christian denominations. Its four sessions held in the Vatican basilica offered the world the spectacle of the most massive assemblage of bishops, archbishops, cardinals, and patriarchs ever seen—not to mention all the ecclesial experts, bureaucrats, and hangers-on who attempted to interpret and steer the council. Journalists from all over the world arrived to report on the council's proceedings. The media would play an important role in the council, informing many bishops what the Latin discourses in the aula were about, discussing the politics behind the scenes, explaining the theological issues involved, and heightening expectations. Contrary to usual ecclesial procedure the "progressive party" made appeal to the press to overcome obstacles placed in its path by the "conservative party" grouped around the Roman Curia, past masters of the politics of delay and referral. To update the bishops on theological questions both progressives and conservatives offered theological lectures by experts to enlighten and confirm those of their persuasion and encourage waverers to join their fold. Thus the anomaly was effected that the successors of the Apostles, teachers of the church, were being instructed by theologians about the faith. Certainly progressives employed the media and lectures more

effectively than conservatives since they carried most of their points. Circumstances also moved them to co-opt the media to their advantage since the conservatives were entrenched in the committees preparing the original schemata and in the Roman Curia, which had developed a worldwide network of ecclesial contacts and relied on Catholic loyalty to the pope to support their programs. It seemed at first to the conservatives neither necessary nor useful to go outside tried and true methods of persuasion until their flank was turned by the progressives' use of the media. The media were happy to go along with the progressives not only because thereby they were let into the inner workings of the council behind the customary veil of curial secrecy but also because the heightening of conflict and change sells newspapers and produces higher ratings. A peek into the human foibles and antagonisms behind the shrouding incense always attracts curiosity. The conservatives found themselves at a disadvantage not only on account of their late start in developing contacts with the press but also because their theology, stressing the hierarchical structure of the church's magisterium, prevented them from approving the democratic techniques to mold opinion which their opponents exploited. John XXIII's word "*aggiornamento*" became the press's slogan to describe the council and its intention: to bring the church into accord with the modern world.

The Student's Companion to the Theologians, First Edition. Edited by Ian S. Markham.
© 2013 Blackwell Publishing Ltd. Published 2013 by Blackwell Publishing Ltd.

The Council's Eve

By 1960 the Catholic Church probably enjoyed a moral authority unprecedented in the previous 200 years, perhaps in the previous 500 years. In convoking the council Pope John XXIII presented the church as "the most authoritative voice, interpreter and affirmer of the moral order, and champion of the right and duties of all human beings and of all political communities" (1996b, 847). Despite the ravages of the Enlightenment and the French Revolution, the church had not only survived and grown in numbers throughout the world but also maintained clarity of vision and consistency of practice. The world had seen the collapse of Nazism and fascism, secular ideologies against which the church had warned and fought. Her perceptive, early condemnations of atheistic communism had fortified the West's resolve against Stalinism and Maoism, whose honeyed promises had seduced academics. That France and Italy had not succumbed in elections to communism nor Germany to socialism immediately after the war—nor Spain earlier—was attributed to her robust resolve to organize and inspire the masses. Once condemned for aligning herself with the *ancien régime*, she had emerged in time as a supporter of democracy. She was still widely praised for her condemnations of racism and the wartime protection offered to Jews. Her charitable postwar labors for the wounded, displaced, homeless, and hungry were roundly appreciated. It was hardly possible to imagine the moral and social rebuilding of Europe without her mighty contributions. Her international vision and preaching banked the fires of national prejudices which had incited three centuries of war. Not by chance the leading statesmen of Europe were convinced Catholics, most of whom favored a greater unification of the continent in economic and political matters as well as militant resistance to communism. The postwar era had seen a revival of religious conviction and practice in Europe, and in the United States, the leader of the anti-communist struggle, Catholics were achieving a status undreamed of a generation previously. The old anti-American charge, so long a prejudice in the nation's history, had shriveled in view of enthusiastic Catholic support for the war effort and the struggle against communism.

Without public expense Catholic schools were producing well-educated, patriotic citizens, who melded into the general population; Catholic hospitals dominated the health-care scene in most of the United States; and Catholic social doctrine had won a favorable hearing not only among labor unions but also in Congress where New Deal legislation had contributed to the support of the family. Catholic associations were promoting Catholic values in the public square. Inside the church seminaries and religious houses overflowed with candidates. With the lowering of prejudice, the debilitating effect of liberal theology upon mainline Protestant denominations, and the retreat of fundamentalism not only did Bishop Sheen top TV ratings but also almost two million Americans converted to Catholicism between the war's end and 1960. In the postwar economic boom increasing numbers of Catholics were entering the middle class and sharing the optimism of the late 1950s. With John Kennedy's election American Catholics thought that they had finally arrived and were ready to teach the rest of the church about the advantages of American democracy.

Intellectually, the church thought herself well prepared to meet the postwar era. No longer was there need of condemnations directed against Enlightenment and Idealistic philosophies. In practice and theory they had disqualified themselves. Philosophers had grown hesitant about constructing world visions and even about the powers of human intelligence to know reality. Aside from communism, still a menace, ideologies had passed out of favor, and many thinkers acknowledged the limits of science and the realm of mystery. Furthermore, the church considered herself intellectually equipped to debate her opponents. Theologians need not borrow eclectically from current philosophies in order to win a hearing for the Christian message. The revival of Thomism, vigorously promoted by Leo XIII and his successors, had given believers an intelligent worldview that with its balanced sanity might attract and persuade any searcher for truth. Historical studies had revealed the subtlety of medieval thinkers, and such first-class minds as Maritain and Gilson, highly appreciated at secular universities, had trained cadres of disciples enthusiastic in promoting the *philosophia perennis*. Upon that philosophical foundation was constructed a theology accepting revealed truths guaranteed by the authority of Christ and the church. Internally the church was well organized with a clear hierarchical structure defined in the 1917 Code of Canon Law, Cardinal Gasparri's masterpiece. The lines of jurisdictional authority let all believers find their places on their pilgrimage to salvation and learn how they might arrive there. Clarity in doctrine and authority generated a willingness to sacrifice for the Church's well-being and the world's conversion. A tremendous *esprit de corps* joined Catholics to each other everywhere and bound all of them to the pope and the hierarchy.

Pope John's Call

On the whole, church members shared in the tremendous optimism of the times when on January 25, 1959 Pope John XXIII stunned the College of Cardinals with his intention to summon a new ecumenical council. Although the pope saw a crisis in the weakening of spiritual values before a spreading practical materialism, he did not agree with prophets of doom. Instead he saw an opportunity for the church to "discern the signs of the times" and contribute to "a new order of human relations." Despite warring ideologies and questions raised by scientific progress, the human race was moving toward greater integration. To the solution of its problems, he thought, the church might contribute by bringing the vivifying energies of the gospel and her counsel.

Only against the optimism of the time can the postconciliar turmoil be appreciated. For what happened was not the victory of northern European theology over a Mediterranean mindset (Wiltgen, 1967), nor the victory of progressive over conservative forces (Rynne, 1968), nor a break from the past into a new era of ecclesial self-understanding (Alberigo, 1997–2003), much less the church's capitulation to modernism (Archbishop Lefebvre). Such theories fail to explain how all the conciliar decrees were approved by overwhelming majorities of the bishops present. Admittedly Paul VI heeded the complaints of conservative prelates and intervened at decisive moments to influence the composition of some documents. But it is scarcely imaginable that a whole assembly of aged bishops should suddenly take it upon themselves to alter the church's faith in which they had been schooled, to which they had dedicated their lives, and for which many were suffering persecution, because a new vision of the universe suddenly enlightened them. At the council's opening John XXIII had defined its first duty: "The sacred deposit of Christian doctrine should be guarded and taught more efficaciously." That "sacred patrimony of truth received from the Fathers" was to be handed on "pure and integral, without any attenuation or distortion" (1966a, 862f.). Yet upon returning to their dioceses many bishops were nonplussed by the alleged changes which they were accused of introducing into the church. The council actually marked the encounter and compromise of two principal theologies which sought to remain faithful to Christ's message while making it more intelligible to their contemporaries and dealing with some theological problems (Philips, 1967; Ratzinger, 1968). Besides preserving tradition, the council was challenged by the pope "to look to the present, to the new conditions and new forms of life introduced into the modern world which have opened new avenues to the Catholic apostolate." Authentic doctrine was to be expounded through "the literary forms of modern thought": "The substance of the ancient doctrine of the deposit of faith is one thing, and the way in which it is presented is another. And it is the latter that must be taken into great consideration with patience if necessary, everything being measured in the forms and proportions of a magisterium which is predominantly pastoral in character" (1966a, 862, 865).

The council was caught in the pincers of time. How can the past be preserved when new words, which represent new thoughts, must be found for it? That was the basic intellectual problem of the council for the two competing theological currents. Conservatives emphasized integral preservation, progressives the need for adaptation. Concern for truth and service to God's people rather than power politics produced the council's documents. Because of the compromise's novelty, however, and because human beings seek rational consistency, even in matters of faith, the delicate balance between the competing visions of the faith was not always maintained in the postconciliar era as the novel elements, highlighted by progressive theologians and the press, were interpreted and exaggerated in the "spirit of Vatican II."

The church's remarkable unity, to which Pope John appealed as he called the council to increase the sanctification of the church's members and "rebuild the visible unity of all Christians which would properly satisfy the wishes of the Divine Redeemer" (1966b, 845), was not very visible a decade after the council.

Although John XXIII said that his unexpected summoning of the council had stricken his audience silent "as if by a flash of heavenly light," his predecessor, Pius XII, had ordered some preliminary studies about a council's possibility. Good reasons prompted such an initiative. Ecumenical councils were usually called to resolve disputes threatening the church's unity in faith or to overcome schism, but Vatican I sought to shore up the Church's defenses vis-à-vis secularism and rationalism. For this reason no major battle or schism followed in its wake aside from a few German dissenters who established the Old Catholic Church with Bismarck's encouragement. Actually the papal magisterium's purging of professorial heresies in the previous 50 years had anticipatorily strengthened its position (McCool, 1977). Less dissent was foreseen with Vatican II since Vatican I had established the authority structure so firmly that revolt against church doctrine or authority hardly seemed possible. Yet there was work to be done. Vatican I's discussion on the church had been prematurely aborted by the Piedmontese army's menacing invasion of the Papal States. The Council fathers had handled the reason–faith relation as well as papal jurisdiction and infallibility. The intended discussion about bishops had been postponed indefinitely. Was it not time to treat that issue in more detail after almost a century of theological research and reflection? Furthermore, with the church no longer tied to European monarchies and expanding her missions in all quarters of the globe, should she not reassess her relation to the world? Without any pressing dogmatic issues John XXIII envisioned a pastoral council to update church teaching, invite "separated brethren" to ecclesial unity, and welcome all men to Christ.

The Debate

Before the council convened, theological commissions were formed of Roman experts close to the Curia and others in order to compose preliminary schemata.

The Preparatory Theological Commission prepared two dogmatic texts, *On the Sources of Revelation* and *On the Church*. From them emerged the council's two dogmatic constitutions, but only after great debate, papal interventions, and much rewriting. At a critical early moment, when the majority of Council fathers wished to reject *On the Sources* for its lack of pastoral concern but could not muster the requisite two-thirds majority to send it back for rewriting, John XXIII intervened, siding with the majority and remanding the document to a new conciliar committee. When internal divisions brought that committee to the point of abandoning the project, Paul VI's insistence kept them at their labors, which ultimately produced *Dei Verbum*. Papal support of the majority likewise facilitated the drastic revision of the schema on the church, and Paul VI satisfied the minority by adding a "preliminary explanatory note" to *Lumen Gentium*. Those debates on these two dogmatic constitutions honed the council's theological vision, which resulted in 14 additional constitutions, decrees, and declarations.

Although various theological currents were operative within the majority and the minority positions, the council is best understood through the contrast between the older conceptualist theology, which embraced Cajetanian Thomists, Suarezians, and Scotists, and more recent forces working for "renewal." The former wished to maintain and strengthen the theological structure elaborated at Trent and Vatican I, which stayed generally within the parameters of baroque theology. The "new theology" seeking changes appealed to the authority of the church fathers, St Thomas, and other medieval doctors as well as to the needs of preaching in the modern world. Although the latter thought that it could solve diverse theological difficulties besetting the former, underlying both positions were different philosophies of being. Both sides agreed on the dogmas of faith, but their interpretation depended on a philosophy. Since God has no difficulty in revealing himself, theological difficulties must arise from human understandings of revelation. Insofar as human beings seek to be consistent in their comprehension of revelation—God does not contradict himself—a philosophy, i.e., an attempt at consistent reasoning about reality, must be presupposed. Depending on whether the human intellect is understood as grasping being, i.e., reality, in a concept or a judgment (or intuition), diverse theologies result. That question is the speculative hinge on which the two theologies of Vatican II diverged. The contrast between conceptualist and transcendental interpretations of St Thomas's thought provides the hermeneutical key to the council. We present them in rough outline, overlooking the subtle distinction of their talented proponents (McDermott, 1988, 1991).

Conceptualist Thomism

If being can be grasped in a concept, however analogous, all of reality can be conceptualized. The intellect operates principally as a passive faculty receiving abstractions effected by the illumination of the active intellect. It receives impressions from without and does not constitute them; hence the external sensible world is known objectively in and through concepts. Since concepts result from a process of abstraction, intelligibility is attributed primarily to form, a form that is opposed to the unintelligibility of matter, which is responsible for the "here and now" of individuality. As form is superior to the matter it informs, so the soul is superior ontologically to the body. Yet because the proper and proportionate object of the intellect is the essence, or nature, of a material reality, the soul knows itself only by reflection upon an already completed act of knowing. Furthermore, since the intellect is primarily passive, it can be contrasted to the will, the faculty of spiritual striving, in terms of their diverse formal objects, the true and the good. Then, insofar as the will depends on the intellect and the intellect knows by abstractions, a distance between the will and the concrete object of choice is achieved which grounds freedom of indifference. The will "steps back," as it were, from the possible objects of choice before engaging itself. Then the choice is neither forced (due to the distance won by abstraction) nor arbitrary (since the intellect offers a reason), but occurs in the mutual causality of intellect and will.

Such an understanding of the intellect's natural production of concepts permits a clear distinction of natural and supernatural orders. Revelation proclaims that the elect shall one day see God face to face (1 Cor. 13:12; 1 John 3:2). This immediate vision of God, whereby God, bypassing the senses, takes the place of the *species impressa* (the formal abstraction not yet recognized as the explicitly universal concept, the *species expressa*), is obviously beyond a creature's natural powers. As pure gift, it becomes the touchstone of the supernatural. It and all that lead to it are supernatural; that includes faith, hope, and charity as well as all the mysteries to be believed, the graces to be received, and whatever else Christ performed or instituted for our salvation.

Intellectually human beings have access to supernatural salvation through faith. If the mind knows in and through concepts, the object of faith must be true and is offered in conceptual form, in propositions uniting concepts. Since faith responds to a supernatural revelation, its assent surpasses the capabilities of the natural human intellect. Lest the assent be judged irrational, *praeambula fidei*, or rational arguments for the fact of revelation, were developed in apologetics. The authority of the divine messenger was proven by the fulfillment of prophecies and the accomplishment of miracles, by which God bore testimony to his messenger. Hence a prophet was primarily one who foretold the future (Jesus Christ) and scripture tended to be taken literally since God revealed propositions. This emphasis on literalism derived also from Protestants who insisted on the literal, or historical, sense of scripture in interdenominational debates.

In this theology the role of apologetics was central and ecclesiology was intimately linked to it since the believer had to be concerned with the identification of the authentic supernatural authority. Among the many churches and sects claiming to transmit Christ's message, whose conceptually formulated doctrines were contradictory, there could be only one true church distinguished by the creed's marks: one, holy, catholic, and apostolic. Foreseeing confusion resulting from human sin and error, Christ established a hierarchical institution endowed with his authority to preserve and interpret his revelation and to administer properly the sacraments. Authority was indispensable, and conceptual clarity illuminated the various ranks of the hierarchical pyramid to which the permanent deposit of faith had been entrusted. Some hierarchical elements were essential constituents of the Church *de jure divino*, i.e., by divine institution, which could not be altered. The hierarchy taught, ruled, and sanctified with Christ's authority. The laity learned, obeyed, contributed financially, and grew in holiness. Not surprisingly ecclesiology tended to merge with canon law, which regulated relations among various holders of authority. Only one peak of the supernatural pyramid could be acknowledged; otherwise the clarity of revelation and its interpretation would be imperiled. The pope enjoyed infallibility in doctrine as well as jurisdictional primacy. Furthermore, reflecting the clear distinction between natural and supernatural orders, the church claimed freedom from the state and, in case of conflict, primacy over it. All are required to believe in God for their salvation (Heb. 11:6; Rom. 10:10–17). Since belief is impossible without accepting Christ's authority, which he transmitted to the church, there is in principle no salvation outside the church.

While such an ecclesiology has been labeled authoritarian, juridical, and triumphalistic, a more benign judgment might describe a church entrusted with authority by Christ, concerned with clarity in doctrine and morals, and convinced that the message of Christ would ultimately prevail. In the nineteenth century the church did not need to proclaim herself the church of the poor since she was regularly suffering persecution. Under attack by the world, she required clear lines of command, fidelity, unity of vision, and unanimity of action; assurance of final victory meant a great deal to the huddled masses of believers yearning to be free, who found salvation only in the cross.

The apologetics leading to faith was indispensable. All depended on the witnesses' authority. Only on authority was God's word accepted as God's word. There was a tendency to literalism since words represent concepts which grasp reality and human beings could not presume to judge God's supernatural ways of speaking. Moreover, the supernatural breaks in from without. This interruption into the human was due to the utterly transcendent object of faith, the sinful condition which rendered our need of salvation absolute, and the fact of historically mediated revelation. Because of their experience of sin people recognized their inability to find a solution to the intellectual and moral problems of life. They had to go outside themselves to discover saving revelation in history.

From the analysis of faith emanated a straightforward theological method. First, dogmatic theology studied scripture and tradition, revelation's sources, to ascertain the exact content of the faith to which assent had been given. Generally the "regressive method" was used: since the Holy Spirit conserves the church continually in truth, one should start with present church teaching and seek its grounding in past witnesses, allowing even the *lacunae* of historical witnesses to favor present doctrine. Upon the content of faith thus established speculative theology set to work. Though its task was admittedly impossible, understanding supernatural mysteries beyond human understanding and deducing conclusions from them, theologians zealously and insightfully used analogy liberally, showing similarities between the truths of reason and faith, among the truths of faith, and between the truths of faith and their final end, the beatific vision. Since all theologians accepted propositional dogmas on authority, but the mysteries contained therein exceeded reason, pluralism in their interpretation was inevitable. Speculative theology also employed conceptualist presuppositions to illumine theology's content, applying Aristotelian categories to faith's mysteries. Those categories were stretched at times almost beyond recognition since the primacy of faith was respected. For example, Christ's eucharistic presence was understood as transubstantiation, i.e., a change of substance, even though he became personally present in two substances and the natural accidents of bread and wine remained without a natural substrate. Similarly, the un-Aristotelian notion of person differed in Trinity, "subsistent relation," and christology, "individual substance of a rational nature," and the agency in Christ's miracles was attributed not to his person but to the divine nature, which used the humanity instrumentally. Again, the reliance on efficient causality to explain sacramental causality and to relate God's omnipotent operation to human freedom generated some bitter disputes. Theologians willingly lived with such discrepancies because faith's propositions surpassed human insight and were accepted on authority. Besides, they thought that their philosophical presuppositions were required to refute Luther, fideism, and rationalism in accord with Trent and Vatican I.

Overcoming Past Opponents

Against the threefold Lutheran assertion: *sola fide, sola gratia, sola Scriptura*, the Council of Trent insisted also on charity, human freedom, and tradition. Influenced by late medieval thought and Protestant insistence on the literal sense, Trent saw the faith was grounded also in tradition, widely conceived as oral truths revealed to the Apostles. Whereas Luther's Augustinian anthropology located freedom in the individual's dynamic will which original sin perversely turned from God and rendered incapable of any good deed unless God's omnipotent attraction overcame its perversion, Trent insisted on free co-operation with grace and responsibility for its rejection (DS 1521, 1525, 1528f., 1554–11556, 1559). This seemed to call for a clear distinction of nature and grace: nature was only wounded, not thoroughly corrupted, by original sin. Hence freedom, conceived primarily as freedom of indifference, was capable of directing its own dynamism, co-operating with grace or rejecting it (DS 1530, 1535–1539, 1561). Such a freedom actively accepted faith, God's gift, and worked through charity. Given the goodness of nature, grace might build upon it, using the church and sacraments as instruments mediating grace (DS 1604, 1606–1609, 1767f., 1774). Subsequent battles against Baius, Jansenius, and their disciples, who employed an Augustinian anthropology, cemented the nature–grace distinction in Catholic theology.

Vatican I relied on the same distinction to rebut the rationalism and fideism stemming from the Enlightenment and Idealism (DS 3015–16). Reason and faith correspond epistemologically to nature and revelation. So the council affirmed the possibility of knowing God with certitude "by the natural light of human reason from created realities" (DS 3004). Since God ordained human beings to the supernatural end revealed in scripture and tradition, they were called to believe what surpassed the powers of unaided reason, viz., God's revelation of "Himself and the eternal decrees of His will" (DS 3004–06). Grace illumined and moved them to supernatural faith on the basis of the revealing God's authority. Corresponding to the grace–nature relation, faith's obedience was "in harmony with reason," for God, author of both orders who can neither deceive nor be deceived, provided "external proofs of His revelation, viz., divine facts, and especially miracles and prophecies" as "most certain signs of divine revelation, well fitted to the intelligence of all" (DS 3008–10, 3017, 3019). To the Catholic Church revelation had been entrusted. She not only was responsible for its preservation and infallible interpretation but was also herself a "motive of credibility" by her wondrous propagation, holiness, spiritual fruitfulness, unity, and stability (DS 3007, 3013f., 3017f., 3020). The council also defined specifically that the pope enjoyed infallibility in irreformably defining faith and morals as well as divinely instituted jurisdictional primacy over the whole church and every member (DS 3055, 3058, 3064, 3074).

The Difficulties

Despite authority's backing, time revealed weaknesses in conceptualist theology. For one, the continuity between faith and the beatific vision, the touchstone of the supernatural, was not clear. Supernatural revelation was historical while the vision occurred outside time. Second, the vision marked the highest actualization of the human intellect whereas in the act of faith the insight into the mystery affirmed was at a minimum. Third, in the vision intellectual subjectivity took precedence over faith's objective content in defining the supernatural. Fourth, the vision was conceived as the highest type of intellectual clarity, obviating the need of faith (despite 1 Cor. 13:13); somehow the intuition contained all the clarity of concepts while utterly surpassing them. The very notion of an intuitive grasp of the infinite God seemed to Suarezians impossible for finite human knowing which is always bound to a *species expressa*. Thomists simply admitted the mystery, responding that otherwise we could not see God as he is, face to face.

For its part the conceptualist analysis of faith proved too much or too little. So strong were the arguments for the fact of revelation, which evoked at least moral certitude, that only idiots or persons of ill will might apparently reject faith; no room seemed left for freedom or grace. Conversely, if the rational proofs were insufficient, freedom would choose faith without sufficient reason; then grace would immorally demand that the intellect affirm as true what it could not know to be true. Finally, demanding faith for salvation seemed in conflict with justice, the basis of the natural moral order: how could God condemn a person to hell who committed no personal sin?

Besides these inherent tensions the magisterium had introduced others in the intervening years. Pius

XII issued two encyclicals in 1943, *Mystici Corporis* and *Divino afflante Spiritu*. The former identified the visible Catholic Church with the Body of Christ. Historical research had revealed the centrality of this image from St Paul to the medieval doctors, and Pius used it to stress the interior bonding of believers to Christ and among themselves by grace. Though membership was limited to Catholics in union with the hierarchy, the church was no longer seen primarily as an instructional institution. The latter encyclical urged exegetes to study the biblical authors' literary genres in their historical contexts to comprehend better scripture's meaning. Thereby exegetes were freed from the necessity of defending the literal sense and might explore the implications of form-criticism, which, developed by Protestants, concentrated more on the meaning of scripture for believers than on its historical veracity. The final difficulty arose when in 1950 Pius XII defined infallibly the Blessed Virgin's corporeal assumption into heaven. Scripture did not witness explicitly to this dogma and no document before the sixth century mentioned it. While it was possible to imagine six centuries of solely oral tradition, the imagination was taxed. Conceptualist theologians had debated theories of dogmatic development, but they were constrained by the limits of their epistemology: if dogmatic propositions are explicit and supernatural, how can the natural mind deduce anything from them? With the Assumption's proclamation the theories' insufficiencies became acute (Schoof, 1970). Faithful theologians accepted the dogma on authority but they sought new ways of justifying their acceptance. Then J. Geiselmann (1966), while acknowledging that the fathers of Trent considered tradition a separate source alongside scripture, questioned whether that understanding was actually contained in their decrees.

Historical studies, on which conceptualist theologians depended to provide faith's content, also undermined the conceptualist superstructure. Central terms of conciliar definitions, like *homoousios*, *hypostasis*, and transubstantiation, had only been hammered out through acrimonious debates over the centuries. The council fathers must have understood something of these supernatural mysteries in defining them. Furthermore, the theological pluralism among orthodox fathers and medieval doctors was stunning. Though the fathers maintained human freedom's

co-operation with grace, they never employed the natural–supernatural distinction, which became common usage only in the thirteenth century. St Thomas himself propounded the paradoxical doctrine of the natural desire for the beatific vision. Indeed, he held that truth was found in judgment, and a newly discovered autograph of his, *In Boethii de Trinitate*, declared that being's metaphysical abstraction occurred through an existential judgment, not a concept. Neither did he commit himself to the analogy of proportionality but employed Platonic accents in his ontology and grace treatises. The conceptualist theology was beset by difficulties, but in 1950 Pius had also issued *Humani generis*, insisting on the natural–supernatural distinction. Too much seemed to be lost without it.

The Council's Texts

Conceptualist theologians tried to use Vatican II to shore up their positions. The council was expected to consider the church; the Preparatory Theological Commission also presented a schema on revelation. The contrast of these rejected preparatory schemata with *Dei Verbum* and *Lumen Gentium* highlights the theological changes wrought by Vatican II.

Revelation

On the Sources of Revelation affirmed that revelation comes to the church through scripture and tradition, a double source whose common root is the preaching authorized by Christ. The divine tradition preserved in the church contains everything about faith and morals which the Apostles received and passed on; only through this living tradition could some truths be known, especially those concerning scripture's inspiration, canonicity, and integrity. The living magisterium, "the proximate and universal norm of belief," preserves and authentically interprets the deposit of faith, judging what pertains to faith and morals directly or indirectly as well as explicating "what is contained in both sources only obscurely or, as it were, implicitly" (3–6, 27). The second chapter asserted that God, the principal author, internally inspired the sacred authors, his instruments, to "conceive correctly in mind and commit faithfully to writing all those things and only those things which He intended." They were individually inspired, and the inspiration extended to every part of scripture. Since truth is its author, "all error in anything whatsoever, religious or profane," is excluded from it. Nonetheless its truth and historical fidelity must be properly understood by attending to the "customary, natural ways of thinking, saying, or narrating" in use in the sacred authors' intellectual milieu. This accords with the divine condescension whereby the Word assumed human, weak flesh in willing to be like us in all but sin (7–14). The next two chapters treated Old and New Testaments. The Old bore prophetic witness to the New's grace and salvation, ultimately to Christ. The contents of the former are incomplete, especially on moral matters, and have to be compared to Christ's gospel and submitted to the magisterium for correct interpretation. Nonetheless the inspiration of the human authors remains intact (16–18). The historicity of the New Testament is strongly upheld since the Gospels "sincerely pass on what Jesus, the Son of God living among men for their eternal salvation, really did and taught"; the names of the evangelists are defended as is the "objective, historical truth of the facts of the life of our Lord Jesus Christ," especially the infancy narrative, signs, and miracles as well as his resurrection and ascension. Even if the reporting was not literally exact, all those denying the "force and substance" of Christ's words are condemned, as are those claiming a discrepancy between Christ's teachings and the Apostles' (19–23). The final chapter maintained that the church always preserved the correct meaning of scripture. Hence it defended the Vulgate against any error in faith or morals even while encouraging bishops to provide approved translations for the people. Exegetes were urged to employ new discoveries for "a more penetrating understanding of the literal sense" and theologians were to expand their teaching with the correct interpretation of scripture "since Sacred Scripture together with tradition is, as it were, the soul of all theological doctrine" (24–29).

The final version of *Dei Verbum* repeats many affirmations of Vatican I and *On the Sources*: natural knowledge of God, God's revelation of himself and the eternal decrees of his will, the obedience of faith, God as author inspiring scripture, the Old Testament

preparing for Christ, the magisterium as scripture's authentic interpreter, etc. Yet additions and subtle shifts of emphasis profoundly alter the result. Revelation consists not just of propositions but of deeds and words intrinsically bound together (2, 6, 17). Scripture and tradition, though necessary, are not described as two separate sources. They are united in source (gospel) and goal (sanctification) and coalesce into the single deposit of God's Word. They are so intricately bound to each other and the magisterium for the salvation of souls that one cannot stand without the others (8–10). Though authentic teacher, the magisterium is no longer the proximate norm of faith; rather scripture and tradition together are "the supreme rule" of the church's faith, for she serves the Word of God and is not superior to it. Indeed she grows in her understanding of it as the Spirit guides her into the full truth. The gospel is not identified with books; it is first preached and then written as the "fourfold gospel." Though the scripture without error transmits the truths confided to it for our salvation, inerrancy in all religious and profane matters is not claimed. Scripture's various literary forms present the truth differently (10–12, 21). Though the Gospels faithfully transmit the "honest truth" about what Jesus said and did for our salvation, their authors selected and synthesized the message, in the form of preaching, in view of the churches' circumstances (18–19). No statement directly contradicts conceptualist theology, but the interpretation of tradition as the dynamic process sustaining the gospel can easily be substituted for tradition as a separate source, especially when Jesus is presented as "simultaneously mediator and fullness of all revelation," the mystery of salvation present in scripture which, parallel to the Eucharist, nourishes believers (2, 21, 24, 26).

Ecclesiology

"Mystery" is also central to *Lumen Gentium*, changing theological parameters. The schema *De Ecclesia* had treated the church in the traditional apologetic-juridical mode, touching in order the church's nature, her membership and the need of belonging in order to attain salvation, the episcopate, residential bishops, states of perfection, the laity, the magisterium, authority and obedience, church–state relations, the necessity of preaching the gospel to all peoples everywhere, and ecumenism. *Lumen Gentium*'s radically revised order of presentation manifests a profound change of emphasis. Grounded in the Trinity's design of salvation fulfilled and revealed in Jesus Christ, the church belongs to that salvific mystery. She is described as "a people brought into unity from the unity of the Father, the Son, and the Holy Spirit" and "a type of sacrament, i.e., a sign and instrument of communion with God and of unity among all men" (1–4). This notion is novel since conceptualist theology reserved the term sacrament for the seven instruments of grace established by Christ. Instead of defining the church in clear, juridical terminology, *Lumen Gentium* employs various biblical "images" or "figures" before considering the main image, the Body of Christ. "In that body the life of Christ is communicated to those who believe and who, through the sacraments, are united in hidden and real way to Christ in His Passion and glorification" (6–7). Interior life and unity are emphasized. Only later is this "community of faith, hope, and charity" identified as a visible hierarchical organization forming one complex reality from a human and a divine element." This "sole Church of Christ," one, holy, catholic, and apostolic, is said to "subsist in the Catholic Church" (8). Why did the Council not simply write, "This sole Church of Christ is the Catholic Church"? Rivers of ink still flow over the meaning of *subsistit in* (von Teuffenbach, 2002; Becker, 2006; Sullivan, 2006).

Doubtless the church's internal, invisible life enjoys a priority over the external, hierarchical structure; sacrament precedes juridical institution. The remaining text confirms this change: before Chapter 3 presents the Hierarchical Church, Chapter 2 considers the People of God as a whole. The hierarchy is subordinated to the whole people as a means toward salvation. Moreover, in stressing the continuity between Old and New Testaments, the human element in the "pilgrim Church" is highlighted. Subordinate to and complementary of "Body of Christ," "people of God" brings out the continuity and difference between Old and New Covenants. It also opens to Protestant theology, whose stress on God's absolute transcendence resists binding him definitively to any human structure. Yet, as Grillmeier pointed out (1967), the

people's eschatological status distinguishes *Lumen Gentium*'s use from the Protestant interpretation. Two further shifts of emphasis quickly follow. First, the equality of all believers precedes hierarchical distinctions. All believers are priests and prophets, all alike called to holiness. Correspondingly, diversity among particular churches and believers is understood as a richness adorning the unity, not a fall from ideal uniformity. That prepared the appreciation of Eastern Churches in *Orientalium Ecclesiarum*. Second, though Christian fullness is predicated of the Catholic Church alone, non-Catholic Christians are "in some real way joined to us in the Holy Spirit" and non-Christians and non-believers are related to that fullness in varying degrees (14–16). The distinction between "true faith based on authority" and unbelief is not employed. On this basis the council established positions on the church–world relation (*Gaudium et spes*), religious freedom (*Dignitatis humanae*), missionary activity (*Ad gentes*), ecumenism (*Unitatis reintegratio*), Catholic–Jewish relations (*Nostra aetate*), and the communications media (*Inter mirifica*).

Chapter 3 states that as a collegial body the bishops possess "supreme and full authority over the universal Church." This authority is recognized as ordinary and immediately given by God, not dependent upon the pope, even if he also maintains an immediate jurisdictional authority over all bishops and faithful and bishops cannot exercise their authority apart from the pope. Similarly, infallibility is no longer a special prerogative of the pope, which he shares with ecumenical councils; rather the bishops' and the pope's infallibility is comprised within the church's infallibility. The council privileged the church as a whole, laity, clergy, and pope, before considering her various constituent, hierarchical elements. The monarchical papacy has retreated.

This emphasis on personal and universal instead of structural and particular recurs regarding the church's sanctity. Whereas conceptualists deemed the church holy due to the sacraments, which communicate sanctifying grace, and the many saints produced by that grace, especially as witnessed in religious life, the new emphasis on the people of God moved the council to write: "The Church, clasping sinners to her bosom, at once holy and always in need of purification, follows constantly the path of penance and renewal" (8).

Chapter 4 treats the laity before vowed religious life; the traditional state of perfection is handled in Chapter 6 only after the universal call to holiness was expounded in Chapter 5: "All Christians in any state or walk of life are called to the fullness of Christian life and to the perfection of love" (40). These themes were expanded in other conciliar documents: on the laity (*Apostolicam actuositatem*), religious orders (*Perfectae caritatis*), priests (*Presbyterorum Ordinis*), and bishops (*Christus Dominus*). A concluding chapter on the Pilgrim Church stresses her transitoriness and imperfection. "The Church … will receive her perfection only in the glory of heaven." Though the final age of the world has begun and the church's sanctity is real, it is still imperfect (48). Where is the apologetics depicting the church as already offering the full, visible realization of the unity, holiness, catholicity, and apostolicity intended by Christ for his church? Only a different theology can account for the shift from emphasizing institutional fullness to growing personal appropriation of the mystery of salvation.

Transcendental Thomism

Transcendental Thomists located truth in a judgment or insight, of which the concept is only a part. The mind therefore goes beyond the concept to reach reality; thus are concepts relativized. Moreover truth is realized not in the passive intellect receiving a concept, but in the activity of the judging intellect. The knower's activity contributes to truth's constitution; there is no objectivity unless over subjectivity. Knowledge consists in existential identity of knower and known, not in comparing forms. Since judgment is a reflexive act, in knowing the material other the intellect is immediately present to itself. Its movement, *qua* movement, implies a goal. It moves toward the true as its own good; as the formal objects, the good and the true, coalesce, intellect and will unite into one spiritual dynamism. The deepest truth is most free. Not freedom of indifference, but engaged, Augustinian freedom is directed toward or away from its proper goal, and it has to be liberated to attain its goal. Moreover, since a judgment synthesizes the material object with its spiritual meaning, body and soul, sensation and intellection, are understood as a basic unity, each implying the other. Matter and spirit refer to each other, and matter implies relation to other bodies; hence incarnate spirit can only be itself in relation to all of reality: God and material creation. The "in-itself" of conceptualist natures has given way to a whole web of relations.

The spiritual dynamism's goal cannot be finite. Once limitation is recognized, the mind immediately transcends it. Nothing finite can satisfy the intellect's natural desire to know reality as it seeks knowledge's final ground. Only the infinite God, not a concept of him, can sate the intellect's craving. As knowledge's condition of possibility he is affirmed in every true judgment. But God in himself is Trinity, a supernatural mystery. Thence arises the paradoxical natural desire for the supernatural. Augustine's longing for the Trinitarian God is built into human nature. Since human thought primordially refers to God as its ground, the analogy of proportion is preferred, and the analogous, based upon the oscillation between being's infinity and concrete instances, is previous to the univocal concept. Concepts have their place only within the movement of the existential judgment.

While concepts ground clear distinctions, transcendental judgments transcend them toward a higher unity: God and man, true and good, intellect and will, body and soul, subject and object, natural and supernatural tend to be amalgamated. Not that the value of concepts is denied; without concepts thought is not possible. The best transcendental thinkers tried to preserve concepts and all necessary distinctions but did not absolutize them. They subtly shifted from unity to diversity and back again according to need. But on the whole, unity or amalgamation prevailed. Other changes followed. Since the spiritual dynamism was basic to reality, final causality took precedence over efficient causality. Subjectivity assumed a dominant role since only over it was reality attained. The concrete and existential, to which judgment refers, prevailed over the abstract and essential. The supernatural was no longer an intruder from without but the intrinsic completion of the universe's concrete order. These changes of emphasis allowed the new theology to resolve many of the problems besetting the conceptualist theology but also entailed novel dilemmas.

For the act of faith the transcendental theology explained how the external sign is linked to the internal grace to produce a single certitude and how the assent of faith is most certain and free. For the intellect is a synthetic power, i.e., expressing itself in a judgment joining its components. The natural world of facts serves as signs, or clues, of a higher significance. As two detectives can observe the same phenomena, yet only the more intelligent perceives the unified pattern, so in matters of faith there can be similarity of representational elements with differences of interpretation. One sees and interprets correctly, the other does not. Faith's act results from the mutual causality of perception and perceived. The sign is seen as significant only within a greater meaning, and the meaning is revealed only through the sign. Thus the natural order serves as a sign of the supernatural order which envelops, surpasses, and perfects it. The same intellectual movement joins freedom and certitude, for it is a basic desire or love to possess itself and God. Intellect and will mutually affect each other; thus practical judgment and voluntary election unite in the voluntary election as the supernatural elevation simultaneously expands the soul's fundamental love. Love and insight grow concomitantly. A revealed external sign is required to prevent the soul from being misled by any affective tendency whatever. Thus the unity of external sign and interior assent is preserved. Faith is free since the grace calling for free homage may be rejected, and faith is reasonable since the perceived sign applies the witness of the natural order to the recognized truth. Finally, because God alone gives the grace to perceive the supernatural meaning, the soul recognizes God's authority in accepting faith.

From those foundations many conclusions can follow. Grace, God's presence, is given to all not only because God wills that all be saved (1 Tim. 2:4) but also because by nature all are ordained to the beatific vision and anticipatorily participate in that goal. Since all are immediately self-conscious, they are aware unthematically, i.e., non-conceptually, of God. Hence (uncreated) grace can be experienced unthematically and through the church's preaching anonymous Christians can be led to explicit faith. Apologetics becomes fundamental theology wherein the individual's experience is analyzed to reveal how it accords with the Christian message which brings it to full flowering. Grace comes to its clearest expression in Christ's death and resurrection; since human nature is visible

and social, grace elevates nature and finds a fitting expression not only in Christ but also in the church, the visible sign of grace already received. Christ's humanity and the church can both be understood as sacraments, visible expressions of interior union with God. Although the full expression is found in the Catholic Church, others participating in grace can be oriented to it and saved by unthematic faith in Christ. For faith is primarily a response to the revealing God; it is personal more than propositional. Dogmas are understood as finite articulations of the human encounter with the infinite God. Since they do not exhaust the mystery, they can be reformulated in ways better adapted to convey the gospel message to new generations. Development of dogma is explained as progressive articulations of the encounter with God mediated by Jesus and the church through word (scripture in tradition) and sacrament. The church, in union with the resurrected Christ directly and though history, remains the irrevocable sign of God's victory over death and sin, and her magisterium functions as the arbiter of theological language.

Difficulties

The more intelligent transcendental Thomists carefully preserved a concept of being within the dynamism; without concepts judgments are literally inconceivable. Since concepts preserve diversity, wise theologians fell back upon them to uphold necessary distinctions. Thus their method enabled them to affirm what the church taught and to resolve various problems in conceptualist theology. Unfortunately, after the council many less intelligent disciples emphasized the novelty of the documents and, thinking to effect "theological progress," relied on the dynamism's transcendence to relativize finite expressions and institutions. Even Christ's unique mediatorship was denied. But Catholic theology cannot be reduced to rational systematization; it consists in a balancing of truths and perspectives. That is why oscillation or paradox was fundamental to transcendental Thomism. Its basic tensions could not be denied. In the act of faith, "natural" sign be identified if objectivity is known only over subjectivity and the subject stands under grace? If the intellect is naturally oriented to the God of grace, how does the supernatural expand the soul's fundamental love and how can the dynamism be free to accept a supernatural expansion? Though the link to external reality in the sign is preserved, the need of any particular historical sign is not clear. If anything, even a blade of grass, as Rousselot wrote (1910), can serve as the occasion for the spirit's transcendence in grace, what need is there of Christ's historical particularity? Then there is a fundamental ontological conundrum: if the natural desire for God needs grace to attain its end, nature in itself is frustrated; if it does not need grace, then Jesus is not needed. In the former case Catholic theology approaches Barth's dialectic or Bultmann's "nevertheless"; in the latter, secular naturalism results. Furthermore, since God is affirmed and chosen in every intellectual-voluntary act, sin, the rejection of God, seems impossible. Rahner calls it a "real absolute contradiction," yet affirms its possibility (1976, 106). Finally with the transcendence of concepts all finite intelligibility depends upon God's infinite mystery and universal concepts are relativized. This leads to confusion not only in dogma but also in morality (McDermott, 1999). How can the magisterium be infallible if every statement is revisable, never definitive? It is easy to see how confusion entered the Catholic Church and splintered theological unity after Vatican II, especially when Western society was convulsing under protests against Vietnam and racism, the sexual revolution, and drugged euphoria.

What Did the Council Achieve?

Without doubt the council destroyed the hegemony of conceptualist theology by attacking two cardinal issues: the relation of reason and faith in *Dei Verbum* and the position of the church in *Lumen gentium*. The first questioned the adequacy of the natural-supernatural distinction as well as the distinct sources of revelation. The second touched a neuralgic point since ecclesiology stood at the culmination of apologetics and the beginning of dogmatic theology. Once the church was no longer understood primarily as an authoritative hierarchy, the repercussions upon apologetics and dogma had to follow. The reintroduction of a strong Augustinian emphasis into Catholic theology facilitated dialogue with Protestants, even as the retained

"nature" permitted her to talk with the world. The church need not be primarily defensive, concerned merely with preserving intact the deposit of faith. But did the church subscribe to transcendental Thomism?

Transcendental Thomism is a variegated movement. There were at least three different understandings of the church as sacrament before the council (McDermott, 2006). Within 10 years of the council's termination many of its leading theological protagonists had gone into mutual opposition, some seeing it as the first step in a radical rethinking of Christianity, others recalling the need of continuity with tradition. The council itself deliberately refrained from endorsing any particular theological system (Moeller, 1966a, 1966b). As we indicated, it made compromises right down the line between two principal theologies. That was not ill advised. While the conceptualist theology tended to absolutize finite intelligibility and structures, transcendental theology tended to relativize them before infinite mystery. The most intelligent representatives of both schools recognized the need for balance: concept and judgment, essence and existence, form and matter, nature and grace. There is diversity within unity because the infinite and the finite cannot be opposed as if they contradicted each other. Indeed the basic sacramental structure of Catholicism confirms the juncture of infinite and finite, God and man, in Jesus, the Eucharist, and the church, each in an analogous way. That central mystery cannot be encompassed or controlled by any rational systematization. Rather it is open to God's omnipotence (infinity of willing) and man's freedom (finite willing).

The apparent opposition between conceptualist and transcendental theologies is due to their foundations in natures. As necessary principles of activity, natures develop according to inherent laws; in classical philosophy the necessary laws of thought were grounded in the objectivity of the natural order. Conceptualist thinkers built the natural order upon natures, and transcendental thinkers based their system upon the necessity inherent in the natural intellect's judgment. Modernity has stressed human freedom beyond natures in order technologically to control nature. It relativized natures before the arbitrariness of individual choice, leading to historical and cultural relativism as well as arbitrary "political correctness." Unintentionally Vatican II brought the

Catholic Church into the modern world by inoculating her with modernity's intellectual confusion. Paradoxically, this opening to history may also be the way to her deepest identity and the world's salvation. For Christ is the absolute in history; his union with humanity is not natural but hypostatic, personal. Neither conceptualist nor transcendental theology elaborated consistently the relation between person and nature in Christ and the Trinity. That is the principal task for Christian theology, for person joins relation

with "in-itself" (Ratzinger, 1990). Providentially, in his magisterial *The Acting Person* K. Wojtyla located freedom squarely in the person, not the natural will, and saw that persons possess themselves by losing themselves in love. As pope he wrote many encyclicals from that conviction. "Person" can reconcile freedom and nature, God and man, unity and diversity in the mystery of the incarnation. That synthesis still to be accomplished may be the ultimate achievement of Vatican II (cf. McDermott, 2004).

References

Alberigo, Guiseppe, ed. 1997–2006. *History of Vatican II*, 5 vols. English edition edited by Joseph A. Komonchak. Maryknoll: Orbis.

Becker, Karl J. 2006. "The Church and Vatican II's '*Subsistit in*' Terminology," *Origins* 35: 514–22.

Geiselmann, Johannes R. 1966. *The Meaning of Tradition*, trans. W. J. O'Hara. New York: Herder and Herder.

Grillmeier, Aloys. 1967. "The People of God." In *Commentary on the Documents of Vatican II*, ed. Herbert Vorgrimler, 1: 153–85. New York: Herder and Herder.

John XXIII. 1966a. *Gaudet Mater Ecclesia* (October 11, 1962). In *Constitutiones Decreta Declarationes*, ed. General Secretariat of Vatican II. Vatican: Vatican Press, pp. 854–72.

John XXIII. 1966b. *Humanae Salutis* (December 25, 1961). In *Constitutiones Decreta Declarationes*, ed. General Secretariat of Vatican II, pp. 839–53.

McCool, Gerald A. 1977. *Catholic Theology in the Nineteenth Century*. New York: Seabury.

McDermott, John M. 1988. "Faithful and Critical Reason in Theology." In *Excellence in Seminary Education*, ed. Stephen Minkiel, Ronald Lawler, and Francis Lescoe. Erie: Gannon University.

McDermott, John M. 1990. "Metaphysical Conundrums at the Root of Moral Disagreement," *Gregorianum* 71: 713–42.

McDermott, John M. 1991. "The Methodological Shift in Twentieth Century Thomism," *Seminarium* 31: 245–66.

McDermott, John M. 1999. "The Context of *Veritatis Splendor*." In *Prophecy and Diplomacy: The Moral Doctrine of John Paul II*, ed. John J. Conley and Joseph W. Koterski. New York: Fordham University, pp. 115–72.

McDermott, John M. 2002. "Faith, Reason, and Freedom," *Irish Theological Quarterly* 67: 307–32.

McDermott, John M. 2006. "Vatican II and the Theologians on the Church as Sacrament," *Irish Theological Quarterly* 71: 143–78.

McDermott, John M. 2007. "*Lumen Gentium*: The Once and Future Constitution." In *After Forty Years: Vatican Council II's Diverse Legacy*, ed. Kenneth D. Whitehead. South Bend: St. Augustine's, pp. 134–63.

Moeller, Charles. 1966a. "History of *Lumen Gentium's* Structure and Idea." In *Vatican II: An Interfaith Appraisal*, ed. John H. Miller. Notre Dame: University of Notre Dame, pp. 123–52.

Moeller, Charles. 1966b. "Session IV Discussion." In *Vatican II: An Interfaith Appraisal*, ed. John H. Miller. Notre Dame: University of Notre Dame, pp. 176–84.

Philips, Gérard. 1967. "Dogmatic Constitution on the Church: History of the Constitution." In *Commentary on the Documents of Vatican II*, ed. Herbert Vorgrimler, 1:105–37. New York: Herder and Herder.

Rahner, Karl. 1976. *Grundkurs des Glaubens*. Freiburg: Herder.

Ratzinger, Joseph. 1968. "Dogmatic Constitution on Divine Revelation: Origin and Background." In *Commentary on the Documents of Vatican II*, ed. Herbert Vorgrimler, 3:155–66. New York: Herder and Herder.

Ratzinger, Joseph. 1990. "Concerning the Notion of Person in Theology," *Communio* 17: 439–54.

Rousselot, Pierre. 1910. "Les Yeux de la foi," *Recherches des Science Religieuse* 1: 241–59, 444–75.

Rynne, Xavier. 1968. *Vatican Council II*. New York: Farrar, Straus and Giroux.

Schoof, T. Mark. 1970. *A Survey of Catholic Theology 1800–1970*, trans. N. D. Smith. Glen Rock: Paulist Newman.

Sullivan, Francis A. 2006. "Quaestio Disputata: A Response to Karl Becker, S. J., on the Meaning of *Subsistit in*," *Theological Studies* 67: 395–409.

von Teuffenbach, Alexandra. 2002. *Die Bedeutung des "Subsistit in" (LG 8)*. Munich: Utz.

Wiltgen, Ralph M. 1967. *The Rhine Flows into the Tiber*. New York: Hawthorn Books.

Wojtyla, Karol. 1979. *The Acting Person*, trans. Andrzej Potocki. Dordrecht: D. Reidel.

Keith Ward (1938–)

Ian S. Markham

Keith Ward is best known for his remarkable exercise in a systematic theology which takes comparative theology very seriously.

I. Life

Keith Ward was born in northern England in 1938. He describes himself as "naturally religious, in the sense that I seemed to apprehend a spiritual presence (or presences) both in the natural world and in music" (Ward in Bartel, 2003, 190). However, he also lived in an "in between" space—a space between the "natural feelings of my heart and the critical questions of my mind" (ibid.).

He trained as a philosopher (collecting a BA from the University of Wales) and becoming a Lecturer in Logic at the University of Glasgow. For much of this period, he describes himself as an atheist; yet he also sees the "tide turning" (an allusion to his BBC series and book *The Turn of the Tide*, 1986) and a growing convergence between modern physics and faith. So it was that when he was at King's College, London, he became a priest in the Church of England in 1972.

He then held a succession of senior professorial chairs in the United Kingdom—F. D. Maurice Professor of Moral and Social Theology, followed by the Professor of History and Philosophy of Religion (both at King's College, London), then the Regius Professor of Divinity at the University of Oxford in 1991. He held this chair until his retirement from Oxford University in 2004.

II. Theology

To understand Ward's method, one must begin with the logician at the University of Glasgow. Ward is first and foremost a good competent philosopher, able to use the most rigorous of philosophical tools. This has shaped many of his often unspoken assumptions. It meant that as Ward developed his interests in theological questions, he saw the goal of theological study as the quest for a coherent and comprehensive description of the ways things are. He is a critical realist, and he uses traditional criteria to determine whether a particular account is true. He writes:

> There are some very basic rational criteria which can be brought to bear upon all claims to truth, in religion as elsewhere. Rationality involves the use of intelligent capacities, including the capacity to register information correctly, to compare similar pieces of information, to deduce and infer in accordance with rules of logic and relate means to ends effectively. A rational person can act on a consciously formulated principle in order to attain an intended goal … Such simple forms of reasoning are necessary to any form of intelligently ordered social life. They are not, and cannot be, culturally relative. (Ward, 1994, 319)

The Student's Companion to the Theologians, First Edition. Edited by Ian S. Markham.
© 2013 Blackwell Publishing Ltd. Published 2013 by Blackwell Publishing Ltd.

This means in practice that an account must be internally coherent; if it is coherent, then it is a matter of evidence, explanatory power, and plausibility. He is impatient with those who want to describe different and incommensurable traditions with different rationalities. He explains that

> if one asks to what "tradition" these basic criteria of rationality—self-consistency, coherence with other knowledge, and adequacy to available data—belong, the answer must be that they belong to the tradition of being human, as such … [T]hey are principles of rationality which are built into the necessary structure of human social life, and thus function as desirable ideals for any community that wishes to survive for any length of time. (Ward, 1994, 320)

It is at this point he understands—even if he does entirely agree with—the Richard Swinburne project. Richard Swinburne's initial trilogy—*The Coherence of Theism*, *The Existence of God*, and *Faith and Reason*—works with the traditional philosophical paradigm. You demonstrate first the coherence of God, then provide good arguments for the existence of God, and finally demonstrate the relationship of this approach with faith. *Rational Theology and the Creativity of God* (1982) is the best example of Ward working within the Swinburne framework. He writes: "These two tasks—of expounding the idea of God, and of establishing the rationality and moral importance of belief in God—go together. Without a clear idea of God, one cannot be sure of what, exactly, one is looking for reasons to accept. And without a clear account of the reasons for belief, one cannot be sure of what it is that one has established as the conclusion of those reasonings" (Ward, 1982, 1). Here Ward argues from the assumption of intelligibility to theism at the same time as providing an account of God which is internally coherent.

In terms of philosophical competence, Ward could have easily joined those Christian analytical philosophers of religion who have set themselves the task of defending the central doctrines of the Christian faith, of whom Swinburne is the leading British example. However, he moved away from this approach and turned instead to one much more sympathetic to religious studies and traditional theology.

One factor in Ward's distant relationship with analytical philosophy of religion was his unfashionable

support for certain Wittgensteinian insights. One of his early works, *Concept of God*, clearly shows a debt to Wittgenstein. He returns to Wittgenstein in *Religion and Revelation* (1994). Here he identifies with Wittgenstein's sense that there are certain "frameworks" that are not justified rationally but simply assumed. Ward writes:

> Worship and prayer, for example, are natural practices by which humans relate to the world of their experience in specific ways. They do not, as such, stand in need of justification, for they are rooted in basic attitudes of awe, reverence, gratitude and dependence, which show themselves in human behaviour. They form the basis for developing sets of concepts which aim to provide illuminating descriptions of how the world is and of how humans ought to live. At that stage they become subject to rational enquiry and assessment. (Ward, 1996a, 11)

So Ward's more sophisticated account of religious language, coupled with his Wittgensteinian sympathy with the community-orientated nature of religious discourse, meant that he never reduced the theological task to the reproduction of key doctrines in symbolic logic. Therefore Ward's methodology never resulted in Swinburne's rather crude simplification of theological ideas. He understands Swinburne's wish to simplify and clarify religious language, but feels that the confusing nature of elements of the Christian narrative is there for a purpose. Ward, in short, lives with a much greater sense of mystery than Swinburne would ever tolerate.

For Ward then, his methodology involves taking a framework of belief and exploring (a) the coherence of the beliefs within that framework and (b) the arguments for and against those beliefs. He does so, sensitive to the distinctive nature of theological discourse. Ward creates a methodology for comparative theology, which does not simply describe, but engages constructively and distinctively with the worldviews with a goal of discerning the truth about God and God's relationship with the world. So he does not surrender to incommensurable rationalities that make these traditions unable to speak to each other; nor does he allow one tradition to simply be defined and explained by a different one. Instead he shares the traditional philosopher's conviction that the human gift of rationality does give us the equipment to understand each other. However, conversely, he also allows the distinctive "music" or "dance" of the theological discourse to thrive. Ramanuja, for example, does not always work with clear premises leading to appropriate conclusions as a result of strict deductive logic. Keith Ward has both the rationality that makes engagement possible and the sensitivity to the distinctive nature of the discourse that makes engagement meaningful.

Turning now to methodology, it is clear that his understanding of Christ has been modified in three of his books: *Divine Action* (1990), *A Vision to Pursue* (1991), and *Religion and Revelation* (1994). Ward explains the movement from *Divine Action* to *A Vision to Pursue* in his introduction to *A Vision to Pursue*. Since he became a Christian, his instinct was to see Jesus as a human being "who obeyed God fully, knew and loved him intimately, and as a result was able to bring God close to others or even act in the place of God in regard to other people. He was a man wholly transparent to God, perhaps, and thus a perfected vehicle of the divine love" (Ward, 1991, 49). However, he explained that he wanted to explore the classical doctrine of the incarnation: he could see certain advantages, and therefore set out to defend an ontological doctrine of the incarnation in *Divine Action*. This is the philosopher Ward speaking: he seems to be saying that *Divine Action* was in part an exploration of a "conceptual possibility" (i.e., the attempt to formulate a good case for a logically possible position). *Divine Action* defends a kenotic version of the incarnation. Yet even here, he acknowledged the major difficulty that would provoke *A Vision to Pursue*. He writes:

> The intellectual coherence of the doctrine of incarnation, its apparent confirmation by continued experience of the Lordship of Christ in the Church, and its fruitfulness in suggesting illuminating ways of understanding both the nature of God and of human experience in general, all combine to place the gospel accounts within a framework of interpretation which makes them strong enough to bear the doctrine which has historically grown from reflection upon them. But one major problem remains to be faced. The earliest followers of Jesus saw themselves as living in the "last days," and Jesus as the culminating act of God in history. But the world did not end, and the figure of Jesus has now receded into the past. (Ward, 1990, 252)

Although, in *Divine Action*, the problem is resolved by examining the redemption of all time in the eschaton, the problem of Jesus' mistaken knowledge provides the main argument against an "ontological" incarnation in *A Vision to Pursue*. However, he seems to move back to a more incarnational position in *Religion and Revelation*. In a footnote, he explains that any reader of *A Vision to Pursue* "will note a much more pronounced incarnational emphasis in the present work. I have become convinced that such an emphasis is necessary and possible, given a relatively small amendments of the previous analysis" (Ward, 1994, 240, fn.75). For Ward there was greater consistency than his critics had recognized. He was right; he continued to reject a Jesus who was omniscient, omnipotent, and consciously pre-existent. Instead he becomes an advocate of an enhypostatic view of incarnation. Ward explains thus: "What the life-perfectly-united-to-God shows is the nature and purpose of God. Jesus has a free mind and will, which makes its own decisions and performs its own creative actions. He is united to God in such a way that, in freely obeying his distinctive calling, he expresses what God is, becoming a living revelation of Supreme value." In short, Jesus is a person completely interpenetrated by the Divine Word.

One must grant that on christology there is modification. However, methodologically, there are three factors operating here: a respect for the classical definition of Christ, a desire to find a coherent and plausible account of the incarnation which is compatible with the evidence available in the New Testament, and the necessity to have a christology that is not simply compatible with the expectation that we learn of God from non-Christian sources but makes it an imperative.

Thus his engagement with other faith traditions has introduced a distinctive twist to the Ward methodology. He became an advocate of an "open orthodoxy" (Ward, 1994, 2) (sometimes described as an "open theology"), "which will be true to the main orthodox Christian tradition, yet which will be open to a fruitful interaction with other traditions, and with the developing corpus of scientific knowledge" (Ward, 1994, 1). "Open Orthodoxy" makes possible "a committed, open, and developing understanding of faith in the contemporary world" (ibid.).

Now it is not entirely clear whether this label is supposed to be descriptive or prescriptive: whether Ward believes that the tradition, at its best, *is* "open" or whether the tradition *ought* to be "open." On the descriptive side, Aquinas is treated as an example of a theologian who took his "interpretative clues from philosophical or cultural factors not confined to Christianity" (Ward, 1994, 37). Yet his description of "open orthodoxy," which by the end of the book is called "open theology," seems rather more prescriptive. Ward writes:

> One might perhaps speak of an "open theology", which can be characterised by six main features. It will seek a convergence of common core beliefs, clarifying the deep arguments which underlie diverse cultural traditions. It will seek to learn from complementary beliefs in other traditions, expecting that there are forms of revelation one's own tradition does not express. It will be prepared to reinterpret its beliefs in the light of new, well-established factual and moral beliefs. It will accept the full right of diverse belief-systems to exist, as long as they do not cause avoidable injury or harm to innocent sentient beings. It will encourage a dialogue with conflicting and dissenting views, being prepared to confront its own tradition with critical questions arising out of such views. And it will try to develop a sensitivity to the historical and cultural contexts of the formulation of its own beliefs, with a preparedness to continue developing new insights in new cultural situations. (Ward, 1996a, 339–40)

This seems prescriptive because, as he admits himself, "no theology is wholly open or wholly closed" (Ward, 1996, 340).

The important point is that Ward's open theology emerges from a commitment to the Christian tradition. This enables Ward to sound both traditional and liberal because he believes that the tradition, at its best and perhaps unconsciously, is liberal. By liberal, I mean the tradition is committed to openness and change. Comparative theology emerges from his commitment to the Christian tradition.

This is the reason why it is wrong to link Ward, and therefore any theology of engagement, too closely with John Hick. John Hick argues that comparative theology will depend on a "pluralist theology of other religions," which involves a Copernican revolution from a christocentric tradition to a theocentric one. Instead of exclusivism (Jesus is the only way to be saved) or inclusivism (others are saved through Jesus without realizing it), Hick wants us to cross the Rubicon and become pluralists (all religions are equally salvific). Ward does not see Christ as a problem for a theocentric understanding of religions and is disinclined to cross the Rubicon. Instead Ward underpins his open theology with "soft pluralism." Ward is unhappy with Hick's pluralism because it seems to rest on a "pragmatic theory of truth" (Ward, 1994, 310). Ward does want to talk about more or less adequate accounts of ultimate reality and maintains that all traditions contain some false beliefs. He rejects the label "inclusivist" because an inclusivist assumes that his or her tradition includes the best of other traditions, while a soft pluralist believes that other traditions have insights not known (or perhaps not known sufficiently well) within Christianity.

Ward's "open theology" approach has been applied to four areas. The first is "revelation" (volume 1, 1994); the second is "creation" (volume 2, 1996a); the third is human nature (volume 3, 1998); and the fourth is community (volume 4, 2000). The results are interesting. First, he captures well the diversity of each tradition and the legitimate connections that can be made across traditions. So, to take an example, the study on human nature shows how the non-dualistic school of Vedanta, Advaita, which holds the view that human beings are essentially spiritual, is also found in certain strands of "Western religious thought which have Neo-platonic roots" (Ward, 1998, 1). Second, for Ward, one must first understand the other before offering an analysis. In this way he then finds that the exercise of understanding provokes an insight which he insists the Christian tradition must take seriously. This is close to my concept of "overhearing." For example, Ward looks at three major interpretations of rebirth within Hindu orthodoxy. Although he notes the problems (for example, Vaishnava rejects the scientific hypothesis of evolution because it is incompatible with the rebirth hypothesis), he insists that, "the idea of rebirth does enshrine a hope for the possibility of spiritual progress and development, even for those whose earthly lives seem to make such a hope impossible. That is a hope that must be basic for any religion of devotion to a truly gracious and loving God, and there must be some way of providing for it in any religion of grace" (Ward, 1998, 75).

Ward's achievement is this remarkable "comparative systematic theology." It stands alone in its comprehensive nature and scope. All those interested in this work need to relate to his distinctive methodology. And there are five elements to that methodology. First, Ward is a critical realist: the task for the theologian is to provide a coherent account of faith based on sound reasons and compatible with other insights in other areas. Second, he insists that there is no neutral vantage point for evaluation of traditions, yet strongly rejects any talk of different rationalities within different traditions. This is in part shaped by his Wittgensteinian sympathies. Third, the theological task must take other religious traditions seriously. Comparative theology is a historically self-conscious development of traditional Christian methodology. Fourth, comparative theology assumes that it is possible to arrive at more or less adequate descriptions of ultimate reality; Ward is therefore a "soft pluralist." Fifth, the results of comparative theology are (a) greater understanding, (b) connections within and across traditions, and (c) the illumination of certain issues that then need to be subsequently accommodated into any adequate Christian theology.

III. Significance

Keith Ward's primary contribution is in the realm of comparative theology. He provides a system by which the insights of other faith traditions can be taken seriously, while not losing sight of the truth project. John Hick captures this when he writes of Keith Ward: "I see him as being as open to the reality and profound value of other world faiths as is possible whilst remaining within the borders of basic Christian orthodoxy" (Hick in Bartel, 2003, 25). In this respect, Ward represents a vitally important movement; he is a Christian who wants to engage constructively with the other, while continuing to work within the bounds of Christian orthodoxy. Given that the dream of a world of Hick-type pluralists (all of whom are agnostic about the truth claims within their own religions) is not going to come about, then this really is the hope for constructive theological engagement between persons from different faith traditions.

However, Ward is also a popular author. He is widely read by Christians who are seeking to understand their faith in the light of modernity and science. He was one of the first to take issue with the atheist Richard Dawkins (Ward, 1996b). He has written a whole set of accessible books on philosophy and faith that are deeply attractive to the person who wants to think and, at the same time, believe.

References

Bartel, T. W. 2003. *Comparative Theology: Essays for Keith Ward*. London: SPCK.

Ward, Keith. 1974. *The Concept of God*. Oxford: Blackwell.

Ward, Keith. 1982. *Rational Theology and the Creativity of God*. Oxford: Blackwell.

Ward, Keith. 1990. *Divine Action*. London: Collins.

Ward, Keith. 1991. *A Vision to Pursue*. London: SCM Press.

Ward, Keith. 1994. *Religion and Revelation: A Theology of Revelation in the World Religions*. Oxford: Clarendon Press.

Ward, Keith. 1996a. *Religion and Creation*. Oxford: Clarendon Press.

Ward, Keith. 1996b. *God, Chance and Necessity*. Oxford: Oneworld Publication.

Ward, Keith. 1998. *Religion and Human Nature*. Oxford: Clarendon Press.

Ward, Keith. 2000. *Religion and Community*. Oxford: Clarendon Press.

Glossary

adoptionism: the view that at some point in Jesus' life, God "adopted" him as a son (some say baptism, others say the resurrection).

agnostics: at a popular level, the term describes people who are not sure whether God exists. More technically, an agnostic is a person who thinks that we can never know the truth about metaphysics.

Anabaptists: literally re-baptizers. A nickname used to describe those Christians who emerged in the sixteenth and seventeenth centuries and taught that infant baptism is wrong and one should only be baptized as a believer.

apocalypticism: expectations around the "end of the age."

Apollinarianism: the view that Jesus was not completely human.

atheists: people who do not believe in the existence of God. Some atheists are also "secular humanists" (i.e., people who believe that society should be free from religious influences and affirm the importance and value of humanity).

atonement: "at-one"-ment; the claim that with the death of Jesus on the cross we are made one with God. There are various atonement theories that seek to explain how the death of Jesus makes a difference.

catechism: from a Greek word meaning "to make hear or to instruct"; an outline of Christian doctrine.

Chalcedon/Chalcedonian: this refers to an ecumenical Council of the Church which was called in 451 CE to think through the precise relationships of the human and divine natures in the incarnation.

contingent existence: a type of existence which could be otherwise.

correlation: the attempt to bring the questions posed by living in line with the answers offered by the Christian tradition.

Council of Trent (1545–63): held by Roman Catholics in response to Protestantism. Considered by Roman Catholics a major reforming council.

deductive argument: the movement from true premises to a conclusion that inescapably follows.

deism: the belief in a creator God who then does not interfere with the world. Very popular in the seventeenth and eighteenth centuries in England. There are other versions of deism that include a belief in providence.

dispensationalism: the doctrine that the history of God's treatment of humanity can be divided into different periods.

The Student's Companion to the Theologians, First Edition. Edited by Ian S. Markham.
© 2013 Blackwell Publishing Ltd. Published 2013 by Blackwell Publishing Ltd.

docetism: the view that Christ was not actually human, but simply appeared to be.

ecclesiology: the study of the church.

ecumenism/ecumenical movement: literally, from the Greek, the whole world. The term is used to describe the attempt to bring all the major churches together.

empirical: the emphasis on the data collected from sense experience (what we see, touch, taste, hear, and smell).

encyclical: a letter traditionally sent by a bishop; in Roman Catholic circles it is now confined to a letter sent by the pope.

Enlightenment: this describes a period of European history that includes a range of writers including John Locke, David Hume, Voltaire, Rousseau, and supremely Kant. The themes emerging from this period include the importance of reason, the willingness to question authority, and the importance of science.

epistemic distance: the distance which is necessary to enable humanity not to be overwhelmed by the presence of God.

epistemology: the science of knowing.

eschatology: the study of views about the "end of the age."

evidential form of the problem of evil: the claim that the problem of evil does not necessarily demonstrate that theism is incoherent, but it does point to the idea that theism is unlikely to be true.

existentialism: a primarily European approach to philosophy which stresses the centrality of human experience – a strong reaction to classical philosophy, which emphasizes the disinterested rational observer. Thinkers as diverse as Kierkegaard, Nietzsche, and Sartre are often counted as part of this movement.

fideism: literally "faith." This term is often used in the debate around the relationship between faith and reason to describe those approaches that emphasize the non-rational nature of Christian belief.

filioque: the clause "and the son," which was inserted into the Nicene creed by the Western church, is known as the "*filioque* clause." Instead of the Holy Spirit simply proceeding from the Father, the Western church wanted to talk about the Holy Spirit proceeding from both the Father and the Son. In 1054, the Orthodox churches separated from the Roman Catholic churches partly because of a disagreement over the *filioque* clause, with the Orthodox churches very unhappy with the change to the creed.

fundamentalist/fundamentalism: from 1910 to 1913, a series of pamphlets were published called "The Fundamentals," which called for American evangelicals to reaffirm the basics of "biblical inerrancy," "substitutionary atonement," among other doctrines.

genetic fallacy: the view that to identify a social or psychological genesis for a view or position does not then preclude the possibility that the view or position is true.

Gnosticism: within early Christianity, the Gnostics were an important movement. The word comes from the Greek, meaning "knowledge." This was a very diverse movement, but one shared feature was a commitment to a secret, often esoteric, knowledge that members could discover.

God of the gaps: the view that God explains those aspects of creation that science cannot explain.

hell: a place of punishment after death.

hereditary sin: the view that original sin is inherited and transmitted from generation to generation.

heresy: a view condemned by the church as incompatible with the truth believed to be orthodox.

homoousios: lit. "of one substance." At the Council of Nicaea (325 CE), this described the relationship between the Father and the Son within the Trinity. Nicaea affirmed that the Son was everything that the Father was. The Council rejected the term *homoiousios* (of like substance) because they wanted equality between the Father and the Son.

humanism: a term that has evolved to mean a belief in the importance of people which does not depend on religion.

immutability: changeless, which captures the claim that God does not change.

incarnation: the claim that God was in a human person. In Christian doctrine it involves the claim that Jesus was both completely God and completely human.

inductive argument: the movement from true premises to a conclusion which in all probability is true.

justification: derived from the Greek word for "made righteous"; a key theme of Luther's theology. God has made us righteous with God; it is not for us to seek salvation through works.

kenotic: the view that when God became human, God "emptied" himself of his divine attributes.

liturgy: lit. "the work of the people"; a term to describe structured worship.

Logos: Greek for "word"; used at the start of John's Gospel to describe the incarnation: Jesus was the Eternal Word made flesh.

metaphysics: literally, beyond physics. Any attempt to describe ultimate reality.

misogyny: the hatred of women.

monophysitism: the view that in Christ there was just a single nature, not a dual nature.

monotheism: A belief in one God.

myth: various meanings. At the popular level, it is the idea of a story that is untrue; at the more technical level, it is a story whose truth might be found in poetry rather than history.

natural theology: a theological method that starts with human reason and seeks to establish the existence of God through argument.

necessary existence: a complex notion, which has a variety of different meanings, all of which stress the impossibility of non-existence.

Neoplatonic: a tradition that is derived from Plato (429 to 347 BCE) and a major influence on the early church. The tradition develops from Plotinus (205–70 CE) and was important for the work of Augustine of Hippo.

noumenal: a technical term used in philosophy and central to the work of Immanuel Kant, which describes the world as it is in "itself."

omnipotence: the doctrine that God is all-powerful.

omniscience: the doctrine that God is all-knowing.

original sin: the view that all humanity is born in a state of alienation from God.

panentheism: a belief that God and the world are identified together, but God is more than the world.

pantheism: a belief that God and the world should be identified together.

patriarchy: the rule of men.

phenomenal: a technical term in philosophy which describes the world as "it appears to mind."

polytheism: a belief in many gods.

postcolonialism: movements that take seriously the challenge of colonialism.

predestination: some Christians affirm God's sovereignty over creation such that God has ordained all those who will be saved. In Augustine this took the view that God ordains the Christian to salvation, while in Calvin we find a doctrine of double-predestination, which involves some being ordained to salvation and others to damnation.

purgatory: traditionally understood in Roman Catholic theology as the place where those who die in the "grace of God" can receive due punishment for their venial sins (as opposed mortal sins).

rapture: the belief that the second coming of Jesus will be marked by a first stage when the true church will disappear and meet Christ in the skies.

relativism: the view that certain disagreements (especially religious and moral) are unresolvable and one's perspective will be determined by one's culture.

resurrection: the claim that both the body and the spirit of a person survives death.

revisionism: the view that the theological task is to revise our understanding of the Christian drama in the light of justice issues, modern knowledge, and insights from other faith traditions.

sacraments: term used to describe certain basic Christian practices (Eucharist and baptism; or for Roman Catholics an additional five). Traditionally defined as "an outward and visible sign of an inward and spiritual grace" (Book of Common Prayer).

secularization: the process that has seen in Western Europe a decline in the significance of religious institutions in society.

sheol: a Hebrew term which describes the place of the departed. The term occurs in the Hebrew Bible.

soteriology: the study of "salvation."

soul: understood in several different ways to describe the "spirit" or "essence" of a person that survives death.

subordinationism: the heresy that the Son is less important (subordinate) to the Father.

theism: a belief in a personal God.

theodicy: an attempt to justify why God allows evil and suffering in his creation.

transubstantiation: the doctrine that the bread and the wine become the body and blood of Jesus.

tritheism: a belief that there is no fundamental unity to God; instead there are three divine persons.

Index

The Student's Companion to the Theologians, First Edition. Edited by Ian S. Markham.
© 2013 Blackwell Publishing Ltd. Published 2013 by Blackwell Publishing Ltd.